Auditing & Assurance Services

Second International Edition

Auditing & Assurance Services

Second International Edition

Aasmund Eilifsen, William F. Messier Jr,
Steven M. Glover, Douglas W. Prawitt

McGraw-Hill
Higher Education

London Boston Burr Ridge, IL Dubuque, IA Madison, WI New York San Francisco
St. Louis Bangkok Bogotá Caracas Kuala Lumpur Lisbon Madrid Mexico City Milan
Montreal New Delhi Santiago Seoul Singapore Sydney Taipei Toronto

Auditing & Assurance Services *Second International Edition*
Aasmund Eilifsen, William F. Messier Jr, Steven M. Glover, Douglas F. Prawitt
ISBN-13 978-0-07-712250-8
ISBN-10 0-07-712250-X

McGraw-Hill
Higher Education

Published by McGraw-Hill Education
Shoppenhangers Road
Maidenhead
Berkshire
SL6 2QL
Telephone: 44 (0) 1628 502 500
Fax: 44 (0) 1628 770 224
Website: www.mcgraw-hill.co.uk

British Library Cataloguing in Publication Data

A catalogue record for this book is available from the British Library

Library of Congress Cataloguing in Publication Data

The Library of Congress data for this book has been applied for from the Library of Congress

Senior Acquisitions Editor: Mark Kavanagh
Development Editor: Karen Harlow
Marketing Manager: Vanessa Boddington
Senior Production Editor: James Bishop

Cover design by ego creative ltd
Printed and bound in Great Britain by Bell & Bain Ltd, Glasgow

ISBN-13 978-0-07-712250-8

ISBN-10 0-07-712250-X

Mixed Sources
Product group from well-managed
forests and other controlled sources
www.fsc.org Cert no. TT-COC-002769
© 1996 Forest Stewardship Council

The **McGraw·Hill** Companies

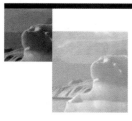

Dedication

This book is dedicated to Bente, Christoffer, Sigrid, Lars Eirik, Kristian and Gustav.
—Aasmund Eilifsen

This book is dedicated to Teddie, Stacy, Mark, Bob, Brandon and Zachary.
—William F. Messier, Jr

This book is dedicated to Tina, Jessica, Andrew, Jennifer, Anna, Wayne and Penny.
—Steven M. Glover

This book is dedicated to Meryll, Nathan, Matthew, Natalie, Emily, AnnaLisa, Leah, George and Diana.
—Douglas F. Prawitt

Brief Table of Contents

Preface   xiii
Guided Tour   xv
Website   xvii
Acknowledgements   xx
About the Authors   xxi

PART I   Introduction to Assurance and Financial Statement Auditing

1   An Introduction to Assurance and Financial Statement Auditing   3
2   The Financial Statement Auditing Environment   39

PART II   Basic Auditing Concepts: Risk Assessment, Materiality and Evidence

3   Risk Assessment and Materiality   75
4   Audit Evidence and Audit Documentation   113

PART III   Planning the Audit and Internal Control

5   Audit Planning and Types of Audit Tests   143
6   Internal Control in a Financial Statement Audit   185
7   Auditing Internal Control Over Financial Reporting   222

PART IV   Statistical and Non-Statistical Sampling Tools for Auditing

8   Audit Sampling: An Overview and Application to Tests of Controls   257
9   Audit Sampling: An Application to Substantive Tests of Account Balances   291

PART V   Auditing Business Processes

10   Auditing the Revenue Process   329
11   Auditing the Purchasing Process   373
12   Auditing the Human Resource Management Process   408
13   Auditing the Inventory Management Process   431
14   Auditing the Financing/Investing Process: Prepaid Expenses; Intangible Assets and
     Goodwill, and Property, Plant and Equipment   459
15   Auditing the Financing/Investing Process: Long-Term Liabilities, Stockholders' Equity
     and Income Statement Accounts   481
16   Auditing the Financing/Investing Process: Cash and Investments   499

PART VI   Completing the Audit and Reporting Responsibilities

17   Completing the Audit Engagement   525
18   Reports on Audited Financial Statements   550

PART VII   Professional Responsibilities

19   Professional Ethics, Independence and Quality Control   577

PART VIII *Assurance, Related Services and Internal Auditing*

20 Assurance, Related Services and Internal Auditing 615

Index *650*

Detailed Table of Contents

Preface   xiii
Guided Tour   xv
Website   xvii
Acknowledgements   xx
About the Authors   xxi

PART I *Introduction to Assurance and Financial Statement Auditing*

1   **An Introduction to Assurance and Financial Statement Auditing**   3
    The Study of Auditing   5
    The Demand for Auditing and Assurance   5
    An Assurance Analogy: The Case of the
    Building Surveyor   8
    Auditing and Assurance Defined   10
    Fundamental Concepts in Conducting a
    Financial Statement Audit   11
    Sampling: Inferences Based on Limited
    Observations   14
    The Audit Process   14
    Conclusion   20
    Key Terms   21
    Review Questions   22
    Problems   22
    Discussion Case   23
    Internet Assignments   24
    EarthWear Annual Report 2009
    (see colour section)

2   **The Financial Statement Auditing Environment**   39
    A Time of Challenge and Change for
    Auditors   40
    Auditors' Legal Liability   43
    International Organizations that Affect the
    Accounting Profession   44
    Auditing Standards   49
    Society's Expectations and the Auditor's
    Responsibilities   53
    Ethics, Independence and the IFAC Code of
    Ethics for Professional Accountants   54
    Audit Firms   54
    Types of Services Offered by Audit Firms   56
    Types of Auditors   58

The Context of Financial Statement
Auditing   60
A Model of Business   61
A Model of Business Processes: Five
Components   62
Management Assertions   64
Conclusion   65
Key Terms   66
Review Questions   67
Problems   68
Discussion Cases   68
Internet Assignments   70

PART II *Basic Auditing Concepts: Risk Assessment, Materiality and Evidence*

3   **Risk Assessment and Materiality**   75
    Audit Risk   76
    The Audit Risk Model   77
    The Auditor's Risk Assessment Process   80
    Evaluate the Entity's Risk Assessment
    Process   86
    Assessing the Risk of Material Misstatements
    Due to Error or Fraud   86
    The Auditor's Response to the Results of the
    Risk Assessments   92
    Evaluation of Audit Test Results   93
    Documentation of the Auditor's Risk
    Assessment and Response   94
    Communications about Fraud to
    Management, Those Charged with
    Governance and Others   96
    Materiality   96
    Advanced Module: Auditing of Accounting
    Estimates, Including Fair Value Accounting
    Estimates   102
    Key Terms   105
    Review Questions   106
    Problems   107
    Discussion Cases   110
    Internet Assignment   111

4   **Audit Evidence and Audit Documentation**   113
    The Relationship of Audit Evidence to the
    Audit Report   114

Management Assertions	115
Audit Procedures	120
The Concept of Audit Evidence	120
Audit Procedures for Obtaining Audit Evidence	123
Reliability of the Types of Evidence	127
Audit Documentation	128
Key Terms	134
Review Questions	135
Problems	135
Discussion Cases	138
Internet Assignment	139

PART III *Planning the Audit and Internal Control*

5	**Audit Planning and Types of Audit Tests**	**143**
	Client Acceptance and Continuance	146
	Establishing an Understanding with the Client	147
	Preliminary Engagement Activities	150
	Planning the Audit	151
	Types of Audit Tests	156
	Substantive Analytical Procedures	157
	The Audit Testing Hierarchy	168
	Advanced Module 1: Selected Financial Ratios Useful as Analytical Procedures	172
	Advanced Module 2: Special Considerations in the Audit of Group Financial Statements	175
	Key Terms	178
	Review Questions	179
	Problems	179
	Discussion Cases	182
	Internet Assignments	183
6	**Internal Control in a Financial Statement Audit**	**185**
	Introduction	187
	Internal Control: An Overview	188
	The COSO Framework	189
	Planning an Audit Strategy	195
	Obtain an Understanding of Internal Control	198
	Assessing Control Risk	203
	Substantive Procedures	205
	Timing of Audit Procedures	206
	Auditing Accounting Applications Processed by Service Organizations	208
	Communication of Deficiencies in Internal Control	209

Advanced Module 1: Types of Control in an IT Environment	210
Advanced Module 2: Computer-Assisted Audit Techniques	213
Advanced Module 3: Flowcharting Techniques	215
Key Terms	216
Review Questions	217
Problems	217
Discussion Cases	220

7	**Auditing Internal Control Over Financial Reporting**	**222**
	Management Responsibilities under Section 404	224
	Auditor Responsibilities under Section 404 and AS5	224
	Internal Control over Financial Reporting Defined	224
	Internal Control Deficiencies Defined	225
	Management's Assessment Process	226
	Performing an Audit of ICFR	230
	Planning the Audit of ICFR	231
	Using a Top-Down Approach	233
	Test the Design and Operating Effectiveness of Controls	235
	Evaluating Identified Control Deficiencies	238
	Remediation of a Material Weakness	240
	Written Representations	241
	Auditor Documentation Requirements	241
	Auditing Reporting on ICFR	241
	Other Reporting Issues	245
	Additional Required Communications in an Audit of ICFR	246
	Advanced Module: Special Considerations for an Audit of Internal Control	247
	Key Terms	248
	Review Questions	249
	Problems	249
	Internet Assignments	254

PART IV *Statistical and Non-Statistical Sampling Tools for Auditing*

8	**Audit Sampling: An Overview and Application to Tests of Controls**	**257**
	What If You Were an Apple Inspector?	259
	Introduction	260
	Definitions and Key Concepts	261
	Types of Auditing Sampling	264

Attribute Sampling Applied to Tests of
Controls   265
Non-Statistical Sampling for Tests of
Controls   282
Conclusion   283
Advanced Module: Considering the Effect of
the Population Size   284
Key Terms   284
Review Questions   285
Problems   285
Discussion Case   289

9   **Audit Sampling: An Application to Substantive
    Tests of Account Balances**   291
    Sampling for Substantive Tests of Details of
    Account Balances   293
    Monetary-Unit Sampling   294
    Non-Statistical Sampling for Tests of
    Account Balances   307
    The Rise and Fall of Statistical Audit
    Sampling   312
    Advanced Module: Classical Variables
    Sampling   312
    Key Terms   318
    Review Questions   319
    Problems   319
    Discussion Cases   323

PART V *Auditing Business Processes*

10 **Auditing the Revenue Process**   329
    Revenue Recognition   331
    Overview of the Revenue Process   334
    Inherent Risk Assessment   343
    Control Risk Assessment   344
    Control Activities and Tests of Controls:
    Revenue Transactions   346
    Control Activities and Tests of Controls:
    Cash Receipts Transactions   350
    Control Activities and Tests of Controls:
    Sales Returns and Allowances
    Transactions   353
    Relating the Assessed Level of Control Risk
    to Substantive Procedures   354
    Auditing Accounts Receivable and Related
    Accounts   354
    Substantive Analytical Procedures   355
    Tests of Details of Classes of Transactions,
    Account Balances, and Disclosures   356
    The Confirmation Process: Accounts
    Receivable   362
    Auditing Other Receivables   366

Evaluating the Audit Findings: Accounts
Receivable and Related Accounts   366
Key Terms   367
Review Questions   367
Problems   368
Discussion Case   371
Internet Assignment   371

11 **Auditing the Purchasing Process**   373
    Expense and Liability Recognition   376
    Overview of the Purchasing Process   377
    Inherent Risk Assessment   384
    Control Risk Assessment   384
    Control Activities and Tests of Controls:
    Purchase Transactions   387
    Control Activities and Tests of Controls:
    Cash Disbursement Transactions   390
    Control Activities and Tests of Controls:
    Purchase Return Transactions   393
    Relating the Assessed Level of Control Risk
    to Substantive Procedures   393
    Auditing Accounts Payable and Accrued
    Expenses   394
    Substantive Analytical Procedures   394
    Tests of Details of Classes of Transactions,
    Account Balances and Disclosures   395
    Accounts Payable Confirmations   399
    Evaluating the Audit Findings: Accounts
    Payable and Related Accounts   401
    Key Terms   401
    Review Questions   402
    Problems   402
    Discussion Case   406
    Internet Assignments   407

12 **Auditing the Human Resource Management
    Process**   408
    Overview of the Human Resource
    Management Process   410
    Inherent Risk Assessment   416
    Control Risk Assessment   416
    Control Activities and Tests of Controls:
    Payroll Transactions   418
    Relating the Assessed Level of Control Risk
    to Substantive Procedures   420
    Auditing Payroll-Related Accounts   420
    Substantive Analytical Procedures   420
    Tests of Details of Classes of Transactions,
    Account Balances and Disclosures   421
    Evaluating the Audit Findings:
    Payroll-Related Accounts   425
    Key Terms   425

Review Questions 426
Problems 426
Discussion Cases 429
Internet Assignment 430

13 Auditing the Inventory Management Process 431
Overview of the Inventory Management Process 433
Inherent Risk Assessment 438
Control Risk Assessment 440
Control Activities and Tests of Controls: Inventory Transactions 441
Relating the Assessed Level of Control Risk to Substantive Procedures 444
Auditing Inventory 444
Substantive Analytical Procedures 445
Auditing Standard Costs 446
Observing Physical Inventory 447
Tests of Details of Classes of Transactions, Account Balances and Disclosures 448
Evaluating the Audit Findings: Inventory 452
Key Terms 453
Review Questions 453
Problems 454
Discussion Case 457
Internet Assignment 458

14 Auditing the Financing/Investing Process: Prepaid Expenses; Intangible Assets and Goodwill; and Property, Plant and Equipment 459
Auditing Prepaid Expenses 461
Inherent Risk Assessment: Prepaid Expenses 461
Control Risk Assessment: Prepaid Expenses 462
Substantive Procedures: Prepaid Insurance 462
Auditing Intangible Assets and Goodwill 464
Inherent Risk Assessment: Intangible Assets and Goodwill 464
Control Risk Assessment: Intangible Assets and Goodwill 465
Substantive Procedures: Intangible Assets and Goodwill 465
Auditing the Property Management Process 467
Inherent Risk Assessment: Property Management Process 468
Control Risk Assessment: Property Management Process 470
Substantive Procedures: Property, Plant and Equipment 471

Evaluating the Audit Findings: Property, Plant and Equipment 475
Key Terms 475
Review Questions 476
Problems 476
Discussion Case 479
Internet Assignment 479

15 Auditing the Financing/Investing Process: Long-Term Liabilities, Stockholders' Equity and Income Statement Accounts 481
Auditing Long-Term Debt 483
Inherent Risk Assessment: Long-Term Debt 484
Control Risk Assessment: Long-Term Debt 484
Substantive Procedures: Long-Term Debt 486
Auditing Stockholders' Equity 489
Control Risk Assessment: Stockholders' Equity 489
Auditing Equity Capital Accounts 490
Auditing Dividends 491
Auditing Retained Earnings 492
Auditing Income Statement Accounts 492
Assessing Control Risk for Business Processes: Income Statement Accounts 492
Substantive Test: Income Statement Accounts 493
Key Terms 494
Review Questions 494
Problems 495
Discussion Cases 497
Internet Assignment 498

16 Auditing the Financing/Investing Process: Cash and Investments 499
Auditing Cash 501
Types of Bank Accounts 502
Control Risk Assessment: Cash 503
Substantive Procedures: Cash 503
Auditing Investments 512
Control Risk Assessment: Investments 512
Substantive Procedures: Investments 514
Key Terms 517
Review Questions 517
Problems 518
Internet Assignment 522

PART VI *Completing the Audit and Reporting Responsibilities*

17 Completing the Audit Engagement 525
Review for Contingencies 527

Commitments *530*
Review for Subsequent Events *531*
Final Evidence Evaluation Processes *533*
Communications with Those Charged with
Governance and Management *539*
Key Terms *540*
Review Questions *541*
Problems *541*
Discussion Cases *546*
Internet Assignment *548*

18 Reports on Audited Financial Statements *550*
Reporting on the Financial Statement Audit:
The Audit Report with an Unmodified
Opinion *553*
An Emphasis of Matter Paragraph
or Other Matter Paragraph Added
in the Audit Report *554*
Audit Reports with Modified Opinion *556*
Discussion of Conditions Requiring Audit
Reports with Modified Opinion *558*
Special Reporting Issues *562*
Reporting on Comparative Information *562*
Other Information in Documents Containing
Audited Financial Statements *564*
Reporting on Specialized Areas *565*
Key Terms *568*
Review Questions *569*
Problems *569*
Discussion Case *572*
Internet Assignment *573*

PART VII *Professional Responsibilities*

**19 Professional Ethics, Independence and Quality
Control** *577*
Ethics and Ethical Professional
Behaviour *579*
IFAC Code of Ethics for Professional
Accountants *582*

Independence: Audit and Review
Engagements *591*
Professional Ethics for Professional
Accountants in Business *601*
Auditor Independence in the EU *602*
Quality Control Systems *602*
Quality Assurance Programmes *605*
Key Terms *605*
Review Questions *606*
Problems *607*
Discussion Cases *609*
Internet Assignments *611*

PART VIII *Assurance, Related Services and
Internal Auditing*

**20 Assurance, Related Services and Internal Au-
diting** *615*
Assurance Services *616*
The IAASB International Framework for
Assurance Engagements *617*
The IAASB Assurance Standards and
Assurance Level *622*
Review of Historical Financial
Information *623*
Assurance Engagements Other Than Audits
or Reviews of Historical Financial
Information *625*
Related Services *634*
Internal Auditing *637*
Key Terms *644*
Review Questions *645*
Problems *646*
Discussion Cases *646*
Internet Assignments *647*

Index *650*

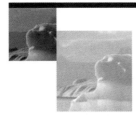

Preface

As we all know, this decade has brought possibly the most far-reaching changes in the history of modern financial markets and the international financial statement auditing environment. In the face of the challenges presented during this unprecedented period, we are committed to providing lecturers and students with the most complete and up-to-date materials possible so their hard work and energy in teaching and studying represents an investment in the latest, most current concepts. We are confident that the changes made in this edition will make it easier for lecturers to teach effectively and for students to learn more efficiently.

What's new in the Second International Edition?

Although the auditing environment has become even more complex and demanding, at the same time it is increasingly important that students gain a deep understanding and working knowledge of fundamental auditing concepts and how they are applied. We have worked hard to make this book the most 'student-friendly' auditing book on the market. In this new international edition we have focused on making the book even clearer and easier to understand and on encouraging students to think more clearly and deeply about what they are studying. This is accomplished primarily by:

(1) Introducing 'stop and think' and 'pause to test your intuition' phrases at key places throughout the chapters to encourage students to internalize key concepts more fully
(2) Clarifying explanations and adding easy-to-understand examples throughout the book
(3) Making several chapters more concise, and enhancing the focus on key concepts by deleting non-central detail
(4) Improving end-of-chapter and supplementary materials throughout the book and on the website by clarifying or replacing existing questions and problems.

This Second International Edition also contains important updates to reflect the recent landmark changes in the international professional standards. The International Federation of Accountants (IFAC) and its boards are established as the global leaders in professional standards. The international professional standards are the basis for the conduct of audits all over the world. In 2009 the International Auditing and Assurance Standards Board (IAASB) completed its comprehensive programme to update and enhance the clarity of the set of International Standards on Auditing (ISAs). The 36 updated and clarified ISAs include substantive new requirements and introduced significant changes to audits. The implementation and appropriate application of the clarified ISAs is critical for the success of the auditing profession in the coming years.

Education and professional training of auditors worldwide need to take action at the earliest opportunity to deal with the new set of clarified ISAs and the clarified International Standard on Quality Control. The new ISAs are integrated throughout all the chapters in this book. Because of their increasing complexity and importance to the audit process, this Second International Edition also includes extended discussions of auditing of accounting estimates, including fair value accounting estimates; and auditing of group financial statements. Additionally, in 2009 the International Ethics Standards Board for Accountants (IESBA) issued a revised and stringent Code of Ethics for Professional Accountants. The Code of Ethics clearly identifies the requirements and establishes acceptable behaviour for professional accountants around the world.

How does Auditing & Assurance Services Second International Edition prepare students for the accounting profession?

The recent implosion of financial markets has had a significant effect on the auditing profession. Upon graduation students will need to operate in this new, ever-changing environment. It is therefore crucial to learn from the most up-to-date resources. Once again, the author team of *Auditing & Assurance Services Second International Edition* is dedicated to providing the most current professional content and real-world application, as well as helping prepare students for the licensing requirements. This book combines a genuine international perspective and relevant international regulatory requirements with the conceptual and systematic approach to auditing inherent in the 7th edition of *Auditing & Assurance Services: A Systematic Approach* (Messier, Glover and Prawitt, 2010). In this Second International Edition we continue to reinforce the fundamental values central to the first edition, as follows.

International Approach. The book has a genuine international perspective on auditing. Auditing network firms operate globally and cross borders, and professional practice and regulation are driven by international events and initiatives. Thus, students and practising auditors need to understand how the international environment shapes the profession and international professional standards. The International Federation of Accountants (IFAC) and its boards are consolidated as *the* global standard setter. In 2004 the International Auditing and Assurance Standards Board (IAASB) launched an ambitious project designed to improve the clarity of its pronouncements. In 2009 IAASB completed its clarity project and released 36 updated and clarified International Standards on Auditing (ISAs) and a clarified International Standard on Quality Control. IAASB decided that all clarified standards would become effective for audits of financial statements for periods beginning on or after 15 December 2009. Members of the Forum of Firms, an association of over 20 of the largest international networks of audit firms, began to use the clarified ISAs swiftly. Countries and jurisdictions all over the world implement and apply these clarified ISAs. The ISAs are integrated into this book and numerous international real-world cases are inserted to illustrate concepts and application of the standards. In addition, separate chapters cover international assurance and related services engagement standards, and the revised Code of Ethics for Professional Accountants.

Student Engagement. The authors believe students are best served by acquiring a strong understanding of the basic concepts that underlie the audit process and how to apply those concepts to various audit and assurance services. The primary purpose for an auditing text is not to serve as a reference manual but to facilitate student learning, and this text is written accordingly. The text is accessible to students through straightforward writing and the use of engaging, relevant real-world examples, illustrations and analogies. The text explicitly encourages students to think through fundamental concepts and to avoid trying to learn auditing through rote memorization. New to this edition, students are prompted by the text to 'stop and think' at important points in the text, in order to help them apply the principles covered. Consistent with this aim, the text's early chapters avoid immersing students in unnecessary detail about such topics as independence and reporting requirements, focusing instead on students' understanding of fundamental audit concepts. Additionally, the case involving EarthWear Clothiers, a mail-order retailer, has been updated and integrated throughout the book. Finally, the addition of 'practice insights' throughout the book engages students and helps them understand the practical nature of auditing.

A Systematic Approach. The underlying concepts of auditing and the audit process are basically universal. The text continues to take a systematic approach to the audit process by first introducing the three underlying concepts: audit risk, materiality and evidence. The assessment of control risk is then described, followed by discussion of the nature, timing and extent of evidence necessary to reach the appropriate level of detection risk. These concepts are then applied to each major business process and related account balances using a risk-based approach.

Decision Making. In covering these important concepts and their applications, the book focuses on critical judgements and decision-making processes followed by auditors. Much of auditing practice involves the application of auditor judgement. If a student understands these basic concepts and how to apply them to an audit engagement, he or she will be more effective in today's dynamic audit environment.

Thank you for your support of this text and the many compliments we have received regarding the First International Edition. We are gratified by the enthusiastic response the text has received as we have done our best to create a clear, easy-reading, student-friendly auditing textbook. We welcome your suggestions and hope you will be impressed with the updates we have made in this Second International Edition.

Aasmund Eilifsen, William F. Messier Jr, Steven M. Glover, Douglas F. Prawitt

Guided Tour

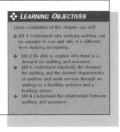

Learning Objectives and Relevant Accounting and Auditing Pronouncements

Each chapter opens with a set of learning objectives, summarizing what you should learn from each chapter. There is also a list of relevant pronouncements.

Figures, Tables and Exhibits

Each chapter provides a number of figures, tables and exhibits to help you to visualize the various models, and to illustrate and summarize important concepts.

Key Terms

Each chapter ends with a summary of the key terms used and their definitions. These words are also highlighted at the relevant point in the chapter.

Practice Insight boxes

These brief insights into practice demonstrate the realities of auditing in the real world.

Review Questions

These questions encourage you to review and apply the knowledge you have acquired from each chapter. They are pitched at different levels.

Problems

This end-of-chapter feature is the perfect way to practise the techniques you have been taught and apply the methodology to real-world situations.

Discussion Cases

Detailed questions based on real-world examples are posed at the end of every chapter to test understanding.

Internet Assignments

With a wealth of information available on the Internet, these exercises challenge you to find it and make use of it. They are designed to familiarize you with important websites.

Technology to enhance learning and teaching

Visit **www.mcgraw-hill.co.uk/textbooks/eilifsen** today

Online Learning Centre (OLC)

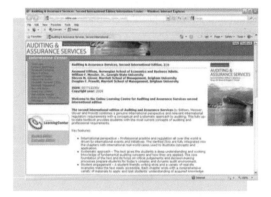

After completing each chapter, log on to the supporting Online Learning Centre website. Take advantage of the study tools offered to reinforce the material you have read in the text, and to develop your knowledge of auditing in a fun and effective way.

Resources for lecturers include:

- *PowerPoint slides*
- *Solutions to questions and problems in the book*
- *Instructors' Manual*

Also available for students:

- *Weblinks*
- *PowerPoint slides*

Custom Publishing Solutions: Let us help make our content your solution

At McGraw-Hill Education our aim is to help lecturers to find the most suitable content for their needs delivered to their students in the most appropriate way. Our **custom publishing solutions** offer the ideal combination of content delivered in the way which best suits students and lecturers.

Our custom publishing programme offers lecturers the opportunity to select just the chapters or sections of material they wish to deliver to their students from a database called Primis at www.primisonline.com

Primis contains over two million pages of content from:

● textbooks
● professional books
● case books – Harvard Articles, Insead, Ivey, Darden, Thunderbird and BusinessWeek
● Taking Sides – debate materials

Across the following imprints:

● McGraw-Hill Education
● Open University Press
● Harvard Business School Press
● US and European material

There is also the option to include additional material authored by lecturers in the custom product – this does not necessarily have to be in English.

We will take care of everything from start to finish in the process of developing and delivering a custom product to ensure that lecturers and students receive exactly the material needed in the most suitable way.

With a Custom Publishing Solution, students enjoy the best selection of material deemed to be the most suitable for learning everything they need for their courses – something of real value to support their learning. Teachers are able to use exactly the material they want, in the way they want, to support their teaching on the course.

Please contact your local McGraw-Hill representative with any questions or alternatively contact Warren Eels **e:** warren_eels@mcgraw-hill.com.

Make the grade!

30% off any Study Skills book!

Our Study Skills books are packed with practical advice and tips that are easy to put into practice and will really improve the way you study. Topics include:

- techniques to help you pass exams
- advice to improve your essay writing
- help in putting together the perfect seminar presentation
- tips on how to balance studying and your personal life.

www.openup.co.uk/studyskills

Visit our website to read helpful hints about essays, exams, dissertations and much more.

Special offer! As a valued customer, buy online and receive 30% off any of our Study Skills books by entering the promo code **getahead**

Acknowledgements

Publisher Acknowledgements

Our thanks go to the following reviewers for their comments at various stages in the text's development:

Caroline Aggestam, Copenhagen Business School
Bernice Beukes, University of Pretoria, South Africa
Joost van Buuren, Nyenrode Business University
Christine Cheong, Temasek Polytechnic, Singapore
Frank Conaty, NUI Galway
John Dunn, University of Strathclyde
David Godsell, University of Kent
Bijan Hesni, University of Westminster
Claus Holm, University of Aarhus
Olafur Kristinsson, University of Iceland
Brian Leigh, Manchester Metropolitan University
Anna Noteborg, Erasmus University Rotterdam
Ann Vanstraelen, Maastricht University
Bent Warming-Rasmussen, University of Southern Denmark, Kolding
Mike Woodrow, Lancaster University
Henning Zulch, University of Leipzig

Author Acknowledgements

First and foremost, we would like to thank our families for their continuous support. We would like to acknowledge the International Auditing and Assurance Standards Board for quotations from international professional standards, and the International Ethics Standards Board for Accountants for quotations from the Code of Ethics for Professional Accountants. Finally, we would like to extend our gratitude to Director Roger Kjelløkken of PricewaterhouseCoopers for his careful reading of and feedback on the text, and Professor Atle Johnsen at the Department of Accounting, Auditing, and Law, Norwegian School of Economics and Business Administration, for all our valuable discussions on accounting issues.

About the Authors

Professor Aasmund Eilifsen is Director of the Graduate Auditing Program and Professor in Auditing at the Department of Accounting, Auditing, and Law, Norwegian School of Economics and Business Administration. He received his PhD from the same institution. He was a visiting faculty member at the University of Washington, Seattle, and the University of Florida, Gainesville. He has been a member of the European Accounting Association's (EAA) Standing Scientific Committee and serves at the Scientific Committee of the European Auditing Research Network (EARNet). Professor Eilifsen is on the editorial boards of *Auditing: A Journal of Practice & Theory*, the *International Journal of Accounting* and the *International Journal of Auditing.* He has authored or co-authored over 25 articles in journals and books, primarily in the areas of auditor judgement and decision making, audit education and audit practice. Professor Eilifsen has since 1999 served as the Academic Member on the Norwegian Auditing Standards Committee and holds a part-time position as adviser at the Norwegian Institute of Public Accountants. He has also served as an expert witness in audit litigation cases.

Professor William F. Messier, Jr holds the Kenneth and Tracy Knauss Endowed Chair in Accounting at the Department of Accounting, University of Nevada, Las Vegas. He is also the PricewaterhouseCoopers Professor II at the Department of Accounting, Auditing, and Law at the Norwegian School of Economics and Business Administration. Professor Messier holds a BBA, from Siena College, an MS from Clarkson University, and an MBA and DBA from Indiana University. He is a CPA in Florida and has held faculty positions at the University of Florida (Price Waterhouse Professor) and Georgia State University (Deloitte & Touche Professor). Professor Messier was a visiting faculty member at SDA Bocconi in Milan and the University of Michigan. Professor Messier served as the Academic Member of the AICPA's Auditing Standards Board and as Chair of the AICPA's International Auditing Standards Subcommittee. He is a Past-Editor of *Auditing: A Journal of Practice & Theory* and formerly President of the Auditing Section of the American Accounting Association. Professor Messier was the recipient of the AAA Auditing Section's Outstanding Educator Award (2009) and the Distinguished Service in Auditing Award (2008). He has also served as an expert witness in a number of audit litigation cases.

Professor Steven M. Glover is the Mary & Ellis Professor of Accounting at the Marriott School of Management, Brigham Young University. Professor Glover is a CPA in Utah and holds a PhD and BS from the University of Washington and an AA in Business from BYU – Idaho. He previously worked as an auditor for KPMG LLP and as a director in the national office of PricewaterhouseCoopers LLP. Professor Glover serves on the audit committee of a non-profit organization and has served on the board of advisers for technology companies, and he actively consults with public companies and public accounting firms. He has also served as an expert witness. Professor Glover is the President Elect of the Auditing Section of the American Accounting Association. He has been on auditing-related task forces of the AICPA. Professor Glover is on the editorial boards of *Auditing: A Journal of Practice & Theory, The Accounting Review* and *Accounting Horizons.* He has authored or co-authored over 25 articles and books primarily focused in the areas of auditor decision making, audit education and audit practice.

Professor Douglas F. Prawitt is the Glen Ardis Professor of Accountancy at the Marriott School of Management, Brigham Young University. Professor Prawitt is a CPA in Utah. He holds a PhD from the University of Arizona, and BS and MAcc degrees from Brigham Young University. Professor Prawitt was awarded the Marriott School's Teaching Excellence and Outstanding Researcher awards in 1998 and 2000. He received the Merrill J. Bateman Student Choice Teaching Award in 2002 and BYU's Wesley P. Lloyd Award for Distinction in Graduate Education in 2006. He consults actively with international and local public accounting firms. Over the past five years he has worked extensively with the Committee of Sponsoring Organizations (COSO) on the COSO *Enterprise Risk Management Framework* and Internal Control over Financial Reporting – Guidance for Smaller Public Companies projects. Professor Prawitt has also served in several capacities with the American Accounting Association and is on the editorial boards of *Auditing: A Journal of Practice & Theory, Behavioral Research in Accounting* and *Accounting Horizons.* He has authored or co-authored over 25 articles and books, primarily in the areas of auditor judgement and decision making, audit education and audit practice. Finally, he served a three-year appointment to the AICPA Auditing Standards Board from 2005–2008.

PART I
Introduction to Assurance and Financial Statement Auditing

PART CONTENTS

1 An Introduction to Assurance and Financial Statement Auditing
2 The Financial Statement Auditing Environment

An Introduction to Assurance and Financial Statement Auditing

❖ LEARNING OBJECTIVES

Upon completion of this chapter you will

- ❖ **LO1** Understand why studying auditing can be valuable to you and why it is different from studying accounting.
- ❖ **LO2** Be able to explain why there is a demand for auditing and assurance.
- ❖ **LO3** Understand intuitively the demand for auditing and the desired characteristics of auditors and audit services through an analogy to a building surveyor and a building survey.
- ❖ **LO4** Understand the relationships between auditing and assurance.

- ❖ **LO5** Know the basic definition and three fundamental concepts of a financial statement audit.
- ❖ **LO6** Understand why on most audit engagements an auditor tests only a sample of transactions that occurred.
- ❖ **LO7** Be able to describe the basic financial statement auditing process and the phases in which an audit is carried out.
- ❖ **LO8** Know what an audit report is and the nature of an audit report with an unmodified opinion.
- ❖ **LO9** Understand why auditing demands logic, reasoning and resourcefulness.

❖ RELEVANT ACCOUNTING AND AUDITING PRONOUNCEMENTS

IAASB, International Framework for Assurance Engagements

ISA 200, Overall Objectives of the Independent Auditor and the Conduct of an Audit in Accordance with International Standards on Auditing

ISA 300, Planning an Audit of Financial Statements

ISA 315, Identifying and Assessing the Risks of Material Misstatement through Understanding the Entity and Its Environment

ISA 320, Materiality in Planning and Performing an Audit

ISA 330, The Auditor's Responses to Assessed Risks

ISA 450, Evaluation of Misstatements Identified during the Audit

ISA 500, Audit Evidence

ISA 700, Forming an Opinion and Reporting on Financial Statements

AS YOU WILL LEARN in this chapter, auditing consists of a set of practical conceptual tools that help a person to find, organize and evaluate evidence about the assertions of another party. The demand for capable accountants and auditors of high integrity has never been greater. Opportunities for auditors are plentiful and rewarding, and can lead to attractive career opportunities in other areas. Those who practise as auditors often later go into financial management, becoming controllers, chief financial officers (CFOs) and even chief executive officers (CEOs). But even those who do not plan to become an auditor can benefit greatly from an understanding of financial statement auditing and its underlying concepts. Learning these tools will be valuable to any business decision maker.

While opportunities in auditing are great, the last several years have been challenging for the accounting profession. In the early 2000s, a series of high-profile accounting frauds all over the world began to cause investors to doubt the integrity of the financial reporting system, including the role of the external auditor. The global nature of capital markets and businesses, as well as the accounting profession made the loss of trust a genuine international issue. To restore investor confidence, a series of regulatory initiatives were taken at international, regional and national levels. At the global level the *International Auditing and Assurance Standards Board* (IAASB) launched a landmark reformation project of the set of *International Standards on Auditing* (ISAs). The project is now completed. The ISAs and their audit implications are discussed throughout the text. While the scandals, public scrutiny and new regulation have been painful for accountants and auditors, the events of the last several years have also been a powerful reminder of just how critical the roles of accounting and auditing are in our society.

We live in a time when the amount of information available for decision makers via electronic databases, the Internet and other sources is rapidly expanding, and there is a great need for the information to be understandable, relevant, reliable and timely. High-quality information is necessary if managers, investors, creditors, employees, regulatory bodies and others are to make informed decisions. Auditing and assurance services play an important role in ensuring the quality of business information.

The following examples present situations where auditing enters into economic transactions and increases the confidence of an entity's financial statements:

> ❝ Bente Jacobsen has together with other volunteers been operating a not-for-profit centre that provides assistance to abused women and their children. The centre has financed most of its operations from private contributions. Recently, the centre applied to the government for a substantial grant to accommodate more women. In completing the grant application, it was discovered that recipients of grants must have their financial statements audited to ensure that funds are being used appropriately. The centre hired an independent auditor to audit its financial statements. Based on the centre's activities, the intended use of the funds, and the auditor's report, the grant was approved.

> Walter Johnson is the sole owner of a small auto parts distributor. His profitable store has been financed from operations and personal savings. Mr Johnson plans to expand his operations by opening two more stores. He approaches the local bank for the necessary financing and provides the loan officer with his unaudited financial statements. The loan officer informs him that to become eligible for a loan the bank

needs financial statements audited by an independent auditor. Based on financial performance and audited financial statements the bank grants Mr Johnson the loan he applied for.

Search & Transfer is developing computer software. The company was started five years ago by a group of software engineers. Search & Transfer's revenues and profits increased by 25 per cent in each of the last two years. To finance further growth and to make its shares more liquid the company decided to have its shares listed at the stock exchange. However, to give investors greater confidence in investing in stock all listed companies are required to have their financial statements audited. Search & Transfer hired a major audit firm and later its shares were successfully listed at the stock exchange. *,,*

These situations show the importance of auditing to both private and public enterprise. By adding an audit to each situation, the users of the financial statements have additional assurance that the financial statements do not contain material misstatements or omissions, and they will be more willing to rely on those statements.

Most readers of an introductory auditing text initially have little understanding of what auditing and assurance entail. Thus, we start by helping you understand in general terms why there is a demand for auditing and assurance services. We then compare auditing to other well-known forms of assurance to provide an intuitive understanding of the role auditing plays in economic transactions. Finally, we define auditing and assurance, and give you an overview of the financial statement auditing process.

❖ THE STUDY OF AUDITING

LO1

You will find that the study of auditing is different from any of the other accounting courses you have taken, and for good reason. Most accounting courses focus on learning the rules, techniques and computations required to prepare and analyse financial information. Auditing focuses on learning the analytical and logical skills necessary to evaluate the relevance and reliability of the systems and processes responsible for recording and summarizing that information, as well as the information itself. As such, you will find the study of auditing to be much more conceptual in nature than your other accounting courses. This is simply due to the nature of auditing. Thus, we will periodically prompt you to 'stop and think' about the concepts being discussed throughout the book. Seeking to thoroughly understand and apply principles as you read them will greatly improve your success in studying auditing.

Learning auditing essentially helps you understand how to gather and assess evidence so you can evaluate assertions (or claims) made by others. This text is filled with the tools and techniques used by financial statement auditors in practice. You will find that the 'tool kit' used by auditors consists of a coherent logical framework, together with tools and techniques useful for analysing financial data and gathering evidence about others' assertions. Acquiring and learning to use this conceptual tool kit can be valuable in a variety of settings, including practising as an auditor, running a small business, providing consulting services and even making executive business decisions. An important implication is that learning this framework makes the study of auditing valuable to future accountants and business decision makers, whether or not they plan to become auditors.

While we are convinced the concepts and techniques covered in this book will be useful to you regardless of your career path, our experience is that students frequently fall into the trap of defining auditing in terms of memorized lists of rules, tools and techniques. The study of auditing and the related rules, tools and techniques will make a lot more sense if you can first build up your intuition of why audits are needed, what an auditor does, and the necessary characteristics of audits and auditors.

Reliable information is important for managers, investors, creditors, regulatory bodies and others to make informed decisions. Auditing helps ensure that information is understandable, relevant, reliable and timely. You will find that the concepts behind financial statement auditing provide a useful tool kit that can improve the reliability of information for decision makers of all kinds.

❖ THE DEMAND FOR AUDITING AND ASSURANCE[i]

LO2

Why would an entity decide to spend money on an audit? This is an important question in view of the fact that many of the largest companies spend substantial amounts each year on their annual audit. Some might answer that audits are required by law. While true in certain circumstances, this answer is far too simplistic. Audits are often utilized in situations where they are not required by law, and audits were in demand long before laws required them. In fact, evidence shows that some forms of accounting and auditing existed in Greece as early as 500 BC.[ii] However, the development of the corporate form of business and the expanding world economy over the last 200 years have given rise to an explosion in the demand for the assurance provided by auditors.

Principals and Agents

The demand for auditing can be understood through the need for accountability when business owners hire others to manage their business, as is typical in modern corporations. Until the late eighteenth and early nineteenth centuries, most organizations were relatively small and were owned and operated as sole proprietorships or partnerships. Because businesses were generally run by their owners, there was limited accountability to outside parties. The birth of modern accounting and auditing occurred during the Industrial Revolution, when companies became larger and needed to raise capital to finance expansion.[iii] Over time, securities markets developed, enabling companies to raise the investment capital necessary to expand to new markets, to finance expensive research, and to fund the buildings, technology and equipment needed to deliver a product to market. A capital market allows a public company to sell small pieces of ownership (i.e. stocks/shares) or to borrow money in the form of thousands of small loans (i.e. bonds) so that vast amounts of capital can be raised from a wide variety of investors and creditors. A *public company* is a company that sells its stocks or bonds to the public, giving the public a valid interest in the proper use of, or stewardship over, the company's resources. Thus, the growth of the modern corporation led to diverse groups of owners who are not directly involved in running the business (stockholders) and the use of professional managers hired by the owners to run the corporation on a day-to-day basis. In this setting, the managers serve as *agents* for the owners (sometimes referred to as *principals*) and fulfil a *stewardship* function by managing the corporation's assets.

Accounting and auditing play important roles in this principal–agent relationship. We will first explain the roles of accounting and auditing from a conceptual perspective. Then we will use an analogy involving a building surveyor to illustrate the concepts. It is important to understand that the relationship between an owner and manager often results in **information asymmetry** between the two parties. *Information asymmetry* means that the manager generally has more information about the 'true' financial position and results of operations of the entity than does the absentee owner. Before continuing, stop and consider the following questions. What negative consequences could this information asymmetry have for the absentee owner? How do the perspectives and motives of the manager and absentee owner differ?

Because their goals may not coincide, there is a natural *conflict of interest* between the manager and the absentee owner. If both parties seek to maximize their self-interest, the manager may not always act in the best interest of the owner. For example, the risk exists that a manager may spend funds on excessive personal benefits or favour entity growth at the expense of stockholders values. Or the manager might manipulate the reported performance in order to inflate the price of the company's stock to earn larger bonuses and sell stock holdings at artificially high prices. The owner can attempt to protect him or herself against the possibility of improper use of resources by reducing the manager's compensation by the amount of company resources that the owner expects the manager to consume. But rather than accept reduced compensation, the manager may agree to some type of monitoring provisions in his or her employment contract, providing assurance to the owner that he or she will not misuse resources. For example, the two parties may agree that the manager will periodically report on how well he or she has managed the owner's assets. Of course, a set of criteria is needed to govern the form and content of the manager's reports. In other words, reporting of this financial information to the owner must follow some set of agreed-upon accounting principles. As you can see, one primary role of accounting information is to hold the manager accountable to the owner – hence the word 'accounting'.

The Role of Auditing

Of course, reporting according to an agreed-upon set of accounting principles does not solve the problem by itself. Because the manager is responsible for reporting on the results of his or her own actions, which the absentee owner cannot directly observe, the manager is in a position to manipulate the reports. Again, the owner adjusts for this possibility by assuming that the manager will manipulate the reports to his or her benefit and by reducing the manager's compensation accordingly. It is at this point that the demand for auditing arises. If the manager is honest, it may very well be in the manager's interest to hire an auditor to monitor his or her activities. The owner likely will be willing to invest more in the business and to pay the manager more if the manager can be held accountable for how he or she uses the owner's invested resources. Note that as the amount of capital involved and the number of potential owners increase, the potential impact of accountability also increases. The auditor's role is to determine whether the reports prepared by the manager conform to the contract's provisions, including the agreed-upon accounting principles. Thus, the auditor's verification of the financial information adds credibility to the report and reduces *information risk*, or the risk that information circulated by a company will be false or misleading. Reducing information risk potentially benefits both the owner and the manager. While other forms of monitoring might be possible, the extensive presence of auditing in such situations suggests that auditing is a cost-effective monitoring device. Figure 1–1 provides an overview of this agency relationship.

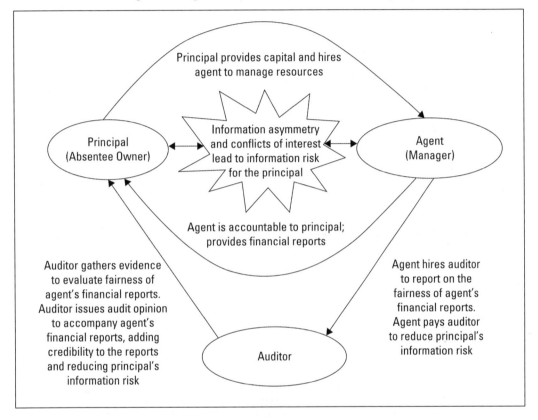

Figure 1–1 Overview of the Principal–Agent Relationship Leading to the Demand for Auditing

While the setting we have outlined is very simple, understanding the basics of the owner–manager relationship is helpful in understanding the concepts underlying the demand for auditing. The principal–agent model is a powerful conceptual tool that can be extrapolated to much more complex employment and other contractual arrangements, and these same ideas apply to other relationships that involve the entity. For example, how can a lender prevent management from taking the borrowed funds and using them inappropriately? One way is to place restrictive covenants in the debt agreement that must be complied with by the entity and its management. Again, this arrangement gives rise to a demand for auditing of information produced by management.

Legal audit requirements reflect lawmakers' and, in that sense, society's preferences for an audit. While laws and regulations account for some of the demand for auditing, they do not account for all of it. Auditing is demanded because it plays a valuable role in monitoring the contractual relationships between the entity and its stockholders, managers, employees and creditors. As a result, they are able to add credibility to information produced by management. The role of the independent auditor is discussed in more detail in Chapter 2.

❖ AN ASSURANCE ANALOGY: THE CASE OF THE BUILDING SURVEYOR

LO3

Before we discuss financial statement auditors further, let us consider a context that often involves an 'auditor' or assurance provider as an analogy: buying an older home. This analogy will help illustrate the concepts we have just covered. In the purchase of an existing house, *information asymmetry* is usually present because the seller typically has more information about the house than does the buyer. There is also a natural *conflict of interest* between the buyer and the seller. Sellers generally prefer a higher selling price to a lower one, and may be motivated to overstate the positive characteristics, and to understate or remain silent about the negative characteristics of the property they have for sale. In other words, there is *information risk* to the buyer.

Seller Assertions, Information Asymmetry and Surveyor Characteristics

To support the asking price, sellers typically make *assertions* about their property. For instance, the seller of an older home might declare that the roof is watertight, that the foundation is sound, that there is no rot or pest damage, and that the plumbing and electrical systems are in good working order. Fortunately, many sellers are honest and forthcoming, but this is not always the case. The problem is that the buyer often does not know if she or he is dealing with an honest seller or if the seller has the necessary expertise to evaluate all the structural or mechanical aspects of the property. Lacking the necessary expertise to validate the seller's assertions, the buyer can logically reduce information risk by hiring a building surveyor. Before moving on, imagine for a moment that you are buying a house and are wisely considering hiring a surveyor. Test your intuition – what characteristics would you like your surveyor to possess? In Table 1–1 we have listed several characteristics we think would be desirable.

Table 1–1   Important Characteristics of Building Surveyors and Surveys

Desirable characteristics of building surveyors
- Competent – they possess the required training, expertise and experience to evaluate the property for sale.
- Objective – they have no reason to side with the seller; they are independent of the seller's influence.
- Honest – they will conduct themselves with integrity, and they will share all of their findings with the buyer.
- Sceptical – they will not simply take the seller's assertions at face value; they will conduct their own analysis and testing.
- Responsible and/or liable – they should stand behind their assessment with a guarantee and/or be subject to litigation if they fail to act with due care.

Desirable characteristics of a building survey
- Timely – the results of the service are reported in time to benefit the decision maker.
- Reasonably priced – the costs of the services must not exceed the benefits. For this to occur the service provider will likely need to focus attention on the most important and risky assertions and likely cannot provide absolute assurance.
- Complete – the service addresses all of the most important and risky assertions made by the seller.
- Effective – the service provides some degree of certainty that it will uncover significant risks or problems.
- Systematic and reliable – the service is based on a systematic process, and the conclusions are based on reliable evidence. In other words, another comparable surveyor would likely find similar things and come to similar conclusions.
- Informative – the service provides a sense of how likely mechanical or structural failure is in the near future and provides an estimate of the cost to repair known defects or failures.

Desired Characteristics of the Building Survey

Now that you have identified some of the characteristics of a good surveyor, consider the key characteristics of the service he or she will provide. Are some of the seller's assertions more important than others? For instance, you are probably not equally concerned with the assertion that there is no structural rot and the assertion that the lightbulbs in the bathroom are relatively new. Depending on what you are willing to pay, the survey could theoretically range from the extremes of driving past the house to taking the home entirely apart, board by board. How thorough do you want the surveyor to be? Do you want the surveyor to issue a 'pass–fail' grade or would you like more details, such as costs of necessary repairs? As you can see, there are many factors to take into account in deciding on the nature and extent of the assurance service you want to buy. In Table 1–1 we have also listed what we think are desirable characteristics of the service provided by a building surveyor.

Table 1–1 contains concepts that are in fact fundamental to most forms of survey (and all financial statement audits). Certainly home surveys and other assurance services must focus on the assertions that are most important, and they must be conducted in a timely and cost-effective manner. Some assertions are more important than others because of their potential risk or cost. For example, a building surveyor should recognize the signs that indicate an increased risk of a leaky roof. If those signs are present, he or she should investigate further, because damage caused by a leaky roof can be very expensive to repair. At the same time, just because the seller asserts that he or she recently lubricated all the door and window hinges does not mean it would be wise to pay the surveyor to validate this assertion. Before going on, stop and think for a moment about how the building survey example might relate to a financial statement audit.

Relating the Building Survey Analogy to Financial Statement Auditing

Now that we have discussed some of the basic characteristics of surveyors and their services, let us consider how these relate to financial statement auditors. As noted previously, the demand for the assurance provided by a building surveyor comes from information asymmetry and conflicts of interest between the buyer and the seller. One important difference between our building surveyor example and financial statement auditing is that the buyer of a home typically hires the surveyor. In other words, the buyer identifies and hires the surveyor rather than using someone that the seller recommends – presumably because by hiring a surveyor directly, they increase the likelihood that the surveyor will be objective and independent.

However, as was discussed previously, there are some important differences in most financial statement audit settings that shift the model so that the companies selling stocks or bonds to the public typically hire and pay the auditor, rather than the other way around. To raise capital in the marketplace, companies often sell many small parcels of stocks and bonds to small investors. Suppose a financial statement audit of a given company would cost €500,000. Under such circumstances, it obviously does not make sense for each individual investor to pay for an audit. Instead, the company hires and pays for the auditor because a reputable independent auditor's opinion can provide assurance to thousands of potential investors. By purchasing the assurance provided by an audit, the company can sell its stocks and bonds to prospective owners and creditors at more favourable prices, significantly reducing the cost of capital. In fact, studies indicate that audits save companies large amounts in costs of obtaining capital.

Given that the seller of stocks and bonds typically hires the auditor, consider just how crucial a strong reputation is to an independent auditor. Four large, international audit firms dominate the audits of large and public companies. One reason these firms dominate the audits of large companies is because they have well-known names and strong reputations. Entities who buy assurance from these firms know that potential investors and creditors will recognize the audit firm's name and reputation, and feel assured that they therefore face reduced information risk.

The fact that the entity being audited typically hires the auditor also highlights just how important auditor objectivity and independence are to the investing public. In fact, Arthur Andersen, the once highly regarded member of the former 'Big 5' international audit firms, arguably failed in 2002 at least in part because the firm lost its reputation as a high-quality, objective auditor whose opinion could be relied upon by investors and creditors. Later in the book we will discuss some recent changes enacted to strengthen the independence of financial statement auditors, including changes in the regulatory framework and restrictions of auditors' provision of consulting services to their audit clients.

Management Assertions and Financial Statements

We have seen that home sellers make a number of different assertions about which a home buyer might want independent assurance. What assertions does a seller of stocks or bonds make? Some of the most important assertions entities make to investors are implicit in the entities' financial statements. Immediately after this chapter you will find a set of financial statements for EarthWear, a hypothetical seller of high-quality outdoor clothing. We will use EarthWear examples and exercises throughout the book to illustrate important audit concepts and techniques. Let us consider what assertions EarthWear makes to potential investors when it publishes its financial statements. For example, EarthWear lists the asset account 'Cash' on its balance sheet and indicates that the account's year-end balance was €48.9 million. Pause and consider for a moment what assertions the company is making about cash. An obvious answer is that EarthWear is asserting the cash really exists. EarthWear is also implicitly asserting that the cash amount is fairly and accurately recorded, that all cash is included, and that no other parties have valid claims to the cash. Such assertions are implicit for each account in the financial statements.

Obviously, information asymmetry exists between the managers of EarthWear and potential investors. The interests of EarthWear managers and investors may also conflict. For example, if managers are overly optimistic or if they wish to inflate their bonus compensation, they may unintentionally or intentionally overstate the company's profit and assets (e.g. by understating the allowance for doubtful accounts or by claiming to have more cash than they really have).

One of the main tasks of the auditor is to collect sufficient appropriate evidence that management's assertions regarding the financial statements are correct. If you were asked to audit EarthWear, how would you go about collecting evidence for the cash account? The process is logical and intuitive. First, you would carefully consider the most important assertions the company is making about the account, and then you would decide what evidence you would need to substantiate the truthfulness of each important assertion. For example, to ensure the cash exists, you might call the bank, examine bank statements or send a letter to the bank requesting confirmation of the balance. To ensure the cash has not been pledged or restricted, you might review the minutes of key management meetings to look for discussions on this issue. Once you have finished auditing the important assertions relating to the accounts contained in the company's financial statements, you will need to report your findings to the company's shareholders and to the investing public because EarthWear is publicly traded.

Instead of EarthWear's auditor, imagine you are a prospective investor in EarthWear. As an investor, would the reputation of the company's auditor matter to you? What if the audit engagement partner were related to EarthWear's president? Would you want to know that the audit firm used a well-recognized audit approach to gather sufficient appropriate evidence? What form of report would you expect? These questions lead to characteristics of auditors and audit services that are quite similar to those relating to building surveyors and the building survey.

We hope the analogy of building surveyors and auditors as assurance providers has helped you understand the basic intuition behind the necessary characteristics of auditors and auditing and why auditing is in demand, even when it is not required by law. We will refer back to this analogy occasionally throughout the book to remind you of this basic intuition. Before you memorize lists of standards, techniques or concepts, we encourage you to consider how the information relates to your basic understanding of important characteristics of 'information inspectors' and the services they offer. Keep the big picture in mind!

❖ AUDITING AND ASSURANCE DEFINED

LO4

In addition to auditing, the professional literature refers to the more general concept of assurance. An audit of financial statements is a specialized form of an assurance engagement. Assurance engagements, however, also include engagements beyond audits, for example assurance of non-financial information such as an entity's reporting on its environmental performance. Many times the terms audit and assurance are used interchangeably because they are related, and, at a general level, they encompass the same process: *the evaluation of evidence to determine the correspondence of some information to a set of criteria, and the issuance of a report to indicate the degree of correspondence.*

Auditing

A widely cited definition of auditing is the following:

> **Auditing** *is a systematic process of objectively obtaining and evaluating evidence regarding assertions about economic actions and events to ascertain the degree of correspondence between those assertions and established criteria and communicating the results to interested users.*[iv]

A number of phrases in this definition deserve attention. The phrase 'systematic process' implies that there should be a well-planned and thorough approach for conducting an audit. This plan involves 'objectively obtaining and evaluating evidence'. Two activities are involved here. The auditor must *objectively search for* and *evaluate* the relevance and validity of evidence. While the type, quantity and reliability of evidence may vary between audits, the process of obtaining and evaluating evidence makes up most of the auditor's activities on an audit.

As our analogy between building survey and auditing illustrates, the evidence gathered by the auditor must relate to 'assertions about economic actions and events'. The auditor compares the evidence gathered to assertions about economic activity in order to assess 'the degree of correspondence between those assertions and established criteria'. While numerous sets of criteria are available for measuring the degree of correspondence in various settings, a financial reporting framework such as the International Financial Reporting Standards (IFRS)[v] serves as the auditor's basis for assessing management's assertions in the context of a financial statement audit.

The last important phrase, 'communicating the results to interested users', is concerned with the type of report the auditor provides to the intended users. In financial statement audits, very specific types of reports are prescribed by auditing standards to communicate the auditor's findings. We briefly introduce audit reports later in this chapter.

Assurance

Auditors have a reputation for independence and objectivity. As a result, various users in the past requested that auditors provide assurance on information beyond historical financial information, but traditional auditing standards did not provide for such services. The international standard setters responded to this demand by establishing a framework for assurance engagements and standards for non-audit assurance engagements.

An assurance engagement is defined as follows:

> An **assurance engagement** *is an engagement in which a practitioner expresses a conclusion designed to enhance the degree of confidence of the intended users other than the responsible party about the outcome of the evaluation or measurement of a subject matter against criteria.*[vi]

Because assurance engagements also include other engagements than audits, the term *practitioner* is used instead of auditor. The definition of an assurance engagement is broader than the one previously discussed for an audit. The *subject matter* of an assurance engagement may take many forms, including an entity's financial or non-financial performance (e.g. environmental performance) or performance of systems and processes (e.g. effectiveness of internal control). However, the practitioner's role is similar to that in an audit; he or she must determine the correspondence of the subject matter information to criteria. The subject matter information is the outcome of the evaluation or measurement of the subject matter, for example an entity's published environmental report. Criteria are the benchmarks used to evaluate or measure the subject matter, for example established guidelines for environmental reporting. The practitioner gathers sufficient appropriate evidence to provide a reasonable basis for expressing a conclusion on the subject matter information in an assurance report. The intended users are those for whom the practitioner prepares the assurance report. Before you continue, consider the following questions. What are the subject matter information and the criteria in a financial statement audit? Which party is responsible for subject matter information in an audit?

This text focuses primarily on financial statement auditing because it represents the major assurance service offered by audit firms. In addition, in many instances, the approach, concepts, methods and techniques used for financial statement audits also apply to other assurance engagements. The reader should keep in mind that a financial statement audit is a specialized form of assurance engagement. Chapter 20 covers in detail assurance engagements beyond financial statements audits.

❖ FUNDAMENTAL CONCEPTS IN CONDUCTING A FINANCIAL STATEMENT AUDIT

LO5

Figure 1–2 presents a simplified overview of the process for a financial statement audit. The auditor gathers evidence about the business transactions that have occurred ('economic activity and events') and about management (the preparer of the financial statements). The auditor uses this evidence to compare the assertions contained in the financial statements to the criteria used by management in preparing them (i.e. the **applicable financial reporting framework** such as IFRSs). The auditor's report communicates to the user the degree of correspondence between the assertions and the criteria.

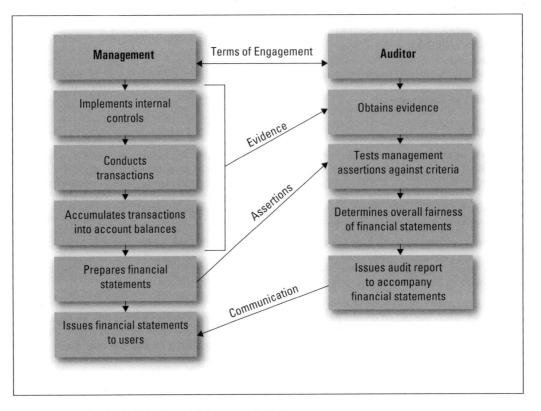

Figure 1–2 An Overview of the Financial Statement Audit Process

The conceptual and procedural details of a financial statement audit build on three fundamental concepts: audit risk, materiality and evidence relating to management's **financial statement assertions**. The auditor's assessments of audit risk and materiality influence the nature, timing, and extent of the audit work to be performed (referred to as the *scope* of the audit). This section briefly discusses the concepts of audit risk, materiality and evidence. Chapters 3 and 4 cover these concepts in greater depth.

Audit Risk

The first major concept involved in auditing is audit risk, which is the risk that the auditor may give an unmodified ('clean') opinion on financial statements that are materially misstated.

> **Audit risk** *is the risk that the auditor expresses an inappropriate audit opinion when the financial statements are materially misstated.*[vii]

The auditor's report states that the audit provides only reasonable assurance that the financial statements do not contain material misstatements. The term reasonable assurance implies some risk that a material misstatement could be present in the financial statements and the auditor will fail to detect it. The auditor plans and conducts the audit to achieve an acceptably low level of audit risk. The auditor controls the level of audit risk by the effectiveness and extent of the audit work conducted. The more effective and extensive the audit work, the lower the risk that a misstatement will go undetected and that the auditor will issue an inappropriate report. However, the concept of reasonable assurance means that an auditor could conduct an audit in accordance with professional auditing standards and issue an unmodified opinion, and the financial statements might still contain material misstatements. A building surveyor cannot absolutely guarantee the absence of problems without taking apart a house board by board, which of course is highly impractical. Similarly, due to cost considerations and the sheer impossibility of investigating every item reflected in an entity's financial statements, the risk that an auditor will mistakenly issue an unmodified opinion on financial statements that are in fact materially misstated cannot be driven to zero. Even careful and competent auditors can offer only reasonable, rather than absolute, assurance.

Practice Insight 1.1

Auditors must understand the risks associated with rapidly changing technology and how those risks apply to a given client. For example, audit risk may be different for a client with a sophisticated electronic business system than for a client with a traditional accounting information system. Professional expertise and judgement are critical when evaluating the technologies and systems used by the audit client.

Materiality

The second major concept involved in auditing is **materiality**. The auditor's consideration of materiality is a matter of **professional judgement**. It reflects the auditor's perception of the financial information needs of users of the financial statements. The international standards on auditing refer to the materiality concept as follows:

> **Misstatements**, *including omissions, are considered to be material if they, individually or in the aggregate, could reasonably be expected to influence the economic decisions of users taken on the basis of the financial statements. Judgements about materiality are made in light of surrounding circumstances, and are affected by the size or nature of a misstatement, or a combination of both.*[viii]

The focus is on the users of the financial statements. In planning the engagement, the auditor assesses the magnitude of a misstatement that may affect the users' decisions. This assessment helps the auditor determine the nature, timing and extent of audit procedures. Relating the concept of materiality to our building surveyor analogy is rather intuitive – a building surveyor will not validate the remaining life of lightbulbs or thoroughly test every cabinet hinge or drawer glide. These items are not critical to the buyer's decision.

While determining materiality is influenced by a number of factors, a common rule of thumb is that total (aggregated) misstatements of more than 5 per cent of profit (net income) before tax would cause financial statements to be materially misstated. Suppose the auditor decides that the financial statements of a client can be materially misstated if total misstatements exceed €400,000. The auditor would design audit procedures to test accounts to a sufficient level of detail. When testing is complete for all accounts, the auditor will issue an unmodified audit opinion if the uncorrected misstatements in all the accounts in total add up to less than overall materiality of €400,000.

As we shall see later in this chapter, the wording of the auditor's report with an unmodified opinion includes the phrase 'the financial statements present fairly *in all material respects*'. This is the manner in which the auditor communicates the notion of materiality to the users of the auditor's report. Keep in mind, as we explained in connection with the concept of audit risk, there can be no guarantee that the auditor will uncover *all* material misstatements. The auditor can only provide **reasonable assurance** that all material misstatements are detected; in the context of financial statement auditing, reasonable assurance has been defined to mean a high, but not absolute level of assurance. The auditor provides no assurance that immaterial misstatements will be detected.

Evidence Regarding Management Assertions

The third major concept involved in auditing is *evidence regarding management's assertions*. Most of the auditor's work in arriving at an opinion on the financial statements consists of obtaining and evaluating evidence. Chapters 2 and 4 contain more detail about the specific assertions relevant to financial statement auditing. **Audit evidence** consists of the underlying accounting data and any additional information available to the auditor, whether originating from the client or externally.[ix]

As illustrated earlier in our discussion about EarthWear, management's assertions are used as a framework to guide the collection of audit evidence. The assertions, in conjunction with the assessment of materiality and audit risk, are used by the auditor to determine the nature, timing and extent of evidence to be gathered. Once the auditor has obtained sufficient appropriate evidence that the management assertions can be relied upon for each significant account and disclosure, reasonable assurance is provided that the financial statements are fairly presented.

In obtaining and evaluating the appropriateness of audit evidence, the auditor is concerned with the relevance and reliability of the evidence. *Relevance* refers to whether the evidence relates to the specific management assertion being tested. *Reliability* refers to the diagnosticity of the evidence. In other words, can a particular type of evidence be relied upon to signal the true state of the account balance or assertion being examined? Using the building surveyor example, inspecting the foundations of a house would not give us relevant evidence about whether the roof leaks. Likewise, the seller's opinion of the home's roof would not be as reliable as that of the surveyor, because the seller has an incentive to deceive the buyer.

The auditor seldom has the luxury of obtaining completely convincing evidence about the true state of a particular assertion. In most situations, the auditor is able to obtain only enough evidence to be persuaded that the assertion is fairly stated. Additionally, for many parts of an audit, the auditor examines only a sample of the transactions processed during the period.

❖ SAMPLING: INFERENCES BASED ON LIMITED OBSERVATIONS

LO6

You might ask why the auditor relies on concepts such as audit risk and materiality in designing an audit. Why not test all transactions that occurred during the period so that audit risk can be driven to zero, even for immaterial misstatements? The main reason is the cost and feasibility of such an audit. In a small business, the auditor might be able to examine all transactions that occurred during the period and still issue the audit report in a reasonable amount of time. However, it is unlikely that the owner of the business could afford to pay for such an extensive audit. For a large organization, the sheer volume of transactions, which might well reach into the millions, prevents the auditor from examining every transaction. Thus, just as with a building surveyor, there is a trade-off between the exactness or precision of the audit and its cost.

To deal with the problem of not being able to examine every transaction, the auditor uses (1) his or her knowledge about the transactions and/or (2) a sampling approach to examine a subset of the transactions. Many times the auditor is aware of items in an account balance that are likely to contain misstatements based on previous audits, a solid understanding of the client's internal control system or knowledge of the client's industry. For example, the auditor's prior knowledge may indicate that transactions with certain types of customers are relatively likely to contain misstatements. The auditor can use this knowledge to specifically select those transactions (e.g. specific accounts receivable) for examination. When the auditor has no special knowledge about which particular transactions or items may be misstated, he or she uses sampling procedures that increase the likelihood of obtaining a sample that is *representative* of the population of transactions or account items. In such cases, the auditor uses the laws of probability to make inferences about potential misstatements based on examining a sample of transactions or items.

The size of the auditor's sample is a function of materiality and desired level of assurance for the account or assertion being examined. There is an *inverse* relation between sample size and materiality, and a direct relation between sample size and desired level of assurance. For example, if an auditor assesses materiality for an account to be a small amount, a larger sample will be needed than if materiality were a larger amount. This occurs because the auditor must gather more evidence (a larger sample) to have a reasonable likelihood of detecting smaller errors. You can think of materiality as the 'fineness of the auditor's filter'. A lower materiality amount requires the auditor to use a finer filter in order to detect smaller errors, and it takes more work to create a finer filter. Similarly, as the desired level of assurance increases for a given materiality amount, the sample size necessary to test an assertion becomes greater.

❖ THE AUDIT PROCESS

LO7

This section provides an overview of how auditors go about the process of auditing financial statements and then presents the major phases that the auditor performs during a financial statement audit. Later chapters provide detailed coverage of the process and the phases of the audit.

Overview of the Financial Statement Auditing Process

Consider the auditor's task from a logical perspective. The end product of a financial statement auditor's work is an audit opinion indicating whether or not the client's financial statements are free of material misstatement. What might an auditor do to obtain the information needed to develop and support that opinion? The auditor must first obtain a thorough understanding of the client, its business and its industry. The auditor must understand the risks the client faces, how it is dealing with those risks, and what remaining risks are most likely to result in a material misstatement in the financial statements. Armed with this understanding, the auditor plans procedures that will produce evidence helpful in developing and supporting an opinion on the financial statements.

To understand this process intuitively, consider what financial statements are made of. From your financial accounting courses, you know that accounting systems capture, record and summarize individual transactions. Entities, of course, must design and implement controls to ensure that those transactions are initiated, captured, recorded and summarized appropriately. These individual transactions are grouped and summarized into various account balances and, finally, financial statements are formed by organizing meaningful collections of those account balances. We have just identified three stages in the accounting process that take place in the preparation of financial statements: *internal controls* are implemented to ensure appropriate capturing and recording of *individual transactions*, which are then collected into ending *account balances*. This summary might seem like an oversimplification, but it will help you understand the stages of a client's accounting process on which auditors focus to collect evidence.

Keep in mind that the auditor's job ultimately is to express an opinion on *whether the financial statements are fairly stated*. It makes sense, then, that the auditor can design procedures to collect *direct* information about the ending account balances that make up the financial statements. For example, an auditor might confirm the ending balance of the cash account by contacting the client's bank, or the auditor might verify the ending balance of the inventory account by physically examining individual inventory items that make up the ending balance. But, remember, account balances are made up of *individual transactions* that occurred over the past year (or beyond). If the auditor designs procedures to test whether the transactions were actually captured and handled properly, the auditor can obtain indirect information about whether the ending account balances are likely to be fairly stated. This information is clearly one step removed from the ending account balances themselves. But we can even back up one more step. If the auditor designs procedures to test whether the entity's *internal control* over financial transactions is effective, the auditor can obtain additional indirect information regarding whether the account balances are fairly stated. Take a moment to think through the logic in this last step; if controls are effective, then the transactions will probably be captured and summarized properly, which means in turn that the account balances are likely to be free of material misstatement. Thus, information about internal control is even more indirect than information about transactions, but it is useful information nonetheless! In fact, while it is indirect, evidence about internal control is usually a relatively cost-effective form of audit evidence.

In summary, the auditor can collect evidence in each of three different stages in a client's accounting system to help determine whether the financial statements are fairly stated: (1) *the internal control* put in place by the client to ensure proper handling of transactions (e.g. evaluate and test the controls); (2) the *transactions* that affect each account balance (e.g. examine a sample of the transactions that happened during the period); and (3) the ending *account balances* themselves (e.g. examine a sample of the items that make up an ending account balance at year end). Evidence that relates directly to ending account balances is usually the highest quality, but also the costliest evidence. Thus, an auditor will usually rely on a combination of evidence from all three stages in forming an audit opinion regarding the fairness of the financial statements. On which of these three areas it is best to focus depends on the circumstances, and this is generally left to the auditor's discretion. Chapter 4 addresses in more detail the types of procedures and types of evidence available to the auditor.

Major Phases of the Audit

The audit process can be broken down into a number of audit phases (see Figure 1–3). While the figure suggests that these phases are sequential, they are actually quite iterative and interrelated in nature. Phases often include audit procedures designed for one purpose that provide evidence for other purposes, and sometimes audit procedures accomplish purposes in more than one phase. Figure 1–3 shows the specific chapters where each of these phases is discussed in detail.

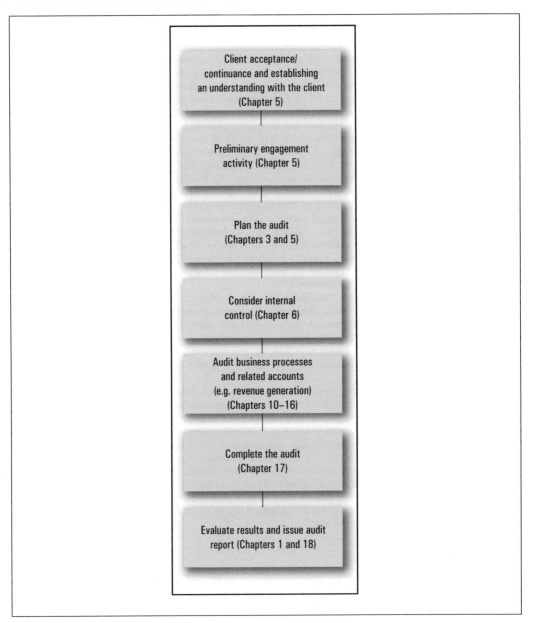

Figure 1–3 Major Phases of an Audit

Client Acceptance/Continuance and Establishing an Understanding with the Client

Professional standards require that audit firms establish policies and procedures for deciding whether to accept new clients and to retain current clients. The purpose of such policies is to minimize the likelihood that an auditor will be associated with clients who lack integrity. If an auditor is associated with a client who lacks integrity, the risk increases that material misstatements may exist and not be detected by the auditor. This can lead to lawsuits brought by users of the financial statements. For a prospective new client, auditors would ordinarily confer with the predecessor auditor and frequently conduct background checks on top management. The knowledge that the auditor gathers during the acceptance/continuance process provides valuable understanding of the entity and its environment, thus helping the auditor assess risk and plan the audit. Once the acceptance/continuance decision has been made, the auditor establishes an understanding with the client regarding the services to be performed and the terms of the engagement. Such terms would include, for example, the responsibilities of each party, the assistance to be provided by client personnel and internal auditors, the timing of the engagement and the expected audit fees.

Preliminary Engagement Activities

There are generally two preliminary engagement activities: (1) determining the audit engagement team requirements and (2) ensuring that the audit firm and engagement team are in compliance with ethical requirements, including being independent of the entity subject to the audit.

The auditor starts by updating his or her understanding of the entity and its environment. The auditor's understanding of the entity and its environment should include information about each of the following categories:

- Industry, regulatory and other external factors.
- Nature of the entity.
- Accounting policies.
- Objectives, strategies and related business risks.
- Financial performance measures.
- Internal control.

Because the understanding of the entity and its environment is used to assess the **risk of material misstatement** and to set the scope of the audit, the auditor should perform risk assessment procedures to support that understanding (e.g. inquiring of personnel, reading business plans and strategies).

The engagement partner or manager ensures that the audit team is composed of team members who have the appropriate audit and industry experience for the engagement. The partner or manager also determines whether the audit will require information technology (IT) or other types of experts (e.g. actuaries or appraisers).

The independence of the auditor from the client in terms of freedom from prohibited relationships that might threaten the auditor's objectivity must also be established up front. Chapter 5 addresses the preliminary engagement activities of the audit process in more detail.

Plan the Audit

Proper planning is important to ensure that the audit is conducted in an effective and efficient manner. In order to plan the audit properly, the audit team must make a preliminary assessment of the client's business risks and determine materiality. The audit team relies on these judgements to then assess risk relating to the likelihood of material misstatements in the financial statements. Chapter 3 discusses both of these concepts.

In planning the audit, the auditor should be guided by (1) the procedures performed to gain and document an understanding of the entity and (2) the results of the risk assessment process. As part of the planning process, the auditor may conduct preliminary analytical procedures (such as ratio analysis) to identify specific transactions or account balances that should receive special attention due to an increased risk of material misstatement. Audit planning should take into account the auditor's understanding of the entity's internal control system (discussed next). The outcome of the auditor's planning process is a written plan that sets forth the overall audit strategy and the nature, extent and timing of the audit work. Chapters 3 and 5 cover the issues that are involved in this phase of the audit.

Consider Internal Control

Internal control is designed and affected by an entity's board of directors or other body charged with governance, management and other personnel to provide reasonable assurance regarding the achievement of objectives in the following categories: (1) reliability of financial reporting; (2) effectiveness and efficiency of operations; and (3) compliance with applicable laws and regulations. When obtaining an understanding of the entity and its environment, the auditor should gain an understanding of internal control to help the auditor assess risk and identify areas where financial statements might be misstated. Chapter 6 provides detailed coverage of internal control in a financial statement audit. Later chapters apply the process of considering internal control in the context of various business processes.

Practice Insight 1.2

In the USA the Sarbanes–Oxley Act of 2002 was passed in response to a series of business scandals (e.g. Enron and WorldCom). The Act requires the auditor to report on public companies' internal control over financial reporting. Because of its relevance for many international auditing practices, Chapter 7 in the book covers the details of this USA-specific requirement. The purpose of an audit in accordance with the International Standards on Auditing is, however, *not* to express an opinion on the effectiveness of the internal control over financial reporting control.

Audit Business Processes and Related Accounts

The auditor typically assesses the risk of material misstatement by examining the entity's business processes or accounting cycles (e.g. purchasing process or revenue process). The auditor then determines the audit procedures that are necessary to reduce the risk of material misstatement to a low level for the financial statement accounts affected by a particular business process. Individual audit procedures are directed towards specific assertions in the account balances that are likely to be misstated. For example, if the auditor is concerned about the possibility of obsolete inventory, the auditor could conduct lower-of-cost-or-value tests to determine if the inventory on hand is properly valued. On most engagements, actually conducting the planned audit tests comprises most of the time spent on a financial statement audit.

Complete the Audit

After the auditor has finished gathering evidence relating to financial statement assertions, the sufficiency of the evidence gathered is evaluated. The auditor must obtain sufficient appropriate evidence in order to reach and justify a conclusion on the fairness of the financial statements. In this phase, the auditor also assesses the possibility of contingent liabilities, such as lawsuits, and searches for any events subsequent to the balance sheet date that may impact the financial statements. Chapter 17 covers each of these issues in detail.

Evaluate Results and Issue Audit Report

LO8

The final phase in the audit process is to evaluate results and choose the appropriate audit report to issue. The audit report, also referred to as the audit opinion, is the main product or output of the audit. Just as the report of a building surveyor communicates the surveyor's findings to a prospective buyer, the audit report communicates the auditor's findings to the users of the financial statements.

During and at the completion of the audit, the auditor requests the client to correct the identified misstatements. If at the end of the audit any remaining uncorrected misstatements are judged to be material, the auditor issues an audit report that expresses and explains that the financial statements are materially misstated. If the uncorrected misstatements do not cause the financial statements to be materially misstated, the auditor may issue an audit report with an unmodified (i.e. 'clean') opinion. In this context, *unmodified* means that because the auditor has concluded that the financial statements are free from material misstatements, the auditor does not find it necessary to *modify* his or her opinion about the fairness of the financial statements.

The Audit Report with an Unmodified Opinion

The audit report with an **unmodified opinion** is by far the most common type of report issued. While it is fairly common for the auditor to find misstatements needing correction, audit clients are ordinarily willing to make the necessary adjustments to receive a 'clean' opinion. Exhibit 1–1 presents an audit report issued on EarthWear Clothiers' consolidated financial statements. The left margin refers to the standard elements of an audit report with an unmodified opinion.

Exhibit 1–1	The Auditor's Report with an Unmodified Opinion
Title:	INDEPENDENT AUDITOR'S REPORT
Addressee:	*To the Shareholders of EarthWear Clothiers*
Introductory paragraph:	We have audited the accompanying consolidated financial statements of EarthWear Clothiers and its subsidiaries, which comprise the consolidated balance sheet as at 31 December 2009, and the consolidated income statement, statement of changes in equity and cash flow statement for the year then ended, and a summary of significant accounting policies and other explanatory information.
Management's responsibility paragraph:	*Management's Responsibility for the Consolidated Financial Statements* Management is responsible for the preparation and fair presentation of these consolidated financial statements in accordance with International Financial Reporting Standards, and for such internal control as management determines is necessary to enable the preparation of consolidated financial statements that are free from material misstatement, whether due to fraud or error.
Auditor's responsibility paragraph:	*Auditor's Responsibility* Our responsibility is to express an opinion on these consolidated financial statements based on our audit. We conducted our audit in accordance with International Standards on Auditing. Those standards require that we comply with ethical requirements and plan and perform the audit to obtain reasonable assurance about whether the consolidated financial statements are free from material misstatement. An audit involves performing procedures to obtain audit evidence about the amounts and disclosures in the consolidated financial statements. The procedures selected depend on the auditor's judgement, including the assessment of the risks of material misstatement of the consolidated financial statements, whether due to fraud or error. In making those risk assessments, the auditor considers internal control relevant to the entity's preparation and fair presentation of the consolidated financial statements in order to design audit procedures that are appropriate in the circumstances, but not for the purpose of expressing an opinion on the effectiveness of the entity's internal control. An audit also includes evaluating the appropriateness of accounting policies used and the reasonableness of accounting estimates made by management, as well as evaluating the overall presentation of the consolidated financial statements. We believe that the audit evidence we have obtained is sufficient and appropriate to provide a basis for our audit opinion.
Auditor's opinion paragraph:	*Opinion* In our opinion, the consolidated financial statements present fairly, in all material respects, the financial position of EarthWear Clothiers and its subsidiaries as at 31 December 2009, and their financial performance and cash flows for the year then ended in accordance with International Financial Reporting Standards.
Auditor's signature:	Willis & Adams International *M. J. Willis* M. J. Willis, Partner
Date of the auditor's report:	15 February 2010
Auditor's address:	Europolis

Take a moment to read through the report. You will see that the title refers to the independence of the auditor issuing the audit report. The report is addressed to the individual or group that is the intended recipient of the report. The body of the report begins with an introductory paragraph indicating the financial statements covered by the report. The second paragraph states that the preparation and fair presentation of the financial statements in accordance with the International Financial Reporting Standards are the responsibility of management.

In the third paragraph the auditor states that his or her responsibility is to express an opinion on the financial statements based on the audit, and communicates to the users, in very general terms, what an audit entails. In addition, to convey to users that the audit was conducted in accordance with the International Standards on Auditing, including compliance with ethical requirements, it emphasizes the fact that the audit provides only reasonable assurance that the financial statements contain no material misstatements. The paragraph communicates that the procedures selected to obtain evidence depend on the auditor's judgements. This includes assessments of the risks of material misstatements and considerations of internal control relevant to a financial statement audit in making these assessments. The paragraph also discloses that the audit covers an evaluation of the appropriateness of accounting policies and the reasonableness of accounting estimates, as well as an evaluation of the overall financial statement presentation. Finally, the paragraph asserts the auditor's belief that the audit evidence obtained provides a basis for the audit opinion.

The fourth paragraph contains the auditor's opinion concerning the fairness of the financial statements based on the audit evidence. Note two important phrases contained in this paragraph. First, the phrase 'present fairly … in accordance with International Financial Reporting Standards' indicates the criteria against which the auditor assesses management assertions. Second, the opinion paragraph contains the phrase 'in all material respects', emphasizing the concept of materiality.

Finally, the audit report is signed, dated and the auditor's address is disclosed. The date of the auditor's report informs the reader that the auditor has considered the effect of events and transactions of which the auditor became aware and that occurred up to that date.

An audit report may sometimes after the opinion paragraph include a paragraph that draws the user's attention to a specific matter that does not affect the auditor's opinion. For example, the auditor may add an emphasis of matter paragraph to highlight the disclosure in the financial statements of the existence of a material uncertainty about the entity's ability to continue as a going concern. In Chapter 18, you will learn more about such additional communication to users in the audit report.

Audit Reports with Modified Opinion

For an audit opinion to be unmodified (i.e. 'clean') there must be no limitations imposed on the auditor's procedures to obtain sufficient appropriate evidence *or* departure from the applicable financial reporting framework that cause the financial statements to be materially misstated. If the financial statements are materially misstated, the auditor issues an audit report with a modified opinion. The report appropriately conveys to the reader the nature of the opinion and the reasons why the opinion is modified.

For example, suppose a client's financial statements contain a misstatement that the auditor considers material and the client refuses to correct the misstatement. The auditor will likely *modify* the opinion, expressing that the financial statements are fairly presented *except for* the misstatement identified by the auditor. If the significance of the effect on the financial statements of the material misstatement, however, is pervasive, the auditor will issue an audit report with an *adverse* opinion, indicating that the *financial statements are not presented fairly* and should not be relied upon. Similar types of opinions are available to the auditor when the modified opinion is caused by the auditor's inability to obtain sufficient appropriate evidence to conclude on the financial statements. While it is important for you to be familiar with the basic elements of the audit report as part of understanding an overview of the audit process, we cover the different types of financial statement audit reports in detail in Chapter 18. Our experience is that students find it more intuitive to learn the fundamental concepts of auditing and how an audit is conducted before being immersed in the details of audit reporting.

The audit report represents the culmination of the audit process and is the auditor's primary venue for communicating his or her opinion about a client's financial statements with outside parties. An example of an audit report with an unmodified ('clean') opinion (Exhibit 1–1) is included in this chapter to give you a basic idea of what the most common type of audit report looks like.

❖ CONCLUSION

LO9

You can see from this chapter that a good financial statement auditor needs to understand not only accounting but also the concepts and techniques of gathering and evaluating evidence to assess management's financial statement assertions. In addition, an auditor needs a deep understanding of business in general, as well as of the specific industries in which his or her clients operate. This is why professionals with auditing experience frequently have attractive opportunities to move into other areas of business and management. Chief executive officers, business owners, chief financial officers, consultants and controllers are often former auditors.

This chapter is designed to help you develop an intuitive understanding of basic auditing concepts. As you study auditing, you will need to commit some details to memory. But you will understand and appreciate the details of the auditing process much more fully if you have a good grasp of the underlying concepts – why financial statement auditing is in demand, what it is, and the basic process by which it is carried out.

Keep in mind that auditing is a fundamentally logical process of thinking and reasoning – do not hesitate to exercise your common sense and reasoning skills! You will benefit much more from your reading of this text if you study it with a reasoning, inquisitive approach, rather than merely attempting to memorize details. As you learn new auditing concepts, take some time to understand the underlying logic and how the concepts interrelate with other concepts. As you learn about auditing procedures, ask yourself how and why the procedure might yield relevant evidence, and try to think of other ways you might obtain useful evidence. Rote memorization alone is not a good way to study auditing!

Being a good auditor sometimes requires imagination and innovation. For example, an auditor was faced with figuring out how to verify a client's assertion regarding the existence of an inventory. The problem was that the 'inventory' consisted of thousands of head of tame reindeer grazing on a mountain plateau covering hundreds of square kilometres. There was no standard procedure manual for the auditor to refer to – he simply had to figure out an effective and efficient way to obtain persuasive evidence that the reindeer existed in the numbers asserted by the herd's management.

In the end, the auditor decided to charter a small aeroplane to fly over the mountain plateau and take photographs. The auditor was able to obtain a count of the reindeer from the photos. He also evaluated veterinary records to see if the number of required annual vaccinations approximated the number of reindeer counted in the photographs. Finally, he did some calculations based on average calf birth and death rates, taking into account recorded purchases and sales of reindeer during the year. Using this combination of procedures, the auditor was able to obtain persuasive evidence supporting management's assertion regarding inventory (and got an aeroplane ride in the process!).

We hope this example helps illustrate why you will need to approach the study of auditing differently from that of most other accounting courses. As you learn the concepts and techniques of auditing, you are not only acquiring the tools to become an effective financial statement auditor but also a conceptual tool kit that can be useful to you in many different settings and contexts.

❶ Key Terms

Applicable financial reporting framework. The financial reporting framework adopted in the preparation of the financial statements.

Assurance engagement. An engagement in which a practitioner expresses a conclusion designed to enhance the degree of confidence of the intended users other than the responsible party about the outcome of the evaluation or measurement of a subject matter against criteria.

Audit evidence. All the information used by the auditor in arriving at the conclusions on which the audit opinion is based, and includes the information contained in the accounting records underlying the financial statements and other information.

Audit risk. The risk that the auditor expresses an inappropriate audit opinion when the financial statements are materially misstated.

Auditing. A systematic process of: (1) objectively obtaining and evaluating evidence regarding assertions about economic actions and events to ascertain the degree of correspondence between those assertions and established criteria; and (2) communicating the results to interested users.

Financial statement assertions. Representations by management, explicit or otherwise, that are embodied in the financial statements.

Information asymmetry. The concept that the manager generally has more information about the true financial position and results of operations of the entity than the absentee owner does.

Materiality. Misstatements, including omissions, that individually or in the aggregate, could reasonably be expected to influence the economic decisions of users taken on the basis of the financial statements. Judgements about materiality are made in light of surrounding circumstances, and are affected by the size or nature of a misstatement, or a combination of both.

Misstatement. A difference between the amount, classification, presentation or disclosure of a reported financial statement item and the amount, classification, presentation or disclosure that is required for the item to be in accordance with the applicable financial reporting framework. Misstatements can arise from error or fraud.

Professional judgement. The application of relevant training, knowledge and experience, within the context provided by auditing, accounting and ethical standards, in making informed decisions about the courses of action that are appropriate in the circumstances of the audit engagement.

Reasonable assurance. The concept that an audit done in accordance with auditing standards may fail to detect a material misstatement in a client's financial statements. In an auditing context this term has been defined to mean a high, but not absolute level of assurance.

Risk of material misstatement. The risk that the entity's financial statements will contain a material misstatement whether caused by error or fraud.

Unmodified opinion. The auditor's opinion that the financial statements present fairly, in all material respects, in accordance with the applicable financial reporting framework (i.e. a 'clean' opinion).

? Review Questions

LO1 1–1 Why is studying auditing different from studying other accounting topics? How might understanding auditing concepts prove useful for consultants, business managers and other business decision makers?

LO2 1–2 Discuss why there is a demand for auditing services in a free-market economy. What evidence suggests that auditing would be demanded even if it were not required by government regulation?

LO2 1–3 Why are there natural conflicts of interest in the agency relationship between the manager and the absentee owner?

LO3 1–4 Why is independence such an important standard for auditors? How does independence relate to the agency relationship between owners and managers?

LO4 1–5 Define *auditing* and an *assurance engagement*.

LO4 1–6 What does the phrase 'systematic process' mean in the definition of auditing?

LO5 1–7 Define *audit risk* and *materiality*. How are these concepts reflected in the auditor's report?

LO6 1–8 Briefly describe why on most audit engagements an auditor tests only a sample of the transactions that occurred.

LO7 1–9 What are the major phases of an audit?

LO7 1–10 The auditor's understanding of the entity and its environment should include knowledge of which categories of information?

LO8 1–11 Identify the elements of the audit report with an unmodified opinion.

LO9 1–12 Briefly discuss why auditors must often exercise creativity and innovation in auditing financial statements. Give an example different from the one offered in the text.

✎ Problems

LO1,2,3 1–13 You recently attended your five-year university reunion. At the main reception, you encountered an old friend, Lee Larsen, who recently graduated from law school and is now practising with a large law firm in town. When you told him that you were an independent auditor and employed by a regional audit firm, he made the following statement: 'You know, if a legal audit requirement did not exist, no one would be interested in having an audit performed. You auditors are just creatures of regulation.'

Required:

Draft a memo that highlights your thoughts about Lee's statement that auditors are 'creatures of regulation'. Be sure to consider relevant evidence of a demand for auditing services outside of legal and regulatory requirements in your memo, and focus on the value that auditing provides.

LO2,3 1–14 Greenbloom Garden Centres is a small, privately held corporation that has two stores. The Greenbloom family owns 100 per cent of the company's stock, and family members manage the operations. Sales at the company's stores have been growing rapidly, and there appears to be a market for the company's sales concept – providing bulk garden equipment and supplies at low prices. The controller prepares the company's financial statements, which are not audited. The company has no debt but is considering expanding to other cities. Such expansion may require long-term borrowings and is likely to reduce the family's day-to-day control of the operations. The family does not intend to sell stock in the company.

Required:

Discuss the factors that may make an audit necessary and potentially valuable for the company. Be sure to consider the concept of information risk.

LO3,5   1–15   You were recently hired by the audit firm of Honson & Hansen. Within two weeks, you were sent to the first-year staff training course. The instructor asked you to prepare answers to the following questions.

a How is audit evidence defined?
b How should audit evidence relate to assertions and to the audit report?
c What characteristics of evidence should an auditor be concerned with when searching for and evaluating audit evidence?

LO7   1–16   John Josephs, an audit manager for Tip, Acanoe & Tylerto, was asked to speak at a dinner meeting of the local Small Business Association. The president of the association has suggested that he talk about the various phases of the audit process. John has asked you, his trusted assistant, to prepare an outline for his speech. He suggests that you answer the following.

a List and describe the various phases of an audit.
b Describe how audit procedures designed for one purpose might provide evidence for other purposes. Give an example.
c One of the phases involves understanding an entity's internal control. Why might the members of the association be particularly interested in the work conducted by auditors in this phase of the audit?

LO8   1–17   Using the audit report included in Chapter 1, identify and record the phrases or words that indicate to the users that the audited financial statements are not an 'exact' representation of the results of operations and financial position of a company.

Discussion Case

LO1,3,5,8,9   1–18   In a report, the Office of Auditor General gave the following results based on an examination of seven banks in financial difficulties.

The early warning system provided by bank reporting to regulators is seriously flawed. The quarterly reports of the seven banks with financial difficulties did not provide the regulators with sufficiently advance warning of the true magnitude of the deterioration in the banks' financial condition. By 1 July loss reserves should have been increased from €0.5 billion to €2.4 billion. A major portion of the €1.9 billion deterioration in asset values was not reported because deficiencies in the financial reporting framework allowed bank management to unduly delay the recognition of losses and mask the need for early regulatory intervention.

None of the seven failed banks did obtain an independent audit of their quarterly reports. Without an audit of such reports, a troubled institution's management can more easily delay warning and conceal its financial difficulties.

The corporate governance system upon which successful regulation depends is seriously flawed. Of the seven banks, six had serious internal control problems that contributed significantly to their losses. Had these problems been corrected, the losses could have been prevented or limited.

Audits of quarterly reports would improve early warning of financial difficulties. In addition, the roles of both management and the auditors would be strengthened if they were required to assume responsibility for assessing and reporting on the condition of internal control, a significant cause of bank failures.

Required:

Describe in one or two concise, informative paragraphs how audits of the quarterly reports by external auditors could have prevented or limited the losses incurred.

 Internet Assignments

LO8 1–19   Many companies post their financial statements and auditor's report on their home pages, generally under a heading labelled 'investor relations'. Use one of the Internet search engines to do the following:

a Search the World Wide Web for the home page of one or more companies and review their financial statements, including their auditor's reports. Identify the auditing standards followed by the companies' auditors. For example, BMW's home page (www.bmwgroup.com) allows a visitor to download the financial statements as a .pdf file.
b Compare the audit report for company (e.g. BMW) with the EarthWear's audit report in Exhibit 1–1.

LO1,9 1–20   Using an Internet browser, identify five Internet sites that contain accounting or auditing resources. For each site identified, prepare a brief summary of the types of information that are available. For example, the International Federation of Accountants' (IFAC) home page (www.ifac.org) contains extensive information on the organization's activities.

Notes

i   See G.L. Sundem, R.E. Dukes and J.A. Elliott, *The Value of Information and Audits*, Coopers & Lybrand, New York, 1996, for a more detailed discussion of the demand for accounting information and auditing.
ii   G.J. Costouros, 'Auditing in the Athenian State of the Golden Age (500–300 BC)', *The Accounting Historian Journal* (Spring 1978), pp. 41–50.
iii   See M. Chatfield, *A History of Accounting Thought*, Dryden Press, Hinsdale, IL, 1974, for a discussion of the historical development of accounting and auditing. For more on the birth of auditing and development of audit regulation in European countries see R. Quick, S. Turley and M. Willekens (eds), *Auditing, Trust and Governance – Developing Regulation in Europe*, Routledge, Oxford, 2008.
iv   American Accounting Association, Committee on Basic Auditing Concepts, *A Statement of Basic Auditing Concepts*, AAA, Sarasota, FL, 1973.
v   The International Accounting Standards Board (IASB) publishes standards in a series of pronouncements called International Financial Reporting Standards (IFRSs). The IASB has also adopted the body of international accounting standards issued by its predecessor standard-setting body the International Accounting Standards Committee (IASC). Those pronouncements continue to be designated International Accounting Standards (IASs). When this book refers to a specific financial reporting framework it refers to international accounting standards, i.e. IFRSs/IASs.
vi   International Auditing and Assurance Standards Board (IAASB), *International Framework for Assurance Engagements*, 2009.
vii   International Standard on Auditing (ISA) 200, *Overall Objectives of the Independent Auditor and the Conduct of an Audit in Accordance with International Standards on Auditing*.
viii   International Standard on Auditing (ISA) 320, *Materiality in Planning and Performing an Audit*.
ix   International Standard on Auditing (ISA) 500, *Audit Evidence*.

EarthWear
2009

Annual Report

Company History and Operations

EarthWear Clothiers was founded in Europolis, by Tor Engan and Calvin Rogers in 1993 to make high-quality clothing for outdoor sports, such as hiking, skiing, fly-fishing, and white-water kayaking. Over the years, the company's product lines have grown to include casual clothing, accessories, shoes and soft luggage. EarthWear offers its products through three retailing options: catalogues; retail outlets; and its website.

The company strives to provide excellent, high-quality products at reasonable prices. EarthWear has a commitment to excellence in customer service and an unconditional guarantee. The company is also conscious of its environmental responsibilities. All company facilities are insulated, recycle and conserve power. The company continuously monitors the environmental impact of its products. The company believes that many of its customers share this concern for the environment.

The company offers its products principally through regular mailings of its monthly catalogues. EarthWear has seven outlet stores in the USA, six in Germany and France, five in the UK, two in Denmark, Sweden and Japan. The company also offers its products over the Internet. During 2009, the Company expanded its global presence by launching sites in Belgium, Finland, Hungary, Ireland, Italy, Norway, Poland, Singapore, Slovenia and Spain. Currently, revenue from catalogue sales, retail outlets and the website are 74 per cent, 5 per cent and 21 per cent respectively. Management expects that Internet sales will grow significantly in the future, perhaps replacing catalogues as the major source of sales.

EarthWear went public on the Euro Stock Exchange (ESE) in 2002 and is listed on the NASDAQ (USA) from 2007.

COMPANY GROWTH STRATEGY

EarthWear's growth strategy has three elements. First, the company attempts to increase sales by expanding its customer base and by increasing sales to existing customers through improved product offerings. Second, the company seeks to generate additional sales by targeted mailings of special issues of its catalogues and by offering its products through its website. Third, the company is pursuing additional opportunities to expand its merchandising skills internationally.

CATALOGS AND SALES OPERATIONS

During 2009 the company mailed 12 issues of its regular monthly catalogue with an average of 75 pages per issue. Worldwide, the company mailed approximately 160 million full-price catalogues. EarthWear views each catalogue issue as a unique opportunity to communicate with its customers. Products are described in visual and editorial detail, and the company uses such techniques as background stories and distinctive covers to stimulate the readers' interest.

Each issue of the regular catalogue offers certain basic product lines for men and women. The regular catalogue also offers seasonal merchandise. In addition, EarthWear mails two end-of-season clearance catalogues. The company mails its catalogues to prospective customers who are identified based on lists of magazine subscribers and lists of households meeting certain demographic criteria. In addition, the company identifies prospective new customers through its national advertising campaign.

In 2001 the company introduced its first business specialty catalogue, which offered its products to groups and companies for corporate incentive programmes. EarthWear's embroidery capabilities allow for the design and monogram of unique logos or emblems for groups and companies. In 2009 the company mailed five issues of its corporate sales catalogues.

The international business segment includes operations in seven countries, and various Internet sites. Catalogues mailed in those countries are written in the local languages and denominated in local currencies. EarthWear has launched local websites in each of these countries in their respective languages and currencies.

CUSTOMER DATABASE

A principal factor in the company's success has been the development of its own list of active customers. At the end of 2009 the company's mailing list consisted of about 21.1 million persons, approximately 7 million of whom were viewed as customers because they had made at least one purchase from the company within the last 24 months.

The company routinely updates and refines the database before mailing catalogues to monitor customer interest as reflected in criteria such as the regency, frequency, amount and product type of purchases.

EarthWear believes that its customer database has desirable demographic characteristics and is well suited to the products offered in the company's catalogues. A survey conducted by the company in seven countries during 2008 indicated that approximately 50 per cent of its customers were in the 35–54 age group and had median incomes of €62,000.

The company advertises to build its reputation and to attract new customers. In 2009 this advertising campaign appeared in about 70 international and national magazines and publications, as well as on nine national television networks. EarthWear also advertises on a number of Internet search engines and websites.

PRODUCT DEVELOPMENT

EarthWear concentrates on clothing and other products that are aimed at customers interested in outdoor activities. The company products are styled and quality crafted to meet the changing tastes of the company's customers rather than to mimic the changing fads of the fashion world. At the same time, the company seeks to maintain customer interest by developing new products, improving existing core products, and reinforcing its value positioning.

The company continues to incorporate innovations in fabric, construction, and detail that add value and excitement and differentiate EarthWear from the competition. In order to ensure that products are manufactured to the company's quality standards at reasonable prices, product managers, designers and quality assurance specialists develop the company's own products.

EarthWear deals directly with its suppliers and seeks to avoid intermediaries. All goods are produced by independent manufacturers except for most of its soft luggage, which is assembled at the company's facilities. During 2009 the company purchased merchandise from approximately 300 domestic and foreign manufacturers. In 2009, one manufacturer and one intermediary accounted for about 14 and 29 per cent of the company's received merchandise, respectively. In 2009 about 80 per cent of the company's merchandise was imported, mainly from Asia, (Bangladesh, China, India, Indonesia and Malaysia). The company will continue to take advantage of worldwide sourcing without sacrificing customer service or quality standards.

Order Entry, Fulfillment, and Delivery

EarthWear has toll-free telephone numbers that customers can call 24 hours a day, seven days a week to place orders or to request a catalogue. Approximately 90 per cent of catalogue orders are placed by telephone. Telephone calls are answered by the company's well-trained sales representatives, who utilize online computer terminals to enter customer orders and to retrieve information about product characteristics and availability. The company's main international telephone centre is located in Mumbai, India. Other telephone centres are located in Boise, USA; London, England; Tokyo, Japan; and Mannheim, Germany.

The company's order entry and fulfilment system permits shipment of in-stock orders on the following day, but orders requiring monogramming or inseaming typically require one or two extra days. The company's sales representatives enter orders into an online order entry and inventory control system. Customers using the company's Internet site see colour photos of the products, their availability and prices. When ordering a product over the Internet, the customer completes a computer screen that requests information on product code, size, colour and so on. When the customer finishes shopping for products, he or she enters delivery and credit card information into a computer-based form.

Orders are generally shipped by United Parcel Service (UPS) or comparable services at various tiered rates that depend on the total monetary value of each customer's order. Other expedited delivery services are available at additional charge.

MERCHANDISE LIQUIDATION Liquidations (sales of overstock and end-of-season merchandise at reduced prices) were approximately 12 per cent, 11 per cent and 8 per cent of net sales in 2009, 2008 and 2007, respectively. Most liquidation sales were made through catalogues and other print media. The balance was sold principally through the company's outlet retail stores.

COMPETITION The company's principal competitors are retail stores, including specialty shops, department stores and other catalogue companies. The company may also face increased competition from other retailers as the number of television shopping channels and the variety of merchandise offered over the Internet increase. The apparel retail business in general is intensely competitive. EarthWear competes principally on the basis of merchandise value (quality and price), its established customer list, and customer service, including fast order fulfilment and its unqualified guarantee.

TRADEMARKS The company uses the trademarks of 'EarthWear' and 'EWC' on products and catalogues.

SEASONALITY OF BUSINESS The company's business is highly seasonal. Historically, a disproportionate amount of the company's net sales and most of its profits have been realized during the fourth quarter. If the company's sales were materially different from seasonal norms during the fourth quarter, the company's annual operating results could be materially affected. Accordingly, results for the individual quarters do not necessarily indicate results to be expected for the entire year. In 2009, 37 per cent of the company's total revenue came in the fourth quarter.

EMPLOYEES The company believes that its skilled and dedicated workforce is one of its key resources. The majority of employees are covered by collective bargaining agreements, and the company considers its employee relations to be excellent. As a result of the highly seasonal nature of the company's business, the size of the company's workforce varies, ranging from approximately 3,500 to 5,300 individuals in 2009. During the peak winter season of 2009 approximately 2,700 of the company's 5,300 employees were temporary employees.

EXECUTIVE OFFICERS OF THE COMPANY

Tor Engan, 65, is chairman of the board and former chief executive officer. Mr Engan was one of the two original founders of EarthWear. He stepped down as chief executive officer in December 2006.

Calvin J. Rogers, 57, is president and chief executive officer of the company. Mr Rogers was one of the two original founders of the company. He assumed his present position in December 2006.

Stefan Anderson, 56, is executive vice president and chief operating officer. Mr Anderson joined the company as chief operating officer in June 2001. He was promoted to vice president in October 2004. Mr Anderson was previously employed by Eddie Bauer in various capacities.

Linda S. McDaniel, 45, is senior vice president of sales. She joined the company in July 2003. Ms Hansen served as divisional vice president, merchandising, with Patagonia between 1998 and 2001. Ms Hansen was the president and chief executive officer for Mountain Goat Sports from 2001 until 2003. She has been serving as a director of the company since November 2004.

James C. ('JC') Watts, 45, is senior vice president and chief financial officer. Mr Watts joined the company in May 2005, assuming his current position. He was previously employed by Artic Department Stores.

Mary Ellen Tornesello, 47, is senior vice president of operations. Ms Tornesello joined the company in 2000 as operations manager. She served as vice president of operations from 2001 until 2003, at which time she assumed her present position.

EarthWear

Market information The shares of the company are listed and traded on the Euro Stock Exchange (ESE) and on NASDAQ. The high and low prices of the company's common shares for 2009 were €52.50 and €21.75 per share. The closing price of the company's shares on 31 December 2009 was €40.25 per share.

Shareholders As of 31 December 2009, the number of shareholders of record of common stock of the company was 2,120.

Independent Auditors The company has been audited by Willis & Adams International since establishment in 1993.

Financial Reporting Framework EarthWear prepares consolidated financial statements reports in accordance with the International Financial Reporting Standards (IFRSs) issued by the International Accounting Standards Board (IASB).

EARTHWEAR CLOTHIERS

Consolidated Income Statements
(In € thousands, except per share data)

	For the period ended 31 December		
	2009	2008	2007
Net Sales (note D)	€ 950,484	€ 857,885	€ 891,394
Cost of sales	(546,393)	(472,739)	(490,530)
Gross Profit	404,091	385,146	400,864
Selling, general, and administrative expenses	(364,012)	(334,994)	(353,890)
Non-recurring charge	——	1,153	(8,190)
Other	(4,798)	(1,090)	(1,592)
Profit from operations	35,281	50,215	37,192
Finance cost (interest expense)	(983)	(1,229)	(5,027)
Finance income	1,459	573	10
Profit before tax	35,757	49,559	32,175
Income tax expense	(13,230)	(18,337)	(11,905)
Profit for the year	22,527	31,222	20,270
Basic earnings per share	1.15	1.60	1.02
Diluted earnings per share	1.14	1.56	1.01
Basic weighted average shares outstanding	19,531	19,555	19,806
Diluted weighted average shares outstanding	19,774	20,055	19,996

EARTHWEAR CLOTHIERS
Consolidated Balance Sheets
(In € thousands)

	31 December	
Assets	**2009**	2008
Current assets:		
Cash and cash equivalents	€ 48,978	€ 49,668
Receivables, net	12,875	11,539
Inventory (note D)	122,337	105,425
Prepaid advertising (note D)	11,458	10,772
Other prepaid expenses	13,447	10,710
Total current assets	209,095	188,115
Non-current assets:		
Property, plant and equipment, at cost		
Land and buildings	70,918	66,804
Fixtures and equipment	67,513	66,876
Computer hardware and software	64,986	47,466
Leasehold improvements	3,010	2,894
Total property, plant, and equipment	206,426	184,040
Less accumulated depreciation and amortization (note D)	85,986	76,256
Property, plant, and equipment, net	120,440	107,784
Goodwill (note D)	423	628
Total assets	€ 329,959	€ 296,527
Liabilities and equity		
Current liabilities:		
Lines of credit (note F)	€ 11,011	€ 7,621
Accounts payable	62,509	48,432
Reserve for returns (note D)	5,890	5,115
Provisions	26,738	28,440
Accrued profit sharing	1,532	1,794
Income taxes payable	8,588	6,666
Total current liabilities (note G)	116,268	98,067
Deferred income taxes payable:	9,469	5,926
Equity:		
Issued capital, 26,121 shares issued (note E)	261	261
Share premium	26,200	24,711
Deferred compensation	(79)	(153)
Foreign currency translation adjustments	588	
Unrealized gain on forward contracts	3,295	1,739
Retained earnings	317,907	295,380
Treasury stock, 6,546 and 6,706 shares at cost, respectively (note E)	(143,950)	(129,462)
Total equity	204,222	192,535
Total liabilities and equity	€ 329,959	€ 296,527

EARTHWEAR CLOTHIERS

Consolidated Statements of Changes in Equity

(In € thousands)

	Issued Capital	Share Premium	Deferred Compensation	Accumulated Foreign Currency Translation Adjustments	Accumulated Unrealized Gain on Forward Contracts	Retained Earnings	Treasury Stock	Total
Balance 31 December 2006	€ 261	€ 22,657	(€ 681)	€ 569		€243,888	(€108,931)	€157,763
Purchase of treasury shares							(23,112)	(23,112)
Issuance of treasury shares							1,199	1,199
Tax benefit of shares options exercised		349						349
Deferred compensation expense			424					424
Profit for the year						20,270		20,270
Foreign currency translation adjustments				733				733
Balance 31 December 2007	€ 261	€ 23,006	(€ 257)	€ 1,302		€264,158	(€130,844)	€157,626
Purchase of treasury shares							(2,935)	(2,935)
Issuance of treasury shares							4,317	4,317
Tax benefit of shares options exercised		1,765						1,765
Deferred compensation expense			103					103
Profit for the year						31,222		31,222
Foreign currency translation adjustments				437				437
Balance 31 December 2008	€ 261	€ 24,771	(€ 154)	€ 1,739		€295,380	(€129,463)	€192,534
Purchase of treasury shares							(18,192)	(18,192)
Issuance of treasury shares							3,704	3,704
Tax benefit of shares options exercised		1,429						1,429
Deferred compensation expense			75					75
Profit for the year						22,527		22,527
Foreign currency translation adjustments				(1,151)				(1,151)
Unrealized gain on forward contracts					3,295			3,295
Balance 31 December 2009	**€ 261**	**€ 26,200**	**(€79)**	**€ 588**	**€ 3,295**	**€ 317,907**	**(€143,950)**	**€204,222**

EARTHWEAR CLOTHIERS

Consolidated Statements of Cash Flows

(In € thousands)

	For the period ended 31 December		
Cash flows from (used for) operating activities:	**2009**	2008	2007
Profit for the year	**€ 22,527**	€ 31,222	€ 20,270
Adjustments to reconcile profit for the year to net cash flows from operating activities:			
Non-recurring charge		(1,153)	8,190
Depreciation and amortization	**15,231**	13,465	12,175
Deferred compensation expense	**75**	103	424
Deferred income taxes	**3,340**	5,376	(3,866)
Loss on disposal of fixed assets	**€ 284**	602	381
Changes in assets and liabilities excluding the effects of divestitures:			
Receivables, net	**(1,336)**	2,165	(3,666)
Inventory	**(16,912)**	37,370	13,954
Prepaid advertising	**(686)**	3,110	(1,849)
Other prepaid expenses	**(2,534)**	1,152	(1,628)
Accounts payable	**14,078**	(8,718)	2,716
Reserve for returns	**775**	439	692
Provisions	**(709)**	(4,982)	4,545
Accrued profit sharing	**(262)**	328	(1,320)
Income taxes payable	**1,923**	(2,810)	(3,834)
Tax benefit of stock options	**1,429**	1,765	349
Other	**2,144**	437	733
Net cash from (used for) operating activities	**39,367**	79,871	48,269
Cash flows from (used for) investing activities:			
Cash paid for capital additions	**(28,959)**	(18,208)	(30,388)
Net cash flows used for investing activities	**(28,959)**	(18,208)	(30,388)
Cash flows from (used for) financing activities:			
Proceeds from (payment of) short-term debt	**3,390**	(17,692)	4,228
Purchases of treasury shares	**(18,192)**	(2,935)	(23,112)
Issuance of treasury shares	**3,704**	4,317	1,199
Net cash flows used for financing activities	**(11,097)**	(16,310)	(17,685)
Net increase (decrease) in cash and cash equivalents	**(690)**	45,352	197
Cash equivalents at 1 January	**49,668**	4,317	4,120
Cash equivalents at 31 December	**€ 48,978**	€ 49,668	€ 4,317
Supplemental cash flow disclosures:			
Interest paid	**€ 987**	€ 1,229	€ 5,000
Income taxes paid	**6,278**	13,701	18,107

EARTHWEAR CLOTHIERS

Five-Year Consolidated Financial Summary (unaudited)

(In € thousands, except per share data)

| | For the period ended 31 December | | | | |
	2009	2008	2007	2006	2005
Income statement data:					
Net Sales	**950,484**	857,885	891,394	821,359	503,434
Profit before tax	**35,757**	49,559	32,175	66,186	38,212
Percent of net sales	**3.8%**	5.8%	3.6%	8.1%	7.6%
Profit for the year	**22,527**	31,222	20,270	41,698	22,929
Per share of issued capital:					
Basic earnings per share	**1.15**	1.60	1.02	2.01	1.54
Diluted earnings per share	**1.14**	1.56	1.01	2.00	1.53
Common shares outstanding	**19,531**	19,555	19,806	20,703	14,599
Balance sheet data:					
Current assets	**209,095**	188,115	191,297	194,445	122,418
Current liabilities	**116,268**	98,067	133,434	118,308	65,505
PPE and goodwill	**120,863**	108,412	105,051	87,312	46,658
Total assets	**329,959**	296,527	296,347	281,757	170,121
Non-current liabilities	**9,469**	5,926	5,286	5,686	4,211
Total equity	**204,222**	192,535	157,627	157,763	100,405
Other data:					
Net working capital	**92,827**	90,048	57,863	76,136	56,913
Capital expenditures	**28,959**	18,208	30,388	31,348	8,316
Depreciation and amortization expense	**15,231**	13,465	12,175	9,833	6,101
Return on average shareholders' investment	**11%**	18%	13%	28%	24%
Return on average assets	**7%**	11%	7%	16%	15%

PROFIT FOR THE YEAR

NET SALES

BASIC EARNINGS PER SHARE

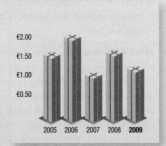

NOTE A: NATURE OF BUSINESS

EarthWear markets high-quality clothing for outdoor sports, casual clothing, accessories, shoes and soft luggage. The company manages its business in three operating segments consisting of core, business-to-business and international. The company's primary market is Europe; other markets include Japan, and the USA.

NOTE B: BASIS OF PREPARATION

The consolidated financial statements have been prepared based on a historical cost basis, except for derivatives that have been measured at fair value.

NOTE C: STATEMENT OF COMPLIANCE

The consolidated financial statements of EarthWear have been prepared in accordance with International Financial Reporting Standards (IFRSs).

NOTE D: SUMMARY OF SIGNIFICANT ACCOUNTING POLICIES

BASIS OF CONSOLIDATION The consolidated financial statements include the financial statements of EarthWear and its subsidiaries after elimination of intercompany balances and transactions.

USE OF ESTIMATES The preparation of financial statements in accordance with IFRSs requires management to make estimates and assumptions that affect the reported amounts of assets and liabilities and disclosure of contingent assets and liabilities at the date of the financial statements and the reported amounts of revenues and expenses during the reporting periods. Actual results may differ from these estimates.

REVENUE RECOGNITION The company recognizes revenue at the time of shipment for catalogue and E-commerce sales and at the point for sale for stores. The company provides a reserve for returns.

RESERVE FOR LOSSES ON CUSTOMER RETURNS At the time of sale, the company provides a reserve equal to the gross profit on projected merchandise returns, based on prior returns experience.

INVENTORY Inventory is measured using the first-in, first-out (FIFO) method and valued at the lower of cost and net realizable value.

ADVERTISING The company expenses the costs of advertising for magazines, television, radio and other media the first time the advertising takes place, except for direct-response advertising, which is capitalized and amortized over its expected period of future benefits. Direct-response advertising consists primarily of catalogue production and mailing costs, which are generally amortized within three months from the date catalogues are mailed.

DEPRECIATION Depreciation expense is calculated using the straight-line method over the estimated useful lives of the assets, which are 20 to 30 years for buildings and land improvements and 5 to 10 years for leasehold improvements and furniture, fixtures, equipment and software. The company allocates one half year of depreciation to the year of addition or retirement.

GOODWILL Goodwill is tested annually for impairment and carried at cost less accumulated impairment losses.

FINANCIAL INSTRUMENTS WITH OFF-BALANCE-SHEET RISK The company uses import letters of credit to purchase foreign-sourced merchandise. The letters of credit are primarily Euro-denominated and are issued through third party financial institutions to guarantee payment for such merchandise within the agreed-upon time periods. At 31 December 2009, the company had outstanding letters of credit of approximately €23 million, all of which had expiration dates of less than one year.

FOREIGN CURRENCY TRANSLATIONS AND TRANSACTIONS Financial statements of the foreign subsidiaries are translated into Euros.

NOTE C: STOCKHOLDERS' EQUITY

The company currently is authorized to issue 70 million shares of €0.01 par value common shares.

TREASURY SHARES The company's board of directors has authorized the purchase of a total of 12.7 million shares of the company's common shares. A total of 6.5 million and 6.7 million had been purchased as of 31 December 2009 and 2008, respectively.

SHARE-BASED PAYMENT TRANSACTIONS The company has a restricted share-based payment plan. Under the provisions of the plan, a committee of the company's board may award shares of the company's common shares to its officers and key employees. Such shares vest over a 10-year period on a straight-line basis.

The granting of these awards has been recorded as deferred compensation based on the fair market value of the shares at the date of the grant. Compensation expense under these plans is recorded as shares vest.

[1]THE FULL SET OF NOTES IS NOT INCLUDED.

The company has 3.5 million shares that may be issued pursuant to the exercise of options granted under the company's stock option plan. Options are granted at the discretion of a committee of the company's board of directors to officers and key employees of the company.

Equity settled awards are accounted for in accordance with IFRS 2, share-based payment.

NOTE F: LINES OF CREDIT

The company has unsecured domestic lines of credit with various European banks totalling €150 million. There were €23.4 million amounts outstanding at 31 December 2009 compared to €20.2 million outstanding at 31 December 2008. In addition, the company has unsecured lines of credit with USA banks totalling the equivalent of €30 million for its wholly owned subsidiaries. At 31 December 2009, €11 million was outstanding at interest rates averaging 4.6 per cent, compared with €7.6 million at 31 December 2008.

NOTE G: LONG TERM DEBT

There was no long-term debt at 31 December 2009 and 2008.

NOTE H: LEASES

The company leases store and office space and equipment under various lease arrangements. The leases are accounted for as operating leases.

NOTE I: RETIREMENT PLANS

The company has a retirement plan that covers most regular employees and provides for annual contributions at the discretion of the board of directors.

MANAGEMENT'S DISCUSSION AND ANALYSIS: RESULTS OF OPERATIONS FOR 2009 COMPARED TO 2008

TOTAL REVENUE INCREASED BY 3.2 PERCENT Total revenue for the year just ended was €950.5 million, compared with €857.9 million in the prior year, an increase of 3.2 per cent. Seasonally strong sales resulted in a higher level of back orders during the fourth quarter and a first-time fulfilment rate of 85 per cent for the year as a whole, slightly below the prior year's rate. Overall merchandise sales growth was primarily attributable to changes in circulation, which included adding back our end-of-year catalogue and our January full-price catalogue, shifting the timing of our autumn/winter mailings, increased page circulation and improved merchandise selection and creative presentations.

PROFIT FOR THE YEAR DECREASED Profit for the year 2009 was €22.5 million, down 27.8 per cent from the €31.2 million earned in 2008. Diluted earnings per share for the year just ended were €1.14, compared with €1.56 per share for the prior year. The diluted weighted average number of common shares outstanding was 19.8 million for 2009 and 20.1 million for 2008.

GROSS PROFIT MARGIN Gross profit for the year just ended was €404 million, or 42.5 per cent of total revenue, compared with €385 million, or 44.9 per cent of total revenue, for the prior year. Liquidations were about 11 per cent of net merchandise sales in 2009, compared with 12 per cent in the prior year. In 2009, the cost of inventory purchases was down 2.0 per cent, compared with deflation of 2.7 per cent in 2008. This reduction was a result of improved sourcing.

SELLING, GENERAL AND ADMINISTRATIVE EXPENSES Selling, general and administrative (SG&A) expenses increased 9.2 per cent to €364 million in 2009, compared with €334 million in the prior year. As a percentage of sales, SG&A was 38.3 per cent in 2009 and 39.1 per cent in the prior year. The absolute increase in the SG&A ratio was the result of higher sales, higher catalogue costs associated with increased page circulation, as well as higher information services expenses as we continue to invest in the Internet and upgrade systems capabilities. The cost of producing and mailing catalogues represented about 39 per cent and 38 per cent of total SG&A in 2009 and 2008, respectively.

CREDIT LINES AND CAPITAL EXPENDITURES Interest expense on lines of credit was down in 2009 due to lower average borrowing levels. Interest expense decreased to €1.0 million in 2009, compared to €1.2 million in 2008. We spent €29 million in cash on capital expenditures, which included €20 million for computer hardware and software. In addition, the company acquired a new aeroplane by exchanging two of its own aircraft in 2009. Also, we purchased about €18 million in treasury shares. No long-term debt was outstanding at year-end 2009. Depreciation and amortization expense was €15.2 million, up 13.1 per cent from the prior year, mainly due to computer software. Rental expense was €10.4 million, up 3.4 per cent from 2008, primarily due to additional computer hardware.

INDEPENDENT AUDITOR'S REPORT

To the Shareholders of EarthWear Clothiers

We have audited the accompanying consolidated financial statements of EarthWear Clothiers and its subsidiaries, which comprise the consolidated balance sheet as at 31 December 2009, and the consolidated income statement, statement of changes in equity and cash flow statement for the year then ended, and a summary of significant accounting policies and other explanatory information.

Management's Responsibility for the Consolidated Financial Statements

Management is responsible for the preparation and fair presentation of these consolidated financial statements in accordance with International Financial Reporting Standards, and for such internal control as management determines is necessary to enable the preparation of consolidated financial statements that are free from material misstatement, whether due to fraud or error.

Auditor's Responsibility

Our responsibility is to express an opinion on these consolidated financial statements based on our audit. We conducted our audit in accordance with International Standards on Auditing. Those standards require that we comply with ethical requirements and plan and perform the audit to obtain reasonable assurance about whether the consolidated financial statements are free from material misstatement.

An audit involves performing procedures to obtain audit evidence about the amounts and disclosures in the consolidated financial statements. The procedures selected depend on the auditor's judgement, including the assessment of the risks of material misstatement of the consolidated financial statements, whether due to fraud or error. In making those risk assessments, the auditor considers internal control relevant to the entity's preparation and fair presentation of the consolidated financial statements in order to design audit procedures that are appropriate in the circumstances, but not for the purpose of expressing an opinion on the effectiveness of the entity's internal control. An audit also includes evaluating the appropriateness of accounting policies used and the reasonableness of accounting estimates made by management, as well as evaluating the overall presentation of the consolidated financial statements.

We believe that the audit evidence we have obtained is sufficient and appropriate to provide a basis for our audit opinion.

Opinion

In our opinion, the consolidated financial statements present fairly, in all material respects, the financial position of EarthWear Clothiers and its subsidiaries as at 31 December 2009, and their financial performance and cash flows for the year then ended in accordance with International Financial Reporting Standards.

Willis & Adams International
M. J. Willis
M. J. Willis, Partner

15 February 2010

Europolis

CHAPTER 2

The Financial Statement Auditing Environment

❖ *RELEVANT ACCOUNTING AND AUDITING PRONOUNCEMENTS*

EU, EU 8th Directive on Statutory Audits of Annual Accounts and Consolidated Accounts, 2006

IAASB, International Framework for Assurance Engagements

ISA 200, Overall Objectives of the Independent Auditor and the Conduct of an Audit in Accordance with International Standards on Auditing

ISA 240, The Auditor's Responsibilities Relating to Fraud in an Audit of Financial Statements

ISA 315, Identifying and Assessing the Risks of Material Misstatement through Understanding the Entity and Its Environment

ISA 500, Audit Evidence

THIS CHAPTER covers the context or environment in which auditors function, starting with an overview of the far-reaching changes in the accounting profession over the past several years. The chapter then addresses auditors' legal liability and explains how it affects the accounting profession and the audit markets. The accounting profession operates globally and is increasingly governed by international organizations and initiatives taken at the international level. The chapter discusses the International Federation of Accountants (IFAC) and other major international organizations and explains how they impact the accounting profession worldwide. The chapter proceeds by expanding on the standard-setting process of the International Auditing and Assurance Standards Board (IAASB). The IAASB completed in 2009 a comprehensive project to clarify the International Standards on Auditing (ISAs). The chapter explains the structure of the clarified ISAs and the responsibility of the auditor inherent in the ISAs. This discussion is followed by a closer look at management's and auditor's responsibility for the **financial statements**. Ethical behaviour and reputation play key roles in shaping the accounting profession and its environment. The chapter explains how the accounting profession worldwide is governed by the IFAC Code of Ethics for Professional Accountants. The chapter then sets the focus on the organization and composition of audit firms and the various categories of services they offer, followed by a discussion of the different types of auditors. One of the most important and useful skills auditors develop is the ability to quickly understand and analyse various business models, strategies and processes, and to identify key risks relevant to a particular client. Further, these elements largely shape the context in which auditing is performed. Accordingly, the chapter introduces a high-level model of business and then offers a model of business processes that is useful for organizing an audit. The chapter concludes on the concept of management assertions introduced in Chapter 1. These assertions will in the next chapters prove to be quite powerful and underlie much of what auditors do.

❖ A TIME OF CHALLENGE AND CHANGE FOR AUDITORS

LO1

The environment in which auditors work has been dramatically reshaped by the events taking place in the business world during the past several years. In fact, the profession has gone through a period of almost unprecedented change, including changes in regulation and public oversight, professional standards, and organization of audit firms. Because of the global nature of the events leading up to these changes, the primary initiatives for and responses to changes were taken at the international level. This section briefly discusses some of the issues and controversies that led up to the many changes experienced by the profession. While the profession has undergone profound changes, the events of the past several years have served to solidify the crucial role of accounting and auditing in protecting public interests.

During the economic boom of the late 1990s and early 2000s, audit firms aggressively sought opportunities to market a variety of high-margin non-audit services to their audit clients. The consulting revenue of the largest audit firms grew extremely quickly, until in many instances consulting revenues from audit clients greatly exceeded the fee for the external audit. Exhibit 2–1 provides examples of audit and non-audit fees reported for 2001.

Exhibit 2–1 Examples of Audit and Non-Audit Fees in 2001			
	Types of Fees (in € millions)		
Company	*Auditor*	*Statutory Audit*	*Non-audit*
Barclays	PricewaterhouseCoopers	8	52
BP	Ernst & Young	24	59
HBOS	KPMG	11	36
Shell	KPMG/PricewaterhouseCoopers	18	32
Vodafone	Deloitte	6	34
Unilever	PricewaterhouseCoopers	16	76
Source: Annual reports 2001. Non-audit fees may include fees for audit-related services.			

A Series of Scandals

Starting in October 2001 with the investigation of the accounting practices of the Houston-based energy giant Enron, a series of high-profile accounting scandals hit the USA, Europe and the rest of the world. The scandals involved corporate giants (e.g. Adelphia, Ahold, Parmalat, Tyco, WorldCom and Xerox), global brokerage firms (e.g. Merrill Lynch), mutual funds (e.g. Piper Jaffray) and several of the large audit firms. Most countries experienced incidences of corporate financial scandals and accounting **frauds**. Events unfolding in one country often turned out to have international spillover effects. The series of scandals caused a general crisis of confidence in the integrity of the entire system of corporate accountability, including the role of auditors and the effectiveness of the auditing process. The global nature of capital markets, businesses and major audit firms made the loss of confidence a genuine international issue.

The Enron accounting fraud is the most infamous in recent history because it led to the demise of one of the large audit firms, Arthur Andersen, caught tremendous media interest, and triggered outrage among investors, creditors, regulators, politicians and the public. The investigation of the accounting practices of Enron quickly uncovered massive financial deception that had been going on for several years. The company released an earnings restatement for previous years, disclosing billions of dollars in overstated earnings and previously undisclosed debt obligations. Arthur Andersen, the auditor of Enron, immediately became embroiled in the controversy, because the firm had failed to report the vast extent of Enron's improper accounting. Many argued that this failure came about at least in part because Andersen was paid tens of millions of dollars in separate fees for consulting and internal auditing services, which amounted to more than the fee for the external audit. In August 2002, Andersen stopped providing audits and began to dismantle its business. Andersen's collapse resulted from the firm's loss of reputation brought about by a string of audit failures and by the firm's indictment and subsequent conviction on charges of obstruction of justice. Though the conviction was overturned by the US Supreme Court a few years later, the fatal damage had been done. Ironically, for most of Andersen's 89 years of existence it enjoyed a sterling reputation as one of the world's biggest and most respected audit firms.

Practice Insight 2.1

In 1952, Arthur Edward Andersen was inducted into the Accounting Hall of Fame for his contributions to the accounting profession. Mr Andersen was known for his honesty and integrity and his motto was 'Think Straight – Talk Straight'. He often exhorted his employees to 'do the right thing'. Mr Andersen was the founder of the firm known as Arthur Andersen & Company, for which he served as senior partner until his death in January 1947.

In Europe the dairy-food giant Parmalat, once considered the jewel of Italian capitalism, became known for one of the largest and most brazen frauds in history. Exhibit 2–2 illustrates the Parmalat scandal.

Exhibit 2–2 The Parmalat Scandal

The Italian dairy giant Parmalat (Parmalat Finanziaria S.p.A.) was one of Europe's largest and most global food companies. The company was founded by Calisto Tanzi in the 1960s in the northern Italian city Parma. Parmalat had by 2003 grown global, selling long-lasting milk and other dairy products in 30 countries and employing 36,000 people. The Tanzi family owned 51 per cent of the company. Parmalat was raising money by selling huge amounts of bonds to the public. Leading global banks were the bond placers.

In December 2003 Parmalat had difficulty making a €150 million bond payment. This was alarming since Parmalat had been reported to hold a bank account in the Bank of America (BAC) of €3.95 billion through its offshore subsidiary Bonlat. On 19 December BAC reported that no such account existed. Parmalat was forced into bankruptcy proceedings on 27 December 2003. The same day Parmalat's founder and former CEO Tanzi was arrested on suspicion of fraud, embezzlement, false accounting and misleading investors.

Until 1999 the Italian arm of mid-tier international audit firm Grant Thornton was Parmalat's principal auditor. Following the Italian rule of mandatory rotation of audit firms every nine years, the Parmalat group switched to the Italian unit of Deloitte & Touche, as principal auditor in 1999. Grant Thornton, however, continued to audit Parmalat subsidiaries, including the subsidiary Bonlat where the scandal began.

When Grant Thornton audited the Bonlat bank account with a BAC, the auditor received a letter on a BAC letterhead confirming the existence of the account. The confirmation letter, however, had been forged by Parmalat. This prompted the questions if Grant Thornton acted properly in the confirmation process and if Deloitte & Touche behaved properly as the group auditor.

The Italian prosecutors soon discovered that financial fraud had been going on for 15 years and that the company as of the end September 2003 had understated its reported debt of €6.4 billion by at least €7.9 billion. Investigations uncovered what appeared to be a large and intricate accounting fraud. The charges included fraudulent transfers of uncollectible and impaired receivables to 'nominee' entities where their diminished or non-existent value was hidden, fraudulent use of the same nominee entities to fabricate non-existent financial operations intended to offset losses of its operating subsidiaries, and fraudulent transfers of money to various businesses owned and operated by Tanzi family members. The charges reflect that Parmalat may have engaged in one of the largest and most brazen corporate financial frauds in history.

Parmalat continues operations under new management and is relisted on the Milan Stock Exchange. In August 2004 Parmalat filed a lawsuit seeking $10 billion in damages from the two audit firms, Deloitte & Touche and Grant Thornton. Parmalat also filed lawsuits against, or is targeting, a number of financial institutions, including Banca Nazionale del Lavoro, Bank of America, Credit Suisse First Boston, Citigroup, UBS and Deutsche Bank. In January 2007 Parmalat reached an agreement with Deloitte & Touche under which the audit firm paid €112 million. So far Parmalat has in total recovered €650 million. Unsettled claims against others amount to €27 billion in Italy and €10 billion in the USA.

Sources: 'How Parmalat Went Sour', *Business Week* (12 January 2004); 'Statement on Behalf of Deloitte Italy Regarding Parmalat', Deloitte (2004); 'Europe's Corporate Governance: Parma Splat', *The Economist* (15 January 2004); 'Parmalat Files €250m Suit against CSFB', *Financial Times* (20 August 2004); 'Statement from Grant Thornton International 18 August 2004', Grant Thornton (2004); 'Parmalat: All You Need to Know about the Collapse of the Italian Dairy Giant', *Guardian* (6 October 2004); 'SEC Charges Parmalat with Financial Fraud', US Securities and Exchange Commission (2003); and 'SEC Alleged Additional Violations by Parmalat Finanziaria, S.p.A., and Simultaneously Settles Civil Action', US Securities and Exchange Commission (2004); 'Deloitte Settles $149m Parmalat Suit', *Financial Times* (13 January 2007), and 'Italian Food Buon Appetito', *The Economist* (20 January 2007).

Regulation[i]

The fundamental function of auditing in the economy and its role of serving the public interest have for a long time implied substantial government involvement and regulation of the auditing sector. The degree of regulation has varied among countries, from a fairly self-regulated profession to a strongly governmentally regulated auditing sector. Individual countries and jurisdictions found their own balance of self-regulation by the profession and regulation by the government. Following the corporate scandals and the undermining of public confidence in the financial reporting and auditing process, a reconsideration of the regulatory systems and measures took place. Overall, this resulted in stricter regulation and stronger public oversight. For example, in the USA the Sarbanes–Oxley Act of 2002 (commonly known as SOX) transferred authority to set auditing standards for public company audits from the profession to the Public Company Accounting Oversight Board (PCAOB). Although less dramatic than the shifts in the USA regulations, the European Union (EU) 8th Directive on Statutory Audits of 2006 tightens the regulation and public oversight of the auditing sector in EU member states. While various countries and jurisdictions may not rely on the same balance between regulation by the government and self-regulation of the profession, a clear shift throughout the world towards more regulation and public oversight of the accounting profession is evident. Further, the international convergence processes of regulatory systems and professional standards have gained momentum. Specifically, the International Standards on Auditing have become more comprehensive and are today established as global auditing standards.

Back to Basics

It would be difficult to overemphasize the impact of the events of the late 1990s and early 2000s. The accounting profession around the globe has been through a fundamental shift from being largely self-regulated to being regulated. Regulations have consistently been initiated at the international level and the international professional standards have achieved widespread adoption. Audit firms, restricted from providing many non-audit services for audit clients, reorganized or sold their consulting divisions and began to refocus their efforts and attention once again on their core services: the financial statement audit. While these changes caused pain and turmoil, they served to highlight and reaffirm the essential importance of auditing in our economic system and the accounting profession was powerfully reminded of the importance of integrity and professionalism in protecting the public interest.

❖ AUDITORS' LEGAL LIABILITY

LO2

Chapter 1 presented an economic view of auditing, and we provided a building surveyor analogy to illustrate the concepts. The auditor (or surveyor) adds value to the principal–agent relationship by providing an objective, independent opinion on the quality of the information reported. However, what prevents the auditor from cooperating with management and issuing an unmodified opinion on financial statements that are materially misstated? The main deterrent, other than an individual's ethical principles, is the threat of legal liability. If a client or a third party suffers loss from such fraudulent behaviour, the auditor's personal wealth and professional reputation will be affected by litigation.

Legal liability regimes of auditors and auditors' exposure to litigation vary between countries and jurisdictions. Legal liability rules differ according to which actions the auditor can be held liable for, which third parties auditors are liable to, joint and several liability or proportional liability, existence of legal liability caps and allowance to contract liability caps, and rules for allocation of litigation costs between parties. Joint and several liability of the auditor and the audited entity towards third parties provides less protection in lawsuits than proportional liability since the auditor's liability will go beyond his or her proportional share of the damage. The plaintiffs may claim damages from the auditor regardless of the degree of involvement of the auditor. The joint and several legal liability doctrine is most common in member states in the EU. In some countries (e.g. Austria, Belgium, Germany, Greece and Slovenia) auditors' liability is legally capped, i.e. the auditor is jointly and severally liable with the company only up to the cap provided. The UK allows contractual caps between a company and its auditor subject to shareholders' approval. The number of corporate failures, auditors' liability insurance coverage, and the general litigation climate will also be factors affecting auditors' litigation risk exposure.

For 2007, the six largest US audit firms paid 15.1 per cent of audit-related revenue as litigation and practice protection costs. While showing a rising trend, the comparable costs are lower in the EU.[ii] Costs involved in dealing with claims may be considerable and cases often take long time to resolve.

Although auditors' legal liability is considered an important driver to provide audit quality, concerns has been raised that the litigation risk for audit firms may have adverse effects on the concentration and choice of available auditors in the audit market for listed companies. This market at present comprises limited players. The largest audit firms, known as the 'Big 4' firms (Deloitte, Ernst & Young, KPMG and PricewaterhouseCoopers), exclusively serve or dominate large company audit assignments. Litigation risk exposure is perceived as a barrier to market entry by other audit firms. (Audit firms are discussed in a later section in this chapter.) In recent years this barrier has risen because the availability of auditor liability insurance for higher limits has fallen. The concern is aggravated by the fact that the number of suppliers could be reduced even further as a result of existing and potential future damage claims against the large audit firms. Bear in mind the collapse in 2002 of Arthur Andersen and that the then Big 5 became the Big 4. To summarize, companies need access to high-quality audits at reasonable costs, and audit firms' litigation exposure may preclude the supply of such audit services because of high market concentration and barriers to market entry. This is the background for the debate and initiatives on liability reforms that take place in various jurisdictions and forums.

The European Commission (EC) issued in 2008 a Recommendation concerning the limitation of the liability of statutory auditors.[iii] The Recommendation is a response to the increasing trend of litigation and lack of sufficient insurance cover in the auditing sector in the EU. It aims to protect European capital markets by ensuring that audit firms remain available to carry out audits on companies listed in the EU. The Recommendation leaves it to member states to decide on the appropriate method for limiting liability, and proposes the following measurers to limit liability:

- Establishment of a maximum financial amount or of a formula allowing for the calculation of such an amount (legal liability cap).
- Establishment of a set of principles by virtue of which a statutory auditor or an audit firm is not liable beyond its actual contribution to the loss suffered by a claimant and is accordingly not jointly and severally liable with other wrongdoers (proportional liability).
- Provision allowing any company to be audited and the statutory auditor or audit firm to determine a limitation of liability in an agreement (contractual liability cap).

A fundamental challenge for legislators' decisions on the legal liability regime of auditors is to strike a proper balance between the need for well-functioning audit markets, fair compensation to damaged parties, and to maintain strong auditor incentives to provide audit quality, including to avoid auditors' negligence.

Practice Insight 2.2

The 'deep pocket' syndrome?

Auditors assert that joint and several liability systems are unjust and that they are considered by plaintiffs as an insurance against any deficiencies on the part of companies in their financial statements. Auditors can only give a reasonable assurance that financial statements provide a true and fair view of the company's financial position. The opinion of an auditor cannot provide an absolute assurance and is not required to do so under law.

A liability regime under which an auditor is liable for any damage caused by the failure of the audit client might create the expectation among potential plaintiffs that auditors are gatekeepers against corporate fraud or other corporate malpractice. Joint and several liability reinforces this 'expectation gap' on the side of investors. But it is neither efficient nor equitable for the market to operate on the expectation that the financial deficiencies of a company will be compensated for by the company's audit firm. Moreover, it is arguable that the existing regime decreases the incentive for companies to prevent corporate malpractice.

Joint and several liability is particularly relevant where the audited company becomes bankrupt, since creditors and liquidators are seeking further avenues for compensation. Major audit firms risk being treated as offering 'deep pockets' although this is very questionable since in recent years the amount of claims has increased significantly and the available insurance has sharply decreased.

Source: European Commission, Directorate General for Internal Market and Services (2007), *Commission Staff Working Paper: Consultation on Auditors' Liability and Its Impact on the European Capital Markets*.

◆ INTERNATIONAL ORGANIZATIONS THAT AFFECT THE
LO3 ACCOUNTING PROFESSION

In addition to legislators, a number of international, regional and national organizations affect the practice of auditing within a specific country or jurisdiction. The following section discusses the activities of some the most influential organizations at the international level.

At the global scene, the International Federation of Accountants (IFAC) is the prime issuer of pronouncements on auditing matters. The IFAC's International Auditing and Assurance Standards Board (IAASB) issues the International Standards on Auditing (ISAs). The IAASB and the ISAs are discussed in more detail in a section later in the chapter. The International Accounting Standards Board (IASB) issues the International Financial Reporting Standards (IFRSs). The IFRSs have gained widespread acceptance throughout the world. The International Organization of Securities Commissions (IOSCO) assembles securities commissions worldwide. The IOSCO is important for the global acceptance of the international financial reporting and auditing standards. The International Organization of Supreme Audit Institutions (INTOSAI) organizes national Supreme Audit Institutions (Offices of Auditor General) and is involved in international standard-setting. The EU regulates audit matters in its member states. The EU also plays an important role for the acceptance of the international standards. From 2005 the International Financial Reporting Standards (as adopted by the EU) have been the required financial reporting framework in the EU for consolidated accounts for listed companies. The EU has decided that statutory audits in the EU shall adhere to the ISAs. Finally, the USA regulatory environment is presented. The US accounting and auditing standards affect and are affected by the international standards, but the USA remains a separate regulatory environment.

International Federation of Accountants (IFAC)[iv]

The International Federation of Accountants (IFAC) was established in 1977 and is a global organization of national accountancy bodies. It has more than 157 member bodies and associates in 123 countries around the world. Membership of IFAC member bodies comprises more than 2.5 million accountants in public and private practice. The IFAC's mission is:

> To serve the public interest, strengthen the accountancy profession worldwide and contribute to the development of international economies by establishing and promoting adherence to high-quality professional standards, furthering international convergence of such standards, and speaking out on public interest issues where the profession's expertise is most relevant.

A Public Interest Oversight Board (PIOB) oversees the auditing and assurance, ethics and education standard-setting activities of the International Auditing and Assurance Standards Board (IAASB), the International Ethics Standards Board for Accountants (IESBA), and the International Accounting Education Standards Board (IAESB). Before a standard is final the PIOB must approve that the standard-setting has followed a due process, including that the standard-setting was sufficiently responsive to the needs and perceptions of various stakeholders, with the primary emphasis on investors, regulators and corporate users. The PIOB also oversees the IFAC's Compliance Advisory Panel and thereby IFAC members' endeavours to incorporate the international standards. Members of the PIOB are nominated by regulators and related organizations. A Consultative Advisory Group (CAG) for each of the standard-setting boards serves to provide further public interest input into the standard-setting process.

The IFAC's structure and governance reflect its public interest mission and are designed to promote public oversight, consultation with stakeholders, accountability, and issuance of and compliance with high-quality professional standards. Figure 2–1 and the following text provide an overview of the IFAC's structure, governance and activities.

- *IFAC Council.* The IFAC Council is responsible for deciding on constitutional questions and electing the IFAC Board. The Council comprises one representative from each member body and meets once a year.
- *IFAC Board.* The IFAC Board recommends to the Council the strategic course of the IFAC with respect to policy-making, major initiatives and fostering relations with international organizations and governments. The Board is committed to maintain the three public interest standard-setting boards in auditing and assurance (IAASB), ethics (IESBA) and education (IAESB), their Consultative Advisory Group (CAG) and the Compliance Advisory Panel (CAP). In doing so, the IFAC Board provides the authority for those boards to issue standards. Subject to the approval of the PIOB the IFAC Board determines the Terms of References (the 'constitution') of all boards and committees, and for the CAGs. The IFAC Boards authority includes issuing Statements of Membership Obligations (SMOs) that establish requirements for IFAC members to promote, incorporate and assist in implementing the international standards.
- *IFAC Nominating Committee.* The IFAC Nominating Committee makes recommendations regarding the composition of the IFAC's boards and committees. The Committee's nominations to the public interest standard-setting boards in auditing and assurance (IAASB), ethics (IESBA) and education (IAESB) are subject to the approval of the PIOB.
- *IFAC Leadership Group.* The IFAC Leadership Group includes the IFAC President, Deputy President, Chief Executive, the Chairs of the IAASB, the Transnational Auditors Committee (TAC), the Forum of Firms (FOF), and up to four other members designated by the IFAC Board. It works with the Monitoring Group and addresses issues related to the regulation of the profession.

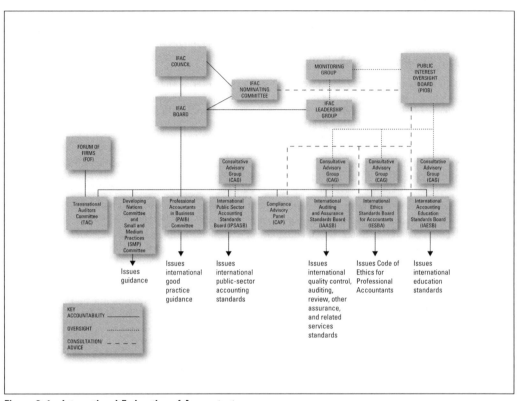

Figure 2–1   International Federation of Accountants

Source: Adapted from International Federation of Accountants, 2009.

- *Public Interest Oversight Board* (PIOB). The Public Interest Oversight Board (PIOB) is an independent body charged with the oversight of the public interest standard-setting boards in auditing and assurance (IAASB), ethics (IESBA) and education (IAESB), their respective Consultative Advisory Group (CAG) and the Compliance Advisory Panel (CAP). The PIOB reviews and approves the standard-setting board's Terms of Reference and evaluates the boards' due process in standard-setting. It also oversees the work of IFAC's Nominating Committee and approves the committee's nominations to the boards and their CAG. The PIOB's ten members are nominated by the International Organization of Securities Commissions, the Basel Committee on Banking Supervision, the International Association of Insurance Supervisors, the World Bank and the European Commission.

- *Monitoring Group.* The Monitoring Group comprises the regulators and related organization that nominate the members of the PIOB. It evaluates the governance processes of the IFAC and the operations of the PIOB.

- *Consultative Advisory Group* (CAG). A Consultative Advisory Group (CAG) is established for each standard-setting board in auditing and assurance (IAASB), ethics (IESBA) and education (IAESB), as well as for the International Public Sector Accounting Standards Board (IPSASB). CAGs are an integral and important part of the boards' formal process of consultation; CAG members provide advice to the boards on many issues, including the boards' agenda and project priorities. The international financial regulatory community and other organizations involved in the financial reporting process are members of the CAGs.

- *Forum of Firms* (FOF). The Forum of Firms (FOF) is an organization of international firms that perform audits of financial statements that are used across national borders. The objective of the FOF is to promote consistent and high-quality standards of financial reporting and auditing practices worldwide. The work of the FOF is primarily conducted by the Transnational Auditors Committee (TAC).

- *Transnational Auditors Committee* (TAC). The Transnational Auditors Committee (TAC) is the executive arm of FOF. Specific responsibilities of TAC include identifying audit practice issues and qualified candidates to serve on IFAC standard-setting boards. TAC is important in supporting activities and providing expertise to the standard-setting boards and other IFAC committees.

- *Developing Nations Committee.* The Developing Nations Committee represents and addresses the interests of developing nations. Its activities include seeking resources and assistance from IFAC member bodies and other organizations to develop the accountant profession in developing nations.
- *Small and Medium Practices (SMP) Committee.* The Small and Medium Practices (SMP) Committee is established to ensure that the IFAC's and its boards give consideration in the standards-setting to issues relevant to small and medium-sized accounting practices and small and medium-sized entities. The SMP Committee issues guidance to support the use of ISAs in the audit of small and medium-sized entities.
- *Professional Accountants in Business (PAIB) Committee.* The Professional Accountants in Business (PAIB) Committee develops good practice guidelines on issues affecting professional accountants in business, including guidelines on corporate code of conduct and governance in organizations. Professional accountants in business work in commerce, industry, the public sector, education and the not-for-profit sector.
- *International Public Sector Accounting Standards Board* (IPSASB). The International Public Sector Accounting Standards Board (IPSASB) focuses on the accounting and financial reporting needs of governments and related governmental agencies. Its main task is to issue International Public Sector Accounting Standards (IPSASs), which are based largely on the International Financial Reporting Standards issued by the International Accounting Standards Board.
- *Compliance Advisory Panel* (CAP). The Compliance Advisory Panel is the IFAC's instrument to oversee the implementation and operation of the Member Body Compliance Programme. This programme is set up to assess member body's regulatory and standard-setting framework and their self-assessment. The Statements of Membership Obligations (SMOs) are the foundation of the Member Body Compliance Programme.
- *International Auditing and Assurance Standards Board* (IAASB). The International Auditing and Assurance Standards Board is an independent standard-setting body under the auspices of the IFAC and subject to the oversight of the PIOB. The IAASB develops and issues the international standards on quality control, auditing, review, other assurance and related services. (The standard-setting of IAASB is discussed in a later section in this chapter.)
- *International Ethics Standards Board for Accountants* (IESBA). The International Ethics Standards Board for Accountants (IESBA) is an independent standard-setting body under the auspices of the IFAC and subject to the oversight of the PIOB. It develops and issues ethical standards and guidance for use by professional accountants. The issue of the Code of Ethics for Professional Accountants is the IESBA's main task. The Code establishes ethical requirements for professional accountants and provides a conceptual framework for all professional accountants to ensure compliance with fundamental principles of professional ethics. The Code serves as the foundation for codes of ethics developed and enforced by IFAC member bodies. (The IFAC's Code of Ethics for Professional Accountants is discussed in a later section in this chapter and in detail in Chapter 19.)
- *International Accounting Education Standards Board* (IAESB). The International Accounting Education Standards Board (IAESB) is an independent standard-setting body under the auspices of the IFAC and subject to the oversight of the PIOB. The IAESB develops and issues guidance to accounting education around the world. International Education Standards (IESs) express the benchmarks that IFAC member bodies are expected to meet in the preparation and continual development of professional accountants. They establish the essential elements of the content and process of education and development. Additional international education guidelines (IEGs) interpret and expand on matters related to the education standards.

The IFAC's activities also include the appointment of special task forces to address specific issues, and issuance of various reports, papers and practice guidance. For example, as a result of the financial crisis that hit globally in 2008, the IAASB issued two so-called Audit Practice Alerts on auditing fair values and audit considerations in respect of going concern.

The European regional body of IFAC, the Fédération des Experts Comptables Européens (FEE), organizes the professional accountancy bodies in Europe.[v] The FEE's activities cover accounting, auditing, ethics, public-sector accounting, capital markets, environmental issues and regulation of the profession. The organization strongly supports compliance with ISAs throughout Europe. The FEE commands substantial expertise in auditing matters and contributes to audit-sector initiatives taken by the EU. Other regional accounting organizations of the IFAC with parallel activities to the FEE are the Confederation of Asian and Pacific Accountants (CAPA), the Eastern Central and Southern African Federation of Accountants (ECSAFA), and the Interamerican Accounting Association (IAA).

International Accounting Standards Board (IASB)[vi]

The International Accounting Standards Board (IASB) is an independent, privately funded accounting standard-setter that develops international accounting standards for financial statements. The IASB publishes its standards in a series of pronouncements called International Financial Reporting Standards (IFRSs). It has also adopted the body of accounting standards issued by its predecessor, the International Accounting Standards Committee (IASC). Those pronouncements continue to be designated International Accounting Standards (IASs).

Some countries or jurisdictions have adopted the IFRSs as their national financial reporting framework. Other countries have developed national accounting regulations and practices. The IFRSs are generally influential on these national regulations. The EU requires the IFRSs (as adopted by the EU) to be applied to the preparation of consolidated accounts for listed companies in member states. EU member states can opt to adopt the IFRSs for other entities.

The IFAC and the IAASB strongly support the work of the IASB in the setting and promotion of the IFRSs. The ISAs, however, are also designed to be applied to financial reporting frameworks other than the IFRSs.

When this book refers to a specific financial reporting framework and its standards, it refers to the IFRSs. However, this auditing textbook is also relevant for audits of financial statements prepared in accordance with relevant financial reporting frameworks other than that of the IFRS.

International Organization of Securities Commissions (IOSCO)[vii]

The International Organization of Securities Commissions (IOSCO) organizes national securities commissions around the world. Members of IOSCO cooperate to promote high standards of regulation in order to maintain just, efficient and sound capital markets. The IOSCO has a close dialogue with major standard-setters, including the IAASB through its Consultative Advisory Group. The IOSCO is a member of the Monitoring Group that evaluates the governance processes of the IFAC and nominates members of the Public Interest Oversight Board.

International Organization of Supreme Audit Institutions (INTOSAI)[viii]

The International Organization of Supreme Audit Institutions (INTOSAI) assembles Supreme Audit Institutions (Offices of Auditor General) at a global level. The INTOSAI issues standards for government auditing. It cooperates closely with IFAC boards and committees in projects relevant to the public sector and interacts with the IAASB through its representation in the IAASB's Consultative Advisory Group. The ISAs are also relevant for the public-sector and include considerations specific to the audits of public-sector entities.

European Union (EU)

The European Union (EU) consists of 27 member states. The EU Council and the European Parliament take legislative decisions within the EU. National governments are represented within the Council. The European Parliament is directly elected by EU citizens.

The European Commission (EC) takes policy initiatives and makes proposals for new legislation and regulations for the EU, including for the auditing sector. In addition, the Commission acts as the EU's executive body and as the guardian of the EU treaties to ensure that European legislation is applied correctly. The Commission is organized in Directorates-General and Services. The Directorate-General for Internal Market and Services is responsible for company law and financial reporting, including auditing matters.

Historically, there has been a lack of harmonization at the EU level concerning the statutory audit. Concerns were raised that this could have adverse effects on audit quality and caused a handicap in improving the access of European companies to the international capital markets. Against this background, the EU concluded there was a need for further action. The corporate scandals reinforced the need for EU initiatives on statutory audits.

In 2006 the EU issued a new EU 8th Directive on Statutory Audits.[ix] At the time of writing (2009), the member states are in the process of transposition of the Directive into national laws.

The Directive sets out principles for public oversight, criteria for external quality assurance programmes (systems), and principles of auditors' independence for statutory auditors and audit firms. Member states are required to establish audit oversight boards which will be responsible for matters such as approval and registration of audit firms, and investigative and, if necessary, disciplinary actions against audit firms. The Directive refers to the Commission's Recommendation on a set of fundamental principles of auditors' independence (2002). To supplement the Directive, the Commission issued in 2008 a Recommendation on external quality assurance for auditing of public-interest entities. (The independence of auditors and quality assurance are discussed in Chapter 19.) The Directive led to the creation of two new EU bodies to coordinate and implement oversight and regulation within the EU: the European Group of Auditors' Oversight Bodies (EGAOB) and the Audit Regulatory Committee (AuRC).

The Directive introduces stricter requirements for public-interest entities such as listed companies and financial institutions, and for the audit of these. Public-interest entities are required to establish an audit committee. (See Practice Insight 2.6 in the section on corporate governance later in this chapter.) The Directive requires statutory auditors and audit firms that audit public-interest entities to publish on their websites an annual transparency report on specified audit firm information. (See Practice Insight 2.4 in the section on audit firms later in this chapter.)

The Directive states that it is important to ensure consistently high quality in all statutory audits required by Community law. Member states shall require statutory auditors and audit firms to carry out statutory audits in compliance with international auditing standards (i.e. the ISAs) adopted by the Commission. The Directive subjects the adoption of the ISAs to conditions such as their quality and whether they are conducive to the European public good. As of the time of writing of this text (2009) it is not clear how and when the ISAs will be adopted for statutory audits in the EU.

Finally, the Directive provides a basis for cooperation between regulators in the EU and with regulators in third countries, such as the USA Public Company Accounting Oversight Board (PCAOB) discussed in the next section.

The Regulatory Environment in the USA

The Securities and Exchange Commission (SEC) is a government agency that regulates disclosure of information for an initial public offering of securities and ongoing reporting by companies whose securities are listed and traded on a US stock exchange. The SEC has responsibility and authority to oversee the establishment of accounting and auditing standards for public companies.

The quasi-governmental Public Company Accounting Oversight Board (PCAOB), created by the Sarbanes–Oxley Act of 2002, is a regulatory body overseen by the SEC.[x] The Sarbanes–Oxley Act essentially transferred authority for standard setting, inspection, investigation and enforcement for public company audits from the profession to the PCAOB.

The Financial Accounting Standards Board (FASB) is a privately funded body whose mission is to establish US standards for financial accounting and reporting. The Statements of Financial Accounting Standards (SFAS) and interpretations issued by the FASB are recognized as 'US GAAP' (Generally Accepted Accounting Principles) by the SEC, the PCAOB and the accounting profession (the American Institute of Certified Public Accountants – AICPA).

The American Institute of Certified Public Accountants (AICPA) organizes the US accounting profession. Until 2003, the Auditing Standards Board (ASB) was responsible for establishing auditing standards in the USA. The ASB is sponsored by the AICPA. The Sarbanes–Oxley Act gave the PCAOB the authority to either set auditing standards for public company audits itself or to delegate that role to another party. The PCAOB chose to take on the standard-setting role in-house. The ASB continues, however, to promulgate standards that guide audit practice and related services to non-publicly traded companies. At the time of the writing (2009), with the exception of the PCAOB requirement for an integrated audit of internal control and financial statements (see Chapter 7) and some PCAOB modifications to the ASB's standards, the standards of the ASB and the PCAOB are quite similar. This is because the PCAOB adopted the ASB's auditing standards that existed at April 2003. Since the ASBs cooperates closely with the IAASB in developing auditing standards, it implies that US auditing standards are not fundamentally different from the ISAs. An aspect of auditing standard-setting that will be particularly important for you to follow is the convergence of US auditing standards with the ISAs. A common view is that the IAASB has taken the hegemony as the world's leading auditing standard-setter.

❖ AUDITING STANDARDS

LO4

❖

LO5

Auditing standards serve as a guideline for and a measure of the quality of the auditor's performance. Auditing standards help ensure that financial statement audits are conducted in a thorough and systematic way that produces reliable conclusions. The International Auditing and Assurance Standards Board (IAASB) develops and issues the international standards on auditing, as well as the international standards on quality control, review, other assurance and related services. These standards are established as global standards and the standards are applied by auditors all over the world. This book refers extensively to the IAASB's international standards in the text.

International Auditing and Assurance Standards Board (IAASB)

The International Auditing and Assurance Standards Board (IAASB) is a standard-setting board established by the International Federation of Accountants. The IFAC Nominating Committee makes recommendations on members of IAASB. The recommendations are subject to the approval of the independent Public Interest Oversight Board (PIOB) that oversees the IFAC's activities. The PIOB evaluates the due process of the standard-setting of the IAASB, including that the standard-setting was sufficiently responsive to the needs and perceptions of various stakeholders. The IFAC's Statement of Membership Obligation 3 obliges IFAC member bodies to incorporate IAASB standards into their national standards. The PIOB oversees IFAC members' implementation of the international standards.

The IAASB issues international standards on *quality control* (International Standards on Quality Control, ISQCs), *auditing* (International Standards on Auditing, ISAs), *review* (International Standards on Review Engagements, ISREs), *other assurance* (International Standards on Assurance Engagements, ISAEs) and *related services* (International Standards on Related Services, ISRSs). The standards for audits, reviews, other assurance engagements and related services (i.e. ISAs, ISREs, ISAEs and ISRSs) are collectively referred to as the IAASB's **engagement standards**. The IAASB has also issued an *International Framework for Assurance Engagements*. Figure 2–2 illustrates the hierarchy and structure of the IAASB standards.

Figure 2–2 Structure of IAASB standards

International Standards on Quality Control are applied for all engagements falling under IAASB engagement standards. *Quality Control for Firms That Perform Audits and Reviews of Financial Statements, and Other Assurance and Related Services Engagements* (ISQC 1) establishes the audit firm's responsibilities for its system of quality control. (ISQC 1 is discussed in Chapter 19.)

The International Framework for Assurance Engagements defines and describes the objectives and elements of an assurance engagement. An assurance engagement is an audit, review and other assurance engagement. A **review engagement** provides, in contrast to an audit, not reasonable assurance but the lower, limited assurance that the historical financial information does present fairly. Entities' interim financial statements are often reviewed rather than audited. *Other assurance engagements* are engagements that meet the assurance framework's definition of an assurance engagement, but are *not* an engagement to audit or review historical financial information. An example of such other assurance engagement would be if the auditor assures the entity's reporting on its environmental performance. Reporting on environmental performance typically includes non-financial information.

IAASB *related services engagements* are covered by the quality control standards, but are not assurance engagements because the auditor does not provide any assurance in a related services engagement. The International Standards on Related Services (ISRSs) cover compilation and agreed-upon procedures. In a **compilation engagement** the auditor is presenting financial information that is the representation of management without undertaking to express any assurance on the information. An **agreed-upon procedures engagement** is one in which an auditor is engaged by a client to issue a report of factual findings based on specific agreed procedures performed on financial information, i.e. without expressing any assurance. (Chapter 20 discusses in detail reviews, other assurance engagements and related services engagements.)

International Standards on Auditing (ISAs)

The International Standards on Auditing (ISAs) apply to audits of financial statements of entities of all sizes and in all sectors of the economy. In the interpretation of the ISAs and in making informed decisions required in an audit, the auditor applies his or her knowledge and experience to the facts and circumstances of the audit engagement. Such *professional judgement* is essential to the proper conduct of an audit and needs to be exercised throughout the audit. Keep in mind that the auditor never has sufficient evidence to 'guarantee' that the financial statements do not contain material misstatements. An audit conducted in accordance with ISAs is designed to provide **reasonable assurance** that the financial statements taken as a whole are free from material misstatement.

In 2004 IAASB started a comprehensive project to enhance the clarity of the ISAs. This project involved the application of new drafting conventions to all ISAs, either as part of a substantive revision of the standard or through a redrafting. In early 2009 the clarity project was completed. The IAASB has decided that the 36 updated and clarified ISAs are effective for audits of financial statements for periods beginning on or after 15 December 2009. Table 2–1 lists the 36 clarified ISAs.

Table 2–1	International Standards on Auditing
200–299	**General Principles and Responsibilities**:
ISA 200	Overall Objectives of the Independent Auditor and the Conduct of an Audit in Accordance with International Standards on Auditing
ISA 210	Agreeing the Terms of Audit Engagements
ISA 220	Quality Control for an Audit of Financial Statements
ISA 230	Audit Documentation
ISA 240	The Auditor's Responsibilities Relating to Fraud in an Audit of Financial Statements
ISA 250	Consideration of Laws and Regulations in an Audit of Financial Statements
ISA 260	Communication with Those Charged with Governance
ISA 265	Communicating Deficiencies in Internal Control to Those Charged with Governance and Management
300–499	**Risk Assessment and Response to Assessed Risks**
ISA 300	Planning an Audit of Financial Statements
ISA 315	Identifying and Assessing the Risks of Material Misstatement through Understanding the Entity and Its Environment
ISA 320	Materiality in Planning and Performing an Audit
ISA 330	The Auditor's Responses to Assessed Risks
ISA 402	Audit Considerations Relating to an Entity Using a Service Organization
ISA 450	Evaluation of Misstatements Identified during the Audit
500–599	**Audit Evidence**
ISA 500	Audit Evidence
ISA 501	Audit Evidence – Specific Considerations for Selected Items
ISA 505	External Confirmations
ISA 510	Initial Audit Engagements – Opening Balances
ISA 520	Analytical Procedures
ISA 530	Audit Sampling
ISA 540	Auditing Accounting Estimates, Including Fair Value Accounting Estimates, and Related Disclosures
ISA 550	Related Parties
ISA 560	Subsequent Events
ISA 570	Going Concern
ISA 580	Written Representations
600–699	**Using Work of Others**
ISA 600	Special Considerations – Audits of Group Financial Statements (Including the Work of Component Auditors)
ISA 610	Using the Work of Internal Auditors
ISA 620	Using the Work of an Auditor's Expert

700–799	**Audit Conclusions and Reporting**
ISA 700	Forming an Opinion and Reporting on Financial Statements
ISA 705	Modifications to the Opinion in the Independent Auditor's Report
ISA 706	Emphasis of Matter Paragraphs and Other Matter Paragraphs in the Independent Auditor's Report
ISA 710	Comparative Information – Corresponding Figures and Comparative Financial Statements
ISA 720	The Auditor's Responsibilities Relating to Other Information in Documents Containing Audited Financial Statements
800–899	**Specialized Areas**
ISA 800	Special Considerations – Audits of Financial Statements Prepared in Accordance with Special Purpose Frameworks
ISA 805	Special Considerations – Audits of Single Financial Statements and Specific Elements, Accounts or Items of a Financial Statement
ISA 810	Engagements to Report on Summary Financial Statements

Taken together the ISAs provide the standards for the auditor's work in fulfilling the *overall objectives* of the auditor in an audit of financial statements, that is:

(a) *To obtain reasonable assurance about whether the financial statements as a whole are free from material misstatement, whether due to fraud or error, thereby enabling the auditor to express an opinion on whether the financial statements are prepared, in all material respects, in accordance with an applicable financial reporting framework; and (b) to report on the financial statements, and communicate as required by the ISAs, in accordance with the auditor's findings.* (ISA 200, para. 11)

Some ISAs deal with the auditor's general responsibilities and others with the application of those responsibilities to specific topics. For example, ISA 500, *Audit Evidence,* deals with the auditor's general responsibility to perform audit procedures to obtain audit evidence while ISA 520, *Analytical Procedures,* deals with the auditor's responsibility to perform **analytical procedures** (i.e. a specific type of audit procedure) to obtain audit evidence. Before continuing, stop and observe how the ISAs are numbered and grouped into categories, and how this relates to the phases of the auditing process.

A clarified ISA is organized into sections (not all ISAs contain sections of introductory material and definitions):

- Introductory material.
- Objectives.
- Definitions.
- Requirements.
- Application and other explanatory material.

The *introductory material* provides context essential to a proper understanding of the ISAs. Introductory material may include information regarding the purpose, scope and subject matter of the ISAs.

The *objective* or objectives of the ISAs provide the context in which the requirements of the ISAs are set. Objectives are to be understood in the context of the overall objectives of the auditor in the audit. The auditor uses the objectives in planning and performing the audit, having regard to the interrelationships among the ISAs. The objectives assist the auditor to determine whether any audit procedures in addition to those required by the ISAs are necessary in pursuance of the objectives stated in the ISAs, and to evaluate whether sufficient appropriate audit evidence has been obtained. If an objective in a relevant ISA cannot be achieved, the auditor shall evaluate whether this prevents him or her from achieving the overall objectives of the audit, and consider as appropriate consequences for the audit opinion.

To promote consistent application and interpretation of the ISAs an ISA may include *definitions* of certain terms used in the ISA. Unless otherwise indicated, those terms will carry the same meanings throughout all ISAs.

The *requirements* of the ISAs are designed to enable the auditor to achieve the objectives of the ISAs, and thereby the overall objectives of the auditor. The requirements are expressed using the word 'shall'. The auditor complies with the requirements of an ISA in all cases where they are *relevant* in the circumstances of the audit. An ISA is relevant (or not relevant) to the audit when the circumstances addressed by the ISA (do not) exist. For example, if an entity does not have an internal audit function, ISA 610 *Using the Work of Internal Auditors* is not relevant. In *exceptional circumstances,* the auditor may judge it necessary to depart from a relevant requirement in an ISA and perform alternative audit procedures to achieve the aim of that requirement. The need for the auditor to depart from a relevant requirement is expected to arise only where the requirement is for a specific procedure to be performed and, in the specific circumstances of the audit, that procedure would be ineffective in achieving the aim of the requirement. In such exceptional circumstances, the auditor documents the reasons for the departure and how the alternative audit procedures performed achieve the aim of that requirement.

The *application and other explanatory material* contained in an ISA is an integral part of the ISA. This means that the auditor shall have an understanding of the entire text of an ISA, including its application and other explanatory material, to understand its objectives and to apply its requirements properly. The application and other explanatory material provides further explanation of and guidance for carrying out the requirements of the ISA, such as examples of procedures that may be appropriate in the circumstances. Such guidance is, however, not intended in itself to impose a requirement. An ISA may also include appendices. These form part of the application and other explanatory material, and are therefore also an integral part of the ISA.

The application and other explanatory material may include additional considerations specific to audits of smaller entities and public-sector entities. These additional considerations assist in the application of the requirements of the ISA in the audit of such entities. They do not, however, limit or reduce the responsibility of the auditor to apply and comply with the requirements of the ISAs.

As discussed, the auditor shall comply with all ISAs relevant to the audit. Further, the auditor shall not represent compliance with ISAs in the auditor's report unless the auditor has complied fully with *all* of those ISAs relevant to the audit.

The ISAs do not override the local laws or regulations that govern the audit of historical financial statements. In the event that such law or regulation differs from the ISAs, an audit conducted only in accordance with law or regulation will not automatically comply with ISAs. The auditor may conduct the audit in accordance with both the ISAs and the auditing standards of a specific jurisdiction or country. In such cases, in addition to complying with each of the ISAs relevant to the audit, it may be necessary for the auditor to perform additional audit procedures in order to comply with the relevant standards of that jurisdiction or country.

In an audit in accordance with the ISAs, the auditor shall comply with relevant ethical requirements, including those pertaining to independence.

❖ SOCIETY'S EXPECTATIONS AND THE AUDITOR'S RESPONSIBILITIES

LO6

Financial statement audits play an important role in the functioning of our economy, and thus our society expects auditors to exercise professional judgement and maintain professional scepticism in their work. **Professional judgement** means that the auditor, within the context provided by auditing and ethical standards, applies relevant training, knowledge and experience in making informed decisions during the audit. **Professional scepticism** means an attitude that includes a questioning mind and a critical assessment of audit evidence. If the auditor fails to exercise professional judgement and to maintain professional scepticism, he or she may be held liable.

Many readers of financial statements believe that auditors are ultimately responsible for the financial statements or at least that they have a responsibility to detect *all* errors and fraud. This is simply not true. While auditors must exercise professional judgement and maintain professional scepticism in their work, the financial statements ultimately are the responsibility of management (note that the assertions are called *management assertions*). It is important to remember that while auditors do have important responsibilities, *management* is primarily responsible for the fairness of the entity's financial statements.

Auditing standards (ISA 240) provide the following responsibility to detect errors and fraud for auditors:

> *An auditor conducting an audit in accordance with ISAs is responsible for obtaining reasonable assurance that the financial statements taken as a whole are free from material misstatement, whether caused by fraud or error. Owing to the inherent limitations of an audit, there is an unavoidable risk that some material misstatements of the financial statements may not be detected, even though the audit is properly planned and performed in accordance with the ISAs.*

Pause for a moment and be sure you understand that the subsequent discovery of a material misstatement of the financial statements resulting from errors or fraud does not by itself indicate a failure to conduct an audit in accordance with ISAs, but also that the inherent limitations of an audit are not a justification for the auditor to be satisfied with less-than-persuasive audit evidence. Whether the auditor has performed an audit in accordance with ISAs is determined by the audit procedures performed in the circumstances, the sufficiency and appropriateness of the audit evidence obtained as a result thereof, and the suitability of the auditor's report based on an evaluation of that evidence in light of the overall objectives of the auditor.

The auditor's responsibility to provide reasonable assurance with respect to errors and fraud clearly shapes the auditor's environment. More information on the auditor's responsibility for errors and fraud is contained in Chapters 3.

Practice Insight 2.3

There is an expectation by users of financial statements that the auditor will form an opinion on the financial statements within a reasonable period of time and at a reasonable cost, recognizing that it is impracticable to address all information that may exist or to pursue every matter exhaustively on the assumption that information is in error or fraudulent until proved otherwise (ISA 200).

ETHICS, INDEPENDENCE AND THE IFAC CODE OF ETHICS FOR PROFESSIONAL ACCOUNTANTS

LO7

As envisioned ethical behaviour and independence on the part of the auditor are vital to the audit function. The demand for auditing arose from the need for a competent, independent person to monitor the contractual arrangements between principal and agent. If an auditor is incompetent or lacks independence, the parties to the contract will place little or no value on the service provided.

Ethics refers to a system or code of conduct based on moral duties and obligations that indicates how we should behave. *Professionalism* refers to the conduct, aims, or qualities that characterize or mark a profession or professional person.[xi] Most professions (e.g. medicine, law and accounting) operate under some type of code of ethics or code of conduct. The IFAC Code of Ethics for Professional Accountants issued by the International Ethics Standards Board for Accountants establishes acceptable behaviour for professional accountants around the world. No IFAC member body or firm is allowed to apply less stringent standards than those stated in the Code unless prohibited from complying with a certain part of the Code by law or regulation. Part A of the Code defines the fundamental ethical principles for behaviour and the conceptual framework for applying those principles. The fundamental principles are integrity, objectivity, professional competence and due care, confidentiality, and professional behaviour. The conceptual framework should assist the professional accountant to identify, evaluate and respond to threats to compliance with the fundamental principles. Part B and C of the Code illustrate how the conceptual framework contained in Part A is applied in specific situations, including in Part B in situations where independence may be challenged. A distinction is made between *independence of mind* and *independence in appearance*. An auditor must not only be independent of mind but also avoid actions and circumstances that may appear to affect independence. If an auditor is perceived as not being independent, users may lose confidence in the auditor's ability to report objectively and truthfully on financial statements. The IFAC Code of Ethics is an important element worldwide of the environment in which the auditors work.

Auditors are frequently faced with situations that may test their professionalism, ethical character and independence. For example, auditors' independence is tested when clients engage in *opinion shopping* – that is, when clients seek the views of other auditors, hoping they will agree with the client's desired accounting treatment. Clients sometimes attempt to influence the auditor to go along with the desired accounting treatment by threatening to change auditors. Chapter 19 contains an in-depth discussion of professional ethics and the IFAC Code of Ethics for Professional Accountants.

AUDIT FIRMS

LO8

Small organizations can be audited by a single auditor, operating as the sole owner of an audit firm. However, auditing larger businesses and other organizations requires significantly more resources than a single auditor can provide. Thus, audit firms range in size from a single proprietor to thousands of owners (or 'partners') and thousands of professional and administrative staff employees. Audit firms typically offer a variety of professional services in addition to financial statement audits.

Organization and Composition

Audit firms are organized as proprietorships, general or limited liability partnerships, or corporations. Not all countries allow the audit firms to structure themselves using the corporate form. Structuring audit firms as proprietorships and general partnerships offers additional protection for users of their services because such organizational structures, unlike a corporation, do not provide limited liability for the owners or partners. In such cases, aggrieved parties can seek recourse not only against the audit firm's assets but also against the personal assets of individual partners. This lends additional credibility to the services provided to the users because the individual auditor is willing to risk the loss of his or her personal wealth. Because of litigation against auditors, audit firms tend to organize as corporations when possible.

Audit firms are often categorized by size. The largest firms are the 'Big 4': Ernst & Young, Deloitte, KPMG and PricewaterhouseCoopers. Big 4 firms audit most of the world's larger corporations. These large international organizations are able to serve clients throughout the world by tapping into their worldwide audit network. As illustrated in Exhibit 2–3 Big 4 annual global revenues range from about $23 billion to over $28 billion. They may employ more than 160,000 people. Following the Big 4 in size are several so-called 'mid-tier' international audit network (association) firms. The global revenue of the largest of these firms, BDO International, is over $5 billion.

Exhibit 2–3 Annual Global Revenue of Major Audit Network Firms*		
Audit Firm	*Revenue*	*Growth Rate*
PricewaterhouseCoopers	28.2	14
Deloitte	27.4	19
Ernst & Young	24.5	16
KPMG	22.7	15
BDO International	5.1	9
Grant Thornton International	4.0	14
RSM International	3.6	19
Praxity	3.2	14
Baker Tilly International	3.0	18
Crowe Horwath International	2.9	19
* Annual total global revenue in $ billion for year ending in 2008. (The audit firms differ in year end.) *Source: World Accounting Intelligence* (2009).		

Other audit firms operate primarily within a few countries or one country. These firms may, however, be significant providers of audits and other professional services within their markets. Finally, there are thousands of regional and local audit firms that have one or a few offices. These audit firms provide audit, tax, consulting and accounting services, generally to smaller entities.

Audits beyond the very small ones are usually conducted by teams of auditors. The typical audit engagement team is composed of, in order of authority, a partner, a manager, one or two seniors, and several staff members. Audit teams for large international entities are typically made up of several partners and managers and many seniors and staff. The lead engagement partner has the authority and decision-making responsibility for auditing matters, including the issuance of the audit report. Table 2–2 summarizes the duties performed by each member of the audit team.

Table 2–2 Selected Duties of Audit Team Members	
Audit Team Member	*Selected Duties*
Partner	• Reaching agreement with the client on the scope of the service to be provided.
	• Ensuring that the audit is properly planned.
	• Ensuring that the audit team has the required skills and experience.
	• Supervising the audit team and reviewing the working papers.
	• Signing the audit report.
Manager	• Ensuring that the audit is properly planned, including scheduling of team members.
	• Reviewing the working papers, financial statements, and audit report.
	• Dealing with invoicing and ensuring collection of payment for services.
	• Informing the partner about any auditing or accounting problems encountered.
Senior/In-charge	• Assisting in the development of the audit plan.
	• Preparing budgets.
	• Assigning audit tasks to associates and directing the day-to-day performance of the audit.
	• Supervising and reviewing the work of the associate.
	• Informing the manager about any auditing or accounting problems encountered.
Associate/Staff	• Performing the audit procedures assigned to them.
	• Preparing adequate and appropriate documentation of completed work.
	• Informing the senior about any auditing or accounting problems encountered.

Practice Insight 2.4

The EU 8th Directive on Statutory Audits requires auditors and audit firms that audit public-interest entities to publish an annual *transparency report*. The report should include disclosure on the audit firm's legal and governance structure (and if applicable for the network the audit firm belongs to), internal quality control system, last quality assurance review, public-interest entity clients, independence practices, fees by categories, and compensation scheme for audit partners.

TYPES OF SERVICES OFFERED BY AUDIT FIRMS

LO9

In addition to the financial statement audit, audit firms offer non-audit assurance services, related services, tax services, advisory services and accounting services, as well as a number of other specialized services. In this section, examples of these services are briefly discussed. A number of the services discussed in the following may be provided by different types of auditors as well as by non-auditors such consultants and lawyers.

Non-Audit Assurance Services

Opportunities where auditors can provide assurance services typically arise from the need for management to be accountable to employees, shareholders, customers and the public. In this section, examples of non-audit assurance services are briefly discussed. (Chapter 20 offers a detailed discussion of non-audit assurance engagements.)

Review

Small and medium-sized entities that are not required to have an audit may engage an auditor to review their financial statements, for example a review of the financial statements may be needed as part of loan application. Further, listed companies may have their interim financial information reviewed, ordinarily by their financial statement auditor. The scope of a review is substantially less than an audit. The procedures in a review consist primarily of applying analytical procedures and making enquiries to management. The review provides a basis to express a conclusion whether anything has come to the auditor's attention that causes him or her to believe that the financial information is not in accordance with the **applicable financial reporting framework**. In a review the auditor gives limited assurance that the financial information do present fairly.

Other Assurance Services

Audit firms offer assurance services beyond audits and reviews. These services may cover information on a wide variety of subject matters. For example, assurance may be provided on the entity's reporting of prospective financial information, sustainability performance, effectiveness of internal controls, or compliance with laws and regulations. To illustrate, a growing number of companies publish sustainability reports that contain information on their environmental, social and economic performance. The users of such reports may be concerned about the credibility of such reporting. An assurance provider such as an audit firm can add credibility to sustainability reports. (See Chapter 20 for a detailed discussion of assurance of sustainability reporting and other non-traditional assurance engagements.)

Related Services

Related services are either agreed-upon procedures regarding financial information or a compilation of financial information. An agreed-upon procedures engagement is one in which an auditor is engaged by a client to issue a report of factual findings based on specific procedures performed on the subject matter. In a compilation engagement the auditor is engaged to use accounting expertise to collect, classify and summarize financial information. (Related services are discussed in Chapter 20.)

Other Services

In addition to various assurance engagements (including audits of financial statements and reviews) and related services, audit firms typically perform three other broad categories of services: (1) tax services, (2) advisory services and (3) accounting services. These three services, together with audits of financial statements, ordinarily generate most of the audit firms' revenues. Exhibit 2–4 presents the practice mix of the major international audit firms by revenues. The audit firm's service portfolio may also include a variety of other specialized services. Forensic audit is an example of such specialized service and is discussed in the following.

Exhibit 2–4 Global Practice Mix of Services by Major Audit Network Firms (Revenue*)				
Audit firm	Total	Audit/Assurance	Tax	Advisory/Consulting
PricewaterhouseCoopers	28.2	13.8	7.5	6.9
Deloitte	27.4	12.7	6.0	8.7
Ernst & Young	24.5	16.3	6.1	2.1
KPMG	22.7	10.7	4.7	7.3
BDO International	5.1	2.9	1.0	1.2
Grant Thornton International	4.0	2.1	0.9	1.0
RSM International	3.6	1.8	1.0	0.8
Praxity	3.2	2.0	0.7	0.5
Baker Tilly International	3.0	1.5	0.7	0.8
Crowe Horwath International	2.9	1.6	0.6	0.7

* Annual global revenue in $ billion for year ending in 2008. (Audit firms differ in year end.)
Audit/Assurance may include accounting services. Advisory/ Consulting for Deloitte includes financial advisory services ($2.4) and consulting services ($6.3). Audit/Assurance for Ernst & Young includes assurance and advisory business services, and their Advisory/Consulting is transaction advisor services. Advisory/Consulting for BDO International includes other revenues ($0.15). Advisory/Consulting for Crowe Horwath International includes management consulting, corporate finance, corporate recovery/insolvency and other.
Sources: Home pages or direct from the audit firms.

Tax Services

Audit firms have tax departments that assist clients with preparing and filing tax returns, provide advice on tax and estate planning and provide representation on tax issues before the tax authorities or tax courts. In addition to auditors tax departments engage lawyers.

Advisory Services

Advisory services are consulting activities that may involve providing advice and assistance concerning an entity's organization, personnel, finances, operations, systems or other activities. Because of independence and other issues, a number of the major firms have reorganized or sold their consulting practices. However, the audit firms continue to perform advisory services to non-audit clients and to audit clients if appropriate.

Accounting Services

Audit firms may perform a number of accounting services in addition to compilation services for non-audit clients. These services include bookkeeping, payroll processing and preparing financial statements.

Forensic Audits

A forensic audit's purpose is the detection or deterrence of fraudulent activities. The use of auditors to conduct forensic audits has increased significantly in recent years. Some examples where a forensic audit might be conducted include:

- Business or employee fraud.
- Criminal investigations.
- Shareholder and partnership disputes.
- Business economic losses.
- Matrimonial disputes.

For example, in a business fraud engagement, an audit might involve tracing expenditures or identifying and recovering assets. Exhibit 2–5 describes a forensic audit conducted by a major audit firm for the board of directors of Lernout & Hauspie Speech Products NV. Some audit firms specialize in forensic audit services.

Exhibit 2–5 PricewaterhouseCoopers Issues Report on Fraudulent Activities at Lernout & Hauspie

Lernout & Hauspie Speech Products NV (L&H), headquartered in Leper, Belgium, was a leader in speech translation software. L&H went public and at one time had a market capitalization of nearly $6 billion. In 2000, inflated reported revenues claims in Asia of the high-flying company caught the attention of securities regulators in Belgium and the USA. Subsequently, the company filed for bankruptcy in both Belgium and the USA.

At the request of the company's new management, PricewaterhouseCoopers (PwC) was hired to conduct a forensic audit of the accounting fraud. PwC discovered that most of the fraud occurred in L&H's Korean unit. In an effort to obtain bonuses based on sales targets, the managers of the Korean unit went to great lengths to fool L&H's auditor, KPMG. The PwC auditors reported that the Korean unit used two types of schemes to perpetrate the fraud. One involved factoring of receivables with banks to obtain cash to disguise the fact that the receivables were not valid. L&H Korea gave the banks side letters that provided that the money would be given back if the banks could not collect them. These side letters were concealed from KPMG. The second scheme arose after KPMG questioned why L&H Korea was not collecting more of its outstanding receivables. L&H Korea had its customers transfer their contracts to third parties, who then took out bank loans to pay L&H Korea. L&H Korea provided the collateral for the loans. PwC reported that nearly 70 per cent of the $160 million in sales booked in the Korean unit of L&H were fictitious.

Sources: M. Maremont, J. Elsinger and J. Carreyrou, 'How High-Tech Dream at Lernout & Houspie Crumbled in a Scandal', *Wall Street Journal* (7 December 2000), pp. A1, A18; J. Carreyrou and M. Maremont, 'Lernout Unit Engaged in Massive Fraud to Fool Auditors, New Inquiry Concludes', *Wall Street Journal* (6 April 2001), p. A3; and J. Carreyrou, 'Lernout Unit Booked Fictitious Sales, Says Probe', *Wall Street Journal* (9 April 2001), p. B2.

 # TYPES OF AUDITORS

LO10

A number of different types of auditors can be identified; however, most can be classified under four headings: external auditors, internal auditors, government auditors and forensic auditors. One important requirement for each type of auditor is independence, in some form, from the entity being audited. As described below, each different type of auditor usually specializes in a particular type of audit work. However, they each often provide a number of the types of services described in the previous section.

External Auditors

External auditors are often referred to as *independent auditors* or *professional accountants in public practice*. Such auditors are called 'external' because they are not employed by the entity being audited. In this book, the terms *external auditor, independent auditor, professional accountants in public practice, practitioner* or simply *auditor* will be used interchangeably. A *statutory auditor* is an external auditor approved to carry out an audit of the financial statements required by law. Typically, auditors hold some form of licence or authorization. For instance, they are certified, chartered, registered or state-authorized.

External auditors audit financial statements for publicly traded and private companies, partnerships, municipalities, other types of entities and individuals. They may also conduct other services for such entities. However, regulation and codes of ethics restrict some types of services such as certain advisory services that an external auditor can provide to financial statement audit clients.

The professional qualifications to act as an auditor are regulated. The requirements for licensing vary among nations and jurisdictions. Typically a university or college degree with selected courses in topics such as accounting, auditing, business administration, and business and tax law is required. Before a licence is granted, a period of professional practice is ordinarily needed. To keep the licence, continuing professional education requirements apply. The EU 8th Directive on Statutory Audits sets the minimum educational and professional practice requirements for statutory auditors in member states. The IFAC's International Accounting Education Standards Board issues international guidance to accounting education.

Internal Auditors

Auditors that are employees of individual companies, government bodies and other entities are called internal auditors. In major corporations, internal audit staff may be very large and the director of internal auditing is usually a major position within the entity.

The Institute of Internal Auditors (IIA) is the global organization supporting internal auditors. Its mission is to be 'the primary international professional association, organized on a worldwide basis, dedicated to the promotion and development of the practice of internal auditing'. The IIA has developed a set of standards to be followed by internal auditors and has established a certification programme. An individual who meets the certification requirements established by the IIA, including passing a uniform written examination, can become a certified internal auditor (CIA).[xii] Many internal auditors also hold a licence as external auditor.

The Institute of Internal Auditors (IIA) defines **internal auditing** as 'an independent, objective assurance and consulting activity designed to add value and improve an organization's operations. It helps an organization accomplish its objectives by bringing a systematic, disciplined approach to evaluate and improve the effectiveness of risk management, control, and governance processes.'

Internal auditors may conduct financial, internal control, compliance, operational and forensic audits, as well as consulting within their organizations. They in some cases may assist the external auditors with the annual financial statement audit. Chapter 20 offers more detail on the IIA and the internal auditing profession.

Government Auditors

Government auditors are employed by national or local governmental institutions and public bodies. The majority of government auditors provide assurance on compliance and operational performance, ordinarily termed compliance audits and operational performance audits. A compliance audit determines the extent to which rules, policies, laws or government regulations are followed by the entity being audited, for example an examination of tax returns of individuals and companies by the tax law enforcement authorities for compliance with the tax laws. An operational performance audit involves a systematic review of part or all of an organization's activities to evaluate whether resources are being used effectively and efficiently.

At the national level most countries have established an Office of Auditor General (Supreme Audit Institution). Such offices are normally empowered by the constitution and are responsible to parliament or a similar legislative institution. Offices of Auditor General monitor the use of public funds, conduct assurance of activities, financial transactions and accounts of the government. They may also assist

Parliament by performing special audits, surveys and investigations. The fact that they report directly to Parliament provides the Offices of Auditor General with an organizational arrangement that ensures objectivity and independence.

Most regional and local governments and municipals also have audit offices that perform functions similar to the Office of the Auditor General. Such offices include tax auditors that ensure that individuals and organizations are complying with tax laws. Finally, there are international organizations that support the government audit profession such as the International Organization of Supreme Audit Institutions (INTOSAI).

Forensic Auditors

Forensic auditors are employed by corporations, government agencies, audit firms, and consulting and investigative services firms. They are trained in detecting, investigating and deterring fraud and white-collar crime (see the discussion of forensic auditing earlier in the chapter). Some examples of situations where forensic auditors have been involved include:

- Reconstructing incomplete accounting records to settle an insurance claim over inventory valuation.
- Probing money-laundering activities by reconstructing cash transactions.
- Investigating and documenting embezzlement and negotiating insurance settlements.

The Association of Certified Fraud Examiners (ACFE) is the global organization supporting forensic auditors.[xiii.] The ACFE is a 40,000-member professional organization dedicated to educating certified fraud examiners (CFEs), who are trained in the specialized aspects of detecting, investigating and deterring fraud and white-collar crime.

The ACFE offers a certification programme for individuals wanting to become CFEs. Individuals interested in becoming a CFE must pass the Uniform CFE Examination. Certified fraud examiners come from various professional backgrounds, including auditors, accountants, fraud investigators, loss prevention specialists, lawyers, educators and criminologists. They gather evidence, take statements, write reports and assist in investigating fraud in its varied forms.

❖ THE CONTEXT OF FINANCIAL STATEMENT AUDITING

LO11

The chapter has so far explained how the corporate scandals, the regulatory environment and the nature of audit firms affect the accounting profession and auditing. This section is designed to help you understand how the audit client's business, industry and economic environment shape the context in which auditing takes place and directly affect how the audit is performed.

Business as the Primary Context of Auditing

In studying subsequent chapters, you will be building your auditing tool kit. How you apply auditing tools on any particular engagement will depend greatly on the nature of the client's business. For example, if you are auditing a computer hardware manufacturer, one of your concerns will be whether your client has inventories that are not selling quickly and are becoming obsolete due to industry innovation. Such inventory might not be properly valued on the client's financial records. If you are auditing a jeweller you will probably not be as worried about obsolescence, but you will still be interested in whether the diamonds and other gems in inventory are valued properly. You may need to hire a qualified gemologist to help you assess the valuation assertion, and you would certainly want to keep up on the dynamics of the international diamond and gem markets. The point is that the context provided by the client's business greatly impacts the auditor and the audit, and is thus a primary component of the environment in which financial statement auditing is conducted. While every business is different, business organizations can be conceptualized or modelled in common ways. The next section describes the essential characteristics of a business: governance, objectives, strategies, processes, risks, controls and reporting.

> **Practice Insight 2.5**
>
> The nature of a client's business can have a dramatic effect on the nature of the auditor's work and work environment. For example, an auditor working at a meat-packing client will have very different experiences from an auditor working at a banking client. Further, many auditors eventually specialize in certain industries and acquire significant expertise in those industries. This expertise and specialization often leads to attractive employment opportunities as a member of management. Thus, in choosing which firm (or which office of a large firm) at which to seek a job, new auditors are well advised to consider carefully whether the firm (or office) has a significant presence in the industries in which the prospective auditor is most interested.

❖ A MODEL OF BUSINESS

LO12

Business organizations exist to create value for their stakeholders. To form a business enterprise, entrepreneurs decide on an appropriate organizational form (e.g. corporation or partnership) and hire managers to manage the resources that have been made available to the enterprise through investment or lending.

Corporate Governance

Due to the way resources are invested and managed in the modern business world, a system of *corporate governance* is necessary, through which managers are overseen and supervised. Simply defined, **corporate governance** consists of all the people, processes and activities in place to help ensure proper stewardship over an entity's assets. Good corporate governance ensures that those managing an entity properly utilize their time, talents and the entity's resources in the best interest of owners and other stakeholders, and that they faithfully report the economic condition and performance of the enterprise.

Those charged with governance are person(s) or organization(s) with responsibility for overseeing the strategic direction of the entity and obligations related to the accountability of the entity. The structures of corporate governance vary from country to country, reflecting cultural and legal backgrounds. For example, in some countries, the supervision function and the executive function are legally separated into different bodies (a 'two-tier board' structure), such as a supervisory (wholly or mainly non-executive) board and a management board. In other countries, both functions are the legal responsibility of a single board (a 'one-tier board' structure) such as a **board of directors**. Management is person(s) with executive responsibility for the conduct of the entity's operations. In small entities those charged with governance are often the same individual(s) as management. For example, the role of those charged with governance is undertaken by the owner-manager where there are no other owners. Since governance structures vary by country and by entity characteristics, this book ordinarily refers to *those charged with governance* instead of specific governing bodies. Auditing standards require the auditor to make a number of important communications of audit matters to those charged with governance (see Chapters 5 and 17).

An **audit committee** exists to assist the governing body in meeting its responsibilities with respect to financial reporting. In an increasing number of countries and jurisdictions an audit committee is a mandatory requirement for listed companies and financial institutions. For example, the EU 8th Directive on Statutory Audits requires public-interest entities to establish an audit committee. (See Practice Insight 2.6.) Companies may also establish audit committees on a voluntary basis. The composition of the audit committee may vary and the committee's responsibilities may differ. In a 'one-tier' board structure, an audit committee is normally a subcommittee of the board of directors that has overall responsible for the financial reporting and disclosure process. Members of the audit committee may be required to be independent and have competence in accounting and auditing. 'Independent' ordinarily means not receiving, other than for service on the audit committee, any consulting, advisory or other compensatory fee, and not being affiliated with the company. The audit committee may be directly responsible for the appointment, compensation and oversight of the work of the audit firm engaged by the company. Further, audit and non-audit services provided by its auditor may require pre-approval by the audit committee. Through the link with the audit committee and other interactions with those charged with governance, and through the audit of the financial statements, auditors play an important role in facilitating effective corporate governance.

In many countries best practice corporate governance codes or guidance have been developed for listed companies, for example the UK Combined Code on Corporate Governance. At the global level the Organisation for Economic Co-operation and Development (OECD), in 2004, issued *Principles of Corporate Governance* to improve corporate governance. The Professional Accountants in Business Committee of IFAC issues guidance on good corporate governance.

Practice Insight 2.6

The EU 8th Directive on Statutory Audits requires public-interest entities to have an audit committee. The statutory auditor shall report to the audit committee on key matters arising from the statutory audit, and in particular on material weaknesses in internal control in relation to the financial reporting process.

The audit committee shall:

- Monitor the financial reporting process.
- Monitor the effectiveness of the company's internal control, internal audit where applicable, and risk management systems.
- Monitor the statutory audit of the annual and consolidated account.
- Review and monitor the independence of the statutory auditor or audit firm, and in particular the provision of additional services to the audited entity.

Objectives, Strategies, Processes, Controls, Transactions and Reports

Management, with guidance and direction from those charged with governance (e.g. the board of directors), decides on a set of *objectives*, along with *strategies* designed to achieve those objectives. The organization then undertakes certain *processes* in order to implement its strategies. The organization must also assess and manage risks that may threaten the achievement of its objectives. While the processes implemented in business organizations are as varied as the different types of businesses themselves, most business enterprises establish processes that fit in five broad *process categories*, sometimes known as *cycles*. The five categories that characterize the processes of most businesses are the *revenue process*, the *purchasing process*, the *human resource management process*, the *inventory management process* and the *financing process*. Each process involves a variety of important transactions.

The enterprise must design and implement *accounting information systems* to capture the details of those transactions. It must also design and implement a *system of internal control* to ensure that the transactions are handled and recorded appropriately and that its resources are protected. The accounting information system must be capable of producing financial reports, which summarize the effects of the organization's transactions on its account balances and which are used to establish management accountability to outside owners. The next section provides a brief overview of the five process categories listed above. Auditors often rely on this process model to divide the audit of a business's financial statements into manageable pieces. Chapters 10 through to 16 go into considerable detail regarding how these processes typically function and how they are used to organize an audit.

❖ A MODEL OF BUSINESS PROCESSES: FIVE COMPONENTS

LO13

Figure 2–3 illustrates the five basic **business processes** into which auditors typically organize a financial statement audit in context with the overall business model presented in the previous section. Let us briefly discuss each of the five processes.

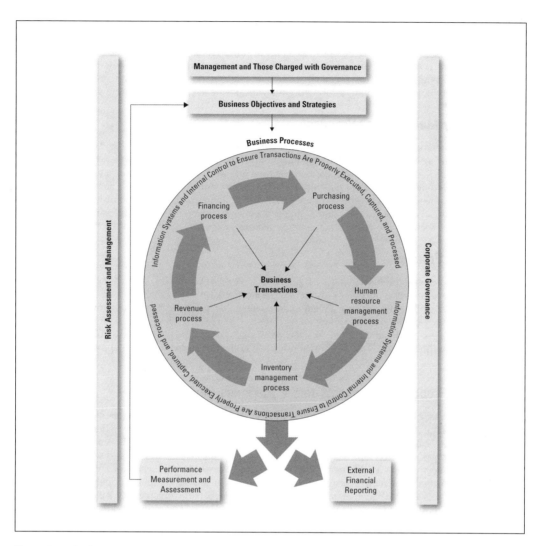

Figure 2–3   An Overview of Business

The Financing Process

Businesses obtain capital through borrowing or soliciting investments from owners, and typically invest in assets such as land, buildings and equipment in accordance with their strategies. As part of this process, businesses also need to repay lenders and provide a return on owner investments. These types of transactions are all part of the financing process. For example, EarthWear tends not to rely on long-term debt financing. Instead, it primarily uses capital provided by shareholders to invest in long-term assets such as its headquarters building, retail stores, and various order and distribution centres.

The Purchasing Process

Businesses must acquire goods and services to support the sale of their own goods or services. For example, EarthWear must purchase inventory to sell to its customers. The company must also purchase office supplies, needed services, and many other items to support its activities.

The Human Resource Management Process

Business organizations hire personnel to perform various functions in accordance with the enterprise's mission and strategy. At EarthWear this process starts with the establishment of sound policies for hiring, training, evaluating, counselling, promoting, compensating and terminating employees. The main transaction in this process that affects the financial statement accounts is a payroll transaction, which usually begins with an employee performing a job and ends with payment being made to the employee.

The Inventory Management Process

This process varies widely between different types of businesses. Service providers (such as auditors, lawyers or advertising agencies) rarely have significant inventories to manage, since their primary resources typically consist of information, knowledge, and the time and effort of people. Manufacturers, wholesalers and retailers, including EarthWear, all typically have significant, numerous and often complex transactions belonging to the inventory management process. While the actual purchasing of finished goods or raw materials inventories is included in the purchasing process (see above), the inventory management process for a manufacturer includes the cost-accounting transactions to accumulate and allocate costs to inventory.

The Revenue Process

Businesses generate revenue through sales of goods or services to customers, and collect the proceeds of those sales in cash, either immediately or through collections on receivables. For example, EarthWear retails high-quality clothing for outdoor activities. To create value for its customers, employees and owners, EarthWear must successfully process orders for, and deliver its clothing to, customers. It must also collect cash on those sales, either at the point of sale or through later billing and collection of receivables. Management establishes controls to ensure that sales and collection transactions are appropriately handled and recorded.

Relating the Process Components to the Business Model

Pause for a moment and take another look at Figure 2–3. How might the components of our model differ for a client in automobile manufacturing versus banking, and how might those differences affect the auditor's work? How might differences in these components affect the risk of material misstatement in the financial statements? Management establishes processes in the five categories discussed above to implement the organization's strategies and achieve its objectives. Management then identifies risks, or possible threats to the achievement of established objectives (including compliance with applicable laws and regulations and reliable external reporting), and ensures that the organization's system of internal control mitigates those risks to acceptable levels. The organization's accounting information system must be capable of reliably measuring the performance of the business to assess whether objectives are being met and to comply with external reporting requirements. Financial statements, which are affected by all the different components of our business model, represent an important output of the entity's efforts to measure the organization's performance and an important form of external reporting and accountability.

 MANAGEMENT ASSERTIONS

LO14

In Chapter 1, we introduced the concept that the financial statements issued by management contain both explicit and implicit **assertions**. Table 2–3 summarizes and explains management assertions. Take a few minutes to examine and understand these assertions – you will see over the next several chapters that this simple conceptual tool is actually quite powerful and underlies much of what auditors do.

Table 2–3   Summary of Management Assertions by Category

Assertions about classes of transactions and events for the period under audit
- **Occurrence** – transactions and events that have been recorded have occurred and pertain to the entity.
- **Completeness** – all transactions and events that should have been recorded have been recorded.
- **Authorization** – all transactions and events have been properly authorized.*
- **Accuracy** – amounts and other data relating to recorded transactions and events have been recorded appropriately.
- **Cut-off** – transactions and events have been recorded in the correct accounting period.
- **Classification** – transactions and events have been recorded in the proper accounts.

Assertions about account balances at the period end
- **Existence** – assets, liabilities and equity interests exist.
- **Rights and obligations** – the entity holds or controls the rights to assets, and liabilities are the obligations of the entity.
- **Completeness** – all assets, liabilities and equity interests that should have been recorded have been recorded.
- **Valuation and allocation** – assets, liabilities and equity interests are included in the financial statements at appropriate amounts and any resulting valuation or allocation adjustments are appropriately recorded.

Assertions about presentation and disclosure
- **Occurrence and rights and obligations** – disclosed events, transactions and other matters have occurred and pertain to the entity.
- **Completeness** – all disclosures that should have been included in the financial statements have been included.
- **Classification and understandability** – financial information is appropriately presented and described, and disclosures are clearly expressed.
- **Accuracy and valuation** – financial and other information are disclosed fairly and at appropriate amounts.

*The International Standards on Auditing (ISA 315) do not list authorization as a financial statement assertion. We list authorization as a separate assertion about classes of transactions for instructional purposes.

The presentation explicitly recognizes that auditors evaluate management assertions as they are applied to three aspects of information reflected in the financial statements: transactions, account balances, and presentation and disclosure. For example, management asserts, among other things, that transactions relating to inventory actually *occurred*, that they are *complete* (i.e. no valid transactions were left out), that they are *classified* properly (e.g. as an asset rather than an expense), and that they are recorded *accurately* and in the correct period. Similarly, management asserts that the inventory represented in the inventory account balance *exists*, that the entity *owns* the inventory, that the balance is *complete*, and that the inventory is properly *valued*. Finally, management asserts that the financial statements properly *classify* and *present* the inventory (e.g. inventory is appropriately listed as a current asset on the balance sheet) and that all required *disclosures* having to do with inventory (e.g. a note to the financial statements indicating that the company uses the FIFO – first in first out – inventory method) are *complete, accurate* and *understandable*. Understanding the assertions in terms of transactions, account balances, and presentation and disclosure is helpful because the three categories help the auditor focus on the different types of audit procedures needed to test the assertions in the three different categories. Chapter 5 discusses the types of procedures available to the auditor in more detail.

Although all balance-related assertions apply to nearly every account, not every assertion is equally important for each account. Recognizing the assertions that deserve the most emphasis depends on an understanding of the business and of the particular type of account being audited. For example, auditors typically consider the completeness assertion to be the most important assertion for liability accounts for two reasons. First, when all obligations are not properly included in the liability account, the result is an understatement of liabilities and often an overstatement of profit (net income). Second, management is more likely to have an incentive to understate a liability than to overstate it.

Pause and test your intuition: why might auditors consider existence to be a crucial assertion for accounts receivable? Why would they normally consider existence to be more important than completeness for receivables?

CONCLUSION

Chapter 1 explained why assurance is in demand, defined what auditing is, and laid out the phases through which financial statement auditing is carried out. This chapter explains the broader context in which financial statement auditing takes place. To fully understand auditing, you must be aware of the factors that shape the auditing environment, including the dramatic events over the past several years that led to fundamental change; auditors' legal liability; professional, regulatory and standard setting bodies that govern the accounting profession; auditing standards and how they affect auditor's responsibilities; and codes of ethics and the core value of auditor's independence; as well as how these factors all relate to the auditor's public interest function. You must also understand the nature of the audit firms within which auditors organize themselves to conduct audits of entities of various sizes and to provide a wide range of other services. Finally, you must understand how the client's economic business environment and business processes as well as management's assertions in the financial statements fundamentally and directly impact how auditing is done. This chapter provides an introduction to the complex and ever-changing environment in which financial statement auditing is performed.

🔓 Key Terms

Advisory services. Consulting services that may provide advice and assistance concerning an entity's organization, personnel, finances, operations, systems or other activities.

Agreed-upon procedures engagement. Specific procedures of an audit nature to which the auditor and the entity and any appropriate third parties have agreed and to report on factual findings.

Analytical procedures. Evaluations of financial information through analysis of plausible relationships among both financial and non-financial data.

Applicable financial reporting framework. The financial reporting framework adopted by management and, where appropriate, those charged with governance in the preparation of the financial statements that is acceptable in view of the nature of the entity and the objective of the financial statements, or that is required by law or regulation.

Assertions. Representations by management, explicit or otherwise, that are embodied in the financial statements, as used by the auditor to consider the different types of potential misstatements that may occur.

Audit committee. A committee ordinarily consisting of members of the board of directors, charged with overseeing the entity's system of internal control, internal and external auditors, and the financial reporting process. Members typically must be independent of management.

Board of directors. Persons elected by the shareholders of a corporation to oversee management and to direct the affairs of the corporation.

Business processes. Processes implemented by management to achieve entity objectives. Business processes are typically organized into the following categories: revenue; purchasing; human resource management; inventory management; and financing processes.

Compilation engagement. An engagement in which accounting expertise, as opposed to auditing expertise, is used to collect, classify and summarize financial information.

Corporate governance. The oversight mechanisms in place to help ensure the proper stewardship over an entity's assets. Management and those charged with governance (e.g. the board of directors, the supervisory board, the audit committee) play primary roles and the independent auditor plays a key facilitating role.

Engagement standards (IAASB). Standards for audits, reviews, other assurance engagements and related services.

Ethics. A system or code of conduct based on moral duties and obligations, which indicates how an individual should behave.

Financial statements. A structured representation of historical financial information, including related notes, intended to communicate an entity's economic resources or obligations at a point in time or the changes therein for a period of time in accordance with a financial reporting framework. The related notes ordinarily comprise a summary of significant accounting policies and other explanatory information. The term can refer to a complete set of financial statements, but it can also refer to a single financial statement, for example a balance sheet, or an income statement, and related explanatory notes.

Fraud. Intentional misstatement that can be classified as fraudulent financial reporting and/or misappropriation of assets.

Internal auditing. An appraisal activity established within an entity as a service to the entity. Its functions include, among other things, examining, evaluating and monitoring the adequacy and effectiveness of internal control.

Professional scepticism. An attitude that includes a questioning mind, being alert to conditions that may indicate possible misstatement due to errors or fraud, and a critical assessment of audit evidence.

Professional judgement. The application of relevant training, knowledge and experience, within the context provided by auditing, accounting and ethical standards, in making informed decisions about the courses of action that are appropriate in the circumstances of the audit engagement.

Reasonable assurance. A term which implies that engagement client assurance risk is reduced to an acceptably low level in the circumstances of the engagement. In the context of an audit of financial statements, a high, but not absolute, level of assurance.

Review engagement. An assurance engagement that enables an auditor to state whether, on the basis of procedures that do not provide all the evidence that would be required in an audit, anything has come to the auditor's attention that causes the auditor to believe that the financial statements are not prepared, in all material respects, in accordance with an applicable financial reporting framework.

Those charged with governance. The persons or person with responsibility for overseeing the strategic direction of the entity and obligations related to the accountability of the entity, including overseeing the financial reporting process.

? REVIEW QUESTIONS

LO1	2–1	Briefly discuss the key events that led up to the significant changes that have taken place in the auditing profession over the past several years.
LO1	2–2	Discuss how the events that have so dramatically affected auditors and the accounting profession since the Enron and Parmalat scandals may in some senses be 'healthy' for the profession.
LO2	2–3	What is meant by joint and several liability? Contrast this legal doctrine with the doctrine of proportional liability.
LO3	2–4	What are the functions of the PIOB in the IFAC's governance and standard-setting activities?
LO3	2–5	What role do the IASB, IOSCO and INTOSAI play, and how do these organizations affect the ISAs acceptance as global auditing standards?
LO4	2–6	List the five categories of standards issued by the IAASB. Which of these are designated engagement standards and which are designated assurance standards?
LO5	2–7	List the sections an ISA is organized into and how the sections relate to each other.
LO6	2–8	Compare and contrast management's responsibility for the entity's financial statements with the auditor's responsibilities for detecting errors and fraud in the financial statements.
LO7	2–9	Why is independence such an important standard for auditors? How does auditor independence relate to the agency relationship between owners and managers discussed in Chapter 1?
LO9	2–10	What are the main services offered by audit firms?
LO10	2–11	List the various types of auditors.
LO12	2–12	Briefly discuss each of the components of the high-level model of business offered in the chapter (i.e. corporate governance, objectives, strategies, processes, etc.). Why might understanding the characteristics of a client's business in each of these areas be important for a financial statement auditor?
LO12,13	2–13	What roles do information systems and systems of internal control play in the high-level model of business discussed in the chapter, and why might it be important for an auditor to understand these roles?
LO14	2–14	How might the three categories of management assertions provide a powerful tool for the financial statement auditor?

Problems

LO5,6,7 **2–15** Dale Boucher, the owner of a small electronics firm, asked Sally Jones, independent auditor, to conduct an audit of the company's records. Boucher told Jones that the audit was to be completed in time to submit audited financial statements to a bank as part of a loan application. Jones immediately accepted the engagement and agreed to provide an auditor's report within one month. Boucher agreed to pay Jones her normal audit fee plus a percentage of the loan if it was granted.

Jones hired two recent accounting graduates to conduct the audit, and spent several hours telling them exactly what to do. She told the new hires not to spend time considering the internal control but to concentrate on proving the mathematical accuracy of the general and subsidiary ledgers and summarizing the data in the accounting records that supported Boucher's financial statements. The new hires followed Jones's instructions and after two weeks gave Jones the financial statements excluding notes. Jones reviewed the statements and prepared an audit report with an unmodified opinion. The report did not refer to any auditing standards, and no audit procedures were conducted to evaluate the appropriateness of accounting policies used and the reasonableness of accounting estimates made.

Required:

Indicate how the action(s) of Jones resulted in failure to comply with auditing standards and ethical requirements.
(AICPA, adapted)

LO9,10 **2–16** Various types of auditors offer and perform a wide range of assurance services such as audit of financial statements, review of financial information, assurance on compliance with laws and regulations, assurance on financial forecasts, assurance on the effectiveness of internal control, forensic audits and operational audits.

Required:

For each of the following descriptions, indicate which type of assurance service best characterizes the nature of the service being conducted. Also indicate which type of auditor (external auditor, internal auditor, government auditor, or forensic auditor is likely to perform the engagement.

a *Evaluate the policies and procedures of the Medical Control Agency in terms of bringing new drugs to market.*
b *Determine the fair presentation of Ajax Chemical's balance sheet, income statement and statement of cash flows.*
c *Review the payment procedures of the Accounts Payable Department for a large manufacturer.*
d *Evalute if the internal controls of the entity comply with the criteria of COSO (Committee of Sponsoring Organizations of the Treadway Commission) framework.*
e *Evaluate the feasibility of forecasted rental income for a planned student housing project.*
f *Evaluate a company's computer services department in terms of the efficient and effective use of corporate resources.*
g *Control the partnership tax return of a real estate development company.*
h *Investigate the possibility of payroll fraud in a pension fund.*

Discussion Cases

LO7,9 **2–17** **Part I: Merry-Go-Round** (MGR), a clothing retailer located primarily in shopping malls, was founded in 1968.[xiv] By the early 1990s, the company had gone public and had expanded to approximately 1500 stores, 150,000 employees and $1 billion in annual sales. The company's locations in malls targeted the youth and teen market. The company was listed by *Forbes* magazine as one of the top 25 companies in the late 1980s. However, in the early 1990s, the company faced many challenges. One of its co-founders died, and the other left to pursue unrelated business interests. The company faced stiff competition from other retailers (e.g. Gap and Banana Republic), fashion trends changed and mall traffic declined. Sales fell, and experts speculated that MGR failed to anticipate key industry trends and lost sight of its customer market. To try to regain its strong position, the company acquired Chess King, Inc., a struggling chain of men's clothing stores located in malls, in 1993.

The company's sales continued to fall and, later in 1993, it brought back one of its co-founders to manage the company and wrote down a significant amount of inventory. However, this inventory write-down caused the company to violate loan covenants. Facing bankruptcy, the company, based on the advice of its newly hired law firm Swidler and Berlin, hired turnaround specialists from Ernst & Young (E&Y) to help overcome the financial crisis and develop a long-term business plan. However, the company's decline continued, and it filed for Chapter 11 reorganization in 1994. In 1996, the remaining assets were sold for pennies on the dollar.

Subsequently, a group of 9000 creditors (including former employees and stockholders) began litigation against parties it deemed responsible for their losses. These parties included E&Y, which the creditors sued for $4 billion in punitive and compensatory damages (E&Y's fees from MGR totalled $4.5 million).

The lawsuit alleged that E&Y's incompetence was the main cause of MGR's decline and demise. The lawsuit alleged in part that:

- The turnaround team did not act fast enough.
- The leader of the team took an eight-day vacation at a critical point during the engagement.
- The cost-cutting strategy called for only $11 million in annual savings, despite the fact that the company was projected to lose up to $200 million in 1994.
- While store closings were key to MGR's survival, by 1995 only 230 of 1434 stores had been closed and MGR still operated two stores in some malls.
- The turnaround team included inexperienced personnel – a retired consultant, a partner with little experience in the USA and with retail firms, and two recent college graduates.
- E&Y charged exorbitant hourly rates and charged unreasonable expenses (e.g. charges included reimbursement for a dinner for three of the consultants totalling in excess of $200).
- E&Y denied any wrongdoing, but in April 1999 agreed to pay $185 million to settle with the injured parties.

Required:

Should there be specific professional standards for independent auditors who consult? Given that non-auditors who consult do not have formal professional standards, describe the advantages and disadvantages that result from such standards.

LO7 **2–18** **Part II: Merry-Go-Round**. Additional charges made against E&Y include the following (recall that MGR hired E&Y for turnaround consulting services):

- E&Y had a close relationship with Rouse Co., one of MGR's primary landlords (E&Y was soliciting business from Rouse and provided significant tax services).
- Swidler (the law firm that recommended E&Y to MGR) and E&Y had participated in at least 12 different business arrangements, some of which resulted in Swidler receiving significant fees from E&Y.
- E&Y did not disclose either of these relationships to MGR.

Required:

a Do you think that E&Y acted unethically given it had these relationships?

b How could these relationships have affected E&Y's advice to MGR? In other words, refer to the charges above and speculate as to whether any of the charges against E&Y may have stemmed from the relationships described above.

Internet Assignments

LO3,4   2–19   Go to the IFAC's home site (www.ifac.org).

a Use the links to 'About IFAC' and 'Membership' and learn about IFAC member(s) from your home country (and other members).

b Use the link to 'Standard-Setting Boards' and learn more about the standard-setting boards. Use the link to 'IAASB Clarity Center' on the IAASB home site and learn more about the clarity standard project and clarified standards.

c Use the link to 'Exposure Drafts and Consultation Papers' and learn about outstanding exposure drafts.

d Use the link to 'Site Map' and become familiar with the IFAC's home site.

e Go to the PIOB's home site and learn more about its responsibilities, its members and the organizations that nominate the PIOB members (www.ipiob.org/).

LO3,8,9   2–20   The major international audit firms (cf. Exhibit 2–3) have global (and normally regional and national) home sites accessible on the Internet. Use an Internet search engine to access the audit firms' home sites and do the following (for a number of the audit firms):

a Which services do the audit firms offer?

b Where do the audit firms have locations?

c Collect financial information about the audit firms.

d Collect information about the audit firms' employees (number, positions, etc.).

e Learn about the audit firms' publications.

f Do the audit firms publish transparency reports?

g Are the audit firms members of the IFAC's Forum of Firms? (Hint: go to the IFAC's home site and FOF.)

LO2,4,6,8   2–21   In 2006 the CEOs of six of the major international audit networks published 'Global Capital Markets and the Global Economy: A Vision From the CEOs of the International Audit Networks'. Download the report from the Internet (www.gti.org/files/CEO_vision.pdf) and discuss the following:

a What are the audit firms' arguments for a single global set of standards?

b Which suggestions have the audit firms to confront the 'expectation gap' regarding fraud?

c What are the firms' view on the effects of auditors' legal liability on the concentration in the auditing profession?

Notes

i   For an discussion of global regulation see C. Humphrey and P. Moizer, 'Understanding Regulation in its Global Context', in *Auditing, Trust and Governance – Developing Regulation in Europe* (eds R. Quick, S. Turely and M. Willekens), Routledge, Oxford, 2008.

ii London Economics in association with Professor Ralf Ewert, Goethe University, Frankfurt am Main, Germany: 'Study on the Economic Impact of Auditors' Liability Regimes', September 2006, (http://ec.europa.eu/internal_market/auditing/liability/index_en.htm).

iii European Commission (2008), *Commission Recommendation of 5 June 2008 Concerning the Limitation of the Civil Liability of Statutory Auditors and Audit Firms.* (http://eur-lex.europa.eu/LexUriServ/LexUriServ.do?uri=OJ:L:2008:162:0039:0040:EN:PDF).

iv See the IFAC's home page for more information on the IFAC (www.ifac.org/). For an analysis of IFAC's structures and governance processes see A. Loft, C. Humphrey and S. Turley (2006), 'In Pursuit of Global Regulation – Changing Governance and Accountability Structures at the International Federation of Accountants (IFAC), *Accounting Auditing & Accountability Journal* (3), pp. 428–451.

v See the FEE's home page for more information on the FEE (www.fee.be/).

vi See the IASB's home page for more information on the IASB (www.iasb.org/home).

vii See the IOSCO's home page for more information on the IOSCO (www.iosco.org/).

viii See the INTOSAI's home page for more information on the INTOSAI (www.intosai.org/).

ix The European Economic Area (EEA) unites the 27 EU member states and the three EEA European Free Trade Association (EFTA) states, Iceland, Liechtenstein and Norway, into an internal market governed by the same basic rules. This implies that EU regulatory measures of auditing discussed in the current text also are relevant to Iceland, Liechtenstein and Norway.

x See the PCAOB's website for more information about the PCAOB (www.pcaobus.org).

xi S.M. Mintz, *Cases in Accounting Ethics and Professionalism*, 3rd edn, McGraw-Hill, New York, 1997.

xii See the IIA's home page for more information on the IIA and the certified internal auditor programme (www.theiia.org).

xiii See the ACFE's home page for more information on the association and the CFE programme (www.acfe.org).

xiv The following articles were sources for the information in the case: E. MacDonald, 'Ernst & Young Will Pay $185 Million to Settle Claims of Merry-Go-Round', *Wall Street Journal*, 29 April 1999; E. McDonald and S. J. Paltrow, 'Merry-Go-Round: Ernst & Young Advised the Client, but Not about Everything – It Didn't Reveal Business Ties Alleged to Pose Conflict with Its Consulting Job – Settlement for $185 Million', *Wall Street Journal*, 8 August 1999, p. A1.

PART II

Basic Auditing Concepts: Risk Assessment, Materiality and Evidence

PART CONTENTS

3 Risk Assessment and Materiality
4 Audit Evidence and Audit Documentation

CHAPTER 3

Risk Assessment and Materiality

❖ LEARNING OBJECTIVES

Upon completion of this chapter you will

- ❖ **LO1** Understand the concept of audit risk.
- ❖ **LO2** Learn the form and components of the audit risk model.
- ❖ **LO3** Understand how to use the audit risk model.
- ❖ **LO4** Learn the limitations of the audit risk model.
- ❖ **LO5** Understand the auditor's risk assessment process.
- ❖ **LO6** Know the factors that determine the auditor's assessment of the risk of material misstatement.
- ❖ **LO7** Learn how to respond to the results of the risk assessments.
- ❖ **LO8** Learn how to evaluate the results of the audit tests.
- ❖ **LO9** Understand the documentation requirements for risk assessments and responses.
- ❖ **LO10** Learn the auditor's communication requirements to management, those charged with governance and others.
- ❖ **LO11** Understand the concept of materiality.
- ❖ **LO12** Know the steps to applying materiality in an audit.
- ❖ **LO13** Apply the materiality steps to an example (EarthWear).
- ❖ **LO14** Understand how to audit accounting estimates, including fair value accounting estimates and related disclosures.

❖ RELEVANT ACCOUNTING AND AUDITING PRONOUNCEMENTS

IASB, IAS 1, Presentation of Financial Statements

IASB, IAS 8, Accounting Policies, Changes in Accounting Estimates and Errors

ISA 200, Overall Objectives of the Independent Auditor and the Conduct of an Audit in Accordance with International Standards on Auditing

ISA 240, The Auditor's Responsibilities Relating to Fraud in an Audit of Financial Statements

ISA 250, Consideration of Laws and Regulations in an Audit of Financial Statements

ISA 260, Communication with Those Charged with Governance

ISA 300, Planning an Audit of Financial Statements

ISA 315, Identifying and Assessing the Risks of Material Misstatement through Understanding the Entity and Its Environment

ISA 320, Materiality in Planning and Performing an Audit

ISA 330, The Auditor's Responses to Assessed Risks

ISA 450, Evaluation of Misstatements Identified during the Audit

ISA 500, Audit Evidence

ISA 530, Audit Sampling

ISA 540, Auditing Accounting Estimates, Including Fair Value Accounting Estimates, and Related Disclosures

ISA 580, Written Representations

ISA 700, Forming an Opinion and Reporting on Financial Statements

---

IN CHAPTER 1 the three fundamental concepts that underlie the conduct of a financial statement audit were briefly discussed. This chapter provides detailed coverage of two of those concepts: **audit risk** and **materiality**. Audit risk and materiality significantly impact the auditor's evidence decisions. The auditor considers both concepts in planning the nature, timing and extent of **audit procedures**, and in evaluating the results of those procedures.

The audit risk model serves as a framework for assessing audit risk. The auditor follows a risk assessment process to identify the risk of material misstatement in the financial statement accounts. The risk of material misstatement is composed of two components of the audit risk model: **inherent risk** and **control risk**. The risk of material misstatement is used to determine the acceptable level of **detection risk** and to plan the auditing procedures to be performed. The auditor restricts audit risk at the account balance level in such a way that, at the end of the engagement, he or she can express an opinion on the financial statements, taken as a whole, at an acceptably low level of audit risk.

In planning the audit the auditor determines materiality for the financial statements as a whole and, if appropriate, materiality for particular classes of transactions, account balances or disclosure. The auditor considers materiality from how **misstatements** could reasonably be expected to influence the economic decisions of users taken on the basis of the financial statements. Judgements about materiality are made in light of surrounding circumstances, and are affected by the size or nature of a misstatement. In applying materiality on an audit the auditor follows a three-step process.

Accounting estimates, including fair value accounting estimates, and related disclosures have become more prevalent in current financial reporting frameworks. The auditor's risk assessment process as well as the evaluation of materiality of misstatements covers accounting estimates. The *Advanced Module* section at the end of this chapter offers a detailed discussion of auditing of accounting estimates.

❖ AUDIT RISK

LO1

Audit risk is the first fundamental concept that underlies the audit process. Because of the nature of audit evidence and the characteristics of management fraud, an auditor can only provide reasonable assurance, as opposed to absolute assurance, that the financial statements are free from material misstatement. The term 'reasonable assurance' is used in the paragraph of the audit report describing the auditor's responsibility to inform the reader that there is some level of risk that the audit did not detect *all* material misstatements. Audit risk is defined as follows:

> **Audit risk** *is the risk that the auditor expresses an inappropriate audit opinion when the financial statements are materially misstated.*

In simple terms, audit risk is the risk that an auditor will issue an unmodified opinion on materially misstated financial statements. The auditor should perform the audit to reduce audit risk to a sufficiently low level for expressing an opinion on the overall financial statements.

While the auditor is ultimately concerned with audit risk at the financial statement level, as a practical matter audit risk must be considered at more detailed levels through the course of the audit, including the class of transactions, account balance or disclosure level. For ease of presentation, we will use the term *assertion* to refer to consideration of audit risk at these lower levels. In other words, consideration of audit risk at the assertion level means that the auditor must consider the risk that he or she will conclude that an assertion for a particular class of transactions (e.g. classification of capital lease transactions), a particular account balance (e.g. existence of accounts receivable) or a particular disclosure (e.g. valuation of amounts disclosed in a note dealing with stock compensation) is fairly stated, when in fact it is materially misstated.

Thus, at the assertion level, audit risk consists of:

1   The risk that the relevant assertions related to classes of transactions, balances or disclosures contain misstatements that could be material to the financial statements when aggregated with misstatements in other classes, balances or disclosures (inherent risk and control risk).
2   The risk that the auditor will not detect such misstatements (detection risk).

In other words, audit risk is the combination of these two elements—that the client's financial statements will contain material misstatements and that the auditor will fail to detect any such misstatements.

In addition to audit risk, an auditor is subject to *business risk* in his or her professional practice, which can be defined as:

Auditor's business risk *is the risk that the auditor is exposed to loss or injury to professional practice from litigation, adverse publicity or other events arising in connection with financial statements audited and reported on.*

For example, an auditor may conduct an audit in accordance with auditing standards and still be sued by the client or a third party. Although the auditor has complied with professional standards and may ultimately win the lawsuit, his or her professional reputation may be damaged in the process by the negative publicity.

Auditor's business risk cannot be directly controlled by the auditor, although some control can be exercised through the careful acceptance and continuance of clients. Audit risk, on the other hand, can be directly controlled by manipulating detection risk. The auditor manipulates detection risk by changing the scope of the auditor's test procedures (see Practice Insight 3.1). As the next section demonstrates, the *audit risk model* provides a framework for auditors to follow in planning audit procedures and evaluating audit results.

Practice Insight 3.1

When auditors use the term 'scope', they are referring to the *nature, timing* and *extent* of audit procedures, where nature refers to the type of evidence; timing refers to when the evidence will be examined; and extent refers to how much of the type of evidence will be gathered.

❖ THE AUDIT RISK MODEL

LO2

The auditor considers audit risk at the relevant assertion level because this directly assists the auditor to plan the appropriate audit procedures for those transactions, accounts or disclosures. The risk that the relevant assertions are misstated consists of two components:

1   *Inherent risk* (IR) is the susceptibility of an assertion about a class of transactions, account balance or disclosure to a misstatement that could be material, either individually or when aggregated with other misstatements, before consideration of any related controls. In other words, IR is the likelihood that a material misstatement exists in the financial statements without the consideration of internal control.
2   *Control risk* (CR) is the risk that a misstatement that could occur in an assertion about a class of transactions, account balance or disclosure and that could be material, either individually or when aggregated with other misstatements, will not be prevented, or detected and corrected, on a timely basis by the entity's internal control. CR is a function of the effectiveness of the design and operation of internal control in achieving the entity's objectives relevant to preparation of the entity's financial statements. Some CR will always exist because of the inherent limitations of internal control.

Inherent risk and control risk exist independently of the audit. In other words, the levels of inherent risk and control risk are functions of the entity and its environment. The auditor has little or no control over these risks. Auditing standards refer to the combination of IR and CR as the *risk of material misstatement* (RMM). Some auditors refer to this combination as 'client risk' because it stems from decisions made by the client (e.g. what kinds of business transactions to engage in, how much to invest in internal controls). To properly assess CR, the auditor must understand the client's controls and perform audit procedures to determine if the controls are operating effectively. You will learn about controls and tests of controls in a financial statement audit in Chapter 6.

Detection risk (DR) is the risk that the auditor will not detect a misstatement that exists in a relevant assertion that could be material either individually or when aggregated with other misstatements. Detection risk is determined by the effectiveness of the audit procedure and how well the audit procedure is applied by the auditor. Thus, detection risk cannot be reduced to zero because the auditor seldom examines 100 per cent of the account balance or class of transactions (sampling risk). In addition, the auditor's work is subject to *non-sampling risk*. Non-sampling risk is the risk that the auditor might select an inappropriate audit procedure, misapply the appropriate audit procedure or misinterpret the audit results. Non-sampling risk can be reduced through adequate planning, proper assignment of audit staff to the engagement team, the application of **professional scepticism**, supervision and review of the audit work performed, and supervision and conduct of a firm's audit practice in accordance with appropriate quality control standards.[i]

Detection risk has an inverse relationship to inherent risk and control risk. For example, if an auditor judges a client's inherent risk and control risk to be high, the auditor should set a low level of detection risk in order to achieve the planned level of audit risk. Conversely, if inherent risk and control risk are low, the auditor can accept higher detection risk.

The audit risk model can be specified as:

$$AR = RMM \times DR$$

This model expresses the general relationship of audit risk and the risks associated with the auditor's assessments of risk of material misstatement (inherent risk and control risk) and the risks that substantive tests will fail to detect a material misstatement in a relevant assertion (detection risk).

The determination of audit risk and the use of the audit risk model involve considerable judgement on the part of the auditor. The audit risk model assists the auditor in determining the scope of auditing procedures for a relevant assertion in a class of transactions, account balance or disclosure. Auditing standards do not provide specific guidance on what is an acceptable low level of audit risk.

The auditor's assessment of audit risk and its component risks (RMM and DR) is a matter of **professional judgement**. At the completion of the audit, the *actual* or *achieved* level of audit risk is *not* known with certainty by the auditor. If the auditor assesses the *achieved* audit risk as being less than or equal to the *planned* level of audit risk, an unmodified opinion can be issued. If the assessment of the achieved level of audit risk is greater than the planned level, the auditor should either conduct additional audit work or modify the audit opinion. In either case, the judgements involved are often highly subjective.

❖ Use of the Audit Risk Model

LO3

The audit risk model is not intended to be a precise formula that includes all factors influencing the assessment of audit risk. However, auditors find the logic that underlies the model useful when planning risk levels (and thus making scoping decisions) for audit procedures. The discussion that follows concerning the audit risk model is limited to its use as an audit planning tool. Three steps are involved in the auditor's use of the audit risk model at the assertion level:

1 Setting a planned level of audit risk.
2 Assessing the risk of material misstatement.
3 Solving the audit risk equation for the appropriate level of detection risk.

Practice Insight 3.2

Auditing standards allow the auditor to directly assess the *RMM*, or to separately assess the two components of *RMM*, i.e. *IR* and *CR*. This choice is typically built in to each audit firm's methodology.

In applying the audit risk model in this manner, the auditor determines or assesses each component of the model using either quantitative or qualitative terms. In step 1, the auditor sets audit risk for each class of transactions, account balance or disclosure in such a way that, at the completion of the engagement, an opinion can be issued on the financial statements with an acceptable low level of audit risk. Step 2 requires that the auditor assess the risk of material misstatement (see Practice Insight 3.2). To assess the risk of material misstatement, the auditor evaluates the entity's business risks and how those business risks could lead to material misstatements. Figure 3–1 shows the relationship of the assessment of the entity's business risks and risk of material misstatement to the audit risk model. The assessment of business risks is described in detail in the next two sections of the chapter. In step 3, the auditor determines the appropriate level of detection risk by solving the audit risk model as follows:

$$AR = RMM \times DR$$
$$DR = AR/RMM$$

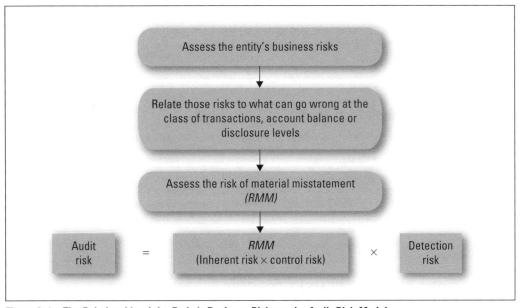

Figure 3–1   The Relationship of the Entity's Business Risks to the Audit Risk Model

The auditor uses the planned level of detection risk to design the audit procedures that will reduce audit risk to an acceptable low level. However, even if the risk of material misstatement is judged to be very low, the auditor must still perform some substantive procedures before concluding that an account balance is not materially misstated. Auditing standards include this caveat because of the imprecision that may occur in assessing the risk of material misstatement.

Consider the following numerical example:

> Suppose that the auditor has determined that the planned audit risk for the accounts receivable balance should be set at .05 based on the significance of the account to the financial statements. By establishing a relatively low level of audit risk, the auditor is minimizing the possibility that the account may contain a material misstatement. Assume further that the auditor assesses the risk of material misstatement for accounts receivable to be .60. Substituting the values for AR and RMM into the equation indicates that the auditor should set DR at approximately .08 (DR = .05/.60) for testing the accounts receivable balance. Thus, the auditor establishes the **scope of the audit** for accounts receivable so that there is only an 8 per cent chance that a material misstatement, if present, is not detected.

Due to the subjectivity involved in judging the audit risk model's components, many audit firms find it more appropriate to use qualitative terms, rather than percentages, in the model. For example, planned audit risk might be classified into two categories: *very low* and *low*. Auditing standards state that audit risk must be reduced to at least a low level. Likewise, the risk of material misstatement and detection risk might be classified into three categories (e.g. *low*, *moderate* or *high*). The logic behind the audit risk model is the same whether the auditor uses percentages or qualitative terms. When using qualitative terms, audit risk is set using one of the category choices. Similarly, the auditor selects the category for the risk of material misstatement that is most appropriate under the circumstances. The specified combination of audit risk and risk of material misstatement is then used to determine the appropriate level of detection risk. Following are three examples of the use of a qualitative approach to the audit risk model.

Example	AR	RMM	DR
1	Very low	High	Low
2	Low	Moderate	Moderate
3	Very low	Low	High

In the first example the auditor has determined that a very low level of audit risk is appropriate for this account because of its importance to the financial statement. The auditor has assessed the risk of material misstatement as high, indicating that there is a high risk of a material misstatement that was not prevented, or detected and corrected by the internal control system. Given a very low level of audit risk and a high level of risk of material misstatement, the auditor would set detection risk as low. A low assessment for detection risk implies that the auditor will conduct a more detailed investigation of this account than if the assessment of detection risk were high. Before you continue, think about the other two examples in the chart above. What does the implied DR level mean about how much evidence must be gathered during the audit? Would a lower DR lead you to gather more or less audit evidence?

❖ Limitations of the Audit Risk Model

LO4

Standard setters developed the audit risk model as a *planning* tool. However, the model has a number of limitations that must be considered by auditors and their firms when the model is used to *revise* an audit plan or to *evaluate* audit results.[ii] In those instances, the *actual* or *achieved* level of audit risk may be smaller or greater than the audit risk indicated by the formula. This can occur because the auditor *assesses* the risk of material misstatement, and such an assessment may be higher or lower than the *actual* risk of material misstatement that exists for the client. Inaccurate assessments are likely to result in a flawed determination of detection risk. Thus, the desired level of audit risk may not actually be achieved. In addition, the audit risk model also does not specifically consider non-sampling risk. While the audit risk model has limitations, it serves as an important tool that auditors can use for planning an audit engagement.

❖ THE AUDITOR'S RISK ASSESSMENT PROCESS

LO5

To properly assess the risks of material misstatement the auditor performs **risk assessment procedures**. The auditor should obtain an understanding of management's objectives and strategies, and the related business risks that may result in material misstatement of the financial statements. The following sections discuss management's strategies, objectives and business risks. We then discuss the auditor's risk assessment process.

Management's Strategies, Objectives and Business Risks

Strategies are the operational approaches used by management to achieve objectives. To achieve their business objectives, managers pursue strategies, such as being the low-cost or high-quality provider of a product. Typical business objectives include growth in market share, first-rate reputation and excellent service. **Business risks** are threats to management's ability to achieve its objectives. Business risks are risks that result from significant conditions, events, circumstances, and actions or inactions that may adversely affect management's ability to execute its strategies and to achieve its objectives, or through the setting of inappropriate objectives or strategies. Business activities, strategies, objectives and the business environment are ever changing, and the dynamic and complex nature of business causes business risks. For example, risks arise from the development of a new product because the product may fail or because flaws in the product may result in lawsuits or damage to the company's reputation. Management is responsible for identifying such risks and responding to them. Usually, management develops approaches to address business risks by implementing a risk assessment process.

Business Risks and the Risk of Material Misstatement

Business risk is a broader concept than the risk of material misstatement. However, most business risks have the potential to affect the financial statements either immediately or in the long run. Auditors need to identify business risks and understand the potential misstatements that may result. Before you continue, pause and consider how a specific business risk could lead to misstatements in the financial statements. For example, consider a client who sells goods to a declining customer base. What risks does this client face? How will these risks impact the audit? This client faces pressure to maintain historical profit margins, which increases the risk of misstatement associated with the valuation of assets such as receivables. However, the same risk may also have longer-term implications for the company's overall health if the economy remains depressed. In such a case, the auditor would consider the likelihood that the client will not remain financially viable and whether the going-concern assumption is still appropriate.

Understanding the Entity and Its Environment

Figure 1–2 presented an overview of the audit process. This process starts by obtaining an understanding of the entity and its environment. Obtaining an understanding of the entity and its environment is a continuous, dynamic process of gathering, updating and analysing information throughout the audit. The goal of this step is to assess the business risks faced by the entity. Based on the auditor's understanding of the entity's business risks and how those risks are controlled or not controlled by the entity, the auditor assesses the risk of material misstatement at the assertion level. Figure 3–2 provides an overview of the auditor's assessments of business risks and the risk of material misstatement (i.e. the auditor's risk assessment process). Unless otherwise stated in the text, the risk of material misstatement refers to misstatements caused by **error** or **fraud**.

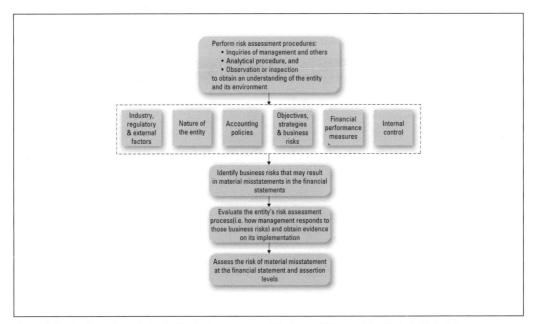

Figure 3–2 An Overview of the Auditor's Assessment of Business Risks and the Risk of Material Misstatements

The auditor's understanding of the entity and its environment includes knowledge about the following categories:

- Industry, regulatory and other external factors.
- Nature of the entity.
- Accounting policies.
- Objectives and strategies, and related business risks.
- Financial performance measures.
- Internal control.

In obtaining knowledge about each of these categories, the auditor should be particularly alert for the following conditions and events that may indicate the existence of business risks:

- Significant changes in the entity such as large acquisitions, reorganizations or other unusual events.
- Significant changes in the industry in which the entity operates.
- Significant new products or services, or significant new lines of business.
- New locations.
- Significant changes in the IT environment.
- Operations in areas with unstable economies.
- High degree of complex regulation.

Industry, Regulatory and Other External Factors

Industry, regulatory and other external factors are relevant to the auditor's understanding of the entity. Obtaining an understanding of these factors assists the auditor in identifying risks of material misstatements. Some industries are subject to risks of material misstatement as a result of unique accounting estimates. For example, a property and casualty insurance company needs to establish loss reserves based on historical data that may be subject to misstatement. Table 3–1 presents examples of industry, regulatory and other external factors that should be considered by the auditor.

Table 3–1   Industry, Regulatory and Other External Factors
Industry conditions
• The market and competition, including demand, capacity and price competition.
• Cyclical or seasonal activity.
• Product technology relating to the entity's products.
• Energy supply and cost.
Regulatory environment
• Accounting principles and industry-specific practices.
• Regulatory framework for a regulated industry.
• Legislation and regulation that significantly affect the entity's operations.
• Taxation (corporate and other).
• Government policies currently affecting the conduct of the entity's business.
• Environmental requirements affecting the industry and the entity's business.
Other external factors
• General level of economic activity (e.g. recession, growth).
• Interest rates and availability of financing.
• Inflation and currency revaluation.

Nature of the Entity

Obtaining an understanding of the nature of the entity includes obtaining an understanding of the following:

- The entity's organizational structure and management personnel.
- The sources of funding of the entity's operations and investment activities, including the entity's capital structure, non-capital funding and other debt instruments.
- The entity's investments.
- The entity's operating characteristics, including its size and complexity.
- The sources of the entity's earnings, including the relative profitability of key products and services.
- Key supplier and customer relationships.

- Financial reporting, including accounting for fair values.

An understanding of the nature of an entity gives the auditor a better idea of what potential misstatements might be found in the financial statements. For example, the applicable financial reporting framework may require or permit a variety of fair value measurements and disclosures. To assess the risk of material misstatement the auditor should understand the requirements of the reporting framework relevant to fair value accounting. Take a moment to think about the importance of fair values in current financial reporting frameworks, and how fair value measurements may involve estimation uncertainty and give rise to risk of material misstatement.

Practice Insight 3.3

Auditors are expected to understand the accounting principles and rules relating to accounting on the basis of fair value, including disclosures, and to give appropriate consideration to the audit of fair values. Auditing of fair values may be particularly challenging in times of market uncertainty and illiquid markets.

Accounting Policies

The auditor should evaluate whether the entity's **accounting policies** are appropriate for the business, and consistent with the applicable financial reporting framework and accounting policies used in the relevant industry. For example, the auditors evaluate if EarthWear's policy to capitalize and amortize cost of direct-response advertising such as catalogue production is consistent with the requirements in the financial reporting framework and industry norms. An understanding of the entity's selection and application of accounting policies may encompass such matters as:

- The methods the entity uses to account for significant and unusual transactions.
- The entity's revenue recognition policies.
- The effect of significant accounting policies in controversial or emerging areas for which there is a lack of authoritative guidance or consensus.
- Changes in the entity's accounting policies.
- Financial reporting standards and laws and regulations that are new to the entity, and when and how the entity will adopt such requirements.

The fact that an audit covers accounting policies and accounting estimates is expressed to users of the financial statements by the sentence, 'An audit also includes evaluating the appropriateness of accounting policies used and the reasonableness of accounting estimates made by management, as well as evaluating the overall presentation of the financial statements', contained in the auditor responsibility paragraph of the auditor's report (refer to Exhibit 1–1).

Objectives, Strategies and Related Business Risks

As discussed previously, the auditor must identify and understand the entity's objectives and strategies used to achieve its objectives, and the business risks associated with those objectives and strategies. Table 3–2 provides examples of business risks the auditor considers when developing an understanding of the entity's objectives and strategies.

Table 3–2 Examples of Business Risks that the Auditor Considers When Developing an Understanding of the Entity's Objectives and Strategies
• Industry developments.
• New products and services.
• Expansion of the business.
• New accounting requirements.
• Regulatory requirements.
• Current and prospective financing requirements.
• Use of IT.
• Effects of implementing a strategy, particularly any effects that will lead to new accounting requirements.

Smaller entities often do not set their objectives and strategies, or manage the related business risks, through formal plans or processes. In many cases there may be no documentation of such matters. In such entities the auditor's understanding is ordinarily obtained through inquiries of management and observation of how the entity responds to such matters.

Financial Performance Measures

Internally generated information used by management to measure and review the entity's financial performance may include:

- Key performance indicators (KPIs).
- Budgets.
- Variance analysis.
- Subsidiary information and divisional, departmental or other level performance reports.
- Comparisons of an entity's performance with that of competitors.

External parties (e.g. analysts and credit rating agencies) may also measure and review the entity's financial performance. Internal measures provide management with information about progress towards meeting the entity's objectives. Thus, a deviation in the entity's performance measures may indicate a risk of misstatement in the related financial statement information. When the auditor intends to make use of the entity's performance measures for the purpose of the audit, the auditor should consider whether the information provided is reliable and trustworthy, and whether it is sufficiently detailed or precise. Both internal and external information is useful to the auditor's understanding of the entity and its environment.

Smaller entities ordinarily do not have formal processes to measure and review the entity's financial performance. Management nevertheless often relies on certain key indicators which knowledge and experience of the business suggest are reliable bases for evaluating financial performance and taking appropriate action.

Internal Control

Internal control is the label given to the entity's policies and procedures designed to provide reasonable assurance about the achievement of the entity's objectives. Internal control is implemented by the client's board of directors (or other body charged with governance), management and other personnel. Because of the significance of internal control to the financial statement audit, it will be covered in great detail in Chapter 6. To provide you with an introduction to the concept of internal control, here are several examples of policies and procedures that may be a part of an entity's internal control:

- Active and qualified board of directors and audit committee with members independent from the company.
- Effective risk assessment process.
- Competent and objective internal audit personnel.
- Proper authorization of transactions (e.g. a supervisor must approve all purchases over €5,000).
- Procedures to ensure assets exist (e.g. inventory counts).
- Monitoring of controls (e.g. supervisor observes the procedures at the loading dock to ensure control procedures are properly followed).

The auditor should understand and assess the effectiveness of internal control. The auditor uses the understanding of internal control to identify types of potential misstatements; consider factors that affect the risks of material misstatement; and design appropriate audit procedures.

Auditor's Risk Assessment Procedures

The auditor obtains an understanding of the entity and its environment by performing the following risk assessment procedures: inquiries of management and others; analytical procedures; and observation and inspection.

Inquiries of Management and Others

The auditor obtains information about the entity and its environment through inquiry of management, individuals responsible for financial reporting and other personnel within the entity. For example, the auditor makes inquiries of management about changes in circumstances that may give rise to new, or the need to revise existing, accounting estimates. As another example, the auditor inquires of management about the entity's related parties and related party transactions. Making inquiries of others *within* the entity may be useful in providing the auditor with a perspective different from that of management and those responsible for financial reporting. The auditor might make inquiries of:

- The board of directors, audit committee or others charged with governance.
- Internal audit personnel.
- Employees involved in initiating, processing or recording complex or unusual transactions.
- In-house legal counsel.
- Production, marketing, sales and other personnel.

For example, inquiries directed to internal audit personnel might relate to their activities concerning the design and operating effectiveness of the entity's internal controls. The auditor might also inquire of the in-house legal counsel about issues such as litigation, compliance with laws and regulations, and the meaning of contract terms.

The auditor might also inquire of others *outside* the entity. For example, the auditor may consider it is appropriate to make inquiries of customers, suppliers or valuation experts. Such discussions may provide information that will assist the auditor in uncovering the fraud. For example, customers may report that they received large quantities of unordered products from the audit client just before year end. This would be an indicator of overstated revenues.

Analytical Procedures

Analytical procedures are evaluations of financial information through analysis of plausible relationships among both financial and non-financial data. Auditing standards require that the auditor conducts analytical procedures in planning the audit. Such preliminary analytical procedures assist the auditor in understanding the entity and its environment, and in identifying areas that may represent specific risks relevant to the audit. Analytical procedures can be helpful in identifying the existence of unusual transactions or events and amounts, ratios and trends that might have implications for audit planning. In performing such analytical procedures, the auditor should develop expectations about plausible relationships that are expected to exist, based on the understanding of the entity and its environment. However, the results of such high-level analytical procedures provide only a broad initial indication about whether a material misstatement may exist. Analytical procedures are discussed in more detail in Chapter 5.

Observation and Inspection

Observation and inspection include audit procedures such as:

- Observation of entity activities and operations.
- Inspection of documents (e.g. business plans and strategies), records and internal control manuals.
- Reading reports prepared by management, those charged with governance, and internal audit.
- Visits to the entity's premises and plant facilities.
- Tracing transactions through the information system relevant to financial reporting, which may be performed as part of a walk-through.

The auditor may also read about industry developments and trends, read the current year's interim financial statements, and review regulatory or financial publications. Table 3–3 presents sources where the auditor can obtain information for developing an understanding of the entity and its environment.

Table 3–3   Sources of Information for Understanding the Entity and Its Environment
● Cumulative knowledge and experience obtained from prior audits.
● Procedures performed in client acceptance and continuance process.
● Knowledge obtained from performing interim procedures.
● Consulting, tax or other engagements performed for the entity.
● Communications with predecessor auditors.
● Published annual reports and interim reports to shareholders, if applicable.
● Discussions with management.
● Minutes of board of director's and/or audit committee's meetings.
● Entity's business/strategic plans, budgets or other documentation.
● Reports prepared by analysts, banks, underwriters, rating agencies and the like.
● Individuals knowledgeable about the industry, such as the engagement team members for clients in a similar business/industry.
● Audit firm – generated industry guidance, databases and practice aids, where applicable.
● Government statistics.
● Economic and financial journals.
● Industry or trade journals.
● Client press releases, publications and brochures.
● Internal audit reports.

EVALUATE THE ENTITY'S RISK ASSESSMENT PROCESS

Management has a responsibility to identify, control and mitigate business risks that may affect the entity's ability to achieve its objectives. The auditor should obtain information on the entity's risk assessment process and whether it is operating effectively. If the entity's response to the identified risk is adequate, the risk of material misstatement may be reduced. However, if the entity's response to the identified risk is inadequate, the auditor's assessment of the risk of material misstatement may increase. If the entity does not respond adequately to business risks, the auditor will have to develop tests to determine if any misstatements are present in the related class of transactions or account balance. Chapter 6 provides detailed coverage of the entity's risk assessment management process.

❖ ASSESSING THE RISK OF MATERIAL MISSTATEMENT DUE TO ERROR
LO6   OR FRAUD[III]

Based on knowledge of the entity and its environment, the auditor should assess the risk of material misstatement at the assertion level and determine the audit procedures that are necessary based on that **risk assessment** (see Fig. 3–2). At this point in the risk assessment process, the auditor has identified the entity's business risks. To assess the risk of material misstatement, the auditor must then consider how the identified risks could result in a material misstatement in the financial statements. This includes considering whether the magnitude and likelihood of the risk could result in a material misstatement. For example, the entity's risk assessment process may have identified product obsolescence as a business risk that could result in a material misstatement to the inventory and cost-of-goods accounts. However, the entity's risk assessment process has determined that there is a low likelihood that such a misstatement could occur because the entity has installed strong controls that track inventory levels and market pricing.

This section will first review the types and causes of misstatements, and then focuses primarily on assessing the risk of material misstatement due to fraud, sometimes referred to as the *fraud risk assessment*.

Types and Causes of Misstatements[iv]

Misstatements can result from error or fraud. The term *error* refers to *unintentional* misstatements of amounts or disclosures in financial statements. The term *fraud* refers to an *intentional* act by one or more individuals among management, those charged with governance, employees or third parties, involving the use of deception to obtain an unjust or illegal advantage. Thus, the primary distinction between error and fraud is whether the misstatement was intentional or unintentional. Unfortunately, it is often difficult to determine intent. For example, suppose the auditor detects a misstatement in an account that requires an estimate, such as bad debt expense; it may be difficult to determine whether the misstatement was intentional.

A misstatement due to error or fraud is defined as follows:

A misstatement *due to error or fraud is a difference between the amount, classification, or presentation of a reported financial statement element, account or item and the amount, classification or presentation that would have been reported under the applicable financial reporting framework.*

Misstatements from error and fraud may result from:

- An inaccuracy in gathering or processing data from which the financial statements are prepared.
- An omission of an amount or disclosure.
- An incorrect accounting estimate arising from overlooking or clear misinterpretation of facts.
- Management's selection and application of accounting policies that the auditor considers inappropriate or judgements concerning accounting estimates that the auditor considers unreasonable, including related disclosures.

Fraud can be classified into two types: (1) misstatements arising from fraudulent financial reporting; and (2) misstatements arising from misappropriation of assets.

Misstatements arising from fraudulent financial reporting are intentional misstatements or omissions of amounts or disclosures in financial statements intended to deceive financial statement users. Fraudulent financial reporting may involve acts such as the following:

- Manipulation, falsification or alteration of accounting records or supporting documents from which financial statements are prepared.
- Misrepresentation in, or intentional omission from, the financial statements of events, transactions or other significant information.
- Intentional misapplication of accounting policies relating to amounts, classification, manner of presentation or disclosure.

Misstatements arising from misappropriation of assets (sometimes referred to as *defalcation*) involve the theft of an entity's assets where the theft causes the financial statements to be misstated. Examples of misappropriation include:

- Embezzling cash received.
- Stealing assets.
- Causing the entity to pay for goods or services not received.

Misappropriation of assets may be accompanied by false or misleading records or documents, possibly created by circumventing controls, and may involve one or more individuals among management, employees or third parties.

To assist the auditor in evaluating misstatements identified during the audit auditing standards distinguish between **factual misstatements**, **judgemental misstatements** and **projected misstatements**:

- Factual misstatements are misstatements about which there is no doubt.
- Judgemental misstatements are differences arising from the selection or application of accounting policies that the auditor considers inappropriate, or the judgements of management concerning accounting estimates that the auditor considers unreasonable.
- Projected misstatements are the auditor's best estimate of misstatements in populations, involving the projection of misstatements identified in audit samples to the entire populations from which the samples were drawn (see Chapter 9).

The Fraud Risk Identification Process

The auditor performs the following steps to obtain information to identify the risks of material misstatement due to fraud:

● Discussion among the audit engagement members regarding the risks of material misstatement due to fraud.
● Inquire of management, those charged with governance and others about their views on the risks of fraud and how it is addressed.
● Consider any unusual or unexpected relationships that have been identified in performing analytical procedures in planning the audit, including procedures related to revenue accounts.

The following two sections address the first two points.

Discussion among the Audit Engagement Team

Auditing standards (ISA 240 and ISA 315) require that the engagement team have discussions about the entity's financial statements' susceptibility to material misstatements. In planning the audit, the engagement partner or manager should communicate with members of the engagement team regarding the potential for material misstatement due to fraud. This brainstorming session can be held separately, or concurrently, with the discussion required as part of understanding the entity and its environment (ISA 315, para. 10). The engagement partner or manager should determine which audit engagement members should be included in the communication, how it should occur and the extent of the communication. The objectives of the brainstorming meeting are to:

● Share insights about the entity and its environment, and the entity's business risks.
● Provide an opportunity for the team members to discuss how and where the entity might be susceptible to fraud.
● Emphasize the importance of maintaining professional scepticism throughout the audit regarding the potential for material misstatement due to fraud.

Engagement team members should be encouraged to communicate and share information obtained throughout the audit that may affect the assessment of risks of material misstatement or the auditor's responses to those risks. Small audits are often carried out entirely by the engagement partner. In such situations, the engagement partner, having personally conducted the planning of the audit, considers the susceptibility of the entity's financial statements to material misstatement due to fraud.

The auditor should conduct the audit with professional scepticism. Professional scepticism includes a questioning mind and a critical assessment of audit evidence. For example, the auditor should be alert to audit evidence that contradicts other audit evidence obtained and information that brings into question the reliability of documents and responses to inquiries to be used as audit evidence. The auditor should conduct the engagement assuming there is a possibility that a material misstatement due to fraud could be present, regardless of any prior beliefs or past experience with the entity and regardless of the auditor's belief about management's honesty and integrity. Pretend for a moment that you are a member of the engagement team assigned to the EarthWear audit and are thus participating in the fraud brainstorming session concerning EarthWear. What are one or two of the external/internal influences that might create pressure for EarthWear to commit fraud? (See Table 3–4.)

Inquiries of Management and Others

The auditor should inquire about management's knowledge of fraud within the entity. The auditor should also understand the programmes and controls that management has established to mitigate specific risk factors and how well management monitors those programmes and controls. Some of the inquiry would take place when the auditor obtains an understanding of the entity and its environment.

Those charged with governance in the entity, such as the board of directors, the audit committee or other body with equivalent authority and responsibility should assume an active role in oversight of the assessment of the risk of fraud. The auditor should obtain an understanding of how the board of directors exercises its oversight activities, including direct inquiry of the board of directors. When the entity has an internal audit function, the auditor also should inquire of internal audit personnel about their assessment of the risk of fraud, including whether management has satisfactorily responded to internal audit findings during the year.

The auditor should also consider inquiries from others within the entity and third parties. For example, the auditor also may consider making inquiries of third parties, such as vendors, customers or regulators. It can be uncomfortable to inquire about potentially fraudulent activities; however, it is much more uncomfortable to fail to detect a material fraud.

Conditions Indicative of Fraud and Fraud Risk Factors

Three conditions are generally present when material misstatements due to fraud occur:

1   Management or other employees have an *incentive* or are under *pressure* that provides a reason to commit fraud.
2   Circumstances exist that provide an *opportunity* for a fraud to be carried out.
3   Those involved are able to *rationalize* committing a fraudulent act. Some individuals possess an *attitude*, character or set of ethical values that allow them to knowingly and intentionally commit a dishonest act.

These three conditions are sometimes referred to as the fraud risk triangle. Even honest individuals can commit fraud in an environment where sufficient pressure is being exerted on them. The greater the incentive or pressure, the more likely an individual will be able to rationalize the acceptability of committing fraud. Withholding evidence or misrepresenting information through falsified documentation, including forgery, may conceal fraud. Fraud also may be concealed through collusion among management, employees or third parties.

Management has the ability to perpetrate fraud because it is in a position to directly or indirectly manipulate the accounting records and prepare fraudulent financial reports. In most cases, fraudulent financial reporting also involves some management override of controls.

Because of the characteristics of fraud, particularly those involving concealment through collusion; withheld, misrepresented or falsified documentation; and the ability of management to override or instruct others to override controls, an auditor may unknowingly rely on audit evidence that appears to be valid, but in fact is false and fraudulent.

Thus, **fraud risk factors** related to fraudulent financial reporting and misappropriation of assets can be classified among the three conditions generally present when fraud exists:

- An *incentive/pressure* to perpetrate fraud.
- An *opportunity* to carry out the fraud.
- An *attitude/rationalization* to justify the fraudulent action.

Fraudulent Financial Reporting

Tables 3–4 to 3–6 present the risk factors related to each category of conditions for the potential for fraudulent financial reporting. Table 3–4 contains numerous risk factors that, if present, may suggest that management and others have incentives to manipulate financial reporting. For example, the entity may be facing increased competition that results in declining profit margins. Similarly, in the high-technology sector, rapid changes in technology can affect the profitability and the fair market value of products. Entities that have recurring operating losses and negative cash flow from operations may face bankruptcy, foreclosure or takeover. In each of these situations, management may have incentives to manipulate reported earnings. Management (or those charged with governance) may also be facing pressures to maintain the entity's reported earnings to meet analysts' forecasts because their bonuses or personal wealth are tied to the entity's stock price. Exhibit 3–1 illustrates the massive fraudulent financial reporting in Satyam Computer Services Limited – India's Enron.

Table 3–4   Risk Factors Relating to Incentives/Pressures to Report Fraudulently

● Financial stability or profitability is threatened by economic, industry, or entity operating conditions, such as:
    ● High degree of competition or market saturation, accompanied by declining margins.
    ● High vulnerability to rapid changes, such as changes in technology, product obsolescence or interest rates.
    ● Significant declines in customer demand and increasing business failures in either the industry or overall economy.
    ● Operating losses making the threat of bankruptcy, foreclosure or hostile takeover imminent.
    ● Rapid growth or unusual profitability, especially compared with that of other companies in the same industry.
    ● New accounting, statutory or regulatory requirements.

- Excessive pressure exists for management to meet requirements or expectations of third parties due to:
  - Profitability or trend level expectations of investment analysts, institutional investors, significant creditors or other external parties.
  - Need to obtain additional debt or equity financing to stay competitive.
- The personal financial situation of management or those charged with governance is threatened by the entity's financial performance.

Exhibit 3–1   Satyam Computer Services Limited – India's Enron

On 7 January 2009, B. Ramalinga Raju, Chairman and Founder of Satyam, sent a letter to the Board of Directors informing them that he had carried out a massive financial statement fraud. In his letter, Raju stated that the fraud 'attained unmanageable proportions as the size of the company operations grew'. Satyam was India's fourth largest technology company. Its stock traded on the NYSE and it was audited by Price Waterhouse, a separate legal entity within the PricewaterhouseCoopers global business network. Some of the companies for which Satyam does outsourcing work include Citicorp, Caterpillar and Coca-Cola. Ironically, Satyam means 'truth' in Sanskrit.

For the year ended 31 March 2008, Satyam reported sales of $2.1 billion and profits of $427.6 million. However, Mr Raju's letter indicated that in the quarter ended 30 September 2008, Satyam reported $555 million in sales instead of the true figure of $434 million. The company reported $136 million in profit, but the real amount was $12.5 million. Accounts receivable were reported at $545.6 million but Mr Raju indicated in reality they totalled only $444.8 million. Most importantly, Satyam reported $1.1 billion in available cash, but had only $66 million on hand. More than $1 billion of Satyam's cash was either missing or never existed!

The Indian government ousted the Board of Directors and Price Waterhouse was removed as the company's auditors. KPMG and Deloitte were hired as the new auditors.

Investigators determined that Satyam's account-balance statements and letters of confirmation of account balances at HSBC Holdings PLC of the UK, Citigroup Inc. of the US, and HDFC Bank and ICICI Bank Ltd. of India were forgeries.

Selected sources: B.R. Raju, Letter to Satyam's Board of Directors (7 January 2009); 'India's Enron: Scandal hits India's flagship industry', *The Economist* (8 January 2009); 'Pricewaterhouse Defends Its Audit Procedures', *Wall Street Journal* (9 January 2009); 'The Satyam Scandal: Offshore Inmates' – India Struggles to Get to Grips with a Bewildering Corporate Fraud', *The Economist* (15 January 2009); 'Satyam Bank Documents at Issue', *Wall Street Journal* (20 January 2009); and 'Satyam Founder Accused of Falsely Inflating Size of Staff', *Wall Street Journal* (23 January 2009).

Management must also have the opportunity to commit the fraud. Table 3–5 lists the opportunities that may be available to management or those charged with governance to perpetuate fraudulent financial reporting. For example, assets, liabilities, revenues or expenses may be based on subjective estimates that may be difficult for the auditor to corroborate. Two examples of such situations are the recognition of income on long-term contracts when the percentage of completion method is used, and establishing the amount of loan loss reserves for a financial institution. Another opportunity for fraudulent financial reporting is when a single person or small group dominates management. Dominance by one individual may lead to processing accounting transactions that are not consistent with the entity's controls.

Table 3–5   Risk Factors Relating to Opportunities to Report Fraudulently

- The nature of the industry or the entity's operations provide opportunities to engage in fraudulent financial reporting due to:
  - Significant related-party transactions.
  - Assets, liabilities, revenue, or expenses based on significant estimates that involve subjective judgements or uncertainties that are difficult to corroborate.
  - Significant, unusual or highly complex transactions.
- There is ineffective monitoring of management.
- There is a complex or unstable organizational structure.
- Internal control components are deficient.

Risk factors reflective of attitudes/rationalizations by board members or others charged with governance, management or employees may allow them to engage in and/or justify fraudulent financial reporting. Table 3–6 lists a number of attitudes or rationalizations that may be used to justify fraudulent financial reporting. For example, the entity may have weak ethical standards for management behaviour or poor communication channels for reporting such behaviour.

Table 3–6 Risk Factors Relating to Attitudes/Rationalizations to Report Fraudulently
• Ineffective communication implementation, support and enforcement of the entity's values or ethical standards by management, or the communication of inappropriate values or ethical standards.
• Non-financial management's excessive participation in, or preoccupation with, the selection of accounting policies or the determination of significant estimates.
• Known history of violations of securities laws or other laws and regulations, or claims against the entity, its senior management, or those charged with governance alleging fraud or violations of laws and regulations.
• Excessive interest by management in maintaining or increasing the entity's stock price or earnings trend.
• A practice by management of committing to analysts, creditors and other third parties to achieve aggressive or unrealistic forecasts.
• Recurring attempts by management to justify marginal or inappropriate accounting on the basis of materiality.

Misappropriation of Assets

Risk factors that relate to misstatements arising from misappropriation of assets also are classified along the three conditions generally present when fraud exists. Some of the risk factors related to misstatements arising from fraudulent financial reporting also may be present when misstatements arising from misappropriation of assets exist (see Exhibit 3–2). Table 3–7 presents the risk factors related to each category of conditions for the potential of misappropriation of assets. For example, an employee may have financial problems that create an incentive to misappropriate the cash. In order for the employee who has financial problems to misappropriate cash, he or she must have access to the cash. This is likely to occur only when there is inadequate segregation of duties or poor oversight by personnel responsible for the asset. Lastly, an employee who has access to assets susceptible to misappropriation may have a change in behaviour or lifestyle that may indicate he or she has misappropriated assets.

Table 3–7 Risk Factors Relating to the Misappropriation of Assets
Incentive/Pressures
• Personal financial obligations may create pressure for management or employees with access to cash or other assets susceptible to theft to misappropriate those assets.
• Adverse relationships between the entity and employees with access to cash or other assets susceptible to theft may motivate those employees to misappropriate those assets.
Opportunities
• Certain characteristics or circumstances may increase the susceptibility of assets to misappropriation. For example, large amounts of cash on hand or processed.
• Inadequate internal control over assets may increase the susceptibility of misappropriation of those assets. For example, misappropriation of assets may exist because there is inadequate management oversight of employees responsible for assets.
Attitudes/Rationalization
• Disregard for the need for monitoring or reducing risks related to misappropriation of assets.
• Disregard for internal control over misappropriation of assets by overriding existing controls or by failing to correct known internal control deficiencies.
• Changes in behaviour or lifestyle that may indicate assets have been misappropriated.

Exhibit 3–2 illustrates a misappropriation of assets of historical dimensions: the Madoff $50 billion fraud.

Exhibit 3–2   Madoff 's $50 Billion Ponzi Scheme

In early December 2008, Bernie Madoff told his two sons that his investment advisory business, Bernard Madoff Investment Securities (BMIS), was basically a giant Ponzi scheme. Madoff had falsely represented to investors that returns were being earned on their accounts at BMIS and that he was investing their money in securities. In fact, Madoff paid earlier investors with funds raised from later investors. Authorities believe that the fraud may date back at least three decades. Madoff estimated the losses from the fraud at as much as $50 billion. Madoff's investors included many famous individuals and charities, some of whom lost their life savings.

While Madoff told prosecutors that he had acted alone, one of the major issues is how much others may have been involved. Others include the value of any remaining assets in BMIS, whether Madoff hid some of the assets, and how much of his personal assets can be used to pay off investors.

Selected sources: Securities and Exchange Commission Complaint, United States District Court Southern District Of New York (11 December 2008); 'US: Madoff had $173 Million in Checks', *Wall Street Journal* (9 January 2009); 'Madoff Brother, at Arm's Length?', *Wall Street Journal* (10–11 January 2009); 'Sons' Roles in Spotlight', *Wall Street Journal* (24–25 January 2009); 'The Madoff Affair: Going Down Quietly – History's Biggest Swindler Faces Life Behind Bars But Keeps Mum', *The Economist* (12 March 2009).

❖ THE AUDITOR'S RESPONSE TO THE RESULTS OF THE RISK ASSESSMENTS

LO7

Figure 3–3 provides an overview of how the auditor responds to the results of the risk assessments. Once the risks of material misstatement have been identified, the auditor determines whether they relate more pervasively to the overall financial statements and potentially affect many relevant assertions or whether the identified risks relate to specific relevant assertions, related to classes of transactions, account balances and disclosures. To respond appropriately to financial statement level risks, the auditor's response may be a reconsideration of the overall audit approach. The response to such pervasive risks may include:

● Emphasizing to the engagement team the need to maintain professional scepticism in gathering and evaluating audit evidence.
● Assigning more experienced staff or those with specialized skills, or using experts.
● Providing more supervision.
● Incorporating additional elements of unpredictability in the selection of audit procedures to be performed.

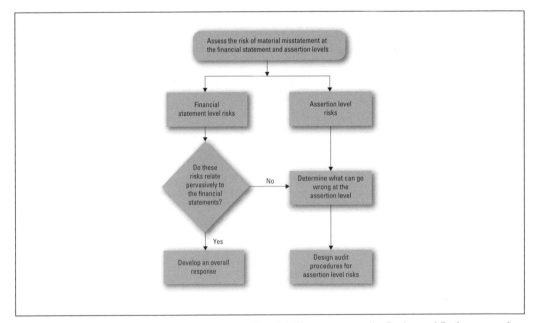

Figure 3–3   Relating the Assessment of the Risk of Material Misstatement to the Design and Performance of Audit Procedures

When the risks relate to a single assertion or set of assertions for the same business process or account, the auditor should consider the entity's internal controls. As discussed in Chapter 6, the auditor needs to consider the design and operation of controls within a business process to determine if they prevent, or detect and correct misstatements. If the controls are properly designed, and the auditor intends to rely on those controls, the auditor will test the operating effectiveness of the controls. Depending on the operating effectiveness of the entity's controls, the auditor will design and perform substantive tests directed at the potential misstatements that may result from the identified risks.

As part of the risk assessment process, the auditor should determine which of the risks identified require special audit consideration. Such risks are referred to as **significant risks** (ISA 315, paras 27–29). The auditor uses professional judgement to determine which risks are significant, and uses that judgement to determine whether the nature of the risk, the likely magnitude of the potential misstatement including the possibility that the risk may give rise to multiple misstatements, and the likelihood of the risk occurring are such that they require special audit consideration. Examples of the types of items that may result in significant risks include:

- Assertions identified with fraud risk factors.
- Non-routine or unsystematically processed transactions.
- Significant accounting estimates and judgements.
- Highly complex transactions.
- Significant transactions with related parties.
- Significant transactions outside the normal course of business of the entity, or that otherwise appear to be unusual.
- Application of new accounting standards.
- Revenue recognition in certain industries or for certain types of transactions.
- Industry-specific issues.

The auditor always treats assessed risks of material misstatement due to fraud as significant risks (ISA 240 para. 27). Accounting estimates having high estimation uncertainty such as estimates highly dependent upon judgement give rise to significant risks. (The section on the *Advanced Module* later in this chapter discusses auditing of accounting estimates in detail.)

When the auditor has determined that a significant risk exists, the auditor should, to the extent not already done, obtain an understanding of the entity's controls, including control activities, *relevant to that risk* (ISA 315 para. 29). The auditor should always perform substantive procedures that *directly respond* to the significant risk at assertion (ISA 330 para. 21). For example, for accounting estimates that give rise to significant risks the auditor should perform specific substantive procedures including evaluation of the reasonableness of management's assumptions and how estimation uncertainty has been addressed. When the auditor plans to rely on controls over a significant risk, the auditor tests those controls in the current period (ISA 330 para. 15).

> ### Practice Insight 3.4
>
> Auditing standards state that the auditor should presume that there is a fraud risk involving improper revenue recognition on every audit engagement. The auditor must evaluate the types of revenue or revenue transactions that are subject to such a risk.

❖ EVALUATION OF AUDIT TEST RESULTS

LO8

As the audit progresses and at the completion of the audit the auditor evaluates the effect of the identified misstatements on the audit. The auditor requests, on a timely basis, management to correct misstatements. At the completion of the audit the auditor determines if the remaining uncorrected misstatements would cause the financial statements to be materially misstated. If the individual or aggregate uncorrected misstatements are greater than materiality, the auditor would have to issue a qualified or adverse opinion. When the uncorrected misstatements are evaluated immaterial and the relevant qualitative aspects of the entity's accounting practices and financial statements presentation do not imply otherwise, the auditor can conclude that the financial statements as a whole are free from material misstatement. (Chapter 18 discusses in detail the auditor's forming of an audit opinion, including evaluations related to relevant qualitative aspects of the entity's accounting practices and financial statements.)

If the auditor has determined that the misstatement is or may be the result of fraud, and either has determined that the effect could be material to the financial statements or has been unable to evaluate whether the effect is material, the auditor should:

● Attempt to obtain audit evidence to determine whether, in fact, material fraud has occurred and, if so, its effect.
● Consider the implications for other aspects of the audit.
● Discuss the matter and the approach to further investigation with an appropriate level of management that is at least one level above those involved in committing the fraud and with senior management.
● If appropriate, suggest that the client consult with legal counsel.

If the results of the audit tests indicate a significant risk of fraud, the auditor should consider withdrawing from the engagement and communicating the reasons for withdrawal to those charged with governance (i.e. the board of directors, the audit committee or others with equivalent authority and responsibility).

❖ DOCUMENTATION OF THE AUDITOR'S RISK ASSESSMENT AND RESPONSE

LO9

The auditor has extensive documentation requirements for risk assessment (including fraud risk assessment) and audit responses to identified risks. For example, the auditor should document the risk of material misstatement for all material accounts and classes of transactions in terms of the related assertions. The level of risk may be described as quantitative or qualitative (high, medium or low). Exhibit 3–3 shows the use of a questionnaire to document the nature of the entity. Briefly review this exhibit. After considering the responses listed on the document, how would this information guide the planning of your audit? Other areas of documentation include the following:

● The nature and results of the communication among engagement personnel that occurred in planning the audit regarding the risks of material misstatement.
● The steps performed in obtaining knowledge about the entity's business and its environment. The documentation should include:
  – The risks identified.
  – An evaluation of management's response to such risks.
  – The auditor's assessment of the risk of error or fraud after considering the entity's response.
● The nature, timing and extent of the procedures performed in response to the risks of material misstatement due to fraud and the results of that work.
● Fraud risks or other conditions that caused the auditor to believe that additional audit procedures or other responses were required to address such risks or other conditions.
● The nature of the communications about fraud made to management, those charged with governance, and others.
● The basis for the auditor's conclusions about the reasonableness of accounting estimates that give rise to significant risks.

Exhibit 3–3 A Partial Questionnaire for Documenting the Understanding of EarthWear Clothiers and its Environment		
CLIENT NAME: EARTHWEAR CLOTHIERS		**Completed by:**
Entity and Environment Category: Nature of the Entity		**Reviewed by:**
Year ended: 31 December 2009		
Risk Factors	*Description/Response*	*Any Remaining Risk*
What are the entity's major sources of revenue, including the nature of its products and or services?	EarthWear Clothiers generates revenue mainly through the sale of high-quality clothing for outdoor sports, such as hiking, skiing, fly-fishing and white-water kayaking. The company's product lines also include casual clothes, accessories, shoes and soft luggage. These sales are made mainly through the company's freephone number and over its Internet websites, In 2009, Internet sales accounted for 21 per cent of total revenue.	No. The company uses conservative methods to record revenue and provides an adequate reserve for returned merchandise.

Who are the entity's key customers?	The company's key customers are the 21.1 million persons on its mailing list, approximately 7 million of whom are viewed as 'current customers' because they have purchased from the company in the last 24 months. Market research as of January 2008 indicates that approximately 50 per cent of customers are in the 35–54 age group and had a median income of €62,000. Almost two-thirds are in professional or managerial positions.	No.
Who are the entity's key suppliers?	During 2009, the company had purchase orders for merchandise from about 300 domestic and foreign manufacturers, including intermediaries (agents). One manufacturer and one intermediary accounted for about 14 and 29 per cent of the company's received merchandise euros, respectively, in 2009. In 2009, about 80 per cent of the merchandise was imported, mainly from Asia. The company will continue to take advantage of worldwide sourcing without sacrificing customer service or quality standards.	Yes. The company would be subject to some risk in finding alternative sourcing if this manufacturer and or intermediary experiences prolonged work stoppages or economic problems. The availability and cost of certain foreign products may be affected by trade policies, economic events and the value of the euro relative to other currencies.
What is the entity's organizational structure?	The company has a well-developed organizational structure with clear lines of authority among the various operating departments and staff functions. The organizational structure is appropriate for EarthWear's activities.	No.
Where are its major locations?	Europolis is the main corporate location. EarthWear has its main international phone centre in Mumbai. Other centres are in the UK, Germany and Japan. During 2009, EarthWear expanded its global Internet presence by launching sites in ten more countries.	Yes. The USA and Italy have restrictive trade laws where companies get a certain degree of protection from the government when their markets are threatened. Political uncertainty in less developed countries could affect EarthWear's sales activities in these countries.
What are the entity's major assets?	The major assets of the company are inventory; property, plant and equipment; and its customer mailing list.	No.
What are the entity's major liabilities?	The company has no long-term debt. However, it maintains a line of credit for financing purchases during the peak purchasing season.	No. The company has cash flow to meet its current obligations.
What are the entity's financial characteristics including financing sources and current and prospective financial condition?	The company uses its line of credit to meet its normal financing activities. Overall the company's financial condition is good.	No.
Are there any potential related parties?	No.	No.
Are there any individually significant events and transactions such as acquisitions or disposals of subsidiaries, businesses, or product lines during the year?	The expansion of the company's Internet presence to ten more countries.	Yes. Restrictive trade laws.
Does the entity have any major uncertainties or contingencies?	No.	No.

◈ COMMUNICATIONS ABOUT FRAUD TO MANAGEMENT, THOSE CHARGED WITH
LO10 **GOVERNANCE AND OTHERS**

Whenever the auditor has found evidence that a fraud may exist, that matter should be brought to the attention of an appropriate level of management. Fraud involving senior management and fraud that causes a material misstatement of the financial statements should be reported direct to those charged with governance, for example the board of directors or the audit committee, if any. In addition, the auditor should reach an understanding with those charged with governance regarding the expected nature and extent of communications about misappropriations perpetrated by lower-level employees.

The disclosure of fraud to parties other than the client's senior management and those charged with governance ordinarily is not part of the auditor's responsibility and ordinarily would be precluded by the auditor's ethical or legal obligations of confidentiality. The auditor's legal responsibilities vary by country, and in certain circumstances the duty of confidentiality may be overridden by statute, the law or courts of law. For example, in some countries, the auditor of a financial institution has a statutory duty to report the occurrence of fraud to supervisory authorities. Also, in some countries the auditor has a duty to report misstatements to authorities in those cases where management and those charged with governance fail to take corrective action. The IFAC Code of Ethics for Professional Accountants provides guidance on circumstances where auditors should disclose confidential information or when such disclosure may be appropriate (see Chapter 19 for a discussion of the IFAC Code of Ethics and the auditor's obligations of confidentiality).

◈ MATERIALITY[v]

LO11

The auditor's consideration of materiality on an audit is a matter of *professional judgement*. It reflects the auditor's perception of how misstatements could reasonably be expected to influence the economic decisions of users of the financial statements. The applicable financial reporting framework often discusses materiality.[vi] Such discussion in the context of the preparation and presentation of financial statement provides a frame of reference to the auditor in determining a materiality. Although financial reporting frameworks may discuss materiality in different terms, they generally explain the materiality concept as follows:

> *Misstatements, including omissions, are considered to be material if they, individually or in the aggregate, could reasonably be expected to influence the economic decisions of users taken on the basis of the financial statements. Judgements about materiality are made in light of surrounding circumstances, and are affected by the size or nature of a misstatement, or a combination of both. (ISA 320)*

Auditing standards refer to users as a group, not specific individual users, and provide guidance to auditors' professional judgements in assessing the common financial information needs of such users of financial statements. It is reasonable for the auditor to assume that users:

- Have a reasonable knowledge of business and economic activities and accounting, and a willingness to study the information in the financial statements with reasonable diligence.
- Understand that financial statements are prepared and audited to levels of materiality.
- Recognize the uncertainties inherent in the measurement of amounts based on the use of estimates, judgement, and the consideration of future events.
- Make reasonable economic decisions on the basis of the information in the financial statements (ISA 320, para. 4).

The concept of materiality is applied by the auditor (1) in *planning* and *performing* the audit; and (2) in *evaluating* the effect of **identified misstatements** on the audit and in *evaluating* the effect of **uncorrected misstatements** on the financial statements and in forming the opinion in the auditor's report.

The following sections present an approach to assessing materiality, which is then followed by an example. The presentation is based on the general approach provided by auditing standards (ISA 320 and ISA 450). While the policies and procedures of individual audit firms may differ in some respects, the approach presented here provides the reader with a basic framework for understanding the consideration of materiality in an audit.

❖ Steps in Applying Materiality

LO12 Figure 3–4 presents the three major steps in the application of materiality to an audit. Steps 1 and 2 are normally performed early in the engagement as part of planning the audit. Step 3 is performed usually prior to, or when the auditor evaluates the evidence at the completion of the audit to determine if it supports the fair presentation of the financial statements.

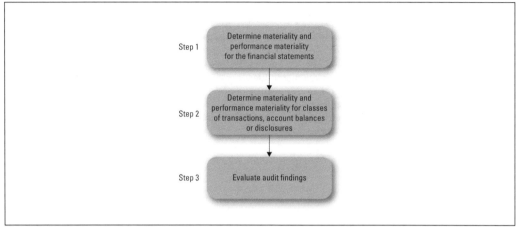

Figure 3–4   Steps in Applying Materiality on an Audit

Step 1: Determine Materiality and Performance Materiality for the Financial Statements

In Step 1 the auditor first establishes the materiality level for the financial statements as a whole, and then determines a lower amount, **performance materiality**, to establish the scope for the audit procedures.

Materiality is the maximum amount by which the auditor believes the financial statements could be misstated and still *not* reasonably be expected to affect the decisions of users taken on the basis of the financial statements. Materiality, however, is a relative, not an absolute, concept. For example, €5,000 might be considered highly material for a small sole proprietorship, but this amount would clearly be immaterial for a large multinational company. Thus, the relative size of the company being audited affects materiality.

A *percentage* is often applied to a chosen *benchmark* as a starting point in determining materiality. Factors that may affect the identification of an appropriate benchmark include the following:

● The elements of the financial statements such as assets, liabilities, equity, revenue and expenses.
● Whether there are items on which the attention of the users of the particular entity's financial statements tends to be focused.
● The nature of the entity, where the entity is in its life cycle, and the industry and economic environment in which the entity operates.
● The entity's ownership structure and the way it is financed.
● The relative volatility of the benchmark (ISA 320, para. A3).

Examples of benchmarks that might be appropriate include categories of reported income such as total revenues, total expenses, gross profit and profit before tax. Profit before tax from continuing operations is often used for profit-oriented entity. Net asset value or total equity might be suitable as a benchmark for asset-based entities (e.g. investment funds). For small owner-managed entities a benchmark such as profit before the owner's remuneration and tax might be suitable. Lastly, for a not-for-profit entity, total revenues or total expenses might be appropriate benchmarks.

Determining a percentage to be applied to a chosen benchmark also involves the exercise of professional judgement. A common rule of thumb is to use 5 per cent of profit before tax for profit-oriented entities. However, if current-year profit before tax is not stable, the entity is close to breaking even or experiencing a loss, auditors might use an average of the previous years' profit or another base. For example, suppose that an entity has profit before taxes of €3,000,000 one year and the auditor decides that 5 per cent of that amount, €150,000, would be material. Suppose, in the following year, the entity's profit before taxes falls to €250,000 due to a temporary decrease in sales prices for its products. If the auditor uses the 5 per cent factor, the materiality would be €12,500 (€250,000 × 0.05), and a much more extensive audit would be required. Thus, using an average of the prior three years' profit or another base such as total assets or total revenues may provide a more stable benchmark from year to year. The percentage applied to total assets or total revenues will ordinarily be lower than the percentage applied to profit before tax.

At the planning stage the auditor should also determine *performance materiality*. Performance materiality is determined for the purposes of assessing the risks of material misstatement and determining the nature, timing and extent of further audit procedures. Performance materiality is set at a *lower* amount than materiality to provide a *margin* for possible undetected misstatements. This reduces the risk that the aggregate of uncorrected and undetected misstatements will exceed materiality for the financial statements. Undetected misstatements could exist because of the presence of sampling risk and non-sampling risk. Performance materiality judgements may be affected by factors such as the auditor's understanding of the entity, and the nature and extent of misstatements identified in previous audits and thereby the auditor's expectations in relation to misstatements in the current period.

The auditor's documentations should include the amount and factors considered in determination of materiality, performance materiality and, if determined, the materiality level or levels for particular classes of transactions, account balances or disclosures (Step 2).

Step 2: Determine Materiality and Performance Materiality for Classes of Transactions, Account Balances or Disclosures

In Step 2 the auditor establishes, if appropriate, materiality levels for particular classes of transactions, account balances or disclosure. Auditing standards require that the auditor *in the specific circumstances of the entity* determines lesser amounts than materiality for the financial statements as a whole for particular classes of transactions, account balances or disclosures. The auditor concludes on this matter based on his or her expectations on how misstatements in classes of transactions, account balances or disclosures reasonably could influence the economic decisions of users taken on the basis of the financial statements. Factors indicating the need to determine lesser materiality levels for particular classes of transactions, account balances or disclosures include:

- Whether law, regulation or the applicable financial reporting framework affect users' expectations regarding the measurement or disclosure of certain items, for example related party transactions and the remuneration of management and those charged with governance.
- The key disclosures in relation to the industry in which the entity operates, for example research and development costs for a pharmaceutical company.
- Whether attention is focused on a particular aspect of the entity's business that is separately disclosed in the financial statements, for example a newly acquired business.

To summarize, the auditor *may or may not* conclude that it is appropriate to determine materiality levels to be applied to particular classes of transactions, account balances or disclosures. If, however, the auditor concludes that such determination is appropriate based on the financial information needs of the users of the financial statements, the auditor will when evaluating audit findings compare whether the determined materiality levels for the particular classes of transactions, account balances or disclosures have been exceeded (Step 3).

For the purpose of establishing the scope of audit procedures the auditor may also find it appropriate to determine performance materiality for classes of transactions, account balances or disclosures. Again, the lower performance materiality provides a margin for undetected misstatements, thereby reducing the risk that the aggregate of undetected and uncorrected misstatements could be material.

Practice Insight 3.5

The specific policies and procedures of the individual audit firm on materiality may differ in some respects, for example in allocating materiality to individual elements of financial statements. Some firms do not practise such allocation, while other firms may systematically allocate materiality to accounts and classes of transactions for planning purposes. For example, a computational benchmark may be to allocate 50 to 75 per cent of materiality for the financial statements to an account, depending on relevant qualitative factors in the circumstances. Obviously, this approach results in an allocation of combined allocated materiality that is greater than materiality for the financial statements. There are a number of reasons why such allocation makes sense from an audit planning perspective. For instance, not all accounts will be misstated by the full amount of their allocation, and when misstatements are identified in an account, the auditors typically perform additional procedures in that, and related, accounts.

As the *audit progresses* the auditor should revise materiality when becoming aware of new information that would have caused the auditor to have determined a different amount initially. For example, if during the audit it appears as though actual financial results are likely to be substantially different from the anticipated period-end financial results that were used initially to determine materiality, the auditor revises that materiality. When this occurs, the auditor should document the reasons for using a different materiality level.

Step 3: Evaluate Audit Findings

Step 3 is completed near the end of the audit, when the auditor evaluates all the evidence that has been gathered. Based on the results of the audit procedures conducted, the auditor aggregates identified misstatements, other than those that are judged clearly trivial. Matters are clearly trivial when the auditor expects that the accumulation of such amounts would not have a material effect on the financial statements.

As discussed in a prior section in this chapter, identified misstatements may be classified as factual misstatements, judgemental misstatements (the *Advanced Module* section at the end of this chapter discusses judgemental misstatements related to accounting estimates) and projected misstatements (discussed in Chapter 9). In evaluating the effect of the *identified* misstatements on the *audit*, the auditor compares the aggregate identified misstatement with materiality, including appropriate materiality levels for classes of transactions, account balances and disclosures. If the identified misstatement approaches materiality, there may be greater than an acceptable low level of risk that the identified misstatement and possible undetected misstatements in aggregate could exceed materiality. In such cases the auditor should determine whether the overall *audit strategy* and *audit plan* are appropriate. Further, the nature of identified misstatements and the circumstances of their occurrence may indicate that other misstatements may exist. For example, other misstatements may exist when auditor identifies a misstatement that arose from a breakdown in internal control or from the entity's application of an inappropriate valuation method. If such misstatements could be material when aggregated with misstatements accumulated during the audit, the auditor should also determine whether the overall audit strategy and audit plan need to be revised.

The auditor *communicates* on a timely basis, ordinarily as a continual and interactive process, identifies misstatements accumulated during the audit with the appropriate level of *management* and requests management to correct those misstatements. If management refuses to correct misstatements communicated, the auditor obtains an understanding of management's reasons for not making the corrections. Such understanding is taken into account when evaluating whether the financial statements are free from material misstatement. The auditor communicates any uncorrected misstatements and the effect that they may have on the audit opinion to *those charged with governance*, and requests uncorrected misstatements to be corrected. Finally, the auditor requests a *written representation* from management and, where appropriate, those charged with governance whether they believe the effects of any remaining uncorrected misstatements are immaterial. Pause for a moment, and consider how these requirements and procedures may encourage the entity to correct identified misstatements.

In evaluating the effect of *uncorrected* misstatements on the financial statements, the auditor determines whether the uncorrected misstatements are material, either individually or when aggregated with other misstatements. When appropriate, the auditor also determines if the uncorrected misstatements for particular classes of transactions, account balances and disclosures are material (cf. Step 2). In the process the auditor considers the size and nature of the misstatements as well as the particular circumstances of their occurrence. For example, a client may have illegally paid a commissioned agent to secure a sales contract. While the amount of the illegal payment may be immaterial to the financial statements, the disclosure of the illegal act may result in loss of the contract and substantial penalties that may be material. Table 3–8 presents a list of examples of circumstances that may be considered in evaluating materiality of uncorrected misstatements. Such circumstances may cause the auditor to evaluate misstatement as material, individually or when considered together with other misstatement accumulated during the audit, even if they are lower than materiality levels set at Steps 1 and 2.

Table 3–8   Examples of Circumstances that May Affect Evaluating Materiality of Uncorrected Misstatements

- Whether the misstatement involves fraud or illegal acts, for example the concealment of an unlawful transaction.
- Whether the misstatement has the effect of increasing management's compensation, for example by ensuring that the requirements for the award of bonuses are satisfied.
- Whether the misstatement relates to items involving particular parties such as related parties.
- Whether the misstatement affects compliance with regulatory requirements, for example information required by supervisory authorities.
- Whether the misstatement affects compliance with contractual requirements, for example with loan covenants.
- Whether the misstatement affects ratios, financial statements items or disclosure used to evaluate the entity, for example segment information.
- Whether the misstatement masks a change in earnings or other trends.
- Whether the misstatement is a misclassification between balance sheet line items or affects the income statement.
- Whether the misstatement relates to the incorrect selection or application of an accounting policy that has an immaterial effect on the current period's financial statements but is likely to have a material effect on future periods' financial statements.
- Whether the misstatement affects other information that will be communicated in documents containing the audited financial statements, for example in the annual report.

The auditor also considers the effect of uncorrected misstatements related to prior periods on the current period. (Discussion Case 3–23 covers the auditor's consideration of prior periods' uncorrected misstatements in the evaluation of current-year audit results.)

When uncorrected misstatements are evaluated material, the auditor should issue a qualified or adverse opinion because the financial statements do not present fairly in all material respects. When the uncorrected misstatements are evaluated immaterial and the relevant qualitative aspects of the entity's accounting practices and financial statements do not imply otherwise (refer to Chapter 18 for a discussion of relevant qualitative aspects), the auditor can conclude that the financial statements as a whole are free from material misstatement.

The auditor should *document* the amount below which misstatements would be regarded as clearly trivial; all identified misstatements during the audit and whether they have been corrected; and the auditor's conclusion as to whether uncorrected misstatements are material and the basis for that conclusion.

Practice Insight 3.6

If an individual misstatement is judged to be material, auditing standards consider it is unlikely that it can be offset by other misstatements (ISA 450). For example, if revenue has been materially overstated, the financial statements as a whole will be materially misstated, even if the effect of the misstatement on earnings is completely offset by an equivalent overstatement of expenses. It may be appropriate to offset misstatements within the same account balance or class of transactions; however, the risk that further undetected misstatements may exist is considered before concluding that offsetting even immaterial misstatements is appropriate.

Determining whether a classification misstatement is material involves the evaluation of qualitative considerations. There may be circumstances where the auditor concludes that a classification misstatement is not material in the context of the financial statements as a whole, even though it may exceed the materiality level or levels applied in evaluating other misstatements.

❖ An Example

LO13   In this example, the three steps for applying materiality are illustrated, using financial information for EarthWear Clothiers for the year ended 31 December 2009. This financial information is taken from the case illustration included in Chapter 1.

Step 1: Determine Materiality and Performance Materiality for the Financial Statements

EarthWear Clothiers' net profit before taxes is €36 million (rounded). Assume that the auditors, Willis & Adams, have decided that 5 per cent of this benchmark is appropriate for materiality for the financial statements as a whole. Thus, they determine materiality for the financial statements as a whole to be €1,800,000 (€36,000,000 × .05) For the purpose of establishing the scope of audit procedures the auditors set performance materiality at €1,700,000.

Step 2: Determine Materiality and Performance Materiality for Classes of Transactions, Account Balances or Disclosures

In our example, for simplicity of presentation, we assume that EarthWear's auditors determine that €900,000 is the materiality level for each account and class of transactions, i.e. €900,000 is relevant amount for evaluating the materiality of audit findings in accounts and class of transactions.

Step 3: Evaluate Audit Findings

Auditing standards require that the auditor document all identified misstatements accumulated during the audit. Exhibit 3–4 presents an example of a working paper that can be used to aggregate the effects of misstatements identified during the audit. Assume that during the course of the audit the auditor identified four misstatements. In the example, misstatements are compared to the materiality for the financial statements as well as the materiality levels set for each account and class of transactions. For example, the first misstatement indicates a factual misstatement in the accrual of payroll expense and bonuses. The total misstatement of accrued payroll is €215,000. The second entry is based on the results of a statistical sampling application for inventory. The statistical results indicated a projected misstatement of €312,500. In this example no identified misstatements in individual accounts or class of transactions are larger than their materiality of €900,000, and the total identified misstatements are less than materiality for the financial statement as a whole. Before concluding on the effect of the identified misstatements on the *audit*, the auditors consider if the nature and circumstances related to identified misstatements indicate further possible misstatements. For example, the auditors consider further possible misstatements that may be due to sampling.

Exhibit 3–4 Example Working Paper for Proposed Adjusting Entries					
EARTHWEAR CLOTHIERS					
Schedule of Proposed Adjusting Entries 31/12/09					
Working Paper Ref.	Proposed Adjusting Entry	Assets	Liabilities	Equity	Revenues	Expenses
N10	Payroll expense					75,000
	Bonuses					140,000
	Provisions		215,000			
	To accrue payroll through 31/12 and recognize 2009 bonuses					
F20	Cost of sales					312,500
	Inventory	(312,500)				
	To adjust ending inventory based on sample results					
F22	Inventory	227,450				
	Accounts payable		227,450			
	To record inventory in transit at 31/12					
R15	Accounts receivable	79,850				
	Sales				79,850	
	To record sales cut-off errors at 31/12					
	Total	€(5,200)	€442,450		€79,850	€527,500

Materiality for classes of transactions and account balances = €900,000.

Conclusion: Based on the above analysis, the account balances for EarthWear Clothiers are fairly stated in accordance with the applicable financial reporting framework.

Although not considered material, Willis & Adams will request management to correct the identified misstatements. If the aggregate of the uncorrected misstatements were in excess of materiality for the financial statement as a whole or the uncorrected misstatements in an account or class of transactions were in excess of their set materiality, the auditor would have to issue a qualified or adverse opinion.

❖ ADVANCED MODULE: AUDITING OF ACCOUNTING ESTIMATES, INCLUDING
LO14 **FAIR VALUE ACCOUNTING ESTIMATES**

ISA 540 *Auditing Accounting Estimates, Including Fair Value Accounting Estimates, and Related Disclosures* deals with the overreaching process on how the auditor obtains sufficient appropriate audit evidence as to whether accounting estimates are *reasonable* and related disclosures are *adequate*. ISA 540 tailors the requirements in other ISAs to the auditing of accounting estimates. Particularly, the standard expands on how accounting estimates are integrated in the auditor's assessment and response to risks of material misstatements and evaluation of audit findings.

This chapter discusses auditing of accounting estimates in relevant sections. When relevant, the business process chapters (Chapters 10–16) as well as other chapters include discussions of auditing of accounting estimates. This *Advanced Module* offers a discussion of auditing of accounting estimates in more detail.

Accounting estimates are financial statements items that cannot be measured precisely, but can only be estimated. The estimation may relate to forecasting the outcome of a transaction, event or condition, giving rise to the need for the accounting estimate, such as when estimating the allowance for uncollectable accounts. The estimation of the allowance for uncollectable accounts is affected by such factors as the client's credit-granting and cash-collection policies, and the financial strength of the client's customers. In fair value accounting, estimates are expressed in terms of the value of a current transaction or financial statement item based on conditions prevalent at the measurement date. The *fair value accounting estimate* of a financial statement item may be the prevalent estimated market price of a particular type of asset or liability. The value of a current transaction is the prevalent estimated price at which the transaction would occur rather than settlement at some past or future date. Such an estimate may sometimes be an assumed hypothetical current transaction between knowledgeable, willing parties in an arm's length transaction. For example, the estimate may relate to the fair values at the acquisition date and subsequent periods of goodwill and intangible assets acquired in a business combination.

Auditing standards define accounting estimates as follows:

> **Accounting estimates** *is an approximation of a monetary amount in the absence of a precise means of measurement. This term is used for an amount measured at fair value where there is estimation uncertainty, as well as for other amounts that require estimation.*

Examples of situations where accounting estimates, other than fair value accounting estimates, may be required include:

- Allowance for uncollectable accounts including loan loss reserves.
- Inventory obsolescence.
- Warranty obligations.
- Depreciation method and asset useful life.
- Provisions.
- Pensions.
- Construction contracts and other long-term contracts.
- Litigation outcomes.

Examples of situations where fair value accounting estimates may be required include:

- Financial instruments.
- Share-based payments.
- Property, plant and equipment.
- Goodwill and intangible assets acquired in a business combination.
- Non-monetary exchanges.

Fair value accounting estimates may also be required to evaluate and determine possible impairment of an asset or liability.

The nature and reliability of information available to management to support the making of an accounting estimate vary widely. This affects the degree of **estimation uncertainty** associated with accounting estimates and therefore the risk of material misstatement of accounting estimates. Some accounting estimates, however, involve relatively low estimation uncertainty and may give rise to lower risks of material misstatements. This includes accounting estimates that are frequently made and updated because they relate to routine transactions, estimates derived from data that are readily available, such as published interest rate data, and fair value accounting estimates where there is an active market that provides readily available and reliable information on the prices at which actual exchanges occur. In contrast, other accounting estimates may have relatively high estimation uncertainty, particularly when they are based on significant and uncertain assumptions such as the outcome of litigation, and fair value measurements in inactive markets, or where models for calculating fair values and their assumptions are not reliable or readily available.

Identifying and Assessing the Risks of Material Misstatements for Accounting Estimates

In obtaining an understanding of the entity and its environment in order to provide a basis for identification and assessment of risks of material misstatement of accounting estimates, the auditor obtains an understanding of:

- The requirements of the applicable financial framework relevant to accounting estimates, including related disclosures.
- How management identifies those transactions, events and conditions that may give rise to the need for accounting estimates to be recognized or disclosed in the financial statements.
- How management makes the accounting estimates and an understanding of the data on which they are based, including methods and, where applicable, the model used, as well as change or need for change in methods used; relevant controls; the assumptions underlying the accounting estimate; whether management has used an expert; and whether and, if so, how management has assessed the effect of estimation uncertainty.

A review of the outcome of prior-period accounting estimates is also part of the auditor's understanding for identification and assessment of accounting estimates in the current period.

In identifying and assessing the risks of material misstatement the auditor evaluates the degree of *estimation uncertainty* associated with an accounting estimate. The degree of estimation uncertainty may be influenced by factors such:

- The extent to which the accounting estimate depends on judgement.
- The sensitivity of the accounting estimate to changes in assumptions.
- The existence of recognized measurement techniques that may mitigate the estimation uncertainty.
- The length of the forecast period, and the relevance of data drawn from past events to forecast future events.
- The availability of reliable data from external sources.
- The extent to which the accounting estimate is based on observable or unobservable inputs.

If an accounting estimate has high estimation uncertainty, it gives rise to a significant risk. Auditing standards guide extensively on how the auditor identifies and assesses the risk of material misstatements of accounting estimates, including assessment of accounting estimate uncertainty and what is constituting a high estimation uncertainty (ISA 540, paras A12–A51).

Responses to the Assessed Risks of Material Misstatements for Accounting Estimates

Based on the assessed risks of material misstatement of the accounting estimates the auditor *determines* (1) whether management has appropriately applied the requirements of the applicable financial reporting framework relevant to the accounting estimate, and (2) whether the methods for making the accounting estimates are appropriate and have been applied consistently, as well as the appropriateness of any changes in method.

In responding to assessed risks of material misstatement of accounting estimates, the auditor takes into account the nature of the accounting estimate. For example, for the allowance for doubtful accounts, an effective procedure for the auditor may be to review subsequent cash collections in combination with other procedures. Other appropriate responses than to base audit evidence on events occurring up to the date of the auditor's report include testing how management made the accounting estimate and the data on which it is based, testing the operating effectiveness of the controls over how management made the accounting estimate, and developing a point estimate or a range to evaluate management's point accounting estimate. An accounting estimate that gives rise to a significant risk requires further substantive procedures related to how management has addressed the estimation uncertainty, management's decision to recognize or not recognize the accounting estimate in the financial statements, and the selected measurement basis for the accounting estimate. Auditing standards provide extensive guidance for the auditor's response to assessed risk of material misstatement of accounting estimates, including responses to significant risks (ISA 540, paras A52–A115).

Evaluating the Reasonableness of Accounting Estimates, and Concluding

Based on the audit evidence the auditor evaluates whether the accounting estimate is reasonable or is misstated, and whether the disclosure is adequate. For instance, the auditor may have concluded that it is appropriate to use a range for evaluation of management's point estimate. In this situation the auditor has narrowed the range, based on audit evidence available, until all outcomes within the range are considered reasonable. Ordinarily, a range that has been narrowed to be equal to or less than performance materiality is adequate. In evaluating the reasonableness of management's point estimate the auditor determines whether the range supports the recorded estimate by management. To illustrate, where audit evidence supports the auditor's use of a point estimate, the difference between the auditor's point estimate and management's point estimate constitutes a judgemental misstatement. Where the auditor has concluded that using a *range* is appropriate, a management point estimate that lies outside the auditor's range is not supported by audit evidence. In such cases, the misstatement is no less than the difference between management's point estimate and the nearest point of the auditor's range. For example, suppose that the auditor concludes, based on the evidence, that the allowance for doubtful accounts should be between €210,000 and €270,000. If management's recorded estimate falls within this range (say €250,000), the auditor may conclude that the recorded amount is reasonable and no difference would be aggregated. If the recorded estimate falls outside this range (say €190,000), the difference between the recorded amount and the amount at the nearest point of the auditor's range (€20,000) would at minimum be aggregated as a judgemental misstatement.

Although auditing standards assist the auditor to form an appropriate conclusion about the reasonableness of accounting estimates and adequacy of related disclosures, the *reliability* of audit evidence may be a fundamental challenge in the auditing of accounting estimates. This become evident in fair value estimates when market information is either not available or sufficient information is difficult to obtain, such as when markets are not active. Inactive markets lead to the use of valuation models for estimation purposes rather than valuation by market prices. Market changes such as increased uncertainty may cause inactive and illiquid markets. Changes in markets may, however, also require changes in valuation approaches, including of the model choice and model assumptions. Consequently, in such situations the auditor should consider the degree of consistency in and relevance of valuation approach and assumptions. It may be necessary for the auditor to look at a broader set of sources of evidence to accumulate sufficient appropriate evidence. For example, the auditor may decide to use the work of an auditor's expert. It may also become an issue whether the measurement of the accounting estimate is sufficiently reliable to meet the recognition criteria of the applicable financial reporting framework.

During the audit the auditor reviews the judgements and decisions made by management, including the making of accounting estimates, to identify whether there are *indicators of possible management bias*. For example, an indicator of possible **management bias** would be management's selection of significant assumptions underlying accounting estimates that yield a point estimate favourable for management objectives. Indicators of possible management bias may affect the auditor's conclusion as to whether the auditor's risk assessment and related responses remain appropriate. The auditor may also need to consider the implications of the presence of such indicators for the rest of the audit and the audit opinion.

Before ending this module, pause for a moment and reflect on the following challenges for preparers and auditors in considering fair value accounting estimates, particularly in times and markets with high uncertainty:[vii]

- The measurement objective, as fair value accounting estimates are expressed in terms of the value of a current transaction or financial statement item based on conditions prevalent at the measurement date.
- The need to incorporate judgements concerning significant assumptions that may be made by others such as experts employed or engaged by the entity or the auditor.
- The availability (or lack thereof) of information or evidence and its reliability.
- The breadth of assets and liabilities to which fair value accounting may be, or is required to be, applied.
- The choice and sophistication of acceptable valuation techniques and models.

● The need for appropriate disclosure in the financial statements about measurement methods and uncertainty, especially when relevant markets are illiquid.

🔐 Key Terms

Accounting estimate. An approximation of a monetary amount in the absence of a precise means of measurement. This term is used for an amount measured at fair value where there is estimation uncertainty, as well as for other amounts that require estimation.

Accounting policies (IAS 8). The specific principles, bases, conventions, rules and practices applied by an entity in preparing and presenting financial statements.

Analytical procedures. Evaluations of financial information through analysis of plausible relationships among both financial and non-financial data.

Audit procedures. Specific acts performed as the auditor gathers evidence to determine if specific audit assertions are being met.

Audit risk. The risk that the auditor expresses an inappropriate audit opinion when the financial statements are materially misstated. Audit risk is a function of the risks of material misstatement and detection risk.

Auditor's business risk. The risk that the auditor is exposed to loss or injury to professional practice from litigation, adverse publicity, or other events arising in connection with financial statements audited and reported on.

Business risks (clients). Risks resulting from significant conditions, events, circumstances, actions or inactions that may adversely affect the entity's ability to execute its strategies and to achieve its objectives.

Control risk. The risk that material misstatements that could occur will not be prevented, or detected and corrected by internal controls.

Detection risk. The risk that the auditor will not detect a material misstatement that exists in the financial statements.

Error. An unintentional misstatement or omission of an amount or a disclosure.

Estimation uncertainty. The susceptibility of an accounting estimate and related disclosures to an inherent lack of precision in its measurement.

Factual misstatements. Misstatements about which there is no doubt.

Fair value. The amount for which an asset could be exchanged, or a liability settled, between knowledgeable, willing parties in an arm's length transaction.

Fraud. Intentional misstatement that can be classified as fraudulent financial reporting and/or misappropriation of assets.

Fraud risk factors. Events or conditions that indicate an incentive or pressure to commit fraud or provide an opportunity to commit fraud.

Identified misstatements. The aggregate of factual misstatements, judgemental misstatements and projected misstatements.

Inherent risk. The susceptibility of an assertion to material misstatement, assuming no related controls.

Judgemental misstatements. Differences arising from the judgements of management concerning accounting estimates that the auditor considers unreasonable, or the selection or application of accounting policies that the auditor considers inappropriate.

Management bias. A lack of neutrality by management in the preparation and presentation of information.

Materiality. Misstatements, including omissions, that individually or in the aggregate, could reasonably be expected to influence the economic decisions of users taken on the basis of the financial statements. Judgements about materiality are made in light of surrounding circumstances, and are affected by the size or nature of a misstatement, or a combination of both.

Misstatements. A difference between the amount, classification, presentation or disclosure of a reported financial statement item and the amount, classification, presentation or disclosure that is required for the item to be in accordance with the applicable financial reporting framework. Misstatements can arise from error or fraud.

Performance materiality. The amount or amounts set by the auditor at less than materiality for the financial statements as a whole to reduce to an appropriately low level the probability that the aggregate of uncorrected and undetected misstatements exceeds materiality for the financial statements as a whole. If applicable, performance materiality also refers to the amount or amounts set by the auditor at less than the materiality level or levels for particular classes of transactions, account balances or disclosures.

Professional judgement. The application of relevant training, knowledge and experience, within the context provided by auditing, accounting and ethical standards, in making informed decisions about the courses of action that are appropriate in the circumstances of the audit engagement.

Professional scepticism. An attitude that includes a questioning mind, being alert to conditions which may indicate possible misstatement due to error or fraud, and a critical assessment of audit evidence.

Projected misstatements. Best estimate of misstatements in populations, involving the projection of misstatements identified in audit samples to the entire populations from which the samples were drawn.

Risk assessment. The identification, analysis, and management of risks relevant to the preparation of financial statements that are fairly presented in accordance with the applicable financial reporting framework.

Risk assessment procedures. The audit procedures performed to obtain an understanding of the entity and its environment, including the entity's internal control.

Scope of the audit. Refers to the nature, timing and extent of audit procedures, where nature refers to the type of evidence; timing refers to when the evidence will be gathered; and extent refers to how much of the type of evidence will be evaluated.

Significant risk. An identified and assessed risk of material misstatement that in the auditor's judgement requires special audit consideration.

Uncorrected misstatements. Misstatements that the auditor has accumulated during the audit and that have not been corrected.

? Review Questions

LO1	3–1	Distinguish between audit risk and auditor's business risk.
LO1,2	3–2	How do inherent risk and control risk differ from detection risk?
LO4	3–3	What are some limitations of the audit risk model?
LO2	3–4	Distinguish between sampling and non-sampling risk.
LO5,6	3–5	In understanding the entity and its environment, the auditor gathers knowledge about which categories of information?
LO5,6	3–6	Give three examples of conditions and events that may indicate the existence of (client) business risks.
LO5,6	3–7	Distinguish between error and fraud. Give three examples of each.
LO11,12	3–8	Why is it important for audit firms to develop policies and procedures for establishing materiality?
LO12	3–9	List and describe the three major steps in applying materiality to an audit.
LO12	3–10	While net profit before taxes is frequently used for calculating materiality, discuss circumstances when total assets or revenues might be better bases for calculating materiality.
LO11,12	3–11	Why do auditors determine and apply performance materiality?
LO11,12,13	3–12	List four circumstances that may affect the auditor's evaluation of materiality of uncorrected misstatements.

Problems

LO1,2,3,11,12 **3–13**   The auditor should consider audit risk and materiality when planning an audit.

Required:

a   *Define audit risk and materiality.*
b   *Describe the components of audit risk (e.g. inherent risk, control risk and detection risk).*
c   *Explain how these components are interrelated.*
d   *Discuss how the auditor determines materiality for the financial statements.*

(AICPA, adapted)

LO1,2,3   **3–14**   The audit firm of Lumley & Lu uses a quantitative approach to implementing the audit risk model. Calculate detection risk for each of the following hypothetical clients.

Client No.	Audit Risk	Risk of Material Misstatement	Detection Risk
1	5%	20%	
2	5%	50%	
3	10%	15%	
4	10%	40%	

LO1,2,3   **3–15**   The audit firm of Quigley & Associates uses a qualitative approach to implementing the audit risk model. Audit risk is categorized using two terms: very low and low. The risk of material misstatement and detection risk are categorized using three terms: low; moderate; and high. Calculate detection risk for each of the following hypothetical clients.

Client No.	Audit Risk	Risk of Material Misstatement	Detection Risk
1	Low	Moderate	
2	Very low	High	
3	Low	Low	
4	Very low	Moderate	

LO1,2,3   **3–16**   Assume that you are the new audit senior on the LV Drug Corporation (LVD) engagement. LVD is a pharmaceutical company that has three successful drugs and a number of drugs in progress in its research and development pipeline. You are considering detection risk at the financial statement level and it is important to identify the inherent risks and control risks that LVD has and how they relate to audit risk.

Required:

For each of the following factors, indicate whether it is an inherent risk or a control risk factor, and its effect on detection risk. In answering this question, assume that each factor is independent of the others.

a   *LVD is a publicly traded company.*
b   *Dr Jones is the major shareholder of LVD and its CEO.*
c   *Dr Jones has unusual influence over the board of directors.*
d   *Your firm has audited LVD for the last four years.*
e   *There has been high turnover of key accounting personnel during the last two years.*
f   *The internal audit function reports to the audit committee.*
g   *LVD signed an exclusive distribution contract with another pharmaceutical company to distribute its latest blockbuster drug – Xarmdon.*
h   *During the current year, LVD began leasing a manufacturing facility that is owned by Forge Limited Partners. Dr Jones is a partner in Forge.*

    i   *LVD has been the subject of lawsuits by users of Framadon, who claim that the drug affects their liver function. LVD is confident that there are no side effects from the use of Framadon.*

    j   *The Medical Control Agency has begun an investigation into LVD's compliance procedures over its drug testing on human subjects.*

LO1,2,3   **3–17**   When planning a financial statement audit, an auditor must understand audit risk and its components. The firm of Pack & Peck evaluates the risk of material misstatement (RMM) by disaggregating RMM into its two components: inherent risk and control risk.

Required:

For each illustration, select the component of audit risk that is most directly illustrated. The components of audit risk may be used once, more than once or not at all.

Components of Audit Risk:

a   *Control risk.*
b   *Detection risk.*
c   *Inherent risk.*

Illustration	Component of Audit Risk
1. A client fails to discover employee fraud on a timely basis because bank accounts are not reconciled monthly.	
2. Cash is more susceptible to theft than an inventory of coal.	
3. Confirmation of receivables by an auditor fails to detect a material misstatement.	
4. Disbursements have occurred without proper approval.	
5. There is inadequate segregation of duties.	
6. A necessary substantive audit procedure is omitted.	
7. Notes receivable are susceptible to material misstatement, assuming there are no related internal controls.	
8. Technological developments make a major product obsolete.	
9. XYZ Company, a client, lacks sufficient working capital to continue operations.	

LO3,5,6   **3–18**   For each of the following situations, explain how risk of material misstatement should be assessed and what effect that assessment will have on detection risk.

    a   Johnson is a fast-growing trucking company. The company is publicly held, but Ivan Johnson and his sons control 55 per cent of the stock. Ivan Johnson is chairman of the board and CEO. He personally makes all major decisions with little consultation with the board of directors. Most of the directors, however, are either members of the Johnson family or long-standing friends. The board basically rubber-stamps Ivan Johnson's decisions.

    b   MaxiWrite Corporation is one of several companies engaged in the manufacture of high-speed, high-capacity data storage devices. The industry is very competitive and subject to quick changes in technology. MaxiWrite's operating results would place the company in the second quartile in terms of profitability and financial position. The company has never been the leader in the industry, with its products typically slightly behind the industry leaders in terms of performance.

c   The Focus Bank has been your client for the past two years. During that period you have had numerous arguments with the president and the controller over a number of accounting issues. The major issue is related to the bank's reserve for loan losses and the value of collateral. Your prior audits have indicated that a significant adjustment is required each year to the loan loss reserves.

LO5,6,9   **3–19**   Management fraud (e.g. fraudulent financial reporting) is a relatively rare event. However, when it does occur, the frauds (i.e. Enron and Parmalat) can have a significant effect on shareholders, employees and other parties. ISA 240 provides the relevant guidance for auditors.

Required:

a   *What is the auditor's responsibility for detecting fraud?*
b   *Describe the three conditions that are generally present when fraud occurs.*
c   *What are the objectives of the 'brainstorming' meeting that is held among the audit engagement team members?*
d   *What is the required documentation for identified risk factors?*

LO5,6   **3–20**   Assume that your firm is considering accepting NewSkin Pharma as a new audit client. NewSkin is a startup biotech firm that has publicly traded stock. Your audit partner has asked you to perform some preliminary work for the firm's client acceptance process.

Required:

a   *Prepare a list of business risks that NewSkin is likely to face as a startup biotech firm.*
b   *Choose two of these risks and consider how they might affect your decision to accept NewSkin as a client.*

LO12,13   **3–21**   For each of the following scenarios determine materiality and evaluate audit findings. Justify your decisions.

Scenario 1:

Murphy & Johnson is a manufacturer of small motors for lawnmowers, tractors and snowmobiles. The components of its financial statements are (1) net profit = €21 million, (2) total assets = €550 million, and (3) total revenues = €775 million.

During the course of the audit, Murphy & Johnson's audit firm detected two misstatements that aggregated to an overstatement of net profit of €1.25 million.

Scenario 2:

Delta Investments provides a group of mutual funds for investors. The elements of its financial statements are (1) net profit = €40 million, (2) total assets = €4.3 billion, and (3) total revenues = €900 million.

During the course of the audit, Delta's audit firm detected two misstatements that aggregated to an overstatement of net profit of €5.75 million.

Scenario 3:

Swell Computers manufacturers desktop and laptop computers. The elements of the financial statements are: (1) net profit = €500,000, (2) total assets = €2.2 billion, and (3) total revenues = €7 billion.

During the course of the audit, Swell's audit firm detected one misstatement that resulted in an overstatement of net profit by €1.5 million.

Discussion Cases

LO5,6   3–22   **CarProof.** CarProof is a public company founded in 2000 to manufacture and sell speciality auto products mainly relating to paint protection and rust proofing. By 2007, the CarProof board of directors felt that the company's products had fully matured and that it needed to diversify. CarProof aggressively sought out new products and in March 2008 it acquired the formula and patent of a specialized motor lubricant (Run-Smooth) from SIM. In addition, the company purchased 15 per cent of SIM's outstanding common stock. At the time of the stock purchase, Steve Matthews owned 100 per cent of SIM; he retained ownership of 85 per cent of SIM after CarProof's 15 per cent purchase. In December 2008, the board of directors appointed Mr Matthews to be president of CarProof.

Run-Smooth is unlike conventional motor lubricants. Its innovative molecular structure accounts for what management believes is its superior performance. Although it is more expensive to produce and has a higher selling price than its conventional competitors, management believes that it will reduce maintenance costs and extend the life of equipment in which it is used.

CarProof's main competitor is a very successful multinational conglomerate that has excellent customer recognition of its products and a large distribution network. To create a market niche for Run-Smooth, CarProof's management is targeting commercial businesses that service vehicle fleets and industrial equipment.

CarProof's existing facilities were not adequate to produce Run-Smooth in commercial quantities. In June 2009 CarProof commenced construction of a new plant. After lengthy negotiation it received a €900,000 grant from the government. The terms of the grant require CarProof to maintain certain employment levels over the next three years or the grant must be repaid. The new facilities became operational on 1 December 2009. CarProof financed its recent expansion with a bank loan. Management is considering issuing additional stock later in 2010 to address the company's cash flow problems.

CarProof's auditors resigned in February 2010, after which Steve Matthews contacted your firm. The previous auditors informed Mr Matthews that they disagreed with CarProof's valuation of deferred development costs for Run-Smooth.

It is now 20 April 2010 and you and a partner in your firm have just met with Steve Matthews to discuss the services your firm can provide to CarProof for the year ending 31 March 2010. During your meeting, you collected the following information:

● CarProof has incurred substantial losses during the past three fiscal years.
● There have been significant orders of Run-Smooth received to date.
● CarProof has commenced a lawsuit against its major competitor for patent infringement and industrial espionage. Management has evidence that it believes will result in a successful action, and wishes to record the estimated gain on settlement of €4 million. Although no court date has been set, legal correspondence shows that the competitor intends 'to fight this action to the highest court'.
● Deferred development costs of €2 million represent material, labour and subcontract costs incurred during 2008 and 2009 to evaluate the Run-Smooth product and prepare it for market. CarProof has not taken any amortization to date but thinks that a period of 20 years would be appropriate.
● Royalties of €0.25 per litre of Run-Smooth produced are to be paid annually to SIM.
● The €3.514 million bank loan is secured by a floating charge over all corporate assets. The loan agreement requires CarProof to undergo an annual environmental assessment of its old and new blending facilities.

As you return to the office, the partner tells you that he is interested in having CarProof as an audit client. He wants a memo from you covering in detail the audit and (Client) business risks you see arising from this potential engagement.

Required:

Prepare the memo requested by the audit partner.

LO11,12,13   3–23   Wyly Waste Management. ISA 450 *Evaluation of Misstatements Identified during the Audit* requires the auditor to evaluate the effect of uncorrected misstatements related to prior periods on the current period. The auditing standard acknowledges that there are different acceptable approaches to the auditor's evaluation of such uncorrected misstatements on the current period's financial statements. ISA 450 does not mandate the use of one approach over another, but recognizes that using the same evaluation approach provides consistency from period to period (ISA 450, para. A18).

Two different acceptable approaches to the evaluation of prior periods uncorrected misstatements are:

1   *Iron curtain method (balance sheet view)* – this approach quantifies the misstatement based on the amount required to correct the misstatement in the balance sheet at the year end irrespective of the misstatement's year of origination.

2   *Rollover method (income statement view)* – this approach quantifies the misstatement based on the amount of the error that originates in the current-year income statement. This approach ignores the effects of correcting the portion of the current-year balance sheet misstatements that originated in prior years (i.e. it ignores the 'carryover effects' of prior-year misstatements).

Your firm is auditor of Wyly Waste Management (WWM). Materiality for the audit is €100,000. Shortly after the end of the year, WWM's CFO is meeting with your audit partner to review the preliminary results of the audit. Your partner presents a copy of the draft unadjusted misstatement summary to the CFO, which contains one misstatement.

During the year, WWM did not capitalize individual expenditures of less than €10,000, which is in accordance with its company policy. In the past, WWM's capital expenditures have been relatively constant each period and the expensing of the items has not caused any material errors. In the prior two years, the expensed items totalled €7,500 and €5,000 respectively. However, in the current year, WWM undertook significant development of a new waste disposal plant. As a result, WWM incurred eight capital expenditures of less than €10,000 each that were not capitalized. These purchases totalled €75,000.

Required:

a   *Quantify the misstatement using both the iron curtain approach and the rollover approach. Should your partner require WWM to correct the financial statements in the current year for the expensed items before being willing to issue an unmodified audit opinion?*

b   *Suppose the facts were changed and the expensed items for the prior two years totalled €22,500 and €15,000, respectively. Quantify the misstatement using both the iron curtain approach and the rollover approach. Should your partner require WWM to correct the financial statements in the current year for the expensed items before being willing to issue an unmodified audit opinion; and if a correction is required, by what amount?*

◯ Internet Assignment

LO5,6,7   3–24   Auditors are required to obtain and support an understanding of the entity and its environment in order to identify business risks. Much of the information needed to identify the risks can be obtained from the company's annual report. Many companies publish these documents on their website. Additionally, industry information on these companies can be obtained from websites such as Yahoo! (http://yahoo.marketguide.com).

a In groups (of two or three members) complete the questionnaire (except for the business process section) for a real-world company assigned by your instructor. There may be some questions asked on the questionnaire that you will be unable to answer. If you cannot answer a question, respond 'information not available'.

b The measurement and performance section asks for information on the entity's key performance indicators (KPIs). Identify what you think the KPIs are for the company assigned, and how the company compares to its industry averages and major competitors. Prepare tables for this data and a memo of your analyses.

Risk Response Table			
Business Risks	Audit Area Affected	Assertion	Response

Notes

[i] See T.B. Bell, M.E. Peecher and I. Solomon, *The 21st Public Company Audit: Conceptual Elements of KPMG's Global Audit Methodology*, KPMG, 2005, for a detailed discussion of the importance of recognizing the potential for non-sampling risk when conducting an audit.

[ii] See B.E. Cushing and J.K. Loebbecke (1983), 'Analytical Approaches to Audit Risk: A Survey and Analysis', *Auditing: A Journal of Practice and Theory*, Fall, pp. 23–41; W.R. Kinney, Jr (1983), 'A Note on Compounding Probabilities in Auditing', *Auditing: A Journal of Practice and Theory*, Spring, pp. 13–22; and W.R. Kinney, Jr (1989), 'Achieved Audit Risk and the Audit Outcome Space', *Auditing: A Journal of Practice and Theory*, pp. 67–84, for more detailed discussions of the limitations of the audit risk model.

[iii] See recent surveys by KPMG (*KPMG Forensic: Integrity Survey 2005–2006*, KPMG LLP, New York: 2005) and PwC (4th biennial *Global Economic Crime Survey 2007*, PwC, New York: 2007) for information on the incidence of fraud.

[iv] See A. Eilifsen and W.F. Messier, Jr (2000), 'Auditor Detection of Misstatements: A Review and Integration of Empirical Research', *A Journal of Accounting Literature* (19), pp 1–43, for a detailed review of research studies that have examined auditor-detected misstatements.

[v] See W.F. Messier, Jr, N. Martinov and A. Eilifsen, 'A Review and Integration of Empirical Research on Materiality: Two Decades Later', *Auditing: A Journal of Practice & Theory* (November 2005), pp. 153–87, for a discussion of materiality research.

[vi] For example, International Accounting Standards (IAS) 1, *Presentation of Financial Statements* provides the following definition of materiality: '*Omissions or misstatements of items are material if they could, individually or collectively, influence the economic decisions of users taken on the basis of the financial statements. Materiality depends on the size and nature of the omission or misstatement judged in the surrounding circumstances. The size or nature of the item, or a combination of both, could be the determining factor.*'

[vii] IAASB (October 2008) *Staff Audit Practice Alert. Challenges in Auditing Fair Value Accounting Estimates in the Current Market Environment*, http://web.ifac.org/download/Staff_Audit_Practice_Alert.pdf.

CHAPTER 4

Audit Evidence and Audit Documentation

❖ LEARNING OBJECTIVES

Upon completion of this chapter you will

❖ **LO1** Understand the relationship between audit evidence and the auditor's report.

❖ **LO2** Know management assertions about classes of transactions and events for the period under audit, assertions about account balances at the period end, and assertions about presentation and disclosure.

❖ **LO3** Know why audit procedures are performed.

❖ **LO4** Learn the basic concepts of audit evidence.

❖ **LO5** Know the audit procedures used for obtaining audit evidence.

❖ **LO6** Understand the reliability of the types of evidence.

❖ **LO7** Understand the objectives of audit documentation.

❖ **LO8** Develop an understanding of the content, types, organization and ownership of audit documentation.

❖ RELEVANT ACCOUNTING AND AUDITING PRONOUNCEMENTS

ISQC 1, Quality Control for Firms That Perform Audits and Reviews of Financial Statements, and Other Assurance and Related Services Engagements

ISA 230, Audit Documentation

ISA 240, The Auditor's Responsibilities Relating to Fraud in an Audit of Financial Statements

ISA 300, Planning an Audit of Financial Statements

ISA 315, Identifying and Assessing the Risks of Material Misstatement through Understanding the Entity and Its Environment

ISA 320, Materiality in Planning and Performing an Audit

ISA 330, The Auditor's Responses to Assessed Risks

ISA 450, Evaluation of Misstatements Identified during the Audit

ISA 500, Audit Evidence

ISA 505, External Confirmations

ISA 520, Analytical Procedures

THIS CHAPTER covers the third of the three fundamental audit concepts introduced in Chapter 1: **audit evidence**. Audit evidence is all the information used by the auditor in arriving at the conclusions on which the audit opinion is based, including the information contained in the accounting records underlying the financial statements and other information. In Chapter 1, we indicated that auditing is essentially a set of conceptual tools that guide an auditor in collecting and evaluating evidence regarding others' assertions, and we assured you that these conceptual tools are extremely useful in a variety of settings. We encourage you to keep this perspective in mind as you study Chapter 4. While this chapter does contain some lists you will probably want to commit to memory (e.g. management assertions and characteristics of audit evidence), remember that these are not just lists – they constitute powerful conceptual tools that can help you in almost any setting that requires you to collect and evaluate evidence. Understanding the nature and characteristics of evidence is fundamental to effective auditing and is a key part of the conceptual tool kit we hope to help you acquire as you go through this book.

On a typical audit most of the auditor's work involves obtaining and evaluating evidence using procedures such as inspection of records and confirmations to test the fair presentation of the financial statements. To perform this task effectively and efficiently, an auditor must thoroughly understand the important aspects of audit evidence. This includes understanding how audit evidence relates to financial statement assertions and the auditor's report, the sufficiency and appropriateness of evidence, types of **audit procedures** and the documentation of evidence in the working papers. Each of these topics is covered in this chapter.

❖ THE RELATIONSHIP OF AUDIT EVIDENCE TO THE AUDIT REPORT

LO1

Auditing standards provide the basic framework for the auditor's understanding of audit evidence and its use in supporting his or her opinion on the financial statements. The auditor gathers evidence by conducting audit procedures to test management assertions. This evidence serves as the support for the auditor's opinion about whether the financial statements are fairly presented. Figure 4–1 presents an overview of the relationships among the financial statements, management assertions about elements of the financial statements, audit procedures and the audit report. More specifically, the financial statements reflect management's assertions about the various financial statement elements. The auditor tests management's assertions by conducting audit procedures that provide evidence on whether each relevant management assertion is supported. When the evidence supports management's assertions, the auditor can issue an audit report with an unmodified opinion.

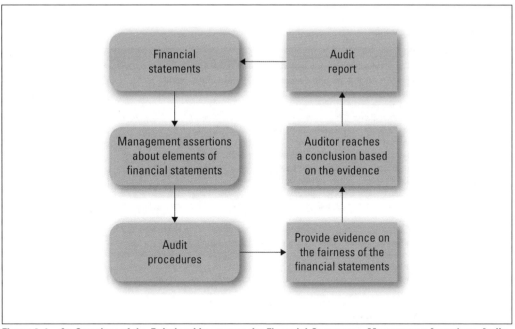

Figure 4–1   An Overview of the Relationships among the Financial Statements, Management Assertions, Audit Procedures and the Audit Report

Auditors typically divide financial statements into elements or segments in order to manage the audit. An element can be a financial statement account or a business process. As indicated in Chapter 2, the basic processes of most businesses are the *revenue process* the *purchasing process*, the *human resource management process*, the *inventory management process* and the *financing/investing process*. Sometimes business processes are referred to as transaction cycles (e.g. the revenue cycle). Each process may involve a number of important transactions. Business processes support functions such as sales and services, materials acquisition, production and distribution, human resource management and treasury management. This text focuses on business processes and their related transactions and financial statement accounts. Examining business processes and their related accounts allows the auditor to gather evidence by examining the processing of related transactions through the information system from their origin to their ultimate disposition in the accounting journals and ledgers. Later chapters in this text cover each of the major business processes that auditors typically encounter on an engagement.

❖ MANAGEMENT ASSERTIONS

LO2

Management is responsible for the fair presentation of the financial statements. **Assertions** are representations by management, explicit or otherwise, that are embodied in the financial statements, as used by the auditor to consider the different types of potential misstatements that may occur (ISA 315, para. 4(a)). In other words, assertions are expressed or implied representations by management regarding the recognition, measurement, presentation and disclosure of information in the financial statements and related disclosures. For example, when the balance sheet contains a line item for accounts receivable of €5 million, management asserts that those receivables exist and have a net realizable value of €5 million. Management also asserts that the accounts receivable balance arose from selling goods or services on credit in the normal course of business. As another example, take a moment and consider what the relevant management assertions are when the financial statements show a net sales figure of €10 million. Here, management asserts that the sales exist (existence assertion), were all conducted within the current time frame (cut-off assertion) and have been recorded in their correct amounts (accuracy assertion). Under current auditing standards, management assertions fall into the following categories:

- Assertions about classes of transactions and events for the period under audit.
- Assertions about account balances at the period end.

● Assertions about presentation and disclosure.

Table 4–1 presents the definitions of each assertion by category while Table 4–2 shows how the assertions are related across categories.

Table 4–1 Definitions of Management Assertions by Category
Assertions about classes of transactions and events for the period under audit
● **Occurrence** – transactions and events that have been recorded have occurred and pertain to the entity (sometimes referred to as validity).
● **Completeness** – all transactions and events that should have been recorded have been recorded.
● **Authorization** – all transactions and events have been properly authorized.
● **Accuracy** – amounts and other data relating to recorded transactions and events have been recorded appropriately.
● **Cut-off** – transactions and events have been recorded in the correct accounting period.
● **Classification** – transactions and events have been recorded in the proper accounts.
Assertions about account balances at the period end
● **Existence** – assets, liabilities and equity interests exist.
● **Rights and obligations** – the entity holds or controls the rights to assets, and liabilities are the obligations of the entity.
● **Completeness** – all assets, liabilities and equity interests that should have been recorded have been recorded.
● **Valuation and allocation** – assets, liabilities and equity interests are included in the financial statements at appropriate amounts, and any resulting valuation or allocation adjustments are appropriately recorded.
Assertions about presentation and disclosure
● **Occurrence and rights and obligations** – disclosed events, transactions and other matters have occurred and pertain to the entity.
● **Completeness** – all disclosures that should have been included in the financial statements have been included.
● **Classification and understandability** – financial information is appropriately presented and described, and disclosures are clearly expressed.
● **Accuracy and valuation** – financial and other information are disclosed fairly and at appropriate amounts.

Table 4–2 Summary of Management Assertions by Category			
	Categories of Assertions		
	Classes of Transactions and Events during the Period	*Account Balances at the End of the Period*	*Presentation and Disclosure*
Occurrence/Existence	Transactions and events that have been recorded have occurred and pertain to the entity.	Assets, liabilities and equity interests exist.	Disclosed events and transactions have occurred and pertain to the entity.
Rights and Obligations	–	The entity holds or controls the rights to assets, and liabilities are the obligations of the entity.	–
Completeness	All transactions and events that should have been recorded have been recorded.	All assets, liabilities and equity interests that should have been recorded have been recorded.	All disclosures that should have been included in the financial statements have been included.
Authorization	All transactions and events that should have been recorded have been authorized.	–	–
Accuracy/Valuation and Allocation	Amounts and other data relating to recorded transactions and events have been recorded appropriately.	Assets, liabilities and equity interests are included in the financial statements at appropriate amounts, and any resulting valuation or allocation adjustments are recorded appropriately.	Financial and other information is disclosed fairly and at appropriate amounts.
Cut-off	Transactions and events have been recorded in the correct accounting period.	–	–

| Classification and Understandability | Transactions and events have been recorded in the proper accounts. | – | Financial information is appropriately presented and described, and disclosures are expressed clearly. |

Pay close attention to the wording of the assertions as defined and described below. The way auditors use certain words as they relate to assertions may differ somewhat from your everyday usage of the terms, and part of mastering auditing is learning the language of auditors.

Assertions about Classes of Transactions and Events during the Period

Assertions about classes of transactions and events relate to the transactions that flow through a particular business process and accumulate in one or more financial statement accounts. Auditors perform audit procedures to gather evidence that tests relevant assertions related to those transactions. Transaction-related assertions help the auditor conceptualize, plan and perform those audit procedures.

Occurrence

The occurrence assertion relates to whether all recorded transactions and events have occurred and pertain to the entity. For example, management asserts that all revenue transactions recorded during the period were valid transactions. Occurrence is sometimes also referred to as validity. Take a minute and consider this assertion further. For which accounts would an auditor worry that the client might record transactions that did not occur? The occurrence assertion is relevant for revenue transactions because the client might have incentives to record fictitious transactions.

Completeness

The completeness assertion relates to whether all transactions and events that occurred during the period have been recorded. For example, if a client fails to record a valid revenue transaction, the revenue account will be understated. Note that the auditor's concern with the completeness assertion is opposite to the concern for occurrence. Failure to meet the completeness assertion results in an understatement in the related account, while failure to meet the occurrence assertion results in an overstatement in the account.

Authorization

The authorization assertion relates to whether all transactions have been properly authorized. For example, the purchase of a a significant new manufacturing facility should be approved by the board of directors.

Accuracy

The accuracy assertion addresses whether amounts and other data relating to recorded transactions and events have been recorded appropriately. For example, a sale to a customer that is recorded at an incorrect amount due to omission of an applicable discount would be considered a valid but inaccurate sales transaction.

The applicable financial reporting framework establishes the appropriate method for recording a transaction or event. For example, the international accounting standards state that the amount recorded for the cost of a new machine includes all directly attributable costs necessary to bring the machine to its required working condition.

Cut-off

The cut-off assertion relates to whether transactions and events have been recorded in the correct accounting period. The auditor's procedures must ensure that transactions occurring near year end are recorded in the financial statements in the proper period. For example, the auditor may want to test proper cut-off of revenue transactions at 31 December 2009. The auditor can examine a sample of shipping documents and sales invoices for a few days before and after year end to test whether the sales transactions are recorded in the proper period. The objective is to determine that all 2009 sales and no 2010 sales have been recorded in 2009. Thus, the auditor examines the shipping documents to ensure that no 2010 sales have been recorded in 2009 and that no 2009 sales are recorded in 2010.

Classification

The classification assertion is concerned with whether transactions and events have been recorded in the proper accounts. For example, management asserts that all direct cost transactions related to inventory have been properly classified in either inventory or as part of cost of sales. As another example, purchases are properly recorded as either assets or expenses, as appropriate.

Auditing standards allow the auditor to use the set of assertions as shown here or to express them differently. For example, the auditor may combine the assertions about transactions and events with assertions about account balances, or the auditor may subdivide individual assertions.

It is useful for the auditor to understand how internal controls relate to assertions embodied in the financial statements. *Authorization* of transactions is an important aspect of the design and effectiveness of internal control that may relate to multiple financial statement assertions such as occurrence, completeness and accuracy. In this book we discuss proper authorization of transactions as a separate assertion, together with those financial statement assertions listed in auditing standards' guidance. We have found that such explicit discussion makes it easier to understand the role of proper authorization and how it relates to the direct financial statement assertions.

Assertions about Account Balances at the Period End

Assertions about account balances relate directly to the ending balances of the accounts included in the financial statements. Auditors perform audit procedures to gather evidence relating to assertions relevant to those account balances. Balance-related assertions help the auditor conceptualize, plan and perform such audit procedures.

Existence

The assertion about existence addresses whether ending balances of assets, liabilities and equity interests included in the financial statements actually exist at the date of the financial statements. For example, management asserts that inventory shown on the balance sheet exists and is available for sale.

Rights and Obligations

The assertions about rights and obligations address whether the entity holds or controls the rights to assets included on the financial statements, and that liabilities are the obligations of the entity. For example, management asserts that the entity has legal title or rights of ownership to the inventory shown on the balance sheet. Similarly, amounts capitalized for leases reflect assertions that the entity has rights to leased property and that the corresponding lease liability represents an obligation of the entity.

Completeness

The assertion about completeness addresses whether all assets, liabilities and equity interests that should have been included as ending balances on the financial statements have been included. For example, management implicitly asserts that the ending balance shown for accounts payable on the balance sheet includes all such liabilities as of the balance sheet date.

Valuation and Allocation

Assertions about valuation or allocation address whether assets, liabilities and equity interests included in the financial statements are at appropriate amounts, and any resulting valuation or allocation adjustments are appropriately recorded. For example, management asserts that inventory is carried at the lower of cost or net realizable value on the balance sheet. Similarly, management asserts that the cost of property, plant and equipment is systematically allocated to appropriate accounting periods by recognizing depreciation expense.

Assertions about Presentation and Disclosure

This category of assertions relates to presentation of information in the financial statements and disclosures in the notes that are directly related to a specific transaction or account balance (e.g. disclosure related to property, plant and equipment) and those that apply to the financial statements in general (e.g. the note for the summary of significant accounting policies). Auditors perform audit procedures to gather evidence relating to assertions relevant to presentation and disclosure.

Occurrence and Rights and Obligations

The assertions about occurrence and rights and obligations address whether disclosed events, transactions and other matters have occurred and pertain to the entity. For example, when management presents capitalized lease transactions on the balance sheet as leased assets, the related liabilities as long-term debt, and the related note, it is asserting that a lease transaction occurred, it has a right to the leased asset and it owes the related lease obligation to the lessor. In addition, there is a note disclosure that provides additional information on the lease such as a description of the leasing arrangement.

Completeness

The completeness assertion in this category relates to whether all disclosures that should have been included in the financial statements have been included. Therefore, management asserts that no material disclosures have been omitted from the notes and other disclosures accompanying the financial statements.

Classification and Understandability

The assertions related to classification and understandability address whether the financial information is appropriately presented and described, and disclosures are clearly expressed. For example, management asserts that the portion of long-term debt shown as a current liability will mature in the current year. Similarly, management asserts that all major restrictions on the entity resulting from debt covenants are disclosed in notes and are able to be understood by the users of the financial statements.

Accuracy and Valuation

The accuracy and valuation assertions address whether financial and other information is disclosed fairly and at appropriate amounts. For example, when management discloses the fair value of securities, it is asserting that these financial instruments are properly valued in accordance with the applicable financial reporting framework. In addition, management may disclose in a note other information related to financial instruments.

Before we discuss important characteristics of evidence available to the auditor, pause for a moment to consider the usefulness of the sets of management assertions we have just discussed. The assertions collectively provide a road map for the auditor in determining what evidence to collect regarding various transactions, account balances and required financial statement disclosures. The auditor determines the type of evidence to gather by considering what possible misstatements could occur. Table 4–3 shows the management assertions for the accounts receivable balance. It also shows some of the misstatements that might occur if management's assertions are not correct. For example, the existence assertion might not be met if the accounts receivable balance includes fictitious customers. Management assertions also guide the auditor in designing audit procedures to collect the needed evidence, as well as assisting the auditor in evaluating the appropriateness and sufficiency of the evidence. For example, once the auditor is comfortable that he or she has gathered sufficient appropriate evidence relating to each balance-related assertion for the accounts payable account, the auditor can rest assured that no important aspect of that account has been neglected. The management assertions help the auditor focus his or her attention on all the various aspects of transactions, account balances and required disclosures that need to be considered. As such, the three sets of management assertions constitute a powerful conceptual tool in the auditor's toolbox.

Table 4–3 Management Assertions, Possible Misstatements and Illustrative Audit Procedures		
Management Assertions about the Accounts Receivable Element of the Financial Statements	*Possible Misstatement*	*Example Audit Procedures for Accounts Receivable*
Existence	Fictitious customer	Confirm accounts receivable
Rights and obligations	Receivables have been sold or factored	Inquire of management whether receivables have been sold
Completeness	Customer accounts are not recorded	Agree total of accounts receivable subsidiary ledger to accounts receivable control account
Valuation and allocation	Delinquent customer carried at full amount	Test the adequacy of the allowance for doubtful accounts

 # AUDIT PROCEDURES

LO3

Audit procedures are specific acts performed by the auditor to gather evidence to determine if specific assertions are being met. Audit procedures are performed to:

- Obtain an understanding of the entity and its environment, including its internal control, to assess the risks of material misstatement at the financial statement and assertion levels. Such audit procedures are referred to as *risk assessment procedures*. These procedures were discussed in Chapter 3.
- Test the operating effectiveness of controls in preventing, or detecting and correcting, material misstatements at the assertion level. Audit procedures performed for this purpose are referred to as *tests of controls*. Tests of controls are discussed in Chapters 5 and 6.
- Detect material misstatements at the assertion level. Such audit procedures are referred to as *substantive procedures*. Substantive procedures include tests of details of classes of transactions, account balances and disclosures, and substantive analytical procedures. Substantive procedures are discussed in detail in Chapter 5 and in each business process chapter.

A set of audit procedures prepared to test assertions for an element of the financial statements is part of the *audit plan*. Table 4–3 illustrates an audit procedure for each assertion related to the audit of accounts receivable. The reader should note that there is *not* a one-to-one relationship between assertions and audit procedures. In some instances more than one audit procedure is required to test an assertion. Conversely, in some cases an audit procedure provides evidence for more than one assertion. Note that the assertions do not change whether information is processed manually or electronically. However, the methods of applying audit procedures may be influenced by the method of information processing. Examples of audit procedures used to test various account balances will be presented in later chapters.

 # THE CONCEPTS OF AUDIT EVIDENCE

LO4

Audit evidence is all the information used by the auditor in arriving at the conclusions on which the audit opinion is based, and includes the information contained in the **accounting records** underlying the financial statements and other information. A solid understanding of the characteristics of evidence is obviously an important conceptual tool for auditors as well as for professionals in a variety of other settings. The following concepts of audit evidence are important to understanding the conduct of the audit:

- The nature of audit evidence.
- The sufficiency and appropriateness of audit evidence.
- The evaluation of audit evidence.

The Nature of Audit Evidence

Evidence is the information gathered or used by the auditor to support his or her opinion. The *nature* of the evidence refers to the form or type of information, which includes accounting records and other available information. *Accounting records* include the records of initial entries and supporting records, such as cheques and records of electronic fund transfers; invoices; contracts; the general and subsidiary ledgers, journal entries and other adjustments to the financial statements that are not reflected in formal journal entries; and records such as work sheets and spreadsheets supporting cost allocations, computations, reconciliations and disclosures. Many times these entries in the accounting records are initiated, recorded, processed and reported in electronic form. *Other information* that the auditor may use as audit evidence includes minutes of meetings; confirmations from third parties; analysts' reports; comparable data about competitors (benchmarking); controls manuals; information obtained by the auditor from such audit procedures as inquiry, observation and inspection; and other information developed by, or available to, the auditor that permits the auditor to reach conclusions through valid reasoning.

For some entities, accounting records and other information may be available only in electronic form. Thus, source documents such as purchase orders, bills of lading, invoices and cheques are replaced with electronic messages or electronic images. Two common examples are electronic data interchange (EDI) and image-processing systems. A client that uses EDI may process sales or purchase transactions electronically. For example, the client's EDI system can contact a vendor electronically when supplies of a part run low. The vendor will then ship the goods to the client and send an invoice electronically. The client can authorize its bank to make an electronic payment directly to the vendor's bank account. In an image-processing system, documents are scanned and converted to electronic images to facilitate storage and reference, and the source documents may not be retained after conversion. In such systems, electronic evidence may exist at only a certain point in time and may not be retrievable later. This may require the auditor to select sample items several times during the year rather than at year end.

The Sufficiency and Appropriateness of Audit Evidence

Sufficiency is the measure of the *quantity* of audit evidence. *Appropriateness* is a measure of the *quality* of audit evidence. Sufficiency and appropriateness of audit evidence are interrelated. The auditor must consider both concepts when assessing risks and designing audit procedures.

The quantity of audit evidence needed is affected by the risk of misstatement and by the quality of the audit evidence gathered. Thus, the greater the risk of misstatement, the more audit evidence is likely to be required to meet the audit test. And the higher the quality of the evidence, the less evidence that may be required to meet the audit test. Accordingly, there is an inverse relationship between the sufficiency and appropriateness of audit evidence.

In most instances, the auditor relies on evidence that is *persuasive* rather than *convincing* in forming an opinion on a set of financial statements. This occurs for two reasons. First, because an audit must be completed in a reasonable amount of time and at a reasonable cost, the auditor examines only a sample of the transactions that compose the account balance or class of transactions. Thus, the auditor reaches a conclusion about the account or class of transactions based on a subset of the available evidence.

Second, due to the nature of evidence, auditors must often rely on evidence that is not perfectly reliable. As discussed in the next section, the types of audit evidence have different degrees of reliability, and even highly reliable evidence has weaknesses. For example, an auditor can physically examine inventory, but such evidence will not ensure that obsolescence is not a problem. Therefore, the nature of the evidence obtained by the auditor seldom provides absolute assurance about an assertion.

Evidence is considered appropriate when it provides information that is both relevant and reliable.

Relevance

The **relevance of audit evidence** refers to its relationship to the assertion or to the objective of the control being tested. If the auditor relies on evidence that is unrelated to the assertion, he or she may reach an incorrect conclusion about the assertion. For example, suppose the auditor wants to check the completeness assertion for recording sales transactions; that is, are all goods shipped to customers recorded in the sales journal? A normal audit procedure for testing this assertion is to trace a sample of shipping documents (such as bills of lading) to the related sales invoices and entries in the sales journal. If the auditor samples the population of sales invoices issued during the period, the evidence would not relate to the completeness assertion (that is, the auditor would not detect shipments made that are not billed or recorded). The auditor should check the log of prenumbered bills of lading, after ascertaining that such documents were issued for all customer shipments. Any conclusion based on the population of sales invoices would not be based on evidence relevant to testing the completeness assertion.

Reliability

The **reliability** (or validity) **of evidence** refers to whether a particular type of evidence can be relied upon to signal the true state of an assertion. Because of varied circumstances on audit engagements, it is difficult to generalize about the reliability of various types of evidence. However, the reliability of evidence is influenced by its source and by its nature, and is dependent on the individual circumstances under which it is obtained.

- *Knowledgeable independent source of the evidence.* Evidence obtained directly by the auditor from a knowledgeable independent source outside the entity is usually viewed as more reliable than evidence obtained solely from within the entity. Thus, a confirmation of the client's bank balance received directly by the auditor would be viewed as more reliable than examination of the cash receipts journal and cash balance as recorded in the general ledger. Additionally, evidence that is obtained from the client, but that has been subjected to verification by a knowledgeable independent source, is viewed as more reliable than evidence obtained solely from within the entity. For example, a cancelled cheque held by the client would be more reliable than a duplicate copy of the cheque because the cancelled cheque would be endorsed by the payee and cleared through the bank – in other words, it has been verified by an independent source.

- *Effectiveness of internal control.* A major objective of a client's internal control is to generate reliable information to assist management decision making. As part of the audit, the effectiveness of the client's internal control is assessed. When the auditor assesses the client's internal control as effective (that is, low control risk), evidence generated by that accounting system is viewed as reliable. Conversely, if internal control is assessed as ineffective (that is, high control risk), the evidence from the accounting system would not be considered reliable. Thus, the more effective the client's internal control, the more assurance it provides about the reliability of audit evidence.

- *Auditor's direct personal knowledge.* Evidence obtained directly by the auditor (e.g. observation of the performance of a control) is generally considered to be more reliable than evidence obtained indirectly or by inference (e.g. inquiry about the performance of a control). For example, an auditor's physical inspection of a client's inventory is considered to be relatively reliable because the auditor has direct personal knowledge regarding the inventory. There are, of course, exceptions to this general rule. For example, if an auditor examined an inventory composed of diamonds or speciality computer chips, the auditor may lack the expertise to appropriately assess the validity and valuation of such inventory items. In such cases, the auditor may need the skill and knowledge of an expert to assist with the inventory audit.

- *Documentary evidence.* Audit evidence is more reliable when it exists in documentary form, whether paper, electronic, or other medium. Thus, a written record of a board of directors meeting is more reliable than a subsequent oral representation of the matters discussed.

- *Original documents.* Audit evidence provided by original documents is more reliable than audit evidence provided by photocopies or facsimiles. An auditor's examination of an original, signed copy of a lease agreement is more reliable than a photocopy.

Determining the sufficiency and appropriateness of evidence are two of the more critical decisions the auditor faces on an engagement. Before continuing, take a moment to consider which of the following sources of evidence are more reliable:

- Inquiry of an accounts receivable clerk regarding the accounts receivable balance *or* an account receivable confirmations sent to a sample of customers.
- Physical examination of lumber inventory performed by the external auditor *or* physical examination of inventory performed by internal auditors.

The Evaluation of Audit Evidence

The ability to evaluate evidence appropriately is another important skill an auditor must develop. Proper evaluation of evidence requires that the auditor understands the types of evidence that are available and their relative reliability or diagnosticity. The auditor must be capable of assessing when a sufficient amount of appropriate evidence has been obtained in order to determine the fairness of management's assertions.

In evaluating evidence, an auditor should be *thorough* in searching for evidence and *unbiased* in its evaluation. For example, suppose an auditor decides to mail accounts receivable confirmations to 50 of the largest customers of a client that has a total of 5,000 customer accounts receivable. Even if some of the 50 customers do not respond directly to the auditor, the auditor must gather sufficient evidence on each of the 50 accounts, which could include searching for subsequent cash receipts, shipping documents, invoices, and so forth. In evaluating evidence, the auditor must remain objective and must not allow the evaluation of the evidence to be biased by other considerations. To illustrate, in evaluating a client's response to an audit inquiry, the auditor must not allow any personal factors (e.g. the client is likeable and friendly) to influence the evaluation of the client's response.

◆ AUDIT PROCEDURES FOR OBTAINING AUDIT EVIDENCE

LO5

In conducting audit procedures, the auditor examines various types of audit evidence. Evidence is commonly categorized into the following types:

- Inspection of records or documents.
- Inspection of tangible assets.
- Observation.
- Inquiry.
- Confirmation.
- Recalculation.
- Reperformance.
- Analytical procedures.
- Scanning.

Inspection of Records or Documents

Inspection of records or documents consists of examining internal or external records or documents that are in paper form, electronic form or other media. On most audit engagements, inspection of records or documents makes up the bulk of the evidence gathered by the auditor. Two issues are important in discussing inspection of records or documents: the reliability of such evidence and its relationship to specific assertions.

Reliability of Records or Documents

A previous section noted the independence of the source of evidence as a factor that affected the reliability of audit evidence. In particular, evidence obtained from a knowledgeable source outside the entity is generally considered more reliable than evidence obtained solely from within the entity. Typically a distinction is made between internal and external documents. *Internal documents* are generated and maintained within the entity; that is, these documents have not been seen by any party outside the client's organization. Examples include duplicate copies of sales invoices and shipping documents, materials requisition forms, and work sheets for overhead cost allocation. *External documents* are of two forms: documents originating within the entity but circulated to independent sources outside the entity, and documents generated outside the entity but included in the client's accounting records. Examples of the first include remittance advices returned with cash receipts from customer payment, while examples of the second include bank statements and vendors' invoices.

In general, external documentary evidence is viewed as more reliable than internal evidence because a third party either initiated or reviewed it. However, the difference in reliability between internal and external documents depends on a number of factors, including the reliability of controls over preparation and storage of internal documents, and various factors affecting the reliability of external documents.

Documentary Evidence Related to Assertions

The second issue concerning records or documents relates directly to the occurrence and completeness assertions, and to the *direction of testing* taken when documentary evidence is examined. Figure 4–2 presents an overview of this relationship.

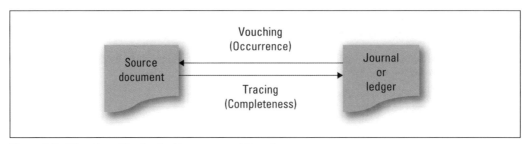

Figure 4–2 Direction of Testing for Occurance and Completeness

The *direction of testing* between the accounting records and source documents (such as sales invoices or shipping documents) is important when testing the occurrence and completeness assertions. *Vouching* refers to first selecting an item for testing from the accounting journals or ledgers, and then examining the underlying source document. Thus, the direction of testing is from the journals or ledgers back to the source documents. This approach provides evidence that items included in the accounting records have *occurred* (or are valid transactions). For example, an auditor may want to examine a sample of sales transactions from the sales journal to ensure that sales are not fictitious. If adequate source documents exist for each sales transaction selected from the sales journal, the auditor can conclude that each sale was valid. *Tracing* refers to first selecting an accounting transaction (a source document) and then following it into the journal or ledger. The direction of testing in this case is from the source documents to the journals or ledgers. Testing in this direction ensures that transactions that occurred are recorded (*completeness*) in the accounting records. For example, if the auditor selects a sample of shipping documents and traces them to the related sales invoices and then to the sales journal, he or she would have evidence on the completeness of sales. Take a few moments to be sure you understand how the direction of testing relates to the completeness and occurrence assertions. This is an important concept for auditors to understand. To help you better understand this concept, review each of the following examples and determine (1) if you are vouching or tracing, and (2) how that relates to either the occurrence or completeness assertion:

- Selecting a sample of transactions in the purchases journal and ensuring that they are supported by receiving documents.
- Selecting a sample of inventory tags used during the observation of the entity's physical inventory count and ensuring that they agree with the inventory ledger.

Inspection of Tangible Assets

Inspection of tangible assets consists of physical examination of the assets. Inspection is a relatively reliable type of evidence that involves the auditor inspecting or counting a tangible asset. An audit engagement includes many situations in which the auditor physically examines an entity's assets. Some examples might be counting cash on hand, examining inventory or marketable securities, and examining tangible fixed assets. This type of evidence primarily provides assurance that the asset exists. In some instances, such as examining inventory, physical examination may provide evidence on valuation by identifying items that are obsolete or slow-moving. However, physical examination provides little or no assurance on the rights and obligations assertions.

Observation

Observation consists of looking at a process or procedure being performed by others. The actions being observed typically do not leave an audit trail that can be tested by examining records or documents. Examples include observation of the counting of inventories by the entity's personnel, and observation of the performance of control activities. Observation provides audit evidence about the performance of a process or procedure but is limited to the point in time at which the observation takes place. It is also limited by the fact that the client personnel may act differently when the auditor is not observing them. Observation is useful in helping auditors understand client processes, but is generally not considered very reliable and thus generally requires additional corroboration by the auditor. Corroborating evidence includes data or documents from the accounting records and other documentary information (e.g. contracts and written confirmations).

Students often confuse the technical auditing definition of the term **observation** with the common usage of the word. As a result, students will use the term *observation* to describe such audit procedures as inspection of tangible assets or documents and records. However, as we discussed above, 'observation' in the auditing sense consists of looking at a *process or procedure being performed by others*. Technical terms or jargon serve an important role in efficient professional communication, and you will want to develop the proper vocabulary. Just as technical accounting terms such as *revenue* and *income* are not used interchangeably by professional accountants, professional auditors do not use 'observation' and 'inspection' interchangeably.

Inquiry

Inquiry consists of seeking information of knowledgeable persons (both financial and non-financial) throughout the entity or outside the entity. Inquiry is an important audit procedure that is used extensively throughout the audit and often is complementary to performing other audit procedures. For example, much of the audit work conducted to understand the entity and its environment, including internal control, involves inquiry.

Inquiries may range from formal written inquiries to informal oral inquiries. Evaluating responses to inquiries is an integral part of the inquiry process. Table 4–4 provides guidance for conducting and evaluating inquiries.

Table 4–4   Techniques for Conducting and Evaluating Inquiries
In conducting an inquiry, the auditor should:
● Consider the knowledge, objectivity, experience, responsibility and qualifications of the individual to be questioned.
● Ask clear, concise and relevant questions.
● Use open or closed questions appropriately.
● Listen actively and effectively.
● Consider the reactions and responses, and ask follow-up questions.
● Evaluate the response.

Responses to inquiries may provide the auditor with information not previously possessed or with corroborative audit evidence. Alternatively, responses might provide information that differs significantly from other information that the auditor has obtained, for example information regarding the possibility of management override of controls. The reliability of audit evidence obtained from responses to inquiries is also affected by the training, knowledge and experience of the auditor performing the inquiry because the auditor analyses and assesses responses while performing the inquiry and refines subsequent inquiries according to the circumstances. In some cases, the nature of the response may be so significant that the auditor requests a written representation from the source.

Inquiry alone ordinarily does not provide sufficient audit evidence, and the auditor will gather additional corroborative evidence to support the response.

Confirmation

Confirmation is the process of obtaining a representation of information or of an existing condition directly from a third party. Confirmations are also used to obtain audit evidence about the absence of certain conditions, for example the absence of a 'side agreement' that may influence revenue recognition. Auditors usually use the term *inquiry* to refer to unwritten questions asked of the client or of a third party, and the term *confirmation* to refer to written requests for a written response from a third party.

The reliability of evidence obtained through confirmations is directly affected by factors such as:

● The form of the confirmation.
● Prior experience with the entity.

- The nature of the information being confirmed.
- The intended respondent.

Confirmations are used extensively on audits; they generally provide reliable evidence for the existence assertion and, in testing certain financial statement elements (such as accounts payable), can provide evidence about the completeness assertion. Evidence about other assertions can also be obtained through the use of confirmations. For example, an auditor can send a confirmation to a consignee to verify that a client's inventory has been consigned. The returned confirmation provides evidence that the client owns the inventory (rights and obligations assertion). Table 4–5 lists selected amounts and information confirmed by auditors. Accounts receivable, accounts payable and bank confirmations, as well as the requirements and guidance in ISA 505 *External Confirmations*, are discussed in more detail in later chapters.

Table 4–5 Amounts and Information Frequently Confirmed by Auditors	
Amounts or Information Confirmed	*Source of Confirmation*
Cash balance	Bank
Accounts receivable	Individual customers
Inventory on consignment	Consignee
Accounts payable	Individual vendors
Bonds payable	Bondholders/trustee
Common stock outstanding	Registrar/transfer agent
Insurance coverage	Insurance company
Collateral for loan	Creditor

Recalculation

Recalculation consists of checking the mathematical accuracy of documents or records. Recalculation can be performed through the use of information technology (e.g. by obtaining an electronic file from the entity and using **computer-assisted audit techniques** (**CAATs**) to check the accuracy of the summarization of the file). Specific examples of this type of procedure include recalculation of depreciation expense on fixed assets and recalculation of accrued interest. Recalculation also includes footing, crossfooting, reconciling subsidiary ledgers to account balances and testing postings from journals to ledgers. Because the auditor creates this type of evidence, it is normally viewed as highly reliable.

Reperformance

Reperformance involves the independent execution by the auditor of procedures or controls that were originally performed by company personnel. For example, the auditor may reperform the ageing of accounts receivable. Because the auditor creates this type of evidence, it is normally viewed as highly reliable.

Analytical Procedures

Analytical procedures are an important type of evidence on an audit. They consist of evaluations of financial information made by a study of plausible relationships among both financial and non-financial data (ISA 520). For example, the current-year accounts' receivable balance can be compared to the prior years' balances after adjusting for any increase or decrease in sales and other economic factors. Similarly, the auditor might compare the current-year gross margin percentage to the gross margin percentage for the previous five years. The auditor makes such comparisons either to identify accounts that may contain material misstatements and require more investigation, or as a reasonableness test of the account balance. Analytical procedures are an effective and efficient form of evidence.

The reliability of analytical procedures is a function of: (1) the availability and reliability of the data used in the calculations; (2) the plausibility and predictability of the relationship being tested; and (3) the precision of the expectation and the rigour of the investigation. Because of the importance of this type of evidence in auditing, analytical procedures are covered in greater detail in Chapter 5.

Scanning

Scanning is the review of accounting data to identify significant or unusual items. This includes the identification of anomalous individual items within account balances or other client data through the scanning or analysis of entries in transaction listings, subsidiary ledgers, general ledger control accounts, adjusting entries, suspense accounts, reconciliations and other detailed reports. Scanning includes searching for large and unusual items in the accounting records (e.g. non-standard journal entries), as well as reviewing transaction data (e.g. expense accounts, adjusting journal entries) for indications of errors that have occurred. It might be used in conjunction with analytical procedures but also as a stand-alone procedure. Scanning can be performed either manually or through the use of CAATs.

 RELIABILITY OF THE TYPES OF EVIDENCE

LO6

Table 4–6 presents a hierarchy of the reliability of the types of evidence. Inspection of tangible assets, reperformance and recalculation are generally considered of high reliability because the auditor has direct knowledge about them. Inspection of records or documents, confirmation and analytical procedures, and scanning are generally considered to be of medium reliability. The reliability of inspection of records or documents depends primarily on whether a document is internal or external, and the reliability of confirmation is affected by the four factors listed previously. The reliability of analytical procedures may be affected by the availability and reliability of the data. Finally, observation and inquiry are generally low-reliability types of evidence because both require further corroboration by the auditor.

Table 4–6 General Guidelines for the Reliability Hierarchy by Evidence Type	
*General Reliability Relationship**	*Types of Evidence*
Higher	Inspection of tangible assets, reperformance, recalculation
↕	Inspection of records or documents, confirmation, analytical procedures, scanning
Lower	Observation, inquiry
* This figure illustrates general hierarchical guidelines. The reliability of the evidence will depend on the facts and circumstances. For example, confirmations may be highly reliable in some circumstances.	

The reader should understand, however, that the levels of reliability shown in Table 4–6 are general guidelines. The reliability of the types of evidence may vary considerably across entities, and may be subject to a number of exceptions. For example, in some circumstances, confirmations may be viewed as a highly reliable source of evidence. This may be true when a confirmation is sent to an independent third party who is highly qualified to respond to the auditor's request for information. Inquiries of client personnel or management provide another example.

Practice Insight 4.1

If audit evidence obtained from one source is inconsistent with that obtained from another, or if the auditor has doubts about the reliability of information to be used as audit evidence, the auditor should perform the audit procedures necessary to resolve the matter and should assess the effect, if any, on other aspects of the audit.

AUDIT DOCUMENTATION

❖ Objectives of Audit Documentation

LO7

Audit documentation consists of the record of audit procedures performed, relevant audit evidence obtained, and conclusions the auditor reached (ISA 230, para. 6(a)). Audit documentation also facilitates the planning, performance and supervision of the engagement, and provides the basis for the review and inspection of the quality of the work by providing written documentation of the evidence supporting the auditor's significant conclusions.

You can think of audit documentation as the 'story' of the audit. It should allow the reader to understand easily the issues and risks, the assertions tested, the audit procedures performed to gather evidence, the findings and the conclusion. The basic characteristics of good audit documentation are similar to good documentation in other fields (e.g. medical and legal research).

Audit documentation is also referred to as working papers or the audit file. The audit file contains the records that comprise the audit documentation. While some working papers may be prepared in hard-copy format, audit software is normally used to prepare and store them.

ISA 230 *Audit Documentation* deals with the auditor's responsibility to prepare audit documentation. Other ISAs contain specific documentation requirements that are intended to clarify the application of ISA 230 in the particular circumstances of those other ISAs. This text discusses a number of these specific requirements in the relevant chapters.

ISA 230 stipulates that working papers have two functions: (1) to provide a sufficient and appropriate record of the basis for the auditor's report; and (2) to provide evidence that the audit was planned and performed in accordance with ISAs and applicable legal and regulatory requirements (ISA 230, para. 5). The form, content and extent of audit documentation are a function of the circumstances of the specific engagement such as the size and complexity of the entity, and the audit methodology and tools used in the audit.

Support for the Audit Report

When the engagement is complete, the auditor must decide on the appropriate type of report to issue. The basis for this decision rests in the audit evidence gathered, and the conclusions reached and documented in the working papers. The working papers also document that the scope of the audit was adequate for the report issued. Information on the correspondence of the financial statements with the applicable financial reporting framework is also included in the working papers.

Compliance with ISAs

Audit documentation provides evidence that the audit complies with the ISAs. The planning of the engagement, along with the execution of the audit plan, is contained in the working papers. However, it is neither necessary nor practicable for the auditor to document every matter considered, or professional judgement made, in an audit.

❖ Content of Audit Documentation

LO8

Audit documentation is the principal record of auditing procedures applied, evidence obtained and conclusions reached by the auditor in the engagement. The documentation is also the focal point for reviewing the work of subordinates and quality control reviewers as well as monitoring inspection by external parties for regulatory or other purposes.

The auditor should consider the following factors when determining the form, content and extent of the documentation for a particular audit area or auditing procedure:

- The nature of auditing procedures to be performed.
- The identified risks of material misstatement.
- The extent of judgement involved in performing the work and evaluating the results.
- The significance of the evidence obtained.
- The nature and extent of exceptions identified.
- The need to document a conclusion or the basis for a conclusion not readily determinable from the documentation of the work performed or evidence obtained.

Auditing standards use the ability of *'an experienced auditor'* to understand the aduit performed, as a point of reference for the level of documentation. In this context an experienced auditor means an individual with practical audit experience who has a reasonable understanding of audit processes, ISAs and applicable legal and regulatory requirements, the business environment in which the entity operates, and auditing and financial reporting issues relevant to the entity's industry. Audit documentation should enable an experienced auditor, having no previous connection with the audit, to understand:

- The nature, timing, extent of the audit procedures performed to comply with ISAs and applicable legal and regulatory requirements.
- The results of the audit procedures performed and the audit evidence obtained.
- S*ignificant matters* arising during the audit, the conclusions reached thereon, and significant professional judgements made in reaching those conclusions (ISA 230, para. 8).

When documenting the auditing procedures performed and evidence obtained, the auditor should *identify* the items tested. In addition the auditor should record who performed the audit work and the date such work was completed, as well as the person who reviewed the work and the date of such review. Table 4–7 presents the documentation requirements for items tested by the auditor.

Table 4–7 Documentation Requirements for Items Tested
The identification of the items tested may be satisfied by indicating the source from which the items were selected and the specific selection criteria: • If an audit sample is selected from a population of documents, the documentation should include identifying characteristics (e.g. the specific payroll payment numbers of the items included in the sample).   • If all items over a specific monetary amount are selected from a population of documents, the documentation need describe only the scope and the identification of the population (e.g. all vouchers over €10,000 from the July voucher register).   • If a systematic sample is selected from a population of documents, the documentation need only provide an identification of the source of the documents and an indication of the starting point and the sampling interval (e.g. a systematic sample of sales invoices was selected from the sales journal for the period from 1 January to 1 October, starting with invoice number 375 and selecting every fiftieth invoice).

Judging the *significance of a matter* requires an objective analysis of the facts and circumstances. Examples of significant matters are shown in Table 4–8.

Table 4–8 Examples of Significant Matters that Require Documentation
• Matters that give rise to significant risks.   • Results of audit procedures indicating (1) that the financial information or disclosures could be materially misstated; or (2) a need to revise the auditor's previous assessment of the risks of material misstatement and the auditor's responses to those risks.   • Circumstances that cause the auditor significant difficulty in applying necessary audit procedures.   • Findings that could result in a modification of the auditor's opinion or the inclusion of an emphasis of matter paragraph in the auditor's report.

An important factor in determining the form, content and extent of audit documentation of significant matters is the extent of *professional judgement* exercised in performing the work and evaluating the results. For example, it would be appropriate to document the basis for the auditor's conclusion on the reasonableness of significant accounting estimates.

The auditor should document *discussions of significant matters* with management, those charged with governance, and others, including the nature of the significant matters discussed and when and with whom the discussions took place (ISA 230, para. 10).

Most audit firms maintain audit documentation in two types of files: permanent and current. Permanent files contain historical data about the client that are of continuing relevance to the audit. Current files, on the other hand, include information and data related specifically to the current year's engagement. Table 4–9 shows examples of the types of information included in each type of file.

Table 4–9   Examples of Information Included in Permanent and Current Files

Permanent File

- Copies of, or excerpts from, the corporate charter.
- Chart of accounts.
- Organizational chart.
- Accounting manual.
- Copies of important contracts (pension contracts, union contracts, leases, etc.).
- Documentation of internal control (e.g. flowcharts).
- Terms of stock and bond issues.
- Prior years' analytical procedure results.

Current File

- Copy of financial statements and auditor's report.
- Overall audit strategy and audit plan.
- Copies of, or excerpts from, minutes of important board and committee meetings.
- Working trial balance.
- Adjusting and reclassification of journal entries.
- Working papers supporting financial statement accounts.

❖ Examples of Audit Documentation

LO8

Audit documentation comes in a variety of types. The more common audit documentation includes the overall audit strategy and audit plan, working trial balance, account analysis and listings, audit memoranda, and adjusting and reclassification entries.

Overall Audit Strategy and Audit Plan

The overall audit strategy contains the strategy to be followed by the auditor in conducting the audit. This document outlines the auditor's understanding of the client and the potential audit risks. It contains the basic framework for how the audit resources (budgeted audit hours) are to be allocated to various parts of the engagement. The audit plan contains the audit procedures that will be conducted by the auditor. Generally, each business process and account balance has a separate audit plan.

Working Trial Balance

The working trial balance links the amounts in the financial statements to the audit working papers. Exhibit 4–1 illustrates a partial working trial balance for EarthWear Clothiers. In addition to a column for account name, the trial balance contains columns for working paper references, the prior year's balances, the unadjusted current-year balances, and columns for adjusting and reclassification entries. The last column would agree to the amounts contained in the financial statements after combining common account balances. A lead schedule is then used to show the detailed general ledger accounts that make up a financial statement category (cash, accounts receivable, and so on). For example, the trial balance would contain only one line for 'cash and cash equivalents' and the 'C lead' schedule would list all general ledger cash accounts. This approach is described in more detail later in the chapter.

Exhibit 4–1   An Example of a Partial Working Trial Balance

EARTHWEAR CLOTHIERS
Partial Working Trial Balance
31 December 2009

Account Description	W/P Ref.	Balance 31/12/08	Balance 31/12/09	Adjustments DR	Adjustments CR	Adjusted T/B	Reclassification DR	Reclassification CR	Financial Statements
Cash and cash equivalents	C lead	€49,668	€48,978						
Receivables	E lead	11,539	12,875						
Inventory	F lead	105,425	122,337						
Prepaid advertising	G lead	10,772	11,458						

Account Analysis and Listings

Account analysis working papers generally include the *activity* in a particular account for the period. For example, Exhibit 4–2 shows the analysis of legal and audit expense for EarthWear Clothiers for the year ended 31 December 2009. Listings represent a schedule of items remaining in the ending balance of an account and are often called *trial balances*. For example, the auditor may obtain a listing of all amounts owed to vendors that make up the accounts payable balance as of the end of the year. This listing would represent a trial balance of unpaid vendors' invoices.

Exhibit 4–2	Example of an Account Analysis Working Paper			

T20
GMP
4/2/10

EARTHWEAR CLOTHIERS
Analysis of Legal and Audit Expense
31/12/09

Date	Payee	Amount	Explanation
1 Feb.	Katz & Fritz	€28,500.00V	For services related to a patent infringement suit by Gough Mfg. Co. Lawsuit was dismissed.
10 April	Willis & Adams International	950,000.00V	Annual audit fee.
1 Oct.	Katz & Fritz	26,200.00V	Legal fee for patent infringement suit against Weshant.
20 Oct.	Smoothe, Sylk, Fiels, Goode & Associates	2,100.00V	Legal services for a purchase contract with McDonald Merchandise.
Total		1,006,800.00	
		F T/B	

Tick Mark Legend
V = Examined payees' bills for amount and description.
F = Footed.
T/B = Agreed to trial balance.
Conclusion: Based on the audit work performed, EarthWear's legal and audit expense account is not materially misstated.

Audit Memoranda

Much of the auditor's work is documented in written memoranda. These include discussions of items such as internal controls, inventory observation, errors identified and problems encountered during the audit.

Adjusting and Reclassification Entries

The audit documentation should also include the adjusting and reclassification entries identified by the auditor or client. Adjusting entries are made to correct misstatements in the client's records. For example, if the auditor discovered that certain inventory items were improperly valued, an adjusting entry would be proposed to correct the amount of misstatement. Adjusting entries are posted in both the client's records and the working trial balance.

Reclassification entries are made to properly present information on the financial statements. A reclassification entry affects income statement accounts or balance sheet accounts, but not both. For example, a reclassification entry might be necessary to present as a current liability the current portion of long-term debt.

❖ Format of Audit Documentation

LO8

Audit documentation may be prepared in both hard copy and electronically. Most auditors now use personal computers and have electronic documentation programs. Whether the documentation is prepared manually or electronically, the manner in which it is formatted usually contains three general characteristics.

Heading

All audit documentation should have a proper heading. The heading should include the name of the client, the title of the working paper and the client's year-end date. Exhibit 4–2 shows a working paper with a proper heading.

Indexing and Cross-Referencing

The audit documents must be organized so that members of the engagement team or firm can find relevant audit evidence. Some firms use a lettering system; other firms use some type of numbering system. For example, the general working papers may be labelled 'A', internal control systems working papers 'B', cash working papers 'C', and so on. When the auditor performs audit work on one working paper and supporting information is obtained from another working paper, the auditor cross-references (it can be 'linked' in audit software) the information on each working paper. This process of indexing and cross-referencing provides a trail from the financial statements to the individual audit documents that a reviewer can easily follow. Indexing and cross-referencing are discussed further in the next section.

Tick Marks

Auditors use *tick marks* to document work performed. Tick marks are simply notations that are made by the auditor near, or next to, an item or amount on an audit document. The tick mark symbol is typically explained or defined at the bottom of the audit document, although many firms use a standard set of tick marks. Exhibit 4–2 shows some examples of tick marks. In this example of documentation, the tick mark 'V' indicates that the auditor examined the bills sent to the client by the payee for proper amount and description.

Many audit firms document their conclusions about an individual account or other elements of the financial statements. Exhibit 4–2 shows an example of how an auditor might document a conclusion about an individual account.

Organization of Audit Documentation

LO8

The audit documentation needs to be organized so that any member of the engagement team (and others) can find the audit evidence that supports each financial statement account. While auditing standards do not dictate how this should be accomplished, the following discussion presents a general approach that is commonly used.

The financial statements contain the accounts and amounts covered by the auditor's report. These accounts come from the working trial balance, which summarizes the general ledger accounts contained on each lead schedule. Each lead schedule includes the general ledger accounts that make up the financial statement account. Different types of audit documentation (account analysis, listings, confirmations, and so on) are then used to support each of the general ledger accounts. Each of these audit documents is indexed, and all important amounts are cross-referenced between audit documents.

Figure 4–3 presents an example of how audit documents could be organized to support the cash account. Note that the €15,000 shown on the balance sheet agrees to the working trial balance. The 'A lead' schedule in turn contains the three general ledger accounts that are included in the €15,000 balance. Audit documents then support each of the general ledger accounts. For example, the audit documents indexed 'A2' provide the audit evidence supporting the general cash balance of €12,000. Also note that each important amount is cross-referenced. For example, the balance per bank of €14,000 on 'A2' is referenced to 'A2.1' and the cash balance on 'A2.1' is referenced back to 'A2'.

Ownership of Audit Documentation

LO8

Audit documentation is the property of the auditor. This includes not only audit documents prepared by the auditor but also audit documents prepared by the client at the request of the auditor. Although the auditor owns the audit documents, they cannot be shown, except under certain circumstances, to anyone without the client's consent. Chapter 19 discusses the auditor's ethical considerations concerning the confidentiality of client information.

The auditor should assemble the final audit file on a timely basis and retain the audit files for a number of years after the date of the audit report.

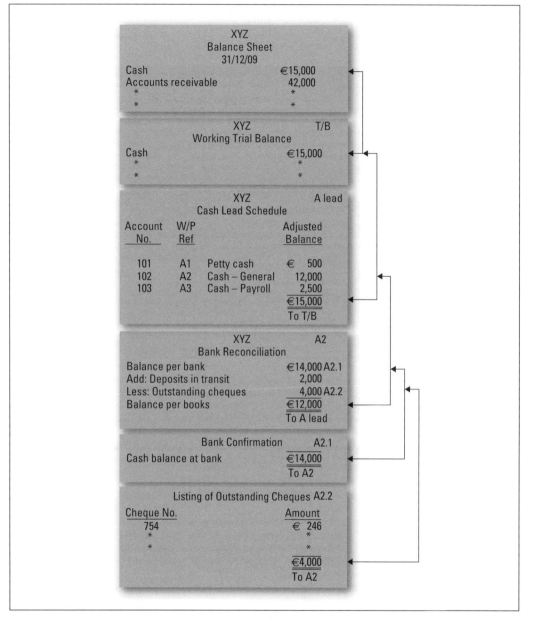

Figure 4–3 An Example of the Organization of Audit Documents

Audit Document Archiving and Retention

The International Standard on Quality Control (ISQC) 1 requires firms to establish policies and procedures for the timely completion of the assembly of audit files, ordinarily not more than 60 days after the date of the auditor's report (ISQC 1, paras 52 and A50). Changes should not be made to the audit documentation during this final assembly process unless they are administrative in nature. Examples of such administrative routines are cross-referencing working papers and deleting or discarding superseded documentation. After the assembly of the final audit file has been completed, the auditor should not delete or discard audit documentation of any nature before the end of its retention period.

The destruction of documents and the indictment of Arthur Andersen in the Enron audit set the spotlight on the practice of archiving and retaining audit documentation. Exhibit 4–3 describes Arthur Andersen's federal indictment and conviction on obstruction of justice charges for deletions and alterations of audit documentation related to the Enron audit. The indictment and conviction ultimately led to the failure of Arthur Andersen.

Exhibit 4–3   The Wholesale Destruction of Documents and the Indictment of Arthur Andersen

On 14 March 2002, a federal grand jury indicted Arthur Andersen, initiating the first criminal charge in the Enron bankruptcy. The one-count indictment, alleging obstruction of justice, read that for a one-month span in October and early November 2001, 'Andersen … did knowingly, intentionally, and corruptly persuade' employees to 'alter, destroy, mutilate, and conceal'. The indictment charged that Arthur Andersen employees 'were instructed by Andersen partners and others to destroy immediately documentation relating to Enron and told to work overtime if necessary to accomplish the destruction'. The indictment also called the destruction an 'unparalleled initiative to shred physical documentation and delete computer files. Tons of paper relating to the Enron audit was promptly shredded as part of the orchestrated document destruction. The shredder at the Andersen office at the Enron building was used virtually constantly and, to handle the overload, dozens of large trunks filled with Enron documents were sent to Andersen's main Houston office to be shredded.'

In November 2001, the SEC served Andersen with the anticipated subpoena relating to its work for Enron. In response, members of the Andersen team on the Enron audit were alerted finally that there could be 'no more shredding' because the firm had been 'officially served' for documents. During the trial, the only major issue of dispute between the government and defence was whether anyone at Arthur Andersen acted with intent to impede the regulatory proceeding prior to being 'officially served'. The fate of Arthur Andersen hung on this single issue. Arthur Andersen's specialists on securities regulation maintained that the firm never considered the possibility of a federal inquiry in fall 2001 at a time others in the firm were destroying documents related to Enron.

In June 2002, the federal jury convicted Arthur Andersen of obstruction of justice after ten days of deliberation. Ironically, in interviews, jurors said that they reached their decision because an Arthur Andersen lawyer had ordered critical deletions to an internal memorandum, rather than because of the firm's wholesale destruction of Enron-related documents (*New York Times*, 15 June 2002).

On 31 May 2005, the Supreme Court overturned Arthur Andersen's conviction. The court ruled unanimously that the Houston jury that found Arthur Andersen LLP guilty of obstruction of justice was given overly broad instructions by the federal judge who presided at the trial. However, this ruling came too late to save Arthur Andersen.

Quality control standards require the firm to establish policies and procedures for the retention of engagement documentation for a period sufficient to meet the needs of the firm or as required by law or regulation (ISQC 1, para. 54). The needs of the firm for retention of engagement documentation, and the period of such retention, will vary with the nature of the engagement and the firm's circumstances, but would ordinarily be no shorter than five years from the date of the auditor's report.

🔓 Key Terms

Accounting records. The records of initial entries and supporting records, such as cheques and records of electronic fund transfers; invoices; contracts; the general and subsidiary ledgers, journal entries and other adjustments to the financial statements that are not reflected in formal journal entries; and records such as work sheets and spreadsheets supporting cost allocations, computations, reconciliations and disclosures.

Analytical procedures. Evaluations of financial information through analysis of plausible relationships among both financial and non-financial data.

Assertions. Representations by management, explicit or otherwise, that are embodied in the financial statements, as used by the auditor to consider the different types of potential misstatements that may occur.

Audit documentation (**working papers**). The auditor's principal record of audit procedures performed, relevant audit evidence obtained, and conclusions the auditor reached. It also facilitates the planning, performance and supervision of the engagement, and provides the basis for the review and inspection of the quality of the work by providing written documentation of the evidence supporting the auditor's significant conclusions.

Audit evidence. All the information used by the auditor in arriving at the conclusions on which the audit opinion is based, and includes the information contained in the accounting records underlying the financial statements and other information such as minutes of meetings;

confirmations from third parties; industry analysts' reports; controls manuals; information obtained by the auditor through audit procedures such as inquiry, observation, and inspection.

Audit procedures. Specific acts performed by the auditor in gathering evidence to determine if specific assertions are being met.

Computer-assisted audit techniques (CAATs). Applications of auditing procedures using the computer as an audit tool.

Confirmation. Audit evidence obtained as a direct written response to the auditor from a third party (the confirming party), in paper form, or by electronic or other medium.

Inquiry. Seeking information of knowledgeable persons, both financial and non-financial, throughout the entity or outside the entity.

Inspection of records or documents. Examination of internal or external records or documents that are in paper form, electronic form or other media.

Inspection of tangible assets. Physical examination of the tangible assets.

Observation. Watching a process or procedure being performed by others.

Recalculation. Determination of the mathematical accuracy of documents or records.

Relevance of audit evidence. The relevance of audit evidence refers to its relationship to the assertion or to the objective of the control being tested.

Reliability of evidence. The diagnosticity of evidence; that is, whether the type of evidence can be relied on to signal the true state of the assertion.

Reperformance. The auditor's independent execution of procedures or controls that were originally performed as part of the entity's internal control, either manually or through the use of computer-assisted audit techniques.

Scanning. Reviewing accounting data to identify significant or unusual items; including the identification of anomalous individual items within account balances or other client data through the scanning or analysis of entries in transaction listings, subsidiary ledgers, general ledger control accounts, adjusting entries, suspense accounts, reconciliations and other detailed reports.

? Review Questions

LO1	4–1	Explain why the auditor divides the financial statements into elements or segments in order to test management's assertions.
LO1	4–2	How do management assertions relate to the financial statements?
LO2	4–3	List and define the assertions about classes of transactions and events for the period under audit.
LO2	4–4	List and define the assertions about account balances at the period end.
LO4	4–5	Define audit evidence. Provide an example of evidence from accounting records and other information.
LO4	4–6	Explain why in most instances audit evidence is persuasive rather than convincing.
LO5	4–7	List and define the audit procedures for obtaining audit evidence.
LO5,6	4–8	In a situation that uses inspection of records and documents as a type of evidence, distinguish between vouching and tracing in terms of the direction of testing and the assertions being tested.
LO5,6	4–9	Why is it necessary to obtain corroborating evidence for inquiry and for observation?
LO6	4–10	Discuss the relative reliability of evidence from the different types of audit procedures.
LO8	4–11	Why are indexing and cross-referencing important to the documentation of audit working papers?

✐ Problems

| LO2 | 4–12 | Management makes assertions about elements of the financial statements. Match the management assertions shown in the following left-hand column with the proper description of the assertion shown in the right-hand column. |

Management Assertion	Description
a Existence	**1** The accounts and transactions that should be included are included; thus, the financial statements are complete.
b Rights and obligations	**2** Assets, liabilities, equity interests, revenues and expenses are appropriately valued and are allocated to the proper accounting period.
c Completeness	**3** The assets are the rights of the entity, and the liabilities are its obligations.
d Valuation and allocation	**4** The assets and liabilities exist, and the recorded transactions have occurred.

LO2   **4–13**   Management assertions about classes of transactions are:

     a   Occurrence.
     b   Completeness.
     c   Authorization.
     d   Accuracy.
     e   Cut-off.
     f   Classification.

Required:

For each management assertion, indicate an example of a misstatement that could occur for revenue transactions.

LO5   **4–14**   For each of the following specific audit procedures, indicate the type of audit procedure it represents: (1) inspection of records or documents; (2) inspection of tangible assets; (3) observation; (4) inquiry; (5) confirmation; (6) recalculation; (7) reperformance; (8) analytical procedures; and (9) scanning.

     a   Sending a written request to the client's customers requesting that they report the amount owed to the client.
     b   Examining large sales invoices for a period of two days before and after year end to determine if sales are recorded in the proper period.
     c   Agreeing the total of the accounts receivable subsidiary ledger to the accounts receivable general ledger account.
     d   Discussing the adequacy of the allowance for doubtful accounts with the credit manager.
     e   Comparing the current-year gross profit percentage with the gross profit percentage for the last four years.
     f   Examining a new plastic extrusion machine to ensure that this major acquisition was received.
     g   Watching the client's warehouse personnel count the raw materials inventory.
     h   Performing test counts of the warehouse personnel's count of the raw material.
     i   Obtaining a letter from the client's lawyer indicating that there were no lawsuits in progress against the client.
     j   Tracing the prices used by the client's billing programme for pricing sales invoices to the client's approved price list.
     k   Reviewing the general ledger for unusual adjusting entries.

LO2,5   **4–15**   For each of the audit procedures listed in Problem 4–14, identify the category (assertions about classes of transactions and events or assertions about account balances) and the primary assertion being tested.

LO1,4,5,7   **4–16**   **a**   ISA 300 requires that the auditor plan the audit so that the engagement will be performed in an effective manner. An effective tool that aids the auditor in adequately planning is *an audit plan*.

Required:

Describe an audit plan and the purposes it serves.

b Procedures relate to acts that the auditor performs while trying to gather evidence. Procedures specifically refer to the methods or techniques the auditor uses in conducting the examination.

Required:

List at least eight different types of procedures an auditor would use in examining financial statements. For example, a type of procedure an auditor would use frequently is the observation of activities and conditions. Do not discuss specific accounts.

(AICPA, adapted)

LO5,6 **4–17** Evidence comes in various types and has different degrees of reliability. Following are some statements that compare various types of evidence.

a A bank confirmation versus observation of the segregation of duties between cash receipts and recording payment in the accounts receivable subsidiary ledger.

b An auditor's recalculation of depreciation versus examination of raw material requisitions.

c A bank statement included in the client's records versus shipping documents.

d Physical inspection of common stock certificates held for investment versus physical examination of inventory components for a personal computer.

Required:

For each situation, indicate whether the first or second type of evidence is more reliable. Provide a rationale for your choice.

LO5,6 **4–18** Inspection of records and documents relates to the auditor's examination of client accounting records and other information. One issue that affects the reliability of documentary evidence is whether the documents are *internal* or *external*. Following are examples of documentary evidence:

1 Duplicate copies of sales invoices.
2 Purchase orders.
3 Bank statements.
4 Remittance advices.
5 Vendors' invoices.
6 Materials requisition forms.
7 Overhead cost allocation sheets.
8 Shipping documents.
9 Payroll cheques.
10 Long-term debt agreements.

Required:

a *Classify each document as internal or external evidence.*
b *Classify each document as to its reliability (high, moderate or low).*

LO5,6 **4–19** The confirmation process is the process of obtaining and evaluating a direct written communication from a third party in response to a request for information about a particular item affecting financial statement assertions.

Required:

a *List the factors that affect the reliability of confirmations.*
b *In the Parmalat fraud (see Exhibit 2–2) the confirmation of a €3.95 billion account in Bank of America was forgery. Auditing standards state that 'an audit rarely involves the authentication of documentation, nor is the auditor*

trained as or expected to be an expert in such authentication'. What steps could Parmalat's auditors have taken to ensure that bank confirmations were reliable?

c *Refer back to EarthWear Clothiers' financial statements included after Chapter 1. Identify any information on EarthWear's financial statements that might be verified through the use of confirmations.*

LO7,8   **4–20**   Audit documentation is the auditor's record of work performed and conclusions reached on an audit engagement.

Required:

a *What are the purposes of audit documentation?*
b *List and describe the various types of audit documents.*
c *What factors affect the auditor's judgement about the nature and extent of audit documentation for a particular engagement?*

Discussion Cases

LO4,5,6   **4–21**   **Part I.** Lernout & Hauspie (L & H) was the world's leading provider of speech and language technology products, solutions and services to businesses and individuals worldwide. Both Microsoft and Intel invested millions in L & H. However, accounting scandals and fraud allegations sent the company's stock crashing, and forced the firm to seek bankruptcy protection in Belgium and the USA. The following selected information pertains to L & H's sales and accounts receivable:

- Consolidated revenue increased 184 per cent from the 1997 fiscal year to the 1998 fiscal year.
- Revenue in South Korea, which has a reputation as a difficult market for foreign companies to enter, increased from $97,000 in the first quarter of 1999 to approximately $59 million in the first quarter of 2000.
- In the second quarter of 2000, sales grew by 104 per cent but accounts receivable grew by 128 per cent.
- Average days outstanding increased from 138 days in 1998 to 160 days for the six-month period ended 30 June 2000.

Required:

a *Based on the above information, which assertion(s) for sales should the auditor be most concerned with? Why?*
b *Based on the above information, which assertion(s) for accounts receivable should the auditor be most concerned with? Why?*
c *What audit evidence should the auditor gather to verify the assertion(s) for sales and accounts receivable? Be specific as to how each type of evidence relates to the assertions you mentioned in parts a and b of this question.*

Part II. L & H's auditor did not confirm accounts receivable from customers in South Korea. However, *Wall Street Journal* contacted 18 of L & H's South Korean customers and learned the following:

- Three out of 18 customers listed by L & H stated that they were not L & H customers.
- Three others indicated that their purchases from L & H were smaller than those reported by L & H.

Required:

a *If L & H's auditor had confirmed these receivables and received such responses, what additional evidence could they have gathered to try to obtain an accurate figure for sales to and accounts receivable from customers in South Korea?*

b *If you were L & H's auditor and you had received such responses from South Korean customers, how likely would you be to use inquiry of the client as an audit procedure? Why?*

Sources: M. Maremont, J. Eisinger and J. Carreyrou, 'How High-Tech Dream at Lernout & Hauspie Crumbled in a Scandal', *Wall Street Journal* (7 December 2000), pp. A1, A18; J. Carreyrou and M. Maremont, 'Lernout Unit Engaged in Massive Fraud to Fool Auditors, New Inquiry Concludes', *Wall Street Journal* (6 April 2001), p. A3; and J. Carreyrou, 'Lernout Unit Booked Fictitious Sales, Says Probe', *Wall Street Journal* (9 April 2001), p. B2.

LO4,5,6 **4–22** Bentley Bros. Book Company publishes more than 250 fiction and non-fiction titles. The company sells most of its books to major retail stores.

Your firm was just selected as the new auditors for Bentley Bros., and you have been appointed as the audit manager for the engagement based on your prior industry experience. The prior auditors were removed because the client felt that it was not receiving adequate service. The prior auditors have indicated to you that the change in auditors did not result from any disagreements over accounting or auditing issues.

Your preliminary review of the company's financial statements indicates that the account for allowance for return of unsold books has high estimation uncertainty giving rise to a significant risk. Consistent with industry practice, retailers are allowed to return unsold books for full credit. You know from your prior experience with other book publishers that the return rate for individual book titles can range from 30 to 50 per cent. The client develops its allowance for return of unsold books based on internally generated records; that is, it maintains detailed records of all book returns by title.

Required:

a *Discuss how you would assess the reliability of the client's records for developing the allowance for return of unsold books.*
b *Discuss how you would determine the return rate for relatively new titles.*
c *Consider whether any external evidence can be obtained that would provide additional evidence on the reasonableness of the account.*

Internet Assignment

LO4,5,6 **4–23** Use one of the Internet browsers to search for the following terms:

- Electronic data interchange.
- Image-processing systems.

Prepare a memo describing EDI and image-processing systems. Discuss the implications of each for the auditor's consideration of audit evidence.

PART III
Planning the Audit and Internal Control

PART CONTENTS

5 Audit Planning and Types of Audit Tests
6 Internal Control in a Financial Statement Audit
7 Auditing Internal Control over Financial Reporting

CHAPTER 5

Audit Planning and Types of Audit Tests

❖ LEARNING OBJECTIVES

Upon completion of this chapter you will

- ❖ **LO1** Understand the auditor's requirements for client acceptance and continuance.
- ❖ **LO2** Know what is required to establish an understanding with the client.
- ❖ **LO3** Know the types of information that are included in an engagement letter.
- ❖ **LO4** Understand how the work of the internal auditors may modify the audit procedures to be performed.
- ❖ **LO5** Know how the external auditors relate to those charged with governance.
- ❖ **LO6** Understand the steps that are involved in the preliminary engagement activities.

- ❖ **LO7** Know the steps that are performed in planning an audit engagement.
- ❖ **LO8** Know the types of audit tests.
- ❖ **LO9** Learn the purposes and types of analytical procedures.
- ❖ **LO10** Understand the audit testing hierarchy.
- ❖ **LO11** Be familiar with financial ratios that are useful as analytical procedures.
- ❖ **LO12** Understand special considerations in the audit of group financial statements.

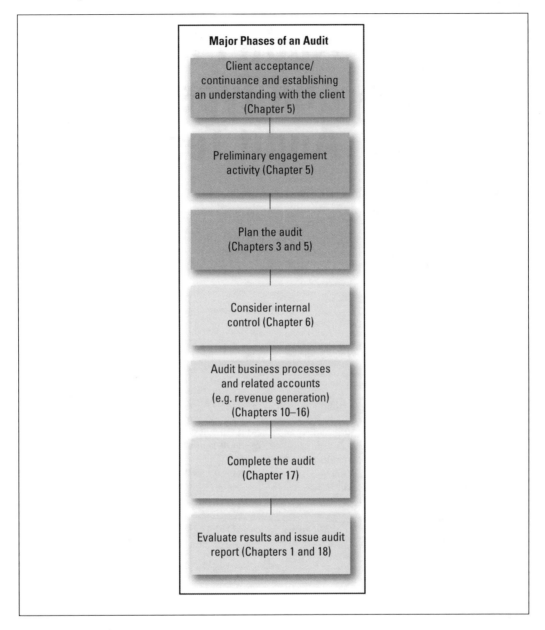

Major Phases of an Audit

Client acceptance/
continuance and establishing
an understanding with the client
(Chapter 5)

Preliminary engagement
activity (Chapter 5)

Plan the audit
(Chapters 3 and 5)

Consider internal
control (Chapter 6)

Audit business processes
and related accounts
(e.g. revenue generation)
(Chapters 10–16)

Complete the audit
(Chapter 17)

Evaluate results and issue audit
report (Chapters 1 and 18)

❖ RELEVANT ACCOUNTING AND AUDITING PRONOUNCEMENTS

IASB, IAS 24, Related Party Disclosures

IFAC, Code of Ethics for Professional Accountants

ISQC 1, Quality Control for Firms That Perform Audits and Reviews of Financial Statements, and Other Assurance and Related Services Engagements

ISA 200, Overall Objectives of the Independent Auditor and the Conduct of an Audit in Accordance with International Standards on Auditing

ISA 210, Agreeing the Terms of Audit Engagements

ISA 220, Quality Control for an Audit of Financial Statements

ISA 230, Audit Documentation

ISA 240, The Auditor's Responsibilities Relating to Fraud in an Audit of Financial Statements

ISA 250, Consideration of Laws and Regulations in an Audit of Financial Statements

ISA 260, Communication with Those Charged with Governance

ISA 265, Communicating Deficiencies in Internal Control to Those Charged with Governance and Management

ISA 300, Planning an Audit of Financial Statements

ISA 315, Identifying and Assessing the Risks of Material Misstatement through Understanding the Entity and Its Environment

ISA 320, Materiality in Planning and Performing an Audit

ISA 330, The Auditor's Responses to Assessed Risks

ISA 450, Evaluation of Misstatements Identified during the Audit

ISA 500, Audit Evidence

ISA 510, Initial Audit Engagements-Opening Balances

ISA 520, Analytical Procedures

ISA 530, Audit Sampling

ISA 540, Auditing Accounting Estimates, Including Fair Value Accounting Estimates, and Related Disclosures

ISA 550, Related Parties

ISA 600, Special Considerations-Audits of Group Financial Statements (Including the Work of Component Auditors)

ISA 610, Using the Work of Internal Auditors

ISA 620, Using the Work of an Auditor's Expert

AUDITING STANDARDS require that the audit be properly planned. Planning an audit includes establishing the overall audit strategy for the engagement and developing an audit plan, which includes risk assessment procedures and planned audit responses to the risks of material misstatement. If the audit is not properly planned, the auditor may issue an incorrect audit report or conduct an inefficient audit. The audit starts with the initial appointment or reappointment of the auditor by the client or audit committee. Next, the auditor performs a number of activities that go into developing an overall audit strategy.

This chapter covers the following phases of the audit identified in Chapter 1 (Fig. 1–3):

● Client acceptance and continuance, and establishing an understanding with the client.
● Preliminary engagement activities.
● Planning the audit.

It then reviews the major types of audit **tests** and covers analytical procedures. Analytical procedures are required to be performed as part of the planning of the audit and as part of wrapping up the audit. They are also often useful for providing substantive audit evidence during the conduct of the audit of business processes and related accounts. *Advanced Module 1* presents ratios that are useful for analytical procedures. *Advanced Module 2* discusses special considerations in the audit of group financial statements.

CLIENT ACCEPTANCE AND CONTINUANCE

LO1

The first phase of the audit process that relates to audit planning is client acceptance and continuance (see Fig. 5–1). The extent of effort that goes into evaluating a new client is normally much greater than the decision to continue an existing client. With a continuing client the auditor possesses extensive knowledge about the entity and its environment.

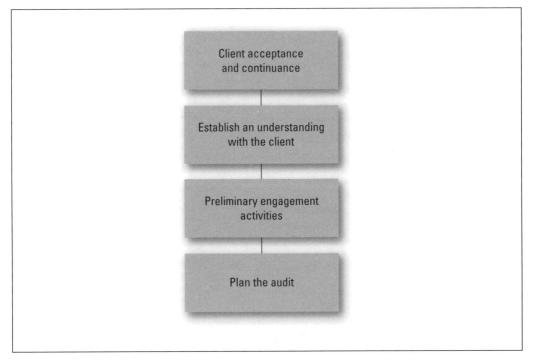

Figure 5–1   The Phases of an Audit That Relate to Audit Planning

Prospective Client Acceptance

Audit firms should investigate a prospective client prior to accepting an engagement. Table 5–1 lists procedures that a firm might conduct to evaluate a prospective client. Performance of such procedures would normally be documented in a memo or by completion of a client acceptance questionnaire or checklist.

Table 5–1 Procedures for Evaluating a Prospective Client
1   Obtain and review available financial information (annual reports, interim financial statements, income tax returns, etc.).
2   Inquire of third parties about any information concerning the integrity of the prospective client and its management. (Such inquiries should be directed to the prospective client's bankers and lawyers, credit agencies and other members of the business community who may have such knowledge.)
3   Unless prohibited by law or regulation, communicate with the predecessor auditor about whether there were any disagreements about accounting policies, audit procedures or similar significant matters.
4   Consider whether the prospective client has any circumstances that will require special attention or that may represent unusual business or audit risks, such as litigation or going-concern problems.
5   Determine if the firm is independent of the client and able to provide the desired service.
6   Determine if the firm has the necessary technical skills and knowledge of the industry to complete the engagement.
7   Determine if acceptance of the client would violate any applicable regulatory or ethical requirements such as those in the IFAC Code of Ethics for Professional Accountants.

When the prospective client has previously been audited, auditing standards (ISA 300) require that the successor (incoming) auditor communicates with the predecessor (previous) auditor, in compliance with relevant legal and ethical responsibilities and requirements. The confidentiality principle in the IFAC Code of Ethics for Professional Accountants (IFAC Code of Ethics) requires that the professional accountant refrains from disclosing any confidential client information *without* the specific consent of the client, unless there is a legal or professional duty to disclose (Chapter 19 provides further details). The legal and regulatory responsibilities and requirements for communication between the successor and predecessor auditor differ among jurisdictions. For example, the successor auditor may have a legal duty to inquire the predecessor auditor on certain matters about the appointment and the predecessor auditor may have a legal duty to respond. The communication may include information about questions related to the integrity of **management**; disagreements with management over accounting and auditing issues; communications with those charged with **governance** regarding fraud, non-compliance with laws and regulations or internal control deficiencies; and the predecessor's understanding of the reason for the change in auditors. Such information may help the successor auditor determine whether to accept the appointment. In other cases there may be legal or regulatory constraints on the communication between the successor and predecessor auditor. Subject to any such constraint and given the consent of the client, the predecessor auditor ordinarily advises the successor auditor whether there are any professional reasons not to accept the appointment.

In the unusual case where the prospective client refuses to permit the predecessor auditor to respond, the successor auditor should have reservations about accepting the client. Such a situation should raise serious questions about management's motivations and integrity. In addition, if the client has unusual business risks such as possible going-concern issues, the auditor is not likely to accept the prospective client because the auditor's own business risk may be too high.

After accepting the engagement, the successor auditor may need information on opening balances in order to issue an unmodified opinion. The successor auditor should ordinarily request that the client authorize the predecessor auditor to permit a review of his or her working papers. In most instances, the predecessor auditor will allow the successor auditor to make copies of any working papers of continuing interest (for example, details of selected balance sheet accounts).

If the client has not previously been audited, the audit firm might complete all the procedures listed in Table 5–1, except for the communication with the predecessor auditor. The auditor should review the prospective client's financial information and carefully assess the integrity of management as well as the principal owners and those charged with governance in the entity, for example by communicating with the entity's bankers and lawyers, as well as other members of the business community. Larger audit firms may have full-time staff that complete background checks and monitor news of major clients.

Continuing Client Retention

Audit firms need to evaluate periodically whether to retain their current clients. This evaluation may take place at or near the completion of an audit or when some significant event occurs. Conflicts over accounting and auditing issues or disputes over fees may lead an audit firm to disassociate itself from a client.

❖ ESTABLISHING AN UNDERSTANDING WITH THE CLIENT

LO2

The auditor should establish an understanding with the client about the terms of the engagement. This understanding reduces the risk that either party may misinterpret what is expected or required of the other party. The terms of the engagement, which are documented in the engagement letter, should include the objectives of the engagement, management's responsibilities, the auditor's responsibilities, and the limitations of the engagement. In establishing an understanding with the client, three topics should be discussed: (1) the engagement letter; (2) the internal auditors; and (3) those charged with governance.

❖ The Engagement Letter

LO3

An **engagement letter** formalizes the arrangement reached between the auditor and the client. This letter serves as a contract, outlining the responsibilities of both parties and preventing misunderstandings between the two parties. Auditing standards (ISA 210) require that the agreed terms of the audit engagement are recorded in an audit engagement letter or other suitable form of written agreement. Exhibit 5–1 shows a sample engagement letter for EarthWear.

Exhibit 5–1 A Sample Engagement Letter: EarthWear Clothiers

Willis & Adams International	1 April 2009

Mr Calvin J. Rogers
EarthWear Clothiers
PO Box 787
Europolis

The Objective and Scope of the Audit

You have requested that we audit the financial statements of EarthWear Clothiers, which comprise the balance sheet as of 31 December 2009, and the income statement, statement of changes in equity and cash flow statement for the year then ended, and a summary of significant accounting policies and other explanatory information. We are pleased to confirm our acceptance and our understanding of this audit engagement by means of this letter. Our audit will be conducted with the objective of our expressing an opinion on the financial statements.

Our Responsibilities and Limitations

We will conduct our audit in accordance with International Standards on Auditing (ISAs). Those standards require that we comply with ethical requirements and plan and perform the audit to obtain reasonable assurance about whether the financial statements are free from material misstatement. An audit involves performing procedures to obtain audit evidence about the amounts and disclosures in the financial statements. The procedures selected depend on the auditor's judgement, including the assessment of the risks of material misstatement of the financial statements, whether due to error or fraud. An audit also includes evaluating the appropriateness of accounting policies used and the reasonableness of accounting estimates made by management, as well as evaluating the overall presentation of the financial statements.

Because of the inherent limitations of an audit, together with the inherent limitations of internal control, there is an unavoidable risk that some material misstatements may not be detected, even though the audit is properly planned and performed in accordance with ISAs.

In making our risk assessments, we consider internal control relevant to the entity's preparation of the financial statements in order to design audit procedures that are appropriate in the circumstances, but not for the purpose of expressing an opinion on the effectiveness of the entity's internal control. However, we will communicate to management in writing concerning any significant deficiencies in internal control relevant to the audit of the financial statements that we have identified during the audit.

Management's Responsibilities

Our audit will be conducted on the basis that management acknowledges and understands that it has responsibility:

(a)   For the preparation and fair presentation of the financial statements in accordance with International Financial Reporting Standards;

(b)   For such internal control as management determines is necessary to enable the preparation of financial statements that are free from material misstatement, whether due to error or fraud; and

(c)   To provide us with:

  (i)   Access to all information of which management is aware that is relevant to the preparation of the financial statements such as records, documentation and other matters;

  (ii)   Additional information that we may request from management for the purpose of the audit; and

  (iii) Unrestricted access to persons within the entity from whom we determine it necessary to obtain audit evidence.

As part of our audit process, we will request from management written confirmation concerning representations made to us in connection with the audit.

We look forward to full cooperation from your staff during our audit.

Fees

Our fees are based on the time required by the individuals assigned to the engagement plus out-of-pocket expenses. Individual hourly rates vary according to the degree of responsibility involved and the experience and skill required. We estimate our fees for this audit of the financial statements will be €500,000, exclusive of out-of-pocket expenses. This estimate takes into account the agreed-upon level of preparation and assistance from company personnel; we will advise management should this not be provided or should any other circumstances arise which may cause actual time to exceed that estimate. Invoices rendered are due and payable upon receipt.

Reporting

We form an opinion on the financial statements based on conclusions drawn from the audit evidence obtained. We expect to issue an audit report expressing an unmodified opinion that the financial statements are prepared, in all material respects, in accordance with International Financial Reporting Standards. The form and content of our report may need to be amended in the light of our audit findings.

This engagement letter reflects the entire agreement between us relating to the services covered by this letter. It replaces and supersedes any previous proposals, correspondence, and understandings, whether written or oral. The agreements of EarthWear Clothiers and Willis & Adams International contained in this engagement letter will be effective for future years unless it is terminated, amended or superseded.

If you have any questions, please contact us.

Please sign and return the attached copy of this letter to indicate your acknowledgement of, and agreement with, the arrangements for our audit of the financial statements including our respective responsibilities.

Willis & Adams International

M. J. Willis

M. J. Willis, Partner

Acknowledged and agreed on behalf of EarthWear Clothiers by

Calvin J. Rogers

Calvin J. Rogers, Chief Executive Officer

3 April 2009

In addition to the items mentioned in the sample engagement letter in Exhibit 5–1, the engagement letter may include:

- Arrangements involving the use of experts or internal auditors.
- Explanation of the auditor's responsibilities to communicate audit matters of governance interest with those charged with governance (e.g. the board of directors).
- Any limitation of the liability of the auditor or client.
- Arrangements to be made with the predecessor auditor in the case of an initial audit.
- Additional services to be provided relating to regulatory requirements.
- Arrangements regarding other services (e.g. assurance, tax or consulting services).

An engagement letter communicates clearly the respective responsibilities of the client and the auditor. This is specifically valuable in the audit of small entities where typical owner-managers may not be fully aware of their own responsibilities or those of their auditor. For example, the auditor would in such a case include in the engagement letter details of anticipated matters on which management representations will be obtained.

❖ Internal Auditors

LO4

When the client has **internal auditors**, the external auditor may use the work of the internal auditors to modify the audit precedures to be performed. The auditor first needs to obtain an understanding of the **internal audit function**, including information about the activities that it performs. The auditor next must determine whether any of these activities are likely to be relevant to the audit of the financial statements. A major issue for the external auditor is assessing the *competence* and *objectivity* of the internal auditors and determining the effect if any of their work on the external audit procedures. Table 5–2 presents factors that the auditor should consider when assessing the competence and objectivity of the internal auditors.

Table 5–2 Factors for Assessing the Competence and Objectivity of Internal Auditors

Competence

- Educational level and professional experience.
- Professional certification and continuing education.
- Audit policies, procedures and checklists.
- Practices regarding their assignments.
- The supervision and review of their audit activities.
- The quality of their working paper documentation, reports and recommendations.
- Evaluation of their performance.

Objectivity

- The organizational status of the internal auditor responsible for the internal audit function (e.g. the internal auditor reports to and has direct access to those charge with governance).
- Policies to maintain internal auditors' objectivity about the areas audited (e.g. internal auditors are prohibited from auditing areas to which they have recently been assigned).
- To what extent management acts on the recommendations of the internal audit function, and how such action is evidenced.

In addition to competence and objectivity, the external auditor should also assess the effectiveness of the communication with the internal auditors.

The internal auditors' work may affect the nature, timing and extent of the audit procedures performed by the external auditor. For example, as part of their regular work, internal auditors may review, assess and monitor the entity's controls that are included in the accounting system. If the internal auditors are sufficiently competent and objective, the external auditor may use the internal auditors' work to reduce the scope of audit work. The materiality of the account balance or class of transactions and its related audit risk may also determine how much the external auditor can rely on the internal auditors' work. When the external auditor intends to use specific work of the internal auditors, he or she should evaluate and perform **audit procedures** on that work to confirm its adequacy for the external audit purposes. For example, such procedures may include observation of procedures performed by the internal auditors. When internal auditors provide *direct* assistance to the external auditor in carrying out external audit procedures (not allowed in all jurisdictions), the auditor should supervise, review, evaluate and test the internal auditors' work.

Practice Insight 5.1

From the Internal Audit's Report in Danske (Danish) Bank Annual Report 2008

Basis of opinion. We conducted our audit in accordance with the executive order of the Danish Financial Supervisory Authority on auditing financial enterprises and financial groups and in accordance with Danish auditing standards. These standards require that we plan and perform the audit to obtain reasonable assurance that the annual report is free from material misstatement. The audit comprised all significant areas and risk areas and was conducted in accordance with the division of duties agreed with the external auditors, enabling the external auditors to the widest possible extent to base their audit on the work performed by the internal auditors.

Copenhagen, 5 February 2009.

Source: www.danskebank.com/en-uk/ir/Documents/2008/Q4/Annualreport2008.pdf

---

❖ Those Charged with Governance

LO5

Those charged with governance are person(s) with responsibility for overseeing the strategic direction of the entity and obligations related to the accountability of the entity. This includes overseeing the financial reporting process. The external auditor needs to identify and communicate with those charged with governance.

The primary bodies responsible for governance are the supervisory board in countries with a two-tier board structure and the board of directors in countries with a single board structure. An audit committee may be established to oversee the internal and external auditing work done for the organization. (See Chapter 2 for a discussion of corporate governance.)

At the outset of the audit the auditor establishes a constructive working relationship with those charged with governance in the entity. The auditor will meet or by other means communicate with those charged with governance before the engagement starts, to establish a communication process and discuss matters such as the auditor's responsibilities and significant accounting policies of the entity. The auditor's communication with those charged with governance also includes an overview of the planned scope and timing of the audit and the auditor's compliance with independence requirements.

The auditor is required to make a number of important communications of audit matters to those charged with governance during or at the end of the engagement (ISA 260). Most of the communications are made at the completion of the engagement. Chapter 17 covers them in detail.

❖ PRELIMINARY ENGAGEMENT ACTIVITIES

LO6

There are generally two preliminary engagement activities: (1) determining the audit engagement team requirements; and (2) ensuring that the audit firm and engagement team are in compliance with ethical requirements, including independence.

Determine the Audit Engagement Team Requirements

Audit firms need to ensure that their engagements are completed by auditors having the proper degree of technical training and proficiency given the circumstances of the clients. Factors that should be considered in determining staffing requirements include engagement size and complexity, level of risk, any special expertise, personnel availability and timing of the work to be performed. For example, if the engagement involves a high level of risk, the firm should staff the engagement with more experienced auditors. Similarly, if the audit involves a specialized industry (banking, insurance and so on) or if the client uses sophisticated IT processing or holds financial instruments, the firm must ensure that members of the engagement team possess the requisite expertise. Generally, a time budget for the planned work is prepared in order to assist with the staffing requirements and to schedule the fieldwork.

Assess Compliance with Ethical Requirements, including Independence

Auditing standards require that the auditor complies with relevant ethical requirements, including those pertaining to independence (ISA 200). The ethical requirements ordinarily comprise the IFAC Code of Ethics for Professional Accountants together with any national requirements that are more restrictive. Part B, section 290 of the IFAC Code of Ethics provides independence provisions related to audit and review engagements (see Chapter 19).

Quality control standards require the firm to establish policies and procedures designed to provide it with reasonable assurance that the firm and its personnel comply with the relevant ethical requirements and that independence is maintained (ISQC 1). A firm can document compliance with this policy by having all personnel complete an annual independence questionnaire or report. This questionnaire requests information about the auditor's financial or business relationships with the firm's clients. Under certain circumstances, family members' financial or business relationships are attributable to the auditor. For example, if the spouse of an auditor participating in an engagement was an accounting supervisor for the client, independence would be considered impaired.

At the engagement level, the **engagement partner** should ensure that all individuals assigned to the engagement are independent of the client (ISA 220). This can be accomplished by reviewing the annual independence reports for each member of the engagement team, or through the firm's independent database.

Another area of concern related to independence is overdue client fees. If an account receivable from a client takes on the characteristics of a loan, the auditor's independence may be impaired. Many audit firms adopt a policy of not completing the current audit until all of the prior year's fees have been paid.

Finally, the firm must be concerned when it also provides non-assurance services for an audit client such as consulting. While the provision of non-assurance services to an audit client does not necessarily impair independence, the auditor must in such a situation apply the threat and safeguard approach inherent in the IFAC Code of Ethics (see Chapter 19).

❖ PLANNING THE AUDIT

LO7

Engagement **planning** involves all the issues the auditor should consider in developing an **overall audit strategy** for conducting the audit. In determining the audit strategy, the auditor should determine the scope of the engagement, ascertain the reporting objectives to plan the timing of the audit, consider the factors that will determine the focus of the engagement team's efforts (determination of appropriate materiality levels, areas of high risk of material misstatement, etc.). Developing the audit strategy helps the auditor determine what resources are needed to perform the engagement.

Once the audit strategy has been established, the auditor develops an **audit plan**. The audit plan is more detailed than the audit strategy. In the audit plan, the auditor documents a description of: (1) the nature, timing and extent of the planned risk assessment procedures to be used; (2) the nature, timing and extent of planned further audit procedures at the assertion level for each class of transactions, account balance and disclosure and (3) a description of other audit procedures to be performed in order to comply with auditing standards. Basically, the audit plan should consider how to conduct the audit in an effective and efficient manner.

When preparing the audit plan, the auditor should be guided by the results of the risk assessment procedures performed to gain the understanding of the entity. Additional steps that should be performed include:

- Assess business risks and establish materiality.
- Assess the need for experts.
- Consider the possibility of non-compliance with laws and regulations (illegal acts).
- Identify related parties.
- Conduct preliminary analytical procedures.
- Consider additional value-added services.

Assess Business Risks and Establish Materiality

Chapter 3 provided a detailed discussion of the process used to assess the client's business risks and to establish materiality. The auditor restricts audit risk at the account balance level in such a way that, at the end of the engagement, he or she can express an opinion on the financial statements, taken as a whole, at an acceptably low level of audit risk. The audit risk model serves as a framework for this process. The auditor obtains an understanding of the entity and its environment. Based on this understanding, the auditor identifies those business risks that may result in material misstatements. The auditor evaluates the client's response to those business risks and ensures that those responses have been adequately implemented. Based on this information, the auditor assesses the level of risk of material misstatement of assertions in relation to financial statement accounts. The risk of material misstatement is used to determine the acceptable level of detection risk and to plan the auditing procedures to be performed. The auditor considers materiality from the perspective of how misstatements could reasonably be expected to influence the economic decisions of users, and follows a three-step process in applying materiality on an audit. You should consider returning to Chapter 3 to review the important issues related to these concepts.

Assess the Need for Experts

A major consideration in planning the audit is the need for experts. Auditing standards (ISA 620) define an **auditor's expert** as an individual or organization possessing expertise in a field other than accounting or auditing, whose work in that field is used by the auditor to assist the auditor in obtaining sufficient appropriate audit evidence. An auditor's expert may be either an internal (partner or staff of the auditor's firm) expert or an external (not employed by the auditor's firm) expert. This would include experts in finance, tax, valuation, pension and information technology. Such experts may assist the auditor with measuring fair values, valuing financial instruments, determination of physical quantities, amounts derived from specialized techniques, or interpretations of regulations or agreements. The use of an IT expert is a significant aspect of most audit engagements. When deciding whether an IT expert is to be used, a primary concern is the extent to which IT is used in processing accounting information. The presence of complex information technology may require the use of an IT expert. Chapter 6 covers these issues in more detail.

The auditor is still ultimately responsible for work performed by the expert. In relying on the expert, the auditor should evaluate the competence and objectivity of the expert, audit the inputs used by the expert (e.g. census data for actuary) and reconcile the output (e.g. an estimate should be found in the financial statements or disclosures), and review the expert work for reasonableness, including the reasonableness of assumptions.

Consider the Possibility of Non-Compliance with Laws and Regulations

The term **non-compliance acts** refers to acts of omission or commission by the entity, either intentional or unintentional, which are contrary to the prevailing laws or regulations. In some instances, fraud may also consist of non-compliance acts (see Chapter 3). Ordinarily, the further removed non-compliance is from the events and transactions reflected in the financial statements, the less likely the auditor is to become aware of it or to recognize the non-compliance.

Auditing standards (ISA 250) distinguish between provisions of laws and regulations that have a *direct* effect on the financial statements and those that have *indirect* effects. For example, tax and pension laws and regulations that may affect the amount of revenue recognized under a government contract fall into the direct effect category. The auditor's responsibility for detecting non-compliance with the provisions of those laws and regulations generally recognized as having a direct effect on the determination of material amounts and disclosures in the financial statements is the same as that for error or fraud.

Other non-compliance, such as violations of an operating licence, occupational safety and health regulations, environmental regulations, employment regulations and fair competition regulations, may be fundamental to the operating aspects of the entity or to avoid penalties, but only *indirectly* affect the amounts in the financial statements. For non-compliance with such laws and regulations the auditor's responsibility is limited to perform specified audit procedures such as inquiry of management and inspection of correspondence to help identify instances of non-compliance. During the audit, however, the auditor should be aware that non-compliance acts may have occurred.

Table 5–3 presents some examples of specific information or circumstances that indicate the possibility of a non-compliance act. For example, the business world has seen a number of instances where payments of sales commissions or agent's fees were really bribes to secure contracts. When the auditor becomes aware of such a possible non-compliance act, he or she should obtain an understanding of the nature of the act, the circumstances in which it occurred, and sufficient other information to evaluate its effects on the financial statements. The auditor should then discuss the matter with the appropriate level of management. If management does not provide satisfactory information, the auditor should consult with the client's legal counsel and apply additional audit procedures, if necessary.

Table 5–3 Information or Circumstances that May Indicate a Non-Compliance Act
• Unauthorized transactions, improperly recorded transactions, or transactions not recorded in a complete or timely manner.
• An investigation by a government body, an enforcement proceeding, or payment of unusual fines or penalties.
• Violations of laws or regulations cited in reports of examinations by regulatory authorities.
• Large payments for unspecified services to consultants, affiliates or employees.
• Sales commissions or agents' fees that appear excessive.
• Large payments in cash or bank cashiers' cheques.
• Unexplained payments to government officials.
• Failure to file tax returns or pay government duties.

If a non-compliance act has occurred or is likely to have occurred, the auditor should consider its implications for other aspects of the audit, particularly the reliability of management representations. The auditor should ensure that those charged with governance are adequately informed about non-compliance with laws and regulations. The auditor should also recognize that, under the circumstances noted previously, he or she may have a duty to notify parties outside the client such as regulatory and enforcement authorities. For example, in many countries the auditor must report suspicion of money laundering to competent authorities.

Identify Related Parties[i]

The applicable financial reporting framework ordinarily defines a related party to the reporting entity, and establishes specific accounting and disclosure requirements for related party relationships, transactions and balances. For example, International Accounting Standard (IAS) 24 *Related Party Disclosures* includes a detailed definition of a related party. A related party would typically be within one of these three categories:

1 A person or other entity that has control or significant influence, directly or indirectly through one or more intermediaries, over the reporting entity.
2 Another entity over which the reporting entity has control or significant influence, directly or indirectly through one or more intermediaries.
3 Another entity that is under common control with the reporting entity through having common controlling ownership, owners who are close family members, or common key management.

Auditors should attempt to identify all related parties during the planning phase of the audit (ISA 550). It is important to identify related party transactions because the transaction may not be 'at **arm's length**'. For example, the client may lease property from an entity owned by the chief executive officer at lease rates in excess of prevailing market rates. The auditor can identify related parties by accessing the entity's information system for related party relationships or requesting a list of related parties from management. Once related parties have been identified, audit personnel should be provided with the names so that transactions with such parties are identified and investigated. During the audit, the auditor maintains alertness for related party information when reviewing records and documents such as:

• Minutes of meetings of shareholders, management and those charged with governance.
• Entity income tax returns.
• Shareholder registers to identify the entity's principal shareholders.
• Statements of conflicts of interest from management and those charged with governance.
• Records of the entity's investments and those of its pension plans.
• Contracts and agreements with key management or those charged with governance.
• Significant contracts and agreements not in the entity's ordinary course of business.
• Internal auditors' reports.
• Documents associated with the entity's filings with a securities regulator.

Related party relationships are also a regular feature of many entities that are owned and managed by an individual or by a family. The auditor's in-depth knowledge of the small entity may, however, be of assistance in the identification of related parties and transactions with related parties.

Conduct Preliminary Analytical Procedures

Analytical procedures are defined as consisting of evaluations of financial information through analysis of plausible relationships among both financial and non-financial data (ISA 520). Auditing standards require that the auditor applies analytical procedures at the planning phase for all audits. The main objectives of preliminary analytical procedures at this point are: (1) to understand the client's business and transactions; and (2) to identify financial statement accounts that are likely to contain errors. By identifying where errors are likely, the auditor can allocate more resources to investigate those accounts. Suppose, for example, that an auditor computes a client's inventory turnover ratio for the last five years as follows:

$$\text{Inventory turnover} = \frac{\text{Cost of goods sold}}{\text{Inventory}}$$

The results of this analysis show the following trend, which is compared to industry data:

	2005	2006	2007	2008	2009
Client	8.9	8.8	8.5	8.0	7.9
Industry	8.8	8.7	8.8	8.6	8.6

The client's inventory turnover ratio in this case has declined steadily over the five-year period, while the industry turnover ratio shows only a minor decline over the same period. The auditor might suspect that the client's inventory contains slow-moving or obsolete inventory. The auditor would then plan additional testing for selected assertions such as valuation, completeness and existence.

Consider Additional Value-Added Services

As part of the planning process, the auditor should look for opportunities to recommend additional value-added services. Traditionally, value-added services have included tax planning, transaction support, IT consultancy and internal reporting processes. With auditors taking a more global view of the entity and its environment, there are new opportunities to provide valuable services for the client. For example, the auditor can provide recommendations based on the assessment of the entity's business risks. With the knowledge gathered through assessing business risks, the auditor can provide important feedback to management and those charged with governance on the strengths and weaknesses of business processes, strategic planning and emerging trends. Proper consideration of value-added services during the planning process should alert the audit engagement team to proactively identify opportunities to improve client service. Of course, auditors are limited in the types of consulting services they can offer their audit clients (see Chapter 19).

Document Overall Audit Strategy and Audit Plan

The auditor should document the overall audit strategy and audit plan. This involves documenting the decisions about the nature, timing and extent of audit tests. At this stage, the auditor compiles his or her knowledge about the client's business objectives, strategies, and related business and audit risks. The auditor records how the client is managing its risks (i.e. through internal control processes) and then documents the effect of the risks and controls on the planned audit procedures. Auditors ensure they have addressed the risks they identified in their understanding of the risk assessment process by documenting the linkage from the client's business objectives and strategy to audit plans. The form of documentation varies from firm to firm, but a simple illustration using EarthWear might look as follows:

Business Objectives and Strategy	Business Risks	Account(s)/ (Assertions)	Audit Risks	Controls	Effect on Audit Plan
Increase market share through sales at new locations (e.g. during the current year websites were developed for ten more countries)	Restrictive trade laws may affect sales tactics Strong consumer protection in several European countries	*Revenue:* accuracy and valuation	Overstated due to pricing issues	EwC has installed a special group to track compliance with local and international laws	Observe and test group's policies and procedures (see work paper R-11)
	Political uncertainly in less developed countries (LDCs)	*Reserve for returns:* completeness	Understated due to failure to properly track returns in new locations	EwC has placed more frequent review of returns in new locations	Extend audit work on EwC's return tracking with emphasis on new locations (see work paper R-15)
	Currency risks	*Gains/losses from currency hedging:* valuation and accuracy	Gains/losses not properly calculated or accrued on hedging activity	EwC has strong controls in the Treasury Department to account for hedging activities	Increase the number of hedging contracts tested with particular emphasis on contracts in unstable currencies (see work paper S-14)

The overall audit strategy and audit plan are documented in a written plan (ISA 300). Exhibit 5–2 presents a partial audit plan for substantive tests of accounts receivable. The types of audit tests are discussed in the next section.

Exhibit 5–2 A Partial Audit Plan for Substantive Procedures Testing of Accounts Receivable

Audit Procedures.	W/P Ref	Completed by	Date
1 Obtain the 31 December 2009, aged accounts receivable trial balance and			
a Foot the trial balance and agree total to accounts receivable control account.			
b Randomly select 30 accounts from the aged trial balance; agree the information per the aged trial balance to the original sales invoice and determine if the invoice was included in the appropriate ageing category.			
2 Confirm accounts receivable using a monetary-unit sampling plan. Set the desired confidence level = 90%, tolerable misstatement = €50,000, and expected misstatement = €20,000.			
a For all responses with exceptions, follow up on the cause of the error.			
b For all non-responses, examine subsequent cash receipts and or supporting documents.			
c Summarize the sampling test results.			
d Summarize the confirmation results.			
3 Test sales cut-off by identifying the last shipping advice for the year and examining five large sales for three days before and after year end.			
4 Test the reasonableness of the allowance for doubtful accounts by the following:			
a Test the reasonableness using past percentages on bad debts.			
b For any large account in the aged trial balance greater than 90 days old, test for subsequent cash receipts.			
c For the following financial ratios, compare the current year to the trend of the prior three years results and internal budgets:			
• Number of days outstanding in receivable.			
• Ageing of receivables.			
• Write-offs as a percentage of sales.			
• Bad debt expense as a percentage of sales.			
5 Prepare a memo summarizing the tests, results and conclusions.			

TYPES OF AUDIT TESTS

LO8

There are three general types of audit tests:

1 Risk assessment procedures.
2 Tests of controls.
3 Substantive procedures.

Risk Assessment Procedures

Auditor risk assessment procedures are used to obtain an understanding of the entity and its environment, including its internal control. Risk assessment procedures include inquiries of management and others, analytical procedures, and observation and inspection. Such procedures are used to assess the risks of material misstatement at the financial statement and assertion levels. Risk assessment procedures were covered in depth in Chapter 3.

Tests of Controls

Tests of controls are audit procedures performed to test the *operating effectiveness* of controls in preventing, or detecting and correcting material misstatements at the relevant assertion level. The following audit procedures are examples of tests of controls:

● Inquiries of appropriate management, supervisory and staff personnel.
● Inspection of documents, reports and electronic files.
● Observation of the application of specific controls.
● Walk-throughs, which involve tracing a transaction from its origination to its inclusion in the financial statements through a combination of audit procedures including inquiry, observation and inspection.
● Reperformance of the application of the control by the auditor.

For example, in evaluating the design of an automated IT application control and determining whether it has been implemented, the auditor may make inquiries of entity personnel and inspect relevant systems documentation, reports or other documents. Table 5–4 provides additional examples of controls that are normally present in the processing of revenue transactions and tests of controls that the auditor might use to test the operation of the controls. While always an option, tests of controls are necessary in two circumstances. When the auditor's risk assessment includes an expectation of the operating effectiveness of controls, the auditor is required to test those controls to support the risk assessment. In addition, when substantive procedures alone do not provide sufficient appropriate audit evidence, the auditor is required to perform tests of controls to obtain audit evidence about their operating effectiveness. For example, the auditor may find it impossible to design effective substantive procedures when an entity conducts its business using IT and no documentation of transactions is produced or maintained, other than through the IT system. Tests of controls will be discussed further in Chapter 6.

Table 5–4 Examples of Internal Controls and Tests of Controls

Internal Controls	Tests of Controls
Create a separation of duties between the shipping function and the order entry and billing functions.	Observe and evaluate whether shipping personnel have access to the order entry or billing activities.
Credit Department personnel initial sales orders, indicating credit approval.	Inspect a sample of sales orders for presence of initials of Credit Department personnel.
Billing Department personnel account for the numerical sequence of sales invoices.	Inquire of Billing Department personnel about missing sales invoice numbers.
Agree sales invoices to shipping document and customer order for product types, price and quantity.	Recompute the information on a sample of sales invoices.

Substantive Procedures

Substantive procedures detect material misstatements (that is, monetary errors) in a transaction class, account balance and disclosure element of the financial statements. There are two categories of substantive procedures: (1) tests of details of classes of transactions, account balances and disclosures; and (2) substantive analytical procedures.

Tests of details of classes of transactions, account balances and disclosures

Tests of details are usually categorized into two types: (1) **substantive tests of transactions** and (2) **tests of details of account balances and disclosures**. Substantive tests of transactions test for errors or fraud in individual transactions. For example, an auditor may examine a large purchase of inventory by testing that the cost of the goods included on the vendor's invoice is properly recorded in the inventory and accounts payable accounts. This gives the auditor evidence about the occurrence, completeness and accuracy assertions.

Tests of details of account balances and disclosures focus on the items that are contained in the financial statement account balances and disclosures. These important tests establish whether any material misstatements are included in the accounts or disclosures in the financial statements. For example, the auditor may want to test accounts receivable. To detail test the balance of accounts receivable, the auditor is likely to send confirmations to a sample of customers in order to gather evidence about the existence assertion. Such tests also provide evidence regarding the transaction assertions of accuracy and cut-off.

Substantive Analytical Procedures

Because of the importance of substantive analytical procedures, they are discussed in more detail in the next section.

Dual-Purpose Tests

Tests of controls check the operating effectiveness of controls, while substantive tests of transactions are concerned with monetary misstatements. However, it often makes more sense to design audit procedures to conduct both test of controls or a substantive test of transactions simultaneously on the same document. For example, in Table 5–4, the last control procedure shown is agreement of sales invoices to shipping documents and customer orders for product type, price and quantity. The test of controls shown is to recompute the information on a sample of sales invoices. While this test primarily checks the effectiveness of the control, it also provides evidence on whether the sales invoice contains the wrong quantity, product type or price. **Dual-purpose tests** can also improve the efficiency of the audit.

This text discusses tests of controls within each business process. Substantive tests of transactions are discussed along with the other substantive tests when the financial statement accounts affected by the business process are discussed. You should remember, however, that in most audit situations substantive tests of transactions are conducted at the same time as tests of controls.

SUBSTANTIVE ANALYTICAL PROCEDURES

Analytical Procedures

Auditing standards define analytical procedures as consisting of evaluations of financial information through analysis of plausible relationships among both financial and non-financial data. An important aspect of the definition of analytical procedures is that they involve a comparison of recorded values with *expectations* developed by the auditor. Analytical procedures can facilitate an effective audit by helping the auditor understand the client's business, directing attention to high-risk areas, identifying audit issues that might not be otherwise apparent, providing audit evidence, and assisting in the evaluation of audit results.

Purposes of Analytical Procedures

Analytical procedures are used for three purposes:

1 *Preliminary analytical procedures* are used to assist the auditor to better understand the business, and to plan the nature, timing and extent of audit procedures.
2 *Substantive analytical procedures* are used as a substantive procedure to obtain evidence about particular assertions related to account balances or classes of transactions.
3 *Final analytical procedures* are used as an overall review of the financial information in the final review stage of the audit.

Auditing standards require the use of analytical procedures for the first and third purposes. However, analytical procedures are also commonly used to gather substantive evidence because they are effective at detecting misstatements.[ii] Analytical procedures are also relatively inexpensive tests to perform.

The purpose of the analytical procedures, and the facts and circumstances will dictate the type of analytical procedure used to form an expectation and the techniques involved in investigating a significant difference. Analytical procedures may range from the use of simple trend analysis to the use of complex regression models. The discussion of analytical procedures in this chapter is limited to the following three types of analytical procedure:

1   Trend analysis – the examination of changes in an account over time.
2   Ratio analysis – the comparison, across time or to a benchmark, of relationships between financial statement accounts or between an account and non-financial data.
3   Reasonableness analysis – development of a model to form an expectation using financial data, non-financial data, or both, to test account balances or changes in account balances between accounting periods.

The use of regression analysis as an analytical procedure is covered in auditing texts devoted to statistical auditing methods.[iii]

Preliminary analytical procedures were discussed earlier in this chapter.

Substantive Analytical Procedures

Figure 5–2 presents an overview of the auditor's decision process when using substantive analytical procedures to collect audit evidence. While the overall process is similar for the other two purposes of analytical procedures (i.e. preliminary and final analytical procedures), we will identify important differences as we discuss each step in the process.

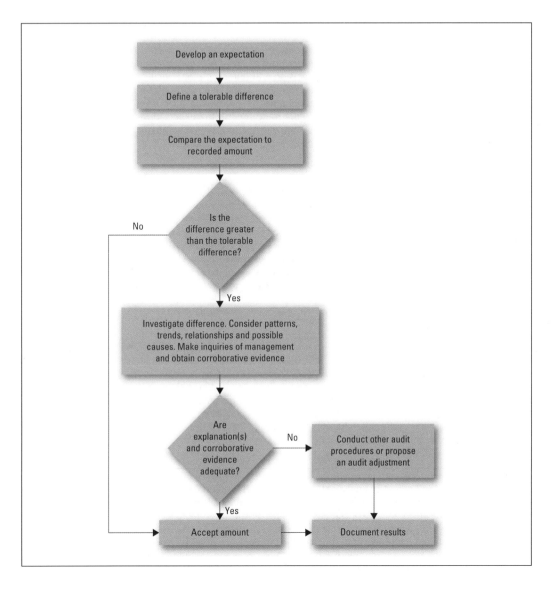

Figure 5–2 Overview of the Auditor's Decision Process for Substantive Analytical Procedures

Develop an Expectation

The first step in the decision process is to develop an expectation for the amount or account balance. This is the most important step in performing analytical procedures. Auditing standards require the auditor to have an expectation whenever analytical procedures are used. An expectation can be developed using any of the types of analytical procedures discussed previously using information available from a variety of sources, such as:

- Financial and operating data.
- Budgets and forecasts.
- Industry publications.
- Competitor information.
- Management's analyses.
- Analyst's reports.

Precision of the Expectation

The quality of an expectation is referred to as the *precision* of the expectation. Precision is a measure of the potential effectiveness of an analytical procedure; it represents the degree of reliance that can be placed on the procedure. Precision is a measure of how closely the expectation approximates the 'correct' but unknown amount. The degree of desired precision will differ with the specific purpose of the analytical procedure. The precision of the expectation is a function of the materiality and required detection risk for the assertion being tested. If the assertion being tested requires a low level of detection risk, the expectation needs to be very precise. However, the more precise the expectation, the more extensive and expensive the audit procedures used to develop the expectation, which results in a cost–benefit trade-off.

The following four factors affect the precision of analytical procedures.

DISAGGREGATION

The more detailed the level at which an expectation is formed, the greater the precision. For example, expectations formed using monthly data will be more precise than expectations formed using annual data. Similarly, expectations formed at an individual product level will be more precise than expectations formed for all products combined. Preliminary and final analytical procedures are often conducted at relatively high levels of aggregation. However, analytical procedures conducted to provide substantive evidence normally cannot be performed at aggregated levels (e.g. annual data, total revenues). Misstatements are difficult to detect when analysing data at aggregate levels, due to offsetting trends or activities that can mask risks and misstatements. Examples later in the chapter illustrate this concept.

THE PLAUSIBILITY AND PREDICTABILITY OF THE RELATIONSHIP BEING STUDIED

As indicated previously, analytical procedures involve the study of plausible relationships among financial and non-financial data. The primary concern with plausibility is simply whether the relationship used to test the assertion makes sense. For example, it is usually plausible to expect that an increase in sales should lead to an increase in accounts receivable. Many factors, including changes in the business or industry, influence the predictability of relationships among financial and non-financial data. Income statement items tend to be more predictable than balance sheet items because income statement accounts involve transactions over a period of time, whereas balance sheet accounts represent amounts at a specific point in time. The more plausible and predictable the relationship, the more precise the expectation.

DATA RELIABILITY

The ability to develop precise expectations is influenced by the reliability of the available data. For example, the nature and extent of analytical procedures at the planning stage of the audit of a small entity may be limited by the lack of reliable interim or monthly financial information at that point in time. The reliability of data for developing expectations depends on the three factors discussed in Chapter 4 under the appropriateness of audit evidence (e.g. the independence of the source of the evidence, the effectiveness of internal controls, and the auditor's direct personal knowledge). In addition, data for analytical procedures are more reliable if the data were subjected to audit in the current or prior periods, and when the expectation is developed from multiple sources of data.

TYPE OF ANALYTICAL PROCEDURE USED TO FORM AN EXPECTATION

The three types of analytical procedures discussed earlier (trend, ratio and reasonableness analysis) represent different ways to form an expectation. In general, trend analysis is the least precise method used and reasonableness analysis is the most precise. All three types are used for substantive analytical procedures but reasonableness analysis is not commonly used for preliminary or final analytical procedures. Table 5–5 provides the definitions of the types of analytical procedures, and then we present several examples.

Table 5–5 Definitions of the Types of Analytical Procedures Used to Form Expectations*

Trend analysis is the analysis of changes in an account over time. Simple trend analyses compare last year's account balance (the 'expectation') with the current balance. Trend analysis can also encompass multiple time periods and includes comparing recorded trends with budget amounts and with competitor and industry information. The number of time periods used is a function of predictability and desired precision. The more stable the operations over time, the more predictable the relationship and the more appropriate the use of multiple periods. Generally, the more time periods used and the more disaggregated the data, the more precise the expectation. Because trend analysis relies on a single predictor (i.e. prior period information for an account balance), it does not normally yield as precise an expectation as the other two types.

Ratio analysis is the comparison, across time or to a benchmark, of relationships between financial statement accounts (e.g. return on equity) or between an account and non-financial data (e.g. cost per square metre or sales per item). Ratio analysis also includes 'common-size' analysis, which is the conversion of financial statement amounts to percentages. Industry or competitor ratios are often used to benchmark the client's performance. *Advanced Module 1* illustrates selected financial ratios useful in analytical procedures. Ratio analysis is often more effective at identifying risks and potential misstatements than trend analysis because comparisons of relationships between accounts and operating data are more likely to identify unusual patterns than is an analysis focused only on an individual account. As with trend analysis, to gather substantive evidence effectively, ratio analysis should be performed on disaggregated data (e.g. by product, location or month) over multiple periods where applicable.

Reasonableness analysis involves forming an expectation using a model. In many cases, a simple model may be sufficient. For example, ticket revenue can be modelled by taking average attendance by average ticket price. Similarly, depreciation expense can be modelled by taking book value divided by average useful life for a class of assets. Because it forms an explicit expectation, reasonableness analysis typically forms a more precise expectation than trend or ratio analysis. Of course, the precision of an expectation formed with a reasonableness test depends on the other factors influencing precision (i.e. disaggregation, predictability and reliability).

* Regression analysis is another type of analytical procedure. Because it involves relatively complex statistical modelling in audit settings, we do not discuss it in this text. See note iii for further information.

Examples of Expectations Formed by Analytical Procedures

Proper application of analytical procedures requires that the auditor has knowledge of the client's business and industry. Without such knowledge, the auditor may be unable to develop appropriate expectations or properly evaluate the results of the procedures. The auditor can use a number of different analytical procedures to form expectations. Some common examples include the following.

Comparison of Current-Year Financial Information with Comparable Prior Period(s) after Consideration of Known Changes

This is perhaps the most commonly used analytical procedure. The comparison of financial statement amounts can be done using absolute amounts (i.e. trend analysis) or by converting the financial statement amounts to 'common-size' financial statements (ratio analysis). Exhibit 5–3 presents an example of common-size income statements for EarthWear for 2009–07. An auditor may compare the amounts shown for the three years and investigate those amounts that are out of line by some predetermined cut-off percentage or absolute amount. Before continuing, pause for a moment and consider the financial data presented in Exhibit 5–3. Using your developing skills as an auditor, consider one or two trends or ratios that would cause you as an auditor to pause and want to investigate further.

Exhibit 5–3 Common-Size Income Statements for EarthWear Clothiers (in thousands)

	2009		2008		2007	
Net Sales	€950,484	100.00%	€857,885	100.00%	€891,394	100.00%
Cost of sales	(546,393)	–57.49%	(472,739)	-55.11%	(490,530)	–55.03%
Gross Profit	404,091	42.51%	385,146	44.89%	400,864	44.97%
Selling, general and administrative expenses	(364,012)	–38.30%	(334,994)	–39.05%	(353,890)	–39.70%
Non-recurring charge	–		1,153	0.14%	(8,190)	–0.92%
Other	(4,798)	–0.50%	(1,090)	–0.13%	(1,592)	–0.18%
Profit from Operations	35,281	3.71%	50,215	5.85%	37,192	4.17%
Finance cost (interest expense)	(983)	–0.10%	(1,229)	–0.14%	(5,027)	–0.56%
Finance income	1,459	0.15%	573	0.07%	10	0.00%

31 December

Profit before tax	35,757	3.76%	49,559	5.78%	32,175	3.61%
Income tax expense	(13,230)	-1.39%	(18,337)	-2.14%	(11,905)	-1.34%
Profit for the Year	**€22,527**	**2.37%**	**€31,222**	**3.64%**	**€20,270**	**2.27%**
Basic Earnings per Share	**1.15**		**1.60**		**1.02**	
Diluted Earnings per Share	**1.14**		**1.56**		**1.01**	
Basic weighted average shares outstanding	19,531		19,555		19,806	
Diluted weighted average shares outstanding	19,774		20,055		19,996	

For example, the auditor can compare the current-year gross profit balance with the prior year's balance. Referring to Exhibit 5–3, we see that gross profit from 2008 to 2009 has increased in absolute amounts from €385.1 million to €404.1 million but decreased in percentage terms from 44.89 to 42.51 per cent. Because this type of analytical procedure is typically performed on the aggregated company-wide financial statements, the expectation that the current-year gross profit percentage will be the same as that of the prior year is relatively imprecise. Thus, it is typically used for planning and final review purposes, but is not considered particularly useful for providing substantive evidence about a particular account balance or class of transactions. At planning, the auditor would investigate this increase in cost of sales which resulted in the decline in gross profit, and adjust the planned audit procedures to address risks associated with the increase. To illustrate the effect of conducting analytical procedures at aggregated company-wide levels, consider what effect this decline in gross profit percentage has on profit from operations. Recall from Chapter 3 that materiality for EarthWear was set at €1,800,000 for the financial statements and €900,000 for each account and class of transactions. Profit from operations declined from €50.2 million to €35.3 million. The 2.38 percentage point (44.89 to 42.51) decrease in gross profit resulted in profit from operations being approximately €22.62 million lower than expected (sales = €950.5 × .0238). However, this analysis does not provide appropriate evidence to explain the increase in cost of sales. The auditor would have to perform additional procedures to corroborate the increase in cost of sales. This simple example highlights that it is difficult to obtain useful audit evidence from high-level company-wide analytical procedures because the expectations are typically not sufficiently precise. In other words, whether or not the auditor observes a significant difference using a year-to-year comparison may be useful for planning purposes, but it would provide little or no audit evidence because of the imprecision of the expectation.

Comparison of Current-Year Financial Information with Budgets, Projections and Forecasts

This technique is usually performed using trend analysis and is similar to the previous example except that the current-year budget, projection or forecast represents the expectation (rather than the expectation being provided by prior year data). For example, the auditor can test the fairness of advertising expense by comparing the current year amount to the client's budget and investigating differences.

Relationships among Elements of Financial Information within the Current Period

There are many examples of one element in the financial statements directly relating to another element. This is particularly true for the association between certain balance sheet accounts and their related income or expense accounts. In these situations, reasonableness analysis is typically used to model the association. Taking this information into account, consider some of the relationships between income statement and balance sheet accounts you would expect to see in a growing company. Ask yourself what the relationship would normally be between sales and accounts receivable? What about between property, plant and equipment (PP&E) and depreciation expense? For example, there should be a relationship between the balance for long-term debt and interest expense. The auditor can model interest expense by multiplying the average long-term debt for the period by the period's average interest rate. This estimate of interest expense can be compared to the balance of interest expense shown on the trial balance. Later in the chapter we present a comprehensive example of an interest expense reasonableness test for EarthWear Clothiers.

Comparison of the Client's Financial Information with Industry Data

The auditor can compare the client's financial ratios (receivable turnover, inventory turnover, and so on) to industry averages. The industry information can serve as a benchmark for assessing how well the client's financial position and performance compare with other companies in the industry. Dun & Bradstreet and Standard & Poor's, among others publish this type of industry data. Exhibit 5–4 contains an extract of industry data for mail-order houses. *Advanced Module 1* to this chapter illustrates several ratios used in ratio analysis.

Exhibit 5–4 An Example of Industry Data Available from Published Sources

Mail-Order Houses
Annual Statement

	% of Total Assets
Cash & Equivalents	16.1
Trade Receivables – (net)	11.1
Inventory	38
All Other Current Assets	4.8
Total Current Assets	**69.9**
Fixed Assets (net)	12.8
Intangibles (net)	9.5
All Other Non-Current Assets	7.8
Total Assets	**100**
Notes Payable-Short Term	11.6
Cur. Mat.-L/T/D	3.1
Trade Payables	22.5
Income Taxes Payable	0.3
All Other Current Liabilities	12.7
Total Current Liabilities	**50.2**
Long-Term Debt	11.8
Deferred Taxes	0.6
All Other Non-Current Liabilities	6.9
Net Worth	30.6
Total Liabilities & Net Worth	**100**

	% of Net Sales
Net Sales	100
Gross Profit	43.1
Operating Expenses	39.5
Operating Profit	3.7
All Other Expenses (net)	0.8
Profit Before Taxes	2.9
Net Sales (€)	**€12,385,152,000.0**
Total Assets (€)	**€5,015,679,000.0**

	Quartile		
RATIOS	Upper	Medium	Lower
Solvency:			
Quick	1.2	0.4	0.1
Current	2.8	1.5	1.1
Fixed / Net Worth	0.1	0.3	2
Debt / Net Worth	0.7	1.7	19.5
Earnings before interest and taxes	15.9	3.9	1.4
Efficiency:			
Sales / Receivables	44.5	67.6	24.4
Sales / Net Working Capital	6.8	13.7	54
Cost of Sales / Inventory	9.3	4.7	3.1

Cost of Sales / Payables	19.9	10.6	5.8
Profitability:			
% Profit before Taxes / Tangible Net Worth	60.9	31.1	9.4
% Profit before Taxes / Total Assets	20.5	8.1	1.1
Sales / Net Fixed Assets	121.9	37.6	14.9
Sales / Total Assets	4.5	3.2	2.2
Source: RMA eStatement Studies			

Relationships of Financial Information to Non-Financial Information

The auditor may have relevant non-financial information available for comparison purposes or for developing estimates of the client's financial information. This might include such items as cost per employee, sales per square metre, utility expense per hour, and so on. For example, in a telecommunications company, the auditor can multiply the number of cell phone subscribers by the average billing rate to test a client's total revenue. Other examples include computing the average number of days a product is in inventory or developing an expectation for commission expense by multiplying commissioned sales by the average commission rate and comparing this estimate to the client's recorded commission expense.

Practice Insight 5.2

Using non-financial information in analytical procedures can be an effective way to identify potential frauds because while perpetrators of fraud can manage financial numbers, it is difficult or impossible to manage non-financial data (e.g. square metres, days in the calendar year, numbers of employees). For example, auditors could compare a client's actual square footage of warehouse space with the amount of square footage that would be required to store the inventory as listed on the books.

Plotting Trends over Multiple Periods

It can be very beneficial to plot or graph trends over several periods. Figure 5–3 provides a monthly plot of ending inventory for a three-year period. Suppose the auditor is auditing year-ending inventory for year 3 and that years 1 and 2 have been previously audited. The pattern of previously audited financial information suggests some inventory 'spikes' every six months. These spikes may be due to inventory buildup around busy seasons (e.g. holidays). The star at the end of year 3 indicates the auditor's expectation based on the past trends. The auditor would investigate the cause of the large increase in ending inventory at the end of year 3. Note that the potentially problematic spikes would not have shown up at all if the auditor had just plotted year-end inventory balances rather than monthly balances! Again, using detailed data is critical in enhancing precision.

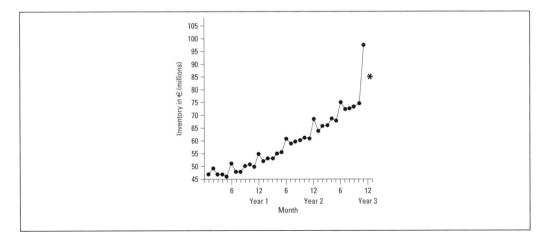

Figure 5–3 An Illustration of a Monthly Plot of Ending Inventory (in € millions)

The foregoing discussion and examples have all related to the first step in the analytical procedures decision process (see Fig. 5–2). The first step is the most important step in performing effective substantive analytical procedures.

Define a Tolerable Difference

The second step in the analytical procedures decision process (see Fig. 5–2) is to define a tolerable difference. Since the expectation developed by the auditor will rarely be identical to the client's recorded amount, the auditor must decide the amount of difference that would require further investigation. The size of the tolerable difference depends on the significance of the account, the desired degree of reliance on the substantive analytical procedure, the level of disaggregation in the amount being tested, and the precision of the expectation. The amount of difference that can be tolerated will always be lower than materiality for the financial statements, and when testing an entire account with a substantive analytical procedure, tolerable differences will be equal or less than materiality for the account. For example, the auditors may use rules of thumb such as, 'tolerable difference is 5 per cent of the client's recorded amount, but not to exceed materiality for the account'.

Compare the Expectation to the Recorded Amount

The next step in the analytical procedures decision process (Fig. 5–2) is to determine if the amount of difference between the auditor's expectation and the recorded amount exceeds the auditor's predetermined 'tolerable difference'. If the observed difference is less than the tolerable difference, the auditor accepts the account. If not, the auditor must investigate the difference using other audit procedures.

Investigate Differences Greater Than the Tolerable Difference

The fourth step in the analytical procedures decision process (Fig. 5–2) is the investigation of significant differences and the formation of conclusions. Differences identified by substantive analytical procedures indicate an increased likelihood of misstatements. The more precise the expectation, the greater the likelihood that the difference is actually a misstatement. Inquiry of the client is frequently an important aspect of the investigation of differences. Nevertheless, client inquiry should not be the sole support for an explanation without quantification and corroboration (discussed below). There are four possible causes of significant differences – accounting changes, economic conditions or events, error, and fraud. In most instances, the cause of an identified difference involves a legitimate accounting change or an economic condition or event. However, even when a significant difference is due to error or fraud, the client may provide a plausible, yet ultimately untrue, business explanation. Thus, the effectiveness of substantive analytical procedures in identifying material misstatements is enhanced when auditors develop potential explanations *before* obtaining the client's explanation. By doing this, the auditor is better able to exercise appropriate professional scepticism and challenge the client's explanation, if necessary.

The development of potential explanations need not be time-consuming. Auditors typically re-examine and understand the various relationships in the financial and non-financial data. Then, based on their previous experience with the client, other audit work performed and discussions with other members of the engagement team, they develop potential explanations for the observed difference. The independent consideration of potential explanations is more important for more significant accounts and when a higher degree of assurance is desired from substantive analytical procedures.

Explanations for significant differences observed for substantive analytical procedures must be followed up and resolved through quantification, corroboration and evaluation.

Quantification

It is usually not practicable to identify an explanation for the exact amount of a difference between an analytical procedure's expectation and the client's recorded amount. However, auditors should quantify the portion of the difference that can be explained. Quantification involves determining whether the explanation or error can explain the observed difference. This may require the recalculation of the expectation after considering the additional information. For example, a client may offer the explanation that the significant increase in inventory over the prior year is due to a 12 per cent increase in raw materials prices. The auditor should compute the effects of the raw materials price increase and determine the extent to which the price increase explains (or does not explain) the increase in the overall inventory account.

Corroboration

Auditors must corroborate explanations for unexpected differences by obtaining sufficient appropriate audit evidence linking the explanation to the difference and substantiating that the information supporting the explanation is reliable. This evidence should be of the same quality as the evidence obtained to support tests of details. Such evidence could vary from simply comparing the explanation to the auditor's knowledge from other areas, to employing other detailed tests to confirm or refute the explanation. Common corroborating procedures include examination of supporting evidence, inquiries of independent persons, and evaluating evidence obtained from other auditing procedures.

Evaluation

The key mindset behind effectively performing substantive analytical procedures is one of appropriate professional scepticism, combined with the desire to obtain sufficient appropriate audit evidence, similar to other auditing procedures. The auditor should evaluate the results of the substantive analytical procedures to conclude whether the desired level of assurance has been achieved. If the auditor obtains evidence that a misstatement exists and can be sufficiently quantified, the auditor makes note of his or her proposed adjustment to the client's financial statements. Towards the end of the audit, all such proposed adjustments, if not already corrected, are accumulated, summarized and evaluated before being presented to the client (Chapter 17 provides further details).

If the auditor concludes that the substantive analytical procedure performed did not provide the desired level of assurance, additional substantive analytical procedures and/or tests of details should be performed to achieve the desired assurance.

The Investigation of Differences for Planning and Final Analytical Procedures

The way in which differences are investigated diverges in important ways for preliminary and final analytical procedures. At planning, the auditor is not required to obtain corroborative evidence because preliminary analytical procedures are not intended to provide substantive audit evidence regarding specific assertions. Rather, the auditor normally determines whether the planned audit procedures need to be revised in light of the results of preliminary analytical procedures. For example, to address the increased risk posed by the spike in inventory illustrated in Figure 5–3, the auditor may decide to expand the number of items tested during the observation of the year-end physical inventory count.

When conducting final analytical procedures, the auditor investigates unexpected differences by first going to the working papers to determine if sufficient appropriate evidence has already been gathered to explain the difference (rather than going to the client for an explanation). If the auditor cannot find sufficient evidence within the working papers, then the auditor would formulate possible explanations, conduct additional testing and seek an explanation from the client.

Comprehensive EarthWear Example

Suppose we want to use substantive analytical procedures to test the reasonableness of interest expense reported by EarthWear Clothiers (i.e. a 'reasonableness test'). Consider the following example.

> EarthWear's 2009 income statement shows €983,000 of interest expense. To conduct a substantive analytical procedure on this account, the auditor could develop an expectation using reasonableness analysis by building a model in the following manner. Obtain the ending monthly balance for the short-term line of credit from the monthly bank loan statement and calculate the average monthly ending balance. Trace the monthly loan balances to the general ledger. Determine the average interest rate for the year for the short-term line of credit based on the bank's published rate in the monthly bank loan statement. Multiply the average monthly balance previously calculated by the average interest rate, and compare the result to the recorded interest expense. Suppose that the auditor obtained the following information from EarthWear's general ledger:

Month	Balance (in € thousands)
January	21,500
February	18,600
March	18,100
April	17,900
May	16,100
June	15,500
July	14,200
August	20,200
September	34,500
October	28,100
November	15,200
December	11,000
Total	230,900
Average	19,240

> Further, assume that interest rates recorded on the loan statements have remained stable over the year, fluctuating between 5 and 5.5 per cent. If the auditor uses 5.25 per cent as the average interest rate, the expectation for interest expense is €1,010,100 (€19,240,000 × 0.0525).

As shown in Fig. 5–2, once an expectation is developed, the next step is to determine the tolerable difference. Because interest expense is a predictable account, the information used to form the expectation is deemed reliable. When the substantive analytical procedure will be the primary substantive test, the auditor forms a fairly precise expectation and will define a more precise tolerable difference than the full materiality for the account. Accordingly, the tolerable difference is set at 5 per cent of recorded interest expense, or €49,150 (0.05 × €983,000). The next step is to compare the expectation of €1,010,100 to the recorded value of €983,000 to determine if the difference is greater than can be tolerated. Because the difference between the auditor's expectation and the recorded amount, €27,100, is less than the tolerable difference, the auditor would accept the interest expense account as fairly stated. However, if the difference between the recorded amount and the expectation is greater than the tolerable difference, the auditor will need to investigate the difference. In the example above, the auditor would probably examine loan activity within each month to determine if there was significant variation in the balance that was not accounted for by the month-end model used to form the expectation. If the difference could still not be explained, the auditor would inquire of management about the cause of the difference. If the client provides a plausible explanation (e.g. interest expense reported in the financial statements also includes interest paid for other short-term loans that were only outstanding for a few days at a time), auditing standards require the auditor to obtain corroborating evidence. If the client's explanation and the corroborating evidence are not adequate, or if no corroborative evidence is available, the auditor will need to conduct additional audit procedures. If the explanation and evidence are adequate for resolving the difference, the auditor can accept the amount as being fairly presented.

As with other audit procedures, when analytical procedures are used to gather substantive evidence, the auditor's purpose is to evaluate one or more assertions. For example, in the interest expense example, the auditor is testing primarily the completeness and valuation assertions. The effectiveness and efficiency of substantive analytical procedures in identifying material misstatements depend on:

- The plausibility and predictability of the relationship.
- The availability and reliability of the data used.
- The precision of the expectation.
- The rigour and sufficiency of the investigation of observed differences (if greater than tolerable difference).
- The nature of the assertion.

We have already discussed all but the last item in the above list.

The Nature of the Assertion

Substantive analytical procedures can be used to test all transactions and balance assertions except rights and obligations. However, they may be more effective at identifying certain types of misstatements than testing individual transactions. For example, they may be more effective at detecting omissions (completeness assertion) than providing detailed documentary evidence. The key points are that: (1) some assertions are more amenable to examination through analytical procedures than others; and (2) the auditor must ensure that the analytical procedure performed is appropriate for the assertion being examined.

Documentation Requirements

When a substantive analytical procedure is used as the principal substantive procedure for a significant financial statement assertion, the auditor should document all of the following:

- The expectation and how it was developed.
- Results of the comparison of the expectation to the recorded amounts or ratios developed from recorded amounts.
- Any additional auditing procedures performed in response to significant unexpected differences arising from the analytical procedure and the results of such additional procedures.

Final Analytical Procedures

The objective of analytical procedures at the overall review stage of an audit is to assist the auditor in assessing the conclusions reached and evaluating the overall financial statement presentation. This requires reviewing the trial balance, financial statements and notes in order to: (1) judge the adequacy of the evidence gathered to support any unusual or unexpected balances investigated during the audit; and (2) determine if any other unusual balances or relationships have not been investigated.

In the first instance, appropriate evidence in the working papers should support any differences from the auditor's expectations. For example, the auditor can compare the audited balances from the current year with the audited balances from the prior year. If there is a material difference, the auditor's working papers should explain the difference. In the second instance, this comparison of audited values may reveal some unusual items that have not been investigated and explained. Assuming that the difference between the auditor's expectation and the recorded amount is material, the auditor will have to perform additional audit work before an audit report can be issued.

THE AUDIT TESTING HIERARCHY

LO10

The risk-based audit approach we have discussed so far in the text is often referred to as a 'top-down' approach, where the auditor obtains an understanding of the client's business objectives and strategies, identifies business and audit risks, documents an understanding of internal control, and then gathers sufficient appropriate audit evidence using a combination of tests of controls, substantive analytical procedures and tests of details to support the audit opinion.

Now that we have discussed evidence (Chapter 4) and introduced you to the types of audit tests (risk assessment procedures, tests of controls, substantive analytical procedures and tests of details), you are ready to be introduced to the thought process auditors use in choosing audit tests, and in what order. The overall decision approach used to gather evidence is depicted in Figure 5–4 and is referred to in later chapters as the *audit testing hierarchy*.

The audit testing hierarchy starts with tests of controls and substantive analytical procedures. Starting with controls and substantive analytical procedures is generally both more effective and more efficient than starting with tests of details.

- *Applying the audit testing hierarchy is more effective.* The auditor's understanding and testing of controls will influence the nature, timing and extent of substantive testing, and will enhance the auditor's ability to home in on areas where misstatements are more likely to be found. If controls are highly effective, less extensive substantive procedures (i.e. substantive analytical procedures and tests of details) will need to be performed. Similarly, substantive analytical procedures can direct attention to higher-risk areas where the auditor can design and conduct focused tests of details.
- *Applying the audit testing hierarchy is more efficient.* Generally, tests of controls and substantive analytical procedures are less costly to perform than are tests of details. This is usually because tests of controls and substantive analytical procedures provide assurance on multiple transactions. In other words, by testing controls and related processes, the auditor generally gains a degree of assurance over thousands or even millions of transactions. Furthermore, substantive analytical procedures often provide evidence related to more than one assertion and often more than one balance or class of transactions. On the other hand, tests of details often only obtain assurance related to one or two specific assertions pertaining to the specific transaction(s) or balance tested.

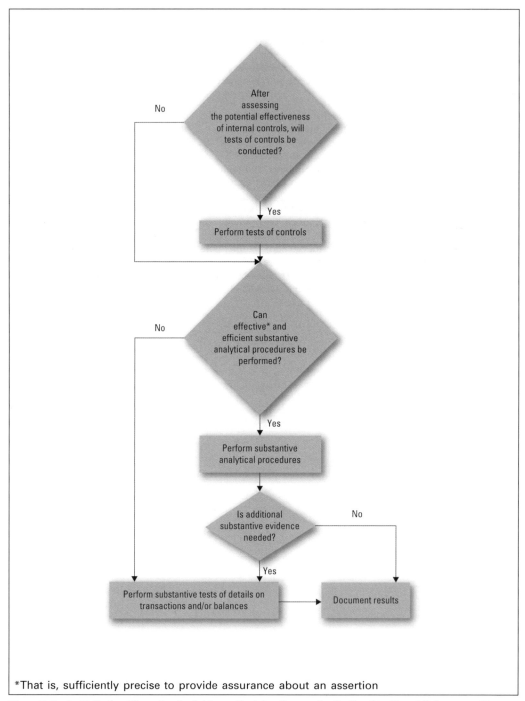

Figure 5–4   Audit Testing Hierarchy: An Evidence Decision Process for Testing Significant Balances or Classes of Transactions

Auditing standards require that auditors perform substantive procedures for each material account balances and classes of transactions regardless of the assessed level of control risk. In other words, assurance obtained solely from testing controls is not sufficient for material balances and classes of transactions. Substantive procedures include substantive analytical procedures and tests of details. For this reason, Figure 5–4 depicts that either substantive analytical procedures, tests of details, or both, will always be conducted for each material accounts or classes of transactions. For high-risk areas or highly material accounts, the auditors will almost always perform some tests of details in addition to tests of controls and substantive analytical procedures.

The decision process depicted in Figure 5–4 recognizes that for some assertions, tests of details may be the only form of testing used, because in some cases it is more efficient and effective to move directly to tests of details. Examples of situations where the auditor might move directly to tests of details include a low volume of large transactions (e.g. two large notes payable issued) and poor controls resulting in client data that are unreliable for use in substantive analytical procedures.

An 'Assurance Bucket' Analogy

We have found that an analogy often helps students understand and visualize how an auditor decides on the proper mix of testing and evidence. Figure 5–5 illustrates what we call the 'assurance bucket.' The assurance bucket must be filled with sufficient appropriate evidence to obtain the level of assurance necessary to support the auditor's opinion. Following the top-down audit testing hierarchy means that auditors first begin to fill the bucket with evidence from the risk assessment procedures. In Figure 5–5, after completing risk assessment procedures, the auditor sees that the assurance bucket for a particular account and assertion is about 20 per cent full. The auditor would next conduct control testing. In our example, control testing might add about another 30 per cent to the bucket. How would the auditor know just how full the bucket is after testing controls? This is clearly a very subjective evaluation, and it is a matter of professional judgement.

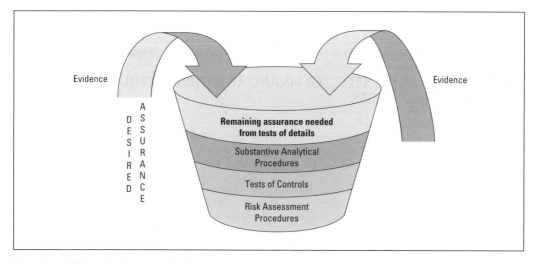

Figure 5–5 Filling the Assurance Bucket

The auditor next performs substantive analytical procedures and adds the assurance gained from these procedures to the bucket. In Figure 5–5 the bucket is now about 70 per cent full. In this illustration, the auditor would need to top up the assurance bucket with evidence obtained through tests of details.

For lower-risk, well-controlled accounts, the assurance bucket may be entirely filled with tests of controls and substantive analytical procedures. For other accounts or assertions, the bucket may be filled primarily with tests of details.

The size of the assurance bucket can vary, depending on the auditor's risk assessment and the assertion being tested. Obviously, certain assertions will be more important or present bigger risks for some accounts than for others. For instance, existence (or validity) is typically more important for accounts receivable than it is for accounts payable. After the auditor has determined the risks associated with the assertions for an account balance, she or he can determine the size of the assurance buckets (i.e. how much assurance is needed) and then begin filling the buckets by applying the audit testing hierarchy. Figure 5–6 illustrates these concepts for accounts payable. Note that the largest bucket is for the *completeness* assertion, because with liability accounts the auditor is primarily concerned with potential understatement errors. The example in Figure 5–6 also illustrates that some assertions may be filled entirely with tests of details (e.g. rights and obligations) and that others may not require any tests of details (e.g. existence). Again, these are subjective matters that require considerable professional judgement.

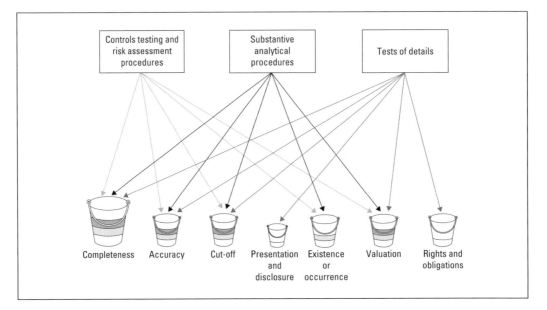

Figure 5–6   Accounts Payable Example of Filling the Assurance Buckets for Each Assertion

ADVANCED MODULE 1: SELECTED FINANCIAL RATIOS USEFUL AS
LO11 **ANALYTICAL PROCEDURES**

A number of financial ratios are used by auditors as analytical procedures. These ratios are typically broken down into four categories: short-term liquidity; activity; profitability; and coverage ratios. Although the ratios discussed apply to most entities, auditors may also use other industry-specific ratios. As follows, each ratio is calculated for EarthWear Clothiers for the year ended 31 December 2009.

A few points are worth mentioning before the financial ratios are discussed. First, in many instances, the auditor may compare the client's ratios with industry averages (see Exhibit 5–4). While the industry averages serve as useful benchmarks, certain limitations should be recognized. Because the industry ratios are averages, they may not capture operating or geographical factors that may be specific to the client. The use of different accounting policies for valuing inventory or calculating depreciation may also result in differences from industry averages for certain ratios. Finally, the industry data may not be available in sufficient detail for a particular client. For example, if the auditor was looking for industry information on a company that operated solely in the wireless industry, such industry ratio data might be combined with other companies within the telecommunications industry.

Second, audit research has shown that material misstatements may not significantly affect certain ratios.[iv] This is particularly true for activity ratios. Third, the auditor must be careful not to evaluate a financial ratio in isolation. In certain cases, a ratio may be favourable because its components are unfavourable. If related ratios are not examined, the auditor may draw an incorrect conclusion. For example, suppose that a client's days outstanding in accounts receivable is getting larger and the inventory turnover ratio is getting smaller. The negative trend in these ratios may indicate that accounts receivable are getting older and that some inventory may be obsolete. However, both of these factors positively affect the current ratio. If the auditor calculates only the current ratio, he or she may reach an incorrect conclusion about the entity's ability to meet current obligations.

Short-Term Liquidity Ratios

Short-term liquidity ratios indicate the entity's ability to meet its current obligations. Three ratios commonly used for this purpose are the current ratio, quick (or acid test) ratio and the operating cash flow ratio.

Current Ratio

The current ratio is calculated as follows:

$$\text{Current ratio} = \frac{\text{Current assets}}{\text{Current liabilities}} = \frac{209,095}{116,268} = 1.80$$

It includes all current assets and current liabilities and is usually considered acceptable if it is 2 to 1 or better. Generally, a high current ratio indicates an entity's ability to pay current obligations. However, if current assets include old accounts receivable or obsolete inventory, this ratio can be distorted.

Quick Ratio

The quick ratio includes only assets that are most readily convertible to cash and is calculated as follows:

$$\text{Quick ratio} = \frac{\text{Liquid assets}}{\text{Current liabilities}} = \frac{48,978 + 12,875}{116,268} = 0.53$$

Thus, inventories and prepaid items are not included in the numerator of the quick ratio. The quick ratio may provide a better picture of the entity's liquidity position if inventory contains obsolete or slow-moving items. A ratio greater than 1 generally indicates that the entity's liquid assets are sufficient to meet the cash requirements for paying current liabilities.

Operating Cash Flow Ratio

The operating cash flow ratio measures the entity's ability to cover its current liabilities with cash generated from operations and is calculated as follows:

$$\text{Operating cash flow ratio} = \frac{\text{Cash flow from operations}}{\text{Current liabilities}} = \frac{39,367}{116,268} = 0.34$$

The operating cash flow ratio uses the cash flows as opposed to assets to measure short-term liquidity. It provides a longer-term measure of the entity's ability to meet its current liabilities. If cash flow from operations is small or negative, the entity is likely to need alternative sources of cash, such as additional borrowings or sales of assets, to meet its obligations.

Activity Ratios

Activity ratios indicate how effectively the entity's assets are managed. Only ratios related to accounts receivable and inventory are discussed here because for most wholesale, retail or manufacturing companies these two accounts represent the assets that have high activity. Activity ratios may also be effective in helping the auditor determine if these accounts contain material misstatements.

Receivables Turnover and Days Outstanding in Accounts Receivable

These two ratios provide information on the activity and age of accounts receivable. The receivables turnover ratio and days outstanding in accounts receivable are calculated as follows:

$$\text{Receivables turnover} = \frac{\text{Credit sales}}{\text{Receivables}} = \frac{950,484}{12,875} = 73.8$$

$$\text{Days outstanding in accounts receivable} = \frac{365 \text{ days}}{\text{Receivables turnover}} = 4.94 \text{ days}$$

The receivables turnover ratio indicates how many times accounts receivable are turned over during a year. However, the days outstanding in accounts receivable may be easier to interpret because this ratio can be compared to the client's terms of trade. For example, if an entity's terms of trade are 2/10, net/30, the auditor would expect that if management was doing a good job of managing receivables, the value for this ratio would be 30 days or less. If the auditor calculates the days outstanding to be 43 days, he or she might suspect that the account contains a material amount of bad debts. Comparing the days outstanding to industry data may be helpful in detecting a slowdown in payments by customers, which is affecting the entire industry. EarthWear's ratio is 4.94 days because most sales are paid by credit card.

Inventory Turnover and Days of Inventory on Hand

These activity ratios provide information on the inventory and are calculated as follows:

$$\text{Inventory turnover} = \frac{\text{Cost of goods sold}}{\text{Inventory}} = \frac{546{,}393}{122{,}337} = 4.47$$

$$\text{Days of inventory on hand} = \frac{365 \text{ days}}{\text{Inventory turnover}} = 81.7 \text{ days}$$

Inventory turnover indicates the frequency with which inventory is consumed in a year. The higher the ratio, the better the entity is at liquidating inventory. This ratio can easily be compared to industry standards. Suppose that the auditor calculates the inventory turnover to be 4.7 times a year. If the industry average is 8.2 times a year, the auditor might suspect that inventory contains obsolete or slow-moving goods. The days of inventory on hand measures how much inventory the entity has available for sale to customers.

Profitability Ratios

Profitability ratios indicate the entity's success or failure for a given period. A number of ratios measure the profitability of an entity, and each ratio should be interpreted by comparison to industry data.

Gross Profit Percentage

The gross profit percentage ratio is generally a good indicator of potential misstatements and is calculated as follows:

$$\text{Gross profit percentage} = \frac{\text{Gross profit}}{\text{Net sales}} = \frac{404{,}091}{950{,}484} = 42.5\%$$

If this ratio varies significantly from previous years or differs significantly from industry data, the entity's financial data may contain errors. Numerous errors can affect this ratio. For example, if the client has failed to record sales, the gross profit percentage will be less than in previous years. Similarly, any errors that affect the inventory account can distort this ratio. For example, if the client has omitted goods from the ending inventory, this ratio will be smaller than in previous years.

Profit Margin

The profit margin ratio is calculated as follows:

$$\text{Profit margin} = \frac{\text{Profit for the year}}{\text{Net sales}} = \frac{22{,}527}{950{,}484} = 2.4\%$$

While the gross profit percentage ratio measures profitability after cost of goods sold is deducted, the profit margin ratio measures the entity's profitability after all expenses are considered. Significant fluctuations in this ratio may indicate that misstatements exist in the selling, general or administrative expense accounts.

Return on Assets

This ratio is calculated as follows:

$$\text{Return on assets} = \frac{\text{Profit for the year}}{\text{Total assets}} = \frac{22{,}527}{329{,}959} = 6.8\%$$

This ratio indicates the return earned on the resources invested by both the stockholders and the creditors.

Return on Equity

The return on equity ratio is calculated as follows:

$$\text{Return on equity} = \frac{\text{Profit for the year}}{\text{Total equity}} = \frac{22{,}527}{204{,}222} = 11.0\%$$

This ratio is similar to the return on assets ratio except that it shows only the return on the resources contributed by the stockholders.

Coverage Ratios

Coverage ratios provide information on the long-term solvency of the entity. These ratios give the auditor important information on the ability of the entity to continue as a going concern.

Debt to Equity

This ratio is calculated as follows:

$$\text{Debt to equity} = \frac{\text{Short-term debt} + \text{Long-term debt}}{\text{Total equity}} = \frac{116{,}268 + 0}{204{,}222} = 0.569\%$$

This ratio indicates what portion of the entity's capital comes from debt. The lower the ratio, the less debt pressure on the entity. If the entity's debt to equity ratio is large relative to the industry's, it may indicate that the entity is too highly leveraged and may not be able to meet its debt obligations on a long-term basis.

Times Interest Earned

This ratio is calculated as follows:

$$\text{Times interest earned} = \frac{\text{Profit for the year} + \text{Interest expense}}{\text{Interest expense}}$$

$$= \frac{22{,}527 + 983}{983} = 23.9$$

The times interest earned ratio indicates the ability of current operations to pay the interest that is due on the entity's debt obligations. The more times that interest is earned, the better the entity's ability to service the interest on long-term debt.

 ## ADVANCED MODULE 2: SPECIAL CONSIDERATIONS IN THE AUDIT OF GROUP
LO12 FINANCIAL STATEMENTS

A group consists of components. A **component** is an entity or business activity for which financial information is included in the group financial statements (ISA 600), e.g. a subsidiary or a joint venture. The work performed by the **group engagement team** on a component is determined by the *significance* of the component and the involvement of *component auditors*. A **component auditor** is an auditor who, at the request of the group engagement team, performs work on financial information related to a component for the group audit. The group engagement partner is the auditor responsible for the group audit and for the audit report on the group financial statements.

As part of the client acceptance process the group engagement team obtains an understanding of the group, its components and their environments. This includes obtaining an understanding of the group-wide controls and the consolidation process. Auditing standards require the group engagement team to identify components that are likely to be *significant components*. A significant component is:

1   A component that is of individual financial significance to the group, or

2 A component that, due to its specific nature or circumstances, is likely to include significant risks of material misstatement of the group financial statements.

The risks of material misstatement of the group financial statements ordinarily increase with the size of the component. For example, the group engagement team may consider that components exceeding 15 per cent of group assets are significant components. In other circumstances, a component may not be of individual financial significance, but expose the group to a significant risk of material misstatement such as a component responsible for foreign exchange trading. Figure 5–7 outlines how the significance of the component affects the work to be performed on the financial information of the component.

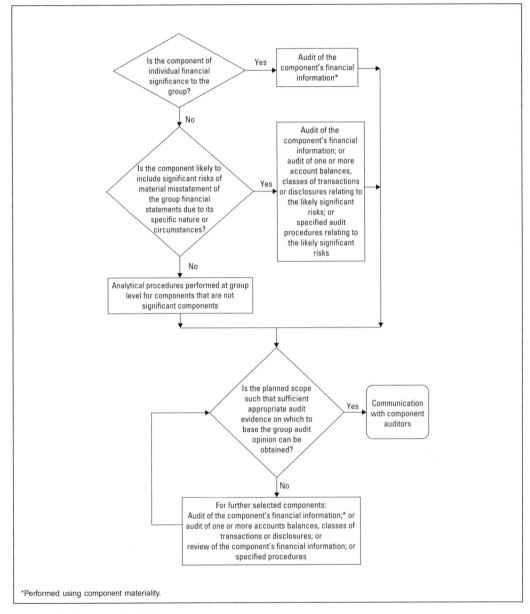

Source: IAASB, ISA 600 (2009).

Figure 5–7   Significance of the Component and the Work Performed

When the component is of individual financial significance to the group, an audit of the component's financial information is performed. When the component is likely to include significant risks, the component's financial information is either audited; relevant financial accounts balances, classes of transactions or disclosures are audited; or specified audit procedures relating to the significant risks are applied. An audit of the financial information of a component uses component materiality that will be lower than the materiality for the group financial statements as a whole. For not significant components the group engagement team performs analytical procedures at group level. For any component, irrespective of its significance, additional work may be performed to obtain sufficient appropriate evidence, draw conclusions and form an opinion on the group financial statements.

The group engagement team is involved when component auditors perform work on its behalf on the financial information of the components. When a component auditor performs an audit of the financial information of a significant component, the group engagement team should be involved in the risk assessment process. The group engagement team may be involved in further audit procedures, in particular when significant risks have been identified in the component on which the component auditor performs work.

When the group engagement team plans to request a component auditor to perform work on the financial information of a component, the group engagement team should obtain an understanding of the following:

1   Whether the component auditor understands and will comply with the ethical requirements that are relevant to the group audit and, in particular, is independent.
2   The component auditor's professional competence.
3   Whether the group engagement team will be able to be involved in the work of the component auditor to the extent necessary to obtain sufficient appropriate audit evidence.
4   Whether the component auditor operates in a regulatory environment that actively oversees auditors (ISA 600, para. 19).

The engagement team establishes the overall group audit strategy and develops a group audit plan, including when appropriate determines component materiality. The group engagement team communicates with the component auditor, ordinarily in a *letter of instructions*, on matters such as the work to be performed, the use to be made of that work, and the form and content of the communication process between the parties. A component auditor's *confirmation letter* is often obtained to confirm the parties' common understanding, including of the work performed by the component auditor and its use for the group audit. The group engagement team communicates with group management and those charged with governance of the group on matters such as identified deficiencies in internal control and fraud. The communication with those charged with governance also includes matters related to the nature and the work of the component auditors as well as any limitations on the group audit.

If the group engagement team is unable to obtain sufficient appropriate evidence on a component, the group engagement partner should consider the implications for the group audit opinion. For example, such inability may relate to limitations of access to financial information, management and the auditor of a foreign associate significant to the group, resulting in a qualified group audit opinion.

Practice Insight 5.3

Refer back to Exhibit 2–2, the Parmalat scandal. In 1999 the Italian unit of Deloitte & Touche replaced the Italian arm of Grant Thornton as Parmalat's principal auditor. Grant Thornton, however, continued to audit Parmalat subsidiaries, including the subsidiary Bonlat where the scandal began. The dairy group's 2002 financial statements disclosed that Grant Thornton did audit work on 49 per cent of its assets. Deloitte & Touche was relying heavily on Grant Thornton's report, which accepted a confirmation letter, seemingly from Bank of America, confirming that Bonlat held €3.95 billion in cash and investment in an account at the bank.

🔒 Key Terms

Analytical procedures. Evaluations of financial information through analysis of plausible relationships among both financial and non-financial data. Analytical procedures encompass such investigation as is necessary of identified fluctuations or relationships that are inconsistent with other relevant information or that differ from expected values by a significant amount.

Arm's length (transaction). A transaction conducted on such terms and conditions as between a willing buyer and a willing seller who are unrelated and are acting independently of each other and pursuing their own best interests.

Audit plan. Converts the overall audit strategy into a more detailed plan, and includes the nature, timing and extent of audit procedures to be performed.

Audit procedures. Specific acts performed as the auditor gathers evidence to determine if specific audit assertions are being met.

Auditor's expert. An individual or organization possessing expertise in a field other than accounting or auditing, whose work in that field is used by the auditor to assist the auditor in obtaining sufficient appropriate audit evidence.

Component. An entity or business activity for which group or component management prepares financial information that should be included in the group financial statements.

Component auditor. An auditor who, at the request of the group engagement team, performs work on financial information related to a component for the group audit.

Dual-purpose tests. Tests of transactions that both evaluate the effectiveness of controls and detect monetary errors.

Engagement letter. A letter that formalizes the contract between the auditor and the client, and outlines the responsibilities of both parties.

Engagement partner. The partner or other person in the firm who is responsible for the engagement and its performance, and for the report that is issued on behalf of the firm, and who, where required, has the appropriate authority from a professional, legal or regulatory body.

Governance. Describes the role of persons entrusted with the supervision, control and direction of an entity.

Group engagement team. Partners, including the group engagement partner, and staff who establish the overall group audit strategy, communicate with component auditors, perform work on the consolidation process, and evaluate the conclusions drawn from the audit evidence as the basis for forming an opinion on the group financial statements.

Internal audit function. An appraisal activity established or provided as a service to the entity. Its functions include, among other things, examining, evaluating and monitoring the adequacy and effectiveness of internal control.

Internal auditors. Those individuals who perform the activities of the internal audit function. Internal auditors may belong to an internal audit department or equivalent function.

Management. The person(s) who have executive responsibility for the conduct of the entity's operations, including preparing the financial statements, overseen by those charged with governance.

Non-compliance acts (illegal acts). Acts of omission or commission by the entity, either intentional or unintentional, which are contrary to the prevailing laws or regulations.

Overall audit strategy. The auditor's plan for the expected conduct, organization and staffing of the audit. Sets the scope, timing and direction of the audit, and guides the development of the more detailed audit plan.

Planning. Involves establishing the overall audit strategy for the engagement and developing an audit plan.

Substantive procedures. Audit procedures performed to detect material misstatements at the assertion level, and including substantive analytical procedures and tests of details of classes of transactions, account balances, and disclosures.

Test. The application of procedures to some or all items in a population.

Tests of controls. Audit procedures performed to obtain audit evidence about the operating effectiveness of controls in preventing, or detecting and correcting, material misstatements at the assertion level.

Tests of details of account balances and disclosures. Substantive tests that concentrate on the details of items contained in the account balance and disclosure.

Tests of details of transactions (substantive tests of transactions). Tests to detect errors or fraud in individual transactions.

Those charged with governance. Those persons or person with responsibility for overseeing the strategic direction of the entity and obligations related to the accountability of the entity, including overseeing the financial reporting process.

? Review Questions

LO1	5–1	What types of inquiries about a prospective client should an auditor make to third parties?
LO1	5–2	What type of information should be requested by the successor auditor from the predecessor auditor?
LO2,3	5–3	What is the purpose of an engagement letter? List the important information that the engagement letter should contain.
LO4	5–4	What factors should an external auditor use to assess the competence and objectivity of internal auditors?
LO5	5–5	Who are those charged with governance, and what are their responsibilities?
LO6,7	5–6	List the matters an auditor should consider when developing an audit plan.
LO7	5–7	List five circumstances that may indicate that a non-compliance with laws or regulations (illegal act) may have occurred.
LO7	5–8	List three audit procedures that may be used to identify transactions with related parties.
LO8	5–9	What are the three general types of audit tests? Define each type of audit test and give two examples of each.
LO9	5–10	What are the purposes for using preliminary analytical procedures?
LO9	5–11	When discussing the use of analytical procedures, what is meant by the 'precision of the expectation'? In applying this notion to an analytical procedure, how might an auditor calculate a tolerable difference?
LO9	5–12	Significant differences between the auditor's expectation and the client's book value require explanation through quantification, corroboration and evaluation. Explain each of these terms.
LO10	5–13	Why does the 'audit testing hierarchy' begin with tests of controls and substantive analytical procedures?
LO10	5–14	Consider the 'assurance bucket' analogy. Why are some of the buckets larger than others for particular assertions or accounts?
LO11	5–15	List and discuss the four categories of financial ratios that are presented in the chapter.

✎ Problems

LO1,3	5–16	The audit committee of the board of directors of Unicorn Corporation asked Tish & Field, independent auditors, to audit Unicorn's financial statements for the year ended 31 December 2009. Tish & Field explained the need to make an inquiry of the predecessor auditor and requested permission to do so. Unicorn's management agreed and authorized the predecessor auditor to respond fully to Tish & Field's inquiries.

Required:

a What information should Tish & Field obtain during its inquiry of the predecessor auditor prior to accepting the engagement?

b What other audit procedures should Tish & Field perform in evaluating Unicorn as a potential client?

c After a satisfactory communication with the predecessor auditor, Tish & Field drafted an engagement letter that was mailed to the audit committee of the board of directors of Unicorn Corporation. The engagement letter clearly set forth the arrangements concerning the involvement of the predecessor auditor and other matters. What other matters would Tish & Field generally have included in the engagement letter?

(AICPA, adapted)

LO2,6,7   **5–17**   Parker is the in-charge auditor for the upcoming annual audit of FGH Company, a continuing audit client. Parker will supervise two assistants on the engagement and will visit the client before the fieldwork begins.

Parker has completed the engagement letter and established an understanding with the Chief Internal Auditor on the assistance to be provided by the internal audit function.

Required:

List the preliminary engagement and planning activities that Parker needs to complete.

(AICPA, adapted)

LO2,3   **5–18**   An independent auditor has been asked to audit the financial statements of a new client. All preliminary verbal discussions and inquiries among the auditors, the company, the predecessor auditor and all other necessary parties have been completed. The auditor is now preparing an engagement letter.

Required:

a List the items that should be included in the typical engagement letter in these circumstances.

b Describe the benefits derived from preparing an engagement letter.

(AICPA, adapted)

LO5   **5–19**   The use of audit committees has become widespread. Independent auditors have become increasingly involved with audit committees, and consequently have become familiar with their nature and function.

Required:

a Describe what an audit committee is.

b Identify the reasons why audit committees have been formed and are currently in operation.

c Describe the functions of an audit committee.

(AICPA, adapted)

LO7,8   **5–20**   Exhibit 5–2 contains a partial audit plan for substantive tests of accounts receivable.

Required:

For audit procedures 1–4, identify the primary assertion being tested.

LO9   **5–21**   Analytical procedures consist of evaluations of financial information made by a study of plausible relationships among both financial and non-financial data. They range from simple comparisons to the use of complex models involving many relationships and elements of data. They compare recorded amounts, or ratios developed from recorded amounts, to expectations developed by the auditor.

Required:

a   Describe the purposes of analytical procedures.
b   Identify the sources of information from which an auditor develops expectations.
c   Describe the factors that influence an auditor's consideration of the reliability of data for the purpose of testing assertions.

(AICPA, adapted)

LO9   **5–22**   At 31 December 2009, EarthWear has €5,890,000 in a liability account labelled 'Reserve for returns'. The notes to the financial statements contain the following policy: 'At the time of sale, the company provides a reserve equal to the gross profit on projected merchandise returns, based on prior returns experience.' EarthWear has indicated that returns for sales that are six months old are negligible, and gross profit percentage for the year is 42.5 per cent. EarthWear has also provided the following information on sales for the last six months of the year:

Month	Monthly Sales (€000s)	Historical Return Rate
July	73,300	0.004
August	82,800	0.006
September	93,500	0.010
October	110,200	0.015
November	158,200	0.025
December	202,500	0.032

Required:

a   Using the information given, develop an expectation for the reserve for returns account. Because the rate of return varies based on the time that has passed since the date of sale, do not use an average historical return rate.
b   Determine a tolerable difference for your analytical procedure.
c   Compare your expectation to the book value and determine if it is greater than tolerable difference.
d   Independent of your answer to part c, what procedures should the auditor perform if the difference between the expectation and the book value is greater than tolerable difference?

LO9,11   **5–23**   Arthur, independent auditor, is auditing The Home Improvement Store as of 31 December 2010. As with all audit engagements, Arthur's initial procedures are to analyse the client's financial data by reviewing trends in significant ratios and comparing the company's performance with the industry so that he better understands the business and can determine where to concentrate his audit efforts. As part of Arthur's audit of The Home Improvement Store, he performed analytical procedures by calculating the following ratios and obtaining related industry data.

	The Home Improvement Store					Industry				
	2006	2007	2008	2009	2010	2006	2007	2008	2009	2010
Quick Ratio	0.67	0.73	1.38	0.45	0.29	0.79	0.81	0.87	0.91	1.08
Days of Inventory on Hand	62.73	75.15	82.40	84.02	80.52	82.26	79.89	86.86	84.13	75.04
Inventory/ Current Assets	53.48%	45.51%	48.42%	62.28%	80.81%	58.04%	56.44%	60.19%	60.92%	50.33%

Return on Assets	16.10%	9.75%	5.70%	2.16%	6.05%	6.98%	8.87%	7.05%	5.06%	11.73%
Debt to Equity	0.02	0.07	1.47	2.36	0.72	0.44	0.31	0.56	0.53	0.57

Required:

Compare The Home Improvement Store's ratios with those of its industry. You may want to reference Advanced Module 1 in this chapter for more information regarding the ratios used in the analytical procedure. For each ratio provided in the table above:

a *Indicate the potential risks the ratio and/or historical patterns may present.*
b *Indicate one or two plausible explanations for why The Home Improvement Store's ratios or historical patterns differ from those of the industry.*

Discussion Cases

LO7,8   5–24   Forestcrest Woollen Mills is a closely held company that has existed since 1920. The company manufactures high-quality woollen cloth for men's and women's outerwear. Your firm has audited Forestcrest for 15 years.

Five years ago, Forestcrest signed a consent decree with the Environmental Protection Agency. The company had been convicted of dumping pollutants (such as bleaching and dyeing chemicals) into the local river. The consent decree provided that Forestcrest construct a water treatment facility within eight years.

You are conducting the current year audit, and you notice that there has been virtually no activity in the water treatment facility construction account. Your discussion with the controller produces the following comment: 'Because of increased competition and lower sales volume, our cash flow has decreased below normal levels. You had better talk to the president about the treatment facility.'

The president (and majority shareholder) tells you the following: 'Given the current cash flow levels, we had two choices: lay off people or stop work on the facility. This is a rural area with few other job opportunities for our people. I decided to stop work on the water treatment facility. I don't think that the state will fine us or close us down.' When you ask the president if the company will be able to comply with the consent decree, he informs you that he is uncertain.

Required:

a *Discuss the implications of this situation for the audit and audit report.*
b *Would your answer change if these events occurred in the seventh year after the signing of the consent decree?*

LO9   5–25   The auditors for City Football Club are conducting their audit for the fiscal year ended 31 December 2009. Specifically, the audit firm is now focusing on the audit of revenue from October to December 2009 of home football games in the national league. While planning the audit of sales of football tickets, one of their newer staff people observed that, in prior years, many hours were spent auditing revenue. This staff associate pointed out that perhaps the firm could apply analytical procedures to evaluate whether it appears that the revenue account is properly stated.

The staff associate noted that information for a typical home game could be used to estimate revenues for the relevant period. October to December consisted of seven home games – one against the league's most merited team, Athletic, and six games against other opponents. One of these games is against United, the in-city arch-rival. All of these games were played during the day, except for the late evening game against Palace.

The auditors will base their estimate on the game played against Rovers. This game is considered to be an average home game for City. The following information concerning that game is available:

Total attendance   24,000 (stadium capacity is 40,000)

This attendance figure includes the 500 free seats described below, and the 24,000 figure should be used as a basis for all further calculations.

Ticket prices
Box seats   €12 per ticket
End-zone seats   8 per ticket
Upper-deck seats   5 per ticket

At the game against Rovers, total attendance was allocated among the different seats as follows:

Box seats   70%
End-zone seats   20%
Upper-deck seats   10%

Based on information obtained in prior-year audits, the following assumptions are made to assist in estimating revenue for the other games:

● Attendance for the Athletic game was expected to be 30 per cent higher than total attendance for an average game, with the mix of seats purchased expected to be the same as for a regular game; however, tickets are priced 20 per cent higher than for a normal game.
● The game against United was expected to draw 20 per cent more fans than a normal game, with 75 per cent of these extra fans buying box seats and the other 25 per cent purchasing upper-deck seats.
● To make up for extra costs associated with the late-evening game, ticket prices were increased by 10 per cent each; however, attendance was also expected to be 5 per cent lower than for a normal game, with each type of seating suffering a 5 per cent decline.
● At every game 500 box seats are given away free to players' family and friends. This number is expected to be the same for all home games.

Required:

1   *Based on the information above, develop an expectation for ticket revenue for the seven home football games.*
2   *Reported ticket revenue was €2,200,000. Is the difference between your estimate and reported ticket revenue large enough to prompt further consideration? Why or why not? If further consideration is warranted, provide possible explanations for the difference between estimated and actual football ticket revenue. What evidence could you gather to verify each of your explanations?*
3   *Under what conditions are substantive analytical procedures likely to be effective in a situation such as that described in this problem?*

ⓘ Internet Assignments

LO4	**5–26**	Visit the Institute of Internal Auditors (IIA) home page (www.theiia.org) and familiarize yourself with the information contained there. Search the site for information about the IIA's requirements for the objectivity and independence of internal auditors.
LO7	**5–27**	EarthWear Clothiers makes high-quality clothing for outdoor sports. It sells most of its products through mail order. Use the Internet to obtain information about the retail mail-order industry.

Notes

i　E.A. Gordon, E. Henry, T.J. Louwers and B.J. Reed, 'Auditing Related Party Transactions: A Literature Overview and Research Synthesis', *Accounting Horizons* (March 2007), pp. 81–102, for a review a research on related parties.

ii　A. Eilifsen and W.F. Messier, Jr (2000), 'Auditor Detection of Misstatements: A Review and Integration of Empirical Research', *Journal of Accounting Literature* (19), pp. 1–43, reviews the audit research on this issue.

iii　See A.D. Bailey, Jr, *Statistical Auditing: Review, Concepts, and Problems*, Harcourt Brace Jovanovich, New York, 1981, Chapter 10, for a detailed discussion of regression analysis applied to auditing.

iv　See W.R. Kinney, Jr, 'Attention-Directing Analytical Review Using Accounting Ratios: A Case Study', *Auditing: A Journal of Practice and Theory* (Spring 1987), pp. 59–73, for a discussion of this limitation of analytical procedures.

CHAPTER 6

Internal Control in a Financial Statement Audit

❖ LEARNING OBJECTIVES

Upon completion of this chapter you will

- ❖ **LO1** Understand the importance of internal control to management and auditors.
- ❖ **LO2** Know the definition of internal control.
- ❖ **LO3** Know what controls are relevant to the audit.
- ❖ **LO4** Understand the effect of information technology on internal control.
- ❖ **LO5** Be familiar with the components of internal control.
- ❖ **LO6** Understand how to plan an audit strategy.
- ❖ **LO7** Know how to develop an understanding of an entity's internal control.
- ❖ **LO8** Be familiar with the tools available for documenting the understanding of internal control.
- ❖ **LO9** Know how to assess the level of control risk.

- ❖ **LO10** Know the types of tests of controls.
- ❖ **LO11** Understand audit strategies for the nature, timing and extent of substantive procedures based on different levels of detection risk.
- ❖ **LO12** Understand the considerations for the timing of audit procedures.
- ❖ **LO13** Be familiar with how to assess control risk when an entity's accounting transactions are processed by a service organization.
- ❖ **LO14** Understand the auditor's communication of deficiencies in internal control.
- ❖ **LO15** Be familiar with and understand general and application controls.
- ❖ **LO16** Be familiar with computer-assisted audit techniques.
- ❖ **LO17** Understand how to flowchart a business process.

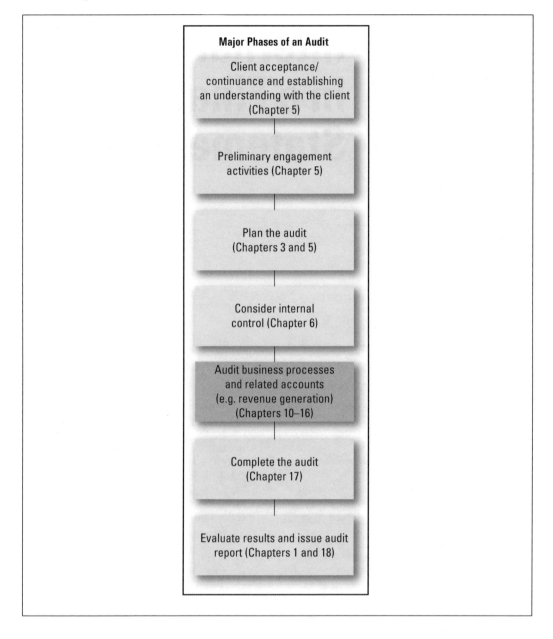

❖ RELEVANT ACCOUNTING AND AUDITING PRONOUNCEMENTS

COSO, Internal Control – Integrated Framework, 1992

COSO, Enterprise Risk Management – Integrated Framework, 2004

COSO, Internal Control over Financial Reporting – Guidance for Smaller Public Companies, 2006

COSO, Guidance on Monitoring Internal Control Systems, 2009

ISA 230, Audit Documentation

ISA 240, The Auditor's Responsibilities Relating to Fraud in an Audit of Financial Statements

ISA 260, Communication with Those Charged with Governance

ISA 265, Communicating Deficiencies in Internal Control to Those Charged with Governance and Management

ISA 300, Planning an Audit of Financial Statements

ISA 315, Identifying and Assessing the Risks of Material Misstatement through Understanding the Entity and Its Environment

ISA 320, Materiality in Planning and Performing an Audit

ISA 330, The Auditor's Responses to Assessed Risks

ISA 402, Audit Considerations Relating to an Entity Using a Service Organization

ISA 450, Evaluation of Misstatements Identified during the Audit

ISA 500, Audit Evidence

ISA 520, Analytical Procedures

ISA 620, Using the Work of an Auditor's Expert

IN CHAPTER 3, we noted that a major part of the auditor's understanding of the entity and its environment involves knowledge about the entity's internal control. In Chapter 5, we introduced you to the concepts of the assurance testing hierarchy and the 'assurance bucket', which indicate that the auditor typically obtains assurance from tests of controls before substantive procedures. This chapter provides detailed coverage of the auditor's assessment of **control risk**. It addresses the importance of internal control and its components, as well as how evaluating internal control relates to substantive testing. The chapter covers the COSO (Committee of Sponsoring Organizations of the Treadway Commission) framework and how the auditor's consideration of a client's internal control impacts the financial statement audit. This chapter also discusses the timing of audit procedures, service organizations and the required communications of deficiencies in internal control. Finally, the chapter offers *Advanced Modules* on: (1) types of controls in an IT environment; (2) computer-assisted audit techniques; and (3) flowcharting techniques.

❖ INTRODUCTION

LO1

Internal control plays an important role in how management meets its stewardship or agency responsibilities. Management has the responsibility to maintain controls that provide reasonable assurance that adequate control exists over the entity's assets and records. Strong internal control ensures that assets and records are properly safeguarded. Management also needs a control system that generates reliable information for decision making. If the information system does not generate reliable information, management may be unable to make informed decisions about issues such as product pricing, cost of production and profit information.

The auditor needs assurance about the reliability of the data generated by the information system in terms of how it affects the fairness of the financial statements and how well the assets and records of the entity are safeguarded. The auditor uses risk assessment procedures to obtain an understanding of the entity's internal control. The auditor uses this understanding of internal control to identify the types of potential misstatements, ascertain factors that affect the risk of material misstatement, and design tests of controls and substantive procedures. As we discussed previously, there is an inverse relationship between the reliability of internal control and the amount of substantive evidence required of the auditor. In other words, when the auditor is filling the assurance bucket for an assertion (see Chapter 5, Fig. 5–5), obtaining more controls evidence means he or she needs to obtain less substantive evidence to top it up.

As we shall see in this chapter, the auditor's understanding of internal control is a major factor in determining the overall audit strategy. After providing an overview of internal control and the COSO framework, we discuss the auditor's responsibilities for internal control under two major topics: (1) obtaining an understanding of internal control; and (2) assessing control risk.

INTERNAL CONTROL: AN OVERVIEW

Definition of Internal Control

LO2

According to COSO's *Internal Control – Integrated Framework*, internal control is designed and effected by those charged with governance in the entity (e.g. an entity's board of directors or audit committee), management and other personnel to provide *reasonable assurance* about the achievement of the entity's objectives in the following categories: (1) reliability of financial reporting; (2) effectiveness and efficiency of operations; and (3) compliance with applicable laws and regulations. Auditing standards refer to this definition.

Internal control over the safeguarding of assets against unauthorized acquisition, use or disposition is also important, and may include controls relating to financial reporting and operations objectives.

Controls Relevant to the Audit

LO3

While an entity's internal controls address objectives in each category, not all of these objectives and their related internal controls are relevant to a financial statement audit. Generally, internal controls pertaining to the preparation of financial statements for external purposes are relevant. Controls relating to operations and compliance objectives may be relevant when they relate to data the auditor uses to apply auditing procedures. For example, the internal controls that relate to operating statistics may be utilized by the auditor as data for analytical procedures. On the other hand, some controls that relate to management's planning or operating decisions may not be relevant. In summary, the controls relevant to the audit are those that are likely to prevent, or detect and correct, material misstatements in the financial statement assertions.

The Effect of Information Technology on Internal Control

LO4

The extent of an entity's use of information technology (IT) can affect internal control. The use of IT affects the way that transactions are initiated, authorized, recorded, processed and reported.

Controls in most information systems consist of a combination of manual controls and automated controls. In such systems, manual controls may be independent of, or dependent on, IT. Manual controls may also use information produced by IT, or they may be limited to monitoring the functioning of IT and automated controls and to handling exceptions. An entity's mix of manual and automated controls varies with the nature and complexity of the entity's use of IT.

Table 6–1 lists the benefits and risks of using IT for an entity's internal control. The risks to internal control vary depending on the nature and characteristics of the entity's information system. For example, where multiple users may access a common database, a lack of control at a single user entry point may compromise the security of the entire database. This may result in improper changes to or destruction of data. When IT personnel or users are given, or can gain, access beyond that necessary to perform their assigned duties, a breakdown in segregation of duties can occur. This may result in unauthorized transactions or changes to programs or data.

Table 6–1 Potential Benefits and Risks to an Entity's Internal Control from IT

Benefits
- Consistent application of predefined business rules and performance of complex calculations in processing large volumes of transactions or data.
- Enhancement of the timeliness, availability and accuracy of information.
- Facilitation of additional analysis of information.
- Enhancement of the ability to monitor the performance of the entity's activities and its policies and procedures.
- Reduction in the risk that controls will be circumvented.
- Enhancement of the ability to achieve effective segregation of duties by implementing security controls in applications, databases and operating systems.

Risks
- Reliance on systems or programs that inaccurately process data, process inaccurate data, or both.
- Unauthorized access to data that may result in destruction of data or improper changes to data, including the recording of unauthorized or non-existent transactions or inaccurate recording of transactions.
- Unauthorized changes to data in master files.
- Unauthorized changes to systems or programs.
- Failure to make necessary changes to systems or programs.
- Inappropriate manual intervention.
- Potential loss of data.

Practice Insight 6.1

A common challenge that increases control risk is the fact that many clients have a large variety of technological platforms, software and hardware. Companies that have grown through merger and acquisition frequently band the legacy systems together rather than replace one or both systems. The resulting montage of servers, computers, off-the-shelf and custom-programmed software, and so on, creates a complex and potentially risk-prone **IT environment**.

THE COSO FRAMEWORK

Components of Internal Control

LO5 Internal control as defined by the COSO framework consists of five components:

1 The control environment.
2 The entity's risk assessment process.
3 The information system and related business processes relevant to financial reporting and communication.
4 Control activities.
5 Monitoring of controls.

Table 6–2 defines each of the components, while Figure 6–1 shows how the categories of objectives of internal control, including safeguarding of assets, relate to the five components. You can see that each of the five components impacts each of the objectives. However, as mentioned above, the auditor is mainly concerned with how the five components affect the financial reporting objective. In terms of safeguarding assets, the auditor is generally concerned with controls that are relevant to the reliability of financial reporting. For example, access controls, such as passwords, that limit access to data and programs that process transactions may be relevant to the audit.

Table 6–2 Components of Internal Control

Control environment. The control environment sets the tone of an organization, influencing the control consciousness of its people. It is the foundation for effective internal control, providing discipline and structure. The control environment includes the attitudes, awareness, policies and actions of management and those charged with governance concerning the entity's internal control and its importance in the entity.

The entity's risk assessment process. The process for identifying and responding to business risks and the results thereof. For financial reporting purposes, the entity's risk assessment process includes how management identifies risks relevant to the preparation of financial statements that are fairly presented in accordance with the applicable financial reporting framework, estimates their significance, assesses the likelihood of their occurrence and decides upon actions to manage them.

The entity's information system and related business processes relevant to financial reporting and communication. The information system relevant to financial reporting objectives, which includes the accounting system, consists of the procedures, whether automated or manual, and records established to initiate, authorize, record, process and report entity transactions, and to maintain accountability for the related assets, liabilities and equity. Communication involves providing an understanding of individual roles and responsibilities pertaining to internal control over financial reporting.

Control activities. Control activities are the policies and procedures that help ensure that management directives are carried out, for example that necessary actions are taken to address risks to achievement of the entity's objectives. Control activities, whether automated or manual, have various objectives and are applied at various organizational and functional levels.

Monitoring of controls. A process to assess the quality of internal control performance over time. It involves assessing the design and operation of controls on a timely basis and taking necessary corrective actions.

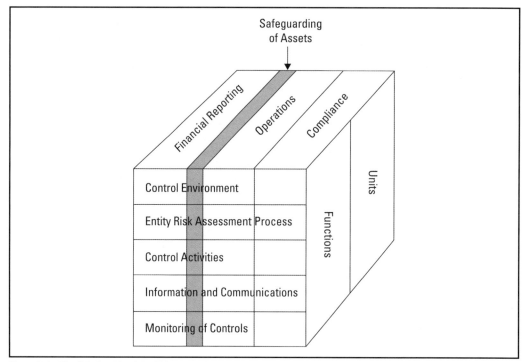

Figure 6–1   The Relationship of the Objectives of Internal Control to the Five Components of Internal Control

Control Environment

The **control environment** sets the tone of an organization, influencing the control consciousness of its people. It is the foundation for all other components of internal control, providing discipline and structure.

The importance of control to an entity is reflected in the overall attitude to, awareness of and actions of those charged with governance, management and owners regarding control. The control environment can be thought of as an umbrella that covers the entire entity, and establishes the framework for implementing the entity's accounting systems and internal controls. Factors that affect the control environment are shown in Table 6–3.

Table 6–3 Factors Affecting the Control Environment
• Communication and enforcement of integrity and ethical values.
• A commitment to competence.
• Participation by those charged with governance.
• Management's philosophy and operating style.
• Organizational structure.
• Assignment of authority and responsibility.
• Human resource policies and practices.

Communication and Enforcement of Integrity and Ethical Values

The effectiveness of an entity's internal controls is influenced by the integrity and ethical values of the individuals who create, administer and monitor the controls. An entity needs to establish ethical and behavioural standards that are communicated to employees and are reinforced by day-to-day practice. For example, management should remove incentives or opportunities that might lead personnel to engage in dishonest, illegal or unethical acts. Some examples of incentives that may lead to unethical behaviour are pressures to meet unrealistic performance targets, and performance-dependent rewards. Examples of opportunities include an ineffective board of directors, a weak internal audit function and insignificant penalties for improper behaviour. Management can best communicate integrity and ethical behaviour within an entity by example and through the use of policy statements, codes of conduct and training.

A Commitment to Competence

Competence is the knowledge and skills necessary to accomplish the tasks that define an individual's job. Management must specify the competence level for a particular job and translate it into the required level of knowledge and skills. For example, an entity should have a formal or informal job description for each job. Management then must hire employees who have the appropriate competence for their jobs. Good human resource policies (discussed later in this section) help to attract and retain competent and trustworthy employees.

Participation by Those Charged with Governance[i]

Those charged with governance, such as the board of directors, the supervisory board and the audit committee, significantly influence the control consciousness of the entity. Those charged with governance must take their fiduciary responsibilities seriously and actively oversee the entity's accounting and reporting policies and procedures. Factors that affect the effectiveness of those charged with governance include the following:

- Its independence from management.
- The experience and stature of its members.
- The extent of its involvement with and scrutiny of the entity's activities.
- The appropriateness of its actions.
- The information it receives.
- The degree to which difficult questions are raised and pursued with management.
- Its interaction with the internal and external auditors.

Management's Philosophy and Operating Style

Establishing, maintaining and monitoring the entity's internal controls are management's responsibility. Management's philosophy and operating style can significantly affect the quality of internal control. Characteristics that may signal important information to the auditor about management's philosophy and operating style include the following:

- Management's approach to taking and monitoring business risks.
- Management's attitudes and actions towards financial reporting (conservative or aggressive accounting policies, and the conscientiousness and conservatism with which **accounting estimates** are developed).
- Management's attitudes towards information processing and accounting functions and personnel.

Organizational Structure

The organizational structure defines how authority and responsibility are delegated and monitored. It provides the framework within which an entity's activities for achieving entitywide objectives are planned, executed, controlled and reviewed. An entity develops an organizational structure suited to its needs. Establishing a relevant organizational structure includes considering key areas of authority and responsibility and appropriate lines of reporting.

The appropriateness of an entity's organizational structure depends on its size and the nature of its activities. Factors such as the level of technology in the entity's industry and external influences such as regulation play a major role in the type of organizational structure used. For example, an entity in a high-technology industry may need an organizational structure that can respond quickly to technological changes in the marketplace. Similarly, an entity that operates in a highly regulated industry, such as banking, may be required to maintain a very tightly controlled organizational structure in order to comply with laws and regulations.

Assignment of Authority and Responsibility

This control environment factor includes how authority and responsibility for operating activities are assigned, and how reporting relationships and authorization hierarchies are established. It includes policies regarding acceptable business practices, knowledge and experience of key personnel, and resources provided for carrying out duties. It also includes policies and communications directed at ensuring that all personnel understand the entity's objectives, know how their individual actions interrelate and contribute to those objectives, and recognize how and for what they will be held accountable.

An entity can use a number of controls to meet the requirements of this control environment factor. For example, the entity can have a well-specified organizational chart that indicates lines of authority and responsibility. Further, management and supervisory personnel should have job descriptions that include their control-related responsibilities.

Human Resource Policies and Procedures

The quality of internal control is a direct function of the quality of the personnel operating the system. The entity should have sound personnel policies for hiring, orienting, training, evaluating, counselling, promoting, compensating and taking remedial action. For example, in hiring employees, standards that emphasize seeking the most qualified individuals, with emphasis on educational background, prior work experience, and evidence of integrity and ethical behaviour, demonstrate an entity's commitment to employing competent and trustworthy people. Research into the causes of errors in accounting systems has shown personnel-related issues to be a major cause of error.[ii]

The Entity's Risk Assessment Process

An **entity's risk assessment process** is its process for identifying and responding to business risks. This process includes how management identifies risks relevant to the preparation of financial statements, estimates their significance, assesses the likelihood of their occurrence and decides upon actions to manage them. For example, the entity's risk assessment process may address how the entity identifies and analyses significant estimates recorded in the financial statements.

This risk assessment process should consider external and internal events and circumstances that may arise and adversely affect the entity's ability to initiate, authorize, record, process and report financial data consistent with the assertions of management in the financial statements. Once risks have been identified, management should consider their significance, the likelihood of their occurrence and how they should be managed. Management should initiate plans, programmes or actions to address specific risks. In some instances, management may accept the consequences of a possible risk because of the costs to remediate or other considerations. Client business risks can arise or change due to the following circumstances:

- *Changes in the operating environment.* Changes in the regulatory or operating environment can alter competitive pressures and create significantly different risks.
- *New personnel.* New personnel may have a different focus on or understanding of internal control.
- *New or revamped information systems.* Significant and rapid changes in information systems can change the risk relating to internal control.
- *Rapid growth.* Significant and rapid expansion of operations can strain controls and increase the risk of a breakdown of controls.
- *New technology.* Incorporating new technologies into production processes or information systems may change the risk associated with internal control.
- *New business models, products, or activities.* Entering business areas or transactions with which an entity has little experience may introduce new risk associated with internal control.
- *Corporate restructurings.* Restructuring may be accompanied by staff reductions and changes in supervision and segregation of duties that may change the risk associated with internal control.
- *Expanded international operations.* The expansion or acquisition of international operations carries new and often unique risks that may impact internal control.
- *New accounting pronouncements.* Adopting new accounting policies or changing accounting policies may affect the risk involved in preparing financial statements.

Information Systems and Communication

An information system consists of infrastructure (physical and hardware components), software, people, procedures (manual and automated) and data. The **information system relevant to the financial reporting** objective includes the accounting system, and consists of procedures (whether automated or manual) and records established to initiate, authorize, record, process and report an entity's transactions, and to maintain accountability for the related assets and liabilities. An effective accounting system gives appropriate consideration to establishing methods and records that will:

● Identify and record all valid transactions.
● Describe on a timely basis the transactions in sufficient detail to permit proper classification of transactions for financial reporting.
● Measure the value of transactions in a manner that permits recording their proper monetary value in the financial statements.
● Determine the time period in which transactions occurred to permit recording of transactions in the proper accounting period.
● Properly present the transactions and related disclosures in the financial statements.

Communication involves providing an understanding of individual roles and responsibilities pertaining to internal control over financial reporting. It includes the extent to which personnel understand how their activities in the financial reporting information system relate to the work of others and the means of reporting exceptions to an appropriate higher level within the entity. Policy manuals, accounting and reporting manuals, and memoranda communicate policies and procedures to the entity's personnel. Communications can also be made electronically, orally or through the actions of management.

Control Activities

Control activities are the policies and procedures that help ensure that management's directives are carried out and are implemented to address risks identified in the risk assessment process. Control activities include a range of activities, including approvals, authorizations, verifications, reconciliations, reviews of operating performance and segregation of duties. They occur throughout the organization, at all levels and in all functions. Control activities are commonly categorized into the following four types:

1 Performance reviews.
2 Information processing controls, including authorization and document-based controls.
3 Physical controls.
4 Segregation of duties.

Performance Reviews

A strong accounting system should have controls that independently check the performance of the individuals or processes in the system. For example, senior management should review actual performance versus budgets, forecasts, prior periods and competitors. Similarly, managers running functions or activities should review performance reports. For example, a manager responsible for a bank's consumer loans should review loan reports by type, checking summarizations and identifying trends, and relating results to economic statistics and targets. Lastly, persons within the entity should review and analyse the relationships among both financial and non-financial data (e.g. key performance indicators – KPIs), investigate any unusual items, and take corrective actions when necessary.

Information Processing Controls

These controls are performed to check accuracy, completeness and authorization of transactions. Data entered are subject to online edit checks or matching to approved control files. For example, a customer's order is accepted only after reference to an approved customer file and credit limit. In addition, development of new systems and changes to existing ones are controlled, as is access to data, files and programs. The two broad categories of information systems control activities are general controls and application controls. **General controls** relate to the overall information processing environment and include controls over data centre and network operations; system software acquisition, change and maintenance; access security; and application system acquisition, development and maintenance. For example, an entity's controls for developing new programs for existing accounting systems should include adequate documentation and testing before implementation. **Application controls** apply to the processing of individual applications and help ensure the occurrence (validity), completeness and accuracy of transaction processing. General and application controls are covered in more detail in *Advanced Module 1* at the end of this chapter.

Physical Controls

These controls include the physical security of assets (e.g. equipment, inventories, securities, cash and other assets), and the periodic counting and comparison with amounts shown in control records.

Segregation of Duties

It is important for an entity to segregate the authorization of transactions, recording of transactions and custody of the related assets. Independent performance of each of these functions reduces the opportunity for any one person to be in a position to both perpetrate and conceal errors or fraud in the normal course of his or her duties. For example, if an employee receives payment from customers on account and has access to the accounts receivable subsidiary ledger, it is possible for that employee to misappropriate the cash and cover the shortage in the accounting records. Pause for a moment and consider: why is it important that different individuals perform the duties of authorization, recording and custody? What could happen, for example, if an individual were responsible for both the receipt of customer payments and their recording in the accounts receivable ledger?

Monitoring of Controls

This monitoring component has received increased attention in recent years. In 2009, COSO issued *Guidance on Monitoring Internal Control Systems*, an integral part of its framework. **Monitoring of controls** is a process that assesses the quality of internal control performance over time. To provide reasonable assurance that an entity's objectives will be achieved, management should monitor controls to determine whether they are operating effectively. Since risks change over time, management needs to monitor whether controls need to be redesigned when risks change. Figure 6–2 shows how monitoring applies to the other four components of internal control.

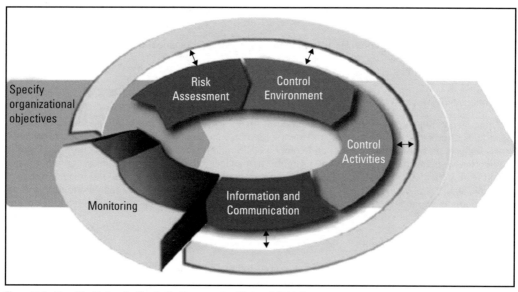

Figure 6–2   How Monitoring Applies to the Components of Internal Control
Source: COSO, *Guidance on Monitoring Internal Control Systems* (Vol. 1, page 4)

Effective monitoring involves: (1) establishing a baseline for control effectiveness; (2) designing and executing monitoring procedures that are based on the significance of business risks relative to the entity's objectives; and (3) assessing and reporting results including follow-up on corrective actions.

Monitoring can be done through ongoing activities or separate evaluations. Ongoing monitoring procedures are built into the normal, recurring activities of the entity, and include regular management and supervisory activities. Management can use internal auditors or personnel performing similar functions to monitor the operating effectiveness of internal control. For example, management might review whether bank reconciliations are being prepared on a timely basis and reviewed by the internal auditors. In many entities, the information system produces much of the information used in monitoring. If management assumes that data used for monitoring are accurate, errors may exist in the information, potentially leading management to incorrect conclusions. Take a moment to think about other examples of monitoring controls.

❖ PLANNING AN AUDIT STRATEGY

LO6

The audit risk model states that $AR = RMM \times DR$ where $RMM = IR \times CR$. In this definition, the auditor's assessment of RMM must consider the level of CR in applying the audit risk model. How the auditor determines the appropriate level of CR is described in the remainder of this chapter. Figure 6–3 presents a flowchart of the auditor's decision process when considering internal control. As we discussed in Chapter 3, the auditor must assess the risk of material misstatement (refer to Figure 3–1). The information gathered by performing risk assessment procedures is used to evaluate the *design* of controls and to determine whether the controls have been *implemented*. This is the first step in Figure 6–3. The auditor then documents this understanding of the internal controls. With a recurring engagement, the auditor is likely to possess substantial knowledge about the client's internal controls and may be able to choose an audit strategy after only updating the understanding of the entity's internal control. For a new client, the auditor may delay making a judgement about an audit strategy until a more detailed understanding of internal control is obtained.

The next step for the auditor is whether or not to rely on the controls. When the auditor's risk assessment procedures indicate that the controls are not properly designed or not implemented, the auditor will not rely on the controls. In this instance, the auditor will set control risk at maximum and use substantive procedures to reduce the risk of material misstatement to an acceptably low level (i.e. the assurance bucket is filled almost entirely with substantive evidence). When the auditor's risk assessment procedures suggest that the controls are properly designed and implemented, the auditor will probably rely on the controls. If the auditor intends to rely on the controls, tests of controls are required to be performed to obtain audit evidence that the controls are operating effectively. The auditor will make an assessment of control risk based on the results of the tests of controls.

To assist your comprehension of how the auditor uses the understanding and assessment of internal control to determine the nature, timing and extent of audit procedures, we describe only two audit strategies: a **substantive strategy** and a **reliance strategy**. However, keep in mind that there is no single strategy for the entire audit; rather the auditor establishes a strategy for individual business processes (such as revenue or purchasing) or by specific assertion (occurrence, completeness, and so on) within a business process. Furthermore, even when auditors follow a reliance strategy, the amount of assurance obtained by controls testing will vary from assertion to assertion. In other words, a reliance strategy just means the auditor intends to begin filling the assurance bucket with test of controls evidence, but the percentage of the bucket filled with controls evidence will differ between assertions and across accounts in the various business processes. Finally, it is important to understand that auditing standards require some substantive evidence for all significant accounts and assertions. Thus, a reliance strategy reduces but does not eliminate the need to gather some substantive evidence.

Practice Insight 6.2

In some situations the auditor may find it necessary to rely on evidence stored by the client in electronic form. In such situations a reliance strategy may be required due to the importance of controls in maintaining the integrity of the electronic evidence. Examples include the following:

- An entity that initiates orders using **electronic data interchange** (**EDI**) for goods based on predetermined decision rules and pays the related payables based on system-generated information regarding receipt of goods. No other documentation is produced or maintained.
- An entity that provides electronic services to customers, such as an Internet service provider or a telephone company, and uses IT to log services provided to users, initiate bills for the services, process the billing transactions, and automatically record such amounts in electronic accounting records.

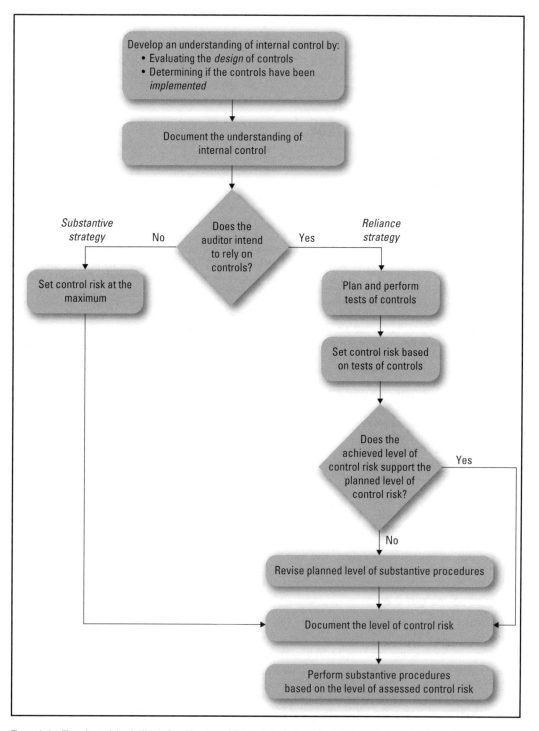

Figure 6–3   Flowchart of the Auditor's Consideration of Internal Control and its Relation to Substantive Procedures

Substantive Strategy

A substantive audit strategy means that the auditor has decided not to rely on the entity's controls and instead use substantive procedures as the main source of evidence about the assertions in the financial statements. As Figure 6–3 shows, a substantive strategy still requires the auditor to have a sufficient understanding of the client's internal controls to know whether they are properly designed and implemented. This knowledge includes an understanding of the five components of internal control.

The auditor may decide to follow a substantive strategy for some or all assertions because of one or all of the following factors:

- The implemented controls do not pertain to the assertion the auditor is considering.
- The implemented controls are assessed as ineffective.
- Testing the operating effectiveness of the controls would be inefficient.

The auditor next documents the level of control risk at the maximum. Finally, substantive procedures are designed and performed based on the assessment of a maximum level of control risk. Therefore, when the auditor follows a substantive strategy, the assurance bucket (refer to Fig. 5–5) is filled with some evidence from the risk assessment procedures and an extensive amount of evidence from substantive procedures (i.e. substantive analytical procedures and tests of details).

Auditing standards point out that the auditor needs to be satisfied that performing only substantive procedures would be effective in restricting detection risk to an acceptable level. For example, the auditor may determine that performing only substantive procedures would be effective and more efficient than performing tests of controls for an entity that has a limited number of long-term debt transactions because corroborating evidence can be obtained by examining the loan agreements and confirming relevant information.

Reliance Strategy

A reliance strategy means that the auditor intends to rely on the entity's controls. If a reliance strategy is followed, the auditor may need a more detailed understanding of internal control to develop a preliminary or 'planned' assessment of control risk. The auditor will then plan and perform tests of controls. The auditor uses the test results to assess the 'achieved' level of control risk. If test results indicate that achieved control risk is higher than planned, the auditor will normally increase the planned substantive procedures and document the revised control risk assessment. If the planned level of control risk is supported, no revisions of the planned substantive procedures are required. The level of control risk is documented, and substantive procedures are then performed. Keep in mind that there may be different degrees of control reliance for different business processes or assertions within a process.

From a practical standpoint, the level of control risk is normally set in terms of the assertions about classes of transactions and events for the period under audit. Table 6–4 presents the assertions related to transactions and events that were discussed in Chapter 4 and control activities that are normally in place for each assertion to protect against material misstatements. For example, the use and tracking of prenumbered documents is a control activity typically found in each business process to ensure occurrence and completeness. In a revenue process, accounting for prenumbered shipping documents provides reasonable assurance that all revenue is recorded (completeness). Similarly, reconciliation of the accounts receivable subledger to the general ledger accounts receivable account provides a control to help ensure that the occurrence assertion is met. Later chapters show these control activities for each business process.

Table 6–4 Assertions about Classes of Transactions and Events and Related Control Activities	
Assertion	*Control Activities*
Occurrence	Segregation of duties.
	Prenumbered documents that are accounted for.
	Daily or monthly reconciliation of subsidiary records with independent review.
Completeness	Prenumbered documents that are accounted for.
	Segregation of duties.
	Daily or monthly reconciliation of subsidiary records with independent review.
Accuracy	Internal verification of amounts and calculations.
	Monthly reconciliation of subsidiary records by an independent person.
Authorization	General and specific authorization of transactions at important control points.
Cut-off	Procedures for prompt recording of transactions.
	Internal review and verification.
Classification	Chart of accounts.
	Internal review and verification.

◆ OBTAIN AN UNDERSTANDING OF INTERNAL CONTROL

Overview

Auditing standards require the auditor to obtain an understanding of each of the five components of internal control in order to plan the audit. This understanding includes knowledge about the design of relevant controls and whether they have been placed in operation by the entity. The auditor uses this knowledge to:

- Identify the types of potential misstatement.
- Pinpoint the factors that affect the risk of material misstatement.
- Design tests of controls and substantive procedures.

In deciding on the nature and extent of the understanding of internal control needed for the audit, the auditor should consider the complexity and sophistication of the entity's operations and systems, including the extent to which the entity relies on manual controls or on automated controls. The auditor may determine that the engagement team needs an IT expert. In determining whether an IT expert is needed, the following factors should be considered:

- The complexity of the entity's IT systems and controls, and the manner in which they are used in conducting the entity's business.
- The significance of changes made to existing systems, or the implementation of new systems.
- The extent to which data are shared among systems.
- The extent of the entity's participation in **electronic commerce**.
- The entity's use of emerging technologies.
- The significance of audit evidence that is available only in electronic form.

The IT expert can be used to assist the engagement team in a number of ways. For example, the IT expert can inquire of the entity's IT personnel about how data and transactions are initiated, authorized, recorded, processed and reported, and how IT controls are designed; inspect systems documentation; observe the operation of IT controls; and plan and perform tests of IT controls. The auditor should have sufficient IT-related knowledge to communicate the assertions to the IT expert, to evaluate whether the specified procedures meet the auditor's objectives and to evaluate the results of the audit procedures completed by the IT expert.

To properly understand a client's internal control, an auditor must understand the five components of internal control. The auditor may use the following audit procedures to learn about internal control:

- Inquiry of appropriate management, supervisory and staff personnel.
- Inspection of entity documents and reports.
- Observation of entity activities and operations.

Understanding the Control Environment

The auditor should gain sufficient knowledge about the control environment to understand management's and those charged with governance's attitude, awareness and actions concerning the control environment, considering both the substance of controls and their collective effect. This includes knowledge of the factors contained in Table 6–3. Exhibit 6–1 presents a questionnaire that includes the type of information the auditor would document about EarthWear's control environment.[iii] Pause for a moment and review Exhibit 6–1. Do any possible control risks jump out at you from this questionnaire? Do you believe that any of the responses merit further inquiry? How would an auditor obtain this information?

Exhibit 6–1 Excerpt from a Questionnaire for Documenting the Auditor's Understanding of the Control Environment

CONTROL ENVIRONMENT QUESTIONNAIRE

Client: EarthWear Clothiers   Balance Sheet Date: 31/12/2009

Completed by: SAA Date: 30/9/09   Reviewed by: DRM Date: 15/10/09

COMMUNICATION AND ENFORCEMENT OF INTEGRITY AND ETHICAL VALUES

The effectiveness of controls cannot rise above the integrity and ethical values of the people who create, administer and monitor them. Integrity and ethical values are essential elements of the control environment, affecting the design, administration and monitoring of other components. Integrity and ethical behaviour are the product of the entity's ethical and behavioural standards, how they are communicated and how they are reinforced in practice.

	Yes, No, N/A	Comments
Have appropriate entity policies regarding matters as acceptable business practices, conflicts of interest and codes of conduct been established, and are they adequately communicated?	Yes	*The permanent work papers contain a copy of EarthWear's conflict-of-interest policy.*
Does management demonstrate the appropriate 'tone at the top', including explicit moral guidance about what is right or wrong?	Yes	*EarthWear's management maintains high moral and ethical standards and expects employees to act accordingly.*
Are everyday dealings with customers, suppliers, employees and other parties based on honesty and fairness?	Yes	*EarthWear's management maintains a high degree of integrity in dealing with customers, suppliers, employees and other parties; it requires employees and agents to act accordingly.*
Does management document or investigate deviations from established controls?	Yes	*To our knowledge, management has not attempted to override controls. Employees are encouraged to report attempts to bypass controls to appropriate individuals within the organization.*

COMMITMENT TO COMPETENCE

Competence is the knowledge and skills necessary to accomplish tasks that define the individual's job. Commitment to competence includes management's consideration of the competence levels for particular jobs and how those levels translate into requisite skills and knowledge.

Does the company maintain formal or informal job descriptions or other means of defining tasks that comprise particular jobs?	Yes	*EarthWear has formal written job descriptions for all supervisory personnel, and job duties for non-supervisory personnel are clearly communicated.*
Does management determine to an adequate extent the knowledge and skills needed to perform particular jobs?	Yes	*The job descriptions specify the knowledge and skills needed. The Human Resources Department uses this information in hiring, training and promotion decisions.*
Does evidence exist that employees have the requisite knowledge and skills to perform their job?	Yes	*Our prior experiences with EarthWear personnel indicate that they have the necessary knowledge and skills.*

Understanding the Entity's Risk Assessment Process

The auditor should obtain sufficient information about the entity's risk assessment process to understand how management considers risks relevant to financial reporting objectives and decides what to do to address those risks. For example, suppose a client operates in the oil industry, where there is always some risk of environmental damage. The auditor should obtain sufficient knowledge about how the client manages its environmental risks, because environmental accidents can result in costly litigation against the entity.

Understanding the Information System and Communications

The auditor should obtain sufficient knowledge of the information system to understand the following:

- The classes of transactions in the entity's operations that are significant to the financial statements.
- The procedures, both automated and manual, by which transactions are initiated, authorized, recorded, processed and reported from their occurrence to their inclusion in the financial statements.
- The related accounting records, whether electronic or manual, supporting information and specific accounts in the financial statements that are involved in initiating, authorizing, recording, processing and reporting transactions.
- How the information system captures other events and conditions that are significant to the financial statements.

● The financial reporting process used to prepare the entity's financial statements, including significant accounting estimates and disclosures.

The auditor must learn about each business process that affects significant account balances in the financial statements. This includes understanding how transactions are initiated and authorized, how documents and records are generated, and how the documents and records flow to the general ledger and financial statements. Understanding the information system also requires knowing how IT is used for data processing.

The auditor should understand the procedures used by the entity to prepare financial statements and related disclosures. Such procedures include:

● The procedures used to enter transaction totals into the general ledger.
● The procedures used to initiate, authorize, record and process journal entries in the general ledger.
● Other procedures used to record recurring and non-recurring adjustments to the financial statements.
● The procedures to combine and consolidate general ledger data.
● The procedures to prepare financial statements and disclosures.

In addition, the auditor should obtain sufficient knowledge of how the entity communicates financial reporting roles and responsibilities, and significant matters relating to financial reporting.

Understanding Control Activities

As the auditor learns about the other components of external control, he or she is also likely to obtain information about control activities. For example, in examining the information system that pertains to accounts receivable, the auditor is likely to see how the entity grants credit to customers.

The extent of the auditor's understanding of control activities is a function of the audit strategy adopted. When the auditor decides to follow a substantive strategy approach, little work is done on understanding control activities. When a reliance strategy is followed, the auditor has to understand the control activities that relate to assertions for which a lower level of control risk is expected. Auditors normally use walk-throughs to develop an understanding of control activities.

Understanding Monitoring of Controls

The auditor should obtain an understanding of the major types of activities that the entity uses to monitor internal control, including the sources of the information related to those activities, and how those activities are used to initiate corrective actions to its controls.

◆ Documenting the Understanding of Internal Control

LO8

Auditing standards require that the auditor documents the understanding of the entity's internal control components. A number of tools are available to the auditor for documenting the understanding of internal control. These include:

● The entity's procedures manuals and organizational charts.
● Narrative description.
● Internal control questionnaires.
● Flowcharts.

Procedures Manuals and Organizational Charts

Many organizations prepare procedures manuals that document the entity's policies and procedures. Portions of such manuals may include documentation of the accounting systems and related control activities. The entity's organizational chart presents the designated lines of authority and responsibility. Copies of both of these documents can help the auditor document his or her understanding of the internal control system.

Narrative Description

The understanding of internal control may be documented in a memorandum. This documentation approach is most appropriate when the entity has a simple internal control system.

Internal Control Questionnaires

Internal control questionnaires are one of many types of questionnaires used by auditors. Questionnaires provide a systematic means for the auditor to investigate areas such as internal control. An internal control questionnaire is generally used for entities with relatively complex internal control. It contains questions about the important factors or characteristics of the five internal control components. Exhibit 6–1 provides an example of the use of such questionnaires. The auditor's responses to the questions provide the documentation for his or her understanding.

Flowcharts

Flowcharts provide a diagrammatic representation, or 'picture', of the entity's accounting system. The flowchart outlines the configuration of the system in terms of functions, documents, processes and reports. This documentation facilitates an auditor's analysis of the system's strengths and weaknesses. Figure 6–4 presents a simple example of a flowchart for the order entry portion of a revenue process. *Advanced Module 3* to this chapter provides detailed coverage of flowcharting techniques. Flowcharts are used extensively in this book to represent accounting systems.

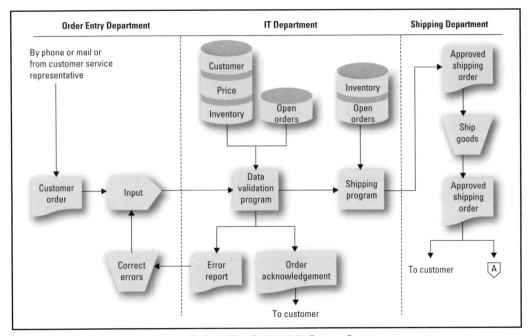

Figure 6–4 An Example of a Flowchart for the Order Entry Portion of the Revenue Process

On many engagements, auditors combine these tools to document their understanding of the components of internal control. The combination depends on the complexity of the entity's internal control system. For example, in a complex information system where a large volume of transactions occur electronically, the auditor may document the control environment, the entity's risk assessment process, and monitor activities using a memorandum and internal control questionnaire. Documentation of the information system and communication component, as well as control activities, may be accomplished through the use of an internal control questionnaire and a flowchart. For a small entity with a simple information system, documentation using a memorandum may be sufficient.

The Effect of Entity Size on Internal Control

The size of an entity may affect how the various components of internal control are implemented. While large entities may be able to implement the components in the fashion just described, small to mid-size entities may use alternative approaches and still achieve effective internal control. For example, a large entity may sometimes have a written code of ethics, while a small or mid-size entity may not. However, a small entity may achieve a similar objective by developing a culture that emphasizes integrity and ethical behaviour through oral communication and the example of the owner-manager.

While the basic concepts of the five components should be present in all entities, they are likely to be less formal in a small or mid-size entity than in a large entity. For example, in a small entity, the owner-manager's involvement in day-to-day activities can provide a highly effective control that identifies and monitors risks that may affect the entity. A small entity can also have effective communication channels due to its size, the fact that there are fewer levels in the organizational hierarchy, and management's greater visibility. The monitoring component can also be effective in a small to mid-size entity as a result of management's close involvement in operations. For example, the owner may review all daily cash disbursements to ensure that only authorized payments are made to vendors. By being involved in day-to-day operations, management may be better able to identify variances from expectations and inaccuracies in financial data.

The Limitations of an Entity's Internal Control

An internal control system should be designed and operated to provide reasonable assurance that an entity's objectives are being achieved. The concept of reasonable assurance recognizes that the cost of an entity's internal control system should not exceed the benefits that are expected to be derived. Balancing the cost of controls with the related benefits requires considerable estimation and judgement on the part of management. The effectiveness of any internal control system is subject to certain inherent limitations, including management override of internal control, personnel errors or mistakes, and collusion. For example, in a recent survey by PricewaterhouseCoopers (PwC) (see Fig. 6–5), 'insufficient controls' and 'able to use authority to override control' were two of the major corporate causes cited for why fraud occurred.

Management Override of Internal Control

In some cases, an entity's controls may be overridden by management. For example, a senior-level manager can require a lower-level employee to record entries in the accounting records that are not consistent with the substance of the transactions and that violate the entity's controls. The lower-level employee may record the transaction, even though he or she knows that it violates the entity's controls, out of fear of losing his or her job. In another example, management may enter into side agreements with customers that alter the terms and conditions of the entity's standard sales contract in ways that would preclude revenue recognition.

The auditor is particularly concerned when senior management is involved in such activities because it raises serious questions about management's integrity. Violations of control activities by senior management, however, are often particularly difficult to detect with normal audit procedures.

Human Errors or Mistakes

The internal control system is only as effective as the personnel who implement and perform the controls. Breakdowns in internal control can occur because of human failures such as simple errors or mistakes. For example, errors may occur in designing, maintaining or monitoring automated controls. If IT personnel do not completely understand how a revenue system processes sales transactions, they may erroneously design changes to the system to process sales for a new line of products.

Collusion

The effectiveness of segregation of duties lies in individuals performing only their assigned tasks or in the performance of one person being checked by another. There is always a risk that collusion between individuals will destroy the effectiveness of segregation of duties. For example, an individual who receives cash receipts from customers can collude with the one who records those receipts in the customers' records to steal cash from the entity.

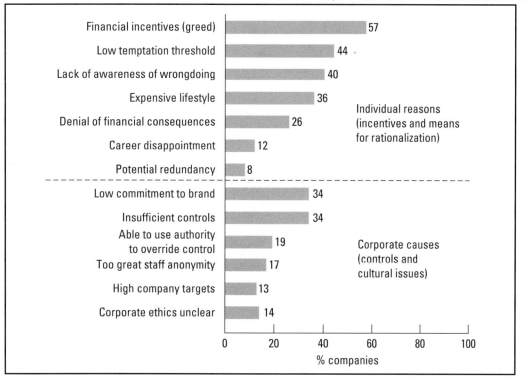

Figure 6–5   Reasons Cited by Companies for why Fraud Occurred
Source: PricewaterhouseCoopers, *Economic Crime: People, Culture And Controls.*
The 4ᵗʰ biennial Global Economic Crime Survey, 2007.

 ## ASSESSING CONTROL RISK

LO9

Assessing control risk is the process of evaluating the effectiveness of an entity's internal control in preventing, or detecting and correcting, material misstatements in the financial statements. As discussed earlier, the auditor can set control risk at the maximum (a substantive strategy) or at a lower level (a reliance strategy). As shown in Figure 6–3, when the auditor sets control risk at the maximum, he or she documents control risk assessment and performs substantive procedures. The discussion in this section focuses on the situation where the auditor plans to set control risk below the maximum (i.e. a reliance strategy). To set control risk below the maximum, the auditor must:

- Identify specific controls that will be relied upon.
- Perform tests of controls.
- Conclude on the achieved level of control risk.

Identifying Specific Controls that Will Be Relied Upon

The auditor's understanding of internal control is used to identify the controls that are likely to prevent, or detect and correct, material misstatements in specific assertions. In identifying controls to be relied upon, the auditor should consider that the controls could have a pervasive effect on many assertions. For example, the conclusion that an entity's control environment is highly effective may influence the auditor's decision about the number of an entity's locations at which auditing procedures are to be performed. Alternatively, some controls only affect an individual assertion contained in a financial statement account. For example, a credit check performed on a customer's order specifically related to the valuation assertion for the accounts receivable balance.

Advanced Module 1 at the end of the chapter provides a discussion of the types of general and application controls that should be considered by the auditor. General controls are pervasive to all information systems while application controls relate to a specific business process such as sales or purchasing. It is important to note that the reliability of application controls, especially those that are automated, are affected by the reliability of the general controls. For example, if there were no general controls over program changes, it would be possible for a programmer to make inappropriate changes to controls in an information system.

❖ Performing Tests of Controls

Tests of controls are audit procedures designed to evaluate the effectiveness of controls in preventing, or detecting and correcting, material misstatements at the relevant assertion level. Tests of controls are performed in order to provide evidence to support the lower level of control risk. Tests of controls directed towards the effectiveness of the design of a control are concerned with evaluating whether that control is suitably designed to prevent, or detect and correct, material misstatements. Tests of controls directed towards operating effectiveness are concerned with assessing how the control was applied, the consistency with which it was applied during the audit period, and by whom it was applied.

Procedures that are used for tests of controls are listed below, together with an example illustrating how the auditor might apply each:

Types of Tests of Controls	Examples
Inquiry of appropriate entity personnel.	Inquiry of credit manager about the policies for writing off uncollectible accounts.
Inspection of documents, reports or electronic files indicating the performance of the control.	Inspect bank reconciliations prepared by the internal auditors.
Observation of the application of the control.	Observe the application of controls surrounding the handling of cash to ensure that there is proper segregation of duties.
Reperformance of the application of the control by the auditor.	Reperform the authorization control used for granting credit.

A combination of these procedures may be necessary to evaluate the effectiveness of the design or operation of a control. For example, auditors perform walk-throughs of a client's business process (i.e. revenue) where they 'walk' a sales transaction from its origination (customer order) to its inclusion in the financial statements. While performing the walk-through, the auditor will inquire of, and observe, client personnel, and inspect relevant documents.

The operating effectiveness of the control can be affected by whether the control is performed manually or is automated. If the control is performed manually, it may be subject to human errors or mistakes in its application. If properly designed, automated controls should operate more consistently, and the auditor usually does not need to test as many instances of an automated control's operation because automated application controls should function consistently unless the program is changed. To test automated controls, the auditor may need to use techniques that are different from those used to test manual controls. For example, **computer-assisted audit techniques** (**CAATs**) may be used to test automated controls. The *Advanced Module 2* to this chapter offers a brief discussion of computer-assisted audit techniques.

Concluding on the Achieved Level of Control Risk

After the tests of controls have been completed, the auditor should reach a conclusion on the *achieved level of control risk*. The auditor uses the achieved level of control risk and the assessed level of inherent risk to assess the risk of material misstatement and to then determine the level of detection risk needed to bring audit risk to an acceptable low level. The level of detection risk is used to determine the nature, timing and extent of substantive tests.

Figure 6–3 shows the decision process followed by the auditor upon completing the planned tests of controls. If the tests of controls are consistent with the auditor's planned assessment of control risk, no revision in the nature, timing or extent of substantive procedures is necessary. On the other hand, if the tests of controls indicate that the controls are not operating as preliminarily assessed, this means that the achieved level of control risk is higher than the planned level, and the nature, timing and extent of planned substantive procedures will have to be modified.

Documenting the Achieved Level of Control Risk

The auditor should document the achieved level of control risk for the controls evaluated. The auditor's assessment of the level of control risk can be documented using a structured working paper, an internal control questionnaire or a memorandum.

An Example

Table 6–5 presents two account balances from EarthWear Clothiers' financial statements that differ in terms of their nature, size and complexity. The differences in these characteristics result in different levels of understanding of internal control and different control risk assessments. Before reading further, review Table 6–5 and its information. Why would an auditor decide to follow a substantive strategy for the prepaid advertising account but a reliance strategy for the inventory account?

Table 6–5 An Example of How Account Characteristics Affect the Auditor's Understanding of Internal Control, Control Risk Assessment and Planned Substantive Procedures				
EarthWear Account Balance	*Account Characteristics*	*Extent of Understanding Needed to Plan the Audit*	*Control Risk Assessment*	*Planned Substantive Procedures*
Inventory (€122,337,000)	• Material balance. • Numerous transactions from a large product base. • Significant inherent disk related to overstock and out-of-style products. • Complex computer processing.	• Entity control environment factors. • Risk assessment factors. • Monitoring activities. • Significant classes of transactions. • Inventory pricing policies. • Initiation, processing and recording of transactions. • Control activities to be relied upon.	• Control risk is assesed as *low* because tests of controls conducted on relevant controls in the purchasing and inventory cycles were consistent with the planned assessment of control risk.	Substantive procedures will include: • Physical examination of inventory. • Computer-assisted audit techniques to audit the inventory compilation.
Prepaid advertising (€11,458,000)	• Significant balance. • Few transactions. • Little or no inherent risk. • Simple accounting procedures.	• Entity control environmental factors. • Nature of the account balance. • Monitoring activities.	• Control risk is assessed at the *maximum* because there are few transactions and the procedures for amortizing advertising expenditures are simple, a substantive strategy is selected.	• Substantive procedures will recalculate the amortization of the advertising expenditures.

In this example, inventory is a material account balance that is composed of numerous products. This account also contains significant inherent risk, and the data for this account are generated by a complex computer system. For inventory, the auditor must understand the control environment factors, risk assessment factors, monitoring activities, significant classes of transactions, inventory pricing policies, the flow of transactions, and what control activities will be relied upon. The auditor will use the audit procedures discussed earlier in the chapter to obtain an understanding of internal control for inventory. In contrast, while prepaid advertising is a significant account, it contains few transactions. There is little or no inherent risk and the accounting records are simple, so the knowledge needed about the client's risk assessment, information system and communication, and monitoring regarding this account is minimal. In this instance, the auditor needs only to understand the control environment factors, the nature of the account balance, and the client's monitoring activities. Limited knowledge of the client's control activities is necessary for this account. Audit procedures for the prepaid advertising account would probably be limited to recalculation of amortization of advertising.

 ## SUBSTANTIVE PROCEDURES

LO11

The last step in the decision process under either strategy is performing substantive procedures. As discussed in Chapter 5, substantive procedures include substantive analytical procedures and tests of details.

Table 6–6 presents two examples of how the nature, timing and extent of substantive procedures may vary as a function of the detection risk level for the purchasing process and inventory account. Assume that audit risk is set low for both clients but that client 1 has a high level of risk of material misstatement (inherent risk and control risk), while client 2 has a low level of risk of material misstatement. The use of the audit risk model results in setting detection risk at low for client 1 and high for client 2. For client 1, to achieve a low detection risk the auditor must (1) obtain more reliable types of evidence, such as confirmation and reperformance, (2) conduct most of the audit work at year end (as such tests are usually considered to be stronger than tests done at an interim date), and (3) make the tests more extensive (larger sample size). This is because the auditor must fill the assurance bucket almost entirely with substantive evidence. In contrast, client 2 has a high detection risk, which means that (1) less reliable types of evidence, such as analytical procedures, can be obtained, (2) most of the audit work can be conducted at an interim date, and (3) tests of the inventory account would involve a smaller sample size. Another major difference between the two strategies involves the physical examination of the inventory on hand. For the low-detection-risk strategy, physical inventory would be examined at year end because the control risk was assessed to be high. For the high-detection-risk strategy, the auditor can examine the physical inventory at an interim date because the control risk assessment indicates little risk of material misstatement.

Table 6–6 Audit Strategies for the Nature, Timing and Extent of Substantive Procedures Based on Different Levels of Detection Risk for Inventory

Low-Detection-Risk Strategy – Client 1

Nature	Audit tests for all significant audit assertions using the following types of audit procedures:
	• Physical examination (conducted at year end).
	• Review of external documents.
	• Confirmation.
	• Reperformance.
Timing	All significant work completed at year end.
Extent	Extensive testing of significant accounts or transactions.

High-Detection-Risk Strategy – Client 2

Nature	Corroborative audit tests using the following types of audit tests:
	• Physical examination (conducted at an interim date).
	• Analytical procedures.
	• Substantive tests of transactions and balances.
Timing	Interim and year end.
Extent	Limited testing of accounts or transactions.

❖ TIMING OF AUDIT PROCEDURES

LO12

Audit procedures may be conducted at an interim date or at year end. Figure 6–6 presents a timeline for planning and performing a mid-size to large audit for an entity such as EarthWear Clothiers with a 31/12/09 year end. In this example, the audit is planned and preliminary analytical procedures are conducted around 31/5/09. The interim tests of controls are conducted some time during the time frame 31/7/09 to 30/11/09. Substantive procedures are planned for the time frame 30/11/09 to 15/2/10, when the audit report is to be issued. The auditor's considerations of conducting tests of controls and substantive tests at an interim date are discussed in turn.

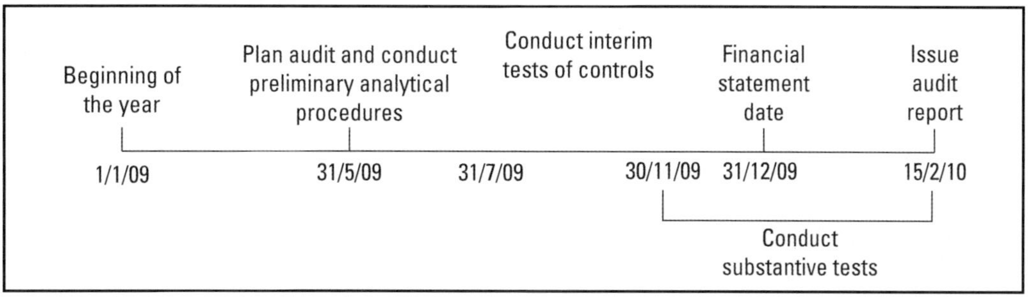

Figure 6–6   A Timeline for Planning and Performing the Audit of EarthWear Clothiers

Interim Tests of Controls

An auditor might test controls at an interim date because the assertion being tested may not be significant, the control has been effective in prior audits, or it may be more efficient to conduct the tests at that time. A reason why it may be more efficient to conduct interim tests of controls is that staff accountants may be less busy at the time, and it may minimize the amount of overtime needed at year end. Additionally, if the controls are found not to be operating effectively, testing them at an interim date gives the auditor more time to reassess the control risk and modify the audit plan. It also gives the auditor time to inform management so that likely misstatements can be located and corrected before the rest of the audit is performed.

An important question the auditor must address is the need for additional audit work in the period following the interim testing period. For example, suppose the auditor examines a sample of sales transactions for the period 1/1/09 to 31/8/09. What testing, if any, should the auditor conduct for the period 1/9/09 to 31/12/09? In making this decision, the auditor should consider factors such as the significance of the assertion, the evaluation of the design and operation of the relevant controls, the results of tests of controls, the length of the remaining period, and the planned substantive procedures in determining the nature and extent of audit work for the remaining period. At a minimum, the auditor would inquire about the nature and extent of changes in policies, procedures or personnel that occurred subsequent to the interim period. If significant changes have occurred, or if the results of tests of controls are unfavourable, the auditor may need to conduct additional audit procedures for the remaining period.

Interim Substantive Procedures

Conducting substantive procedures only at an interim date may increase the risk that material misstatements are present in the financial statements. The auditor can control for this potential problem by considering when it is appropriate to examine an account at an interim date, and by performing selected audit procedures for the period between the interim date and the year end.

The auditor should consider the following factors when substantive procedures are to be completed at an interim date:

- The control environment and other relevant controls.
- The availability of information at a later date that is necessary for the auditor's procedures (e.g. information stored electronically for a limited period of time).
- The objective of the substantive procedure.
- The assessed risk of material misstatement.
- The nature of the class of transactions or account balance and relevant assertions.
- The ability of the auditor to reduce the risk that misstatements existing at the period's end are not detected by performing appropriate substantive procedures or substantive procedures combined with tests of controls to cover the remaining period.

For example, if the entity's accounting system has control deficiencies that result in a high level of assessed control risk, it is unlikely that the auditor would conduct substantive procedures at an interim date. In this instance, the auditor has little assurance that the accounting system will generate accurate information during the remaining period.

When the auditor conducts substantive procedures of an account at an interim date, some additional substantive procedures are ordinarily conducted in the remaining period. Generally, this would include comparing the year-end account balance with the interim account balance. It might also involve conducting analytical procedures or reviewing related journals and ledgers for large or unusual transactions. If misstatements are detected during interim testing, the auditor will have to revise the planned substantive procedures for the remaining period or perform some additional substantive procedures at year end.

Practice Insight 6.3

Auditing standards (ISA 330) require that if the auditor plans to use audit evidence about the operating effectiveness of controls obtained in *prior audits*, audit evidence should be obtained about whether changes that affect those controls' continuing relevance have occurred subsequent to the prior audit. To confirm the understanding of those specific controls the auditor performs inquiry in combination with observation or inspection. If changes in the specific controls that affect their continuing relevance have occurred, the operating effectiveness of such controls should be tested in the current audit. If changes in the specific controls have not occurred, the auditor should test the operating effectiveness of such controls *at least once in every third audit* and test some controls each audit. Where the auditor plans to rely on the operating effectiveness of the internal controls to mitigate a *significant risk*, however, tests of those controls should be performed in the current period.

❖ AUDITING ACCOUNTING APPLICATIONS PROCESSED BY
LO13 **SERVICE ORGANIZATIONS**

In some instances, a client may have some or all of its accounting transactions processed by an outside service organization. Often such service organizations are IT service centres that process transactions such as payroll and the related accounting reports. Auditing standards provide guidance to the auditor when a client uses a service organization to process certain transactions (ISA 402).

When a client obtains services from a service organization, those services are part of an entity's information system relevant to financial reporting if they affect any of the following:

● The classes of transactions of the client that are significant to the client's financial statements.
● The accounting processing involved from the initiation of the transactions to their inclusion in the financial statements, including electronic means used to transmit, process, maintain and access information.
● The accounting records, supporting information and specific accounts in the financial statements involved in the processing and reporting of the client's transactions.
● The financial reporting process used to prepare the client's financial statements, including significant accounting estimates and disclosures.
● Controls surrounding journal entries, including non-standard journal entries used to record non-recurring, unusual transactions or adjustments.

The significance of the controls of the service organization to those of the client depends primarily on the nature and materiality of the transactions it processes for the client and the degree of interaction between its activities and those of the client. For example, if the client initiates transactions and the service organization executes and does the accounting processing of those transactions, there is a high degree of interaction.

Because the client's transactions are subjected to the controls of the service organization, one of the auditor's concerns is the internal control system in place at the service organization. The auditor's understanding of the client's internal control components may include controls placed in operation by the client and the service organization.

After obtaining an understanding of internal control, the auditor identifies controls that are applied by the client or the service organization that will allow an assessment of reduced control risk. The auditor may obtain evidence to support the lower assessment of control risk by tests of controls at the service organization or using another auditor to perform tests of controls at the service organization on his or her behalf.

Because service organizations process data for many customers, it is not uncommon for them to have an auditor issue an assurance report on their operations. Such assurance reports can be distributed to the auditors of a service organization's customers. A service organization's auditor can issue one of two types of report. A *type 1 report* is a description of the service organization's controls and an assessment of whether they are suitably designed to achieve specified internal control objectives and implemented. A *type 2 report* goes further by including tests of the operating effectiveness of the relevant controls and thus that they provide reasonable assurance that the related control objectives were achieved during the period. An auditor may reduce control risk below the maximum on the basis of service auditor's assurance report that includes tests of the controls.

❖ COMMUNICATION OF DEFICIENCIES IN INTERNAL CONTROL

LO14

A **deficiency in internal control** exists if (1) a control is designed, implemented or operated in such a way that it is *unable* to prevent, or detect and correct, misstatements in the financial statements on a timely basis; or (2) a control necessary to prevent, or detect and correct, misstatements in the financial statements on a timely basis is *missing*. A *significant control deficiency* (individually or in combination with other deficiencies) in internal control occurs if, in the auditor's professional judgement, it is of sufficient importance to merit the attention of those charged with governance. Auditing standards (ISA 265) require that the auditor communicates in writing significant control deficiencies to those charged with governance and management. The auditor should also communicate to management other control deficiencies judged to be of sufficient importance to merit management's attention.

Deficiencies in internal control may be identified as part of the auditor's consideration of the five components of internal control during the risk assessment process or at any other stage of the audit. The auditor should determine, on the basis of the audit work performed, whether he or she has identified one or more control deficiencies and whether they constitute significant control deficiencies. Table 6–7 presents examples of indicators of **significant deficiencies in internal control**.

Table 6–7 Examples of Indicators of Significant Deficiencies in Internal Control
• Evidence of ineffective aspects of the control environment, such as:
– Indications that significant transactions in which management is financially interested are not being appropriately scrutinized by those charged with governance.
– Identification of management fraud, whether or not material, that was not prevented by the entity's internal control.
– Management's failure to implement appropriate remedial action on significant deficiencies previously communicated.
• Absence of a risk assessment process within the entity where such a process would ordinarily be expected to have been established.
• Evidence of an ineffective entity risk assessment process, such as management's failure to identify a risk of material misstatement that the auditor would expect the entity's risk assessment process to have identified.
• Evidence of an ineffective response to identified significant risks (e.g. absence of controls over such a risk).
• Misstatements detected by the auditor's procedures that were not prevented, or detected and corrected, by the entity's internal control.
• Restatement of previously issued financial statements to reflect the correction of a material misstatement due to error or fraud.
• Evidence of management's inability to oversee the preparation of the financial statements (ISA 265, para. A7).

Practice Insight 6.4

The significance of a deficiency, or a combination of deficiencies, in internal control depends not only on whether a misstatement has actually occurred, but also on the likelihood that a misstatement could occur and the potential magnitude of the misstatement. Significant deficiencies may therefore exist even though the auditor has not identified misstatements during the audit.

❖ ADVANCED MODULE 1: TYPES OF CONTROLS IN AN IT ENVIRONMENT

LO15

There are two broad categories of information systems control activities: general controls and application controls. *General controls* relate to the overall information processing environment and have a *pervasive* effect on the entity's computer operations. General controls are sometimes referred to as supervisory, management or information technology controls. *Application controls* apply to the processing of specific computer applications and are part of the computer programs used in the accounting system (for example, revenues or purchasing).

General Controls

General controls include controls over:

- Data centre and network operations.
- System software acquisition, change and maintenance.
- Access security.
- Application system acquisition, development and maintenance.

Data Centre and Network Operations Controls

Data centre and network operations controls include controls over computer and network operations, data preparation, work flow control and library functions. Important controls over computer and network operations should prevent unauthorized access to the network programs, files and systems documentation by computer operators. In IT systems, traditional controls such as rotation of operator duties and mandatory vacations should be implemented. The operating systems log, which documents all program and operator activities, should be regularly reviewed to ensure that operators have not performed any unauthorized activities.

Controls over data preparation include proper entry of data into an application system and proper oversight of error correction. Controls over work flow include scheduling of application programs, proper setup for programs and use of the correct files. The library function needs controls to ensure that: (1) the correct files are provided for specific applications; (2) files are properly maintained; and (3) backup and recovery procedures exist.

Systems Software Acquisition, Change and Maintenance Controls

Systems software are computer programs that control the computer functions and allow the application programs to run. These programs include operating systems, library and security packages, and database management systems. For example, the operating system controls the operations of the computer and allocates computer resources among the application programs. The operating system also detects and corrects processing errors. The entity should have strong controls that ensure proper approval for purchases of new system software and adequate controls over changes and maintenance of existing systems software. Generally, an approval process similar to the one described below for application systems can accomplish this.

Access and Security Controls

These general controls are concerned with: (1) physical protection of computer equipment, software, and data; and (2) loss of assets and information through theft or unauthorized use. Security controls include locating the computer facilities in a separate building or in a secure part of a building. They also include limiting access to the computer facilities through the use of locked doors, with authorized personnel being admitted through use of a conventional key, an authorization card or physical recognition. Control must also be enforced within the computer facility. For example, programmers must not be allowed access to the computer room; this restriction will prevent them from making unauthorized modifications to systems and application programs.

There must also be adequate protection against events such as fire and water damage, electrical problems and sabotage. Proper construction of computer facilities can minimize the damage from such events. In order to ensure that the entity's operations are not interrupted by such events, the entity should have an operational disaster recovery plan, which may include an off-site backup location for processing critical applications.

Unauthorized access to programs or data can cause loss of assets and information. Physical control over programs and data can be maintained by a separate library function that controls access and use of files. In IT systems with online, real-time database systems and telecommunications technologies, programs and data can be accessed from outside the computer facility. Access controls in IT systems should thus include physical security over remote terminals, authorization controls that limit access only to authorized information, firewalls, user identification controls such as passwords, and data communication controls such as encryption of data. Without such controls, an unauthorized user could access the system, with a resulting loss of assets or a decrease in the reliability of data.

Application Systems Acquisition, Development and Maintenance Controls

These controls are critical for ensuring the reliability of information processing. The ability to audit accounting systems is greatly improved if: (1) the entity follows common policies and procedures for systems acquisition or development; (2) the internal and/or external auditors are involved in the acquisition or development process; and (3) proper user, system operator and program documentation is provided for each application. For example, having internal or external auditors involved early in the design of the system can ensure that proper controls are built into the system.[iv]

The entity should establish written policies and procedures for planning, acquiring or developing and implementing new systems. Normally, a request for a new system is submitted by the user department to the IT department or an information services committee. A feasibility study may be conducted that includes cost–benefit analysis, hardware and software needs, and the system's impact on current applications and operations. Next, the system is acquired or designed, programmed, tested and implemented. Last, the entity should prepare good documentation, including flowcharts, file layouts, source code listings and operator instructions. This level of documentation is necessary for the auditors to understand the accounting systems, including application controls, so that tests of controls and substantive testing can be properly planned and conducted.

The entity must also have strong controls to ensure that once programs are placed into operation, all authorized changes are made and unauthorized changes are prevented. Although not as detailed, the controls for program changes are similar to those followed for new systems development. From the auditor's perspective, the important issue here is whether changes to programs are properly authorized, tested and implemented.

Application Controls

Application controls apply to the processing of individual accounting applications, such as sales or payroll, and help ensure the completeness and accuracy of transaction processing, authorization and validity. Although application controls are typically discussed under the categories of input, processing and output controls, changes in technology have blurred the distinctions among input, processing and output. For example, many of the data validation checks that were once performed as part of production programs are now accomplished with sophisticated editing routines and intelligent data entry equipment. As a result, application controls are discussed under the following categories:

- Data capture controls.
- Data validation controls.
- Processing controls.
- Output controls.
- Error controls.

Data Capture Controls

Data capture controls must ensure that: (1) all transactions are recorded in the application system; (2) transactions are recorded only once; and (3) rejected transactions are identified, controlled, corrected and re-entered into the system. Thus, data capture controls are concerned primarily with *occurrence*, *completeness* and *accuracy assertions*. For example, checking that all transactions are recorded in the system relates to the completeness objective.

There are three ways of capturing data in an information system: (1) source documentation; (2) direct data entry; or (3) a combination of the two. When source documents are present, batch processing is an effective way of controlling data capture. Batching is simply the process of grouping similar transactions for data entry. It is important that each batch be well controlled. This can be accomplished by assigning each batch a unique number and recording it in a batch register or log. A cover sheet should also be attached to each batch with spaces for recording the batch number, the date, the signatures of various persons who processed the batch, and information on errors detected. To ensure complete processing of all transactions in a batch, some type of batch total should be used.

Direct data entry, on the other hand, involves online processing of the data with no source documents. The combination method may involve entry of the data from source documents directly through online processing. If direct data entry or a combination of source documents and direct data entry is used, the system should create a *transaction log*. The log should contain a detailed record of each transaction, including date and time of entry, terminal and operator identification and a unique number (such as customer order number).

Data Validation Controls

These controls can be applied at various stages, depending on the entity's IT capabilities, and are mainly concerned with the accuracy assertion. When source documents are batch processed, the data are taken from source documents and transcribed to tape or disk. The data are then validated by an edit program or by routines that are part of the production programs. When the data are entered directly into offline storage through an intelligent terminal or directly into a validation program with subsequent (delayed or real-time) processing into the application system, each individual transaction should be subjected to a number of programmed edit checks. Table 6–8 lists common validation tests. For example, a payroll application program may have a limit test that subjects any employee payroll transaction involving more than 80 hours worked to review before processing.

Table 6–8 Common Data Validation Controls	
Data Validation Control	*Description*
Limit test	A test to ensure that a numerical value does not exceed some predetermined value.
Range test	A check to ensure that the value in a field falls within an allowable range of values.
Sequence check	A check to determine if input data are in proper numerical or alphabetical sequence.
Existence (validity) test	A test of an ID number or code by comparison to a file or table containing valid ID numbers or codes.
Field test	A check on a field to ensure that it contains either all numeric or alphabetic characters.
Sign test	A check to ensure that the data in a field have the proper arithmetic sign.
Check-digit verification	A numeric value computed to provide assurance that the original value was not altered.

Some entities use turnaround documents to improve data accuracy. *Turnaround documents* are output documents from the application that are used as source documents in later processing. For example, a monthly statement sent to a customer may contain two parts; one part of the monthly statement is kept by the customer, while the other part is returned with the payment. The latter part of the statement contains encoded information that can be processed using various input devices. By using a turnaround document, the entity does not have to re-enter the data, thus avoiding data capture and data validation errors.

With direct data (online) entry, accuracy can be improved by special validation routines that may be programmed to *prompt* the data entry personnel. Here the system requests the desired input data and then waits for an acceptable response before requesting the next piece of input data. In many cases, the screen displays the document format with blanks that are completed by data entry personnel. The validation routine should include a completeness test to ensure that all data items are completed before processing. Airline reservation systems and catalogue retailers (like EarthWear) that take telephone orders use this type of entry system. Entering data over an entity's website can be controlled in a similar manner.

Processing Controls

These are controls that ensure proper processing of transactions. In some information systems, many of the controls discussed under data validation may be performed as part of data processing. General controls play an important role in providing assurance about the quality of processing controls. If the entity has strong general controls (such as application systems acquisition, development and maintenance controls;

library controls; personnel practices; and separation of duties), it is likely that programs will be properly written and tested, correct files will be used for processing and unauthorized access to the system will be limited.

Output Controls

Output includes reports, checks, documents and other printed or displayed (on terminal screens) information. Controls over output from computer systems are important application controls. The main concern here is that computer output may be distributed or displayed to unauthorized users. A number of controls should be present to minimize the unauthorized use of output. A report distribution log should contain a schedule of when reports are prepared, the names of individuals who are to receive the report, and the date of distribution. Some type of transmittal sheet indicating the intended recipients' names and addresses should be attached to each copy of the output. A release form may be part of the transmittal sheet and should be signed by the individual acknowledging receipt of the report.

The data control group should be responsible for reviewing the output for reasonableness, and reconciling the control or batch totals to the output. The user departments should also review the output for completeness and accuracy because they may be the only ones with sufficient knowledge to recognize certain types of errors.

Error Controls

Errors can be identified at any point in the system. While most transaction errors should be identified by data capture and data validation controls, some errors may be identified by processing or output controls. After identification, errors must be corrected and resubmitted to the application system at the correct point in processing. Error controls help ensure that errors are handled appropriately. For example, if a transaction is entered with an incorrect customer number, it should be rejected by a validity test. After the customer number is corrected, it should be resubmitted into the system. Errors that result from processing transactions (such as data entry errors) should be corrected and resubmitted by the data centre control group. Errors that occur outside the IT department (like omitted or invalid data) should be corrected by the appropriate user department and resubmitted. This segregation of duties prevents the data centre control group from processing invalid transactions.

❖ ADVANCED MODULE 2: COMPUTER-ASSISTED AUDIT TECHNIQUES

LO16

Most major audit firms have groups of auditors specializing in information technology. They often use computer-assisted audit techniques (CAATs) to assist the auditor in testing transactions, account balances and application controls. Many of these controls are embedded into the client's computer programs and can thus be tested via CAATs. Additionally, the auditor may also gain great efficiencies by using CAATs to execute substantive procedures when the information is maintained in machine-readable form. The following types of CAATs are discussed:

- Generalized audit software.
- Custom audit software.
- Test data.

Other techniques (parallel simulation, integrated test facility and concurrent auditing techniques) are discussed in advanced IT auditing books.[v]

Generalized Audit Software

Generalized audit software (GAS) includes programs that allow the auditor to perform tests on computer files and databases. Audit Command Language (ACL) is an example of a GAS program that is commonly used in practice. Generalized audit software was developed so that auditors would be able to conduct similar computer-assisted audit techniques in different IT environments. For example, GAS permits an auditor to select and prepare accounts receivable confirmations from a variety of computer systems. This type of software provides a high-level computer language that allows the auditor to easily perform various functions on a client's computer files and databases. A sample of functions that can be performed by GAS is shown in Table 6–9.

Table 6–9 Functions Performed by Generalized Audit Software	
Function	Description
File or database access	Reads and extracts data from a client's computer files or databases for further audit testing.
Selection operators	Select from files or databases transactions that meet certain criteria.
Arithmetic functions	Perform a variety of arithmetic calculations (addition, subtraction and so on) on transactions, files and databases.
Statistical analyses	Provide functions supporting various types of audit sampling.
Report generation	Prepares various types of documents and reports.

GAS offers several advantages: (1) it is easy to use; (2) limited IT expertise or programming skills are required; (3) the time required to develop the application is usually short; and (4) an entire population can be examined, eliminating the need for sampling in some instances. Among the disadvantages of GAS are that: (1) it involves auditing *after* the client has processed the data rather than while the data are being processed; (2) it provides a limited ability to verify programming logic because its application is usually directed to testing client files or databases; and (3) it is limited to audit procedures that can be conducted on data available in electronic form.

Custom Audit Software

Custom audit software is generally written by auditors for specific audit tasks. Such programs are necessary when the entity's computer system is not compatible with the auditor's GAS or when the auditor wants to conduct some testing that may not be possible with the GAS. It may also be more efficient to prepare custom programs if they will be used in future audits of the entity or if they may be used on similar engagements. The major disadvantages of custom software are that: (1) it is expensive to develop; (2) it may require a long development time; and (3) it may require extensive modification if the client changes its accounting application programs.

Inventory observation and testing provide a good example of where such a program might be useful. Suppose a client maintains computerized perpetual inventory records that are updated by the sales and purchasing systems. Further assume that the client conducts a physical inventory count once a year, at which time the perpetual records are corrected. At the time of the physical inventory count, the client's employees record the physical counts on special computer forms that are optically scanned to create a physical inventory file. The quantities on hand are priced using an approved price file. What results from this analysis is the inventory balance used for updating the perpetual records and the financial statements.

The auditors who observe the client's physical inventory count record the results on special computer forms that are optically scanned and used as input to the custom program. The custom program performs the following audit procedures: (1) traces the test counts into the client's perpetual inventory file and prints out any exceptions; (2) performs a complete mathematical test, including extensions, footings, crossfootings and use of approved prices; (3) summarizes the inventory by type; and (4) prints out items in excess of a predetermined amount for review.

Test Data

The auditor uses test data for testing the application controls in the client's computer programs. In using this method, the auditor first creates a set of simulated data (that is, test data) for processing. The data should include both valid and invalid data. After calculating the expected results of processing the test data, the auditor uses the client's computer and application programs to process the data.

The valid data should be properly processed, while the invalid data should be identified as errors. The results of this processing are compared to the auditor's predetermined results. This technique can be used to check:

- Data validation controls and error detection routines.
- Processing logic controls.
- Arithmetic calculations.
- The inclusion of transactions in records, files and reports.

The objective of using the test data method is to ensure the accuracy of the computer processing of transactions.

The main advantage of the test data method is that it provides direct evidence on the effectiveness of the controls included in the client's application programs. However, the test data method has a number of potential disadvantages. First, it can be very time-consuming to create the test data. Second, the auditor may not be certain that all relevant conditions or controls are tested. The use of special computer programs called *test data generators* may help alleviate these potential disadvantages. Third, the auditor must be certain that the test data are processed using the client's regular production programs. This concern can be alleviated if the client's general controls for program changes, access and library functions are reliable. Last, the auditor must be sure to remove the valid test data from the client's files.

ADVANCED MODULE 3: FLOWCHARTING TECHNIQUES

LO17

From the auditor's perspective, a flowchart is a diagrammatic representation of the entity's accounting system. The information systems literature typically discusses three types of flowcharts: document flowcharts, systems flowcharts and program flowcharts. A *document flowchart* (or data flow diagramming) represents the flow of documents among departments in the entity. A *systems flowchart* extends this approach by including the processing steps, including computer processing, in the flowchart. A *program flowchart* illustrates the operations performed by the computer in executing a program. Flowcharts that are typically used by audit firms combine document and systems flowcharting techniques. Such flowcharts show the path from the origination of the transactions to their recording in the accounting journals and ledgers. While there are some general guidelines on preparing flowcharts for documenting accounting systems, the reader should understand that audit firms often modify these techniques to correspond with their firm's audit approaches and technologies.

Following are a number of common guidelines that are used in preparing flowcharts.

Symbols

A standard set of symbols is used to represent documents and processes. Figure 6–7 presents examples of the more commonly used symbols. Note that the symbols are divided into three groups: input/output symbols; processing symbols; and data flow and storage symbols.

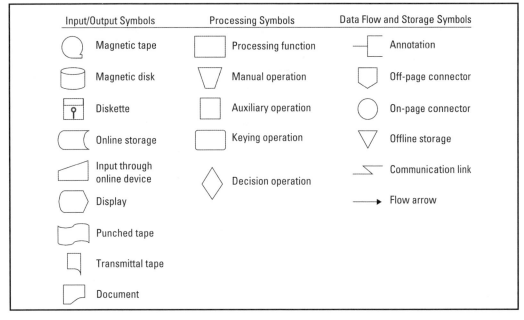

Figure 6–7   Flowcharting Symbols

Organization and Flow

A well-designed flowchart should start in the upper-left part of the page and proceed to the lower-right part of the page. When it is necessary to show the movement of a document or report back to a previous function, an on-page connector should be used. When the flowchart continues to a subsequent page, the movement of documents or reports can be handled by using an off-page connector. Flow arrows show the movement of documents, records or information. When processes or activities cannot be fully represented by flowchart symbols, the auditor should supplement the flowchart with written comments. This can be accomplished by using the annotation symbol or just writing the comment directly on the flowchart.

A flowchart is typically designed along the lines of the entity's departments or functions. It is thus important to indicate the delineation of activities between the departments or functions. As shown in Figure 6–4, this can be accomplished by using a vertical dashed line.

🔑 Key Terms

Accounting estimate. An approximation of a monetary amount in the absence of a precise means of measurement.

Application controls. Controls that apply to the processing of specific computer applications and are part of the computer programs used in the accounting system.

Computer-assisted audit techniques (CAATs). Computer programs that allow auditors to test computer files and databases.

Control activities. The policies and procedures that help ensure that management's directives are carried out.

Control environment. Includes the governance and management functions, and the attitudes, awareness and actions of those charged with governance and management concerning the entity's internal control and its importance in the entity.

Control risk. The risk that material misstatements that could occur will not be prevented, or detected and corrected by internal controls.

Deficiency in internal control. A control designed, implemented or operated in such a way that it is unable to prevent, or detect and correct, misstatements on a timely basis; or a control necessary to prevent, or detect and correct, misstatements on a timely basis that is missing.

Electronic commerce (Internet). Business transactions between individuals and organizations that occur without paper documents, using computers and telecommunication networks.

Electronic data interchange (EDI). The transmission of business transactions over telecommunications networks.

Entity's risk assessment process. A component of internal control that is the entity's process for identifying business risks relevant to financial reporting objectives and deciding about actions to address those risks, and the results thereof.

General controls. Controls that relate to the overall information processing environment and have a pervasive effect on the entity's computer operations.

Information system relevant to financial reporting. A component of internal control that includes the financial reporting system, and consists of the procedures and records established to initiate, authorize, record, process and report entity transactions (as well as events and conditions) and to maintain accountability for the related assets, liabilities and equity.

Internal control. The process designed, implemented and maintained by those charged with governance, management and other personnel to provide reasonable assurance about the achievement of an entity's objectives with regard to reliability of financial reporting, effectiveness and efficiency of operations, and compliance with applicable laws and regulations.

IT environment. The policies and procedures that the entity implements and the IT infrastructure (hardware, operating systems, etc.) and application software that it uses to support business operations and achieve business strategies.

Monitoring of controls. A process that assesses the quality of internal control performance over time.

Reliance strategy. The auditor's decision to rely on the entity's controls, test those controls and reduce the substantive tests of the financial statement accounts.

Significant deficiency in internal control. A deficiency or combination of deficiencies in internal control that in the auditor's professional judgement is of sufficient importance to merit the attention of those charged with governance.

Substantive strategy. The auditor's decision not to rely on the entity's controls and to audit the related financial statement accounts by relying more on substantive procedures.

Tests of controls. Audit procedures designed to evaluate the operating effectiveness of controls in preventing, or detecting and correcting, material misstatements at the assertion level.

? Review Questions

LO1,2,3	6–1	What are management's incentives for establishing and maintaining strong internal control? What are the auditor's main concerns with internal control?
LO4	6–2	What are the potential benefits and risks to an entity's internal control from information technology?
LO5	6–3	Describe the five components of internal control.
LO5	6–4	What are the factors that affect the control environment?
LO5,7	6–5	What is meant by the concept of reasonable assurance in terms of internal control? What are the inherent limitations of internal control?
LO6	6–6	What are the major differences between a substantive strategy and a reliance strategy when the auditor considers internal control in planning an audit?
LO7	6–7	Why must the auditor obtain an understanding of internal control?
LO8	6–8	List the tools that can document the understanding of internal control.
LO10	6–9	Describe five procedures that can be used for tests of controls.
LO11,12	6–10	What factors should the auditor consider when substantive procedures are to be completed at an interim date? If the auditor conducts substantive procedures at an interim date, what audit procedures would normally be completed for the remaining period?
LO14	6–11	What is the auditor's responsibility for communicating deficiencies in internal control?
LO16	6–12	Distinguish between generalized and custom audit software. List the functions that can be performed by generalized audit software.

✎ Problems

LO2,5,6,9   6–13   An auditor should obtain sufficient understanding of each component of an entity's internal control system to plan the audit of the entity's financial statements and to assess control risk for the assertions embodied in the transaction class, account balance and disclosure elements of the financial statements.

Required:

a   *Define internal control.*
b   *For what purpose should an auditor's understanding of the internal control components be used in planning an audit?*
c   *What are an auditor's documentation requirements concerning an entity's internal control system and the assessed level of control risk?*

LO5,7   6–14   Johnson, independent auditor, has been engaged to audit the financial statements of Rose. Before assessing control risk, Johnson is required to obtain an understanding of Rose's control environment.

Required:

a   *Identify additional control environment factors (excluding the factor illustrated in the following example) that set the tone of an organization, influencing the control consciousness of its people.*
b   *For each control environment factor identified in part a, describe the components and why each component would be of interest to the auditor.*

Use the following format.

Communication and Enforcement of Integrity and Ethical Values:

The effectiveness of controls cannot rise above the integrity and ethical values of the people who create, administer and monitor them. Integrity and ethical values are essential elements of the control environment, affecting the design, administration and monitoring of other components. Integrity and ethical behaviour are the product of the entity's ethical and behavioural standards, how they are communicated and how they are reinforced in practice.

LO4   **6–15**   Assume that you are an audit senior in charge of planning the audit of a client that your firm has audited for the previous four years. During the audit planning meeting with the manager and partner in charge of the engagement, the partner noted that the client recently adopted an IT-based accounting system to replace its manual system. The manager and partner have limited experience with IT-based accounting systems and are relying on you to help them understand the audit implications of the client's change. Consequently, they have asked you to respond to a few concerns regarding automated accounting systems.

Required:

a   *In previous years, the audit firm has relied heavily on substantive procedures as a source of audit evidence for this client. Given that the client now has changed its accounting system, what are some of the factors that you should consider when deciding whether to move to a reliance strategy?*
b   *Under what conditions should the audit firm consider engaging an IT expert to assist in the evaluation? If the firm hires an IT expert, what information should the auditors ask the expert to provide?*
c   *How are the five components of the client's internal control affected by the client's change to an IT-based accounting system?*

LO8   **6–16**   Auditors use various tools to document their understanding of an entity's internal control system, including narrative descriptions, internal control questionnaires and flowcharts.

Required:

a   *Identify the relative strengths of each tool.*
b   *Briefly describe how the complexity of an entity's internal control system affects the use of the various tools.*

LO11,12   **6–17**   Cook, independent auditor, has been engaged to audit the financial statements of General Department Stores, a continuing audit client, which is a chain of medium-sized retail stores. General's fiscal year will end on 30 June 2009, and General's management has asked Cook to issue the auditor's report by 1 August 2009. Cook will not have sufficient time to perform all of the necessary fieldwork in July 2009 but will have time to perform most of the fieldwork as of an interim date, 30 April 2009.

After the accounts are tested at the interim date, Cook will also perform substantive procedures covering the transactions of the final two months of the year. This will be necessary to extend Cook's conclusions to the balance sheet date.

Required:

a   *Describe the factors Cook should consider before applying substantive procedures to General's balance sheet accounts at 30 April 2009.*
b   *For accounts tested at 30 April 2009, describe how Cook should design the substantive procedures covering the balances as of 30 June 2009, and the transactions of the final two months of the year.*

(AICPA, adapted)

LO14   **6–18**   Ken Smith, the partner in charge of the audit of Houghton Enterprises, identified the following deficiencies in internal control during the audit of the 31 December 2009 financial statements:

1   Controls for granting credit to new customers were not adequate. In particular, the credit department did not adequately check the creditworthiness of customers with an outside credit agency.

2   There were inadequate physical safeguards over the company's inventory. No safeguards prevented employees from stealing high-value inventory parts.

Required:

How should Smith communicate the identified deficiencies in internal control?

LO16   **6–19**   Auditors use various audit techniques to gather evidence when a client's accounting information is processed using IT. Select the audit procedure from the following list and enter it in the appropriate place on the grid.

Audit procedure:

1   Test data method
2   Custom audit software
3   Auditing around the computer
4   Generalized audit software

Description of Audit Technique	Audit Technique
a Program written by the auditor to perform a specific task for a particular client.	
b The auditor's auditing of the inputs and outputs of the system without verification of the processing of the data.	
c Processing fictitious and real data separately through the client's IT system.	

LO16   **6–20**   Brown, independent auditor, is auditing the financial statements of Big Z Wholesaling, a continuing audit client, for the year ended 31 January 2009. On 5 January 2009, Brown observed the tagging and counting of Big Z's physical inventory and made appropriate test counts. These test counts have been recorded on a computer file. As in prior years, Big Z gave Brown two computer files. One file represents the perpetual inventory (first-in, first-out) records for the year ended 31 January 2009. The other file represents the January 5 physical inventory count.

Assume:

1   Brown issued an unmodified opinion on the prior year's financial statements.

2   All inventory is purchased for resale and located in a single warehouse.

3   Brown has appropriate computerized audit software.

4   The perpetual inventory file contains the following information in item number sequence:

     a   Beginning balances at 1 February 2008: item number, item description, total quantity and price.

     b   For each item purchased during the year: date received, receiving report number, vendor item number, item description, quantity and total euro amount.

     c   For each item sold during the year: date shipped, invoice number, item number, item description, quantity and euro amount.

     d   For each item adjusted for physical inventory count differences: date, item number, item description, quantity and euro amount.

5   The physical inventory file contains the following information in item number sequence: tag number, item number, item description and count quantity.

Required:

Describe the substantive auditing procedures Brown may consider performing with computerized audit software using Big Z's two computer files and Brown's computer file of test counts. The substantive auditing procedures described may indicate the reports to be printed out for Brown's follow-up by subsequent application of manual procedures. Do not describe subsequent manual auditing procedures. (Group the procedures by those using (1) the perpetual inventory file and (2) the physical inventory and test count files.)

Discussion Cases

LO5,6   6–21   You are the engagement partner of the client Fish Farms. The company operates salmon farms in Canada and Chile, mainly supplying the American and Asian markets with fresh and frozen salmon. You have the following information of the stock of salmon (biomass).

1   Lists with details of numbers and weight of live salmon in net cages in open water and smolt (small salmon) in closed fresh-water tanks on land.
2   Daily market prices for harvested salmon of various sizes.
3   Production cost of salmon of all sizes. Seventy per cent of the production costs of salmon relates to feeding.

It takes two to five years for smolt to grow to market-ready salmon. Fish Farms has designed and implemented strong controls that keep track of the number and weight of salmon during production and at harvesting. Smolt are counted when migrated from fresh water to cages in the sea. All harvested fish are counted and weighed. Dead fish are immediately removed from cages and counted. The weight of the fish during production is an estimate based on the relationship between expected growth rates and feed consumption. The net cages are large and the salmon are constantly in motion. Salmon are easily stressed and cannot be removed from the cages before they are harvested.

Required:

a   *What are the assertions you consider to be most critical in the audit of the stock of salmon (biomass) of Fish Farms?*
b   *You plan to rely on the internal controls when appropriate. To prepare for a meeting with your audit team write a short memo explaining why you consider a reliance strategy.*
c   *Give examples of tests of controls you plan to perform in the audit of the stock of salmon (biomass).*

LO5,6   6–22   Preview Company, a diversified manufacturer, has five divisions. Preview has historically allowed its divisions to operate autonomously. Corporate intervention occurred only when planned results were not obtained. Corporate management has high integrity, but the board of directors is not very active. Preview has a policy of hiring competent people. The company has a code of conduct, but there is little monitoring of compliance by employees. Management is fairly conservative in terms of accounting policies and practices, but employee compensation packages depend highly on performance. Preview Company does not have an internal audit department, and it relies on your firm to review the controls in each division.

Chip Harris is the general manager of the Fabricator Division. The Fabricator Division produces a variety of standardized parts for small appliances. Harris has been the general manager for the last seven years, and each year he has been able to improve the profitability of the division. He is compensated based largely on the division's profitability. Much of the improvement in profitability has come through aggressive cost-cutting, including a substantial reduction in control activities over inventory.

During the last year a new competitor has entered Fabricator's markets and has offered substantial price reductions in order to grab market share. Harris has responded to the competitor's actions by matching the price cuts in the hope of maintaining market share. Harris is very concerned because he cannot see any other areas where costs can be reduced so that the division's growth and profitability can be maintained. If profitability is not maintained, his salary and bonus will be reduced.

Harris has decided that one way to make the division more profitable is to manipulate inventory because it represents a large amount of the division's balance sheet. He also knows that controls over inventory are weak. He views this inventory manipulation as a short-term solution to the profit decline due to the competitor's price cutting. Harris is certain that once the competitor stops cutting prices or goes bankrupt, the misstatements in inventory can be corrected with little impact on the bottom line.

Required:

a Evaluate the strengths and weaknesses of Preview Company's control environment.

b What factors in Preview Company's control environment have led to and facilitated Harris's manipulation of inventory?

(Used with permission of the PricewaterhouseCoopers LLP Foundation).

Notes

i   See PricewaterhouseCoopers, *2009 Current Developments For Directors*, PricewaterhouseCoopers, New York, 2009, for a discussion of audit committees and corporate governance. Also see information published by KPMG's Audit Committee Institute (www.kpmg.com/aci).

ii A. Eilifsen and W.F. Messier, Jr (2000) 'Auditor Detection of Misstatements: A Review and Integration of Empirical Research', *Journal of Accounting Literature* (19), pp. 1–43, reviews research studies that have examined the causes of auditor-detected misstatements. For example, A. Wright and R.H. Ashton, 'Identifying Audit Adjustments with Attention-Directing Procedures', *Accounting Review* (October 1989), pp. 710–28, find that approximately 55 per cent of the errors detected by auditors resulted from personnel problems, insufficient accounting knowledge and judgement errors.

iii Exhibit 6–1 shows how the understanding of internal control can be developed and documented using a separate internal control questionnaire. Some or all of the information on the components of the entity's internal control may be captured as part of the auditor's understanding of the entity and its environment (see Chapter 3).

iv Note that external auditor involvement in the information systems acquisition and development process for an audit client may be limited when such involvement cause a self-review threat. See the discussion of IFAC Code of Ethics for Professional Accountants in Chapter 19 for further details.

v   For example, see J.D. Warren, Jr, L.W. Edelson, X.L. Parker and R.M. Thurun, *Handbook of IT Auditing* RIA Group/WG&L, Boston, MA, 1998.

CHAPTER 7

Auditing Internal Control Over Financial Reporting

❖ LEARNING OBJECTIVES

Upon completion of this chapter you will

❖ **LO1** Understand management's responsibilities for reporting on internal control under Section 404 of the Sarbanes–Oxley Act.

❖ **LO2** Understand the auditor's responsibilities for reporting on internal control under Section 404 of the Sarbanes–Oxley Act.

❖ **LO3** Know the definition of internal control over financial reporting (ICFR).

❖ **LO4** Be able to explain the differences between a control deficiency, a significant deficiency and a material weakness.

❖ **LO5** Understand management's assessment process.

❖ **LO6** Know how auditors conduct an audit of ICFR.

❖ **LO7** Understand how the auditor plans the audit of ICFR.

❖ **LO8** Be able to describe the top-down, risk-based approach that auditors use for an audit of ICFR.

❖ **LO9** Understand how to test the design and operating effectiveness of controls.

❖ **LO10** Understand how to evaluate identified control deficiencies.

❖ **LO11** Understand how remediation affects audit reporting.

❖ **LO12** Know the written representations that the auditor must obtain from management.

❖ **LO13** Be familiar with the auditor's documentation requirements.

❖ **LO14** Understand auditor reporting for the audit of ICFR.

❖ **LO15** Know the auditor's communication responsibilities on an audit of ICFR.

❖ **LO16** Understand how to obtain assurance on controls at a service organization that processes transactions for the entity.

❖ **LO17** Know management's and the auditor's responsibilities for controls that provide reasonable assurance for safeguarding company assets.

❖ RELEVANT ACCOUNTING AND AUDITING PRONOUNCEMENTS

FASB ASC Topic 450, Contingencies

AICPA, AU 314, Understanding the Entity and Its Environment and Assessing the Risks of Material Misstatement

AICPA, AU 316, Consideration of Fraud in a Financial Statement Audit

AICPA, AU 322, The Auditor's Consideration of the Internal Audit Function in an Audit of Financial Statements

AICPA, AU 324, Service Organizations

COSO, Internal Control – Integrated Framework, 1992

COSO, Enterprise Risk Management – Integrated Framework, 2004

COSO, Guidance on Monitoring Internal Control Systems, 2009

PCAOB Auditing Standard No. 3, Audit Documentation (AS3)

PCAOB Auditing Standard No. 4, Reporting on Whether a Previously Reported Material Weakness Continues to Exist (AS4)

PCAOB Auditing Standard No. 5, An Audit of Internal Control Over Financial Reporting That Is Integrated with An Audit of Financial Statements (AS5)

PCAOB Proposed Auditing Standards Related to the Auditor's Assessment of and Response to Risk, PCAOB Release No. 2008–006 (21 October 2008)

Securities and Exchange Commission, Commission Guidance Regarding Management's Report on Internal Control Over Financial Reporting Under Section 13(a) or 15(d) of the Securities Exchange Act of 1934. (SEC 2007)

CHAPTER 7 has a different focus than the rest of the chapters in this international textbook on auditing and assurance. It covers the reporting requirements for an audit of internal control over financial reporting (ICFR) as required by the US Sarbanes–Oxley Act 2002. The chapter is of interest for an international audience because a large number of international auditing practices are involved in complying with the Sarbanes–Oxley Act and because the US requirement for an audit of ICFR influences and serves as a reference for many regulatory initiatives on internal control taken outside the USA.

Non-US auditors are involved in assisting companies in complying with the requirements of the Sarbanes–Oxley Act, including auditing ICFR. A large number of non-US companies are registered and file reports with the US Securities and Exchange Commission (SEC). These companies are ordinarily audited by non-US audit practices. Further, many US public companies have their foreign subsidiaries audited by non-US audit practices.

The increased focus on considerations and communications related to internal control is a global phenomenon. The regulatory initiatives taken vary by jurisdiction. For example, the EU 8th Directive on Statutory Audits of 2006 requires the statutory auditor of a public-interest entity to report to the audit committee on material weaknesses in internal control in relation to the financial reporting process. The International Standards on Auditing (ISAs) have expanded the auditor's responsibility to consider internal control and communicate control deficiencies in a financial statement audit. The purpose of an audit in accordance with the ISAs is, however, *not* to express an opinion on the effectiveness of ICFR. At the international level an engagement to assure the effectiveness of the internal control should be performed in accordance with the international standards on assurance engagements. (See Chapter 20 for a detailed discussion of assurance.)

The Sarbanes–Oxley Act 2002 was passed in response to a series of business scandals (e.g. Enron and WorldCom). A common question being asked at the time was, 'Why did these companies' systems of internal control fail to prevent these frauds?' Failure of internal control over financial reporting was one of the major concerns addressed by Congress in the Sarbanes–Oxley Act, which imposes unprecedented requirements on both management and auditors of public companies. Section 404 of the Act requires that management report on the effectiveness of its ICFR and that its auditor also provides an attestation on the effectiveness of ICFR based on standards issued by the Public Company Accounting Oversight Board (PCAOB).

In 2004, the PCAOB issued Auditing Standard No. 2, *An Audit of Internal Control over Financial Reporting Performed in Conjunction with an Audit of Financial Statements* (AS2), to provide guidance for the audit engagements referred to in Section 404. After the issuance of AS2, the SEC and the PCAOB monitored the implementation of its requirements. Based on this monitoring, the SEC issued guidance for management and the PCAOB issued AS5, which superseded AS2, for auditors. These documents require that management and their auditors follow a top-down, risk-based approach to evaluating ICFR.

This chapter covers what management must do in order to issue a report that the entity's ICFR is effective and how the entity's auditor performs an audit regarding the effectiveness of ICFR. The material covered in this chapter applies to companies subject to the reporting requirements of Section 404 of the Sarbanes–Oxley Act 2002 (i.e. most public companies registered in the USA).

◆ MANAGEMENT RESPONSIBILITIES UNDER SECTION 404

LO1

Section 404 of the Sarbanes–Oxley Act requires management of a publicly traded company to issue a report that accepts responsibility for establishing and maintaining adequate internal control over financial reporting and also assert as to whether ICFR is effective as of the end of the fiscal year. Note that the Act provides no guidance on what constitutes adequate internal control. Thus, the SEC and PCAOB were left to address the issue of adequacy. Further, the assessment is to be made as of a specific point in time – that is, 'as of' the end of the fiscal year. Therefore, management's assessment does not cover the entire year. This has implications for the timing of both management's and the auditor's work, and the handling of any control deficiencies discovered during the year. Most importantly, the 'as of' nature of the assessment in many cases allows management to remediate deficiencies discovered prior to year end and still receive an unqualified opinion on ICFR. It also has implications for the use of the auditor's internal control work for financial statement audit purposes.

Management must comply with the following requirements in order for its registered public accounting firm (external auditor) to complete an audit of ICFR:

● Accept responsibility for the effectiveness of the entity's ICFR.
● Evaluate the effectiveness of the entity's ICFR using suitable control criteria.
● Support the evaluation with sufficient evidence, including documentation.
● Present a written assessment regarding the effectiveness of the entity's ICFR 'as of' the end of the entity's most recent fiscal year.

Each of these steps is discussed below. Recognize, however, that the second and third bullet points require a substantial investment of time, energy and money on the part of the entity.

◆ AUDITOR RESPONSIBILITIES UNDER SECTION 404 AND AS5

LO2

Section 404 requires the entity's auditor to audit management's assertion about the effectiveness of ICFR. AS5 states that the auditor must conduct the audits of financial statements and ICFR in an integrated way because each audit provides the auditor with information relevant to the evaluation of the results of the other. AS5 makes it clear that while the two audits are to be integrated, they have different objectives. The auditor's objective in an audit of ICFR is 'to express an opinion on the effectiveness of the company's internal control over financial reporting' (AS5, para. 3), while the objective in a financial statement audit is to express an opinion on whether the financial statements are fairly stated in accordance with generally accepted accounting principles (GAAP).

To form a basis for expressing an opinion on the effectiveness of ICFR, the auditor must plan and perform the audit to obtain *reasonable assurance* about whether the entity maintained, in all material respects, effective internal control 'as of' the date specified in management's assessment. Reasonable assurance in this context recognizes that no system of internal control is perfect and that there is a remote likelihood that material misstatements will not be prevented or detected on a timely basis, even if controls are, in fact, effective (AS5, para. 3). While reasonable assurance is not absolute assurance, in this context it indicates a high level of assurance.

◆ INTERNAL CONTROL OVER FINANCIAL REPORTING DEFINED

LO3

Chapter 6 presented the COSO definition of internal control. For purposes of both management's assessment and the audit of internal control, the PCAOB defines ICFR as:

> *A process designed by, or under the supervision of, the company's principal executive and principal financial officers, or persons performing similar functions, and effected by the company's board of directors, management, and other personnel, to provide reasonable*

assurance regarding the reliability of financial reporting and the preparation of financial statements for external purposes in accordance with GAAP, and includes those policies and procedures that:

(1) *Pertain to the maintenance of records that, in reasonable detail, accurately and fairly reflect the transactions and dispositions of the assets of the company;*

(2) *Provide reasonable assurance that transactions are recorded as necessary to permit preparation of financial statements in accordance with generally accepted accounting principles, and that receipts and expenditures of the company are being made only in accordance with authorizations of management and directors of the company; and*

(3) *Provide reasonable assurance regarding prevention or timely detection of unauthorized acquisition, use or disposition of the company's assets that could have a material effect on the financial statements. (AS5, para. A5)*

This definition makes it clear that the CEO and CFO are responsible for the reliability of ICFR and the preparation of the financial statements. It is the responsibility of the board of directors and management to implement an effective internal control system. You will note that the objectives of internal control in the PCAOB's definition are much more specific than the objectives listed in the COSO definition. Items (1) and (2) relate directly to controls for initiating, authorizing, recording, processing and reporting significant accounts and disclosures and related assertions embodied in the financial statements. Item (3) concerns controls over safeguarding of assets.

❖ INTERNAL CONTROL DEFICIENCIES DEFINED

LO4
Control Deficiency

For managements and auditors to assess whether ICFR is effective, it is necessary to define what constitutes a control deficiency and to define different levels of severity. While the PCAOB's definitions in this area are somewhat technical, it is important that you invest the time and energy to understand them.

A **control deficiency** exists when the *design or operation* of a control does not allow management or employees, in the normal course of performing their assigned functions, to prevent or detect misstatements on a timely basis. A *design deficiency* exists when (1) a control necessary to meet the relevant **control objective** is missing, or (2) an existing control is not properly designed so that, even if the control operates as designed, the control objective would not be met. A deficiency in *operation* exists when a properly designed control does not operate as designed or when the person performing the control does not possess the necessary authority or qualifications to perform the control effectively (AS5, para. 3).

Material Weakness

The focus of the audit of ICFR is on deficiencies that are serious enough that there is a reasonable possibility that a material misstatement of the financial statements could result. Accordingly, the PCAOB defines a **material weakness** as a deficiency, or combination of deficiencies, in ICFR, such that there is a *reasonable possibility* that a *material* misstatement of the annual or interim financial statements will not be prevented or detected on a timely basis (AS5, para. A7).

Significant Deficiency

A **significant deficiency** is a control deficiency, or combination of control deficiencies, in ICFR that is less severe than a material weakness, yet important enough to merit attention by those responsible for oversight of the company's financial reporting (AS5, para. A11).

Likelihood and Magnitude

According to the above definitions, in judging the significance of a control deficiency, management and the auditor must consider two dimensions of the control deficiency: *likelihood* and *magnitude* of misstatements that could result from the control deficiency. The definition of material weakness includes the phrase 'reasonable possibility'. The term *reasonable possibility* is to be interpreted using the guidance in FASB ASC Topic 450, *Contingencies.* Accordingly, the likelihood of an event is a 'reasonable possibility' if it is either reasonably possible or probable. While this guidance is helpful, these concepts are clearly subjective and require the application of considerable professional judgement.

Determining the magnitude of a financial statement misstatement that might result from a control deficiency also requires a great deal of professional judgement. In making such judgements, the auditor should be satisfied that a 'prudent official' would be likely to concur. In determining whether it is reasonably possible that a financial statement misstatement resulting from a deficiency is material the auditor relies on the same concept of materiality as is used in determining financial statement materiality. Figure 7–1 represents how likelihood and magnitude relate to each other in the determination of whether a control deficiency rises to the level of a significant deficiency or a material weakness.

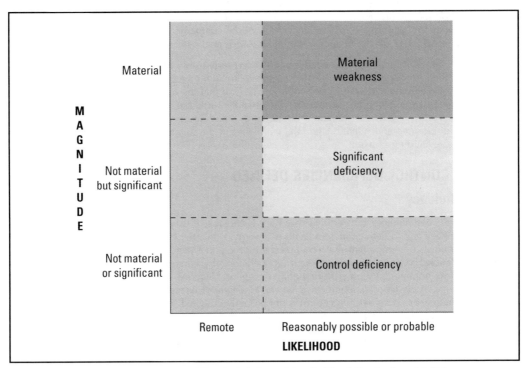

Figure 7–1 The Relationship of Likelihood and Magnitude in Determining the Materiality of a Control Deficiency

Later in the chapter we discuss how the auditor applies the concepts of likelihood and materiality in an audit of ICFR.

Practice Insight 7.1

Before deciding whether a significant deficiency or material weakness exists, AS5 requires the auditor to evaluate the effectiveness of compensating controls. To have a mitigating effect, the compensating control should operate at a level of precision that would prevent or detect a misstatement that could be material (AS5, para. 68).

 ## MANAGEMENT'S ASSESSMENT PROCESS

LO5

In order to issue a report on the effectiveness of internal control, management needs to first design and implement an effective system of ICFR and then develop an ongoing assessment process. To assist management, the SEC issued guidance for evaluating and assessing ICFR. We do not provide detailed coverage of the SEC's guidance since this chapter focuses primarily on the external auditor's responsibilities. The reader should refer to the SEC's guidance for more detail.

The SEC's guidance provides a top-down, risk-based approach for management to follow in evaluating and assessing ICFR. The purpose of management's evaluation of ICFR is to provide management with a reasonable basis for its assessment as to whether any material weaknesses in ICFR exist 'as of' the end of the period. The evaluation process has three steps:

1   Identify financial reporting risks and related controls.
2   Evaluate evidence about the operating effectiveness of ICFR.
3   Consider which locations to include in the evaluation.

Once the evaluation process is complete, management must address its reporting responsibilities.

Framework Used by Management to Conduct Its Assessment

Management is required to base its assessment of the effectiveness of the entity's ICFR on a suitable, recognized control framework established by a body of experts that follows due-process procedures. In the USA, most entities use the framework developed by COSO in the early 1990s (COSO, *Internal Control – Integrated Framework*). Some may use the new COSO, Enterprise Risk Management framework (*Enterprise Risk Management – Integrated Framework*), which subsumes and builds on the COSO internal control framework. Other suitable frameworks have been published in other countries. Review Chapter 6 for a discussion of the COSO framework.

Identify Financial Reporting Risks and Related Controls

Management must first identify and assess *financial reporting risks*; that is, the risk that a misstatement could result in a material misstatement of the financial statements. How management identifies financial reporting risks will vary based on the characteristics of the entity. Such characteristics include the size, complexity and organizational structure of the entity, and its processes and financial reporting environment.

Management then identifies controls that are in place to address the financial reporting risks. In addition to specific controls that address financial reporting risks, management also evaluates whether there are controls in place to address entity-level and other pervasive elements of ICFR. **Entity-level controls** can have a pervasive effect on the entity's ability to meet the COSO control criteria. Table 7–1 presents examples of entity-level controls.

Table 7–1   Examples of Entity-Level Controls
• Controls within the control environment (e.g. tone at the top, assignment of authority and responsibility, consistent policies and procedures, and company-wide programmes, such as codes of conduct and fraud prevention, that apply to all locations and business units).
• Controls over management override.
• The entity's risk assessment process.
• Centralized processing and controls, including shared service environments.
• Controls to monitor results of operations.
• Controls to monitor other controls, including activities of the internal audit function, the audit committee and self-assessment programs.
• Controls over period-end financial reporting process.
• Policies that address significant business control and risk management practices.
Source: AS5, para. 24

Management should then consider the effect of information technology general controls that are necessary for proper and consistent operation of other technology-based controls designed to address financial reporting risks. Lastly, management must obtain and document reasonable evidential support for its assessment.

Evaluate Evidence About the Operating Effectiveness of ICFR

The evaluation of the operating effectiveness of a control considers whether the control is operating as designed, and whether the person performing the control possesses the necessary authority and competence to perform the control effectively. Management should focus its evaluation on areas that pose the highest risk to ICFR. As the risk of control failure increases, management will need more evidence to support its conclusion about the operating effectiveness of the control. Table 7–2 shows controls that are typically included for testing.

Table 7–2   Controls Typically Included for Testing
● Controls over initiating, authorizing, recording, processing and reporting significant accounts and disclosures and related assertions embodied in the financial statements.
● Controls over the selection and application of accounting policies that are in conformity with GAAP.
● Antifraud programs and controls.
● Controls, including IT general controls, on which other controls are dependent.
● Controls over significant non-routine and non-systematic transactions, such as accounts involving judgements and estimates.
● Entity-level controls (see Table 7–1).

Evidence on the operating effectiveness of a control may be obtained from direct testing of the control, ongoing monitoring, or both. Direct tests of controls are usually performed on a periodic basis by individuals with a high degree of objectivity (e.g. internal auditors) with respect to the control being tested. Ongoing monitoring includes self-assessment procedures and procedures to analyse performance measures (key performance indicators) designed to track the performance of the control.

Management's assessment must be supported by evidence that provides reasonable support for its assessment. The nature and extent of this evidence will vary based on the assessed level of ICFR risk for controls over each of its financial reporting elements.

Consider Which Locations to Include in the Evaluation

Management should generally include all of its locations and business units when considering financial reporting risks. However, the approach followed by management in choosing which locations to include in its assessment of internal control is a function of the presence of entity-level controls and the financial reporting risk at the individual locations or business units. If financial reporting risks are adequately addressed by entity-level controls, then the evaluation approach for the locations and business units would focus on those entity-level controls. When controls that are necessary to address financial reporting risks operate at more than one location or business unit, management needs to evaluate evidence of the operation of the controls at the individual locations or business units.

If management determines that financial reporting risks for the controls that operate at individual locations or business units are low, management may rely on self-assessment processes in conjunction with entity-level controls for their assessment. When management determines that the financial reporting risks for the controls at an individual location are high, management will normally need to directly test the operation of the controls at that location. Take a moment and think about how a large multinational corporation would accomplish such a task.

Reporting Considerations

In determining its reporting responsibilities, management first evaluates the severity of the control deficiencies identified. Similar to the approach taken by the auditor, management considers the likelihood of and degree to which the financial statements could be misstated by the control failure. If management determines that no material weaknesses exist, they can conclude that the company's ICFR was effective. Exhibit 7–1 provides an example management report.

Exhibit 7–1 An Example of Management's Report on Internal Control Over Financial Reporting

Management is responsible for establishing and maintaining adequate internal control over financial reporting of the company. Internal control over financial reporting is a process designed to provide reasonable assurance regarding the reliability of financial reporting and the preparation of financial statements for external purposes in accordance with accounting principles generally accepted in the United States of America.

The company's internal control over financial reporting includes those policies and procedures that (i) pertain to the maintenance of records that, in reasonable detail, accurately and fairly reflect the transactions and dispositions of the assets of the company; (ii) provide reasonable assurance that transactions are recorded as necessary to permit preparation of financial statements in accordance with accounting principles generally accepted in the United States of America, and that receipts and expenditures of the company are being made only in accordance with authorizations of management and directors of the company; and (iii) provide reasonable assurance regarding prevention or timely detection of unauthorized acquisition, use, or disposition of the company's assets that could have a material effect on the financial statements.

Because of its inherent limitations, internal control over financial reporting may not prevent or detect misstatements. Also, projections of any evaluation of effectiveness to future periods are subject to the risk that controls may become inadequate because of changes in conditions, or that the degree of compliance with the policies or procedures may deteriorate.

Management conducted an evaluation of the effectiveness of internal control over financial reporting based on the framework in Internal Control – Integrated Framework issued by the Committee of Sponsoring Organizations of the Treadway Commission (COSO). Based on this evaluation, management concluded that the company's internal control over financial reporting was effective as of December 31, 2008.

Samuel J. Palmisano
Chairman of the Board,
President and Chief Executive Officer
February 24, 2009

Mark Loughridge
Senior Vice President,
Chief Financial Officer
February 24, 2009

Source: IBM's Form 10K

If a control deficiency is determined to be a material weakness, management must disclose the material weakness in its assessment of the effectiveness of ICFR on an annual basis. The disclosure about the material weakness(es) should include the following:

- The nature of the material weakness(es).
- Its impact on the company's financial reporting and its ICFR.
- Management's current plans, if any, for remediating the material weakness.

Exhibit 7–2 presents an example of management's disclosure of a material weakness. Any control deficiency that is considered a significant deficiency or material weakness should be reported to the audit committee and the external auditor.

Exhibit 7–2 An Example of the Disclosure of a Material Weakness by AIG's Management

As of December 31, 2007, controls over the AIGFP super senior credit default swap portfolio valuation process and oversight thereof were not effective. AIG had insufficient resources to design and carry out effective controls to prevent or detect errors and to determine appropriate disclosures on a timely basis with respect to the processes and models introduced in the fourth quarter of 2007. As a result, AIG had not fully developed its controls to assess, on a timely basis, the relevance to its valuation of all third party information. Also, controls to permit the appropriate oversight and monitoring of the AIGFP super senior credit default swap portfolio valuation process, including timely sharing of information at the appropriate levels of the organization, did not operate effectively. As a result, controls over the AIGFP super senior credit default swap portfolio valuation process and oversight thereof were not adequate to prevent or detect misstatements in the accuracy of management's fair value estimates and disclosures on a timely basis, resulting in adjustments for purposes of AIG's December 31, 2007 consolidated financial statements. In addition, this deficiency could result in a misstatement in management's fair value estimates or disclosures that could be material to AIG's annual or interim consolidated financial statements that would not be prevented or detected on a timely basis.

Solely as a result of the material weakness in internal control over the fair value valuation of the AIGFP super senior credit default swap portfolio described above, AIG management has concluded that, as of December 31, 2007, AIG's internal control over financial reporting was not effective based on the criteria in *Internal Control – Integrated Framework* issued by the COSO.

Source: AIG's Form 10K

Management's assessment process involves special consideration of two topics. These topics must also be considered by the auditor during the audit of ICFR. The two topics are:

1   Service organizations.
2   Safeguarding assets.

The *Advanced Module* at the end of the chapter discusses each of these topics in detail.

Management Documentation

The SEC's guidance allows considerable flexibility to management in how it documents reasonable support for its assessment. However, reasonable support would include the basis for management's assessment and conclusion. Such documentation would include the design of the controls management has placed in operation to adequately address identified financial reporting risks, including the entity-level and other pervasive elements necessary for effective ICFR. The guidance does not require management to identify and document every control in a process or to document the business processes impacting ICFR. Instead, documentation should focus on those controls management concludes are adequate to address the entity's financial reporting risks.

Documentation of ICFR may take many forms, such as paper, electronic files or other media. It also includes a variety of information, such as policy manuals, process models, flowcharts, job descriptions, documents and forms.

❖ PERFORMING AN AUDIT OF ICFR

LO6

While the audit of ICFR and the audit of financial statements have different objectives, the auditor must plan and perform the audit work to achieve the objectives of both audits as an integrated audit. In planning the integrated audit, the auditor should design tests of controls to accomplish the objectives of both audits simultaneously. The purpose of tests of controls in an audit of ICFR is to provide evidence on the effectiveness of the entity's controls over financial reporting 'as of' the end of the reporting period. The purpose of tests of controls in an audit of financial statements is to assist the auditor in assessing control risk, which in turn affects the nature, timing and extent of the auditor's substantive tests.

The auditor should incorporate the results of tests of controls in the audit of ICFR into the tests of controls for the audit of the financial statements, and should use those results for determining the nature, timing and extent of substantive procedures. Similarly, the auditor should consider the results of substantive procedures on the conclusions about the effectiveness of ICFR. For example, if a misstatement is detected by substantive procedures, the auditor should consider how and why the controls failed to detect the misstatement and whether the control deficiency might affect the opinion on the audit of ICFR.

Figure 7–2 shows the steps involved in performing an audit of ICFR. While Figure 7–2 suggests a sequential process, the audit of ICFR involves an iterative process of gathering, updating and analysing information.

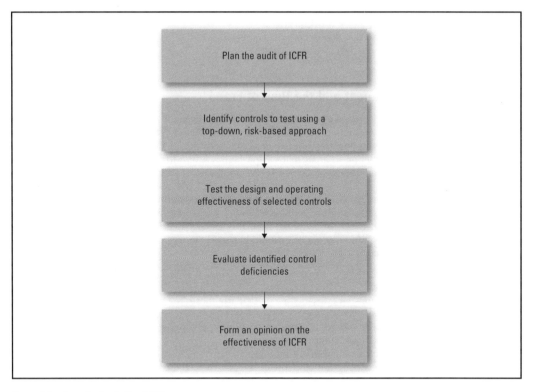

Figure 7–2   Steps in the Audit of ICFR

 PLANNING THE AUDIT OF ICFR

LO7   The process for planning an audit of ICFR should be integrated with planning the financial statement audit. Table 7–3 contains some of the factors that may affect the planning of an audit of ICFR. A number of these factors are similar to those discussed in Chapter 5.

Table 7–3   Factors that May Affect Planning an Audit of ICFR
• Knowledge of the entity's ICFR obtained during other engagements.
• Matters affecting the industry in which the entity operates, such as financial reporting practices, economic conditions, laws and regulations, and technological changes.
• Matters relating to the entity's business, including its organization, operating characteristics and capital structure.
• The extent of recent changes in the entity, its operations or its ICFR.
• Preliminary judgements about materiality, risk and other factors relating to the determination of material weaknesses.
• Control deficiencies previously communicated to the audit committee or management.
• Legal or regulatory matters of which the entity is aware.
• The type and extent of available evidence related to the effectiveness of the entity's ICFR.
• Preliminary judgements about the effectiveness of ICFR.
• Public information about the entity relevant to the evaluation of the likelihood of material financial statement misstatements and the effectiveness of the entity's ICFR.
• Knowledge about risks related to the entity evaluated as part of the auditor's client acceptance and retention evaluation.
• The relative complexity of the entity's operations.
Source: AS5, para. 39

In planning an audit of ICFR the auditor considers the following activities:

- The role of risk assessment and the risk of fraud.
- Scaling the audit.
- Using the work of others.
- Materiality.

The Role of Risk Assessment and the Risk of Fraud

A major premise of AS5 is that risk assessment underlies the entire audit of ICFR. In other words, there should be a direct relationship between the risk that a material weakness could exist in a particular area of the internal controls of the entity and the amount of audit work that is devoted to that area. Thus, the auditor should devote more attention to areas that have a high risk of a material weakness. This process is very similar to the risk assessment process followed by the auditor in the audit of financial statements (refer to Chapter 3).

A major part of risk assessment is assessing the risk of fraud. In considering the risk of fraud for the ICFR portion of the integrated audit, the auditor should refer to the work done as part of the audit of financial statements to comply with Statement on Auditing Standards (SAS) No. 99, *Consideration of Fraud in a Financial Statement Audit* (AU 316). The auditor should evaluate the risk of material misstatement due to fraud and the risk of management override of controls.

AS5 (para. 14) points out that the following controls might address the risk of fraud and management override:

- Controls over significant, unusual transactions, particularly those that result in late or unusual journal entries.
- Controls over journal entries and adjustments made in the period-end financial reporting process.
- Controls over related-party transactions.
- Controls related to significant management estimates.
- Controls that mitigate incentives for, and pressures on, management to falsify or inappropriately manage financial results.

Scaling the Audit

AS5 (para. 13) specifies that the 'size and complexity of the company, its business processes, and business units, may affect the way in which the company achieves many of its control objectives'. Allowing the concepts behind achieving effective internal control to be appropriately scaled to companies of different size and complexity is an extension of the risk-based approach required by AS5. AS5 explicitly recognizes and allows for the idea that a small, less-complex entity might achieve its control objectives differently from a large, complex entity.

Using the Work of Others

AS5 allows the auditor to use the work performed by, or receive direct assistance from, internal auditors, company personnel, and third parties working for management or the audit committee.

If the work of others is to be used, the auditor should assess the competence and objectivity of the persons whose work will be used. AS5 refers to AU 322, *The Auditor's Consideration of the Internal Audit Function in an Audit of Financial Statements*, for relevant guidance in assessing competence and objectivity. We previously discussed how the internal auditor's work may affect the audit procedures performed by the external auditor in Chapter 5. Table 5–2 provides the factors for assessing competence and objectivity.

The risk associated with the control being tested also plays a role in using the work of others. As the risk associated with the control increases, the auditor should perform more of the work. For example, the auditor will rely less on the work of others for a control relating to transactions that involve subjective judgements or that are highly susceptible to manipulation than for a control that relates to routine, objective transactions.

Materiality

In planning the audit of ICFR and determining the magnitude of a control deficiency, the auditor should use the same materiality considerations that were used for planning the audit of financial statements.

USING A TOP-DOWN APPROACH

LO8

The auditor should use a top-down approach to the audit of ICFR. As outlined in Figure 7–3, the auditor first identifies the entity-level controls. Next the auditor identifies the significant accounts and disclosures, and understands where the likely sources of misstatements occur. Based on this information, the auditor selects which controls to test.

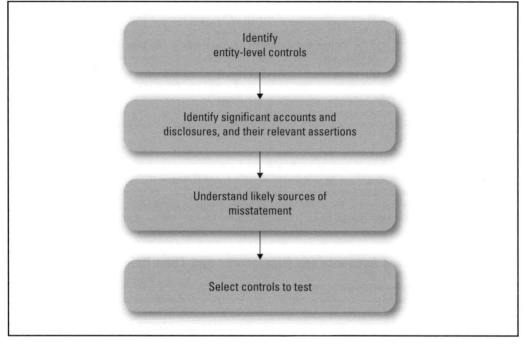

Figure 7–3   Top-Down, Risk-Based Approach to the Audit of ICFR
Source: **AS5, paras 21–41**

Identify Entity-Level Controls

Table 7–1 contains a list of entity-level controls. Entity-level controls can have a pervasive effect on the entity's ability to meet the COSO control criteria and, as a result, the auditor must test their effectiveness. The auditor's evaluation of the entity-level controls can result in increasing or decreasing the testing performed on other controls. AS5 (para. 23) points out that entity-level controls vary in nature and precision.

Two categories of entity-level controls require evaluation by the auditor: (1) the control environment and (2) the period-end financial reporting process.

Control Environment

Because of its importance to effective ICFR, the auditor must evaluate the control environment. In particular, the auditor should assess whether:

● Management's philosophy and operating style promote effective ICFR.
● Sound integrity and ethical values, particularly of top management, are developed and understood.
● The board or audit committee understands and exercises oversight responsibility over financial reporting and internal control.

Period-End Financial Reporting Process

The period-end financial reporting process is important to the auditor's opinion on ICFR and to financial statement reporting. The period-end financial reporting process controls include procedures used to enter transaction totals into the general ledger; select and apply accounting policies; initiate, authorize, record and process period-end journal entries in the general ledger; record recurring and non-recurring adjustments to the annual and quarterly financial statements; and prepare annual and quarterly financial statements and related disclosures. Even though these controls operate after the 'as of' year-end reporting date, they are used to support the auditor's 'as of' date opinion.

The auditor's evaluation of the period-end financial reporting process includes the inputs, procedures performed and outputs of the processes the company uses to produce its annual and quarterly financial statements. The auditor should also consider the extent of IT involvement in each period-end financial reporting process, who participates from management, the number of locations involved, types of adjusting and consolidating entries, and the nature and extent of the oversight of the process by management, the board of directors and the audit committee. The auditor's understanding of the entity's period-end financial reporting process and how it interrelates with the entity's other significant processes helps the auditor identify and test controls that are most relevant to financial statement risks. For example, it is common for entities to manually compile summary information for financial reporting purposes based on detailed financial information taken from accounting information systems. In some cases, entities use hundreds or even thousands of computer spreadsheets to summarize massive amounts of detailed data into financial statement accounts.

Due to the nature of spreadsheets and the operating environment in a typical organization, there is a heightened risk that controls over spreadsheets will not be effective. The external auditor must evaluate management's IT spreadsheet policy to determine the risks associated with its spreadsheet information. Because the data in spreadsheets can easily be changed, they are subject to increased inherent risk (input errors, logic errors, interface errors, etc.). The level of control over a spreadsheet should be relative to its use, complexity and required reliability of the information. Ideally, the IT department should manage spreadsheets, so that there is central control, but this is not often the case.

Identifying Significant Accounts and Disclosures and Their Relevant Assertions

The auditor should identify significant accounts and disclosures and their relevant assertions. **Relevant assertions** are financial statement assertions (see Chapter 4) that have a reasonable possibility of containing a misstatement that would cause the financial statements to be materially misstated. To identify significant accounts and disclosures and their relevant assertions, the auditor uses the following risk factors:

- Size and composition of the account.
- Susceptibility to misstatement due to errors or fraud.
- Volume of activity, complexity and homogeneity of the individual transactions processed through the account or reflected in the disclosure.
- Nature of the account or disclosure.
- Accounting and reporting complexities associated with the account or disclosure.
- Exposure to losses in the account.
- Possibility of significant contingent liabilities arising from the activities reflected in the account or disclosure.
- Existence of related-party transactions in the account.
- Changes from the prior period in account or disclosure characteristics (AS5, para. 29).

The risk factors that the auditor evaluates for an audit of ICFR are essentially the same as those used in the audit of financial statements.

Understanding Likely Sources of Misstatements

In order to understand the likely sources of potential misstatements the auditor needs to do the following:

- Understand the flow of transactions related to the relevant assertions, including how these transactions are initiated, authorized, processed and recorded.
- Identify the points within the entity's processes at which a misstatement – including a misstatement due to fraud – could arise that, individually or in combination with other misstatements, would be material.
- Identify the controls that management has implemented to address these potential misstatements.
- Identify the controls that management has implemented over the prevention or timely detection of unauthorized acquisition, use or disposition of the company's assets that could result in a material misstatement of the financial statements (AS5, para. 34).

Performing a **walk-through** is often the best way to identify sources of misstatements. To perform a walk-through, the auditor traces a transaction from origination through the entity's processes and information system until it is reflected in the entity's financial reports. It should encompass the entire information flow through the subprocesses of initiating, authorizing, recording, processing and reporting individual transactions for each of the significant processes identified. Walk-throughs help the auditor in confirming his or her understanding of control design and transaction process flow, as well as in determining whether all points at which misstatements could occur have been identified, evaluating the effectiveness of the design of controls, and confirming whether controls have been placed in operation.

In performing the walk-through, the auditor should make inquiries of relevant personnel involved in significant aspects of the process or controls. The auditor should use probing questions to determine client personnel's understanding of what is required by the controls and to determine whether the processing procedures are performed as understood and on a timely basis. These questions typically include inquiries on how exceptions are handled, how 'hand-offs' are properly accomplished between previous and succeeding processes, and who performs the control when an employee is sick or absent. These questions help corroborate the client's design and transaction flow documentation. Walk-through inquiries should include questions designed to identify abuse of controls (i.e. inappropriate management override) or indicators of fraud.

Select Controls to Test

The auditor does not need to test all controls – only those that are important to the auditor's conclusion about whether the entity's controls sufficiently address the assessed risk of misstatement to each relevant assertion, often referred to as key controls. Identifying the controls to be tested is a subjective task that requires professional judgement. Table 7–4 provides a list of factors that the auditor should consider in deciding which controls to test. The auditor should evaluate whether to test preventive controls, detective controls or a combination of both. For example, a monthly reconciliation (a detective control) might detect an out-of-balance situation resulting from an unauthorized transaction being initiated due to an ineffective authorization procedure (a preventive control). When determining whether the detective control is effective, the auditor should evaluate whether the detective control is sufficient to achieve the control objective to which the preventive control relates.

Table 7–4   Factors Commonly Considered When Identifying Controls to Test

- Points at which errors or fraud could occur.
- The nature of the controls implemented by management.
- The significance of each control in achieving the objectives of the control criteria and whether more than one control achieves a particular objective or whether more than one control is necessary to achieve a particular objective.
- The risk that the controls might not be operating effectively. Factors that affect whether the control might not be operating effectively include the following:
    - Whether there have been changes in the volume or nature of transactions that might adversely affect control design or operating effectiveness.
    - Whether there have been changes in the design of controls.
    - The degree to which the control relies on the effectiveness of other controls (e.g. the control environment or IT general controls).
    - Whether there have been changes in key personnel who perform the control or monitor its performance.
    - Whether the control relies on performance by an individual or is automated.
    - The complexity of the control.

In selecting the controls to test, the auditor must make decisions similar to management in deciding which locations or business units to include for testing. Thus, the choice of which locations to include in the assessment of internal control is based on the presence of entity-level controls and the financial reporting risk at an individual location or business unit.

TEST THE DESIGN AND OPERATING EFFECTIVENESS OF CONTROLS

Evaluating Design Effectiveness of Controls

LO9

Controls are effectively designed when they prevent or detect errors or fraud that could result in material misstatements in the financial statements. Once key controls are identified, the auditor evaluates design effectiveness through inquiry, observation, walk-throughs, inspection of relevant documentation, and subjective evaluations of whether the controls are likely to prevent or detect errors or fraud that could result in misstatements assuming they are operated as prescribed by qualified persons. The procedures performed by the auditor to test and evaluate design effectiveness might in some cases also provide some evidence about operating effectiveness.

Testing and Evaluating Operating Effectiveness of Controls

An auditor evaluates the operating effectiveness of a control by determining whether the control is operating as designed and whether the person performing the control possesses the necessary authority and competence to perform the control effectively. In testing the operating effectiveness of controls, the auditor needs to consider the scope (nature, timing and extent) of testing. For each control selected for testing, the evidence necessary to persuade the auditor that the control is effective depends on the risk that a material weakness would result. As the risk associated with the control being tested increases, the quality and/or quantity of the evidence that the auditor should obtain also increases. Table 7–5 presents the factors that affect the risk associated with a control.

Table 7–5 Factors that Affect the Risk Associated with a Control
• The nature and materiality of misstatements that the control is intended to prevent or detect.
• The inherent risk associated with the related account(s) and assertion(s).
• Whether there have been changes in the volume or nature of transactions that might adversely affect control design or operating effectiveness.
• Whether the account has a history of errors.
• The effectiveness of entity-level controls, especially controls that monitor other controls.
• The nature of the control and the frequency with which it operates.
• The degree to which the control relies on the effectiveness of other controls.
• The competence of the personnel who perform the control or monitor its performance and whether there have been changes in key personnel who perform the control or monitor its performance.
• Whether the control relies on performance by an individual or is automated.
• The complexity of the control and the significance of the judgements that must be made in connection with its operation.

Nature of Testing

Tests of controls for operating effectiveness include such procedures as inquiry of appropriate personnel, inspection of relevant documentation, observation of the entity's operations and reperformance of the application of the control. In many instances, a combination of these procedures is necessary to ensure that a control is operating effectively.

Inquiry is used extensively throughout the audit of internal control. Because inquiry alone does not provide sufficient evidence to support the operating effectiveness of a control, the auditor should perform additional tests of controls. For example, suppose an entity implements a control whereby its sales manager reviews and investigates a report listing invoices with unusually high or low gross margins. Inquiry of the sales manager as to whether he or she investigates discrepancies would not be sufficient evidence to ensure that the control is working effectively. The auditor should corroborate the sales manager's responses by performing other procedures, such as inspecting reports generated by the performance of the control and evaluating whether appropriate actions were taken.

The type of control often affects the nature of control testing the auditor can perform. For example, an entity may have a control that requires a signature (digital or otherwise) on a voucher package to indicate that the signer approved it. However, the presence of a signature does not necessarily mean that the person carefully reviewed the package before signing. As a result, the quality of the evidence regarding the effective operation of the control might not be sufficiently persuasive. In order to gain more persuasive evidence, the auditor could reperform the control by checking the voucher package for accuracy and completeness, essentially repeating the steps taken to initially perform the control. The auditor might also inquire of the person responsible for approving voucher packages regarding what he or she looks for when approving packages and ask to see documentation of the errors that have been found and rectified in the recent past.

Timing of Tests of Controls

The auditor must perform tests of controls over a period of time that is adequate to determine whether the significant controls are operating effectively 'as of' the date indicated in management's report. The period of time over which the auditor performs tests of controls will vary with the nature of the controls and the frequency with which they are applied. Some controls operate continuously (e.g. controls over the processing of routine sales transactions), while other controls operate only occasionally (e.g. monthly bank reconciliations). Routine transactions typically involve routine processing controls, such as verification of data entry, edit checks and validation controls, completeness controls, and so forth. For non-routine transactions, especially those involving estimation, review and approval controls are usually considered more critical. In some cases, controls may operate after the 'as of' date specified in management's report. For example, controls over a December 31 period-end financial reporting process normally operate in January of the following year.

In many instances, the auditor obtains evidence about the operating effectiveness of controls at an interim date for reporting on internal control even though the auditor's report on the effectiveness of internal control is for an 'as of' date. For example, the auditor might test controls over the revenue process for the first nine months of the year. The auditor will then need to determine what additional evidence is needed concerning the operating effectiveness of the controls for the remaining three-month period. In deciding what additional evidence is needed, the auditor considers the specific controls tested prior to the 'as of' date and the results of those tests, the sufficiency of the evidence of effectiveness obtained, the length of the remaining period, and the possibility that there have been significant changes in internal control subsequent to the interim date (AS5, para. 56). For controls over significant non-routine transactions, controls over accounts or processes with a high degree of subjectivity or judgement in measurement, or controls over the recording of period-end adjustments, the auditor should perform tests closer to the 'as of' date.

If management implements changes to the entity's controls to make them more effective or efficient prior to the date specified in management's report, the auditor might not need to evaluate the superseded controls.

Extent of Tests of Controls

AS5 does not provide any detailed guidance on what constitutes a sufficient sample for testing the operating effectiveness of the control. This is left to the auditor as a matter of professional judgement.

The auditor should consider the following factors when deciding on the extent of testing:

- *Nature of the control.* Manual controls should be subjected to more extensive testing than automated controls in view of the greater variability inherent in controls involving people.
- *Frequency of operation.* Generally, the more frequently a manual control operates, the greater the number of operations of the control the auditor should test.
- *Importance of the control.* The more important the control, the more extensively it should be tested.

Most public accounting firms have developed firm-wide guidance for the sample sizes used to test for various types of controls. Chapter 8 provides guidance on using statistical and non-statistical sampling for tests of controls.

AS5 provides guidance on incorporating knowledge obtained from prior years' audits into the decision-making process for determining the nature, timing and extent of testing for the current year audit. Factors that may affect the risk associated with a control in the current year include:

- The nature, timing and extent of procedures performed in previous audits.
- The results of the previous years' testing of the control.
- Whether there have been changes in the control or the process in which it operates since the previous audit (AS5, para. 58).

For example, if the results for testing a particular control were favourable in the prior year, and no changes were made to the control, the auditor might assess the risk for the control lower and reduce the extent of testing in the current year. If the controls are automated, the auditor might consider using a benchmarking strategy.[i] Benchmarking strategy is an approach that allows the auditor to conclude that a previously tested automated control continues to be effective based on indicators of whether there has been any change in the operation of the control rather than on repeating the full extent of the prior detail testing work.

❖ EVALUATING IDENTIFIED CONTROL DEFICIENCIES

LO10

The auditor is required to evaluate the severity of each control deficiency (AS5, para. 62). The assessment of the significance of a control deficiency depends on the *potential* for a misstatement, not on whether a misstatement has actually occurred. As discussed earlier, the severity of a control deficiency depends on two factors:

1   Whether there is a reasonable possibility that the company's controls will fail to prevent or detect a misstatement of an account balance or disclosure (likelihood).
2   The magnitude of the potential misstatement resulting from the deficiency or deficiencies (magnitude).

Table 7–6 presents the risk factors that affect whether there is a reasonable possibility that a control deficiency, or a combination of control deficiencies, will result in a misstatement of an account balance or disclosure.

Table 7–6   Risk Factors that Affect Whether There is a Reasonable Possibility that a Control Deficiency (or a Combination of Control Deficiencies) Will Result in a Misstatement of an Account Balance or Disclosure
● The nature of the financial statement accounts, disclosures and assertions involved.
● The susceptibility of the related asset or liability to loss or fraud.
● The subjectivity, complexity or extent of judgement required to determine the amount involved.
● The interaction or relationship of the control with other controls, including whether they are interdependent or redundant.
● The interaction of the deficiencies.
● The possible future consequences of the deficiency.
Source: AS5, para. 65

Factors that affect whether the magnitude of the misstatement might result in a material weakness include:

● The financial statement amounts or total of transactions exposed to the deficiency.
● The volume of activity in the account balance or class of transactions exposed to the deficiency that has occurred in the current period or that is expected in future periods.

Table 7–7 presents indicators of material weaknesses in ICFR.

Table 7–7   Indicators of Material Weaknesses
● Identification of fraud, whether or not material, committed by senior management.
● Restatement of previously issued financial statements to reflect the correction of a material misstatement.
● Identification by the auditor of a material misstatement of financial statements in the current period in circumstances that indicate that the misstatement would not have been detected by the company's ICFR.
● Ineffective oversight of the company's external financial reporting and ICFR by the company's audit committee.
Source: AS5, para. 69

AS5 provides the following guidance on assessing the severity of a control deficiency:

When evaluating the severity of a deficiency, or combination of deficiencies, the auditor also should determine the level of detail and degree of assurance that would satisfy prudent officials in the conduct of their own affairs that they have reasonable assurance that transactions are recorded as necessary to permit the preparation of financial statements in conformity with generally accepted accounting principles. If the auditor determines that a deficiency, or combination of deficiencies, might prevent prudent officials in the conduct of their own affairs from concluding that they have reasonable assurance that transactions are recorded as necessary to permit the preparation of financial statements in conformity with generally accepted accounting principles, then the auditor should treat the deficiency, or combination of deficiencies, as an indicator of a material weakness. (AS5, para. 70)

You will note that applying this guidance requires a good deal of judgement on the part of the auditor.

An Example

Exhibit 7–3 presents a detailed example of an auditor's tests of the design and operating effectiveness for a daily IT-dependent manual control.

Exhibit 7–3   An Example of an Auditor's Tests of a Daily Information Technology–Dependent Manual Control

Bill Boyd is manager for Emets & Shinn, the independent registered public accounting firm for Petheridge Packing Company (PPC). Based on discussions with PPC personnel and review of company documentation, the auditor learns that PPC had the following procedures in place over the entire period to account for cash received in the bank lockbox:

- The company receives from the bank an electronic file listing cash received from customers.

- The IT system applies cash received in the lockbox to individual customer accounts.

- Any cash received in the lockbox and not applied to a customer's account is listed on an exception report called the 'unapplied cash exception report'.

The application of cash to a customer's account is a *programmed application control*, while the review and follow-up of unapplied cash from the exception report is a *manual control*.

Boyd wants to determine whether misstatements in cash (primarily relating to the existence assertion) and accounts receivable (existence, valuation, and completeness) would be prevented or detected on a timely basis. In order to test these objectives, Boyd decides to test the manual control.

Nature, Timing and Extent of Procedures

Objectives of Test   To determine whether there is a listing of non-matching cash items on the exception report.

Boyd decides to perform the following tests of controls to ensure the *operating effectiveness* of the control for the review and follow-up on the daily unapplied cash exception report.

1   Inquired of company personnel about the procedures in place to ensure that all unapplied items are resolved, the time frame in which such resolution takes place, and whether unapplied items are handled properly within the system.

    Findings: Boyd discussed these matters with the employee responsible for reviewing and resolving the daily unapplied cash exception reports. Boyd learned that items appearing on the daily unapplied cash exception report must be manually entered into the system. The employee typically performs the resolution procedures the next business day. In most cases, items that appear on the daily unapplied cash exception report relate to payments made by a customer who failed to reference an invoice number or purchase order number, or to underpayments of an invoice due to quantity or pricing discrepancies.

2   Reperformed the control.

    Findings: Boyd selected 25 daily unapplied cash exception reports from the period January to September and reperformed the follow-up procedures that the employee performed. Boyd inspected the documents and sources of information used in the follow-up and determined that the transaction was properly corrected in the system. He also scanned other daily unapplied cash exception reports to determine that the control was performed throughout the period of intended reliance.

3   Follow-up tests: because the tests were performed at an interim date, Boyd asked entity personnel about the procedures in place at year end. The procedures had not changed from the interim period; therefore, Boyd observed that the controls were still in place by scanning daily unapplied cash exception reports to determine the control was performed on a timely basis during the period from September to year end. No exceptions were noted.

Based on the audit procedures, Boyd concluded that the employee was clearing exceptions in a timely manner and that the control was operating effectively as of year end.

Following are examples of control deficiencies that may represent significant deficiencies or material weaknesses. For each control deficiency, indicate whether it is a significant deficiency or material weakness. Justify your decision. After you have tried on your own to assess the situation, look at the solution to see how well you did!

Scenario 1

Murray Company processes a significant number of routine inter-company transactions on a monthly basis. Individual intercompany transactions are not material and primarily relate to balance sheet activity; for example, cash transfers between business units to finance normal operations.

A formal management policy requires monthly reconciliation of inter-company accounts and confirmation of balances between business units. However, there is no process in place to ensure performance of these procedures. As a result, detailed reconciliations of inter-company accounts are not performed on a timely basis. Management does perform monthly procedures to investigate selected large-dollar inter-company account differences. In addition, management prepares a detailed monthly variance analysis of operating expenses to assess their reasonableness.

Scenario 2

Ragunandan Company processes a significant number of inter-company transactions on a monthly basis. Inter-company transactions relate to a wide range of activities, including transfers of inventory with inter-company profit between business units, allocation of research and development costs to business units, and corporate charges. Individual inter-company transactions are frequently material.

A formal management policy requires monthly reconciliation of inter-company accounts and confirmation of balances between business units. However, there is no process in place to ensure that these procedures are performed on a consistent basis. As a result, reconciliations of inter-company accounts are not performed on a timely basis, and differences in inter-company accounts are frequent and significant. Management does not perform any alternative controls to investigate significant inter-company account differences.

Solution: Scenario 1

Based only on these facts, the auditor should determine that this control deficiency represents a significant deficiency for the following reasons. The magnitude of a financial statement misstatement resulting from this deficiency would reasonably be expected to not be material but significant because individual inter-company transactions are not material, and the compensating controls operating monthly should detect a material misstatement. Furthermore, the transactions are primarily restricted to balance sheet accounts. However, the compensating detective controls are designed only to detect material misstatements. The controls do not address the detection of misstatements that are significant but not material. Therefore, the likelihood that a misstatement could occur is reasonably possible.

Solution: Scenario 2

Based only on these facts, the auditor should determine that this deficiency represents a material weakness for the following reasons. The magnitude of a financial statement misstatement resulting from this deficiency would reasonably be expected to be material, because individual inter-company transactions are frequently material and relate to a wide range of activities. Additionally, actual unreconciled differences in inter-company accounts have been, and are, material. The likelihood of such a misstatement is reasonably possible because such misstatements have frequently occurred and compensating controls are not effective, either because they are not properly designed or are not operating effectively. Taken together, the magnitude and likelihood of misstatement of the financial statements resulting from this internal control deficiency meet the definition of a material weakness.

❖ REMEDIATION OF A MATERIAL WEAKNESS

LO11

When an entity determines that it has a material weakness, it should take steps to correct it. This is referred to as **remediation**. If the material weakness cannot be corrected and/or properly tested before the 'as of' date, management and the auditor would issue reports that the ICFR is not operating effectively. If management corrects a material weakness before the 'as of' date, there must be sufficient time for both management and the auditor to adequately test the operating effectiveness of the control. If there is not sufficient time, then neither management nor the auditor can conclude that ICFR is effective. If there is sufficient time to remediate the material weakness and the testing shows that the new control is operating effectively, management and the auditor can issue a report that ICFR is operating effectively. Management would make the following type of disclosure in its FORM 10-K:

The Company has been actively engaged in the implementation of remediation efforts to address the material weakness in controls over income tax accounting that was in existence at December 31, 2008. These remediation efforts are specifically designed to address the material weakness identified by management. As a result of its assessment of the effectiveness of internal control over financial reporting, management determined that as of December 31, 2009, the material weakness relating to the controls over income tax accounting no longer existed.

 ## WRITTEN REPRESENTATIONS

LO12

In addition to the management representations obtained as part of a financial statement audit (see Chapter 17), the auditor obtains written representations from management related to the audit of ICFR. Table 7–8 presents a typical set of management representations made to the auditor related to the audit of internal control. Failure to obtain written representations from management, including management's refusal to furnish them, constitutes a limitation on the scope of the audit sufficient to preclude an unqualified opinion. While the required representations are typically drafted by the auditor, they are addressed to the auditor and are signed (and worded as if written) by the CEO and CFO.

Table 7–8   Written Representations Made by Management to the Auditor
• Management is responsible for establishing and maintaining effective ICFR.
• Management has performed an evaluation and made an assessment of the effectiveness of the company's ICFR and specifying the control criteria.
• Management did not rely on work performed by the auditor in forming its assessment of the effectiveness of ICFR.
• Management's conclusion about the effectiveness of the entity's ICFR based on the control criteria as of a specified date.
• Management has disclosed to the auditor all deficiencies in the design or operation of ICFR identified as part of management's evaluation, and has identified all such deficiencies that it believes to be significant deficiencies or material weaknesses.
• Descriptions of any material fraud and any other fraud that, although not material, involves senior management or management or other employees who have a significant role in the company's ICFR.
• Control deficiencies identified and communicated to the audit committee during previous engagements have (or have not) been resolved (and specifically identifying any that have not).
• Descriptions of any changes in ICFR or other factors that might significantly affect ICFR, including any corrective actions taken by management with regard to significant deficiencies and material weaknesses.
Source: AS5, para. 75

 ## AUDITOR DOCUMENTATION REQUIREMENTS

LO13

The auditor should document the processes, procedures, judgements and results relating to the audit of internal control. The auditor's documentation must include the auditor's understanding and evaluation of the design of each of the components of the entity's ICFR. The auditor also documents the process used to determine the points at which misstatements could occur within significant accounts and disclosures. The auditor must document the extent to which he or she relied upon work performed by others. Finally, the auditor must describe the evaluation of any deficiencies discovered, as well as any other findings, that could result in a modification to the auditor's report.

AUDITOR REPORTING ON ICFR

LO14

After auditing the effectiveness of a client's internal control, an auditor issues an unqualified opinion if the client's internal control is designed and operating effectively in all material respects. Significant deficiencies do not require a departure from an unqualified opinion because they relate to possible financial statement misstatements that are less than material. If the scope of the auditor's work is limited, a disclaimer of opinion is issued on the effectiveness of ICFR. If a material weakness is identified, the auditor issues an adverse opinion. Figure 7–4 gives an overview of the types of audit reports relating to the effectiveness of ICFR.

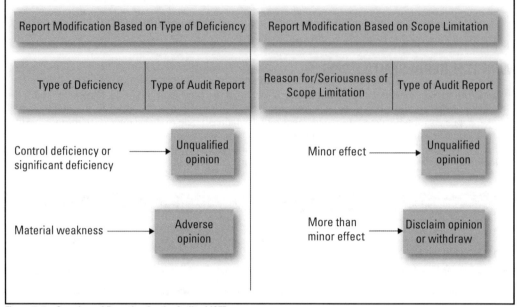

Figure 7–4   Overview of Reporting for the Audit of ICFR

Elements of the Auditor's Report

The auditor's report on the effectiveness of internal control has a number of required elements. The report identifies management's conclusion about the effectiveness of the company's ICFR and states that the assessment on which management's conclusion is based is the responsibility of management. The report defines ICFR and indicates that the standards of the PCAOB require that the auditor plan and perform the audit to obtain reasonable assurance about whether effective ICFR was maintained in all material respects. The report goes on to explain in general terms what an audit of ICFR entails and explicitly addresses the fact that even effective internal control cannot guarantee that misstatements will be prevented or detected and corrected. Finally, the report concludes with the auditor's opinion on whether the company maintained, in all material respects, effective ICFR 'as of' the end of the period.

The auditor may choose to issue separate reports on the company's financial statements and ICFR, or may issue a combined report. Under either approach, the date of the two reports should be the same. The following sections explain the unqualified report, the adverse report for material weaknesses, and the disclaimer of opinion for scope limitations.

Unqualified Report

An unqualified opinion regarding the effectiveness of the client's ICFR provides reasonable assurance that the client's controls are designed and operating effectively in all material respects 'as of' the balance sheet date. The phrase 'all material respects' means that the client's ICFR is free of any material weakness. An unqualified opinion can be issued even in the presence of significant deficiencies. Exhibit 7–4 presents an example of an auditor's unqualified report that is presented separately from the auditor's report on the financial statements. Note that the report includes an explanatory paragraph referring to the financial statement audit report. The last paragraph of the separate report on the financial statement would also include an explanatory paragraph referring to the audit of ICFR and indicating that an unqualified opinion was issued with respect to the effectiveness of internal control.

Exhibit 7–4 An Example of a Separate Report Giving an Unqualified Opinion on the Effectiveness of ICFR

Report of Independent Registered Public Accounting Firm

[Introductory Paragraph]

We have audited EarthWear Clothiers' internal control over financial reporting as of December 31, 2009, based on criteria established in *Internal Control – Integrated Framework*, issued by the Committee of Sponsoring Organizations of the Treadway Commission (COSO). EarthWear Clothiers' management is responsible for maintaining effective internal control over financial reporting and for its assessment of the effectiveness of internal control over financial reporting. Our responsibility is to express an opinion on the company's internal control over financial reporting based on our audit.

[Scope Paragraph]

We conducted our audit in accordance with the standards of the Public Company Accounting Oversight Board (United States). Those standards require that we plan and perform the audit to obtain reasonable assurance about whether effective internal control over financial reporting was maintained in all material respects. Our audit included obtaining an understanding of internal control over financial reporting, testing and evaluating the design and operating effectiveness of internal control, and performing such other procedures as we considered necessary in the circumstances. We believe that our audit provides a reasonable basis for our opinion.

[Definition Paragraph]

A company's internal control over financial reporting is a process designed to provide reasonable assurance regarding the reliability of financial reporting and the preparation of financial statements for external purposes in accordance with generally accepted accounting principles. A company's internal control over financial reporting includes those policies and procedures that (1) pertain to the maintenance of records that, in reasonable detail, accurately and fairly reflect the transactions and dispositions of the assets of the company; (2) provide reasonable assurance that transactions are recorded as necessary to permit preparation of financial statements in accordance with generally accepted accounting principles, and that receipts and expenditures of the company are being made only in accordance with authorizations of management and directors of the company; and (3) provide reasonable assurance regarding prevention or timely detection of unauthorized acquisition, use, or disposition of the company's assets that could have a material effect on the financial statements.

[Inherent Limitations Paragraph]

Because of its inherent limitations, internal control over financial reporting may not prevent or detect misstatements. Also, projections of any evaluation of effectiveness to future periods are subject to the risk that controls may become inadequate because of changes in conditions or that the degree of compliance with the policies or procedures may deteriorate.

[Opinion Paragraph]

In our opinion, EarthWear Clothiers maintained, in all material respects, effective internal control over financial reporting as of December 31, 2009, based on criteria established in *Internal Control – Integrated Framework*, issued by the Committee of Sponsoring Organizations of the Treadway Commission (COSO).

[Explanatory Paragraph]

We have also audited, in accordance with the standards of the Public Company Accounting Oversight Board (United States), the consolidated financial statements of EarthWear Clothiers, and our report dated February 15, 2010, expressed an unqualified opinion.

Willis & Adams International
Europolis
February 15, 2010

Exhibit 7–5 presents an example of a *combined report* for EarthWear Clothiers that gives an unqualified opinion on both the financial statement audit and the audit of ICFR. When the auditor elects to issue a combined report, the report may address multiple reporting periods for the financial statements presented but will address only the end of the most recent fiscal year for the effectiveness of internal control.

Exhibit 7–5 An Example of a Combined Report Expressing an Unqualified Opinion on Financial Statements and an Unqualified Opinion on the Effectiveness of ICFR

Report of Independent Registered Public Accounting Firm

[Introductory paragraph]

We have audited the accompanying balance sheets of EarthWear Clothiers as of December 31, 2009 and 2008, and the related statements of income, stockholders' equity and comprehensive income, and cash flows for each of the years in the three-year period ended December 31, 2009. We also have audited EarthWear Clothiers' internal control over financial reporting as of December 31, 2009, based on criteria established in Internal Control – Integrated Framework issued by the Committee of Sponsoring Organizations of the Treadway Commission (COSO). EarthWear Clothiers' management is responsible for these financial statements, for maintaining effective internal control over financial reporting, and for its assessment of the effectiveness of internal control over financial reporting, included in the accompanying Management Report on the Financial Statements and Internal Control. Our responsibility is to express an opinion on these financial statements and an opinion on the effectiveness of the company's internal control over financial reporting based on our audits.

[Scope paragraph]

We conducted our audits in accordance with the standards of the Public Company Accounting Oversight Board (United States). Those standards require that we plan and perform the audits to obtain reasonable assurance about whether the financial statements are free of material misstatement and whether effective internal control over financial reporting was maintained in all material respects. Our audit of financial statements included examining, on a test basis, evidence supporting the amounts and disclosures in the financial statements, assessing the accounting principles used and significant estimates made by management, and evaluating the overall financial statement presentation. Our audit of internal control over financial reporting included obtaining an understanding of internal control over financial reporting, testing and evaluating the design and operating effectiveness of internal control, and performing such other procedures as we considered necessary in the circumstances. We believe that our audits provide a reasonable basis for our opinions.

[Definition paragraph]

A company's internal control over financial reporting is a process designed to provide reasonable assurance regarding the reliability of financial reporting and the preparation of financial statements for external purposes in accordance with generally accepted accounting principles. A company's internal control over financial reporting includes those policies and procedures that (1) pertain to the maintenance of records that, in reasonable detail, accurately and fairly reflect the transactions and dispositions of the assets of the company; (2) provide reasonable assurance that transactions are recorded as necessary to permit preparation of financial statements in accordance with generally accepted accounting principles, and that receipts and expenditures of the company are being made only in accordance with authorizations of management and directors of the company; and (3) provide reasonable assurance regarding prevention or timely detection of unauthorized acquisition, use, or disposition of the company's assets that could have a material effect on the financial statements.

[Inherent limitations paragraph]

Because of its inherent limitations, internal control over financial reporting may not prevent or detect misstatements. Also, projections of any evaluation of effectiveness to future periods are subject to the risk that controls may become inadequate because of changes in conditions, or that the degree of compliance with the policies or procedures may deteriorate.

[Opinion paragraph]

In our opinion, the financial statements referred to above present fairly, in all material respects, the financial position of EarthWear Clothiers as of December 31, 2009 and 2008, and the results of its operations and its cash flows for each of the years in the three-year period ended December, 31 2009, in conformity with accounting principles generally accepted in the United States of America. Also, in our opinion, EarthWear Clothiers maintained, in all material respects, effective internal control over financial reporting as of December 31, 2009, based on criteria established in *Internal Control – Integrated Framework* issued by the Committee of Sponsoring Organizations of the Treadway Commission (COSO).

Willis & Adams International
Europolis
February 15, 2010

Adverse Report for a Material Weakness

The presence of a material weakness at the end of the period necessitates an adverse assessment by management and an adverse opinion by the auditor. An adverse report includes a definition of a material weakness and a description of the particular material weakness identified in the client's system of internal control, along with the auditor's opinion that the client has not maintained effective ICFR 'as of' the report date. See Exhibit 7–6 for an example of an adverse report.

Exhibit 7–6   An Example of an Adverse Opinion on the Effectiveness of ICFR Because of the Existence of a Material Weakness

Report of Independent Registered Public Accounting Firm
[Standard Wording for the Introductory, Scope, Definition and Inherent Limitations Paragraphs]
[Explanatory Paragraph]

A material weakness is a deficiency, or a combination of deficiencies, in internal control over financial reporting, such that there is a reasonable possibility that a material misstatement of the company's annual or interim financial statements will not be prevented or detected on a timely basis. The following material weakness has been identified and included in management's assessment. Treadron had an inadequate system for recording cash receipts, which could have prevented the Company from recording cash receipts on accounts receivable completely and properly. Therefore, cash received could have been diverted for unauthorized use, lost, or otherwise not properly recorded to accounts receivable. This material weakness was considered in determining the nature, timing, and extent of audit tests applied in our audit of the 2009 financial statements, and this report does not affect our report dated February 15, 2010, on those financial statements.

[Opinion Paragraph]

In our opinion, because of the effect of the material weakness described above on the achievement of the objectives of the control criteria, Treadron Company has not maintained effective internal control over financial reporting as of December 31, 2009, based on criteria established in *Internal Control – Integrated Framework*, issued by the Committee of Sponsoring Organizations of the Treadway Commission (COSO).

Mortensen & Mortensen
Houston, Texas
March 15, 2010

> ### Practice Insight 7.2
>
> In 2004, the first year of compliance with Rule 404 of the Sarbanes–Oxley Act, about 15.9 per cent of all auditor reports were adverse with respect to the effectiveness of internal control over financial reporting. In year 2005, the rate of adverse reports had fallen to slightly less than 10 per cent. Keep in mind, though, that the smallest public companies were granted a delay in the effective date of Rule 404. The results of their 404 audits will not be known for some time, but it is expected that the rate of adverse reports for these smaller public companies might be significantly higher than for the larger companies that have already been through the process.

It is possible for the auditor to issue an adverse opinion on internal control while at the same time issuing an unqualified opinion on the financial statement audit. Such a conclusion is reached when a client's internal control is not effective at preventing or detecting material errors, but the auditor concludes (based on substantive procedures) that the client's financial statements do not contain material misstatements. Such circumstances can arise when an identified material weakness does not actually result in a misstatement in the financial statements or when a material weakness does result in a material misstatement but the client corrects the misstatement prior to issuing the financial statements.

Whether or not the auditor's opinion on the financial statements is affected by the adverse opinion on the effectiveness of ICFR, the report on ICFR (or the combined report) should indicate that the weakness was considered in determining the nature, timing and extent of financial statement audit tests in the paragraph that describes the material weakness. Such disclosure is important to ensure that users of the auditor's report on the financial statements understand why the auditor issued an unqualified opinion on those statements.

> ### Practice Insight 7.3
>
> In the first two years of Sarbanes–Oxley compliance, approximately 75 per cent of the material weaknesses reported were identified when the auditor discovered a material misstatement while conducting substantive audit procedures. When a material misstatement is discovered, the auditor does a 'root cause analysis' to find out why the client's internal control over financial reporting failed to prevent or detect the misstatement. Such an analysis usually leads to the identification of a material weakness.

Disclosure is also important when the auditor's opinion on the financial statements *is* affected by the adverse opinion on the effectiveness of internal control. In such a circumstance, the report on ICFR (or the combined report) should similarly indicate that the material weakness was considered in determining the nature, timing and extent of procedures performed as part of the financial statement audit.

Disclaimer for Scope Limitation

The auditor can express an unqualified opinion on the effectiveness of ICFR only if the auditor has been able to apply all the procedures necessary in the circumstances. If the scope of the auditor's work is limited because of circumstances beyond the control of management or the auditor, the auditor should disclaim an opinion or withdraw from the engagement. The auditor's decision depends on an assessment of the importance of the omitted procedure(s) to his or her ability to form an opinion.

OTHER REPORTING ISSUES

Management's Report Incomplete or Improperly Presented

If the auditor determines that elements of management's annual report on ICFR are incomplete or improperly presented, the auditor should modify his or her report to include an explanatory paragraph describing the reasons for this determination.

The Auditor Decides to Refer to the Report of Other Auditors

On some engagements parts of the audit may be completed by another public accounting firm. In such circumstances, the auditor must decide whether to refer to work performed by the other auditor. The decision is based on factors similar to those considered by the auditor who uses the work and reports of other independent auditors when reporting on a company's financial statements. If the auditor decides to make reference to the report of the other auditor as a basis, in part, for his or her opinion, the auditor should refer to the report of the other auditor in describing the scope of the audit and in expressing the opinion (AS5, paras C8–C14).

Subsequent Events

The auditor has a responsibility to report on any changes in internal control that might affect financial reporting between the end of the reporting period and the date of the auditor's report. The auditor's treatment of a subsequent event depends on whether the event reveals information about a material weakness that existed 'as of' the end of the reporting period, or whether the event creates or reveals information about a new condition that did not exist 'as of' the end of the reporting period.

Management's Report Contains Additional Information

Management may include additional information in its report on ICFR. For example, management may include disclosures about corrective actions taken by the company after the date of management's assessment, the company's plans to implement new controls, or a statement that management believes the cost of correcting a material weakness would exceed the benefits to be derived from implementing new controls. The auditor should disclaim an opinion on such information and include the following language as the last paragraph of the report:

> We do not express an opinion or any other form of assurance on management's statement referring to the costs and related benefits of implementing new controls.

If the auditor believes that the additional information contains a material misstatement of fact, he or she should discuss the matter with management. If the auditor concludes that a material misstatement of fact remains after discussing it with management, he or she should notify the audit committee in writing. The auditor also should consider consulting the auditor's legal counsel about further actions to be taken, including the auditor's responsibility under the Securities Exchange Act of 1934 (AS5, para. C14).

Reporting on a Remediated Material Weakness at an Interim Date

The PCAOB Auditing Standard No. 4 provides direction for auditors in reporting on whether a material weakness continues to exist at an interim date. As a result of this standard, rather than making a client wait 12 months to receive a clean opinion regarding its ICFR in the next year-end report, the auditor can provide an interim opinion once management has remediated the material weakness. This standard allows auditors to attest on a timely basis as to whether a client has eliminated the cause of a previously issued adverse opinion regarding its ICFR.

❖ ADDITIONAL REQUIRED COMMUNICATIONS IN AN AUDIT OF ICFR

LO15

The auditor has a number of communication responsibilities under AS5. The auditor must communicate in writing to management and the audit committee all significant deficiencies and material weaknesses identified during the audit. The written communication should be made prior to the issuance of the auditor's report on ICFR. The auditor's communication should distinguish clearly between those matters considered to be significant deficiencies and those considered to be material weaknesses. If a significant deficiency or material weakness exists because the oversight by the company's audit committee is ineffective, the auditor must communicate that specific significant deficiency or material weakness in writing to the board of directors.

In addition, the auditor should communicate to management, in writing, all control deficiencies (deficiencies in internal control that are not material or significant – see Figure 7–1) identified during the audit, and inform the audit committee when such a communication has been made. Keep in mind that the auditor's role is to identify material weaknesses. The auditor is not required to perform procedures to identify control deficiencies that do not rise to the level of a material weakness.

The auditor's written communication about control deficiencies states that the communication is intended solely for the information and use of the board of directors, audit committee, management and others within the organization. When governmental authorities require the entity to furnish such a report, a specific reference to such regulatory agencies may be made in the report. These written communications also include the definitions of control deficiencies, significant deficiencies and material weaknesses, and clearly identify the types of deficiencies being communicated. The auditor's communication may indicate that no material weaknesses were identified if none were found. However, because the auditor's procedures were geared towards detecting material weaknesses, the auditor may not represent that no significant deficiencies were noted during an audit of internal control.

When auditing ICFR, the auditor may become aware of fraud or other possible illegal acts. If the matter involves fraud, it must be brought to the attention of the appropriate level of management. If the fraud involves senior management, the auditor must communicate the matter directly to the audit committee. If the matter involves other possible illegal acts, the auditor must be assured that the audit committee is adequately informed, unless the matter is clearly inconsequential. When timely communication is important, the auditor communicates such matters during the course of the audit rather than at the end of the engagement.

ADVANCED MODULE: SPECIAL CONSIDERATIONS FOR AN AUDIT OF INTERNAL CONTROL

The PCAOB specifies two areas that require special consideration by management and the auditor during an audit of ICFR:

1 Service organizations.
2 Safeguarding assets.

❖ Use of Service Organizations

LO16

Many companies use service organizations to process transactions. If the service organization's services make up part of a company's information system, then they are considered part of the information and communication component of the company's ICFR. Thus, both management and the auditor must consider the activities of the service organization.

Management and the auditor should perform the following procedures with respect to the activities performed by the service organization: (1) obtain an understanding of the controls at the service organization that are relevant to the entity's internal control and the controls at the user organization over the activities of the service organization; and (2) obtain evidence that the controls that are relevant to management's assessment and the auditor's opinion are operating effectively.

Evidence about the operating effectiveness of controls that are relevant to management's assessment and the auditor's opinion may be obtained by performing tests of the user organization's controls over the activities of the service organization, performing tests of controls at the service organization, or obtaining a service auditor's report on the design and operating effectiveness of controls placed in operation at the service organization (often referred to as a 'SAS No. 70 report'). If a service auditor's report on controls placed in operation and tests of operating effectiveness is available, management and the auditor separately evaluate whether this report provides sufficient evidence to support the assessment and opinion. Important factors that management and the auditor should consider include the scope of the examination, the controls tested, the results of those tests of controls, and the service auditor's opinion on the operating effectiveness of the controls. Management and the auditor should also make inquiries concerning the service auditor's reputation, competence and independence.

When a significant period of time has elapsed between the time period covered by the tests of controls in the service auditor's report and the date of management's assessment, additional procedures should be performed.

If the auditor concludes that additional evidence about the operating effectiveness of controls at the service organization is required, the auditor should perform additional procedures. For example, the auditor might investigate whether management has taken actions to monitor or evaluate the quality of the service provider and evaluate the results of such actions. The auditor might also contact the service organization to obtain specific information, or request that a service auditor be engaged to perform procedures that will supply the necessary information. Finally, the auditor might even visit the service organization and perform such procedures first hand. Based on the evidence obtained, management and the auditor should determine whether they have obtained sufficient evidence to obtain the reasonable assurance necessary for their assessment and opinion, respectively.

❖ Safeguarding of Assets

LO17

Safeguarding of assets is defined in AS5 as policies and procedures that 'provide reasonable assurance regarding prevention or timely detection of unauthorized acquisition, use or disposition of the company's assets that could have a material effect on the financial statements'. This definition is consistent with the definition in the COSO framework. For example, a company could have safeguarding controls over inventory tags (preventive controls) and perform timely periodic physical inventory counts (detective control) for its quarterly and annual financial reporting dates. Given that the definitions of material weakness and significant deficiency relate to the likelihood of misstatement of the financial statements, the failure of the inventory tag control will not result in a significant deficiency or material weakness if the physical inventory count prevents a misstatement of the financial statements. Therefore, the COSO definition indicates that although losses might occur, controls over financial reporting are effective if they provide reasonable assurance that those losses are properly reflected in the financial statements.

🔓 Key Terms

Control deficiency. A weakness in the design or operation of a control such that management or employees, in the normal course of performing their assigned functions, fail to prevent or detect misstatements on a timely basis.

Control objective. An objective for ICFR generally relates to a relevant financial statement assertion and states a criterion for evaluating whether the company's control activities in a specific area provide reasonable assurance that a misstatement or omission in that relevant assertion is prevented or detected by controls on a timely basis.

Entity-level controls. Controls that have a pervasive effect on the entity's system of internal control such as controls related to the control environment (for example, management's philosophy and operating style, integrity and ethical values; board or audit committee oversight; and assignment of authority and responsibility); controls over management override; the company's risk assessment process; centralized processing and controls, including shared service environments; controls to monitor results of operations; controls to monitor other controls, including activities of the internal audit function, the audit committee and self-assessment programs; controls over the period-end financial reporting process; and policies that address significant business control and risk management practices.

Material weakness. A deficiency, or a combination of deficiencies, in ICFR, such that there is a reasonable possibility that a material misstatement of the company's annual or interim financial statements will not be prevented or detected on a timely basis.

Relevant assertion. A financial statement assertion that has a reasonable possibility of containing a misstatement or misstatements that would cause the financial statements to be materially misstated.

Remediation. The process of correcting a material weakness as part of management's assessment of the effectiveness of ICFR.

Safeguarding of assets. Those policies and procedures that provide reasonable assurance regarding prevention or timely detection of unauthorized acquisition, use or disposition of the company's assets that could have a material effect on the financial statements.

Significant deficiency. A deficiency, or a combination of deficiencies, in ICFR that is less severe than a material weakness, yet important enough to merit attention by those responsible for oversight of the company's financial reporting.

Walk-through. A transaction being traced by an auditor from origination through the entity's information system until it is reflected in the entity's financial reports. It encompasses the entire process of initiating, authorizing, recording, processing and reporting individual transactions and controls for each of the significant processes identified.

? Review Questions

LO1,2   **7–1**   Briefly summarize management's and the auditor's basic responsibilities under Section 404 of the Sarbanes–Oxley Act 2002.

LO4   **7–2**   Discuss how the terms *likelihood* and *magnitude* play a role in evaluating the significance of a control deficiency.

LO5   **7–3**   The first element in management's process for assessing the effectiveness of internal control is determining which controls should be tested. Identify the controls that would typically be tested by management.

LO5,8   **7–4**   Describe how management and the auditor decide on which locations or business units to test.

LO5   **7–5**   Management must document its assessment of internal control. What would such documentation include?

LO6   **7–6**   List the steps in the auditor's process for an audit of ICFR.

LO7   **7–7**   How does the auditor evaluate the competence and objectivity of others who perform work for management?

LO7,8   **7–8**   Describe the steps in obtaining an understanding of ICFR using a top-down, risk-based approach.

LO8   **7–9**   The period-end financial reporting process controls are always important. What are those controls and what should the auditor's evaluation of those controls include?

LO8   **7–10**   A walk-through involves tracing a transaction through the information system. What types of evidence does a walk-through provide to the auditor?

LO10   **7–11**   AS5 indicates that certain circumstances are indicators of a material weakness. What are these circumstances, and why do you think the PCAOB assessed them as being of such importance?

LO11   **7–12**   Describe what is meant when management remediates a material weakness. If a material weakness is remediated before the 'as of' date and sufficiently tested, what can management assert about ICFR?

LO13   **7–13**   What are the auditor's documentation requirements for an audit of ICFR?

LO14   **7–14**   What are the types of reports that an auditor can issue for an audit of ICFR? Briefly identify the circumstances justifying each type of report.

LO14   **7–15**   Under what circumstances would an auditor give an adverse opinion on the effectiveness of a client's ICFR?

LO14   **7–16**   Under what circumstances would an auditor disclaim an opinion on the effectiveness of a client's ICFR?

LO16   **7–17**   What should the auditor do when a significant period of time has elapsed between the service organization auditor's report and the date of management's assessment?

✒ Problems

LO6,7,8   **7–18**   Following are three examples of controls for accounts that you have determined are significant for the audit of ICFR. For each control, determine the nature, timing and extent of testing of the design and operating effectiveness.

Refer to Exhibit 7–3 for a way to format your answer.

Control 1. Monthly Manual Reconciliation: Through discussions with company personnel and review of company documentation, you find that company personnel reconcile the accounts receivable subsidiary ledger to the general ledger on a monthly basis. To determine whether misstatements in accounts receivable (existence, valuation and completeness) would be detected on a timely basis, you decide to test the control provided by the monthly reconciliation process.

Control 2. Daily Manual Preventive Control: Through discussions with company personnel, you learn that company personnel make a cash disbursement only after they have matched the vendor invoice to the receiver and purchase order.

To determine whether misstatements in cash (existence) and accounts payable (existence, valuation and completeness) would be prevented on a timely basis, you decide to test the control over making a cash disbursement only after matching the invoice with the receiver and purchase.

Control 3. Programmed Preventive Control and Weekly Information Technology-Dependent Manual Detective Control: Through discussions with company personnel, you learn that the company's computer system performs a three-way match of the receiving report, purchase order and invoice. If there are any exceptions, the system produces a list of unmatched items that employees review and follow up weekly. The computer match is a programmed application control, and the review and follow-up of the unmatched items report is a manual detective control. To determine whether misstatements in cash and accounts payable–inventory would be prevented or detected on a timely basis, you decide to test the programmed application control of matching the receiver, purchase order, and invoice, as well as the review and follow-up control over unmatched items.

LO4,6,10   **7–19**   Following are examples of control deficiencies that may represent significant deficiencies or material weaknesses. For each control deficiency, indicate whether it is a significant deficiency or material weakness. Justify your decision.

a   The company uses a standard sales contract for most transactions. Individual sales transactions are not material to the entity. Sales personnel are allowed to modify sales contract terms. The company's accounting function reviews significant or unusual modifications to the sales contract terms, but does not review changes in the standard shipping terms. The changes in the standard shipping terms could require a delay in the timing of revenue recognition. Management reviews gross margins on a monthly basis and investigates any significant or unusual relationships. In addition, management reviews the reasonableness of inventory levels at the end of each accounting period. The entity has experienced limited situations in which revenue has been inappropriately recorded in advance of shipment, but amounts have not been material.

b   The company has a standard sales contract, but sales personnel frequently modify the terms of the contract. The nature of the modifications can affect the timing and amount of revenue recognized. Individual sales transactions are frequently material to the entity, and the gross margin can vary significantly for each transaction. The company does not have procedures in place for the accounting function to regularly review modifications to sales contract terms. Although management reviews gross margins on a monthly basis, the significant differences in gross margins on individual transactions make it difficult for management to identify potential misstatements. Improper revenue recognition has occurred, and the amounts have been material.

c   The company has a standard sales contract, but sales personnel frequently modify the terms of the contract. Sales personnel frequently grant unauthorized and unrecorded sales discounts to customers without the knowledge of the accounting department. These amounts are deducted by customers in paying their invoices and are recorded as outstanding balances on the accounts receivable ageing. Although these amounts are individually insignificant, when added up they are material and have occurred regularly over the past few years.

LO4,6,10   **7–20**   Following are examples of control deficiencies that may represent significant deficiencies or material weaknesses. For each of the following scenarios, indicate whether the deficiency is a significant deficiency or material weakness. Justify your decision.

    a   During its assessment of ICFR, the management of Lorenz Corporation and its auditors identified the following control deficiencies that individually represent significant deficiencies:

- Inadequate segregation of duties over certain information system access controls.
- Several instances of transactions that were not properly recorded in subsidiary ledgers. While the transactions that were not recorded properly were not material, the gross amount of the transactions of that type totalled up to an amount several times materiality.
- A lack of timely reconciliations of the account balances affected by the improperly recorded transactions.

    b   During its assessment of ICFR, management of First Coast BankCorp and its auditors identified the following deficiencies that individually represent significant deficiencies: the design of controls over the estimation of credit losses (a critical accounting estimate); the operating effectiveness of controls for initiating, processing and reviewing adjustments to the allowance for credit losses; and the operating effectiveness of controls designed to prevent and detect the improper recognition of interest income. In addition, during the past year, First Coast experienced a significant level of growth in the loan balances that were subjected to the controls governing credit loss estimation and revenue recognition, and further growth is expected in the upcoming year.

LO4,10,14   **7–21**   For each of the following independent situations, indicate the type of report on ICFR you would issue. Justify your report choice.

    a   Johnson Company's management does not have an adequate antifraud program or controls.
    b   Tap, Tap, & Associates completed the integrated audit of Maxim Corporation. It did not identify any control deficiencies during its audit.
    c   During the audit of Fritz, Inc., Boyd & Company discovered a material misstatement that was not discovered by Fritz's internal control system.
    d   Scoles Manufacturing Company does not have adequate controls over non-routine sales transactions.
    e   Lee, Leis, & Monk (LL&M) performs the audit of Freedom Insurance Company. LL&M has determined that Freedom has an ineffective regulatory compliance function.

LO4,10,14   **7–22**   For each of the following independent situations, indicate the type of report on ICFR you would issue. Justify your report choice.

    a   Hansen, Inc., has restated previously issued financial statements to reflect the correction of a misstatement.
    b   Shu & Han Engineering does not have effective oversight of the company's external financial reporting.
    c   Kim Semiconductor has an ineffective audit committee.
    d   The internal audit function at Smith Components, a very large manufacturing company, was ineffective. The company's auditor has determined that the internal audit function needed to be effective in order for the company to have an effective monitoring component.
    e   The auditors of Benron identified significant financial statement fraud by the company's chief financial officer.
    f   Conroy Trucking Company has an ineffective control environment.
    g   Edwards & Eddins, independent auditors, communicated significant deficiencies to Waste Disposal's management and the audit committee for the last two years. At the end of the current year, these significant deficiencies remain uncorrected.

LO10,14   **7–23**   For each of the following independent situations relating to the audit of ICFR, indicate the reason for and the type of audit report you would issue.

a During the audit of Wood Pharmaceuticals, you are surprised to find several control deficiencies in the company's internal control. You determine that there is a reasonable possibility that any one of them could result in a misstatement that is significant. Although the odds are extremely low that the deficiencies, singly or taken together, will result in a material misstatement of the company's financial statements, the large number of problems causes you concern. Management's written assessment concludes that the company's ICFR was effective 'as of' the report date.

b You agreed to perform an audit for Rodriguez & Co., after the client's year end. Due to time constraints, your audit firm could not complete a full audit of ICFR. However, the evidence you did collect suggests that the company has exceptionally strong ICFR. You seriously doubt that a material weakness would have been found if time had permitted a more thorough audit. Management's written assessment concludes that the company's ICFR was effective 'as of' the report date.

c George & Diana Company's internal audit function identified a material weakness in the company's ICFR. The client corrected this weakness about four months prior to the end of the annual reporting period. Management reassessed controls in the area and found them effective. After re-evaluating and retesting the relevant controls, you believe the controls to have been effective for a sufficient period of time to provide adequate evidence that they were designed and operating effectively 'as of' the end of the client's reporting period. Management's written assessment concludes that the company's ICFR was effective 'as of' the report date.

d Reynolds' Distilleries identified what you agree is a material weakness and made an adverse assessment in its report on ICFR. The company had not corrected the material weakness 'as of' the end of the reporting period.

e Cindy & David Company's management identified a material weakness in the company's ICFR during its assessment process. The client corrected this weakness about a month prior to the end of the annual reporting period. Management reassessed controls in the area, and believes they were effective 'as of' the end of the reporting period. After re-evaluating and retesting the relevant controls, you agree that the new controls are well designed, but since the controls over this particular area are applied only once at the end of each month (i.e. the controls have only operated twice since being corrected), you do not believe you have sufficient audit evidence to assess their operating effectiveness. Management's written assessment concludes that the company's internal control was effective 'as of' the report date.

f During the audit of ICFR for Big Al & Larry Industries, you discover several control deficiencies. You determine that there is more than a reasonable possibility that any one of them could result in a financial statement misstatement. Although you do not believe that any of the deficiencies taken individually will result in a material misstatement, you believe there is a moderately low likelihood that, taken together, the deficiencies could produce a material misstatement. Management's written assessment concludes that the company's internal control was effective 'as of' the report date.

LO10,14   **7–24**   For each of the following independent situations, indicate the type of report on ICFR you would issue. Justify your report choice.

a The management's report on ICFR issued by Graham Granary, Inc., includes disclosures about corrective actions taken by the company after the date of management's assessment and the company's plans to implement new controls.

b Meryll Company's management identified a material weakness prior to the 'as of' date and implemented controls to correct it. Management believes that the new controls have been operating for a sufficient period of time to determine that they are designed and operating effectively. However, Meryll's auditor disagrees with the sufficiency of the time period for testing the operating effectiveness of the controls.

LO10,14   **7-25**   Assume that scenario a in Problem 7–20 is a material weakness. Prepare a draft of the auditor's report for an audit of ICFR. Assume that Lorenz's auditor is issuing a separate report on internal control.

LO10,14   **7-26**   Assume that scenario b in Problem 7–20 is a material weakness. Prepare a draft of the auditor's report for an audit of ICFR. Assume that First Coast's auditor is issuing a combined report for the financial statement audit and audit of internal control.

LO10,14   **7-27**   The following audit report was drafted by a junior staff accountant of Lipske & Griffin, CPAs, at the completion of the audit of Douglas Company's ICFR. The report was submitted to the engagement partner, who reviewed matters thoroughly and properly concluded that there was a material weakness in the client's ICFR. Douglas's management agreed and wrote an assessment indicating that the company's ICFR was not effective 'as of' the end of the reporting period. Sufficient appropriate evidence was obtained during the financial statement audit to provide reasonable assurance that the overall financial statements present fairly in accordance with GAAP.

Required:

Identify the errors and omissions contained in the auditor's report as drafted by the staff accountant. Group the errors and omissions by paragraph, where applicable. Do not redraft the report.

Report of Independent Registered Public Accounting Firm

[Introductory paragraph]

We have audited management's assessment, included in the accompanying Management Report on the Financial Statements and Internal Control, that Douglas did not maintain effective internal control over financial reporting as of December 31, 2009, based on criteria established in *Enterprise Risk Management – Integrated Framework* issued by the Committee of Sponsoring Organizations of the Treadway Commission (COSO). Douglas's management is responsible for maintaining effective internal control over financial reporting and for its assessment of the effectiveness of internal control over financial reporting. Our responsibility is to express an opinion on management's assessment and an opinion on the effectiveness of the company's internal control over financial reporting based on our audit.

[Scope paragraph]

We conducted our audit in accordance with generally accepted auditing standards (United States). Those standards require that we plan and perform the audit to obtain assurance about whether effective internal control was maintained. Our audit included obtaining an understanding of internal control over financial reporting, evaluating management's assessment, testing and evaluating the operating effectiveness of internal control, and performing such other procedures as we considered necessary in the circumstances. We believe that our audit provides a reasonable basis for our opinion.

[Definition paragraph]

A company's internal control over financial reporting is a process designed to provide assurance regarding the reliability of financial reporting and the preparation of financial statements for external purposes in accordance with generally accepted auditing principles. A company's internal control over financial reporting includes those policies and procedures that (1) pertain to the maintenance of records that, in reasonable detail, accurately and fairly reflect the transactions and dispositions of the assets of the company; (2) provide assurance that transactions are recorded as necessary to permit preparation of financial statements in accordance with generally accepted auditing principles, and that receipts and expenditures of the company are being made only in accordance with authorizations of management and directors of the company; and (3) provide assurance regarding prevention or timely detection of unauthorized acquisition, use, or disposition of the company's assets that could have an inconsequential effect on the financial statements.

[Inherent limitations paragraph]

Because of its inherent limitations, internal control over financial reporting will prevent or detect misstatements. Also, projections of any evaluation of effectiveness to future periods are subject to the risk that controls may become inadequate because of changes in conditions, or that the degree of compliance with the policies or procedures may deteriorate.

[Opinion paragraph]

In our opinion, management's assessment that Douglas maintained ineffective internal control over financial reporting as of December 31, 2009, is fairly stated, in all material respects, based on criteria established in *Enterprise Risk Management – Integrated Framework* issued by the Committee of Sponsoring Organizations of the Treadway Commission (COSO). We therefore express an adverse opinion on management's assessment. Also in our opinion, Douglas maintained, in all material respects, effective internal control over financial reporting as of December 31, 2009, based on criteria established in *Enterprise Risk Management – Integrated Framework* issued by the Committee of Sponsoring Organizations of the Treadway Commission (COSO), except for one material weakness, which results in our issuing a qualified opinion on Douglas's internal control over financial reporting.

[Explanatory paragraph]

We have also audited, in accordance with generally accepted accounting standards (United States), the consolidated financial statements of Douglas, and our report dated February 15, 2010, expressed a qualified opinion.

Lipske & Griffin, CPAs
Mapleton, Arizona
March 11, 2010

Internet Assignments

LO4,10,14   7–28   Search the Internet (e.g. a company's website or sec.gov), and find an audit report for a company's audit of internal control over financial reporting. Determine whether the company used the combined or separate format.

LO4,14   7–29   Search the Internet (e.g. a company's website or sec.gov), and find an audit report for a company's audit of internal control over financial reporting that expresses an adverse opinion with respect to the effectiveness of internal control.

Notes

i   For a discussion of how the auditor might use a benchmarking strategy, refer to AS5, paras B28–B33.

PART IV

Statistical and Non-Statistical Sampling Tools for Auditing

PART CONTENTS

8 Audit Sampling: An Overview and Application to Tests of Controls
9 Audit Sampling: An Application to Substantive Tests of Account Balances

CHAPTER

8

Audit Sampling: An Overview and Application to Tests of Controls

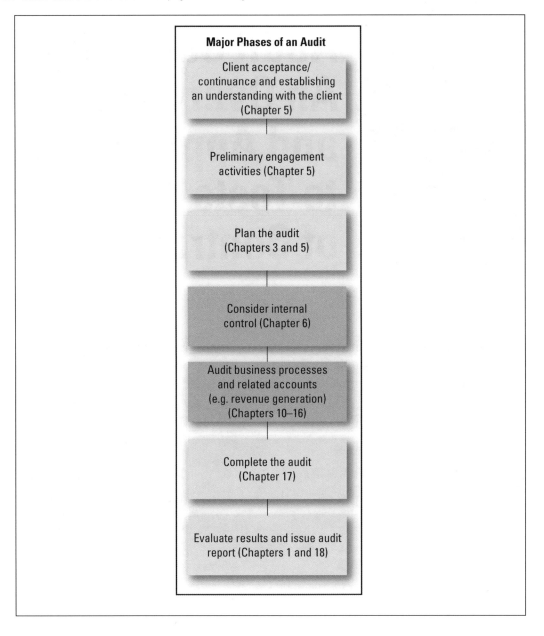

❖ *RELEVANT ACCOUNTING AND AUDITING PRONOUNCEMENTS*

AICPA, *Audit Sampling* (Audit Guide), AICPA, New York, 2008

ISA 230, Audit Documentation

ISA 240, The Auditor's Responsibilities Relating to Fraud in an Audit of Financial Statements

ISA 265, Communicating Deficiencies in Internal Control to Those Charged with Governance and Management

ISA 300, Planning an Audit of Financial Statements

ISA 315, Identifying and Assessing the Risks of Material Misstatement through Understanding the Entity and Its Environment

ISA 320, Materiality in Planning and Performing an Audit

ISA 330, The Auditor's Responses to Assessed Risks

ISA 450, Evaluation of Misstatements Identified during the Audit

ISA 500, Audit Evidence

ISA 530, Audit Sampling

IN THE NEXT TWO chapters we examine how auditors apply sampling theory to gather evidence to confirm or disconfirm management's assertions. Sampling and statistics in general are topics that make many people feel uncomfortable. Before getting into technical audit sampling and statistical terms, we have found that it is useful for students to consider some of the basic concepts of sampling in a non-technical context.

WHAT IF YOU WERE AN APPLE INSPECTOR?

Please imagine that you have just taken a job as an apple inspector for Best Apples – a large apple grower. You are replacing a previous inspector who was recently fired for lack of due care, and your new employer has made it clear that you must meet high performance standards to make it through your probationary period. Best Apples owns and operates many apple orchards and sells its apples to major fruit processors (hereafter 'buyers') whose products include fresh apples, apple sauce and apple juice. Best Apples makes large shipments of apples to buyers on a daily basis during harvest season; each shipment contains approximately 1,500 bushels from various orchards. Each bushel (about 35 litres) contains 100 to 150 apples. The bushel indicates which orchard the apples came from. Your job is to manually inspect the quality of apples just prior to shipment. Obviously, there is neither the time nor need to inspect every apple, so you will examine a sample of apples.

Imagine it is your first day on the job; consider for a moment what information about the apples, your employer or the buyer, you would like to know before you begin your inspections. Among other things, before beginning your inspection, it would be useful to know the answers to the following questions:

- For what purpose will the current shipment be used (e.g. fresh apples, sauce or juice)?
- The definition of a defect – what constitutes a bad apple?
- Tolerable defect percentage – what percentage of defective apples will the buyers accept in a shipment?
- What has Best Apples' historical defect percentage been?
- Have growing conditions (e.g. weather, pests) been normal this year?
- What happens if we send a shipment that contains an unacceptably high percentage of defects?
- Level of assurance or confidence – how confident do I need to be in my testing results?
- What quality controls and processes does Best Apples have in place?
- Are the defect percentages the same for all orchards?

Suppose you receive satisfactory answers to these questions and you begin your testing. The primary purpose of sampling is to draw inferences about the whole population based on the results of testing only a subset of the **population**. You draw a sample of 20 apples and find 1 defective apple. Projecting your sample defect rate to the total population suggests a shipment defect rate of 5 per cent (1/20). While 5 per cent is your best estimate based on your sample results, will you be positive that you have determined the correct defect rate for the entire shipment? The obvious answer is no, because there is a chance the shipment defect rate could be higher or lower than your sample rate of 5 per cent. The uncertainty associated with sampling is known as sampling risk. Whenever inspectors or auditors test less than the entire population, there is a risk that the sample results will not be similar to what the results would be if the inspector were to test the entire population. In other words, sampling risk is the risk that the results of a sample are not representative of the population.

Sampling theory allows us to measure the risk associated with sampling. For example, if we know a buyer would accept up to 10 per cent defective apples in a shipment, we can compute the risk that the actual shipment defect rate is higher than 10 per cent (you will learn how to make such evaluations in this chapter). For a sample of 20 apples with 1 defective apple there is approximately a 40 per cent chance that the actual shipment defect rate exceeds the buyer's tolerable defect rate of 10 per cent. Inspectors and auditors can reduce sampling risk by taking larger samples. In the extreme, if you tested 100 per cent of the apples in a shipment, then there would be no sampling risk because you would know with certainty the true shipment defect rate. While it would not be economical for you to inspect every apple, you could increase your sample size to reduce the risk that the shipment will contain an unacceptably high rate of defects. If you examine a sample of 100 apples and find 5 defects, sampling theory indicates that you would face only approximately a 6 per cent chance that the true shipment defect rate exceeds the buyer's tolerable rate of 10 per cent. So an important concept in audit sampling is that by increasing sample size, you can reduce uncertainty and risk.

The converse of sampling risk is *confidence level*. In other words, while both samples discussed above yielded a defect rate of 5 per cent (1/20 and 5/100), with the larger sample you can be approximately 94 per cent confident (100 per cent – 6 per cent sampling risk) that the shipment is acceptable. The smaller sample allows you to be only 60 per cent confident (100 per cent – 40 per cent sampling risk). We will continue to refer back to this apple inspector example as we introduce sampling terms and concepts in this chapter.

This chapter has two overall objectives: (1) to provide an introduction and overview of audit sampling; and (2) to apply statistical and non-statistical sampling techniques to tests of controls. In Chapter 9 we cover statistical and non-statistical sampling techniques for substantive tests of account balances.

❖ INTRODUCTION

LO1

In the early days of auditing, it was not unusual for the independent auditor to examine all of the records of the company being audited.[i] However, as companies grew in size and complexity, it became uneconomical to examine all of the accounting records and supporting documents. Auditors found it necessary to draw conclusions about the fairness of a company's financial statements based on an examination of a subset of the records and transactions. As a result, the auditor provides reasonable, not absolute, assurance that the financial statements are fairly presented. The justification for accepting some uncertainty is the trade-off between the cost of examining all of the data and the cost of making an incorrect decision based on a sample of the data. As noted in Chapter 1, this concept of reasonable assurance is addressed in the auditor's report.

Auditing standards recognize and permit both statistical and non-statistical methods of audit sampling. Research suggests that non-statistical methods are the most common in practice.[ii] Later in the chapter we discuss some reasons why **non-statistical sampling** has become more common in practice. Both non-statistical and statistical methods are based on the same fundamental sampling theories. In fact, the steps and techniques used for these two sampling approaches are far more similar than they are different. To properly apply a non-statistical sampling approach, it is necessary to understand the underlying statistical principles; thus, we cover statistical sampling before we discuss non-statistical sampling.

Occasionally, students will ask if recent advances in technology have or will eliminate the need for audit sampling. Two advances have reduced the number of times auditors need to apply sampling techniques to gather audit evidence. First, many companies have developed well-controlled, automated accounting systems that can process routine transactions with no or very few errors. Rather than rely on audit sampling to test routine transactions processed by these automated information systems, auditors test the processing software control configurations and general computer controls (e.g. restricted access, program change management) associated with the automated controls. Second, the advent of powerful audit software such as Audit Command Language (ACL) allows auditors, in some situations, to download and examine electronic client data rather than sample.

While technology has reduced the number of situations where audit sampling is necessary, technology will never eliminate the need for auditors to rely on sampling to some degree because: (1) many control processes require human involvement to operate effectively (e.g. reconciliations, review and resolution of a system's generated exception reports); (2) many testing procedures require the auditor to physically examine an asset (e.g. inventory) or inspect characteristics of a transaction or balance (e.g. terms in a contract); and (3) in many cases auditors are required to obtain and examine evidence from third parties (e.g. letters confirming accounts receivable balances from client customers). These situations require the auditor's 'hands-on' attention. When the number of items or transactions in these populations is large, it is not economical for auditors to test 100 per cent of the population; instead they use sampling to gather sufficient audit evidence.

DEFINITIONS AND KEY CONCEPTS

Audit Sampling

Auditing standards define **audit sampling** as the application of an audit procedure to less than 100 per cent of the items within a population of audit relevance such that all sampling units have a chance of selection in order to provide the auditor with a reasonable basis on which to draw conclusions about the entire population (ISA 530, para. 5 (a)). The auditor's alternatives to audit sampling are selecting all items in a population (100 per cent examination) or selecting specific items from a population (for example, all items over a certain amount).

 ## Sampling Risk

LO2

When sampling is used by an auditor, an element of uncertainty enters into the auditor's conclusions. This element of uncertainty, referred to as **sampling risk**, was discussed briefly under detection risk in Chapter 3 and in the apple inspector example at the beginning of this chapter. Sampling risk refers to the possibility that the sample drawn is not representative of the population and that, as a result, the auditor will reach an incorrect conclusion about the account balance or class of transactions based on the sample. When using audit sampling techniques to obtain evidence, the auditor must always accept some sampling risk. Sampling risk is one reason why auditors must accept some detection and audit risk, as discussed in Chapter 3.

Due to sampling risk, the auditor faces the chance that sampling may lead to one of two possible types of decision errors: (1) deciding that the population tested is not acceptable when in reality it is; 2) deciding that the population tested is acceptable when in reality it is not. In statistical terms, these errors are known as Type I and Type II errors, respectively. More formally, Type I and Type II errors are defined as follows:

- *Risk of incorrect rejection (Type I)*. In testing an internal control, this is the risk that the sample supports a conclusion that the control is not operating effectively when, in truth, it is operating effectively. When an auditor is evaluating the level of reliance that can be placed on a control in the context of a financial statement audit, this risk is also commonly referred to as the *risk of underreliance* or the *risk of assessing control risk too high*.
  In substantive testing, this is the risk that the sample supports the conclusion that the recorded account balance is materially misstated when it is actually not materially misstated.

- *Risk of incorrect acceptance (Type II)*. In testing a control, this is the risk that the sample supports a conclusion that the control is operating effectively when, in truth, it is not operating effectively. When an auditor is evaluating the level of reliance that can be placed on a control in the context of a financial statement audit, this risk is also commonly referred to as the *risk of overreliance* or the *risk of assessing control risk too low*.
  In substantive testing, this is the risk that the sample supports the conclusion that the recorded account balance is not materially misstated when it is actually materially misstated.

The **risk of incorrect rejection** (a Type I decision error) relates to the *efficiency* of the audit. This type of decision error can result in the auditor conducting more audit work than necessary in order to reach the correct conclusion. The **risk of incorrect acceptance** (a Type II decision error) relates to the *effectiveness* of the audit. This type of decision error can result in the auditor failing to detect a material misstatement in the financial statements. This can lead to litigation against the auditor by parties that rely on the financial statements. Because of the potentially severe consequences of a Type II decision error, auditors design their sampling applications to keep this risk to an acceptably low level. Auditors typically focus only on Type II decision errors in determining their sample sizes, because Type I decision errors affect efficiency and not effectiveness and because, by controlling for the risk of Type II errors, they also obtain relatively good coverage for the risk of Type I errors. For these reasons, in this chapter we do not address the potential implications on sampling applications of Type I errors.

Audit sampling can also involve **non-sampling risk**. Non-sampling risk is the risk of auditor error, and arises from the possibility that the auditor may sample the wrong population to test an assertion, fail to detect a misstatement when applying an audit procedure, or misinterpret an audit result. When applying audit sampling to substantive tests of details, both sampling and non-sampling risk make up the auditor's detection risk (see Chapter 3). While **statistical sampling** allows the auditor to quantify and control sampling risk, no sampling method allows the auditor to measure non-sampling risk. The uncertainty related to non-sampling risk can be controlled by adequate training, proper planning and effective supervision.

Three Important Factors

In the preface to this chapter, we asked you to imagine that you were an apple inspector and we asked you to consider what information you would like to have before you began testing apples. While you would want answers to all the questions listed there, you will find that three of the factors listed are the most important inputs to determine sample sizes for all types of audit sampling. These three inputs are: (1) desired level of assurance in the results (or confidence level); (2) acceptable defect rate (or tolerable error); and (3) historical defect rate (or expected error).

Confidence Level

The first input, *confidence level*, is the complement of sampling risk. For example, as an apple inspector you have to accept some risk that the shipment defect percentage is higher than your sample defect percentage, and higher than the defect rate the buyer will tolerate. You would determine your acceptable level of sampling risk by considering the amount of reliance to be placed on your tests and the consequences of a decision error. The more the reliance placed on your inspection (versus other testing or quality control measures) and the more severe the consequences of a Type II decision error (e.g. the buyer will stop doing business with your company if you mistakenly accept and send a failed shipment), the less risk you will want to accept and the more confident you will want to be in your testing. Auditors, like inspectors, focus on both risk and confidence level. In statistical terminology, a confidence level represents the probability that a given interval includes the true but unknown measure of the characteristic of interest. For example, to place reliance on a control, an auditor may want to be 95 per cent confident that the control operates effectively at least 97 per cent of the time (or fails to operate no more than 3 per cent of the time). Because risk is the complement of confidence level, auditors can either set confidence level or sampling risk. For example, the auditor may set sampling risk for a particular sampling application at 5 per cent, which results in a confidence level of 95 per cent. Confidence level and sampling risk are related to sample size: the larger the sample, the higher the confidence level and the lower the sampling risk.

Tolerable and Expected Error

Once the **desired confidence level** is established, the appropriate sample size is determined largely by how much *tolerable error* exceeds *expected error*. The smaller the difference between these two variables, the more precise the sampling results must be, and therefore the larger the sample size needed. For example, assume that during your interview for the apple inspector position you were told that the historical shipment defect rate has averaged 3 per cent ±2 per cent and the buyers typically can accept up to 10 per cent defective apples. However, as you are planning your sample on the first day of work, you learn that poor weather this year has resulted in an expected defect rate of 7 per cent ±3 per cent. All else being equal, the new information will require a larger sample size because now there is a smaller margin for error, or smaller difference between tolerable and expected error. This is because there is less room to accommodate sampling risk in the interval between 7 and 10 per cent than there is in the interval between 3 and 10 per cent. Similarly, even assuming the historical rate stayed at 3 per cent, if a customer reduced their acceptance defect level from 10 per cent to 6 per cent the margin for error would be smaller. It does not matter which of the two factors causes a change in the difference between tolerable and expected error to be smaller; the critical factor is how large the difference is between the defect rate (or error) that is expected and the defect rate (or error) that can be tolerated.

In typical statistical sampling terminology, the term *precision* relates to how close a sample estimate is to the population characteristic being estimated, given a specified sampling risk. Thus, precision at the planning stage of an audit sampling application is the difference between the *expected* and the **tolerable deviation rate** or misstatement. The term **allowance for sampling risk** is used to reflect the concept of precision in a sampling application. For example, if an auditor expected that a control would have a 2 per cent deviation (failure) rate and he or she was willing to tolerate a deviation rate of 5 per cent, the allowance for sampling risk would be 3 per cent. Remember that in order to successfully apply audit sampling to gather audit evidence, auditors must be able to 'tolerate' some deviations (for controls testing) or misstatement (for substantive testing) to provide an allowance for sampling risk. The only way to completely remove this risk is to test all the items in a population.

❖ Audit Evidence Choices That Do and Do Not Involve Sampling

LO3 In assessing the risk of material misstatement, or in auditing an account balance or a class of transactions, the auditor seldom relies on a single test. Generally, the auditor applies a number of audit procedures in order to reach a conclusion. Some audit procedures involve sampling as defined by auditing standards, while others do not involve sampling. Table 8–1 indicates the types of evidence that are commonly gathered using audit sampling as well as types where sampling is generally not used.

Table 8–1 Relationship between Evidence Types and Audit Sampling	
Type of Evidence	*Audit Sampling Commonly Used*
Inspection of tangible assets	Yes
Inspection of records or documents	Yes
Reperformance	Yes
Recalculation	Yes
Confirmation	Yes
Analytical procedures	No
Scanning	No
Inquiry	No
Observation	No

We have already covered the types of evidence in earlier chapters, but here are some examples of typical sampling applications.

- *Inspection of tangible assets.* An auditor typically attends a client's year-end inventory count. Because the number of inventory items can be very large, the auditor may use audit sampling to select inventory items to physically inspect and count.
- *Inspection of records or documents.* A control may require that before transfer of payment to a vendor, the payables clerk must match an approved purchase order to an approved receiving report and vendor invoice, and indicate an acceptable match by initialling the disbursement document stapled to the other three documents. For large companies, this sort of control would be performed many times a day. The auditors can gather evidence on the effectiveness of the control by testing a sample of the documentation packages.
- *Reperformance.* In assessing the competence and objectivity of the client's work, the auditor may reperform a sample of the tests performed by the client.
- *Confirmation.* A common technique to gather evidence that accounts receivable balances exist and are accurately recorded is to send letters to customers asking them to confirm their balance. Rather than send a letter to all customers, the auditor can select a sample of customers.

Testing All Items with a Particular Characteristic

Table 8–1 indicates that sampling is commonly used to gather evidence of the first five types. It is also common for auditors to use other testing approaches instead of sampling or in combination with sampling to gather evidence. For example, when an account or class of transactions is made up of a few large items, the auditor may examine all the items in the account or class of transactions. Because the entire class or balance is subjected to a 100 per cent examination, such an audit procedure does not involve sampling. More common than testing 100 per cent of the items in an account balance or class of transactions is a technique in which the auditor tests all items with a particular characteristic of interest based on risk or monetary value. For example, if the auditor is aware of certain transactions that look unusual or present greater risk, the auditor should examine all these items rather than applying audit sampling.

Similarly, if a relatively small number of large transactions make up a relatively large percentage of an account or class of transactions, auditors will typically test all the transactions greater than a particular monetary amount. As an illustration, an auditor may decide to audit all 15 individual accounts receivable balances greater than €100,000, because these large customers make up 70 per cent of the total account balance. For the remaining 30 per cent of the total account balance consisting of individual customer account balances less than €100,000, the auditor could apply audit sampling. Alternatively, the auditor could decide to apply substantive analytical procedures to the part of the total receivables balance consisting of individual customer accounts under €100,000, or may even decide to apply no audit procedures to this part of the total account because he or she deems that an acceptably low risk of material misstatement exists in this group. In these latter two instances, the auditor is not using sampling.

Testing Only One or a Few Items

Automated information systems process transactions consistently unless the system or programs are changed. When testing automated IT controls, the auditor may decide to test one or a few of each type of transactions at a point in time. In conjunction with that test of the automated controls the auditor may test general controls over changes to the system and program in order to provide evidence that the automated controls have been operating over the audit period. This type of test of automated IT control does not involve audit sampling.

TYPES OF AUDIT SAMPLING

❖ Non-Statistical versus Statistical Sampling

LO4

There are two general approaches to audit sampling: *non-statistical* and *statistical*. In non-statistical sampling, the auditor does not use statistical techniques to determine the sample size, select the sample and/or measure sampling risk when evaluating results. Statistical sampling, on the other hand, uses the laws of probability to compute sample size and evaluate the sample results, thereby permitting the auditor to use the most efficient sample size and to quantify the sampling risk for the purpose of reaching a statistical conclusion about the population. Both approaches require the use of the auditor's professional judgement to plan, perform and evaluate the sample evidence. The major advantages of statistical sampling are that it helps the auditor: (1) design an efficient sample; (2) measure the sufficiency of evidence obtained; and (3) quantify sampling risk. The disadvantages of statistical sampling include additional costs of: (1) training auditors in the proper use of sampling techniques; (2) designing and conducting the sampling application; and (3) lack of consistent application across engagement teams due to the complexity of the underlying concepts.

With a non-statistical sampling application, the auditor must rely on his or her professional judgement, in combination with audit firm guidance and knowledge of the underlying statistical sampling theories, to reach a conclusion about the audit test. Therefore, to properly apply non-statistical sampling, auditors' judgement and their firm's sampling guidance must be grounded in statistical sampling theory. In fact, auditing standards indicate that the sample sizes for statistical and non-statistical sampling should be comparable (ISA 530, para. A9). Thus, a disadvantage of non-statistical sampling is that auditor judgement may diverge significantly from sampling theory, resulting in testing that is not as effective as statistical sampling. Most firms address this concern by providing their auditors with non-statistical sampling guidance and procedures that are easy to use, encourage consistency in sampling applications across engagement teams, and are grounded in sampling theory. Non-statistical audit sampling can be simpler to use and more consistently applied than statistical sampling because some of the more difficult statistical decisions can be made by experts. The experts' decisions are then built into the audit firm's guidance and decision aids.

This chapter and Chapter 9 provide detailed coverage of both statistical and non-statistical sampling. Even though non-statistical sampling is very common in practice, we cover statistical sampling first because statistical theory provides the foundation for both sampling approaches.

Types of Statistical Sampling Techniques

Auditors use three major types of statistical sampling techniques: **attribute sampling**, **monetary-unit sampling** and **classical variables sampling**.

Attribute Sampling

Attribute sampling is used to estimate the proportion of a population that possesses a specified characteristic. The most common use of attribute sampling is for tests of controls. In this case, the auditor wants to determine the deviation rate for a control implemented within the client's accounting system. For example, the auditor may want to gather evidence that a credit check is performed on customer orders before shipment. Measurement of the deviation rate provides evidence about whether the control is operating effectively to process accounting transactions properly and therefore provides support for the auditor's set level of control risk. Attribute sampling may also be used with a substantive test of transactions when such a test is conducted with a test of controls as a dual-purpose test.

Monetary-Unit Sampling

Monetary-unit sampling uses attribute-sampling theory and techniques to estimate the monetary amount of misstatement for a class of transactions or an account balance. Variations of monetary-unit sampling are known as *probability-proportional-to-size sampling* and *cumulative monetary amount sampling*. Auditors use this sampling technique extensively because it has a number of advantages over classical variables sampling. Monetary-unit sampling builds upon attribute-sampling theory to express a conclusion in monetary amounts. You will learn about monetary-unit sampling in Chapter 9.

Classical Variables Sampling

Classical variables sampling includes the sampling techniques typically taught in an undergraduate statistics class. While auditors sometimes use variables sampling to estimate the monetary value of a class of transactions or account balance, it is more frequently used to determine whether an account is materially misstated. Classical variables sampling is covered in the *Advanced Module* in Chapter 9.

Regardless of the approach or type of sampling, auditing standards contain requirements that auditors must follow when planning, selecting a sample for, and performing and evaluating the audit sampling applications. We will refer to these requirements as we discuss the different approaches and types of audit sampling.

The remainder of this chapter presents an application of statistical attribute sampling to tests of controls, followed by a discussion of non-statistical sampling applied to tests of controls.

> ### Practice Insight 8.1
>
> In this chapter the focus is on tests of controls for purpose to determine the degree of reliance that can be placed on controls for a financial statement audit. The text is also relevant for tests of controls for other purposes such as assurance of an entity's internal control (see Chapter 20), including auditing internal control over financial reporting as required by the Sarbanes–Oxley Act in the USA for public companies (see Chapter 7).

❖ ATTRIBUTE SAMPLING APPLIED TO TESTS OF CONTROLS

LO5

LO6

LO7

Attribute sampling is a statistical sampling method used to estimate the proportion of a characteristic in a population. In applying this technique to tests of controls, the auditor normally attempts to determine the operating effectiveness of a control in terms of deviations from a prescribed internal control.

In conducting a statistical sample for a test of controls, auditing standards (ISA 530) require the auditor to properly plan, perform and evaluate the sampling application, and adequately document each phase of the sampling application in the working papers. The following sections discuss the steps that are included in the three phases of an attribute-sampling application. Table 8–2 lists the steps involved in the three phases of an attribute-sampling application.

Table 8–2 Steps in Attribute-Sampling
Planning
1. Determine the test objectives.
2. Define the population characteristics:
● Define the sampling population.
● Define the sampling unit.
● Define the control deviation conditions.
3. Determine the sample size, using the following inputs:
● The desired confidence level or risk of incorrect acceptance.
● The tolerable deviation rate.
● The expected population deviation rate.
Performance
4. Select sample items.
5. Perform the auditing procedures:
● Understand and analyse any deviations observed.
Evaluation
6. Calculate the sample deviation rate and the computed upper deviation rate.
7. Draw final conclusions.

Calabro Wireless, Illustration

Audit tests for the audit of Calabro Wireless Services will be used to demonstrate an attribute-sampling application. Calabro is a business services company that uses wireless communications technology to develop solutions for businesses. The company emphasizes its systems, reliability, solution-oriented marketing and high level of customer service. The company provides high-quality, low-cost service to the marketplace. In recent years the company has experienced annual subscriber growth of about 20 per cent per year. Andrew Judd is the audit senior on the Calabro audit and his firm has audited Calabro for ten years. The auditors have developed an understanding of Calabro's revenue process and have decided to rely on selected controls to reduce control risk below the maximum for the current-year financial statement audit.

Planning

Proper planning of an attribute-sampling application involves completing a number of important steps. Each of these steps, in turn, requires the use of professional judgement on the part of the auditor. The following subsections document Judd's sampling plan on the Calabro Wireless Services audit. Typically, an audit firm uses a formal working paper or template to document the steps in the sampling plan.

Step 1: Determine the Test Objectives

Auditing standards require that sampling applications be well planned and take into consideration the relationship of the sample to the objective(s) of the test. The objective of attribute sampling when used for tests of controls in a financial statement audit is to determine the degree of reliance that can be placed on controls. Thus, the auditor assesses the deviation or error rate that exists for each control selected for testing. Audit sampling for tests of controls is generally appropriate when the application of the control leaves documentary evidence (e.g. initials of approval).

In the Calabro audit, the objective of the test is to determine if Calabro's revenue process is functioning as documented. Judd, the audit senior, wants to determine if the controls identified concerning credit authorization, contract approval and proper pricing are operating effectively, and thus allow control risk to be set below the maximum.

Calabro's revenue transactions arise in the following manner:

> Subscribers may lease a wireless device (an electronic pager or mobile phone) from the company or purchase a wireless device and pay only an access fee for the company's wireless communication system. Each subscriber enters into a service contract with the company,

which provides for the payment of the access fee and the purchase or lease of one or more wireless devices. Contracts with customers with large numbers of devices are typically for three- to five-year terms, while contracts for smaller quantities are typically for one-year terms with renewal options at the end of the terms.

For this sampling application, Judd has decided to rely on three controls in Calabro's revenue process. The three control activities and their definitions are as follows:

1 **Sales and service contracts are properly authorized for credit approval.** *Calabro's credit department personnel check the creditworthiness of new customers and establish a credit limit based on that evaluation. For existing customers, the amount of the new sale or lease is added to the existing accounts receivable balance, and the total is compared to the customer's credit limit. If the amount is less than the credit limit, the transaction is processed. If the total is more than the credit limit, the transaction is subjected to review by the credit manager before the sale is approved.*

2 **Sales are not recorded without an approved sales and lease contract.** *Calabro's revenue process contains a control that no revenue transactions are to be recorded unless an approved sales or lease contract is sent to the billing department.*

3 **Sales and lease contracts are properly priced.** *Calabro's revenue process also includes a control that requires billing department personnel to use an authorized price list for the sale of wireless devices. Access and lease fees are determined based on a fee structure that includes volume discounts for large-unit subscribers.*

Step 2: Define the Population Characteristics

To achieve the test objectives, the auditor must carefully consider the characteristics of the sampling population.

Define the Sampling Population

All or a subset of the items that constitute the class of transactions (or account balance when not testing controls) make up the sampling population. The auditor must determine that the population from which the sample is selected is appropriate for the specific assertion, because sample results can be projected only to the population from which the sample was selected. For example, suppose the auditor is interested in examining the effectiveness of a control designed to ensure that all shipments to customers are billed by testing whether all shipments were, in fact, billed. If the auditor uses the population of sales invoices as the sampling population, he or she is not likely to detect goods shipped but not billed, because the population of sales invoices includes only sales that were billed. In this example, the correct sampling population for testing the completeness assertion would be the population of all shipped goods as documented by bills of lading.

There is a natural tendency to designate an entire class of transactions (or all the items in an account balance) as the population. However, the sample population should be restricted to the transactions and time period under the same system of controls that are relevant to the assertions being tested. For example, if the testing will be conducted in October for a calendar-year-end client, the sampling population can be defined as all transactions in the first nine months of the year. The results of the sampling application in this case would apply only to the nine-month period tested. However, the auditor must also consider whether to conduct additional tests in the remaining period under audit through to year end. (See Chapters 5 for discussions of what auditors do to 'roll forward' testing between an interim date and year end.)

Once the population has been defined, the auditor must determine that the physical representation (referred to as the *frame*) of the population is complete. This determination is typically made by comparing the frame, for example an accounts receivable listing, to the general ledger or by examining and accounting for the numerical sequence of prenumbered sales invoice documents. Because the auditor selects the sample from the frame, any conclusions relate only to that physical representation of the population. If the frame and the population differ, the auditor might draw the wrong conclusion about the population. In the example above, if the frame and the population differ, the sales journal (the frame) would not include all sales transactions during the period of interest (the population).

For the audit of Calabro's revenue process, Judd has decided the population will include all sales and leases recorded in the entire year. The physical representation of the population is the numeric file of sales and lease contracts maintained in the sales department. Based on a review of the client's procedures for completeness, which includes accounting for prenumbered documents, Judd has determined that the frame is complete. The population of sales and lease transactions for the year contains 125,000 items that are numbered from 1 to 125,000.

Define the Sampling Unit

The individual members of the sampling population are called the **sampling units**. In the apple inspector example, the sampling unit is an individual apple. In auditing, a sampling unit may be a document, an entry, or a line item. Each sampling unit makes up one item in the population. The sampling unit should be defined in relation to the control being tested.

The sampling unit for the test of controls in the Calabro audit is defined as the sales or lease contract. Judd can perform all tests for the controls selected by examining this set of documents.

Define the Control Deviation Conditions

For tests of controls, a deviation is a departure from adequate performance of the internal control. It is important for the auditor to define carefully what is considered a deviation. Thinking back to the apple inspector example, before you begin your inspection, you need to know what constitutes a 'bad' apple: does it take a minor blemish or significant damage to conclude that an apple is defective?

Judd has defined control deviations for each of the internal controls being assessed as follows:

1   **Sales and service contracts are properly authorized for credit approval.** *A deviation in this test is defined as the failure of Calabro's credit department personnel to follow proper credit approval procedures for new and existing customers.*
2   **Sales are not recorded without an approved sales and lease contract.** *For this control, a deviation is defined as the absence of an approved sales or lease contract.*
3   **Sales and lease contracts are properly priced.** *A deviation in this case is the use of an unauthorized price for a wireless device or an incorrect access or lease fee.*

Step 3: Determine the Sample Size

Considerable judgement is required in determining the appropriate values for the inputs that are used to compute sample size. The three key inputs to determining the sample are the same as those discussed earlier: the desired confidence level, tolerable deviation rate, and **expected population deviation rate**. Auditing standards require that auditors give adequate consideration to the appropriate value of these inputs. Because of the difficulty of making these input judgements, determining the sample size is typically the most difficult step of an audit sampling application.

Desired Confidence Level

As discussed earlier in the chapter, the complement of the confidence level is the risk that the sample results will support a conclusion that the control is functioning effectively when in truth it is not (i.e. the risk of incorrect acceptance). In a financial statement audit, this can result in assessing control risk too low. This risk influences the effectiveness of the audit. If the auditor sets control risk too low and overrelies on the controls, the level of substantive procedures may be too low to detect material misstatements that may be present in the financial statement account. This is because when control risk inappropriately decreases, the auditor increases the acceptable level of detection risk associated with substantive testing to compensate (see discussion of the audit risk model in Chapter 3). Thus, if control risk is mistakenly set at a low level, detection risk will be set too high. This increases the risk that the auditor will fail to detect a material misstatement if one exists in the account.

In setting the desired confidence level and acceptable level of risk, the auditor considers the significance of the account and the importance of the assertion on which the control provides assurance, as well as the degree of reliance to be placed on the control. Generally, when the auditor has decided to rely on controls, the confidence level is set at 90 or 95 per cent, meaning that the auditor is willing to accept a 10 or 5 per cent risk of accepting the control as effective when in fact it is not. However, the auditor must remember that there is a direct relationship between the confidence level and sample size: The more confident the auditor would like to be (and the less risk he or she is willing to accept), the larger the sample size must be, all else being equal. For example, in the illustration that follows, the effect on the sample size is substantial (a 21 per cent increase) when the desired confidence level increases from 90 to 95 per cent.

Desired Confidence Level	Sample Size[iii]
90%	77
95%	93

Thus, the auditor must balance effectiveness concerns with efficiency concerns when setting the desired confidence level and acceptable risk of incorrect acceptance.

Tolerable Deviation Rate

The tolerable deviation rate is the maximum deviation rate from a prescribed control that the auditor is willing to accept and still consider the control effective (i.e. the control activity would be relied on).

It can seem odd to students that auditors will actually 'tolerate' any deviations in a control. There are two reasons auditors will tolerate deviations and still consider a control to be effective. The first reason is technical and relates to sampling risk. Remember that for an auditor (or an apple inspector) to use sampling to gather evidence there must be some margin for error, because there is a risk that the sample deviation rate differs from the population deviation rate. Even if there are no deviations in a sample, there must still be an allowance (or upper confidence limit) for sampling risk. Just as in the apple inspector example, the only way to know with certainty what the shipment defect rate actually is would be to inspect all the apples.

The second reason auditors are willing to tolerate some control deviations relates to the purpose and application of controls. To be effective, most controls do not need to operate 100 per cent of the time so long as the times the control fails to operate are not predictable and the person(s) performing the control investigates processing exceptions observed during the proper application of the control. By way of analogy, suppose you have battery-operated smoke detectors in your apartment or house and one of the alarms starts to signal a low battery. The fact that a day or two passes between the removal of the old battery and installation of a new one does not render the system of controls ineffective for the entire period you have lived in the apartment or house. The risk of fire is pretty remote, even if there were no smoke detectors at all. Also, if one detector is not working, you have other smoke detectors that will sound if smoke appears. Obviously, if all the smoke detectors are disabled for long periods of time, the system of fire detection is not effective and the risk of injury due to fire increases. Similarly, when a control fails to operate, it usually does not result in a monetary misstatement to the financial statements, because most transactions are properly input and processed (i.e. actual inherent risk is less than 100 per cent) and there are other compensating controls or processes that might detect a misstatement should one occur. Furthermore, if the operator of the control investigates processing exceptions that are discovered, he or she can research the cause and potential implications of the exception(s) and take corrective actions if necessary.

To be effective, a control does need to operate effectively a reasonably high percentage of the time. Table 8–3 provides some examples of the relationship between the assessed importance of a control and the tolerable deviation rate.

Table 8–3 Examples of Tolerable Deviation Rates for Assessed Importance of a Control	
Assessed Importance of a Control	Tolerable Deviation Rate
Highly important	3–5%
Moderately important	6–10%

A low tolerable deviation rate (such as 3 to 5 per cent) is used when the auditor plans to test the effectiveness of a highly important control. A higher tolerable deviation rate (6 to 10 per cent) is used when the auditor plans to test the effectiveness of a moderately important control.

The tolerable deviation rate is *inversely* related to the sample size. The lower the tolerable deviation rate, the larger the sample size. Recall that in testing controls, the key determinant of sample size is the amount by which tolerable deviation rate exceeds the expected deviation rate. For example, assuming a desired confidence level of 95 per cent, an expected population deviation rate of 0 per cent and a large population, the effect of tolerable deviation rate on sample size is:

Tolerable Deviation Rate	Sample Size
2%	149
6%	49
10%	29

Expected Population Deviation Rate

The expected population deviation rate is the rate the auditor expects to exist in the population. Some level of deviation is commonly expected because the controls that auditors typically use sampling to test will be dependent on some human involvement (e.g. matching documents, credit approval, following up on system-generated exception reports), and humans are not perfect. The auditor can develop this expectation based on prior years' results or on a pilot sample. If the auditor believes that the expected population deviation rate exceeds the tolerable deviation rate, the statistical testing should not be performed because in such a situation no amount of sampling can reduce the population deviation rate below the tolerable rate. Instead, the auditor should perform additional substantive procedures rather than relying on the control.

The expected population deviation rate has a direct relationship to sample size; the larger the expected population deviation rate, the larger the sample size, all else equal. For example, assuming a desired confidence level of 95 per cent, a tolerable deviation rate of 5 per cent and a large population, the effect of the expected population deviation rate on sample size is:

Expected Population Deviation Rate	Sample Size
1%	93
1.5%	124
2%	181
3%	*
* Sample size is too large to be cost-effective for most audit applications.	

The dramatic effect of expected population deviation rate on sample size highlights the importance of a good estimate of the expected deviation rate. It is perplexing to some that an estimate of the expected population deviation rate is required as an input to determine sample size – after all, is not the whole purpose of testing a sample to estimate the deviation rate in the population? The reason an estimate is necessary relates back to the notion of precision, or by how much the tolerable deviation rate exceeds the estimated deviation rate, as discussed earlier in the chapter. Recall the apple inspector illustration where the buyer's tolerable defect rate was 10 per cent and poor weather increased the expected defect rate from a historical rate of 3 per cent ±2 per cent to 7 per cent ±3 per cent. All else being equal, the increase in expected defect rate will require a larger sample size, because there is now less room for sampling risk to be accommodated, and thus the sampling conclusion needs to be more precise. Just as the historical defect rate is an important input for apple inspection, a good estimate of the expected population deviation rate is very important for attribute sampling because the statistical sample size will be just large enough such that if the auditor observes the deviation rate she or he expects or lower, the sampling application will support a conclusion that the control is operating effectively. Similarly, if the auditor observes a higher deviation rate than the expected rate used in the sample size calculation, this usually means the sample results are unacceptable. As such, it is wise to be conservative when estimating the expected population deviation rate so that the sample size will be adequate even if the population deviation rate is larger than the auditor initially thought it would be.

Table 8–4 shows Judd's decision for each of the parameters required to determine sample size. Judd decides to set the desired confidence level at 95 per cent (i.e. the risk of incorrect acceptance is 5 per cent), the tolerable deviation rate at 6 per cent, and the expected population deviation rate at 1 per cent for control 1. For control 1, Judd has planned a high confidence level (see Table 8–3). A similar strategy is followed for control 3. For control 2, Judd has planned a moderate confidence level because he plans to place less reliance on the control. In this sampling plan, the effect of the population size can be ignored because the population is very large. The effect of population size on attribute sampling is discussed below.

Table 8–4 The Auditor's Decisions for Sample Size in Calabro Wireless Example

Parameters	Control* 1	2	3
Desired confidence level	95%	90%	95%
Tolerable deviation rate	6%	8%	5%
Expected population deviation rate	1%	2%	1%
Sample size from table	78	48	93

* Control 1: Sales or lease contracts are properly authorized for credit approval.
Control 2: Sales are not recorded without an approved sales and lease contract.
Control 3: Sales and lease contracts are properly priced.

Tables 8–5 and 8–6 are used to determine the sample size for each of the controls. For control 1, Judd uses Table 8–5 to determine the sample size because the desired confidence level is 95 per cent. Judd identifies the column for a 6 per cent tolerable deviation rate and reads down that column until the row for a 1 per cent expected population deviation rate is found. The sample size for control 1 is 78 items. For control 2, Judd uses Table 8–6 because the desired confidence level is 90 per cent. Reading down the 8 per cent tolerable deviation rate column until the 2 per cent expected population deviation rate is found, Judd determines that the sample size is 48. Finally, the sample size for control 3 is 93. This is found by using Table 8–5 and reading down the 5 per cent tolerable deviation rate column until the 1 per cent expected deviation rate row is reached.

Table 8–5 Statistical Sample Sizes for Attribute Sampling – 95 per cent Desired Confidence Level (i.e. 5 per cent Risk of Incorrect Acceptance)

Expected Population Deviation Rate	Tolerable Deviation Rate 2%	3%	4%	5%	6%	7%	8%	9%	10%	15%	20%
0.00%	149(0)	99(0)	74(0)	59(0)	49(0)	42(0)	36(0)	32(0)	29(0)	19(0)	14(0)
.25	236(1)	157(1)	117(1)	93(1)	78(1)	66(1)	58(1)	51(1)	46(1)	30(1)	22(1)
.50	*	157(1)	117(1)	93(1)	78(1)	66(1)	58(1)	51(1)	46(1)	30(1)	22(1)
.75	*	208(2)	117(1)	93(1)	78(1)	66(1)	58(1)	51(1)	46(1)	30(1)	22(1)
1.00	*	*	156(2)	93(1)	78(1)	66(1)	58(1)	51(1)	46(1)	30(1)	22(1)
1.25	*	*	156(2)	124(2)	78(1)	66(1)	58(1)	51(1)	46(1)	30(1)	22(1)
1.50	*	*	192(3)	124(2)	103(2)	66(1)	58(1)	51(1)	46(1)	30(1)	22(1)
1.75	*	*	227(4)	153(3)	103(2)	88(2)	77(2)	51(1)	46(1)	30(1)	22(1)
2.00	*	*	*	181(4)	127(3)	88(2)	77(2)	68(2)	46(1)	30(1)	22(1)
2.25	*	*	*	208(5)	127(3)	88(2)	77(2)	68(2)	61(2)	30(1)	22(1)
2.50	*	*	*	*	150(4)	109(3)	77(2)	68(2)	61(2)	30(1)	22(1)
2.75	*	*	*	*	173(5)	109(3)	95(3)	68(2)	61(2)	30(1)	22(1)
3.00	*	*	*	*	195(6)	129(4)	95(3)	84(3)	61(2)	30(1)	22(1)
3.25	*	*	*	*	*	148(5)	112(4)	84(3)	61(2)	30(1)	22(1)
3.50	*	*	*	*	*	167(6)	112(4)	84(3)	76(3)	40(2)	22(1)
3.75	*	*	*	*	*	185(7)	129(5)	100(4)	76(3)	40(2)	22(1)
4.00	*	*	*	*	*	*	146(6)	100(4)	89(4)	40(2)	22(1)
5.00	*	*	*	*	*	*	*	158(8)	116(6)	40(2)	30(2)
6.00	*	*	*	*	*	*	*	*	179(11)	50(3)	30(2)
7.00	*	*	*	*	*	*	*	*	*	68(5)	37(3)

* Sample size is too large to be cost-effective for most audit applications. The number in parentheses represents the maximum number of deviations in a sample of that size that allows the auditor to conclude that the tolerable deviation rate is not exceeded.

Table 8–6 Statistical Sample Sizes for Attribute Sampling – 90 per cent Desired Confidence Level (i.e. 10 per cent Risk of Incorrect Acceptance)

Expected Population Deviation Rate	Tolerable Deviation Rate										
	2%	3%	4%	5%	6%	7%	8%	9%	10%	15%	20%
0.00%	144(0)	76(0)	57(0)	45(0)	38(0)	32(0)	28(0)	25(0)	22(0)	15(0)	11(0)
.25	194(1)	129(1)	96(1)	77(1)	64(1)	55(1)	48(1)	42(1)	38(1)	25(1)	18(1)
.50	194(1)	129(1)	96(1)	77(1)	64(1)	55(1)	48(1)	42(1)	38(1)	25(1)	18(1)
.75	265(2)	129(1)	96(1)	77(1)	64(1)	55(1)	48(1)	42(1)	38(1)	25(1)	18(1)
1.00	*	176(2)	96(1)	77(1)	64(1)	55(1)	48(1)	42(1)	38(1)	25(1)	18(1)
1.25	*	221(3)	132(2)	77(1)	64(1)	55(1)	48(1)	42(1)	38(1)	25(1)	18(1)
1.50	*	*	132(2)	105(2)	64(1)	55(1)	48(1)	42(1)	38(1)	25(1)	18(1)
1.75	*	*	166(3)	105(2)	88(2)	55(1)	48(1)	42(1)	38(1)	25(1)	18(1)
2.00	*	*	198(4)	132(3)	88(2)	75(2)	48(1)	42(1)	38(1)	25(1)	18(1)
2.25	*	*	*	132(3)	88(2)	75(2)	65(2)	42(1)	38(1)	25(1)	18(1)
2.50	*	*	*	158(4)	110(3)	75(2)	65(2)	58(2)	38(1)	25(1)	18(1)
2.75	*	*	*	209(6)	132(4)	94(3)	65(2)	58(2)	52(2)	25(1)	18(1)
3.00	*	*	*	*	132(4)	94(3)	65(2)	58(2)	52(2)	25(1)	18(1)
3.25	*	*	*	*	153(5)	113(4)	82(3)	58(2)	52(2)	25(1)	18(1)
3.50	*	*	*	*	194(7)	113(4)	82(3)	73(3)	52(2)	25(1)	18(1)
3.75	*	*	*	*	*	131(5)	98(4)	73(3)	52(2)	25(1)	18(1)
4.00	*	*	*	*	*	149(6)	98(4)	73(3)	65(3)	25(1)	18(1)
5.00	*	*	*	*	*	*	160(8)	115(6)	78(4)	34(2)	18(1)
6.00	*	*	*	*	*	*	*	182(11)	116(7)	43(3)	25(2)
7.00	*	*	*	*	*	*	*	*	199(14)	52(4)	25(2)

* Sample size is too large to be cost-effective for most audit applications. The number in parentheses represents the maximum number of deviations in a sample of that size that allows the auditor to conclude that the tolerable deviation rate is not exceeded.

Significant areas of Tables 8–5 and 8–6 are covered by asterisks. The corresponding note at the bottom of the tables states, 'Sample size is too large to be cost-effective for most audit applications.' Another way to explain the cause of the asterisks is insufficient precision. Recall that to apply sampling there must be sufficient margin for error. When tolerable and estimated deviation rates are too close together, sample sizes will become too large to be practical or are simply not computable because there is insufficient allowance for sampling risk. Furthermore, in some instances where an asterisk appears in the tables, the expected population deviation rate is greater than the tolerable deviation rate; audit sampling obviously is not appropriate in such situations because there is no allowance for sampling risk.

Auditors often establish one sample size for all controls tested within a business process. This is particularly true when all the tests of controls are to be conducted on the same sampling units. The auditor would use the largest sample size. Therefore, in this example, the auditor may decide to use a sample size of 93 to test the three controls. However, we will assume that the auditor in the Calabro example used the sample sizes shown in Table 8–4.

Computing Sample Size with ACL Software

Exhibit 8–1 shows the screen display from ACL™ for Windows software for determining the sample size for control 3.[iv] The auditor opens a client workbook, chooses the 'Sampling' button on the menu and selects 'Calculate Sample Size'. The size window is then displayed and the auditor enters the relevant data. Since this is attribute sampling, the auditor selects 'Record' for type of sampling. The auditor enters '95' for 'Confidence', '125000' for 'Population' size (you do not include commas when entering values in ACL), and the 'Upper Error Limit' of 5 per cent (i.e. tolerable deviation rate) and 'Expected Error Rate' of 1 per cent (i.e. expected population deviation rate). This produces a sample size of 95 that is slightly larger than the amount determined using the tables.

Exhibit 8–1 Sample Screens from ACL™ Software

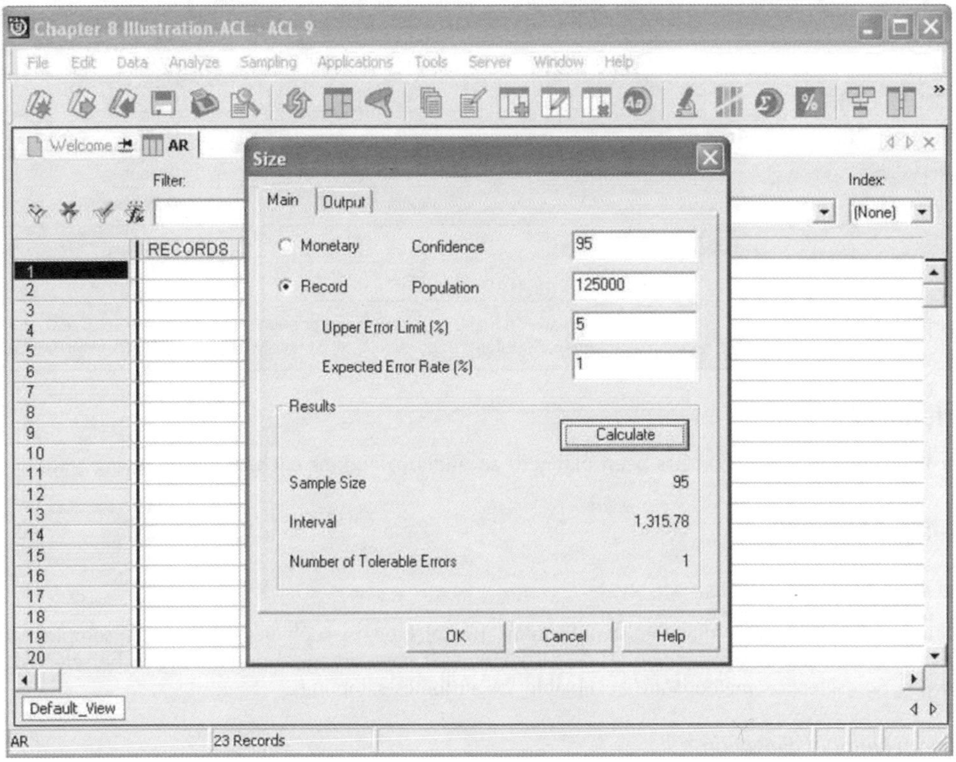

Population Size

Students and auditors are often surprised that the size of the population is not an important factor in determining sample size for attribute sampling. The population size has little or no effect on the sample size, unless the population is relatively small, say less than 500 items. In fact, so long as the population is made up of similar items under the same system of controls, it does not matter if the population is 100,000 items, 1 million items, 100 million items or more; the sample size is the same. Popular audit sampling programs, like ACL, completely ignore the effects of population size when computing sample size for attribute sampling. Because most of the populations that auditors test are larger than a few hundred items, and because assuming large population sample size does not reduce the effectiveness of the sampling application, we ignore the effects of population size in this chapter. However, in the *Advanced Module* in this chapter we include a brief discussion of how sample sizes can be adjusted for smaller populations and we provide a small population sample size table developed by the profession for testing controls that operate infrequently (i.e. quarterly, monthly, weekly).

Table 8–7 summarizes the effects of the four factors on the size of the sample to be selected.

Table 8–7 The Effect of Sample Selection Factors on Sample Size

Factor	Relationship to Sample Size	Examples	
		Change in Factor	Effect on Sample
Desired confidence level	Direct	Lower	Decrease
		Higher	Increase
Tolerable deviation rate	Inverse	Lower	Increase
		Higher	Decrease
Expected population deviation rate	Direct	Lower	Decrease
		Higher	Increase
Population size	Decreases sample size only when population size is small (e.g. 500 or fewer items). Therefore, population size generally has no effect on sample size.		

Performance

After the sampling application has been planned, an auditor performs each of the following steps.

Sample Selection

Step 4: Select Sample Items

Auditing standards require that the sample items be selected in such a way that the sample can be expected to represent the population. Thus, all items must have an equal opportunity to be selected. The following two selection methods are acceptable for attributes sampling.

Random-Number Selection

The auditor may select a random sample using random numbers generated by a spreadsheet application or audit sampling software. Using this method of selection, every item in the population (such as a document or customer account) has the same probability of being selected as every other sampling unit in the population. Statistical sampling requires that the auditor be able to measure the probability of selecting the sampling units selected. Thus, random-number selection is used in many statistical sampling applications. Auditors typically use unrestricted random sampling without replacement for sampling applications. This means that once an item is selected, it is removed from the frame and cannot be selected a second time. Given the auditor's objectives, it seems sensible for an auditor to include an item only once in the sample. Random numbers can be obtained from random number tables or software such as MS Excel or ACL. For the Calabro audit, Judd used MS Excel to generate 93 (the sample size determined by using the tables) random numbers between 1 and 125,000 and collected sales and lease contracts corresponding to those random numbers for testing.

Obtaining Random Numbers from ACL Software

Exhibit 8–2 shows an example of the output from the random-number generator in ACL. The auditor chooses the 'Tools' button on the menu and selects 'Generate Random Numbers'. The random window is then displayed and the auditor enters the relevant data. The sample size of 95 is entered for 'Number'. The 'Seed' is used to start the random-number process. If no value is entered into ACL, then ACL automatically creates a random seed. The auditor then enters the range of the invoice number sequence (1 to 125,001).[v] The 'Unique' and 'Sorted' items should be checked so that each random number is unique and the output is produced in sequence. Rather than using random numbers, if the population data is available in electronic format, ACL or spreadsheet programs like MS Excel can randomly select the sample records directly from the population.

Exhibit 8–2 An Example of a Random Sample Drawn from ACL™

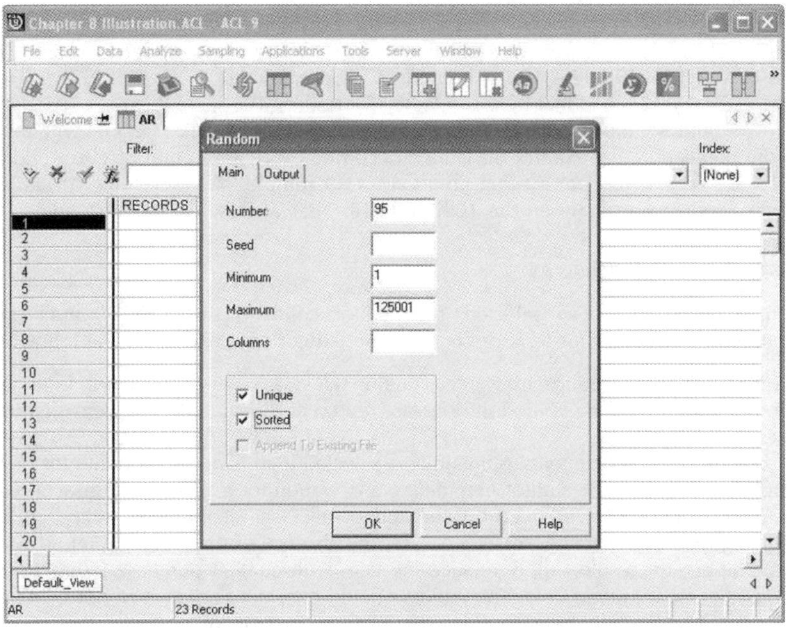

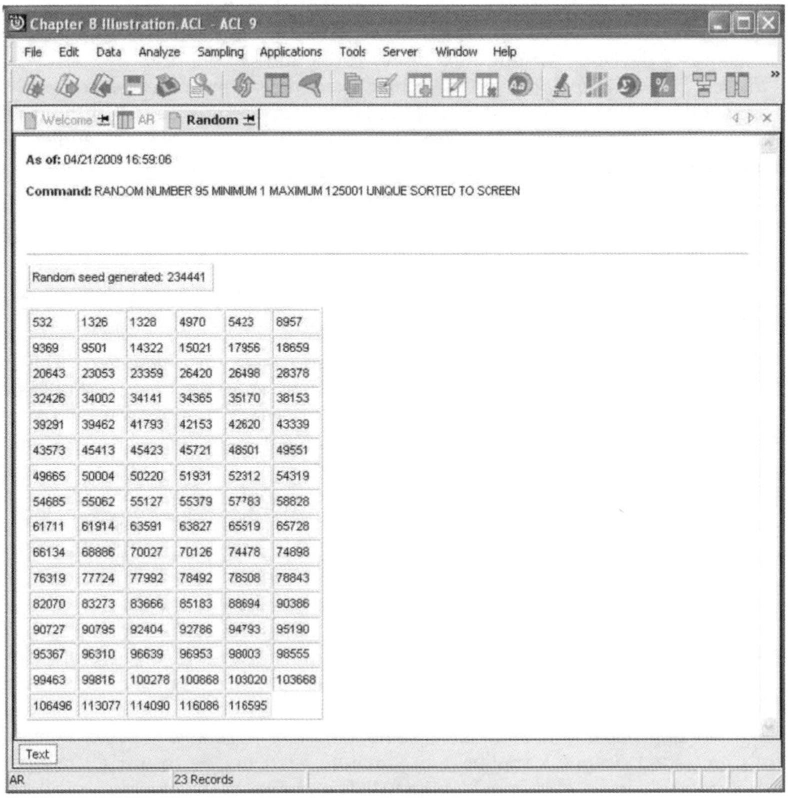

Systematic Selection

When using a systematic selection approach to select a sample, the auditor determines a sampling interval by dividing the sampling population by the sample size. A starting number is selected in the first interval, and then every *n*th item is selected. When a random starting point is used, systematic selection provides a sample where every sampling unit has an equal chance of being selected. For example, suppose the auditor wishes to select 100 items from a population of 15,000 items numbered 1 to 15,000. The sampling interval in this case is 150 (15,000 ÷ 100). The auditor chooses a random number in the first interval (i.e. between 1 and 150), say 125, and that item is selected for testing. The second item is 275 (125 + 150), the third item is 425, and so on. To avoid the possibility that a systematic sample will miss systematic deviations in the population (e.g. control deviations occurring every 300th unit or every Friday afternoon), the auditor can use several random starting points. In our example, after selecting 10 items, the auditor could use a new random start between the 10th and 11th interval to select the 11th item.

Step 5: Perform the Audit Procedures

After the sample items have been selected, the auditor conducts the planned audit procedures. In conducting the audit procedures for tests of controls, the auditor may encounter the following situations:

- *Voided documents.* The auditor may occasionally select a voided document in a sample. If the transaction has been properly voided, it does not represent a deviation. The item should be replaced with a new sample item.
- *Unused or inapplicable documents.* Sometimes a selected item is not appropriate for the definition of the control. For example, the auditor may define a deviation for a purchase transaction as a vendor's bill not supported by a receiving report. If the auditor selects a telephone or utility bill, there will not be a receiving report to examine. In such a case, the absence of the receiving report would not be a deviation. The auditor would simply replace the item with another purchase transaction.
- *Inability to examine a sample item.* The auditor should consider the effect of not being able to apply a planned audit procedure to a sample item. For most tests of controls, the auditor examines documents for evidence of the performance of the control. If the auditor is unable to examine a document or to use an alternative procedure to test whether the control was adequately performed, the sample item is a deviation for purposes of evaluating the sample results.
- *Stopping the test before completion.* If a large number of deviations are detected early in the tests of controls, the auditor should consider stopping the test as soon as it is clear that the results of the test will not support the planned assessed level of control risk. In such a case, the auditor would rely on other internal controls or set control risk at the maximum for the audit assertion affected, and appropriately enhance the related substantive tests.

Whenever a deviation is observed in controls, the auditor should investigate the nature, cause and consequence of the exception.

Understand and Analyse Deviations Observed

The auditor should evaluate the qualitative aspects of the deviations identified. This involves two considerations. First, the nature of each deviation, and its cause and consequences, should be considered. For example, the auditor should determine if a deviation represents an unintentional error or a fraud and whether the deviation actually resulted in a monetary misstatement to the financial statements. The auditor should also attempt to determine whether a deviation resulted from a cause such as misunderstanding of instructions or carelessness. Understanding the nature and cause of a deviation helps the auditor better assess control risk and evaluate whether the deviation(s) represent control deficiencies. Second, the auditor should consider how the deviations may impact the other phases of the audit. For example, suppose that deviations found in a test of the revenue process resulted from improper granting of credit. As a result, the risk that the valuation assertion was not met for accounts receivable would increase, and the auditor would therefore increase substantive procedures for the allowance for uncollectible accounts.

In the Calabro example, Judd examines each of the sample items for the presence of a deviation. Thus, for control 1, Judd tests the 78 sales and lease contracts (sample size from the table) for proper credit authorization procedures by credit department personnel. The results of the audit procedures can be documented in a working paper similar to the example shown in Exhibit 8–3. As noted earlier, when multiple controls are tested on one sampling unit, auditors often decide to test all controls for the full sample when such testing can be efficiently conducted. The choice of whether to test all controls for the full sample is a matter of risk management. The argument supporting this approach is that since the auditor is physically inspecting the documentation in the full sample, the auditor may want to reduce the risk that deficiencies go undetected in the documents examined for the full sample. The concern is that at some future date a litigation event may identify deviations in sample items 79 to 93 for control 1, and those deviations seem readily apparent to the courts based only on a cursory review of the documents. In legal terms, if the auditor failed to detect a deviation that a jury believes a professional auditor should have detected, then the risk that the auditor could be successfully sued for negligence increases.

Exhibit 8–3 A Sample Working Paper for Recording the Results of Tests of Controls

				B20 DLJ 3/2/10
	CALABRO WIRELESS SERVICES **Controls Tested – Revenue Process** **31/12/09**			
		Control Activity		
Sample Item	*Sales and Lease Transaction Number*	*1*	*2*	*3*
1	35381	✔	✔	✔
2	82765	E	✔	✔
•		•	•	•
•		•	•	•
48	1347	✔	✔	✔
49	1283	E		✔
•		•	•	•
•		•	•	•
77	52140	✔		✔
78	88878	✔		✔
•				•
•				•
91	107409			✔
92	17080			✔
93	122891			✔
Number of deviations		2	0	0
Sample size from tables		78	48	93
Sample deviation rate		2.6%	0%	0%
Desired confidence level		95%	90%	95%
Computed upper deviation rate from tables		8.2%	5.0%	3.3%
Tolerable deviation rate		6%	8%	5%
Auditor's decision		Does not support reliance	Supports reliance	Supports reliance

Tick Mark Legend
✔ = Sales or lease contract examined for proper performance of control activity. No exception.
E = Control *not* performed properly.

Before calculating the sample results and drawing final conclusions on the sampling plan, Judd investigates the nature and cause of the exceptions. Judd also considers whether the deviations may impact the other phases of the audit. In the current example, two deviations were detected for control 1, which relates to proper authorization of credit. Judd's investigation indicates that both deviations had occurred when sales in excess of credit limits were made to existing customers. Further investigation disclosed that the sales manager instead of the credit manager had approved the sale. Judd now knows the nature and cause of the errors. The effect of the control deviations is likely to be an increase in the amount of audit work conducted on the allowance for uncollectible accounts.

After the audit procedures have been completed, the auditor proceeds with his or her evaluation of the sample results.

Evaluation

Step 6: Calculate the Sample Deviation and Computed Upper Deviation Rates

After completing the audit procedures, the auditor summarizes the deviations for each control tested and evaluates the results. Determining the sample results for an attribute-sampling application can be accomplished by the use of a computer program or attribute-sampling tables. The auditor calculates the sample deviation rate and the computed upper deviation rate. The sample deviation rate is simply the number of deviations found in the sample divided by the number of items in the sample. This calculation projects the sample results to the population and is required by auditing standards. For example, if two deviations were found in a sample of 50, the sample deviation rate would be 4 per cent (2 ÷ 50). In attribute sampling, the sample deviation rate represents the auditor's best estimate of the population deviation rate. However, because this result is based on a sample, the auditor does not know the true population deviation rate and must consider an allowance for sampling risk.

In evaluating the results of testing a control, the auditor is normally concerned only with whether the true deviation rate exceeds the tolerable deviation rate. Because the auditor does not know the true deviation rate, he or she calculates a *computed upper deviation rate*. The computed upper deviation rate is the sum of the sample deviation rate and an appropriate allowance for sampling risk. This sum represents an upper limit on how high the population deviation rate might actually be, at a controlled level of sampling risk (e.g. 5 or 10 per cent). In other words, at the 95 per cent confidence level, there is only a 5 per cent chance that the true population deviation rate exceeds the computed upper deviation rate. This is sometimes referred to as the *upper-limit approach*.

Exhibit 8–3 shows the results of the tests of the three controls for the Calabro audit. Judd calculates the sample deviation rate and the computed upper deviation rate for each control tested. To determine the computed upper deviation rate, Judd uses either Table 8–8 or Table 8–9, depending on the desired confidence level for the test. A 95 per cent confidence level is desired for control 1, thus Judd uses Table 8–8 in the following way. The column for the actual number of deviations found (2 deviations) is read down until the appropriate row for sample size is found. If the exact sample size is not found, the closest smaller sample size is used. This approach provides a conservative (larger) computed upper deviation rate. For control 1, the row for a sample size of 75 is used. The computed upper deviation rate for control 1 is 8.2 per cent. Thus, for control 1, the sample deviation rate is 2.6 per cent and the allowance for sampling risk is 5.6 per cent (8.2 – 2.6). For control 2, Table 8–9 is used because the desired confidence level is 90 per cent. In this case, no deviations were found, so the sample deviation rate is 0 per cent and the upper computed deviation rate is 5 per cent (rounding the sample size down to 45). No control deviations were found for control 3; therefore, the sample deviation rate is 0 per cent. Table 8–8 shows a computed upper deviation rate of 3.3 per cent (rounding the sample size down to 90). In other words, even though the auditor's best estimate based on the results of the testing is that the population contains no deviations, the allowance for sampling risk associated with the sample tested is 3.3 per cent.

Table 8–8 Statistical Sample Results Evaluation Table (Computed Upper Deviation Rates) for Attribute Sampling – 95 per cent Desired Confidence Level

Sample Size	Actual Number of Deviations Found										
	0	1	2	3	4	5	6	7	8	9	10
25	11.3	17.6	*	*	*	*	*	*	*	*	*
30	9.5	14.9	19.6	*	*	*	*	*	*	*	*
35	8.3	12.9	17.0	*	*	*	*	*	*	*	*
40	7.3	11.4	15.0	18.3	*	*	*	*	*	*	*
45	6.5	10.2	13.4	16.4	19.2	*	*	*	*	*	*
50	5.9	9.2	12.1	14.8	17.4	19.9	*	*	*	*	*
55	5.4	8.4	11.1	13.5	15.9	18.2	*	*	*	*	*
60	4.9	7.7	10.2	12.5	14.7	16.8	18.8	*	*	*	*
65	4.6	7.1	9.4	11.5	13.6	15.5	17.4	19.3	*	*	*
70	4.2	6.6	8.8	10.8	12.6	14.5	16.3	18.0	19.7	*	*
75	4.0	6.2	8.2	10.1	11.8	13.6	15.2	16.9	18.5	20.0	*
80	3.7	5.8	7.7	9.5	11.1	12.7	14.3	15.9	17.4	18.9	*
90	3.3	5.2	6.9	8.4	9.9	11.4	12.8	14.2	15.5	16.8	18.2
100	3.0	4.7	6.2	7.6	9.0	10.3	11.5	12.8	14.0	15.2	16.4
125	2.4	3.8	5.0	6.1	7.2	8.3	9.3	10.3	11.3	12.3	13.2
150	2.0	3.2	4.2	5.1	6.0	6.9	7.8	8.6	9.5	10.3	11.1
200	1.5	2.4	3.2	3.9	4.6	5.2	5.9	6.5	7.2	7.8	8.4

* Over 20 per cent.

Table 8–9 Statistical Sample Results Evaluation Table (Computed Upper Deviation Rates) for Attribute Sampling – 90 per cent Desired Confidence Level

Sample Size	Actual Number of Deviations Found										
	0	1	2	3	4	5	6	7	8	9	10
20	10.9	18.1	*	*	*	*	*	*	*	*	*
25	8.8	14.7	19.9	*	*	*	*	*	*	*	*
30	7.4	12.4	16.8	*	*	*	*	*	*	*	*
35	6.4	10.7	14.5	18.1	*	*	*	*	*	*	*
40	5.6	9.4	12.8	16.0	19.0	*	*	*	*	*	*
45	5.0	8.4	11.4	14.3	17.0	19.7	*	*	*	*	*
50	4.6	7.6	10.3	12.9	15.4	17.8	*	*	*	*	*
55	4.1	6.9	9.4	11.8	14.1	16.3	18.4	*	*	*	*
60	3.8	6.4	8.7	10.8	12.9	15.0	16.9	18.9	*	*	*
70	3.3	5.5	7.5	9.3	11.1	12.9	14.6	16.3	17.9	19.6	*
80	2.9	4.8	6.6	8.2	9.8	11.3	12.8	14.3	15.8	17.2	18.6
90	2.6	4.3	5.9	7.3	8.7	10.1	11.5	12.8	14.1	15.4	16.6
100	2.3	3.9	5.3	6.6	7.9	9.1	10.3	11.5	12.7	13.9	15.0
120	2.0	3.3	4.4	5.5	6.6	7.6	8.7	9.7	10.7	11.6	12.6
160	1.5	2.5	3.3	4.2	5.0	5.8	6.5	7.3	8.0	8.8	9.5
200	1.2	2.0	2.7	3.4	4.0	4.6	5.3	5.9	6.5	7.1	7.6

* Over 20 per cent

The upper limit represents the upper one-sided confidence limit for the population deviation rate based on the sample size, the number of deviations and the planned level of confidence. In evaluating the results of testing a control, the auditor is normally concerned only with whether the true deviation rate exceeds the tolerable deviation rate. Therefore, the auditor is generally concerned only with how *high* the population deviation rate might be; it does not matter how *low* the population deviation rate might be.

Exhibit 8–4 Evaluation Results from ACL™

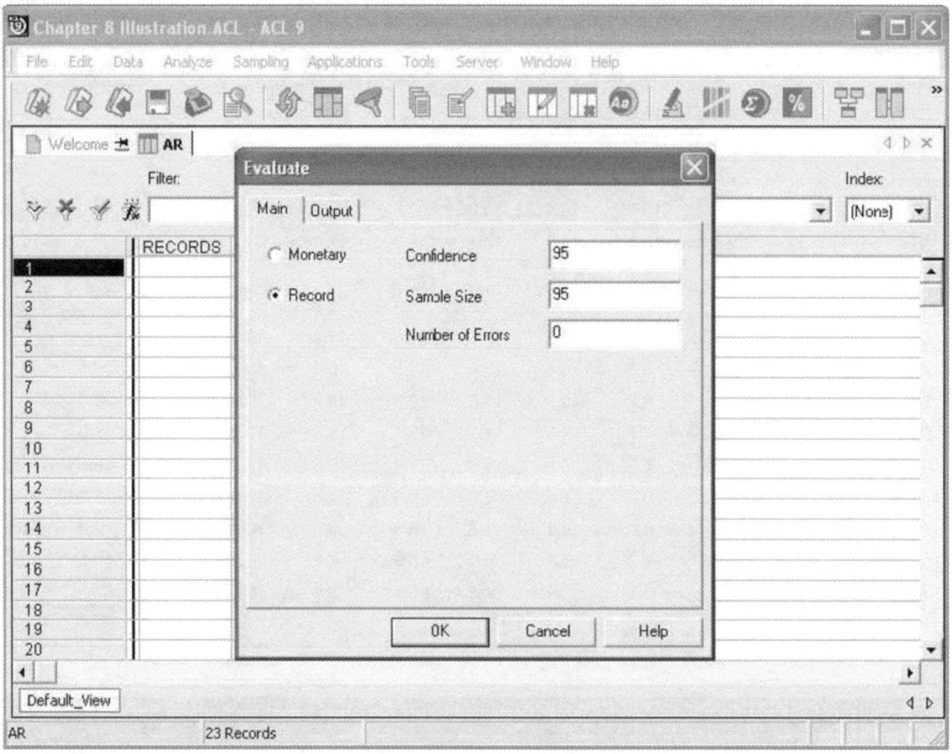

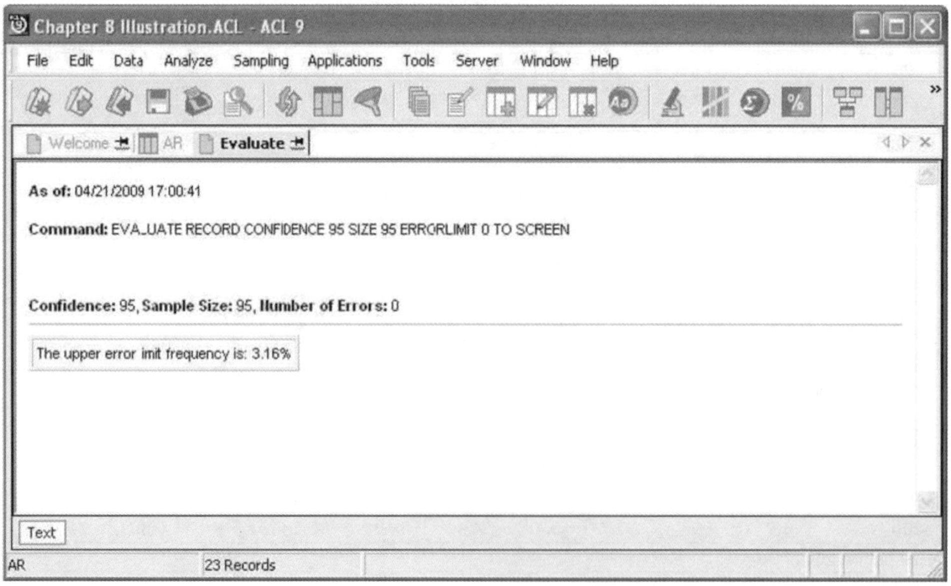

Computing Upper Deviation Rate with ACL Software

Exhibit 8–4 shows the output from ACL for control 3. The auditor chooses the 'Sampling' button on the menu bar and selects 'Evaluate Error'. The evaluate window is then displayed, and the auditor enters the relevant data for control 3: 'Confidence' is 95 per cent, 'Sample Size' is 95 (based on ACL sample size computation), and 0 'Number of Errors'. The estimated upper limit error frequency (i.e. computed upper deviation rate) is 3.16 per cent.

Step 7: Draw Final Conclusions

In drawing a conclusion about the statistical sampling application for tests of controls, the auditor compares the tolerable deviation rate to the computed upper deviation rate. If the computed upper deviation rate is less than the tolerable deviation rate, the auditor can conclude that the controls can be relied upon. If the computed upper deviation rate exceeds the tolerable deviation rate, the auditor will normally conclude that the controls are not operating at an acceptable level. The auditor must evaluate if a control deficiency should be communicated to those charged with governance and management (see Chapter 6).

For a financial statement audit, the final conclusion about control risk for the accounting system being tested is based on the auditor's professional judgement of the sample results and other relevant tests of controls such as inquiry and observation. If the auditor concludes that the evidence supports the planned level of control risk, no modifications of the planned substantive procedures are necessary. On the other hand, if the planned level of control risk is not supported by the sample results and other tests of controls, the auditor should either: (1) test other control activities that could support the planned level of control risk; or (2) increase the assessed level of control risk and modify the nature, extent or timing of substantive procedures.

Table 8–10 shows the auditor's risks when evaluating sample evidence on the planned level of control risk. If the evidence supports the planned level of control risk and the internal control is reliable, the auditor has made a correct decision. Similarly, if the evidence does not support the planned level of control risk and the internal control is not reliable, a correct decision has been made. The other two combinations result in decision errors by the auditor. If the evidence supports the planned level of control risk and the internal control is not reliable, the auditor will have incorrectly accepted the control as effective and overrelied on internal control (Type II error). This results in the auditor establishing detection risk too high and leads to a lower level of evidence being gathered through substantive procedures. Thus, the auditor's risk of not detecting material misstatement is increased. This can lead to a lawsuit against the auditor. If the evidence does not support the planned level of control risk and the internal control is reliable (Type I error), the auditor will have incorrectly rejected the control and detection risk will have been set too low. Thus, a higher level of evidence will be gathered by substantive procedures, leading to over-auditing and an inefficient audit.

Table 8–10 The Auditor's Risks When Evaluating Sample Evidence on the Planned Level of Control Risk		
Auditor's Decision Based on Sample Evidence	*True State of Internal Control*	
	Reliable	*Not Reliable*
Supports the planned level of control risk	Correct decision	Risk of incorrect acceptance (Type II)
Does not support the planned level of control risk	Risk of incorrect rejection (Type I)	Correct decision

For the Calabro audit, Exhibit 8–3 shows that the sample evidence does not support the operating effectiveness of control 1 (credit authorization) because the computed upper deviation rate (8.2 per cent) exceeds the tolerable deviation rate (6 per cent). For control 1, the sample deviation rate was 2.6 per cent and the allowance for sampling risk was 5.6 per cent. In this example, there appear to be no other controls or other evidence to support the operating effectiveness of control 1. Thus, Judd increases both the assessed level of control risk and the substantive procedures related to the valuation assertion.

Judd's sample evidence supports the reliability of controls 2 and 3 because the computed upper deviation rates are less than the tolerable deviation rates.

❖ NON-STATISTICAL SAMPLING FOR TESTS OF CONTROLS

LO8

When conducting a non-statistical sampling application for tests of controls, the auditor considers each of the steps shown in Table 8–2. The differences between non-statistical and statistical sampling occur in any or all of the following steps:

- Determining the sample size.
- Selecting the sample items.
- Calculating the computed upper deviation rate.

Determining the Sample Size

When a non-statistical sampling application is used in determining sample size, the auditor should consider the desired confidence, the tolerable deviation rate and the expected population deviation rate. While the auditor is not required to use a statistical formula or table to determine sample size, auditing standards indicate that sample sizes for non-statistical and statistical applications should be comparable. In other words, 'non-statistical' does not justify an auditor in using sample sizes that are too small to provide sufficient evidence. Non-statistical sample sizes are determined by applying professional judgement and guidance in audit firm policy.

A number of audit firms establish guidelines for non-statistical sample sizes for tests of controls. Typically, audit firms' non-statistical guidelines are consistent with sampling theory and are designed to provide two primary benefits: (1) to simplify the judgements required by field auditors by having experts at firm headquarters make firm-wide judgements; and (2) to improve consistency in sampling applications within and across engagement teams. For example, a firm might establish guidelines as follows:

Desired Level of Controls Reliance	Sample Size
Low	15–20
Moderate	25–35
High	40–60

In developing non-statistical sampling guidelines like those above, the firm's experts have decided what confidence levels achieve low, moderate and high assurance (say 70–75, 80–85 and 90–95 per cent confidence respectively). The experts have decided reasonable levels of tolerable deviation rates (say 5 to 10 per cent), and they have decided to base an initial sample on zero expected deviations. Following this guidance, if one or more deviations are found in the sample, the auditor needs to expand the sample or increase the assessed level of control risk.

Selecting the Sample Items

While random-sample or systematic-sample (with a random start) selection is required for statistical sampling, non-statistical sampling allows the use of those selection methods as well as other selection methods such as *haphazard sampling*. When a haphazard selection approach is used, sampling units are selected without any conscious bias – that is, without a special reason for including or omitting items from the sample. This does not imply that the items are selected in a careless manner; rather, the sampling units are selected to represent the population. Haphazard selection may be useful for non-statistical sampling, but it should not be used for statistical sampling because the auditor cannot measure the probability of an item being selected. When using audit sampling, the auditor should avoid distorting the sample by selecting only items that are unusual or large, or items that are the first or last items in the frame, because the auditor needs a sample that represents the population in order to draw inferences about the population from the sample. This is not to say that selection of unusual, large or risky events, transactions or balances should be avoided in other audit procedures that do not involve audit sampling. On the contrary, the auditor should focus specific audit procedures on all such items and not turn the selection of these items over to chance, which is required for audit sampling.

Calculating the Computed Upper Deviation Rate

With a non-statistical sample, the auditor can calculate the sample deviation rate but cannot quantify the computed upper deviation rate and the sampling risk associated with the test. Auditing standards provide the following guidance for evaluating the sampling results for tests of controls:

> For tests of controls, an unexpectedly high sample deviation rate may lead to an increase in the assessed risk of material misstatement, unless further audit evidence substantiating the initial assessment is obtained. If the auditor concludes that audit sampling has not provided a reasonable basis for conclusions about the population that has been tested, the auditor might extend the sample size, test an alternative control or modify related substantive procedures.[vi]

The AICPA Audit Guide, *Audit Sampling*, provides the following advice for considering sampling risk in a non-statistical test of controls:

> An auditor using non-statistical sampling uses judgement to consider the allowance for sampling risk. For example, when the rate of deviation from the prescribed control exceeds the expected rate used to plan the sample, the auditor usually concludes that there is unacceptably high sampling risk and he or she typically would increase the assessed level of control risk or consider further whether to rely at all on the control.[vii]

Suppose an auditor planned a non-statistical sampling application by setting the desired confidence level at 'high' (i.e. 90 to 95 per cent), the expected population deviation rate at 1.5 per cent, and the tolerable deviation rate at 8 per cent. Assume the auditor judgementally determines to select a sample size of 50 items and makes the selections haphazardly. If the auditor detects no control deviations, the sample deviation rate is 0 per cent. In this instance, the sample deviation rate, 0 per cent, is less than the expected population deviation rate, 1.5 per cent, and there is an acceptable risk that the true population deviation rate exceeds the tolerable deviation rate.

Assume that one control deviation had been detected. The sample deviation rate is 2 per cent, which is greater than the expected population deviation rate (1.5 per cent). Now there is an unacceptably high risk that the true population deviation rate exceeds the tolerable deviation rate. Referring to the statistical evaluation table illustrates why the results of the non-statistical sample are not likely to support the effectiveness of the control. Table 8–8 shows that if one deviation is found in a sample of 50 items, the computed upper deviation rate is 9.2 per cent. This exceeds the tolerable deviation rate of 8 per cent.

Students and auditors are sometimes confused by what causes a sampling approach to be 'non-statistical'. An approach is non-statistical if: (1) judgement is used to determine the sample size; (2) a haphazard sample selection technique is used; and/or (3) the sample results are evaluated judgementally. A non-statistical approach can involve random selection and a judgemental evaluation. While haphazardly selected samples cannot be statistically evaluated, any randomly drawn sample can be statistically evaluated – even if the auditor labels the approach 'non-statistical' and even if the sample size was not statistically derived. This is an important point because it highlights the need for auditors to understand the key concepts of sampling theory even if they are using a non-statistical approach. Remember, if an auditor randomly selects a sample and then evaluates the results judgementally, the quality of his or her judgement can be evaluated against statistical theory by outside experts.

CONCLUSION

The use of sampling is common in auditing because of the need to gather evidence over large populations of client data in a cost-effective manner. In this chapter we discussed the basic concepts that are relevant to all forms of audit sampling, such as sampling risk. Whenever auditors use sampling techniques, they face the risk that their sample is not representative of the population, which could lead them to draw the wrong conclusions. Statistical theory allows auditors to measure this risk and manage it by taking the appropriate sample size. In this chapter we focused primarily on statistical attributes sampling for tests of controls, and we provided a step-by-step approach to planning a sample, executing the sample testing and evaluating the results from the sample. The steps were illustrated using both statistical tables and the audit software ACL. Non-statistical sampling is commonly used in practice, but it is important to remember that non-statistical approaches must be founded in statistical theory.

In Chapter 9, you will learn about statistical and non-statistical sampling techniques auditors use to gather substantive evidence.

ADVANCED MODULE: CONSIDERING THE EFFECT OF THE POPULATION SIZE

The population size generally has little or no effect on the sample size. If the population contains more than 500 units, the effect on the sample size is negligible.

The attribute-sampling tables presented earlier in this chapter assume a large population. When the population size is smaller than 500, the sample size taken from the tables can be adjusted by using the finite population correction factor as follows:

$$\text{Finite population correction factor} = \sqrt{1 - \frac{n}{N}}$$

where

n = the sample size from the tables
N = the number of units in the population

For example, the sample size for desired confidence of 90 per cent, a tolerable deviation rate of 10 per cent, and expected population deviation rate of 1 per cent is 39 when population size is 1,000. If the population size were 100, the sample size of 39 could be adjusted as follows:

$$\text{Sample size} = n \sqrt{1 - \frac{n}{N}}$$

$$= 39 \sqrt{1 - \frac{39}{100}} = 31$$

Some controls may operate only weekly, monthly or quarterly. For infrequent controls some auditors use samples sizes provided in the following table:

Small Population Sample Size Table[viii]	
Control Frequency and Population Size	*Sample Size*
Quarterly (4)	2
Monthly (12)	2–4
Semi-monthly (24)	3–8
Weekly (52)	5–9

Key Terms

Allowance for sampling risk. The uncertainty that results from sampling; the difference between the expected mean of the population and the tolerable deviation or misstatement.

Attribute sampling. Sampling used to estimate the proportion of a population that possesses a specified characteristic.

Audit sampling. The application of audit procedures to less than 100 per cent of items within a population of audit relevance such that all sampling units have a chance of selection in order to provide the auditor with a reasonable basis on which to draw conclusions about the entire population.

Classical variables sampling. The use of normal distribution theory to estimate the monetary amount of misstatement for a class of transactions or an account balance.

Desired confidence level. The probability that the true but unknown measure of the characteristic of interest is within specified limits.

Expected population deviation rate. The deviation rate that the auditor expects to exist in the population.

Monetary-unit sampling. Attribute-sampling techniques used to estimate the monetary amount of misstatement for a class of transactions or an account balance.

Non-sampling risk. The possibility that the auditor may use inappropriate audit procedures, fail to detect a misstatement when applying an audit procedure, or misinterpret an audit result.

Non-statistical sampling. Audit sampling that relies on the auditor's judgement to select the sample (typically of comparable size to a statistically based sampling approach) and/or evaluate the results for the purpose of reaching a conclusion about the population.

Population. The entire set of data from which a sample is selected and about which the auditor wishes to draw conclusions.

Risk of incorrect acceptance. The risk that the sample supports the conclusion that the control is operating effectively when it is not, or that the recorded account balance is not materially misstated when it is materially misstated.

Risk of incorrect rejection. The risk that the sample supports the conclusion that the control is not operating effectively when it actually is, or that recorded account balance is materially misstated when it is not materially misstated.

Sampling risk. The possibility that the sample drawn is not representative of the population and that, as a result, the auditor reaches an incorrect conclusion about the reliability of the control, the account balance or class of transactions based on the sample.

Sampling unit. The individual member of the population being sampled.

Statistical sampling. Sampling that uses the laws of probability to select and evaluate the results of an audit sample, thereby permitting the auditor to quantify the sampling risk for the purpose of reaching a conclusion about the population.

Tolerable deviation rate. The maximum deviation rate from a prescribed control that the auditor is willing to accept without altering the planned assessed level of control risk.

? Review Questions

LO1	8–1	Define audit sampling. Why do auditors sample instead of examine every transaction?
LO2	8–2	Distinguish between Type I and Type II errors. What terms are used to describe these errors when the auditor is conducting tests of controls and substantive tests? What costs are potentially incurred by auditors when such decision errors occur?
LO3	8–3	List audit evidence choices that do not involve sampling and provide an example of a situation where an auditor would not use audit sampling.
LO4	8–4	Distinguish between non-statistical and statistical sampling. What are the advantages and disadvantages of using statistical sampling?
LO6,7	8–5	Define attribute sampling. Why is this sampling technique appropriate for tests of controls?
LO6,7,8	8–6	How does the timing of controls testing affect the population definition?
LO7	8–7	List the four factors that enter into the sample size decision. What is the relationship between sample size and each of these factors?
LO6,7,8	8–8	In performing certain audit procedures the auditor may encounter voided documents, inapplicable documents, missing documents, or the auditor may stop testing before examining all the items selected for the sample. How should each of these situations be handled within the attribute-sampling application?
LO6,7,8	8–9	The auditor should evaluate the qualitative aspects of deviations found in a sampling application. What are the purposes of evaluating the qualitative aspects of deviations?
LO8	8–10	How should the results of a non-statistical test of controls sample be evaluated in terms of considering sampling risk?

✏ Problems

LO1,2	8–11	Audit sampling is defined as applying an audit procedure to less than

100 per cent of the population such that all sampling units have a chance of selection. When an auditor uses sampling, an element of uncertainty enters into the auditor's conclusions.

Required:

a *Explain the auditor's justification for accepting the uncertainties that are inherent in the sampling process.*

b *Discuss the uncertainties that collectively embody the concept of audit risk.*

c *Discuss the nature of sampling risk and non-sampling risk. Include the effect of sampling risk on tests of controls.*

LO2,3,4   **8–12**

a. Attribute sampling.	1. The possibility that the sample drawn is not representative of the population and leads to an incorrect conclusion.
b. Desired confidence Level.	2. Relies on the auditor's judgement to determine sample size and evaluate the results.
c. Allowance for sampling risk.	3. The maximum deviation rate from a prescribed control that an auditor is willing to accept.
d. Sampling risk.	4. All or a subset of the items that constitute the class of transactions.
e. Sampling population.	5. The probability that the true but unknown measure of the characteristic of interest is within specified limits.
f. Non-statistical sampling.	6. Used to estimate the proportion of a population that possesses a certain characteristic.
g. Tolerable deviation rate.	7. The difference between the expected and the tolerable deviation rate.

Required:

Match the term to the definition.

LO6,7   **8–13**   Following is a set of situations that may or may not involve sampling.

1   An auditor is examining loan receivables at a local bank. The population of loans contains two strata. One stratum is composed of 25 loans that are each greater than €1 million. The second stratum contains 450 loans that are less than €1 million. The auditor has decided to test all loans greater than €1 million and 15 loans less than €1 million.

2   Assume the same facts as number 1 except that the auditor decides to apply analytical procedures to the second stratum of loans.

3   An auditor has haphazardly selected 30 sales invoices to be examined for proper pricing of the goods purchased by the customer.

4   The prepaid insurance account is made up of four policies that total €45,000. The auditor has decided that this account is immaterial and decides that no policies will be examined.

Required:

Indicate which situations involve audit sampling (statistical or non-statistical) and why.

LO6,7   **8–14**   Jenny Jacobs, independent auditor, is planning to use attribute sampling in order to determine the degree of reliance to be placed on an audit client's system of internal control over sales. Jacobs has begun to develop an outline of the main steps in the sampling plan as follows:

1   State the test objectives (for example, to test the reliability of internal controls over sales).

2   Define the population (the period covered by the test, the sampling unit, the completeness of the population).

3   Define the sampling unit (for example, client copies of sales invoices).

Required:

a   *What are the remaining steps in the outline that Jacobs should include in the statistical test of sales invoices?*

b   *What are the advantages of using statistical audit sampling?*

(AICPA, adapted)

LO6   **8–15**   Determine the sample size for each of the control activities shown in the following table (assuming a large population):

Parameters	Control Activity			
	1	2	3	4
Risk of incorrect acceptance	5%	5%	10%	10%
Tolerable deviation rate	4%	5%	7%	8%
Expected population deviation rate	1%	2%	3%	4%
Sample size				

LO6   **8–16**   Using the sample sizes determined in Problem 8–15 and the number of deviations shown here, determine the sample deviation rate, the computed upper deviation rate, and the auditor's conclusion (i.e. testing results do or do not support operating effectiveness of the control) for each control activity.

Results	Control Activity			
	1	2	3	4
Number of deviations	0	5	4	3
Sample size				
Sample deviation rate				
Computed upper deviation rate				
Auditor's conclusion				

LO6   **8–17**   Determine the sample size for each of the control activities shown in the following table:

Parameters	Control Activity			
	1	2	3	4
Risk of incorrect acceptance	5%	5%	10%	10%
Tolerable deviation rate	6%	7%	4%	3%
Expected population deviation rate	2%	2%	1%	0%
Sample size				

LO6   **8–18**   Using the sample sizes determined in Problem 8–17 and the number of deviations shown here, determine the sample deviation rate, computed upper deviation rate, and the auditor's conclusion (i.e. testing results do or do not support operating effectiveness of the control) for each control activity.

Results	Control Activity			
	1	2	3	4
Number of deviations	4	2	2	0
Sample size				
Sample deviation rate				
Computed upper deviation rate				
Auditor's conclusion				

LO8 **8–19** Calgari Clothing Company manufactures high-quality silk ties that are marketed under a number of trademark names. Joe & Vandervelte have been the company's auditors for five years. Lisa Austen, the senior-in-charge of the audit, has reviewed Calgari's controls over purchasing and inventory, and she determined that a number of controls can be relied upon to reduce control risk. Austen has decided to test two control activities over purchases and inventory: (1) purchase orders are agreed to receiving reports and vendor's invoices for product, quantity and price; and (2) inventory is transferred to raw material stores using an approved, prenumbered receiving report.

Austen decided to use a non-statistical sampling approach based on the following judgements for each control activity and has judgementally decided to use a sample size of 75 purchase orders for control 1 and 30 receiving reports for control 2.

Parameters	Control Activity	
	1	2
Desired confidence	95%	90%
Tolerable deviation rate	7%	9%
Expected population deviation rate	2%	2.5%

After completing the examination of the sample items, Austen noted one deviation for each control activity.

Required:

What conclusion should Austen reach about each control activity? Justify your answer.

LO8 **8–20** Nathan Matthews conducted a test of controls where the tolerable deviation rate was set at 6 per cent and the expected population deviation rate was 3 per cent. Using a sample size of 150, Matthews performed the planned test of controls. He found six deviations in the sample and he calculated the computed upper deviation rate to be 7.8 per cent.

Required:

a *Based on the sample results, what allowance for sampling risk is included in the computed upper deviation rate of 7.8?*

b *Assume that Matthews preliminarily assessed control risk as 'low'. Given the results above, the auditor could decide to do one of three things: (1) increase the sample size; (2) increase the preliminary assessment of control risk; or (3) not adjust the preliminary assessment of control risk. Describe how Matthews could justify each of those three actions.*

LO8 **8–21** Doug Iceberge, senior-in-charge of the audit of Fisher Industries, has decided to test the following two controls for Fisher's revenue process.

1 All sales invoices are supported by proper documentation – that is, a sales order and a shipping document.

2 All sales invoices are mathematically correct.

Iceberge has decided to use a non-statistical sampling approach based on the following judgements for each control and has judgementally decided to use a sample size of 50 sales invoice packets.

Parameters	Control Activity	
	1	2
Desired confidence level	95%	90%
Risk of assessing control risk too low	5%	10%
Tolerable deviation rate	6%	8%
Expected population deviation rate	3%	3%

After completing the examination of the 50 sample items, Iceberge noted one deviation for control 1 and two deviations for control 2.

Required:

What should Iceberge conclude about each control? Justify your answer.

Discussion Case

LO2,5,6   8–22   Baker, independent auditor, was engaged to audit Mill Company's financial statements for the year ended 30 September. After studying Mill's internal control, Baker decided to obtain evidence about the effectiveness of both the design and the operation of the controls that may support a low assessed level of control risk concerning Mill's shipping and billing functions. During the prior years' audits, Baker had used non-statistical sampling, but for the current year Baker used a statistical sample in the tests of controls to eliminate the need for judgement.

Baker wanted to assess control risk at a low level, so a tolerable deviation rate of 20 per cent was established. To estimate the population deviation rate and the computed upper deviation rate, Baker decided to apply a sampling technique of attribute sampling that would use an expected population deviation rate of 3 per cent for the 8,000 shipping documents and to defer consideration of the allowable risk of assessing control risk too low until the sample results were evaluated. Baker used the tolerable deviation rate, the population size, and the expected population deviation rate to determine that a sample size of 80 would be sufficient. When it was subsequently determined that the actual population was about 10,000 shipping documents, Baker increased the sample size to 100.

Baker's objective was to ascertain whether Mill's shipments had been properly billed. Baker took a sample of 100 invoices by selecting the first 25 invoices from the first month of each quarter. Baker then compared the invoices to the corresponding prenumbered shipping documents.

When Baker tested the sample, eight deviations were discovered. Additionally, one shipment that should have been billed at €10,443 was actually billed at €10,434. Baker considered this €9 to be immaterial and did not count it as an error.

In evaluating the sample results, Baker made the initial determination that a 5 per cent risk of assessing control risk too low was desired and, using the appropriate statistical sampling table, determined that for eight observed deviations from a sample size of 100, the computed upper deviation rate was 14 per cent. Baker then calculated the allowance for sampling risk to be 5 per cent, the difference between the actual sample deviation rate (8 per cent) and the expected error rate (3 per cent). Baker reasoned that the actual sample deviation rate (8 per cent) plus the allowance for sampling risk (5 per cent) was less than the computed upper deviation rate (14 per cent); therefore, the sample supported a low level of control risk.

Required:

Describe each incorrect assumption, statement and inappropriate application of attribute sampling in Baker's procedures.

(AICPA, adapted)

Notes

i   See the introduction to the American Institute of Certified Public Accountants, *Audit Sampling* (AICPA Audit Guide), AICPA, New York, 2008, for a discussion of the development of sampling in auditing.

ii   See N. Hitzig, 'Audit Sampling: A Survey of Current Practice', *CPA Journal* (1995), pp. 54–57; and W.F. Messier, Jr, S.J. Kachelmeier and K. Jensen, 'An Experimental Assessment of Recent Professional Developments in Nonstatistical Sampling Guidance', *Auditing: A Journal of Practice & Theory* (2001), pp. 81–96.

iii   The sample sizes assume a tolerable deviation rate of 5 per cent, an expected population deviation rate of 1 per cent and a large population.

iv   This material is used with the permission of ACL Services Limited. The authors are grateful to the company for allowing the use of this material.

v   Each random number generated by ACL will be greater than or equal to the minimum value and less than the maximum value you specify. No random number will be equal to the maximum value. For this reason the maximum range is input as 125,001.

vi   Adapted from ISA 530, paras A21 and A23.

vii   Adapted from American Institute of Certified Public Accountants, *Audit Sampling* (Audit Guide), AICPA, New York, 2008.

viii   This is Table 3.5 from the American Institute of Certified Public Accountants, *Audit Sampling* (AICPA Audit Guide), AICPA, New York, 2008.

CHAPTER

9

Audit Sampling: An Application to Substantive Tests of Account Balances

❖ LEARNING OBJECTIVES

Upon completion of this chapter you will

- ❖ **LO1** Understand the similarities and differences between audit sampling for tests of controls and substantive tests of details of account balances.
- ❖ **LO2** Learn to apply monetary-unit sampling.
- ❖ **LO3** Work through an extended example of monetary-unit sampling.

- ❖ **LO4** Learn to apply non-statistical sampling techniques.
- ❖ **LO5** Learn to apply classical variables sampling.
- ❖ **LO6** Work through an example of classical variables difference estimation.

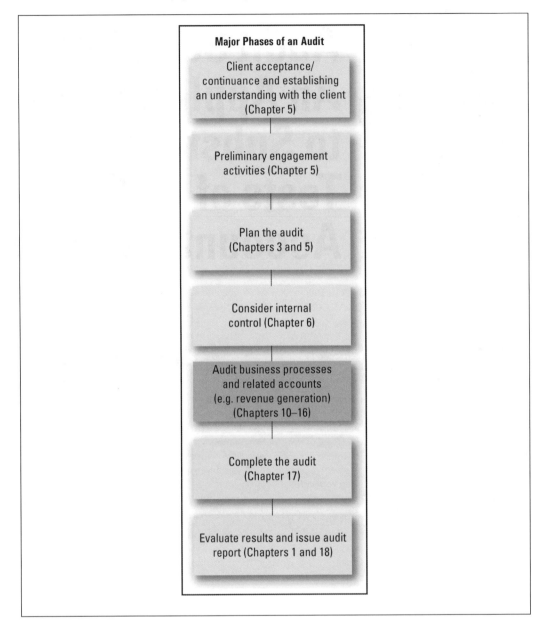

> ## ❖ RELEVANT ACCOUNTING AND AUDITING PRONOUNCEMENTS
>
> **AICPA,** *Audit Sampling* (Audit Guide), AICPA, New York, 2008
>
> **SA 230,** Audit Documentation
>
> **ISA 240,** The Auditor's Responsibilities Relating to Fraud in an Audit of Financial Statements
>
> **ISA 300,** Planning an Audit of Financial Statements
>
> **ISA 315,** Identifying and Assessing the Risks of Material Misstatement through Understanding the Entity and Its Environment
>
> **ISA 320,** Materiality in Planning and Performing an Audit
>
> **ISA 450,** Evaluation of Misstatements Identified during the Audit
>
> **ISA 500,** Audit Evidence
>
> **ISA 530,** Audit Sampling

THIS CHAPTER demonstrates the application of audit sampling to substantive tests of details of account balances. In Chapter 8, attribute sampling was used to determine whether controls were operating effectively and could therefore be relied on by the auditor to generate accurate accounting information. Thus, the objective of attribute sampling was to determine the reliability of the client's controls. In this chapter, the purpose of the sampling application is to determine if a financial statement account is fairly stated.

Two statistical sampling techniques, **monetary-unit sampling** and **classical variables sampling**, and non-statistical sampling are demonstrated in this chapter. While both statistical sampling methods can provide sufficient appropriate evidence, monetary-unit sampling may be more practical for most audit applications. The chapter starts with an introduction of monetary-unit sampling and an extended example. Non-statistical sampling is then covered. The *Advanced Module* contains a discussion and example of classical variables sampling.

❖ SAMPLING FOR SUBSTANTIVE TESTS OF DETAILS OF ACCOUNT BALANCES

LO1

The basic statistical concepts discussed in Chapter 8 are also applicable for sampling approaches used to test account balances. Three important determinants of sample size are desired confidence level, **tolerable misstatement** and estimated misstatement. Misstatements discovered in the audit sample must be projected to the population, and there must be an **allowance for sampling risk**.

In the preface to Chapter 8, we asked you to imagine that you were an apple inspector. We did this to illustrate some of the basic concepts of **audit sampling** before covering the technical details. Before we get into the details of audit sampling for substantive tests, we want you to use your developing professional judgement and understanding of sampling to evaluate the sampling results related to a test of the inventory balance provided below. Suppose the misstatement of €2,000 represents differences between the auditor's inventory test count and the amount in the client's records based on the client's inventory counting procedures:

Book value of the inventory account balance	€3,000,000
Book value of items sampled	€ 100,000
Audited value of items sampled	€ 98,000
Total amount of misstatement observed in audit sample	€ 2,000

The purpose of audit sampling is to draw inferences about the entire population (the reported inventory account balance in the example above) from the results of a sample. Using just the information provided above, what is your best estimate of the misstatement in the inventory account balance? In Chapter 8 our best estimate of the population deviation rate for control testing was the sample deviation rate. Similarly, when using audit sampling to test account balances, we will want to project the misstatement observed in the sample to the population. In the example above, the observed misstatement could be projected to the population by computing the ratio of misstatement to the total euros sampled: 2 per cent (€2,000 ÷ €100,000). Applying this ratio to the entire account balance produces a *best estimate* or *projected misstatement* in the inventory account of €60,000 (2% × €3,000,000). If your best estimate is that the account is overstated by €60,000, do you believe the account is fairly stated? The answer to this question, like many questions in auditing is, 'it depends'. It depends in part on the amount of misstatement that can be tolerated for the inventory account. If the amount of misstatement that can be tolerated for this account is €50,000, then we cannot conclude that the account is fairly stated because our best estimate (or projected misstatement) is higher than the amount we can tolerate. What if tolerable misstatement was €110,000; would you conclude that the account is fairly stated? The answer is again, 'it depends'. Whenever sampling is used, the evaluation must include an allowance for sampling risk. When sampling is used to estimate monetary misstatement, an upper and lower **confidence bound** or misstatement limit must be established as an allowance for sampling risk. In the above example, the misstatement in the population could be €60,000, but it also might be higher or lower because the estimate is based on a sample. If tolerable misstatement is €110,000, and the upper limit on the account's possible misstatement is less than €110,000, then the account is considered fairly stated. The size of the upper limit on misstatement is largely dependent on the sample size, which is also directly related to the desired confidence level.

You may remember from your statistics courses using concepts such as 'standard deviation' and a 'normal distribution' (i.e. 'Z scores' or confidence coefficients) to compute *confidence limits* and *intervals*. This traditional statistical approach is used for classical variables sampling, which is covered in the *Advanced Module*. Before personal computers were commonly available, the mathematical complexity of classical variable sampling was problematic for auditors. In response, auditors developed an audit sampling approach for testing balances called monetary-unit sampling. Monetary-unit sampling is based on attribute-sampling concepts. While the computations involved in classical variables sampling can now easily be performed with a personal computer or handheld calculator, auditors have found that monetary-unit sampling provides other important advantages. For this reason, popular audit sampling software, such as ACL, include monetary-unit sampling but not classical variables sampling. However, monetary-unit sampling is not the best approach to use for all substantive tests of details; therefore, in this chapter we also cover non-statistical sampling and classical variables sampling.

❖ MONETARY-UNIT SAMPLING

LO2

Monetary-unit sampling (MUS) uses attribute-sampling theory to express a conclusion in euro (or other currency) amounts rather than as a rate of occurrence. Monetary-unit sampling was developed by auditors to overcome the computational complexity of other statistical sampling techniques and because most accounting populations contain relatively little misstatement. The statistical estimators of potential misstatement involved in classical variables sampling (see the *Advanced Module*) are not very effective in populations with little misstatement. Monetary-unit sampling is commonly used by auditors to test accounts such as accounts receivable, loans receivable, investment securities, and inventory. While MUS is based on attribute-sampling theory, the fact that MUS is designed to test monetary amounts (e.g. euros, dollars, yen or pesos) rather than internal control effectiveness causes important differences in these techniques. The differences are driven by the characteristics of control deviations and monetary misstatements. In attribute sampling, the control either works or it does not. Thus, all items sampled are either correct or a deviation. Attributes sampling provides an estimate and upper limit on the percentage of the time that a control is failing. With MUS, the sampling item tested may be valid and posted to the correct account in the correct period, but the euro amount may not be accurately recorded. For instance, an invoice for €2,565 might be entered into the accounting system as €2,655. In this case there is a misstatement, but the misstatement is only about 3.5 per cent of the transaction. A direct application of attribute sampling to monetary items would treat all misstatements as deviations or 100 per cent misstatements. However, doing so would not result in a useful estimate of the monetary amount of the misstatement in the population. Monetary-unit sampling begins with attribute-sampling concepts as a foundation but takes into consideration misstatement amounts observed in each **sampling unit** when computing the best estimate of the population misstatement and formulating the confidence limits around this estimated misstatement. Over the years academics, audit firms and software programmers (e.g. ACL) have developed slightly different MUS approaches and enhancements. However, the underlying concepts in all MUS approaches are similar to those discussed in this chapter.

To summarize, the basic underlying concepts of MUS are straightforward. Monetary-unit sampling uses attribute-sampling theory to estimate the *percentage* of monetary units in a population that might be misstated and then multiplies this percentage by an estimate of *how much* the euros are misstated. Keep these basic concepts in mind as you study MUS in this chapter.

Monetary-unit sampling is designed primarily to test for *overstatement* errors. However, it can accommodate understatement errors if special considerations are made during the evaluation of the sample results. Monetary-unit sampling is most appropriate for low-error-rate populations because it provides as effective a test as classical variables sampling does but has a more efficient sample size. Following are some advantages and disadvantages of MUS.

Advantages

- When the auditor expects few to no misstatements, MUS usually results in a smaller sample size than classical variables sampling.
- The calculation of the sample size and the evaluation of the sample results are *not* based on the variation (or standard deviation) in the population. The standard deviation is required to compute the sample size for a classical variables sampling application because it relies on the central limit theorem.
- When applied using a probability-proportional-to-size sample selection procedure, as outlined in this text, MUS automatically results in a stratified sample because sampled items are selected in proportion to their euro amounts. Thus, larger euro items have a higher probability of being selected. With classical variables sampling, the population must be stratified in order to focus on larger items.

Disadvantages

- The selection of zero or negative balances generally requires special design consideration. For example, if examining zero balances is important (searching for unrecorded liabilities in accounts payable), the auditor must test those items separately because such items will not be selected using a probability-proportional-to-size selection method. Alternatively, if an account such as accounts receivable contains credit balances, the auditor should segregate those items and test them separately.
- The general approach to MUS assumes that the audited amount of the sample item is not in error by more than 100 per cent. If the auditor detects items that are in error by more than 100 per cent, special adjustments will be necessary when calculating sample results. For example, suppose an accounts receivable account contains a *debit* balance book value of €1,500. If the auditor determines that the correct value for the account should be a *credit* balance of €3,000, the account will be in error by 300 per cent. Such an item would require special consideration when the auditor projects the amount of misstatement.
- When more than one or two misstatements are detected using a MUS approach, the sample results calculations as shown in the textbook may overstate the allowance for sampling risk. This occurs because the methods used to determine the amount of misstatement are conservative. Thus, an auditor is more likely to reject an acceptable recorded book value and overaudit.[i]

Applying Monetary-Unit Sampling

In Chapter 8 the general considerations when using sampling for substantive tests were discussed along with the steps in a sampling application. In conducting MUS for substantive tests of details of account balances, the auditor follows the same basic steps outlined in Chapter 8 for attribute sampling. Table 9–1 lists each step by the three phases in the sampling application. Again, the auditor is required to use substantial judgement and should adequately document the sampling application in the audit working papers.

Table 9–1 Steps in a Monetary-Unit Sampling Application
Planning
1. Determine the test objectives.
2. Define the population characteristics: <ul><li>Define the population.</li><li>Define the sampling unit.</li><li>Define a misstatement.</li></ul>
3. Determine the sample size, using the following inputs: <ul><li>The desired confidence level or acceptable risk of incorrect acceptance.</li><li>The tolerable misstatement.</li><li>The expected population misstatement.</li><li>Population size.</li></ul>

Performance

4. Select sample items.

5. Perform the auditing procedures:

- Understand and analyse any misstatements observed.

Evaluation

6. Calculate the projected misstatement and the upper limit on misstatement.

7. Draw final conclusions.

Planning

Step 1: Determine the Test Objectives

Sampling may be used for substantive testing to: (1) test the reasonableness of assertions about a financial statement amount (e.g. accuracy, existence); or (2) develop an estimate of some amount. The first use, which is the most frequent application of sampling as a substantive procedure in a financial statement audit, tests the assertion or hypothesis that a financial statement account is fairly stated. The second use is less frequent but is occasionally used to develop an estimate of an amount as part of a consulting engagement or in some cases to provide evidence on a client estimate (e.g. sales returns for a new product). The discussion in this chapter is limited to the use of audit sampling to test the assertion that an account or monetary population is fairly stated. The objective of MUS for substantive tests of details is to test the assertion that no material misstatements exist in an account balance, a class of transactions, or a disclosure element of the financial statements.

Step 2: Define the Population Characteristics

To achieve the test objectives, the auditor must carefully consider the characteristics of the sampling population.

Define the Population

The auditor must define the population so that the selected sample is appropriate for the assertions being tested, because sample results can be projected only to the population from which the sample was selected. For example, if the auditor is concerned about goods shipped but not billed, the population of shipping documents rather than sales invoices is the appropriate population for drawing the sample.

For MUS, the population is defined as the monetary value of an account balance, such as accounts receivable, investment securities or inventory. As with attribute sampling, once the population has been defined, the auditor must determine that the physical representation, or *frame*, of the population is complete. For example, if the auditor is testing the accounts receivable account, he or she would foot the accounts receivable subsidiary ledger and agree the total to the general ledger account to verify the completeness of the frame. Because the auditor selects the sample from the frame, any conclusions about the population relate only to that frame, which is the physical representation of the population. If the frame and the intended sampling population differ, the auditor might very well draw an incorrect conclusion about the population.

Practice Insight 9.1

When using ACL, or any other auditing tool, remember to examine the underlying source documents. For example, many companies rely on spreadsheets as a tool in their financial reporting. The risk associated with a spreadsheet depends on its complexity and the developer's spreadsheet proficiency. The samples chosen will be only as dependable as the underlying documentation.

Define the Sampling Unit

With MUS, an *individual euro* represents the sampling unit. In fact, this is where monetary-unit sampling gets its name. For example, if the population to be sampled is the accounts receivable balance of €2.5 million, then there are 2.5 million sampling units in the population. However, because the accounts receivable balance is organized by customer or transaction (e.g. customer account or invoice number) and not individual euros, the auditor does not audit the individual euro but the account or transaction that contains the selected euro. In other words, while the sampling unit is an individual euro in a customer account (or invoice), the auditor cannot very well audit a single euro; instead, the auditor will audit the entire customer account (or transaction) that contains the selected euro. The customer account or transaction that contains the selected euro is called the *logical unit*. In essence, by selecting a euro contained in a customer account (or transaction), the auditor by extension selects the logical unit that contains the selected monetary unit to audit.

Define a Misstatement

For MUS a misstatement is defined as the difference between monetary amounts in the client's records and amounts supported by audit evidence. A clear misstatement definition is important because definitions that are too narrow or too broad may result in inefficient or ineffective testing. For example, if an accounts receivable confirmation letter from a customer reports a difference between the customer records and the client's records, it would not be considered a misstatement if the difference is explainable and supportable by the circumstances, such as timing differences (e.g. the customer mistakenly confirms a balance as of 31 January when the confirmation letter requests the customer's balance as of the 31 December year end) and other documentation supports the client's recorded value.

Step 3: Determine the Sample Size

Considerable judgement is required in determining the appropriate values for the inputs used to compute an MUS sample size. The following four factors must be considered.

Desired Confidence Level or Acceptable Risk of Incorrect Acceptance

There is a *direct* relationship between the confidence level and sample size. The basic idea is fairly simple: to increase confidence, more work is required, which is reflected in a larger sample size. Confidence levels and the **risk of incorrect acceptance** are complements. If the auditor wants to be 95 per cent confident in the sampling conclusion, then he or she must be willing to accept a 5 per cent risk of incorrect acceptance. The risk of incorrect acceptance is the risk that the sample supports the conclusion that the recorded account balance is fairly stated when in fact it is not (a Type II error). This risk relates to the effectiveness of the audit. In determining an acceptable risk of incorrect acceptance, the auditor should consider the components of the audit risk model: the acceptable level of audit risk and risk of material misstatement. For practical purposes, the acceptable risk of incorrect acceptance is the same as *detection risk (DR)* after considering the assessed level of detection risk based on other substantive procedures such as substantive analytical procedures. If the auditor incorrectly accepts an account balance as being fairly stated when it is actually materially misstated, he or she will allow the issuance of financial statements that are not fairly presented. The users of those financial statements may then sue the auditor for damages that result from relying on those financial statements. There is an *inverse* relationship between the risk of incorrect acceptance and sample size. The lower the acceptable risk for incorrect acceptance, the larger the sample size must be.

Tolerable Misstatement

Tolerable misstatement is the maximum amount by which the account or class of transactions can be misstated and still be acceptable to the auditor as being fairly presented. The auditor determines tolerable misstatement in order to address the risk that the aggregate of individuality immaterial misstatements may cause the financial statements to be materially misstated and provide a margin for possible undetected misstatements. Tolerable misstatement is the application of performance materiality, as discussed in Chapter 3, to a particular sampling procedure. Tolerable misstatement may be the same amount or an amount lower than performance materiality.

Audit sampling techniques designed to test the assertion that an account is fairly stated cannot be performed unless tolerable misstatement exceeds expected misstatement by a sufficient amount, because there must always be room for an allowance for sampling risk between the two measures. Tolerable misstatement is also inversely related to sample size – the lower the amount of tolerable misstatement, the more precise the test the auditor needs, and the larger the sample size must be.

Expected Population Misstatement

The **expected misstatement** is the euro amount of misstatement that the auditor believes exists in the population. The auditor can develop this expectation based on the assessment of inherent risk, prior years' results, a pilot sample, the results of related substantive procedures, or the results of tests of controls. As the expected misstatement approaches the tolerable misstatement, the auditor needs more precise information from the sample. Therefore, there is a direct relationship to sample size: the larger the expected misstatement, the larger the sample size must be.

Population Size

Population size is directly related to sample size. Because MUS populations are made up of individual euros, populations tested with MUS are usually large. As such, some MUS approaches, like the one we demonstrate below using the attributes tables in Chapter 8, do not use population size directly as an input for sample size determination, but population size is used in the conversion of tolerable and expected misstatements to percentages. However, for approaches like the one used in ACL, population size is a direct input to determine sample size.

Table 9–2 summarizes the effects of the four factors on sample size.

Table 9–2 The Effect of Sample Selection Factors on Sample Size			
Factor	Relationship to Sample Size	Examples	
		Change in Factor	Effect on Sample
Desired confidence level	Direct	Lower	Decrease
		Higher	Increase
Tolerable misstatement	Inverse	Lower	Increase
		Higher	Decrease
Expected misstatement	Direct	Lower	Decrease
		Higher	Increase

Computing Sample Sizes Using the Attribute-Sampling Tables

A monetary-unit sample size can be determined by using the attribute sample size tables shown in Chapter 8. The auditor first determines the desired confidence level and then converts the tolerable misstatement and the expected misstatement to percentages of the book value of the balance tested. For example, suppose the auditor has established a tolerable misstatement of €125,000 and an expected misstatement of €25,000 for an accounts receivable account with a book value of €2,500,000. The tolerable misstatement would be 5 per cent (€125,000 ÷ €2,500,000), and the expected misstatement would be 1 per cent (€25,000 ÷ €2,500,000). If the desired confidence level is 95 per cent (for a risk of incorrect acceptance of 5 per cent), the auditor would use Table 8–5 in Chapter 8. In this example, the sample size is 93. Be sure you can identify how the sample size was determined using Table 8–5 before moving on.

Computing Sample Sizes Using ACL

Software programs like ACL can also be used to determine sample size. Exhibit 9–1 shows the computation of sample size for the previous example using ACL software. To compute sample size, you open a workbook file (for sample size calculations, it can be any workbook file) and then select 'Calculate Sample Size' from the 'Sampling' menu. In the sample size dialogue box, select 'Monetary' for MUS. Enter the desired 'Confidence', which in our example is 95 per cent (input into ACL as 95). Enter the 'Population', €2,500,000 in our example (input in ACL as 2500000). Enter 'Materiality' or tolerable misstatement of €125,000 (input as 125000), and finally 'Expected Total Errors' or expected misstatement of €25,000 (input as 25000), and then hit the 'Calculate' button. Note that with ACL the auditor enters tolerable and expected misstatement in euros rather than in percentage terms, as we did with attribute sampling in Chapter 8. The result is a sample size of 92, which is slightly smaller than the size determined using the tables.[ii]

Exhibit 9–1 Sample Size Calculation Using ACL™ Software

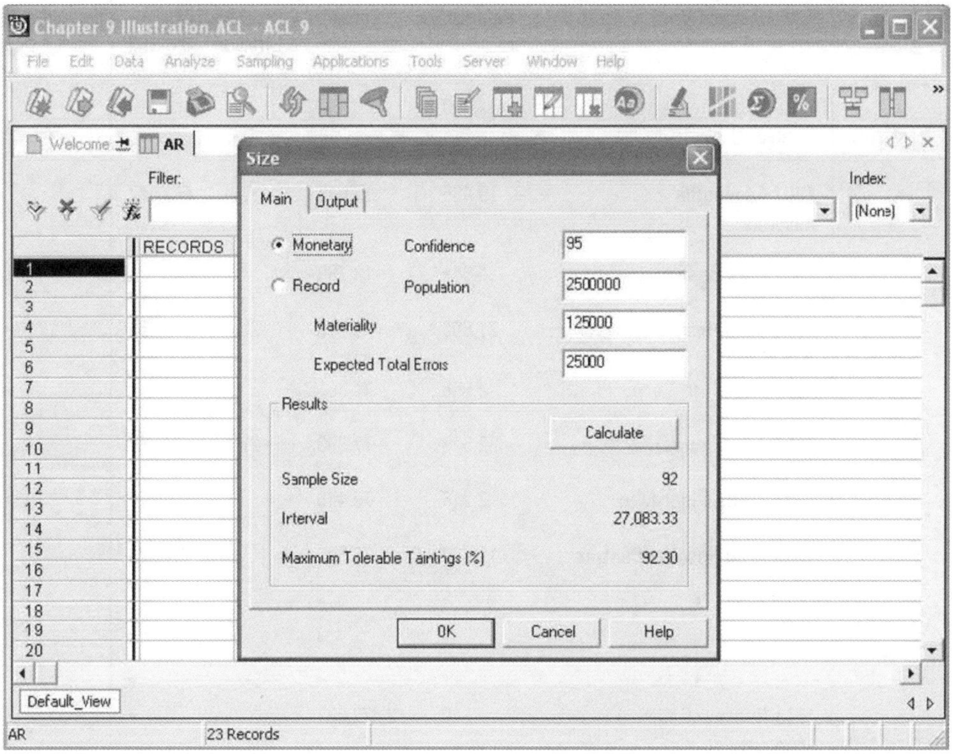

While the underlying concepts and sample sizes produced by the attribute-sampling tables in Chapter 8 and ACL are similar, ACL uses a different approach to compute sample sizes. Rather than first solve for sample size and then compute the sampling interval (discussed in the next section), ACL first computes the sampling interval (i.e. the interval in Exhibit 9–1 is defined as every 27,083rd euro) using factors based on the proportion of expected misstatement to tolerable misstatement and a statistical value associated with the desired confidence level. ACL then divides the population by the sampling interval to determine the sample size.

Performance

Step 4: Select Sample Items

In selecting the sample items, the auditor attempts to draw the sample in such a way that it accurately represents the population. The auditor selects a sample for MUS by using a systematic selection approach called *probability-proportionate-to-size selection*, often with the help of a computer program such as ACL. Probability proportionate-to-size sample selection uses an interval to select sample items. Keep in mind that MUS defines an individual euro (or other monetary unit) as the sampling unit. The sampling interval can be determined by dividing the book value of the population by the sample size. Because the first sampling item is randomly selected within the first interval, each individual euro in the population has an equal chance of being selected. Figure 9–1 provides an example of how probability-proportionate-to-size selection is applied.

Customer Number and Name (Logical Unit)	Customer Balance	Cumulative Euros	Sample Items (Random start €3,977, interval €26,882)	
1001 Ace Emergency Centre	€2,350	€2,350		
1002 Admington Hospital	15,495	17,845	(1)	€3,977
1003 Jess Base	945	18,780		
1004 Good Hospital Corp.	21,893	40,683	(2)	30,859
1005 Jen Mara Corp.	3,968	44,651		
1006 Axa Corporation	32,549	77,200	(3)	57,741
1007 Green River Mtg	2,246	79,446		
1008 Bead Hospital Centres	11,860	91,306	(4)	84,623
•	•	•		•
•	•	•		•
•	•	•		•
1213 Andrew Call Medical	0	2,472,032		•
1214 Lilly Health	26,945	2,498,977	(93)	€2,477,121
1215 Jayne Ann Corp.	1,023	€2,500,000		
Total accounts receivable	€2,500,000			

Figure 9–1   An Example of Probability-Proportionate-to-Size Selection

In Figure 9–1, the total book value of the client's accounts receivable balance is €2,500,000, and the auditor determined a sample size of 93. The sampling interval will be €26,882 (€2,500,000 ÷ 93). To select a probability-proportionate-to-size sample, the auditor arranges the client's accounts receivable records in some order (e.g. by customer number or alphabetically) and then creates a column of cumulative euros. In Figure 9–1, the customer records are arranged by customer number. The auditor obtains a random number between 1 and the size of the sampling interval (€26,882) by using computer software such as ACL or MS Excel. The random number becomes the first sample item selected, and then the sampling interval is added to determine the second sampling item and so on for every 26,882th euro in the population. In the example illustrated in Figure 9–1, the random start is €3,977, and the customer account that contains the 3,977th euro is selected for testing. In this case, Admington Hospital, with a balance of €15,495, is selected for testing. The auditor then adds the sampling interval, either manually or with the aid of a computer program, through the population and selects each logical unit that contains the computed amount.[iii] Following this process, the second customer account selected would be Good Hospital Corp., which contains the 30,859th euro (€3,977 + 26,882) and has a balance of €21,893. The third account would be Axa Corporation, which contains the 57,741th euro (€30,859 + 26,882), and so on until the entire population has been subjected to sampling and 93 units have been selected.

The advantage of using this approach to selecting the sample is that while each euro in the population has an equal chance of being selected, *logical units* containing more euros have a higher chance of being selected; hence the name, 'probability-proportionate-to-size' sample selection. Note that all logical units with a book value larger than the sampling interval (such as Axa Corporation and Lilly Health) are certain to be selected using this method. From an audit perspective, this approach guarantees that all individually significant accounts are examined and that, in general, the sample will be made up of larger accounts. This approach is particularly appropriate when the auditor is primarily concerned about overstatements and larger overstatements are expected to be found in larger logical units (such as with accounts receivable). If the auditor is primarily concerned about understatements or unrecorded amounts, other selection techniques (e.g. random or specific identification) should be used. Let us check your understanding. In the example in Figure 9–1, what is the probability that customer 1213, Andrew Call Medical (with a zero balance), will be selected? The probability is zero, because the customer's balance is zero.

When the logical unit, a customer account in this example, exceeds the sampling interval, more than one sampling unit may be selected from the same logical unit. If this happens, the logical unit is included only once when the sample results are evaluated. Thus, the number of logical units examined may be less than the computed sample size, which is another advantage of this selection technique. In fact, once the auditor has used the computed sample size to determine an interval, the computed sample size is not used again in an MUS application. As you will see later, rather than use the computed sample size in the evaluation of results, the auditor uses the sampling interval.

Step 5: Perform the Audit Procedures

After the sample items have been selected, the auditor conducts the planned audit procedures on the logical units containing the selected sampling units. In some instances, the auditor may not be able to conduct the planned procedures on a particular logical unit (e.g. customer account). This may occur, for example, because a supporting document is missing. Unless other evidence is available, such items should be considered misstatements. The auditor must also be careful to conduct the audit procedures so as to avoid non-sampling errors caused by carelessness, poor supervision or mistaken judgement. After all the audit procedures have been completed, the auditor evaluates the sample results.

Evaluation

The evaluation phase of the sampling application includes the following steps.

Step 6: Calculate the Projected Misstatement and the Upper Limit on Misstatement

The misstatements detected in the sample must be projected to the population. As mentioned earlier, an MUS application is designed primarily to test for overstatement errors. The projection of the errors to the population is referred to as the **projected misstatement** (ACL refers to this as the *most likely error*); it is comparable to the sample deviation rate or best estimate in Chapter 8. The auditor calculates an allowance for sampling risk and adds it to the projected misstatement. The total of the projected misstatement and the allowance for sampling risk is referred to as the **upper misstatement limit** (ACL refers to this as the *upper error limit*). These computations are somewhat involved, so rather than talk about them in abstract terms, we will explain them using an example.

An Extended Example

LO3

An example is used to demonstrate the computation and evaluation of projected and upper misstatement limit (UML) of a monetary-unit sampling application. The following information relates to the audit of a client's accounts receivable balance:

Example Information

- Book value = €2,500,000
- Tolerable misstatement = €125,000
- Sample size = 93
- Desired confidence level = 95 per cent
- Expected amount of misstatement = €25,000
- Sampling interval = €26,882

The calculations of sample size and sampling interval using the attributes sampling tables were shown previously. Assume further that, based on the auditor's understanding of the business and previous experience auditing this account, the auditor is primarily concerned with overstatements.

Basic Precision

As you learned in Chapter 8 with attributes sampling, even when the auditor observes no control deviations, the allowance for sampling risk still results in a computed upper deviation limit. The same is true for MUS; if no misstatements are found in the sample, the projection or best estimate of the population misstatement would be zero euros. However, even with zero projected misstatements, an allowance for sampling risk must be computed, which will result in an upper misstatement limit that is greater than zero. This allowance for sampling risk when no misstatements are observed is referred to as the *basic precision*. If the appropriate sample size was computed and used to derive the sampling interval and no misstatements were found in the logical units tested, then the auditor would be guaranteed that the upper misstatement limit would be less than or equal to the tolerable misstatement used to compute the sample size.

In evaluating MUS results, the sampling interval and the desired level of confidence are two of the important factors, along with the MUS misstatement factors in Table 9–3. In the example, the sampling interval is €26,882 and the desired level of confidence is 95 per cent. For basic precision use the factor associated with zero misstatements in Table 9–3. The misstatement factor is 3.0. The upper misstatement limit (and basic precision) is thus €80,646 (3.0 × €26,882). The basic precision essentially assumes any undetected misstatements in the population are misstated by 100 per cent. This is a very conservative, but justifiable assumption given the high potential cost of underestimating the amount of misstatement in a client's financial statements.

Table 9–3 Monetary Unit Sampling Misstatement Factors for Sample Evaluation[iv]

Number of Misstatements	90% Desired Confidence Level		95% Desired Confidence Level	
	Misstatement Factor	Incremental Increase	Misstatement Factor	Incremental Increase
0	2.3	0.0	3.0	0.0
1	3.9	1.6	4.7	1.7
2	5.3	1.4	6.2	1.5
3	6.6	1.3	7.6	1.4
4	7.9	1.3	9.0	1.4
5	9.1	1.2	10.3	1.3
6	10.3	1.2	11.5	1.2

In practice, auditors use firm-specific MUS guidance or software programs like ACL to determine MUS sample sizes and to evaluate MUS results. Although firms and software developers use different algorithms and assumptions in computing MUS misstatement limits, the underlying theory and ultimate conclusions are similar. Before demonstrating how to evaluate MUS results with ACL, we demonstrate how to manually complete the calculations. Demonstrating the manual calculation will help you better understand output from packages like ACL.

Misstatements Detected

Assume that the auditor sent confirmations to the customers selected from the client's accounts receivable account using a sampling interval of €26,882 as illustrated in Figure 9–1 and that all but four customers returned confirmations indicating the client's records are correct. Based on document inspection and inquiry of the client, the four detected misstatements appear to be unintentional processing errors. For example, discounts granted were not recorded or in the case of Learn Heart Centres the merchandise was returned prior to year end, but the credit was not processed until the subsequent period. The following table lists the misstatements detected:

Customer	Book Value	Audit Value	Difference	Tainting Factor (column 4 ÷ column 2)
Good Hospital	€21,893	€18,609	€3,284	0.15
Marva Medical Supply	6,705	4,023	2,682	0.40
Learn Heart Centres	15,000	0	15,000	1.00
Axa Corporation	32,549	30,049	2,500	Not applicable*
* Book value is greater than sampling interval.				

Overstatement Misstatements Detected

If misstatements are found in the sample, the auditor needs to calculate a projected misstatement and an allowance for sampling risk. Because in an MUS sample each selected euro 'represents' a group of euros in the population, the percentage of misstatement in the logical unit represents the percentage of misstatement in the sampling interval from which the euro was selected. Three types of situations can occur with detected misstatements.

1 *The logical unit is equal to or greater than the sampling interval.* In this situation, the projected misstatement is equal to the actual misstatement detected in the logical unit. For example, the Axa Corporation account in Figure 9–1 contained a balance of €32,549, which is larger than the sampling interval of €26,882. In the example, the projected misstatement associated with this account would be €2,500, and no sampling risk is added. No allowance for sampling risk is necessary for these large accounts because all accounts larger than the sampling interval will automatically be selected by an MUS sampling approach using probability-proportional-to-size selection. Since all the euros in the large accounts are audited, there is no risk of additional potential misstatement associated with large accounts (logical units).

2 *The logical unit's book value is less than the sampling interval, and it is misstated by less than 100 per cent.* This is the most common situation. The percentage of misstatement in the logical unit is referred to as the *tainting factor*. The tainting factor is calculated using the following formula:

$$\text{Tainting factor} = \frac{\text{Book value} - \text{Audit value}}{\text{Book value}}$$

For example, the Good Hospital Corp. account is overstated by €3,284. Thus, the tainting factor for the account would be 0.15 [(€21,893 – €18,609) ÷ €21,893]. The projected misstatement for the interval containing this logical unit would be €4,032 (0.15 × €26,882). The tainting factor associated with the interval containing the Marva Medical Supply account is 0.40 [(€6,705 – €4,023) ÷ 6,705], and the projected misstatement for the interval is €10,753 (0.40 × €26,882). An allowance for sampling risk would be added to these projected misstatements as illustrated below.

3 *The book value of the logical unit is less than the sampling interval, and it is 100 per cent misstated.* Because the logical unit represents the group of euros in the sampling interval, the sampling interval is assumed to be 100 per cent in error. In the above example, the audited value for Learn Heart Centres is €0. The projected error for the interval containing this logical unit is €26,882, which is determined by multiplying the percentage misstated (100 per cent) by the size of the sampling interval (€26,882). An allowance for sampling risk would be added to this amount as illustrated below.

Computing Upper Misstatement Limit Manually

To compute the upper misstatement limit (UML), the auditor first computes basic precision and then ranks the detected misstatements based on the size of the tainting factor from the largest tainting factor to the smallest. Projected and upper misstatement limits are computed using the computed tainting factor and the appropriate misstatement factor from Table 9–3. Finally, misstatements detected in logical units greater than the sampling interval are added.

Customer Name	Tainting Factor	Sampling Interval	Projected Misstatement (columns 2 × 3)	95% Misstatement Factor or Increment (from Table 9–3)	Upper Misstatement Limit (columns 2 × 3 × 5)
Basic Precision	1.00	€26,882	NA	3.0	€80,646
Learn Heart Centres	1.00	26,882	26,882	1.7 (4.7 – 3.0)	45,700
Marva Medical	0.40	26,882	10,753	1.5 (6.2 – 4.7)	16,130
Good Hospital	0.15	26,882	4,032	1.4 (7.6 – 6.2)	5,645
Add misstatements detected in logical units greater than the sampling interval:					
Axa Corporation	NA	26,882	2,500	NA	2,500
Upper Misstatement Limit					€150,621

NA = not applicable.

The UML in this case is €150,621, and is calculated as follows. First, basic precision, €80,646, is computed by multiplying the sampling interval by the misstatement factor from Table 9–3, (€26,882 × 3.0). The €80,646 represents the **sampling risk** that exists even if no misstatements are observed in the sample. Remember, because we are basing our conclusions on a sample, we cannot be sure there are no misstatements in the population even if we find none in the sample.

Second, logical units smaller than the interval where misstatements are detected, Learn Heart Centres, Marva Medical and Good Hospital, are ranked according to the size of their tainting factor from largest to smallest.

Third, the projected misstatements for Learn Heart Centres, Marva Medical and Good Hospital are calculated. Projected misstatement is computed by multiplying the sampling interval by the tainting factor (column 2 × column 3). This calculation is based on the assumption that the euro selected for testing represents the sampling interval. In turn, it is assumed that the extent of misstatement in the logical unit that contains the sampled euro represents the amount of misstatement in the sampling interval.

Next, for the intervals containing the Learn Heart Centres, Marva Medical and Good Hospital accounts, an allowance for sampling risk is added to the projected misstatement by multiplying the projected misstatement by the incremental change in the misstatement factor for the desired confidence level. In this example, the desired confidence is 95 per cent, so the misstatement factors are taken from the appropriate column in Table 9–3. For basic precision, the factor, 3.0, is taken from the 'Misstatement Factor' column of Table 9–3 (95 per cent confidence) because it is the first 'layer' of the UML calculation.

For the first misstatement observed, Learn Heart Centres, the misstatement factor from Table 9–3 (95 per cent confidence) is 4.7. However, the misstatement factors in Table 9–3 are cumulative. In other words, the factor for 1 misstatement, 4.7, includes the sampling risk associated with zero misstatements (i.e. it includes the misstatement factor 3.0). Since basic precision already includes the factor for zero misstatements, only the increase or *increment* is used for the first misstatement, and likewise for subsequent misstatements. The incremental change is calculated by simply subtracting the misstatement factor for the current number of misstatements from the factor for the previous number of misstatements (i.e. 4.7 – 3.0 = 1.7). Thus, for Learn Heart Centres, the projected misstatement is €26,882, and the UML is €45,700 (1.7 × €26,882) as illustrated in the table above. The difference between the projected misstatement and the UML is the allowance for sampling risk. Thus, the allowance for sampling risk for Learn Heart Centres is €18,818 (€45,700 – €26,882). Before you proceed verify that for the third misstatement observed, Good Hospital, the UML is €5,645 and the allowance for sampling risk is €1,613.

Ranking the logical units by their tainting factors leads to a UML that is conservative because the largest tainting factor is multiplied by the largest incremental change in the misstatement factor. This conservative approach means there is a higher risk that an acceptable account balance will be rejected by the auditor.

Finally, misstatements detected in logical units that are greater than the sampling interval are added to the upper limit. As noted earlier, the reason misstatements from logical units greater than the sampling interval do not require projection or the consideration of sampling risk is because all accounts larger than the sampling interval will automatically be selected by a probability-proportionate-to-size sampling approach. Since all the euros in the large accounts are audited, there is no sampling risk associated with large accounts (logical units). Thus, in the example above, the misstatement detected in Axa Corporation's balance, €2,500 (€32,549 − €30,049) is simply added to the upper misstatement.

Step 7: Draw Final Conclusions

For this example, the final decision on whether the accounts receivable balance is materially misstated is made by comparing the tolerable misstatement to the UML. If the UML is less than or equal to the tolerable misstatement, the evidence supports the conclusion that the account balance is not materially misstated. In this case the UML of €150,621 is more than the tolerable misstatement of €125,000. Because the UML exceeds the tolerable misstatement of €125,000, the auditor has evidence that there is an unacceptably high risk that accounts receivable is materially misstated.

The auditor now has four options. First, the sample size can be increased. While this approach is possible in theory, it is not practical in many audit settings. Second, other substantive procedures can be performed. This approach might be followed if the auditor's qualitative analysis of the detected misstatements indicates that there is a systematic problem with the population. For example, the auditor might determine that three of the misstatements occurred in the pricing of one particular product line sold by the client. In this instance, he or she might design a substantive procedure that examines the pricing of all sales in that product line. Third, the auditor can request that the client adjusts the accounts receivable balance. In our example, the minimum adjustment would be €25,621 (€150,621 − €125,000). If the client adjusts the account by €25,621, the UML will be equal to or less than the tolerable misstatement at a 5 per cent risk of incorrect acceptance. Finally, if the client refuses to adjust the account, the auditor would issue a qualified or adverse opinion (this situation would be extremely rare).

Table 9–4 illustrates the risks auditors face when evaluating an account balance based on sample evidence. If the evidence supports the fairness of the account balance based on the sample evidence and the account is not materially misstated, the auditor has made a correct decision. If the evidence does not support the fairness of the account based on the sample evidence and the account is materially misstated, a correct decision has also been made. The other two combinations result in decision errors by the auditor. If the evidence does not support the fairness of the account when it is in reality not materially misstated (Type I error), the auditor have incorrectly rejected the account. This can lead to over-auditing and an inefficient audit. If the evidence supports the account as fairly stated when the account actually contains a material misstatement, the auditor will have incorrectly accepted the account (Type II error). Keep in mind, however, that the auditor almost never finds out the 'true' account balance unless later events, such as lawsuits against the auditor for issuing a report on misleading financial statements, require an examination of the entire population.

Table 9–4 The Auditor's Risks When Evaluating a Financial Statement Account Based on Sample Evidence

Auditor's Decision Based on Sample Evidence	True State of Financial Statement Account	
	Not Materially Misstated	*Materially Misstated*
Supports the fairness of the account balance	Correct decision	Risk of incorrect acceptance (Type II)
Does not support the fairness of the account balance	Risk of incorrect rejection (Type I)	Correct decision

Computing Projected Misstatement and Upper Misstatement Limit Using ACL

Exhibit 9–2 shows the evaluation of the sample results using ACL software. The UML is calculated to be €152,744. To use ACL to evaluate sample results, open a workbook file (for sample evaluation calculations, it can be any workbook file) and then select 'Evaluate Error' from the 'Sampling' menu. In the sample size dialogue box, select 'Monetary' for MUS. Enter the desired confidence level, which in our example is 95 per cent. Enter the sampling interval, in our example €26,882 (input into ACL as 26882). Enter book values followed by misstatement amount in the 'Errors' box. When using ACL, the order in which misstatements are input does not affect the results. In comparing the manually computed UML, €150,621 (illustrated earlier), to ACL's UML, we see that the upper limit on basic precision is identical, as are projected misstatements in the manual calculation to the 'Most Likely Error' in ACL. Similarly, the

Exhibit 9–2 Sample Results with Overstatement Misstatements Using ACL™ Software

	Item	Error	Most Likely Error	Upper Error Limit
Basic Precision				80,646.00
	15,000.00	15,000.00	26,882.00	47,043.50
	6,705.00	2,682.00	10,752.80	16,666.84
	21,893.00	3,284.00	4,032.36	5,887.25
	32,549.00	2,500.00	2,500.00	2,500.00
Totals			44,167.16	152,743.59

addition of misstatements from logical units greater than the sampling interval is the same for both methods. However, ACL uses a different underlying statistical distribution to estimate the UML than does the manual approach we illustrated.

You should also be aware that alternative methods of calculating the upper limit on misstatement are available and used by some audit firms. These alternative methods will produce UMLs that are somewhat different from those shown here. For example, some of these methods correct for the overstatement of sampling risk.

Practice Insight 9.2

Audit firms typically develop standardized documentation templates for audit sampling applications to ensure all steps in the process are completed and documented in a consistent manner.

The Effect of Understatement Misstatements

The methodology used earlier for computing the UML is based on the auditor's assumption, at the time of planning the sampling application, that all errors in the population are overstatements. Recall that MUS is not particularly effective at detecting understatements because under an MUS approach the probability of selecting a smaller account is proportionately lower than the probability of selecting a larger account. Thus, an understated account is, by definition, less likely to be selected than an overstated account. In the extreme, an account could be missing or it could be 100 per cent understated and recorded at a value of €0; in either case the probability of the account being selected for audit will be zero. When understatement errors are detected, different approaches can be used. When understatements are entered into ACL, ACL adjusts the total 'most likely error' downwards, but does not adjust the 'upper-error limit'. To demonstrate this approach, assume that the auditor detected the four overstatement misstatements shown in the previous example and that the following understatement misstatement was also detected.

Customer	Book Value	Audit Value	Differ-ence	Tainting Factor (column 4 ÷ column 2)
Wayne County Medical	€2,000	€2,200	−200	−0.10

Exhibit 9–3 shows the evaluation of the sample results, including the understatement misstatement, using ACL software. Note that the UML is still €152,744, but that 'most likely error' is now reduced by the projected understatement €2,688 (0.10 × €26,882).

Some auditors also adjust down the UML by the projected understatement to obtain a *net* upper misstatement limit.[v] This approach is followed when the auditor believes that the overall misstatement in the population is in the direction of overstatement. The understatements identified are used to adjust the UML.

Using the UML computed in Exhibit 9–3, the adjusted or net UML is €150,056 (€152,744 − €2,688). Using the previous decision rule, the auditor would still conclude that the account was materially misstated because the net UML of €150,056 is more than the tolerable misstatement of €125,000.

❖ NON-STATISTICAL SAMPLING FOR TESTS OF ACCOUNT BALANCES[vi]

LO4

When conducting a **non-statistical sampling** application for testing an account balance, the auditor considers each of the steps shown in Table 9–1. The sampling unit for non-statistical sampling is normally a customer account, an individual transaction or a line item on a transaction. When a non-statistical sampling application is used, the following items need further explanation:

- Identifying individually significant items.
- Determining the sample size.
- Selecting sample items.
- Calculating the sample results.

Exhibit 9–3 Sample Results with Under- and Overstatements Using ACL™ Software

Chapter 9 Illustration.ACL – ACL 9

File Edit Data Analyze Sampling Applications Tools Server Window Help

Welcome AR

Filter: Index:
                                                                                 (None)

Evaluate

Main | Output

- Monetary   Confidence   95

- Record   Interval   26882

                  Item amount, Error

        Errors   21893, 3284
                  6705, 2682
                  15000, 15000
                  32549, 2500
                  2000, -200

        OK   Cancel   Help

RECORDS

Default_View

AR   23 Records

Chapter 9 Illustration.ACL – ACL 9

File Edit Data Analyze Sampling Applications Tools Server Window Help

Welcome AR **Evaluate**

As of: 04/21/2009 17:04:53

Command: EVALUATE MONETARY CONFIDENCE 95 ERRORLIMIT 21893, 3284,6705, 2682,15000, 15000,32549, 2500,2000, -200 INTERVAL 26882 TO SCREEN

Confidence: 95, Interval: 26882

	Item	Error	Most Likely Error	Upper Error Limit
Basic Precision				80,646.00
	15,000.00	15,000.00	26,882.00	47,043.50
	6,705.00	2,682.00	10,752.80	16,666.84
	21,893.00	3,284.00	4,032.36	5,887.25
	32,549.00	2,500.00	2,500.00	2,500.00
	2,000.00	-200.00	-2,688.20	0.00
Totals			41,478.96	152,743.59

Text

AR   23 Records

Identifying Individually Significant Items

In many non-statistical sampling applications, the auditor determines which items should be tested individually and which items should be subjected to sampling. The items that will be tested individually are items that may contain potential misstatements that individually exceed the tolerable misstatement. These items are tested 100 per cent because the auditor is not willing to accept any sampling risk. For example, an auditor using non-statistical sampling may be examining a client's accounts receivable balance in which 10 customer accounts are greater than tolerable misstatement. The auditor would test all 10 large accounts, and supposing that those 10 made up 40 per cent of the account balance, the auditor would apply non-statistical audit sampling to the remaining customer accounts making up the other 60 per cent of the balance. Testing all individually significant items produces an emphasis on large items similar to probability-proportionate-to-size selection. Recall that probability-proportionate-to-size selection guarantees that all items greater than the sampling interval will be included in the sample.

Determining the Sample Size

When determining the sample size, the auditor should consider the level of desired confidence, the risk of material misstatement, the tolerable and expected misstatements, and the population size. While an auditor may determine a non-statistical sample size by using professional judgement, auditing standards indicate that the sample sizes for statistical and non-statistical sampling should be similar. Thus, it is common for firms to develop guidance for non-statistical sampling based on statistical theory such as the formula provided below, which was adapted from the AICPA Audit Guide *Audit Sampling*:[vii]

$$\text{Sample size} = \left(\frac{\text{Sampling population book value}}{\text{Tolerable } - \text{ Expected misstatement}} \right) \times \text{Confidence factor}$$

The 'sampling population book value' excludes the amount of items to be individually audited. The confidence factor is identified by determining the level of desired confidence (largely driven by the amount of other relevant audit evidence in the 'assurance bucket'; see Chapter 5) and the risk of material misstatement (i.e. inherent and control risk). Table 9–5 contains the confidence factors for various combinations of desired confidence and risk assessment.

Table 9–5 Confidence Factors for Non-Statistical Sampling			
	Desired Level of Confidence		
Assessment of Risk of Material Misstatement	High	Moderate	Low
High	3.0	2.3	2.0
Moderate	2.3	1.6	1.2
Low	2.0	1.2	1.0

Selecting Sample Items

When any form of audit sampling is used to gather evidence, auditing standards require that the sample items be selected in such a way that the sample can be expected to represent the population. While some form of random sample or systematic selection (e.g. probability proportionate to size) is required for **statistical sampling**, auditing standards allow the use of these selection methods, as well as other selection methods including haphazard sampling when using non-statistical sampling. As discussed in Chapter 8, haphazard selection allows the auditor to 'randomly' select items judgementally (i.e. with no conscious biases or reasons for including or omitting items from the sample). This does not imply that the items are selected in a careless manner; rather, the sampling units are selected such that they will be representative of the population. The reason haphazard selection is not appropriate for statistical sampling is because people are not very good at being truly random, no matter how hard we may try. For example, the first item on a report or computer screen may never be selected because it does not feel 'random' to the auditor to select the very first item. Such biases mean that each item in the population did not have an equal chance of being selected.

Calculating the Sample Results

Auditing standards require that the auditor projects the amount of misstatement found in the sample to the population. The AICPA guide, *Audit Sampling*, describes two acceptable methods of projecting the amount of misstatement found in a non-statistical sample.

The first method of projecting the sample results to the population is to apply the misstatement ratio observed in the sample to the population. For example, if the auditor finds misstatements of €1,500 in a sample totalling €15,000, the misstatement ratio in the sample is 10 per cent (1,500 ÷ 15,000) and that ratio is applied to the population. If the total population is €200,000, then projected misstatement using the ratio approach will be €20,000 (10% × €200,000). This method of projection is often referred to as *ratio projection*, and it is used with both non-statistical sampling and classical variables statistical sampling (see the *Advanced Module* at the end of this chapter). Ratio projection is used when the euro amount of misstatement is expected to relate to the euro amount of items tested.

The second method, referred to as *difference projection*, projects the average misstatement of each item in the sample to all items in the population and is used when the misstatement is expected to be relatively constant for all items in the population regardless of their euro size. Difference estimation is the name of a sampling technique that uses information about misstatements to determine sample size, projected misstatement, and confidence bounds. Difference estimation is illustrated in the *Advanced Module*.

In evaluating the results of a non-statistical sample, the auditor uses professional judgement and experience to draw a conclusion. If the sample is drawn haphazardly (versus randomly), the allowance for sampling risk cannot be statistically quantified within a specified level of confidence. Auditing standards provide the following guidance for evaluating the sampling results for tests of details:

> An unexpectedly high misstatement amount in a sample may cause the auditor to believe that a class of transactions or account balance is materially misstated, in the absence of further audit evidence that no material misstatement exists.
>
> The projected misstatement is the auditor's best estimate of misstatement in the population. When the projected misstatement exceeds tolerable misstatement, the sample does not provide a reasonable basis for conclusions about the population that has been tested. The closer the projected misstatement is to tolerable misstatement, the more likely that actual misstatement in the population may exceed tolerable misstatement.
>
> Also if the projected misstatement is greater than the auditor's expectations of misstatement used to determine the sample size, the auditor may conclude that there is an unacceptable sampling risk that the actual misstatement in the population exceeds the tolerable misstatement.[viii]

The AICPA *Audit Sampling* guide provides the following direction:

> If the total projected misstatement is less than the tolerable misstatement for the account balance or class of transactions, the auditor then should consider the risk that such a result might be obtained even though the true monetary misstatement for the population exceeds tolerable misstatement. In other words, the auditor should consider the risk (for instance, sampling risk) that there might be other, undetected misstatements remaining in the population examined that might indicate a material misstatement exists. Alternatively, the auditor may compare the projected misstatement to the expected misstatement used in determining the sample size. When projected misstatement exceeds the expected misstatement, the sample may not have achieved an adequate allowance for sampling risk.

As noted in Chapter 8, students and auditors are sometimes unclear as to the factors that cause a sampling approach to be 'non-statistical'. An approach is non-statistical if: (1) judgement is used to determine the sample size; (2) a haphazard sample selection technique is used; and/or (3) because the sample results are evaluated judgementally. A non-statistical approach can involve random selection and a judgemental evaluation. While haphazardly selected samples cannot be statistically evaluated, any randomly drawn sample can be statistically evaluated – even if the auditor labels the approach 'non-statistical' and even if the sample size was not statistically derived. This is an important point because it highlights the need for auditors to understand the key concepts of sampling theory *even if they are using a non-statistical approach*. If an auditor randomly selects a sample and evaluates the results judgementally, the quality of his or her judgement can be compared to statistical theory by an outside expert.

An Example of Non-Statistical Sampling

This example extends the example shown in Chapter 8 for the tests of controls of the revenue process for Calabro Wireless Services. The audit senior, Andrew Judd, has decided to design a *non-statistical* sampling application to examine the accounts receivable balance of Calabro Wireless Services at 31 December 2009. As of 31 December, there were 11,800 accounts receivable accounts with a balance of €3,717,900 and the population is composed of the following strata:

Number and Size of Accounts	Book Value of Stratum
15 accounts > €25,000	€550,000
250 accounts > €3,000	850,500
11,535 accounts < €3,000	2,317,400

Judd has made the following decisions:

- Based on the results of the tests of controls, the risk of material misstatement is assessed as low.
- The tolerable misstatement for accounts receivable is €55,000, and the expected misstatement is €15,000.
- The desired level of confidence is moderate based on the other audit evidence already gathered.
- All customer account balances greater than €25,000 will be audited.

Based on these decisions, the sample size is determined as follows. First, individually significant items are deducted from the account balance, leaving a balance of €3,167,900 (€3,717,900 – €550,000) to be sampled. Second, the sample size for the remaining balance is determined using the non-statistical sample size formula:

$$\text{Sample size} = \left(\frac{€3,167,900}{€55,000 - €15,000} \right) \times 1.2 = 95$$

The confidence factor of 1.2 is determined by using Table 9–5 and a 'Low' assessment for risk of material misstatement and 'Moderate' level of desired confidence. The 95 sample items are divided between the two strata based on the recorded amount for each stratum. Accordingly, 26 [(€850,500 ÷ €3,167,900) × 95] of the 95 are allocated to the stratum of accounts greater than €3,000 and 69 to the stratum of accounts less than €3,000. The total number of items tested is 110, composed of 15 individually significant accounts tested 100 per cent and a sample of 95 items.

Judd mailed positive confirmations to each of the 110 accounts selected for testing. Either the confirmations were returned to Judd, or he was able to use alternative procedures to determine that the receivables were valid. Four customers indicated that their accounts were overstated, and Judd determined that the misstatements had resulted from unintentional errors by client personnel. The results of the sample are summarized as follows.

Stratum	Book Value of Stratum	Book Value of Sample	Audit Value of Sample	Amount of Overstatement
>€25,000	€550,000	€550,000	€549,500	€500
> €3,000	850,500	425,000	423,000	2,000
< €3,000	2,317,400	92,000	91,750	250

Based on analysis of the misstatements found, Judd concluded that the amount of misstatement in the population was likely to correlate to the total euro amount of the items in the population and not to the number of items in the population. Thus, he decided to use ratio projection (applying the ratio of misstatement in the sampling strata) to compute projected misstatement. His projection of the misstatements follows:

Stratum	Amount of Misstatement	Ratio of Misstatements in Stratum Tested	Projected Misstatement
>€25,000	€500	Not Applicable – 100% Tested	€500
> €3,000	2,000	(€2,000 ÷ €425,000) × €850,500	4,002
< €3,000	250	(€250 ÷ €92,000) × €2,317,400	6,298
Total Projected Misstatement			€10,800

The total projected misstatement is €10,800. Judd should conclude that there is an acceptably low risk that the true misstatement exceeds the tolerable misstatement because the projected misstatement of €10,800 is less than the expected misstatement of €15,000.

Before reaching a final conclusion on the fair presentation of Calabro's accounts receivable balance, Judd would consider the qualitative characteristics of the misstatements detected and the results of other auditing procedures. If these steps are successfully completed, Judd can conclude that the accounts receivable balance is fairly presented in accordance with the applicable financial reporting framework.

THE RISE AND FALL OF STATISTICAL AUDIT SAMPLING

Non-statistical audit sampling is very common in practice. In the 1970s–1980s, statistical sampling was more common than it is today. In fact, many audit firms developed proprietary statistical audit sampling software packages. Why did statistical sampling fall out of favour? We believe there were two primary reasons.

First, firms found that some auditors were over-relying on statistical sampling techniques to the exclusion of good judgement. As we discussed earlier, if the auditor can use knowledge and expertise to identify high-risk transactions or balances (e.g. large unusual items, transactions near period end, transactions in an area where material misstatements have been discovered in the past), then it is better to target those risky items and test 100 per cent of them rather than to turn the selection procedure over to chance as is required by audit sampling.

The second reason relates to poor linkage between the applied audit setting and traditional statistical sampling applications. In most scientific statistical applications, a high degree of confidence, say 95 to 99 per cent, is required. However, in an audit context, sampling is often used to just top off the 'assurance bucket' (see Chapter 5), which already contains evidence from risk assessment procedures, tests of controls, substantive analytical procedures, and other audit testing. Thus, in some instances, the auditors only needed a low or moderate level of confidence or assurance (e.g. 70 to 80 per cent). Experienced auditors understood this intuitively but did not always have the knowledge to appropriately apply statistical sampling in an audit context. Thus, some of the audit firms simply moved to non-statistical sampling with guidance based on judgement. With the increased scrutiny on audit firms in the last few years, the large firms have updated their non-statistical sampling approaches to be more consistent with statistical theory.

❖ ADVANCED MODULE: CLASSICAL VARIABLES SAMPLING

LO5

Classical variables sampling uses normal distribution theory to evaluate the characteristics of a population based on sample data. This approach to audit sampling is similar to the techniques taught in college or university introductory statistics courses. While this is not a statistics book, we do want to discuss briefly how distribution theory is helpful for audit sampling. In Figure 9–2 you will see two normally distributed, bell-shaped curves that depict sampling distributions. The mean or average of the distributions is €10,000. Auditors most commonly use classical variables sampling to estimate the size of misstatement, so in our example let us say the €10,000 represents the size of the total misstatement in an account or population. The flatter, wider distribution in Figure 9–2 is based on a sample size of 50, and the taller, thinner distribution is based on a sample of size 200. Both sampling distributions are taken from the same underlying population.

The sampling distributions are formed by plotting the projected misstatements yielded by an infinite number of audit samples of the same size taken from the same underlying population. For example, the height of the flatter distribution at €9,000 represents the number (or per cent) of times a sample of size 50 would return a projected misstatement of €9,000.

Rather than actually take an infinite number of samples of the same size to form a picture of the distribution, the distribution is modelled using the mathematical properties of the normal distribution. Thus,

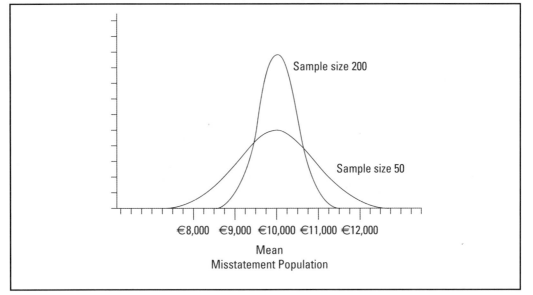

Figure 9–2   Normally Distributed Sampling Distributions

a sampling distribution is really a theoretical distribution that models how the means of an infinite number of hypothetical samples of a given sample size would be distributed. A sampling distribution is useful because it allows us to estimate the probability of observing *any single* sample result. Two important features of sampling distributions are very useful for auditors:

● The mean of the sampling distribution will be equal to the true mean of the underlying population. Thus, Figure 9–2 tells us that the true mean misstatement in the population is €10,000.
● The area under the curve can be used to quantify likelihoods. For example, the standard error for the flatter curve is €1,000. If we look at the area covered by two standard errors above and two standard errors below the mean (i.e. the area under the curve between €8,000 and €12,000), we know that the area captures about 95 per cent of all observed sample results. This is simply a mathematical property of a bell-shaped distribution.

Considering the first feature listed above, if auditors did actually take an infinite or even a very large number of samples of, say, size 50, they could determine with near certainty the amount of misstatement in an account. That seems easy enough – except that taking an infinite number or even 500 samples of size 50 is not economically practical. Instead, the auditor will only take one sample of size 50 and will use the results of that single sample to estimate the actual misstatement in the population. Given this audit approach, what information does distribution theory provide to an auditor that only takes one sample? Distribution theory can be very useful, even when the auditor is only drawing one sample because the theory allows for an uncertain, but informed, prediction to be made about the underlying population.

Referring to the flatter distribution in Figure 9–2, which sampling outcome is more likely, a projected sample misstatement result of €10,000 or €12,000? The height of the curve in the middle indicates values around the mean of the distribution will be more commonly observed than values in the tails of the distribution. Because the most likely projected misstatement is one that is near the true misstatement, the auditor considers the observed projected sample misstatement as the best estimate of the true misstatement in the population. While the sample projection is the best estimate, the auditor understands there is uncertainty or sampling risk. Referring again to Figure 9–2, the most likely sample result is a projected misstatement at or near €10,000, but is it possible the auditor could draw a random sample of 50 that yields a projected misstatement of €8,000? Yes, due to sampling risk, it is possible to draw a non-representative sample. However, observing a projected misstatement of €8,000 from a sample of 50 is not very likely given that the 'true' population misstatement is €10,000. Now, consider the same question but with a sample size of 200 instead of 50. Could a sample of 200 produce a projected misstatement of €8,000? Again it is possible, but because the distribution for a sample of 200 is taller and tighter than the distribution for a sample of 50, it is much less likely that the auditor will get a projected misstatement result of €8,000 from a sample size of 200. The basic idea is simple: As the sample size increases, the results from the sample are increasingly likely to approximate the true population mean. In the extreme, if the sample size equalled the size of the population, the sample mean would exactly equal the true population mean.

Distribution theory allows auditors to quantify sampling risk through the use of *confidence bounds*, which are used to form what is commonly called a *confidence interval*. Referring to the flatter distribution in Figure 9–2, if the auditor wants to be 95 per cent confident that his or her sample results include the true population misstatement, he or she would add and subtract two standard errors to and from the sample projected misstatement. For example, if the auditor takes a sample of 50 and computes a projected misstatement of €11,250, the auditor can be 95 per cent confident that the interval between €9,250 and €13,250 (€11,250 ± €2,000) contains the true population misstatement. Thus, even though auditors do not know for sure which part of the actual sampling distribution their sample results come from (because they do not actually take an infinite number of samples to form the distribution), they use normal distribution theory to compute an interval of values that is likely to contain the true population value.

The computational complexity of calculating classical variables sampling results, in particular computing the standard deviation, made it a difficult technique for auditors to use before electronic calculators and personal computers were common on audit engagements. This complexity was one of the factors that led to the development of MUS. Another important reason MUS was developed is that most accounting populations contain relatively little misstatement, and the estimators used to compute sample size and potential misstatement for some classical variables sampling techniques (e.g. difference estimation) are not effective in populations with little or no misstatement. Therefore, MUS is used in practice because of the advantages discussed earlier in the chapter.

Classical variables sampling can easily handle both overstatement and understatement errors. It is most appropriate for populations that contain a moderate to high rate of misstatement. Some applications of this sampling approach include auditing accounts receivable in which unapplied credits exist or a relatively large amount of misstatement is expected, and inventory in which significant audit differences are expected between test counts and pricing tests. Following are some of the advantages and disadvantages of classical variables sampling.

Advantages

- When the auditor expects a relatively large number of differences between book and audited values, classical variables sampling will normally result in a smaller sample size than monetary-unit sampling.
- Classical variables sampling techniques are effective for both overstatements and understatements. No special evaluation considerations are necessary if the sample data include both types of misstatements.
- The selection of zero balances generally does not require special sample design considerations because the sampling unit will be not an individual euro but rather an account or a transaction, or a line item.

Disadvantages

- When using the approach to evaluate likely misstatement in an account or population, some classical variables sampling techniques (e.g. difference estimation) do not work well when little to no misstatement is expected.
- In order to determine the sample size for the technique illustrated in this text, the auditor must estimate the standard deviation of the audit differences. Since this value is unknown, auditors often use a surrogate such as the standard deviation of the recorded values in the population. However, this approach tends to overstate the standard deviation of the differences because recorded values tend to be more variable than audit differences in most accounting populations.
- If few misstatements are detected in the sample data, the true variance tends to be underestimated, and the resulting projection of the misstatements and the related confidence limits are not likely to be reliable.

A number of classical variables sampling techniques are available to the auditor for projecting the sample results to the population. These include mean per unit, difference, ratio and regression techniques.

These techniques differ basically on the assumed relationship between the book value and the audit value. We demonstrated ratio projection in the prior section on non-statistical sampling. In this section we illustrate how the classical variables sampling technique known as difference estimation is used to determine sample size, project misstatement, and compute confidence bounds.[ix]

◆ Applying Classical Variables Sampling

LO6 The discussion in this section focuses on the special features that apply to classical variables sampling. A detailed example is included to demonstrate the application of classical variables sampling.

Defining the Sampling Unit

When an auditor uses classical variables sampling techniques, the sampling unit can be a customer account, an individual transaction, or a line item. For example, in auditing accounts receivable, the auditor can define the sampling unit to be a customer's account balance or an individual sales invoice included in the account balance.

Determining the Sample Size

The following formula can be used to determine the sample size for a classical variables sample:

$$\text{Sample size} = \left[\frac{\text{Population size (in sampling units)} \times \text{CC} \times \text{SD}}{\text{Tolerable misstatement} - \text{Estimated misstatement}} \right]^2$$

where

CC = Confidence coefficient
SD = Estimated standard deviation of audit differences

Table 9–6 shows the confidence coefficient values for various levels of desired confidence. The risk of incorrect acceptance is the risk that the auditor will mistakenly accept a population as fairly stated when the true population misstatement is greater than tolerable misstatement, and is the complement of the level of confidence. For example, at a confidence level of 95 per cent, the risk of incorrect acceptance is 5 per cent (1 − 95).[x]

Table 9–6 Confidence Coefficient Values	
Desired Level of Confidence	*Confidence Coefficient*
95%	1.96
90%	1.64
80%	1.28
70%	1.04

The following example demonstrates how to determine sample size using this formula. Assume that the auditor has decided to apply classical variables sampling to a client's accounts receivable account. Based on the results of testing internal controls over the revenue process, the auditor expects to find a moderate level of misstatement in accounts receivable due mainly to improper pricing of products on sales invoices. The year-end balance for accounts receivable contains 5,500 customer accounts and has a book value of €5,500,000. The tolerable misstatement for accounts receivable has been established at €50,000, and the expected misstatement has been estimated at €20,000. The auditor would like a high level of assurance from the test and has set the desired confidence level at 95 per cent (**risk of incorrect rejection** of 5 per cent). Based on the results of last year's audit work, the standard deviation of audit differences is set at €31. Using these parameters, a sample size of 125 is calculated (rounding up):

$$\text{Sample size} = \left(\frac{5,500 \times 1.96 \times €31}{€50,000 - €20,000} \right)^2 = 125$$

In calculating the sample size, the confidence coefficient value (CC) for the desired level of confidence is taken from Table 9–6. The CC for a 95 per cent confidence level is 1.96.

Selecting the Sample

Sample selection for classical variables sampling normally relies on random-selection techniques. If the sampling unit is defined to be a customer account, the accounts to be examined can be selected randomly from the aged trial balance of accounts receivable. In this example, a random sample of 125 customer accounts is selected.

Calculating the Sample Results

Difference projection computes the sample projected misstatement by projecting the average misstatement of each item in the sample to all items in the population. Continuing with the prior example, assume that the auditor has confirmed 125 individual customer accounts receivable, and that confirmation evidence and alternative procedures, performed for customers who did not reply, results in the determination that 30 customer accounts contain misstatements. Table 9–7 presents the details of the 30 misstatements and the data necessary for calculating the sample results. The difference between the book value and the audited value is shown in the fifth column. The sixth column contains the square of each difference. The sum of these squared differences is needed to calculate the standard deviation.

Table 9–7 Summary of Misstatements Detected					
Sample Item Number	Account Number	Book Value	Audit Value	Audit Difference	(Audit Difference)²
1	3892	€1,221.92	€1,216.40	€5.52	€30.47
4	1982	2,219.25	2,201.34	17.91	320.77
8	893	1,212.00	1,204.34	7.66	58.68
9	25	5,201.51	5,190.21	17.11	292.75
13	1703	7,205.40	7,188.29	−11.00	121.00
19	4258	3,685.62	3,725.62	−40.00	1,600.00
22	765	58.30	50.64	7.66	58.65
34	1256	17,895.15	17,840.30	54.85	3,008.52
36	3241	542.95	525.98	16.97	287.98
45	895	895.24	823.70	71.54	5,117.97
47	187	10,478.60	10,526.40	−47.80	2,284.84
55	4316	95.00	90.00	5.00	25.00
57	2278	1,903.51	1,875.00	28.51	812.82
59	1843	185.23	200.25	−15.02	225.60
61	64	4,759.65	4,725.32	34.33	1,178.55
69	2371	2,549.61	2,540.26	9.35	87.42
70	1982	12,716.50	12,684.23	32.27	1,041.35
72	2350	361.45	375.50	14.05	197.40
75	349	11,279.40	11,250.40	29.00	841.00
87	2451	74.23	95.40	−21.17	448.17
88	3179	871.58	837.96	33.62	1,130.30
91	1839	571.13	590.00	−18.87	−356.08
93	4080	9,467.24	9,504.50	−37.26	1,388.31
97	13	45.20	40.75	4.45	19.80
100	1162	524.90	515.15	9.75	95.06
101	985	7,429.09	7,356.21	72.88	5,311.49
108	304	12,119.60	12,043.60	76.00	5,776.00
110	1977	25.89	26.89	−1.00	1.00
115	1947	1,982.71	2,025.87	−43.16	1,862.79
118	1842	6,429.35	6,384.20	45.15	2,038.52
Total		€123,995.91	€123,665.71	€330.20	€36,018.32

The first calculation is that of the mean misstatement in an individual account, which is calculated as follows:

$$\text{Mean mistatement per sampling item } = \frac{\text{Total audit difference}}{\text{Sample size}}$$

$$= \frac{€330.20}{125} = €2.65$$

Thus, the average misstatement in a customer account based on the sample data is an overstatement of €2.65.

The mean misstatement must then be projected to the population. The projected mean misstatement for the population is an overstatement of €14,575, which is determined as follows:

$$\text{Projected population misstatement } = \text{Population size (in sampling units)}$$

$$\times \text{ Mean misstatement per sampling item}$$

$$= 5,500 \times €2.65 = €14,575$$

The projected population misstatement is the auditor's 'best estimate' of the misstatement present in the account. However, the auditor is relying on a sample, and the resulting uncertainty must be recognized by calculating an allowance for sampling risk. The allowance for sampling risk is represented by the confidence bound. To calculate the confidence bound, the auditor first calculates the standard deviation of audit differences (SD), by using the following formula:

$$SD = \sqrt{\left[\frac{\text{Total squared audit differences } - (\text{Sample size} \times \text{Mean difference per sampling items}^2)}{\text{Sample size } - 1} \right]}$$

$$= \sqrt{\left[\frac{€36,018.32 - (125 \times 2.65^2)}{125 - 1} \right]} = €16.83$$

In our example, the standard deviation is €16.83. The confidence bound is then calculated using the following formula:

$$\text{Confidence bound} = \text{Population size (in sampling units)} \quad \times CC \times \frac{SD}{\sqrt{(\text{Sample size})}}$$

$$5,500 \times (1.96) \times \frac{€16.83}{\sqrt{125}} = €16,228$$

In calculating the confidence bound, the auditor uses the confidence coefficient (CC) value for the desired level of confidence.[xi] In our example, the confidence bound is €16,228. The auditor then calculates a confidence interval as follows:

$$\text{Confidence interval } = \text{Projected population misstatement} \pm \text{Confidence bound}$$

$$\text{Confidence interval} = €14,575 \pm €16,228$$

where €30,803 is the upper limit and − €1,653 is the lower limit. The auditor can be 95 per cent confident that the actual misstatement in the population is between the upper and lower limits. Since the auditor can tolerate €50,000 misstatement (either understatement or overstatement), the auditor can accept the population as fairly stated.

The auditor decides that the evidence supports or does not support the account balance by determining whether the upper and lower limits are within tolerable misstatement. If both limits are within the bounds of tolerable misstatement, the evidence supports the conclusion that the account is not materially misstated. If either limit is outside the bounds of tolerable misstatement, the evidence does not support the conclusion that the account is materially correct. In our example, the upper and lower limits are within the bounds of tolerable misstatement and the auditor can conclude the account is fairly stated. Figure 9–3 displays this result.

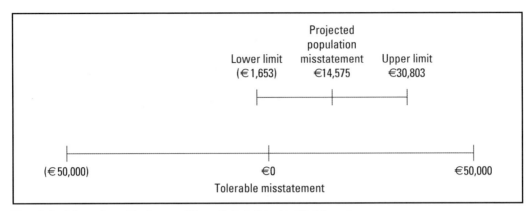

Figure 9–3 A Comparison of the Lower and Upper Limits to Tolerable Misstatement

When the evidence indicates that the account may be materially misstated, the auditor must consider the same four options discussed under monetary-unit sampling: (1) increase sample size; (2) perform additional substantive procedures; (3) adjust the account; or (4) issue a qualified or adverse opinion.

🔑 Key Terms

Allowance for sampling risk. The uncertainty that results from sampling; the difference between the expected mean of the population and the tolerable deviation or misstatement.

Audit sampling. The application of audit procedures to less than 100 per cent of items within a population of audit relevance such that all sampling units have a chance of selection in order to provide the auditor with a reasonable basis on which to draw conclusions about the entire population.

Classical variables sampling. The use of normal distribution theory to estimate the monetary amount of misstatement for a class of transactions or an account balance.

Confidence bound. A measure of sampling risk added and subtracted to the projected misstatement to form a confidence interval.

Expected misstatement. The amount of misstatement that the auditor believes exists in the population.

Monetary-unit sampling (MUS). Attribute-sampling techniques used to estimate the monetary amount of misstatement for a class of transactions or an account balance.

Non-statistical sampling. Audit sampling that relies on the auditor's judgement to determine the sample size, select the sample, and/or evaluate the results for the purpose of reaching a conclusion about the population.

Projected misstatement. The extrapolation of sample results to the population. The projected misstatement represents the auditor's 'best estimate' of the misstatement in the sampling population.

Risk of incorrect acceptance. The risk that the sample supports the conclusion that the recorded account balance is not materially misstated when it is materially misstated.

Risk of incorrect rejection. The risk that the sample supports the conclusion that the recorded account balance is materially misstated when it is not materially misstated.

Sampling risk. The possibility that the sample drawn is not representative of the population and that, as a result, the auditor reaches an incorrect conclusion about the account balance or class of transactions based on the sample.

Sampling unit. The individual member of the population being sampled.

Statistical sampling. Sampling that uses the laws of probability to select and evaluate the results of an audit sample, thereby permitting the auditor to quantify the sampling risk for the purpose of reaching a conclusion about the population.

Tolerable misstatement. The maximum amount by which an account or class of transactions can be misstated and still be acceptable to the auditor as being fairly presented.

Upper misstatement limit. The total of the projected misstatement plus the allowance for sampling risk.

Review Questions

LO1	9–1	List the steps in a statistical sampling application for substantive testing.
LO1	9–2	How is the sampling unit defined when monetary-unit sampling is used for statistical sampling? How is the sampling unit defined when classical variables sampling is used?
LO1	9–3	How are the desired confidence level, the tolerable misstatement and the expected misstatement related to sample size?
LO2	9–4	Identify the advantages and disadvantages of monetary-unit sampling.
LO2,3	9–5	How does the use of probability-proportional-to-size selection provide an increased chance of sampling larger items?
LO2,3	9–6	What is the decision rule for determining the acceptability of sample results when monetary-unit sampling is used?
LO1,4	9–7	How do the desired confidence level, risk of material misstatement, and tolerable and expected misstatements affect the sample size in a non-statistical sampling application?
LO4	9–8	Describe the two methods suggested for projecting a non-statistical sample result. How does an auditor determine which method should be used?
LO5	9–9	What are the advantages and disadvantages of classical variables sampling?
LO5,6	9–10	What is the decision rule for determining the acceptability of sample results when classical variables sampling is used?

Problems

LO1,2,5   9–11   Edwards has decided to use monetary-unit sampling (MUS) in the audit of a client's accounts receivable balance. Few, if any, misstatements of account balance overstatement are expected.

Required:

a   *Identify the advantages of using monetary-unit sampling over classical variables sampling.*

b   *Calculate the sample size and the sampling interval Edwards should use for the following information:*

Tolerable misstatement €15,000
Expected misstatement €6,000
Desired confidence level 95%
Recorded amount of accounts receivable €300,000

c   *Calculate the upper misstatement limit (UML) assuming that the following three misstatements were discovered in a MUS sample.*

Misstatment Number	Book Value	Audit Value
1	€400	€320
2	500	0
3	3,000	2,500

(AICPA, adapted)

LO2,3   **9–12**   The firm of Le and Lysius was conducting the audit of Coomes Moulding Corporation for the fiscal year ended 31 October. Michelle Le, the partner in charge of the audit, decides that MUS is the appropriate sampling technique to use in order to audit Coomes's inventory account. The balance in the inventory at 31 October was €4,250,000. Michelle has established the following: risk of incorrect acceptance = 5 per cent (i.e. the desired confidence level of 95 per cent), tolerable misstatement = €212,500, and expected misstatement = €63,750.

Required:

a   Calculate the sample size and sampling interval.

b   Hon Zhu, staff accountant, performed the audit procedures listed in the inventory audit plan for each sample item. Calculate the upper limit on misstatement based on the following misstatements. What should Hon conclude about Coomes's inventory account?

Misstatment Number	Book Value	Audit Value
1	€6,000	€2,000
2	24,000	20,000
3	140,000	65,000

LO2,3   **9–13**   McMullen and Mulligan, independent auditors, were conducting the audit of Cusick Machine Tool Company for the year ended 31 December. Jim Sigmund, senior-in-charge of the audit, plans to use MUS to audit Cusick's inventory account. The balance at 31 December was €9,000,000.

Required:

a   Based on the following information, compute the required MUS sample size:

Tolerable misstatement = €360,000

Expected misstatement = €90,000

Risk of incorrect acceptance = 5%

b   Nancy Van Pelt, staff accountant, used the sample items selected in part a and performed the audit procedures listed in the inventory audit plan. She notes the following misstatements:

Misstatement Number	Book Value	Audit Value
1	€10,000	€7,500
2	9,000	6,000
3	60,000	0
4	800	640

Using this information, calculate the upper misstatement limit. What conclusion should Van Pelt make concerning the inventory?

c   Assume that, in addition to the four misstatements identified in part b, Van Pelt had identified the following two understatements:

Misstatement Number	Book Value	Audit Value
5	€6,000	€6,500
6	750	800

Calculate the net projected population misstatement.

LO4   **9–14**   The audit firm of Johnson and Johnson has decided to design a non-statistical sample to examine the accounts receivable balance of Francisco Fragrances at 31 October. As of 31 October, there were 1,500 accounts receivable accounts with a balance of €5.5 million. The accounts receivable population can be segregated into the following strata:

Number and Size of Accounts	Book Value of Stratum
10 accounts > €50,000	€750,000
440 accounts > €5,000	3,000,000
1,050 accounts < €5,000	1,750,000

Jonathan L. Gren, senior-in-charge of the audit, has made the following decisions:

- Based on the results of the tests of controls and risk assessment procedures, a low assessment is made for the risk of material misstatement.
- The desired confidence level is moderate.
- The tolerable misstatement for accounts receivable is €155,000, and the expected misstatement is €55,000.
- All the balances greater than €50,000 will be audited.

Required:

a   *Using the non-statistical sampling formula included in the textbook, compute the suggested sample size for this test.*

b   *Gren confirmed the accounts receivable accounts selected and noted the following results:*

Stratum	Book Value of Stratum	Book Value of Sample	Audit Value of Sample	Amount of Overstatement
> €50,000	€750,000	€750,000	€746,500	€3,500
> €5,000	3,000,000	910,000	894,750	15,250
< €5,000	1,750,000	70,000	68,450	1,550

Using ratio projection, what is the total projected misstatement? What conclusion should Gren make concerning the accounts receivable balance?

LO5,6   **9–15**   Mining mogul Steve Wilsey hired the audit firm of Joe Wang Associates to conduct an audit of his new acquisition, Cougar Goldust. The gold inventory was scheduled to be taken on 30 November. The perpetual records show only the *weight* of the gold in various inventory bins. Wang has decided to use a variables sampling approach (difference estimation) to determine the correct weight of the gold on hand. (Note that the pricing of the inventory is straightforward because the market value on 30 November determines the price for balance sheet purposes.) There are 4,000 bins in the Cougar warehouse. The bins will serve as the sampling units. Wang's desired level of confidence is 90 per cent. The tolerable misstatement is set at 35,000 ounces, and the expected misstatement is 10,000 ounces. The perpetual record shows 700,000 ounces on hand.

Required:

[Note: Parts a and b are independent of each other.]

a *Compute the preliminary sample size. The estimated standard deviation is 25 ounces.*

b *Assume that Wang examined a sample of 100 bins. The following information summarizes the results of the sample data gathered by Wang:*

Difference Number	Recorded Weight	Audited Weight	Audit Difference	(Audit Difference)²
1	445	440	5	25
2	174	170	4	16
*	*	*	*	*
*	*	*	*	*
*	*	*	*	*
29	217	215	2	4
30	96	97	(1)	1
Total	24,000	23,600	400	17,856

Compute the sample results and indicate what conclusion Wang should make concerning the inventory balance.

LO5,6   **9–16**   You are in charge of the audit of Hipp Supply Company for the year ended 31 December. In prior years, your firm observed the inventory and tested compilation and pricing. Various misstatements were always found. About 10 per cent of the euro value of the inventory is usually tested.

This year you have established the tolerable misstatement to be €5,000. The client's book value is €97,500. The client has 960 inventory items, the number of which has been determined by examining inventory codes. Each item will be tagged with a prenumbered inventory tag numbered from 1 to 960. You plan to evaluate the results using classical variables sampling (difference estimation).

Assume you have selected a sample of 100 items randomly. For each sample item, audit tests are performed to make sure that the physical count is correct, the pricing is accurate, and the extensions of unit price and quantity are correct. The results are summarized as follows:

Inventory Tag Number	Book Value	Audit Value	Audit Difference	(Audit Difference)²
6	€100	€100	€0	€0
42	85	85	0	0
46	120	120	0	0
51	420	450	(30)	900
55	18	18	0	0
56	10	10	0	0
*	*	*	*	*
*	*	*	*	*
*	*	*	*	*
851	25	25	0	0
854	152	150	2	4
857	85	85	0	0
862	76	86	(10)	100
Total	€10,147	€9,666	€481	€8,895

There were 50 differences, making up the net difference of €481. The recorded total of the client's inventory sheets is €97,500.

Required:

Determine the results of the audit tests using a desired confidence level of 90 per cent. Indicate whether the evidence supports the fair presentation of the inventory account.

Discussion Cases

LO1,2,5   **9–17**   Mead, independent auditor, was engaged to audit Jiffy Company's financial statements for the year ended 31 August. Mead is applying sampling procedures.

During the prior years' audits Mead used classical variables sampling in performing tests of controls on Jiffy's accounts receivable. For the current year Mead decided to use monetary-unit sampling in confirming accounts receivable because MUS uses each account in the population as a separate sampling unit. Mead expected to discover many overstatements but presumed that the MUS sample would still be smaller than the corresponding size for classical variables sampling.

Mead reasoned that the MUS sample would automatically result in a stratified sample because each account would have an equal chance of being selected for confirmation. Additionally, the selection of negative (credit) balances would be facilitated without special considerations.

Mead computed the sample size using the risk of incorrect acceptance, the total recorded book amount of the receivables and the number of misstated accounts allowed. Mead divided the total recorded book amount of the receivables by the sample size to determine the sampling interval. Mead then calculated the standard deviation of the euro amounts of the accounts selected for evaluation of the receivables.

Mead's calculated sample size was 60, and the sampling interval was determined to be €10,000. However, only 58 different accounts were selected because two accounts were so large that the sampling interval caused each of them to be selected twice. Mead proceeded to send confirmation requests to 55 of the 58 customers. Three selected accounts each had insignificant recorded balances under €20. Mead ignored these three small accounts and substituted the three largest accounts that had not been selected in the sample. Each of these accounts had a balance in excess of €7,000, so Mead sent confirmation requests to those customers.

The confirmation process revealed two differences. One account with an audited amount of €3,000 had been recorded at €4,000. Mead projected this to be a €1,000 misstatement. Another account with an audited amount of €2,000 had been recorded at €1,900. Mead did not count the €100 difference because the purpose of the test was to detect overstatements.

In evaluating the sample results, Mead determined that the accounts receivable balance was not overstated because the projected misstatement was less than the allowance for sampling risk.

Required:

Describe each incorrect assumption, statement and inappropriate application of sampling in Mead's procedures.

(AICPA, adapted)

LO1,4   **9–18**   Doug Stevens, independent auditor, is interested in testing the fairness of the ending inventory balance at an audit client, Morris Co. Doug has relatively little experience using statistical sampling methods and, quite frankly, does not like to turn anything over to random chance – especially the selection of items to test. Doug used a judgemental method of selecting items for testing. The method involves testing the inventory-item balances that he deems most risky or most likely to be misstated. Doug identified items to test based on size of balance, findings from prior years, age of inventory, description and professional judgement.

He selected 26 items with a total book value of €720,000. In his 'sample', he found a combined €80,000 in overstatement errors. The book value of inventory on the client's records is €1,090,000. Overall materiality for the engagement is €500,000. Doug's policy is to use 50 per cent or less of overall materiality as tolerable misstatement for any one account.

Required:

a   *What is your opinion of Doug's method of selecting his 'sample'?*

b   *Evaluate Doug's results. Does he have sufficient evidence to conclude that the balance is fairly stated?*

Notes

i   There are alternative methods that overcome this disadvantage. However, these methods are more complex. See D.A. Leslie, A.D. Teitlebaum and R.J. Anderson, *Dollar Unit Sampling: A Practical Guide for Auditors*, Copp, Clark and Pitman, Toronto, 1979, and W.L. Felix, Jr, R.A. Grimlund, F.J. Koster and R.S. Roussey, 'Arthur Andersen's New Monetary-Unit Sampling Approach', *Auditing: A Journal of Practice & Theory* (Fall 1990), pp. 1–16, for a discussion of alternative approaches.

ii   ACL software uses a different underlying statistical distribution than the attributes sampling tables, which in this case resulted in a slightly smaller sample size (see note iv).

iii   The 'Sample Records' command in ACL's sampling menu can also be used to select a probability-proportionate-to-size sample.

iv   The misstatement factors in Table 9–3 are based on computed upper deviation rate factors used in attribute sampling (binomial distribution). In MUS, the sampling interval and the tainting factor are used in the evaluation and not the original computed sample size. When the population is large and misstatement rate low (both common for MUS applications using accounting data) the limiting form of the binomial distribution is the Poisson distribution, which only requires the level of confidence to determine the appropriate misstatement factor to compute the upper misstatement limit (see Leslie *et al.*, *Dollar Unit Sampling*). The Poisson distribution factors are nearly identical to the misstatement factors in Table 9–3. ACL uses the Poisson factors, which explains the slight differences in sample sizes and upper limits compared to the manual approach using the attribute sampling tables. Note that, in evaluating MUS results, ACL does not require sample or population size because the interval, tainting factor and desired confidence provide all the necessary information for evaluation (see Exhibit 9–2).

v   See Leslie *et al.*, *Dollar Unit Sampling*. Alternative approaches are also used in practice. For example, if the direction of the errors in the population is unknown, a two-sided confidence interval can be constructed by separating the understatements and calculating a lower limit on misstatements. See A.D. Bailey, Jr, *Statistical Auditing: Review, Concepts, and Problems*, Harcourt Brace Jovanovich, New York, 1981, for a discussion of this approach.

vi   The approach presented here for non-statistical sampling is based on the American Institute of Certified Public Accountants, *Audit Sampling* (Audit Guide), AICPA, New York, 2008.

vii   This formula is based on the statistical theory underlying monetary-unit sampling. This approach will yield lower confidence levels as expected misstatement becomes larger relative to tolerable misstatement.

viii   Adapted from ISA 530, paras A21 and A22. The guidance from ISA 530 referred to, paras does not include the extremely rare circumstance when a misstatement has been established as an anomaly. An anomaly is a misstatement that is demonstrably not representative of misstatements in a population. An anomaly may be excluded when projecting misstatements to the population, but considered in addition to the projection of the non-anomalous misstatements.

ix   See D.M. Roberts, *Statistical Auditing*, AICPA, New York, 1978, or see A.D. Bailey, Jr, *Statistical Auditing: Review, Concepts, and Problems*, Harcourt Brace Jovanovich, New York, 1981, for a discussion of the other classical variables sampling techniques.

x   Because an account can only be over- or understated, but not both, the risk of incorrect acceptance is commonly referred to in the technical literature as a *one-tailed test*. However, when an auditor uses a sample to evaluate the fairness of an account, she or he does not know with certainty the size or direction of the actual misstatement; therefore it is appropriate to use the traditional two-tailed values of the confidence coefficient as shown in Table 9–6. The confidence coefficient associated with the risk of incorrect rejection can also be included in the sample size computation. If this risk is included in the formula, the sample size will be larger. In practice, the risk of incorrect rejection is typically not considered because it deals with efficiency and not effectiveness. When an account is incorrectly rejected due to a non-representative sample, the auditor typically performs more work, which will provide evidence that the account is fairly stated. Auditors have determined that it is more costly to increase all sample sizes to control for the risk of incorrect rejection than it is to simply perform additional procedures when they believe an account is rejected incorrectly.

[xi]   Note that the CC value simply represents the number of standard errors the auditor would like to use in establishing the confidence bounds around the sample result. The sample mean ±1 standard error results in about a 65 per cent confidence interval, ±2 standard errors results in about a 95 per cent confidence interval, and ± 3 standard errors results in about a 99 per cent confidence interval.

PART **V**

AUDITING
BUSINESS PROCESSES

PART CONTENTS

10 Auditing the Revenue Process
11 Auditing the Purchasing Process
12 Auditing the Human Resource Management Process
13 Auditing the Inventory Management Process
14 Auditing the Financing/Investing Process: Prepaid Expenses; Intangible Assets and Goodwill; and Property, Plant and Equipment
15 Auditing the Financing/Investing Process: Long-Term Liabilities, Stockholders' Equity and Income Statement Accounts
16 Auditing the Financing/Investing Process: Cash and Investments

CHAPTER 10

Auditing the Revenue Process

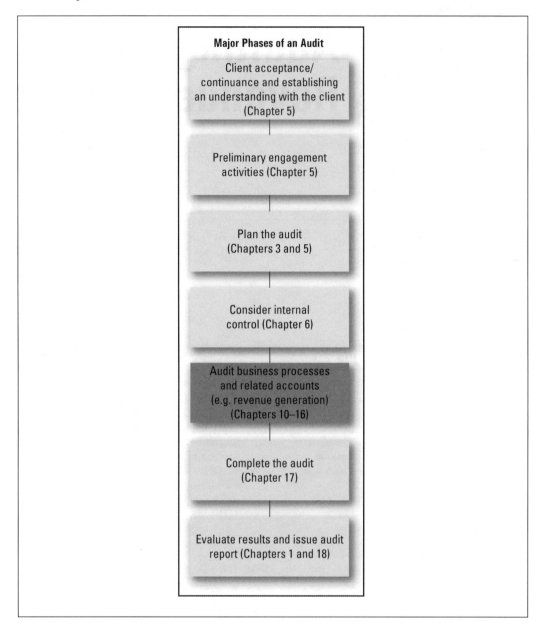

❖ *RELEVANT ACCOUNTING AND AUDITING PRONOUNCEMENTS*

COSO, Internal Control – Integrated Framework, 1992

COSO, Enterprise Risk Management – Integrated Framework, 2004

COSO, Internal Control over Financial Reporting – Guidance for Smaller Public Companies, 2006

COSO, Guidance on Monitoring Internal Control Systems, 2009

IASB, IAS 18, Revenue

ISA 230, Audit Documentation

ISA 240, The Auditor's Responsibilities Relating to Fraud in an Audit of Financial Statements

ISA 315, Identifying and Assessing the Risks of Material Misstatement through Understanding the Entity and Its Environment

ISA 320, Materiality in Planning and Performing an Audit

ISA 330, The Auditor's Responses to Assessed Risks

ISA 450, Evaluation of Misstatements Identified during the Audit

ISA 500, Audit Evidence

ISA 505, External Confirmations

ISA 520, Analytical Procedures

ISA 540, Auditing Accounting Estimates, Including Fair Value Accounting Estimates, and Related Disclosures

AUDITORS GENERALLY divide an entity's information system into business processes or transaction cycles. Using this approach, the auditor is able to gather evidence by examining the processing of related transactions from their origin to their ultimate disposition in accounting journals and ledgers. We first introduced the concept of viewing business from a process perspective in Chapter 2. Figure 10–1 summarizes a model of business centring on business processes or transaction cycles. As the figure shows, the five basic processes are: (1) the revenue process; (2) the purchasing process; (3) the human resource management process; (4) the inventory management process; and (5) the financing process. Auditors divide the financial statement elements into business processes or cycles in order to manage the audit better.

In this chapter, the concepts and techniques learned in the previous chapters are applied to determine the risk of material misstatement (i.e. setting the level of inherent risk and control risk) for the revenue process and related accounts. The revenue process focuses on the sale of goods and services to customers. For virtually all entities, the revenue and purchasing processes represent the two major business processes that affect the financial statements.

The chapter starts by reviewing the basic concepts related to revenue recognition. An overview of the revenue process is then presented as an aid to provide you with an understanding of the process. This is followed by a discussion of the specific factors that affect the assessment of inherent risk for the revenue process and the auditor's assessment of control risk. The remainder of the chapter discusses the test of controls and substantive procedures the auditor conducts to reach the appropriate level of detection risk for the accounts affected by the revenue process. While the main emphasis is on accounts receivable, the discussion also covers the allowance for uncollectable accounts, bad-debt expense, and sales returns and allowances. Because the cash account is affected by other business processes, it is covered separately in Chapter 16.

REVENUE RECOGNITION

LO1

Revenue recognition is reviewed at the beginning of this chapter because knowledge of this underlying concept is fundamental to auditing the revenue process. Additionally, revenue must be recognized in accordance with the applicable financial reporting framework in order for an auditor to issue an unmodified opinion. A revenue-producing transaction generally consists of the sale of a product or the rendering of a service. The International Accounting Standards Board (IASB)[i] defines revenue in the International Accounting Standard (IAS) 18 *Revenue* as:

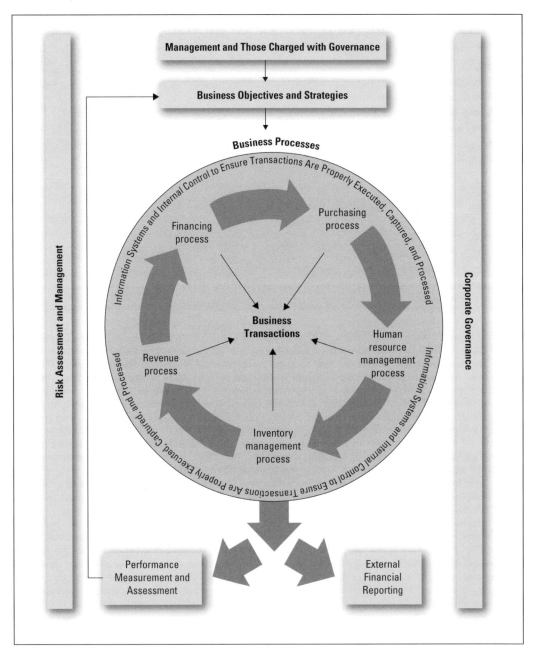

Figure 10–1   An Overview of Business

The gross inflow of economic benefits during the period arising in the course of the ordinary activities of an entity when those inflows result in increases in equity, other than increases relating to contributions from equity participants (para. 7).

IAS 18 states that revenue shall be measured at the fair value of the consideration received or receivable. Fair value is the amount for which an asset could be exchanged, or a liability settled, between knowledgeable, willing parties in an arm's length transaction. Auditing standards (ISA 540) provide guidance on auditing fair value measurements and disclosures.

In general, the entity receives cash or claims to cash for the goods or services provided. Claims to cash are usually referred to as trade accounts receivable. The primary issue in accounting for revenue is determining when to recognize (record) revenue in the income statement. As a general rule revenue is recognized when the earnings process is complete. IAS 18 states that revenue is recognized when it is probable that future economic benefits will flow to the entity and these benefits can be measured reliably. Thus, revenues from the sale of goods are recognized once delivery has taken place, the risk has been transferred and the entity has established a receivable due by customer.

The international accounting standard provides the following criteria for revenue recognition:

- The entity has transferred to the buyer the significant risks and rewards of ownership of the goods.
- The entity retains neither continuing managerial involvement to the degree usually associated with ownership nor effective control over the goods sold.
- The amount of revenue can be measured reliably.
- It is probable that the economic benefits associated with the transaction will flow to the entity.
- The costs incurred or to be incurred in respect of the transaction can be measured reliably.

The two first criteria may be more difficult than the others and require more attention by management and the auditor. The assessment of when an entity has transferred the significant risks and rewards of ownership to the buyer requires an examination of the circumstances of the transaction. In most cases, the transfer of the risks and rewards of ownership coincides with the transfer of the legal title or the passing of possession to the buyer. This is the case for most retail sales. If the entity retains significant risks of ownership, the transaction is not a sale and revenue is not recognized. For example, if the seller transfers goods to the buyer and the seller has an obligation to repurchase goods, no sale is recognized as substantially all the risks and rewards are retained by the seller.

Revenue recognition continues to pose a significant audit risk to auditors and has resulted in questions about the integrity of the financial reporting process. In fact, the auditing standard on fraud states that the auditor should presume that there is a risk of material misstatement due to fraud relating to revenue recognition (ISA 240, para. 27).

The auditor should be alert to the following activities that are fraud risks related to revenue recognition:

- Side agreements are arrangements that are used to alter the terms and conditions of recorded sales in order to entice customers to accept delivery of goods and services.
- Channel stuffing (also known as *trade loading*) is a marketing practice that suppliers sometimes use to boost sales by inducing distributors to buy substantially more inventory than they can promptly resell.
- Related-party transactions require special consideration because related parties may be difficult to identify, and such transactions may pose significant 'substance over form' issues.
- Bill and hold sales (also called parked inventory schemes) are sales where the customer agrees to purchase the goods but the seller retains physical possession until the customer requests shipments. Unless certain conditions are met, such an arrangement does not qualify as a sale because delivery has not occurred.

For most entities, this revenue recognition process occurs over a short period of time (days, weeks or months), but in certain industries, such as construction or defence, the revenue recognition process may extend over a period of years.

An entity's revenue recognition policies affect how transactions are processed and how they are accounted for in the financial statements. Thus, an auditor must understand an entity's revenue recognition policies in order to audit the revenue process.

Practice Insight 10.1

According to the Association of Certified Fraud Examiners, there are eight common methods for committing financial statement fraud. These include:

1 Early revenue recognition.
2 Holding the books open past the accounting period.
3 Fictitious sales.
4 Failure to record returns.
5 Fraud in the percentage of completion method.
6 Related-party transactions.
7 Overstating receivables and inventory.
8 Liability and expense omissions.

❖ OVERVIEW OF THE REVENUE PROCESS

LO2

In this section an overview of the revenue process for EarthWear Clothiers is presented, beginning with an order from a customer, proceeding to the exchange of goods or services for a promise to pay, and ending with the receipt of cash. Exhibit 10–1 describes EarthWear's revenue process. Before proceeding, take a moment to review this exhibit. Do any risks seem especially apparent? If so, how might these risks impact the nature, timing and extent of your audit procedures?

Figure 10–2 presents the flowchart of EarthWear's revenue process (excluding sales from company stores), which will provide a framework for discussing controls and tests of controls in more detail. The discussion of the revenue process in this chapter can be applied equally well to manufacturing, wholesale and service organizations. It should be kept in mind, however, that an accounting system must be tailored to meet the specific needs of an entity. Therefore, the reader should concentrate on understanding the basic concepts presented so that they can be applied to specific revenue systems.

Exhibit 10–1   Description of EarthWear's Revenue Process

EarthWear provides 24-hour toll-free telephone numbers that may be called seven days a week to place orders. Telephone calls are answered by the company's sales representatives, who use online computer terminals to enter customer orders and to retrieve information about product characteristics and availability. The company's sales representatives enter orders into an online order entry and inventory control system. Customers using the company's Internet site complete a computer screen that requests information on product code, size, colour, and so forth. When the customer finishes shopping for products, he or she enters delivery and credit card information into a computer-based form.

Computer order processing is performed each night on a batch basis, at which time shipping tickets are printed with bar codes for optical scanning. Inventory is picked based on the location of individual products rather than orders, followed by computerized sorting and transporting of goods to multiple packing stations and shipping zones. The computerized inventory control system also handles items that customers return. Orders are generally shipped by United Parcel Service (UPS) or comparable services at various tiered rates, depending upon the total euro value of each customer's order. Other expedited delivery services are available for additional charges.

With the exception of sales to groups and companies for corporate incentive programmes, customers pay in cash (in stores) or with credit cards. EarthWear's major bank is reimbursed directly by credit card companies, usually within three days. Group and corporate accounts are granted credit by the credit department. When group or corporate orders are received from new customers, the credit department performs a credit check following corporate policies. A credit authorization form is completed with the credit limit entered into the customer database. When a group or corporate order is received from an existing customer, the order is entered, and the data validation program performs a credit check by comparing the sum of the existing order and the customer's balance to the customer's credit limit.

The reader should also notice that the revenue process shown in Figure 10–2 interacts with the inventory management process. Many accounting systems integrate the revenue, purchasing, human resources and inventory processes. The flowcharts used in this text to represent those processes show the points where the processes interact with one another. As entities use more advanced IT technology, it is becoming easier to integrate the information flow among the various accounting processes.

We now discuss the following topics related to the revenue process:

● Types of transactions and financial statement accounts affected.
● Types of documents and records.
● The major functions

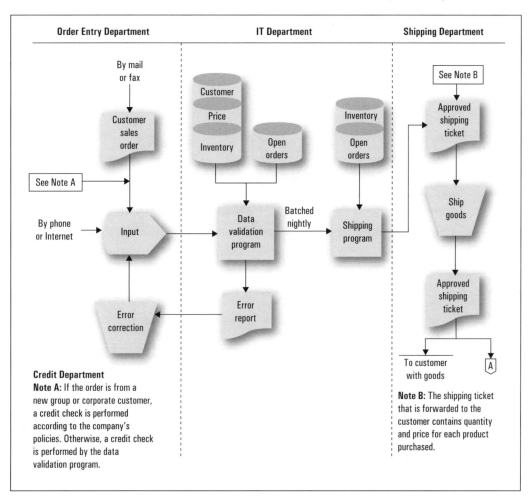

Figure 10–2   Flowchart of the Revenue Process: EarthWear Clothiers (continued on p. 336)

- The key segregation of duties.

◆ Types of Transactions and Financial Statement Accounts Affected

LO3

Three types of transactions are typically processed by the revenue process:

- The sale of goods or rendering of a service for cash or credit.
- The receipt of cash from the customer in payment for the goods or services.
- The return of goods by the customer for credit or cash.

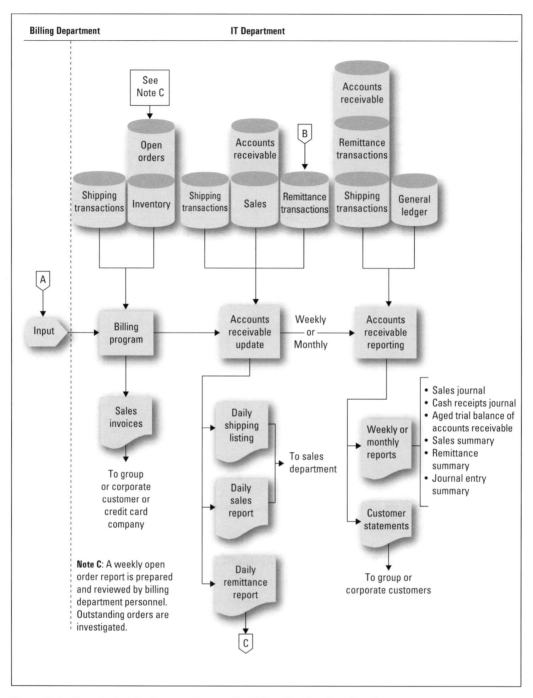

Figure 10–2 Flowchart of the Revenue Process: EarthWear Clothiers (continued)

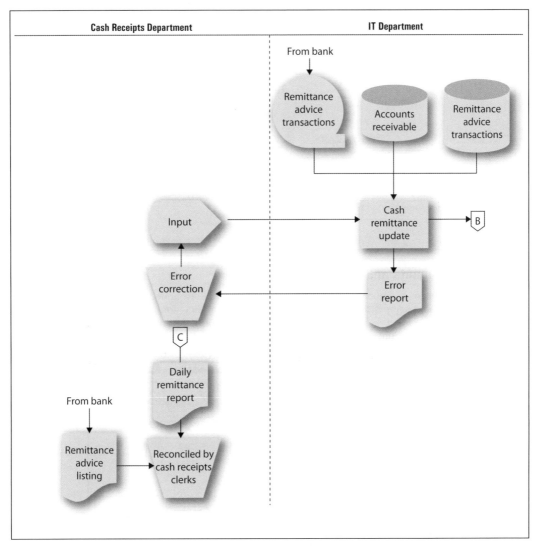

Figure 10–2   Flowchart of the Revenue Process: EarthWear Clothiers (continued)

The key controls involved in each of these transactions are discussed later in the chapter. For some entities, other types of transactions that may occur as part of the revenue process include scrap sales, inter-company sales and related-party sales. The auditor should be aware of how these transactions are processed and their related controls when they represent material amounts in the financial statements.

The revenue process affects numerous accounts in the financial statements. The most significant accounts affected by each type of transaction are as follows:

Type of Transaction	Account Affected
Sales transactions	Trade accounts receivable
	Sales
	Allowance for uncollectable accounts
	Bad-debt expense
Cash receipts transactions	Cash
	Trade accounts receivable
	Cash discounts
Sales return and allowance transactions	Sales returns
	Sales allowances
	Trade accounts receivable

❖ Types of Documents and Records

LO4

Table 10–1 lists the more important documents and records that are normally contained in the revenue process. Each of these items is discussed briefly in the order that they normally occur in the process. The reader should keep in mind that in advanced IT systems some of these documents and records may exist for only a short period of time or may be maintained only in machine-readable form.

Table 10–1 Documents and Records Included in the Revenue Process	
Customer sales order.	Accounts receivable subsidiary ledger.
Credit approval form.	Aged trial balance of accounts receivable.
Open-order report.	Remittance advice.
Shipping document.	Cash receipts journal.
Sales invoice.	Credit memorandum.
Sales journal.	Write-off authorization.
Customer statement.	

Customer Sales Order

This document contains the details of the type and quantity of products or services ordered by the customer, and customer information. Customer sales orders may be prepared and forwarded by a salesperson, mailed or faxed, or received by phone or over the Internet. In the EarthWear example (Fig. 10–2), order entry personnel enter the mailed or faxed information from customer sales orders into the revenue system. Phone or Internet sales are entered directly into the data validation program.

Credit Approval Form

When a customer purchases products on credit from the client for the first time, the client should have a formal procedure for investigating the creditworthiness of the customer. The result of this procedure should be documented on some type of credit approval form. When the customer plans to purchase additional products in the future, this procedure should be used to establish the customer's credit limit. The amount of the credit limit should be documented on the approval form. When credit limits are included in the client's customer files, the approval forms represent the source documents authorizing the amounts contained in the information system. EarthWear follows such a policy for its group and corporate customers (see Exhibit 10–1).

Open-Order Report

This is a report of all customer orders for which processing has not been completed. In the typical revenue process, once a customer's order has been accepted, the order is entered into the system. After the goods have been shipped and billed, the order should be noted as filled. This report should be reviewed daily or weekly, and old orders should be investigated to determine if any goods have been shipped but not billed or to determine why orders have not been filled. Figure 10–2 shows that EarthWear has an open-order file. Note C indicates that an open-order report is prepared weekly and reviewed by billing department personnel for long overdue orders.

Shipping Document

A shipping document must be prepared any time goods are shipped to a customer. This document generally serves as a *bill of lading*, and contains information on the type of product shipped, the quantity shipped and other relevant information. In some revenue systems, the shipping document and bill of lading are separate documents. A copy of the shipping document is sent to the customer, while another copy of the shipping document is used to initiate the billing process. Figure 10–2 shows that EarthWear follows a similar process using a shipping ticket.

Sales Invoice

This document is used to bill the customer. The sales invoice contains information on the type of product or service, the quantity, the price and the terms of trade. The original sales invoice is usually forwarded to the customer, and copies are distributed to other departments within the organization. The sales invoice is typically the source document that signals the recognition of revenue. Many entities bill customers electronically, for example customers signup for receiving E-invoicing via email or receive invoices via EDI. Online billing is faster and normally cheaper than sending invoices by mail. Seller and customers may also integrate IT systems to the extent the need for invoices are eliminated. The majority of EarthWear's sales are made to customers using credit cards, and they do not receive a bill direct from the company. However, the shipping ticket that accompanies the goods contains the quantity and prices for products purchased. That amount shows up on the customer's credit card statement.

Sales Journal

Once a sales invoice has been issued, the sale needs to be recorded in the accounting records. The sales journal is used to record the necessary information for each sales transaction. Depending on the complexity of the entity's operation, the sales journal may contain information classified by type of sale (for example, product line, inter-company sales, related parties). The sales journal contains columns for debiting accounts receivable and crediting the various sales accounts. EarthWear maintains such a journal.

Customer Statement

Such a document may be mailed to a customer periodically, for example monthly. It contains the details of all sales, cash receipts and credit memorandum transactions processed through the customer's account for the period. EarthWear prepares monthly statements only for group or corporate customers who have accounts receivable with the company.

Accounts Receivable Subsidiary Ledger

The accounts receivable subsidiary ledger contains an account and the details of transactions with each customer. A transaction recorded in the sales journal and cash receipts journal is posted to the appropriate customer's account in the accounts receivable subsidiary ledger. For IT systems such as EarthWear's, this information is maintained in the accounts receivable file (see Fig. 10–2).

Aged Trial Balance of Accounts Receivable

This report, which is normally prepared weekly or monthly, summarizes all the customer balances in the accounts receivable subsidiary ledger. Customers' balances are reported in categories (such as less than 30 days, 30–60 days, 60–90 days, more than 90 days old) based on the time expired since the date of the sales invoice. The aged trial balance of accounts receivable is used to monitor the collection of receivables and to ensure that the details of the accounts receivable subsidiary ledger agree with the general ledger control account. The auditor uses this report for conducting much of the substantive audit work in accounts receivable. EarthWear prepares an aged trial balance of accounts receivable for group and corporate customers.

Remittance Advice

Such a document may be forwarded with the customer's bill and returned with the customer's payment for goods or services. A remittance advice contains information regarding which invoices are being paid by the customer. Entities may use turnaround documents, where a portion of the sales invoice serves as a remittance advice that is returned with the customer's payment. When electronic funds transfer is made direct to the seller's bank, a remittance advice listing is forwarded to the seller. E-invoices and documents such as bank giros that include identifying data such as bank account numbers, customer's account, reference numbers and bank codes are specifically designed to facilitate such E-payment transfers. EarthWear receives remittance advices from group and corporate customers after the payment has been processed by the company's bank. Payments from credit card companies are also made direct to the bank, and a remittance advice listing is forwarded to EarthWear.

Cash Receipts Journal

This journal is used to record the entity's cash receipts. The cash receipts journal contains columns for debiting cash, crediting accounts receivable, and crediting other accounts such as scrap sales or interest income. EarthWear maintains such a journal.

Credit Memorandum

This document is used to record credits for the return of goods in a customer's account or to record allowances that will be issued to the customer. Its form is generally similar to that of a sales invoice, and it may be processed through the system in the same way as a sales invoice. Exhibit 10–2 describes how EarthWear handles goods returned from customers. The process of customer returns is not shown in the revenue flowchart (Fig. 10–2).

Exhibit 10–2   Description of EarthWear Clothiers' Process for Handling Customer Returns
In order to receive credit for returned goods, customers must mail the goods to EarthWear's receiving department. There the goods are inspected, and a receiving document, which also serves as a credit memorandum, is prepared. Credit memoranda are entered into the revenue process along with the normal batching of customer orders. The customer receives either a replacement product, a cash refund, or a credit to his or her credit card.
The returned goods are placed back into inventory if they are not defective or damaged. If the goods are defective or damaged they are listed as 'seconds' and sold at reduced prices. The inventory records are updated to reflect either the original cost or the reduced price.

Write-Off Authorization

This document authorizes the write-off of an uncollectable account. It is normally initiated in the credit department, with final approval for the write-off coming from the treasurer. Depending on the entity's accounting system, this type of transaction may be processed separately or as part of the normal stream of sales transactions. EarthWear has negligible bad debts because most sales are made by credit card. Any bad debts related to group or corporate sales are written off by the credit department after approval by the treasurer.

The Major Functions

LO5

The principal objective of the revenue process is selling the entity's goods or services at prices and terms that are consistent with management's policies. Table 10–2 summarizes the functions that normally take place in a typical revenue process.

Table 10–2 Functions in the Revenue Process	
Order entry	Acceptance of customer orders for goods and services into the system in accordance with management criteria.
Credit authorization	Appropriate approval of customer orders for creditworthiness.
Shipping	Shipping of goods that has been authorized.
Billing	Issuance of sales invoices to customers for goods shipped or services provided; also, processing of billing adjustments for allowances discounts and returns.
Cash receipts	Processing of the receipt of cash from customers.
Accounts receivable	Recording of all sales invoices, collections and credit memoranda in individual customer accounts.
General ledger	Proper accumulation, classification and summarization of revenues, collections and receivables in the financial statement accounts.

Order Entry

The initial function in the revenue process is the entry of new sales orders into the system. It is important that sales or services be consistent with management's authorization criteria before entry into the revenue process. In most entities, there is a separate order entry department (see Fig. 10–2).

Credit Authorization

The credit authorization function must determine that the customer is able to pay for the goods or services. Failure to perform this function properly may result in bad-debt losses. In many entities, customers have preset credit limits. The credit authorization function must ensure that the credit limit is not exceeded without additional authorization. Where credit limits are programmed into the information system, a sale that causes a customer's balance to exceed the authorized credit limit should not be processed. The system should also generate an exception report or review by the credit function prior to further processing. Periodically, each customer's credit limits should be reviewed to ensure that the amount is consistent with the customer's ability to pay.

The credit authorization function also has responsibility for monitoring customer payments. An aged trial balance of accounts receivable should be prepared and reviewed by the credit function. Payment should be requested from customers who are delinquent in paying for goods or services. The credit function is usually responsible for preparing a report of customer accounts that may require write-off as bad debts. However, the final approval for writing off an account should come from an officer of the company who is not responsible for credit or collections. If the authorization for bad-debt write-off is part of the credit function, it is possible for credit personnel who have access to cash receipts to conceal misappropriation of cash by writing off customers' balances. In many organizations, the treasurer approves the write-off of customer accounts because this individual is responsible for cash management activities and the treasurer's department is usually separate from the credit function. In some entities, the accounts written off are turned over to a collection agency for continuing collection efforts. By following this procedure, an entity discourages the use of fictitious bad-debt write-offs to conceal the misappropriation of cash. Many entities have a separate credit department.

Shipping

Goods should not be shipped, nor should services be provided, without proper authorization. The main control that authorizes shipment of goods or performance of services is payment or proper credit approval for the transaction. The shipping function must also ensure that customer orders are filled with the correct product and quantities. To ensure timely billing of customers, completed orders must be promptly forwarded to the billing function. The shipping function is often completed within a separate shipping department.

Billing

The main responsibility of the billing function is to ensure that all goods shipped and all services provided are billed at authorized prices and terms. The entity's controls should prevent goods from being shipped to customers who are not being billed. In an IT system, an open-order report should be prepared and reviewed for orders that have not been filled on a timely basis. In other systems, all prenumbered shipping documents should be accounted for and matched to their related sales invoices. Any open or unmatched transactions should be investigated by billing department or sales department personnel.

The billing function is also responsible for handling goods returned for credit. The key control here is that a credit memorandum should not be issued unless the goods have been returned. A receiving document should first be issued by the receiving department to acknowledge receipt of the returned goods.

Cash Receipts

The collection function must ensure that all cash collections are properly identified and promptly deposited intact at the bank. In a growing number of countries electronic payments instruments such as credit cards, bank cards and payments via PC/Internet now totally dominate paper-based instruments. In some countries cheques still have significant usage. In cross-border transfers the use of cheques is more common. Thus, entities may receive a combination of electronic payments and cheques from customers, although electronic fund transfers (EFT) increasingly dominate.

In E-payment transfers payment identifying data are simultaneously communicated to the seller. Neither seller nor customer may need separate receipts, as the necessary identifying data are printed on their account statements. Each transaction is ordinarily subjected to programmed validation data checks such as data entry checks. For example, the system requests the desired data and then waits for an acceptable response before requesting the next piece of input data. Electronic cross-country transfer of money via Internet is becoming more common as well. For example, the use of International Bank Account Number (IBAN) provides a means of electronic cross-country payments parallel to the domestic interbank systems.

In a paper-based system companies may use a so-called lockbox system, in which customers' payments are sent direct to the entity's bank. The bank then forwards a file of cash receipts transactions and remittance advices to the entity. In situations where payments are sent direct to the entity, the cheques should be restrictively endorsed and a 'prelisting' or control listing prepared. All cheques should be deposited daily.

Accounts Receivable

The accounts receivable function is responsible for ensuring that all billings, adjustments and cash receipts are properly recorded in customers' accounts receivable records. Any entries in customers' accounts should be made from authorized source documents such as sales invoices, remittance advices and credit memoranda. In an IT system, the entries to customers' accounts receivable records may be made direct as part of the normal processing of these transactions. The use of control totals and daily activity reports provides the control for ensuring that all transactions are properly recorded. The accounts receivable function is normally performed within the billing department or a separate accounts receivable department.

General Ledger

The main objective of the general ledger function in terms of a revenue process is to ensure that all revenues, collections and receivables are properly accumulated, classified and summarized in the accounts. In an IT system, the use of control or summary totals ensures that this function is performed correctly. One important function is the reconciliation of the accounts receivable subsidiary ledger to the general ledger control account. The general ledger function is also normally responsible for mailing the monthly customer account statements.

◆ Key Segregation of Duties

LO6

One of the most important controls in any accounting system is proper segregation of duties. This is particularly important in the revenue process because of the potential for theft and fraud. Therefore, individuals involved in the order entry, credit, shipping or billing functions should not have access to the accounts receivable records, the general ledger or any cash receipts activities. If IT is used extensively in the revenue application, there should be proper segregation of duties in the IT department. Table 10–3 contains some of the key segregation of duties for the revenue process, as well as examples of possible errors or fraud that can result from conflicts in duties.

·Table 10–3 Key Segregation of Duties in the Revenue Process, and Possible Errors or Fraud

Segregation of Duties	Possible Errors or Fraud Resulting from Conflicts of Duties
The credit function should be segregated from the billing function	If one individual has the ability to grant credit to a customer and also has responsibility for billing that customer, it is possible for sales to be made to customers who are not creditworthy. This can result in bad debts.
The shipping function should be segregated from the billing function	If one individual who is responsible for shipping goods is also involved in the billing function, it is possible for unauthorized shipments to be made and for the usual billing procedures to be circumvented. This can result in unrecorded sales transactions and theft of goods.
The accounts receivable function should be segregated from the general ledger function	If one individual is responsible for the accounts receivable records and also for the general ledger, it is possible for that individual to conceal unauthorized shipments. This can result in unrecorded sales transactions and theft of goods.
The cash receipts function should be segregated from the accounts receivable function	If one individual has access to both the cash receipts and the accounts receivable records, it is possible for cash to be diverted and the shortage of cash in the accounting records to be covered. This can result in theft of the entity's cash.

Table 10–4 shows the proper segregation of duties for individual revenue functions across the various departments that process revenue transactions. Using this table, briefly analyse EarthWear's flowchart as shown in Fig. 10–2. Evaluate whether EarthWear has sufficient segregation of duties and if not, what could happen as a result.

Table 10–4 Segregation of Duties for Revenue and Accounts Receivable Functions by Department

Revenue and Accounts Receivable Functions	Order Entry	Credit	Shipping	Accounts Receivable	Cash Receipts	IT	Treasurer
Receiving and preparing customer order	X						
Approving credit		X					
Shipping goods to customer and completing shipping document			X				
Preparing customer invoice				X		X	
Updating accounts receivable records for sales				X		X	
Receiving customer's remittance					X		
Updating accounts receivable for remittances				X		X	
Preparing accounts receivable aged trial balance				X		X	
Authorization of accounts receivable write-off							X

❖ INHERENT RISK ASSESSMENT

LO7

In examining the revenue process, the auditor should consider the inherent risk factors that may affect both the revenue and cash receipts transactions, and the financial statement accounts affected by those transactions. Most business risks are viewed as inherent risks. The assessment of the potential effects of inherent risk factors is one of the inputs for the risk of material misstatement. Chapter 3 pointed out the three conditions (incentive/pressure, opportunity and attitude) that are generally present when fraud occurs. Four specific inherent risk factors that may affect the revenue process are the following:

- Industry-related factors.
- The complexity and contentiousness of revenue recognition issues.
- The difficulty of auditing transactions and account balances.
- Misstatements detected in prior audits.

Industry-Related Factors

Factors such as the profitability and health of the industry in which an entity operates, the level of competition within the industry and the industry's rate of technological change affect the potential for misstatements in the revenue process. For example, if the industry is experiencing a lack of demand for its products, the entity may be faced with a declining sales volume, which can lead to operating losses and poor cash flow. Similarly, competition within the industry can affect the entity's pricing policies, credit terms and product warranties. If such industry-related factors are present, management may engage in activities that can result in misstatements.

The level of governmental regulation within the industry may also affect sales activity. While all industries are regulated by legislation restricting unfair trade practices such as price fixing, a number of industries are more highly regulated. For example, banks and insurance companies are subject to regulations that may limit an entity's operations. The products developed and sold by pharmaceutical companies are normally regulated by medicines control agencies. Finally, most countries have consumer protection legislation that may affect product warranties, returns, financing and product liability. Industry-related factors directly impact the auditor's assessment of inherent risk for **assertions** such as authorization and accuracy.

The Complexity and Contentiousness of Revenue Recognition Issues

For most entities the recognition of revenue is not a major problem because revenue is recognized when a product is shipped or a service is provided. However, for some entities the recognition of revenue may involve complex calculations. Examples include recognition of revenue on long-term construction contracts, long-term service contracts, lease contracts and instalment sales. Briefly consider EarthWear and its revenue process. Does EarthWear's typical sales process indicate a higher or lower risk of material misstatement due to improper revenue recognition? In some cases, there may be disputes between the auditor and management over when revenue, expenses and related profits should be recognized. In such circumstances, the auditor should assess the risk of material misstatement to be high. Revenue recognition may also have a significant impact on the cut-off and accuracy assertions.

The Difficulty of Auditing Transactions and Account Balances

Accounts that are difficult to audit can pose inherent risk problems for the auditor. For example, management's estimate for the allowance for uncollectable accounts and sales returns can be difficult to audit because of the subjectivity that may be involved in determining its proper value. The risk of a material misstatement for these estimates is a function of factors such as the complexity of the customer base and the reliability of the data available to test the accounts. For example, the only evidence available to determine the collectability of a customer's account may be past payment history or a credit agency report. Such evidence is not as reliable as payments by the customer.

Misstatements Detected in Prior Audits

As discussed in earlier chapters, the presence of misstatements in previous audits is a good indicator that misstatements are likely to be present during the current audit. With a continuing engagement, the auditor has the results of prior years' audits to help in assessing the potential for misstatements in the revenue process.

CONTROL RISK ASSESSMENT

LO8

The concepts involved in control risk assessment were discussed in Chapter 6. The following sections apply the approach outlined there to the revenue process. For discussion purposes, it is assumed that the auditor has decided to follow a reliance strategy for the revenue process. Figure 10–3 summarizes the three steps for setting control risk when a **reliance strategy** is being followed. Each of these steps is briefly reviewed within the context of the revenue process.

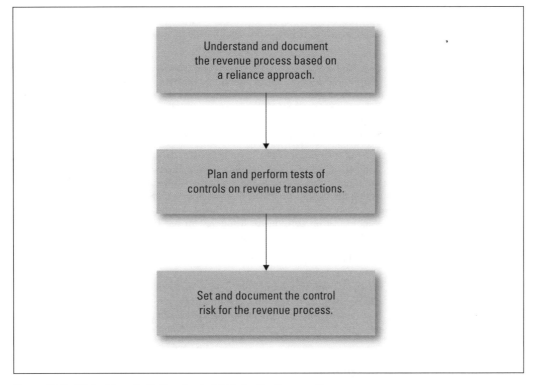

Figure 10–3   Major Steps in Setting Control Risk for the Revenue Process

Understand and Document Internal Control

In order to assess the control risk for the revenue process, the auditor must understand the five components of internal control.

Control Environment

Table 6–3 in Chapter 6 listed the factors that are important in understanding the control environment (e.g. integrity and ethical values, commitment to competence). Because these factors have a pervasive effect on all accounting applications, understanding the control environment is generally completed on an overall entity basis. The auditor should, however, consider how the various control environment factors may affect the individual accounting applications. In the remaining discussion of the revenue process, it is assumed that the control environment factors, including general IT controls, are reliable.

The Entity's Risk Assessment Process

The auditor must understand how management considers risks that are relevant to the revenue process, estimates their significance, assesses the likelihood of their occurrence and decides what actions to take to address those risks. Some of these risks include competition, rapid growth and new technology. Each of these factors can represent a serious risk to an entity's internal controls over the revenue process.

Control Activities

When a reliance strategy is adopted for the revenue process, the auditor needs to understand the controls that exist to ensure that management's objectives are being met. More specifically, the auditor identifies what controls ensure that the assertions for transactions and events are being met. The auditor's understanding of the revenue process can be documented using procedures manuals, narrative descriptions, internal control questionnaires and flowcharts.

Information Systems and Communication

For each major class of transactions in the revenue process, the auditor needs to obtain the following knowledge:

- The process by which sales, cash receipts, and sales returns and allowances transactions are initiated.
- The accounting records, supporting documents and accounts that are involved in processing sales, cash receipts, and sales returns and allowances transactions.
- The flow of each type of transaction from initiation to inclusion in the financial statements, including computer processing of the data.
- The process used to prepare estimates for accounts such as the allowance for uncollectable accounts and sales returns.

The auditor can develop an understanding of an accounting (information) system such as the revenue process by conducting a walk-through. This involves the auditor's 'walking' a transaction through the accounting system and documenting the various functions that process it. In the case of a continuing audit, the auditor has the prior years' systems documentation to assist in the walk-through, although the possibility of changes in the system must be considered. If the system has been changed substantially, or the audit is for a new client, the auditor should prepare new documentation of the system.

Monitoring of Controls

The auditor needs to understand the client's monitoring of controls in the revenue process. This includes understanding how management assesses the design and operation of controls in the revenue process. It also involves understanding how supervisory personnel within the system review the personnel who perform the controls and evaluate the performance of the entity's IT function, as well as the effectiveness of controls.

Plan and Perform Tests of Controls

The auditor should systematically examine the client's revenue process to identify relevant controls that help to prevent, or detect and correct, material misstatements. Because these controls are relied upon in order to set control risk below the maximum, the auditor conducts **tests of controls** to ensure that the controls in the revenue process operate effectively. Audit procedures used to test controls in the revenue process include inquiry of client personnel, inspection of documents and records, observation of the operation of the control, walk-throughs, and reperformance by the auditor of the **control activities**.

Subsequent sections examine tests of controls for each major type of transaction in the revenue process more specifically. Chapter 8 presented sampling approaches to conducting tests of controls.

Set and Document the Control Risk

Once the tests of controls in the revenue process have been completed, the auditor sets the *achieved* level of control risk. If the results of the tests of controls support the planned level of control risk, the auditor conducts the planned level of substantive procedures for the related account balances. If the results of the tests of controls do not support the planned level of control risk, the auditor sets control risk at a level higher than planned. Additional substantive procedures in the accounts affected by the revenue process must then be conducted.

The auditor should document the achieved level of control risk. The level of control risk for the revenue process can be set using either quantitative amounts or qualitative terms such as 'low', 'medium' and 'high'. The documentation of the achieved level of control risk for the revenue process would include documentation of the accounting system such as the flowchart included in Fig. 10–2, the results of the tests of controls and a memorandum indicating the overall conclusions about control risk.

CONTROL ACTIVITIES AND TESTS OF CONTROLS: REVENUE TRANSACTIONS

LO9

Table 10–5 presents the assertions about transactions and events that were discussed in Chapters 2, 4 and 6. Table 10–6 summarizes the assertions for revenue transactions along with some examples of possible misstatements. For each of these misstatements we have included one or two possible control activities that management could implement to mitigate the risk, as well as some example tests of controls that the auditor could use to test those controls. This table (and similar tables in later chapters) is not an exhaustive list of misstatements, control activities or tests of controls for revenue transactions; rather it provides some specific examples by assertion to help you understand the underlying concepts. Most of these controls exist within EarthWear's revenue process (Fig. 10–2).

Table 10–5 Assertions about Classes of Transactions and Events for the Period under Audit	
Occurrence	All revenue and cash receipt transactions and events that have been recorded have occurred and pertain to the entity.
Completeness	All revenue and cash receipt transactions and events that should have been recorded have been recorded.
Authorization	All revenue and cash receipt transactions and events are properly authorized.
Accuracy	Amounts and other data relating to recorded revenue and cash receipt transactions and events have been recorded appropriately and properly accumulated from journals and ledgers.
Cut-off	All revenue and cash receipt transactions and events have been recorded in the correct accounting period.
Classification	All revenue and cash receipt transactions and events have been recorded in the proper accounts.

The auditor's decision process on planning and performing tests of controls involves considering the assertions and the possible misstatements that can occur if internal control does not operate effectively. The auditor evaluates the client's accounting system to determine the controls that will prevent, or detect and correct, such misstatements. When controls are present and the auditor decides to rely on them, they must be tested to evaluate their effectiveness. For example, suppose the auditor's evaluation of the entity's revenue process indicates that monthly statements are mailed to customers by the accounts receivable department with complaints being handled by the billing department. This control is intended to prevent the recording of fictitious sales transactions. The auditor can review and test the client's procedures for mailing customer statements and handling complaints. If no exceptions or an immaterial number are noted, the auditor has evidence that the control is operating effectively.

Each of the assertions shown in Table 10–6 for revenue transactions is discussed mainly in terms of control activities and tests of controls. The column for test of controls includes both manual tests and computer-assisted audit techniques (CAATs). The choice of which type of test of controls is appropriate for a particular assertion will be a function of the following:

- The volume of transactions or data.
- The nature and complexity of the systems by which the entity processes and controls information.
- The nature of the available evidence, including audit evidence in electronic form.

Table 10–6 Summary of Assertions, Possible Misstatements, Example Control Activities, and Example Tests of Controls for Revenue Transactions			
Assertion	Possible Misstatement	Example Control Activity	Example Test of Controls
Occurrence	Fictitious revenue.	Segregation of duties.	Observation and evaluation of proper segregation of duties.
	Revenue recorded, goods not shipped, or services not performed.	Sales recorded only with approved customer order and shipping document.	Testing of a sample of sales invoices for the presence of authorized customer order and shipping document; if IT application, examination of application controls.
		Accounting for numerical sequences of sales invoices.	Review and testing of client procedures (control activities) for accounting for numerical sequence of sales invoices; if IT application, examination of application controls.
		Monthly customer statements; complaints handled independently.	Review and testing of client procedures for mailing and handling complaints about monthly statements.

Completeness	Goods shipped or services performed, revenue not recorded.	Accounting for numerical sequences of shipping documents and sales invoices.	Review and testing of client's procedures for accounting for numerical sequence of shipping documents and sales invoices; if IT application, examination of application controls.
		Shipping documents matched to sales invoices.	Tracing of a sample of shipping documents to their respective sales invoices and to the sales journal.
		Sales invoices reconciled to daily sales report.	Testing of a sample of daily reconciliations.
		An open-order file that is maintained currently and reviewed periodically.	Examination of the open-order file for unfilled orders.
Authorization	Goods shipped or services performed for a customer who is a bad credit risk.	Proper client's procedures for authorizing credit and shipment of goods.	Review of client's procedures for granting credit. Examination of sales orders for evidence of proper credit approval; if IT application, examination of application controls for credit limits.
	Shipments made or services performed at unauthorized prices or on unauthorized terms.	Authorized price list and specified terms of trade.	Comparison of prices and terms on sales invoices to authorized price list and terms of trade; if IT application, examination of application controls for authorized prices and terms.
Accuracy	Revenue transaction recorded at an incorrect monetary amount.	Authorized price list and specified terms of trade Each sales invoice agreed to shipping document and customer order for product type and quantity; mathematical accuracy of sales invoice verified.	Same as above. Examination of sales invoice for evidence that client personnel verified mathematical accuracy. Recomputation of the information on a sample of sales invoices; if IT application, examination of application controls and consideration of use of computer-assisted audit techniques.
	Revenue transactions not posted correctly to the sales journal or customers' accounts in accounts receivable subsidiary ledger.	Sales invoices reconciled to daily sales report Daily postings to sales journal reconciled with posting to subsidiary ledger.	Examination of reconciliation of sales invoices to daily sales report. Examination of reconciliation of entries to sales journal with entries to subsidiary ledger.
	Amounts from sales journal not posted correctly to general journal.	Subsidiary ledger reconciled to general ledger control account Monthly customer statements with independent review of complaints.	Review of reconciliation of subsidiary ledger to general ledger control account. Review and testing of client procedures for mailing and handling complaints related to monthly statements.
Cut-off	Revenue transactions recorded in the wrong period.	All shipping documents forwarded to the billing function daily Daily billing of goods shipped.	Comparison of the dates on sales invoices with the dates of the relevant shipping documents. Comparison of the dates on sales invoices with the dates they were recorded in the sales journal.
Classification	Revenue transaction not properly classified.	Chart of accounts. Proper codes for different types of products or services.	Review of sales journal and general ledger for proper classification. Examination of sales invoices for proper classification; if IT application, testing of application controls for proper codes.

The following sections also include a discussion of control activities and tests of controls that are relevant for EarthWear's revenue process.

Occurrence of Revenue Transactions

Auditors are concerned about the occurrence assertion for revenue transactions because clients are more likely to overstate sales than to understate them. The auditor is concerned about two major types of material misstatements: sales to fictitious customers, and recording of revenue when goods have not been shipped or services have not been performed. In other words, the auditor needs assurance that all recorded revenue transactions are *valid*. The controls shown in Table 10–6 are designed to reduce the risk that revenue is recorded before goods are shipped or services are performed. The major control for preventing fictitious sales is proper segregation of duties between the shipping function and the order entry and billing functions. If these functions are not properly segregated, unauthorized shipments can be made to fictitious customers by circumvention of normal billing control activities. Requiring an approved customer sales order and shipping document before revenue is recognized also minimizes the recording of fictitious sales in a client's records. Accounting for the numerical sequence of sales invoices can be accomplished manually or by computer. The use of monthly customer statements also reduces the risk of revenue being recorded before goods are shipped or services are performed because customers are unlikely to recognize an obligation to pay in such a circumstance. Figure 10–2 shows that EarthWear's revenue process includes these control activities where applicable.

For each of the controls shown, a corresponding test of control is indicated. For example, the auditor can observe and evaluate the segregation of duties. The auditor can also examine a sample of sales invoices for the presence of an authorized customer order and shipping document for each one. In an IT environment, such as EarthWear's revenue process, the auditor can test the **application controls** to ensure that revenue is recorded only after an approved customer order has been entered and the goods shipped.

Completeness of Revenue Transactions

The major misstatement that concerns both management and the auditor is that goods are shipped or services are performed and no revenue is recognized. Failure to recognize revenue means that the customer may not be billed for goods or services and the client does not receive payment. Control activities that ensure that the completeness assertion is being met include accounting for the numerical sequence of shipping documents and sales invoices, matching shipping documents with sales invoices, reconciling the sales invoices to the daily sales report, and maintaining and reviewing the open-order file. For example, EarthWear (Fig. 10–2) reconciles the batch totals of orders entered and provides a reconciliation of the daily shipping listing and the daily sales report. Additionally, the open-order file is reviewed periodically with follow-up on any order older than some predetermined date.

Tests of controls for these control activities are listed in Table 10–6. For example, to test the control that shipping documents are matched to sales invoices, the auditor could select a sample of bills of lading and trace each one to its respective sales invoice and to the sales journal. If all bills of lading in the sample were matched to sales invoices and included in the sales journal, the auditor would have evidence that all goods shipped are being billed. The auditor could also use a generalized audit software package to print the items in the open-order file that are older than the client's predetermined time frame for completing a transaction. These transactions would then be investigated to determine why the sales were not completed.

Authorization of Revenue Transactions

Possible misstatements due to improper authorization include shipping goods to or performing services for customers who are bad credit risks and making sales at unauthorized prices or terms. As discussed earlier in this chapter, management should establish procedures for authorizing credit, prices and terms. Additionally, no goods should be shipped without a properly authorized sales order. Table 10–6 lists a number of tests of controls for this assertion. In a computerized revenue process such as EarthWear's, the auditor may need to review the application controls and use CAATs to test the proper authorization of revenue transactions.

Accuracy of Revenue Transactions

Accuracy is an important assertion because revenue transactions that are not processed accurately result in misstatements that directly affect the amounts reported in the financial statements. Again, the presence of an authorized price list and terms of trade reduces the risk of inaccuracies. There should also be controls that ensure proper verification of the information contained on the sales invoice, including type of goods and quantities shipped, prices, and terms. The sales invoice should also be verified for mathematical accuracy before being sent to the customer. In a manual system, the sales invoice may contain the initials of the client personnel who verified the mathematical accuracy. In an IT application such as EarthWear's, most of these controls would be programmed. For example, the price list is maintained in a master file. However, the client still needs controls to ensure that the authorized price list is updated promptly and that only authorized changes are made to the master file. The auditor can verify the application controls by using CAATs.

The accuracy assertion also includes the possibility that transactions are not properly summarized from source documents or posted properly from journals to the subsidiary and general ledgers. In the revenue process, control totals should be utilized to reconcile sales invoices to the daily sales report and the daily recordings in the sales journal should be reconciled with the posting to the accounts receivable subsidiary ledger. The accounts receivable subsidiary ledger should periodically be reconciled to the general ledger control account. In a properly designed computerized revenue system, such controls are programmed and reconciled by the control groups in the IT department and the user departments. The auditor can examine and test the application controls and various reconciliations. The use of monthly customer statements may also identify posting errors.

Cut-off of Revenue Transactions

If the client does not have adequate controls to ensure that revenue transactions are recorded on a timely basis, sales may be recorded in the wrong accounting period. The client should require that all shipping documents be forwarded to the billing function daily. The auditor can test this control by comparing the date on a bill of lading with the date on the respective sales invoice and the date the sales invoice was recorded in the sales journal. In EarthWear's revenue process, the shipping department forwards the approved shipping order to the billing department for entry into the billing program. In such a system, sales should be billed and recorded within one or two days of shipment.

Classification of Revenue Transactions

The use of a chart of accounts and proper codes for recording transactions should provide adequate assurance about this assertion. The auditor can review the sales journal and general ledger for proper classification, and can test sales invoices for proper classification by examining programmed controls to ensure that sales invoices are coded by type of product or service.

◆ CONTROL ACTIVITIES AND TESTS OF CONTROLS: CASH RECEIPTS
LO9 TRANSACTIONS

Table 10–7 summarizes the assertions for cash receipts transactions along with some examples of possible misstatements. For each of these misstatements we have included one or two possible control activities that management could implement to mitigate the risk, as well as some example tests of controls that the auditor could use to test those controls. This table is not an exhaustive list of misstatements, control activities or tests of controls for cash receipts transactions; rather it provides some specific examples by assertion to help you understand the underlying concepts. In assessing the control risk for cash receipts transactions, the auditor follows the same decision process as described for revenue transactions. Each of the assertions shown in Table 10–7 is discussed with an emphasis on the control activities and tests of controls. The substantive audit procedures for cash are covered in Chapter 16.

Table 10–7 Summary of Assertions, Possible Misstatements, Example Control Activities, and Example Tests of Controls for Cash Receipts Transactions

Assertion	Possible Misstatement	Example Control Activity	Example Tests of Controls
Occurrence	Cash receipts recorded but not received or deposited	Use of electronic cash receipts transfer Segregation of duties	Examine application controls for electronic cash receipts transfer. Observation and evaluation of proper segregation of duties.
		Bank reconciliations prepared regularly and independently reviewed	Review of bank reconciliation for indication of independent review.
Completeness	Cash receipts received or deposited but not recorded	Same control activities as above Daily cash receipts reconciled with posting to accounts receivable subsidiary ledger	Same tests of controls as above. Testing of the reconciliation of daily cash receipts with posting to accounts receivable subsidiary ledger.
		Customer statements prepared on a regular basis; complaints handled independently	Inquiry of client personnel about handling of customer statements and examination of resolution of complaints.
Authorization	Cash discounts not properly taken	Client's procedures specifying policies and controls for cash discounts	Review and test client's procedures to control proper cash discounts.
Accuracy	Cash receipts recorded at incorrect amount	Daily remittance report reconciled to control listing of remittance advices	Review and testing of reconciliation.
		Bank statement reconciled regularly and independently reviewed	Examination of bank reconciliation for independent review.
Cut-off	Cash receipts recorded in wrong period	Cash receipts at, before, and after an accounting period are reconciled to ensure recording in appropriate period	Review and testing of reconciliation.
Classification	Cash receipts posted to wrong customer account	Daily remittance report reconciled daily with postings to cash receipts journal and accounts receivable subsidiary ledger	Review and testing of reconciliation; if IT application, testing of application controls for posting.
		Monthly customer statements with independent review of complaints	Review and testing of client procedures for mailing statements and handling complaints from customers.
	Cash receipts not properly posted to general ledger accounts	Monthly cash receipts journal agreed to general ledger posting Accounts receivable subsidiary ledger reconciled to general ledger control account	Review of posting from cash receipts journal to the general ledger. Examination of reconciliation of accounts receivable subsidiary ledger to general ledger control account.
	Cash receipts recorded in wrong financial statement account	Chart of accounts	Tracing of cash receipts from listing to cash receipts journal for proper classification. Review of cash receipts journal for unusual items.

Payments instruments for cash receipts may be electronic based such as cards or online transfers via PC/Internet, or paper based such as cheques. As discussed, many countries today have well-developed or are increasingly moving towards E-payment systems for transfer of money. Information technology information processing controls and the auditor's examination of these, often by the use of CAATs and with the assistance of an IT expert are applicable when customers pay electronically. (See *Advanced Modules* in Chapter 6 for a detailed discussion of information processing controls in an IT environment and the use of

CAATs.) Recall that in the discussion of the revenue cycle we have assumed the control environmental factors, including general IT controls, are reliable. Electronic cash receipts transfer and effective application controls of processing of cash receipts reduce the risk of misstatements such as misstatements caused by clerical errors in the deposit process and theft of cash receipts.

Occurrence of Cash Receipts Transactions

The possible misstatement that concerns the auditor when considering the occurrence assertion is that cash receipts are recorded but not deposited in the client's bank account. A strong control that prevents such misstatements exists when cash receipts are transferred electronically; preventing the client's employees from having access to cash. The cash is deposited by the customer in the client's account, and the bank forwards the remittance advices and a file of the cash receipts transactions to the client for processing. If paper-based instruments such as cheques are used, proper segregation of duties between the cash receipts function and the accounts receivable function (or a lockbox system where the customers' cash receipts are mailed directly to the client's bank) will normally be preventive. Finally, preparation of bank reconciliations that are independently reviewed reduces the possibility that cash receipts will be recorded but not deposited. Table 10–7 lists the tests of controls the auditor could conduct to assess the effectiveness of the client's controls over the occurrence assertion.

Completeness of Cash Receipts Transactions

An important control related to the completeness assertion that all cash receipts received or deposits made are recorded is reconciliation of the daily cash receipts with the amounts posted to customers' accounts in the accounts receivable subsidiary ledger. An example of this control is shown in EarthWear's system, where the total of the remittance advices is reconciled with the daily remittance report by the cash receipts department. Additionally, reconciliation of received customer statements with customers' accounts will ensure that deposited cash receipts are recorded.

When electronic transfer of cash receipts is used, a strong control exists to ensure that cash receipts are not stolen or lost before recording. In a paper-based system proper segregation of duties between the cash receipts function and the accounts receivable function or a lockbox system are controls for ensuring that cash or cheques are not stolen or lost before being recorded in the cash receipts records. When a lockbox system is not used, cheques should be restrictively endorsed when received, and a daily cash listing should be prepared.

In terms of tests of controls, the controls conducted for the occurrence assertion also provide some evidence about completeness. In addition, the reconciliation of the daily cash receipts and customers' statements with the postings to the accounts receivable subsidiary ledger can be tested by the auditor on a sample basis. For cheques, the auditor can observe the client's personnel endorsing the cheques and preparing the cash listing.

When the client does not have adequate segregation of duties or if collusion is suspected, the possibility of defalcation is increased. An employee who has access to both the cash receipts and the accounts receivable records has the ability to steal cash and manipulate the accounting records to hide the misstatement. This is sometimes referred to as **lapping**. When lapping is used, the perpetrator covers the cash shortage by applying cash from one customer's account against another customer's account. For example, suppose customer 1 has a balance of €5,000 and makes a €3,000 cash payment on the account. A client's employee who has access to both the cash receipts and the accounts receivable records can convert the €3,000 payment to his or her personal use. The theft of the cash can be covered in the following way: the €3,000 payment is not reflected in the customer's account. When a payment is subsequently received from customer 2, the payment is deposited in the client's cash account but applied to customer 1's accounts receivable account. Now the shortage of cash is reflected in customer 2's accounts receivable account. The client employee who stole the cash keeps hiding the theft by shifting the €3,000 difference from one customer's accounts receivable account to another's. If cash is stolen *before* it is recorded as just described, the fraud is difficult and time-consuming for the auditor to detect. If the auditor suspects that this has occurred, the individual cash receipts have to be traced to the customers' accounts receivable accounts to ensure that each cash receipt has been posted to the correct account. If a cash receipt is posted to a different account, this may indicate that someone is applying cash to different accounts to cover a cash shortage. However, if duties are not properly segregated, that person may also be able to hide the theft through use of a credit memorandum, bad-debt write-off, or no recognition of the revenue transaction. For example, the employee could issue a credit memorandum for €3,000 against the customer's accounts receivable account to cover the €3,000 difference.

Authorization of Cash Discounts

Terms of trade generally include discounts for payment within a specified period as a way of encouraging customers to pay on time. Controls in the accounting system should ensure that management's policies concerning cash discounts are followed. For example, the client may establish terms of trade of 2/10, net/30 days. Customers paying within 10 days are then entitled to a 2 per cent discount. When the cash is received, client personnel should check to be sure that the customer is complying with the payment terms. The auditor can test this control for a sample of receipts transactions by examining signatures for such compliance check.

Accuracy of Cash Transactions

There are several reasons why cash receipts might be recorded at an incorrect amount. For example, the wrong amount could be recorded from the remittance advice, or the receipt could be incorrectly processed during data entry. The controls listed in Table 10–7 provide reasonable assurance that such errors would be detected and corrected. The corresponding tests of controls involve examining and testing the various reconciliations that take place in this part of the revenue process.

The other major misstatements that can occur for the accuracy assertion are cash receipts being posted to the wrong customer account or the wrong general ledger account. This last misstatement should not be confused with the misstatement discussed under the classification assertion. For the classification assertion, the misstatement results from the wrong financial statement accounts being credited in the cash receipts journal. The misstatement related to the accuracy assertion involves posting to the accounts receivable subsidiary ledger or from the totals in the cash receipts journal to the general ledger accounts.

The use of monthly customer statements provides a check on posting to the correct customer account because a customer who has made a payment and whose monthly statement does not reflect it will complain to the client. The other controls mainly involve the use of various reconciliations that ensure that cash receipts transactions are properly summarized and posted to the general ledger. Tests of controls that may be used by the auditor are presented for each control activity shown in Table 10–7.

Cut-off of Cash Receipts Transactions

If the client uses electronic fund transfer, a lockbox system, or if cash is deposited daily in the client's bank, there is a small possibility of cash being recorded in the wrong period. Thus, generally the auditor has little concern with this type of misstatement.

Classification of Cash Receipts

The auditor seldom has major concerns about cash receipts being recorded in the wrong financial statement account. The major control for preventing cash from being recorded in the wrong account is a chart of accounts. The auditor's concern is with applying appropriate account codes to the individual cash receipts, especially cash receipts from unusual sources such as scrap sales, notes receivable and proceeds from sales of equipment. The auditor can trace a sample of remittance advices to the cash receipts journal to ensure proper classification. The cash receipts journal can also be reviewed for unusual items.

LO9

CONTROL ACTIVITIES AND TESTS OF CONTROLS: SALES RETURNS AND ALLOWANCES TRANSACTIONS

For most entities, sales returns and allowances transactions are few and do not represent a material amount in the financial statements. As a result, this text does not cover them in as much detail as revenue or cash receipts transactions. However, credit memoranda that are used to process sales returns and allowances transactions can also be used to cover an unauthorized shipment of goods or conceal a misappropriation of cash.

Two important controls should be present regarding the processing of credit memoranda. First, each credit memorandum should be approved by someone other than the individual who initiated it. This provides proper segregation of duties between access to the customer's record and authorization for issuing a credit memorandum. Second, a credit for returned goods should be supported by a receiving document indicating that the goods have been returned. The auditor can perform tests of controls on credit memoranda by examining a sample of credit memoranda for proper approval and the presence of the respective receiving documents. For a credit memorandum issued for a reason other than a return of goods, approval by an appropriate individual is the critical control. See Exhibit 10–2 for a discussion of the control activities used by EarthWear to control sales returns.

For entities with few or immaterial sales returns and allowances transactions, the auditor may decide only to gain an understanding of how such transactions are processed and not to conduct tests of controls. Substantive analytical procedures (discussed later in this chapter) can then be used to provide sufficient evidence on the fairness of the sales returns and allowances account.

◆ RELATING THE ASSESSED LEVEL OF CONTROL RISK TO SUBSTANTIVE
LO10 PROCEDURES

The results of the auditor's testing of internal control for the revenue process directly impact detection risk and therefore the level of substantive procedures that will be required for the accounts affected by this process. This includes balance sheet accounts such as accounts receivable, allowance for uncollectable accounts, and cash, as well as income statement accounts such as sales, bad-debt expense, and sales returns and allowances.

When the results of testing controls support the planned level of control risk, the auditor can conduct substantive procedures of these accounts at the planned level. If the results of testing controls indicate that the control risk can be further reduced, the auditor can increase the detection risk. This might lead to a reduction in the amount or the mix of the substantive procedures. For example, if the tests of controls indicate that control risk is lower than planned, the auditor might plan to perform more substantive **analytical procedures** and fewer tests of details of account balances. However, if the results of the tests of controls do not support the planned level of control risk, the detection risk will have to be set lower. This normally leads to an increase in the amount of substantive procedures. For example, if controls for the occurrence assertion are weaker than planned for revenue transactions, the auditor might increase the number of accounts receivable confirmations mailed to customers.

AUDITING ACCOUNTS RECEIVABLE AND RELATED ACCOUNTS

The auditor uses substantive procedures to detect material misstatements in accounts receivable and related accounts.

As discussed in Chapter 5, there are two categories of substantive procedures: (1) substantive analytical procedures; and (2) tests of details of classes of transactions, account balances and disclosures. Substantive analytical procedures are used to examine plausible relationships among accounts receivable and related accounts. This includes disaggregated analytical procedures for revenue. Tests of details focus on transactions, account balances or disclosures. In the revenue process, **tests of details of transactions** (also called **substantive tests of transactions**) focus mainly on the sales and cash receipts transactions. Tests of details of account balances concentrate on the detailed amounts or estimates that make up the ending balance for accounts receivable and related accounts. **Tests of details of disclosures** are concerned with the presentation and disclosures related to accounts receivable and related accounts.

Table 10–5 presented the assertions for revenue and cash receipt transactions and events. Table 10–8 lists the assertions for account balances and disclosures as they apply to accounts receivable and related accounts. The reader should note that the auditor may test assertions related to transactions (substantive tests of transactions) in conjunction with testing internal control. If the tests of controls indicate that the controls are not operating effectively, the auditor may need to test transactions closer to year end or the balance sheet date.

Table 10–8 Management Assertions about Account Balances and Disclosures for Accounts Receivable and Related Accounts

Assertions about account balances at the period end

- **Existence.** Recorded accounts receivable and related accounts exist.
- **Rights and obligations.** The entity holds or controls the rights to accounts receivable and related accounts, and any liabilities related to those accounts are the obligations of the entity.
- **Completeness.** All accounts receivable and related accounts that should have been recorded have been recorded.
- **Valuation and allocation.** Accounts receivable and related accounts are included in the financial statements at appropriate amounts, and any resulting valuation or allocation adjustments are appropriately recorded.

Assertions about presentation and disclosure

- **Occurrence and rights and obligations.** All disclosed events, transactions and other matters relating to accounts receivable and related accounts have occurred and pertain to the entity.
- **Completeness.** All disclosures relating to accounts receivable and related accounts that should have been included in the financial statements have been included.
- **Classification and understandability.** Financial information relating to accounts receivable and related accounts is appropriately presented and described, and disclosures are clearly expressed.
- **Accuracy and valuation.** Financial and other information relating to accounts receivable and related accounts are disclosed fairly and at appropriate amounts.

We discuss substantive analytical procedures first because, after control testing, the assurance 'bucket' is usually filled with evidence from substantive analytical procedures before tests of details.

❖ SUBSTANTIVE ANALYTICAL PROCEDURES

LO11

Substantive analytical procedures are useful audit tests for examining the fairness of accounts such as sales, accounts receivable, allowance for uncollectable accounts, bad-debt expense, and sales returns and allowances because such tests provide sufficient evidence at low cost. Table 10–9 lists examples of substantive analytical procedures that are useful in auditing accounts receivable and related accounts. Many of the analytical procedures listed in Table 10–9 could also be used for preliminary analytical procedures at the planning stage or as a final analytical procedure at the completion of the audit. Table 10–9 is not an exhaustive list of substantive analytical procedures for accounts receivable and related accounts; rather it provides some specific examples by account to help you understand the underlying concepts.

For example, what evidence might be provided by comparing this year's gross profit percentage with that of previous years? Further, what might it mean if this year's percentage is significantly *less* than last year's? What if it is significantly *more* than last year's? This comparison of gross profit percentage to previous years' or industry data may provide valuable evidence on unrecorded revenue (an understatement) or fictitious revenue (an overstatement) and related accounts receivable when this ratio is significantly higher or lower than previous years' or industry data. This ratio may also provide information on changes in pricing policies.

Table 10–9 Examples of Substantive Analytical Procedures Used in Testing Accounts Receivable and Related Accounts	
Example Substantive Analytical Procedure	*Possible Misstatement Detected*
Revenue	
Comparison of gross profit percentage by product line with previous years' and industry data	Unrecorded (understated) revenue
	Fictitious (overstated) revenue
Comparison of reported revenue to budgeted revenue	Changes in pricing policies
Analysis of the ratio of sales in the last month or week to total sales for the quarter or year	Product-pricing problems
Comparison of revenues recorded daily for periods shortly before and after the end of the audit period for unusual fluctuations such as an increase just before and a decrease just after the end of the period	
Comparison of details of units shipped with revenues and production records and consideration of whether revenues are reasonable compared to levels of production and average sales price	

Comparison of the number of weeks of inventory in distribution channels with prior periods for unusual increases that may indicate channel stuffing

Comparison of percentages and trends of sales into the distributor channel with industry and competitors' sales trends, if known

Accounts Receivable, Allowance for Uncollectable Accounts, and Bad-Debt Expense

Comparison of receivables turnover and days outstanding in accounts receivable to previous years' and/or industry data	Under- or overstatement of allowance for uncollectable accounts and bad-debt expense
Comparison of ageing categories on aged trial balance of accounts receivables to previous years	
Comparison of bad-debt expense as a percentage of revenue to previous years' and/or industry data	
Comparison of the allowance for uncollectable accounts as a percentage of accounts receivable or credit sales to previous years' and/or industry data	
Examination of large customer accounts individually and comparison to previous year	

Sales Returns and Allowances and Sales Commissions

Comparison of sales returns as a percentage of revenue to previous years' or industry data	Under- or overstatement of sales returns
Comparison of sales discounts as a percentage of revenue to previous years' and/or industry data	Under- or overstatement of sales discounts
Estimation of sales commission expense by multiplying net revenue by average commission rate and comparison of recorded sales commission expense	Under- or overstatement of sales commission expense and related accrual

The five ratios shown under the 'Accounts Receivable' subheading in Table 10–9 provide evidence on whether accounts receivable properly reflect net realizable value. Each ratio aids the auditor in assessing the fairness of the allowance for uncollectable accounts, which in turn affects the fairness of accounts receivable and bad-debt expense. The days outstanding in accounts receivable ratio for EarthWear provides a good example of a substantive analytical procedure that provides strong evidential support for the accurate valuation of accounts receivable. The days outstanding in accounts receivable ratio is 4.91 and 4.94 days for 2008 and 2009, suggesting that EarthWear collects its accounts receivable quickly. This result is consistent with the majority of the company's sales being made with credit cards. EarthWear is reimbursed in three to five days by its credit card providers. Given the relative size of accounts receivable and this result indicating that receivables are collected so quickly, EarthWear's auditors may do no further audit work on accounts receivable and instead rely on evidence gathered regarding cash receipts and the ending cash balance. Pretend for a moment that 2009's days outstanding in accounts receivable ratio increased substantially. How might this impact the nature, timing and extent of your audit procedures? What types of EarthWear's customers would be the source of the bad debt problems?

Last, comparing the ratio of sales returns or sales discounts to revenue with previous years' and industry data provides the auditor with evidence on whether all sales returns or sales discounts have been recorded. The auditor can also estimate sales commission expense by multiplying the average commission rate by net sales and comparing that amount with recorded commission expense. In many situations, the auditor may be able to accept the sales returns, sales discounts and sales commission expense as fairly presented without conducting any additional substantive tests if such substantive analytical procedures produce results that are consistent with the auditor's expectations.

◆ TESTS OF DETAILS OF CLASSES OF TRANSACTIONS, ACCOUNT BALANCES AND DISCLOSURES
LO12

LO13

Table 10–10 presents the assertions for accounts receivable, allowance for uncollectable accounts and bad-debt expense along with related tests of transactions, account balances and disclosures. This table should not be construed as an exhaustive list of substantive audit procedures for accounts receivable and related accounts.

Table 10–10 Summary of Assertions and Related Tests of Transactions, Account Balances and Disclosures: Accounts Receivable, Allowance for Uncollectable Accounts and Bad-Debt Expense

Assertions about Classes of Transactions	Substantive Tests of Transaction*
Occurrence	For a sample of sales transactions recorded in the sales journal, vouching of the sales invoices back to customer orders and shipping documents
Completeness	Tracing of a sample of shipping documents to the details of the sales invoices and to the sales journal and customers' accounts receivable subsidiary ledger
Authorization and accuracy	Comparison of prices and terms on a sample of sales invoices with authorized price list and terms of trade
Cut-off	Comparison of the dates on a sample of sales invoices with the dates of shipment and with the dates they were recorded in the sales journal
Classification	Examine a sample of sales invoices for proper classification into revenue accounts
Assertions about Account Balances	*Tests of Details of Account Balances*
Existence	Confirmation of selected accounts receivable Performance of alternative procedures for accounts receivable confirmation exceptions and non-responses
Rights and obligations	Review of bank confirmations for any liens on receivables Inquiry of management, review of any loan agreements and review of board of directors' minutes for any indication that the accounts receivable have been sold
Completeness	Obtaining of aged trial balance of accounts receivable and agreeing total to general ledger control accounts Review results of testing the completeness assertion for assessing control risk; tracing of shipping documents into sales journal and to accounts receivable subsidiary ledger if such testing was not performed as a test of controls
Valuation and allocation	Examination of the results of confirmations of selected accounts receivable Examination of the adequacy of the allowance for uncollectable accounts
Assertions about Presentation and Disclosure	*Tests of Details of Disclosures*
Occurrence, and rights and obligations	Determine whether any receivables have been pledged, assigned or discounted. Determine if such items require disclosure
Completeness	Complete financial reporting checklist to ensure that all financial statement disclosures related to accounts receivable and related accounts have been disclosed
Classification and understandability	Review of aged trial balance for material credits, long-term receivables and non-trade receivables. Determine whether such items require separate disclosure on the balance sheet Read notes to ensure that required disclosures are understandable
Accuracy and valuation	Read notes and other information to ensure that the information is accurate and properly presented at the appropriate amounts

* Each of these substantive tests of transactions could be conducted as a test of controls or a dual-purpose test. Of these six assertions, the cut-off assertion is the one that is most often to be conducted as a substantive procedure.

Tests of details of transactions (substantive tests of transactions) are tests conducted to detect monetary misstatements in the individual transactions processed through all accounting applications. Often the auditor conducts substantive tests of transactions at the same time as tests of controls. Thus, it is often difficult to distinguish a substantive test of transactions from a test of controls because the specific audit procedure may both test the operation of a control activity and a test for monetary misstatement. If the controls are not operating effectively or if the auditor did not rely on those controls, substantive tests of transactions may be necessary for the auditor to reach an appropriate level of evidence. The cut-off assertion is the one that is most often conducted as a substantive procedure.

Table 10–10 also presents the assertions for account balances and disclosures. For each assertion, one or more tests of details are presented. In the following subsection, we discuss how the auditor approaches the audit of each important assertion for accounts receivable and related accounts. We begin with the completeness assertion for the accounts receivable balance because the auditor must establish that the detailed records that support the account to be audited agree with the general ledger account. Note that we do not cover each assertion listed in Table 10–10 because they are not applicable to EarthWear or they would have been conducted as tests of controls.

Completeness and Accuracy

The auditor's concern with completeness is whether all accounts receivable have been included in the accounts receivable subsidiary ledger and the general ledger accounts receivable account. The reconciliation of the aged trial balance to the general ledger account should detect an omission of a receivable from *either* the accounts receivable subsidiary ledger or the general ledger account. If the client's accounting system contains proper control totals and reconciliations, such errors should be detected and corrected by the relevant control activities for accuracy and completeness. For example, in EarthWear's revenue process (Fig. 10–2), control totals exist for daily shipping and billing. Personnel in the billing department would be responsible for reconciling the two totals. If such control activities do not exist in a client's accounting system, or if they are not operating effectively, the auditor will have to trace a sample of shipping documents to sales invoices, the sales journal, and the accounts receivable subsidiary ledger to ensure that the transactions were included in the accounting records.

This process followed by the auditor is to agree the accounts receivable subsidiary ledger of customer accounts to the general ledger accounts receivable (control) account. This is typically accomplished by obtaining a copy of the aged trial balance of accounts receivable and comparing the total balance with the general ledger accounts receivable account balance. Exhibit 10–3 presents an aged trial balance of accounts receivable working paper for Calabro Wireless Services. An aged trial balance of the subsidiary ledger is used because the auditor will need this type of data to examine the allowance for uncollectable accounts.

Exhibit 10–3	Example of an Aged Trial Balance of Accounts Receivable Working Paper				
	CALABRO WIRELESS SERVICES				E10
	Aged Trial Balance – Accounts Receivable				DLJ
	31/12/09				15/2/2010
Customer Name	Total	*≤ 30 Days*	*31–60 Days*	*61–90 Days*	*> 90 Days*
Abbott Construction	€10,945¥	€9,542	€1,403		
Acton Labs	9,705		5,205	€4,500	
•	•	•	•	•	•
•	•	•	•	•	•
•	•	•	•	•	•
Wright Industries	29,875¥	18,875	11,000		
Zorcon	4,340				€4,340
Total	€3,717,900	€2,044,895	€1,301,215	€260,253	€111,537
	F T/B	F	F	F	F

F = Footed.
T/B = Agreed to trial balance.
¥ = Customer account traced to subsidiary ledger; agreed to total and proper ageing tested.

The auditor must also have assurance that the detail making up the aged trial balance is accurate. This can be accomplished in a number of ways. One approach involves mainly manual audit procedures. First, the aged trial balance is footed and crossfooted. *Footing* and *crossfooting* mean that each column of the trial balance is added, and the column totals are then added to ensure that they agree with the total balance for the account. Then a sample of customer accounts included in the aged trial balance is selected for testing. For each selected customer account, the auditor vouches the customer's balance back to the subsidiary ledger detail, and verifies the total amount and the amounts included in each column for proper ageing. A second approach involves the use of CAATs. If the **general controls** over IT are adequate, the auditor can use a generalized audit software package to examine the accuracy of the aged trial balance generated by the client's accounting system.

Cut-off

The cut-off assertion attempts to determine whether all revenue transactions and related accounts receivable are recorded in the proper period. While the auditor can obtain assurance about the cut-off assertion for sales by conducting tests of controls, in most cases, cut-off tests are conducted as substantive tests of transactions or as a dual-purpose test. Additionally, sales cut-off is coordinated with inventory cut-off because the shipment of goods normally indicates that the earnings process is complete. The auditor wants assurance that if goods have been shipped in the current period, the resulting sale has been recorded, and also that if the sales have been recorded, the corresponding inventory has been removed from the accounting records. In addition, the auditor needs to determine if there is proper cut-off for sales returns.

If there is not a proper cut-off of revenue transactions, both revenue and accounts receivable will be misstated for the current and following years. In most instances, errors related to sales cut-off are unintentional and are due to delays in recognizing the shipment of goods or the recognition of the sale. In other instances, the client may intentionally fail to recognize revenue transactions in the current period or may recognize sales from the next period in the current period (see Problem 10–17). The first situation can occur by the revenue transactions not being recorded in the sales journal until the next period. For example, sales that take place on the last two days of the current year are recorded as sales in the next year by delaying entry until the current-year sales journal is closed. The second situation is generally accomplished by leaving the sales journal 'open' and recognizing sales from the first few days of the next period as current-period sales.

The client's accounting system should have controls that ensure timely recording of revenue transactions. The results of tests of controls, if performed, should provide evidence of the cut-off assertion. Additionally, the client should have end-of-period control activities for ensuring a proper sales cut-off between accounting periods.

The test of sales cut-off is straightforward. The auditor first identifies the number of the last shipping document issued in the current period. Then a sample of sales invoices and their related shipping documents is selected for a few days just prior to, and subsequent to, the end of the period. Assuming that sales are recorded at the time of shipment (free-on-board (FOB)-shipping point), sales invoices representing goods shipped prior to year end should be recorded in the current period, and invoices for goods shipped subsequent to year end should be recorded as sales in the next period. Any transaction recorded in the wrong period should be corrected by the client. For example, suppose the last shipping document issued in the current period was numbered 10,540. None of the recorded revenue transactions sampled from a few days prior to year end should have related shipping document numbers higher than 10,540, and none of the sampled revenue transactions recorded in the first few days of the subsequent period should have related shipping document numbers lower than 10,540. In an IT system such tests are still necessary because a delay in entering data may occur, or management may manipulate the recognition of the transactions.

The processing of sales returns may differ across entities. When sales returns are not material, or if they occur irregularly, the entity may recognize a sales return at the time the goods are returned. However, for entities like EarthWear, sales returns may represent a material amount or may occur regularly. In this instance, the client may estimate an allowance for sales returns. When sales returns represent a material amount, the auditor needs to test for proper cut-off.

Substantive analytical procedures may be used to test cut-off for sales returns. The ratio of sales returns to sales may indicate to the auditor that sales returns are consistent with expectations and therefore that the sales returns cut-off is adequate. If the auditor decides to conduct more detailed tests, the receiving documents used to acknowledge receipt of the returned goods must be examined. Using procedures similar to those for testing sales cut-off, the auditor selects a sample of receiving documents for a few days prior to and subsequent to the end of the period. The receiving documents are traced to the related credit memoranda. Sales returns recorded in the wrong period should be corrected, if material.

Existence

The existence of accounts receivable is one of the more important assertions because the auditor wants assurance that this account balance is not overstated through the inclusion of fictitious customer accounts or amounts (see Exhibit 10–4). The major audit procedure for testing the existence assertion for accounts receivable is confirmation of customers' account balances. If a customer does not respond to the auditor's confirmation request, additional audit procedures may be necessary. The confirmation process is discussed later in this chapter.

Exhibit 10–4	Fictitious Customers

ComRoad AG was a small Münich-based telematic network provider listed at the Neuer Markt of Deutsche Börse. The company had a history of reporting earnings and turnover far beyond target figures. In April 2002 the new auditor of ComRoad, Rödl & Partner, announced that 63 per cent, 86 per cent and 97 per cent of the total revenues reported in 1998, 1999 and 2000, respectively, were earned through its subsidiary VT Electronics Ltd, Hong Kong. Rödl & Partner pointed out that they could not find any basis that actual revenues were realized with this firm or that this company actually existed at any point in time. The predecessor auditor of ComRoad, KPMG, subsequently withdrew its opinions for 1998–2000.

Sources: 'Company Accounts – Badly in Need of Repair', *The Economist* (2 May 2002); 'Preliminary Findings from the Special Audit of the 1998 through 2000 Financial Statements', ComRoad AG (23 April 2002); 'KPMG Widerruft Bestätigungsvermerke für ComROAD-Jahresanschlüsse 1998 bis 2000', KPMG (24 April 2002).

Rights and Obligations

The auditor must determine whether the accounts receivable are owned by the entity because accounts receivable that have been sold should not be included in the entity's financial statements. For most audit engagements, this does not represent a problem because the client owns all the receivables. However, in some instances a client may sell its accounts receivable. The auditor can detect such an action by reviewing bank confirmations, cash receipts for payments from organizations that factor accounts receivable, or corporate minutes for authorization of the sale or assignment of receivables.

Valuation and Allocation

The major valuation issue related to accounts receivable is concerned with the net realizable value of accounts receivable. The auditor is concerned with determining that the allowance for uncollectable accounts, and thus bad-debt expense, is fairly stated. The allowance for uncollectable accounts is affected by internal factors such as the client's credit-granting and cash collection policies, and external factors such as the state of the economy, conditions in the client's industry and the financial strength of the client's customers. Auditing standards (ISA 540) require the auditor to evaluate whether the estimate for allowance for uncollectable accounts is either reasonable or is misstated.

In verifying the adequacy of the allowance for uncollectable accounts, the auditor starts by assessing the client's policies for granting credit and collecting cash. If the client establishes strict standards for granting credit, the likelihood of a large number of bad debts is reduced. Generally, the auditor assesses the adequacy of the allowance account by first examining the aged trial balance for amounts that have been outstanding for a long time. The probability of collecting these accounts can be assessed by discussing them with the credit manager, examining the customers' financial statements, obtaining credit reports (such as from Dun & Bradstreet), or reviewing the customers' communications with the client related to payment.

The second step in assessing the adequacy of the allowance account involves examining the client's prior experience with bad debts. The problem with examining only delinquent accounts is that no consideration is given to accounts that are current but that may result in bad debts. By maintaining good statistics on bad debts, the client can determine what percentage of each ageing category will become uncollectable. The auditor can test these percentages for reasonableness. Following is an example of how this approach would work.

Suppose Calabro Wireless Services developed the following historical data on bad debts:

Ageing Category	Percentage as Bad Debts
≤ 30 days	0.001
31–60 days	0.025
61–90 days	0.140
> 90 days	0.550

The allowance for uncollectable accounts can be determined in the following manner, using the data from Exhibit 10–3:

≤ 30 days	31–60 days	61–90 days	> 90 days	Total
€2,044,895	€1,301,215	€260,253	€111,537	€3,717,900
× 0.001	× 0.025	× 0.14	× 0.55	
€2,045	€32,530	€36,435	€61,345	€132,355

Suppose that the balance in the allowance for doubtful accounts on Calabro's general ledger is €135,300. This general ledger balance appears reasonable, given the auditor's calculation of €132,355. If the percentage for bad debts in the 31–60 days column was 5 per cent instead of 2.5 per cent, would your conclusion change? What if it was 7.5 per cent? While determining the proper amount for the allowance for uncollectible accounts may seem relatively straightforward, considerable judgement on the part of the auditor is involved. As mentioned, the auditor must evaluate the collectibility of individual problem accounts and consider whether the historically derived percentages are reasonable, given the current economic and industry conditions.

Classification and Understandability

The major issues related to the presentation and disclosure assertion about classification are: (1) identifying and reclassifying any material credits contained in accounts receivable; (2) segregating short-term and long-term receivables; and (3) ensuring that different types of receivables are properly classified. In many entities, when a customer pays in advance or a credit is issued, the amount is credited to the customer's accounts receivable account. The auditor should determine the amount of such credits and, if material, reclassify them as either a deposit or another type of liability. The second issue requires that the auditor identifies and separates short-term receivables from long-term receivables. Long-term receivables should not be included with trade accounts receivable. The auditor must also ensure that non-trade receivables are properly separated from trade accounts receivable. For example, receivables from officers, employees or related parties should not be included with trade accounts receivable because users might be misled if such receivables are combined.

Other Presentation and Disclosure Assertions

Disclosure is important for accounts receivable and related accounts. While management is responsible for the financial statements, the auditor must ensure that all necessary disclosures are made. Most audit firms use some type of financial statement reporting checklist to ensure that all necessary disclosures are made for each account (completeness). Table 10–11 presents examples of disclosure items for the revenue process and related financial statement accounts. Exhibit 10–5 presents two examples of common disclosures for revenue-related accounts. The first disclosure relates to the basis for recognizing revenue. This disclosure is normally included in a note that describes significant accounting policies. The second example presents disclosure of related-party transactions. Disclosures about related-party transactions normally discuss the nature of the transactions, the amounts and whether the transactions were similar in terms to those for unrelated parties.

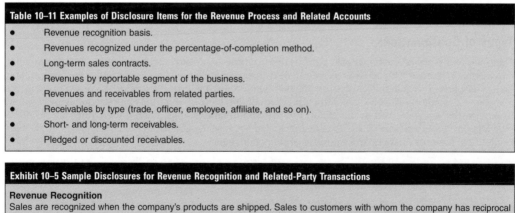

Table 10–11 Examples of Disclosure Items for the Revenue Process and Related Accounts

- Revenue recognition basis.
- Revenues recognized under the percentage-of-completion method.
- Long-term sales contracts.
- Revenues by reportable segment of the business.
- Revenues and receivables from related parties.
- Receivables by type (trade, officer, employee, affiliate, and so on).
- Short- and long-term receivables.
- Pledged or discounted receivables.

Exhibit 10–5 Sample Disclosures for Revenue Recognition and Related-Party Transactions

Revenue Recognition
Sales are recognized when the company's products are shipped. Sales to customers with whom the company has reciprocal purchase agreements are accounted for in the same manner as inter-company transactions and are eliminated in the financial statements.

Related-Party Transactions
The company's chairman of the board is also chairman of the board of Dyco Industries. Net sales to Dyco were €990,000 and €1,244,000 for the two years ended 2009 and 2008. Accounts receivable from Dyco were €243,000 and €489,000 at 31 December 2009 and 2008, respectively. The company believes that the terms of sale were substantially the same as those available to unrelated parties for similar products.

❖ THE CONFIRMATION PROCESS: ACCOUNTS RECEIVABLE

LO14

External **confirmation** is audit evidence obtained as a direct written response to the auditor from a third party (the confirming party), in paper form, or by electronic or other medium (ISA 505). In deciding to what extent to use external confirmations the auditor considers the materiality of the account, the assessment of risk of material misstatement in the account, and effectiveness of external confirmations as an audit procedure. For example, external confirmations may not be used because the account is immaterial, the auditor's assessment of inherent risk and control risk may be low and evidence gathered from other substantive tests is sufficient to reduce audit risk to an acceptably low level, or the use of external confirmations is not considered effective based on prior experience of low response rate or unreliable responses. External confirmations are, however, ordinarily used in relation to accounts receivable.

Confirmations can address more than one assertion. However, confirmations normally provide different levels of assurance for different assertions. Accounts receivable confirmations are generally a good source of evidence for testing the existence assertion. If the customer confirms the amount owed to the client, the auditor has appropriate evidence that the account receivable is valid.[ii] Accounts receivable confirmations may also provide evidence on the cut-off, completeness, and valuation and allocation assertions. For example, a customer's confirmation of the monetary amount owed provides some evidence on the valuation assertion.

A number of factors affect the reliability of accounts receivable confirmations. The auditor should consider each of the following factors when using confirmations to test accounts receivable:

- The type of confirmation request.
- Prior experience with the client or similar engagements.
- The intended respondent.

The types of confirmations are discussed in the next section. The auditor should consider prior experience with the client in terms of confirmation response rates, misstatements identified and the accuracy of returned confirmations when assessing the reliability of accounts receivable confirmations. For example, if response rates were low in prior audits, the auditor might consider obtaining evidence using alternative procedures. The intended respondents to accounts receivable confirmations may vary from individuals with little accounting knowledge to large corporations with highly qualified accounting personnel. The auditor should consider each respondent's competence, knowledge, ability and objectivity when assessing the reliability of confirmation requests. For example, if an auditor is confirming accounts receivable for a small retail organization, it is possible that the respondents may not have the knowledge or ability to respond appropriately to the confirmation request. On the other hand, if confirmations are sent to medium-sized or large corporations with well-controlled accounts payable systems, the information received in response to such confirmation requests is likely to be reliable. However, some large organizations and government agencies do not respond to confirmations because it may be difficult to accumulate the necessary data since they are on a voucher system. Such non-responses must be tested using procedures discussed later in the chapter.

Types of Confirmations

There are two types of confirmations: *positive* and *negative*. A positive accounts receivable confirmation requests that customers indicate whether they agree with the amount due to the client stated in the confirmation. Thus, a response is required regardless of whether the customer believes the amount is correct or incorrect. Sometimes an auditor will use a 'blank' form of positive confirmation, in which the request requires the customer to provide the amount owed to the client. **Positive confirmations** are generally used when an account's individual balances are large or if errors are anticipated because the control risk has been judged to be high. Exhibit 10–6 presents an example of a positive confirmation request.

Exhibit 10–6 Example of a Positive Confirmation Request

CALABRO WIRELESS SERVICES

Wright Industries
PO Box XXX
City

Dear Customers:

Please examine the accompanying statement carefully and either confirm its correctness or report any differences to our auditors

   Abbott & Johnson
   PO Box XXX
   City

who are auditing our financial statements.
   Your prompt attention to this request will be appreciated. An envelope is enclosed for your reply. Please do not send your payments to the auditors.

Sincerely,
Jan Rodriguez
Controller, Calabro Wireless Services

Confirmation:
The balance receivable from us for €29,875 as of 31 December 2009 is correct except as noted below:

_____

_____

Wright Industries
Date _____   By _____

A **negative confirmation** requests that customers respond only when they disagree with the amount due to the client. An example of a negative confirmation request is shown in Exhibit 10–7. Negative confirmation requests are used when there are many accounts with small balances, control risk is assessed to be low and the auditor believes that the customers will devote adequate attention to the confirmation. On many audit engagements, a combination of positive and negative confirmations is used to test accounts receivable because of materiality considerations and a mix of customers. For example, positive confirmations may be sent to selected large-monetary customer accounts and negative confirmations sent to a sample of small-monetary customer accounts.

Exhibit 10–7 Example of a Negative Confirmation Request

CALABRO WIRELESS SERVICES

Zorcon
PO Box XXX
City

Dear Customers:

Please examine the accompanying statement carefully. If it does NOT agree with your records, please report any differences directly to our auditors

   Abbott & Johnson
   PO Box XXX
   City

who are auditing our financial statements.
   Your prompt attention to this request will be appreciated. An envelope is enclosed for your reply. Please do not send your payments to the auditors.

Sincerely,
Jan Rodriguez
Controller, Calabro Wireless Services

Because positive accounts receivable confirmations require that customers respond to the auditor, any amounts for which responses are not received must be verified by the auditor using alternative procedures. Negative accounts receivable confirmations require a response only when the information about the customer's balance is incorrect. Therefore, a non-response to a negative confirmation request is generally assumed to represent a valid accounts receivable. This can be a major drawback to the use of negative confirmations.

The accuracy of the accounts receivable confirmation request can generally be improved if a copy of the customer's monthly statement is enclosed with the confirmation request.

Timing

Accounts receivable may be confirmed at an interim date or at year end. Such considerations were discussed in Chapter 6. The confirmation request should be sent soon after the end of the accounting period in order to maximize the response rate. Sending the confirmations at the end of the accounting period reduces the chance of timing differences arising due to processing of purchases and cash disbursements by the customers.

Confirmation Procedures

The auditor must maintain control over the accounts receivable confirmations so as to minimize the possibility that direct communication between the customers and the auditor is biased by interception or alteration of the receivable confirmation by the client. For control purposes, the auditor should mail the confirmations outside the client's facilities. Direct mailing from the audit firm's office generally provides the best control. To ensure that any confirmations that are undeliverable by the post office are returned to the auditors and not the client, the confirmations should be mailed in envelopes with the audit firm's address listed as the return address. The envelope used by customers for returning the confirmation response should also be addressed to the audit firm. The fact that undeliverable confirmations are returned directly to the auditor also provides some assurance that fictitious customers are identified.

The auditor should maintain a record of the confirmations mailed and those returned. When positive confirmations are used, the auditor generally follows up with second, and possibly third, requests to customers who do not reply, in an attempt to increase the response rate to the confirmation requests. In some cases, a customer may respond using electronic media (such as email or fax) or orally. In such situations the auditor should verify the source and contents of the communication. For example, a fax response may be verified by a telephone call to the respondent, and an oral response can be verified by requesting a written communication from the respondent.

Each confirmation exception (that is, difference between the recorded balance and the balance confirmed by the customer) should be carefully examined by the auditor to determine the reason for the difference. In many cases, exceptions result from what are referred to as *timing differences*. Such differences occur because of delays in recording transactions in either the client's or the customer's records. For example, the client may ship goods to a customer on the last day of the period and record it as a current period sale. The customer will probably receive and record the goods as a purchase in the next period. Such situations are not errors and result only because of a delay in recording the transaction. Table 10–12 presents some examples of exceptions and their potential causes.

Table 10–12 Examples of Exceptions to Confirmation Requests

Type of Difference	Potential Cause
Goods not received by customer	Timing difference
	Goods delivered to wrong customer
	Invoice sent to wrong customer
	Fictitious sale
Payment not recorded in client's records	Timing difference
	Payment applied to wrong customer account
	Cash misappropriated
Goods returned for credit by customer	Timing difference
Processing error	Incorrect quantity or price
	Recording error
Amount in dispute	Price of goods in dispute
	Goods do not meet specifications
	Goods damaged in transit

The need to maintain control over accounts receivable confirmations and responses does not preclude the use of internal auditors in the confirmation process. For example, internal auditors may confirm accounts receivable as part of their normal duties, or they may directly assist the auditor in performing accounts receivable confirmations as part of the annual audit. If internal auditors are used in this capacity, their work should be supervised, reviewed, evaluated and tested by the external auditor.

Practice Insight 10.2

According to auditing standards properly controlled electronic confirmations may be considered to be reliable audit evidence. If the auditor is satisfied that the electronic confirmation process is secure and properly controlled, and the confirmation is directly from a third party who is a bona fide authorized respondent, electronic confirmations may be considered as an appropriate, valid confirmation responses. Various means might be used to validate the sender of electronic information and the respondent's authorization to confirm the requested information. For example, the use of encryption and electronic digital signatures may improve the security of the electronic confirmation process.

Alternative Procedures

When the auditor does not receive responses to positive confirmations, he or she must apply alternative procedures to determine the existence and valuation of the accounts receivable. Auditors normally send second and third requests; they also perform the following alternative audit procedures:

- Examination of subsequent cash receipts.
- Examination of customer orders, shipping documents and duplicate sales invoices.
- Examination of other client documentation.

Examination of subsequent cash receipts involves checking the accounts receivable subsidiary ledger for payments of the specific sales invoices included in the customer's accounts receivable balances that were outstanding at the date of the confirmation. If the auditor has obtained evidence that the client's controls are strong for recording cash receipts and the amount collected is a significant portion of the accounts receivable balance, the auditor may stop at this point. If the client's controls are weak, the auditor may extend the testing by tracing the payment in the subsidiary ledger to the cash receipts journal and to the bank statement. If the customer has paid for the goods, the auditor has strong evidence concerning the existence and valuation of the accounts receivable.

If a customer has not paid the accounts receivable, the auditor can examine the underlying documentation that supports the revenue transaction. This documentation includes the original customer order, shipping document and duplicate sales invoice. If this documentation indicates that the customer ordered the goods and the goods were shipped, then the auditor would have evidence supporting the validity of the accounts receivable. Last, the auditor may need to examine other correspondence between the client and the customer to obtain adequate evidence on the validity and valuation of the accounts receivable.

❖ AUDITING OTHER RECEIVABLES

LO15

Up to this point the discussion has concentrated on trade accounts receivable. Most entities, however, have other types of receivables that are reported on the balance sheet. Some examples include:

- Receivables from officers and employees.
- Receivables from related parties.
- Notes receivable.

The auditor's concern with satisfying the assertions for these receivables is similar to that for trade accounts receivable. Typically, each of these types of receivables is confirmed and evaluated for collectability. The transactions that result in receivables from related parties are examined to determine if they were at 'arm's length'. Notes receivable would also be confirmed and examined for repayment terms and whether interest income has been properly recognized.

❖ EVALUATING THE AUDIT FINDINGS: ACCOUNTS RECEIVABLE AND
LO16 RELATED ACCOUNTS

When the auditor has completed the planned substantive procedures, all the identified misstatements for accounts receivable should be aggregated. The aggregated identified misstatement is compared to materiality for the financial statements or any lesser materiality amount determined appropriate for the accounts receivable. If the identified misstatement approaches or exceed materiality, or if the nature and the circumstances of identified misstatements indicate that other misstatements exist that when aggregated with misstatements accumulated during the audit, could be material, the auditor should determine if the overall audit strategy and audit plan need to be revised. In some instances, these misstatements may provide additional evidence on control risk. By identifying the cause of the misstatements, the auditor may determine that the original assessment of control risk was too low. For example, the auditor may lower his or her evaluation of the effectiveness of the control for granting credit (that is, may increase control risk) based on a large number of misstatements detected during tests of the allowance for uncollectable accounts. This may impact the auditor's assessment of audit risk.

The auditor should request management to correct identified misstatements. If uncorrected misstatements in accounts receivable and, when considered together with other uncorrected misstatements, are less than materiality, the auditor may accept that the financial statements are fairly presented. Conversely, if the uncorrected misstatement exceeds the materiality, the auditor should conclude that the financial statements are not fairly presented.

For example, in Chapter 3 materiality for accounts receivable for EarthWear was €900,000. Suppose that, after completing the substantive procedures, EarthWear's auditor identified misstatement is €250,000. In this case, the auditor may conclude that EarthWear's accounts receivable are not materially misstated. However, if the identified misstatement is €975,000, materiality for accounts receivable is exceeded. The auditor would determine the nature and circumstances of the misstatement. Additional audit procedures might be required. Such audit procedures would typically be directed at the *systematic* errors detected by the substantive procedures. For example, if the substantive tests of transactions indicated that sales invoices were priced incorrectly, the auditor's additional audit procedures would focus on determining the extent of pricing misstatements. The auditor might conclude that accounts receivable are fairly presented if EarthWear's management adjusts the financial statements by €75,000 (€975,000 – €900,000) or more.

This would result in uncorrected misstatement for accounts receivable being equal to or less than materiality of €900,000. In the final decision on the audit opinion the auditor takes into account other uncorrected misstatements.

🔓 Key Terms

Analytical procedures. Evaluations of financial information through analysis of plausible relationships among both financial and non-financial data.

Application controls. Controls that apply to the processing of specific computer applications and are part of the computer programs used in the accounting system.

Assertions. Representations by management, explicit or otherwise, that are embodied in the financial statements, as used by the auditor to consider the different types of potential misstatements that may occur.

Confirmation. Audit evidence obtained as a direct written response to the auditor from a third party (the confirming party), in paper form, or by electronic or other medium.

Control activities. The policies and procedures that help ensure that management's directives are carried out.

General controls. Controls that relate to the overall information processing environment and have a pervasive effect on the entity's computer operations.

Lapping. The process of covering a cash shortage by applying cash from one customer's accounts receivable against another customer's accounts receivable.

Negative confirmation. A request that the confirming party respond directly to the auditor only if the confirming party disagrees with the information provided in the request.

Positive confirmation. A request that the confirming party respond directly to the auditor indicating whether the confirming party agrees or disagrees with the information in the request, or providing the requested information.

Reliance strategy. The auditor's decision to rely on the entity's controls, test those controls and reduce the substantive tests of the financial statement accounts.

Tests of controls. Audit procedures performed to obtain audit evidence about the operating effectiveness of controls in preventing, or detecting and correcting, material misstatements at the assertion level.

Tests of details of account balances tests of details of disclosures. Tests that concentrate on the details of amounts contained in an account balance and in disclosures.

Tests of details of transactions (substantive tests of transactions). Tests to detect errors or fraud in individual transactions.

❓ Review Questions

LO1	10–1	Accounting standards determine when to recognize revenue. Discuss when revenue should be recognized.
LO5	10–2	Describe the credit function's duties for monitoring customer payments and handling bad debts.
LO6	10–3	When a client does not adequately segregate duties, the possibility of cash being stolen before it is recorded is increased. If the auditor suspects that this type of defalcation is possible, what type of audit procedures can he or she use to test this possibility?
LO7	10–4	The auditor needs to understand how selected inherent risk factors affect the transactions processed by the revenue process. Discuss the potential effect that industry-related factors and misstatements detected in prior periods have on the inherent risk assessment for the revenue process.
LO8	10–5	In understanding the accounting system in the revenue process, the auditor typically performs a walk-through to gain knowledge of the system. What knowledge should the auditor try to obtain about the accounting system?
LO9	10–6	What are the two major controls for sales returns and allowances transactions?

LO11	**10–7**	List four analytical procedures that can be used to test revenue-related accounts. What potential misstatements are indicated by each of these analytical procedures?
LO13	**10–8**	Describe how the auditor verifies the accuracy of the aged trial balance.
LO14	**10–9**	List and discuss the three factors mentioned in the chapter that may affect the reliability of confirmations of accounts receivable.
LO14	**10–10**	Distinguish between positive and negative confirmations. Under what circumstances would positive confirmations be more appropriate than negative confirmations?
LO15	**10–11**	Identify three other types of receivables the auditor should examine. What audit procedures would typically be used to audit other receivables?

Problems

LO1   **10–12**   For each of the following situations indicate how and/or when the client should recognize the revenue. Justify your decision.

1   Your client, Thomson Telecom, maintains an inventory of telecommunications equipment. Bayone Telephone Company placed an order for 10 new transformers valued at €5 million and Thomson delivered them just prior to 31 December. Thompson's normal business practice for this class of customer is to enter into a written sales agreement that requires the signatures of all the authorized representatives of Thomson and its customer before the contract is binding. However, Bayone has not signed the sales agreement because it is awaiting the requisite approval by the legal department. Bayone's purchasing department has orally agreed to the contract and the purchasing manager has assured you that the contract will be approved the first week of next year.

2   Best Products is a retailer of appliances that offers 'layaway' sales to its customers twice a year. Best retains the merchandise, sets it aside in its inventory, and collects a cash deposit from the customer. The customer signs an instalment note at the time the initial deposit is received, but no payments are due until 30 days after delivery.

3   Dave's Discount Stores is a discount retailer who generates revenue from the sale of membership fees it charges customers to shop at its stores. The membership arrangement requires the customer to pay the entire membership fee (usually €48) at the beginning of the arrangement. However, the customer can unilaterally cancel the membership arrangement and receive a refund of the unused portion. Dave's estimates that 35 per cent of the customers will cancel their memberships before the end of the contract.

LO2,5,6,9   **10–13**   The Art Appreciation Society operates a museum for the benefit and enjoyment of the community. During the hours the museum is open to the public, two clerks who are positioned at the entrance collect a €5 admission fee from each non-member patron. Members of the Art Appreciation Society are permitted to enter free of charge upon presentation of their membership cards.

At the end of each day one of the clerks delivers the proceeds to the treasurer. The treasurer counts the cash in the presence of the clerk and places it in a safe. Each Friday afternoon the treasurer and one of the clerks deliver all cash held in the safe to the bank and receive an authenticated deposit slip, which provides the basis for the weekly entry in the cash receipts journal.

The board of directors of the Art Appreciation Society has identified a need to improve the internal control system over cash admission fees. The board has determined that the cost of installing turnstiles or sales booths or otherwise altering the physical layout of the museum would greatly exceed any benefits that might be derived. However, the board has agreed that the sale of admission tickets must be an integral part of its improvement efforts.

Smith has been asked by the board of directors of the Art Appreciation Society to review the internal control over cash admission fees and suggest improvements.

Required:

Indicate deficiencies in the existing internal control system over cash admission fees, which Smith should identify, and recommend one improvement for each of the deficiencies identified. Organize your answer as indicated in the following example:

Deficiencies	Recommendation
1. There is no basis for establishing the documentation of the number of paying patrons.	1. Prenumbered admission tickets should be issued upon payment of the admission fee.

(AICPA, adapted)

LO11,12,13 **10–14** Assertions are expressed or implied representations by management that are reflected in the financial statement elements. The auditor performs audit procedures to gather evidence to test those assertions.

Required:

Your client is All's Fair Appliance Company, an appliance wholesaler. Select the most appropriate audit procedure from the following list and enter the number in the appropriate place on the grid. (An audit procedure may be selected once, more than once, or not at all.)

Audit Procedure:

1 Review of bank confirmations and loan agreements.
2 Review of drafts of the financial statements.
3 Selection of a sample of revenue transactions, and determination that they have been included in the sales journal and accounts receivable subsidiary ledger.
4 Selection of a sample of shipping documents for a few days before and after year end.
5 Confirmation of accounts receivable.
6 Review of ageing of accounts receivable with the credit manager.

Assertion	Audit Procedure
a. Ensure that the entity has legal title to accounts receivable (rights and obligations).	
b. Confirm that recorded accounts receivable include all amounts owed to the client (completeness).	
c. Verify that all accounts receivable are recorded in the correct period (cut-off).	
d. Confirm that the allowance for uncollectable accounts is properly stated (valuation and allocation).	
e. Confirm that recorded accounts receivable are valid (existence).	

LO13,14   **10–15**   Adam Signoff-On, independent auditor, was auditing Defence Industries. Signoff-On sent positive accounts receivable confirmations to a number of Defence's government customers. He received a number of returned confirmations marked 'We do not confirm balances because we are on a voucher system.'

Required:

List three audit procedures that Signoff-On might use to ensure the validity of these accounts.

LO13,14,16   **10–16**   During the year Strang Corporation began to encounter cash-flow difficulties, and a cursory review by management revealed receivable collection problems. Strang's management engaged Stanley, an independent auditor, to perform a special investigation. Stanley studied the billing and collection process and noted the following:

- The accounting department employs one bookkeeper, who receives and opens all incoming mail. This bookkeeper is also responsible for depositing receipts, filing remittance advices on a daily basis, recording receipts in the cash receipts journal, and posting receipts in the individual customer accounts and the general ledger accounts. There are no cash sales. The bookkeeper prepares and controls the mailing of monthly statements to customers.
- The concentration of functions and the receivable collection problems caused Stanley to suspect that a systematic defalcation of customers' payments through a delayed posting of remittances (lapping of accounts receivable) is present. Stanley was surprised to find that no customers complained about receiving erroneous monthly statements.

Required:

Identify the procedures Stanley should perform to determine whether lapping exists. Do not discuss deficiencies in the internal control system.

(AICPA, adapted)

LO13,16   **10–17**   You are engaged to audit the Ferrick Corporation for the year ended 31 December 2009. Only merchandise shipped by the Ferrick Corporation to customers up to and including 30 December 2009 has been eliminated from inventory. The inventory as determined by physical inventory count has been recorded on the books by the company's controller. No perpetual inventory records are maintained. All sales are made on an FOB-shipping point basis. You are to assume that all purchase invoices have been correctly recorded. The following lists of sales invoices are entered in the sales journal for the months of December 2009 and January 2010, respectively.

	Sales Invoice Amount	Sales Invoice Date	Cost of Merchandise Sold	Date Shipped
December 2009				
a.	€3,000	21 Dec.	€2,000	31 Dec.
b.	2,000	31 Dec.	800	13 Dec.
c.	1,000	29 Dec.	600	30 Dec.
d.	4,000	31 Dec.	2,400	9 Jan.
e.	10,000	30 Dec.	5,600	29 Dec.*
January 2010				
f.	€6,000	31 Dec.	€4,000	30 Dec.
g.	4,000	2 Jan.	2,300	2 Jan.
h.	8,000	3 Jan.	5,500	31 Dec.
* Shipped to consignee.				

Required:

You are to ensure that there is proper cut-off of sales and inventory. If an item is not properly recorded, prepare the necessary adjusting entries.

Discussion Case

LO15,16   **10–18**   Friendly Furniture is a manufacturer of fine hardwood furniture. During May, Friendly had a flood due to heavy rains at its major manufacturing facility, which damaged about €525,000 of furniture. Friendly is insured for the property loss at replacement value and carries business interruption insurance for lost production. The company anticipates that the total insurance proceeds will exceed the carrying value of the destroyed furniture, and the cost of repairing the facility will be in the range of €700,000 to €1.75 million. The company believes that the insurance carrier will advance approximately 50 per cent of the expected proceeds some time during July. The company has resumed its operations to about one-half of normal capacity and expects to operate at full capacity by September. The company does not expect to file a formal insurance claim until then because it expects that the entire cost of the business interruption will not be known until September. Friendly expects to receive the proceeds of the settlement from the insurance carrier during its fourth quarter.

Based on the minimum amount of the expected proceeds, Friendly would like to recognize a receivable for the insurance proceeds and to report a gain in its financial statements for the period ended 30 June. The company would also like to allocate a portion of the expected proceeds to cost of products sold.

Required:

a   How much of the expected proceeds from insurance coverage, if any, should Friendly include in its 30 June financial statements?

b   Assuming that Friendly records a receivable from the insurance company at 30 June for the proceeds, what type of audit evidence would the auditor gather to support the amount recorded?

Internet Assignment

10–19   Visit the website of a catalogue retailer similar to EarthWear Clothiers, and determine how it processes sales transactions, recognizes revenue and reserves for returns.

Notes

i   IASB issued in 2008 *Discussion Paper: Preliminary Views on Revenue Recognition in Contracts with Customers.* The discussion paper was been prepared as part of a joint project by the IASB and the USA Financial Accounting Standards Board.

ii   Research has shown that accounts receivable confirmations are not always a reliable source of evidence. See P. Caster, R.J. Elder and D.J. Janvrin, 'A Summary of Research and Enforcement Release Evidence on Confirmation Use and Effectiveness', *Auditing: A Journal of Practice & Theory* (November 2008), pp. 253–80.

CHAPTER

11

Auditing the Purchasing Process

❖ LEARNING OBJECTIVES

Upon completion of this chapter you will

- ❖ **LO1** Understand why knowledge of an entity's expense and liability recognition policies is important to the audit.
- ❖ **LO2** Understand the purchasing process.
- ❖ **LO3** Know the types of transactions in the purchasing process and the financial statement accounts affected.
- ❖ **LO4** Be familiar with the types of documents and records used in the purchasing process.
- ❖ **LO5** Understand the functions in the purchasing process.
- ❖ **LO6** Know the appropriate segregation of duties for the purchasing process.
- ❖ **LO7** Understand the inherent risks relevant to the purchasing process and related accounts.
- ❖ **LO8** Know how to assess control risk for a purchasing process.

- ❖ **LO9** Know the key internal controls and develop relevant tests of controls for purchasing, cash disbursements and purchase return transactions.
- ❖ **LO10** Relate the assessment of control risk to substantive testing.
- ❖ **LO11** Know the substantive analytical procedures used to audit accounts payable and accrued expenses.
- ❖ **LO12** Know the tests of details of transactions used to audit accounts payable and accrued expenses.
- ❖ **LO13** Know the tests of details of account balances and disclosures used to audit accounts payable and accrued expenses.
- ❖ **LO14** Understand how confirmations are used to obtain evidence about accounts payable.
- ❖ **LO15** Understand how to evaluate the audit findings and reach a final conclusion on accounts payable and accrued expenses.

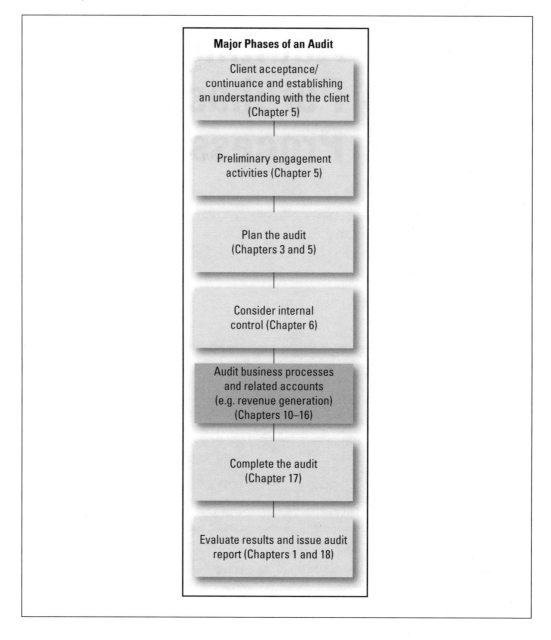

❖ RELEVANT ACCOUNTING AND AUDITING PRONOUNCEMENTS

COSO, Internal Control – Integrated Framework, 1992

COSO, Enterprise Risk Management – Integrated Framework, 2004

COSO, Internal Control over Financial Reporting – Guidance for Smaller Public Companies, 2006

COSO, Guidance on Monitoring Internal Control Systems, 2009

IASB, Framework for the Preparation and Presentation of Financial Statements

IASB, IAS 1, Presentation of Financial Statements

IASB, IAS 24, Related Party Disclosures

ISA 230, Audit Documentation

ISA 240, The Auditor's Responsibilities Relating to Fraud in an Audit of Financial Statements

ISA 315, Identifying and Assessing the Risks of Material Misstatement through Understanding the Entity and Its Environment

ISA 320, Materiality in Planning and Performing an Audit

ISA 330, The Auditor's Responses to Assessed Risks

ISA 450, Evaluation of Misstatements Identified during the Audit

ISA 500, Audit Evidence

ISA 505, External Confirmations

ISA 520, Analytical Procedures

ISA 540, Auditing Accounting Estimates, Including Fair Value Accounting Estimates, and Related Disclosures

ISA 550, Related Parties

ISA 610, Using the Work of Internal Auditors

THE SECOND MAJOR business process focuses on the purchase of and payment for goods and services from outside vendors. The acquisition of goods and services includes the purchase of raw materials, supplies, manufacturing equipment, furniture and fixtures, and payment for repairs and maintenance, utilities and professional services. This process does not include hiring and paying employees or the internal allocation of costs within an entity. Chapter 12 covers the human resource management process.

This chapter begins by reviewing expense and liability recognition concepts with particular emphasis on the categories of expenses. The framework developed in Chapter 10 on the revenue process is used to present the auditor's consideration of internal control. This framework starts with an overview of the purchasing process, including the types of transactions, the documents and records involved, and the functions included in the process. Inherent risk factors that relate directly to the purchasing process are covered next. Assessment of control risk is then presented, followed by a discussion of control activities and tests of controls. The last sections of the chapter cover the audit of accounts payable and accrued expenses, and the major liability accounts affected by the process. Auditing the expense accounts affected by the purchasing process is covered in Chapter 15.

Practice Insight 11.1

The high-profile WorldCom fraud exemplified how expenses may be improperly capitalized as assets to inflate net income. WorldCom inappropriately capitalized as assets costs associated with telephone line maintenance that should have been recorded as period expenses. Some common examples of fraudulent capitalization schemes include software development costs, research and development and start-up costs, interest and advertising costs, recording fictitious fixed assets, and depreciation and amortization schemes.

EXPENSE AND LIABILITY RECOGNITION

LO1

Many transactions processed through a typical purchasing process involve the recognition of an expense and its corresponding liability. As a result, the auditor should understand the basic underlying concepts of expense and liability recognition in order to audit the purchasing process. The International Accounting Standards Board (IASB) *Framework for the Preparation and Presentation of Financial Statements* defines expenses and liability as follows:

> *Expenses are decreases in economic benefits during the accounting period in the form of outflows or depletions of assets or incurrences of liabilities that result in decreases in equity, other than those relating to distributions to equity participants* (para. 70 b).

> *A liability is a present obligation of the entity arising from past events, the settlement of which is expected to result in an outflow from the entity of resources embodying economic benefits* (para. 49 b).

An entity's expense recognition policies and the type of expenses involved affect how the transactions are recorded and accounted for in the financial statements. Expenses may be classified into three categories.

1 Certain expenses can be matched directly with specific transactions or events and are recognized upon recognition of revenue. These types of expenses are referred to as *product costs,* and cost of goods sold includes such expenses.
2 Many expenses are recognized during the period in which cash is spent or liabilities incurred for goods and services that are used up at that time or shortly thereafter. Such expenses cannot be directly related to specific transactions and are assumed to provide no future benefit. These expenses are referred to as *period costs.* Examples of such expenses include administrative salaries and rent expense.
3 Some expenses are allocated by systematic and rational procedures to the periods during which the related assets are expected to provide benefits. Depreciation of plant and equipment is an example of such an expense.

In general, the liabilities normally incurred as part of the purchasing process are trade accounts payable. Other incurred expenses are accrued as liabilities at the end of each accounting period. Most expenses recognized are product or period costs.

The income statement following the international accounting standards either classifies expenses by their nature (for example, depreciation, raw materials, employee benefits, including wages; and advertising) or by their function ('cost of sales' method), whichever provides information that is reliable and more relevant (IAS 1). The functional presentation is used for illustrative purposes in this textbook. This method classifies expenses in the income statement according to their function as part of cost of sales or, for example, as distribution (selling) or administrative expenses. Cost of sales includes product costs and other expenses directly associated with generating sales such as depreciations of assets used in production. Administrative or distribution expenses would include expenses related to these activities and are typically period costs. The classification using the function of expense can provide more relevant information to users than the classification of expenses by nature, but allocating costs to functions may require arbitrary allocations and involve considerable judgement. Following the international accounting standards, entities classifying expenses by function shall disclose additional information on the nature of expenses, including depreciation and amortization expense, and employee benefits expense together with the amount of the net change in inventories for the period.

Accounting for purchasing may involve recognition issues that pose a significant audit risk to auditors. For example, retailers ordinarily get discounts from vendors if they meet sales targets. An important accounting issue is how those discounts are accounted for. The prudent practice is to wait until the targets are met. To inflate earnings, retailers may, however, be inclined to book these payments before they are earned. If the expected level of sales fails to materialize, no discount is due, and the earnings will have been falsely inflated. Exhibit 11–1 illustrates the high-profile accounting scandal of Royal Ahold, where discounts from vendors were falsely recognized in its major subsidiary US Foodservice (see also Exhibit 11–7).

Exhibit 11–1 Royal Ahold's Vendor Receivables: Fraudulent Scheme

Royal Ahold is a long-established Dutch company and one of the word's largest food retailers. During 2002 many analysts expressed concerns over Ahold's accounting practices. Ahold's problems included accounting for volume discounts and rebates at its major subsidiary US Foodservice (USF). A significant portion of Foodservice's operating income was based on vendor payments known as promotional allowances.

On 8 May 2003 Ahold announced that the results of a forensic audit performed by PricewaterhouseCoopers showed that the earnings of USF had been falsely overstated by approximately $880 million during 2000–02. A large part of the restatements were attributed to write-offs of accrued vendor receivables.

On 27 November 2005 Ahold announced that it has reached an agreement with the lead plaintiffs to settle a class action lawsuit* which was pending before the US District Court of the District of Maryland. The $1.1 billion settlement was later approved by the District Court.

On 21 December 2004 and later 18 June 2007 the same US District Court dismissed claims against Ahold's auditor Deloitte: 'Deloitte, despite having been repeatedly lied to by senior USF officers and employee, eventually discovered the fraudulent scheme, in which numerous independent brokers and third-party employees also were complicit, as a result of issuing a substantial number of 'confirms' testing management's representations about the promotional allowances at USF.'

* In a class action, one or more persons called Class Representatives sue on behalf of people who have similar claims. All of these people who have similar claims make up the Class and are Class Members. One court resolves the issues for all Class Members.

Selected sources: 'Retailing – Trouble in Store', *The Economist* (15 May 2003); 'Ahold – Europe's Enron', *The Economist* (27 February 2003); 'Rebuilding Public Confidence in Financial Reporting', IFAC (2003); Royal Ahold Annual Reports (www.ahold.com/en/investors/annual-reports); United States District Court for the District of Maryland, No. 1:03-MD-01539.

❖ OVERVIEW OF THE PURCHASING PROCESS

LO2

A purchase transaction usually begins with a purchase requisition being generated by a department or support function. The purchasing department prepares a purchase order for the purchase of goods or services from a vendor. When the goods are received or the services have been rendered, the entity records a liability to the vendor. Finally, the entity pays the vendor. Exhibit 11–2 describes EarthWear's purchasing system. Before proceeding, take a moment to review this exhibit. Do any risks seem especially apparent? If so, how might these risks impact the nature, timing and extent of your audit procedures?

Exhibit 11–2 Description of EarthWear's Purchasing System

The major purchasing activity for EarthWear involves the purchase of clothing and other products that are styled and quality crafted by the company's design department. All goods are produced by independent manufacturers, except for most of EarthWear's soft luggage. The company purchases merchandise from more than 300 domestic and foreign manufacturers. For many major and most domestic suppliers, goods are ordered and paid for through the company's electronic data interchange (EDI) system. The computerized inventory control system handles the receipt of shipments from manufacturers, permitting faster access to newly arrived merchandise.

Purchases of other goods and services are made in accordance with EarthWear's purchasing authorization policies. Company personnel complete a purchase requisition, which is forwarded to the purchasing department for processing. Purchasing agents obtain competitive bids and enter the information into the purchase order program. A copy of the purchase order is sent to the vendor. Goods are received at the receiving department, where the information is agreed to the purchase order (receiving report). The receiving report is forwarded to the accounts payable department, which matches the receiving report to the purchase order and vendor invoice. The accounts payable department prepares a voucher packet and enters the information into the accounts payable program.

When payment is due on a vendor invoice, the accounts payable program generates a cash disbursement report that is reviewed by the accounts payable department. Items approved for payment are entered into the cash disbursement program, and, if applicable, a cheque is printed. The cheques are sent to the cashier's department for mailing. Final approval for all electronic fund transfers (EFT), including EDI transactions is made by the accounts payable department.

Figure 11–1 presents the flowchart for EarthWear's purchasing system, which serves as a framework for discussing **control activities** (client's control procedures) and **tests of controls**. As mentioned previously, accounting applications are tailored to meet the specific needs of the client. The reader should focus on the basic concepts so that they can be applied to the specific purchasing processes encountered. The following topics related to the purchasing process are covered:

- Types of transactions and financial statement accounts affected.
- Types of documents and records.
- The major functions.
- The key segregation of duties.

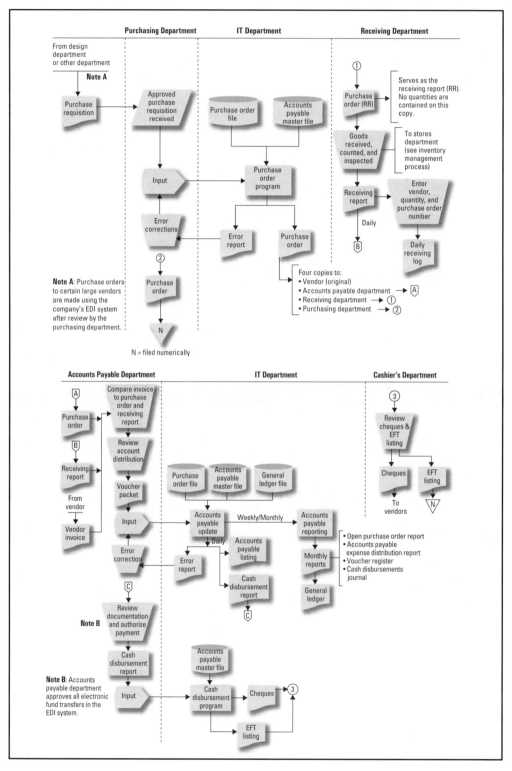

Figure 11–1   Flowchart of the Purchasing Process: EarthWear Clothiers

Types of Transactions and Financial Statement Accounts Affected

LO3 Three types of transactions are processed through the purchasing process:

1 Purchase of goods and services for cash or credit.
2 Payment of the liabilities arising from such purchases.
3 Return of goods to suppliers for cash or credit.

The first type is a purchase transaction that includes acquiring goods and services. The second type is a cash disbursement transaction that involves paying the liabilities that result from purchasing goods and services. The final type is a purchase return transaction, in which goods previously purchased are returned to a supplier for cash or credit.

The purchasing process affects many accounts in the financial statements. The more common accounts affected by each type of transaction are:

Type of Transaction	Account Affected
Purchase transaction	Accounts payable
	Inventory
	Purchases or cost of goods sold
	Various asset and expense accounts
Cash disbursement transaction	Cash
	Accounts payable
	Cash discounts
	Various asset and expense accounts
Purchase return transaction	Purchase returns
	Purchase allowances
	Accounts payable
	Various asset and expense accounts

Types of Documents and Records

LO4 Table 11–1 lists the important documents and records that are normally involved in the purchasing process. Each of these items is briefly discussed here. The use of an advanced IT system may affect the form of the documents and the auditor's approach to testing the purchasing process. For example, goods and services may be primarily paid for through electronic funds transfer, in which client's payments are electronically transferred to the vendor's bank account.

Table 11–1 Documents and Records Involved in the Purchasing Process
Purchase requisition.
Purchase order.
Receiving report.
Vendor invoice.
Voucher.
Voucher register/purchases journal.
Accounts payable subsidiary ledger.
Vendor statement.
Electronic funds transfer and cheques.
Cash disbursements journal.

Purchase Requisition

This document requests goods or services for an authorized individual or department within the entity. Examples of such requests include an order for supplies from an office supervisor and an order for newspaper advertising space from a marketing manager. In EarthWear's purchasing system, the design department would generate purchase requisitions to acquire goods for sale.

Purchase Order

This document includes the description, quality and quantity of, and other information on, the goods or services being purchased. The purchase order also indicates who approved the acquisition and represents the authorization to purchase the goods or services. The purchase order may be mailed, faxed, sent via PC/Internet, or placed by telephone with the supplier or vendor. At EarthWear some purchase orders may be generated by the design department, reviewed by a purchasing agent, and then sent to a vendor using the company's EDI system.

Receiving Report

This document records the receipt of goods. Often, the receiving report is a copy of the purchase order with the quantities omitted. This control activity encourages receiving department personnel to make an adequate, independent count of the goods received. Receiving department personnel record the date, description, quantity, and other information on this document. In some instances, the quality of the goods is determined by receiving department personnel. In other cases, an inspection department determines whether the goods meet the required specifications. The receiving report is important because receiving goods is generally the event that leads to recognition of the liability by the entity.

Vendor Invoice

This document is the bill from the vendor. The vendor invoice includes the description and quantity of the goods shipped or services provided, the price including freight, the terms of trade including cash discounts, and the date billed. Increasingly, vendor invoices are transferred electronically between businesses by email or as part of an EDI system. Highly integrated EDI systems between buyer and supplier may be 'invoiceless'.

Voucher

This document is frequently used by entities to control payment for acquired goods and services. This document serves as the basis for recording a vendor's invoice in the voucher register or purchases journal. In many purchasing systems, such as EarthWear's, the voucher is attached to the purchase requisition, purchase order, receiving report and vendor invoice to create a *voucher packet*. The voucher packet thus contains all the relevant documentation supporting a purchase transaction.

Voucher Register/Purchases Journal

A voucher register is used to record the vouchers for goods and services. The voucher register contains numerous columns for recording the account classifications for the goods or services, including a column for recording credits to accounts payable, and columns for recording debits to asset accounts such as inventory and expense accounts such as repairs and maintenance. The voucher register also contains columns for miscellaneous debits and credits. Some entities use a purchases journal instead of a voucher register. With a purchases journal, either vouchers or vendors' invoices may be used to record the liability. The major difference between a voucher register and a purchases journal is in the way individual vouchers or vendor invoices are summarized. When a voucher register is used, the details of accounts payable are normally represented by a list of unpaid vouchers. With a purchases journal, subsidiary records are normally maintained by the vendor in much the same manner as an accounts receivable subsidiary ledger. However, with computerization of accounts payable records, such distinctions are disappearing. By assigning a vendor number to each voucher, the voucher register can be sorted by vendor to produce a subsidiary ledger for accounts payable.

Accounts Payable Subsidiary Ledger

When a purchases journal is utilized, this subsidiary ledger records the transactions with, and the balance owed to, a vendor. When a voucher register system is used, the subsidiary ledger is a listing of the unpaid vouchers. The total in the subsidiary ledger should equal the balance in the general ledger accounts payable account.

Vendor Statement

This statement may periodically be sent by the vendor to indicate the beginning balance, current period purchases and payments, and the ending balance. The vendor's statement represents the purchase activity recorded on the vendor's records. It may differ from the client's records because of errors or, more often, timing differences due to delays in shipping goods or recording cash receipts. The client verifies the accuracy of its records by comparing vendor statements with the accounts payable records.

Electronic Funds Transfer Listing and Cheques

Goods and services are increasingly paid for through electronic funds transfer. Cheques signed by an authorized individual may also be used to pay for goods or services.

Cash Disbursements Journal

This journal records disbursements, either made electronically or by cheque. The cash disbursements journal contains columns for recording credits to cash and debits to accounts payable and cash discounts. Columns may also record miscellaneous debits and credits. Payments recorded in the cash disbursements journal are also recorded in the voucher register or in the accounts payable subsidiary ledger, depending on which system is used by the entity.

❖ The Major Functions

LO5

The principal business objectives of the purchasing process are acquiring goods and services at the lowest cost consistent with quality and service requirements, and effectively using cash resources to pay for those goods and services. Table 11–2 lists the functions that are normally part of the purchasing process.

Table 11–2 Functions of the Purchasing Process
Requisitioning. Initiation and approval of requests for goods and services by authorized individuals consistent with management criteria.
Purchasing. Approval of purchase orders and proper execution as to price, quantity, quality and vendor.
Receiving. Receipt of properly authorized goods or services.
Invoice processing. Processing of vendor invoices for goods and services received; also, processing of adjustments for allowances, discounts and returns.
Disbursements. Processing of payment to vendors.
Accounts payable. Recording of all vendor invoices, cash disbursements and adjustments in individual vendor accounts.
General ledger. Proper accumulation, classification and summarization of purchases, cash disbursements and payables in the general ledger.

Requisitioning

The initial function in the purchasing process is a request for goods or services by an authorized individual from any department or functional area within the entity (see Fig. 11–1). The important issue is that the request meets the authorization procedures implemented by the entity. One frequent organizational control is the establishment of authorization monetary limits for different levels of employees and executives. For example, department supervisors may be authorized to acquire goods or services up to €1,000, department managers up to €5,000, and divisional heads up to €25,000, while any expenditure greater than €100,000 requires approval by the board of directors.

> ### Practice Insight 11.2
>
> Electronic forms, stored in digital format databases, allow for automatic information routing and integration into other information systems applications. The use of electronic forms is ideal for tracking and managing processes when human oversight, approvals or information input need to be combined with standard elements of information. For example, supplies may be requisitioned by an employee and automatically forwarded to a manager for approval. Once approved, the order may then be input into an EDI translator and forwarded to the appropriate vendor bymeans of a structured XML EDI transaction. Electronic forms add value to the organization, but the auditor must understand these IT systems and test the E-commerce, general and application controls.

Purchasing

The purchasing function executes properly authorized purchase orders. This function is normally performed by a purchasing department (see Fig. 11–1), which is headed by a purchasing manager (or agent) and has one or more buyers responsible for specific goods or services. The purchasing function ensures that goods and services are acquired in appropriate quantities and at the lowest price consistent with quality standards and delivery schedules. Using multiple vendors and requiring competitive bidding are two ways the purchasing function can achieve its objectives.

Receiving

The receiving function is responsible for receiving, counting and inspecting goods received from vendors. The personnel in the receiving department complete a receiving report that is forwarded to the accounts payable function.

Invoice Processing

The accounts payable department (see Fig. 11–1) processes invoices to ensure that all goods and services received are recorded as assets or expenses, and that the corresponding liability is recognized. This function involves matching purchase orders to receiving reports and vendor invoices as to terms, quantities, prices, and extensions. The invoice-processing function also compares the account distributions with established account classifications.

The invoice-processing function is also responsible for purchased goods returned to vendors. Appropriate records and control activities must document the return of the goods and initiate any charges back to the vendor.

Disbursements

The disbursement function is responsible for authorizing electronic funds transfers and preparing and signing cheques for paying vendors. Adequate supporting documentation must verify that the disbursement is for a legitimate business purpose, that the transaction was properly authorized and that the account distribution is appropriate. To reduce the possibility that the invoice will be paid twice, all documentation (such as purchase order, receiving report and vendor invoice) should be marked 'CANCELLED' or 'PAID' by the cashier's department. Finally, electronic transfer should be made, or the cheques should be mailed to the vendor by the cashier's department or treasurer.

When electronic funds transfer or IT is used to prepare cheques, adequate user controls must ensure that only authorized transactions are submitted for payment. Adequate control totals should also be used to agree the amount of payables submitted with the amount of cash disbursed. Payments over a specified limit should be reviewed. For example, in EarthWear's system (see Fig. 11–1), the accounts payable department matches the purchase order to the receiving report and the vendor's invoice. The voucher is then input into the accounts payable program. When the vouchers are due for payment, they are printed out on a cash disbursement report. Accounts payable personnel review the items to be paid and input them into the cash disbursement program.

Practice Insight 11.3

Fraudulent disbursements may include payments made to shell companies or ghost vendors, commission expense schemes, purchases made by employees for personal benefit, duplicate expense reimbursements, and other fictitious expenses.

Accounts Payable

The accounts payable department (see Fig. 11–1) is also responsible for ensuring that all vendor invoices, cash disbursements and adjustments are recorded in the accounts payable records. In IT systems, these entries may be made directly as part of the normal processing of purchase, cash disbursement, or returns and allowances transactions. Proper use of control totals and daily activity reports provides controls for proper recording.

General Ledger

The main objective of the general ledger function for the purchasing process is to ensure that all purchases, cash disbursements and payables are properly accumulated, classified and summarized in the accounts. In an IT system, such as at EarthWear, the use of control or summary totals ensures that this function is performed correctly. The accounting department is normally responsible for this function.

The Key Segregation of Duties

LO6

As discussed in previous chapters, proper segregation of duties is one of the most important control activities in any accounting system. Duties should be assigned so that no one individual can control all phases of processing a transaction in a way that permits errors or fraud to go undetected. Because of the potential for theft and fraud in the purchasing process, individuals responsible for requisitioning, purchasing and receiving should be segregated from the invoice-processing, accounts payable and general ledger functions. If IT is used extensively in the purchasing application, there should be proper segregation of duties in the IT department. Table 11–3 shows the key segregation of duties for the purchasing process, and examples of possible errors or fraud that can result from conflicts in duties.

Table 11–3 Key Segregation of Duties in the Purchasing Process and Possible Errors or Fraud	
Segregation of Duties	*Possible Errors or Fraud Resulting from Conflicts of Duties*
The purchasing function should be segregated from the requisitioning and receiving functions.	If one individual is responsible for the requisition, purchasing and receiving functions, fictitious or unauthorized purchases can be made. This can result in the theft of goods and possibly payment for unauthorized purchases.
The invoice-processing function should be segregated from the accounts payable function.	If one individual is responsible for the invoice-processing and the accounts payable functions, purchase transactions can be processed at the wrong price or terms, or a cash disbursement can be processed for goods or services not received. This can result in overpayment for goods and services or the theft of cash.
The disbursement function should be segregated from the accounts payable function.	If one individual is responsible for the disbursement function and also has access to the accounts payable records, unauthorized payments supported by fictitious documents can be issued, and unauthorized transactions can be recorded. This can result in theft of the entity's cash.
The accounts payable function should be segregated from the general ledger function.	If one individual is responsible for the accounts payable records and also for the general ledger, that individual can conceal any defalcation that would normally be detected by reconciling subsidiary records with the general ledger control account.

Table 11–4 shows the proper segregation of duties for purchasing and accounts payable functions across the various departments that process purchase transactions. Using this table, briefly analyse EarthWear's flowchart as shown in Fig. 11–1. Evaluate whether EarthWear has sufficient segregation of duties and, if not, what errors or fraud could occur because of those conflicts of duties?

Table 11–4 Segregation of Duties for Purchasing and Accounts Payable Functions by Department					
	Department				
Purchasing and Accounts			Accounts		
Payable Function	Purchasing	Receiving	Payable	Cashier	IT
Preparation and approval of purchase order	X				
Receipt, counting and inspection of purchased materials		X			
Receipt of vendor invoices and matching them with supporting documents			X		
Coding (or checking) of account distributions			X		
Updating of accounts payable records			X		X
Preparation of payment to vendors					X
Electronic funds transfer, signing and mailing of vendor cheques				X	
Preparation of voucher register					X
Reconciliation of voucher register to general ledger			X		

INHERENT RISK ASSESSMENT

LO7

At the beginning of the audit of the purchasing process and its related accounts, the auditor should consider the relevant inherent risk factors that may impact the transactions processed and the financial statement accounts. As mentioned previously, most business risks are viewed as inherent risks. The following factors taken from Chapter 3 should be considered by the auditor in assessing the inherent risk for the purchasing process.

Industry-Related Factors

When auditing the purchasing process, the auditor must consider two important industry-related factors in assessing inherent risk: whether the supply of raw materials is adequate and how volatile raw material prices are. If the entity deals with many vendors and prices tend to be relatively stable, there is less risk that the entity's operations will be affected by raw material shortages or that production costs will be difficult to control.

Some industries, however, are subject to such industry-related factors. For example, in the high-technology sector, there have been situations in which an entity has depended on a single vendor to supply a critical component, such as a specialized computer chip. When the vendor has been unable to provide the component, the entity has suffered production shortages and shipping delays that have significantly affected financial performance. Other industries that use commodities such as oil as raw materials may be subject to both shortages and price instability. The auditor needs to assess the effects of such industry-related inherent risk factors in terms of **assertions** such as valuation.

Misstatements Detected in Prior Audits

Generally, the purchasing process and its related accounts are not difficult to audit and do not result in contentious accounting issues. However, auditing research has shown that the purchasing process and its related accounts are likely to contain material misstatements.[i] The auditor's previous experience with the entity's purchasing process should be reviewed as a starting point for determining inherent risk.

CONTROL RISK ASSESSMENT

LO8

The discussion of control risk assessment follows the framework outlined in Chapter 6 on internal control and Chapter 10 on the revenue process. Again it is assumed that the auditor has decided to follow a **reliance strategy**. Figure 11–2 summarizes the major steps involved in setting control risk for the purchasing cycle.

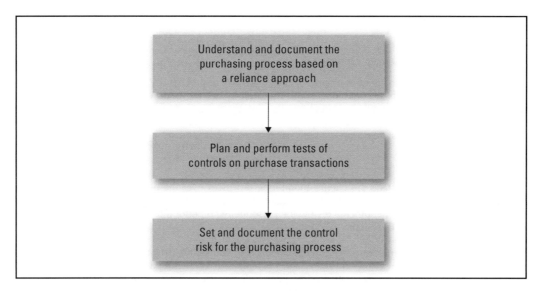

Figure 11–2 Major Steps in Setting Control Risk for the Purchasing Process

Understand and Document Internal Control

In order to set control risk for the purchasing process, the auditor must understand the five components of internal control.

Control Environment

Table 6–3 in Chapter 6 lists factors that affect the control environment. Two factors are particularly important when the auditor considers the control environment and the purchasing process: the entity's organizational structure and its methods of assigning authority and responsibility. The entity's organizational structure for purchasing may impact the auditor's assessment of control risk because control activities are implemented within an organizational structure. Authority and responsibility for purchasing are usually granted via procedures that limit the amount of purchases that can be made by various levels of authority within the entity. The remaining discussions of the purchasing process assume that the control environment factors are reliable.

The Entity's Risk Assessment Process

The auditor must understand how management weighs the risks that are relevant to the purchasing process, estimates their significance, assesses the likelihood of their occurrence and decides what actions to take to address those risks. Some of these risks include a new or revamped information system, rapid growth and new technology. Each of these factors can represent a serious risk to an entity's internal control system over purchases.

Control Activities

When a reliance strategy is adopted for the purchasing process, the auditor needs to understand the controls that exist to ensure that management's objectives are being met. More specifically, the auditor identifies the controls that assure the auditor that the assertions are being met.

Information Systems and Communication

For each major class of transactions in the purchasing process, the auditor again needs to obtain the following information:

- How purchase, cash disbursements and purchase return transactions are initiated.

- The accounting records, supporting documents and accounts that are involved in processing purchases, cash disbursements and purchase return transactions.
- The flow of each type of transaction from initiation to inclusion in the financial statements, including computer processing of the data.
- The process used to estimate accrued liabilities.

The auditor develops an understanding of the purchasing process by conducting a transaction walk-through. In the case of a continuing audit, the auditor has the prior years' documentation of the process to assist in the walk-through, although the possibility of changes in the system must be considered. If the system has been changed substantially or the audit is for a new client, the auditor should prepare new documentation of the system.

Monitoring of Controls

The auditor needs to understand the client's monitoring processes over the purchasing process, including how management assesses the design and operation of controls. It also involves understanding how supervisory personnel within the process review the personnel who perform the controls and evaluating the performance of the entity's IT system.

The auditor can document the purchasing process using procedures manuals, narrative descriptions, internal control questionnaires and flowcharts. For example, the following partial questionnaire could be used to record the auditor's documentation of the information about the controls in the purchasing process. A 'Yes' response would indicate that the control was present.

	Question	Yes	No
1.	Are there written purchasing policies and procedures?		
2.	Are purchase requisitions approved in accordance with management's authorization?		
3.	Are purchases made from approved vendors?		
4.	Are price quotations requested for purchases over an established amount?		
5.	Do purchase orders include adequate descriptions, terms, and instructions?		
6.	Are purchase orders approved by authorized personnel before issuance?		

Plan and Perform Tests of Controls

The auditor systematically analyses the purchasing process in order to identify controls that ensure that material misstatements are either prevented or detected and corrected. The controls can be relied upon by the auditor to reduce the control risk. For example, the client may have formal procedures for authorizing the acquisition of goods and services. The auditor may decide to rely on these controls to reduce the control risk for the authorization assertion. Tests of controls would then be necessary to verify that this control is operating effectively. The auditor would examine a sample of purchase transactions to determine if the acquisition of the goods or services is consistent with the entity's authorization policy.

Set and Document Control Risk

After the controls are tested, the auditor sets the achieved level of control risk. When tests of controls support the planned level of control risk, no modifications are normally necessary to the planned level of detection risk, and the auditor may proceed with the planned substantive procedures. When the tests of controls do not support the planned level of control risk, the auditor must set a higher level of control risk. This results in a lower level of detection risk and leads to more substantive procedures than originally planned.

As discussed earlier, the auditor should establish and document the achieved level of control risk. Documentation of the control risk for the purchasing process might include a flowchart, the results of tests of controls and a memorandum indicating the auditor's overall conclusion about the control risk.

❖ CONTROL ACTIVITIES AND TESTS OF CONTROLS: PURCHASE TRANSACTIONS

Table 11–5 presents the assertions about transactions and events, while Table 11–6 summarizes the assertions for purchase transactions along with some examples of possible misstatements. For each of these misstatements we have included one or two possible control activities that management could implement to mitigate the risk as well as some example tests of controls that the auditor could use to test those controls. This table is not an exhaustive list of misstatements, control activities or tests of controls for purchase transactions; rather it provides some specific examples by assertion to help you understand the underlying concepts. Most of these controls exist within EarthWear's purchasing process (see Fig. 11–1). The following sections also discuss control activities and tests of controls that are relevant for EarthWear's purchasing process.

Table 11–5 Assertions about Classes of Transactions and Events for the Period under Audit

- **Occurrence**. All purchase and cash disbursement transactions and events that have been recorded have occurred and pertain to the entity.
- **Completeness**. All purchase and cash disbursement transactions and events that should have been recorded have been recorded.
- **Authorization**. All purchase and cash disbursement transactions and events are properly authorized.
- **Accuracy**. Amounts and other data relating to recorded purchase and cash disbursement transactions and events have been recorded appropriately and properly accumulated from journals and ledgers.
- **Cut-off**. Purchase and cash disbursement transactions and events have been recorded in the correct accounting period.
- **Classification**. Purchase and cash disbursement transactions and events have been recorded in the proper accounts.

Table 11–6 Summary of Assertions, Possible Misstatements, Example Control Activities and Example Tests of Controls for Purchase Transactions

Assertion	Possible Misstatement	Example Control Activity	Example Test of Controls
Occurrence	Purchase recorded, goods or services not ordered or received	Segregation of duties	Observe and evaluate proper segregation of duties.
		Purchase not recorded without approved purchase order and receiving report	Test a sample of vouchers for the presence of an authorized purchase order and receiving report; if IT application, examine application controls.
		Accounting for numerical sequence of receiving reports and vouchers	Review and test client procedures for accounting for numerical sequence of receiving reports and vouchers; if IT application, examine application controls.
		Cancellation of documents	Examine paid vouchers and supporting documents for indication of cancellation.
Completeness	Purchases made but not recorded	Accounting for numerical sequence of purchase orders, receiving reports, and vouchers	Review client's procedures for accounting for numerical sequence of purchase orders, receiving reports, and vouchers; if IT application, examine application controls.
		Receiving reports matched to vendor invoices and entered in the purchases journal	Trace a sample of receiving reports to their respective vendor invoices and vouchers. Trace a sample of vouchers to the purchases journal.

Authorization	Purchase of goods or services not authorized	Approval of acquisitions consistent with the client's authorization monetary limits	Review client's monetary limits authorization for acquisitions.
		Approved purchase requisition and purchase order	Examine purchase requisitions or purchase orders for proper approval; if IT is used for automatic ordering, examine application controls.
	Purchase of goods or services at unauthorized prices or on unauthorized terms	Competitive bidding procedures followed	Review client's competitive bidding procedures.
Accuracy	Vendor invoice improperly priced or incorrectly calculated	Mathematical accuracy of vendor invoice verified	Recompute the mathematical accuracy of vendor invoice.
		Purchase order agreed to receiving report and vendor's invoice for product, quantity and price	Agree the information on a sample of voucher packets for product, quantity and price.
	Purchase transactions not posted to the purchases journal or the accounts payable subsidiary records	Vouchers reconciled to daily accounts payable listing	Examine reconciliation of vouchers to daily accounts payable report; if IT application, examine application controls.
	Amounts from purchases journal not posted correctly to the general ledger	Daily postings to purchases journal reconciled with postings to accounts payable subsidiary records	Examine reconciliation of entries in purchases journal with entries to accounts payable subsidiary records; if IT application, examine application controls.
Cut-off	Purchase transactions recorded in the wrong period	All receiving reports forwarded to the accounts payable department daily	Compare the dates on receiving reports with the dates on the relevant vouchers.
		Existence of procedures that require recording the purchases as soon as possible after goods or services are received	Compare the dates on vouchers with the dates they were recorded in the purchases journal.
Classification	Purchase transaction not properly classified	Chart of accounts	Review purchases journal and general ledger for reasonableness.

Note: Receiving reports are used to acknowledge the receipt of tangible goods such as raw materials, office supplies and equipment. For services such as utilities and advertising, receiving reports are not used.

Occurrence of Purchase Transactions

The auditor's concern in testing the occurrence of purchase transactions is that fictitious or non-existent purchases may have been recorded in the client's records. If fraudulent transactions are recorded, assets or expenses will be overstated. A liability will also be recorded and a resulting payment made, usually to the individual who initiated the fictitious purchase transactions. Proper segregation of duties is the major control for preventing fictitious purchases. The critical segregation of duties is the separation of the requisitioning and purchasing functions from the accounts payable and disbursement functions. If one individual can both process a purchase order and gain access to the accounting records, there is an increased risk that fictitious purchase transactions will be recorded.

The other control activities shown in Table 11–6 also reduce the risk of purchase transactions being recorded without the goods or services being received. Even with proper segregation of duties, no purchase transaction should be recorded without an approved purchase order and a receiving report. The presence of an approved purchase order ensures that the purchase was authorized, and the presence of a receiving report indicates that the goods were received. In an IT environment, such as EarthWear's, the auditor can test the **application controls** to ensure that purchases are recorded only after an approved purchase order has been entered and the goods received. Accounting for the numerical sequence of receiving reports and vouchers can be accomplished either manually or by using a computer. This control prevents the recording of fictitious purchase transactions through the use of receiving documents or vouchers that are numbered outside the sequence of properly authorized documents. Cancellation of all supporting documents ensures that a purchase transaction is not recorded and paid for a second time. You should keep in mind that there are some types of transactions that are processed through the purchasing process that will not be accompanied by a purchase requisition and receiving report. For example, services for utility and advertising would not use a receiving report.

Completeness of Purchase Transactions

If the client fails to record a purchase that has been made, assets or expenses will be understated and the corresponding accounts payable will also be understated. Controls that ensure that the completeness assertion is being met include accounting for the numerical sequences of purchase orders, receiving reports and vouchers; matching receiving reports with vendor invoices; and reconciling vouchers to the daily accounts payable report. For example, EarthWear uses control totals to reconcile the daily number of vouchers processed with the daily accounts payable listing.

Tests of controls for these control activities are listed in Table 11–6. For example, the auditor can trace a sample of receiving reports to their corresponding vendor invoices and vouchers. The vouchers can then be traced to the voucher register to ensure that each voucher was recorded. Again, these tests can be performed either manually or with CAATs. If each receiving report is matched to a vendor invoice and voucher and the voucher was included in the voucher register, the auditor has a high level of assurance as to the completeness assertion.

The auditor's concern with the completeness assertion also arises when the accounts payable and accrued expenses accounts are audited at year end. If the client has strong controls for the completeness assertion, the auditor can reduce the scope of the search for unrecorded liabilities at year end. This issue is discussed in more detail later in this chapter.

Authorization of Purchase Transactions

Possible misstatements due to improper authorization include the purchase of unauthorized goods and services and the purchase of goods or services at unauthorized prices or terms. The primary control to prevent these misstatements is the use of an authorization schedule or table that stipulates the amount that different levels of employees are authorized to purchase. Tests of controls include examination of purchase requisitions and purchase orders for proper approval consistent with the authorization table. If the client uses a sophisticated production system that reorders goods automatically, the auditor should examine and test the programmed controls. Competitive bidding procedures should be followed to ensure that goods and services are acquired at competitive prices and on competitive terms.

Accuracy of Purchase Transactions

A possible misstatement for the accuracy assertion is that purchase transactions may be recorded at incorrect amounts due to improper pricing or erroneous calculations. The purchase order should contain the expected price for the goods or services being purchased, based on price quotes obtained by the purchasing agents or prices contained in catalogues or published price lists. If the goods or services are purchased under a contract, the price should be stipulated in the contract. For example, an accounts payable clerk should compare the purchase order with the receiving report and vendor invoice (see Fig. 11–1) and investigate significant differences in quantities, prices and freight charges. The accounts payable clerk also checks the mathematical accuracy of the vendor invoice. The auditor's test of controls for this assertion involves reperforming the accounts payable clerk's duties on a sample of voucher packets.

The accuracy assertion is also concerned with proper posting of information to the purchases journal, accounts payable subsidiary records and general ledger. Control totals should be used to reconcile vouchers to the daily accounts payable listing, or else the daily postings to the purchases journal should be reconciled to the accounts payable subsidiary records. In addition, the voucher register or accounts payable subsidiary ledger should be reconciled to the general ledger control account. If these control activities are performed manually, the auditor can review and examine the reconciliations prepared by the client's personnel. In an IT application, such controls would be programmed and reconciled by the control groups in the IT and accounts payable departments. The auditor can examine the programmed controls and review the reconciliations.

Cut-off of Purchase Transactions

The client should have controls to ensure that purchase transactions are recorded promptly and in the proper period. For example, the client's procedures should require that all receiving reports be forwarded to the accounts payable department daily. There should also be a requirement in the accounts payable department that receiving reports be matched on a timely basis with the original purchase order and the related vendor invoice. In EarthWear's system, the receiving department forwards the receiving report to the accounts payable department daily. Within the accounts payable department, the vendor invoices are matched immediately with the original purchase orders and the receiving reports. The auditor can test these control activities by comparing the date on the receiving report with the date on the voucher. There should seldom be a long period between the two dates. The auditor also wants to ensure that the vouchers are recorded in the accounting records in the correct period. This can be tested by comparing the dates on vouchers with the dates the vouchers were recorded in the voucher register.

Classification of Purchase Transactions

Proper classification of purchase transactions is an important assertion for the purchasing process. If purchase transactions are not properly classified, asset and expense accounts will be misstated. Two main controls are used for ensuring that purchase transactions are properly classified. First, the client should use a chart of accounts. Second, there should be independent approval and review of the general ledger accounts charged for the acquisition. A typical procedure is for the department or function that orders the goods or services to indicate which general ledger account to charge. Accounts payable department personnel then review the account distribution for reasonableness (see Fig. 11–1). A test of controls for this assertion involves examining a sample of voucher packets for proper classification.

CONTROL ACTIVITIES AND TESTS OF CONTROLS: CASH DISBURSEMENT TRANSACTIONS

LO9

Table 11–7 summarizes the assertions for cash disbursement transactions along with some examples of possible misstatements. For each of these misstatements we have included one or two possible control activities that management could implement to mitigate the risk as well as some example tests of controls that the auditor could use to test those controls. This table is not an exhaustive list of misstatements, control activities or tests of controls for cash disbursement transactions; rather it provides some specific examples by assertion to help you understand the underlying concepts.

Table 11–7 Summary of Assertions, Possible Misstatements, Example Control Activities and Example Tests of Controls for Cash Disbursement Transactions			
Assertion	*Possible Misstatement*	*Example Control Activity*	*Example Test of Controls*
Occurrence	Cash disbursement recorded but not made	Segregation of duties	Observe and evaluate proper segregation of duties.
		Vendor statements independently reviewed and reconciled to accounts payable records	Review client's procedures for reconciling vendor statements.
		Bank reconciliations prepared and reviewed regularly	Review bank reconciliations for indication of independent review.
Completeness	Cash disbursement made but not recorded	Same as above	Same as above.
		Management reviews listing of cash disbursements prior to release	Examine and test indication of management reviews listing of cash disbursements.

		Daily cash disbursements reconciled to postings to accounts payable subsidiary records	Review client's procedures for reconciling daily cash disbursements with postings to accounts payable subsidiary records; if IT applications, test application controls.
Authorization	Cash disbursement not authorized	Segregation of duties	Evaluate segregation of duties.
		Electronic cash disbursements transfers and cheques prepared only after all source documents have been independently approved	Examine indication of approval on voucher packet.
		Individuals who make electronic cash disbursements transfers and issue cheques are authorized to do so	Review and test client's procedures for authorization.
Accuracy	Cash disbursement recorded at incorrect amount	Daily cash disbursements report reconciled to electronic cash disbursements transfers performed and cheques issued	Review reconciliation.
		Vendor statements reconciled to accounts payable records and independently reviewed	Review reconciliation.
		Bank statements regularly reconciled and independently reviewed	Review bank reconciliations.
	Cash disbursement posted to the wrong vendor account	Vendor statements reconciled and independently reviewed	Review reconciliation.
	Cash disbursements journal not summarized properly or not properly posted to general ledger accounts	Monthly cash disbursements journal agreed to general ledger postings	Review postings from cash disbursements journal to the general ledger.
		Accounts payable subsidiary records reconciled to general ledger control account	Review reconciliation.
Cut-off	Cash disbursement recorded in wrong period	Reconciliation of electronic funds transfer and cheques issued with postings to the cash disbursements journal and accounts payable subsidiary records	Review reconciliations.
Classification	Cash disbursement charged to wrong account	Chart of accounts	Review cash disbursements journal for reasonableness of account distribution.
		Independent approval and review of general ledger account on voucher packet	Review general ledger account code on voucher packet for reasonableness.

In an electronic funds transfer system a variety of IT controls may be used. General authorization controls exist to limit access to information, accounting records and the electronic funds payment systems to authorized personnel. Application controls relate to procedures used to initiate, record, process and report disbursements. These include programmed edit checks to reject invalid disbursements, ensure that disbursements are recorded only once, and to validate for correct amount and account. Monitoring programs may also used to identify and report on all online users and disbursements. Strong **general controls** and application controls are effective in preventing and detecting misstatements. (See also Chapter 6 on controls in an IT environment and Chapter 10 on application controls of cash receipts.)

Occurrence of Cash Disbursement Transactions

For the occurrence assertion, the auditor is concerned with a misstatement caused by a cash disbursement being recorded in the client's records when no payment has actually been made. Electronic disbursement transfer reduces the risk of such misstatements, for example that the payment instrument such as a cheque is lost or stolen before it is mailed. The primary control activities used to prevent occurrence misstatements include proper segregation of duties, independent reconciliation and review of vendor statements and bank reconciliations.

Table 11–7 lists tests of controls that the auditor can use to verify the effectiveness of the client's controls. For example, the auditor can observe and evaluate the client's segregation of duties and review the client's procedures for reconciling vendor statements and bank statements.

Completeness of Cash Disbursement Transactions

The major misstatement related to the completeness assertion is that a cash disbursement is made but not recorded in the client's records. In addition to the control activities used for the occurrence assertion, management's reviews of vendor payments lists and reconciliation of the daily cash disbursements with postings to the accounts payable subsidiary records helps to ensure that all electronic cash disbursements transfers and issued cheques are recorded. The auditor's tests of controls may include reviewing and testing the client's procedures for reviewing vendor payments lists and the client's reconciliation procedures.

Authorization of Cash Disbursement Transactions

Proper segregation of duties reduces the likelihood that unauthorized cash disbursements are made. It is important that an individual who approves a purchase does not have direct access to the cash disbursement for it. In EarthWear's purchasing process, the purchasing department functions are segregated from those of the accounts payable and cashier's departments. The other major control over unauthorized cash disbursements is that payments are not prepared unless all source documents (purchase requisition, purchase order, receiving report, and vendor's invoice) are included in the voucher packet and approved. For EarthWear's purchasing process, a complete voucher packet must be present in order to record the liability and authorize payment. Additionally, access to the electronic funds transfer system and issue of cheques should be controlled and limited to authorized individuals. For example, passwords should be changed regularly for individuals authorized to transfer funds.

Accuracy of Cash Disbursement Transactions

The potential misstatement related to the accuracy assertion is that the payment amount is recorded incorrectly. To detect such errors, the client's personnel should reconcile the total of electronic cash disbursements transfer and the cheques issued on a particular day with the daily cash disbursements report. The client's control activities should regularly require reconciliation of vendor statements to the accounts payable records. Bank reconciliations also provide controls for detecting misstatements caused by cash disbursements being made in incorrect amounts. Each of these reconciliations should be independently reviewed by the client's personnel. The auditor's test of controls involves reviewing the various reconciliations.

Two other possible misstatements are of concern with the accuracy assertion: (1) cash disbursements are posted to the wrong vendor accounts; and (2) the cash disbursements journal is not summarized properly or the wrong general ledger account is posted. The reconciliation of vendors' monthly statements is an effective control activity for detecting payments posted to the wrong vendor accounts. Agreement of the cash disbursements journal to general ledger postings and reconciliation of the accounts payable subsidiary records to the general ledger control account are effective control activities for preventing summarization and posting errors (see Fig. 11–1). The auditor's tests of controls would include checking postings to the general ledger and reviewing the various reconciliations.

Cut-off of Cash Disbursement Transactions

The client should establish procedures to ensure that electronic funds transfers and cheques prepared are recorded on a timely basis in the cash disbursements journal and the accounts payable subsidiary records. When electronic transfers are made or a cheque is prepared in an IT system, a payment is simultaneously recorded in the accounting records by the application programs that control transaction processing. The auditor's tests of controls include reviewing the reconciliation of payment transfers with postings to the cash disbursements journal and accounts payable subsidiary records. The auditor also tests cash disbursements before and after year end to ensure transactions are recorded in the proper period.

Classification of Cash Disbursement Transactions

The auditor's concern with proper classification is that a cash disbursement may be charged to the wrong general ledger account. In most purchasing systems, purchases are usually recorded through the voucher register or purchases journal. Thus, the only entries into the cash disbursements journal are debits to accounts payable and credits to cash. If these procedures are followed, proper classification of cash disbursements is not a major concern.

Sometimes a client pays for goods and services directly from the cash disbursements journal without recording the purchase transaction in the purchases journal. If a client does pay for goods and services directly from the cash disbursements journal, controls must be present to ensure proper classification. The use of a chart of accounts, as well as independent approval and review of the account code on the voucher packet, should provide an adequate control. The auditor can review the cash disbursements journal for reasonableness of account distribution as well as the account codes on a sample of voucher packets.

❖ CONTROL ACTIVITIES AND TESTS OF CONTROLS: PURCHASE
LO9 RETURN TRANSACTIONS

The number and magnitude of purchase return transactions are not material for most entities. However, because of the possibility of manipulation the auditor should, at a minimum, inquire about how the client controls purchase return transactions. When goods are returned to a vendor, the client usually prepares a document (sometimes called a debit memo) that reduces the amount of the vendor's accounts payable. This document is processed through the purchasing process in a manner similar to the processing of a vendor invoice.

Because purchase returns are often few in number and not material, the auditor normally does not test controls of these transactions. Substantive **analytical procedures** are usually performed to test the reasonableness of purchase returns. For example, comparison of purchase returns as a percentage of revenue to prior years' and industry data may disclose any material misstatement in this account.

❖ RELATING THE ASSESSED LEVEL OF CONTROL RISK TO
LO10 SUBSTANTIVE PROCEDURES

The decision process followed by the auditor is similar to that discussed in Chapter 10 for the revenue process. If the results of the tests of controls support the planned level of control risk, the auditor conducts substantive procedures at the planned level. If the results indicate that control risk can be reduced further, the auditor can increase detection risk, which will reduce the nature, timing and extent of substantive procedures needed. However, if the results of the tests of controls do not support the planned level of control risk, detection risk has to be set lower and substantive procedures increased.

The main accounts affected by the auditor's achieved control risk for the purchasing process include accounts payable, accrued expenses and most of the expense accounts in the income statement. Additionally, the tests of controls over purchase transactions affect the assessment of detection risk for other business processes. For example, purchase transactions for the acquisition of inventory and property, plant and equipment are subject to the controls included in the purchasing process. If those controls are reliable, the auditor may be able to increase the detection risk for the affected financial statement accounts and therefore reduce the number of substantive procedures needed.

AUDITING ACCOUNTS PAYABLE AND ACCRUED EXPENSES

The assessments of inherent risk and control risk for the purchasing process are used to determine the level of detection risk for conducting substantive procedures for accounts payable and accrued expenses. Accounts payable generally represent normal recurring trade obligations. Accrued expenses represent expenses that have been incurred during the period but that have not been billed or paid for as of the end of the period; these include accruals for taxes, interest, royalties and professional fees. A number of accrued expenses are also related to payroll. Because there is little difference between accounts payable and accrued expenses, they are covered together in this section.

Substantive analytical procedures and tests of details of classes of transactions, account balances and disclosures are used to test accounts payable and accrued expenses. Substantive analytical procedures are used to examine plausible relationships among accounts payable and accrued expenses. Tests of details focus on transactions, account balances or disclosures. In the purchasing process, **tests of details of transactions** (also called *substantive tests of transactions*) focus mainly on the purchases and cash disbursement transactions. **Tests of details of account balances** concentrate on the detailed amounts or estimates that make up the ending balance for accounts payable and accrued expenses. Tests of details of disclosures are concerned with the presentation and disclosures related to accounts payable and accrued expenses.

Table 11–8 lists the assertions for account balances and disclosures as they apply to accounts payable and accrued expenses. The reader should note that the auditor may test assertions related to transactions (substantive tests of transactions) in conjunction with testing internal controls. If the tests of controls indicate that the controls are not operating effectively, the auditor may need to test transactions at the date the account balance is tested.

Table 11–8 Management Assertions about Account Balances, and Disclosures for Accounts Payable and Accrued Expenses

Assertions about Account Balances at the Period End

- **Existence**. Accounts payable and accrued expenses are valid liabilities.
- **Rights and obligations**. Accounts payable and accrued expenses are the obligations of the entity.
- **Completeness**. All accounts payable and accrued expenses have been recorded.
- **Valuation and allocation**. Accounts payable and accrued expenses are included in the financial statements at appropriate amounts, and any resulting valuation or allocation adjustments are appropriately recorded.

Assertions about Presentation and Disclosure

- **Occurrence and rights and obligations.** All disclosed events, transactions and other matters relating to accounts payable and accrued expenses have occurred and pertain to the entity.
- **Completeness.** All disclosures relating to accounts payable and accrued expenses that should have been included in the financial statements have been included.
- **Classification and understandability.** Financial information relating to accounts payable and accrued expenses is appropriately presented and described, and disclosures are clearly expressed.
- **Accuracy and valuation.** Financial and other information relating to accounts payable and accrued expenses are disclosed fairly and at appropriate amounts.

❖ SUBSTANTIVE ANALYTICAL PROCEDURES

LO11

Substantive analytical procedures can be useful substantive procedures for examining the reasonableness of accounts payable and accrued expenses. Substantive analytical procedures can effectively identify accounts payable and accrual accounts that are misstated, as well as provide evidence regarding the fairness of the recorded accounts. Table 11–9 contains some examples of substantive analytical procedures that can be used in the auditing of accounts payable and accrued expenses. Table 11–9 is not an exhaustive list; rather it provides some specific examples by account to help you understand the underlying concepts. Before moving on, calculate the days outstanding in accounts payable (365 days ÷ payables turnover) using EarthWear's financial statements as presented earlier in the book. Do your findings provide evidence in support of the fair statement of accounts payable or suggest that additional audit work is necessary?

Table 11–9 Examples of Substantive Analytical Procedures used in Auditing Accounts Payable and Accrued Expenses

Example Substantive Analytical Procedure	Possible Misstatement Detected
Compare payables turnover and days outstanding in accounts payable to previous years' and industry data.	Under- or overstatement of liabilities and expenses.
Compare current year balances in accounts payable and accruals with prior years' balances.	Under- or overstatement of liabilities and expenses.
Compare amounts owed to individual vendors in the current year's accounts payable listing to amounts owed in prior years.	Under- or overstatement of liabilities and expenses.
Compare purchase returns and allowances as a percentage of revenue or cost of sales to prior years' and industry data.	Under- or overstatement of purchase returns.

 TESTS OF DETAILS OF CLASSES OF TRANSACTIONS, ACCOUNT BALANCES
LO12 **AND DISCLOSURES**

LO13
Table 11–10 presents examples of tests of details of transactions, account balances and disclosures for assertions related to accounts payable and accrued expenses. This table should not be construed as an exhaustive list of substantive audit procedures for accounts payable and accrued expenses. As discussed previously, tests of details of transactions (substantive tests of transactions) are tests conducted to detect monetary misstatements in the individual transactions processed through all accounting applications, are often conducted at the same time as tests of controls, and are often difficult to distinguish from a test of controls because the specific audit procedure may both test the operation of a control procedure and test for monetary misstatement. Table 11–10 presents a substantive test of transactions for each assertion for purchase transactions. Normally, most of these tests are conducted as tests of controls. However, if the controls are not operating effectively or if the auditor did not rely on those controls, substantive tests of transactions may be necessary for the auditor to reach an appropriate level of evidence. The cut-off assertion is the one that is most often conducted as a substantive procedure.

Table 11–10 Summary of Assertions and Example of Related Tests of Transactions, Account Balances and Disclosures: Accounts Payable and Accrued Expenses

Assertions about Classes of Transactions	Example Substantive Tests of Transaction*
Occurrence	Test a sample of vouchers for the presence of an authorized purchase order and receiving report.
Completeness	Tracing of a sample of vouchers to the purchases journal.
Authorization	Test a sample of purchase requisition for proper authorization.
Accuracy	Recompute the mathematical accuracy of a sample of vendors' invoices.
Cut-off	Compare dates on a sample of vouchers with the dates transactions were recorded in the purchases journal.
	Test transactions around year-end to determine if they are recorded in the proper period.
Classification	Verify classification of charges for a sample of purchases transactions.
Assertions about Account Balances	*Example Tests of Details of Account Balances*
Existence	Vouch selected amounts from the accounts payable listing and schedules for accruals to voucher packets or other supporting documentation.
	Obtain selected vendors' statements and reconcile to vendor accounts.
	Confirmation of selected accounts payable.†
Rights and obligations	Review voucher packets for presence of purchase requisition, purchase order, receiving report and vendor invoice.

Completeness	Obtain listing of accounts payable and agree total to general ledger.[†]
	Search for unrecorded liabilities by inquiring of management and examining post-balance sheet transactions.
	Obtain selected vendors' statements and reconcile to vendor accounts.
	Confirmation of selected accounts payable.[†]
Valuation and allocation	Obtain listing of accounts payable and account analysis schedules for accruals; foot listing and schedules and agree totals to general ledger.[†]
	Trace selected items from the accounts payable listing to the subsidiary records[†] and voucher packets.
	Review results of confirmations of selected accounts payable.
	Obtain selected vendors' statements and reconcile to vendor accounts.
Assertions about Presentation and Disclosure	*Example Tests of Details of Disclosures*
Occurrence and rights and obligations	Inquire about accounts payable and accrued expenses to ensure that they are properly disclosed.
Completeness	Complete financial reporting checklist to ensure that all financial statement disclosures related to accounts payable and accrued expenses have been disclosed.
Classification and understandability	Review of listing of accounts payable for material debits, long-term payables and non-trade payables. Determine whether such items require separate disclosure on the balance sheet.
	Read notes to ensure that required disclosures are understandable.
Accuracy and valuation	Read notes and other information to ensure that the information is accurate and properly presented at the appropriate amounts.

* These tests of details of transactions are commonly conducted as a dual-purpose test (i.e. in conjunction with tests of controls).
† These tests can be conducted manually or using CAATs.

The discussion that follows focuses on tests of details of account balances of accounts payable and accrued expenses. We begin with the completeness assertion for the accounts payable balance because the auditor must establish that the detailed records agree to the general ledger. Note that we do not cover all the assertions listed in Table 11–10 because they are not applicable to EarthWear Clothiers or they would have been conducted as tests of controls.

Completeness and Accuracy

The completeness of accounts payable is first determined by obtaining a listing of accounts payable, footing the listing and agreeing it to the general ledger control account. The items included on this listing are the unpaid individual vouchers (when a voucher system is used) or the balance in the individual vendor accounts in the subsidiary records (when a purchases journal is used). Exhibit 11–3 presents an example of the accounts payable listing for EarthWear in which the information is summarized by vendor from the accounts payable subsidiary ledger. Selected vouchers or vendor accounts are traced to the supporting documents or subsidiary accounts payable records to verify the accuracy of the details making up the listing. For example, the tick mark next to the balance for Aarhus Industries indicates that the auditor has verified the account by tracing the balance to the accounts payable subsidiary records.

Exhibit 11–3 Example of an Accounts Payable Listing Working Paper

N10
DLJ
3/2 /2010

EARTHWEAR CLOTHIERS
Accounts Payable Listing
31/12/09

Vendor Name	Amount Due
Aarhus Industries	€52,758†V
Anderson Clothes	237,344V
.	
.	
.	
.	
Wintersport	122,465†V
Zantec Bros.	7,750
Total	€62,509,740
	F T/B

F = Footed.
† = Traced to accounts payable subsidiary records.
V = Voucher packets examined for transaction validity. No exceptions.
T/B = Agreed to trial balance.

For accrued expense accounts, the auditor obtains a detailed account analysis schedule. For example, Exhibit 11–4 shows an account analysis schedule for accrued real estate taxes. The credits to the accrual account represent the recognition of real estate taxes owed at the end of each month. This amount should agree with the amount of real estate taxes expense shown in the income statement. The debits to the account are payments. This schedule is footed and agreed to the accrued real estate taxes account in the general ledger.

Exhibit 11–4 Account Analysis for the Accrued Real Estate Taxes Account Working Paper

N21
DLJ
5/2/2010

EARTHWEAR CLOTHIERS
Analysis of Accrued Real Estate Taxes
31/12/09

Cash disbursements for real estate tax payments	233,911Γ	Beginning balance	€22,333‡
		12 monthly accruals for real estate taxes	235,245
		Ending balance	€23,667LV
			F

F = Footed.
‡ = Agreed to prior year's working papers.
V = Amount of real estate taxes accrued appears reasonable.
Γ = Payments traced to real estate tax bills and cash disbursements journal.
L = Agreed to general ledger.

The second major test of the completeness assertion is for accounts payable and accruals concerned with unrecorded liabilities. Therefore, auditors frequently conduct extensive tests to ensure that all liabilities are recorded. Such tests are commonly referred to as a *search for unrecorded liabilities*. The following audit procedures may be used as part of the search for unrecorded liabilities:

1   Ask management about control activities used to identify unrecorded liabilities and accruals at the end of an accounting period.
2   Obtain copies of vendors' monthly statements and reconcile the amounts to the client's accounts payable records.
3   Confirm vendor accounts, including accounts with small or zero balances.

4 Vouch large-monetary items from the purchases journal and cash disbursements journal for a limited time after year end; examine the date on each receiving report or vendor invoice to determine if the liability relates to the current audit period.

5 Examine the files of unmatched purchase orders, receiving reports and vendor invoices for any unrecorded liabilities.

Existence

The auditor's major concern with the existence assertion is whether the recorded liabilities are valid obligations of the entity. To verify the validity of liabilities, the auditor can vouch a sample of the items included on the listing of accounts payable, or the accrued account analysis, to voucher packets or other supporting documents. If adequate source documents are present, the auditor has evidence that the amounts represent valid liabilities (see Exhibit 11–3). In some circumstances, the auditor may obtain copies of the monthly vendor statements or send confirmation requests to vendors to test the validity of the liabilities. Confirmation of accounts payable is discussed later in this chapter.

Cut-off

The cut-off assertion attempts to determine whether all purchase transactions and related accounts payable are recorded in the proper period. While the auditor can obtain assurance about the cut-off assertion for purchases by conducting tests of controls, in most cases cut-off tests are conducted as substantive tests of transactions or as a dual-purpose test. On most audits, purchase cut-off is coordinated with the client's physical inventory count. Proper cut-off should also be determined for purchase return transactions.

The client should have control activities to ensure that a proper purchase cut-off takes place. The auditor can test purchase cut-off by first obtaining the number of the last receiving report issued in the current period. A sample of voucher packets is selected for a few days before and after year end. The receiving reports contained in the voucher packets are examined to determine if the receipt of the goods is consistent with the recording of the liability. For example, suppose that the last receiving report issued by EarthWear in 2009 was number 15,755. A voucher packet recorded in the voucher register or accounts payable in 2009 should have a receiving report numbered 15,755 or less. If the auditor finds a voucher packet recorded in 2009 with a receiving report number higher than 15,755, the liability has been recorded in the wrong period. Accounts payable for 2009 should be adjusted and the amount included as a liability in the next period. For voucher packets recorded in 2010, the receiving reports should be numbered 15,756 or higher. If the auditor finds a voucher packet with a receiving report with a number less than 15,756, the liability belongs in the 2009 accounts payable.

Purchase returns seldom represent a material amount in the financial statements. If the client has adequate control activities for processing purchase return transactions, the auditor can use substantive analytical procedures to satisfy the cut-off assertion for purchase returns. For example, the prior year and current-year amounts for purchase returns as a percentage of revenue or cost of sales can be compared. If the results of the substantive analytical procedures are consistent with the auditor's expectation, no further audit work may be necessary.

Rights and Obligations

Generally, there is little risk related to this assertion because clients seldom have an incentive to record liabilities that are not obligations of the entity. Review of the voucher packets for adequate supporting documents relating liabilities to the client provides sufficient evidence to support this assertion.

Valuation

The valuation of individual accounts payable is generally not a difficult assertion to test. Accounts payable are recorded at either the gross amount of the invoice or the net of the cash discount if the entity normally takes a cash discount. The tests of details of account balances noted in Table 11–10 normally provide sufficient evidence as to the proper valuation of accounts payable.

The valuation of accruals depends on the type and nature of the accrued expenses. Most accruals are relatively easy to value, and proper valuation can be tested by examining the underlying source documents. Real estate taxes and interest are examples of accruals that are generally easy to value. In the first case, real estate appraisals or bills usually serve as the basis for the accrual amount (see Exhibit 11–4).

In the second case, the amount of interest accrued relates directly to the amount of debt and the interest rate stipulated in the loan agreement. Other accruals, however, may require the auditor to verify the client's estimates. Auditing standards (ISA 540) provide the auditor with guidance in auditing client's estimates. Examples of such estimates include accruals for vacation pay, pension expense, warranty expense and income taxes.

Classification and Understandability

The major issues related to the presentation and disclosure assertion about classification are (1) identifying and reclassifying any material debits contained in accounts payable; (2) segregating short-term and long-term payables; and (3) ensuring that different types of payables are properly classified. Proper classification can usually be verified by reviewing the accounts payable listing and the general ledger accounts payable account. If material debits are present, they should be reclassified as receivables or as deposits if the amount will be used for future purchases. Any long-term payables should be identified and reclassified to the long-term liability section of the balance sheet. Also, if payables to officers, employees or related parties are material, they should not be included with the trade accounts payable. The auditor should also ensure that accrued expenses are properly classified.

Other Presentation Disclosure Assertions

Even though management is responsible for the financial statements, the auditor must ensure that all necessary financial statement disclosures are made for accounts payable and accrued expenses. Again, a reporting checklist is a useful tool. Table 11–11 presents examples of items that should be disclosed for accounts payable and accrued expenses.

Table 11–11 Examples of Disclosure Items for Purchasing Process and Related Accounts
• Payables by type (trade, officers, employees, affiliates, and so on).
• Short- and long-term payables.
• Long-term purchase contracts, including any unusual or adverse purchase commitments.
• Purchases from and payables to related parties.
• Dependence on a single vendor or a small number of vendors.
• Costs by reportable segment of the business.

Two disclosures are particularly important. The auditor must ensure that all related-party purchase transactions have been identified. If material, such purchase transactions should in general be disclosed. International accounting standards require disclosure of the amount involved in the transaction, as well as the balances to each major category of related parties. The entity should also disclose key management compensation in total and by category of compensation (IAS 24). The other major disclosure issue is purchase commitments. When the client has entered into a formal long-term purchase contract, adequate disclosure of the terms of the contract should be provided in a note. Exhibit 11–5 provides a sample disclosure for a purchase commitment.

Exhibit 11–5 A Sample Disclosure for Purchase Commitments
The company has various agreements that provide for the purchase at market prices of wood chips, bark and other residual fibre from trees.
The company also has an agreement to purchase at market prices through 2013 the entire production of an unbleached kraft paper-making machine at Johnson Forest Products Company. The capacity of this machine is estimated to be 30,000 tons a year.

◆ ACCOUNTS PAYABLE CONFIRMATIONS

LO14

Chapter 10 discussed the **confirmation** process in general and accounts receivable confirmations specifically. This section expands that discussion to include confirmation of accounts payable. Accounts payable confirmations are used less frequently by auditors than accounts receivable confirmations because the auditor can test accounts payable by examining vendor invoices, monthly vendor statements and payments made by the client subsequent to year end. Because vendor invoices and statements originate from sources external to the client, this evidence is viewed as reliable. However, if the client has weak internal control, vendor statements may not be available to examine. In such a case, confirmations may be used as an important source of evidence.

While accounts payable confirmations provide evidence on a number of assertions, they primarily test the completeness assertion. If the client has strong control activities for ensuring that liabilities are recorded, the auditor focuses on confirmation of large-monetary accounts. However, if the auditor has concerns about liabilities not being recorded, regular vendors with small or zero balances and a sample of other accounts may be confirmed in addition to large-monetary accounts. Small- and zero-balance accounts are confirmed because the client may owe such vendors for purchases but the amounts may not be recorded in the client's accounting records.

When confirming accounts payable, auditors generally use a form of **positive confirmation** referred to as a **blank or zero-balance confirmation**. This type of positive confirmation does not state the balance owed. Instead, the confirmation requests that the recipient fill in the amount or furnish other information. Exhibit 11–6 presents an example of an accounts payable confirmation request. Note that the confirmation requests the balance owed and a detailed statement of the account. The confirmation also requests additional information on notes payable and consigned inventory.

Exhibit 11–6 Example of an Accounts Payable Confirmation Request

EARTHWEAR CLOTHIERS

7 January 2010

Zantec Bros.
PO Box XXX
City

Gentlemen:

Our auditors, Willis & Adams International, are conducting an audit of our financial statements as of 31 December 2009. Please confirm to them the amount of our accounts payable. Additionally, please provide the following information as of that date:

1. An itemized statement of our account.
2. A list of any notes payable to you including any discounted notes. Please include the original dates and amounts, due dates and amounts still outstanding.
3. A list of any consigned inventory held by us.

Sincerely,

Sally Jones
Controller, EarthWear Clothiers

Willis & Adams International
PO Box 333
Europolis

We confirm that EarthWear Clothiers' accounts payable balance at

31 December 2009 is _____.

Signature _____   Position _____

Generally, accounts payable confirmations are mailed at year end rather than at an interim date because of the auditor's concerns about unrecorded liabilities. The selection and mailing of accounts payable confirmations should be controlled using the procedures outlined in Chapter 10. When accounts payable confirmations are received, the amounts provided by the vendors must be reconciled with the client's records. Differences are often due to the same types of timing differences noted in Chapter 10 for accounts receivable confirmations. The two major timing differences are due to inventory in transit to the client and cash paid by the client but not yet received by the vendor. Any inconsistencies not due to timing differences normally result in adjustments to the client's records.

Vendors may also owe money to the purchaser, for example if discounts on purchases are based on meeting sales targets. The accounting scandal of the giant Dutch food retailer, Royal Ahold, also involves alleged false audit confirmations of vendors' receivables in its subsidiary US Foodservice. Exhibit 11–7 provides details of the alleged vendors' receivable confirmation fraud (see also Exhibit 11–1 for more on Royal Ahold).

Exhibit 11–7 Royal Ahold's US Foodservice: Charges of False Vendor Confirmations

The US Securities and Exchange Commission's complaints allege that US Foodservice (USF) personnel contacted vendors and urged them to sign and return the false confirmation letters. In some cases USF pressured the vendors; in other cases they provided side letters to the vendors assuring the vendors that they did not owe USF the amounts reflected as outstanding in the confirmation letters. The letters clearly stated that the confirmations were being used in connection with the annual audit and the letters directed the defendants to return the confirmations directly to the company's auditors.

Employees of or agents for vendors which supplied USF aided and abetted the fraud by signing and sending to the company's independent auditors confirmation letters that they knew materially overstated the amounts of promotional allowance income paid or owed to USF. The amounts overstated in the confirmations were often inflated by millions of dollars and by more than 100 per cent.

The complaints allege that USF engaged in a scheme to report earnings equal to or greater than its targets, regardless of the company's true performance. USF inflated its promotional allowance income by at least $700 million for fiscal years 2001 and 2002 and thereby caused Ahold to report materially false operating and net income for these periods. The annual audit confirmation process at USF was systematically corrupted to help keep the fraud from being discovered.

Selected source: US Securities and Exchange Commission, 'Litigation Release' No. 19034/January 13 2005 (www.sec.gov/litigation/litreleases/lr19034.htm).

❖ EVALUATING THE AUDIT FINDINGS: ACCOUNTS PAYABLE AND
LO15 RELATED ACCOUNTS

As discussed in previous chapters, when the auditor has completed the planned substantive procedures, all identified misstatements should be aggregated, that is, factual misstatements, judgemental misstatements and projected misstatements. The aggregated amount of identified misstatement is then compared to materiality, including relevant materiality levels for classes of transactions, account balances and disclosures to determine whether the audit strategy and audit plan are still appropriate. The auditor would again analyse the misstatements identified. For example, if most misstatements identified indicate that accounts payable are not properly valued, the auditor may reassess the control activities used by the client for ensuring proper valuation. If the auditor concludes that the audit risk is unacceptably high, additional audit procedures should be performed.

The auditor should request management to correct identified misstatements. If uncorrected misstatements in accounts payable, and when considered together with other uncorrected misstatements, are less than materiality, the auditor may accept that the financial statements are fairly presented. Conversely, if the uncorrected misstatement exceeds the materiality, the auditor should conclude that the financial statements are not fairly presented.

For example, in Chapter 3, EarthWear's materiality for accounts payable was €900,000. Exhibit 3–4 showed that Willis & Adams identified a misstatement in recording inventory that amounted to a €227,450 understatement of accounts payable. Because this misstatement (€227,450) is considerably less than materiality of €900,000, Willis & Adams may conclude that the audit evidence supports fair presentation. However, if the identified misstatement approaches materiality, there may be a greater than an acceptable low level of risk that the identified misstatement together with possible undetected misstatements in aggregate could exceed materiality. In such a case the auditor would evaluate the effect on the audit. If uncorrected misstatement exceeds materiality for account payable, the auditor would qualify the opinion.

🔒 Key Terms

Analytical procedures. Evaluations of financial information through analysis of plausible relationships among both financial and non-financial data.

Application controls. Controls that apply to the processing of specific computer applications and are part of the computer programs used in the accounting system.

Assertions. Representations by management, explicit or otherwise, that are embodied in the financial statements, as used by the auditor to consider the different types of potential misstatements that may occur.

Blank or zero-balance confirmation. A confirmation request on which the recipient fills in the amount or furnishes the information requested.

Control activities. The policies and procedures that help ensure that management's directives are carried out.

Confirmation. Audit evidence obtained as a direct written response to the auditor from a third party (the confirming party), in paper form, or by electronic or other medium.

General controls. Controls that relate to the overall information-processing environment and have a pervasive effect on the entity's computer operations.

Positive confirmation. A request that the confirming party respond directly to the auditor indicating whether the confirming party agrees or disagrees with the information in the request, or providing the requested information.

Reliance strategy. The auditor's decision to rely on the entity's controls, test those controls and reduce the substantive tests of the financial statement accounts.

Tests of controls. Audit procedures designed to evaluate the operating effectiveness of controls in preventing, or detecting and correcting, material misstatements at the assertion level.

Tests of details of account balances and disclosures. Tests that concentrate on the details of amounts contained in an account balance and related notes.

Tests of details of transactions (substantive tests of transactions). Tests to detect errors or fraud in individual transactions.

? Review Questions

LO1	11–1	Distinguish among the three categories of expenses. Provide an example of each type of expense.
LO2,3	11–2	What major types of transactions occur in the purchasing process? What financial statement accounts are affected by each type of transaction?
LO4	11–3	Briefly describe each of the following documents or records: purchase requisition; purchase order; receiving report; vendor invoice; and voucher. Why would an entity combine all documents related to a purchase transaction into a 'voucher packet'?
LO5,6	11–4	List the key segregation of duties in the purchasing process. What errors or fraud can occur if such duties are not segregated?
LO7	11–5	List two inherent risk factors that directly affect the purchasing process. Why should auditors be concerned about issues such as the supply of raw materials and the volatility of prices?
LO9	11–6	What control activities typically ensure that the occurrence, authorization and completeness assertions are met for a purchase transaction? What tests of controls are performed for each of these assertions?
LO9	11–7	Identify two tests of controls that could be performed using computer-assisted audit techniques (CAATs) for purchase transactions.
LO11	11–8	List two substantive analytical procedures that can test accounts payable. What potential errors or fraud can be identified by each analytical procedure?
LO13	11–9	List the procedures an auditor might use to search for unrecorded liabilities.
LO13	11–10	Identify four possible disclosure issues related to the purchasing process and related accounts.
LO14	11–11	What are the differences between accounts receivable and accounts payable confirmations?

Problems

LO11	11–12	You are the auditor for KPDZ Corporation. You gathered comparative information for inventory and accounts payable, and calculated the days

purchases in accounts payable.

	2008	*2009*
Inventory	€34,270	€57,921
Accounts Payable	€8,295	€10,628
Days Purchases in Accounts Payable (365 days ÷ payables turnover)	44.2 days	44.6 days

Required:

Prepare a list of possible concerns that you might have about potential misstatements in both accounts.

LO2,4,5,6,9 11–13 The flowchart on p. 404 depicts the activities relating to the purchasing, receiving and accounts payable departments of Model Company.

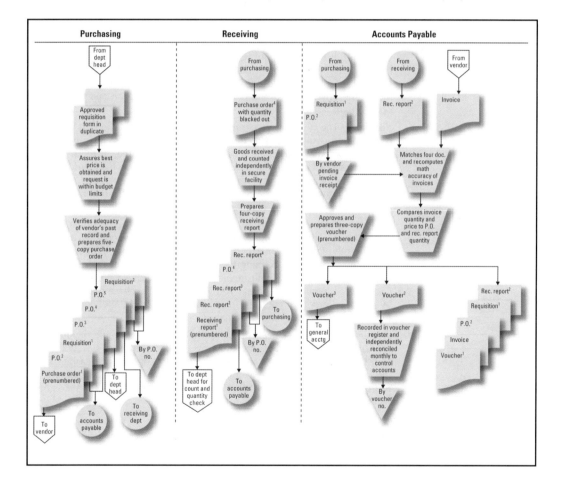

Required:

Based only on the flowchart, describe the control activities that most likely would provide reasonable assurance that specific assertions regarding purchases and accounts payable will be achieved. Do not describe deficiencies in internal control.

(AICPA, adapted)

LO2,5,6,9   **11–14**   In 2009 Kida Company purchased more than €10 million worth of office equipment under its 'special' ordering system, with individual orders ranging from €5,000 to €30,000. 'Special' orders entail low-volume items that have been included in an authorized user's budget. Department heads include in their annual budget requests the types of equipment and their estimated cost. The budget, which limits the types and euro amounts of office equipment a department head can requisition, is approved at the beginning of the year by the board of directors. Department heads prepare purchase requisition forms for equipment and forward them to the purchasing department. Kida's 'special' ordering system functions as follows:

- *Purchasing*: Upon receiving a purchase requisition, one of five buyers verifies that the person requesting the equipment is a department head. The buyer selects the appropriate vendor by searching the various vendor catalogues on file. The buyer then phones the vendor, requests a price quotation and gives the vendor a verbal order. A prenumbered purchase order is processed with the original sent to the vendor, a copy to the department head, a copy to receiving, a copy to accounts payable and a copy filed in the open requisition file. When the buyer is orally informed by the receiving department that the item has been received, the buyer transfers the purchase order from the unfilled file to the filled file. Once a month the buyer reviews the unfilled file to follow up on and expedite open orders.

- *Receiving*: The receiving department receives a copy of the purchase order. When equipment is received, the receiving clerk stamps the purchase order with the date received and, if applicable, in red pen prints any differences between the quantity shown on the purchase order and the quantity received. The receiving clerk forwards the stamped purchase order and equipment to the requisitioning department head and orally notifies the purchasing department.

- *Accounts payable*: Upon receiving a purchase order, the accounts payable clerk files it in the open purchase order file. When a vendor invoice is received, the invoice is matched with the applicable purchase order, and a payable is set up by debiting the equipment account of the department requesting the items. Unpaid invoices are filed by due date, and at the due date a cheque is prepared. The invoice and purchase order are filed by purchase order number in a paid invoice file, and the cheque is then forwarded to the treasurer for signature.

- *Treasurer*: Cheques received daily from the accounts payable department are sorted into two groups: those over €10,000; and those €10,000 and less. Cheques for €10,000 and less are machine-signed. The cashier keeps the key and signature plate to the cheque-signing machine and records all use of the cheque-signing machine. All cheques over €10,000 are signed by the treasurer or the controller.

Required:

a   *Prepare a flowchart of Kida Company's purchasing and cash disbursements system.*

b   *Describe the internal control deficiencies relating to purchases of and payments for 'special' orders of Kida Company for the purchasing, receiving, accounts payable and treasurer functions.*

(AICPA, adapted)

LO11,12,13   **11–15**   Following are audit procedures that are normally conducted in the purchasing process and related accounts.

1   Test a sample of purchase requisitions for proper authorization.

2   Test transactions around year end to determine if they are recorded in the proper period.

3 Review results of confirmation of selected accounts payable.

4 Compare payables turnover to previous years' data

5 Obtain selected vendors' statements and reconcile to vendor accounts.

6 Compare purchase returns and allowances as a percentage of revenue or cost of sales to industry data.

Required:

Identify whether the tests listed above are substantive analytical procedures, tests of details of transactions or tests of details of account balances.

LO11,12,13,14 11–16 Coltrane, independent auditor, is auditing Jang Wholesaling Company's financial statements and is about to perform substantive audit procedures on Jang's trade accounts payable balances. After obtaining an understanding of Jang's internal control for accounts payable, Coltrane assessed control risk below the maximum. Coltrane requested and received from Jang a schedule of the trade accounts payable prepared using the trade accounts payable subsidiary ledger (voucher register).

Required:

Describe the substantive audit procedures Coltrane should apply to Jang's trade accounts payable balances. Do not include procedures that would be applied only in the audit of related-party payables, amounts withheld from employees, and accrued expenses such as pensions and interest.

(AICPA, adapted)

LO13,14   11–17 In obtaining evidence in support of financial statement assertions, the auditor develops specific audit procedures to access those assertions.

Required:

Your client is All's Fair Appliance Company, an appliance wholesaler. Select the most appropriate audit procedure from the list below and enter the number in the appropriate place on the grid. (An audit procedure may be selected once, more than once, or not at all.)

Audit Procedure:

1 Compare selected amounts from the accounts payable listing with the voucher and supporting documents.

2 Review drafts of the financial statements.

3 Search for unrecorded liabilities.

4 Select a sample of receiving documents for a few days before and after year end.

5 Obtain a listing of the accounts payable and agree total to general ledger control account.

Specific Assertion	Audit Procedure
a. Verify that recorded accounts payable include all amounts owed to vendors. (completeness)	
b. Verify that all accounts payable are recorded in the correct period. (Cut-off)	
c. Determine whether accounts payable have been properly accumulated from the journal to the general ledger. (Accuracy)	
d. Determine whether recorded accounts payable are valid. (Existence/occurrence)	

LO12,13 **11–18** You are engaged to perform an audit of the Giordani Corporation for the year ended 31 December 2009. You have decided to perform the following cut-off test for payables and accruals. *Select all items greater than €25,000 for two business days before and after year end from the purchases journal and ensure that all transactions are recorded in the proper period.*

During your firm's observation of Giordani's physical inventory you obtained the following cut-off information: the last receiving report number in 2009 was 49745. Your audit work identified the following items for further investigation:

	Date	RR#	Vendor Name	Amount	Explanation
					Selection from the December 2009 Purchase Journal
a.	30/12	49742	Allen Chem.	€29,875	Chemicals purchased for manufacturing process.
b.	31/12	none	Khan Consulting	€45,000	Payment for consulting services for the three-month period beginning 1 December 2009. The €45,000 was charged to consulting expenses.
c.	31/12	49744	Goff Materials	€205,000	Raw materials used in the manufacturing process.
					Selections from the January 2010 Purchase Journal
d.	2/1	49746	Temper Trucks	€75,985	Purchase of a new forklift.
e.	4/1	49743	Pack Products	€42,000	Paper products used in manufacturing process.
f.	4/1	none	Telecom	€32,450	December 2009 telephone bill.

Required:

For each of the six items provided in the table above, consider whether there is evidence of proper cut-off of payables and accruals (i.e. the transaction is recorded in the proper period). If the item is not properly recorded, prepare the necessary adjusting entries at 31 December 2009. not properly recorded, prepare the necessary adjusting entries.

Discussion Case

LO13,14 **11–19** Mincin is the auditor of the Raleigh Corporation. Mincin is considering the audit work to be performed in the accounts payable area for the current year's engagement. The prior year's working papers show that confirmation requests were mailed to 100 of Raleigh's 1,000 suppliers. The selected suppliers were based on Mincin's sample, which was designed to select accounts with large euro balances. A substantial number of hours was spent by Raleigh and Mincin in resolving relatively minor differences between the confirmation replies and Raleigh's accounting records. Alternative audit procedures were used for suppliers who did not respond to the confirmation requests.

Required:

a *Discuss the accounts payable audit objectives that Mincin must consider in determining the audit procedures to be followed.*

b *Discuss situations in which Mincin should use accounts payable confirmations, and discuss whether Mincin is required to use them.*

c *Discuss why the use of large euro balances as the basis for selecting accounts payable for confirmation might not be the most efficient approach, and indicate what more efficient procedures could select accounts payable for confirmation.*

(AICPA, adapted)

Internet Assignments

11–20   Visit the website of a catalogue retailer similar to EarthWear Clothiers, and determine how it processes purchase transactions and recognizes expenses.

11–21   Visit the SEC's website (www.sec.gov), and identify a company that has recently been cited for financial reporting problems related to the recognition of expenses. Prepare a memo summarizing the expense issues for the company.

Note

i   For example, see A. Eilifsen and W.F. Messier, Jr (2000), 'Auditor Detection of Misstatements: A Review and Integration of Empirical Research', *Journal of Accounting Literature* (19), pp. 1–43, for a detailed review of audit research studies that have examined sources of accounting errors.

CHAPTER

12

Auditing the Human Resource Management Process

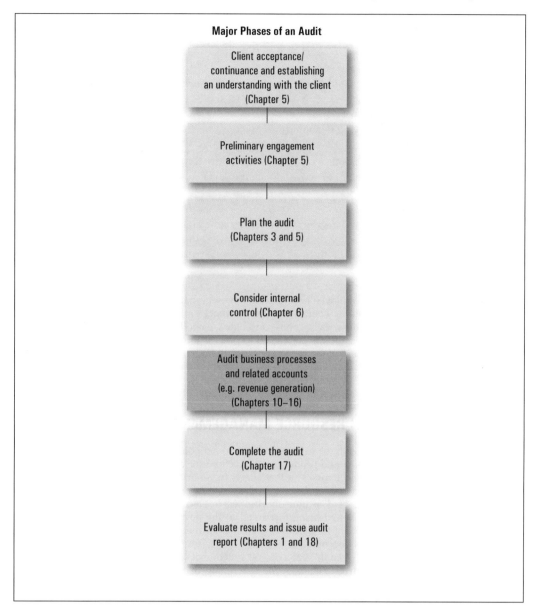

Major Phases of an Audit

Client acceptance/
continuance and establishing
an understanding with the client
(Chapter 5)

Preliminary engagement
activities (Chapter 5)

Plan the audit
(Chapters 3 and 5)

Consider internal
control (Chapter 6)

Audit business processes
and related accounts
(e.g. revenue generation)
(Chapters 10–16)

Complete the audit
(Chapter 17)

Evaluate results and issue audit
report (Chapters 1 and 18)

> ### ❖ RELEVANT ACCOUNTING AND AUDITING PRONOUNCEMENTS
>
> **IASB, IAS 19,** Employee Benefits
> **ISA 230,** Audit Documentation
> **ISA 240,** The Auditor's Responsibilities Relating to Fraud in an Audit of Financial Statements
> **ISA 315,** Identifying and Assessing the Risks of Material Misstatement through Understanding the Entity and Its Environment
> **ISA 320,** Materiality in Planning and Performing an Audit
> **ISA 330,** The Auditor's Procedures in Response to Assessed Risks
> **ISA 402,** Audit Considerations Relating to an Entity Using a Service Organization
> **ISA 450,** Evaluation of Misstatements Identified during the Audit
> **ISA 500,** Audit Evidence
> **ISA 520,** Analytical Procedures
> **ISA 540,** Auditing Accounting Estimates, Including Fair Value Accounting Estimates, and Related Disclosures
> **ISA 620,** Using the Work of an Auditor's Expert

COMPENSATION AND RELATED employee benefit costs represent major expenses for most entities. As a result, organizations tend to have strong control activities for processing payroll transactions. Additionally, because of the routine nature of these transactions, an entity's payroll is normally maintained on an IT system, or an outside service organization is contracted to process the payroll.

This chapter starts with an overview of the human resource management process and then discusses the components of the audit risk model. Specifically, the inherent risks that affect the human resource management process are addressed followed by a discussion of the auditor's control risk assessment. Last, the chapter covers substantive procedures for detection risk for payroll and related accounts.

❖ OVERVIEW OF THE HUMAN RESOURCE MANAGEMENT PROCESS

LO1

The human resource process starts with the establishment of sound policies for hiring, training, evaluating, counselling, promoting, compensating and taking remedial actions for employees. Once an individual has been hired as an employee, the main transaction that affects the financial statement accounts is a payroll (payment) transaction. A payroll transaction usually begins with an employee performing some job and recording the time spent on a time card or time sheet (often in electronic form). The time card or time sheet is approved by a supervisor before being forwarded to the payroll department. The data are then reviewed and sent to the IT department for processing. Finally, payment is made directly to the employee or deposited in the employee's bank account.

Figure 12–1 presents a flowchart of EarthWear's payroll system that serves as a framework for discussing **control activities** and **tests of controls**. Although the description of EarthWear's payroll system is fairly typical, the reader should focus on the basic concepts so that they can be applied to the specific payroll systems encountered. The following topics related to the human resource management process are covered:

- Types of transactions and financial statement accounts affected.
- Types of documents and records.
- The major functions.
- The key segregation of duties.

❖ Types of Transactions and Financial Statement Accounts Affected

LO2

Two main types of transactions are processed through the human resource management process:

1 Payments to employees for services rendered.
2 Accrual and payment of payroll-related liabilities arising from employees' services such as liabilities for payroll taxes.

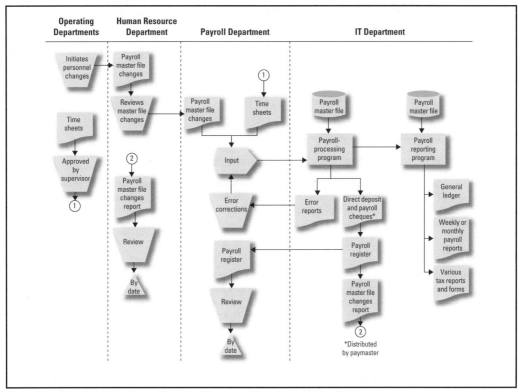

Figure 12–1   Flowchart of the Human Resource Management Process: EarthWear Clothiers

The discussion of internal control focuses on payments to employees, including a description of how such transactions are processed and the key control activities that should be present to ensure that no material misstatements occur. The audit of payroll-related accruals is discussed later in the chapter.

The financial statement accounts that are generally affected by the two types of payroll-related transactions are:

Type of Transaction	Account Affected
Payroll transaction	Cash
	Inventory
	Direct and indirect labour expense accounts
	Various payroll-related liability and expense accounts
Accrued payroll liability transactions	Cash
	Various accruals (such as payroll taxes and pension costs)

❖ Types of Documents and Records

LO3

Table 12–1 lists the important documents and records that are normally involved in the payroll application. Each of these items is briefly discussed here. The use of an IT system may affect the form of the documents and the auditor's approach to testing the payroll application.

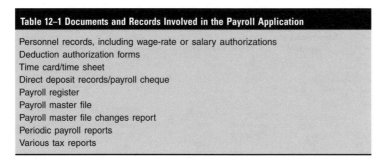

Table 12–1 Documents and Records Involved in the Payroll Application
Personnel records, including wage-rate or salary authorizations
Deduction authorization forms
Time card/time sheet
Direct deposit records/payroll cheque
Payroll register
Payroll master file
Payroll master file changes report
Periodic payroll reports
Various tax reports

Personnel Records, Including Wage-Rate or Salary Authorizations

Personnel records contain information on each employee's work history, including hiring date, wage rate or salary, payroll deduction authorization forms, wage-rate and salary adjustment authorizations, performance evaluations and termination notice, if applicable. Personnel records are normally maintained in the human resource department.

Deduction Authorization Forms

The organization normally makes deductions from the employee's pay. The employee may have to authorize such deductions from his or her pay. The organization uses authorization forms to document such deductions. For example, the employee may complete a form to authorize the withholding of payroll tax. Similar forms may be used for other deductions such as deductions for payments to retirement and health care.

Time Card/Time Sheet

Such documents record the hours worked by the employee, including the time the employee has started and stopped work. In some cases the employee fills in the time worked (typically in an electronic database); in other cases, the employee swipes an employee identification card, or enters an employee identification number into an electronic keypad, when they arrive and leave work, and the time-tracking system records and accumulates the hours worked.

Direct Deposit Records/Payroll Cheque

These records indicate the amount paid to the employee for services rendered. The amount paid is the gross pay less any deductions. In many cases, the employee's pay is directly deposited into the individual's bank account, and the company produces a listing of employees' payments that were transferred to their bank accounts.

Payroll Register

This document, which is also referred to as the *payroll journal*, summarizes all payroll payments issued to employees. A payroll register normally indicates employees' gross pay, deductions and net pay. In an IT environment, the details for this document are maintained in the payroll master file.

Payroll Master File

This computer file maintains all the entity's records related to payroll, including information on each employee such as name, employee identification number, employee number, pay rate, tax rate and any authorized deductions.

Payroll Master File Changes Report

This report contains a record of the changes made to the payroll master file. The human resource department reviews this report to ensure that all authorized changes have been properly made.

Periodic Payroll Reports

At the end of each week or month, a number of summary payroll reports may be prepared. The type of reports prepared depends on the type of organization. A manufacturing entity might have a payroll expense report that showed the allocation of direct labour to various products. EarthWear Clothiers reports a summary of payroll by various job classifications and departments. Department heads use this report to monitor payroll expense variances.

Various Tax Reports

Most companies are required to prepare various payroll tax reports for the government, including reports related to social security taxes.

 # The Major Functions

LO4

The principal objectives of the human resource management process are to (1) record production and other types of payroll costs in the accounts, (2) ensure that payroll costs are for legitimate entity activities, and (3) accrue liabilities for salaries and wages, payroll taxes and various employee benefit programmes. Table 12–2 lists the functions that are normally part of the payroll application.

Table 12–2 Functions in the Payroll Application	
Human resources	Authorization of hiring, firing, wage-rate and salary adjustments, salaries and payroll deductions.
Supervision	Review and approval of employees' attendance and time information; monitoring of employee scheduling, productivity and payroll cost variances.
Timekeeping	Processing of employees' attendance and time information, and coding of account distribution.
Payroll processing	Computation of gross pay, deductions and net pay; recording and summarization of payments and verification of account distribution.
Disbursement	Payment of employees' compensation and benefits.
General ledger	Proper accumulation, classification and summarization of payroll in the general ledger.

Human Resources

The human resources function is responsible for managing personnel needs of the organization. This includes hiring and terminating employees, setting wage rates and salaries, and establishing and monitoring employee benefit programmes. Most large organizations centralize these activities in a human resource department. However, in a small organization, these activities may be combined with the duties of selected operating and administrative personnel. In such organizations, control over human resource activities may not be as strong as when such activities are centralized. The human resource department maintains employees' personnel records. The human resource department may also be responsible for defining job requirements and descriptions, administering union contracts, and developing performance criteria and employee evaluation procedures.

Supervision

Supervisors within operating and supporting departments are responsible for reviewing and approving employees' attendance and time information. When time sheets or other documents are used to record an employee's time worked and job classification, the supervisor approves this information before processing by the payroll function. Additionally, supervisors should monitor labour productivity and labour cost variances. Standardized labour performance measures, such as standard productivity and wage rates, improve the monitoring of payroll costs. Labour cost variances should be investigated by supervisory personnel and communicated to upper-level management. When employees are not required to complete time cards/sheets or job classification documents, the entity needs to have control activities to notify the timekeeping or payroll-processing function about employees' absences and changes in employees' job classifications. This might be accomplished by having the supervisor submit a periodic attendance and job classification report.

Timekeeping

The timekeeping function prepares employees' time information for payroll processing. When payroll cost distribution is determined at the operating department level, the timekeeping function reviews this information before processing. Otherwise, the timekeeping function should be responsible for coding the payroll costs to appropriate accounts. In some organizations, a separate timekeeping department handles these functions. At EarthWear (see Figure 12–1), the operating and supporting departments are responsible for the timekeeping function.

Payroll Processing

The payroll-processing function is responsible for computing gross pay, deductions and net pay. This function is also responsible for recording and summarizing payments, and verifying account distribution. When IT is used to process payroll, as at EarthWear, the entity must have strong **application controls** to ensure proper payroll processing.

Some entities outsource their payroll processing to a third-party service organization. These service organizations can provide a range of services from basic payroll processing to full human resource services from employee hire to retire. When a client uses a third party to process payroll, the auditor will obtain evidence for important **assertions** associated with the data transferred to the service provider. The auditor must also consider the third-party services as part of the client's information system. Because the third-party service organization provides services to many entities, the service organization may obtain an assurance report that the other entity's auditors can rely on. See Chapter 6 for a discussion of auditing accounting applications processed by service organizations.

Disbursement

The disbursement function is responsible for paying employees for services and benefits. When the employee's pay is directly deposited into the individual's bank account, payroll files produced by the IT department serve to electronically transfer the net pay amount to employee's bank accounts. Direct deposit requires strong IT controls, including access security controls and data entry edit controls. Similarly, when payroll cheques are used the disbursement function oversees the preparation and distribution of the cheques. Cheque preparation normally occurs in the IT department. Therefore, it is necessary for the client to have control activities over access to blank cheques and cheque signature plates. Cheques are normally distributed by a paymaster, who is typically a member of the treasurer's department. If payroll disbursements are handled by a third-party service organization, assurance over IT controls may be provided in an assurance report (see Chapter 6).

General Ledger

The general ledger function for the human resource management process is responsible for properly accumulating, classifying and summarizing payroll and benefit transactions in the general ledger. When IT is used to process payroll transactions, control totals can help ensure that this function is performed properly. This function is normally performed by the general accounting department.

❖ The Key Segregation of Duties

LO5

As discussed in prior chapters, proper segregation of duties is one of the most important control activities in any accounting system. Duties should be assigned to individuals in such a way that no one individual can control all phases of processing a transaction, thus permitting misstatements to go undetected. Before reading further, please look back at EarthWear's flowchart in Figure 12–1 in order to identify one or two duties that EarthWear segregates. What might happen if the duties you identified were not segregated?

Individuals responsible for supervision and timekeeping should be segregated from the personnel, payroll-processing and general ledger functions. If IT is used extensively in the payroll application, duties should be properly segregated in the IT department. Table 12–3 contains some of the key segregation of duties for the human resource management process, and examples of possible errors or fraud that can result from conflicts in duties.

Table 12–3   Key Segregation of Duties in the Human Resource Management Process, and Possible Errors or Fraud

Segregation of Duties	Possible Errors or Fraud Resulting from Conflicts of Duties
The supervision function should be segregated from the personnel records and payroll-processing functions.	If one individual is responsible for the supervision, personnel records and payroll-processing functions, fictitious employees can appear on the payroll records or unauthorized payments can be made. This can result in unauthorized payments to existing employees or payments to fictitious employees.
The disbursement function should be segregated from the personnel records, supervision, and payroll-processing functions.	If one individual is responsible for the disbursement function and also has the authority to hire and fire employees, approve time reports, or prepare direct deposit to employees' accounts or prepare payroll cheques, unauthorized disbursements can be made.
The payroll-processing function should be segregated from the general ledger function.	If one individual is responsible for processing payroll transactions and also for the general ledger, that individual can conceal any defalcation that would normally be detected by independent review of accounting entries made to the general ledger.

Table 12–4 shows more detailed segregation of duties for individual payroll functions across the various departments that are involved in processing payroll transactions.

Table 12–4   Segregation of Duties for Payroll Functions by Department

| Payroll Function | Department | | | | | |
	Operating or Supporting	Human Resource	Timekeeping	Payroll	IT	Treasurer
Initiation of wage or salary changes	X					
Initiation of employee hiring and firing	X					
Approval of wage or salary changes		X				
Updating of personnel records		X				
Updating of payroll records		X				
Approval of time sheets and job classification	X					
Review of time data and payroll distribution			X			
Preparation of payroll				X	X	
Preparation of direct deposit and payroll cheques, including signing of cheques					X	
Direct deposit transfers and distribution of payroll cheques						X
Updating of general ledger for payroll activity					X	
Comparison of monthly departmental payroll expense to budget	X					
Calculation and recording of payroll taxes				X		

Returning to your analysis of EarthWear's flowchart (Figure 12–1), we see EarthWear has separated, for example, the supervising function performed by each operating department from the personnel records and the payroll-processing functions, which are performed by the human resources and IT departments respectively. For cheques, EarthWear has also separated processing and preparation of the cheques and distribution. However for direct deposit IT both prepares and transfers. Although not uncommon, the auditor would want to examine and test controls around the payroll preparation and direct deposit processes, particularly controls designed to ensure distributions are made only to valid employees.

INHERENT RISK ASSESSMENT

LO6

With the exception of executive and share-based compensation (see Exhibit 12–1), few inherent risk factors directly affect the human resource management process and its related accounts for non-officers. Some factors the auditor might consider are the effect of economic conditions on payroll costs and the supply of skilled workers. EarthWear is a seasonal business and experiences relatively high turnover in its seasonal employees, with a workforce that fluctuates between 3,500 and 5,300 employees. How might seasonal employee turnover impact the inherent risk assessment for payroll? High turnover will increase the inherent risk assessment due to the level of employee additions and terminations, and the risk associated with processing. For example, there is a greater risk that pay will be inappropriately dispersed to terminated or fictitious employees. Additionally, the presence of labour contracts and labour legislation may also affect the auditor's assessment of inherent risk. Because the payroll system and its related accounts generally contain few inherent risks, the auditor is normally able to set the inherent risk as low.

The inherent risk associated with executive compensation is frequently not set at low because officers may have motive and opportunity to take advantage of their high-ranking offices in the form of excessive compensation. Due to the complexity of accounting and disclosures associated with share-based compensation (e.g. stock options, stock appreciation rights), combined with the degree of judgement and estimation involved in option-valuation models, there can also be substantial inherent risk associated with share-based compensation. Exhibit 12–1 illustrates how backdating of the grant date of corporate executives' stock options was used to benefit their stock appreciation.

Exhibit 12–1   Backdating of the Grant Date of Stock Options

In early 2006 the SEC began a probe to detect possible stock-option abuses; particularly the impeccable timing of granting stock options to corporate executives. Analysis of stock price patterns and grant dates suggested that companies were backdating the grant date of stock options to a low in the stock price so that executives and employees could benefit from sharp stock appreciation. One popular technology company involved in backdating was Apple Inc. In 2006, Apple disclosed that thousands of option grants between 1997 and 2002, including those to CEO Steve Jobs, were improperly dated. The SEC sued Apple's former CFO and general counsel alleging involvement in backdating; the lawsuits were settled out of court for $5.7 million. In a related shareholder lawsuit, Steve Jobs and other Apple executives agreed to settle claims about their alleged participation for $14 million.

Sources: C. Forelle and J. Bandler, 'Stock-Options Criminal Charge: Slush Fund and Fake Employees', *Wall Street Journal* (10 August 2006), p. A1; N. Wingfield and J. Scheck, 'Jobs, Apple Executives Settle Suit', *Wall Street Journal* (11 September 2008).

Practice Insight 12.1

To obtain sufficient appropriate evidence on the fair value of options, the auditor is not required to become an option-pricing expert. If the client is using an approved model (e.g. Black-Scholes-Merton or binomial), the auditor would verify the mathematical accuracy of the client's calculations, tie the output of the model to the financial statements, and tie the known inputs (e.g. term, stock price) to relevant source documents. For forward-looking inputs (e.g. expected volatility, dividends, interest rate), the auditor would perform procedures to test the reasonableness of these inputs. The client should have a verifiable and consistent method to estimate these parameters.

Often the auditor will use the work of a valuation expert to obtain evidence regarding fair value measurements. When an auditor's experts are used, the auditor is required to evaluate the expert's competence, capabilities and objectivity. The auditor also evaluates the adequacy of the expert's work, including the relevance and reasonableness of significant assumptions and methods used by the expert.

CONTROL RISK ASSESSMENT

LO7

The discussion of control risk assessment follows the framework outlined in previous chapters. However, the discussion is not as thorough as the discussion of the revenue or purchasing processes because it is assumed that the reader has now developed a reasonable understanding of the decision process followed by the auditor when setting control risk. Figure 12–2 summarizes the three major steps involved in setting control risk for the human resource management process.

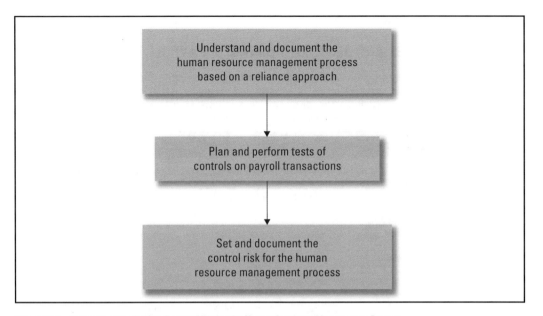

Figure 12–2   Major Steps in Setting Control Risk for the Human Resource Management Process

Understand and Document Internal Control

The level of understanding of the five internal control components should be similar to that obtained for the other processes. The auditor's understanding of the human resource management process is normally gained by conducting a walk-through of the system to gather evidence about the various functions that are involved in processing the transactions through the system. For an ongoing audit, this process merely involves updating prior years' documentation of the payroll system by noting any changes that have occurred. For a new engagement, or if the system has undergone major changes, more time and effort are needed to document the understanding of internal control. The auditor's understanding of internal control for the payroll system should be documented in the working papers using flowcharts, internal control questionnaires and memoranda.

Because the control environment pervasively affects all accounting applications, including the payroll system, two factors shown in Table 6–3 in Chapter 6 should be considered. First, the entity's organizational structure, its personnel practices, and its methods of assigning authority and responsibility must be examined. The proper organizational structure for processing payroll transactions was discussed in the previous section. Second, the entity should have sound policies for hiring, training, promoting and compensating employees. These policies should include specific authority and responsibility for hiring and firing employees, for setting wage rates and making salary changes, and for establishing benefits.

Plan and Perform Tests of Controls

When a **reliance strategy** is followed, the auditor must identify the control activities that ensure that material misstatements are either prevented or detected and corrected. For example, the client may have formal procedures for classifying payroll costs in appropriate accounts. The auditor may decide to rely on this control activity to reduce the control risk for the classification assertion. In this case, the client's procedures for classifying payroll transactions by types of payroll costs should be examined by the auditor.

Set and Document the Control Risk

After the tests of controls are completed, the auditor sets the level of control risk and documents that assessment. The documentation supporting the achieved level of control risk for the payroll system might include a flowchart, the results of tests of controls and a memorandum indicating the overall conclusion about control risk. If control deficiencies are detected and are significant, the auditor communicates these in writing to those charged with governance and management (see Chapter 6).

CONTROL ACTIVITIES AND TESTS OF CONTROLS: PAYROLL TRANSACTIONS

LO8

Table 12–5 summarizes the assertions and possible misstatements for payroll transactions. The table also includes examples of control activities for each assertion and examples of tests of controls that can test the effectiveness of the control activities. The discussion that follows focuses only on the most important assertions for the payroll system. EarthWear's payroll system contains all of the relevant control activities.

Table 12–5 Summary of Assertions, Possible Misstatements, Example Control Activities and Example Tests of Controls for Payroll Transactions

Assertion	Possible Misstatement	Example Control Activity	Example Test of Controls
Occurrence	Payments made to fictitious employees	Segregation of duties	Observe and evaluate proper segregation of duties.
	Payments made to terminated employees	Adequate personnel files	Review and test personnel files.
	Payments made to valid employees who have not worked	Initiation of changes in employment status, wages or salaries, and benefits made by operating departments reported to the office of human resources	Review and test client's procedures for changing employees' records; if IT application, test application controls.
		Time clocks used to record time	Observe employees' use of time clock.
		Time cards approved by supervisors	Inspect time cards presented for approval by supervisor.
		Only employees with valid employee numbers paid	Review and test client's procedures for entering and removing employee numbers from the payroll master file; if IT application, test application controls.
		Use of payroll budgets with review by department supervisors	Review client's budgeting procedures.
Completeness	Employee services provided but not recorded	Prenumbered time cards accounted for by client personnel	Check numerical sequence of time cards; if IT application, test application controls.
		Verification that all employees in the master payroll file submitted a time card for the pay period	Review and test client's verification procedures; if IT application, test application controls.
Authorization	Unauthorized payments made to employees. Payments made to employees at a rate in excess of authorized amount or for unauthorized employee benefits	Authorization procedures for • Hiring and terminating employees • Time worked • Wage, salary, and commission rates • Withholdings • Benefits • Payroll payments	Review and test authorization procedures for each point of authorization in the payroll cycle; if IT application, test application controls.
Accuracy	Employee compensation and payroll deductions computed incorrectly	Verification of payroll amounts and benefit calculations	Review and test client's verification procedures; if IT application, test application controls.

		Review of payroll register for unusual amounts	If IT-prepared, use computer-assisted audit techniques to test computer program logic for calculating amounts.
		Use of payroll budgets with review by department supervisors	Review client's budgeting procedures.
	Payroll transactions not posted correctly to the payroll journal	Changes to master payroll file verified through 'before and after' reports	Test reconciliation of 'before and after' reports to payroll master file; if IT application, test application controls.
	Amounts from payroll journal not posted correctly to general ledger	Payroll master file (payroll register) reconciled to general ledger payroll accounts	Review reconciliation of payroll master file to general ledger payroll accounts; if IT application, test application controls.
Cut-off	Payroll transactions recorded in the wrong period	Notices of additions, terminations and changes to salaries, wages and deductions reported promptly to the payroll processing function, after which the changes are updated promptly on the master payroll file	Review and test client's procedures for changes to master payroll file; if IT application, test application controls.
		All time cards forwarded to the payroll department weekly	Review and test procedures for processing time cards.
		Procedures that require recording payroll liabilities as soon as possible after they are incurred	Review and test procedures for recording payroll liabilities.
Classification	Payroll transactions not properly classified	Chart of accounts	Review chart of accounts.
		Independent approval and review of accounts charged for payroll	Review and test procedures for classifying payroll costs.
		Use of payroll budgets with review by department supervisors	Review client's budgeting procedures.

Occurrence of Payroll Transactions

The auditor wants assurance that payments for payroll-related services are being made to valid employees for time actually worked. Thus, the client needs control activities that prevent payments to fictitious employees and to valid employees who have not worked. Controls must also ensure that payroll payments stop once an employee is terminated. Using your developing auditor expertise, what controls would you expect to see at a company like EarthWear to ensure payments are not made to terminated or fictitious employees? Proper segregation of duties provides the main control against payments to fictitious employees. As noted in Table 12–4, proper segregation of duties among operating and supporting departments, the human resource department and the payroll department minimizes the possibility of fictitious employees existing within the system. The maintenance of adequate personnel files should also prevent such misstatements. For example, a listing of terminated employees could be used to verify that no terminated employees are still listed in the active payroll master file.

The human resource department approves the termination of an employee and ensures that he or she is removed from the master payroll file. Required completion and approval of a time card/time sheet also prevent payments to terminated employees. Proper review and approval of time cards/sheets by supervisors should prevent valid employees from being paid for work not performed.

> **Practice Insight 12.2**
>
> When an external service organization is used to process the audit client's payroll, the controls of the service organization must be understood and tested by the audit firm, or by the service organization auditor (i.e. a *type 2 report* is available), before the controls of the service organization can be relied on (ISA 402).

Finally, when payroll transactions are processed by an IT system, payments should not be prepared unless the employee transaction has a valid employee number. Review and observation are the main tests of controls the auditor uses to examine the control activities shown in Table 12–5.

Authorization of Payroll Transactions

As in the discussion of the authorization assertion for other accounting applications, there are key authorization points within the payroll system. The client should have authorization procedures for hiring and terminating employees, setting pay rates, making withholdings, awarding benefits, making direct deposits to employees' accounts and issuing payroll cheques. For example, the department supervisor should approve the amount of time reported by an employee on his or her time card/sheet. Similarly, hiring and termination of employees and changes in pay rates should be authorized by the human resource department consistent with union contracts or corporate policies. Last, a payroll payment should not be made unless an employee's time card/sheet has been approved and that employee has a valid employee number on the payroll master file.

Accuracy of Payroll Transactions

The main concern related to the accuracy assertion is that an employee's gross pay and payroll deductions may be incorrectly computed. For example, an employee may be paid at an improper rate or payroll deductions may be incorrectly computed. The client should maintain verification procedures to ensure correct payroll and benefit calculations. The auditor can review the client's verification procedures as a test of control. When IT is used to prepare the payroll, the auditor can use computer-assisted audit techniques (CAATs) to test the program logic for proper calculations. In a manual system, or if a service organization is used, the auditor can recompute the payroll calculations for a sample of payroll transactions.

Classification of Payroll Transactions

Because classification is an important assertion for payroll transactions, control activities must ensure that the appropriate payroll accounts are charged. If payroll expense is charged to the wrong accounts, the financial statements may be misstated. For example, if payroll expense is not properly classified between direct and indirect labour, inventory and cost of goods sold may not be valued properly. The use of an adequate chart of accounts is one control activity that helps prevent misclassification. Additionally, the timekeeping function should review the payroll categories assigned by the operating departments. Budgets that compare actual payroll costs to budgeted payroll costs by each category of labour also provide a control over proper classification of payroll. The auditor can review and test the client's control activities for classifying payroll costs.

❖ RELATING THE ASSESSED LEVEL OF CONTROL RISK TO
LO9 SUBSTANTIVE PROCEDURES

If the results of the tests of controls for the payroll system support the planned level of control risk, the auditor conducts substantive procedures of payroll-related accounts at the assessed level. EarthWear, for example, has a strong set of control activities for processing payroll transactions. If the auditor's tests of EarthWear's controls indicate that the controls are operating effectively, then no adjustment of detection risk is necessary. However, if the results of the control tests do not support the planned level of control risk for EarthWear's payroll system, the detection risk will have to be set lower. This would require that the nature and extent of substantive testing of payroll-related accounts be increased.

AUDITING PAYROLL-RELATED ACCOUNTS

Two categories of substantive procedures for auditing payroll expense and payroll-related liabilities are discussed here: (1) substantive **analytical procedures** and (2) tests of details of classes of transactions, account balances and disclosures. Table 12–6 presents the assertions for classes of transactions, events, account balances and disclosures as they apply to payroll expense and payroll-related liabilities, which are often called *accrued payroll* expenses. You should note that the auditor may obtain assurance for assertions related to transactions (substantive tests of transactions) in conjunction with testing the internal controls. If the tests of controls indicate that the controls are not operating effectively, the auditor may need to test transactions at the date the account balance is tested.

Table 12–6 Assertions about Classes of Transactions, Events, Account Balances and Disclosures for Payroll Expense and Payroll-Related Accruals

Assertions about Classes of Transactions and Events:

- **Occurrence**. Payroll transactions and events are valid.
- **Completeness**. All payroll transactions and events have been recorded.
- **Authorization**. All payroll transactions and events are properly authorized.
- **Accuracy**. Payroll transactions have been properly computed, and payroll expense has been properly accumulated from journals and ledgers.
- **Cut-off**. Payroll expense and related accruals are recorded in the correct accounting period.
- **Classification**. Payroll expense and related accruals have been recorded in the proper accounts.

Assertions about Account Balances at the Period End:

- **Existence**. Payroll expense is a valid expense and related accruals are valid liabilities.
- **Rights and obligations**. The payroll-related accruals are the obligations of the entity.
- **Completeness**. All payroll expense and related accruals have been recorded.
- **Valuation and allocation**. Payroll expense and related accruals are included in the financial statements at appropriate amounts, and any resulting valuation or allocation adjustments are appropriately recorded.

Assertions about Presentation and Disclosure:

- **Occurrence and rights and obligations**. All disclosed events, transactions, and other matters relating to payroll expense and related accruals have occurred and pertain to the entity.
- **Completeness**. All disclosures relating to payroll expense and related accruals that should have been included in the financial statements have been included.
- **Classification and understandability**. Financial information relating to payroll expense and related accruals is appropriately presented and described, and disclosures are clearly expressed.
- **Accuracy and valuation**. Financial and other information relating to payroll expense and related accruals are disclosed fairly and at appropriate amounts.

❖ SUBSTANTIVE ANALYTICAL PROCEDURES

LO10

Substantive analytical procedures can be useful substantive tests for examining the reasonableness of payroll expenses and payroll-related accrual accounts. When utilized as part of planning, preliminary analytical procedures can effectively identify payroll expense accounts and accrual accounts that may be misstated. Take a break from reading and think about comparisons and reasonableness tests you could develop to obtain assurance that payroll appears reasonable and that wages payable at the end of the year is accurately stated.

Table 12–7 shows examples of substantive analytical procedures that can be used for auditing payroll. Two examples will help demonstrate their application in practice. First, the auditor can compare budgeted payroll costs with actual payroll costs. Variances due to quantity and wage differences should show up in the client's cost-accounting system (on weekly or monthly reports). If the variances are immaterial, the auditor has some evidence that payroll costs are reasonable. If the variances are material, the auditor should investigate the potential causes of the differences. This substantive analytical procedure also helps the auditor determine the proper valuation of inventory when standard costs are used to value inventory. Second, the auditor can test the reasonableness of certain accrual balances. For example, if accrued wages represent payroll for two days, the auditor can multiply the total weekly payroll by 40 per cent (2 days ÷ 5 days). If the auditor's calculation is close to the accrued amount, no further audit work may be required on the accrued wages account.

Table 12–7 Example Substantive Analytical Procedures for Auditing Payroll Accounts and Payroll-Related Accruals

Example Substantive Analytical Procedures	Possible Misstatement Detected
Payroll Expense Accounts	
Compare current-year balances in the various payroll expense accounts with prior years' balances after adjustment for pay changes and number of employees.	Over- or understatement of payroll expense.
Compare payroll costs as a percentage of sales with prior years' and industry data.	Over- or understatement of payroll expense.
Compare labour utilization rates and statistics with industry data.	Over- or understatement of payroll expense.
Compare budgeted payroll expenses with actual payroll expenses.	Over- or understatement of payroll expense.
Estimate sales commissions by applying commission formulas to recorded sales totals.	Over- or understatement of sales commissions.
Payroll-Related Accrual Accounts	
Compare current-year balances in payroll-related accrual accounts with prior years' balances after adjusting for changes in conditions.	Over- or understatement of accrued liabilities.
Test reasonableness of accrual balances.	Over- or understatement of accrued liabilities.

❖ TESTS OF DETAILS OF CLASSES OF TRANSACTIONS, ACCOUNT BALANCES
LO11 AND DISCLOSURES

❖ Table 12–6 presents the assertions for payroll expense and payroll-related liabilities. The intended purpose
LO12 of tests of details of transactions is to detect monetary misstatements in the individual transactions
processed through the payroll application. As previously mentioned, **tests of details of transactions** are
often conducted in conjunction with tests of controls. Table 12–8 presents examples of tests of details of
transactions, account balances and disclosures for assertions related to payroll. The discussion that follows
focuses on **tests of details of account balances** of payroll expense and accrued payroll liabilities.

Table 12–8 Examples of Payroll Tests of Transactions, Account Balances, and Disclosures

Assertions about Classes of Transactions	Example Substantive Tests of Transactions
Occurrence	Vouche a sample of payroll direct deposits to the master employee list to verify validity.*
Completeness	Tracing of a sample of time cards/sheets to the payroll register.*
Authorization	Test a sample of payroll direct deposits for the presence of an authorized time card/sheet.*
Accuracy	Recompute the mathematical accuracy of a sample of direct deposits: CAATs may be used to test the logic of the computer programs for proper calculation of gross pay, deductions and net pay.
Cut-off	Trace a sample of time cards/sheets before and after period end to the appropriate weekly payroll report, and trace the weekly payroll report to the general ledger to verify payroll transactions are recorded in the proper period.*
Classification	Examine a sample of payroll direct deposits for proper classification into expense accounts.*
Assertions about Account Balances at Period End	**Example Tests of Details of Account Balances**
Existence	Vouch selected amounts from the account analysis schedules for the accruals to supporting documentation (payroll tax returns, corporate benefit policies, etc.).
Rights and obligations	Review supporting documentation to determine that the entity is legally obligated to pay the liability.
	Test a sample of bank reconciliations for the payroll bank account (see Chapter 16).

Completeness	Search for unrecorded liabilities (see Chapter 11).
	Use CAATs to foot weekly payroll reports and reconcile the total to the general ledger (payroll expense and related accruals).
Valuation and allocation	Obtain an account analysis schedule for accrued payroll liabilities; foot schedules and agree total to general ledger.
	Compare amounts accrued to supporting documentation, such as payroll tax returns.
Assertions about Presentation and Disclosure	*Example Tests of Details of Disclosures*
Occurrence, and rights and obligations	Inquire about accruals to ensure that they are properly disclosed.
Completeness	Complete financial reporting checklist to ensure that all financial statement disclosures related to payroll expense and related accruals have been made.
Classification and understandability	Review accrued payroll liabilities for proper classification between short-term and long-term liabilities.
	Read notes to ensure that required disclosures are understandable.
Accuracy and valuation	Review benefit contracts for proper disclosure of pension and postretirement benefits.
	Read notes and other information to ensure that the information is accurate and properly presented at the appropriate amounts.

* These tests of details of transactions are commonly conducted as dual-purpose tests (i.e. in conjunction with tests of controls).

Payroll Expense Accounts

Payroll transactions affect many expense accounts, including direct and indirect manufacturing expense, general and administrative salaries, sales salaries, commissions and payroll tax expenses. Some companies account for such expenses by product line or division. In addition, social security taxes or fringe benefits such as medical and life insurance may be paid at least partly by the organization. If the entity's internal control is reliable, the auditor generally does not need to conduct detailed tests of these payroll expense accounts. On such audits, sufficient evidence can be gathered through an understanding of internal control, tests of controls, tests of details of transactions and substantive analytical procedures. Additional detail testing is necessary only when control deficiencies exist or when the other types of audit tests indicate that material misstatements may be present.

Several payroll expense accounts may still be examined even when control risk is low. For example, it is common to verify the compensation paid to officers of the company because information on executive salaries and bonuses require disclosure. Limits may also be placed on officers' salaries and bonuses as part of lending agreements. If such limits are exceeded, the entity may be in default on the debt. Officers' compensation is also examined because, as noted earlier, officers are in a position to override the control activities and pay themselves more than they are authorized to receive. Officers' compensation expense can be verified by comparing the amounts shown in the payroll records with the amounts authorized in either board of directors' minutes or employment contracts, and by using CAATs to search for other cash payments made to the officer, his or her family or related parties.

Accrued Payroll Liabilities

An entity incurs a number of payroll-related liabilities. In addition to these accrued expenses, the entity also withholds various amounts from an employee's pay. These withholdings may include payroll taxes, medical and life insurance premiums, pension and other miscellaneous deductions. Some examples of accrued payroll liabilities include:

- Accrued wages and salaries.
- Accrued payroll taxes.
- Accrued commissions.
- Accrued bonuses.
- Accrued benefits such as vacation and sick pay.

In auditing accrued payroll liabilities, the auditor is concerned mainly with five audit assertions: *existence, completeness, valuation, cut-off*, and presentation and disclosure assertion of *completeness.* When control risk is low or the amounts in the accounts are relatively small, the auditor can verify accrued payroll liabilities using substantive analytical procedures. For example, the auditor can compare the prior year's balance in each accrual with the current year's balance after considering changing conditions.

For accrued payroll liability accounts for which the control risk is high or whose amounts are material, the auditor can obtain a detailed account analysis schedule. For example, Exhibit 12–2 shows an account analysis schedule for EarthWear's accrued payroll taxes. The credits to the account represent the recognition of payroll tax expense at the end of each pay period. These amounts can be traced to the various payroll tax returns or other documentation filed by the entity and should agree with the amount of payroll tax expense included in the income statement. The debits to the account represent payments made to the relevant tax collection body, for example the municipal treasurer. These payments can be verified by tracing the amounts to the cash disbursements journal.

Exhibit 12–2 Account Analysis for Accrued Payroll Taxes Account			
			N25 DLJ 4/2/10
EARTHWEAR CLOTHIERS **Analysis of Accrued Payroll Taxes** **31/12/09**			
Disbursements for payment of payroll taxes	€253,275£	Beginning balance Weekly accruals for payroll tax expense Ending balance	€9,450 φ 253,540 ✔ €9,715λL F
F = Footed. φ = Traced to prior year's working papers. **L** = Agreed to general ledger. ✔ = Traced three weeks' (19/2, 30/4, and 24/9) payroll expense accruals to weekly payroll records. £ = Traced three payments of payroll taxes to the cash disbursements journal. λ = Recomputed amount of unpaid payroll taxes for two weeks at the end of December 2009.			

An interesting aspect of this type of accrual account is that it periodically 'clears out' the accrued amount. For example, if the client has to make payments for payroll taxes to the government on the fifteenth of each month, the accrued payroll taxes account will have a zero balance after the payment. Thus, at the end of any month, the accrued payroll taxes account should contain only an accrual for payroll taxes since the last payment (approximately two weeks). In many organizations, these costs are broken down into the various types of payroll taxes.

Cut-off

The auditor also wants to determine whether all payroll-related liabilities are recorded in the proper period. An examination of supporting documentation for the accruals provides evidence on the proper period for recording the expense or liability. For example, an examination of the client's life insurance premium invoices should allow the auditor to determine if a proper accrual for life insurance costs has been made in the current period.

Existence and Valuation

The existence and valuation assertions can generally be tested at the same time. The auditor's concerns are whether the recorded liabilities are valid obligations of the entity and whether they are included in the financial statements at the appropriate amount. To verify the existence and valuation of an accrued payroll liability, the auditor can generally vouch the amounts included on the account analysis working paper to supporting documentation such as payroll tax reports. If adequate documentation is present, the auditor has evidence that the amount represents a valid liability. The auditor can usually verify the accuracy of the amounts by recalculating the figures.

Completeness

The auditor wants to make sure that all payroll-related liabilities are recorded. The auditor should be aware of the normal payroll-related taxes that are paid by the entity and therefore should be able to determine if accruals have been made for payroll taxes such as social security taxes. In some instances, the auditor's search for unrecorded liabilities, which was discussed in Chapter 11, may provide evidence that all payroll-related liabilities are recorded.

Presentation and Disclosure: Completeness

The auditor must ensure that all necessary financial statement disclosures for the human resource management process are made. Table 12–9 presents examples of items that ordinarily should be disclosed.

Table 12–9   Sample Disclosure Items for the Human Resource Management Process
Pensions.
Post-retirement benefits.
Share-based payments.
Profit-sharing plans.
Deferred compensation arrangements.

The international accounting standards require substantial disclosure for the human resource management process. International Accounting Standard 19 details disclosure of employee benefits, including pensions, and IFRS 2 deals specifically with disclosure on share-based payment to employees. Although discussion of the audit of these items is beyond the scope of this text, the reader should be aware that such disclosures are important to the fairness of the financial statements.

❖ EVALUATING THE AUDIT FINDINGS: PAYROLL-RELATED ACCOUNTS

LO13

When the auditor has completed the planned substantive procedures of the payroll-related accounts, all the identified misstatements should be aggregated. The aggregated identified misstatement is compared to materiality for the financial statements or any lesser materiality amount determined appropriate for the payroll-related accounts. The auditor determines if the identified misstatements would affect the audit. For example, suppose the auditor's substantive analytical procedures indicate that commissions expense is overstated, the auditor might perform detailed computations of commissions expense.

The auditor again requests the client to correct the identified misstatements and then compares the uncorrected misstatements with materiality to conclude whether the financial statements are fairly stated.

For example, in Chapter 3 materiality for EarthWear's payroll-related accounts was set at €900,000. Exhibit 3–4 showed that Willis & Adams International detected a misstatement in recording payroll expense and bonuses that amounted to a €215,000 understatement of accrued liabilities. Because this misstatement is less than the materiality of €900,000, Willis & Adams can conclude that the audit evidence supports fair presentation. However, if the misstatement was greater than materiality and remained uncorrected, a qualified audit opinion is appropriate.

🔑 Key Terms

Analytical procedures. Evaluations of financial information through analysis of plausible relationships among both financial and non-financial data.
Application controls. Controls that apply to the processing of specific computer applications and are part of the computer programs used in the accounting system.
Assertions. Representations by management, explicit or otherwise, that are embodied in the financial statements, as used by the auditor to consider the different types of potential misstatements that may occur.

Control activities. The policies and procedures that help ensure that management's directives are carried out.

Reliance strategy. The auditor's decision to rely on the entity's controls, test those controls and reduce the substantive tests of the financial statement accounts.

Tests of controls. Audit procedures performed to obtain audit evidence about the operating effectiveness of controls in preventing, or detecting and correcting, material misstatements at the assertion level.

Tests of details of account balances and disclosures. Substantive tests that concentrate on the details of items contained in the account balance and disclosures.

Tests of details of transactions (substantive tests of transactions). Tests to detect errors or fraud in individual transactions.

Review Questions

LO1	12–1	Why is the payroll system of most entities computerized?
LO2	12–2	What are the major types of transactions that occur in the payroll system? What financial statement accounts are affected by each of these types of transactions?
LO3	12–3	Briefly describe each of the following documents or records: payroll register, payroll master file, and payroll master file changes report.
LO4	12–4	What duties are performed within the human resources, timekeeping and payroll-processing functions?
LO5	12–5	List the key segregation of duties in the human resource management process. What errors or fraud can occur if such duties are not segregated?
LO6	12–6	List the inherent risk factors that affect the human resource management process.
LO7,8	12–7	Discuss the two control environment factors that an auditor should consider when examining the human resource management process.
LO8	12–8	What are the key authorization points in a payroll system?
LO8	12–9	Why is it important for the client to establish control activities over the classification of payroll transactions?
LO8,11	12–10	What is an example of a test of control or test of details of transactions that can be performed using CAATs for payroll transactions?
LO10	12–11	List two substantive analytical procedures that can be used to provide audit evidence related to the payroll expense accounts and the payroll-related liabilities.
LO12	12–12	Discuss how an auditor would audit the accrued payroll taxes account.
LO12	12–13	Identify three possible disclosure issues for payroll expense and payroll-related liabilities.

Problems

LO4,5   12–14   You have been hired by Morris & Son to manage its Human Resource Department. As a first step you want to determine personnel needs and assigned duties in order to prevent errors and fraud in the financial statements.

Required:

How many people would you utilize and what duties would you assign to each person hired to best help prevent errors and fraud in the financial statements? Be sure to explain your answer.

LO4,5,7,8   12–15   Audit documentation (working papers) contains a narrative description of a *segment* of the Croyden Factory payroll system and an accompanying flowchart as follows.

Narrative

The internal control system with respect to the personnel department functions well and is not included in the accompanying flowchart.

At the beginning of each workweek, payroll clerk 1 reviews the payroll department files to determine the employment status of factory employees and then prepares time cards and distributes them as each individual arrives at work. This payroll clerk, who is also responsible for custody of the signature stamp machine, verifies the identity of each payee before delivering signed cheques to the foreman.

At the end of each workweek, the foreman distributes the payroll cheques for the preceding workweek. Concurrent with this activity, the foreman reviews the current week's employee time cards, notes the regular and overtime hours worked on a summary form, and initials the time cards. The foreman then delivers all time cards and unclaimed payroll cheques to payroll clerk 2.

Required:

a *Based on the narrative and the flowchart on the next page, what are the deficiencies in internal control?*

b *Based on the narrative and the accompanying flowchart, what inquiries should be made to clarify possible additional deficiencies in internal control? Do not discuss the internal control system of the personnel department.*

(AICPA, adapted)

LO10,11,12 12–16 McCarthy, independent auditor, was engaged to audit the financial statements of Kent Company, a continuing audit client. McCarthy is about to audit Kent's payroll transactions. Kent uses an in-house payroll department to process payroll data and prepare and transfer direct payroll deposits as well as prepare and distribute payroll cheques.

During the planning process, McCarthy determined that the inherent risk of overstatement of payroll expense is high. In addition, McCarthy obtained an understanding of internal control and set the control risk for payroll-related assertions at the maximum level.

Required:

Describe the audit procedures McCarthy should consider performing in the audit of Kent's payroll transactions to address the risk of overstatement. Do not discuss Kent's internal control.

(AICPA, adapted)

LO10,11,12 12–17 James, who was engaged to examine the financial statements of Talbert Corporation, is about to audit payroll. Talbert uses a computer service centre to process weekly payroll as follows.

Each Monday Talbert's payroll clerk inserts data in appropriate spaces on the preprinted service centre-prepared input form and sends it to the service centre via messenger. The service centre extracts new permanent data from the input form and updates its master files. The weekly payroll data are then processed. The weekly payroll register and payroll cheques are printed and delivered by messenger to Talbert on Thursday.

Part of the sample selected for audit by James includes the following input form and payroll register:

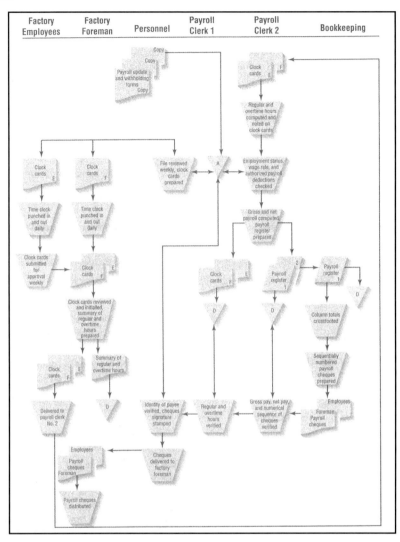

Croyden Factory Payroll System

				Hours		Special Deductions		
TALBERT CORPORATION Payroll Input Week Ending Friday, 27 November 2009								
		Employee Data – Permanent File				Current Week's Payroll Data		
	Name	Identification Number	Deduction Information	Hourly Rate	Regular	Overtime	Bonds	Union	Other
A	Bell	999-99-9991	M-1	€10.00	35	5	€18.75		
B	Carioso	999-99-9992	M-2	10.00	35	4			
C	Deng	999-99-9993	S-1	10.00	35	6	18.75	€4.00	
D	Ellis	999-99-9994	S-1	10.00	35	2		4.00	€50.00
E	Flaherty	999-99-9995	M-4	10.00	35	1		4.00	
F	Gillis	999-99-9996	M-4	10.00	35			4.00	
G	Hua	999-99-9997	M-1	7.00	35	2	18.75	4.00	
H	Jones	999-99-9998	M-2	7.00	35			4.00	25.00
I	King	999-99-9999	S-1	7.00	35	4		4.00	
New Employee:								
J.	Smith	999-99-9990	M-3	7.00	35				

TALBERT CORPORATION
Payroll Register
27 November 2009

			Hours		Payroll			Taxes Withheld					
	Employee	Social Identification Number	Regular	Overtime	Regular	Overtime	Gross Payroll	City	State	County	Other Withheld	Net Pay	Cheque Number
A	Bell	999-99-9991	35	5	€350.00	€75.00	€425.00	€26.05	€76.00	€27.40	€18.75	€276.80	1499
B	Carioso	999-99-9992	35	4	350.00	60.00	410.00	25.13	65.00	23.60		296.27	1500
C	Deng	999-99-9993	35	6	350.00	90.00	440.00	26.97	100.90	28.60	22.75	260.78	1501
D	Ellis	999-99-9994	35	2	350.00	30.00	380.00	23.29	80.50	21.70	54.00	200.51	1502
E	Flaherty	999-99-9995	35	1	350.00	15.00	365.00	22.37	43.50	15.90	4.00	279.23	1503
F	Gillis	999-99-9996	35		350.00		350.00	21.46	41.40	15.00	4.00	268.14	1504
G	Hua	999-99-9997	35	2	245.00	21.00	266.00	16.31	34.80	10.90	22.75	181.24	1505
H	Jones	999-99-9998	35		245.00		245.00	15.02	26.40	8.70	29.00	165.88	1506
I	King	999-99-9999	35	4	245.00	42.00	287.00	17.59	49.40	12.20	4.00	203.81	1507
J	Smith	999-99-9990	35		245.00		245.00	15.02	23.00	7.80		199.18	1508
Total			350	24	€3,080.00	€333.00	€3,413.00	€209.21	€540.90	€171.80	€159.25	€2,331.84	

Required:

a Describe how James should verify the information in the payroll input form shown.

b Describe (but do not perform) the procedures that James should follow in examining the 27 November 2009 payroll register shown.

(AICPA, adapted)

Discussion Cases

LO7,8,9 **12–18** Service Corporation hired an independent computer programmer to develop a simplified payroll application for its newly purchased computer. The programmer developed an online database microcomputer system that minimized the level of knowledge required of the operator. It was based on typing answers to input cues that appeared on the terminal's viewing screen, examples of which follow:

A Access routine:
    1 Operator access number to payroll file?
    2 Are there new employees?

B New employee routine:
    1 Employee name?
    2 Employee number?
    3 Identification number?
    4 Rate per hour?
    5 Single or married?
    6 Number of dependents?
    7 Account distribution?

C Current payroll routine:
    1 Employee number?
    2 Regular hours worked?
    3 Overtime hours worked?
    4 Total employees this payroll period?

The independent auditor is attempting to verify that certain input validation (edit) checks exist to ensure that errors resulting from omissions, invalid entries, or other inaccuracies are detected during the typing of answers to the input cues.

Required:

a Discuss the various types of input validation (edit) controls that the independent auditor would expect to find in the IT system.

b Describe the assurances provided by each identified validation check.

(AICPA, adapted)

LO6,10,12   12–19   A common form of executive compensation is company stock (or options to purchase stock). Designers of these compensation plans argue that by compensating officers with stock, the officers will take actions in the best interest of the shareholders. Critics claim executive compensation is often too high in proportion to average salaries at companies and that the compensation levels motivate officers to take selfish actions.

Required:

a   *Research executive compensation of some well-known companies. (You can find information on executive compensation in annual reports.) Use your best judgement to compute the proportion of executive compensation to average salary (i.e. are executives earning 5 times, or 10 times, or 100 times the average employee). In your opinion, are the executives worth it?*

b   *In your opinion, what are the costs and benefits associated with compensating executives with stock or options to purchase stock?*

c   *What do you believe are the most effective audit procedures to use to identify executive compensation abuse or fraud? Please explain why.*

 Internet Assignment

LO11,12   12–20   Using an Internet browser, search for information on labour costs in the retail catalogue industry (e.g. labour costs as a percentage of sales).

13 Auditing the Inventory Management Process

❖ LEARNING OBJECTIVES

Upon completion of this chapter you will

- ❖ **LO1** Develop an understanding of the inventory management process.
- ❖ **LO2** Be able to identify and describe the types of documents and records used in the inventory management process.
- ❖ **LO3** Understand the functions in the inventory management process.
- ❖ **LO4** Know the appropriate segregation of duties for the inventory management process.
- ❖ **LO5** Be able to identify and evaluate inherent risks relevant to the inventory management process.
- ❖ **LO6** Know how to assess control risk for the inventory system.
- ❖ **LO7** Know key internal controls and develop relevant tests of controls for inventory transactions.

- ❖ **LO8** Understand how to relate the assessment of control risk to substantive procedures.
- ❖ **LO9** Be familiar with substantive analytical procedures used to audit inventory and related accounts.
- ❖ **LO10** Know how to audit standard costs.
- ❖ **LO11** Know how to observe physical inventory.
- ❖ **LO12** Be familiar with tests of details of transactions used to audit inventory and related accounts.
- ❖ **LO13** Be familiar with tests of details of account balances used to audit inventory and related accounts.
- ❖ **LO14** Understand how to evaluate the audit findings and reach a final conclusion on inventory and related accounts.

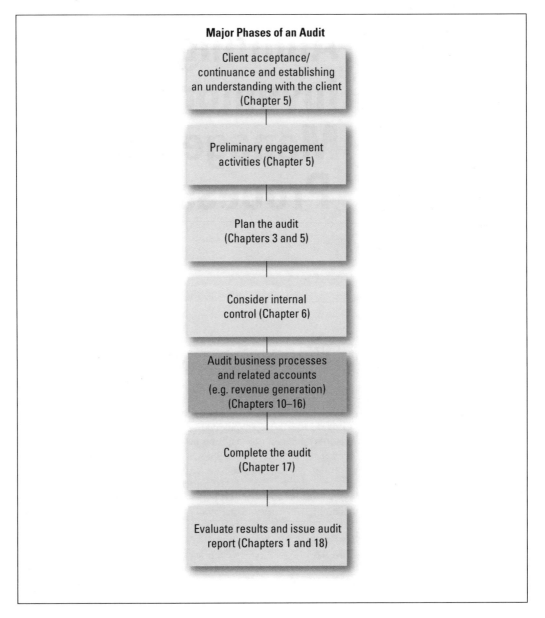

❖ RELEVANT ACCOUNTING AND AUDITING PRONOUNCEMENTS

IASB, IAS 1, Presentation of Financial Statements

IASB, IAS 2, Inventory

ISA 230, Audit Documentation

ISA 240, The Auditor's Responsibilities Relating to Fraud in an Audit of Financial Statements

ISA 315, Identifying and Assessing the Risks of Material Misstatement through Understanding the Entity and Its Environment

ISA 320, Materiality in Planning and Performing an Audit

ISA 330, The Auditor's Responses to Assessed Risks

ISA 450, Evaluation of Misstatements Identified during the Audit

ISA 500, Audit Evidence

ISA 501, Audit Evidence – Specific Considerations for Selected Items

ISA 505, External Confirmations

ISA 520, Analytical Procedures

ISA 540, Auditing Accounting Estimates, Including Fair Value Accounting Estimates, and Related Disclosures

ISA 620, Using the Work of an Auditor's Expert

FOR MOST MANUFACTURING, wholesale, and merchandising (retail) entities, inventory is a major element of the balance sheet. The complexity of auditing inventory may be affected by the degree of processing required to manufacture products. In a merchandising business, products are purchased directly from vendors with little or no additional processing by the entity before sale. In such cases, verifying inventory is relatively straightforward. On the other hand, determining a proper inventory value may be more difficult when the production process involves numerous steps. The presentation in this chapter mainly discusses inventory in terms of a merchandising company. However, the audit approach followed for merchandising entities is easily adapted to other types of inventory processes.

The coverage of the inventory management process follows the components of the audit risk model. An overview of the inventory management process is presented first, followed by discussion of the risk of material misstatement, specifically inherent risk factors and control risk assessment. The last part of the chapter discusses the substantive procedures for inventory with particular emphasis on auditing standard costs and observing physical inventory.

❖ OVERVIEW OF THE INVENTORY MANAGEMENT PROCESS

LO1

The inventory management process is affected by the control activities previously discussed for the revenue, purchasing and payroll processes. Figure 13–1 shows how each of these processes interacts with the inventory management process. The acquisition of and payment for inventory are controlled via the purchasing process. The cost of both direct and indirect labour assigned to inventory is controlled through the payroll process. Last, finished goods are sold and accounted for as part of the revenue process. Thus, the 'cradle-to-grave' cycle for inventory begins when goods are purchased and stored, and ends when the finished goods are shipped to customers.

Inventory can represent one of the most complex parts of the audit. For example, while determining the quantity of inventory on hand is usually an easy audit step to complete, assigning costs to value those quantities is more difficult. Additionally, there may be other troublesome valuation issues related to inventory such as measurement of inventory at the lower of cost or value (net realizable value).

Exhibit 13–1 describes EarthWear's inventory system, while Figure 13–2 flowcharts the system. This description and flowchart provide a framework for discussing the control activities and **tests of controls** for the inventory management process in more detail. However, because of differences in products and their subsequent processing, the inventory system usually differs from one entity to the next. The reader should concentrate on understanding the basic concepts of internal control.

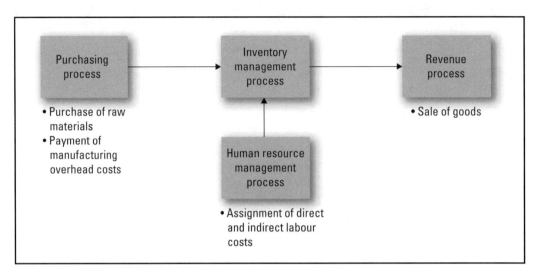

Figure 13–1   The Relationship of the Inventory Management Process to Other Accounting Processes

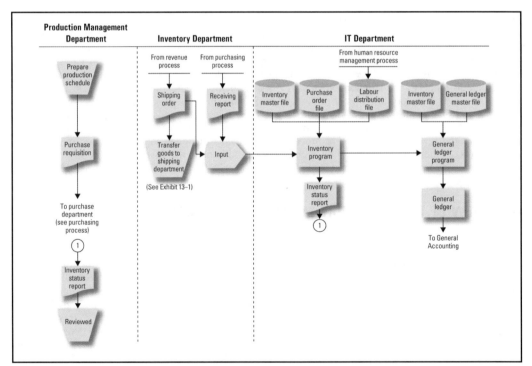

Figure 13–2   Flowchart of the Inventory Management Process: EarthWear Clothiers

---

Exhibit 13–1   Description of EarthWear's Inventory System*

Clothing and other products sold by EarthWear are developed by the company's design department. All goods are produced by independent manufacturers, except for most of EarthWear's soft luggage. The company purchases merchandise from more than 300 domestic and foreign manufacturers. For many major suppliers, goods are ordered and paid for through the company's electronic data interchange (EDI) system. The computerized inventory control system handles the receipt of shipments from manufacturers. Goods are received at the receiving department, where the information is agreed to the purchase order (receiving report) and entered into the inventory control system.

The company's sales representatives enter orders into an online order entry and inventory control system; customers using the company's Internet site complete a computer screen that enters the orders. Computer processing of orders is performed each night on a batch basis, at which time shipping tickets are printed with bar codes for optical scanning. Inventory is picked based on the location of individual products rather than orders, followed by computerized sorting and transporting of goods to multiple packing stations and shipping zones.

* For simplicity of presentation, we have not included inventory processes at EarthWear's outlet stores.
The following topics related to the inventory management process are discussed below:

- Types of documents and records.
- The major functions.
- The key segregation of duties.

 Types of Documents and Records

LO2

Table 13–1 lists the more important documents and records that are normally involved in the inventory system. Not all of these documents are presented in Figure 13–2. They are discussed here to give the reader information on documents and records that might exist in an inventory management process of a manufacturing company. The reader should keep in mind that in an IT system some of these documents and records may exist for only a short time or only in digital form.

Table 13–1   Documents and Records Included in the Inventory Management Process

Production schedule	Production data information
Receiving report	Cost accumulation and variance report
Materials requisition	Inventory status report
Inventory master file	Shipping order

Production Schedule

A production schedule is normally prepared periodically based on the expected demand for the entity's products. The expected demand may be based on the current backlog of orders or on sales forecasts from the sales or marketing department. In EarthWear's system, this schedule is prepared by the design department. Production schedules determine the quantity of goods needed and the time at which they must be ready in order to meet the production scheduling. Many organizations use material requirements planning or just-in-time inventory programs to assist with production planning. Production schedules give the auditor information on the planned level of operating activity.

Receiving Report

The receiving report records the receipt of goods from vendors. This document was discussed as part of the purchasing process. It is reconsidered in the inventory management process because a copy of this document accompanies the goods to the inventory department and is used to update the client's perpetual inventory records. Note in Figure 13–2 that the data from the receiving report are input into the inventory program to update the inventory master file, which contains the information on the client's perpetual records.

Materials Requisition

Materials requisitions are normally used by manufacturing companies to track materials during the production process. Materials requisitions are normally prepared by department personnel as needed for production purposes. For example, the materials requisition is the document that authorizes the release of raw materials from the raw materials department. A copy of the materials requisition may be maintained in the raw materials department, and another copy may accompany the goods to the production departments.

Inventory Master File

The inventory master file contains all the important information related to the entity's inventory, including the perpetual inventory records. In sophisticated inventory systems such as EarthWear's, the inventory master file also contains information on the costs used to value inventory. In a manufacturing company, it would not be unusual for the inventory master file to contain the **standard costs** used to value the inventory at various stages of production.

Production Data Information

In a manufacturing company, production information about the transfer of goods and related cost accumulation at each stage of production should be reported. This information updates the entity's perpetual inventory system. It is also used as input to generate the cost accumulation and variance reports that are produced by the inventory system.

Cost Accumulation and Variance Report

Most inventory control systems in a manufacturing setting produce reports similar to a cost accumulation and variance report. Material, labour and overhead costs are charged to inventory as part of the manufacturing process. The cost accumulation report summarizes the various costs charged to departments and products. The variance reports present the results of inventory processing in terms of actual costs versus standard or budgeted costs. The cost accounting and manufacturing departments review these reports for appropriate charges.

Inventory Status Report

The inventory status report shows the type and amount of products on hand. Such a report is basically a summary of the perpetual inventory records. This report can also be used to determine the status of goods in process. In sophisticated inventory systems, this type of information can be accessed directly through computer terminals or PCs.

Shipping Order

This document was discussed as part of the revenue process. It is reconsidered here because a copy of this document is used to remove goods from the client's perpetual inventory records. Note in Figure 13–2 that the inventory master file is updated when a receiving report is processed or when a shipping order is generated.

The Major Functions

LO3

Table 13–2 summarizes the functions that normally take place in a typical inventory management process.

Table 13–2 Functions in the Inventory Management Process	
Inventory management	Authorization of production activity and maintenance of inventory at appropriate levels; issuance of purchase requisitions to the purchasing department (see Chapter 11 on the purchasing process).
Raw materials stores	Custody of raw materials and issuance of raw materials to manufacturing departments.
Manufacturing	Production of goods.
Finished goods stores	Custody of finished goods and issuance of goods to the shipping department (see Chapter 10 on the revenue process).
Cost accounting	Maintenance of the costs of manufacturing and inventory in cost records.
General ledger	Proper accumulation, classification, and summarization of inventory and related costs in the general ledger.

Inventory Management

At EarthWear, the inventory management function is performed by the design department. This department is responsible for maintaining inventory at appropriate levels. It issues purchase requisitions to the purchasing department and thus represents the point at which the inventory management process integrates with the purchasing process. In a manufacturing company, a production management department would be responsible for managing inventory through planning and scheduling manufacturing activities.

Raw Materials Stores

In a manufacturing company, this function is responsible for the receipt, custody and issuance of raw materials. When goods are received from vendors, they are transferred from the receiving department to the raw materials stores department. Once goods arrive in the raw materials storage area, they must be safeguarded against pilferage or unauthorized use. Finally, when goods are requested for production through the issuance of a materials requisition, this function issues the goods to the appropriate manufacturing department.

Manufacturing

The manufacturing function is responsible for producing the product. From an auditing perspective, there must be adequate control over the physical flow of the goods and proper accumulation of the costs attached to inventory. The manner in which costs are accumulated varies substantially from one entity to another. Entities may produce goods using a job order cost system, a process cost system, or some combination of both.

Finished Goods Stores

This function is responsible for the storage of and control over finished goods. When goods are completed by the manufacturing function, they are transferred to finished goods stores. Again, there must be adequate safeguards against pilferage or unauthorized use. When goods are ordered by a customer, a shipping order is produced by the revenue process and forwarded to the finished goods stores department. The goods are then transferred to the shipping department for shipment to the customer. Because EarthWear is a merchandising company, it maintains only finished goods (see Figure 13–2).

Cost Accounting

This function is responsible for ensuring that costs are properly attached to inventory as goods are processed through the manufacturing function. Cost accounting reviews the cost accumulation and variance reports after such data are processed into the accounting records.

General Ledger

The main objective of the general ledger function is to ensure that all inventory and costs of production are properly accumulated, classified, and summarized in the general ledger accounts. In an IT system, control or summary totals ensure that this function is performed correctly. One important control performed by the general ledger function is the reconciliation of the perpetual inventory records to the general ledger inventory accounts.

◆ The Key Segregation of Duties

LO4
Segregation of duties is a particularly important control in the inventory management process because of the potential for theft and fraud. Therefore, individuals involved in the inventory management and inventory stores functions should not have access to the inventory records, the cost-accounting records or the general ledger. When the inventory accounting records are maintained in an IT environment, there should be proper segregation of duties within the IT department. Table 13–3 shows the key segregation of duties for the inventory management process and examples of possible error or fraud that can result from conflicts in duties. Table 13–4 shows the proper segregation of duties for individual inventory functions across the various departments that control inventory processing. Before reading further, please take a look at EarthWear's flowchart in Figure 13–2 and consider how EarthWear implements segregation of duties.

Table 13–3 Key Segregation of Duties in the Inventory Management Process, and Possible Errors or Fraud

Segregation of Duties	Possible Errors or Fraud Resulting from Conflicts of Duties
The inventory management function should be segregated from the cost-accounting function.	If the individual responsible for inventory management also has access to the cost-accounting records, production and inventory costs can be manipulated. This may lead to an over- or understatement of inventory and net income.
The inventory stores function should be segregated from the cost-accounting function.	If one individual is responsible for both controlling and accounting for inventory, unauthorized shipments can be made or theft of goods can be covered up.
The cost-accounting function should be segregated from the general ledger function.	If one individual is responsible for the inventory records and also for the general ledger, it is possible for that individual to conceal unauthorized shipments. This can result in the theft of goods, leading to an overstatement of inventory.
The responsibility for supervising physical inventory should be separated from the inventory management and inventory stores functions.	If the individual responsible for production management or inventory stores function is also responsible for the physical inventory, it is possible that inventory shortages can be covered up through the adjustment of the inventory records to the physical inventory, resulting in an overstatement of inventory.

Table 13–4 Segregation of Duties for Inventory Functions by Department

	Department				
Inventory Function	Inventory Management	Raw Materials Stores	Finished Goods Stores	Cost Accounting	IT
Preparation of production schedules	X				
Issuance of materials requisitions that accompany goods to the manufacturing department		X			
Updating of cost records with materials, labour and overhead usage				X	X
Updating of inventory records				X	X
Release of goods to the shipping department			X		
Approval and issuance of purchase requisitions	X				

❖ INHERENT RISK ASSESSMENT

LO5

In examining the inventory management process, the auditor needs to consider the inherent risk factors that may affect the transactions processed by the system and the financial statement accounts affected by those transactions. The auditor should consider industry-related factors and operating and engagement characteristics (see Chapter 3) when assessing the possibility of a material misstatement.

Industry-Related Factors

A number of industry factors may indicate the presence of material misstatements in inventory. For example, if industry competition is intense, there may be problems with the proper valuation of inventory in terms of measurement of inventory at the lower of cost or net realizable value.[i] Technology changes in certain industries may also promote material misstatement due to obsolescence (see Exhibit 13–2).

Exhibit 13–2   Digital Cameras Sink Polaroid

Polaroid, the once high-flying company, filed for bankruptcy in October 2001 after it was unable to meet payments on its heavy debt load. In August, the company's auditors, KPMG, raised issue with the company's ability to continue as a going concern. The company, founded by Edward H. Land, was once one of the world's leading photography companies. Its main product was instant colour film that developed when exposed to light. However, since 1995, Polaroid had faced stiff competition from one-hour photo shops and, more recently, from digital cameras. Polaroid was unable to restructure its debt or find a buyer for the company prior to seeking bankruptcy protection. In the years immediately before and after the bankruptcy, Polaroid recorded write-offs of tens of millions of dollars for obsolete inventory.

Sources: J. Bandler, 'Polaroid Sustains Latest Setback as Auditor Questions Its Future', *Wall Street Journal* (10 August 2001), and J. Bandler and M. Pacelle, 'Polaroid is Using Chapter 11 to Seek Buyer', *Wall Street Journal* (15 October 2001).

Engagement and Operating Characteristics

A number of engagement and operating characteristics are important to the assessment of inherent risk for inventory. First, the type of product sold by the client can increase the potential for defalcation. For example, products that are small and of high value, such as jewellery, are more susceptible to theft than large products are. Second, inventory is often difficult to audit, and its valuation may result in disagreements with the client. Finally, the auditor must be alert to possible related-party transactions for acquiring raw materials and selling the finished product. For example, the client may purchase raw materials from a company controlled by the chief executive officer at prices in excess of market value. In such a case, the value of inventory will be overstated, and cash will have been misappropriated from the entity.

Audit research has also shown that there is a relatively high risk that inventory contains material misstatements.[ii] In fact, some of the most notorious accounting frauds in history have involved inventory manipulations. For example, in the 1990s fraudsters at Phar-Mor, a discount store retail chain, recorded a debit to a fraud holding account rather than to cost of goods sold when inventory was sold. Then just before year end, Phar-Mor accountants emptied the contents of the fraud holding account and allocated it to stores as fictitious inventory. Exhibit 13–3 describes the inventory fraud at Centennial Technologies, Inc.

Exhibit 13–3   Inventory Scams at Centennial Technologies

Background

Centennial Technologies designed, manufactured, and marketed an extensive line of PC cards: rugged, lightweight, credit card–sized devices inserted into a dedicated slot in a broad range of electronic equipment that contain microprocessors, such as portable computers, telecommunications equipment and manufacturing equipment. The company's customer list included companies such as Digital Equipment Corporation, Philips Electronics, Sharp Electronics Corporation and Xerox Corporation.

Emanuel Pinez was the CEO of technology highflier Centennial Technologies, Inc., in the mid-1990s. In 1996, Centennial's surging stock graduated to the New York Stock Exchange just two years after going public. It finished 1996 as the best-performing stock on the big board, up a stunning 451 per cent. Just before the fraud was uncovered, analysts still had 'strong buy' recommendations outstanding.

Pinez had an impressive resume, but it turns out much of it was false. After the scandal broke, investors, and the auditors learned what Pinez's wife knew, that he was a 'pathological liar'. For example, as a young man he claimed to have set a world record in an international swimming competition across the English Channel. The reports were published, and Pinez was hailed briefly as a national hero – until the truth came out that there was no such competition or record. Pinez constantly made aggressive estimates regarding Centennial's growth, and in 1996 he began telling investors that Centennial was negotiating an order worth more than $300 million with AT&T (no such deal ever took place or apparently even existed).

Card Scam

Centennial's growth attracted several sophisticated institutional investors, such as Oppenheimer Funds Inc. and Fidelity Investments. Some investors started to crave a first-hand look at Centennial's operations. One investor sent an analyst to meet with Pinez and tour the headquarters in Billerica, Massachusetts. Although the analyst noticed some computer equipment in the administrative offices, he was somewhat surprised that there was none in Pinez's office. During a tour of Centennial's manufacturing facilities, he saw 'a room full of people banging on cards with rubber mallets. I had a bad feeling.' He returned to his firm and 'dumped the Centennial shares immediately'.

In truth, Pinez had enlisted a handful of employees in the company's Billerica manufacturing plant to assemble fake memory cards by simply welding the casings together and leaving out a critical silicon computer chip. These fake cards made their way into inventory and sales.

Flash 98 Scam

In the fourth quarter of 1996 Centennial began shipping a new product called 'Flash 1998'. It was a miniature memory card for notebook computers. Sales for fiscal year 1996 amounted to about $2 million. The company told the auditors that it wanted to keep the details of the card relatively quiet for a few more months for competitive reasons. Pinez indicated that due to design advances developed by Centennial's research and development team, these new cards had an extremely low production cost, about 10 cents, with a sales price of a whopping $500. It turns out there was no such product. All sales were to one company, BBC. The company was run by a close personal friend of Pinez. To fool the auditors into thinking an actual sale took place, Pinez wired $1 million of his own personal funds to a third company, St Jude Management Corp., which then paid Centennial on behalf of BBC for its Flash 98 purchases. After the fraud was uncovered, the auditors, Coopers & Lybrand, claimed that the Flash 98 scam was a 'unique' fraud because it appeared that a product was going out and cash was coming in.

Aftermath

From his prison cell, Pinez denied any wrongdoing and indicated that his actions were undertaken to benefit the company. Pinez attributed his problems to the scrutiny that inevitably comes with success: 'You get lightning when you're very high.'

Sources: M. Beasley, F. Buckless, S. Glover and D. Prawitt, *Auditing Cases: An Interactive Learning Approach*, 4th edn, Prentice Hall, New York, 2008, and J. Auerbach , 'How Centennial Technologies, a Hot Stock, Cooled', *Wall Street Journal* (11 April 1997).

Prior-year misstatements are good indicators of potential misstatements in the current year; thus, auditors should carefully consider if misstatements found in the prior years' audit may be present in the current inventory and plan the audit accordingly.

❖ CONTROL RISK ASSESSMENT

LO6

The auditor may follow a substantive strategy when auditing inventory and cost of goods sold. When this is done, the auditor places no reliance on the control activities in the inventory management process and sets the level of control risk at the maximum. The auditor then relies on substantive procedures to determine the fairness of inventory. Such a strategy may be appropriate when internal control is not adequate.

In many cases, however, the auditor can rely on internal control for inventory. This normally occurs when the client has an integrated cost-accounting/inventory management system. For discussion purposes, it is assumed that the auditor has decided to follow a **reliance strategy**. Figure 13–3 summarizes the three steps for setting the control risk following this strategy. Each of these steps is only briefly reviewed within the context of the inventory management process because it is assumed that the reader now thoroughly understands the control risk setting process followed by auditors.

Understand and Document Internal Control

In order to set the control risk for the inventory management process, the auditor must understand the five internal control components. Two points should be mentioned. First, if the client uses IT for monitoring the flow of goods and accumulating costs, the auditor will need to evaluate both the general IT controls and the inventory **application controls**. Second, the auditor will need a thorough understanding of the process used by the client to value inventory.

Plan and Perform Tests of Controls

In performing this step, the auditor again must identify the relevant control activities within the client's inventory system that ensure that material misstatements are either prevented or detected and corrected. Audit procedures used to test the client's control activities in the inventory management process are discussed in subsequent sections.

Set and Document the Control Risk

Once the controls in the inventory system have been tested, the auditor sets the level of control risk. The auditor should document the achieved level of control risk using either quantitative amounts or qualitative terms. The documentation supporting the achieved level of control risk for the inventory management process might include a flowchart (such as the one shown in Figure 13–2), the results of the tests of controls, and a memorandum indicating the overall conclusions about control risk.

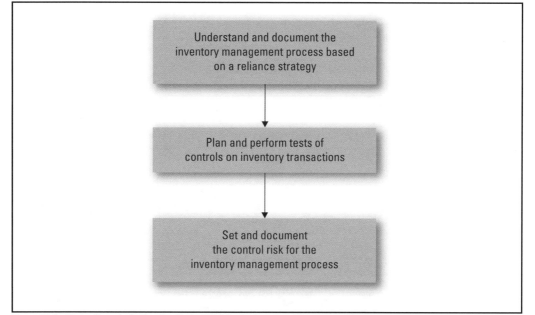

Figure 13–3   Major Steps in Setting the Control Risk in the Inventory Management Process

❖ CONTROL ACTIVITIES AND TESTS OF CONTROLS: INVENTORY TRANSACTIONS

LO7

Table 13–5 provides a summary of the possible misstatements, examples of control activities, and examples of selected tests of controls for inventory transactions. The discussion includes control activities that are present in a manufacturing setting. A number of control activities in the revenue and purchasing processes provide assurance for selected **assertions** for inventory. The discussion that follows is limited to the more important assertions.

Table 13–5   Summary of Assertions, Possible Misstatements, Example Control Activities and Example Tests of Controls for Inventory Transactions

Assertion	Possible Misstatement	Example Activity Control	Example Test of Controls
Occurrence	Fictitious inventory	Segregation of duties	Observe and evaluate proper segregation of duties.
		Inventory transferred to inventory department using an approved, prenumbered receiving report	Review and test procedures for the transfer of inventory.
		Inventory transferred to manufacturing using prenumbered materials requisitions	Review and test procedures for issuing materials to manufacturing departments.
		Accounting for numerical sequence of materials requisitions	Review and test client procedures for accounting for numerical sequence of materials requisitions.
	Inventory recorded but not on hand due to theft	Physical safeguards over inventory	Observe the physical safeguards over inventory.
Complete-ness	Inventory received but not recorded	The same as the control activities for completeness in the purchasing process (see Table 11–6)	The same as the tests of controls performed on the control activities in the purchasing process (see Table 11–6).

	Consigned goods not properly accounted for	Procedures to include goods out on consignment and exclude goods held on consignment	Review and test client's procedures for consignment goods.
Authoriza-tion	Unauthorized production activity, resulting in excess levels of inventory	Preparation and review of authorized purchase or production schedules	Review authorized production schedules.
	Inventory obsolescence	Use of material requirements planning and/or just-in-time inventory systems	Review and test procedures for developing inventory levels and procedures used to control them.
		Review of inventory levels by design department	
Accuracy	Inventory quantities recorded incorrectly	Periodic or annual comparison of goods on hand with amounts shown in perpetual inventory records	Review and test procedures for taking physical inventory.
	Inventory and cost of goods sold not properly costed	Standard costs that are reviewed by management Review of cost accumulation and variance reports	Review and test procedures used to develop standard costs. Review and test cost accumulation and variance reports
	Inventory obsolescence	Inventory management personnel review inventory for obsolete, slow-moving, or excess quantities	Review and test procedures for identifying obsolete, slow-moving, or excess quantities.
	Inventory transactions not posted to the perpetual inventory records		
	Amounts for inventory from purchases journal not posted correctly to the general ledger inventory account	Perpetual inventory records reconciled to general ledger control account monthly	Review the reconciliation of perpetual inventory to general ledger control account.
Cut-off	Inventory transactions recorded in the wrong period	All receiving reports processed daily by the IT department to record the receipt of inventory	Review and test procedures for processing inventory included on receiving reports into the perpetual records.
		All shipping documents processed daily to record the shipment of finished goods	Review and test procedures for removing inventory from perpetual records based on shipment of goods.
Classifica-tion	Inventory transactions not properly classified among raw materials, work in process, and finished goods	Materials requisitions and production data forms used to process goods through manufacturing	Review the procedures and forms used to classify inventory.

Occurrence of Inventory Transactions

The auditor's main concern is that all recorded inventory exists. The major control activity for preventing fictitious inventory transactions from being recorded is proper segregation of duties, in which the inventory management and inventory stores functions are separated from the departments responsible for inventory and cost-accounting records. This control prevents operating personnel from having access to both inventory and the perpetual inventory records. Additionally, prenumbered documents to handle the receipt, transfer and withdrawal of inventory may prevent the recording of fictitious inventory in the accounting records.

The auditor should also be concerned that goods may be stolen. The auditor's concern about theft of goods varies, depending upon the type of product sold or manufactured by the client. Products that are large or cumbersome may be difficult to steal. However, products that are small and of high value, such as jewellery or computer memory chips, are more susceptible to theft. The client should maintain physical safeguards over inventory that are consistent with the susceptibility and value of the goods. What controls does EarthWear have in place to address the occurrence assertion? How would you gather audit evidence regarding the effectiveness of these controls?

Review and observation are the main tests of controls used by the auditor to test the control activities shown in Table 13–5. For example, the auditor can observe and evaluate the employees' segregation of duties. The auditor can also review and test the client's procedures for the transfer of raw materials from the receiving department and their issuance to the manufacturing departments.

Completeness of Inventory Transactions

The control activities for the completeness assertion relate to recording inventory that has been received. Typically, the control activities for this assertion are contained within the purchasing process. These control activities and the related tests of controls were presented in Table 11–6 in Chapter 11. For example, in some instances, additional control activities may be used in the raw materials stores department to ensure that the goods are recorded in the perpetual inventory records. This might include comparing a summary of the receiving reports to the inventory status report.

If goods are consigned, the client must have control activities to ensure that goods held on consignment by other parties are included in inventory and goods held on consignment for others are excluded from inventory. The auditor can review the client's procedures for including or excluding consigned goods.

Authorization of Inventory Transactions

The control activities for the purchase of materials were discussed in Chapter 11 on the purchasing process. The auditor's concern with authorization in the inventory system is with unauthorized purchase or production activity that may lead to excess levels of certain types of finished goods. If such goods can quickly become obsolete, ending inventory may be overstated. The preparation and review of authorized purchase schedules by EarthWear's design department should prevent such misstatements. The use of some type of inventory-planning system, such as a material requirements planning system or a just-in-time inventory system, may also limit unauthorized production.

Accuracy of Inventory Transactions

Accuracy is an important assertion because inventory transactions that are not properly recorded result in misstatements that directly affect the amounts reported in the financial statements for cost of goods sold and inventory. The accurate processing of inventory purchase transactions involves applying the correct price to the actual quantity received. Similarly, when inventory is shipped, accurate processing requires that the actual number of items shipped be removed from inventory and that the proper cost be recorded to cost of goods sold. The use of a perpetual inventory system in conjunction with a periodic or annual physical inventory count should result in the proper quantities of inventory being shown in the client's perpetual inventory records. EarthWear maintains the purchase cost of its products in its master inventory file. Many manufacturing companies use standard cost systems to value their inventory. Standard costs should approximate actual costs, and the presence of large variances is one signal that the inventory may not be valued appropriately. Auditing the client's physical inventory and standard costs is discussed in more detail later in the chapter.

Management should also have controls in place to consider inventory obsolescence. Inventory management personnel should periodically review inventory on hand for obsolete, slow-moving, or excess inventory. Such inventory should be written down to its net realizable value. The auditor can review the client's procedures for identifying obsolete, slow-moving, or excess inventory. EarthWear's design department closely monitors its products to identify any end-of-season merchandise or overstocks, which are then sold at liquidation prices through special catalog inserts.

Cut-off of Inventory Transactions

Inventory transactions recorded in the improper period could affect a number of accounts, as illustrated by this simple inventory computation:

Beginning inventory + Purchases − Cost of goods sold = Ending inventory

The cut-off risks, control activities, and tests of controls associated with inventory transactions were addressed in Chapters 10 and 11, since the sale of inventory involves the revenue process and purchase of inventory involves the purchasing process. For sold (purchased) inventory, a common test of the client's controls to ensure transactions are recorded in a timely manner is to compare the date on the shipping document (receiving report) with the date in the sales journal (payment voucher). There should not be a long period between these two dates. As discussed later, auditors also often focus tests of details on transactions near year end.

It is important to understand that failure to record inventory in the proper period can result in misstatements on both the balance sheet and income statement. For example, if items shipped FOB–destination point are recorded as sold before they are received by the customer, then revenue, costs of goods sold and receivables will be overstated and inventory will be understated.

Classification of Inventory Transactions

Considering what you know about EarthWear's business, how important do you think the classification assertion is for EarthWear's inventory compared to inventory at a manufacturing company? Classification is not an important assertion for EarthWear because all goods are finished and ready for sale. However, in a manufacturing company, the client must have control activities to ensure that inventory is properly classified as raw materials, work in process, or finished goods. This can usually be accomplished by determining which departments in the manufacturing process are included in raw materials, work in process, and finished goods inventory. Thus, by knowing which manufacturing department holds the inventory, the client is able to classify it by type.

◆ RELATING THE ASSESSED LEVEL OF CONTROL RISK TO
LO8 ## SUBSTANTIVE PROCEDURES

The same judgement process is followed in setting control risk in the inventory management process that was used with other processes. For example, EarthWear has strong controls over the processing of inventory transactions. The auditor can rely on those controls if tests of controls indicate that the controls are operating effectively. If the results of the tests of controls for the inventory system do not support the planned level of control risk, the auditor would set control risk higher and set detection risk lower. This would lead to increased substantive procedures.

AUDITING INVENTORY

The discussion of the audit of inventory follows the process outlined in prior chapters. Two categories of substantive procedures are discussed: substantive **analytical procedures** and **tests of details of classes of transactions**, account balances, and disclosures. Table 13–6 presents the assertions for classes of transactions, events, account balances, and disclosures as they apply to inventory. You should note that the auditor may gather evidence about assertions related to transactions (**substantive tests of transactions**) in conjunction with testing the internal controls. If the tests of controls indicate that the controls are not operating effectively, the auditor may need to test transactions at the date the account balance is tested.

Table 13–6	Assertions about Classes of Transactions, Events, Account Balances and Disclosures for Inventory

Assertions about Classes of Transactions and Events:
- **Occurrence.** Inventory transactions and events are valid.
- **Completeness.** All inventory transactions and events have been recorded.
- **Authorization.** All inventory transactions and events are properly authorized.
- **Accuracy.** Inventory transactions have been properly computed, and ending inventory and related revenue and cost of goods sold have been properly accumulated from journals and ledgers.
- **Cut-off.** Inventory receipts and shipments are recorded in the correct accounting period.
- **Classification.** Inventory is recorded in the proper accounts (e.g. raw materials, work in process or finished goods).

Assertions about Account Balances at the Period End:
- **Existence.** Inventory recorded on the books and records actually exists.
- **Rights and obligations.** The entity has the legal right (i.e. ownership) to the recorded inventory.
- **Completeness.** All inventory is recorded.
- **Valuation and allocation.** Inventory is properly recorded in accordance with the applicable financial reporting framework.

Assertions about Presentation and Disclosure:
- **Occurrence and rights and obligations.** All disclosed events, transactions and other matters relating to inventory have occurred and pertain to the entity.
- **Completeness.** All disclosures relating to inventory that should have been included in the financial statements have been included.
- **Classification and understandability.** Financial information relating to inventory is appropriately presented and described, and disclosures are clearly expressed.
- **Accuracy and valuation.** Financial and other information relating to inventory are disclosed fairly and at appropriate amounts.

Practice Insight 13.1

Many companies rely on spreadsheets to support inventory transactions and balances that are recorded into the general ledger and financial statements. Such spreadsheets may include complex calculations with multiple-linked supporting spreadsheets. The importance of the integrity and reliability of the information generated by such spreadsheets increases as the complexity increases from low to high and as usage increases. The auditor should evaluate the controls over the inventory spreadsheets. Because spreadsheets can be generated by multiple users, easily changed, and may lack appropriate controls, the use of spreadsheets can increase inherent risk of misstatement.

SUBSTANTIVE ANALYTICAL PROCEDURES

LO9

Substantive analytical procedures are useful audit tests for examining the reasonableness of inventory and cost of goods sold. When performed as part of audit planning, preliminary analytical procedures can effectively identify whether the inventory and cost of goods sold accounts contain material misstatements. Final analytical procedures are useful as an overall review for inventory and related accounts to identify obsolete, slow-moving and excess inventory. Substantive analytical procedures are useful for obtaining assurance on the valuation assertion for inventory. Such procedures can also identify problems with improper inclusion or exclusion of costs in overhead.

For example, inventory turnover (cost of goods sold ÷ inventory) can be compared over time or to the industry average. From an auditor's perspective, what questions, concerns or risks are suggested by the pattern of data in the table below?

	2007	2008	2009	Industry Average
Inventory	€14,800	€16,500	€26,250	
Inventory Turnover	13	12	9	18

The significant increase in inventory coupled with substantially slower inventory turnover may indicate the presence of slow-moving or obsolete inventory. The auditor would seek an explanation for the pattern from the client and the auditor may need to revise the audit plan for the physical inventory observation and detail testing over the inventory valuation assertion (inventory observation and detail testing are discussed later in the chapter). If inventory turnover is higher than the industry average it may indicate inefficient inventory policies.

Another common analytical procedure involves the gross profit percentages. The gross profit percentage can also be compared to previous years' or industry data and may provide valuable evidence on unrecorded inventory (an understatement) or fictitious inventory (an overstatement). This ratio may also provide information on the proper valuation of inventory. For example, a small or negative gross profit margin may indicate issues related to measurement of inventory at the lower of cost or net realizable value (IAS 2). It is important that the auditor use sufficiently disaggregated analytical procedures in order to identify unusual patterns like the one illustrated in Figure 5–4, in Chapter 5. Table 13–7 lists substantive analytical procedures that are useful in auditing inventory and related accounts at either the planning stage or as an overall review.

Table 13–7 Examples of Substantive Analytical Procedures used in Testing Inventory and Related Accounts	
Example of Substantive Analytical Procedure	*Possible Misstatement Detected*
Compare raw material, finished goods and total inventory turnover to previous years' and industry averages	Obsolete, slow-moving or excess inventory
Compare days outstanding in inventory to previous years' and industry average	Obsolete, slow-moving or excess inventory
Compare gross profit percentage by product line with previous years' and industry data	Unrecorded or fictitious inventory
Compare actual cost of goods sold to budgeted amounts	Over- or understated inventory
Compare current-year standard costs with prior years' after considering current conditions	Over- or understated inventory
Compare actual manufacturing overhead costs with budgeted or standard manufacturing overhead costs	Inclusion or exclusion of overhead costs

Prior to presenting the tests of account balances for inventory, this chapter discusses two significant audit procedures: auditing standard costs and observing physical inventory.

❖ AUDITING STANDARD COSTS

LO10

Many manufacturing entities use a standard cost system to measure performance and to value inventory. If a standard cost system is integrated with the general accounting records, cost accumulation and variance reports are direct outputs of the client's inventory-accounting system.

For accuracy and proper valuation, standard costs should approximate actual costs. To test the standard costs, the auditor should first review the client's policies and procedures for constructing standard costs. Once the policies and procedures are understood, the auditor normally tests the component cost build-up for a representative sample of standard product costs.

Three components make up the cost of producing a product: materials, labour and overhead. For discussion purposes, suppose that Calabro Wireless Services (Calabro company background is provided in Chapter 8) assembles five types of wireless devices. Recall that Calabro is a business services company that uses wireless communications technology to develop solutions for businesses. Assume further that all parts used in the devices are purchased from outside vendors. The process followed in auditing the three components that make up the standard costs for a type of device follows (similar auditing techniques would be used for other clients with production processes).

Materials

Determining the materials costs requires examining the quantity and type of materials included in the product and the price of the materials. The quantity and type of materials are tested by reviewing the engineering specifications for the product. For example, in the case of wireless devices, the auditor can obtain a set of engineering specifications that includes a blueprint and a list of materials needed to manufacture a particular device. The auditor can compare the list of materials with the standard cost documentation used to support the cost accumulation. The prices used on the standard cost documentation can be traced to vendors' invoices as a test of actual costs.

Labour

The determination of labour costs requires evidence about the type and amount of labour needed for production and the labour rate. Following our example, the amount of labour necessary to assemble a wireless device can be determined by reviewing engineering estimates, which may be based on time-and-motion studies or on historical information. The labour rates for each type of labour necessary to assemble a device can be tested by examining a schedule of authorized wages. Labour costs included in inventory are often tested in conjunction with payroll expense.

Overhead

The auditor gathers evidence regarding overhead costs by reviewing the client's method of overhead allocation for reasonableness, compliance with the applicable financial reporting framework, and consistency. The auditor can examine the costs included in overhead to be sure that such costs can appropriately be assigned to the product. The inclusion or exclusion of such costs should be consistent from one period to the next. Using the wireless device example, the auditor would obtain a listing of expense accounts used to make up the overhead pool of costs. The auditor can compare the actual costs for the period to the budgeted costs. The auditor can also compare the costs included in the current year's listing with those in the prior year's listing.

OBSERVING PHYSICAL INVENTORY

LO11

Auditing standards require the auditor's attendance and observation of the entity's physical inventory count (ISA 501). However, the auditor is not required to attend all inventory counts, only when inventory is material. The primary reason for observing the client's physical inventory is to establish the *existence* of the inventory. The observation of the physical inventory also provides evidence on the *accuracy, rights and obligations* and *valuation* assertions. Based on the physical inventory count, the client compiles the physical inventory. While the form of compilation may differ among entities, it normally contains a list of the items by type and quantity, the assigned cost for each item, the inventory value for each item and a total for the inventory.

Prior to the physical count of inventory, the auditor should be familiar with the inventory locations, the major items in inventory, and the client's inventory management processes and instructions for counting inventory. During the observation of the physical inventory count, the auditor should do the following:

- Ensure that no production is scheduled. If production is scheduled, ensure that proper controls are established for movement between departments in order to prevent double counting.
- Ensure that there is no movement of goods during the inventory count. If movement is necessary, the auditor and client personnel must ensure that the goods are not double counted and that all goods are counted.
- Make sure that the client's count teams are following the inventory count instructions. If the count teams are not following the instructions, the auditor should notify the client representative in charge of the area.
- Ensure that inventory tags are issued sequentially to individual departments. For many inventory counts, the goods are marked with multicopy inventory tags. The count teams record the type and quantity of inventory on each tag, and one copy of each tag is then used to compile the inventory. If the client uses another method of counting inventory, such as detailed inventory listings or handheld computers, the auditor should obtain copies of the listings or files prior to the start of the inventory count.
- Perform test counts and record a sample of counts in the working papers. This information will be used to evaluate the accuracy and completeness of the client's inventory compilation.
- Obtain tag control information for testing the client's inventory compilation. Tag control information includes documentation of the numerical sequence of all inventory tags and accounting for all used and unused inventory tags. If inventory listings are used by the client, copies of the listings will accomplish the objective of documenting the entire inventory count.
- Obtain cut-off information, including the number of the last shipping and receiving documents issued on the date of the physical inventory count.

- Observe the condition of the inventory for items that may be obsolete, slow-moving, or carried in excess quantities.
- Inquire about goods held on consignment for others or held on a 'bill-and-hold' basis. Such items should not be included in the client's inventory. The auditor must also request confirmation or perform other appropriate procedures about goods held on consignment for the client. These goods should be included in the inventory count.

If these audit procedures are followed, the auditor has reasonable assurance that a proper inventory count has been taken.

Some companies choose to count their inventory on a cyclical basis throughout the year instead of just once at the end of the year. They may choose to only count part of the warehouse each cycle, but ensure that the entire warehouse is counted at least once each year. If the auditor observes one or more of these interim cycle counts, the client must have a reliable perpetual inventory system so that the auditor can examine activity (on a test basis) between the count date(s) and year end in order to obtain appropriate evidence about the year-end inventory balance.

The auditor's attendance at the inventory count may be impracticable due to factors such as the nature and location of the inventory. For example, the inventory is held in a location that may pose threats to the safety of the auditor. In such cases, the auditor should perform alternative procedures, for example inspection of documentation of the subsequent sale of specific inventory items acquired. If the auditor is unable to perform such procedures, he or she would consider modifying the opinion in the auditor's report as a result of the scope limitation.

Practice Insight 13.2

One of the most effective ways for the auditor to evaluate the possibility of inventory fraud is to physically examine the client's inventory when an inventory count is being performed. But even physical examination procedures do not eliminate the risk of misstatement due to fraud since the client can perpetrate fraud such as:

- Obtaining advance notice of the timing and location of the count, which can permit the client to conceal fictitious inventory at locations not visited.
- Stacking empty containers at a warehouse where container contents are not checked during the count.
- Falsifying shipping documents to show that inventory is in transit from one company location to another.
- Falsifying documents to show that inventory is located at a public warehouse or other location not controlled by the company.

If the auditor does not properly maintain control of a copy of the client's final count sheets to tie into final inventory records the client can also fraudulently overstate inventory by:

- Following the auditor during the count and adding fictitious inventory to items not tested by the auditor; or
- Entering additional quantities on manual and/or electronic inventory sheets that do not exist or adding a digit in front of the actual count.

❖ TESTS OF DETAILS OF CLASSES OF TRANSACTIONS, ACCOUNT BALANCES
LO12 AND DISCLOSURES

Table 13–6 presents the assertions for inventory. The intended purpose of tests of details of transactions is to detect monetary misstatements in the inventory account. The auditor may conduct tests of details of transactions specifically for inventory. However, because the inventory management process interacts with the revenue, purchasing, and human resource management processes, transactions involving the receipt of goods, shipment of goods, and assignment of labour costs are normally tested as part of those processes. For example, receiving department personnel prepare a receiving report that includes the quantity and type of goods received. The receiving report and vendor invoice are then used to record the accounts payable. If the auditor intends to obtain substantive evidence on the perpetual inventory records, the tests of receipt and shipment of goods can be extended by tracing the transactions into the perpetual inventory records.

For example, the receiving report is generally used by the client to record the goods in the perpetual inventory records or inventory master file (see Figure 13–2). The auditor can perform a test of detail of transactions by tracing a sample of receiving reports into the perpetual inventory records. Labour costs can also be traced to individual inventory transactions and into the cost-accounting records.

LO13 As previously mentioned, tests of details of transactions are often conducted in conjunction with tests of controls. Table 13–8 presents examples of tests of details of transactions, account balances, and disclosures for assertions related to inventory. The discussion that follows focuses primarily on **tests of details of account balances** of inventory. Accuracy is the first assertion discussed because the auditor must establish that the detailed records that support the inventory account agree with the general ledger account.

Table 13–8 Examples of Inventory Tests of Transactions, Account Balances and Disclosures	
Assertions about Classes of Transactions	*Example Substantive Tests of Transaction*
Occurrence	Vouch a sample of inventory additions (i.e. purchases) to receiving reports and purchase requisitions.
Completeness	Trace a sample of receiving reports to the inventory records (i.e. master file, status report).
Authorization	Test a sample of inventory shipments to ensure there is an approved shipping ticket and customer sales.
Accuracy	Recompute the mathematical accuracy of a sample of inventory transactions (i.e. price × quantity).
	Audit standard costs or other methods used to price inventory (see discussion in the chapter for the audit procedures used to audit standard costs).
	Trace costs used to price goods in the inventory compilation to standard costs or vendors' invoices.
Cut-off	Trace a sample of time cards before and after period end to the appropriate weekly inventory report, and trace the weekly inventory report to the general ledger to verify inventory transactions are recorded in the proper period.
Classification	Examine a sample of inventory checks for proper classification into expense accounts.
Assertions about Account Balances at Period End	*Example Tests of Details of Account Balances*
Existence	Observe count of physical inventory (see discussion in chapter for proper inventory observation procedures).
Rights and obligations	Verify that inventory held on consignment for others is not included in inventory.
	Verify that 'bill-and-hold' goods are not included in inventory.
Completeness	Trace test counts and tag control information to the inventory compilation.
Valuation and allocation	Obtain a copy of the inventory compilation and agree totals to general ledger.
	Trace test counts and tag control information to the inventory compilation.
	Test mathematical accuracy of extensions and foot the inventory compilation.
	Inquire of management concerning obsolete, slow-moving, or excess inventory.
	Review book-to-physical adjustment for possible misstatements (see Table 13–9).
Assertions about Presentation and Disclosure	*Example Tests of Details of Disclosures*
Occurrence, and rights and obligations	Inquire of management and review any loan agreements and board of directors' minutes for any indication that inventory has been pledged or assigned.
	Inquire of management about issues related to warranty obligations.

Completeness	Complete financial reporting checklist to ensure that all financial statement disclosures related to inventory are made.
Classification and understandability	Review inventory compilation for proper classification among raw materials, work in process and finished goods.
	Read notes to ensure that required disclosures are understandable.
Accuracy and valuation	Determine if the cost method is accurately disclosed.
	Read notes and other information to ensure that the information is accurate and properly presented at the appropriate amounts.

* Many of these tests of details of transactions are commonly conducted as dual-purpose tests (i.e. in conjunction with tests of controls).

Accuracy

Gathering evidence on the accuracy of inventory requires obtaining a copy of the compilation of the physical inventory that shows inventory quantities and prices.

The inventory compilation is footed, and the mathematical extensions of quantity multiplied by price are verified. Additionally, test counts made by the auditor during the physical inventory and tag control information are traced into the compilation.

Many times the client has adjusted the general ledger inventory balance to agree to the physical inventory amounts (referred to as *book-to-physical adjustment*) before the auditor begins the substantive tests of account balances. If the client has made the book-to-physical adjustment, the totals from the compilation for inventory should agree with the general ledger.

When the client maintains a perpetual inventory system, the totals from the inventory compilation should also be agreed to these records. The auditor can use **computer-assisted audit techniques** to accomplish these audit steps. For example, the auditor can use a generalized or custom audit software package to trace costs used to price goods in the inventory compilation to standard cost files. The extensions and footing can also be tested at the same time.

Cut-off

In gathering evidence on the cut-off assertion for inventory, the auditor attempts to determine whether all sales of finished goods and purchases of raw materials are recorded in the proper period. For sales cut-off, the auditor can examine a sample of shipping documents for a few days before and after year end for recording of inventory shipments in the proper period. For purchases cut-off, the auditor can examine a sample of receiving documents for a few days before and after year end for recording of inventory purchases in the proper period. Chapters 10 and 11 discuss sales and purchases cut-off.

Existence

Existence is one of the more important assertions for the inventory account. The auditor's attendance at the entity's physical inventory count is the primary audit step used to verify this assertion. The auditor obtains information regarding existence by observing the inventory count, understanding and testing the client's count procedures addressing validity, and through the auditor's test counts. If the auditor is satisfied with the client's physical inventory count, the auditor has sufficient appropriate evidence on the existence of recorded inventory.

Completeness

The auditor must determine whether all inventory has been included in the inventory compilation and the general ledger inventory account. The tests related to the observation of the physical inventory count provide assurance that all goods on hand are included in inventory. Observing that count teams have placed count tags on all inventory items provides evidence regarding completeness of the count. Tracing test counts and tag control information into the inventory compilation provide assurance that the inventory counted during the physical inventory observation is included in the compilation. In some cases, inventory is held on consignment by others or is stored in public warehouses. The auditor either confirms or performs other appropriate procedures such as attending the consignee's physical count of such inventory (ISA 501).

Practice Insight 13.3

Auditors should investigate significant differences between the physical count and detailed perpetual inventory records before the accounting and inventory records are adjusted to match the physical count. Understanding the nature of the significant difference may indicate problems with either the physical count, the perpetual system or shrinkage (unaccounted reduction in inventory due to theft or damage).

Rights and Obligations

The auditor must determine whether the recorded inventory is actually owned by the entity. Two issues related to ownership can arise. First, the auditor must be sure that the inventory on hand belongs to the client. If the client holds inventory on consignment, such inventory should not be included in the physical inventory. Second, in some industries, goods are sold on a 'bill-and-hold' basis. In such cases, the goods are treated as a sale, but the client holds the goods until the customer needs them. Again, the auditor must be certain that such goods are segregated and not counted at the time of the physical inventory.

Valuation and Allocation

A number of important valuation issues are related to inventory. The first issue relates to the costs used to value the inventory items included in the compilation. When the client, such as EarthWear, purchases inventory, valuation of the inventory can normally be accomplished by vouching the costs to vendors' invoices. When the client uses standard costs, the auditor audits the standard costs as discussed previously. The second valuation issue relates to the lower of cost or net realizable value tests of inventory (IAS 2). The auditor normally performs such tests on large monetary items or on the client's various product lines. At EarthWear, the auditors would likely perform the lower of cost or net realizable value test on merchandise noted by management for liquidation. Write-downs often relates to obsolete, slow-moving, or excess inventory. Inventory management personnel should periodically review inventory on hand for obsolete, slow-moving or excess inventory. Such inventory should be written down to its net realizable value. The auditor can review the client's procedures for identifying obsolete, slow-moving or excess inventory. EarthWear's design department closely monitors its products to identify any end-of-season merchandise or overstocks, which are then sold at liquidation prices through special catalogue inserts. The auditor should ask management their procedures to identify obsolete, slow-moving or excess inventory and if it is determined that such inventory exists the auditor should determine whether the inventory has been properly written down. Note that the international accounting standards require reversal for subsequent increase in value of inventory previously written down (IAS 2). Finally, the auditor should investigate any large adjustments between the amount of inventory shown in the general ledger account and the amount determined from the physical inventory count (book-to-physical adjustments) for possible misstatements. Table 13–9 presents a list of items that may lead to book-to-physical differences.

Table 13–9 Possible Causes of Book-to-Physical Differences

Inventory cut-off errors.

Unreported scrap or spoilage.

Pilferage or theft.

Classification and Understandability

The presentation and disclosure assertion of classification of inventory for EarthWear is not an issue because the company sells only finished products. However, in a manufacturing company, the auditor must determine that inventory is properly classified as raw materials, work in process, or finished goods. In most manufacturing companies, proper classification can be achieved by determining which manufacturing processing department has control of the inventory on the date of the physical count. For example, if inventory tags are used to count inventory and they are assigned numerically to departments, classification can be verified at the physical inventory. The auditor can ensure that each department is using the assigned tags. The tag control information by department can be compared to the information on the inventory compilation to ensure that it is properly classified among raw materials, work in process and finished goods.

Other Presentation and Disclosure Assertions

Several important disclosure issues are related to inventory. Table 13–10 presents some examples of disclosure items for inventory and related accounts. For example, management should disclose the cost method, such as the first in, first out (FIFO) or weighted average methods, used to value inventory. Note that international accounting standards do not permit the use of the last in, first out (LIFO) method (IAS 2). Management should also disclose the components of inventory either on the face of the balance sheet or in the notes. Components of inventories may include merchandise, production supplies, materials, work in progress and finished goods. International accounting standards require detailed disclosure of inventories in the notes, including disclosure of the net change in inventories for the period for entities reporting cost of sales in the income statement. Exhibit 13–4 illustrates financial statement disclosure of accounting policy for inventory.

Table 13–10 Examples of Disclosure Items for Inventory and Related Accounts
Cost method (FIFO or weighted average).
Components of inventory.
Long-term purchase contracts.
Consigned inventory.
Purchases from related parties.
Pledged or assigned inventory.
Expenses from write-downs of inventory or losses on long-term purchase commitments.
Warranty obligations.

Exhibit 13–4 Financial Statement Disclosure for Inventory
Inventories, including work in progress, are valued at the lower of cost or net realizable value less costs to sell after provisions for obsolete inventories. The net realizable value less costs to sell is the estimated selling price in the ordinary course of business, less the estimated cost of completion and estimated costs necessary to make the sale. Inventories are measured using the FIFO method. Finished goods and work in progress include variable costs and fixed costs that can be allocated to goods based on normal capacity.
Obsolete inventories have been fully recognized as impairment losses.

❖ EVALUATING THE AUDIT FINDINGS: INVENTORY

LO14

When the auditor has completed the planned substantive tests of the inventory account, all the identified misstatements should be aggregated. The aggregated identified misstatement is compared to materiality for the financial statements or any lesser materiality amount determined appropriate for the inventory account. If the identified misstatement approaches or exceed materiality, or if the nature and the circumstances of identified misstatements indicate that other misstatements exist that when aggregated with misstatements accumulated during the audit, could be material, the auditor should determine if the overall audit strategy and audit plan are appropriate. For example, identified misstatements may provide additional evidence on the control risk for the inventory management process. If the auditors conclude that the audit risk is unacceptably high, additional audit procedures should be performed.

If uncorrected misstatements in inventory and when considered together with other uncorrected misstatements is less than materiality, the auditor may accept that the financial statements are fairly presented. Conversely, if the uncorrected misstatement exceeds the materiality, the auditor should conclude that the financial statements are not fairly presented.

For example, in Chapter 3, materiality for the inventory account was €900,000. Exhibit 3–4 showed that Willis & Adams International identified two misstatements in inventory: one that resulted in an overstatement of inventory by €312,500 based on a projection of a sample and one misstatement that understated inventory by €227,450 due to inventory in transit. Neither of these misstatements is greater than the materiality and Willis & Adams do not consider it necessary to revise the overall audit strategy and audit plan. However, the auditors would analyse the nature and circumstances of the misstatements identified through the application of substantive procedures. For example, the Willis & Adams would consider further possible misstatements due to sampling.

The auditor requests management to correct all identified misstatements. If uncorrected misstatements, either for the inventory account or for the financial statements, had been greater than the materiality, the evidence would not support fair presentation and the auditor would have to qualify the audit opinion.

🔒 Key Terms

Analytical procedures. Evaluations of financial information through analysis of plausible relationships among both financial and non-financial data.

Application controls. Controls that apply to the processing of specific computer applications and are part of the computer programs used in the accounting system.

Assertions. Representations by management, explicit or otherwise, that are embodied in the financial statements, as used by the auditor to consider the different types of potential misstatements that may occur.

Computer-assisted audit techniques (CAATs). Applications of auditing procedures using the computer as an audit tool.

Reliance strategy. The auditor's decision to rely on the entity's controls, test those controls, and reduce the substantive tests of the financial statement accounts.

Standard costs. Costs assigned to products based on expected costs, which may differ from actual costs.

Tests of controls. Audit procedures designed to evaluate the operating effectiveness of controls in preventing, or detecting and correcting, material misstatements at the assertion level.

Tests of details of account balances and disclosures. Substantive tests that concentrate on the details of items contained in the account balance and disclosure.

Tests of details of transactions (substantive tests of transactions). Tests to detect errors or fraud in individual transactions.

❓ Review Questions

LO1	13–1	Why does inventory represent one of the more complex parts of the audit?
LO1	13–2	How does the inventory management process relate to the revenue, purchasing and payroll processes?
LO2	13–3	Briefly describe each of the following documents or records: production schedule, materials requisition, inventory master file, production data information, and cost accumulation and variance reports.
LO3	13–4	What duties are performed within the inventory management, stores and cost-accounting functions?
LO4	13–5	List the key segregation of duties in the inventory management process. What errors or fraud can occur if such segregation of duties is not present?
LO5	13–6	List the inherent risk factors that affect the inventory management process.
LO6	13–7	List the major steps in setting control risk in the inventory management process.
LO7	13–8	What control activities can a client use to prevent unauthorized inventory production?
LO9	13–9	List three substantive analytical procedures that can test the fairness of inventory and related accounts.
LO10	13–10	Describe how an auditor audits standard costs.
LO11	13–11	List the procedures the auditor should perform during the count of the client's physical inventory.

LO13   13–12   What are some possible causes of book-to-physical inventory differences?

LO13   13–13   List five items for inventory and related accounts that may require disclosure.

Problems

LO1,3,7   13–14   Yardley, independent auditor, prepared the flowchart on the opposite page, which portrays the raw materials purchasing function of one of Yardley's clients, a medium-size manufacturing company, from the preparation of initial documents through the vouching of invoices for payment. The flowchart represents a portion of the work performed on the audit engagement to evaluate internal control.

Required:

Identify and explain the control deficiencies evident from the flowchart. Include the internal control deficiencies resulting from activities performed or not performed. All documents are prenumbered.

(AICPA, adapted)

LO1,6,11,13   13–15   Rasch is the partner-in-charge of the audit of Bonner Distributing Corporation, a wholesaler that owns one warehouse containing 80 per cent of its inventory. Rasch is reviewing the working papers that were prepared to support the firm's opinion on Bonner's financial statements, and Rasch wants to be certain that essential audit tests are well documented.

Required:

a   *What evidence should Rasch find in the working papers to support the fact that the audit was adequately planned and the assistants were properly supervised?*

b   *What substantive tests should Rasch expect to find in the working papers to document management's assertion about completeness as it relates to the inventory quantities at the end of the year?*

(AICPA, adapted)

LO11   13–16   Abbott Corporation does not conduct a complete annual physical count of purchased parts and supplies in its principal warehouse but instead uses statistical sampling to estimate the year-end inventory. Abbott maintains a perpetual inventory record of parts and supplies and believes that statistical sampling is highly effective in determining inventory values and is sufficiently reliable to make a physical count of each item of inventory unnecessary.

Required:

a   *Identify the audit procedures that should be used by the independent auditor that change, or are in addition to, normal required audit procedures when a client utilizes statistical sampling to determine inventory value and does not conduct a 100 per cent annual physical count of inventory items.*

b   *List at least ten normal audit procedures that should be performed to verify physical quantities whenever a client conducts a periodic physical count of all, or part, of its inventory.*

(AICPA, adapted)

LO11,13   13–17   Kachelmeier, independent auditor, is auditing the financial statements of Big Z Wholesaling, a continuing audit client, for the year ended 31 January 2009. On 5 January 2009, Kachelmeier observed the tagging and counting of Big Z's physical inventory and made appropriate test counts. These test counts have been recorded on a computer file. As in prior years, Big Z gave Kachelmeier

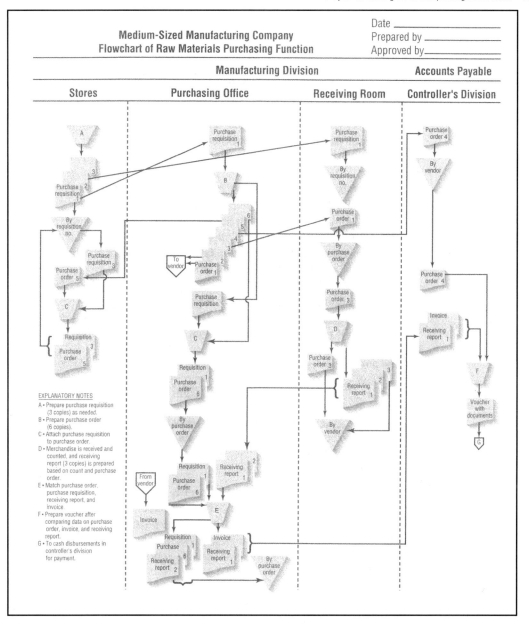

Date _____
Prepared by _____
Approved by _____

Medium-Sized Manufacturing Company
Flowchart of Raw Materials Purchasing Function

EXPLANATORY NOTES
A • Prepare purchase requisition (3 copies) as needed.
B • Prepare purchase order (6 copies).
C • Attach purchase requisition to purchase order.
D • Merchandise is received and counted, and receiving report (3 copies) is prepared based on count and purchase order.
E • Match purchase order, purchase requisition, receiving report, and invoice.
F • Prepare voucher after comparing data on purchase order, invoice, and receiving report.
G • To cash disbursements in controller's division for payment.

two computer files. One file represents the perpetual inventory (FIFO) records for the year ended 31 January 2009. The other file represents the 5 January physical inventory count.

Assume that:

1   Kachelmeier issued an unmodified opinion on the prior year's financial statements.

2   All inventory is purchased for resale and located in a single warehouse.

3   Kachelmeier has appropriate computerized audit software.

4 The perpetual inventory file contains the following information in item number sequence:

- Beginning balances at 1 February 2008: item number, item description, total quantity, and price.

- For each item purchased during the year: date received, receiving report number, vendor item number, item description, quantity, and total monetary amount.

- For each item sold during the year: date shipped, invoice number, item number, item description, quantity, and monetary amount.

- For each item adjusted for physical inventory count differences: date, item number, item description, quantity, and monetary amount.

5 The physical inventory file contains the following information in item number sequence: tag number, item number, item description, and quantity.

Required:

Describe the substantive auditing procedures Kachelmeier may consider performing with computerized audit software using Big Z's two computer files and Kachelmeier's computer file of test counts. The substantive auditing procedures described may indicate the reports to be printed out for Kachelmeier's follow-up by subsequent application of manual procedures. Group the procedures by those using (a) the perpetual inventory file and (b) the physical inventory and test count files. Do not describe subsequent manual auditing procedures.

(AICPA, adapted)

LO11,13   **13–18**   An auditor is examining the financial statements of a wholesale cosmetics distributor with an inventory consisting of thousands of individual items. The distributor keeps its inventory in its own distribution centre and in two public warehouses. An electronic inventory file is maintained on a computer disk, and at the end of each business day the file is updated. Each record of the inventory file contains the following data:

- Item number.
- Location of item.
- Description of item.
- Quantity on hand.
- Cost per item.
- Date of last purchase.
- Date of last sale.
- Quantity sold during year.

The auditor plans to observe the distributor's physical count of inventory as of a given date. The auditor will have available a computer tape of the data on the inventory file on the date of the physical count and a generalized audit software package.

Required:

The auditor is planning to perform basic inventory-auditing procedures. Identify the basic inventory-auditing procedures and describe how the use of the generalized audit software package and the tape of the inventory file data might help the auditor perform such auditing procedures. Organize your answer as follows:

Basic Inventory-Auditing Procedure	How a Generalized Audit Software Package and Tape of the Inventory File Data Might Be Helpful
1. Observation of the physical count, making and recording test counts where applicable	1. By determining which items are to be test counted by selecting a random sample of a representative number of items from the inventory file as of the date of the physical count.

(AICPA, adapted)

LO13   **13–19**   In obtaining audit evidence in support of financial statement assertions, the auditor develops specific audit procedures to address those assertions.

Required:

Your client is Hillmart, a retail department store that purchases all goods directly from wholesalers or manufacturers. Select the most appropriate audit procedure from the list below and enter the number in the appropriate place on the grid. (An audit procedure may be selected once, more than once, or not at all.)

Audit Procedure:

1   Examine current vendor price lists.

2   Review drafts of the financial statements.

3   Select a sample of items during the physical inventory count and determine that they have been included on count sheets.

4   Select a sample of recorded items and examine supporting vendor invoices and contracts.

5   Select a sample of recorded items on count sheets during the physical inventory count and determine that items are on hand.

6   Review loan agreements and minutes of board of directors' meetings.

Specific Assertion	Audit Procedure
a. Ensure that the entity has legal title to inventory (rights and obligations).	
b. Ensure that recorded inventory quantities include all products on hand (completeness).	
c. Verify that inventory has been reduced, when appropriate, to net realizable value.	
d. Verify that the cost of inventory has been properly determined (accuracy).	
e. Verify that the major categories of inventory and their bases of valuation are adequately reported in the financial statements (completeness and accuracy and valuation for presentation and disclosure).	

Discussion Case

LO9,11,13,14 13–20   The following discussion case extends Discussion Case 6–22 in Chapter 6.

Harris decided that the easiest way to make the Fabricator Division appear more profitable was through manipulating the inventory, which was the largest asset on the books. Harris found that by increasing inventory by 2 per cent, income could be increased by 5 per cent. With the weakness in inventory control, he felt it would be easy to overstate inventory. Employees count the goods using count sheets, and Harris was able to add two fictitious sheets during the physical inventory, even though the auditors were present and were observing the inventory. A significant amount of inventory was stored in racks that filled the warehouse. Because of their height and the difficulty of test counting them, Harris was able to cover an overstatement of inventory in the upper racks.

After the count was completed, Harris added four additional count sheets that added €350,000, or 8.6 per cent, to the stated inventory. Harris notified the auditors of the 'omission' of the sheets and convinced them that they represented overlooked legitimate inventory.

The auditors traced the items on these additional sheets to purchase invoices to verify their existence and approved the addition of the €350,000 to the inventory. They did not notify management about the added sheets. In addition, Harris altered other count sheets before sending them to the auditors by changing unit designations (for example, six engine blocks became six 'motors'), raising counts, and adding fictitious line items to completed count sheets. These other fictitious changes added an additional €175,000 to the inflated inventory. None of them was detected by the auditors.

Required:

a   What audit procedures did the auditors apparently not follow that should have detected Harris's fraudulent increase of inventory?

b   What implications would there be to an auditor of failure to detect material fraud as described here?

c   What responsibility did the auditors have to discuss their concerns with those charged with governance?

(Used with the permission of PricewaterhouseCoopers LLP Foundation.)

❶ Internet Assignment

LO9,13   13–21   Using an Internet browser, search for information on inventory turnover and merchandise liquidations in the retail catalogue industry.

Notes

[i]   International accounting standards value inventory at the lower of cost or net realizable value (IAS 2). Net realizable value is the estimated selling price in the ordinary course of business less the estimated costs of completion and the estimated costs necessary to make the sale.

[ii]   A. Eilifsen and W.F. Messier, Jr (2000) 'Auditor Detection of Misstatements: A Review and Integration of Empirical Research', *Journal of Accounting Literature* (19), pp. 1–43.

CHAPTER 14

Auditing the Financing/Investing Process: Prepaid Expenses; Intangible Assets and Goodwill; and Property, Plant and Equipment

❖ LEARNING OBJECTIVES

Upon completion of this chapter you will

- ❖ **LO1** Know the various types of prepaid expenses and intangible assets.
- ❖ **LO2** Understand the auditor's approach to auditing prepaid insurance, intangible assets and goodwill.
- ❖ **LO3** Develop an understanding of the property management process.
- ❖ **LO4** Know the types of transactions in the property management process.
- ❖ **LO5** Be familiar with the inherent risks for property, plant, and equipment.
- ❖ **LO6** Assess control risk for property, plant, and equipment.

- ❖ **LO7** Know the appropriate segregation of duties for property, plant and equipment.
- ❖ **LO8** Know the substantive analytical procedures used to audit property, plant and equipment.
- ❖ **LO9** Identify tests of details of account balances and disclosures used to audit property, plant and equipment.
- ❖ **LO10** Understand how to evaluate the audit findings and reach a final conclusion on property, plant and equipment.

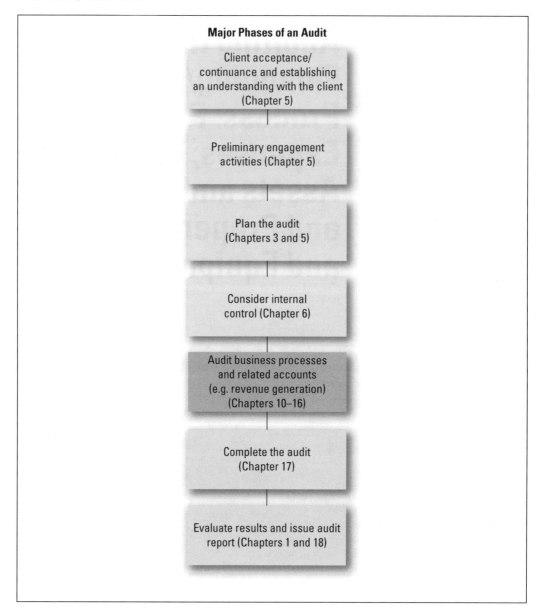

Major Phases of an Audit

Client acceptance/
continuance and establishing
an understanding with the client
(Chapter 5)

Preliminary engagement
activities (Chapter 5)

Plan the audit
(Chapters 3 and 5)

Consider internal
control (Chapter 6)

Audit business processes
and related accounts
(e.g. revenue generation)
(Chapters 10–16)

Complete the audit
(Chapter 17)

Evaluate results and issue audit
report (Chapters 1 and 18)

❖ RELEVANT ACCOUNTING AND AUDITING PRONOUNCEMENTS

IASB, IAS 1, Presentation of Financial Statements

IASB, IAS 16, Property, Plant and Equipment

IASB, IAS 17, Leases

IASB, IAS 36, Impairment of Assets

IASB, IAS 38, Intangible Assets

IASB, IFRS 3, Business Combinations

ISA 230, Audit Documentation

ISA 240, The Auditor's Responsibilities Relating to Fraud in an Audit of Financial Statements

ISA 315, Identifying and Assessing the Risks of Material Misstatement through Understanding the Entity and Its Environment

ISA 320, Materiality in Planning and Performing an Audit

ISA 330, The Auditor's Responses to Assessed Risks

ISA 450, Evaluation of Misstatements Identified during the Audit

ISA 500, Audit Evidence

ISA 505, External Confirmations

ISA 520, Analytical Procedures

ISA 540, Auditing Accounting Estimates, Including Fair Value Accounting Estimates, and Related Disclosures

ISA 620, Using the Work of an Auditor's Expert

THIS CHAPTER EXAMINES the audit of selected asset accounts. Three categories of asset accounts – prepaid expenses; intangibles and **goodwill**;[i] and property, plant and equipment – are used as examples. While the audit approach taken for each category is similar, differences exist between these three categories of asset accounts. For example, while transactions for all three categories are subject to the control activities in the purchasing process, transactions involving intangible assets and goodwill, or property, plant and equipment are likely to be subject to additional control activities because of their complexity or materiality. Additionally, prepaid expenses are normally classified as current assets, while intangibles and goodwill; and property, plant, and equipment are classified as non-current assets.

❖ AUDITING PREPAID EXPENSES

LO1

For many entities, accounts receivable and inventory represent the major current assets included in the financial statements. Also included in most financial statements are accounts that are referred to as *other assets*. When such assets provide economic benefit for less than a year, they are classified as current assets. A common type of other asset is a *prepaid expense*. Examples of prepaid expenses include:

● Prepaid insurance.
● Prepaid rent.
● Prepaid interest.

One major difference between asset accounts such as accounts receivable or inventory and **prepaid expenses** is the materiality of the account balances. On many engagements, prepaid expenses, **intangible assets** and goodwill are not highly material. As a result, substantive **analytical procedures** are often used extensively to verify these account balances.

INHERENT RISK ASSESSMENT: PREPAID EXPENSES

The inherent risk for prepaid expenses such as prepaid insurance would generally be assessed as low because these accounts do not involve any complex or contentious accounting issues. Moreover, misstatements that may have been detected in prior audits would generally be immaterial in amount.

CONTROL RISK ASSESSMENT: PREPAID EXPENSES

Prepaid expenses are typically processed through the purchasing process. Common prepaid expenses include prepaid insurance, prepaid rent, prepaid maintenance or other service, and prepaid interest. The remaining discussion focuses on the prepaid insurance account as an illustration of auditing prepaid expenses because it is encountered on virtually all engagements. Prepaid insurance may relate to an insurance policy on a building or equipment. If, for example, the client borrowed money to purchase equipment, the creditor may have a **lien** on the equipment (i.e. the equipment is used as collateral for the loan). A lien gives the creditor the right to sell the equipment if the client fails to meet the obligations of a loan contract. When there is a lien on a client's building or equipment, the creditor typically requires the client to carry an insurance policy listing the creditor as the beneficiary (i.e. rightful recipient of insurance proceeds).

Part of the auditor's assessment of control risk for prepaid insurance transactions is based on the effectiveness of the control activities in the purchasing process. For example, the control activities in the purchasing process should ensure that new insurance policies are properly authorized and recorded.

Additional control activities may be used to control insurance transactions and information. For example, an *insurance register* may be maintained as a separate record of all insurance policies in force. The insurance register contains important information such as the coverage and expiration date of each policy. This register should be reviewed periodically by an independent person to verify that the entity has insurance coverage consistent with its needs.

The entity also needs to maintain controls over the systematic allocation of prepaid insurance to insurance expense. At the end of each month, client personnel should prepare a journal entry to recognize the expired portion of prepaid insurance. In some cases entities use estimated amounts when recording these journal entries during the year. At the end of the year, the prepaid insurance account is adjusted to reflect the actual amount of unexpired insurance.

❖ SUBSTANTIVE PROCEDURES: PREPAID INSURANCE

LO2

On many audits the auditor can gather sufficient appropriate evidence on prepaid insurance by performing substantive analytical procedures. Tests of details of transactions, if performed at all, are conducted as part of testing the purchasing process. Detailed tests of balances of the prepaid insurance balance are typically necessary only when misstatements are expected.

Substantive Analytical Procedures for Prepaid Insurance

Because there are generally few transactions in the prepaid insurance account and because the amount reported in the financial statements for prepaid insurance is usually immaterial, substantive analytical procedures are effective for verifying the account balance. The following substantive analytical procedures are commonly used to test prepaid insurance:

- Comparing the current-year balance in prepaid insurance and insurance expense with the prior years' balances, taking into account any changes in operations.
- Computing the ratio of insurance expense to assets or sales, and comparing it with the prior years' ratios.
- Computing an estimate of the ending prepaid account balance(s) using the current premium and the amount of time remaining on the policy at the end of the period.

Using the third technique above, do the ending balances in Exhibit 14–1 appear reasonable? Looking at the Fire & Casualty policy, for example, the ending balance of €8,400 does appear reasonable (€8,400 = €33,600 × 3/12).

Tests of Details of the Prepaid Insurance

Tests of details of balances for prepaid insurance and insurance expense may be necessary when the auditor suspects misstatements based on prior years' audits or when substantive analytical procedures indicate that the account balance may be misstated. The auditor begins testing the prepaid insurance account balance by obtaining a schedule from the client that contains a detailed analysis of the policies included in the prepaid insurance account.

Exhibit 14–1 presents a prepaid insurance schedule for EarthWear Clothiers. The accuracy and completeness of this schedule is tested by footing it and tracing the ending balance to the prepaid insurance account in the general ledger. The auditor's work then focuses on testing the existence, completeness, rights and obligations, valuation, and disclosure-classification assertions. No note disclosures are generally necessary for prepaid insurance. These steps, along with other audit work, are documented in Exhibit 14–1.

Exhibit 14–1 Example of an Account Analysis Working Paper for Prepaid Insurance

G10
DLJ
15/2/10

EARTHWEAR CLOTHIERS
Analysis of Prepaid Insurance
31/12/09

Insurance Company	Policy Number	Coverage	Term	Premium	Beginning Balance 1/1/09	Additions	Expense	Ending Balance 31/12/09
Babcock**C**	46–2074	Liability Umbrella Policy	15/1/09 15/1/10					
				€55,000	€2,100	€55,000**V**	€54,800	€2,300 **Y**
Evans & Smith**C**	47801-X7	Fire & Casualty	3/30/09 30/3/10					
				33,600	7,500	33,600**V**	32,700	8,400 **Y**
Nat'l Insurance**C**	8945-X7	Key Executive Term Life Insurance	30/9/09 30/9/10					
				15,000	11,250	15,000**V**	15,000	11,250 **Y**
Total					€20,850¶	€103,600	€102,500**L**	€21,950**LF**
					F	**F**	**F**	**F**

F = Footed and crossfooted.	Reconciliation of insurance expense accounts:
C = Information agreed to insurance company confirmation.	Merchandise overhead insurance expense €69,700**L**
L = Agreed to general ledger.	General and administrative overhead insurance expense 32,800**L**
¶ = Agreed to prior year's working papers.	Total €102,500
V = Agreed to insurance company invoice.	
Y = Amount recomputed by auditor.	

Existence and Completeness

The auditor can test the existence and completeness of insurance policies included in the account analysis by sending a confirmation to the entity's insurance brokers, requesting information on each policy's number, coverage, expiration date and premiums. This is an effective and efficient way of obtaining evidence on these two assertions. An alternative approach is examination of the underlying supporting documents such as the insurance bills and policies. This may be done on a test basis for the policies listed on the schedule. The auditor can also obtain evidence regarding completeness by comparing the detailed policies in the current year's insurance register with the policies included in the prior year's insurance register.

Rights and Obligations

The beneficiary of the policy can be identified by requesting such information on the confirmations sent to the insurance brokers or by examining the insurance policies. If the beneficiary is someone other than the client, this could indicate an unrecorded liability or that another party has a claim against the insured assets.

Valuation

The auditor is concerned with whether the unexpired portion of prepaid insurance, and thus insurance expense, is properly valued. Evidence regarding proper valuation can easily be obtained by recomputing the unexpired portion of insurance after considering the premium paid and the term of the policy. By verifying the unexpired portion of prepaid insurance, the auditor also verifies the total amount of insurance expense. This is shown in Exhibit 14–1.

Classification

The auditor's concern with classification is that the different types of insurance are properly allocated to the various insurance expense accounts. Normally, an examination of the insurance policy's coverage indicates the nature of the insurance. For example, a fire insurance policy on the main manufacturing and administrative facilities should be charged both to the manufacturing overhead insurance expense account and to the general and administrative insurance expense account. Note in Exhibit 14–1 that the various insurance accounts included in the general ledger are reconciled to total insurance expense. One final procedure that the auditor should perform is to ask the client or its insurance broker about the adequacy of the entity's insurance coverage.

❖ AUDITING INTANGIBLE ASSETS AND GOODWILL

LO1,2

Intangible assets are assets that typically provide economic benefit for longer than a year, but lack physical substance. The following list includes examples of five general categories of intangible assets:

1   *Marketing* – trademark, brand name and Internet domain names.
2   *Customer* – customer lists, order backlogs and customer relationships.
3   *Artistic* – items protected by copyright.
4   *Contract* – licenses, franchises and broadcast rights.
5   *Technology* – patented and unpatented technology.

Accounting standards do not allow companies, or are very restrictive, to record internally generated intangibles as assets on the balance sheet.[ii] Rather, intangibles are recorded when the assets are acquired through a purchase or acquisition. This also relates to *goodwill*, which represents the difference between the acquisition price for a company and the fair value of the *identifiable* tangible and intangible assets and liabilities.[iii]

Some intangible assets are amortized over time, while others like broadcast licences, trademarks as well as goodwill are typically considered to have indefinite lives and are not amortized. However, all intangibles would be tested for *impairment* at least annually.[iv]

INHERENT RISK ASSESSMENT: INTANGIBLE ASSETS AND GOODWILL

The nature of the judgements involved in accounting for intangible assets and goodwill raises serious inherent risk considerations. The accounting rules are complex and the transactions are difficult to audit. Pause for a moment and consider EarthWear. If EarthWear were to acquire another successful clothing company, and thus record goodwill, how would that change your audit plan and why? Judgement is required to initially value assets such as trademarks, customer relations, copyrights, customer orders, backlogs (i.e. backlogs represent expected future revenue) and goodwill when one company acquires another. Both the client and the auditor often use valuation **experts** to assist in determining fair values. Considerable judgement is also required to determine useful lives for intangible assets such as patents, copyrights and order backlogs. Finally, asset impairment tests and determining the amount of impairment loss are complex procedures that involve estimation. Accounting standards require different asset impairment tests for different classes of intangible assets. With the judgement and complexity associated with valuation and estimation of intangible assets and goodwill, the auditor is likely to assess the inherent risk as high. For accounting estimates, including for fair value accounting estimates, the auditor evaluates and determines the degree of **estimation uncertainty**. High estimation uncertainty gives rise to a **significant risk**. Significant risks require special audit consideration. For instance, if a highly specialized entity-developed model is used to estimate the fair value of an intangible, a significant risk may exist. In such a situation the auditor may decide to use the work of an **auditor's expert**. The expert may use an independent model to compare its results with those of the model used by management in order to evaluate whether the values determined by management's model are reasonable.

> **Practice Insight 14.1**
>
> An acquired copyright has a remaining legal life of 50 years. An analysis of consumer habits and market trends provides evidence that the copyrighted material will generate net cash inflows for only 30 more years. Following IAS the copyright would be amortized over its 30-year estimated useful life, and reviewed for impairment by assessing at the end of each reporting period whether there is any indication that it may be impaired (IAS 38 *Intangibles Assets Illustrative Examples*). Notice that in order to properly audit a client's impairment testing, the auditor needs expertise in both financial reporting requirements and evidence evaluation.

CONTROL RISK ASSESSMENT: INTANGIBLE ASSETS AND GOODWILL

Management is responsible for making the fair value measurements and disclosures and therefore must establish an accounting and reporting process for determining the fair value measures, selecting the appropriate valuation methods, identifying and supporting significant assumptions used, and preparing the valuation and disclosures in accordance with the applicable financial reporting framework.

Intangible asset and goodwill transactions and initial valuation are typically processed through the client's business acquisition processes. To rely on controls in this process, the auditor needs to understand, document and test the design and operating effectiveness of key controls. For example, the control activities in the business acquisition process should ensure that all identifiable asset categories are separately valued and that any valuation experts used are qualified and objective.

Additional control activities are required for impairment testing. For example, the client's policies and procedures should properly capture and evaluate potential events that may trigger impairment (e.g. significant change in market price or in the way the asset is being used), ensure that all intangible assets and goodwill are tested for impairment at least annually, and verify that the impairment-testing policies and procedures are in compliance with the applicable financial reporting framework. In assessing control risk, the auditor considers factors such as:

- The expertise and experience of those determining the fair value of the asset.
- Controls over the process used to determine fair value measurements, including controls over data and segregation of duties between those committing the client to the purchase and those undertaking the valuation.
- The extent to which the entity engages or employs valuation experts.
- The significant management assumptions used in determining fair value.
- The integrity of change controls and security procedures for valuation models and relevant information systems, including approval processes.

When the auditor determines that an accounting estimate for intangible assets or goodwill gives rise to a significant risk, the auditor should obtain an understanding of the entity's controls related to the significant risk. When the auditor plans to rely on controls over a significant risk, the auditor tests those controls in the current period.

❖ SUBSTANTIVE PROCEDURES: INTANGIBLE ASSETS AND GOODWILL

LO2   ### Substantive Analytical Procedures for Intangible Assets and Goodwill

While analytical procedures help direct the auditor's attention to situations needing additional investigation (e.g. potential asset impairment), unlike with prepaids the principal substantive evidence regarding intangible and goodwill assets is typically obtained via tests of details. Substantive analytical procedures generally are not useful in gathering sufficient appropriate evidence regarding the assertions of primary interest for intangibles and goodwill (valuation, existence, completeness, rights and obligations, and classification). As such, the discussion below is limited to substantive tests of details.

Tests of Details of Intangible Assets and Goodwill

Tests of details associated with valuation and impairment of intangible assets and goodwill are often necessary because the complexity and degree of judgement increase the risk of material misstatement. Further, auditing standards require some substantive evidence for all significant accounts, and, as noted above, substantive analytical procedures are not likely to provide sufficient appropriate evidence for significant transactions involving intangible assets and goodwill. If significant risks exist related to fair value estimates and other accounting estimates for intangible assets and goodwill, the auditor would perform further substantive procedures such as evaluating the reasonableness of significant assumptions made by management.

Existence and Completeness

The auditor normally tests for the existence of intangible assets and goodwill at the time they are acquired. For assets such as patents, copyrights, licences, broadcast rights and trademarks, the auditor would examine legal documentation supporting the validity of the asset. Similarly, customer backlogs can be validated by examining customer order information or by sending confirmations to customers requesting information on their order status.

The auditor's primary concern relative to the completeness assertion for intangible assets and goodwill is to ensure that the client's impairment-testing procedures include all intangible assets and goodwill. To test this assertion, the auditor would obtain a copy of the client's detail listing of intangible assets and goodwill, which should agree with the total amount of intangible assets and goodwill reported on the client's balance sheet. The auditor would also examine the client's impairment documentation to ensure that each asset is subject to the appropriate impairment testing in accordance with the applicable financial reporting framework.

Valuation

It should be no surprise that valuation is the most important assertion associated with intangible assets and goodwill. The initial valuation of intangible assets typically involves an allocation of purchase price in proportion to fair values. Goodwill is a residual, that is the difference between of the cost of acquisition of a company and the fair value of the identifiable tangible and intangible assets and liabilities. Once an intangible asset or goodwill is determined to be impaired, the current fair value must be determined to compute the impairment loss. When there is a market price for the intangible assets, the valuation issues are relatively straightforward. However, in the majority of the situations involving valuation of intangible assets, a readily determined market price is not available.

Accounting standards describe different acceptable valuation methods, but if a market price is not available, all remaining methods rely heavily on assumptions, likelihood assessments and estimation. With the movement towards more fair value accounting, auditors need improved understanding of valuation issues. However, to obtain sufficient appropriate evidence on the valuation of intangible assets and goodwill (either for initial valuation or after an impairment), the auditor is not required to become an expert in valuation. Rather, the auditor will often rely on the help of an expert. When auditor's experts are used to obtain audit evidence, the auditor is required to evaluate the expert's qualifications and objectivity. The auditor also must determine if the valuation model used by the expert is appropriate and consistent with the applicable financial reporting framework, and the auditor must understand and verify the reasonableness of the underlying data and assumptions.

In addition to initial valuation and impairment testing, the auditor would also test the reasonableness of the useful lives used for amortizing intangible assets that have definite lives. For example, even though a patent may have a legal life of 20 years, if the competitive advantages associated with the patent are expected to last only five years, the patent cost should be amortized over a shorter period.

Rights and Obligations

Litigation regarding the rights associated with intangible assets such as trademarks, patents, copyrights, licences and Internet domains is relatively common. The auditor normally examines supporting legal and contractual documentation to verify the client's legal rights to these assets. The auditor also reads the minutes of board of directors meetings and communicates with the client's legal counsel to determine if there is pending litigation regarding legal rights (lawyer's letters are discussed in Chapter 17). As mentioned above, the auditor needs to understand and test the client's business acquisition processes as well as the client's allocation of purchase price to various intangible assets.

Classification

The auditor's concern with classification is that the different types of intangible assets are properly identified and are accounted for separately. A type of intangible asset is a grouping of intangible assets of similar nature and use in an entity's operations such as the five general categories of intangible assets listed earlier in this text.

Practice Insight 14.2

Unprecedented market disruption and economic downturn hit globally in 2008 and changed market outlooks for many companies. This resulted in widespread reporting of impairment losses. Of dramatic proportion, the Royal Bank of Scotland Group reported in 2008 impairment losses of €16.6 billion of goodwill and intangibles. The losses related to prior-year acquisitions, most notably of the Dutch bank ABN AMRO in 2007 and Charter One in the USA in 2004.

AUDITING THE PROPERTY MANAGEMENT PROCESS

LO3

For most entities, property, plant, and equipment represent a material amount in the financial statements. When the audit is an ongoing engagement, the auditor is able to focus his or her efforts on the current year's activity because the assets acquired in earlier years were subjected to audit procedures at the time of acquisition. However, on a new engagement the auditor has to verify the assets that make up the beginning balances in the client's property, plant and equipment accounts.

The size of the entity may also affect the auditor's approach. If the client is relatively small with few asset purchases during the period, it is generally more cost-effective for the auditor to follow a substantive strategy. Following this strategy, the auditor conducts substantive analytical procedures and direct tests of the account balances. Large entities, on the other hand, are likely to have formal procedures for budgeting for and purchasing capital assets. While routine purchases might be processed through the purchasing process, as described in Chapter 11, acquisition or construction of specialized assets may be subject to different requisition and authorization procedures. When an entity has a formal control system over the property management process, the auditor may choose to follow a reliance strategy and test controls.

Types of Transactions

LO4

Four types of property, plant, and equipment transactions may occur:

1 Acquisition of capital assets for cash or non-monetary considerations.
2 Disposition of capital assets through sale, exchange, retirement or abandonment.
3 Depreciation of capital assets over their useful economic life.
4 Leasing of capital assets.

Overview of the Property Management Process

Larger entities generally use IT systems to process property, plant, and equipment transactions, maintain subsidiary records, and produce required reports. Figure 14–1 presents a flowchart of EarthWear's accounting system for the property management process. Transactions are periodically entered both from the purchasing process and through direct input into the system. The property, plant and equipment master file is then updated, and a number of reports are produced. The periodic report for property, plant, and equipment transactions is reviewed for proper recording by the physical plant department. The property, plant and equipment subsidiary ledger is a record of all capital assets owned by the entity. It contains information on the cost of the asset, the date acquired, the method of depreciation and accumulated depreciation. The subsidiary ledger also includes the calculation of depreciation expense for both financial statement and income tax purposes. The general ledger is posted to reflect the new property, plant and equipment transactions and depreciation expense. The subsidiary ledger is reconciled to the general ledger control account monthly.

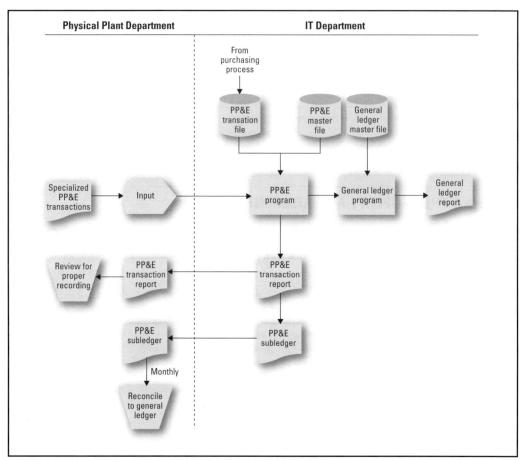

FIGURE 14-1   Flowchart of the Property Management Process: EarthWear Clothiers

❖ INHERENT RISK ASSESSMENT: PROPERTY MANAGEMENT PROCESS

LO5

The assessment of inherent risk for the purchasing process provides a starting point for assessing inherent risk for property, plant and equipment. The following three inherent risk factors classified as operating characteristics require consideration by the auditor:

1   Complex accounting issues.
2   Difficult-to-audit transactions.
3   Misstatements detected in prior audits.

Complex Accounting Issues

A number of different types of property, plant and equipment transactions involve complex accounting issues. Lease accounting, self-constructed assets and capitalized interest are examples of such issues. For example, in the case of a lease transaction the auditor must evaluate the client's decision either to capitalize the lease or to treat it as an operating lease. Because of the complexity of the capitalization decision and the subjectivity involved in assessing the capitalization criteria, it is not uncommon for such transactions to be accounted for incorrectly by the client. For example, EarthWear leases store and office space accounted for as operating leases. Willis & Adams must be sure that these leases do not qualify as capital leases.

Easy and Difficult Transactions to Audit

The majority of additions to property, plant and equipment are relatively easy to audit because they are purchased directly from vendors. For such purchases the auditor is able to obtain evidence for most assertions by examining the source documents. However, transactions involving donated assets, non-monetary exchanges and self-constructed assets are often difficult to audit. For example, it may be difficult to verify the trade-in value of an asset exchanged or to properly audit the cost accumulation of self-constructed assets. The presence of these types of transactions should lead to a higher inherent risk assessment. It is certainly worth noting that one of the largest accounting frauds in history, WorldCom, involved the improper capitalization of operating expenses as property, plant and equipment to overstate income. See Exhibit 14–2 for a more detailed description of the company, the fraud and how the fraud was uncovered.

Exhibit 14–2 WorldCom Overstates PP&E and Net Income

WorldCom started as a mom-and-pop long-distance company in 1983. But in the 1990s, it matured into a powerhouse. In 1997 it shocked the industry with an unsolicited bid to take over MCI, a company more than three times its size. In 1998 *CFO Magazine* named WorldCom's CFO, Scott Sullivan, one of the country's best CFOs. At age 37 he was earning $19.3 million a year. In 1999 WorldCom founder Bernie Ebbers moved the company to Clinton, Mississippi, his old college town, and everything changed. The stock price went through the roof. However, by early 2001, overexuberance for the telecom market had created a glut of companies like WorldCom, and earnings started to fall.

In March 2002, Cynthia Cooper, a WorldCom vice president and head of internal audit was informed by a worried executive in the wireless division that corporate accounting had taken $400 million out of his reserve account and used it to boost WorldCom's income. When Cooper went to WorldCom's external auditors, Arthur Andersen, to inquire about the manoeuvre, she was told matter-of-factly that it was not a problem. When she did not relent, Sullivan angrily told Cooper that everything was fine and she should back off. He was furious at her, according to a person involved in the matter. Says Cooper, 'When someone is hostile, my instinct is to find out why.'

As the weeks went on, Cooper directed her team members to widen their net. Having watched the Enron implosion and Andersen's role in it, she was worried they could not necessarily rely on the accounting firm's audits. So the internal auditors decided to re-audit some areas. She and her team began working late into the night, keeping their project secret. In late May, Cooper and her group discovered a gaping hole in the books. In public reports, the company had classified billions of dollars as property, plant and equipment in 2001, meaning the costs could be stretched out over a number of years into the future. However, these expenditures were for regular fees WorldCom paid to local telephone companies to complete calls and therefore were operating costs, which should be expensed in full each year. It was as if an ordinary person had paid his or her phone bills but written down the payments as if he or she were building a long-term asset, like a phone tower, in his or her backyard. The trick allowed WorldCom to turn a $662 million loss into a $2.4 billion profit in 2001.

Internal audit began looking for ways to somehow justify what it had found in the books. Finally, the internal auditors confronted WorldCom's controller, David Myers, who admitted the accounting could not be justified. Cooper told the audit committee that the company accountants had understated expenses and overstated income. Sullivan was offered the opportunity to present his side of the story, but he could not convince them regarding the propriety of the accounting. Within days, the company fired its famed chief financial officer, Scott Sullivan, and told the world that it had inflated its profits by $3.8 billion. After additional investigation, the number grew to over $9 billion, the largest accounting fraud ever up to that date.

Source: A. Ripley, 'The Night Detective (Persons of the Year)', *Time* (30 December 2002–6 January 2003), p. 36.

Practice Insight 14.3

One way to overstate the net carrying value of plant or equipment is to inappropriately extend the assets' depreciable life. Waste Management used such an approach to fraudulently boost profits. Management has considerable latitude in choosing a depreciation method. Changes to either the useful lives or depreciation methods should be scrutinized for both their purpose and financial effect.

Misstatements Detected in Prior Audits

If the auditor has detected misstatements in prior audits, the assessment of inherent risk should be set higher than if few or no misstatements had been found in the past.[v] For example, in prior years the auditor may have found numerous client misstatements in accumulating costs for valuing self-constructed capital assets. Unless the client has established new control activities over cost accumulation, the auditor should also expect to find misstatements during the current year's audit and therefore set inherent risk as high.

CONTROL RISK ASSESSMENT: PROPERTY MANAGEMENT PROCESS

LO6

Although auditors typically follow a substantive strategy when auditing property management process, an understanding of internal control is required on all audits. The presentation that follows focuses on the major assertions, key control activities, and **tests of controls** that relate directly to the property management process. Other control activities related to the property management process were discussed as part of the purchasing process. Important examples of segregation of duties are also presented.

Occurrence and Authorization

The control activities for the occurrence and authorization assertions are normally part of the purchasing process. Purchase requisitions are initiated in relevant departments and authorized at the appropriate level within the entity. However, large capital asset transactions may be subject to control activities outside the purchasing process. For example, highly specialized technical equipment is likely to be purchased only after passing through a specific capital-budgeting process, which might require that purchase of equipment meet predefined internal rate-of-return criteria. The purchase of equipment may also require that highly skilled engineers approve the technical specifications for the equipment. For such transactions, the auditor may need to examine more than the vendor's invoice to test validity. A review of additional documentation, such as capital-budgeting documents and engineering specifications, may be needed.

Most entities have some type of authorization table based on the size of capital asset transactions. The client should have control activities to ensure that the authorization to purchase capital assets is consistent with the authorization table. For example, the control activities should specify monetary limits at each managerial level to ensure that larger projects are brought to the attention of higher levels of management for approval before commitments are made. Lease transactions should be subject to similar control activities. The entity also needs to have control activities for authorizing the sale or other disposition of capital assets. This should include a level of authorization above the department initiating the disposition. Control activities should also identify assets that are no longer used in operations because they may require different accounting treatment. Finally, all major maintenance or improvement transactions should be properly authorized by an appropriate level of management.

Completeness

Most entities use software to maintain detailed electronic property records (see Figure 14–1). The property, plant and equipment subsidiary ledger usually includes the following information for each capital asset:

- Description, location and ID number.
- Date of acquisition and installed cost.
- Depreciation methods for book and tax purposes, salvage value and estimated useful life.

The control activities used in the purchasing process for ensuring completeness provide some assurance that all capital asset transactions are recorded in the property, plant, and equipment subsidiary ledger and general ledger. One procedure that helps to ensure that this assertion is met is periodic reconciliation of the property, plant, and equipment subsidiary ledger to the general ledger control accounts. Figure 14–1 shows this control activity as it is performed by EarthWear's physical plant department.

Another control activity that an entity may use to ensure that all capital assets are recorded is periodic comparison of the detailed records in the subsidiary ledger with the existing capital assets. This may be done in a number of ways. The client may make a complete physical examination of property, plant and equipment on a periodic or rotating basis, and compare the physical assets to the property, plant and equipment subsidiary ledger. Alternatively, the physical examination may be limited to major capital assets or assets that are subject to loss. In both instances the entity's internal auditors may test the reliability of the subsidiary ledger. Larger entities sometimes employ outside experts to physically examine property, plant and equipment.

 Segregation of Duties

LO7

The existence of adequate segregation of duties for the property management process depends on the volume and significance of the transactions processed. For example, if an entity purchases large quantities of machinery and equipment, or if it has large capital projects under construction, it is likely to have a formal control process. On the other hand, if an entity has few capital asset purchases, it will generally not have a formal control system over such transactions. Table 14–1 shows the key segregation of duties for the property management process, and examples of possible errors or fraud that can result from conflicts in duties.

Table 14–1 Key Segregation of Duties, and Possible Errors or Fraud: Property Management Process	
Segregation of Duties	Possible Errors or Fraud Resulting from Conflicts of Duties
The function of initiating a capital asset acquisition should be segregated from the final approval function.	If one individual is responsible for initiating a capital asset transaction and also has final approval, fictitious or unauthorized purchases of assets can occur. This can result in purchases of unnecessary assets, assets that do not meet the company's quality control standards, or illegal payments to suppliers or contractors.
The property, plant and equipment records function should be segregated from the general ledger function.	If one individual is responsible for the property, plant and equipment records and also for the general ledger functions, that individual can conceal any defalcation that would normally be detected by reconciling subsidiary records with the general ledger control account.
The property, plant and equipment records function should be segregated from the custodial or safeguarding function.	If one individual is responsible for the property, plant and equipment records and also has custodial responsibility for the related assets, tools and equipment can be stolen, and the theft can be concealed by adjustment of the accounting records.
If a periodic physical inventory of property, plant and equipment is taken, the individual responsible for the inventory should be independent of the custodial and record-keeping functions.	If the individual who is responsible for the periodic physical inventory of property, plant and equipment is also responsible for the custodial and record-keeping functions, theft of the entity's capital assets can be concealed.

SUBSTANTIVE PROCEDURES: PROPERTY, PLANT AND EQUIPMENT

As mentioned earlier, when the number of transactions is small, auditors often follow a substantive strategy when auditing property, plant and equipment. Therefore, a detailed discussion of the substantive procedures for property, plant and equipment is provided next. The discussion focuses on substantive analytical procedures and tests of details of transactions, account balances and disclosures.

Substantive Analytical Procedures: Property, Plant and Equipment

LO8
The following list provides examples of substantive analytical procedures that can be used in the audit of property, plant, and equipment:

- Compare prior-periods balances in property, plant and equipment and depreciation expense with current-period balances, taking into account any changes in conditions or asset composition.
- Compute the ratio of depreciation expense to the related property, plant and equipment accounts, and compare to prior years' ratios.
- Compute the ratio of repairs and maintenance expense to the related property, plant and equipment accounts, and compare to prior years' ratios.
- Compute the ratio of insurance expense to the related property, plant and equipment accounts, and compare to prior years' ratios.
- Review capital budgets and compare the amounts spent with amounts budgeted.

For the first two procedures listed above, pause and consider what potential misstatements these procedures may help identify. If, for example, the ratio of depreciation expense to the related property, plant and equipment accounts is less than prior years' and few assets have been disposed of, the auditor might be concerned that depreciation has not been taken on some assets included in the account and additional audit procedures would be performed.

Tests of Details of Transactions, Account Balances and Disclosures: Property, Plant and Equipment

LO9

Table 14–2 summarizes examples of substantive tests for the property, plant, and equipment accounts for each assertion relating to transactions and balances. The discussion that follows focuses on the major audit procedures conducted by the auditor. Completeness and accuracy are discussed first because the auditor must establish that the detailed property, plant and equipment records are accurate, and agree with the general ledger account.

Table 14–2 Examples of Tests of Transactions and Account Balances for Property, Plant and Equipment (PP&E)	
Assertions about Classes of Transactions	*Examples Substantive Tests of Transactions**
Occurrence	Vouch significant additions and dispositions to vendor invoices or other supporting documentation.
	Review lease agreements to ensure that lease transactions are accounted for properly.
Completeness	Trace a sample of purchase requisitions to loading dock reports and to the PP&E records (i.e. transaction and master file).
Authorization	Vouch a sample of PP&E additions to documentation indicating proper authorization.
Accuracy	For assets written off, test amounts charged against income and accumulated depreciation.
Cut-off	Examine the purchases and sales of capital assets for a few days before and after year-end.
Classification	Vouch transactions included in repairs and maintenance for items that should be capitalized.
	Review lease transactions for proper classification between operating and capital leases.
Assertions about Account Balances at Period End	*Examples Tests of Details of Account Balances*
Existence	Verify the existence of major additions by physically inspecting the capital asset.
Rights and obligations	Examine or confirm deeds or title documents for proof of ownership.
Completeness	Obtain a lead schedule of property, plant, and equipment; foot schedule and agree totals to the general ledger.
	Obtain detailed schedules for additions and dispositions of property, plant, and equipment; foot schedule; agree amounts to totals shown on lead schedule.
	Physically examine a sample of capital assets and trace them into the property, plant, and equipment subsidiary ledger.
Valuation and allocation	Evaluate fixed assets for significant write-offs or impairments by performing procedures such as
	• Identify the event or change in circumstance indicating that the carrying value of the asset may not be recoverable.
	• Verify impairment loss by determining recoverable amount and compare to the carrying value.
	• Examine client documentation supporting impairment of write-off.
	Test depreciation calculations for a sample of capital assets.
* These tests of details of transactions are commonly conducted as dual-purpose tests (i.e. in conjunction with tests of controls).	

Completeness and Accuracy

The auditor verifies the accuracy of property, plant, and equipment by obtaining a lead schedule and detailed schedules for additions and dispositions of assets. This lead schedule is footed, and the individual accounts are agreed to the general ledger. The detailed schedules are also tested for accuracy. Exhibit 14–3 presents a lead schedule for EarthWear's property, plant, and equipment. Take a look at Exhibit 14–3 and ask yourself, 'If I were the EarthWear auditor, where would I focus my tests of details?'

Exhibit 14–3 An Example of a Lead Schedule for Property, Plant and Equipment

K Lead
JLJ
15/1/10

EARTHWEAR CLOTHIERS
Lead Sheet – Property, Plant and Equipment
31/12/09

Account	W/P Ref.	Beginning Balance	Additions	Deletions	Ending Balance	Beginning Balance	Additions	Deletions	Ending Balance
		Cost				Accumulated Depreciation			
Land	K10	€6,593,000¶	€2,112,852	€1,786,852	€6,919,000L				
Buildings	K20	60,211,250¶	6,112,600	2,324,950	63,998,900L	€23,638,300¶	€3,411,493	€653,788	€26,396,005L
Fixtures, Computers, and Equipment	K30	114,342,050¶	19,791,763	1,634,988	132,498,825L	51,162,450¶	8,285,360	1,533,398	57,914,462L
Leasehold Improvements	K40	2,894,100¶	780,115	664,595	3,009,620L	€1,455,500¶	413,952	194,019	1,675,433L
Totals		€184,040,400F	€28,797,330	€6,411,385	€206,426,345	€76,266,250F	€12,110,805	€2,381,155	€85,985,900
		F	F	F	F	F	F	F	F

F = Footed and crossfooted.
L = Agreed to general ledger.
¶ = Agreed to prior year's working papers.

The auditor has some assurance about the completeness assertion from the control activities in the purchasing process and, if present, the additional control activities discussed previously in this chapter. If the auditor still has concerns about the completeness assertion, he or she can physically examine a sample of assets and trace them into the property, plant and equipment subsidiary ledger. If the assets are included in the subsidiary ledger, the auditor has sufficient evidence supporting the completeness assertion.

A common cause of an understated **property, plant and equipment** account is the incorrect classification of plant and equipment additions as repairs and maintenance (see the Classification assertion in Table 14-2).

Cut-off

On most engagements, cut-off is tested as part of the audit work in accounts payable and accrued expenses. By examining a sample of vendor invoices from a few days before and after year end, the auditor can determine if capital asset transactions are recorded in the proper period. Inquiry of client personnel and a review of lease transactions for the same period can provide evidence on proper cut-off for leases.

Classification

First, the classification of a transaction into the correct property, plant and equipment account is normally examined as part of the testing of the purchasing process. The auditor's tests of controls and **substantive tests of transactions** provide evidence as to the effectiveness of the control activities for this assertion.

Second, the auditor should examine selected expense accounts such as repairs and maintenance to determine if any capital assets have been incorrectly recorded in these accounts. An account analysis of transactions included in the repairs and maintenance account is obtained, and selected transactions are vouched to supporting documents. In examining the supporting documents, the auditor must determine if the transactions are truly expense items or whether it would be more appropriate to capitalize the costs. For example, the auditor may examine an invoice from a plumbing contractor that shows that the water pipe system for a building has been replaced during the current period. If the amount of this transaction was material and improved the building, it should not be expensed as a repair but rather should be capitalized as a building improvement.

Last, the auditor should examine each material lease agreement to verify that the lease is properly classified as an operating or capital lease.

Existence

Before reading on, use your developing audit knowledge to think of ways, beyond physical inspection, to obtain evidence on the existence of property, plant and equipment.

To test existence, the auditor obtains a listing of all major additions and vouches them to supporting documents such as vendors' invoices. If the purchase was properly authorized and the asset has been received and placed in service, the transaction is valid. In addition, the auditor may want to verify that assets recorded as capital assets actually exist. For major acquisitions, the auditor may physically examine the capital asset.

Similarly, disposition of assets must be properly authorized, and the supporting documentation such as sales receipts should indicate how the disposal took place. Generally, the auditor obtains a schedule of all major dispositions, and verifies that the asset was removed from the property, plant and equipment records. If the disposition is the result of a sale or exchange, the auditor would verify the cash receipt for the sale of the asset or documentation that another asset was received in exchange.

The auditor must also ascertain the validity of lease transactions by examining the lease agreements entered into by the entity. If the lease agreement is properly authorized and the asset is placed in service, the evidence supports the validity of the recorded asset.

Rights and Obligations

The auditor can test for rights or ownership by examining the vendor invoices or other supporting documents. In some instances, the auditor may examine or confirm property deeds or title documents for proof of ownership.

Valuation and Allocation

Capital assets are valued at acquisition cost plus any costs necessary to make the asset operational. The auditor tests the recorded cost of new assets by examining the vendor invoices and other supporting documents used by the client to establish the recorded value of the assets. If the client has material self-constructed assets, the auditor conducts detailed audit work on the construction-in-process account. This includes ensuring that interest is properly capitalized as a cost of the asset (see IAS 23 *Borrowing Cost*).

IAS 36 *Impairment of Assets* requires that long-lived assets be reviewed for impairment whenever events or changes in circumstances indicate that the assets' carrying amount may not be recoverable. The standard defines recoverable amount as the higher of an asset's fair value less costs to sell and its value in use. The best evidence of an asset's fair value less costs to sell is a price in a binding sale agreement in an arm's length transaction. Auditing standards require the auditor to obtain an understanding of the entity's process for determining fair value measurements and based on the assessment of risks of material misstatement, test the fair value measurements (ISA 540). The value in use of an asset involves estimating the future (discounted) cash flows from use and eventual disposition of the assets. IAS 36 provides guidance and illustrations on how to estimate future cash flows, but obviously this area requires substantial judgement and expertise. Typically, the auditor gathers evidence on the valuation of property, plant and equipment through a variety of procedures (e.g. understanding of the business and industry and current events that may lead to impairment, tests of controls over the client's impairment evaluation, inquiry and observation regarding the condition and usefulness of long-lived assets, and tests of details of balances, such as those described in Table 14–2).

The other valuation issue the auditor must address is the recognition of depreciation expense. If the client uses IT to process and account for capital assets, the auditor may be able to use **computer-assisted audit techniques** to verify the calculation of depreciation for various assets. Alternatively, the auditor may recompute the depreciation expense for a sample of capital assets. In making this calculation, the auditor considers the reasonableness of the estimated life of the asset, the depreciation methods used for book and tax purposes, and any expected salvage value.

Disclosure Issues

Table 14–3 shows a number of important items that may require disclosure as part of the audit of property, plant and equipment. Some of these disclosures are made in the 'summary of significant accounting policies' note, while other items may be disclosed in separate notes. Exhibit 14–4 illustrates disclosure accounting policy for impairment of assets.

Table 14–3 Examples of Items Requiring Disclosure: Property, Plant and Equipment
Classes of capital assets and valuation bases.
Depreciation methods and useful lives for financial reporting and tax purposes.
Non-operating assets.
Construction or purchase commitments.
Liens and mortgages.
Acquisition or disposal of major operating facilities.
Capitalized and other lease arrangements.

Exhibit 14–4 Disclosure of Accounting Policy for Impairment of Assets
Assets that have an indefinite useful life, for example goodwill, are not subject to amortization and are tested annually for impairment. Assets that are subject to amortization are reviewed for impairment whenever events or changes in circumstances indicate that the carrying amount may not be recoverable. An impairment loss is recognized for the amount by which the asset's carrying amount exceeds its recoverable amount. The recoverable amount is the higher of an asset's fair value less costs to sell and value in use. For the purposes of assessing impairment, assets are grouped at the lowest levels for which there are separately identifiable cash flows (cash-generating units). Non-financial assets other than goodwill that suffered an impairment are reviewed for possible reversal of the impairment at each reporting date.
Source: PricewaterhouseCoopers, International Financial Reporting Standards, Illustrative Corporate Consolidated Financial Statements 2008.

❖ EVALUATING THE AUDIT FINDINGS: PROPERTY, PLANT AND EQUIPMENT

LO10

The process for evaluating the audit findings for property, plant and equipment is the same as was discussed in previous chapters. The auditor aggregates the identified misstatements and compares this amount to materiality for the financial statements or any lesser materiality amount determined appropriate for the account. If the uncorrected misstatement in the property, plant and equipment accounts, and when considered together with other uncorrected misstatements, is less than materiality, the evidence indicates that the financial statements are not materially misstated. This is the case with EarthWear, as no misstatements were detected for property, plant and equipment (see Exhibit 3–4). The auditors would have requested management to correct any identified misstatements.

🔑 Key Terms

Analytical procedures. Evaluations of financial information through analysis of plausible relationships among both financial and non-financial data.

Auditor's expert. An expert employed or engaged by the auditor to assist the auditor to obtain sufficient appropriate audit evidence, for example in determining fair values of intangible assets.

Computer-assisted audit techniques (CAATs). Applications of auditing procedures using the computer as an audit tool.

Estimation uncertainty. The susceptibility of an accounting estimate and related disclosures to an inherent lack of precision in its measurement.

Expert. A person or organization, possessing expertise in a field other than accounting or auditing.

Goodwill (IFRS 3). An asset representing the future economic benefits arising from other assets acquired in a business combination that are not individually identified and separately recognized.

Intangible assets (IAS 38). An identifiable non-monetary asset without physical substance.

Lien. When a creditor or bank has the right to sell the mortgaged or collateral property of those who fail to meet the obligations of a loan contract.

Prepaid expense. A type of asset that arises on a balance sheet as a result of business making payments for goods and services to be received in the near future. While prepaid expenses are initially recorded as assets, their value is expensed over time as the benefit is received.

Property, plant and equipment (IAS 16). Tangible items that are held for use in the production or supply of goods or services, for rental to others or for administrative purposes; and are expected to be used during more than one period.

Significant risk. An identified and assessed risk of material misstatement that, in the auditor's judgement, requires special audit consideration.

Substantive tests of transactions. Tests to detect errors or fraud in individual transactions.

Tests of controls. Audit procedures designed to evaluate the operating effectiveness of controls in preventing, or detecting and correcting, material misstatements at the assertion level.

Tests of details of account balances and disclosures. Substantive tests that concentrate on the details of items contained in the account balance and disclosure.

? Review Questions

LO1	14–1	Distinguish between prepaid expenses and intangible assets. Give two examples of each.
LO1,2	14–2	Prepaid expenses are generally assessed to have a low inherent risk. Why would intangible assets and goodwill present serious inherent risk consideration?
LO2	14–3	How does the purchasing process affect prepaid insurance and property, plant and equipment transactions?
LO2	14–4	Identify two substantive analytical procedures that can be used to audit prepaid insurance.
LO2	14–5	Confirmation is a useful audit procedure for verifying information related to prepaid insurance. What type of information would be requested from an entity's insurance broker in such an confirmation?
LO2,4	14–6	List four categories of intangible assets and four types of property, plant and equipment transactions.
LO2,5	14–7	Describe two or more factors that the auditor should consider in assessing the inherent risk for (a) intangible assets and (b) the property management process.
LO6	14–8	What is a typical control over authorization of capital asset transactions?
LO7	14–9	What is one of the key segregation of duties for the property management process? What errors or fraud can occur if such segregation is not present?
LO8	14–10	Identify three substantive analytical procedures that can be used to audit property, plant and equipment.
LO9	14–11	What procedures would an auditor use to verify the completeness, rights and obligations, and valuation assertions for property, plant and equipment?

✎ Problems

LO1,2	14–12	Natherson, independent auditor, is engaged to audit the financial statements of Lewis Lumber for the year ended 31 December. Natherson obtained and documented an understanding of internal control relating to the purchasing process and set control risk at the maximum level. Natherson requested and obtained from Lewis a schedule analysing prepaid insurance as of 31 December, and sent confirmation requests to Lewis's insurance broker.

Required:

a *Identify two substantive analytical procedures that Natherson could use to verify prepaid insurance.*

b *What substantive audit procedures should Natherson conduct on the schedule of prepaid insurance?*

LO2	14–13	Taylor, independent auditor, has been engaged to audit the financial statements of Palmer Company, a continuing audit client. Taylor is about to perform substantive audit procedures on Palmer's goodwill (excess of cost over fair value of net assets purchased) and trademark assets that were acquired in prior

years' business combinations. An industry slowdown has occurred recently, and the operations purchased have not met profit expectations.

During the planning process, Taylor determined that there was a high risk that goodwill and the trademark are impaired and may be materially misstated. Taylor obtained an understanding of internal control and set the control risk at the maximum level for the assertions related to intangible assets and goodwill.

Required:

a   Describe the substantive audit procedures Taylor should consider performing in auditing Palmer's goodwill and trademark assets. Do not discuss Palmer's internal controls.

b   If Taylor engages a valuation expert, describe what the auditor's responsibility is if the work of the auditor's expert will be used as audit evidence.

LO6,7   **14–14**   Nakamura, independent auditor, has accepted an engagement to audit the financial statements of Grant Manufacturing Company, a new client. Grant has an adequate control environment and a reasonable segregation of duties. Nakamura is about to set the control risk for the assertions related to Grant's 'property and equipment'.

Required:

Describe the key internal controls related to Grant's property, equipment and related transactions (additions, transfers, major maintenance and repairs, retirements, and dispositions) that Nakamura may consider in setting the control risk.

(AICPA, adapted)

LO4,6,9,10   **14–15**   Gonzales, independent auditor, is the auditor for a manufacturing company with a balance sheet that includes the entry 'Property, plant and equipment'. Gonzales has been asked by the company's management if audit adjustments or reclassifications are required for the following material items that have been included in or excluded from 'Property, plant and equipment':

1   A tract of land was acquired during the year. The land is to be the future site of the client's new headquarters, which will be constructed next year. Commissions were paid to the real estate agent used to acquire the land, and expenditures were made to relocate the previous owner's equipment. These commissions and expenditures were expensed and are excluded from 'Property, plant and equipment'.

2   Clearing costs were incurred to ready the land for construction. These costs were included in 'Property, plant and equipment'.

3   During the land-clearing process, timber and gravel were recovered and sold. The proceeds from the sale were recorded as other income, and are excluded from 'Property, plant and equipment'.

4   A group of machines was purchased under a royalty agreement that provides royalty payments based on units of production from the machines. The costs of the machines, freight costs, unloading charges and royalty payments were capitalized, and are included in 'Property, plant and equipment'.

Required:

a   Describe the general characteristics of assets, such as land, buildings, improvements, machinery, equipment, fixtures, and so on, that should normally be classified as 'Property, plant and equipment', and identify assertions in connection with the examination of 'Property, plant and equipment'. Do not discuss specific audit procedures.

b *Indicate whether each of the items numbered 1 to 4 requires one or more audit adjustments or reclassifications, and explain why such adjustments or reclassifications are required or not required. Organize your answer as follows:*

Item Number	Is Auditing Adjustment or Reclassification Required? (Yes or No)	Reasons Why Audit Adjustments or Reclassifications Are Required or Not Required

(AICPA, adapted)

LO8,9 **14–16** To support financial statement assertions, an auditor develops specific substantive procedures to satisfy or address each assertion.

Required:

Items a to c represent assertions for the property and equipment accounts. Select the most appropriate audit procedure from the following list and enter the number in the appropriate place on the grid. (An audit procedure may be selected once or not at all.)

Audit Procedure:

1 Trace opening balances in the summary schedules to the prior year's audit working papers.

2 Review the provision for depreciation expense, and determine that depreciable lives and methods used in the current year are consistent with those used in the prior year.

3 Determine that the responsibility for maintaining the property and equipment records is segregated from the responsibility for custody of property and equipment.

4 Examine deeds and title insurance certificates.

5 Perform cut-off tests to verify that property and equipment additions are recorded in the proper period.

6 Determine that property and equipment are adequately insured.

7 Physically examine all major property and equipment additions.

	Specific Assertion	Audit Procedure
a.	Verify that the entity has the legal right to property and equipment acquired during the year (rights and obligations).	
b.	Verify that recorded property and equipment represent assets that actually exist at the balance sheet date (existence).	
c.	Verify that net property and equipment are properly valued at the balance sheet date (valuation and allocation).	

(AICPA, adapted)

LO8,9 **14–17** Pierce, an independent auditor, was engaged to examine the financial statements of Wong Construction, for the year ended 31 December. Wong's financial statements reflect a substantial amount of mobile construction equipment used in the firm's operations. The equipment is accounted for in a subsidiary ledger. Pierce developed an understanding of internal control and set the control risk at moderate.

Required:

Identify the substantive audit procedures Pierce should utilize in examining mobile construction equipment and related depreciation in Wong's financial statements.

(AICPA, adapted)

Discussion Case

LO9,10   14–18   On 15 January 2009, Leno, which has a 31 March year end, entered into a transaction to sell the land and building that contained its manufacturing operations, for a total selling price of €19,750,000. The book value of the land and the building was €3,420,000. The final closing was not expected to occur until some time between July 2010 and March 2011.

On 16 March 2009, Leno received an irrevocable letter of credit, issued by a major bank, for €5,000,000, which represented more than 25 per cent of the sales price. Leno would collect the €5,000,000 and would keep the money even if the buyer decided not to complete the transaction. The letter of credit had an option for an extension for up to one year for a total period of two years. At closing, the entire selling price was to be paid in cash.

Leno was going to continue its manufacturing operations in the building and would continue to be responsible for all normal occupancy costs until final closing, when it would move to another location. After the sale, the building would be torn down and replaced by a large office building complex.

Required:

a   *Based on relevant accounting pronouncements, how should Leno account for the transaction at 31 March 2009?*

b   *What additional types of evidence should the auditor examine prior to recognizing any gain on the transaction?*

Internet Assignment

LO3,4,9   14–19   Visit the website of another catalogue retailer similar to EarthWear Clothiers, and determine what useful lives and depreciation methods are used for property, plant and equipment. Compare those methods to EarthWear's, and, if different, consider the implications for using competitor data for preliminary or substantive analytical procedures.

Notes

i   IAS 38 *Intangible Assets* defines an intangible asset as an identifiable non-monetary asset without physical substance. The identifiable criterion is met when the intangible asset is separable (that is, when it can be sold, transferred or licensed), or where it arises from contractual or other legal rights. In the international accounting standards the term identifiable is included to distinguish an intangible asset from goodwill (see note iii). This chapter follows this distinction in the international accounting standards.

ii   IAS 38 *Intangible Assets* allows certain costs arising from the development phase of an internal project to be capitalized as an intangible asset if certain criteria are met. Internally generated goodwill is not recognised as an asset.

iii   IFRS 3 *Business Combinations* defines goodwill as an asset representing the future economic benefits arising from other assets acquired in a business combination that are not individually identified and separately recognized. Goodwill is not subject to amortization (that is, has indefinite life).

iv   IAS 36 *Impairment of Assets* requires that all assets are tested for impairment (that is, possible write down to fair value) at the end of each reporting period where there is an indication that the asset may be impaired. Indefinite lived intangible assets and intangible assets that are not yet available for use as well as goodwill, are also tested for impairment even if there is no impairment indication.

v   Research has shown that property, plant and equipment accounts frequently contain misstatements. See A. Eilifsen and W.F. Messier, Jr (2000) 'Auditor Detection of Misstatements: A Review and Integration of Empirical Research', *Journal of Accounting Literature* (19), pp. 1–43, for a review of the audit research studies that have indicated that property, plant and equipment accounts are likely to contain misstatements.

CHAPTER 15

Auditing the Financing/Investing Process: Long-Term Liabilities, Stockholders' Equity, and Income Statement Accounts

❖ LEARNING OBJECTIVES

Upon completion of this chapter you will

- ❖ **LO1** Understand the types and features of long-term debt.
- ❖ **LO2** Be familiar with assessing control risk for long-term debt.
- ❖ **LO3** Be familiar with key control activities for long-term debt.
- ❖ **LO4** Know how to conduct substantive audit procedures for long-term debt.
- ❖ **LO5** Understand the types of stockholders' equity transactions.
- ❖ **LO6** Be familiar with assessing control risk for stockholders' equity.

- ❖ **LO7** Be familiar with key control activities for stockholders' equity.
- ❖ **LO8** Know the appropriate segregation of duties for stockholders' equity.
- ❖ **LO9** Know how to conduct substantive audit procedures for equity capital.
- ❖ **LO10** Know how to conduct substantive audit procedures for dividends.
- ❖ **LO11** Know how to conduct substantive audit procedures for retained earnings.
- ❖ **LO12** Know how to assess control risk and conduct substantive audit procedures for income statement accounts.

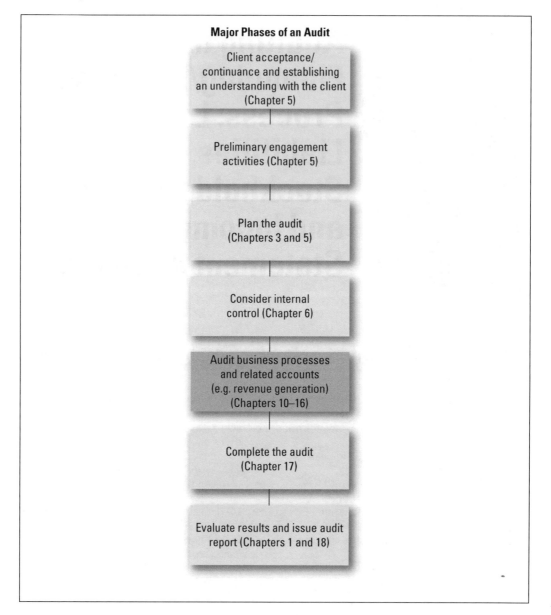

Major Phases of an Audit

Client acceptance/
continuance and establishing
an understanding with the client
(Chapter 5)

Preliminary engagement
activities (Chapter 5)

Plan the audit
(Chapters 3 and 5)

Consider internal
control (Chapter 6)

Audit business processes
and related accounts
(e.g. revenue generation)
(Chapters 10–16)

Complete the audit
(Chapter 17)

Evaluate results and issue audit
report (Chapters 1 and 18)

❖ *RELEVANT ACCOUNTING AND AUDITING PRONOUNCEMENTS*

IASB, IAS 1, Presentation of Financial Statements

IASB, IAS 32, Financial Instruments: Presentation

IASB, IAS 39, Financial Instruments: Recognition and Measurement

IASB, IFRS 7, Financial Instruments: Disclosures

ISA 230, Audit Documentation

ISA 240, The Auditor's Responsibilities Relating to Fraud in an Audit of Financial Statements

ISA 315, Identifying and Assessing the Risks of Material Misstatement through Understanding the Entity and Its Environment

ISA 320, Materiality in Planning and Performing an Audit

ISA 330, The Auditor's Responses to Assessed Risks

ISA 450, Evaluation of Misstatements Identified during the Audit

ISA 500, Audit Evidence

ISA 505, External Confirmations

ISA 520, Analytical Procedures

ISA 540, Auditing Accounting Estimates, Including Fair Value Accounting Estimates, and Related Disclosures

THIS CHAPTER PRESENTS the audit of the financial instruments long-term liabilities and stockholders' equity, as well as the audit of income statement accounts. Long-term debt and equity are the major sources of financing for most entities. A substantive audit strategy is normally followed when long-term liabilities and stockholders' equity accounts are audited, because although the number of transactions is small, each transaction is often highly material. Last, the audit of selected income statement accounts is presented. The discussion of auditing the income statement focuses on how the auditor's work on internal control and substantive analytical procedures provide evidence on income statement accounts and how most income statement accounts are audited when their related balance sheet accounts are audited.

AUDITING LONG-TERM DEBT

LO1

Common types of long-term debt financing include notes, bonds and mortgages. More sophisticated types of debt financing include collateralized mortgage obligations, repurchase and reverse repurchase agreements, interest-rate swaps, financial futures, derivatives (see Exhibit 15–1) and myriad other financial instruments. Accounting for and auditing such sophisticated debt instruments and certain financial instruments with characteristics of both debt and equity can be complex and is beyond the scope of this text. Capitalized lease obligations also represent a form of long-term debt. While the concepts relating to the audit of most types of debt are similar, to simplify our discussion we focus on notes and bonds, including the audit of interest payable and interest expense.

Long-term debt may have a number of features that can affect the audit procedures used. For example, debt may be convertible into stock (shares), or it may be combined with warrants, options or rights that can be exchanged for equity. Debt may be callable under certain conditions, or it may require the establishment of a sinking fund, which is a pool of money set aside for repaying the debt or to repurchase a portion of the existing bonds every year. The sinking fund may be held by a bond trustee to ensure that the funds are used only for bond retirement. Last, debt may be either unsecured or secured by assets of the entity.

The auditor's consideration of long-term debt, however, is no different from that of any other financial statement account. The auditor must be assured that the amounts shown on the balance sheet for the various types of long-term debt are not materially misstated. This assurance extends to the proper recognition of interest expense in the financial statements.

The approach to the audit of long-term debt varies depending on the frequency of the entity's financing activities. For entities that engage in frequent financing activities, the auditor may follow a reliance strategy under which internal control is formally evaluated and **tests of controls** are performed in order to set control risk. However, for the vast majority of entities, it is more efficient for the auditor to follow a substantive strategy and perform a detailed audit of long-term debt and the related interest accounts.

Exhibit 15–1   Derivatives Lead to Losses at AIG

Derivatives are contracts that are written between two parties. The value of a derivative contract to one of the parties and the cost or obligation to the other is derived from the value of an underlying asset, such as currencies, equities, commodities, mortgages, interest rates, or from stock market or other indicators. While derivatives can be used wisely by management to hedge risk, they can also be used to create leverage and thereby greatly increase risk.

AIG (American International Group, Inc.) identified a seemingly low-risk method of capitalizing on the housing boom in the mid-2000s. As the boom grew, fresh capital was needed to provide for the increased demand for home mortgages. A significant source of capital was obtained through the selling of pools of mortgages as bonds to investors (mortgages that are grouped and securitized are known as mortgage-backed securities or asset-backed securities). The mortgage holders selling the securitized bonds wanted a form of insurance that would cover their losses in case homeowners were to default on the underlying mortgages. This 'insurance' was provided in the form of credit-default swaps (CDSs), which is a derivative contract, consisting basically of a promise to pay the value of the mortgage to the holder of the CDS in case of mortgage default. Many banks and institutions sold and purchased CDSs to hedge their exposure to potential losses on their investments in mortgage-backed securities. However, AIG only sold CDSs, which generated significant fee revenue at seemingly little risk ... because everyone knows that housing prices always go up ... well, not quite always, as AIG found out.

AIG's CDS strategy initially paid off handsomely because mortgage defaults are uncommon when home prices are rapidly appreciating. The problem was that the rapid appreciation in home prices actually represented a speculative 'bubble.' When the housing bubble burst and the subprime mortgage market collapsed, homeowners began defaulting on their mortgages in large numbers, and the value of the mortgage-backed securities plummeted. As the value of the bonds dropped, CDS holders demanded that AIG pay up in accordance with the contract. Because AIG had entered the CDS market in such an aggressive manner, the company's exposure to CDS claims was huge. In 2007 and 2008, AIG recognized $11.47 and $28.6 billion, respectively, in charges related to its CDS portfolio, and has survived to the date of this writing only as a result of a massive government bailout.

Source: AIG 2008 Form 10-K.

INHERENT RISK ASSESSMENT: LONG-TERM DEBT

Inherent risk for notes and bonds would normally be assessed as low to moderate because the volume of transactions is low, the accounting is usually not complex, and the client often receives third-party statements or amortization scedules. However, the amounts involved are usually large, and, as noted in the introduction, the financial markets have developed very sophisticated instruments that can introduce an enormous amount of leverage, and that can have characteristics of both debt and equity. The inherent risk associated with these sophisticated instruments is normally high. In this chapter we focus on notes and bonds.

Practice Insight 15.1

It is important for auditors to consider possible off-balance-sheet financing. The determination of whether an entity should be consolidated with its parent company should be evaluated, and special attention should be given to these inherently complex classes of transactions.

Off-balance-sheet entities are often legitimate, however they are also sometimes used to commit fraud. With an off-balance-sheet entity, a parent company need only recognize net assets from the entity on its balance sheet. By doing so, the parent company avoids recording the debt of the entity on its balance sheet. Similarly, the parent records only net profit or losses from the company on its balance sheet, which keeps the expenses of the entity from being disclosed on the parent's income statement. A fraud occurs when a company does not follow financial reporting framework provisions for consolidation and purposefully excludes debt that should be reported in its financial statements.

The high-profile Enron fraud involved abuses of the rules for accounting for off-balance-sheet financing. Enron had off-balance-sheet financing through transactions with 'Special Purpose Entities' (SPEs). Enron did not consolidate these companies because the company claimed that the transactions with these SPEs were arm's length and complied with the accounting standards. This was, however, not the case for some of Enron's transactions involving SPEs because Enron was the underlying guarantor of the SPE debt. In effect, by not consolidating the SPEs, Enron failed to report hundreds of millions in debt.

 # CONTROL RISK ASSESSMENT: LONG-TERM DEBT

LO2

When a substantive strategy is followed, the auditor needs a sufficient understanding of the entity's internal control system over debt transactions to be able to anticipate the types of misstatements that may occur.

The following discussion of control risk assessment for long-term debt focuses on the general types of control activities that should be present to minimize the likelihood of material misstatement. The **assertions** that are of primary concern to the auditor are *occurrence, authorization, completeness, valuation* and *disclosure-classification.*

Assertions and Related Control Activities

LO3

Following are some of the more common controls that should be present for the important assertions for long-term debt.

Occurrence and Authorization

The entity should have controls to ensure that transactions involving long-term financing are properly initiated by authorized individuals. First, adequate documentation must be developed and kept to verify that a note or bond was properly authorized. The presence of adequate documentation, such as a properly signed lending agreement, allows the auditor to determine if the transaction was properly executed. Second, any significant debt commitments should be approved by the board of directors or by executives who have been delegated this authority. Entities that engage in recurring borrowing activities should have both general and specific controls. The board of directors should establish general controls to guide the entity's financing activities. The specific controls for borrowing and repayment may be delegated to an executive, such as the chief financial officer. When the chief financial officer or similar executive is responsible for both executing and accounting for long-term debt transactions, another executive body, such as the finance committee of the board of directors, should provide overall review and approval in the minutes. If the client has proper controls and documentation for debt transactions, it is generally easy for the auditor to obtain evidence on occurrence and authorization at the end of the period.

Completeness

The client should maintain detailed records of long-term debt transactions to ensure that all borrowings and repayments of principal and interest are recorded. One approach to handling detailed debt transactions is to maintain a subsidiary ledger that contains information about all the long-term debt owed by the client. The debt amount recorded in the subsidiary ledger should be reconciled to the general ledger control account regularly.

Valuation

Note and bond transactions are recorded in the accounting records at their face value plus or minus any premium or discount. Premiums or discounts should be amortized using the effective interest method to calculate interest expense. Sometimes an entity incurs 'issuing costs' such as underwriter's fees, legal fees and accounting fees. Such costs should be an integral part of the amortization using the effective interest method. Valuation issues for sophisticated financial instruments are far more complex (see IAS 39 *Financial Instruments: Recognition and Measurement*), especially when fair value measurements are involved. Although the client should have control activities to ensure that long-term debt is properly valued, the client may ask the auditor to assist with recording the debt properly.

Disclosure-Classification

Controls should ensure that the proper disclosures are provided for long-term debt. Common disclosures include: related party transactions, restrictive debt covenants and revolving lines of credit. Controls should also ensure that notes and bonds are properly classified in the financial statements. A major issue is to properly classify as a short-term debt the portion of long-term debt that is due within the next year.

One final issue related to control risk for long-term debt is that the client should have adequate custodial procedures for any unissued notes or bonds to safeguard against loss from theft. Procedures should provide for periodic inspections by an individual who is independent of both the custodial and accounting responsibilities for long-term debt.

Practice Insight 15.2

Because the completeness assertion is more difficult to test, it is particularly important that the auditor use a top-down approach when obtaining evidence on the completeness assertion for liabilities. The auditor must evaluate the incentives, pressures and tone at the top to assess the potential threat for omitted liabilities. Too much focus on transaction-level control activities, to the exclusion of assessing the bigger picture, increases the risk that the auditor will get an inflated sense of comfort and assurance regarding the completeness of the reported liabilities.

❖ SUBSTANTIVE PROCEDURES: LONG-TERM DEBT

LO4

A substantive strategy for auditing long-term debt involves examining any new debt agreements (debt agreements for bonds are called bond or trust indentures), determining the status of prior debt agreements, and confirming balances and other relevant information with outside parties.

Substantive **analytical procedures** are useful in auditing interest expense because of the direct relationship between long-term debt and interest expense. For example, the auditor could estimate interest expense by multiplying the 12 monthly balances for long-term debt by the average monthly interest rate. The reasonableness of interest expense could then be assessed by comparing this estimate to the interest expense amount recorded in the general ledger. If the two amounts are not materially different, the auditor can conclude that interest expense is fairly stated. If the estimated amount of interest expense is materially higher than the recorded amount, the auditor might conclude that the client has failed to record a portion of interest expense. On the other hand, if the recorded amount of interest expense is materially higher than the estimated amount, the client may have failed to record debt. Refer to Chapter 5 for an example of the use of a substantive analytical procedure to test the relationship between EarthWear's short-term line of credit and related interest expense.

Table 15–1 provides examples of tests of transactions and account balances for the key assertions of long-term debt. The following discussion will help you understand the general approach to auditing long-term debt accounts.

Table 15–1 Examples of Tests of Transactions and Account Balances for Long-Term Debt	
Assertions about Classes of Transactions	*Example Substantive Tests of Transactions*˙
Occurrence	Examine copies of new note or bond agreements.
	Examine board of directors' minutes for approval of new lending agreements.
Completeness	Trace large cash receipts and payments to source documents and general ledger (see Chapters 11 and 16).
	Review interest expense for payments to debt holders not listed on the debt analysis schedule.
	Review notes paid or renewed after the balance sheet date to determine if there are unrecorded liabilities at year end.
	Evaluate lease contracts to determine if leases are properly accounted for as an operating or capital lease (i.e. if a lease should be a capital lease, it would likely require recognition of long-term debt).
Authorization	Examine board minutes for evidence of proper authorization of notes or bonds.
Accuracy	Test a sample of receipts and payments.
Cut-off	Review debt activity for a few days before and after year end to determine if the transactions are included in the proper period.
Classification	Examine the due dates on notes or bonds for proper classification between current and long-term debt.
Assertions about Account Balances at Period End	*Example Tests of Details of Account Balances*
Existence	Confirm notes or bonds directly with creditors (in many instances, creditors are banks, insurance companies, or trustees representing the creditors).
Rights and obligations	Examine copies of note and bond agreements.

Completeness	Obtain an analysis of notes payable, bonds payable, and accrued interest payable; foot schedule and agree totals to the general ledger.
	Obtain a bank confirmation that requests specific information on notes from banks (see Chapter 16 for further discussion of bank confirmations).
	Confirm notes or bonds with creditors.
	Inquire of management regarding the existence of off-balance-sheet activities.
	Review board meeting minutes for debt-related activity.
Valuation and allocation	Examine new debt agreements (e.g. bond indentures) to ensure that they were recorded at the proper value.
	Confirm the outstanding balance for notes or bonds and the last date on which interest has been paid.
	Recompute accrued interest payable.
	Verify computation of the amortization of premium or discount.

* These tests of details of transactions are commonly conducted as dual-purpose tests (i.e. in conjunction with tests of controls).

The auditor generally begins the audit of long-term debt by obtaining an analysis schedule for notes payable, bonds payable and accrued interest payable. Exhibit 15–2 presents an example of such a schedule. Because EarthWear does not have long-term debt, the example in Exhibit 15–2 is based on Calabro Wireless Services. If there are numerous transactions during the year, this schedule may include only the debt outstanding at the end of the period. Note that this schedule includes a considerable amount of information on each debt transaction, including the payee, date due, interest rate, original amount, collateral, and paid and accrued interest.

Exhibit 15–2 Analysis Schedule for Auditing Long-Term Debt and Accrued Interest Payable

P10
DLJ
1/2/10

CALABRO WIRELESS SERVICES
Schedule of Long-Term Debt and Accrued Interest Payable
31/12/09

Payee	Due Date	Face Amount	Security	Long-Term Debt				Accrued Interest Payable			
				Beginning Balance	Additions	Payments	Ending Balance	Beginning Balance	Expenses	Paid	Ending Balance
First Bank – Line of credit	1/11/12	€7,000,000	All assets**C**	€200,000	€900,000	€300,000γ	€800,000	€1,875	€22,000λ	€22,815	€1,560
8.75% lease obligation United Insurance Co.	15/12/11	€2,000,000	Communications equipment**C**	238,637		48,230γ	190,407	5,470	17,541λ	18,461	4,550
7% bonds payable – All European Insurance	30/6/14	€10,000,000	Land and buildings**C**	3,100,000		200,000γ	2,900,000	36,850	224,602λ	219,820	41,632
Total				€3,538,637	€900,000	€548,230	€3,890,407**L**	€44,195	€264,643**L**	€261,096	€47,742**L**
				F	**F**	**F**	**F**	**F**	**F**	**F**	**F**

Less current portion of long term debt   424,061✔

€3,466,346

L = Agreed to general ledger.
γ = Traced payments to cash disbursements journal.
λ = Recomputed interest expense.
C = Agreed all information to confirmation.
F = Footed.
✔ = Tested amount of current portion of long-term debt.

Exhibit 15–2 also indicates the audit procedures performed on the details of the debt schedule. Take a break from reading for a moment and look at the tick mark descriptions in Exhibit 15–2; see if you can identify the assertion each procedure is addressing. Evidence is gathered for the most important assertions as follows. Each debt instrument is confirmed with the debt holders and includes a request to verify the amount owed and the last date on which interest has been paid.[i] **Confirmation** of the debt and accrued interest provides evidence on the existence, completeness and valuation assertions. If the client's debt is guaranteed by another party, a confirmation should be sent to the guarantor to confirm the guarantee.

The auditor also examines the due dates for the debt to ensure proper classification between current and long-term liabilities. Last, the auditor examines the debt agreements for any restrictive covenants that require disclosure in the notes. Examples of such covenants include restrictions on the payment of dividends or the issuance of additional debt or equity, and the maintenance of certain financial ratios. Exhibit 15–3 is an example of the disclosure of restrictive covenants.

Exhibit 15–3   Sample Disclosure of Restrictive Loan Covenants

The 7 per cent bond agreement contains provisions (1) limiting funded debt, security interests and other indebtedness; (2) requiring the maintenance of defined working capital and tangible net worth; and (3) imposing restrictions on the payment of cash dividends. The company was in compliance with, or received a waiver regarding, each of the agreements during the year ended 2009. Under the terms of these agreements, €825,000 of retained earnings was available for payment of cash dividends at 31 December 2009.

AUDITING STOCKHOLDERS' EQUITY

LO5

For most entities, stockholders' equity includes common stock, preferred stock, paid-in capital and retained earnings. In recent years, numerous financial instruments have been developed that contain both debt and equity characteristics, and affect the audit of stockholders' equity. A host of stock option and compensation plans also impact the audit of stockholders' equity. A discussion of these complex equity instruments and stock option plans, referred to as share-based payment plans in the international accounting standards, is beyond the scope of this text.

Following are the three major types of transactions that occur in stockholders' equity:

1   *Issuance of stock.* This includes transactions such as sale of stock for cash; the exchange of stock for assets, services, or convertible debt; and issuance of stock for stock splits.
2   *Repurchase of stock.* This includes the re-acquisition of stock (referred to as *treasury stock*) and the retirement of stock.
3   *Payment of dividends.* This includes the payment of cash dividends or issuance of stock dividends.

CONTROL RISK ASSESSMENT: STOCKHOLDERS' EQUITY

LO6

A substantive strategy is most often used to audit stockholders' equity because the number of transactions is usually small. Although control risk can then be set at the maximum, the auditor must still understand the types of controls that are in place to prevent the misstatement of equity transactions.

Large entities, such as listed companies, may use an independent outside agent such as a *registrar*, *transfer agent* and *dividend-disbursing agent* to process and record equity transactions. The registrar is responsible for ensuring that all stock issued complies with the corporate charter and for maintaining the control totals for total shares outstanding. The transfer agent is responsible for preparing stock certificates and maintaining adequate stockholders' records. The dividend-disbursing agent transfers dividend to the stockholders of record. When an entity uses an independent registrar, transfer agent, and dividend-disbursing agent, the auditor may be able to obtain sufficient evidence by confirming the relevant information with those parties.

If an entity uses its own employees to perform the stock transfer and dividend disbursement functions, the auditor needs to perform more detailed testing of the stock-related records and transactions that occurred during the period. Next we will discuss the assertions, control activities and segregation of duties that are relevant when client personnel transfer stock and disburse dividends.

Assertions and Related Control Activities

LO7

Following are the major evidence gathering procedures and assertions for stockholders' equity:

● Verify that stock and dividend transactions comply with the corporate charter (occurrence).

- Verify that all stock and dividend transactions have been properly posted and summarized in the accounting records (accuracy).
- Verify that stock and dividend transactions have been properly approved (authorization).
- Verify that stock and dividend transactions have been properly valued (valuation).

Occurrence

One of the entity's officers, such as the corporate secretary or legal counsel, should ensure that every stock or dividend transaction complies with the corporate charter or any regulatory requirement that affects the entity. This individual should also maintain the stockholders' ledger, which contains the name of each stockholder and the number of shares held by that shareholder.

Accuracy

The control activities for this assertion include reconciliation of the stockholders' records with the number of shares outstanding and reconciliation of dividends paid with the total shares outstanding on the dividend record date.

Authorization

For most entities, the board of directors or stockholders approve stock and dividend transactions. The authorization is normally documented in the minutes of the board of directors' meetings. The auditor can examine the board of directors' minutes for proper authorization.

Valuation

Stock issuances, stock repurchases and dividends should be recorded by the treasurer's department at an amount in accordance with the applicable financial reporting framework. The auditor can recompute the recording of the stock and dividend transactions.

Segregation of Duties

LO8

If the entity has enough personnel, the following segregation of duties should be maintained:

- The individuals responsible for issuing, transferring and cancelling stock certificates should not have any accounting responsibilities.
- The individual responsible for maintaining the detailed stockholders' records should be independent of the maintenance of the general ledger control accounts.
- The individual responsible for maintaining the detailed stockholders' records should not also process cash receipts or disbursements.
- Appropriate segregation of duties should be established among payment and recording of dividend payments.

Pause for a moment and consider what types of problems could occur if there were inadequate segregation of duties in each of the listed areas.

AUDITING EQUITY CAPITAL ACCOUNTS

LO9

The equity capital (capital stock) accounts include common stock, preferred stock and paid-in capital. When auditing the equity capital accounts, including any statement of changes in equity (see IAS 1 *Presentation of Financial Statements*), the auditor is normally concerned with the occurrence, completeness, valuation and completeness of disclosures assertions. The auditor begins the audit of equity capital by obtaining a schedule of all activity in the accounts for the current period. The beginning balance is agreed to the prior year's working papers, and the ending balance is agreed to the general ledger. The majority of the auditor's work then focuses on the current period activity in each account.

Occurrence and Completeness

All valid equity capital transactions must be approved by the board of directors. Therefore, the auditor can obtain assurance on the occurrence of equity capital transactions by tracing the transactions recorded in the current year to the board of directors' minutes. When an outside agent is used by the entity to maintain the stock register and/or a stock certificate book, the auditor confirms the total number of shares outstanding at the end of the period. If the amount of shares listed as outstanding on the confirmation reconciles to the general ledger equity capital accounts, the auditor has evidence that the total number of shares outstanding at the end of the year is correct.

If the entity does not use outside agents, it will maintain a stock register and/or a stock certificate book. The auditor may perform the following procedures:

● Trace the transfers of shares between stockholders to the stock register and/or stock certificate book (accuracy and completeness).
● Foot the shares outstanding in the stock register and/or stock certificate book and agree them to total shares outstanding in the general ledger equity capital accounts (completeness).
● Examine any cancelled stock certificates (occurrence).
● Account for and inspect any unissued stock certificates in the stock certificate book (completeness).

Valuation

When equity capital is issued for cash, the assessment of proper valuation is straightforward. The par, or stated, value for the shares issued is assigned to the respective equity capital account, while the difference between the price and par, or stated, value is allocated to paid-in capital. The auditor can recompute the values assigned to each transaction. The proceeds from the sale of stock are normally traced to the cash receipts records.

The valuation issue is more complex when equity capital is issued in exchange for assets or services, for a merger or acquisition, for convertible securities, or for a stock dividend (see IAS 39). For example, the auditor should evaluate whether any fair value measurements are in accordance with the applicable financial reporting framework (ISA 540).

Completeness of Disclosures

A number of important disclosures are necessary for stockholders' equity. IFRS 7 *Financial Instruments: Disclosure* prescribes the disclosure requirements in the international accounting standards. Table 15–2 contains examples of stockholders' equity disclosures. The normal sources of this information include the corporate charter, minutes of the board of directors' meetings, and contractual agreements.

Table 15–2   Examples of Disclosure Items for Stockholders' Equity
Number of shares authorized, issued and outstanding for each class of stock.
Call privileges, prices and dates for preferred stock.
Stock option or purchase plans.
Restrictions on retained earnings and dividends.
Any completed or pending transactions (such as stock dividends or splits) that may affect stockholders' equity.

AUDITING DIVIDENDS

LO10

Generally, all dividends that are declared and paid will be audited because of concerns with violations of corporate bylaws or debt covenants. When the entity uses an outside agent for dividend-disbursing, the auditor can confirm the amount disbursed to the agent by the entity. This amount is agreed with the amount authorized by the board of directors. The auditor can recompute the dividend amount by multiplying the number of shares outstanding on the record date by the amount of the per share dividend approved by the board of directors. This amount should agree to the amount disbursed to shareholders and accrued at year end. If the auditor is concerned about the client's controls over dividend disbursements, he or she may compare the payee names and amounts paid with the stock register or stock certificate book. The auditor also reviews the entity's compliance with any agreements that restrict the payments of dividends.

AUDITING RETAINED EARNINGS

LO11

Under normal circumstances, retained earnings are affected by the current year's income or loss, as well as cash or stock dividends paid. However, certain accounting standards require that some transactions be made directly to retained earnings. Thus, additional audit procedures are sometimes required. Prior period adjustments, correction of errors, fair value adjustments of certain financial instruments and foreign currency translation are examples of such transactions.

The auditor begins the audit of retained earnings by obtaining a schedule of the account activity for the period. The beginning balance is agreed to the prior year's working papers and financial statements. Net income or loss can be traced to the income statement. The amounts for any cash or stock dividends can be verified as described earlier. If there are any prior-period adjustments, the auditor must be certain that the transactions satisfy the requirements of the relevant accounting standards. Any new appropriations or changes in existing appropriations should be traced to the relevant contractual agreements. Last, the auditor must make sure that all necessary disclosures related to retained earnings are made in the notes. For example, many debt agreements restrict the amount of retained earnings that is available for payment as dividends (see Exhibit 15–3).

AUDITING INCOME STATEMENT ACCOUNTS

LO12

In auditing income statement accounts, the auditor must be satisfied that the revenue and expense accounts are not materially misstated and that they are accounted for in accordance with the applicable financial reporting framework. The income statement is viewed as an important source of information by various users of the financial statements. For example, creditors or potential creditors look to an entity's profitability as one indicator of the entity's ability to repay debt. Potential investors look to the income statement when deciding whether to purchase the entity's stock. Finally, vendors may examine the entity's earnings potential in order to assess whether the entity will be able to pay for goods or services purchased on credit.

The audit of the revenue and expense accounts depends on the extent of work conducted by the auditor on the entity's control system and on the client's balance sheet accounts. For example, the likelihood of material misstatement in the various revenue and expense accounts is a function of the entity's controls. The level of control risk established for the different business processes directly affects the extent of testing that the auditor requires to audit the income statement accounts.

Auditing the income statement includes consideration of the results of audit work conducted in other parts of the audit and completion of additional substantive procedures on selected income statement accounts, including the following:

- The results of testing controls for the various business processes.
- The results of the detailed tests of balance sheet accounts and the related income statement accounts.
- Performance of substantive analytical procedures on income statement accounts.
- Detailed tests of selected income statement accounts.

ASSESSING CONTROL RISK FOR BUSINESS PROCESSES: INCOME STATEMENT ACCOUNTS

In previous chapters, the auditor's approach to setting the control risk for various business processes was discussed. If the control risk is set at the maximum, the auditor does not rely on controls but conducts extensive substantive procedures. When a **reliance strategy** is followed, the auditor conducts tests of controls and **substantive tests of transactions** to determine if the client's controls are operating effectively. If the controls operate effectively, the auditor may reduce the control risk below the maximum.

To better understand the effect of a reduced control risk assessment on the audit of the revenue and expense accounts, consider the income statement accounts affected by the revenue and purchasing business processes. For example, justifiably reduced control risk assessment for the revenue process provides evidence that the sales, accounts receivable, allowance for uncollectible accounts, and sales returns and allowances accounts are not materially misstated. Similarly, a reduced control risk assessment for the purchasing process provides evidence that financial statement accounts such as inventory, property, plant and equipment, accounts payable, and most expense accounts are not materially misstated. The important point here is that the auditor already has reliable evidence on the accounts included in the income statement. The findings for the purchasing process are particularly relevant, since proper controls provide evidence on most of the expense accounts. This allows the auditor to do considerably fewer substantive procedures for these income statement accounts.

SUBSTANTIVE TEST: INCOME STATEMENT ACCOUNTS

Direct Tests of Balance Sheet Accounts

Income statement accounts are normally audited in the course of auditing the related balance sheet accounts. Table 15–3 lists balance sheet accounts and the related income statement accounts that are verified in this manner. For example, when the allowance for uncollectible accounts is audited, bad-debt expense is also tested. Similarly, when auditing notes receivable, the auditor can test interest income.

Table 15–3 Examples of Income Statement Accounts Audited in Conjunction with the Balance Sheet Account	
Balance Sheet Account Audited	*Related Income Statement Account Audited*
Accounts receivable/allowance for uncollectible accounts.	Bad-debt expense.
Notes receivable/investments/accrued interest receivable.	Interest income.
Property, plant and equipment/accumulated depreciation.	Depreciation expense, gain/losses on sales or retirements of assets.
Prepaid insurance.	Insurance expense.
Long-term debt/accrued interest payable.	Interest expense.

Substantive Analytical Procedures for Income Statement Accounts

Substantive analytical procedures can be used extensively to provide assurance on the revenue and expense accounts. The auditing standard on the consideration of fraud risk (ISA 240) indicates that the auditor should ordinarily presume that there is a risk of material misstatement due to fraud relating to revenue recognition. Disaggregated analytical procedures are typically conducted on the revenue account to identify unusual or unexpected relationships that may be indicative of fraud.

One type of substantive analytical procedure involves comparing the current year's euro (or other currency) amount for each revenue and expense account (e.g. by product, business segment or geographic region) with the prior years' balances. Any account that deviates from the prior years' trend by more than a predetermined amount should be investigated. An alternative to this type of substantive analytical procedure involves calculating the ratio of individual expense accounts to net sales and comparing these percentages across years. The auditor can also compare these percentages to industry averages. Individual expense accounts that are judged by the auditor to be out of line are investigated further. While these types of substantive analytical procedures are common, it is important that substantive analytical procedures designed to provide evidence regarding the fairness of revenue or other income statement accounts be conducted at a sufficiently disaggregated (i.e. monthly or weekly data versus annual data, by business segment or product) level to detect potential misstatements. As noted in Chapter 5, even relatively small percentage misstatements in large income statement accounts are often material, thus the need for precise substantive analytical procedures.

Substantive analytical procedures can also be used to provide evidence of *specific* revenue or expense accounts. For example, the auditor can evaluate the reasonableness of sales commissions by using the client's commission schedule and multiplying commission rates by eligible sales. This estimate can be compared to the recorded commission expense. Other examples might include overall reasonableness tests for interest and depreciation expense.

Tests of Selected Account Balances

Even though the auditor has gathered considerable evidence about revenue and expense accounts based on the audit procedures just discussed, the auditor may want to examine some accounts further. For these accounts, the auditor typically analyses in detail the transactions included in each account. The auditor verifies the transactions by examining (vouching) the supporting documentation. Accounts examined in this manner are generally accounts that are not directly affected by a business process, accounts that may contain sensitive information or unusual transactions, or accounts for which detailed information is needed for the tax return or other schedules included with the financial statements. Some examples of such accounts include legal and audit expense, travel and entertainment, charity expense, other income and expenses, and any account containing related-party transactions. Exhibit 15–4 presents an account analysis for EarthWear's legal and audit expense. In auditing this account, the auditor vouches the transactions to the attorneys' invoices. The auditor should examine the invoice not only for the amount but also for information on potential uncertainties, such as lawsuits against the client.

Exhibit 15–4	Example of an Account Analysis Working Paper			

T20
SAA
4/2/10

EARTHWEAR CLOTHIERS
Analysis of Legal and Audit Expense
31/12/09

Date	Payee	Amount	Explanation
2 Feb.	Katz & Fritz	€ 28,500.00V	For services related to a patent infringement suit by Gough Mfg. Co. Lawsuit was dismissed.
10 April	Willis & Adams International	950,000.00V	Annual audit fee.
1 Oct.	Katz & Fritz	26,200.00V	Legal fee for patent infringement suit against Weshant.
20 Oct.	Smoothe, Sylk, Fiels, Goode & Associates	2,100.00V	Legal services for a purchase contract with McDonald Merchandise.
Total		€1,006,800.00	
		F T/B	

Tick Mark Legend
V = Examined payees' bills for amount and description.
F = Footed.
T/B = Agreed to trial balance.
Conclusion: Based on the audit work performed, EarthWear's legal and audit expense account is not materially misstated.

🔐 Key Terms

Analytical procedures. Evaluations of financial information through analysis of plausible relationships among both financial and non-financial data.

Assertions. Representations by management, explicit or otherwise, that are embodied in the financial statements, as used by the auditor to consider the different types of potential misstatements that may occur.

Confirmation. The process of obtaining and evaluating direct communication from a third party in response to a request for information about a particular item affecting financial statement assertions.

Reliance strategy. The auditor's decision to rely on the entity's controls, test those controls, and reduce the substantive tests of the financial statement accounts.

Substantive tests of transactions (tests of details of transactions). Tests to detect errors or fraud in individual transactions.

Tests of controls. Audit procedures performed to test the operating effectiveness of controls in preventing, or detecting and correcting, material misstatements at the assertion level.

Tests of details of account balances and disclosures. Substantive tests that concentrate on the details of items contained in the account balance and disclosure.

❓ Review Questions

LO1,4,5,9 15–1 Why does the auditor generally follow a substantive strategy when auditing long-term debt and capital accounts? Under what conditions might the auditor follow a reliance strategy?

LO2,3 15–2 What are the most important assertions for long-term debt? What documents would normally contain the authorization to issue long-term debt?

LO4	**15–3**	Describe how substantive analytical procedures may be used to provide evidence on the reasonableness of interest expense.
LO4	**15–4**	Confirmations of long-term debt provide evidence about which assertions?
LO8	**15–5**	What is the major segregation of duties that should be maintained when the client does not use an outside agent (for example a registrar or transfer agent) to perform the stock transactions and sufficient personnel are available to perform the stock transactions?
LO9	**15–6**	List two common disclosures for stockholders' equity and why such disclosures are necessary.
LO10,11	**15–7**	Describe common audit procedures used to audit dividends and retained earnings.
LO12	**15–8**	List three substantive analytical procedures that the auditor might use in auditing the income statement.
LO12	**15–9**	Why might the auditor do an account analysis and vouch selected transactions in income statement accounts such as legal expense, travel and entertainment, and other income/expenses?

Problems

LO4   **15–10**   Maslovskaya, independent auditor, has been engaged to examine the financial statements of Broadwall Corporation for the year ended 31 December, 2009. During the year, Broadwall obtained a long-term loan from a local bank pursuant to a financing agreement that provided that:

1   The loan was to be secured by the company's inventory and accounts receivable.

2   The company was not to pay dividends without permission from the bank.

3   Monthly instalment payments were to commence 1 July 2009. In addition, during the year the company borrowed various short-term amounts from the president of the company, including substantial amounts just prior to year end.

Required:

a   *For purposes of the audit of the financial statements of Broadwall Corporation, what procedures should Maslovskaya employ in examining the described loans?*

b   *The loans from the president represent a related-party transaction. What financial statement disclosures do you believe would be appropriate for the loans from the president?*

(AICPA, adapted)

LO4   **15–11**   Your audit client, the Brant Group, reported total interest expense for the year of €2,000. The table below provides the monthly balance of its long-term debt. Interest is paid monthly on the average daily balance during the month. The annual interest rate for the debt is 6%.

Balance of long-term debt	31 Jan	€100,000
Balance of long-term debt	28 Feb	90,000
Balance of long-term debt	31 Mar	80,000
Balance of long-term debt	30 Apr	70,000
Balance of long-term debt	31 May	90,000
Balance of long-term debt	30 June	85,000
Balance of long-term debt	31 July	80,000
Balance of long-term debt	31 Aug	70,000
Balance of long-term debt	30 Sept	60,000
Balance of long-term debt	31 Oct	65,000
Balance of long-term debt	30 Nov	75,000
Balance of long-term debt	31 Dec	50,000

Required:

Based on the data provided, do you consider the reported interest expense fairly stated? Why, or why not?

LO4   **15–12**   The long-term debt working paper below was prepared by client personnel and audited by Andy Fogelman, an audit assistant, during the calendar year 2009 audit of Central Widgets, a continuing audit client. The engagement supervisor is reviewing the working paper thoroughly.

								Initials		Date
				CENTRAL WIDGETS			Prepared By	AF		22/1/10
				Working paper			Approved By			
				21 December 2009						
Lender	Interest Rate	Payment Terms	Collateral	Balance 31/12/08	2009 Borrowings	2009 Reductions	Balance 31/12/09	Interest	Accrued Interest Payable 31/12/09	Comments
First Commercial Bank Φ	12%	Interest only on 25th of month, principal due in full 1/1/13; no prepayment penalty	Inventories	€50,000✔	€300,000**A** 31/1/09	€100,000* 30/6/09	€250,000**CX**	25/12/09	€2,500**NR**	Dividend of €80,000 paid 2/9/09 (W/P N-3) violates a provision of the debt agreement, which thereby permits lender to demand immediate payment; lender has refused to waive this violation.
Lender's Capital Corporation Φ	Prime plus 1%	Interest only on last day of month, principal due in full 5/3/11	2nd mortgage on Park Street Building	100,000✔	50,000**A** 29/2/09	—	200,000**C**	31/12/09	—	Prime rate was 8% to 9% during the year.
Gigantic Building & Loan Association Φ	12%	€5,000 principal plus Interest due on 5th of month, due in full 31/12/18	1st mortgage on Park Street Building	720,000✔	—	60,000	660,000**C**	5/12/09	5,642**R**	Reclassification entry for current portion proposed (see RJE-3).
J. Lott, majority stockholder Φ	0%	Due in full 31/12/12	Unsecured	300,000✔	—	100,000**N** 31/12/09	200,000**C**	—	—	Borrowed additional €100,000 from J. Lott on 7/1/10.
				€1,170,000	€350,000	€260,000	€1,310,000**T/B**		€8,142**T/B**	
				F	**F**	**F**	**F**		**F**	

Tick Mark Legend

C = Confirmed without exception, W/P K-2.
F = Readded, foots correctly.
CX = Confirmed with exception, W/P K-3.
NR = Does not recompute correctly.
A = Agreed to loan agreement, validated bank deposit ticket and board of directors' authorization, W/P W-7.
Φ = Agreed to lender's statements.
N = Agreed to cash disbursements journal
T/B = Traced to working trial balance.
✔ = Agreed to 31/12/08 working papers.
Φ = Agreed interest rate, term, and collateral to copy of note and loan agreement
Φ = Agreed to cancelled check and board of directors' authorization, W/P W-7

Interest costs from long-term debt

Interest expense for year	€281,333**T/B**
Average loan balance outstanding	€1,406,667**R**

Five-year maturities (for disclosure purposes)

Year end	31/12/10	€60,000
	31/12/11	260,000
	31/12/12	260,000
	31/12/13	310,000
	31/12/14	60,000
	Thereafter	360,000
		€1,310,000
		F

Conclusions: Long-term debt, accrued interest payable, and interest expense are correct and complete at 21/12/09.

Required:

There are a number of deficiencies in the working paper. For example, the subject of the working paper is not properly indicated in the title and there is also no indication that the unusually high average interest rate (20% = €281,333/€1,406,667) was noted or investigated. Identify at least five additional deficiencies that the engagement supervisor should discover.

(AICPA, adapted)

LO8,9   **15–13**   Lee, the continuing auditor of Wu, is beginning to audit the common stock and treasury stock accounts. Lee has decided to design substantive procedures without relying on the company's internal control system.

Wu has no par and no stated-value common stock, and it acts as its own registrar and transfer agent. During the past year Wu both issued and reacquired shares of its own common stock, some of which the company still owned at year end. Additional common stock transactions occurred among the shareholders during the year.

Common stock transactions can be traced to individual shareholders' accounts in a subsidiary ledger and to a stock certificate book. The company has not paid any cash or stock dividends. There are no other classes of stock, stock rights, warrants or option plans.

Required:

What substantive audit procedures should Lee apply in examining the common stock and treasury stock accounts?

(AICPA, adapted)

Discussion Case

LO4   **15–14**   On 10 September, Melinda Johnson was auditing the financial statements of a new audit client, Mother Earth Foods, a health-food chain that has a 30 June year end. The company is privately held and has just gone through a leveraged buyout with long-term financing that includes various restrictive covenants.

In order to obtain debt financing, companies often have to agree to certain conditions, some of which may restrict the way in which they conduct their business. If the borrower fails to comply with the stated conditions, it may be considered in default, which would give the lender the right to accelerate the due date of the debt, add other restrictions, waive the default for a stated period, or revise the covenants. Usually there is a grace period during which the borrower can cure the default.

Johnson believes that it is possible that at 31 August Mother Earth was in violation of the debt covenant restrictions, which became effective on that date. The debt covenants require the company to maintain a certain receivable turnover rate. Johnson is not certain, however, because the accounting records, including period-end cut-offs for sales and purchases, have not been well maintained. Nevertheless, Mother Earth's executives assure Johnson that if they were in violation, the company will be able to obtain a waiver or modification of the covenant.

Required:

a   Discuss the audit procedures that Johnson would conduct to determine if Mother Earth violated the debt covenants. How would Johnson determine whether Mother Earth would be able to obtain a waiver, assuming that the company was in violation of the debt covenants?

b   Based on the case scenario and financial accounting pronouncements about the classification of obligations that are callable by the creditor, should Mother Earth continue to classify this debt as non-current? Justify your answer.

Internet Assignment

LO6,7,8,11   15–15   Earlier in this chapter we referred to Enron's accounting for 'Special Purpose Entities' (SPE). In October 2001, Enron reduced shareholders' equity by $1.2 billion because it decided to 'unwind some transactions with limited partnerships with which it had done business'. Questions have been raised about Enron's accounting for these transactions.

Required:

Use the Internet to obtain information about Enron's earnings restatement. Sources of information on this issue can be found at websites for Enron, the SEC (www.sec.gov/), and various news providers (Wall Street Journal). Prepare a memo summarizing the issues related to Enron's accounting. You may relate the discussion to the accounting pronouncements for SPE of the financial reporting framework that is relevant for you.

ISA 240 The Auditor's Responsibilities Relating to Fraud in an Audit of Financial Statements, ISA 315 Identifying and Assessing the Risks of Material Misstatement through Understanding the Entity and Its Environment, ISA 550 Related Parties and ISA 600 Special Considerations-Audits of Group Financial Statements (Including the Work of Component Auditors) refer to transactions with SPE. Prepare a memo summarizing the content of these auditing standards relevant for auditing of transactions with SPE.

Note

[i]   The debt instrument can also be confirmed with the bond trustee, which is a financial institution given fiduciary powers by the debt holder to enforce the terms of the debt instrument. The trustee ensures that interest payments are made on time.

CHAPTER 16

Auditing the Financing/ Investing Process: Cash and Investments

❖ LEARNING OBJECTIVES

Upon completion of this chapter you will

- ❖ **LO1** Understand the relationship of the various business processes to cash.
- ❖ **LO2** Know the different types of bank accounts.
- ❖ **LO3** Know tests of details of transactions used to audit cash.
- ❖ **LO4** Be able to explain tests of details of account balances used to audit cash.
- ❖ **LO5** Know how to audit a bank reconciliation.

- ❖ **LO6** Understand fraud-related audit procedures for cash.
- ❖ **LO7** Understand why clients invest in securities of other entities.
- ❖ **LO8** Be able to explain key controls for investments.
- ❖ **LO9** Know the appropriate segregation of duties for investments.
- ❖ **LO10** Know tests of details of account balances used to audit investments.

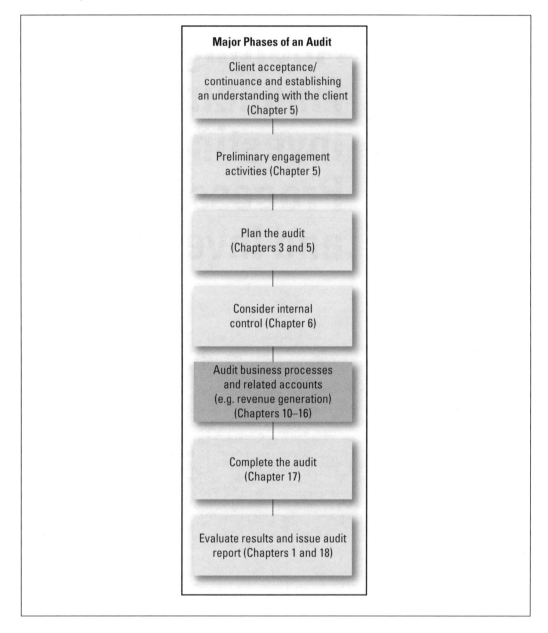

❖ RELEVANT ACCOUNTING AND AUDITING PRONOUNCEMENTS

IASB, IAS 1, Presentation of Financial Statements

IASB, IAS 7, Cash Flow Statements

IASB, IAS 32, Financial Instruments: Presentation

IASB, IAS 39, Financial Instruments: Recognition and Measurement

IASB, IFRS 7, Financial Instruments: Disclosures

ISA 230, Audit Documentation

ISA 240, The Auditor's Responsibilities Relating to Fraud in an Audit of Financial Statements

ISA 315, Identifying and Assessing the Risks of Material Misstatement through Understanding the Entity and Its Environment

ISA 320, Materiality in Planning and Performing an Audit

ISA 330, The Auditor's Responses to Assessed Risks

ISA 450, Evaluation of Misstatements Identified during the Audit

ISA 500, Audit Evidence

ISA 501, Audit Evidence – Specific Considerations for Selected Items

ISA 505, External Confirmations

ISA 520, Analytical Procedures

ISA 540, Auditing Accounting Estimates, Including Fair Value Accounting Estimates, and Related Disclosures

THIS CHAPTER COVERS the audit of cash and investments. These are the last accounts studied in this text because each of the other business processes interacts with cash. Thus, the evidence gathered during the audit of other business processes affects the type and amount of evidence required to audit cash.

Proper management of cash and investments is essential to every entity. The principal goal of cash management is to ensure that sufficient cash is available to meet the entity's needs. Achieving this goal requires good forecasting of cash receipts and disbursements. By using sound cash-forecasting techniques, management can plan to: (1) invest excess cash; and (2) borrow at favourable interest rates when cash is required. Because cash and investments are so liquid, they normally represent critical audit areas.

❖ AUDITING CASH

LO1

The line item 'cash' reported in financial statements represents currency on hand and cash on deposit in bank accounts, including certificates of deposit, time deposits and savings accounts. Frequently, certain **'cash equivalents'** are combined with cash for presentation in the financial statements. IASB IAS 7 *Cash Flow Statements* defines *cash equivalents* as short-term, highly liquid investments that are readily convertible to known amounts of cash or which are subject to an insignificant risk of changes in value (para. 6). Examples of such financial instruments include marketable government securities, commercial paper and money market funds.

Because virtually all accounting transactions pass through the cash account as part of their 'cradle-to-grave' cycle, cash is affected in one way or another by all of the entity's business processes. Figure 16–1 shows the effect each major business process has on the cash account. Although the main source of cash receipts is the revenue process, other sources of cash include: (1) the sale of property, plant and equipment; and (2) the proceeds from issuing long-term debt or equity capital. The main sources of disbursements from cash are the purchasing and human resource management processes. Generally, large payments initiated in the purchasing process are for acquisitions of inventory and property, plant and equipment. Payments on long-term debt and repurchase of stock are other types of cash disbursements.

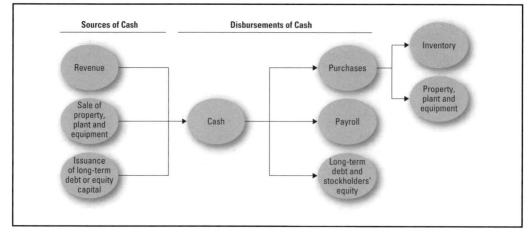

Figure 16–1   The Effects of the Major Accounting Transactions/Business Processes on Cash

Because of the close relationship of cash to the revenue and purchasing processes, issues relating to the inherent risk and control of cash were discussed in Chapters 10 and 11, respectively. Specifically regarding control risk, Table 10–7 summarized the **assertions**, possible misstatements, control activities and **tests of controls** for cash receipt transactions. A similar summary was provided for cash disbursement transactions in Table 11–7. Therefore, we will not repeat the discussion of inherent or control risk for cash receipt and disbursement transactions in this chapter. However, the auditor's assessment of inherent risk and control risk for transactions processed through the revenue and purchasing processes strongly affects the nature and extent of testing for the ending cash balance. Before reading on, stop and think of the inherent and control risk assessments for cash receipts and disbursements. What characteristics of cash increase inherent risk and how would this impact the substantive procedures? What affect does the control risk assessment have on substantive testing for cash? If the control risk assessment is below the maximum for both cash receipts and disbursements, the auditor can reduce the extent of substantive evidence gathered for the cash balances. Be sure this concept makes sense to you before moving on.

❖ TYPES OF BANK ACCOUNTS

LO2

Cash management is an important function in all organizations. In order to optimize its cash flow, an entity implements procedures for accelerating the collection of cash receipts and delaying the payment of cash disbursements, to the extent delay is appropriate. Such procedures allow the entity to earn interest on excess cash or to reduce the cost of cash borrowings.

Management must also be concerned with the control and safekeeping of cash. The use of different types of bank accounts aids in controlling the entity's cash. The following types of bank accounts are typically used:

- General cash account.
- Imprest cash accounts.
- Branch accounts.

It is important to understand each of the different types of bank accounts used. While the audit approach to each type of account is similar, the extent of testing varies from one account to the next. Each type of bank account is briefly discussed.

General Cash Account

The general cash account is the main cash account for most entities. The major source of cash receipts for this account is the revenue process, and the major sources of cash disbursements are the purchasing and human resource management processes. This cash account may also be used for receipts and disbursements from other bank accounts maintained by the entity. For many small entities, this is the only cash account maintained.

Imprest Cash Accounts

An imprest bank account contains a stipulated amount of money to be used for a specific purpose. For example, separate **imprest accounts** may be used for disbursing payroll, payroll taxes and dividend. In the case of payroll, a separate bank account is established for disbursing payroll. Prior to the disbursement of payroll to employees through direct deposit or cheques, funds sufficient to cover payroll are transferred from the general cash account to the payroll imprest account. The payroll is then drawn on this imprest account, which reduces the imprest account balance back to a minimum required to keep the account open and active with the bank. Thus, the payroll account serves as a clearing account for payroll payments and facilitates the disbursement of cash while also helping to maintain adequate control over cash.

Use of imprest accounts also minimizes the time required to reconcile the general cash account.

Branch Accounts

Companies that operate branches in multiple locations may maintain separate accounts at local banks. This allows each branch to pay local expenses and to maintain a banking relationship in the local community. Branch cash accounts can be operated in a number of ways. In some cases, the branch accounts are nothing more than imprest accounts for branch payments in which a minimum balance is maintained. The branch submits periodic cash reports to headquarters, and the branch account receives a transfer from the general cash account. In other cases, the branch account functions as a general cash account by recording both cash receipts and cash disbursements.

For proper control, the branch should be required to submit periodic cash reports to headquarters, and the entity's management should carefully monitor the branch cash requests and account balances.

Practice Insight 16.1

Management ordinarily uses a 'sweep account' cash management strategy to transfer, on a nightly basis, any surplus cash in non-interest-bearing commercial cash accounts to savings or money market accounts in order to earn higher returns on bank accounts.

CONTROL RISK ASSESSMENT: CASH

The reliability of the client's controls over cash receipts and cash disbursements affects the nature and extent of the auditor's tests of details. The preceding chapters discussed a number of important controls for both cash receipts and disbursements. The effective operation of these controls provides strong evidence that the completeness assertion is being met. A major control that directly affects the audit of cash is the completion of a bank reconciliation by client personnel who are independent of the handling and recording of cash receipts and cash disbursements. Such bank reconciliations ensure that the client's books reflect the same balance as the bank's after reconciling items have been considered. Control can be improved further if an independent party such as the internal auditor reviews the bank reconciliation.

If the client has good bank reconciliation procedures that are promptly performed, the auditor may choose to test the client's reconciliation procedures as part of testing controls and thereby reduce the audit work on the ending cash balance.

❖ SUBSTANTIVE PROCEDURES: CASH

LO3

❖

LO4

Substantive Analytical Procedures: Cash

Because of its residual nature, cash does not have a predictable relationship with other financial statement accounts. As a result, the auditor's use of substantive **analytical procedures** for auditing cash is limited to comparisons with prior years' cash balances and to budgeted amounts. This limited applicability of substantive analytical procedures is normally offset by: (1) extensive tests of controls and/or **substantive tests of transactions** for cash receipts and cash disbursements; or (2) extensive tests of the entity's bank reconciliations.

Substantive Tests of Details of Transactions and Balances: Cash

Table 16–1 contains examples of substantive tests of transactions for both cash receipts and cash disbursements. By testing both cash receipts and disbursements, the auditor obtains important evidence about the relevant assertions for the cash account. On most audits, the substantive tests of transactions for cash receipts and cash disbursements are conducted together with the tests of controls for the revenue and purchasing processes, respectively. For example, when the auditor tests a bank reconciliation for independent review by management, a sample of cash receipts and disbursements entries may be traced to cash receipts journal and disbursements journal, respectively.

Table 16–1 Examples of Tests of Details of Transactions for Cash Receipts and Disbursements

Assertions about Classes of Transactions	Examples Substantive Tests of Transactions*	
	Cash Receipts	Cash Disbursements
Occurrence	Vouch a sample of entries in the cash receipts journal to remittance advices, daily deposits and bank statement.	Vouch a sample of entries from the cash disbursements journal to voucher packet, and bank statement.
Completeness	Trace a sample of electronic cash receipts transfers to the cash receipts journal.	Trace a sample of electronic cash disbursements transfers to the cash disbursements journal.
Authorization	For a sample of days, examine the signature on the deposit slip for proper authorization.	Reconcile a sample of electronic cash disbursements transfers with list of payments authorized by management.
Accuracy	For a sample of daily deposits, foot the remittance advices and agree to the cash receipts journal and bank statement.	For a sample of voucher packets, agree amounts in purchase order, receiving report, invoice, electronic cash disbursements transfer and disbursements journal.
	For a sample of weeks, foot the cash receipts journal and agree posting to the general ledger.	For a sample of weeks, foot the cash disbursements journal and agree posting to the general ledger.
Cut-off	Test a sample of cash receipts at, before and after an accounting period for recording in appropriate period.	Test a sample of cash disbursements at, before and after an accounting period for recording in appropriate period.
Classification	Examine a sample of remittance advices for proper account classification.	Examine a sample of electronic cash disbursements transfers for proper account classification.
* These tests of details of transactions are commonly conducted as dual-purpose tests (i.e. in conjunction with tests of controls).		

Balance-Related Assertions

Table 16–2 summarizes the assertions and **tests of details of account balances** for cash accounts. The rights and obligations assertion is not included in Table 16–2 because it is seldom important to the audit of the cash balance. The major audit procedures for each cash account involve tests of the bank reconciliation. The approach to auditing a bank reconciliation is basically the same regardless of the type of bank account being examined. However, the type and extent of the audit work are more detailed for the general cash account because it normally represents a material amount and because of the large amount of activity in the account.

Table 16–2 Examples of Tests of Details of Balances for Cash	
Assertions about Account Balances at Period End	Examples Tests of Details of Account Balances
Existence	Confirm bank account balance with financial institution
Completeness	Test bank reconciliation for each account:
Valuation and Allocation	• Foot the reconciliation
	• Trace balances per book to the general ledger
	• Obtain bank confirmation and trace balance per bank to the bank reconciliation
	• Obtain cut-off bank statement
	• Trace deposits in transit and other reconciling items to cut-off bank statement
	If control risk is high or if fraud is suspected:
	• Perform extended bank reconciliation procedures
	• Perform a proof of cash
	• Test for kiting

❖ Auditing the General Cash Account

LO5

Table 16–2 shows that the main source of evidence for the existence, completeness and valuation assertions is the audit work completed on the bank reconciliation. To audit a cash account, the auditor should obtain the following documents:

- A copy of the bank reconciliation.
- **Confirmation** of account balance information with financial institutions.
- A cut-off bank statement.

Bank Reconciliation Working Paper

Exhibit 16–1 provides an example of a bank reconciliation working paper for EarthWear's general cash account. Note that the difference between the cash balance shown in Exhibit 16–1 and the balance in cash on the financial statements is represented by cash equivalents (marketable government securities and commercial paper). On most audits, the auditor obtains a copy of the bank reconciliation prepared by the client's personnel. The working paper reconciles the balance per the bank with the balance per the books.

Exhibit 16–1 Example of a Bank Reconciliation Working Paper		
		C10 DLJ 15/1/10
	EARTHWEAR CLOTHIERS **Bank Reconciliation** **31/12/09** **General Cash Account**	
Balance per bank: **C11**		€1,854,890**C**
Add:		
Deposits in transit:		
30/12/09	€156,940✔	
31/12/09	340,875✔	497,815
Deduct:		
Outstanding cheques:		
No. 1243	€121,843φ	
No. 1244	232,784φ	
No. 1247	30,431φ	
No. 1250	64,407φ	
No. 1251	123,250φ	(572,715)
Balance per books, unadjusted		1,779,990

Adjustments to books:		
Bank service charges	€250✓	
NSF cheque	7,400✓	
Balance per books, adjusted		(7,650)
		€1,772,340L
		F

F = Footed.
C = Traced balance to bank confirmation.
L = Agreed to cash lead schedule and general ledger.
✓ = Traced amount to cut-off bank statement.
φ = Examined cancelled cheque for proper payee, amount and endorsement.
Note: The controller has signed for the return of the cut-off bank statement.

Reconciling items may include items deposited in the client's bank account, but not recorded in the client's books; items recorded in the client's books, but not deposited in the client's bank account; items disbursed from client's bank account, but not recorded in the client's books; and items recorded in the client's books, but not disbursed from the client's bank account. The major reconciling items are deposits in transit, outstanding cheques and other adjustments, such as bank service charges and any cheque returned because the customer did not have sufficient cash (non-sufficient fund; NSF cheque) in its account to cover payment of the cheque. Note that the reconciling items for entities using primarily electronic fund transfers are normally considerably less than in paper-based systems. For example, in electronic fund transfer systems the cash disbursements transfers from the bank would typically precede or take place simultaneously with the recording, and items recorded in the client's books, but not disbursed from the client's bank account such as those caused by outstanding cheques will not be present.

Bank Confirmation

The auditor generally confirms account balance information with the bank or financial institution that maintains an account for the client. The confirmation form may not require bank personnel to conduct a comprehensive, detailed search of the bank's records beyond the account information requested on the confirmation. However, it may request that bank personnel indicate any other deposits or loans that come to their attention while completing the confirmation. As a result, such confirmation request cannot be relied upon to identify *all* information about a client's bank deposits or loans. If the auditor believes that additional information is needed about a client's arrangements with a financial institution, a more extensive confirmation letter signed by the client should be sent to the official at the financial institution that is responsible for the client's accounts. Details regarding lines of credit and compensating balances are examples of information that might be confirmed in this manner. This issue is discussed later in this chapter.

Bank confirmation requests should be sent and received under the auditor's control. The notorious and massive Parmalat fraud (discussed in Exhibit 2–2) perpetuated through a fictitious €3.95 billion bank confirmation highlights the importance of auditors properly controlling the confirmation process and applying a healthy dose of professional scepticism when evaluating audit evidence even for large and seemingly reputable clients.

Practice Insight 16.2

Parmalat forged a Bank of America confirmation for €3.95 billion and sent it to the company's auditors during the 2002 audit to corroborate the existence of cash. However, the cash did not exist. The forged confirmation was fuzzy and of poor quality because it is alleged that Parmalat officials ran the fake confirmation through the fax machine several times as part of its efforts to hide the fact that the document was a forgery.

Cut-off Bank Statement

A major step in auditing a bank reconciliation is verifying the propriety of the reconciling items such as deposits in transit and outstanding cheques. The auditor obtains a *cut-off bank statement* to test the reconciling items included in the bank reconciliation. A cut-off bank statement normally covers the seven- to ten-day period after the date on which the bank account is reconciled. Any reconciling item should have cleared the client's bank account during the seven- to ten-day period. The auditor obtains this cut-off bank statement by having the client request that the bank sends the statement, including cancelled or substituted cheques, directly to the auditor. When the entity uses electronic fund transfers the bank reconciliation is simpler since transfers are recorded on a timelier basis, normally with not more than a one-day delay.

Tests of the Bank Reconciliation

The auditor typically may use the following audit procedures to test the bank reconciliation:

1 *Verify the mathematical accuracy of the bank reconciliation working paper and agree the balance per the books to the general ledger.* In Exhibit 16–1, the working paper has been footed and the balance per the books as shown on the reconciliation has been agreed to the general ledger.

2 *Agree the bank balance on the bank reconciliation with the balance shown on the bank confirmation.* For example, the bank confirmation shows €1,854,890 and corresponds to the bank reconciliation in Exhibit 16–1.

3 *Trace the deposits in transit on the bank reconciliation to the cut-off bank statement.* Any deposit in transit shown on the bank reconciliation should be listed as a deposit shortly after the end of the period. The tick mark next to the deposits in transit shown in Exhibit 16–1 indicates that the deposits were traced by the auditor to the cut-off bank statement.

4 *Compare the outstanding cheques on the bank reconciliation working paper with the cancelled cheques contained in the cut-off bank statement for proper payee, amount and endorsement.* The auditor should also ensure that no cheques dated prior to 31 December are included with the cut-off bank statement that are not included as outstanding cheques on the bank reconciliation. The tick mark next to the outstanding cheques shown in Exhibit 16–1 indicates that the cheques were traced by the auditor to the cut-off bank statement and that the cancelled cheques were examined for propriety.

5 *Agree any charges included on the bank statement to the bank reconciliation.* In some cases, these charges may result in an adjustment to the client's books. For example, the bank service charges of €250 and the NSF cheque for €7,400 received from a customer shown in Exhibit 16–1 require adjustment of the client's records.

6 *Agree the adjusted book balance to the cash account lead schedule.* The adjusted book balance would be part of the amount included in the financial statements for cash.

❖ Fraud-Related Audit Procedures

LO6

If the client does not have adequate controls over cash or the auditor suspects that some type of fraud or defalcation involving cash has occurred, it may be necessary to extend the normal cash audit procedures. Although many types of fraud, such as forgery or collusion, are difficult to detect, auditing standards (ISA 240) indicate that the auditor has a responsibility to plan and perform the audit to obtain reasonable assurance about whether the financial statements are free of material misstatement, whether caused by error or fraud.

   Three audit procedures that auditors typically use to detect fraudulent activities in the cash accounts are:

1 Extended bank reconciliation procedures.
2 Proof of cash.
3 Tests for kiting.

Extended Bank Reconciliation Procedures

In some instances, an unscrupulous client might use the year-end bank reconciliation to cover cash defalcations. This is usually accomplished by manipulating the reconciling items in the bank reconciliation. For example, suppose a client employee stole €5,000 from the client. The client's cash balance at the bank would then be €5,000 less than reported on the client's books. The employee could hide the €5,000 shortage in the bank reconciliation by including a fictitious deposit in transit. Thus, the typical approach to searching for possible fraud is to extend the bank reconciliation procedures to examine the disposition of the reconciling items included on the prior months' reconciliations and the reconciling items included in the current bank reconciliation.

   For example, assume that the auditor suspected that some type of fraud had been committed. The auditor would examine the November and December bank reconciliations by ensuring that all reconciling items had been properly handled. For deposits in transit on the November bank reconciliation, the auditor would trace the deposits to the November cash receipts journal to verify that they were recorded. The deposits would also be traced to the December bank statement to verify that they were deposited in the bank. Cheques listed as outstanding on the November bank reconciliation would be traced to the November cash disbursements journal, and the cancelled cheques returned with the December bank statement would be examined for propriety. Other reconciling items such as bank charges, NSF cheques and collections of notes by the bank similarly would be traced to the accounting records for proper treatment. The auditor would examine the reconciling items included on the December bank reconciliation in a similar fashion to ensure that such items were not being used to cover a cash defalcation. Further investigation would be required for any reconciling items not properly accounted for. The client's management should be informed if the auditor detects any fraudulent transactions.

While the audit of cash is typically uneventful, certainly it was not in the Parmalat audit (cf. Exhibit 2–2 and Practice Insight 16.2) and it was not for a former auditor we know who arrived at the client's location a day early to audit cash. The surprised CFO, who had been stealing funds from the entity, stood up, turned around and jumped out of the window to his death.

Proof of Cash

A **proof of cash** is used to reconcile the cash receipts and disbursements recorded on the client's books with the cash deposited into and disbursed from the client's bank account for a specific time period. Exhibit 16–2 presents an example of a proof of cash for Calabro Wireless Services for one month, although on some audits a proof of cash is performed for the entire period under audit.

Exhibit 16–2 Example of a Proof of Cash				
				C15 DLJ 15/1/10
CALABRO WIRELESS SERVICES Proof of Cash – General Cash Account 31/12/09				
		December		
	30/11/09	Receipts	Disbursements	31/12/09
Balance per bank	€513,324	€457,822ϕ	€453,387ϕ	€517,759**F**
Deposits in transit:				
30/11/09	114,240	(114,240)		
31/12/09		116,437		116,437
Outstanding cheques:				
30/11/09	(117,385)		(117,385)	
31/12/09			115,312	(115,312)
Bank charges			125	(125)€
NSF cheques		(5,250)		(5,250)€
Balance per books	€510,179	€454,769γ	€451,439μ	€513,509**FL**
	F	**F**	**F**	**F**

F = Footed and crossfooted.
L = Agreed to general ledger.
ϕ = Traced to December bank statement.
γ = Agreed to December cash receipts journal.
μ = Agreed to December cash disbursements journal.
€ = Traced to the 14 January 2010 bank cut-off statement.

Because the proof contains four columns, a proof of cash is commonly referred to as a *four-column proof of cash*. The four columns include:

- A bank reconciliation for the beginning of the period.
- A reconciliation of the cash deposited in the bank with the cash receipts recorded in the cash receipts journal.
- A reconciliation of the cash disbursed through the bank account with the cash disbursements recorded in the cash disbursements journal.
- A bank reconciliation for the end of the period.

The primary purposes of the proof of cash are: (1) to ensure that all cash receipts recorded in the client's cash receipts journal were deposited in the client's bank account; (2) to ensure that all cash disbursements recorded in the client's cash disbursements journal have cleared the client's bank account and (3) to ensure that no bank transactions have been omitted from the client's accounting records. The reader should note that a proof of cash will *not* detect a theft of cash when the cash was stolen *before* it was recorded in the client's books. If the auditor suspects that cash was stolen without being recorded in the client's books, the audit procedures discussed under the completeness assertion for cash receipt transactions in Chapter 10 should be performed.

Practice Insight 16.3

Skimming is the removal of cash from an organization prior to its entry in an accounting system. *Lapping* is one of the most common forms of concealing a skimming scheme. As discussed in Chapter 10, lapping occurs when the perpetrator covers the cash shortage by applying cash from one customer's account against another customer's account. The perpetrator then eliminates the shortage in the accounting records by recording credit memos or write-offs. Thus, to detect lapping, auditors would review the journal entries involving write-offs and credit memos as well as any irregular entries to the cash accounts.

Tests for Kiting

When cash has been stolen by an employee, sometimes the employee will attempt to cover the cash shortage by following a practice known as *kiting*. This involves an employee covering the cash shortage by transferring money from one bank account to another and recording the transactions improperly on the client's books. The employee does this by preparing a cheque on one account before year end but not recording it as a cash disbursement in the account until the next period. The cheque is deposited and recorded as a cash receipt in a second account before year end. The employee makes this deposit close enough to year end so that the cheque will not clear the first bank account before the end of the year. While electronic wire transfers are recorded more rapidly than paper transactions, there is often still a one-day delay, which makes kiting possible even without the use of paper cheques.

One approach that auditors commonly use to test for kiting is the preparation of an *interbank transfer schedule* such as the one shown in Exhibit 16–3. This exhibit provides six examples of the types of cash transfers an auditor might encounter. For example, transfer 2 is an example of a proper cash transfer. A cheque was drawn on the disbursing bank account and recorded as a cash disbursement on 30 December. It was recorded as a cash receipt in the receiving bank account on 30 December and deposited in that account on 31 December. The cheque cleared the disbursing account on 2 January. The auditor would examine this transfer by tracing the cheque to the December cash disbursements and cash receipts journals, and to the 31 December bank reconciliation. Because the cheque cleared the bank on 2 January, it should be listed as an outstanding cheque on the 31 December bank reconciliation for the disbursing bank account. The reader will also notice that transfers 1, 3 and 6 are proper transfers.

Exhibit 16–3 Example of an Interbank Transfer Schedule

| Transfer Number* | Amount | Disbursing Bank Account | | Receiving Bank Account | |
		Recorded in Client's Books	Paid by Bank	Recorded in Client's Books	Received by Bank
1	€15,000	28/12	30/12	28/12	29/12
2	7,500	30/12	2/1	30/12	31/12
3	8,400	31/12	2/1	31/12	2/1
4	10,000	2/1	2/1	30/12	31/12
5	3,000	3/1	3/1	3/1	30/12
6	17,300	2/1	4/1	2/1	2/1

* Explanation for each transfer in determining proper cash cut-off at 31/12:

1. The transfer was made on 28 December and recorded on the books as both a receipt and a disbursement on the same date. The cheque written was deposited on 28 December in the receiving bank account and credited on the bank statement the next day. The cheque cleared the disbursing bank account on 30 December. All dates are in the same accounting period, so there are no questions as to the propriety of the cut-off.
2. This transfer is proper. However, the transfer cheque should appear as an *outstanding cheque* on the reconciliation of the disbursing bank account.
3. Transfer 3 is also proper. In this example, the transfer should appear as a *deposit in transit* on the reconciliation of the receiving bank account and as an outstanding cheque on the reconciliation of the disbursing bank account.
4. This transfer represents kiting because the receipt was recorded on the books in the period prior to that in which the corresponding disbursement was recorded. Cash is overstated by €10,000.

> 5. Transfer 5 is also improper. In this case a deposit was made in the receiving bank in one period without the receipt being made in the books until the subsequent period. Unless this matter is explained on the reconciliation for the receiving bank, the transfer was apparently made to temporarily cover a shortage in that account. While the shortage will become apparent in the accounts as soon as the transfer is recorded in the following period, it will be covered by an unrecorded deposit on the balance sheet date.
> 6. This transfer is proper.

Transfer 4 represents an example of kiting. A cheque was written on the disbursing bank account before year end, but the disbursement was not recorded in the disbursements journal until after year end (2 January). The cheque was deposited in the receiving bank account and recorded as a cash receipt before year end. Thus, the cash shortage in the receiving bank account is covered by a cash deposit from the disbursing bank account, and the net effect is that cash is overstated by €10,000. As noted in Exhibit 16–3, transfer 5 is also improper in that a deposit was made in the receiving bank in one period without the receipt being made in the books until the subsequent period. The matter should be included and explained on the reconciliation for the receiving bank.

In some instances an interbank transfer schedule is used even though control activities are adequate and no fraud is suspected. When a client maintains many cash accounts, cash transfers may be inadvertently mishandled. The use of an interbank transfer schedule provides the auditor with evidence on the proper cut-off for cash transactions.

Auditing a Payroll or Branch Imprest Account

The audit of any imprest cash account such as payroll or a branch account follows the same basic audit steps discussed under the audit of the general cash account. The auditor obtains a bank reconciliation, along with a bank confirmation and a cut-off bank statement. However, the audit testing is less extensive for two reasons. First, the imprest balance in the account is generally not material. For example, an imprest payroll or branch account may contain a minimum balance, of say €100, required by the bank to keep the account open and active except for the short time after a payroll deposit and before the related payroll disbursements have cleared. Second, the types of disbursements from the account are homogeneous. The cheques are for similar types of transactions and for relatively small amounts. For example, there are often limits on individual amounts that can be disbursed or the size of an individual payroll cheque.

Auditing a Petty Cash Fund

Most entities maintain a petty cash fund for paying certain types of expenses or transactions. Although the balance in the fund is not material (hence the word 'petty'), there is a potential for defalcation because a client's employee may be able to process numerous fraudulent transactions through the fund over the course of a year. Auditors seldom perform substantive procedures on the petty cash fund, except when fraud is suspected. However, the auditor may document the controls over the petty cash fund, especially for smaller clients.

Controls Activities: Petty Cash

A petty cash fund should be maintained on an imprest basis by an *independent* custodian. While it is preferable for the custodian not to be involved in any cash functions, this is not possible for many clients. When the petty cash custodian does have other cash-related functions to perform, another supervisory person such as the controller should review the petty cash activity.

Prenumbered petty cash vouchers should be used for withdrawing cash from the fund, and a limit should be placed on the size of reimbursements made from petty cash. Periodically, the petty cash fund is reimbursed from the general cash account for the amount of the vouchers in the fund. Accounts payable clerks should review the vouchers for propriety before replenishing the petty cash fund. Finally, someone independent of the cash function should conduct surprise counts of the petty cash fund.

Audit Tests: Petty Cash

The first step is for the auditor to gain an understanding of the client's controls over petty cash. The adequacy of the client's controls determines the nature and extent of the auditor's work. The audit of petty cash focuses on both the transactions processed through the fund during the period and the balance in the fund. The auditor may select a sample of petty cash reimbursements and examine the propriety of the items paid for by the fund. This may be done as part of the auditor's tests of controls or tests of details of transactions for the cash disbursement functions. The auditor tests the balance in the petty cash fund by counting it. When the count is conducted, the total of cash in the fund plus the vouchers should equal the imprest balance. This count may be done at an interim date or at year end.

Disclosure Issues for Cash

The auditor must consider a number of important financial statement disclosures when auditing cash. Some of the more common disclosure issues are shown in Table 16–3. The auditor's review of the minutes of board of directors' meetings, line-of-credit arrangements, loan agreements and similar documents is the primary source of the information for the financial statement disclosures. In addition, the auditor typically confirms items such as compensating balances required under a bank line of credit.

Table 16–3   Examples of Disclosure Items for Cash
● Accounting policy for defining cash and cash equivalents.
● Any restrictions on cash such as a sinking fund requirement for funds allocated by the entity's board of directors for special purposes.
● Contractual obligations to maintain compensating balances.
● Cash balances restricted by foreign exchange controls.
● Letters of credit.

Exhibit 16–4 illustrates a letter for confirmation of compensating balances, while Exhibit 16–5 presents an example of note disclosures for compensating balances.

Exhibit 16–4   Illustrative Letter for Confirmation of Compensating Balances
<div align="center">**CALABRO WIRELESS SERVICES**</div>
31 December 2009
Mr John L. Gren First Europe Bank PO Box XXX City
Dear Mr Gren:
In connection with an audit of the financial statements of Calabro Wireless Services as of 31 December 2009, and for the year then ended, we have advised our independent auditors that as of the close of business on 31 December 2009, there were compensating balance arrangements as described in our agreement dated 30 June 2005. Withdrawal by Calabro Wireless Services of the compensating balance was not legally restricted as of 31 December 2009. The terms of the compensating balance arrangements at 31 December 2009 were: The company has been expected to maintain a compensating balance, as determined from your bank's ledger records without adjustment for estimated average uncollected funds, of 15 per cent of its outstanding loans plus 10 per cent of its unused line of credit. The company was in compliance with, and there have been no changes in, the compensating balance arrangements during the year ended 31 December 2009, and subsequently through the date of this letter. During the year ended 31 December 2009, and subsequently through the date of this letter, no compensating balances were maintained by the company at your bank on behalf of an affiliate, director, officer, or any other third party, and no third party maintained compensating balances at the bank on behalf of the company. Please confirm whether the information about compensating balances presented above is correct by signing below and returning this letter directly to our independent auditors, Abbott & Johnson, PO Box XXX, City.
Sincerely, Calabro Wireless Services BY: *Jan Rodriguez*   Jan Rodriguez, Controller

Dear Abbott & Johnson:

The above information regarding the compensating balance arrangement with this bank agrees with the records of this bank.

BY: *John L. Gren*   Date: 11/1/10
    John L. Gren, Vice President

Exhibit 16–5   Sample Disclosure of Compensating Balances

Lines of Credit:
On 31 December 2005, the company established a line of credit with a bank that provides for unsecured borrowings of €7,000,000 at the bank's prime rate (7 per cent at 31 December 2009). At 31 December 2008 and 2009, €200,000 and €800,000, respectively, had been borrowed under this arrangement. Under the credit arrangement, the company is expected to maintain compensating balances equal to 5 per cent of the borrowings in excess of €500,000. This requirement is generally met through normal operating cash balances, which are not restricted as to withdrawal.

AUDITING INVESTMENTS

LO7

Entities frequently invest in securities of other entities. Such financial investments might include equity securities such as common and preferred stock, debt securities such as notes and bonds, and hybrid securities such as convertible bonds and stocks. The accounting for such financial instruments is affected by factors such as the percentage of the other entity owned, the degree of influence exercised over the entity, the classification of the investment as a current or non-current asset, fair-value considerations, and myriad other factors. IAS 39 *Financial Instruments: Recognition and Measurement* provides detailed guidance on how to account for financial instruments, including relevant guidance to account for financial assets such as investment securities. IAS 32 *Financial Instruments: Presentation* establishes principles for presenting financial instruments. IFRS 7 *Financial Instruments: Disclosures* provide disclosures requirements for financial instruments.

On a general level, the auditor's consideration of investments is no different than for any other financial statement account. That is, the auditor must be assured that the amounts shown on the balance sheet for the various types of investments are not materially misstated. This includes the proper recognition of interest income, dividends and changes in value that must be included in the financial statements.

The inherent risks associated with investments vary with the amount of activity, complexity, and valuation considerations. For example, an investment in stock of a listed company is relatively easy to account for and audit. However, more complex financial instruments, such as derivatives and asset-backed securities, have become increasingly common holdings in investment portfolios. These complex financial instruments often require substantial judgement by management in determining **fair value** measurements. Due to the judgement and complexity associated with these financial instruments, the auditor is likely to assess the inherent risk as high. For an entity that has a large investment portfolio, the auditor is likely to follow a **reliance strategy** in which internal control is formally evaluated and tests of controls are performed in order to set control risk below the maximum. However, for the vast majority of entities, it is more efficient for the auditor to follow a substantive strategy and perform a detailed audit of the investment securities at year-end.

CONTROL RISK ASSESSMENT: INVESTMENTS

LO8

The discussion of investments that follows focuses on the general types of control activities that should be present to minimize the likelihood of a material misstatement. Even when a substantive strategy is followed, the auditor must reasonably understand control over investments in order to anticipate the types of misstatements that may occur and plan the substantive procedures. The main assertions that concern the auditor are occurrence, authorization, completeness, accuracy and classification. Proper segregation of duties is important in ensuring the propriety of investments and will be discussed briefly.

Assertions and Related Control Activities

Following are some of the more common controls that should be present for each of the important assertions for investments.

Occurrence and Authorization

Controls must ensure that the purchase or sale of any investment is properly initiated by authorized individuals. First, the client should have adequate documents to verify that a particular purchase or sale of a security was properly initiated and approved. The presence of adequate documentation allows the auditor to determine the validity of the transaction. Second, the commitment of resources to investment activities should be approved by the board of directors or by an executive who has been delegated this authority. An entity engaging in recurring investment activities should have an entity-wide general investment policy as well as specific procedures and control activities around individual investment transactions. The board of directors should establish general policies to guide the entity's investment activities, while the specific procedures for the purchase and sale of securities may be delegated to an individual executive, investment committee or outside investment advisers. If the client has proper controls for initiating and authorizing securities transactions, it is generally easy for the auditor to verify security transactions at the end of the period.

Completeness

The client should maintain adequate controls to ensure that all securities transactions are recorded, and the auditor should evaluate the design and operating effectiveness of the client's controls. One control for handling the detailed securities transactions is maintenance of a securities ledger that records all securities owned by the client. The client should reconcile the subsidiary ledger to the general ledger control account regularly. Personnel responsible for investment activities should periodically review the securities owned to ensure that all dividends and interest have been received and recorded in the entity's records.

Accuracy and Classification

Some important accuracy and classification issues are related to investment securities. As mentioned previously, IAS 39 and IAS 32 address accounting and reporting for financial instruments, including relevant guidance for investments in equity securities and for investments in debt securities. The standards require that those investments be classified in three categories and accounted for as follows:

- Debt securities that the entity has the positive intent and ability to hold to maturity are classified as *held-to-maturity investments* and reported at amortized cost.
- Debt and equity securities that are bought and held principally for the purpose of selling them in the near term are classified as *trading investments* and reported at fair value, with unrealized gains and losses included in earnings.
- Debt or equity securities not classified as either held-to-maturity or trading securities are classified as *available-for-sale financial assets* and are reported at fair value, with unrealized gains and losses excluded from earnings and reported in a separate element of shareholders' equity.

> ## Practice Insight 16.4
>
> A company can manipulate financial statements by intentionally misclassifying securities or transferring securities to a different class of investment. For example, a company might transfer a security from held-to-maturity to either trading or available-for-sale, which would trigger the recognition of a gain or postpone the recognition of a loss.

The client's controls should ensure that securities are properly classified and that appropriate prices are used to accurately value investments for financial statement.

One final issue related to the control risk for investments is that the client should have adequate custodial procedures to safeguard against theft. When securities are held by the client, they should be stored in a safe or safe-deposit box. Procedures should provide for periodic inspections by an individual independent of both the custodial and accounting responsibilities for securities. If an independent custodian such as a broker maintains securities, the client needs to establish procedures for authorizing the transfer of securities. For example, one approach would require dual authorization by appropriate management personnel.

Segregation of Duties

LO9
Table 16–4 contains some key segregation of duties for investments, and examples of possible errors or fraud that can result from conflicts in duties. However, only entities that engage in a significant number of investment activities are likely to have adequate segregation of duties for all investment activities. When some of the duties noted in Table 16–4 are not segregated, the client should have other compensating controls such as a regular review by a person in a higher level of management of the performance of the duty not segregated.

Table 16–4 Key Segregation of Duties for Investments, and Possible Errors or Fraud	
Segregation of Duties	*Possible Errors or Fraud Resulting from Conflicts of Duties*
The initiation function should be segregated from the final approval function.	If one individual is responsible for both the initiating and approving of securities transactions, fictitious transactions can be made or securities can be stolen.
The valuation-monitoring function should be segregated from the acquisition function.	If one individual is responsible for both acquiring and monitoring the valuation of securities, securities values can be improperly recorded or not reported to management.
Responsibility for maintaining the securities ledger should be separate from that of making entries in the general ledger.	If one individual is responsible for both the securities ledger and the general ledger entries, that individual can conceal any defalcation that would normally be detected by reconciliation of subsidiary records with general ledger control accounts.
Responsibility for custody of the securities should be separate from that of accounting for the securities.	If one individual has access both to securities and to the supporting accounting records, a theft of the securities can be concealed.

SUBSTANTIVE PROCEDURES: INVESTMENTS

LO10
As discussed earlier, it is generally more efficient to follow a substantive strategy for auditing investments. When the control risk is set at the maximum, the auditor conducts extensive substantive procedures to reach the planned level of detection risk. Additionally, because of the nature of the audit work, tests of details of transactions are seldom used as a source of evidence.

Substantive Analytical Procedures: Investments

Substantive analytical procedures such as the following can be used to evaluate the overall reasonableness of investments and related income statement accounts:

- Comparison of the balances in the current year's investment accounts with prior years' balances after consideration of the effects of current-year operating and financing activities on cash and investments.
- Comparison of current-year interest and dividend income with the reported income for prior years and with the expected return on investments.
- Recompute current-year interest income using the face amount of securities held, interest rate and time period held.

Test of Details: Investments

Table 16–5 summarizes audit procedures performed on the investment account for balance and presentation and disclosure assertions. The discussion of the investment account audit procedures focuses on the more important assertions. The procedures shown for the other assertions should be familiar to the reader.

Table 16–5 Examples of Tests of Transactions and Account Balances and Disclosures: Investments	
Assertions about Account Balances at Period End	**Example Test of Details of Account Balances**
Existence	Inspect securities if maintained by client or obtain confirmation from independent custodian.
Rights and obligations	Examine brokers' advices for a sample of securities purchased during the year.
Completeness	Search for purchases of securities by examining transactions for a few days after year end.
	Confirm securities held by independent custodian.
	Review and test securities information to determine if all interest and dividend income has been recorded.
Valuation and allocation	Review brokers' invoices for cost basis of securities purchased.
	Determine basis for valuing investments by tracing values to published quotations for marketable securities.
	Determine whether there has been any permanent impairment in the value of the cost basis of an individual security.
	Examine sales of securities to ensure proper recognition of realized gains or losses.
	Obtain a listing of investments by category (held-to-maturity, trading and available-for-sale); foot listing and agree totals to securities register and general ledger.
Assertions about Presentation and Disclosure	**Example Tests of Details of Disclosures**
Occurrence, and rights and obligations	Determine whether any securities have been pledged as collateral by (1) asking management and (2) reviewing board of directors' minutes, loan agreements and other documents.
Completeness	Determine that all disclosures required by IFRS 7 have been made for investments (both debt and equity securities).
	Complete financial reporting checklist to ensure all financial statement disclosures related to investments are made.
Classification and understandability	Review and inquire of management of proper classification of investments.
	Read notes to ensure that required disclosures are understandable.
Accuracy and valuation	Read notes and other information to ensure that the information is accurate and properly presented at the appropriate amounts.

Existence

The auditor should perform one or more of the following audit procedures when gathering evidence for existence:

- Physical examination.
- Confirmation with the issuer.
- Confirmation with the custodian.
- Confirmation of unsettled transactions with the broker-dealer.
- Confirmation with the counter-party.
- Reading executed partnership or similar agreements.

   If the client maintains custody of the securities, the auditor normally examines the securities. During the physical count, the auditor should note the name, class and description, serial number, maturity date, registration in the name of the client, interest rates or dividend payment dates, and other relevant information about the various securities. The auditor should insist that a representative of the client be present during the physical inspection of securities in order to acknowledge that all securities inspected are returned. If the securities are held in a safe-deposit box and the auditor is unable to inspect and count the securities on the balance sheet date, the auditor should consider having the bank seal the safe-deposit box until the auditor can count the securities at a later date. When the securities are held by an issuer or a custodian such as a broker or investment adviser, the auditor gathers sufficient appropriate evidence for the existence assertion by confirming the existence of the securities. The information contained in the confirmation needs to be reconciled with the client's investment records.

Valuation and Allocation

When securities are initially purchased, they are recorded at their acquisition cost. The auditor can verify the purchase price of a security by examining a broker's invoice or similar document. Debt securities that are to be held to maturity should be valued at their amortized cost. The auditor should have verified the purchase price of the debt at the time of purchase, and the effective interest rate should be used to recognize the interest income, which the auditor can recompute. The fair value of most equity securities is available from market quotations. The auditor can verify these values by tracing them to sources such as brokers, financial journals or other reliable financial publications.

The auditor must also determine if there has been any permanent decline in the value of an investment security. Accounting standards provide guidance for determining whether a decline in value below amortized cost is other than temporary. The following factors are cited in IAS 39 as indicating other-than-temporary impairment of the investment:

- Significant financial difficulty of the issuer or obligor.
- A breach of contract, such as a default or delinquency in interest or principal payments.
- The lender, for economic or legal reasons relating to the borrower's financial difficulty, granting to the borrower a concession that the lender would not otherwise consider.
- It becoming probable that the borrower will enter bankruptcy or other financial reorganization.
- The disappearance of an active market for that financial asset because of financial difficulties.
- Observable data indicating that there is a measurable decrease in the estimated future cash flows from a group of financial assets since the initial recognition of those assets, although the decrease cannot yet be identified with the individual financial assets in the group, including adverse changes in the payment status of borrowers in the group and national or local economic conditions that correlate with defaults on the assets in the group.

If the investment value is determined to be permanently impaired, the security should be written down and a new carrying amount established. Last, the auditor should examine the sale of any security to ensure that proper values were used to record the sale and any realized gain or loss.

Some investments do not have fair values that can be readily obtained from market data and thus require substantial judgement on the part of management. Auditing of fair value estimates is covered in the *Advanced Module* in Chapter 3.

Disclosure Assertions

Two issues are important when the auditor examines the proper classification of investments. First, financial assets such as marketable securities need to be properly classified as held-to-maturity, trading and available-for-sale because both the balance sheet and income statement are affected by misclassification. Second, the financial statement classification requires that all trading securities be reported as current assets. Held-to-maturity securities and individual available-for-sale securities should be classified as current or non-current assets based on whether management expects to convert them to cash within the next 12 months. If the security is expected to be converted to cash within 12 months, it should be classified as a current asset. The auditor should ask management about its plans to sell securities.

The auditor should evaluate both management's intent with regard to an investment and the entity's ability to hold a debt security to maturity. In evaluating management's intent, the auditor considers whether investment activities corroborate or conflict with management's stated intent. The auditor should examine evidence such as written and approved records of investment strategies, records of investment activities, instructions to portfolio managers, and minutes of meetings of the board of directors or the investment committee. In evaluating an entity's ability to hold a debt security to maturity, the auditor considers factors such as the entity's financial position, working capital needs, operating results, debt agreements, guarantees and other relevant contractual obligations, as well as laws and regulations. The auditor should also consider operating and cash flow projections or forecasts when considering the entity's ability to hold the debt security to maturity.

IFRS 7 requires specific disclosures for financial instruments, including relevant disclosure for securities. For example, the terms, conditions and accounting policy for securities and their fair value should be disclosed.

Most of the information necessary for such disclosures is developed as the other assertions are being tested. In addition, the amount of any securities pledged as collateral should be disclosed. To collect such information, the auditor might inquire of management, review the board of directors' minutes, and examine loan agreements and other relevant documents.

ⓘ Key Terms

Analytical procedures. Evaluations of financial information through analysis of plausible relationships among both financial and non-financial data.

Assertions. Representations by management, explicit or otherwise, that are embodied in the financial statements, as used by the auditor to consider the different types of potential misstatements that may occur.

Cash equivalents. Short-term, highly liquid investments that are readily convertible to known amounts of cash or which are subject to an insignificant risk of changes in value (e.g. money market funds and marketable government securities).

Confirmation. Audit evidence obtained as a direct written response to the auditor from a third party (the confirming party), in paper form, or by electronic or other medium.

Fair value. The amount for which an asset could be exchanged, or a liability settled, between knowledgeable, willing parties in an arm's length transaction.

Imprest account. A bank account containing a stipulated amount of money used for limited purposes (e.g. imprest accounts are frequently used for disbursing payroll and dividend).

Proof of cash. A technique used to reconcile the cash receipts and disbursements recorded on the client's books with the cash deposited into and disbursed from the client's bank account for a specific time period.

Reliance strategy. The auditor's decision to rely on the entity's controls, test those controls and reduce the substantive tests of the financial statement accounts.

Substantive tests of transactions. Tests to detect errors or fraud in individual transactions.

Tests of controls. Audit procedures performed to obtain audit evidence about the operating effectiveness of controls in preventing, or detecting and correcting, material misstatements at the assertion level.

Tests of details of account balances and disclosures. Substantive tests that concentrate on the details of items contained in the account balance and disclosure.

? Review Questions

LO1	16–1	How do the client's controls over cash receipts and disbursements affect the nature and extent of the auditor's substantive tests of cash balances?
LO2	16–2	Briefly describe each type of bank account. How does an imprest account help to improve control over cash?
LO3	16–3	Why are analytical procedures of limited use in the audit of the cash balance?
LO4,5	16–4	Why does an auditor obtain a cut-off bank statement when auditing a bank account?
LO6	16–5	List three fraud-related audit procedures for cash.
LO6	16–6	What approach is used by the auditor to test for kiting?
LO8,9	16–7	What are the main transaction-related assertions for investments? Identify the key segregation of investment-related duties and possible errors or fraud that can occur if this segregation is not present.
LO10	16–8	Briefly describe the classification and valuation issues related to investments in debt and equity securities.
LO10	16–9	What two presentation classification issues are important for the audit of investments?

Problems

LO7,8,9 16–10	Cassandra Corporation, a manufacturing company, periodically invests large sums in investment (debt and equity) securities. The investment policy is established by the investment committee of the board of directors, and the treasurer is responsible for carrying out the investment committee's directives. All securities are stored in a bank safe-deposit vault.

The independent auditor's internal control questionnaire with respect to Cassandra's investments in debt and equity securities contains the following three questions:

- Is investment policy established by the investment committee of the board of directors?
- Is the treasurer solely responsible for carrying out the investment committee's directives?
- Are all securities stored in a bank safe-deposit vault?

Required:

In addition to these three questions, what questions should the auditor's internal control questionnaire include with respect to the company's investments in debt and equity securities?

(AICPA, adapted)

LO4,6 16–11	Sevcik Company's auditor received, directly from the banks, confirmations and cut-off statements with related cheques and deposit tickets for Sevcik's three general-purpose bank accounts. The auditor determined that the controls over cash are satisfactory and can be relied upon. The proper cut-off of external cash receipts and disbursements was established. No bank accounts were opened or closed during the year.

Required:

Prepare the audit plan of substantive procedures to verify Sevcik's bank balances. Ignore any other cash accounts.

LO5 16–12	The following client-prepared bank reconciliation is being examined by Zachary Kallick, independent auditor, during the examination of the financial statements of Simmons Company:

SIMMONS COMPANY
Bank Reconciliation
1st National Bank Bank Account
30 September 2009

					Procedure(s)
a.	Select 2 procedures	Balance per bank		€28,375	
b.	Select 5 procedures	Deposits in transit:			
		28/9/09	€4,500		
		30/9/09	1,525	6,025	
				€34,400	
c.	Select 5 procedures	Outstanding cheques:			
		988	31/8/09	2,200	
		1281	26/9/09	675	
		1285	28/9/09	850	
		1289	29/9/09	2,500	
		1292	30/9/09	7,225	(13,450)
				€20,950	
d.	Select 1 procedure	Error:			
		Cheque 1282, written on 25/9/09 for €270, was erroneously charged by bank as €720; bank was notified on 2/10/09.		450	
e.	Select 1 procedure	Balance per books		€21,400	

Required:

Items (a) to (e) represent items an auditor would ordinarily find on a client-prepared bank reconciliation. The following list of audit procedures shows substantive auditing procedures. For each item, select one or more procedures, as indicated, that the auditor most likely would perform to gather evidence in support of that item. (The procedures on the list may be selected once, more than once or not at all.)

Assume that:

- *The client prepared the bank reconciliation on 2/10/09.*
- *The bank reconciliation is mathematically accurate.*
- *The auditor received on 12/10/09 a cut-off bank statement dated 7/10/09 directly from the bank.*
- *The 30/9/09 deposit in transit, outstanding cheques 1281, 1285, 1289 and 1292, and the correction of the error regarding cheque 1282 appear on the cut-off bank statement.*
- *The auditor set control risk concerning the financial statement assertions related to cash at the maximum.*

Audit Procedure:

1   *Trace to cash receipts journal.*
2   *Trace to cash disbursements journal.*
3   *Compare to 30/9/09 general ledger.*
4   *Directly confirm with bank.*
5   *Ascertain reason for unusual delay.*
6   *Inspect supporting documents for reconciling item not appearing on cut-off statement.*
7   *Vouch items on bank reconciliation to cut-off statement.*
8   *Vouch items on the cut-off statement to bank reconciliation.*

(AICPA, adapted)

LO7,8,10 16–13 The schedule that follows was prepared by the controller of World Manufacturing for use by the independent auditors during their examination of World's year-end financial statements. All procedures performed by the audit assistant were noted in the 'Legend' section; the schedule was properly initialled, dated and indexed, and then submitted to a senior member of the audit staff for review. Internal control was reviewed and is considered to be satisfactory.

Required:

a   *What information that is essential to the audit of debt and equity securities is missing from this schedule?*

b   *What essential audit procedures were not noted as having been performed by the audit assistant?*

(AICPA, adapted)

WORLD MANUFACTURING
Marketable Securities
Year Ended 31 December 2009

Description of Security			Serial No.	Face Value of Bonds	General Ledger 1/1	Purchased in 2009	Sold in 2009	Cost	General Ledger 31/12	31/12 Market	Dividend & Interest		
											Pay Date(s)	Amt. Rec.	Accruals 31/12
Corp. Bonds	%	Yr. Due											
A	6	14	21–7	10,000	9,400a				9,400	9,100	15/1	300b,d	
											15/7	300b,d	275
D	4	10	73–0	30,000	27,500a				27,500	26,220	1/12	1,200b,d	100
G	9	15	16–4	5,000	4,000a				4,000	5,080	1/8	450b,d	188
Rc	5	12	08–2	70,000	66,000a		57,000b,c	66,000					
Sc	10	17	07–4	100,000		100,000c,e			100,000	101,250	1/7	5,000b,d	5,000
					106,900a	100,000	57,000	66,000	140,900	141,650		7,250	5,563
					a,f	f	f	f	f,g	f		f	f
Stocks													
P 1,000 shs.			1,044		7,500a				7,500	7,600	1/3	750b,d	
Common											1/6	750b,d	
											1/9	750b,d	
											1/12	750b,d	250
U 50 shs.			8,530		9,700a				9,700	9,800	1/2	800b,d	
Common											1/8	800b,d	667
					17,200				17,200	17,400		4,600	917
					a,f				f,g	f		f	f

Legends and comments relative to above schedule:
a = Beginning balances agreed to 2008 working papers.
b = Traced to cash receipts.
c = Board of directors' minutes examined – purchase and sales approved.
d = Agreed to 1099.
e = Confirmed by tracing to broker's advice.
f = Totals footed.
g = Agreed to general ledger.

LO10   16–14   Phung, independent auditor, has been engaged to audit the financial statements of Vernon Distributors, a continuing audit client, for the year ended 30 September. After obtaining an understanding of Vernon's internal control system, Phung set control risk at the maximum level for all financial statement assertions concerning investments. Phung determined that Vernon is unable to exercise significant influence over any investee and none are related parties. Phung obtained from Vernon detailed analyses of its investments in domestic securities showing:

- The classification among held-to-maturity, trading and available-for-sale securities.

- A description of each security, including the interest rate and maturity date of bonds and the par value and dividend rate of stocks.

- A notation of the location of each security, either in the treasurer's safe or held by an independent custodian.

- The number of shares of stock or face value of bonds held at the beginning and end of the year.

- The beginning and ending balances at cost and at market, and the unamortized premium or discount on bonds.

- Additions to and sales from the portfolios for the year, including date, number of shares, face value of bonds, cost, proceeds, and realized gain or loss.

- Valuation allowances at the beginning and end of the year, and changes therein.

- Accrued investment income for each investment at the beginning and end of the year, and income earned and collected during the year.

Phung then prepared the following partial audit plan of substantive audit procedures:

1   Foot and crossfoot the analyses.

2 Trace the 30 September balances to the general ledger and financial statements.

3 Vouche the beginning balances to the prior year's working papers.

4 Obtain positive confirmation of the investments held by any independent custodian as of the balance sheet date.

5 Determine that income from investments has been properly recorded as accrued or collected by reference to published sources, by computation and by tracing to recorded amounts.

6 For investments in non-public entities, compare carrying value to information in the most recently available audited financial statements.

7 Determine that all transfers among held-to-maturity, trading and available-for-sale securities have been properly authorized and recorded.

8 Determine that any other-than-temporary decline in the price of an investment has been properly recorded.

Required:

a *For procedures 4 to 8, identify the primary financial statement assertion relative to investments that would be addressed by each procedure.*

b *Describe three additional substantive auditing procedures Phung should consider in auditing Vernon's investments.*

(AICPA, adapted)

LO10   **16–15**   To support financial statement assertions, an auditor develops specific audit procedures to satisfy or accomplish each assertion.

Required:

Items a through b represent assertions for investments. Select the most appropriate procedure from the following list and enter the number in the appropriate place on the grid. (An audit procedure may be selected once or not at all.)

Audit Procedure:

1 *Vouche opening balances in the subsidiary ledgers to the prior year's audit working papers.*

2 *Determine that employees who are authorized to sell investments do not have access to cash.*

3 *Examine supporting documents for a sample of investment transactions to verify that prenumbered documents are used.*

4 *Determine that any impairments in the price of investments have been properly recorded.*

5 *Verify that transfers from the current to the non-current investment portfolio have been properly recorded.*

6 *Obtain positive confirmations as of the balance sheet date of investments held by independent custodians.*

7 *Trace investment transactions to minutes of board of directors' meetings to determine that transactions were properly authorized.*

Specific Assertion		Audit Procedure
a.	Verify that investments are properly described and classified in the financial statements (presentation and disclosure-classification).	
b.	Verify that recorded investments represent investments actually owned at the balance sheet date (rights and obligations).	
c.	Verify that investments are properly valued at the lower of cost or value at the balance sheet date (valuation and allocation).	

(AICPA, adapted)

Internet Assignment

LO7,10   16–16   Visit the home pages of two major companies in the country you live in, and review their financial statements for information on how they account for investment securities and the amounts of those securities.

PART VI

Completing the Audit and Reporting Responsibilities

PART CONTENTS

Chapter **17** Completing the Audit Engagement
Chapter **18** Reports on Audited Financial Statements

Completing the Audit Engagement

❖ *LEARNING OBJECTIVES*

Upon completion of this chapter you will

❖ **LO1** Be able to explain the audit issues related to contingencies.

❖ **LO2** Know the audit procedures used to identify contingencies.

❖ **LO3** Understand the audit issues related to a legal letter.

❖ **LO4** Be able to explain why the auditor must be concerned with commitments.

❖ **LO5** Know the types of subsequent events.

❖ **LO6** Understand the auditor's responsibility regarding subsequent events.

❖ **LO7** Know the audit procedures used to identify subsequent events.

❖ **LO8** Know the audit steps included in the auditor's final evidence evaluation process.

❖ **LO9** Be able to explain how auditors identify and assess going-concern problems.

❖ **LO10** Understand the auditor's communication with those charged with governance and management and the matters that should be addressed.

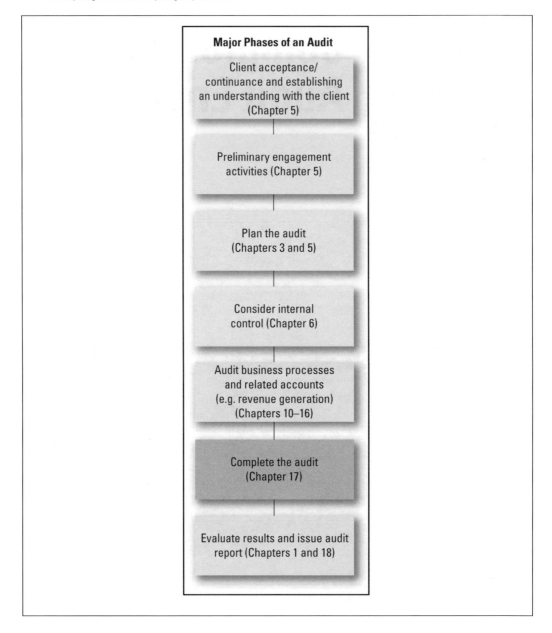

❖ RELEVANT ACCOUNTING AND AUDITING PRONOUNCEMENTS

IASB, IAS 1, Presentation of Financial Statements

IASB, IAS 10, Events after the Balance Sheet Date

IASB, IAS 37, Provisions, Contingent Liabilities and Contingent Assets

ISA 220, Quality Control for an Audit of Financial Statements

ISA 230, Audit Documentation

ISA 240, The Auditor's Responsibilities Relating to Fraud in an Audit of Financial Statements

ISA 260, Communication with Those Charged with Governance

ISA 265, Communicating Deficiencies in Internal Control to Those Charged with Governance and Management

ISA 330, The Auditor's Responses to Assessed Risks

ISA 500, Audit Evidence

ISA 501, Audit Evidence – Specific Considerations for Selected Items

ISA 505, External Confirmations

ISA 520, Analytical Procedures

ISA 540, Auditing Accounting Estimates, Including Fair Value Accounting Estimates, and Related Disclosures

ISA 550, Related Parties

ISA 560, Subsequent Events

ISA 570, Going Concern

ISA 580, Written Representations

ISA 700, Forming an Opinion and Reporting on Financial Statements

ONCE THE VARIOUS business processes and related financial statement accounts have been audited, the evidence is summarized and evaluated. Before determining the appropriate audit report, the auditor considers a number of additional issues that may impact the financial statements. This chapter discusses the following topics associated with completing the audit:

- Review for contingencies.
- Commitments.
- Review for subsequent events.
- Final evidence evaluation processes.
- Communications with those charged with governance and management.

REVIEW FOR CONTINGENCIES

LO1

Liabilities differ in their uncertainty about timing and amount. Most liabilities are legally enforceable and arise under contractual arrangements for amounts borrowed, amounts owed for assets purchased or services obtained. Other liabilities are uncertain because the possible outflow of resources from the entity will ultimately be resolved when some future event occurs or fails to occur. We refer to such liabilities as contingencies. Examples of contingencies include:

- Pending or threatened litigation.
- Actual or possible claims and assessments.
- Income tax disputes.
- Product warranties or defects.
- Guarantees of obligations to others.
- Agreements to repurchase receivables that have been sold.

It is important to the auditor to identify and understand contingencies because they may require recognition and/or disclosure in the financial statements. For example, application of International Accounting Standard (IAS) 37 *Provisions, Contingent Liabilities and Contingent Assets* to contingencies would imply the following:[i]

- *Probable.* A contingency that more likely than not will occur and that can be measured reliably should be recognized in the financial statements and requires disclosure.
- *Neither probable nor remote.* A contingency that less likely than not will occur but where the likelihood of occurrence is not remote (slight) requires disclosure.
- *Remote.* A contingency where the likelihood of occurrence is remote (slight) does not require disclosure.

Exhibit 17–1 presents an example of disclosure of a contingency taken from the annual report of a company you are already familiar with from Chapter 11: Royal Ahold. The contingency relates to legal proceedings as a result of accounting irregularities in Ahold's subsidiary US Foodservice (cf. Exhibits 11–1 and 11–7). Recall from Exhibit 11–1 that Ahold in November 2005 entered into an agreement with the lead plaintiffs for the sum of $1.1 billion. After you have read Exhibit 17–1, pause and consider how much judgement is involved on the part of management and the auditor in making and assessing the reasonableness of this type of disclosure. This is just one example of how both accounting and auditing involve a great deal of subjectivity and professional judgement.

Exhibit 17–1   Example of Note Disclosure for a Contingency: Royal Ahold Legal Proceedings

On 17 February 2004, the lead plaintiffs in the Securities Action served their consolidated amended complaint. The plaintiffs claim violations of Sections 20(a) and 10(b) of the U.S. Securities Exchange Act of 1934, as amended (the 'Exchange Act'), and Rule 10b-5 promulgated there under, and violations of Sections 11, 12(a)(2) and 15 of the U.S. Securities Act of 1933, as amended (the 'Securities Act'), by Ahold and certain of its current and/or former officers, directors, associates, auditors and underwriters. As a result of its contractual relationships with the banks that acted as underwriters of some of Ahold's securities offerings, Ahold may be obligated to indemnify the underwriters for certain legal fees and certain judgements that may be obtained against them. The consolidated amended complaint does not specify the amount of compensatory damages sought; however, the plaintiffs allege that the class has suffered billions of dollars in damages. The scope of the class is unknown at this time because a class has not been certified.

On 14 May 2004, Ahold moved to dismiss certain defendants and counts and to strike certain allegations of the consolidated amended complaint and the other defendants have moved to dismiss the entire Securities Action. On 21 December 2004, the court decided the motions to dismiss. The court dismissed the complaint against Ahold U.S.A., Ahold U.S.A. Holdings, Inc., Ahold's auditors and underwriters (with leave to re-plead certain claims against the underwriters) and certain of Ahold's current and former officers and directors. The court further dismissed the Securities Act claims (with leave to re-plead the Section 12(a)(2) claims against Ahold) and all claims that pre-date 30 July 1999 against all defendants. The remaining claims are the Section 10(b) and Rule 10b-5 claims against Ahold and U.S. Foodservice. The Securities Action is currently in the discovery phase, with trial anticipated in early 2007. At this point it is impossible to estimate Ahold's potential exposure in the Securities Action, but if the case goes to trial or Ahold would enter into a settlement, an adverse outcome of the trial or the settlement would likely involve an amount that is material.

Source: Royal Ahold Annual Report 2004.

Audit Procedures for Identifying Contingencies

LO2

Examples of procedures that may help the auditor identify contingencies include:

1   Reading the minutes of meetings of **those charged with governance** (e.g. the board of directors and audit committee).
2   Reviewing contracts, loan agreements, leases and correspondence from government bodies.
3   Reviewing tax returns, tax liability and tax authorities' reports.
4   Confirming or otherwise documenting guarantees and letters of credit obtained from financial and lending institutions.
5   Inspecting other documents for possible guarantees or other similar arrangements.

For example, the auditor usually reads the minutes of the board of directors' meetings for identification and approval of major transactions. Normally, the board of directors would discuss any material uncertainty that might exist for the entity. Similarly, the auditor examines the entity's income tax expense and accrued tax liability. The audit procedures for this account include determining if the tax authorities have audited the entity's prior year's tax returns. If so, the auditor should examine the tax authorities' report for any additional taxes assessed and determine whether the entity will contest the additional assessment.

In addition, near the completion of the engagement the auditor conducts *specific* audit procedures to identify contingencies. Such procedures include:

1   *Inquiry of and discussion with management about its policies and procedures for identifying, evaluating and accounting for contingencies.* Management has the responsibility for establishing policies and procedures to identify, evaluate, and account for contingencies. Large entities may

implement such policies and procedures as part of their risk assessment process. Smaller entities, however, may rely on legal counsel and other parties to identify and account for contingencies.

2 *Examining documents in the entity's records such as correspondence and invoices from lawyers for pending or threatened lawsuits.* Even though the amount of the legal expense account may be immaterial, the auditor normally examines the transactions in the account (see Chapter 15). The purpose of this examination is to identify actual or potential litigation against the client. The account analysis can also be used to develop a list of lawyers who have been consulted by the entity.

3 *Obtaining a* **legal letter** *that describes and evaluates any litigation, claims or assessments.* Legal letters are discussed in the next section.

4 *Obtaining written representation from management that all litigation, asserted and unasserted claims, and assessments have been disclosed in accordance with the applicable financial reporting framework.* This information is obtained in a **representation letter** furnished by the client. Representation letters are discussed later in this chapter.

❖ Legal Letters

LO3

A letter of inquiry (referred to as a *legal letter*) sent to the client's lawyers is the primary means to obtain corroborating evidence provided by management to the auditor about litigation, claims and assessments. Auditors typically analyse legal expense for the entire period and then ask management to send a legal letter to each lawyer who has been consulted by managment. In certain circumstances, the auditor may meet with the lawyers, for example if there is disagreement between management and the lawyers. Table 17–1 provides examples of types of litigation that the auditor may encounter.

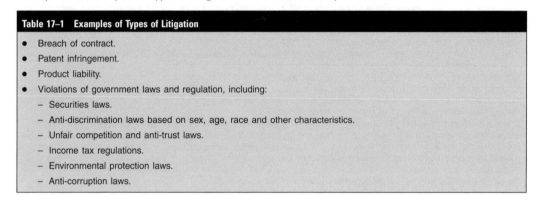

Table 17–1   Examples of Types of Litigation

- Breach of contract.
- Patent infringement.
- Product liability.
- Violations of government laws and regulation, including:
  - Securities laws.
  - Anti-discrimination laws based on sex, age, race and other characteristics.
  - Unfair competition and anti-trust laws.
  - Income tax regulations.
  - Environmental protection laws.
  - Anti-corruption laws.

A legal letter prepared by management and sent to the entity's lawyers may request information about a number of items, including the following:

- A list of any pending or threatened litigation, or any probable but as yet unasserted claims, on which the lawyer has devoted substantial attention or for which there is more than a remote possibility of an unfavourable outcome.
- A request that the lawyer describes and evaluates each pending or threatened litigation, including the progress of the case, the action the entity plans to take, the likelihood of unfavourable outcome, and the amount or range of potential loss.
- A request that the lawyer confirms the reasonableness of management's assessments and if the management's information is considered incomplete or incorrect.
- A request that the lawyer indicates if his or her response is limited in any way and the reasons for such limitations.

Exhibit 17–2 presents an example of a legal letter of EarthWear. Lawyers are generally willing to provide evidence on actual or pending litigation. However, they are sometimes reluctant to provide information on unasserted claims or assessments. An unasserted claim or assessment is one in which the injured party or potential claimant has not yet notified the entity of a possible claim or assessment. For example, suppose there is a cave-in at one of a coal-mining entity's mines and a number of miners are killed. Suppose further that a subsequent investigation shows that the client had failed to install proper safety equipment. The entity's fiscal year may end, and the financial statements for the period that includes the accident may be released. Although the families of the employees have not yet initiated or threatened litigation, an unasserted claim may very well exist at the financial statement date. In this case, the entity's lawyers may be reluctant to provide the auditor with information about the unasserted claims because of client–lawyer privilege. The lawyers may also be concerned that disclosing the unasserted claim in the financial statements may actually encourage a lawsuit or make it more difficult for the entity to defend itself. This type of situation is generally resolved by having the lawyers corroborate management's understanding of their professional responsibility involving unasserted claims and assessments. Refer to the third paragraph in the legal letter shown in Exhibit 17–2 for the manner in which the client requests the lawyers to communicate to the auditor. In general, disclosing an unasserted claim is not required unless it is probable that the claim will be asserted and there is more than a remote possibility that the outcome will prove to be unfavourable.

Exhibit 17–2 Example of a Legal Letter

EARTHWEAR CLOTHIERS

15 January 2010
Katz & Fritz
PO Box 402
City

In connection with an audit of our financial statements for the year ended 31 December 2009, please furnish our auditors, Willis & Adams International, PO Box 333, Europolis, with the information requested below concerning contingencies involving matters with respect to which you have devoted substantial attention on behalf of the company in the form of legal consultation or representation. For the purposes of your response to this letter, we believe that as to each contingency an amount in excess of €25,000 would be material, and in the aggregate €150,000. However, determination of materiality with respect to the overall financial statements cannot be made until our auditors complete their examination. Your response should include matters that existed at 31 December 2009, and during the period from that date up to the date of the audit report, which is anticipated to be on or about 15 February 2010.

Regarding pending or threatened litigations, claims, and assessments, please include in your response: (1) the nature of each matter; (2) the progress of each matter to date; (3) how the company is responding or intends to respond (for example, to contest the case vigorously or seek an out-of court settlement); and (4) an evaluation of the likelihood of an unfavourable outcome and an estimate, if one can be made, of the amount or range of potential loss. Please furnish to our auditors such explanation, if any, that you consider necessary to supplement the foregoing information, including an explanation of the matters as to which your views may differ from those stated.

We understand that in the course of performing legal services for us with respect to a matter recognized to involve an unasserted possible claim or assessment that may call for financial statement disclosure, if you have formed a professional conclusion that we should disclose or consider disclosure concerning such possible claim or assessment, as a matter of professional responsibility to us, you will so advise us and will consult with us concerning the question of such disclosure and the applicable requirements of International Accounting Standard 37 *Provisions, Contingent Liabilities and Contingent Assets*. Please specifically confirm to our auditors that our understanding is correct.

Please specifically identify the nature of and reasons for any limitation on your response.

Sincerely,
Calvin J. Rogers
Chief Executive Officer
EarthWear Clothiers

Lawyers may be unable to respond to the outcome of a matter because the factors in the case do not allow them to reasonably estimate the likelihood of the outcome or to estimate the possible loss. Finally, refusal to furnish information in a legal letter is a limitation on the scope of the audit sufficient to preclude an unmodified opinion.

COMMITMENTS

LO4

Companies often enter long-term commitments to purchase raw materials or to sell their products at a fixed price. For example, an airline might commit to purchase its jet fuel from a supplier at a predetermined price over a given time period. The main purpose of entering into such a purchase or sales contract is to obtain a favourable pricing arrangement or to secure the availability of raw materials. Pause for a moment and consider why an auditor might be concerned with commitments made by a client.

Long-term commitments are usually identified through inquiry of client personnel during the audit of the revenue and purchasing processes and through review of the minutes of board meetings. In most cases, such commitments are disclosed in a note to the financial statements. However, in certain instances the entity may have to recognize a loss on a long-term commitment even though there has been no exchange of goods.

For example, suppose a client produces woollen cloth for use in women's suits and that the company has a 31 December year end. Suppose further that the client enters a noncancellable contract on 30 September 2009 to purchase 1 million kg of wool at €1.00 per kg with delivery on 31 March 2010. At year end (31 December 2009), the auditor compares the current market price of wool with the contract price. If the current price of wool is €1.00 or greater, only note disclosure of the commitment is ordinarily necessary if it is material. However, if the price of wool is less than €1.00, a loss may be necessary to recognize at 31 December 2009. For example, if the current market price of wool is €0.75 per kg, the client would recognize a €250,000 loss (1,000,000 kg × €0.25 per kg) at year end.

❖ REVIEW FOR SUBSEQUENT EVENTS

LO5

Subsequent events are events occurring between the date of the financial statements and the date of the auditor's report, and facts that become known to the auditor after the date of the auditor's report (ISA 560), and may require adjustment or disclosure in the financial statements.

Financial reporting framework ordinarily identifies two types of subsequent events that require consideration by management and evaluation by the auditor:

1   *Type I:* Events that provide additional evidence about conditions that existed at the date of the balance sheet and affect the estimates that are part of the financial statement preparation process. Type I events require adjustment of the financial statements.
2   *Type II:* Events that provide evidence about conditions that did not exist at the date of the balance sheet but arose subsequent to that date. Type II events usually require financial statement disclosure.

Examples of Type I events:

● An uncollectable account receivable resulting from continued deterioration of a customer's financial condition leading to bankruptcy after the balance sheet date.
● The sale of inventories after the balance sheet date giving evidence about their net realizable value at the end of the reporting period.
● The settlement of a lawsuit after the balance sheet date for an amount different from the amount recorded in the year-end financial statements.
● Determination after the balance sheet date of the cost of assets purchased or the proceeds from assets sold before the balance sheet date.

Note that in these examples, additional evidence became available before the financial statements were issued that shed light on estimates previously made in the financial statements. Subsequent events affecting the realization of assets or the settlement of estimated liabilities normally require adjustment of the financial statements.

Examples of Type II events that ordinarily result in disclosure include:

● Purchase or disposal of a business by the entity.
● Sale of equity capital or bond issue by the entity.
● Loss of the entity's manufacturing facility or assets resulting from a casualty such as a fire or flood.
● Commencing major litigation arising solely out of events that occurred after the balance sheet date.

Pause for a moment to test your intuition. You will recall that EarthWear has a 31 December year end. Suppose the tax authorities notified EarthWear on 5 January 2010 that the company had made an error in its prior-year tax return, and as a result had underpaid its 2008 income taxes. If EarthWear settled the claim on 7 February 2010, would the payment be classified as a Type I or Type II event? Once you have articulated your answer to your satisfaction, read on.

The tax payment would be classified as a Type I event because it provides evidence about the underpayment of prior year taxes, a condition that clearly existed prior to the balance sheet date.

❖ Auditor's Responsibility Regarding Subsequent Events

LO6

Auditing standards (ISA 700) state that the auditor's report shall be dated no earlier than the date on which the auditor has obtained sufficient appropriate audit evidence on which to base the auditor's opinion on the financial statements, *including* evidence that: (1) all the statements that comprise the financial statements, including the related notes, have been prepared; and (2) those with the recognized authority (e.g. the board of directors) have asserted that they have taken responsibility for those financial statements (i.e. the financial statements have been approved).

Figure 17–1 presents a diagram of the subsequent-events period for EarthWear. The period from the **date of the financial statements** (31 December 2009) to the **date of the auditor's report** (15 February 2010) is sometimes referred to as the *formal* subsequent-events period. During this time frame, the auditor actively conducts audit procedures related to the current-year audit. Relevant audit procedures for this period are discussed in the next section.

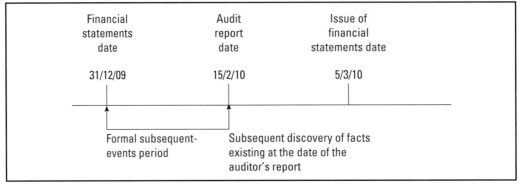

Figure 17–1   Subsequent-Events Period for EarthWear Clothiers

The auditor is not responsible for making any inquiries or conducting any other audit procedures after the date of the audit report. However, facts may come to the auditor's attention after the date of the audit report that might have affected the audit report had he or she known about them. Auditing standards (ISA 560) provide guidance to auditors in this exceptional circumstance.

Let us first concentrate on the period from the date of the audit report (15 February 2010) to the date of the issuance of the financial statements (5 March 2010). The **date the financial statements are issued** is the date that the financial statements and the audit report are made available to third parties. In the situation where a fact becomes known to the auditor that, had it been known to the auditor at the date of the audit report, may have caused the auditor to amend the audit report, the auditor: (1) discusses the matter with management and, where appropriate, those charged with governance; (2) determines whether the financial statements need amendment and, if so, inquires how management intends to address the matter in the financial statements (ISA 560, para. 10).

If management amends the financial statements,[ii] the auditor provides a new audit report on the amended financial statements after having carried out the audit procedures necessary in the circumstances on the amendment and extended other relevant audit procedures to the date of the new audit report.[iii] For example, suppose that EarthWear's auditor Willis & Adams after the date of audit report finds out that a material amount of inventory was not included in the financial statements because of a computer error. The auditor will then perform the necessary audit procedures in the circumstances and provide a new audit report on the amended financial statements. The auditor's responsibility extends to the date of the new audit report. The new audit report would be dated no earlier than the **date of approval of the amended financial statements**.

What about the time frame in Figure 17–1 subsequent to the date of the issuance of the financial statements (5 March 2010)? Recall, after the date of the audit report, the auditor has no obligation to perform any audit procedures regarding the financial statements. Again, the auditor should respond appropriately to a fact that, had it been known to the auditor at that date of the audit report, may have caused the auditor to amend the report. The auditor's response would be similar as the one outlined above for the period from the date of the audit report to the date of the issuance of the financial statements.[iv] The new audit report would, however, include an emphasis of matter paragraph or other matter paragraph that draws the attention to the note to the financial statements discussing the reason for the revision and reissue of the financial statements. Additionally, the auditor would review the steps taken by management to ensure that anyone in receipt of the previously issued financial statements is informed of the situation.

FS   AR
evidence

 Audit Procedures for Subsequent Events up to the Date of the Audit Report

LO7 Auditing standards (ISA 560) require that the auditor performs audit procedures designed to obtain sufficient appropriate audit evidence that all events occurring between the date of the financial statements and the date of the auditor's report, that require adjustment of, or disclosure in, the financial statements have been identified. As you learned from previous chapters, some audit procedures for business processes and their related financial statement accounts are conducted before year end, while others may be conducted subsequent to year end. Some of these audit procedures, such as testing proper sales and purchases cut-off, are applied to transactions *after* the balance sheet date. Such audit procedures may detect subsequent events. In addition, the auditor conducts audit procedures specifically to detect any subsequent events that might have occurred during the period between the balance sheet date and the date of the audit report. These audit procedures include:

- Obtaining an understanding of any procedures management has established to ensure that subsequent events are identified.
- Inquiring of management and, where appropriate, those charged with governance as to whether any subsequent events have occurred which might affect the financial statements. Specific inquires may relate to: (1) the current status of any items in the financial statements that were accounted for based on preliminary or inconclusive data; (2) whether new commitments, borrowings or guarantees have been entered into; (3) whether there have been any developments regarding contingencies; (4) whether any events have occurred that are relevant to the measurement of estimates or provisions made in the financial statements; and (5) whether any events have occurred that are relevant to the recoverability of assets.
- Reading minutes, if any, of the meetings, of the entity's owners, management and those charged with governance, that have been held after the date of the financial statements and inquiring about matters discussed at any such meetings for which minutes are not yet available.
- Reading the entity's latest subsequent interim financial statements, if any.
- Examining the books of original entry (such as sales journal, purchases journal, cash receipts and cash disbursements journals, and general ledger) for the subsequent-events period and investigating any unusual transactions.
- Asking legal counsel about any litigation, claims or assessments against the entity.

 FINAL EVIDENCE EVALUATION PROCESSES

LO8 In addition to the search for unrecorded contingencies and the review for subsequent events, the auditor conducts a number of audit steps before deciding on the appropriate audit report to issue for the entity. These include the following:

- Performance of final analytical procedures.
- Evaluation of the entity's ability to continue as a going concern.
- Obtaining a representation letter.
- Review of working papers.
- Final evaluation of audit results.
- Evaluation of financial statement presentation and disclosure.
- Obtaining a quality control review of the engagement.

Final Analytical Procedures

Auditing standards (ISA 520) require that the auditor perform **analytical procedures** both in planning and at the final review stage of the audit. The objective of conducting analytical procedures near the end of the engagement is to help the auditor assess the conclusions reached on the financial statement elements and evaluate the overall financial statement presentation. These final analytical procedures may include recalculating some of the ratios discussed in the *Advanced Module* in Chapter 5 for planning the audit. However, more frequently, they involve reviewing the adequacy of the evidence gathered in response to unexpected fluctuations in the account balances identified during the planning of the audit and identifying any unusual or unexpected relationships not previously considered. These final analytical procedures may indicate that more evidence is needed for certain account balances.

The auditor performs final analytical procedures to consider the overall reasonableness of the financial statement amounts. In other words, final analytical procedures provide a sort of final, overall 'smell test' by the auditor. In doing this analysis, the auditor re-examines the client's business risks (refer to Chapter 3). For example, the auditor considers the critical issues and significant industry business risks and whether such risks might impact the financial statements. The auditor also assesses the structure and profitability of the industry, and how the client fits within the industry in terms of its profitability and solvency. In other words, the auditor considers whether the financial statement amounts make sense given the auditor's knowledge of the client's business risks.

❖ Going-Concern Considerations

LO9

The going-concern assumption is a fundamental principle in the preparation of financial statements. 'Going concern' in this context means that the 'concern' (i.e. entity) is likely to keep 'going' (i.e. it is likely to be able to keep doing business). Under the going-concern assumption assets and liabilities are recorded on the basis that the entity will be able to realize its assets and discharge its liabilities in the normal course of business.

International Accounting Standard (IAS) 1 states that an entity shall prepare financial statements on a going-concern basis unless management either intends to liquidate the entity or to cease trading, or has no realistic alternative but to do so. The going-concern assessment shall cover at least 12 months from the end of the reporting period. The entity shall disclose material uncertainties related to events or conditions that may cast significant doubt upon the entity's ability to continue as a going concern.

Auditing standards (ISA 570) indicate that the auditor has the responsibility to evaluate management's use of the going-concern assumption in the preparation of the financial statements and conclude whether a material uncertainty exists that may cast significant doubt on the entity's ability to continue as a going concern. While the auditor's going-concern considerations are made during the planning of the engagement, the auditor must also consider the going-concern issue near the end of the engagement.

Steps in the Going-Concern Evaluation

The auditor follows three overall steps in making the going-concern evaluation:

1 Consider whether the results of audit procedures performed during the planning, performance and completion of the audit indicate whether there is significant doubt about the entity's ability to continue as a going concern for the relevant period of time, ordinarily one year.
2 If there is significant doubt, obtain information about management's plans to mitigate the going-concern problem and assess the likelihood that such plans can be successfully implemented.
3 Conclude, in light of management's plans, whether there is significant doubt about the ability of the entity to continue as a going concern; if significant doubt exists, consider the adequacy of the disclosures about the entity's ability to continue and (if disclosure is adequate) include an emphasis of matter paragraph in the audit report.

Let us discuss each of these steps in turn.

Identifying and Assessing Going-Concern Problems

Risk assessment procedures and other ordinary audit procedures are normally sufficient to identify conditions and events that indicate going-concern problems. Examples of audit procedures that are likely to identify these kinds of conditions and events include analytical procedures, review of subsequent events, tests for compliance with debt agreements, reading the minutes of board of directors' (or other relevant governance body) meetings, inquiry of legal counsel, and confirmations with lenders or investors regarding financial arrangements. Conditions or events that may cast doubt about going concern can be categorized into: *negative financial trends*; *other financial difficulties*; *internal matters*; and *external matters*.

Negative financial trends consist of poor results from operations and adverse financial ratios. Analytical procedures during the planning phase of the audit are often particularly helpful in identifying negative financial trends. Table 17–2 lists a number of important financial conditions and ratios that prior audit research has shown to be good indicators of financial distress that can lead to a going-concern problem. If the entity being evaluated meets a number of these financial conditions and has adverse ratios, the auditor may conclude that the entity has a going-concern problem.

Table 17–2 Financial Conditions and Ratios That Indicate Financial Distress	
Financial Conditions	*Ratios*
Recurring operating losses	Net worth/total liabilities
Current-year deficit	Working capital from operations/total liabilities
Accumulated deficits	Current assets/current liabilities
Negative net worth	Total long-term liabilities/total assets
Negative working capital	Total liabilities/total assets
Negative cash flow	Net income before taxes/net sales
Negative income from operations	
Inability to meet interest payments	

Conditions or events that may occur in the other three categories are shown in Table 17–3. Other financial difficulties are particularly important for the going-concern assessment. For example, if an entity has violated certain debt covenants or is in default on its debt, the debt holders may call for immediate payment. In such circumstances, the entity may be unable to meet its cash requirements and may have to seek bankruptcy protection or liquidation. Similarly, internal matters such as work stoppages may have severe consequences on the entity. For example, strikes have sometimes caused entities to go into bankruptcy. Finally, external matters may cause an entity to cease being a going concern. For example, macroeconomic downturns or the loss of even one or two major customers have been known to cause companies to face severe financial difficulties.

Table 17–3 Other Conditions and Events Indicating a Going-Concern Problem		
External Matters	*Internal Matters*	*Other Financial Difficulties*
Legal proceedings	Work stoppages	Default on loans
Loss of a major customer or supplier	Uneconomic long-term commitments	Dividends in arrears
Loss of a key franchise, licence, or patent		Restructuring of debt
	Dependence on the success of one particular project	Denial of trade credit by suppliers
		No additional sources of financing

Consideration of Management's Plans

Once conditions have been identified that indicate significant doubt about the ability of the entity to continue, the auditor should consider management's plans for dealing with the adverse effects of the conditions or events. The auditor should consider the following actions by management:

- Plans to dispose of assets.
- Plans to borrow money or restructure debt.
- Plans to reduce or delay expenditures.
- Plans to increase ownership equity.

For example, management may attempt to sell assets to pay off debt or dispose of operations that are losing money. Management may negotiate with creditors in order to restructure debt or seek additional financing. Frequently, management will develop a plan to reduce wages or cut back the workforce. When evaluating management's plans, the auditor should perform audit procedures to obtain evidence about the elements of the plans and their likelihood of success. This will require examining the assumptions used by management in developing such plans.

If the auditor concludes that there exists a material uncertainty that casts significant doubt about the entity's ability to continue as a going concern, and the disclosure in the financial statements is adequate, the auditor issues an audit report that includes an emphasis of matter paragraph similar to the one shown in Chapter 18 (Exhibit 18–2). The emphasis of matter paragraph highlights the disclosure in the financial statements of the existence of a material uncertainty about the entity's ability to continue as a going concern. If the disclosure in the financial statements is inadequate, the auditor expresses a modified opinion in the audit report (refer to Chapter 18).

Practice Insight 17.1

Neither management nor the auditor can predict future events or conditions that may cause an entity to cease to continue as a going concern. The unexpected severity, speed and consequences of the credit crisis illustrate that fact only too well.

Source: Staff Audit Practice Alert: Audit Considerations in Respect of Going Concern in the Current Economic Environment, IAASB (2009).

Representation Letter

During the course of a financial statement audit, appropriate management makes a number of representations to the auditor as part of the inquiries made to obtain sufficient appropriate evidence. Auditing standards (ISA 580) require that the auditor obtain a *representation letter* from management. The purpose of this letter is to corroborate oral representations made to the auditor and to document the continued appropriateness of those representations. The representation letter also reduces the possibility of misunderstanding between management and the auditor.

For example, during the audit, the auditor may inquire about related parties and conduct specific audit procedures to identify related-party transactions. Even if the results of these audit procedures indicate that such transactions have been properly disclosed, the auditor obtains written representations indicating that management is not aware of any undisclosed related-party transactions. In other instances, evidence may not be available to corroborate management's representations. For example, suppose that management indicates intent to refinance a short-term obligation in the next period and reclassifies it as a long-term liability in the current financial statements. The auditor would obtain written representation from management to confirm that the obligations will be refinanced in the next period. The auditor may also seek confirmation of such financing arrangements from the client's lender.

Exhibit 17–3 presents an example of a representation letter from EarthWear Clothiers. Note the important types of information that management is asked to represent. EarthWear's representation letter includes written representations that are required by ISAs. The representation letter is addressed to the auditor and generally is given the same date as the auditor's report. Normally, the chief executive officer and chief financial officer sign the representation letter. Management's refusal to provide a representation letter results in a scope limitation that is sufficient to preclude an unmodified opinion and is ordinarily sufficient to cause an auditor to disclaim an opinion or withdraw from the engagement.

Exhibit 17–3   Example of a Representation Letter

EARTHWEAR CLOTHIERS

15 February 2010
Willis & Adams International
PO Box 333
Europolis

This representation letter is provided in connection with your audit of the financial statements of EarthWear Clothiers for the year ended 31 December 2009 for the purpose of expressing an opinion as to whether the financial statements are presented fairly, in all material respects, in accordance with International Financial Reporting Standards.
We confirm that:

Financial Statements

- We have fulfilled our responsibilities, as set out in the terms of the audit engagement letter dated 1 April 2009, for the preparation of the financial statements in accordance with International Financial Reporting Standards; in particular the financial statements are fairly presented in accordance therewith.
- All known actual or possible litigation and claims have been appropriately accounted for and disclosed in accordance with the requirements of International Financial Reporting Standards.
- Significant assumptions used by us in making accounting estimates, including those measured at fair value, are reasonable.
- Related-party relationships and transactions have been appropriately accounted for and disclosed in accordance with the requirements of International Financial Reporting Standards.
- All events subsequent to the date of the financial statements and for which International Financial Reporting Standards require adjustment or disclosure have been adjusted or disclosed.
- The effects of uncorrected misstatements are immaterial, both individually and in the aggregate, to the financial statements as a whole. A list of the uncorrected misstatements is attached to the representation letter.

Information Provided

- We have provided you with:
  - ○ Access to all information of which we are aware that is relevant to the preparation of the financial statements such as records, documentation and other matters;
  - ○ Additional information that you have requested from us for the purpose of the audit; and
  - ○ Unrestricted access to persons within the entity from whom you determined it necessary to obtain audit evidence.
- All transactions have been recorded in the accounting records and are reflected in the financial statements.
- We have disclosed to you the results of our assessment of the risk that the financial statements may be materially misstated as a result of fraud.
- We have disclosed to you all information in relation to fraud or suspected fraud that we are aware of and that affects the entity and involves:
  - ○ Management;
  - ○ Employees who have significant roles in internal control; or
  - ○ Others where the fraud could have a material effect on the financial statements.
- We have disclosed to you all information in relation to allegations of fraud, or suspected fraud, affecting the entity's financial statements communicated by employees, former employees, analysts, regulators or others.
- We have disclosed to you all known instances of non-compliance or suspected non-compliance with laws and regulations whose effects should be considered when preparing financial statements.
- We have disclosed to you the identity of the entity's related parties and all the related party relationships and transactions of which we are aware.

Calvin J. Rogers
Chief Executive Officer
James C. Watts
Chief Financial Officer

Source: Adapted from ISA 580 *Written Representations*, IAASB (2009).

Practice Insight 17.2

In practice the management representation letter is typically drafted by the auditor and signed by management, though it is written as a letter addressed to the auditor from management. Practitioners often refer to a letter of representations as a 'rep letter'.

Working Paper Review

All audit work should be reviewed by an audit team member who is senior to the person preparing the **working papers**. Thus, the senior-in-charge should conduct a detailed review of the working papers prepared by staff auditors, and follow up on any unresolved problems or issues. In turn, the manager should review all working papers. The engagement partner normally reviews working papers related to critical audit areas as well as working papers prepared by the manager. In reviewing the working papers, the reviewers must ensure that the working papers document that the audit was properly planned and supervised, that the evidence supports the assertions tested, and that the evidence is sufficient for the type of audit report issued.

Practice Insight 17.3

Auditors must be careful not to leave 'loose ends' in the working papers. Will a regulator or a jury believe that the auditor obtained appropriate sufficient audit evidence if a question is left unanswered or an audit step undocumented? There is a common saying in audit practice: 'If you didn't document it, you didn't do it.'

Final Evaluation of Audit Results

In conjunction with the review of the working papers, the auditor must evaluate the results of the audit tests. The evaluation of the results of the audit is concerned with two issues: (1) the sufficiency of the audit evidence; and (2) the effects of identified misstatements in the financial statements. In evaluating the audit evidence, the auditor determines whether there is sufficient evidence to support each relevant assertion. This evaluation considers evidence obtained to support the assessment of the risk of material misstatement, as well as the evidence gathered to reach the planned level of detection risk (substantive procedures). If this evaluation indicates that the evidence is not sufficient to meet the planned level of audit risk, the auditor may need to gather additional evidence. For example, if the final analytical procedures indicate that inventory may still contain material misstatements, the auditor should gather additional audit evidence on the inventory account balance.

Any misstatements detected during the audit process must be considered in terms of their effects on the financial statements. This involves performing the third step in applying materiality (refer to Chapter 3). In particular, after the auditor has requested management to correct misstatements, the auditor compares the amount of remaining uncorrected misstatements, if any, to the amount of materiality. The auditor also considers the size and nature of the misstatements as well as the particular circumstances of their occurrence.

Exhibit 17–4 is the working paper that was first introduced in Exhibit 3–4. Even though the misstatements shown in Exhibit 17–4, as noted in Chapter 3, are not material, the auditor will request management to correct the identified misstatements. It is normally expected that known misstatements will be corrected. However, the auditor would not necessarily require all proposed adjustments to be booked. For example, suppose the auditor identifies a misstatement in an account receivable for a particular customer in confirming a sample of accounts receivable. She or he is likely to calculate an estimated or projected error in the population of accounts receivable based on the sample results (see Chapter 9). The auditor will normally expect the client to correct the specific customer account found to be in error, but may not require the client to book the full amount of the *projected* error in receivables if the amount is immaterial.

Exhibit 17–4	Example Working Paper for Proposed Adjusting Entries					
	EARTHWEAR CLOTHIERS					
	Schedule of Proposed Adjusting Entries 31/12/09					
Work Paper Ref.	Proposed Adjusting Entry	Assets	Liabilities	Equity	Revenues	Expenses
N10	Payroll expense					75,000
	Bonuses					140,000
	Provisions		215,000			
	To accrue payroll through 31/12 and recognize 2009 bonuses.					
F20	Cost of sales					312,500
	Inventory	(312,500)				
	To adjust ending inventory based on sample results.					
F22	Inventory	227,450				
	Accounts payable		227,450			
	To record inventory in transit at 31/12.					
R15	Accounts receivable	79,850				
	Sales				79,850	
	To record sales cut-off errors at 31/12.					
	Total	€(5,200)	€442,450		€79,850	€527,500

Materiality for classes of transactions and account balances = €900,000 .
Conclusion: Based on the above analysis, the account balances for EarthWear Clothiers are fairly stated in accordance with the applicable financial reporting framework.

> **Practice Insight 17.4**
>
> Determining whether a misstatement is material is not merely a quantitative exercise – the circumstances related to the misstatement can be more important than monetary amount. Auditors are particularly sensitive to misstatements that are *intentional* regardless of their size. If the auditor learns of an intentional misstatement, even when the misstatement is relatively small, he or she may be required to: (1) re-evaluate the degree of audit risk involved in the audit engagement; (2) determine whether to revise the nature, timing, and extent of audit procedures; and (3) consider whether to resign from the engagement.

Evaluating Financial Statement Presentation and Disclosure

The client normally drafts the financial statements, including notes. The auditor reviews the financial statements to ensure compliance with the applicable financial reporting framework, proper presentation of accounts, and inclusion of all necessary disclosures. Most audit firms use some type of financial statement disclosure checklist to assist the auditor in this process.

Engagement Quality Control Review

Audit firms have policies for **engagement quality control review** for audits of financial statements of listed entities and for other audit engagements the firm has determined to have such review. The **engagement quality control reviewer**, normally a partner, is not part of the engagement team. The reviewer should objectively evaluate the significant judgements that the engagement team made and the conclusions it reached in formulating the auditor's report.

Archiving and Retention

As discussed in Chapter 4, legislation and quality control standards require auditors to retain their audit files for a number of years after an audit report is filed. The needs of the firm for retention of engagement documentation, and the period of such retention, will vary with the nature of the engagement and the firm's circumstances, but would ordinarily be no shorter than five years from the date of the auditor's report.

❖ COMMUNICATIONS WITH THOSE CHARGED WITH GOVERNANCE
LO10 AND MANAGEMENT

Auditing standards require that the auditor communicates with those charged with governance (e.g. the board of directors) certain matters related to the audit. Where an audit committee exists, this committee becomes a key element in the communication process. ISA 260 *Communication with Those Charged with Governance* deals with the auditor's responsibility to communicate with those charged with governance. Other ISAs refer to additional matters to be communicated.

The intent of this communication is to encourage a healthy, two-way dialogue about financial reporting matters and to ensure that those charged with governance receive adequate information on significant audit-related issues. The items to be communicated are organized into three categories: the auditor's responsibilities under auditing standards; an overview of the planned scope and timing of the audit; and significant findings from the audit. As shown in Table 17–4, there are several important topics in each of these categories that the auditor should discuss with those charged with governance. (This list is not exhaustive and not all items are relevant when those charged with governance are involved in managing the entity.)

Table 17–4 Examples of Items the Auditor Communicates to Those Charged with Governance

The Auditor's Responsibilities in Relation to the Financial Statement Audit

- The nature of the auditor's responsibility for forming and expressing an opinion on the financial statements that have been prepared by management with the oversight of those charged with governance.
- The fact that the audit of the financial statements does not relieve management or those charged with governance of their responsibilities.

An Overview of the Planned Scope and Timing of the Audit

- The entity's objectives and strategies, and the related business risks that may result in material misstatements.
- How the auditor proposes to address the significant risks of material misstatement, whether due to fraud or error.
- The auditor's approach to internal control relevant to the audit.
- The application of the concept of materiality in the context of an audit.
- The extent to which the auditor will use the work of internal audit, and how the external and internal auditors can best work together.

Significant Findings from the Audit

- The auditor's views about qualitative aspects of the entity's significant accounting practices, including accounting policies, estimates, and financial statement disclosures.
- Significant difficulties, if any, encountered during the audit, for example restrictions imposed on the auditor by management.
- Significant matters, if any, arising from the audit that were discussed, or subject to correspondence with management.
- Significant deficiencies in internal control identified.
- Identified fraud or information that indicates fraud.
- Significant matters in connection with the entity's related parties.
- Events or conditions identified that may cast significant doubt on the entity's ability to continue as a going concern.
- Uncorrected misstatements.
- Expected inclusion of an emphasis of matter paragraph or other matter paragraph in the auditor's report.
- Expected modification of the opinion in the auditor's report.

Communication regarding significant findings from the audit should be in writing when the auditor deems oral communication to be inadequate. Other parts of the communication may be oral or in writing. In the case of listed companies the auditor also prepares a written statement to those charged with governance that the engagement team and others in the firm as appropriate have complied with relevant ethical requirements regarding independence.

Management Letter

In addition to the communications discussed above, the auditor may prepare a *management letter*. Be sure not to confuse the management letter with the management representation letter discussed previously in this chapter. The auditor uses the management letter to make recommendations to the client based on observations during the audit; the letter may include suggested improvements in various areas, such as organizational structure and efficiency issues.

🔑 Key Terms

Analytical procedures. Evaluations of financial information through analysis of plausible relationships among both financial and non-financial data.

Date of approval of the (amended) financial statements. The date on which all the statements that comprise the financial statements, including the related notes, have been prepared and those with the recognized authority have asserted that they have taken responsibility for those financial statements.

Date of the auditor's report. The date the auditor dates the report on the financial statements. The auditor's report is dated no earlier than the date on which the auditor has obtained sufficient appropriate audit evidence on which to base the auditor's opinion on the financial statements, including evidence that all the statements that comprise the financial statements, including the related notes, have been prepared; and those with the recognized authority have asserted that they have taken responsibility for those financial statements.

Date of the financial statements. The date of the end of the latest period covered by the financial statements.

Date the financial statements are issued. The date that audited financial statements and the auditor's report are made available to third parties.

Engagement quality control review. A process designed to provide an objective evaluation, on or before the date of the auditor's report, of the significant judgements the engagement team made and the conclusions it reached in formulating the auditor's report.

Engagement quality control reviewer. A partner, other person in the firm, suitably qualified external person, or a team made up of such individuals, none of whom is part of the engagement team, with sufficient and appropriate experience and authority to objectively evaluate the significant judgements the engagement team made and the conclusions it reached in formulating the auditor's report.

Legal letter. An audit inquiry sent to the client's lawyers in order to obtain or corroborate information about litigation, claims and assessments.

Representation letter. A letter that corroborates oral representations made to the auditor by management and documents the continued appropriateness of such representations.

Subsequent events. Events occurring between the date of the financial statements and the date of the auditor's report, and facts that become known to the auditor after the date of the auditor's report.

Those charged with governance. Those persons or person with responsibility for overseeing the strategic direction of the entity and obligations related to the accountability of the entity, including overseeing the financial reporting process.

Working papers. The material prepared by and for, or obtained and retained by, the auditor in connection with the performance of the audit.

? Review Questions

LO1	17–1	What is meant by a *contingency*? Give four examples of a contingency.
LO3	17–2	What information does the auditor ask the lawyer to provide on pending or threatened litigation?
LO4	17–3	Provide two examples of commitments. Under what conditions may such commitments result in the recognition of a loss in the financial statements?
LO5	17–4	What are the two types of subsequent events relevant to financial statement audits? Give two examples of each type of subsequent event that might materially affect the financial statements.
LO6	17–5	What is the auditor's responsibility regarding subsequent events in the period after the date of the auditor's report?
LO8	17–6	Are analytical procedures required as part of the final overall review of the financial statements? What is the purpose of such analytical procedures?
LO8,9	17–7	List the three overall steps in the going-concern evaluation process.
LO8,9	17–8	What major categories of events or conditions may indicate going-concern problems? Give two examples for each category.
LO8	17–9	Why does the auditor obtain a representation letter from management?
LO8	17–10	Describe the purposes of the engagement quality control review.
LO10	17–11	What categories of items should be included in the auditor's communication with those charged with governance? Give two examples for each category.

✎ Problems

LO1,2,3	17–12	During an audit engagement, Harper, independent auditor, has satisfactorily completed an examination of accounts payable and other liabilities, and now plans to determine whether there are any loss contingencies arising from litigation, claims or assessments.

Required:

What audit procedures should Harper follow with respect to the existence of loss contingencies arising from litigation, claims and assessments? Do not discuss reporting requirements.

(AICPA, adapted)

LO3   **17–13**   Cole & Cole, independent auditors, are auditing the financial statements of Consolidated Industries Company for the year ended 31 December 2009. On 2 April 2010, an inquiry letter to J.J. Young, Consolidated's outside lawyer, was drafted to corroborate the information furnished to Cole by management concerning pending and threatened litigation, claims and assessments, as well as unasserted claims and assessments. On 6 May 2010, C.R. Cao, Consolidated's chief financial officer, gave Cole a draft of the inquiry letter below for Cole's review before mailing it to Young.

6 May 2010
J.J. Young, Lawyer
123 Main Street
Anytown

Dear J.J. Young:

In connection with an audit of our financial statements at 31 December 2009, and for the year then ended, management of the company has prepared, and furnished to our auditors, Cole & Cole, independent auditors, 456 Highway, Anytown, a description and evaluation of certain contingencies, including those set forth below involving matters with respect to which you have been engaged and to which you have devoted substantive attention on behalf of the company in the form of legal consultation or representation. Your response should include matters that existed at 31 December 2009. Because of the confidentiality of all these matters, your response may be limited.

In November 2009 an action was brought against the company by an outside salesman alleging breach of contract for sales commissions and pleading a second cause of action for an accounting with respect to claims for fees and commissions. The salesman's action claims damages of €300,000, but the company believes it has meritorious defences to the claims. The possible exposure of the company to a successful judgement on behalf of the plaintiff is remote.

In July 2009 an action was brought against the company by Industrial Manufacturing Company ('Industrial') alleging patent infringement and seeking damages of €20 million. The action in the District Court resulted in a decision on 16 October 2009, holding that the company had infringed seven Industrial patents and awarding damages of €14 million. The company vigourously denies these allegations and has filed an appeal with the Court of Appeal. The appeal process is expected to take approximately two years, but there is some chance that Industrial may ultimately prevail.

Please furnish to our auditors such explanation, if any, that you consider necessary to supplement the foregoing information, including an explanation of those matters as to which your views may differ from those stated, and an identification of the omission of any pending or threatened litigation, claims and assessments or a statement that the list of such matters is complete. Your response may be quoted or referred to in the financial statements without further correspondence with you.

You also consulted on various other matters considered pending or threatened litigation. However, you may not comment on these matters because publicizing them may alert potential plaintiffs to the strengths of their cases. In addition, various other matters probable of assertion that have some chance of an unfavourable outcome, as of 31 December 2009, are unasserted claims and assessments.

C.R. Cao
Chief Financial Officer

Required:

Describe the omissions, ambiguities, and inappropriate statements and terminology in Cao's letter.

(AICPA, adapted)

LO5,7   **17–14**   Namiki, independent auditor, is auditing the financial statements of Taylor Corporation for the year ended 31 December 2009. Namiki plans to sign the auditor's report about 10 March 2010. Namiki is concerned about events and transactions occurring after 31 December 2009 that may affect the 2009 financial statements.

Required:

a   *What general types of subsequent events require Namiki's consideration and evaluation?*

b   *What auditing procedures should Namiki consider performing to gather evidence concerning subsequent events?*

(AICPA, adapted)

LO5,6,7   **17–15**   For each of the following items, assume that Josh Feldstein, independent auditor, is expressing an opinion on Scornick Company's financial statements for the year ended 31 December 2009; and he now is preparing his opinion to accompany the financial statements. In each item a subsequent event is described. These events were disclosed either in conducted subsequent to year-end audit procedures or in connection with the review of subsequent events.

You are to indicate for each item the required accounting of the event. Each of the five items is independent of the other four and is to be considered separately.

1   A large account receivable from Agronowitz Company was considered partly collectable at 31 December 2009. Agronowitz went out of business on 25 January 2010.

2   The tax court ruled in favour of the company on 25 January 2010. Litigation involved deductions claimed on the 2006 and 2007 tax returns. In accrued taxes payable Scornick had provided for the full amount of the potential disallowances. The tax authorities will not appeal the tax court's ruling.

3   Scornick's Manufacturing Division, whose assets constituted 45 per cent of Scornick's total assets at 31 December 2009, was sold on 1 February 2010. The new owner assumed the bonded indebtedness associated with this property.

4   On 15 January 2010, R.E. Fogler, a major investment adviser, issued a negative report on Scornick's long-term prospects. The market price of Scornick's common stock subsequently declined by 40 per cent.

5   At its 5 January 2010, meeting, Scornick's board of directors voted to increase substantially the advertising budget for the coming year and authorized a change in advertising agencies.

LO8   **17–16**   Arenas, an assistant auditor with the firm of Better & Best, independent auditors, is auditing the financial statements of Tech Consolidated Industries. The firm's audit plan calls for the preparation of a written management representation letter.

Required:

a   *What are the purposes of obtaining the letter?*

b   *To whom should the representation letter be addressed, and when should it be dated? Who should sign the letter, and what would be the effect of his or her refusal to sign the letter?*

c   *In what respects may an auditor's other responsibilities be relieved by obtaining a management representation letter?*

(AICPA, adapted)

LO8   **17–17**

During the examination of the annual financial statements of Amis Manufacturing, the company's president, R. Heinrich, and Luddy, the auditor, reviewed the matters that were to be included in a written representation letter. Upon receipt of the following client representation letter, Luddy contacted Heinrich to state that it was incomplete.

To: E.K. Luddy, Independent Auditor

This representation letter is provided in connection with your audit of the financial statements of Amis Manufacturing as of 31 December 2009 for the purpose of expressing an opinion as to whether the financial statements are presented fairly, in all material respects, in accordance with International Financial Reporting Standards.

We confirm that:

Financial Statements

- All known actual or possible litigation and claims have been appropriately accounted for and disclosed in accordance with the requirements of International Financial Reporting Standards.

- Significant assumptions used by us in making accounting estimates, including those measured at fair value, are reasonable.

- Related party relationships and transactions have been appropriately accounted for and disclosed in accordance with the requirements of International Financial Reporting Standards.

Information Provided

- We have provided you with:
  - Access to all information of which we are aware that is relevant to the preparation of the financial statements such as records, documentation and other matters;
  - Additional information that you have requested from us for the purpose of the audit; and
  - Unrestricted access to persons within the entity from whom you determined it necessary to obtain audit evidence.

- We have disclosed to you the results of our assessment of the risk that the financial statements may be materially misstated as a result of fraud.

- We have disclosed to you the identity of the entity's related parties and all the related-party relationships and transactions of which we are aware.

R. Heinrich,
President Amis Manufacturing
14 March 2010

Required:

Identify the other matters that Heinrich's representation letter should specifically confirm.

(AICPA, adapted)

LO2,3,7,8,10 17–18

Items 1 to 15 represent a series of unrelated statements, questions, excerpts and comments taken from various parts of an auditor's working paper file. Below is a list of the likely sources of the statements, questions, excerpts and comments. Select, as the best answer for each item, the most likely source. Select only one source for each item. A source may be selected once, more than once or not at all.

1   During our audit we discovered evidence of the company's failure to safeguard inventory from loss, damage and misappropriation.

2   The company considers the decline in value of equity securities classified as available-for-sale to be temporary.

3   We have disclosed to you all known instances of non-compliance or suspected non-compliance with laws and regulations whose effects should be considered when preparing financial statements.

4   It is our opinion that the possible liability to the company in this proceeding is nominal in amount.

5   As discussed in Note 4 to the financial statements, the company experienced a net loss for the year ended 31 July 2009, and is currently in default under substantially all of its debt agreements. These matters raise significant doubt about the company's ability to continue as a going concern.

6   During the year under audit, we were advised that management consulted with Better & Best, independent auditors. The purpose of this consultation was to obtain another audit firm's opinion concerning the company's recognition of certain revenue that we believe should be deferred to future periods. Better & Best's opinion was consistent with our opinion, so management did not recognize the revenue in the current year.

7   The company believes that all material expenditures that have been deferred to future periods will be recoverable.

8   Our use of professional judgement and the assessment of audit risk and materiality for the purpose of our audit mean that matters may have existed that would have been assessed differently by you. We make no representation as to the sufficiency or appropriateness of the information in our working papers for your purposes.

9   Indicate in the space provided below whether this information agrees with your records. If there are exceptions, please provide any information that will assist the auditor in reconciling the difference.

10 The company has insufficient expertise and controls over the selection and application of accounting policies that are in accordance with the financial reporting framework.

11 The timetable set by management to complete our audit was unreasonable considering the failure of the company's personnel to complete schedules on a timely basis and delays in providing necessary information.

12 Several employees have disabled the antivirus detection software on their PCs because the software slows the processing of data and occasionally rings false alarms. The company should obtain antivirus software that runs continuously at all system entry points and that cannot be disabled by unauthorized personnel.

13 In connection with an audit of our financial statements, please furnish to our auditors a description and evaluation of any pending or probable litigation against our company of which you are aware.

14 The company has no plans or intentions that may materially affect the carrying value or classification of assets and liabilities.

15 In planning the sampling application, was appropriate consideration given to the relationship of the sample to the assertion and to preliminary judgements about materiality levels?

List of Sources:

A   Practitioner's report on management's assertion about an entity's compliance with specified requirements.

B   Audit inquiry letter to legal counsel.

C   Lawyer's response to audit inquiry letter.

D   Those charged with governance's communication to the auditor.

E   Auditor's communication to those charged with governance.

F   Report on accounting policies.

G   Auditor's engagement letter.

H   Letter for underwriters.

I   Accounts receivable confirmation request.

J   Request for bank cut-off statement.

K   Emphasis of matter paragraph in an auditor's report on financial statements.

L   Engagement control quality reviewer's notes.

M   Management representation letter.

N   Successor auditor's communication with predecessor auditor.

O   Predecessor auditor's communication with successor auditor.

Discussion Cases

LO1,2,3   17–19   In February 2010, Ceramic Crucibles was notified that the environmental authorities were investigating the company's Red River facility to determine if there were any violations of environmental laws. In formulating your opinion on the 2009 financial statements, you determined that, based primarily on management's representations, the investigation did not pose a serious threat to the company's financial well-being.

The company subsequently retained a local law firm to represent it in dealing with the environmental authorities' commission. At the end of 2009, you concluded that the action did not represent a severe threat. However, you have just received the lawyer's letter, which is a little unsettling. It states:

> On 31 January 2010, the National Environmental Protection Authority (NEPA) listed the Red River site on the National Priorities List under the Comprehensive Environmental Response, Compensation, and Liability Act. The site includes property adjoining the western boundary of Ceramic Crucibles' plant in Red River and includes parts of Ceramic Crucibles' property. The NEPA has listed Ceramic Crucibles as one of the three 'potentially responsible parties' ('PRPs') that may be liable for the costs of investigating and cleaning up the site. The NEPA has authorized €400,000 for a 'Remedial Investigation and Feasibility Study' of the site, but that study will not begin until sometime later in 2010. Thus, we do not deem it possible or appropriate at this time to evaluate this matter with regard to potential liability or cost to the company.

You immediately set up a meeting with Dave Buff, Ceramic Crucibles' vice president, Ron Bonner, the company's lawyer, and Margaret Osmond, a lawyer who specializes in NEPA-related issues. At the meeting you ascertain that:

● Ceramic Crucibles bought the Red River facility from TW Industries in 1999.

● TW Industries had operated the facility as a manufacturer of ceramic tiles, and it had used lead extensively in incorporating colour into the tile.

- The site has been placed on the National Priorities List ('the List') apparently because each region must have at least one site on the List. All sites on the List are rated on a composite score that reflects the relative extent of pollution. The Red River site has a rating of 8.3 compared to a rating of no less than 25 for the other sites on the List.

- The most severe lead pollution (based on toxicity) is in an area located on the other side of a levee behind Ceramic Crucibles' facilities.

- Although the area close to the building contains traces of lead pollution, the toxicity in this area is about 50 parts per million (ppm), compared to 19,000 ppm beyond the levee. Although Ceramic Crucibles used lead in colouring its crucibles until about 2001, the lead was locked into a ceramic glaze that met governmental requirements for appliances used in the preparation of food. Apparently, the acids used in determining the leaching properties of lead for NEPA tests are stronger than that used by the national food quality authorities. Since 2001, Ceramic Crucibles has used lead-free mud in its crucibles.

- Affidavits taken from present and former employees of Ceramic Crucibles indicate that no wastewater has been discharged though the levee since Ceramic Crucibles acquired the property in 1999.

- The other PRPs and TW Industries are viable companies that should be in a position to meet their responsibilities resulting from any possible NEPA action.

Materiality for purposes of evaluating a potential loss is €10 million to €13 million. This is based on the assumption that the loss would be deductible for income tax purposes. In that case, the loss would represent a reduction in stockholders' equity of 4.5 per cent to 7.0 per cent. Your best guess is that the company's exposure does not exceed that amount. Further, based on the financial strength of the company and its available lines of credit, you believe such an assessment would not result in financial distress to the company.

The creation of the National Environmental Protection Authority (NEPA) and that of the Comprehensive Environmental Response, Compensation, and Liability Act are a result of the increasing concern of about pollution. An amendment to the Act permits the NEPA to perform the clean-up. NEPA had a national priorities list of 2,700 sites thought to be severely damaged. The average cost of conducting remedial investigation and feasibility studies ranges from €750,000 to €1 million, and such studies may take as long as three years. Clean-up costs are usually another €10 million to €12 million. It is said that the current estimates that €10 billion will be spent to clean up hazardous waste sites may be conservative.

The law requires the NEPA to identify toxic waste sites and request records from PRPs. The PRPs are responsible for the cost of clean-up, but if they lack the funds, the NEPA uses its funds for the clean up. The NEPA has spent €1.3 billion from its trust fund and collected only €65 million from polluters since the passage of the legislation.

Required:

a How would this type of contingency be classified in the accounting literature, and how should it be accounted for?

b Would the amount be material to the financial statements?

c What additional evidence would you gather, and what kinds of representations should you require from the client?

d Should the investigation affect your opinion on those financial statements?

LO8   **17–20**   Medical Products (MPI) was created in 2007 and entered the optical equipment industry. Their made-to-order optical equipment requires large investments in research and development. To fund these needs, MPI made a public share offering, which was completed in 2008. Although the offering was moderately successful, MPI's ambitious management is convinced that they must report a good profit this year (2009) to maintain the current market price of the shares. MPI's president recently stressed this point when he told his controller, Pam Adams, 'If we don't make €1.25 million pre-tax this year, our shares will fall significantly.'

Adams was pleased that even after adjustments for accrued vacation pay, 2009 pre-tax profit was €1.35 million. However, MPI's auditors, Hammer & Bammer (HB), proposed an additional adjustment for inventory valuation that would reduce this profit to €900,000. Hammer & Bammer's proposed adjustment had been discussed during the 2008 audit.

An additional issue discussed in 2008 was MPI's failure to accrue executive vacation pay. At that time HB did not insist on the adjustment because the amount (€20,000) was not material to the 2008 results and because MPI agreed to begin accruing vacation pay in future years. The cumulative accrued executive vacation pay amounts to €300,000 and has been accrued at the end of 2009.

The inventory issue arose in 2007 when MPI purchased €450,000 of specialized computer components to be used with their optical scanners for a special order. The order was subsequently cancelled, and HB proposed to write down this inventory in 2008. Medical Products explained, however, that the components could easily be sold without a loss during 2009, and no adjustment was made. However, the equipment was not sold by the end of 2009, and prospects for future sales were considered non-existent. Hammer & Bammer proposed a write-off of the entire €450,000 in 2009.

The audit partner, Johanna Schmidt, insisted that Adams make the inventory adjustment. Adams tried to convince her that there were other alternatives, but Schmidt was adamant. Adams knew the inventory was worthless, but she reminded Schmidt of the importance of this year's reported income. Adams continued her argument, 'You can't take both the write-down and the vacation accrual in one year; it doesn't fairly present our performance this year. If you insist on taking that write-down, I'm taking back the accrual. Actually, that's a good idea because the executives are such workaholics, they don't take their vacations anyway.'

As Adams calmed down, she said, 'Johanna, let's be reasonable; we like you – and we want to continue our good working relationship with your firm into the future. But we won't have a future unless we put off this accrual for another year.'

Required:

a Should the inventory adjustment be taken in 2009?

b Irrespective of your decision regarding the inventory adjustment, what is your reaction to Adams' suggestion to release the vacation accrual? Should the auditor insist on keeping the accrual of the executives' vacation pay?

c Consider the conflict between Adams and Schmidt. Assuming that Schmidt believes the inventory adjustment and vacation pay accrual must be made and that she does not want to lose MPI as a client, what should she do?

⭕ Internet Assignment

LO1,2   17–21   A number of companies have pending lawsuits or other contingencies reported in their financial statements.

Required:

a *Use an Internet search engine to find information of listed company that report a contingency. Write a paragraph summarizing one of the contingencies found in the financial statements. Did the company disclose the contingency in the notes only, or did they recognize it in the financial statements?*

b *What procedures might the auditors use to search for the contingencies listed in **a**?*

Notes

ⁱ IAS 37 *Provisions, Contingent Liabilities and Contingent Assets* prescribes accounting and disclosure for liabilities, including liabilities that will be resolved by the occurrence or non-occurrence of some future events (i.e. contingencies). The standard uses the term contingent liability only when the liability is not recognized in the financial statement. This book uses the term contingencies for liabilities of a contingent nature, including those requiring recognition in the financial statements. As of writing this book IAS 37 is under revision.

ⁱⁱ In some jurisdictions, management may not be required by law, regulation or the financial reporting framework to issue amended financial statements and, accordingly, the auditor need not provide an amended or new auditor's report. However, if management does not amend the financial statements in circumstances where the auditor believes they need to be amended, then:

(a) If the auditor's report has not yet been provided to the entity, the auditor shall modify the opinion as required by ISA 705 and then provide the auditor's report; or

(b) If the auditor's report has already been provided to the entity, the auditor shall notify management and, unless all of those charged with governance are involved in managing the entity, those charged with governance, not to issue the financial statements to third parties before the necessary amendments have been made. If the financial statements are nevertheless subsequently issued without the necessary amendments, the auditor shall take appropriate action, to seek to prevent reliance on the auditor's report (ISA 560, para. 13).

ⁱⁱⁱ If not prohibit by law or regulation, auditing standards (ISA 560) allow that the amendment of the financial statements are restricted to the effects of the subsequent event or events causing that amendment. In such case, the auditor either:

(a) Amend the auditor's report to include an additional date (dual dating) restricted to that amendment that thereby indicates that the auditor's procedures on subsequent events are restricted solely to the amendment of the financial statements described in the relevant note to the financial statements; or

(b) Provide a new or amended auditor's report that includes a statement in an emphasis of matter paragraph or other matter paragraph that conveys that the auditor's procedures on subsequent events are restricted solely to the amendment of the financial statements as described in the relevant note to the financial statements.

ⁱᵛ As note iii above.

CHAPTER

18

Reports on Audited Financial Statements

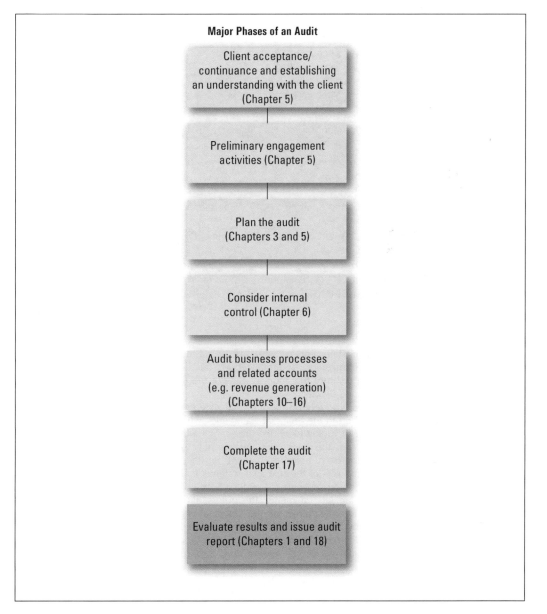

❖ *RELEVANT ACCOUNTING AND AUDITING PRONOUNCEMENTS*

ISA 200, Overall Objectives of the Independent Auditor and the Conduct of an Audit in Accordance with International Standards on Auditing

ISA 450, Evaluation of Misstatements Identified during the Audit

ISA 560, Subsequent Events

ISA 570, Going Concern

ISA 700, Forming an Opinion and Reporting on Financial Statements

ISA 705, Modifications to the Opinion in the Independent Auditor's Report

ISA 706, Emphasis of Matter Paragraphs and Other Matter Paragraphs in the Independent Auditor's Report

ISA 710, Comparative Information – Corresponding Figures and Comparative Financial Statements

ISA 720, The Auditor's Responsibilities Relating to Other Information in Documents Containing Audited Financial Statements

ISA 800, Special Considerations – Audits of Financial Statements Prepared in Accordance with Special Purpose Frameworks

ISA 805, Special Considerations – Audits of Single Financial Statements and Specific Elements, Accounts or Items of a Financial Statement

ISA 810, Engagements to Report on Summary Financial Statements

THE OBJECTIVE OF an audit of financial statements is to enable the auditor to express an opinion in the auditor's report whether the financial statements present fairly, in all material respects, in accordance with the applicable financial reporting framework. Auditor's reports are highly visible and are the auditor's primary venue to communicate the result of the audit to users of the financial statements. Thus, the form and content of the audit report are important.

The audit report enables the users who rely on the financial statements to understand the responsibility of management and the auditor related to the financial statements, what an audit entails and the auditor's opinion on the financial statements, including identified unusual circumstances when they occur. To assist in accomplishing this communication, the auditing standards have adopted a standardized form and wording for audit reports. This approach helps to prevent misunderstandings in the message being communicated by the auditor to the users of the financial statements. At the same time, some argue that the 'boilerplate' nature of the audit report prevents the auditor from conveying subjective information that could be useful to users of the financial statements. Regardless, it is important to keep in mind that management is responsible for the preparation of the financial statements and that the auditor is responsible for expressing an opinion on the financial statements based on the audit.

In the reporting process the auditor considers if it is necessary to add an emphasis of matter paragraph or other matter paragraph in the audit report. The auditor must also conclude if it is necessary to modify the opinion on the financial statements because the financial statements are not free from material misstatements. Auditing standards identify circumstances when it may be necessary to add an emphasis of matter paragraph or other matter paragraph, and when a **modified opinion** is necessary, as well as the nature of the reports.

The last part of this chapter discusses the auditor's reporting responsibility related to special issues. The discussion include auditor's reporting responsibility relating to **comparative information** (prior periods amounts and disclosures included in the financial statement), and **other information** in documents (e.g. the **annual report**) containing the audited financial statements. The chapter concludes with a discussion of reporting on three specialized areas: (1) auditor's reporting on financial statements prepared in accordance with a special purpose framework (e.g. on a tax basis of accounting); (2) auditor's reporting on single financial statements or specific elements of a financial statement (e.g. account receivables); and (3) auditor's reporting on **summary financial statements** derived from audited financial statements.

REPORTING ON THE FINANCIAL STATEMENT AUDIT: THE AUDIT REPORT WITH AN UNMODIFIED OPINION

LO1

An audit report with an **unmodified opinion** is issued when the auditor concludes that the financial statements are prepared, in all material respects, in accordance with the applicable financial reporting framework. In order to form that opinion, the auditor has gathered sufficient appropriate evidence and concluded that **reasonable assurance** is obtained that the financial statements as a whole are free from material misstatement. In concluding, the auditor takes into account whether uncorrected misstatements are material and considerations of qualitative aspects of the entity's accounting practices and financial statements presentation.

Chapter 3 discussed the determination of whether uncorrected misstatements are material. The considerations of the *qualitative aspects* of the entity's accounting practices includes evaluation of the overall financial statements presentation, disclosures, terminology used as well as application and disclosure of accounting policies. When the financial statements are prepared in accordance with a fair presentation framework,[i] this evaluation should also include whether the financial statements achieve fair presentation. In addition to the overall presentation, structure and content of the financial statements, this includes whether the financial statements represent the underlying transactions and events in a manner that achieves fair presentation. Last, the auditor should evaluate indicators of possible bias in management's judgements. For example the auditor may become aware of **management bias** in the making of accounting estimates. The auditor may conclude that the cumulative effect of a lack of neutrality in management's judgements, together with the effect of uncorrected misstatements, causes the financial statements to be materially misstated.

Exhibit 18–1 presents Willis & Adams International's audit report for EarthWear Clothier's consolidated financial statements discussed in Chapter 1. Take the necessary time and be sure you are familiar with the form and content of the report with an unmodified opinion. You will benefit from having a good grasp on this 'baseline' report when you in the next sections of this chapter learn when and how the auditor's reporting deviates from the baseline.

Exhibit 18–1	The Auditor's Report with an Unmodified Opinion
Title:	INDEPENDENT AUDITOR'S REPORT
Addressee:	*To the Shareholders of EarthWear Clothiers*
Introductory paragraph:	We have audited the accompanying consolidated financial statements of EarthWear Clothiers and its subsidiaries, which comprise the consolidated balance sheet as at 31 December 2009, and the consolidated income statement, statement of changes in equity and cash flow statement for the year then ended, and a summary of significant accounting policies and other explanatory information.
Management's responsibility paragraph:	*Management's Responsibility for the Consolidated Financial Statements* Management is responsible for the preparation and fair presentation of these consolidated financial statements in accordance with International Financial Reporting Standards, and for such internal control as management determines is necessary to enable the preparation of consolidated financial statements that are free from material misstatement, whether due to fraud or error.
Auditor's responsibility paragraph:	*Auditor's Responsibility* Our responsibility is to express an opinion on these consolidated financial statements based on our audit. We conducted our audit in accordance with International Standards on Auditing. Those standards require that we comply with ethical requirements and plan and perform the audit to obtain reasonable assurance about whether the consolidated financial statements are free from material misstatement. An audit involves performing procedures to obtain audit evidence about the amounts and disclosures in the consolidated financial statements. The procedures selected depend on the auditor's judgement, including the assessment of the risks of material misstatement of the consolidated financial statements, whether due to fraud or error. In making those risk assessments, the auditor considers internal control relevant to the entity's preparation and fair presentation of the consolidated financial statements in order to design audit procedures that are appropriate in the circumstances, but not for the purpose of expressing an opinion on the effectiveness of the entity's internal control. An audit also includes evaluating the appropriateness of accounting policies used and the reasonableness of accounting estimates made by management, as well as evaluating the overall presentation of the consolidated financial statements. We believe that the audit evidence we have obtained is sufficient and appropriate to provide a basis for our audit opinion.

Auditor's opinion paragraph:	*Opinion* In our opinion, the consolidated financial statements present fairly, in all material respects, the financial position of EarthWear Clothiers and its subsidiaries as at 31 December 2009, and their financial performance and cash flows for the year then ended in accordance with International Financial Reporting Standards.
Auditor's signature:	Willis & Adams International *M. J. Willis* M. J. Willis, Partner
Date of the auditor's report:	15 February 2010
Auditor's address:	Europolis

The auditor uses the phrase 'present fairly, in all material respects' to communicate that he or she has concluded that the financial statements are free from material misstatements. An equivalent phrase to 'present fairly, in all material respects' is 'give a true and fair view of'. If the applicable financial reporting framework does not acknowledge fair presentation, the auditor's opinion uses the phrase 'prepared, in all material respects'. This book generally refers to financial reporting frameworks that acknowledge fair presentation such as IFRSs.

In some jurisdictions the audit may be conducted in accordance with both ISAs and auditing standards of the jurisdiction. The audit report should still, at a minimum, include each of the nine elements in the audit report with an unmodified opinion above. The auditor should refer to both the ISAs and the auditing standards of the jurisdiction. The jurisdiction or country should be disclosed.

In some jurisdictions the auditor is required or permitted, in addition to expressing an opinion on the financial statements, to report on other responsibilities. For example, the auditor may be required to express an opinion on the adequacy of the entity's accounting records and books. These other reporting responsibilities shall be addressed in a separate section in the audit report after the paragraph on the opinion on the financial statements and be sub-titled 'Report on Other Legal and Regulatory Requirements'. Such separation attains comparability of reporting on the financial statements and allows flexibility to deal with local circumstances.

AN EMPHASIS OF MATTER PARAGRAPH OR OTHER MATTER PARAGRAPH ADDED IN THE AUDIT REPORT

LO2

The auditor may in an audit report be required to or judge it necessary to draw users' attention to: (1) a matter, although appropriately presented or disclosed in the financial statements, that is of such importance that it is fundamental to users' understanding of the financial statements; or (2) an other matter that is relevant to users' understanding of the audit, the auditor's responsibilities or the auditor's report. An **emphasis of matter paragraph** included in the audit report refers to a matter appropriately presented or disclosed in the financial statements while an **other matter paragraph** refers to a matter other than those presented or disclosed in the financial statements relevant to users' understanding of the audit, the auditor's responsibilities or the auditor's report.

When the auditor includes an emphasis of matter paragraph in the auditor's report, sufficient appropriate audit evidence has been obtained that the matter is not materially misstated in the financial statements. The emphasis of matter paragraph is included immediately after the opinion paragraph in the audit report and the heading 'Emphasis of Matter' is ordinarily used. The paragraph includes a clear reference to the matter being emphasized and to where relevant disclosures that fully describe the matter can be found in the financial statements. The auditor should indicate that the auditor's opinion is not modified in respect of the matter emphasized.

A basic assumption that underlies financial reporting is that an entity will continue as a going concern (i.e. that it will stay in business). As discussed in Chapter 17, auditing standards (ISA 570) state that the auditor has a responsibility to evaluate whether there is a material uncertainty that may cast significant doubt about the entity's ability to continue as a going concern. When such material uncertainty exists, the auditor considers the possible effects on the financial statements and the related disclosures. If adequate disclosure is made in the financial statements, the audit report should include an emphasis of matter paragraph, such as the one shown in Exhibit 18–2. The emphasis of matter paragraph draws users' attention to the going-concern uncertainty that is adequately disclosed in the financial statements. If the entity's disclosures with respect to the entity's ability to continue as a going concern are inadequate, a departure from the applicable financial reporting framework exists, resulting in a qualified or an **adverse opinion** (discussed later in this chapter).

Exhibit 18–2   Audit Report with Unmodified Opinion and with an Emphasis of Matter Paragraph for Going-Concern Problems

INDEPENDENT AUDITOR'S REPORT

[Standard wording for the introductory, management's responsibility, auditor's responsibility and opinion paragraphs]

Emphasis of Matter

Without qualifying our opinion, we draw attention to Note 7 in the financial statements which indicates that the Company incurred a net loss of €10 million during the year ended 31 December 2009 and, as of that date, the Company's current liabilities exceeded its total assets by €50 million. These conditions, along with other matters as set forth in Note 11, indicate the existence of a material uncertainty that may cast significant doubt about the Company's ability to continue as a going concern.

Source: Adapted from ISA 570 *Going Concern*, IAASB (2009).

In addition to the going-concern situation, the auditor is also required to add an emphasis of matter paragraph or other matter paragraph to communicate to users in a new or amended audit report in the situations where previously issued financial statements were amended and a new or amended audit report is provided (discussed in Chapter 17). A section later in this chapter discusses the use of an emphasis of matter paragraph in the auditor's report on financial statements prepared in accordance with a special purpose framework. Exhibit 18–12 shows an audit report with an emphasis of a matter paragraph alerting the users of the report that the financial statements are prepared on a tax basis of accounting.

There may also be other circumstances where the auditor would consider it necessary to include an emphasis of matter paragraph, but only if the matter is of such importance that it is *fundamental* to users' understanding of the financial statements. Auditing standards (ISA 706) make it clear that a widespread use of emphasis of matter paragraphs diminishes the effectiveness of the auditor's communication of such matters. Additionally, to include more information in an emphasis of matter paragraph than is presented or disclosed in the financial statements may imply that the matter has not been appropriately presented or disclosed in the financial statements. This restricted view on the use of emphasis of matter paragraphs is clearly reflected in the examples given in auditing standards of circumstances where the auditor may consider it necessary to include an emphasis of matter paragraph:

- An uncertainty relating to the future outcome of exceptional litigation or regulatory action.
- Early application (where permitted) of a new accounting standard that has a **pervasive** effect on the financial statements in advance of its effective date.
- A major catastrophe that has had, or continues to have, a significant effect on the entity's financial position.

In addition to an emphasis of matter paragraph, an other matter paragraph may be included in the audit report. The term 'other matter' is used because the matter communicated is a matter other than those that are presented or disclosed in the financial statements. The other matter must relate to the understanding of the audit, the auditor's responsibilities or the auditor's report. An other matter paragraph is headed 'Other Matter' and the paragraph is included in the audit report immediately after the opinion paragraph and any emphasis of matter paragraph. The paragraph should not include information that is required to be provided by management, and the content of an other matter paragraph should reflect clearly that such other matter is not required to be presented and disclosed in the financial statements.

Auditing standards refer to circumstances relevant to users' understanding of the audit, the auditor's responsibilities or the auditor's report where the auditor may consider it necessary to include an other matter paragraph. For example, auditor may include an other matter paragraph if an entity prepares one set of financial statements in accordance with two acceptable financial reporting frameworks and engages the auditor to report on both sets of financial statements. The other matter paragraph should then refer to the fact that another set of financial statements has been prepared by the same entity in accordance with another framework and that the auditor has issued a report on those financial statements. Sections later in this chapter discuss the use of other matter paragraphs in the auditor's report related to comparative financial statements, and to other information in document containing audited financial statements (refer to Exhibit 18–11). Exhibit 18–3 illustrates an audit report with an other matter paragraph related to the circumstance that the prior period **corresponding figures** included in the current period financial statements, were audited by a predecessor auditor.

Exhibit 18–3   Audit Report with an Other Matter Paragraph for Prior Period Corresponding Figures Audited by a Predecessor Auditor

INDEPENDENT AUDITOR'S REPORT

[Standard wording for the introductory, management's responsibility, auditor's responsibility and opinion paragraphs]
Other Matter
The financial statements of Kappa Company for the year ended 31 December 2008 were audited by another auditor who expressed an unmodified opinion on those statements on 31 March 2009.
Source: Adapted from ISA 510 *Initial Engagements – Opening Balances*, IAASB (2009).

If the auditor expects to include an emphasis of matter paragraph or an other matter paragraph in the auditor's report, the auditor communicates with those charged with governance regarding this expectation and the proposed wording of this paragraph.

It is important to understand that the inclusion of an emphasis of matter paragraph or other matter paragraph in the audit report does not affect the auditor's opinion. An emphasis of matter paragraph or other matter paragraph is not a substitute for either disclosures in the financial statements that the applicable financial reporting framework requires management to make, or the auditor's expression of a modified opinion when required by the circumstances. Audit reports with modification of the auditor's opinion are discussed in the next section.

Practice Insight 18.1

The credit crisis and economic downturn have led to a lack of available credit to entities of all sizes, which may affect an entity's ability to continue as a going concern; this and other factors may be relevant in the auditor's evaluation of forecasts prepared by management to support its going-concern assessment.

Consideration of the need for an emphasis of matter paragraph in the auditor's report will be a difficult matter of judgement to be made in the context of the entity's circumstances; the mere existence of the credit crisis, though referred to in the financial statements, does not of itself create the need for an emphasis.

Source: Staff Audit Practice Alert: Audit Considerations in Respect of Going Concern in the Current Economic Environment, IAASB (2009).

AUDIT REPORTS WITH MODIFIED OPINION

While the vast majority of auditors' opinions expressed are unmodified, the auditor can assume differing degrees of responsibility on financial statements by expressing opinions that depart from the unmodified opinion. There are three such types of modified opinions available to the auditor. We next discuss the conditions for expressing opinions that depart from the unmodified opinion, and we then explain the nature of audit reports with modifications in opinion.

❖ Conditions for Modification

LO3

To this point we have been discussing the audit report with an unmodified opinion, without and with additional emphasis of matter paragraph or other matter paragraph. Let us now take a look at the circumstances in which an auditor's opinion might depart from an unmodified or 'clean' opinion. An auditor may be unable to express an unmodified opinion in two situations:

1   *Scope limitation.* A **scope limitation** results from the auditor's inability to obtain sufficient appropriate evidence, such as when management or some set of circumstances prevents the auditor from conducting an audit procedure that the auditor considers necessary.

2   *Departure from applicable financial reporting framework.* A departure from the applicable financial reporting framework exists when the financial statements are prepared or presented in a manner that conflicts with the applicable financial reporting framework, whether due to errors or fraud.

❖ Types of Audit Reports with Modified Opinion

LO4

The three types of audit reports with modified opinions are:

1   *Audit Reports with a Qualified Opinion.* The auditor expresses a **qualified opinion** when the effects of the possible misstatements on the financial statements due to a scope limitation *or* the effects of misstatements on the financial statements due to specific departure from the applicable financial reporting framework, are material but not pervasive. If the auditor decides to qualify an opinion for a scope limitation, the report describes why the limitation arose, and indicates that the financial statements present fairly *except for* the possible effects of the limitation. If the auditor qualifies an opinion for a departure from the applicable financial reporting framework, the report describes the nature of and the impact of a faulty accounting, and indicates that the financial statements present fairly *except for* the effects of the departure. Note that a qualified opinion always uses the words 'except for'.

2   *Audit Reports with a Disclaimer of Opinion.* The auditor disclaims an opinion when the effects of the possible misstatements on financial statements due to a scope limitation are both material and pervasive. In a disclaimer the auditor explains the reasons for withholding an opinion and explicitly indicates that no opinion is expressed.[ii]

3   *Audit Reports with an Adverse Opinion.* The auditor expresses an adverse opinion when the effects of misstatements on the financial statements due to departure from the applicable financial reporting framework are both material and pervasive. In a report with an adverse opinion the auditor explains the nature of the departure and size of the misstatement that relates to specific amounts, and states the opinion that the financial statements do not present fairly in accordance with the applicable financial reporting framework.

The choice of audit opinion depends on both the nature of the condition giving rise to the departure from the unmodified opinion and the **materiality** and pervasiveness of the effects of the misstatements on the financial statements. Figure 18–1 presents an overview of the auditor's opinion options, including the type of modified opinion to be issued under various conditions and the effects of materiality and pervasiveness on the choice of audit opinion. We believe you will find Figure 18–1 to be one of the most helpful figures presented in this text – study it carefully!

❖ The Effects of Materiality and Pervasiveness on Auditor's Opinion

LO5

The concept of materiality plays a major role in the audit, including in the auditor's choice of audit opinion. If the departure or the inability to obtain sufficient appropriate evidence is judged by the auditor to have immaterial effects on the financial statements, an unmodified opinion can be expressed.

When the auditor is faced with a *scope limitation*, the assessment of the omitted procedure(s) should include the nature and magnitude of the potential effects of the unexamined area to the financial statements. If the potential effects relate to many items that could represent a substantial portion of the financial statements, the auditor is likely to issue an audit report with a disclaimer rather than with a qualified opinion. In other words, the *pervasiveness* of the scope limitation's effects on the financial statements determines whether the auditor should issue a qualified opinion or disclaim an opinion. Auditing standards (ISA 705) define pervasive and pervasive effects on the financial statement as follows:

> A term used, in the context of misstatements, to describe the effects on the financial statements of misstatements or the possible effects on the financial statements of misstatements, if any, that are undetected due to an inability to obtain sufficient appropriate audit evidence.
>
> Pervasive effects on the financial statements are those that, in the auditor's judgment:
>
> (i)   Are not confined to specific elements, accounts or items of the financial statements;
> (ii) If so confined, represent or could represent a substantial proportion of the financial statements; or
> (iii) In relation to disclosures, are fundamental to users' understanding of the financial statements.

For example, suppose an auditor is unable to perform certain audit procedures considered necessary in determining the fairness of a client's inventory balance. Assume further that inventory represents approximately 10 per cent of total assets. In such a situation, the auditor would probably consider the item

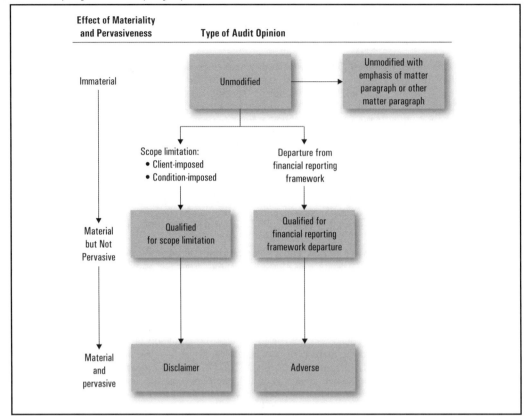

Figure 18–1 An Overview of Audit Opinions

material, but not pervasive, and would most likely issue a qualified opinion. However, if inventory represents a much larger percentage of total assets (such as 30 to 50 per cent), the possible effect on the financial statements is pervasive and would thus lead the auditor to disclaim an opinion on the financial statements.

Judgements concerning the effects of a *departure from the financial reporting framework* are handled similarly. If the departure from the framework is immaterial, the auditor issues an unmodified opinion. If the departure from the framework is material but not pervasive, the auditor issues a qualified opinion. If the departure is material and pervasive, the auditor issues an adverse opinion. For example, suppose that a client accounted for leased assets as operating leases when proper accounting required that the leases be capitalized. If a client had only one small piece of equipment that was treated in such a manner, the auditor would probably issue an unmodified opinion because the item would be immaterial. However, if the client had many leased assets that were accounted for as operating leases instead of capitalized leases, the auditor will normally issue a qualified or adverse opinion, depending on the magnitude of the problem.

DISCUSSION OF CONDITIONS REQUIRING AUDIT REPORTS WITH MODIFIED OPINION

Scope Limitation

A scope limitation results from an inability to obtain sufficient appropriate evidence about some element of the financial statements. This occurs because the auditor is unable to apply all the audit procedures considered necessary. Such restrictions on the scope of the audit may be imposed by the circumstances of the engagement or by the client. An example of a client-imposed limitation occurs when the client requests that the auditor not confirm accounts receivable because of concerns over customer relations. If the auditor is satisfied that the client's reasons for not confirming are legitimate and is unable to apply alternative audit procedures to determine fairness of the receivables, he or she would qualify the opinion or disclaim an opinion depending on the pervasiveness of accounts receivable in the context of the financial statements. Auditors should be particularly cautious when a client limits the scope of the engagement because in such a situation the client may be trying to prevent the auditor from discovering material misstatements. Auditing standards suggest that when restrictions imposed by the client significantly limit the scope of the engagement, the auditor should consider disclaiming an opinion on the financial statements. If the auditor concludes that a qualification of the opinion will be inadequate to communicate the gravity of the situation, the auditor should where practicable and possible under applicable law or regulation withdraw from the audit.

Scope limitations may also arise due to reasons beyond the control of the client such as a fire that destroys accounting records, or from circumstances related to the timing or nature of the auditor's work. If the auditor can overcome such limitations by performing alternative procedures, an audit report with an unmodified opinion can be issued. A number of these types of situations can occur on audit engagements. For example, auditing standards require that the auditor observes the physical inventory count (ISA 501). However, circumstances may prevent the auditor from doing so. Suppose that the auditor is not engaged to conduct the audit until after the end of the period. In such a circumstance, the auditor may not be able to perform a number of audit procedures, including observing the year-end inventory count. If such deficiencies in evidence cannot be overcome by other auditing procedures, the auditor will have to issue a qualified opinion or a disclaimer. Exhibit 18–4 is an example of an audit report with a **disclaimer of opinion** due to this type of scope limitation.

Exhibit 18–4   Audit Report with a Disclaimer of Audit Opinion: Scope Limitation

INDEPENDENT AUDITOR'S REPORT

We were engaged to audit the accompanying financial statements of Kosar Company, which comprise the balance sheet as at 31 December 2009, and the income statement, statement of changes in equity and cash flow statement for the year then ended, and a summary of significant accounting policies and other explanatory information.

[*Standard wording for the management's responsibility paragraph*]

Auditor's Responsibility

Our responsibility is to express an opinion on these financial statements based on conducting the audit in accordance with International Standards on Auditing. Because of the matters described in the Basis for Disclaimer of Opinion paragraph, however, we were not able to obtain sufficient appropriate audit evidence to provide a basis for an audit opinion.

Basis for Disclaimer of Opinion

We were not appointed as auditors of the Company until after 31 December 2009 and thus did not observe the counting of physical inventories at the beginning and end of the year. We were unable to satisfy ourselves by alternative means concerning the inventory quantities held at 31 December 2008 and 2009 which are stated in the balance sheet at €4,250,000 and €4,575,000, respectively. As a result, we were unable to determine whether any adjustments might have been found necessary in respect of recorded or unrecorded inventories, and the elements making up the income statement and the statement of changes in equity and cash flow statement.

Disclaimer of Opinion

Because of the significance of the matters described in the Basis for Disclaimer of Opinion paragraph, we have not been able to obtain sufficient appropriate audit evidence to provide a basis for an audit opinion. Accordingly, we do not express an opinion on the financial statements.

Source: Adapted from ISA 705 *Modifications to the Opinion in the Independent Auditor's Report*, IAASB (2009).

Another example occurs when where the auditor is unable to obtain sufficient appropriate audit evidence regarding an investment in a foreign affiliate. Exhibit 18–5 is an example of an audit report with a qualified opinion for such a scope limitation. The possible effects of the inability to obtain sufficient appropriate audit evidence are deemed to be material but not pervasive to the financial statements.

Exhibit 18–5   Audit Report with a Qualified Opinion: Scope Limitation

INDEPENDENT AUDITOR'S REPORT

[*Standard wording for the introductory and management's responsibility paragraphs*]

Auditor's Responsibility

[*Same wording as for the standard auditor's responsibility paragraph, except for last sentence*]

We believe that the audit evidence we have obtained is sufficient and appropriate to provide a basis for our qualified audit opinion.

Basis for Qualified Opinion

Alfa Company's investment in Beta Company, a foreign associate acquired during the year and accounted for by the equity method, is carried at €12,500,000 on the balance sheet as at 31 December 2009, and Alfa's share of Beta's net income of €1,200,000 is included in Alfa's income for the year then ended. We were unable to obtain sufficient appropriate audit evidence about the carrying amount of Alfa's investment in Beta as at 31 December 2009 and Alfa's share of Beta's net income for the year because we were denied access to the financial information, management, and the auditors of Beta. Consequently, we were unable to determine whether any adjustments to these amounts were necessary.

Qualified Opinion

In our opinion, except for the possible effects of the matter described in the Basis for Qualified Opinion paragraph, the financial statements present fairly, ... [*same wording as for the remainder of the standard opinion paragraph*].

Source: Adapted from ISA 705 *Modifications to the Opinion in the Independent Auditor's Report*, IAASB (2009).

Note that in both examples the paragraph that explains the scope limitation is presented *before* the opinion or disclaimer paragraph. Before you proceed, imagine a situation where that the auditor determines that performing substantive procedures alone is not sufficient to provide audit evidence, but the entity's controls are not effective. Under what conditions would you consider it appropriate to qualify or to disclaim the opinion?

Departure from Applicable Financial Reporting Framework

If the financial statements are materially affected by departure from the applicable financial reporting framework, the auditor should express a qualified or adverse opinion. Such departures include inappropriate selection or application of accounting policies, and inadequate or inappropriate disclosures in the financial statements.

When the financial statements include an accounting policy that is not appropriate, the auditor may issue a qualified or adverse opinion, depending on the materiality and pervasiveness of the misstatements. When the auditor expresses a qualified opinion, a separate paragraph explaining the basis for the opinion is added to the report *before* the opinion paragraph. The basis for opinion paragraph discloses the effects of the departure on the financial statements. Exhibit 18–6 is an example of an audit report with an opinion that has been qualified because a selected accounting policy is inconsistent with the applicable financial reporting framework. In addition the audit report includes an emphasis of matter paragraph for an uncertainty relating to a pending exceptional litigation matter.

Exhibit 18–6   Audit Report with a Qualified Opinion: Departure from the Financial Reporting Framework

INDEPENDENT AUDITOR'S REPORT

[*Standard wording for the introductory and management's responsibility paragraphs*]

Auditor's Responsibility

[*Same wording as for the standard auditor's responsibility paragraph, except for last sentence*]

We believe that the audit evidence we have obtained is sufficient and appropriate to provide a basis for our qualified audit opinion.

Basis for Qualified Opinion

The Company's short-term marketable securities are carried in the balance sheet at €47,570,000. Management has not marked these securities to market but has instead stated them at cost, which constitutes a departure from International Financial Reporting Standards. The Company's records indicate that had management marked the marketable securities to market, the company would have recognized an unrealized loss of €15,460 in the income statement for the year. The carrying amount of the securities in the balance sheet and shareholders' equity at 31 December 2009 would have been reduced by the same amount.

Qualified Opinion

In our opinion, except for the effects of the matter described in the Basis for Qualified Opinion paragraph, the financial statements present fairly, ... [*same wording as for the remainder of the standard opinion paragraph*].

Emphasis of Matter

We draw attention to Note 17 to the financial statements which describes the uncertainty related to the outcome of the lawsuit filed against the company by Gamma Company. Our opinion is not qualified in respect of this matter.
Source: Adapted from ISA 706 *Emphasis of Matter Paragraphs and Other Matter Paragraphs in the Independent Auditor's Report*, IAASB (2009).

If the departure's effect is pervasive on the financial statements, the auditor issues an adverse opinion. When an adverse opinion is issued, the auditor adds a paragraph explaining the basis for the adverse opinion that *precedes* the opinion paragraph. The basis for the adverse opinion paragraph discusses the reasons for the adverse opinion and the effects of the departure on the financial statements. The opinion paragraph is modified to state that the financial statements *do not present fairly* in accordance with the financial reporting framework. Exhibit 18–7 is an example of an audit report with an adverse opinion due to the non-consolidation of a subsidiary. In this example the effects of the misstatement on the financial statements are not determined because it is not practicable to do so.

Exhibit 18–7 Audit Report with an Adverse Opinion: Departure from the Financial Reporting Framework
INDEPENDENT AUDITOR'S REPORT
[*Standard wording for the introductory and management's responsibility paragraphs*]
[*Same wording as for the standard auditor's responsibility paragraph, except for last sentence*]
We believe that the audit evidence we have obtained is sufficient and appropriate to provide a basis for our adverse audit opinion.
Basis for Adverse Opinion
As explained in Note 7, the Delta Company has not consolidated the financial statements of subsidiary Epsilon Company it acquired during 2009 because it has not yet been able to ascertain the fair values of certain of the subsidiary's material assets and liabilities at the acquisition date. This investment is therefore accounted for on a cost basis. Under International Financial Reporting Standards, the subsidiary should have been consolidated because it is controlled by the company. Had Epsilon Company been consolidated, many elements in the accompanying financial statements would have been materially affected. The effects on the financial statements of the failure to consolidate have not been determined.
Adverse Opinion
In our opinion, because of the significance of the matter discussed in the Basis for Adverse Opinion paragraph, the consolidated financial statements do not present fairly the financial position of Delta Company and its subsidiaries as at 31 December 2009 and their financial performance and cash flows for the year then ended in accordance with International Financial Reporting Standards.
Source: Adapted from ISA 705 *Modifications to the Opinion in the Independent Auditor's Report*, IAASB (2009).

If a client fails to disclose information in the financial statements as required by the applicable financial reporting framework, the auditor may issue a qualified or adverse opinion, depending on the materiality and pervasiveness of the omission. The auditor should provide the omitted information in the basis for modification paragraph, if practicable. For example, one situation in which the auditor would modify the opinion but would not have to provide the missing information is where the client has declined to include a cash flow statement. Exhibit 18–8 is a report with a qualified opinion for inadequate disclosure.

Exhibit 18–8 Audit Report with a Qualified Opinion: Inadequate Disclosure
INDEPENDENT AUDITOR'S REPORT
[*Standard wording for the introductory and management's responsibility paragraphs*]
Auditor's Responsibility
[*Same wording as for the standard auditor's responsibility paragraph, except for last sentence*]
We believe that the audit evidence we have obtained is sufficient and appropriate to provide a basis for our qualified audit opinion.
Basis for Qualified Opinion
The Company declined to present a cash flow statement for the year ended 31 December 2009. The omission constitutes a departure from International Financial Reporting Standards.
Qualified Opinion
In our opinion, except for the omission of cash flow statement described in the Basis for Qualified Opinion paragraph, the financial statements present fairly, in all material respects, the financial position of the Zeta Company as at 31 December 2009, and their financial performance then ended in accordance with International Financial Reporting Standards.

When the auditor expects to modify the opinion in the auditor's report, the auditor communicates with those charged with governance the circumstances that led to the expected modification and the proposed wording of the modification.

Finally, as a practical matter, qualified and adverse opinions are quite rare because most clients are willing to make the financial statement adjustments needed in order to obtain a clean opinion.

SPECIAL REPORTING ISSUES

In addition to the types of audit reports just discussed, auditors encounter a number of special reporting issues that affect the auditor's report of audited financial information. Three topics are covered in the remainder of the sections of the chapter:

1   Reports on comparative information.
2   Other information in documents containing audited financial statements.
3   Reports on specialized areas.

❖ REPORTING ON COMPARATIVE INFORMATION

LO6

Ordinarily financial reporting frameworks require comparative information of one or more prior periods in the financial statements. Such information is useful for users of financial statements, for example to identify financial trends and changes in the entity's financial performance over period of time. The auditor should obtain sufficient appropriate audit evidence about whether the comparative information included in the financial statements has been presented, in all material respects, in accordance with the requirements for comparative information in the applicable financial reporting framework.

Comparative information may be corresponding figures or **comparative financial statements**. *Corresponding figures* are comparative information where amounts and other disclosures for the prior periods are an integral part of the current-period financial statements, and are intended to be read only in relation to current-period figures. The level of detail presented in the corresponding figures is determined primarily by its relevance to the current-period figures. *Comparative financial statements* are considered separate financial statements and are included for comparison with the financial statements of the current period. The level of information included in comparative financial statements is comparable with that of the financial statements of the current period.

Auditing standards (ISA 700) require that the auditor in the introductory paragraph of the audit report specifies the date or period covered by each financial statement comprising the audited financial statements (or the financial statement the auditor was engaged to audit if the auditor disclaims the opinion). The paragraph expressing the auditor's opinion includes the same information. For corresponding figures, the audit report ordinarily refers to the financial statements of the current period *only*. For comparative financial statements the audit report refers to each period for which financial statements are presented. Note that to this book generally relates to auditor's reporting on financial statements with corresponding figures which are the most common type of comparative information internationally.

For both types of comparative information the auditor determines whether the financial statements include the comparative information required by the applicable financial reporting framework and whether such information is appropriately classified. The extent of audit procedures performed on comparative information is significantly less than for the audit of the current-period financial statements. Relevant audit procedures include assessment of consistency in application of accounting policies in the prior period with the current period, and agreement of the comparative information with the amounts and disclosure presented in the prior period. When the auditor becomes aware of a possible material misstatement in the prior-year figures when performing the current-period audit, the auditor performs additional appropriate audit procedures (refer to Chapter 17).

Corresponding figures are included as an integral part of the current-period financial statements. When corresponding figures are presented, the audit report ordinarily refers to the financial statements of the current period only. In some circumstances, however, the audit report should also refer to the corresponding figures. For example, this occurs when the auditor's report in the prior period included a modified opinion and the matter which gave rise to the modification is *unresolved*. In this circumstance the auditor should modify the opinion on the current-period financial statements and refer to the corresponding figures in the paragraph that explain the basis for the modification. Exhibit 18–9 illustrates an audit report with a qualified opinion due to that the audit report on the prior period included a qualified opinion and where the matter giving rise to that qualification is unresolved.

Exhibit 18–9   Corresponding Figures: Audit Report with a Qualified Opinion

INDEPENDENT AUDITOR'S REPORT

We have audited the accompanying financial statements of Company, which comprise the balance sheet as at 31 December 2009, and the income statement, statement of changes in equity and cash flow statement for the year then ended, and a summary of significant accounting policies and other explanatory information.

[*Standard wording for the management's responsibility paragraph*]

Auditor's Responsibility

[*Same wording as for the standard auditor's responsibility paragraph, except for last sentence*]

We believe that the audit evidence we have obtained is sufficient and appropriate to provide a basis for our qualified audit opinion.

Basis for Qualified Opinion

As discussed in Note 5 to the financial statements, no depreciation has been provided in the financial statements, which constitutes a departure from International Financial Reporting Standards. This is the result of a decision taken by management at the start of the preceding financial year and caused us to qualify our audit opinion on the financial statements relating to that year. Based on the straight-line method of depreciation and annual rates of 5 per cent for the building and 20 per cent for the equipment, the loss for the year should be increased by 6,000,000 in 2009 and 6,000,000 in 2008, property, plant and equipment should be reduced by accumulated depreciation of 12,000,000 in 2009 and 6,000,000 in 2008, and the accumulated loss should be increased by 12,000,000 in 2009 and 6,000,000 in 2008.

Qualified Opinion

In our opinion, except for the effects of the matter described in the Basis for Qualified Opinion paragraph, the financial statements present fairly, in all material respects, the financial position of the Eta Company as at 31 December 2009, and its financial performance and its cash flows for the year then ended in accordance with International Financial Reporting Standards.

Source: Adapted from ISA 710 *Comparative Information – Corresponding Figures and Comparative Financial Statements*, IAASB (2009).

In Exhibit 18–9 the auditor's opinion on the current period's financial statements is modified because the effects of unresolved matter on the current period's figures are material. When such effects are immaterial, the opinion on the current period's financial statements may nevertheless be of modified because of the effects of the unresolved matter on the comparability of the current period's figures and the corresponding figures. However, when the matter which gave rise to the modified opinion on the prior period is resolved and properly dealt with in the financial statements, the current period audit report does not ordinarily refer to the previous modification.

The prior-period financial statements may be audited by a predecessor auditor. If not prohibited by law or regulation and the auditor decides to do so, the auditor refers to the predecessor auditor's report on the corresponding figures in an other matter paragraph such as illustrated in Exhibit 18–3. If the predecessor's opinion were modified, the reasons therefore are also disclosed. When the prior-period financial statements are not audited, the auditor states in an other matter paragraph that the corresponding figures are unaudited. Such a statement does not, however, relieve the auditor of the requirement to perform appropriate audit procedures regarding opening balances of the current period.

When the comparative information are presented as comparative financial statements, the audit opinion is expressed individually on the financial statements of each period presented. The comparative financial statements are specifically identified in the introductory and opinion paragraph of the audit report. Exhibit 18–10 is an example of an audit report with an unmodified opinion covering comparative financial statements.

Exhibit 18–10   Comparative Financial Statements: Audit Report with an Unmodified Opinion

INDEPENDENT AUDITOR'S REPORT

We have audited the accompanying financial statements of the Psi Company, which comprise the balance sheets as at 31 December 2009 and 2008, and the income statements, statements of changes in equity and cash flow statements for the years then ended, and a summary of significant accounting policies and other explanatory information.

[*Standard wording for the management's responsibility and auditor's responsibility paragraphs*]

Opinion

In our opinion, the financial statements present fairly, in all material respects, the financial position of the Psi Company as of 31 December 2009 and 2008, and of its financial performance and its cash flows for the years then ended in accordance with International Financial Reporting Standards.

The auditor may express a qualified or an adverse opinion, disclaim an opinion, or add an emphasis of matter paragraph or other matter paragraph with respect to one or more financial statements for one or more periods, while issuing a different report on the other financial statements. This follows since the audit report on comparative financial statements applies to the individual financial statements presented. Additionally, when reporting on the prior-period financial statements in connection with the current year's audit, the opinion on such prior-period financial statements may be different from the opinion previously expressed. This may arise when the auditor during the course of the audit of the current period becomes aware of circumstances or events that materially affect the comparative financial statements of a prior period. In such a case the auditor should disclose the substantive reasons for the different opinion in an other matter paragraph.

Similar disclosure requirements in an other matter paragraph as those referred to above for corresponding figures should be made when the comparative financial statements were audited by another auditor, unless the predecessor auditor's report on the prior period's financial statements is reissued with the financial statements. When the prior period financial statements are not audited, the auditor states in an other matter paragraph that the comparative financial statements are unaudited.

❖ OTHER INFORMATION IN DOCUMENTS CONTAINING AUDITED
LO7 FINANCIAL STATEMENTS

A client may publish documents, such as annual reports, that contain other information in addition to the audited financial statements and the audit report. Such 'other information' may be financial and non-financial information. Examples of other information include a report by management or those charged with governance of the entity (for example the board of directors), financial summaries or highlights, financial ratios, names of officers and directors, and selected interim data.

The auditor's reporting responsibility is restricted to information identified in the audit report. In some jurisdictions, however, the auditor is obliged to report, in addition to express an opinion on the financial statements, specifically on certain of the other information published in a document that contains the audited financial statements. For example, the auditor may be responsible to audit elements or the entire report of the board of directors or management published together with the audited financial statements in the annual report. In such circumstances the auditor should apply necessary procedures to assure the relevant other information and report as appropriate.

Auditing standards (ISA 720) provide guidance for the auditor's consideration of other information in documents containing audited financial information. Although the auditor has no obligation to perform any audit procedures to corroborate such other information, the auditor is required to read the other information to identify material inconsistencies, if any, with the audited financial statements. This is required since the credibility of the audited financial statements may be undermined by inconsistencies which may exist between other information in documents containing audited financial information and the audited financial statements and audit report thereon.

For example, the audited financial statements may show a 10 per cent increase in sales and a 5 per cent increase in net income. If the management's report that is included in the annual report states that sales were up 15 per cent and net income increased by 12 per cent, a material **inconsistency** would exist. The auditor would then have to determine whether the financial statements or the management's report require revision. When a revision is necessary in the audited financial statements and the entity refuses to make the revision, the auditor modifies the opinion as appropriate. If the financial statements were correct, the auditor would request that management change the other information. If the other information were not revised, the auditor should include an other matter paragraph in the audit report describing the material inconsistency in the audit report, withhold the audit report, or withdraw from the engagement. Exhibit 18–11 illustrates the use of an other matter paragraph for a material inconsistency related to information in the Chairman's Report contained in the annual report.

Exhibit 18–11 Audit Report with an Other Matter Paragraph for Material Inconsistency
INDEPENDENT AUDITOR'S REPORT
[*Standard wording for the introductory, management's responsibility, auditor's responsibility and opinion paragraphs*]
Other Matter
In the Chairman's Report contained in the Annual Report, it is stated that the Company has realized a relative increase in profitability this year over that of the prior year. While this statement is consistent with regard to earnings before interest, taxes, depreciation and amortization (EBITDA), it is inconsistent with regard to profit for the year, which has decreased from last year.
Source: Adapted from (proposed) ISA 706 *Emphasis of Matter Paragraphs and Other Matter Paragraphs in the Independent Auditor's Report*, IAASB (2005).

The auditor may on reading the other information become aware of an apparent material **misstatement of fact**, i.e. information unrelated to matters appearing in the audited financial statements that is incorrectly stated or presented. A material misstatement of fact may undermine the credibility of the document containing audited financial statements. The auditor discusses such misstatement of fact with management and, if necessary, those charged with governance, and may take further appropriate action.

REPORTING ON SPECIALIZED AREAS

Auditors are sometimes engaged to audit financial statements prepared in accordance with a special purpose framework, or engaged to audit single financial statements or elements of a financial statement. Another specialized area is an engagement to report on summary financial statements derived from the audited financial statements. Auditing standards provide the auditor with specific guidance for such engagements. The following sections discuss the auditor's reporting responsibility related to these three specialized areas.

LO8 Reporting on Financial Statements Prepared in Accordance with a Special Purpose Framework

Up to this point we have referred to applicable financial reporting frameworks that are general purpose frameworks. A **general purpose framework** serves the common financial information needs of a wide range of users, such as for example IFRSs. Sometimes the financial statements are prepared in accordance with a special reporting framework. A special reporting framework is designed to meet the financial information needs of *specific users*, for example regulatory bodies or parties in a contractual relationship.

Examples of special purpose frameworks are:

- *Tax basis.* A tax basis of accounting for a set of financial statements that accompany an entity's tax return.
- *Cash basis.* The cash receipts and disbursements basis of accounting for cash flow information that an entity may be requested to prepare for creditors.
- *Regulatory basis.* The financial reporting provisions established by a regulator to meet the requirements of that regulator.
- *Contract basis.* The financial reporting provisions of a contract, such as a bond indenture, a loan agreement or a project grant.

The auditor must determine the acceptability of the special purpose framework. A key factor in this determination is the financial statements needs of the intended users. Auditing standards (ISA 800) deal with special considerations in the application of the ISAs to an audit of **special purpose financial statements**, including the auditor's reporting responsibility discussed in the following.

The special purpose financial statements may be used for purposes other than those for which they were intended. To avoid misunderstandings, the auditor alerts users of the audit report that the financial statements are prepared in accordance with a **special purpose framework** and, therefore, may not be suitable for another purpose. Exhibit 18–12 is an example of an audit report where the financial statements have been prepared by management of a partnership in accordance with a tax basis of accounting to assist the partners in preparing their individual income tax returns. The audit report includes an emphasis of matter paragraph alerting users of the auditor's report that the financial statements are prepared in accordance with a special purpose framework and that, as a result, the financial statements may not be suitable for another purpose.

Exhibit 18–12   Audit Report for Special Purpose Financial Statements

INDEPENDENT AUDITOR'S REPORT

We have audited the accompanying financial statements of Lamda Partnership, which comprise the balance sheet as at 31 December 2009 and the income statement for the year then ended, and a summary of significant accounting policies and other explanatory information. The financial statements have been prepared by management using the tax basis of accounting in Jurisdiction X.

Management's Responsibility for the Financial Statements

Management is responsible for the preparation of these financial statements in accordance with the tax basis of accounting in Jurisdiction X, and for such internal control as management determines is necessary to enable the preparation of financial statements that are free from material misstatement, whether due to fraud or error.

[Standard wording for the auditor's responsibility paragraph]
Opinion
In our opinion, the financial statements of Lamda Partnership for the year ended 31 December 2009 are prepared, in all material respects, in accordance with the Income Tax Law of Jurisdiction X.
Basis of Accounting and Restriction on Distribution
Without modifying our opinion, we draw attention to Note 1 to the financial statements, which describes the basis of accounting. The financial statements are prepared to assist the partners of Lamda Partnership in preparing their individual income tax returns. As a result, the financial statements may not be suitable for another purpose. Our report is intended solely for Lamda Partnership and its partners and should not be distributed to parties other than Lamda Partnership or its partners.
Source: Adapted from ISA 800 *Special Considerations – Audits of Financial Statements Prepared in Accordance with Special Purpose Frameworks*, IAASB (2009).

Note that in this example the distribution of the report is restricted and management does not have a choice of financial reporting framework. If management has a choice of special purpose frameworks in the preparation of such financial statements, the management's responsibility paragraph also refers to management's responsibility for determining that the framework applied is acceptable in the circumstances.

If the financial statements are not prepared in accordance with the special purpose framework applied, the auditor modifies the opinion as appropriate.

Reporting on Single Financial Statements or Elements of a Financial Statement

LO9

The term financial statements ordinarily refer to a complete set of financial statements. The requirements of the applicable financial reporting framework determine what constitutes a complete set of financial statements. Ordinarily a complete set of financial statements includes a balance sheet, an income statement, a statement of changes in equity, a cash-flow statement and related notes. The related notes ordinarily comprise a summary of significant accounting policies and other explanatory information. In some situations an auditor may be engaged to audit a single financial statement (e.g. the balance sheet) or elements of a financial statement such as accounts and items. This may, for example, relate to reports on rentals, royalties, profit participation, employments bonuses or provision for income taxes. The financial reporting framework applied may be a general purpose or a special purpose framework.

Generally, an audit of specific elements of financial statements is more extensive than if the same information were considered as part of an audit of the complete set of financial statements. Materiality needs to be set in relation to the individual element (or the single financial statement), and the auditor should consider how the element relates to other parts of the financial statements. For example, if the auditor is engaged to audit the entity's accounts receivable, other accounts such as sales and allowance for bad debts should also be considered.

An engagement to express an opinion on a single financial statement or a specific element of a financial statement may be performed as a separate engagement or in conjunction with an engagement to audit the entity's complete set of financial statements. When part of an audit of the entire financial statements, the auditor expresses a separate opinion on each engagement. The auditor cannot express an unmodified opinion on a *single financial statement* of a complete set of financial statements if the auditor has expressed an adverse opinion or disclaimed an opinion on the complete set of financial statements. Only when the opinions are not published together and the specific element does not constitute a major portion of the entity's complete set of financial statements may the auditor express an unmodified opinion on the *element* if an adverse opinion or disclaimed opinion is expressed on the complete set of financial statements.

Suppose an auditor is engaged to issue a special report on gross sales for a client whose rent payment is contingent on the total amount of sales for the period and a fair presentation general purpose framework is applied. The introductory, management's responsibility, auditor's responsibility and opinion paragraphs of the audit report then differ from the standard text only by its references to the account being audited. If a specific purpose framework were applied, an emphasis of matter paragraph would have been added to highlight the use of a specific purpose framework.

Rather than auditing specified elements, an auditor may be engaged to apply only *agreed-upon procedures*. An engagement to apply agreed-upon procedures is one in which the auditor is engaged by a client to issue a *report of factual findings* based on specific, agreed-upon procedures performed regarding the financial information such as a specified element of a financial statement. The report does not express an opinion; it simply reports the results of the procedures that were conducted. Standards on engagements to perform agreed-upon procedures provide the auditor with the guidance for such engagements (discussed in Chapter 20).

❖ Reporting on Summary Financial Statements

LO10   An auditor may be asked to report on summary financial statements derived from financial statements audited in accordance with ISAs by that same auditor. For example, the client may include summary financial statements in the annual report or in other reports. The summary financial statements contain aggregated information and limited disclosure, and are therefore in nature less detailed than the financial statements. They still provide a structured representation consistent with that provided by the financial statements. The criteria for the preparation of summary financial statements may be established by a standards-setting organization or by law or regulation, or developed by management, for example, based on practice in a particular industry.

Auditing standards (ISA 810) provide guidance on auditor's reporting on summary financial statements. Exhibit 18–13 illustrates an auditor's report on summary financial statements with an unmodified opinion. In the example, the summary financial statements are prepared in accordance with criteria developed by management. The auditor has found the applied criteria acceptable and has assured that the criteria are adequately disclosed in the summary financial statements.

Exhibit 18–13   Auditor's Report on Summary Financial Statements

REPORT OF THE INDEPENDENT AUDITOR ON THE SUMMARY FINANCIAL STATEMENTS

The accompanying summary financial statements, which comprise the summary balance sheet as at 31 December 2009, the summary income statement, summary statement of changes in equity and summary cash flow statement for the year then ended, and related notes, are derived from the audited financial statements of Omicron Company for the year ended 31 December 2009. We expressed an unmodified audit opinion on those financial statements in our report dated 15 February 2010.

The summary financial statements do not contain all the disclosures required by International Financial Reporting Standards. Reading the summary financial statements, therefore, is not a substitute for reading the audited financial statements of Omicron Company.

Management's Responsibility for the Summary Financial Statements

Management is responsible for the preparation of a summary of the audited financial statements on the basis described in Note 2.

Auditor's Responsibility

Our responsibility is to express an opinion on the summary financial statements based on our procedures, which were conducted in accordance with International Standard on Auditing (ISA) 810, 'Engagements to Report on Summary Financial Statements'.

Opinion

In our opinion, the summary financial statements derived from the audited financial statements of Omicron Company for the year ended 31 December 2009 are consistent, in all material respects, with those financial statements, on the basis described in Note 2.

Source: Adapted from ISA 810 *Engagements to Report on Summary Financial Statements*, IAASB (2009).

When fair presentation reporting criteria are applied, the auditor's unmodified opinion expresses that the summary financial statements are a fair summary of the audited financial statements.

When the auditor's report on the audited financial statements contains a qualified opinion, an emphasis of matter paragraph or an other matter paragraph, the auditor states this fact in the report of the summary financial statements, and describes their basis and effect thereof on the summary financial statements. When the auditor's report on the audited financial statements includes an adverse opinion or a disclaimer of opinion, the auditor in addition states that, as a result of the adverse opinion or disclaimer of opinion, it is inappropriate to express an opinion on the summary financial statements. If the summary financial statements are not consistent with (not a fair summary of) the audited financial statements, the auditor expresses an adverse opinion on the summary financial statements.

🔑 Key Terms

Adverse opinion. The auditor's opinion that the financial statements do not present fairly in accordance with the applicable financial reporting framework due to departure from the applicable financial reporting framework that materially and pervasively affects the financial statements.

Annual report. A document issued by an entity, ordinarily on an annual basis, which includes its audited financial statements and the auditor's report.

Comparative financial statements. Comparative information where amounts and other disclosures for the prior period are included for comparison with the financial statements of the current period.

Comparative information. The amounts and disclosures included in the financial statements in respect of one or more prior periods in accordance with the applicable financial reporting framework.

Corresponding figures. Comparative information where amounts and other disclosures for the prior period are included as an integral part of the current-period financial statements, and are intended to be read only in relation to the amounts and other disclosures relating to the current period.

Disclaimer of opinion. The auditor expresses no opinion on the financial statements due to a scope limitation that materially and pervasively affects the financial statements.

Emphasis of matter paragraph. A paragraph included in the auditor's report that refers to a matter appropriately presented or disclosed in the financial statements that, in the auditor's judgement, is of such importance that it is fundamental to users' understanding of the financial statements.

General purpose framework. A financial reporting framework designed to meet the common financial information needs of a wide range of users.

Inconsistency. In the context of other information in documents containing the audited financial statements that the other information contradicts information contained in the audited financial statements.

Management bias. A lack of neutrality by management in the preparation and presentation of information.

Materiality. Misstatements, including omissions, that individually or in the aggregate, could reasonably be expected to influence the economic decisions of users taken on the basis of the financial statements. Judgements about materiality are made in light of surrounding circumstances, and are affected by the size or nature of a misstatement, or a combination of both.

Misstatement of fact. Other information in documents containing the audited financial statements that is unrelated to matters appearing in the audited financial statements, and is incorrectly stated or presented.

Modified opinion. A qualified opinion, an adverse opinion or a disclaimer of opinion.

Other information. Financial and non-financial information (other than the financial statements and the auditor's report thereon) which is included, either by law, regulation or custom, in a document containing audited financial statements and the auditor's report thereon.

Other matter paragraph. A paragraph included in the auditor's report that refers to a matter other than those presented or disclosed in the financial statements that, in the auditor's judgement, is relevant to users' understanding of the audit, the auditor's responsibilities or the auditor's report.

Pervasive. In the context of misstatement, the effects on the financial statements of misstatements or the possible effects on the financial statements of misstatements, if any, that are undetected due to an inability to obtain sufficient appropriate audit evidence.

Qualified opinion. The auditor's opinion that due to either a scope limitation or specific departure from the applicable financial reporting framework, the financial statements are materially misstated but the effects of the misstatements on financial statements are not pervasive.

Reasonable assurance. The concept that an audit done in accordance with auditing standards may fail to detect a material misstatement in a client's financial statements. In an auditing context this term has been defined to mean a high, but not absolute level of assurance.

Scope limitation. Auditor's inability to obtain sufficient appropriate evidence that may preclude the auditor from expressing an unmodified opinion.

Special purpose financial statements. Financial statements prepared in accordance with a special purpose framework.

Special purpose framework. A financial reporting framework designed to meet the financial information needs of specific users.

Summary financial statements. Historical financial information that is derived from financial statements but that contains less detail than the financial statements, while still providing a structured representation consistent with that provided by the financial statements of the entity's economic resources or obligations at a point in time or the changes therein for a period of time.

Unmodified opinion. The auditor's opinion that the financial statements present fairly, in all material respects, in accordance with the applicable financial reporting framework (i.e. a 'clean' opinion).

? Review Questions

LO1	18–1	Describe the nine basic elements in an audit report with an unmodified opinion.
LO2	18–2	Explain why the inclusion of an emphasis of matter paragraph or other matter paragraph does not affect the auditor's opinion.
LO2	18–3	Give examples of circumstances that may require an emphasis of matter paragraph or other matter paragraph.
LO3,4	18–4	Give examples of a client-imposed and a condition-imposed scope limitation. Why is a client-imposed limitation generally considered more serious?
LO4	18–5	What are the three types of audit reports with modified opinions and when are these reports used?
LO5	18–6	How do materiality and pervasiveness of the effect on the financial statements of misstatements or the possible misstatements affect the auditor's choice of opinion in the audit report?
LO6	18–7	During 2008 Tosi Corporation entered its first lease transaction, which you have determined is material and meets the criteria for a capitalized lease. Tosi's management chooses to treat the transaction as an operating lease and your audit firm issues an audit report with a modified opinion on the 2008 financial statements of Tosi. Tosi continues its inappropriate accounting policy for leases in 2009. Will your audit report for the financial statements for 2009 refer to the corresponding figures for 2008?
LO7	18–8	What are the auditor's responsibilities for other information included in an entity's annual report?
LO7	18–9	If the auditor determines that other information contained with the audited financial statements includes a material inconsistency and the client refuses to correct the other information, what actions can the auditor take?
LO8,9,10	18–10	List three examples of reporting on specialized areas.
LO8	18–11	List three examples of special purpose frameworks for the preparation of financial statements. Why is it important that the audit report clearly identify the special purpose framework used in the preparation of the financial statements?

✎ Problems

LO1,2,3,4	18–12	For each of the following independent situations, indicate the type of financial statement audit report that you would issue, and briefly explain your reasoning. Assume that each item is significant.

a   The management of Bonner Corporation has decided to exclude the statement of cash flows from its financial statements because it believes that its bankers do not find the statement to be very useful.

b   You are auditing Diverse Carbon, a manufacturer of nerve gas for the military, for the year ended 30 September 2009. On 1 September 2009, one of its manufacturing plants caught fire, releasing nerve gas into the surrounding area. Thirteen people were killed and numerous others paralysed. The company's legal counsel indicates that the company is liable and that the amount of the liability can be reasonably estimated, but the company refuses to disclose this information in the financial statements.

c   During your audit of Cuccia Coal Company, the controller, Tracy Tricks, refuses to allow you to confirm accounts receivable because she is concerned about complaints from her customers. You are unable to satisfy yourself about accounts receivable by other audit procedures and you are concerned about Tracy's true motives.

d   On 31 January 2010, Asare Toy Manufacturing hired your firm to audit the company's financial statements for the year 2009. You were unable to observe the client's inventory on 31 December 2009. However, you were able to satisfy yourself about the inventory balance using other auditing procedures.

e   Gelato Bros. leases its manufacturing facility from a partnership controlled by the chief executive officer and major shareholder of Gelato. Your review of the lease indicates that the rental terms are in excess of rental terms for similar buildings in the area. The company refuses to disclose this related-party transaction in the notes.

f   Johnstone Manufacturing Company has used the double-declining balance method to depreciate its machinery. During the current year, management switched to the straight-line method because it felt that it better represented the utilization of the assets. You concur with its decision. All information is adequately disclosed in the financial statements.

LO1,2,3,4,7   18–13   For each of the following independent situations, indicate the reason for and the type of financial statement audit report that you would issue. Assume that each item is significant.

a   Walker Computers is suing your client, Super Software, for royalties over patent infringement. Super Software's outside legal counsel assures you that Walker's case is completely without merit.

b   In previous years, your client, Merc International, has consolidated its Panamanian subsidiary. Because of restrictions on repatriation of earnings placed on all foreign-owned corporations in Panama, Merc International has decided to account for the subsidiary on the equity basis in the current year. You concur with the change.

c   The accounting records for cash sales of your client, Temptations, are not adequate for audit purposes and you have been unable to obtain reasonable assurance that all cash sales have been properly recorded. The possible effects on the financial statements are material, but not pervasive.

d   Your Eagle Company has in the current year applied a new accounting standard for employees' compensation that will be required to apply next year. The application of the standard has not had a pervasive effect on the financial statements.

e   Upon review of the recent history of the lives of its specialized automobiles, Gas Leak Technology justifiably changed the service lives for depreciation purposes on its autos from five years to three years. This change resulted in a material amount of additional depreciation expense.

f   During the audit of Brannon Bakery Equipment, you found that a material amount of inventory had been excluded from the company's financial statements. After discussing this problem with management, you become convinced that it was an unintentional oversight. Management appropriately corrected the error prior to the completion of your audit.

g   You have detected that the information about this year's sales in the management's report contained in your client's annual report is materially inconsistent with the sales reported in the audited financial statements.

You have determined that the information in the management's report needs revision, but the information has not been revised.

h   East Side Bank's financial condition has been deteriorating for the last five years. Most of its problems result from loans made to real estate developers. Your review of the loan portfolio indicates that there should be a major increase in the loan-loss reserve. Based on your calculations, the proposed write-down of the loans will put East Side Bank into violation of the capital requirements. The client refuses to make the adjustment or to disclose the possible going-concern issue in the notes to the financial statements.

LO2,3,4   **18–14**   Rao audited Devon Worldwide's financial statements for the year ended 31 December 2009. The applicable financial reporting framework is International Financial Reporting Standards. Rao's working papers contain the following information:

The company refused to capitalize certain lease obligations for equipment acquired in 2009. Capitalization of the leases in accordance with IFRSs would have increased assets and liabilities by €312,000 and €387,000, respectively, decreased retained earnings as of 31 December 2009, by €75,000, and decreased net income and earnings per share by €75,000 and €0.75, respectively, for the year then ended. Rao has concluded that the leases should have been capitalized.

After completing the audit on 28 February 2010, Rao concludes that the expression of an adverse opinion is not warranted.

Required:

Prepare the body of Rao's report dated 28 February 2010 addressed to the shareholders.

(AICPA, adapted)

LO8   **18–15**   On 12 March 2010, Brown & Brown, independent auditors, completed the audit of the financial statements of Modern Museum for the year ended 31 December 2009. Modern Museum presents financial statements on a modified cash basis. Assets, liabilities, fund balances, support, revenues and expenses are recognized when cash is received or disbursed, except that Modern includes a provision for depreciation of buildings and equipment. Brown & Brown believes that the special purpose framework applied to prepare Modern's three financial statements is acceptable, and wishes to issue a report on the financial statements. Brown & Brown has gathered sufficient appropriate evidence to be satisfied that the financial statements are presented according to the modified cash basis.

Required:

Draft the audit report to the board of Modern Museum.

(AICPA, adapted)

LO1,3,4   **18–16**   For the year ended 31 December 2009, Friday & Co. ('Friday') independent auditors, audited the financial statements of Kim Company. Friday did not observe the taking of the physical inventory as of 31 December 2008, because that date was prior to its appointment as auditor. Friday was unable to obtain sufficient appropriate evidence regarding inventory by means of other auditing procedures. The effects of the scope limitation on the financial statements were material and pervasive.

The partner-in-charge reviewed the working papers and signed the auditor's report on 18 March 2010.

Required:

Prepare Friday's audit report on the 2009 financial statements.

(AICPA, adapted)

👥 DISCUSSION CASE

LO2   **18–17**   You are auditing the financial statements for your new client, Paper Packaging Corporation, a manufacturer of paper containers, for the year ended 31 December 2009. Paper Packaging's previous auditors issued an audit report that included an emphasis of matter paragraph for a going-concern uncertainty on the 31 December 2008 financial statements for the following reasons:

- Paper Packaging had defaulted on €10 million of unregistered debentures sold to three insurance companies, which were due in 2009, and the default constituted a possible violation of other debt agreements.

- The interest and principal payments due on the remainder of a ten-year credit agreement, which began in 2005, would exceed the cash flows generated from operations in recent years.

- The company had disposed of certain operating units. The proceeds from the sale were subject to possible adjustment through arbitration proceedings, the outcome of which was uncertain at year end.

- Various lawsuits were pending against the company.

- The company was in the midst of tax proceedings as a result of an examination of the company's income tax returns for a period of 12 years.

You find that the status of the above matters is as follows at year end, 31 December 2009:

- The company is still in default on €4.6 million of the debentures due in 2009 but is trying to negotiate a settlement with remaining bondholders. A large number of bondholders have settled their claims at significantly less than par.

- The company has renegotiated the 2005 credit agreement, which provides for a two-year moratorium on principal payments and interest at 8 per cent. It also limits net losses for 2009 and requires a certain level of defined cumulative quarterly operating income to be maintained.

- The arbitration proceedings were resolved in 2009.

- The legal actions were settled in 2009.

- Most of the tax issues have been resolved, and, according to the company's external legal counsel, those remaining will result in a net cash inflow to the company.

At year end Paper Packaging had a cash balance of €5.5 million and expects to generate a net cash flow of €3.2 million in the upcoming fiscal year.

The following information about Paper Packaging's plans for its operations in fiscal year 2010 may also be useful in arriving at a decision.

	Fiscal Year 2010 Budget	Fiscal Year 2009 Actual	Fiscal Year 2009 Budget
Net revenues	€66.2	€60.9	€79.8
Gross margin	34.7	33.6	45.6
Operating expenses	27.9	34.7	31.4
Interest – net	5.1	6.0	5.7
Other income (expenses) – net	(0.8)	2.1	–
Earnings before income taxes	1.5	(5.1)	(0.2)
Cash flows:			

Receipts	69.9	79.7
Disbursements	66.7	96.9
Excess/deficit	3.2	(22.8)

Required (for these questions, you may wish to reference auditing standards – see ISA 570):

a   What should you consider in deciding whether there exists a material going-concern uncertainty?

b   How much influence should the report on the 31 December 2008 financial statements have on your decision?

c   Should your report for the year ended 31 December 2009 include an emphasis of matter paragraph for a going-concern uncertainty? Briefly explain why or why not.

Internet Assignment

LO1,6   18–18   Go to IFAC's home site (www.ifac.org/) and download it's most recent annual report. Read the Independent Auditor's Report for IFAC's financial statements.

a   How does IFAC's audit report differ in form and content from EarthWear's 2009 audit report?

Go to UK Auditing Practice Board (www.frc.org.uk/apb/) and download International Standard on Auditing (UK and Ireland) 700 (revised) The Auditor's Report on Financial Statements.

b   How does the Auditing Practice Board's prescribed audit report (with unmodified opinion) differ in form and content from EarthWear's 2009 audit report?

Notes

i   Auditing standards use the term 'fair presentation framework' to refer to a financial reporting framework that requires compliance with the requirements of the framework and:

(a) Acknowledges explicitly or implicitly that, to achieve fair presentation of the financial statements, it may be necessary for management to provide disclosures beyond those specifically required by the framework; or

(b) Acknowledges explicitly that it may be necessary for management to depart from a requirement of the framework to achieve fair presentation of the financial statements. Such departures are expected to be necessary only in extremely rare circumstances.

The term 'compliance framework' is sometimes used to refer to a financial reporting framework that requires compliance with the requirements of the framework, but does not contain the acknowledgements in (a) or (b) above.

ii   Auditing standards also require the auditor to disclaim an opinion when, *in extremely rare circumstances* involving multiple uncertainties, the auditor concludes that, notwithstanding having obtained sufficient appropriate audit evidence regarding each of the individual uncertainties, it is not possible to form an opinion on the financial statements due to the potential interaction of the uncertainties and their possible cumulative effect on the financial statements. For example, in situations involving multiple material going-concern uncertainties that are significant to the financial statements as a whole, the auditor may consider it appropriate in extremely rare cases to disclaim an opinion on the entity instead of adding an emphasis of matter paragraph.

PART VII
Professional Responsibilities

PART CONTENTS

19 Professional Ethics, Independence and Quality Control

Professional Ethics, Independence and Quality Control

❖ RELEVANT ACCOUNTING AND AUDITING PRONOUNCEMENTS

European Commission, Recommendation on Quality Assurance for the Statutory Audit in the EU: Minimum Requirements, 2000

European Commission, Recommendation on Statutory Auditors' Independence in the EU: A Set of Fundamental Principles, 2002

European Commission, Recommendation on External Quality Assurance for the Statutory Auditors and Audit Firms Auditing Public Interest Entities, 2008

IFAC, SMO 1, Quality Assurance

IESBA, Code of Ethics for Professional Accountants, 2009

IAASB, ISQC 1, Quality Control for Firms That Perform Audits and Reviews of Financial Statements, and Other Assurance and Related Services Engagements

IN THIS CHAPTER we discuss the importance of professional ethics and how accountants comply with the principles and requirements governing ethical behaviour. Independence, arguably the most complicated and controversial aspect of auditor professionalism, is prominently highlighted in this discussion.

We begin by defining ethics and professionalism, and present three basic theories of ethical behaviour within which ethical issues can be evaluated. The following discussion of ethical dilemmas applies those theories to an example.

We then discuss the IFAC Code of Ethics for Professional Accountants. The Code of Ethics establishes fundamental principles of professional ethics for accountants and provides a conceptual framework for applying those principles. The fundamental principles comprise integrity, objectivity, professional competence and due care, confidentiality, and professional behaviour. The conceptual framework approach requires accountants to identify threats to compliance with the fundamental principles and, when necessary, apply safeguards to eliminate or reduce the threats to an acceptable level. Threats are created by circumstances and relationships that could compromise an accountant's ability to comply with the fundamental principles. Safeguards are actions or other measures that may eliminate threats or reduce them to an acceptable level. The Code of Ethics shows how the conceptual framework is applied to situations accountants encounter in practice, including circumstances and relationships that may compromise accountants' independence. One of the circumstances and relationships highlighted is the provision of non-assurance services to an audit client. The nature of the threats to independence is explained and prohibitions described. The presentation of the Code of Ethics concludes with a brief discussion of independence requirements for assurance engagements that are not audit or review engagements, and the application of the conceptual framework for accountants in business. The discussion of the conceptual framework ends with a presentation of the framework's role in EU regulation of statutory auditor's independence.

The last part of the chapter explains how audit firms have established systems of quality control to help ensure quality audits and compliance with professional standards and regulations. Finally, quality assurance programmes of audit firms' practices are discussed.

As you will see from the chapter, codes of ethics and independence requirements are complicated subjects, involving a great deal of technical detail. A sense for the depth of detail involved is essential. However, we encourage you not to lose sight of the big picture. The primary purpose of professional ethics requirements is to establish a minimum level of professionalism to help accountants behave ethically and remain independent of their assurance clients. The essence of even the mind-numbingly detailed independence requirements is that independence of mind and in appearance is critical to the auditor's reputation and the value she or he provides to society. Unfortunately, even practising auditors can get so lost in the detail of the specific requirements that they sometimes lose sight of the fundamental principles on which the requirements are based. If you pursue a career in accounting, you should at least occasionally step back and review the fundamental principles of the Code of Ethics, which involve appropriate professional and moral judgements in all you do, an obligation to honour the public trust and a commitment to perform professional responsibilities with the highest sense of integrity.

❖ ETHICS AND ETHICAL PROFESSIONAL BEHAVIOUR

LO1
Ethics and Professionalism Defined

Ethical conduct is the bedrock of modern civilization – it underpins the successful functioning of nearly every aspect of society, from daily family life to law, medicine, business and government. **Ethics** refers to a system or code of conduct based on moral duties and obligations that indicate how an individual should interact with others in society. A sense for ethics guides individuals to value more than their own self-interest and to recognize and respect the interests of others as well. Our society would fall into chaos if people were devoid of ethics and moral sentiments. Imagine what it would be like if everyone ignored rules of the road, moral standards, obligations, and the rights and interests of others! Life in such a society would be, as the philosopher Hobbes might say, 'solitary, poor, nasty, brutish, and short'.

Ethical conduct is also the bedrock of modern professionalism. **Professionalism**, broadly defined, refers to the conduct, aims or qualities that characterize or mark a profession or professional person.[i] All professions establish rules or codes of ethics or conduct that define ethical (professional) behaviour for members of the profession. These rules are established so that (1) users of the professional services know what to expect when they purchase such services; (2) members of the profession know what behaviour is acceptable; and (3) the profession can use the rules to monitor the actions of its members and apply discipline where appropriate. Consider the medical profession. When you see a doctor for a potentially serious medical condition, you as a user of this professional service have a valid and vital interest in expecting competent and honest behaviour that is free from conflicts of interest. You expect, for example, that the doctor will prescribe the best medication for your condition, rather than one for which the doctor earns a commission. To better meet these expectations, the medical profession requires particular training and certifications, and has a code of professional ethics, the earliest form of which arguably is the Hippocratic oath, written in about 400 BC. An essential distinguishing mark of a profession is that it recognizes its responsibility to place the interests of the public above its own when the two are in conflict.

Recall that in Chapter 1 we discussed the desired characteristics of a building surveyor and concluded that competence, objectivity and integrity are critical. We also discussed the role that auditors, as information inspectors, play in reducing information risk through *independent* verification of management assertions. To be a credible source of objective, independent assurance, the professional must have a solid reputation for competence, and for unquestioned character and integrity. The concepts of ethical behaviour and professional conduct are clearly central to the success of the accounting profession. In fact, those who enter the accounting profession and engage in unethical behaviour will inevitably harm themselves, others, and the profession. The most important concept you will read in this chapter is that of personal responsibility and integrity. As an accountant, auditor, manager or businessperson, you will face numerous difficult ethical issues, and you will experience pressures and temptations. Never forget that your most valuable assets as a professional are integrity and a solid reputation. We encourage you to continually evaluate your choices and behaviour, and commit to a high level of integrity and ethical behaviour as a student, professional and member of society.

Given the importance of reputation, ethical behaviour and professionalism, the accounting profession has developed codes of ethics that guide the behaviour of accounting professionals. At the international level IFAC has issued a *Code of Ethics for Professional Accountants* that guides the behaviour of accounting professionals. The international Code of Ethics and the conceptual framework approach underpinning the Code are discussed later in this chapter, after we discuss a framework for considering ethical issues.

❖ Theories of Ethical Behaviour

LO2
When individuals are confronted with situations that have moral and ethical implications, they do not always agree on the issues at hand, which individuals or groups will be affected and how, or what solutions or courses of actions are available or appropriate for dealing with the situation. Such differences may be caused by differences in the individuals' concepts of fairness and different opinions about the right action to take in a particular situation. Some ethical choices are difficult simply due to the temptation or pressure to pursue one's self-interest, which can cloud judgement regarding what is right or wrong. Other choices are complicated by the sheer difficulty of sorting out the issues and deciphering what might be appropriate or inappropriate actions to take.

S. M. Mintz has suggested that there are three overlapping methods or theories of ethical behaviour that can guide the analysis of ethical issues in accounting.[ii] These theories are (1) *utilitarianism*, (2) a *rights-based approach,* and (3) a *justice-based approach.* No single approach is necessarily better than another. In fact, elements of each theory may be appropriate for resolving ethical dilemmas in different circumstances.

Utilitarian theory recognizes that decision-making involves trade-offs between the benefits and burdens of alternative actions, and it focuses on the consequences of a particular action on the individuals affected. The theory proposes that the interests of all parties affected, not just one's self-interest, should be considered. From this perspective, an action conforms to the principle of utility only if that action will produce more pleasure or happiness (or prevent more pain or unhappiness) than any other possible action. The value of an action is determined solely by the consequences of the action on the welfare of individuals. This is why utilitarianism is sometimes also described as a 'consequentialist' theory. One form of utilitarianism holds that rules have a central position in moral judgement due to the adverse consequences that would likely arise if everyone chose to break them. This approach has significance for auditors, who are expected to follow the Code of Professional Ethics in carrying out their responsibilities. One disadvantage in applying the utilitarian theory to ethical dilemmas is that it is often difficult to measure the potential costs and benefits of the actions to be taken. It may also be difficult to balance the interests of all parties involved when those interests conflict with one another.

The rights-based approach assumes that individuals have certain rights and other individuals have a duty to respect those rights. Thus, a decision maker who follows a theory of rights should undertake an action only if it does not violate the rights of any individual. An obvious disadvantage of the theory of rights is that it may be difficult or impossible to satisfy all rights of all affected parties, especially when those rights conflict. The theory of rights is important to auditors because of their public-interest responsibility. According to the concept known as the 'moral point of view', auditors must be willing to put the interests of other stakeholders, such as investors and creditors, ahead of their own self-interests and those of the audit firm. For example, if a difference of opinion with top management exists over an accounting or reporting issue, the auditor should emphasize the interests of the investors and creditors in deciding what action to take, even if it means losing the client.

The justice-based approach is concerned with issues such as equity, fairness, and impartiality. The theory of justice involves two basic principles.[iii] The first principle posits that each person has a right to have the maximum degree of personal freedom that is still compatible with the liberty of others. The second principle asserts that social and economic actions should be to everyone's advantage and the benefits available to all. For example, someone in a position to accumulate wealth has a moral obligation to make sure that others are not treated unfairly as a result of his or her gains. Mintz argues that decisions made within this theory should fairly and equitably distribute resources among those individuals or groups affected. There may be difficulty in trying to apply this theory in practice because the rights of one or more individuals or groups may be affected when a better distribution of benefits is provided to others. Under this approach, the auditor considers what would be the most just decision in terms of allocation of resources among interested parties.

While none of these theories by itself can provide a perfect ethical framework, note that each emphasizes the need to consider more than one's self-interest, and each can be useful in helping an auditor to solve dilemmas by providing an ethical perspective.

❖ Example: An Ethical Dilemma

LO3 Consider how an auditor might reason through the following simplified situation.

Sun City Bank

Pina, Johnson & Associates has recently been awarded the audit of Sun City Bank for the year just ended. Sun City Bank is now the largest client of the firm, and the fees from this engagement represent a significant portion of the firm's revenues. Upon accepting the Sun City engagement, the firm incurred additional costs by hiring several new employees and a new manager from a larger firm. In bidding on the engagement, Sam Johnson knew that the first-year fees would be just enough to cover the actual cost of the first year's audit, but he hoped that future audit fee increases and fees for other services might lead to a long-term, profitable engagement. Based on his discussions with the predecessor auditors, Johnson knew that there were possible problems with Sun City's loans because of the collateral used for security. Johnson was also concerned that there might be problems with loan-loss reserves due to the effects of the economic slowdown on the tourist industry in Sun City over the last two years. However, Johnson felt that these problems were manageable.

During the current year, the amount included in the loan-loss reserves account was €675,000, approximately the same as the figure for the prior year. The banking regulations require that an amount equal to 1.5 per cent of the loans outstanding be included as a reserve against losses. The €675,000 was slightly above the statutory requirement. However, the audit staff identified two large loans, aggregating to €15 million, that appeared not to be collectable in full. The working papers disclosed that each loan had originated during the current year and that both had been in default for four months. Additionally, the collateral used to secure the loans was worth considerably less than the amount of the loans and was not in accordance with Sun City's loan policy procedures. Based on this information, the staff estimates that about 40 per cent of the €15 million, or €6 million, will not be collected. The staff has also determined that these loans are to entities owned by Patricia Cabot, Sun City's CEO, and some of her business associates.

When Johnson met with Cabot to discuss the two delinquent loans, Cabot assured Johnson that the loans would be paid in full. She told Johnson that the loans had been properly made and that as soon as the economy picked up, payments would be made on the loans. She indicated that no additional reserves were needed and that if Johnson requires such adjustments, his firm might be replaced.

Johnson is concerned that if the loan-loss reserves are increased, Sun City's owners and investors might be hurt financially. Further, if Johnson requires the adjustment, Pina, Johnson & Associates may lose Sun City as a client, his own career goals will be damaged, and the firm may have to lay off professional and staff employees. Johnson believes there could be serious consequences to several different parties whatever decision he makes.

What ethical and professional concerns should Johnson consider in deciding on a course of action? How would Johnson's views differ if the dilemma was viewed with a utilitarian perspective? How about a rights-based or a justice-based approach?

In situations such as this one, an auditor is well advised to think about the ethical issues carefully and from several different perspectives. According to the utilitarian perspective, Johnson should consider the consequences of his actions on all affected parties and whether any rules exist that might require a particular action. He should think not only about the consequences of breaking any applicable rule in the current situation but also what the consequences would be if everyone else also broke the rule. Costs and benefits need to be assessed in terms of the public, Sun City's stockholders, Cabot's reputation and the situation of the audit firm.

Using a rights-based approach, Johnson should consider the rights of the involved parties. If he does so, he will realize that the stockholders' right to fair and accurate information for decision-making purposes would clearly be violated if he does not require an increase in the loan-loss reserves. If Cabot has entered into inappropriate loans at the expense of the stockholders, they will not have received accurate information about Sun City's profitability, liquidity, and so on. Cabot, of course, has no defensible right to misappropriate funds or to report account balances incorrectly.

Finally, from a justice-based perspective, Johnson should think about whether his decision might yield advantages for some at the expense of others, focusing on the protection of those who may otherwise be at a disadvantage. Johnson should avoid favouring the interests of any individual or group, and should not select an action that will confer unfair advantages on some (e.g. the management of Sun City) at the expense of others (e.g. the public). Integrity and objectivity require that Johnson not place his self-interest or that of the client ahead of the public interest. Instead, he must focus on Sun City's shareholders as members of the investing public.

If he does not allow his self-interest to cloud his judgement, Johnson will require the client to book the €6 million adjustment for the delinquent loans, regardless of the consequences to himself or to his firm. But, realistically, Johnson's professionalism is likely to be tested in this situation. After all, he could easily rationalize that there is a good chance the economy will turn around and the loans will be repaid, as promised by Cabot. While he realizes that the loan-loss reserves probably should be increased, he is also likely to be concerned about the possibility of losing this valuable client and the significant investment in new personnel that the firm has made. While it seems fairly clear what action should be taken, the question becomes – as it so often does – does the auditor have the courage to do the right thing?

Auditors *frequently* face ethical pressures, and the issues are often not quite as clear-cut as in the above example. It is important that auditors develop sound moral character so that they can respond appropriately in such situations. Mintz points out that auditors who possess certain 'virtues' or traits of character are more capable of adhering to a moral point of view.[iv] Examples of such virtues include honesty, integrity, impartiality, faithfulness and trustworthiness. These characteristics are embodied in the profession's fundamental principles of professional ethics discussed later in the chapter, and are vital to the continued health of the profession.[v]

Practice Insight 19.1

In the final analysis, individual morality is the basis for effectively dealing with ethical challenges. Moral absolutes or 'bright line' values, such as honesty and fairness, are essential characteristics for members of the accounting profession. Accountants who do not possess these foundational characteristics are likely to do great harm to themselves, the profession and others.

IFAC CODE OF ETHICS FOR PROFESSIONAL ACCOUNTANTS

Introduction

We have argued that the demand for auditing arose from the need for a competent and independent person to monitor the contractual arrangements between principal and agent. The role of the auditor is to reduce information risk through independent assurance of management assertions. To be a credible source of assurance the auditor must be independent. If the auditor has self-serving interests (e.g. due to a financial interest in the client) or is under undue influence of others (e.g. due to a family relationship with client's management), the auditor's independence is impaired and the users of financial statements may no longer trust the auditor's objectivity in assuring the financial statements. Thus, if an auditor lacks independence, users of financial statements will place little or no value on the audit provided.

Regulations to ensure auditors' independence have developed over time. At the end of the 1990s the accounting profession and regulators intensified their search for a well-reasoned and robust operational framework for resolving independence issues. The effort resulted in a *conceptual framework approach* to independence which today is the established approach internationally. The alternative to a conceptual framework approach is a rule-based approach to regulate independence.

The conceptual framework approach requires auditors to identify threats that may compromise independence and, when necessary, apply safeguards to eliminate or reduce the threats to an acceptable level. *Threats* are created by circumstances and relationships that could compromise independence. *Safeguards* are actions or other measures that may eliminate threats or reduce them to an acceptable level. For example, if a member of the audit team has a financial interest in the audit client, such a relationship is a threat to independence. Removing the member from the audit team would be a thinkable safeguard. The auditor's evaluation of the significance of threats and determination of whether threat is reduced to an acceptable level by application of safeguards takes into account what a reasonable and informed *third party* would be likely to conclude. In our example, the auditor may determine it necessary that the audit team member dispose of the financial interest or the firm withdraws from the audit engagement.

The International Federations of Accountants (IFAC) has adopted the conceptual framework approach in the Code of Ethics for Professional Accountants. The conceptual framework is the foundation of the Code of Ethics, and accountants shall apply the framework to comply with the fundamental principles of professional ethics as well as to protect independence. The next sections explain how the Code of Ethics is organized and how the conceptual framework is applied to situations accountants encounter in practice.

Practice Insight 19.2

The distinction between a conceptual framework approach and a rule-based approach is not clear-cut. On the one hand, in a rule-based system common principles may underlie the rules. On the other hand, absolute restrictions and prohibitions are part of a conceptual framework system when such restrictions and prohibitions flow from the application of framework.

Overview of Code of Ethics for Professional Accountants[vi]

LO4

In Chapter 2 we presented the International Federations of Accountants (IFAC) mission to serve public interest, strengthen the accountancy profession worldwide, and establish and promote adherence to high-quality professional standards. We also discussed the IFAC standard-setting body , the International Ethics Standards Board for Accountants (IESBA), and introduced you to the Code of Ethics for Professional Accountants issued by IESBA. The Code of Ethics establishes ethical requirements for professional accountants and provides a conceptual framework to ensure compliance with fundamental principles of ethical behaviour. The Code serves as the foundation for codes of ethics established and enforced by IFAC member bodies. No IFAC member body or firm is permitted to apply less stringent standards than those stated in the Code unless prohibited by law or regulation. Jurisdictions may have additional requirements and guidance that differ from those contained in the Code. Professional accountants in those jurisdictions comply with the more stringent requirements and guidance.

The Code contains three main parts. Part A establishes the fundamental principles of professional ethics and provides a conceptual framework that **professional accountants** shall apply to comply with fundamental principles. Part A applies to all professional accountants. Parts B and C describe how the conceptual framework applies in certain situations encountered by accountants. Part B applies to professional accountants in public practice and Part C to professional accountants in business. The three parts are organized into sections. Table 19–1 gives an overview of the organization and content of the Code of Ethics. Before you look at Table 19–1 it is helpful to have the following definitions in mind:

- **Professional accountant.** An individual who is a member of an IFAC member body.
- **Professional accountant in business.** A professional accountant employed or engaged in an executive or non-executive capacity in such areas as commerce, industry, service, the public sector, education, the not for profit sector, regulatory bodies or professional bodies, or a professional accountant contracted by such entities.
- **Professional accountant in public practice.** A professional accountant, irrespective of functional classification (e.g. audit, tax or consulting) in a firm that provides professional services. This term is also used to refer to a firm of professional accountants in public practice.
- **Professional services.** Services requiring accountancy or related skills performed by a professional accountant including accounting, auditing, taxation, management consulting and financial management services.

Table 19–1   Content of Code of Ethics for Professional Accountants
Part A: General Application of the Code
Section 100 Introduction and Fundamental Principles
Section 110 Integrity
Section 120 Objectivity
Section 130 Professional Competence and Due Care
Section 140 Confidentiality
Section 150 Professional Behaviour
Part B: Professional Accountants in Public Practice
Section 200 Introduction
Section 210 Professional Appointment
Section 220 Conflicts of Interest
Section 230 Second Opinions
Section 240 Fees and Other Types of Remuneration
Section 250 Marketing Professional Services
Section 260 Gifts and Hospitality
Section 270 Custody of Clients Assets
Section 280 Objectivity – All Services
Section 290 Independence – Audit and Review Engagements
Section 291 Independence – Other Assurance Engagements
Part C: Professional Accountants in Business
Section 300 Introduction
Section 310 Potential Conflicts
Section 320 Preparation and Reporting of Information
Section 330 Acting with Sufficient Expertise
Section 340 Financial Interests
Section 350 Inducements
Definitions
Source: Code of Ethics for Professional Accountants, IESBA (2009).

The Code defines a number of other terms and expressions it applies. You are familiar with some of these from your studying of auditing and other are introduced to you in this chapter. It is also helpful to use the Key Terms listed at the end of the chapter. For example, you can learn from the Key Terms that a **public interest entity** is a listed entity, and an entity defined by regulation or legislation as a public interest entity or for which the audit is required by regulation or legislation to be conducted in compliance with the same independence requirements that apply to the audit or listed entities. Recall from Chapter 1 that an **assurance engagement** is designed to enhance intended users' degree of confidence about the outcome of the evaluation or measurement of a subject matter against criteria. An audit is an assurance engagement but there are number of other non-audit assurance engagements. Non-assurance services are professional services such as consulting, tax advisory and legal services.

◆ Fundamental Principles and Conceptual Framework

LO5

Part A of the Code establishes the fundamental principles and the conceptual framework for applying the principles. The fundamental principles the professional accountant is required to comply with are *integrity, objectivity, professional competence and due care, confidentiality,* and *professional behaviour.* Table 19-2 presents the definition of each principle.

Table 19–2 Fundamental Principles
Integrity. A professional accountant shall be straightforward and honest in all professional and business relationships.
Objectivity. A professional accountant shall not allow bias, conflict of interest or undue influence of others to override professional or business judgements.
Professional competence and due care. A professional accountant shall maintain professional knowledge and skill at the level required to ensure that a client or employer receives competent professional services based on current developments in practice, legislation and techniques and act diligently and in accordance with applicable technical and professional standards.
Confidentiality. A professional accountant shall respect the confidentiality of information acquired as a result of professional and business relationships and, therefore, not disclose any such information to third parties without proper and specific authority, unless there is a legal or professional right or duty to disclose, nor use the information for the personal advantage of the professional accountant or third parties.
Professional behaviour. A professional accountant shall comply with relevant laws and regulations and avoid any action that discredits the profession.
Source: Code of Ethics for Professional Accountants, IESBA (2009).

The principle of *integrity* implies that the accountant is straightforward and honest in all professional and business relationships, including fair dealing and truthfulness. Thus, an accountant should make judgements that are consistent with the theories of rights and justice illustrated at the beginning of this chapter. When faced with an ethical dilemma, the accountant should ask, 'What actions would an individual with integrity take, given these facts and circumstances?' Specifically, the Code requires that accountants shall not be associated with reports, returns, communications or other information where they believe that the information contains a materially false or misleading statement. For example, such information could be a material inconsistency or a material misstatement of fact in other information in the annual report containing the financial statements and the audit report (refer to Chapter 18). Generally, when becoming aware of an association with inappropriate information, the accountant shall take steps to be disassociated from that information.

The principle of *objectivity* imposes a responsibility on the accountants not to compromise professional or business judgement because of bias, conflict of interest or the undue influence of others. Relationships or circumstances that bias or unduly influence his or her professional judgement shall be avoided. As a fundamental principle objectivity applies to all accountants and to all professional services provided by accountants in public practice. Accountants in public practice who provide an assurance service shall be independent of the assurance client. Impairment of independence would compromise objectivity.

The principle of *professional competence and due care* requires that the accountant performs his or her professional responsibilities with competence and diligence. Professional competence means the exercise of sound judgement in applying professional knowledge and skill in the performance of services. Such competence shall be attained as well as maintained. Diligence means that the accountant shall observe technical and professional standards.

The principle of *confidentiality* requires that the accountant refrains from disclosing any confidential client information without the specific consent of the client, unless there is a legal or professional duty to disclose. The principle also implies a prohibition on using confidential information to personal advantage or the advantage of third parties. For example, an accountant with multiple clients in the same industry shall not reveal confidential information of one client to another client. Maintenance of confidentiality extends beyond a professional environment, for example in relation to family members.

The last principle of *professional behaviour* requires the accountant to comply with relevant laws and regulations and avoid any action that may bring discredit to the profession. This includes actions which a reasonable and informed third party, having knowledge of all relevant information, would conclude negatively affects the good reputation of the profession. In marketing and promoting themselves and their work, the accountants shall not bring the profession into disrepute, i.e. the accountants shall act with integrity. For example, the accountant shall not make exaggerated claims for the services offered or unsubstantiated comparisons to the work of others accountants.

As illustrated in the audit of Sun City Bank discussed at the beginning of this chapter, accountants may face ethical dilemmas in their practice. An ethical dilemma may arise from a conflict in the application of the fundamental principles. To determine the appropriate course of action in a conflict situation the accountant weighs the consequences of each possible course of action based on the relevant facts, the ethical issues involved and the fundamental principles in conflict. If this does not resolve the matter, the accountant shall consult within the audit firm or employing organization for help in obtaining resolution. The accountant may also obtain professional advice from the relevant professional body or legal advisors. For example, an accountant may have encountered a fraud, the reporting of which could breach the accountant's responsibility to respect confidentiality. The accountant may then obtain legal advice to determine whether there is a requirement to report. If, after exhausting all relevant possibilities, the ethical conflict remains unresolved, the accountant may find it necessary to withdraw from the engagement team or specific assignment. In exceptional cases the accountant would resign from the firm or the employing organization.

The Code lays out the conceptual framework to be applied by accountants. The accountant shall identify, evaluate and address threats to compliance with the fundamental principles. The accountant uses professional judgement in applying the framework. The three steps involved in applying the framework are:

1   Identify threats to compliance with the fundamental principles.
2   Evaluate the significance of the threats identified.
3   Apply safeguards, when necessary, to eliminate the threats or reduce them to an acceptable level.

A threat is created by circumstances and relationships that could compromise an accountant's ability to comply with the fundamental principles. The accountant shall be alert to such circumstances and relationships. Safeguards are actions or other measures that may eliminate threats or reduce them to an acceptable level.

When the accountant identifies threats to compliance with the fundamental principles, he or she evaluates their significance and determines whether they are at an acceptable level or not. The evaluation of a threat includes both qualitative and quantitative factors. In determining if the threats are at an acceptable level or not, the accountant takes into account whether a reasonable and informed *third party* would be likely to conclude, weighing all the specific facts and circumstances available to the professional accountant at that time, that compliance with the fundamental principles is not compromised.

In some situations the threats cannot be eliminated or reduced to an acceptable level, either because the threats are too significant or because appropriate safeguards are not available or cannot be applied. In such situations the accountant shall decline or discontinue the specific professional service involved or, when necessary, resign from the engagement (professional accountants in public practice) or the employing organization (professional accountants in business).

The Code categorizes threats into *self-interest threat, self-review threat, advocacy threat, familiarity threat* and *intimidation threat*. Table 19–3 presents the five categories of threats.

> **Table 19–3 Categories of Threats**
>
> **Self-interest threat.** The threat that a financial or other interest will inappropriately influence the professional accountant's judgement or behaviour.
>
> **Self-review threats.** The threat that a professional accountant will not appropriately evaluate the results of a previous judgement made or service performed by the professional accountant, or by another individual within the professional accountant's firm or employing organization, on which the accountant will rely when forming a judgement as part of providing a current service.
>
> **Advocacy threats.** The threat that a professional accountant will promote a client's or employer's position to the point that the professional accountant's objectivity is compromised.
>
> **Familiarity threats.** The threat that due to a long or close relationship with a client or employer, a professional accountant will be too sympathetic to their interests or too accepting of their work.
>
> **Intimidation threats.** The threat that a professional accountant will be deterred from acting objectively because of actual or perceived pressures, including attempts to exercise undue influence over the professional accountant.
>
> *Source: Code of Ethics for Professional Accountants, IESBA (2009)*

Parts B and Part C of the Code explain how these threats may be created for professional accountants in public practice and professional accountants in business, respectively.

The Code categorizes *safeguards* into two broad groups: (1) those created by the profession, legislation or regulation; and (2) those in the work environment. Safeguards created by the profession, legislation or regulation are common for all professional accountants and include:

- Educational, training and experience requirements for entry into the profession.
- Continuing professional development requirements.
- Corporate governance regulations.
- Professional standards.
- Professional or regulatory monitoring and disciplinary procedures.
- External review by a legally empowered third party of the reports, returns, communications or information produced by a professional accountant.

Safeguards related to the work environment depend on if the professional accountant is in public practice or in business. Thus, these safeguards are discussed separately for the two types of professional accountants. The next section discusses how the conceptual framework applies to situations relevant for professional accountants in public practice.

❖ Professional Ethics for Professional Accountants in Public
LO6 Practice (Practitioners)

Part B of the Code of Ethics applies to professional accountants in public practice. Recall that a *professional accountant in public practice* is professional accountant that provides *professional services* (e.g. auditing, consulting and tax services) in an audit **firm**, and that the term is also used to refer to a firm of professional accountants in public practice. In the following we will use the short form, *practitioner*, when referring to a professional accountant in public practice.

Table 19–1 showed that Part B of the Code covers application of the conceptual framework to the following situations:

- Professional Appointment.
- Conflicts of Interest.
- Second Opinions.
- Fees and Other Types of Remuneration.
- Marketing Professional Services.
- Gifts and Hospitality.
- Custody of Clients' Assets.
- Objectivity – All Services.
- Independence – Audit and Review Engagements.
- Independence – Other Assurance Engagements.

These situations do not cover all the situations that could be encountered by a practitioner that may create threats to compliance with the fundamental principles. The practitioner shall be alert to any situation that may compromise the fundamental principles and apply the framework when necessary.

The nature and significance of the threats may differ for different circumstances, including depending on whether they arise in relation to an audit client and whether the audit client is a public interest entity, to an assurance client that is not an audit client, or to a non-assurance client. Table 19–4 presents examples of circumstances and relationships that may create threats to compliance with the fundamental principles. Take some time to read the table and see if you can explain why these circumstances and relationships create threats. Use your intuition and think of possible safeguards that can eliminate or reduce the threats. We will discuss the circumstances and relationships referred to in Table 19–4 in the text that follows.

Table 19–4 Examples of Circumstances and Relationships That May Create Threats

Self-interest threats

- A member of the audit team having a direct financial interest in the audit client.
- A firm having undue dependence on total fees from an audit client.
- The fee quoted is so low that it may be difficult to perform the engagement in accordance with applicable technical and professional standards for that price.
- A member of the assurance team having a significant close business relationship with an assurance client.
- A member of the audit team entering into employment negotiations with the audit client.

Self-review threats

— Client should prepare these.

- A member of the audit team prepares calculations of current and deferred tax liabilities for an audit client for the purpose of preparing accounting entries.
- A member of the audit team provides recruiting services to an audit client.
- A member of the audit team provides an audit client with accounting and bookkeeping services.
- A member of the assurance team having recently been a director of the assurance client.
- The firm performs internal audit services for the audit client.

Advocacy threats

- The firm promoting shares in an audit client.
- A practitioner acting as an advocate on behalf of an audit client in litigation with third parties.

Familiarity threats

- A member of the assurance team having an immediate family member who is a director of the assurance client.
- A member of the audit team having a close family member who is an employee of the client who is in a position to exert significant influence over the subject matter of the engagement.
- A director of the audit client having recently served as the engagement partner.
- A practitioner accepting gifts or preferential treatment from a client.

Intimidation threats

- A firm being threatened with dismissal from a client engagement.
- A gift from a client is accepted and it is possible that the acceptance of the gift is being made public.
- An audit client indicating that it will not award a planned non-assurance contract to the firm if the firm continues to disagree with the client's accounting treatment for a particular transaction.
- A practitioner feeling pressured to agree with the judgement of a client employee because the employee has more expertise on the matter in question.

Source: Code of Ethics for Professional Accountants, IESBA (2009).

The prior section discussed safeguards created by the profession, legislation or regulation. These were common for all professional accountants. In addition safeguards are created in the accountant's work environment. For practitioners, such safeguards include *firm-wide safeguards, engagement-specific safeguards,* and *safeguards within the client's systems and procedures.* Table 19–5 presents examples in each category of these safeguards. The practitioner cannot rely solely on safeguards within the client's systems and procedures to reduce threats to an acceptable level.

Table 19–5 Examples of Safeguards in the Work Environment

Firm-wide safeguards

- Leadership of the firm that stresses the importance of compliance with the fundamental principles.

- Policies and procedures to implement and monitor quality control of engagements.

- Documented policies regarding the need to identify threats to compliance with the fundamental principles, evaluate the significance of those threats, and apply safeguards to eliminate or reduce the threats to an acceptable level or, when appropriate safeguards are not available or cannot be applied, terminate or decline the relevant engagement.

- Policies and procedures that will enable the identification of interests or relationships between the firm or members of engagement teams and clients.

- Designating a member of senior management to be responsible for overseeing the adequate functioning of the firm's quality control system.

- Published policies and procedures to encourage and empower staff to communicate to senior levels within the firm any issue relating to compliance with the fundamental principles that concerns them.

Engagement-specific safeguards

- Having a practitioner who was not involved with the non-assurance service review the non-assurance work performed or otherwise advise as necessary.

- Consulting an independent third party, such as a another practitioner or a professional regulatory body.

- Discussing ethical issues with those charged with governance of the client.

- Disclosing to those charged with governance of the client the nature of services provided and extent of fees charged.

- Involving another firm to perform or reperform part of the engagement.

- Rotating senior assurance team personnel.

Safeguards within the client's systems and procedures

- The client requires persons other than management to ratify or approve the appointment of a firm to perform an engagement.

- The client has competent employees with experience and seniority to make managerial decisions.

- The client has implemented internal procedures that ensure objective choices in commissioning non-assurance engagements.

- The client has a corporate governance structure that provides appropriate oversight and communications regarding the firm's services.

Source: Code of Ethics for Professional Accountants, IESBA (2009).

We now turn to the situations discussed in the Code that may create threats to the practitioner's compliance with the fundamental principles, and show how the conceptual framework is applied to threats created. We first cover situations that relate to *all* professional services performed by a practitioner (Sections 210–280 of the Code), and then turn to audit and review services and independence requirements (Section 290 of the Code). Finally, we briefly discuss independence and other assurance engagements (Section 291 of the Code).

Professional Appointment

Professional appointment covers three situations:

1   Client acceptance.
2   Engagement acceptance.
3   Changes in professional appointments.

All three situations may create threats that, if not at an acceptable level, shall be mitigated by appropriate safeguards. If it is not possible to reduce the threats to an acceptable level, the practitioner declines to enter into the client relationship, declines the engagement or does not undertake the work.

In a client acceptance situation, threats to the practitioner's integrity or professional behaviour may exist when the potential new client has been involved in tax evasion or questionable financial reporting practice. A possible safeguard in this situation is securing the client's commitment to improve corporate governance practices or internal controls.

In an engagement acceptance situation a self-interest threat to professional competence and due care may exist if the engagement team does not possess the competencies necessary to properly carry out the engagement. Possible safeguards are acquiring knowledge of relevant industries or subject matter, assigning sufficient additional staff with the necessary competencies, and using experts.

Also when changes in a professional appointment occur, threats may be identified. For example, a practitioner may consider tendering for an engagement currently held by another practitioner before knowing all pertinent facts. Such facts may be disagreements between the client and the existing practitioner. Incomplete information may cause a threat to professional competence and due care. A possible safeguard will be a request in the submission of the tender for direct contact with the existing practitioner. Such communication shall adhere to the confidentiality principle.

A practitioner is sometimes asked to undertake work that is complementary or additional to the work of the existing practitioner. Such a situation may give rise to threats to professional competence and due care resulting from, for example, a lack of or incomplete information. Safeguards against such threats include notifying the existing practitioner of the proposed work. This would give the existing practitioner the opportunity to provide the relevant information needed for the proper conduct of the work.

Conflicts of Interest

A practitioner shall take reasonable steps to identify circumstances that could pose a conflict of interest. For example, threats to objectivity and confidentiality may be created when:

- The practitioner and client compete.
- The practitioner performs services for clients whose interests are in conflict.
- The clients are in dispute with each other in relation to the matter or transaction in question.

Depending on the situation giving rise to the conflict, safeguards shall ordinarily include notifying the client or other known relevant parties and obtaining their consent to act.

A possible threat to objectivity or confidentiality exists if a firm competes directly with an (existing or new) client when both parties are offering consulting services. When causing a conflict of interest, the firm in this case notifies the client of the firm's consulting activities, and asks for their consent to perform such activities. Additional safeguards may be the use of separate engagement teams and procedures to prevent access to information (e.g. strict physical separation of such teams, confidential and secure data filing). The outcome may, however, be that it is not appropriate to accept a specific engagement or that resignation from conflicting engagements is required.

The practitioner may request consent from a client to act for another party (which may or may not be an existing client) in respect of a matter where the respective interests are in conflict. If consent has been refused by the client, the practitioner shall not continue to act for one of the parties in the matter giving rise to the conflict of interest.

Second Opinions

A practitioner may be asked to provide a second opinion on the application of accounting, auditing, reporting or other standards or principles to specific circumstances or transactions by or on behalf of a company or an entity that is not an existing client. Such situations may give rise to threats to compliance with the fundamental principles.

For example, there may be a threat to professional competence and due care in circumstances where the second opinion is not based on the same set of facts that were made available to the existing practitioner, or is based on inadequate evidence. The significance of the threat will depend on the circumstances of the request and all the other available facts and assumptions relevant to the expression of a professional judgement. Safeguards include seeking client permission to contact the existing practitioner, describing the limitations surrounding any opinion in communications with the client, and providing the existing practitioner with a copy of the opinion. If the company or entity seeking the opinion will not permit communication with the existing practitioner, the practitioner shall consider whether, taking all the circumstances into account, it is appropriate to provide the opinion sought.

Fees and Other Types of Remuneration

When entering into negotiations regarding professional services, a practitioner may quote whatever fee is deemed to be appropriate. The fact that one practitioner may quote a fee lower than another is not in itself unethical. Nevertheless, there may be threats to compliance with the fundamental principles arising from the level of fees quoted. For example, a self-interest threat to professional competence and due care is created if the fee quoted is so low that it may be difficult to perform the engagement in accordance with applicable technical and professional standards for that price. The significance of such threats will depend on factors such as the level of fee quoted and the services to which it applies. Available safeguards include assigning appropriate time and qualified staff to the task, quality control and procedures, and making the client aware of the terms of the engagement, in particular the basis on which fees are charged and which services are covered by the quoted fee.

Contingent fees are fees calculated on a predetermined basis relating to the outcome or result of a transaction or the result of the work performed. Such fees are commonly used for certain types of non-assurance engagements, but are not allowed for assurance engagements. Contingent fees for non-assurance engagements may give rise to a self-interest threat to objectivity. The significance of such threats will depend on factors such as the nature of the engagement, the range of possible fee amounts, the basis for determining the fee, and whether the outcome or result of the transaction is to be reviewed by an independent third party. Safeguards include an advance written agreement with the client as to the basis of remuneration, disclosure to intended users of the work performed by the practitioner and the basis of remuneration, quality control policies and procedures, and review by an objective third party of the work performed by the practitioner.

In certain circumstances, a practitioner may receive a *referral fee* or *commission* relating to a client. For example, where the practitioner does not provide a specialist service required by a client, a fee may be received for referring a continuing client to another practitioner or other expert for such services. Similarly, a practitioner may pay a referral fee to obtain a client where the client continues as a client of another practitioner but requires specialist services not offered by the existing practitioner. In other situations a practitioner may receive a commission from a third party (e.g. a software vendor) in connection with the sale of goods or services to a client. Possible safeguards when accepting or paying such a referral fee or commission include disclosing to the client any arrangements to pay or receive a referral fee, and obtaining advance agreement from the client for commission arrangements.

In practice a practitioner may purchase all or part of another audit firm on the basis that payments will be made to individuals formerly owning the firm or to their heirs or estates. Such payments are not regarded as referral fees or commissions.

Marketing Professional Services

When a practitioner solicits new work through advertising or other forms of marketing, there may be potential threats to compliance with the fundamental principles. For example, a self-interest threat to compliance with the principle of professional behaviour is created if services, achievements, or products are marketed in a way that may bring the profession into disrepute. As pointed out when discussing the principle of professional behaviour, the practitioners shall be honest and truthful and shall not make exaggerated claims for the services they are able to offer, the qualifications they possess, or experience they have gained; or make disparaging references or unsubstantiated comparisons to the work of others. If the practitioner is in doubt whether a proposed form of advertising or marketing is appropriate, the practitioner shall consult with the relevant professional body.

Gifts and Hospitality

A practitioner, or an **immediate family** member (a spouse, spouse equivalent, or dependent) or **close family** member (parent, child, or sibling who is not an immediate family member) may be offered gifts and hospitality from a client. Such offers ordinarily give rise to threats. For example, self-interest threats to objectivity may be created if a gift from a client is accepted, and intimidation threats to objectivity may result from the possibility of such offers being made public.

The significance of such threats will depend on the nature, value and intent behind the offer. Where gifts or hospitality are offered that a reasonable and informed third party, weighing all the specific facts and circumstances, would consider trivial and inconsequential, a practitioner may conclude that the offer is made in the normal course of business without the specific intent to influence decision-making or to obtain information. In such cases, the practitioner may generally conclude that any threat to compliance with the fundamental principles is at an acceptable level. If, however, the threats cannot be eliminated or reduced to an acceptable level through the application of safeguards, the practitioner shall not accept such an offer.

Custody of Client Assets

A practitioner shall not assume custody of client monies or other assets unless permitted to do so by law and, if so, in compliance with any additional legal duties imposed on a practitioner holding such assets.

The holding of client assets creates threats to compliance with fundamental principles. For example, there is a self-interest threat to professional behaviour and may be a self-interest threat to objectivity arising from holding client assets. To safeguard against such threats, the Code prescribes certain requirements and procedures that the practitioner entrusted with money (or other assets) belonging to others shall follow. The practitioner shall keep such assets separately from personal or firm assets, use such assets only for the purpose for which they are intended; at all times, be ready to account for those assets, and any income, dividends or gains generated, to any persons entitled to such accounting; and comply with all relevant laws and regulations relevant to the holding of and accounting for such assets.

In addition, practitioners shall be aware of threats through association with such assets, for example, if the assets were found to derive from illegal activities, such as money-laundering. As part of client and engagement acceptance procedures for such services, practitioners shall make appropriate inquiries about the source of such assets and shall consider their legal and regulatory obligations. They may also consider seeking legal advice.

Objectivity: All Services

When providing *any* professional service, a practitioner shall consider whether there are threats to compliance with the fundamental principle of objectivity. Such threats may result from having interests in or relationships with a client or directors, officers or employees. For example, a familiarity threat to objectivity may be created from a family or close personal or business relationship.

The existence of threats to objectivity when providing professional services will depend on the particular circumstances of the engagement and the nature of the work that the practitioner is performing. Safeguards include supervisory procedures, discussing the issue with higher levels of management within the firm and with those charged with governance of the client, withdrawing from the engagement team, and terminating the financial or business relationship giving rise to the threat.

A practitioner who provides an assurance service is required to be independent of the assurance client. Independence of mind and in appearance is necessary to enable the practitioner to express a conclusion, and be seen to express a conclusion, without bias, conflict of interest or undue influence of others. We will now turn to independence requirements when the practitioner performs audit and **review engagements**. The Code also covers similar requirements for assurance engagements that are not an audit or review engagement. These are discussed separately.

❖ Independence: Audit and Review Engagements

LO7

Section 290 in the Code addresses the independence requirements for audit and review engagements in which a practitioner expresses a conclusion on financial statements. In a review the practitioner does not obtain all of the evidence that would be required in an audit. The risk of expressing an inappropriate conclusion is reduced to a moderate level in a review rather than to a low level as in an audit. Practitioners may for example review a client's interim reporting. (Review engagements are discussed in detail in Chapter 20.) For presentation purposes, in the Code and the following text, the terms 'audit', 'audit team', 'audit engagement', 'audit client', and 'audit report' includes review, review team, review engagement, review client and review report; and 'firm' includes **network firm**, except where otherwise stated.

The Code requires that practitioners in performing audits (reviews) shall be both independent of mind and in appearance.

- *Independence of Mind.* The state of mind that permits the expression of a conclusion without being affected by influences that compromise professional judgement, thereby allowing an individual to act with integrity and exercise objectivity and professional scepticism.
- *Independence in Appearance.* The avoidance of facts and circumstances that are so significant that a reasonable and informed third party would be likely to conclude, weighing all the specific facts and circumstances, that a firm's, or a member of the audit team's, integrity, objectivity or professional scepticism has been compromised.

Independence of mind, sometimes referred to as independence in fact, is not an observable trait. Independence in appearance relates to a third party's perceptions. These often become the critical when circumstances and relationships are considered incompatible with independence.

The discussion in the following shows how the conceptual framework can be applied to assist firms and members of audit teams in achieving and maintaining independence in situations encountered in practice.

The framework shall, however, also be applied to other situations that threaten independence. The practitioner follows the three steps approach in the framework:

1   Identify threats to independence.
2   Evaluate the significance of the threats identified.
3   Apply safeguards, when necessary, to eliminate the threats or reduce them to an acceptable level.

When the practitioner determines that appropriate safeguards are not available or cannot be applied to eliminate the threats or reduce them to an acceptable level, he or she shall eliminate the circumstance or relationship creating the threats, or decline or terminate the audit engagement.

The practitioner shall document conclusions regarding compliance with independence requirements, and the substance of any relevant discussions that support those conclusions. The Code requires specifically that when safeguards are required to reduce a threat to an acceptable level, the practitioner shall document the nature of the threat and the safeguards in place or applied that reduce the threat to an acceptable level. Additionally, when a threat required significant analysis to determine whether safeguards were necessary and the professional accountant concluded that they were not because the threat was already at an acceptable level, the practitioner shall document the nature of the threat and the rationale for the conclusion.

The following describes specific circumstances and relationships that may create threats to independence, starting with holding a financial interest in an audit client.

Financial Interests

A **financial interest** is an interest in an equity or other security, debenture, loan or other debt instrument of an entity, including rights and obligations to acquire such an interest and derivatives directly related to such interest. Such financial interest in an audit client may create a self-interest threat. For example, the practitioner may be inclined to protect the value of his or her investment in the client where this may be impaired by an audit report with a modified audit opinion. The nature of the financial interest affects the significance of the threat, including:

- Whether the financial interest is direct or indirect.
- The role of the person holding the financial interest.
- The materiality of the financial interest.

A **direct financial interest** is a financial interest owned directly by and under the control of an individual or entity. Financial interests may be held through an intermediary (e.g. a collective investment vehicle, estate or trust). The determination of whether such financial interests are direct or indirect will depend upon whether the beneficial owner has control over the investment vehicle or the ability to influence its investment decisions. When control over the investment vehicle or the ability to influence investment decisions exists, the Code defines that financial interest to be a direct financial interest. Conversely, when the beneficial owner of the financial interest has no control over the investment vehicle or ability to influence its investment decisions, this Code defines that financial interest to be an **indirect financial interest**.

The Code includes circumstances where the self-interest threat created by the financial interest would be so significant that no safeguards could reduce the threat to an acceptable level, i.e. the Code prohibits holding such financial interests.

A *firm* (audit firm or network firm), a *member of the audit team* or a team member's *immediate family* member (i.e. a spouse or dependant) shall not have a direct financial interest or a material indirect financial interest in the audit client. This restriction also applies if one of these parties has a direct or material indirect financial interest in an entity that has a controlling interest in the audit client, and the client is material to the entity. Likewise, no safeguards could ordinarily reduce the threat to an acceptable level if other partners in the office in which the engagement **partner** practices in connection with the audit engagement, or their immediate family members, hold a direct or a material indirect financial interest in that audit client. This extends to other partners and managerial employees who provide non-audit services to the audit client, except those whose involvement is minimal.

Close family (a parent, child or sibling who is not an immediate family) is more distant than immediate family. Consequently, appropriate safeguards may reduce the self-interest to an acceptable level when a member of the audit team's knows that a close family member has a direct or a material indirect financial interest in the audit client. In evaluating the significance of the threat, relevant factors are the nature of the relationship between the member of the audit team and the close family member, and the materiality of the financial interest to the close family member. Potential safeguards would be to remove the individual from the audit team or have the close family dispose the financial interest.

The Code covers several other circumstances when a self-interest may be created, including if the firm, member of the audit team or team member's immediate family has a financial interest in an entity and an audit client also has a financial interest in that entity; and if the firm, member of the audit team or their immediate family has a financial interest in an entity when a director, officer or controlling owner of the audit client is also known to have a financial interest in that entity.

Loans and Guarantees

A loan or a guarantee of a loan from an audit client to a firm, a member of the audit team, or a team member's immediate family may cause a self-interest threat to independence. For example, the practitioner's benefits from a loan on favourable terms from a client may deter the practitioner from taking appropriate action in accordance with the professional standards.

A loan or a guarantee of a loan from an audit client that is a *bank or a similar institution* to a member of the audit team or a team member's immediate family does not create a threat to independence if the loan or guarantee is made under *normal* lending procedures, terms and conditions. Examples of such loans include home mortgages, bank overdrafts, car loans and credit card balances. If such loan or guarantee under normal commercial terms is provided to the *firm*, it may be possible to apply safeguards to reduce the self-interest threat to an acceptable level. An example of such a safeguard is having the work reviewed by a practitioner from a network firm that is neither involved with the audit nor has received the loan. A loan or guarantee *not* held under normal commercial terms from a bank or a similar institution to a firm, a member of the audit team or a team member's immediate family is *not* acceptable.

If a firm, a member of the audit team, or a team member's immediate family has *deposits* or a brokerage account with an audit client that is a bank, broker or similar institution, a threat to independence is not created if the deposit or account is held under normal commercial terms.

If the audit client is *not a bank* or similar institution, it is *not* acceptable for a firm, a member of the audit team or a team member's immediate family to accept a loan or to have borrowing guaranteed, unless the loan or guarantee is immaterial to all the involved parties, including the audit client. Similarly, it is not acceptable for a firm, a member of the audit team or a team member's immediate family, to make or guarantee a loan *to* an audit client, unless the loan or guarantee is immaterial to all parties.

Business Relationships

A close business relationship between a firm, a member of the audit team or a team member's immediate family and the audit client or its management arising from a commercial or common financial interest may cause self-interest or intimidation threats. For example, a common financial interest exists if a member of the audit team has a material financial interest in a joint venture with an officer who performs senior managerial functions for that client. In this situation the practitioner's temptation to protect the joint venture, or the practitioner's perception that the officer may threaten to adversely amend a favourable business relationship may influence or deter the practitioner from acting objectively.

Unless the financial interest is immaterial and the business relationship is insignificant to the firm and the client or its management, no safeguards could reduce the threat to an acceptable level. Therefore such a business relationship shall not be entered into, be reduced to an insignificant level, or terminated. In the case of a member of the audit team, unless such financial interest is immaterial and the relationship is insignificant to that member, the individual shall be removed from the audit team. If the business relationship with the audit client or its management relates to a team member's immediate family, appropriate safeguard may be applied to reduce any threats to an acceptable level.

In the specific case where the business relationship relates to a common interest with the audit client in a closely held entity, threats to independence may also be created.

The purchase of goods and services from an audit client by a firm, a member of the audit team or a team member's immediate family does not generally create a threat to independence in the normal course of business and on an arm's length basis. However, such transactions may be of such a nature or magnitude that they create a self-interest threat. Possible safeguards include eliminating or reducing the magnitude of the transaction and removing the individual from the audit team.

Family and Personal Relationships

Family and personal relationships between a member of the audit team and a director, an officer or certain employees (depending on their role) of the audit client, may create self-interest, familiarity or intimidation threats. For example, the practitioner's wish to maintain a good relationship with family members, the practitioner being too trusting of family, or perceived or actual threats by family, may influence or deter exercising professional scepticism. The existence and significance of the threats depends on a number of factors, including:

- The member's responsibilities on the audit team.
- The role of the family member or other individual within the client.
- The closeness of the relationship.

The member of the audit team is removed from the team (or the firm withdraws from the engagement) when he or she has an *immediate family member* that is (1) a *director* or an *officer* of the audit client, or (2) an *employee* of the audit client in a position to exert *significant influence* over the preparation of the client's accounting records or the financial statements. For example, it is not acceptable that a spouse of a member of the audit team is an employee in a position to exert significant influence over the preparation of client's accounting records.

If the employee of the audit client is in a position to exert significant influence over only the client's financial position, financial performance or cash flows, or is the more distant close family member, appropriate safeguards may be applied to reduce the threats to an acceptable level.

Threats to independence may also be created by a *close relationship* between a member of the audit team and client personnel who are not an immediate or close family member. This relates to a director or officer, or an employee in a position to exert significant influence over the preparation of the client's accounting records or the financial statements.

The Code also covers threats from personal or family relationship between a partner or employee of the firm who is *not* a member of the audit team, and a director or officer of the audit client or an employee in a position to exert significant influence over the preparation of the client's accounting records or the financial statements.

Employment with an Audit Client

In practice it is not uncommon that a former member of the audit team or partner of the firm becomes an employee of the audit client. In such situations self-interest, familiarity or intimidation threats may be created, particularly if the audit client is a public interest entity or significant connections remain between the individual and his or former firm.

Independence is deemed to be compromised if a former member of the audit team or partner of the firm has joined the audit client in a position as a director, an officer or as an employee in a position to exert significant influence over the preparation of the client's accounting records or the financial statements, *and a significant connection remains* between the firm and the individual. Such connection may be that the individual continues to participate or appears to participate in the firm's business or professional activities. If no significant connection remains, appropriate safeguards may be applied to reduce the threats to an acceptable level. For example, the audit plan may be modified or individuals who have sufficient experience in relation to the individual who has joined the client may be assigned to the audit team.

For audit clients that are public interest entities the Code is more restrictive. Assume that a **key audit partner** joins a public interest entity audit client as a director or officer of the entity, or as an employee in a position to exert significant influence over the preparation of the client's accounting records or the financial statements. The Code deems this to comprise independence *unless*, subsequent to the partner ceasing to be a key audit partner, the public interest entity had issued audited financial statements covering a period of not less than 12 months and the partner was not a member of the audit team with respect to the audit of those financial statements.

Temporary Staff Assignments

The lending of staff by a firm to an audit client may create a self-review threat. Such assistance may be given, but only for a short period of time. In addition, the firm's personnel shall not be involved in providing non-assurance services that the Code does not permit or assuming management responsibilities. In all circumstances, the audit client shall be responsible for directing and supervising the activities of the loaned staff.

Recent Service with an Audit Client

To have a former officer, director, or employee of the audit client serve as a member of the audit team may create self-interest, self-review and familiarity threats. This would be particularly true when a member of the audit team has to evaluate elements of the financial statements for which the member had prepared the accounting records while with the client. The Code restricts individuals from assigning to the audit team if, *during the period covered by the audit report,* the individual had served as an officer or director of the audit client, or had been an employee in a position to exert significant influence over the preparation of the client's accounting records or the financial statements. If the service with the audit client was performed prior to the period covered by the audit report, relevant safeguards may be applied to reduce the threats to an acceptable level. For example, the work performed by the individual as a member of the audit team may be reviewed.

Serving as a Director or Officer of Audit Clients

A partner or employee of the firm cannot serve as a director or officer of an audit client. This causes unacceptable self-review and self-interest threats. Therefore, if such an individual were to accept such position while continuing to serve as a partner or employee of the firm, the firm shall decline or withdraw from the audit engagement.

Long Association of Senior Personnel with an Audit Client, Including Partner Rotation

Using the same senior personnel on an audit engagement over a long period of time may create self-interest and familiarity threats. The practitioners shall evaluate threats and apply necessary safeguards. Safeguards may be rotating the senior personnel off the audit team, and regular independent internal or external quality reviews of the engagement. The Code prescribes partner rotation for public interest entity audit clients.

In an audit of a public interest entity, an individual shall not be a key audit partner for more than seven years. After such time, the individual shall not be a member of the engagement team or be a key audit partner for the client for two years. This is referred to as the cooling-off period. During this period, the individual shall not participate in the audit of the entity, provide quality control for the engagement, consult with the engagement team or the client regarding technical or industry-specific issues, transactions or events, or otherwise directly influence the outcome of the engagement.

Provision of Non-Assurance Services to Audit Clients

LO8

Firms have traditionally provided to their audit clients a range of non-assurance services that are consistent with their skills and expertise. The provision of non-assurance services may create threats to independence, particularly self-review, self-interest and advocacy threats. Before the firm accepts an engagement to provide a non-assurance service to an audit client, a determination shall be made as to whether providing such a service would create a threat to independence. Providing certain non-assurance services to an audit client may create a threat to independence so significant that *no safeguards* could reduce the threat to an acceptable level. Accordingly, the firm shall not provide such services or withdraw from the audit engagement. For other non-assurance services the Code guides on evaluation of threats and applicable safeguards. If the threats cannot be reduced to an acceptable level by the application of safeguards, the non-assurance service shall not be provided. In the case that the audit client is a public interest entity, more threats may exist and threats may be more significant, leading to additional restrictions for public interest entities.

The Code addresses a number of specific non-assurance services and circumstances that may threaten independence:

- Preparing accounting records and financial statements.
- Valuation services.
- Taxation services.
- Internal audit services.
- IT systems services.
- Litigation support services.
- Legal services.
- Recruiting services.
- Corporate finance services.

- Fees: relative size of fees, overdue fees and contingent fees.
- Compensation and evaluation policies.
- Gifts and hospitality.
- Actual or threatened litigation.

In evaluating the significance of any threat created by a particular non-assurance service, consideration shall be given to any threat created by providing other related non-assurance services. When specific guidance on a particular non-assurance service or circumstances is not included in the Code, the conceptual framework shall be applied when evaluating the particular circumstances.

Table 19–6 provides examples of safeguards that are particularly relevant in reducing threats created by the provision of non-assurance services to audit clients.

Table 19–6 Examples of Safeguards Related to Provision of Non-Assurance Services to Audit Clients
• Policies and procedures to prohibit professional staff from making management decisions for the audit client, or assuming responsibility for such decisions.
• Discussing independence issues related to the provision of non-assurance services with those charged with governance, such as the audit committee.
• Policies within the audit client regarding the oversight responsibility for provision of non-assurance services by the firm.
• Involving an additional practitioner to advise on the potential impact of the non-assurance engagement on the independence of the member of the audit team and the firm.
• Involving an additional practitioner outside of the firm to provide audit on a discrete aspect of the audit engagement.
• Obtaining the audit client's acknowledgement of responsibility for the results of the work performed by the firm.
• Discussing with those charged with governance the nature and extent of fees charged.
• Making arrangements so that personnel providing non-assurance services do not participate in the audit engagement.

Preparing Accounting Records and Financial Statements

Providing the audit client with accounting and bookkeeping services, such as preparing accounting records or financial statements, creates a self-review threat when the firm subsequently audits the financial statements.

It is the responsibility of management to ensure that accounting records are kept and financial statements are prepared. This responsibility includes:

- Originating or changing journal entries, or determining the account classifications of transactions.
- Preparing or changing source documents or originating data, in electronic or other form, evidencing the occurrence of a transaction.

The practitioner shall not assume management responsibility. Audit firms may, however, provide assistance to management in preparing accounting records or financial statements. The Code discusses three main activities:

1. Activities considered a normal part of the audit process that generally do not threaten independence.
2. Technical assistance and advice on accounting issues that generally do not threaten independence.
3. Services related to the preparation of accounting records and financial statements of a routine or mechanical nature that may create self-review threats.

Examples of activities considered to be a normal part of the audit process involve the application of accounting policies and standards, and proposing adjusting journal entries. Similarly, the financial statement process may involve assisting an audit client in resolving account reconciliation problems or accumulating information for regulatory reporting.

Examples of services of a routine or mechanical nature related to the preparation of accounting records and financial statements include:

- Providing payroll services based on client-originated data.
- Recording transactions for which the client has determined or approved the appropriate account classification.
- Posting transactions coded by the client to the general ledger.
- Posting client-approved entries to the trial balance.

● Preparing financial statements based on information in the trial balance.

Firms may provide such services to an audit client that is not a public interest entity if any self-review threats are reduced to an acceptable level. An example of a safeguard is arranging for such services to be performed by an individual who is not a member of the audit team.

To an audit client that is a *public interest entity* the firm shall ordinarily not provide accounting and bookkeeping services, including payroll services, or prepare financial statements or financial information which forms the basis of the financial statements.

Valuation Services

A valuation comprises the making of assumptions with regard to future developments, the application of appropriate methodologies and techniques, and the combination of both to compute a certain value, or range of values, for an asset, a liability or for a business as a whole. A self-review threat may be created when a firm performs a valuation that is to be incorporated into the client's financial statements. The existence and significance of any threat will depend on factors such as:

● Whether the valuation will have a material effect on the financial statements.
● The extent of the client's involvement in determining and approving the valuation methodology and other significant matters of judgement.
● The availability of established methodologies and professional guidelines.
● For valuations involving standard or established methodologies, the degree of subjectivity inherent in the item.
● The reliability and extent of the underlying data.
● The degree of dependence on future events of a nature that could create significant volatility inherent in the amounts involved.
● The extent and clarity of the disclosures in the financial statements.

Examples of safeguards are that personnel providing the valuation service services do not participate in the audit engagement, or having a professional who was not a member of the audit team to review the audit or the valuation work done.

The firm shall *not* provide a valuation service (or withdraw from the audit engagement) if the valuation service has a *material* effect on the financial statements and the valuation involves a *significant degree of subjectivity.*

For *public interest entity* audit clients the firm shall *not* provide valuation services to an audit client if the valuations would have a *material* effect, separately or in the aggregate, on the financial statements.

Taxation Services

Audit firms provide a broad range of taxation services to audit clients. These may create self-review threats when the service relates to tax matters to be reflected in the financial statements. Advocacy threats may be created when the firm represents an audit client in the resolution of a tax dispute. The Code discusses four categories of taxation services:

1   Tax return preparation.
2   Tax calculations for the purpose of preparing the accounting entries.
3   Tax planning and other tax advisory services.
4   Assistance in the resolution of tax disputes.

Tax return preparation services involve assisting clients with their tax reporting obligations by drafting and completing information. The service does not generally create a threat to independence if management takes responsibility for the returns including any significant judgements made.

Preparing calculations of current and deferred tax liabilities (or assets) for the purpose of preparing accounting entries creates a self-review threat. For *public interest entity* audit clients the firm shall ordinary *not* prepare such tax calculations of entries that are material to the financial statements. For other entities safeguards may be applied to reduce threats to an acceptable level. For example, the firm may use professionals who are not members of the audit team to perform the tax service, or obtain advice on the service from an external tax professional.

Tax planning or other tax advisory services comprise a broad range of services, such as advising the client how to structure its affairs in a tax-efficient manner or advising on the application of a new tax law or regulation. Tax advice may affect matters to be reflected in the financial statements, creating a self-review threat. Factors affecting the significance of such threat and relevant safeguards are similar to those discussed for valuation services. The Code specifies, however, a situation where the firm is not permitted to provide tax advice. This occurs where the effectiveness of the tax advice depends on a particular accounting treatment or presentation in the financial statements, and (a) the audit team has reasonable doubt as to the appropriateness of the related accounting treatment or presentation under the relevant financial reporting framework; and (b) the outcome or consequences of the tax advice will have a material effect on the financial statements. A similar prohibition applies for corporate finance advice (discussed in the following).

An advocacy or self-review threat may be created when the firm represents an audit client in the resolution of a tax dispute. For example, the firm shall not act as an advocate for an audit client before a court in the resolution of a tax matter when the amounts involved are material to the financial statements.

Internal Audit Services

Internal audit services involve assisting the audit client in the performance of its internal audit activities. In providing such services the firm shall not assume management responsibility, for example not set internal audit policies or take responsibility for designing, implementing and maintaining internal control. The Code specifies the conditions to be met to avoid assuming management responsibility in performing internal audit services.

Provision of internal audit services creates a self-review threat to independence if the firm uses the internal audit work in the course of a subsequent external audit. The significance of the threat will depend on factors such as the degree of use of the results of the internal audit service and the materiality of the financial statement amounts involved. For *public interest entity* audit clients the firm shall *not* provide internal audit services that relate to a significant part of the internal controls over financial reporting; financial accounting systems that generate information that is, separately or in the aggregate, significant to the client's accounting records or financial statements; or amounts or disclosures that are, separately or in the aggregate, material to the financial statements.

IT Systems Services

Services related to information technology (IT) systems include the design or implementation of hardware or software systems. The systems may aggregate source data, form part of the internal control over financial reporting or generate information that affects the accounting records or financial statements. Thus, provision of IT systems services may create a self-review threat.

For *public interest entity* audit clients the firm shall *not* provide services involving the design or implementation of IT systems that form a *significant part* of the internal control over financial reporting or generate information that is *significant* to the client's accounting records or financial statements. The Code is less restrictive if the entity is not a public interest entity, but requires specified safeguards to be put in place to ensure that the self-review threat is not too significant.

Litigation Support Services

Litigation support services may include activities such as acting as an expert witness, calculating estimated damages or other amounts that might become receivable or payable as the result of litigation or other legal dispute, and assistance with document management and retrieval. These services may create a self-review or advocacy threat. Where the result of a valuation for litigation support will have a direct effect on the financial statements, the requirements in the Code relating to valuation services are applicable. In the case of other litigation support services, the significance of any threat created shall be evaluated and safeguards applied when necessary to eliminate the threat or reduce it to an acceptable level.

Legal Services

Legal services are defined as any services for which the person providing the services must either be admitted to practice law before the courts of the jurisdiction in which such services are to be provided or have the required legal training to practice law. Providing legal services to an entity that is an audit client may create both self-review and advocacy threats. For example, legal services that support in executing a transaction (e.g. contract support, legal advice, legal due diligence and restructuring) may create self-review threats. The Code advises on relevant factors in evaluating the significance of threats and on applicable safeguards.

The firm is not permitted to act in an advocacy role for an audit client in resolving a dispute or litigation when the amounts involved are material to the financial statements.

Recruiting Services

Audit firms provide recruiting services such as reviewing the professional qualifications of applicants, interviewing candidates and providing advice on their suitability for the post. In providing recruiting services the firm shall not assume management responsibilities, including not acting as a negotiator on the client's behalf or making the hiring decision. Providing recruiting services to an audit client may create self-interest, familiarity or intimidation threats. The significance of the threats will depend on factors such as the nature of the requested assistance and the role of the person to be recruited. Safeguards shall be applied when necessary to reduce the threats to an acceptable level.

Corporate Finance Services

Corporate finance services comprise a broad range of services including assisting in developing corporate strategies, identifying possible targets for the client to acquire, advising on disposal transactions, assisting finance-raising transactions and providing structuring advice. Such services may create advocacy and self-review threats. For example, advice on the structuring of a corporate finance transaction or on financing arrangements may directly affect amounts that will be reported in the financial statements. The Code advises the practitioner how to evaluate the significance of threats and apply relevant safeguards. For example, a safeguard would be to use a professional who is not a member of the audit team to provide the services.

Certain corporate finance services are not permitted, such as services involving promoting, dealing in or underwriting an audit client's shares. In addition, and as referred to in the prior discussion of a similar prohibition of tax advice, the firm is not permitted to provide corporate finance advice where the effectiveness of the corporate finance advice depends on a particular accounting treatment or presentation in the financial statements, and (a) the audit team has reasonable doubt as to the appropriateness of the related accounting treatment or presentation under the relevant financial reporting framework; and (b) the outcome or consequences of the corporate finance advice will have a material effect on the financial statements.

Fees: Relative Size of Fees, Overdue Fees and Contingent Fees

An earlier section in this chapter discussed possible threats to the fundamental principles related to fees and other types of remuneration, including the level of the fee, contingent fees and commissions received from clients. The following discusses how the *relative size of the fee*, *fees overdue* and *contingent fees* relate to threats to independence on an audit engagement.

When the total fees from an audit client represent a large proportion of the total fees of the firm, the dependence on that client and concern about losing the client create a self-interest or intimidation threat. Similar threats are also created when the fees generated from an audit client represent a large proportion of the revenue from an individual partner's clients or a large proportion of the revenue of an individual office of the firm. Relevant safeguards in such situations would be to reduce the dependency on the audit client and quality reviews of the audit performed. For *public interest entity* audit clients the firm is required take specific actions if for two consecutive years the total fees from the client and its related entities represent more than 15 per cent of the total fees received by the firm. In this situation the firm shall disclose to those charged with governance of the audit client the fact that the total of such fees represents more than 15 per cent of the total fees received by the firm, and discuss the safeguards it will be apply to reduce the threat to an acceptable level. The Code prescribed performing an engagement quality control review or equivalent reviews performed as safeguards.

Generally the firm requires payment of audit fees before the audit report is issued. A self-interest threat may be created if fees due from an audit client remain *unpaid* for a long time, especially if a significant part is not paid before the issue of the audit report for the following year. A safeguard would then be to have an additional practitioner who did not take part in the audit engagement to provide advice or review the work performed. The firm shall determine whether the overdue fees might be regarded as being equivalent to a loan to the client and whether, because of the significance of the overdue fees, it is appropriate for the firm to be re-appointed or continue the audit engagement.

Contingent fees are fees calculated on a predetermined basis relating to the outcome of a transaction or the result of the services performed by the firm. A contingent fee is not allowed for audits and other assurance engagements, but may be charged related to a non-assurance service provided to an audit client. This may cause a self-interest threat that is unacceptable. This occurs if one of these situations is present:

- The fee is charged by the firm expressing the opinion on the financial statements, and the fee is material or expected to be material to that firm.
- The fee is charged by a network firm that participates in a significant part of the audit and the fee is material or expected to be material to that firm.
- The outcome of the non-assurance service, and therefore the amount of the fee, is dependent on a future or contemporary judgement related to the audit of a material amount in the financial statements.

For other contingent fee arrangements charged by a firm for a non-assurance service, the Code advises on factors affecting the significance of the threats and on relevant safeguards.

Compensation and Evaluation Policies

A self-interest threat is created when a member of the audit team is evaluated on or compensated for selling non-assurance services to that audit client. The significance of the threat will depend on the proportion of the individual's compensation or performance evaluation that is based on the sale of such services, the role of the individual on the audit team, and whether promotion decisions are influenced by the sale of such services. If the threat is not at an acceptable level, the firm shall either revise the compensation plan or evaluation process for that individual, or apply safeguards to reduce it to an acceptable level. Examples of such safeguards include removing such members from the audit team or having a practitioner review the work of the member of the audit team. A key audit partner is not permitted to be evaluated on or compensated based on that partner's success in selling non-assurance services to the partner's audit client.

Gifts and Hospitality

An earlier section in this chapter discussed threats to the fundamental principles from gifts or hospitality received from a client. By the same arguments, a firm or a member of the audit team shall not accept such gifts or hospitality, unless the value is trivial and inconsequential.

Actual or Threatened Litigation

When litigation takes place, or appears likely, between the firm or a member of the audit team and the audit client, self-interest and intimidation threats are created. For example, management's willingness to make disclosure to the practitioner regarding all aspects relevant to the audit of the business operations may be affected. The significance of the threats created will depend on such factors as the materiality of the litigation and whether the litigation relates to a prior audit engagement. Examples of safeguards are having a professional review of the work performed, or if the litigation involves a member of the audit team, removing that individual from the audit team. If safeguards do not reduce the threats to an acceptable level, the only appropriate action is to withdraw from, or decline, the audit engagement.

Independence for Other Assurance Engagements

Assurance engagements are designed to enhance intended users' degree of confidence about the outcome of the evaluation or measurement of a subject matter against criteria. Compliance with the fundamental principle of objectivity requires being independent when performing assurance engagements.

Part B of the Code of Ethics includes a Section (291) on independence requirements for assurance engagements that are not financial statements audit or review engagements. (Chapter 20 discusses such other assurance engagements in detail.) This section in the Code serves to assist firms and members of assurance teams in applying the conceptual framework approach to achieving and maintaining independence.

There are many matters in the consideration of independence requirements that are relevant for *all* assurance engagements. Thus, many of the same circumstances and relationships discussed previously related to independence requirements for audits and reviews are also discussed in the section in the Code covering other assurance engagements. The meaning of terms and expressions used are the same, including the definition of independence. Threats and safeguards guidance related to the parallel circumstances and relationships in many cases bear close resemblance. However, in specific circumstances the existence and significance of the threats, the effects of applying safeguards and what is an acceptable level of threat may differ. This leads to differences in the appropriate approach to reduce the threats to an acceptable level. Such differences are clearly visible for the provision of non-assurance services. Provision of *specific* non-assurance services is not discussed in the section of the Code covering other assurance engagements.

Threats to independence may, however, be created when a firm provides a non-assurance service related to the subject matter information of an assurance engagement. For example, a self-review threat would be created if the firm developed and prepared prospective financial information and subsequently provided assurance on this information. Consequently, the firm shall evaluate the significance of threats created by the provision of non-assurance services and apply safeguards when necessary to eliminate the threat or reduce it to an acceptable level. However, the nature and significance of the threats may differ depending on whether they arise in relation to the provision of a non-assurance service to an audit client, or to an assurance client that is not an audit client. Threats to independence typically arise more frequently and are of greater significance when a non-assurance service is provided to an audit client. Thus, the provision of non-assurance services to audit clients is more restricted than to non-audit assurance clients.

The reader is referred to the Section 291 in the Code of Ethics for details of independence requirements for assurance engagements. The next section discusses briefly Part C of the Code of Ethics that relates to accountants in business.

Professional Ethics for Professional Accountants in Business

LO9

Professional accountants in business have varied responsibilities and perform a broad range of services. Key roles are providing assurance, facilitating management decision-making and strategic development, and serving as the gatekeeper of corporate integrity. A major challenge is to balance their roles of meeting corporate objectives and shareholders' needs. Accountants in business will often be involved in the preparation and reporting of financial and other information. Thus, in their work the integrity of the numbers produced becomes a key issue. Accountants in business deal with ongoing pressure over ethics, for example related to aggressive earnings management.

Part C of the Code of Ethics shows how the conceptual framework in Part A is applied by professional accountants in business. Recall that a *professional accountant in business* is an accountant holding membership in an IFAC body and is employed or engaged in an executive or non-executive capacity in an organization *other* than an audit firm. Such organizations include commerce, industry, service, the public sector, education, the not-for-profit sector, regulatory bodies, or professional bodies.

Professional accountants in business shall comply with the fundamental principles and apply the conceptual framework when threats to the principles occur. Since they are in business and not in public practice, they are generally less exposed to threats. For example, the independence requirement does primarily relate to accountants that provide assurance services in public practice.

The Code discusses circumstances that may create threats and advises on possible safeguards. For example, an intimidation threat may be created by threat of dismissal of the accountant over a disagreement about the application of an accounting principle. Possible safeguards in such situations are policies and procedures within the employing organization to empower employees to communicate ethical issues of concern to senior level, and consultation with another professional accountant.

The Code focuses on five specific situations that may create threats to compliance with the fundamental principles. These are:

1 Potential conflicts.
2 Preparation and reporting of information.
3 Acting with sufficient expertise.
4 Financial interests.
5 Inducements.

Potential conflicts may be caused by responsibilities to or pressure from the employing organization. For example, a conflict as well as a threat to appropriate preparation of the financial statements is present if the accountant faces pressure from a supervisor to facilitate inappropriate financial reporting. The fundamental principle of professional competence and due care is challenged if the accountant acts without sufficient expertise in undertaking the task. If the accountant holds financial interests in the employing business, self-interest threats to objectivity or confidentiality may be created. As a final example, an accountant being offered inducements such as gifts or preferential treatment may face similar threats. The Code advises on relevant safeguards in these and other circumstances, and prescribes appropriate actions when safeguards cannot reduce the threats to an acceptable level.

◆ AUDITOR INDEPENDENCE IN THE EU

LO10

The EU 8th Directive on Statutory Audits requires member states to ensure that all statutory auditors and audit firms are subject to principles of professional ethics, covering at least their public-interest function, their integrity and objectivity, and their professional competence and due care. The requirements include that statutory auditors and audit firms are independent when carrying out statutory audits. The Directive adheres to the conceptual framework approach and states that the 'the Commission may adopt implementing measures on independence as minimum standards. In doing so, the Commission might take into consideration the principles contained in the Recommendation of 16 May 2002'.

The European Commission's 'Recommendation on Statutory Auditors' Independence in the EU: A Set of Fundamental Principles' of 2002 serves as a benchmark of good practice for EU member states. Member states remain free to establish stricter rules than those laid down in the Recommendation.

The Recommendation follows the conceptual framework approach and its content is similar to that of the IFAC Code of Ethics for Professional Accountants. It is based on the same approach, uses the same concepts, and suggests essentially the same assessments in practical situations. In motivating the preferred approach to ensure auditor's independence the Commission states that:

> A principles-based approach to statutory auditors' independence is preferable to one based on detailed rules because it creates a robust structure within which statutory auditors have to justify their actions. It also provides the audit profession and its regulators with the flexibility to react promptly and effectively to new developments in business and in the audit environment. At the same time, it avoids the highly legalistic and rigid approach to what is and is not permitted which can arise in a rules-based regime. A principles-based approach can cater for the almost infinite variations in individual circumstances that arise in practice and in the different legal environments throughout the EU. Consequently, a principles-based approach will better serve the needs of European capital markets, as well as those of SMEs (small and medium sized enterprises).

Section A of the Recommendation presents the conceptual framework, including the categories of independence threats and safeguards. The statutory auditor shall ensure that independence risk is reduced to an acceptable level by applying safeguards. Section B addresses situations that may compromise independence. The situations covered are similar to those in the Code of Ethics (Section 290). The threats created, safeguards proposed, mandatory safeguards, and prohibitions in the Recommendation are comparable to those in the Code of Ethics. Overall, the application of the Recommendation is expected to result in the same decisions as the application of the Code of Ethics.

QUALITY CONTROL SYSTEMS

Audit firms are required to establish a system of control quality that implements policies and procedures to monitor the firms' practices and ensures that professional standards are being followed. Professional institutes and regulatory bodies have established quality assurance programmes to inspect the firms' quality control systems and its personnel compliance with standards and ethical requirements.

The International Standard on Quality Control ISQC 1 deals with a firm's responsibilities for its **system of quality control** for audits and reviews of financial statements, and other assurance and related services engagements. Quality assurance programmes are established by the professional institutes for their members, by regulatory bodies, or by professional institutes and regulatory bodies in concert. Two principal systems of quality assurance exist: monitoring and peer review. **Monitoring** refers to the situation where staff employed by the professional institute or regulatory bodies manage the quality assurance programme and carry out the inspection. Peer review refers to a system where peers in the profession carry out the reviews.

◆ System of Quality Control

LO11

A firm's system of quality control is designed to provide it with reasonable assurance that the firm and its personnel comply with professional standards and applicable legal and regulatory requirements, and that reports issued by the firm or engagement partners are appropriate in the circumstances (ISQC 1, para. 11). The system of quality control consists of policies and procedures necessary to implement and monitor compliance with those policies. The requirement to establish a system of quality control applies to all firms. A firm's system of quality control, however, has to be tailored to its size, the nature of its practice, its organization, and cost–benefit considerations. For a sole practitioner or small firm, a system of quality control is likely to be much less formal than for a national or international firm. For example, a sole practitioner with three professional staff members may use a simple checklist and conduct periodic informal discussions to monitor his or her firm's compliance with professional standards.[vii] On the other hand, a large international audit firm may develop involved in-house procedures and assign full- or part-time staff to oversee and ensure compliance with the firm's quality control system.

Elements of a System of Quality Control

ISQC 1 identifies the following six elements of firm's system of quality control:

1   Leadership responsibilities for quality within the firm.
2   Relevant ethical requirements.
3   Acceptance and continuance of client relationships and specific engagements.
4   Human resources.
5   Engagement performance.
6   Monitoring.

Table 19–7 defines each of the elements. It should be apparent from the definitions that these elements are interrelated. For example, human resources encompass criteria for capabilities, competence and commitment to ethical principles of the firm's personnel to engagements, which affect specific engagements policies and procedures developed for acceptance and continuance of client relationships as well as to meet engagement performance objectives. It is important for a firm to develop a system of quality control that takes each of these elements into account and to ensure that members of the firm understand the firm's quality control policies and procedures. The quality control policies and procedures should be documented and communicated to the firm's personnel. Such communication describes the quality control policies and procedures and the objectives they are designed to achieve, and includes the message that each individual has a personal responsibility for quality and is expected to comply with these policies and procedures. A firm's quality control policies and the Code of Ethics should be covered in the firm's training programmes.

Table 19–7   Elements of a System of Quality Control

- **Leadership Responsibilities for Quality within the Firm**. Policies and procedures designed to promote an internal culture recognizing that quality is essential in performing engagements.

- **Relevant Ethical Requirements**. Policies and procedures designed to provide the firm with reasonable assurance that the firm and its personnel comply with relevant ethical requirements, including independence requirements, and that it is notified of breaches of independence requirements, and that it is to enable it to take appropriate actions to resolve such situations.

- **Acceptance and Continuance of Client Relationships and Specific Engagements**. Policies and procedures for the acceptance and continuance of client relationships and specific engagements, designed to provide the firm with reasonable assurance that it will only undertake or continue relationships and engagements where the firm:

  (a)   Is competent to perform the engagement and has the capabilities, including time and resources, to do so.
  (b)   Can comply with relevant ethical requirements.
  (c)   Has considered the integrity of the client, and does not have information that would lead it to conclude that the client lacks integrity.

- **Human Resources**. Policies and procedures designed to provide the firm with reasonable assurance that it has sufficient personnel with the competence, capabilities, and commitment to ethical principles necessary to:

  (a)   Perform engagements in accordance with professional standards and applicable legal and regulatory requirements.
  (b)   Enable the firm or engagement partners to issue reports that are appropriate in the circumstances.

- **Engagement Performance**. Policies and procedures designed to provide the firm with reasonable assurance that engagements are performed in accordance with professional standards and applicable legal and regulatory requirements, and that the firm or the engagement partner issue reports that are appropriate in the circumstances.

- **Monitoring**. Established monitoring process designed to provide it with reasonable assurance that the policies and procedures relating to the system of quality control are relevant, adequate, and operating effectively.

Source: ISQC 1 *Quality Control for Firms That Perform Audits and Reviews of Financial Statements, and Other Assurance and Related Services Engagements*, IAASB (2009).

Table 19–8 provides some selected examples of the types of policies or procedures a firm can implement to comply with a sound system of quality control.

Table 19–8   Selected Quality Control Policies and Procedures
Leadership Responsibilities for Quality within the Firm
• Establish the firm's chief executive officer ultimate responsibility for the firm's system of quality control.
• Ensure that person(s) assigned operational responsibility for the firm's system of quality control by the firm's chief executive officer has sufficient and appropriate experience and ability, and the necessary authority, to assume that responsibility.
Ethical Requirements
• Communicate the firm's independence requirements to its personnel and, where applicable, others subject to them.
• Require personnel to promptly notify the firm of circumstances and relationships that create a threat to independence so that appropriate action can be taken.
Acceptance and Continuance of Client Relationships and Specific Engagements
• Obtain such information as the firm considers necessary in the circumstances before accepting an engagement with a new client, when deciding whether to continue an existing engagement, and when considering acceptance of a new engagement with an existing client.
• Require the firm to determine whether it is appropriate to accept the engagement, if a potential conflict of interest is identified in accepting an engagement from a new or an existing client.
Human Resources
• Ensure that the engagement partner has the appropriate competence, capabilities, and authority to perform the role.
• Clearly define and communicate the responsibilities of the engagement partner to that partner.
Engagement Performance
• Ensure that appropriate consultation takes place on difficult or contentious matters.
• Require an engagement quality control review for all audits of financial statements of listed entities.
Monitoring
• Include an ongoing consideration and evaluation of the firm's system of quality control including, on a cyclical basis, inspection of at least one completed engagement for each engagement partner.
• Require that those performing the engagement or the engagement quality control review are not involved in inspecting the engagements.
Source: ISQC 1 *Quality Control for Firms That Perform Audits and Reviews of Financial Statements, and Other Assurance and Related Services Engagements*, IAASB (2009).

The quality control standard requires that the firm continually monitor the relevance, adequacy and operating effectiveness of the system. Ongoing consideration and evaluation of the system of quality control include matters such as the following:

- Inspection procedures of a selection of completed engagements.
- Analysis of:
  - New professional standards and regulatory and legal requirements.
  - Written confirmation of compliance with policies and procedures on independence.
  - Continuing professional development, including training.
  - Decisions related to acceptance and continuance of client relationships and specific engagements.
- Determination of any corrective actions to be taken and improvements to be made in the system.
- Communication to appropriate firm personnel of weaknesses identified in the system, in the level of understanding of the system or compliance with it.
- Follow-up by appropriate firm personnel to ensure that any necessary modifications are promptly made to the quality control policies and procedures.

The firm should evaluate the effect of deficiencies noted as a result of the monitoring process, and communicate the deficiencies and recommendations for appropriate remedial action to relevant engagement partners and other appropriate personnel.

The firm should establish policies and procedures designed to provide it with reasonable assurance that it deals appropriately with: (1) complaints and allegations that the work performed by the firm fails to comply with professional standards and applicable legal and regulatory requirements; and (2) allegations of non-compliance with the firm's system of quality control. As part of this process, the firm should establish clearly defined channels for firm personnel to raise any concerns in a manner that enables them to come forward without fear of reprisals.

❖ Quality Assurance Programmes

LO12 At the national level, professional institutes or regulatory bodies, sometimes in cooperation, have established quality assurance programmes to review and inspect firms' and auditors' practices. The degree of regulator involvement may vary but public oversight of the programmes is common.

A member body of IFAC shall ensure that a mandatory **quality assurance review** programme is in place for its members performing audits of financial statements, as a minimum, for audits of listed entities (SMO 1). The subject of the quality assurance review is either a firm or partner. The objective of a quality assurance review is to determine whether the member is subject to an adequate system of quality control, is in compliance with such system, and has adhered to professional standards and applicable legal and regulatory requirements in performing engagements. The SMO guides on the scope and design of the assurance programme, competence and organization of the quality assurance review team and its procedures, documentation of the reviews, reporting of the results of the reviews, and appropriate corrective and disciplinary actions. A member body shall choose either a cycle or risk-based approach for selecting members for review. When a cycle approach is selected and a firm is the subject of the review, a maximum cycle of three years is adopted. When a partner is the subject, the selected length of the review cycle takes into consideration the quality and effectiveness of the internal inspection programme of the partner's firm.

The EU 8th Directive on Statutory Audits requires that all statutory auditors and audit firms are subject to a quality assurance programme. The programme shall be under public oversight. The scope of the quality assurance review shall include an assessment of compliance with applicable auditing standards and independence requirements, of the quantity and quality of resources spent, of the audit fees charged, and of the internal quality control system of the audit firm. A quality assurance review shall take place at least every six years. In 2000 the European Commission issued a Recommendation on minimum requirements of quality assurance for statutory audits in member states. In 2008 the Commission issued a Recommendation on quality assurance for audits of public interest entities. The Recommendation reduces the flexibility inherent in the Directive on quality assurance for these entities. For audits of public interest entities practising auditors cannot act as inspectors, the public oversight body shall play a more active role in the inspections and assume the ultimate responsibility for the quality assurance programme.

🔐 Key Terms

Assurance engagement. An engagement in which a practitioner (professional accountant in public practice) expresses a conclusion designed to enhance the degree of confidence of the intended users other than the responsible party about the outcome of the evaluation or measurement of a subject matter against criteria.

Close family. A parent, child or sibling who is not an immediate family member.

Contingent fee. A fee calculated on a predetermined basis relating to the outcome of a transaction or the result of the services performed by the firm. A fee that is established by a court or other public authority is not a contingent fee.

Direct financial interest. A financial interest owned directly by and under the control of an individual or entity (including those managed on a discretionary basis by others); or beneficially owned through a collective investment vehicle, estate, trust or other intermediary over which the individual or entity has control, or the ability to influence investment decisions.

Ethics. A system or code of conduct based on moral duties and obligations that indicates how an individual should behave.

Financial interest. An interest in an equity or other security, debenture, loan or other debt instrument of an entity, including rights and obligations to acquire such an interest and derivatives directly related to such interest.

Firm. A sole practitioner, partnership or corporation of professional accountants; an entity that controls such parties, through ownership, management or other means; and An entity controlled by such parties, through ownership, management or other means.

Immediate family. A spouse (or equivalent) or dependant.

Indirect financial interest. A financial interest beneficially owned through a collective investment vehicle, estate, trust or other intermediary over which the individual or entity has no control or ability to influence investment decisions.

Key audit partner. The engagement partner, the individual responsible for the engagement quality control review, and other audit partners, if any, on the engagement team who make key decisions or judgements on significant matters with respect to the audit of the financial statements on which the firm will express an opinion. Depending upon the circumstances and the role of the individuals on the audit, 'other audit partners' may include, for example, audit partners responsible for significant subsidiaries or divisions.

Monitoring (of quality control). A process comprising an ongoing consideration and evaluation of the firm's system of quality control, including a periodic inspection of a selection of completed engagements, designed to enable the firm to obtain reasonable assurance that its system of quality control is operating effectively.

Network. A network is a larger structure that is aimed at cooperation; and that is clearly aimed at profit or cost sharing or shares common ownership, control or management, common quality control policies and procedures, common business strategy, the use of a common brand name, or a significant part of professional resources.

Nework firm. A firm or entity that belongs to a network.

Partner. Any individual with authority to bind the firm with respect to the performance of a professional services engagement.

Professional accountant. An individual who is a member of an IFAC member body.

Professional accountant in business. A professional accountant employed or engaged in an executive or non-executive capacity in such areas as commerce, industry, service, the public sector, education, the not for profit sector, regulatory bodies or professional bodies, or a professional accountant contracted by such entities.

Professional accountant in public practice (practitioner). A professional accountant, irrespective of functional classification (e.g. audit, tax or consulting) in a firm that provides professional services. This term is also used to refer to a firm of professional accountants in public practice.

Professional services. Services requiring accountancy or related skills performed by a professional accountant, including accounting, auditing, taxation, management consulting and financial management services.

Professionalism. The conduct, aims or qualities that characterize or mark a profession or professional person.

Public interest entity. A listed entity, and an entity defined by regulation or legislation as a public interest entity or for which the audit is required by regulation or legislation to be conducted in compliance with the same independence requirements that apply to the audit of listed entities.

Quality assurance review. A review to determine whether the member: (1) is subject to (partner) or has (firm) an adequate system of quality control; (2) is in compliance with such system; and (3) has adhered to professional standards and regulatory and legal requirements in performing engagements.

Review engagement. An assurance engagement that enables an auditor to state whether, on the basis of procedures which do not provide all the evidence that would be required in an audit, anything has come to the auditor's attention that causes the auditor to believe that the financial statements are not prepared, in all material respects, in accordance with an applicable financial reporting framework.

System of quality control. Policies designed to provide a firm with reasonable assurance that: (1) the firm and its personnel comply with professional standards and regulatory and legal requirements; and (2) reports issued by the firm or partners are appropriate in the circumstances, and the procedures necessary to implement and monitor compliance with those policies.

? Review Questions

LO2	**19–1**	Briefly describe the three theories of ethical behaviour that can be used to analyse ethical issues in accounting.
LO4	**19–2**	How is the IFAC Code of Ethics for Professional Accountants organized?

LO5 19–3 What are the five fundamental principles of professional ethics?

LO5,7 19–4 What is meant by an accountant's objectivity and how does independence relate to objectivity?

LO5,6,7 19–5 Why may a self-interest threat to objectivity be created if a gift from a client is accepted?

LO5,6,7 19–6 What is meant by independence of mind and independence in appearance?

LO5,6,7 19–7 Why may a loan from an audit client to a member of the audit team cause a self-interest threat? List two possible safeguards.

LO5,6,7 19–8 Why may a close business relationship between a member of the audit team and the audit client cause self-interest or intimidation threats? List two possible safeguards.

LO5,6,7 19–9 Why may family or personal relationships between a member of the audit team and a director of the audit client create self-interest, familiarity or intimidation threats? List two possible safeguards.

LO5,6,7,8 19–10 List five non-assurance services that may impair independence if provided to an audit client.

LO5,6,7,8 19–11 Can an auditor originate journal entries or determine the account classification of transactions for the audit client?

LO5,6,7,8 19–12 Why may having senior personnel on an audit engagement over a long period of time create self-interest and familiarity threats? List two possible safeguards.

LO11 19–13 What is the purpose of establishing a system of quality control for audit firms? List the six elements of a system of quality control, and provide one example of a policy or procedure related to each element.

LO12 19–14 Why are assurance quality control programmes established?

Problems

LO5,6,7,8 19–15 Dean Wareham, an audit manager, is preparing an offer to provide non-assurance services for a public interest entity audit client in the manufacturing industry. The client is growing rapidly and introducing many new products, yet still has a manual accounting system. The client also has never undertaken any tax planning activities and feels that it pays a higher percentage of its income in taxes than its competitors. Additionally, it is concerned that its monitoring activities are inadequate because it does not have an internal audit department.

Required:

a *Prepare a summary of non-assurance services that Dean can include in his offer that do not violate the Code of Ethics.*

b *How would your answer to part a differ if the client were not a public interest entity?*

LO5,6,7,8 19–16 Each of the following situations involves a possible violation of the Code of Ethics. Indicate whether each situation violates the Code. If it violates the Code, explain why.

a Julia Roberto, a sole practitioner, has provided extensive advisory services for her audit client, Leather and Chains. She has interpreted financial statements, provided forecasts and other analyses, counselled on potential expansion plans, and counselled on banking relationships, but has not made any management decisions.

b Steve Rackwill, practitioner, has been asked by his audit client, Petry Plumbing Supply, to help in the process when implementing a new IT control system. Rackwill will arrange interviews for Petry's hiring of new personnel, and instruct and oversee the training of current client personnel. Petry will make all hiring decisions and supervise employees once they are trained.

c Bob Lanzotti is the partner-in-charge of the audit of Fleet Mobile Homes. Over the years, he has become a golfing buddy of Fleet's CEO, Jim

Harris. During the current year Lanzotti and Harris jointly purchased an exclusive vacation home in Southern Spain. The vacation home represents more than 10 per cent of Lanzotti's personal wealth.

d Kraemeer & Kraemeer recently won the audit of Garvin Clothiers, a large manufacturer of women's clothing. Jock Kraemeer had a substantial investment in Garvin prior to bidding on the engagement. In anticipation of winning the engagement, Kraemeer placed his shares of Garvin stock in a trust.

e Zeker & Associates audits a condominium association in which the parents of a member of the firm own a unit and reside. The unit is material to the parents' net worth, and the member participates in the engagement.

f Jimmy Saad, a sole practitioner, audited Conduit's financial statements for the year ended 30 June 2009, and was issued stock by the client as payment of the audit fee. Saad disposed of the stock before commencing field work planning for the audit of the 30 June 2010 financial statements.

g Dip-It Paint Corporation requires an audit for the current year. However, Dip-It has not paid Allen & Allen the fees due for tax-related services performed two years ago. Dip-It issued Allen & Allen a note for the unpaid fees, and Allen & Allen proceeded with the audit services.

LO5,6,7 **19–17** The questions that follow are based on requirements in Section 290 of the Code of Ethics as it relates to independence and family relationships. Check 'yes' if the situation violates the requirements, 'no' if it does not.

Situation	Yes	No
a A partner's parent is a 5 per cent limited partner in a firm client. Does the parent's direct financial interest in the client impair the firm's independence?		
b A partner assigned to a firm's Brussels office is married to the president of a client for which the firm's Amsterdam office performs audit services. If the partner does not perform services out of or for the Amsterdam office, cannot exercise significant influence over the engagement, and has no involvement with the engagement, such as consulting on accounting or auditing issues, is the firm's independence impaired?		
c A auditor's father acquired a 10 per cent interest in his son's audit client. The investment is material to the father's net worth. If the son is aware of his father's investment and the auditor participates in the audit engagement, is the firm's independence impaired?		
d A audit partner has a brother who owns a 60 per cent interest in an audit client, which is material to the brother's net worth. If the partner participates in the audit engagement but does not know about his brother's investment, is the firm's independence impaired?		

LO5,9 **19–18** Each of the following situations involves a possible violation of the Code of Ethics Part C. For each situation, indicate whether it violates the Code. If it violates the Code, indicate explain why.

a Jack Jackson is a professional accountant in business and controller of Acme Trucking Company. Acme's external auditors have asked Jackson to sign the management representation letter. Jackson has signed the management representation letter, even though he knows that full disclosures have not been made to Acme's external auditors.

b Mary McDermott, professional accountant in business, is employed in the internal audit department of the United Fund of Europe. The United Fund raises money from individuals and distributes it to other organizations. McDermott has audited Children's Charities, an organization that receives funds from United Fund.

c Janet Jett, professional accountant in business, formerly worked for Delta Disk Drive. She is currently interviewing for a new position with Maxiscribe, another manufacturer of disk drives. Jett has agreed to provide confidential information about Delta's trade secrets if she is hired by Maxiscribe.

d Brian Thorough, professional accountant in business, is currently employed as controller of Trans Oil Company. He has discovered that Trans Oil has been illegally paying government employees so that they will not charge Trans Oil with dumping highly toxic chemicals into the rivers. Thorough discloses this information to the office of attorney general.

e Jill Burnett, professional accountant in business, was hired by Cooper Corporation to supervise its accounting department in preparing financial statements and presenting them to senior management. Due to considerable time incurred on other financial activities, Burnett was unable to supervise the accounting staff adequately. It is later discovered that Cooper's financial statements contain false and misleading information.

LO5,6,7,8, 19–19 Perez, a practitioner, has been asked by an audit client to perform a non-recurring engagement involving implementing an IT information and control system. The client requests that, in setting up the new system and during the period prior to conversion to the new system, Perez:

- Counsel on potential expansion of business activity plans.
- Search for and interview new personnel.
- Hire new personnel.
- Train personnel.

In addition, the client requests that, during the three months subsequent to the conversion, Perez:

- Supervise the operation of the new system.
- Monitor client-prepared source documents and make changes in basic IT-generated data as Perez may deem necessary without the concurrence of the client.

Perez responds that he may perform some of the services requested but not all of them.

Required:

a *Which of these services may Perez perform, and which of them may Perez not perform?*

b *Before undertaking this engagement, Perez should inform the client of all significant matters related to the engagement. What are these significant matters that should be included in the engagement letter?*

(AICPA, adapted)

Discussion Cases

LO2,3 19–20 Your supervisor tells you that for the next month you will be working on an audit client with a controller who loves to talk. She explains that the client will want you to spend an hour or so talking about politics, sports and life's mysteries, and you need to keep him happy. She also wants you to follow the time budget which was based on prior years when those in your position would take work home each night to stay on budget. The prior auditors did not record the 'social' time with the client. Will you record all of your time, including 'social' time, or only the time associated with the technical work of the audit?

Required:

1 *Analyse this situation with its possible outcomes using:*
   (a) *The utilitarian theory.*
   (b) *The rights-based approach.*
   (c) *The justice-based approach.*

2 *Which approach do you feel is most appropriate in this situation, and why?*

While completing a test of controls, you appropriately cleared two minor exceptions by examining related documents. The client will need to do some serious digging to find the documents to resolve a third, similar exception and wants to know if you really need the documents. You ask the in-charge senior, and he decides it was probably not a serious potential problem and tells you to sign off to clear the third exception without examining the underlying documents.

Required:

1 *Analyse this situation with its possible outcomes using:*
   (a) *The utilitarian theory.*
   (b) *The rights-based approach.*
   (c) *The justice-based approach.*

2 *Which approach do you feel is most appropriate in this situation, and why?*

LO2,3   **19–21**   Refer back to the hypothetical Sun City Bank case presented in this chapter, and consider each of the following independent situations.

a Suppose that Pina, Johnson & Associates also audited one of the entities who had received one of the large loans that are in dispute. Sam Johnson is not involved with auditing that entity. Is it ethical for Johnson to seek information on the financial condition of that entity from the auditors in his firm? What are the rights of the affected parties in this instance, and what are the costs and benefits of using such information?

b Suppose that Johnson has determined that one of the entities that owes a disputed loan is being investigated for violating environmental laws and may be sued to the point of bankruptcy by the national environmental protection regulatory body. Can Johnson use this information in deciding on the proper loan-loss reserve? What are the ethical considerations?

LO5,6,7,8,9 **19–22**   Schoeck, a practitioner, is considering leaving a position at a major audit firm to join the staff of a local financial institution that does write-up work, tax preparation and planning, and financial planning.

Required:

a *Is the Code of Ethics applied differently to professional accountants that work for a local financial institution that is not owned by practitioner, as compared to a major audit firm?*

b *Do you think the rules should be applied differently to professional accountants depending on the type of entity they work for?*

LO5,6,7,8   19–23   For each of the following scenarios, please indicate whether or not independence-related requirements in the Code of Ethics are being violated. Briefly explain why, or why not.

    a   Adrian Reynolds now works as a junior member of the accounting team at Swiss Precision Tooling, a listed manufacturing company. Three months ago, he worked as a staff auditor for Crowther & Sutherland, a local audit firm, where he worked on the Swiss Precision Tooling audit team. Crowther & Sutherland is still the auditor for Swiss Precision Tooling.

    b   Susana Millar finished working for the audit firm Bircham, Dyson & Bell in August 2006. During that time, she was an engagement review partner on the Unigate Dairies assignment (the engagement period on this audit ended in April 2007). In February 2008, Susana took up a position as controller of Unigate Dairies. Bircham, Dyson & Bell is still the dairy's auditor and plans to finish its current audit assignment in March 2008 (19 months after Susana left the firm).

    c   Janay Butler, a senior auditor, is aware that under the Code of Ethics there are clear limitations on which valuation services her audit firm can perform for an audit client. However, her manager has requested that she appraise some specific large inventory items to verify the client's estimates, which are relied upon by others.

    d   Heath & Associates is the auditor of Halifax Investments, a listed company. Heath makes most of its money by selling non-assurance services to its audit clients, but it ensures every service it provides for Halifax is in accordance with the Code of Ethics and is pre-approved by the company's audit committee. Last year, it billed the following to Halifax: audit fees €0.8 million, tax fees €2.3 million and other fees €5.2 million. No services prohibited by the Code were provided by Heath to Halifax, and the fee figures are appropriately disclosed in Halifax's financial statements.

Internet Assignments

LO5,6   19–24   Visit the home site of audit firms and learn how they are marketing their professional services. Do you think that any firm makes exaggerated claims for their services offered or any other forms of inappropriate marketing?

LO12   19–25   Visit the home site or search information from other sources of the body (bodies) that inspects and reviews audit firms' practices in the country you live in. Investigate the following traits of the quality assurance programme:

- Public oversight of programmes
- Mandatory or voluntary review
- Firms and auditors covered by reviews
- Selection and qualities of reviewers
- Scope and thoroughness of reviews
- Frequencies of reviews
- Public reporting of outcomes of reviews and sanctions imposed
- Sanctions initiated as a result of negative outcomes of reviews

NOTES

[i]   S.M. Mintz, *Cases in Accounting Ethics and Professionalism*, 3rd edn, Irwin/McGraw-Hill, New York, 1997, p. 4.

[ii]   See S.M. Mintz, *Cases in Accounting Ethics and Professionalism*, 1997, for a more detailed discussion of each of these models.

iii   *Theory of Justice* (The Belknap Press of Harvard University Press, Cambridge, MA, 1971).

iv   S.M. Mintz, 'Virtue, Ethics, and Accounting Education', *Issues in Accounting Education* (Fall 1995), pp. 24–31.

v   J.E. Copeland, Jr, 'Ethics as an Imperative', *Accounting Horizons* (March 2005), pp. 35–43.

vi   The text refers to the revised Code of Ethics for Professional Accountants of July 2009. The International Ethics Standards Board for Accountants (IESBA) has developed adaption and implementation materials for the revised Code of Ethics (www.ifac.org/Ethics/Resources.php). The revised Code of Ethics is effective on 1 January 2011, with earlier adoption encouraged.

vii   The IAASB has developed non-authoritative guidance on applying ISQC 1 to quality control for small and medium-sized practices.

PART VIII

Assurance, Related Services and Internal Auditing

PART CONTENTS

20 Assurance, Related Services and Internal Auditing

CHAPTER

20

Assurance, Related Services and Internal Auditing

❖ RELEVANT ACCOUNTING AND AUDITING PRONOUNCEMENTS

AccountAbility, AA1000 Assurance Standard, 2008

COSO, Internal Control – Integrated Framework, 1992

Global Reporting Initiative, G3 Guidelines, 2009

IAASB, International Framework for Assurance Engagements

ISA 610, Using the Work of Internal Auditors

ISRE 2400, Engagements to Review Financial Statements

ISRE 2410, Review of Interim Financial Information Performed by the Independent Auditor of the Entity

ISAE 3000, Assurance Engagements Other than Audits or Reviews of Historical Financial Information

ISAE 3400, The Examination of Prospective Financial Information

ISAE 3402, Assurance Reports on Controls at a Service Organization

ISRS 4400, Engagements to Perform Agreed-Upon Procedures Regarding Financial Information

ISRS 4410, Engagements to Compile Financial Statements

Institute of Internal Auditors, Professional Practices Framework of the Institute of Internal Auditors

---

BECAUSE OF THEIR REPUTATION for competence and objectivity, external auditors for many years have been asked to perform a variety of services beyond the audit of historical financial statements. However, prior to the development of standards specifically relating to non-audit assurance services and related services, auditors found it difficult to provide such services within the bounds of the financial statements auditing standards. To accommodate the demand for services by auditors, the International Federation of Accountants (IFAC) started developing standards beyond auditing standards. These standards for non-audit assurance services and related services are broader or otherwise different in scope than auditing standards so that they can be applied to the array of services being requested of the accounting profession. The International Auditing and Assurance Standards Board (IAASB) *International Framework for Assurance Engagements* covers all assurance engagements, including audits and reviews of historical financial information.

The profession actively sought to expand the opportunities for assurance related services in the late 1990s. The American Institute of Certified Public Accountants (AICPA) 'Elliott Committee' issued a report in 1996 on the potential for providing non-traditional assurance services. The report gained worldwide influence. To support the profession in providing assurance services the IAASB issued a framework for assurance engagements and started a process to revise and expand its standards for non-audit assurance services. While the profession's emphasis on non-traditional assurance services has cooled in the wake of stricter regulation and the subsequent 'back-to-basics' trend, non-audit assurance services constitute a natural part of audit firms' service portfolio.

This chapter starts out with a brief discussion of the Elliott Committee's understanding of the assurance service concept. The IAASB's framework for assurance engagements and standards for non-audit assurance engagements are presented next. This discussion first covers review of historical financial information and then assurance engagements other than audits or reviews. As an example of a viable non-traditional assurance service, assurance on sustainability reporting is discussed, followed by an outline of the general principles on assurance on prospective information. A presentation of the two related services, agreed-upon procedures and compilation, completes the discussion of the IAASB's non-**audit engagement** standards. The last part of the chapter discusses the services and standards relating to internal auditing, an important area that has seen significantly increased emphasis over the past few years.

❖ ASSURANCE SERVICES

LO1

Assurance services may be defined with broad scope. The influential AICPA Special Committee on Assurance Services, 'the **Elliott Committee'**, has defined assurance services as follows:

> **Assurance services** *are independent professional services that improve the quality of information, or its context, for decision makers.*

This definition captures a number of important concepts. First, the definition focuses on decision making. Making good decisions requires quality information, which can be financial or non-financial in nature. Figure 20–1, adapted from the Elliott Committee's report, presents a model for decision making and the role of information in decision-making activities. You will note that information is critical in this decision model. For example, the Elliott Committee points out that three types of information enter into the problem definition stage of the model: (1) environmental information; (2) process monitoring and diagnostic information; and (3) outcome feedback information. An assurance service can help the decision maker search through this information in order to identify which pieces of information are relevant for the required decision.

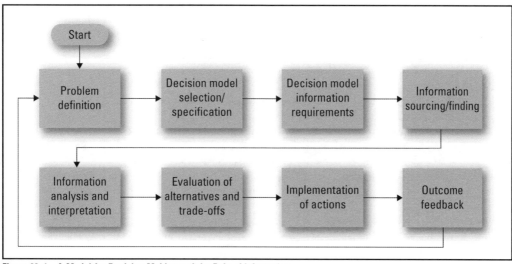

Figure 20–1   A Model for Decision Making and the Role of Information

The second concept in the definition relates to improving the quality of information or its context. In the decision model shown in Figure 20–1, an assurance service can improve quality by increasing confidence in the information's reliability, relevance and timeliness. Context can be improved via the format in which information is presented or through the provision of other relevant benchmarking information.

The third important concept in the definition of assurance services is independence. As we indicated in our earlier discussions of financial statement auditing, independence is the hallmark of the accounting profession. The last concept is professional services, which encompasses the application of professional judgement to the information that is the subject of the assurance service. In summary, assurance services can capture information, improve its quality and enhance its usefulness for decision makers in a way that is free from conflict of interest or bias.

Beyond offering a structured approach to and definition of assurance services, the Elliott Committee argued that the profession should revitalize current assurance services and offer new assurance services to meet the needs and demands of decision makers for information and related assurance. The Committee's view gained widespread support in the profession and initiated a number of initiatives. Audit firms started developing and marketing various assurance products. The IAASB issued a framework for assurance engagements and standards to support the provision of non-audit assurance services. The IAASB *International Framework for Assurance Engagements* is discussed in the next section.

LO2

LO3

THE IAASB INTERNATIONAL FRAMEWORK FOR ASSURANCE ENGAGEMENTS

In developing the international framework for assurance engagements IAASB defined an **assurance engagement** with a more narrow scope than the previous discussed definition of assurance services by the Elliott Committee.[i] Figure 20–2 illustrates the scope of IAASB assurance engagements, and the hierarchy and relationship between IAASB engagement standards. At the top of Figure 20–2 assurance services relate to services in the broad sense as defined by the Elliott Committee. As illustrated by the far right column in Figure 20–2, all services encompassed with the Elliott Committee's definition are not covered by the IAASB assurance engagement framework. For example, engagements that improve the relevance of the information, or its context, are assurance services as defined by the Elliott Committee, but will not necessarily be considered IAASB assurance engagements. The IAASB framework defines and describes the elements and objectives of an assurance engagement, and identifies standards and engagements to which it applies.

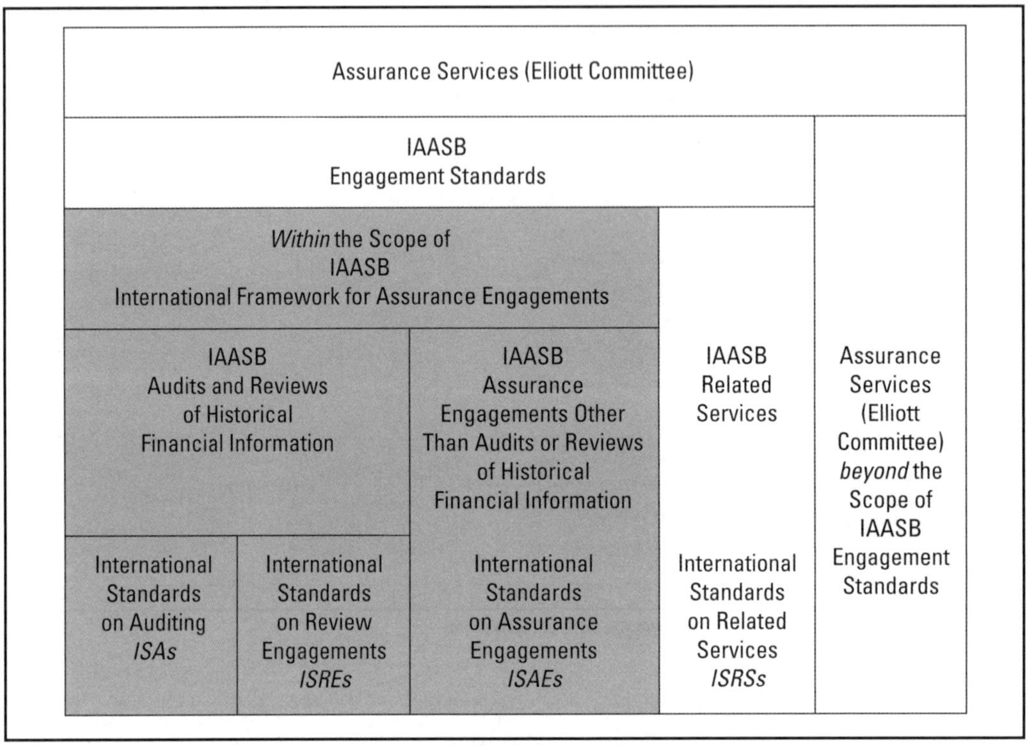

Assurance Services (Elliott Committee)				
IAASB Engagement Standards				
Within the Scope of IAASB International Framework for Assurance Engagements				Assurance Services (Elliott Committee) *beyond* the Scope of IAASB Engagement Standards
IAASB Audits and Reviews of Historical Financial Information		IAASB Assurance Engagements Other Than Audits or Reviews of Historical Financial Information	IAASB Related Services	
International Standards on Auditing *ISAs*	International Standards on Review Engagements *ISREs*	International Standards on Assurance Engagements *ISAEs*	International Standards on Related Services *ISRSs*	

Figure 20–2 Assurance Services and IAASB Engagement Standards

The IAASB *engagement standards* are either within the scope of the IAASB *International Framework for Assurance Engagements* or are *related services standards*. In contrast, related services are within the Elliott Committee's definition of assurance services (cf. Figure 20–2). Related services include performing agreed-upon procedures regarding financial information and compilation of financial information. Such services are not assurance services within the IAASB framework because no assurance is expressed by the practitioner. Related services are discussed in a separate section later in this chapter.

The framework provides guidance for two types of assurance engagements: **reasonable assurance** engagements and **limited assurance** engagements. For assurance engagements regarding historical financial information in particular, reasonable assurance engagements are called audits, and limited assurance engagements are called reviews. The framework also differentiates between, on the one hand, *audits and reviews of historical financial information* and, on the other hand, all *other* assurance engagements.

The IAASB framework defines an assurance engagement as follows:

> **Assurance engagement** *is an engagement in which a practitioner expresses a conclusion designed to enhance the degree of confidence of the intended users other than the responsible party about the outcome of the evaluation or measurement of a subject matter against criteria.*

The *subject matter* of an assurance engagement may take many forms, including an entity's financial or non-financial performance (e.g. historical financial performance or sustainability performance), performance of systems and processes (e.g. effectiveness of internal control), or behaviour (e.g. compliance with laws and regulations). *The subject matter information* is the outcome of the evaluation or measurement of a subject matter that results from applying criteria to the subject matter. *Criteria* are the benchmarks used to evaluate or measure the subject matter. The subject matter information is ordinarily provided to the practitioner in the form of an assertion by the party responsible for the evaluation or measurement. It is the subject matter information about which the practitioner gathers sufficient appropriate evidence to provide a reasonable basis for expressing a conclusion in an assurance report.

For example, in an audit of financial statements the subject matter is the entity's financial position and performance; the subject matter information (assertion) is the financial statements that result from applying the financial reporting framework such as IFRS (the criteria) to measure the financial position and performance. Another example: the subject matter may be the entity's sustainability performance such as environmental and social performance. The subject matter information is then the outcome of the measurement about the sustainability performance such as sustainability key performance indicators (KPIs), ordinarily represented by management's assertion in a sustainability report. Management's assertion results from applying a framework for measuring sustainability performance such as the sustainability reporting guidelines developed by the Global Reporting Initiative (GRI).[ii] (The GRI guidelines are discussed in the section on assurance on sustainability reporting later in this chapter.) Pause for a moment and assume that in an assurance engagement the subject matter is the effectiveness of the entity's internal control. What would be the subject matter information (assertion) and suitable criteria?

The IAASB assurance framework covers two types of assurance engagements: assertion-based engagements and direct reporting engagements. In *assertion-based engagements* the evaluation or measurement of the subject matter is performed by the responsible party, and the subject matter information is in the form of an assertion by the responsible party that is made available to the intended users of the assurance report. Referring back to the examples above, an audit of financial statements and an engagement to assure an entity's sustainability report that accompanies the practitioner's assurance report would be assertion-based engagements. This would also be the case for the assurance of management's assertion about the effectiveness of internal control as long as management's assertion is made available to the intended users, for example in a report by management included in the annual report. In *direct reporting engagements*, the practitioner *either* directly performs the evaluation or measurement of the subject matter *or* obtains a representation from the responsible party that has performed the evaluation or measurement that is *not* available to the intended users. The subject matter information is then provided to the intended users in the practitioner's assurance report. For example, in a direct reporting engagement the practitioner may directly evaluate the effectiveness of the entity's internal control against criteria developed from the COSO framework without any explicit assertion being made by management. Another example of a direct reporting engagement: management presents written assertion about compliance with specific laws and regulations in a representation letter to the practitioner that will not accompany the assurance report. The assurance report then should contain a statement of management's assertion. To summarize, in an assurance engagement the responsible party ordinarily provides the practitioner with a written representation that evaluates or measures the subject matter against the identified criteria. If the representation is not made available to the intended users, it is a not an assertion-based engagement, but a direct reporting engagement. In some other direct reporting engagements, the practitioner may not obtain such an explicit representation and the practitioner then directly performs the evaluation or measurement of the subject matter.

An assurance engagement involves a three-party relationship between: (1) a practitioner; (2) a responsible party; and (3) intended users. A practitioner is a professional accountant in public practice that provides professional services. Because assurance engagements are also engagements other than audits or reviews, the term practitioner is used instead of auditor.

Generally, in an assertion-based engagement the responsible party is responsible for the subject matter information (assertion) as well as the subject matter. For example, this is the case when the entity has engaged a practitioner to perform assurance of its reporting about its own sustainability performance or internal control.[iii] In direct reporting engagements the responsible party may be responsible for the subject matter only.

The intended users are those for whom the practitioner prepares the assurance report. In some cases, the responsible party can be one of the intended users, but cannot be the only one. For example, the framework does not apply if the board of directors of an entity would engage a practitioner to assure the entity's corporate governance practices (which is the responsibility of the board), and report to the board exclusively.

The IAASB framework for assurance engagements is of a *general nature* and sets the scope for the specific assurance standards and of individual assurance engagements. The framework does not provide procedural requirements for the performance of assurance engagements. Such requirements are found in the relevant assurance standards. As Figure 20–2 shows, the assurance framework covers engagements to which *International Standards on Auditing* (ISAs), *International Standards on Review Engagements* (ISREs) and *International Standards on Assurance Engagements* (ISAEs) apply.

Not all professional services performed by practitioners are within the scope of the IAASB assurance framework. Engagements that do not meet the IAASB definition of an assurance engagement are considered non-assurance engagements. As already noted, agreed-upon procedures engagements and **compilation engagements** are non-assurance engagements since the practitioner does not express any assurance in such engagements. Other non-assurance engagements are consulting (advisory) such as management and tax consulting.[iv]

For assurance engagements the subject matter and subject matter information can take many forms, expertise beyond accounting and auditing may be required, the suitability of criteria may vary, and the access to sufficient appropriate evidence may differ. Thus, it is essential that the engagement exhibits certain characteristics before the practitioner can accept the engagement. Table 20–1 presents needed preliminary knowledge of engagement circumstances before the practitioner can accept an assurance engagement.

Table 20–1 Assurance Engagement Acceptance
a   Relevant *ethical* requirements, such as independence and professional competence, will be satisfied.
b   The engagement exhibits all of the following characteristics:
(i)   The subject matter is *appropriate*.
(ii)   The criteria to be used are *suitable* and are available to the intended users.
(iii)   The practitioner has access to *sufficient appropriate* evidence to support the practitioner's conclusion.
(iv)   The practitioner's conclusion, in the form appropriate to either a reasonable assurance engagement or a limited assurance engagement, is to be contained in a *written report*.
(v)   The practitioner is satisfied that there is a *rational purpose* for the engagement.

The IFAC Code of Ethics for Professional Accountants governs the practitioner in performing all assurance engagements. The audit firm must also comply with the international standards on quality control (ISQCs). (Refer to Chapter 19 for a discussion of the IFAC Code of Ethics and ISQC 1.)

A subject matter is *appropriate* if: (1) it is identifiable and capable of consistent evaluation or measurement against the identified criteria; and (2) can be subjected to procedures for gathering sufficient appropriate evidence to support a reasonable assurance or limited assurance conclusion.

To be *suitable*, criteria have to be relevant, complete, reliable, neutral and understandable. For example, the evaluation or measurement of a subject matter on the basis of the practitioner's own expectations, judgements or individual experience would not constitute suitable criteria. Criteria need to be available to the intended users to allow them to understand how the subject matter has been evaluated or measured.

The practitioner should plan and perform an assurance engagement with an attitude of professional scepticism to obtain sufficient appropriate evidence about whether the subject matter information is free of material misstatement. In a *reasonable assurance* engagement sufficient appropriate evidence is obtained as part of a systematic engagement process that includes:

- Obtaining an understanding of the subject matter and other engagement circumstances which, depending on the subject matter, includes obtaining an understanding of internal control.
- Based on that understanding, assessing the risks that the subject matter information may be materially misstated.
- Responding to assessed risks, including developing overall responses and determining the nature, timing and extent of further procedures.
- Performing further procedures clearly linked to the identified risks, using a combination of inspection, observation, confirmation, recalculation, reperformance, analytical procedures, and inquiry. Such further procedures involve substantive procedures, including, where applicable, obtaining corroborating information, and depending on the nature of the subject matter, tests of the operating effectiveness of controls.
- Evaluating the sufficiency and appropriateness of evidence obtained.

The reader should recognize that these elements of the assurance engagement process are similar and generalize those elements discussed in earlier chapters on the audit of the financial statements.

In a *limited assurance* engagement sufficient appropriate evidence is obtained as part of a systematic engagement process that includes obtaining an understanding of the subject matter and other engagement circumstances, but in which procedures are deliberately limited relative to a reasonable assurance engagement.

Assurance engagement risk is defined as follows:

> **Assurance engagement risk** *is the risk that the practitioner expresses an inappropriate conclusion when the subject matter information is materially misstated.*

For all assurance engagements the practitioner may use an assurance risk model composed of the same three components (inherent risk, control risk and detection risk) as the audit risk model discussed in Chapter 3. The assurance risk should be reduced to an acceptable level in the circumstances of the engagement. The level of assurance engagement risk is higher in a limited assurance engagement than in a reasonable assurance engagement.

Practice Insight 20.1

In addition to assurance engagement risk, the practitioner is exposed to the risk of expressing an inappropriate conclusion when the subject matter information is not materially misstated, and risks through loss from litigation, adverse publicity or other events arising in connection with a subject matter reported on (the practitioner's business risk). These risks are not part of assurance engagement risk.

The practitioner provides a *written report* containing a conclusion that conveys the assurance obtained about the subject matter information. A *reasonable assurance* engagement report includes a *positive form* of expression of the conclusion. For example, in an internal control engagement with reasonable assurance the wording may be: 'In our opinion internal control is effective, in all material respects, based on the COSO criteria.' In a *limited assurance* engagement, the practitioner expresses the conclusion in a *negative form*. For example, in an internal control engagement with limited assurance the wording may be: 'Based on our work described in this report, nothing has come to our attention that causes us to believe that internal control is not effective, in all material respects, based on the COSO criteria.'

Both these reporting conclusions are worded in terms of the subject matter (the effectiveness of internal control) and the criteria (COSO). A direct reporting requirement is restricted to such wording because the responsible party makes no assertion or the representation by the responsibly party is not available for intended users. An assertion-based engagement may alternatively be worded in terms of the subject matter information (the responsibly party's assertion). For example, in a reasonable assertion-based assurance engagement the wording may be: 'In our opinion the responsible party's assertion that internal control is effective, in all material respects, based on the COSO criteria, is fairly stated.' Similarly, in a limited assertion-based assurance engagement the wording may be: 'Based on our work described in this report, nothing has come to our attention that causes us to believe that the responsible party's assertion that internal control is effective, in all material respects, based on the COSO criteria, is not fairly stated.' The relevant ISAs, ISREs and ISAEs establish the basic elements of the assurance reports and guide on specific wording.

The assurance report should refrain from an unmodified conclusion if: (1) there is a material limitation of the scope of the practitioner's work; (2) the subject matter information is materially misstated; or (3) when it is discovered after the engagement has been accepted that the criteria are unsuitable or the subject matter is not appropriate for an assurance engagement. The materiality and pervasiveness of the effect of the matter determines if a qualified conclusion, or an adverse conclusion or disclaimer of conclusion is required. Exhibit 20–1 shows a qualified conclusion extracted from the Independent Assurance Report by Deloitte to Unilever's Group Sustainable Development Report 2007. The engagement was carried out as a limited assurance engagement.

Exhibit 20–1   Example of a Qualified Conclusion in a Limited Assurance Engagement on Sustainability Development

What we found: our qualified conclusion

Based on the assurance work performed we have concluded that, for the following five performance indicators:

- Water consumption in m^3 per tonne of production;
- Energy use in GJ per tonne of production;
- Non-hazardous waste in kg per tonne of production;
- Emissions of SO_x from boilers and utilities in kg per tonne of production; and
- Number of fatal accidents,
  nothing came to our attention to suggest that the 2007 data are materially misstated.

In the course of our assurance work for the remaining five indicators:

- Emissions of COD (Chemical Oxygen Demand) in kg per tonne of production;
- CO_2 emissions from energy use in kg per tonne of production;
- Hazardous waste in kg per tonne of production;
- Emissions of ozone-depleting potential in kg per tonne of production; and
- Accident rate: TRFR (Total Recordable Frequency Rate) per 100,000 man-hours,

testing of sample data for individual sites showed that information had not been captured correctly at some sites. Although the individual errors identified were not material to the Group data as a whole, the limited sample meant that it was not possible to extrapolate meaningfully from the sample of sites we visited. Accordingly, despite the fact that we found that the Group level data aggregation and analysis processes appeared to operate effectively, we are not able to conclude as to whether these indicators are materially misstated.

Source: Independent assurance report by Deloitte & Touche LLP to Unilever PLC on the online Group Sustainable Development Report 2007 (www.unilever.com/Images/es_final-assurance-statement-2007_tcm13–125058.pdf).

THE IAASB ASSURANCE STANDARDS AND ASSURANCE LEVEL

LO4

As discussed previously, IAASB assurance engagement standards are organized according to the level of assurance expressed, *reasonable* or *limited* assurance; *and if the engagement is an audit or a review of historical financial information* or *other assurance engagements.* Figure 20–3 illustrates the assurance level provided by IAASB assurance engagements standards. *Reasonable assurance* means that the engagement assurance risk is reduced to an acceptably low level in the circumstances of the engagement. In a reasonable assurance engagement the practitioner expresses the conclusion in the affirmative positive form. Pause for a moment, use your insight from auditing of financial statements and reflect on why reducing the risk to zero to obtain absolute assurance is rarely attainable or cost beneficial.

Assurance Engagements *IAASB Assurance Framework*	Audits and Reviews of Historical Financial Information	Assurance Engagements Other Than Audits or Reviews of Historical Financial Information *ISAE 3000*
Reasonable Assurance Engagements	Audits of Historical Financial Information *ISAs*	Reasonable Assurance Engagements Other Than Audits of Historical Financial Information *ISAE 342*
Limited Assurance Engagements	Reviews of Historical Financial Information *ISREs*	Limited Assurance Engagements Other Than Reviews of Historical Financial Information *ISAE 3400*

Figure 20–3   IAASB Assurance Standards and Assurance Level

In a *limited assurance* engagement the risk is greater than for a reasonable assurance engagement, but still acceptable in the circumstances of the engagement. The practitioner reduces assurance engagement risk by gathering evidence. The nature, timing and extent of procedures for gathering sufficient appropriate evidence in a limited assurance engagement are deliberately limited relative to a reasonable assurance engagement, but at least sufficient for the practitioner to obtain a meaningful level of assurance as the basis for a negative form of expression. To be meaningful, the level of assurance obtained is likely to enhance the intended users' confidence about the subject matter information to a degree that is clearly more than inconsequential. For example, in a limited assurance engagement of historical financial information such as a review, sufficient appropriate evidence is obtained primarily through analytical procedures and inquiries.

Historical financial information is typically financial statements or some element of financial statements. An audit is a reasonable assurance engagement regarding historical financial information, ordinarily financial statements. A review is a limited assurance engagement regarding historical financial information, ordinarily financial statements or interim financial information. Examples of assurance engagements other than audits or reviews of historical financial information are assurance of **prospective financial information** (e.g. financial forecasts), non-financial performance data (e.g. sustainability KPIs), physical characteristics (e.g. capacity of a facility), performance of systems or processes (e.g. effectiveness of internal control), or behaviour (e.g. corporate governance and compliance with regulations).

In 2003 the IAASB issued a general application standard for assurance engagement other than audits or reviews of historical financial information (ISAE 3000). ISAE 3000 covers both reasonable and limited assurance. In practice, many current assurance engagements are conducted with reference to ISAE 3000 such as those engagements reported on in Exhibits 20–1, 20–4, 20–5, 20–6 and 20–7. (ISAE 3000 is discussed in a separate section later in this chapter.) A limited assurance engagement standard on the examination of prospective financial information exists (ISAE 3400). The IAASB has announced its intention to revise ISAE 3400. (Assurance on prospective information is discussed in a later section in this chapter.) In 2009, the IAASB completed a standard on assurance reports on controls at a service organization (ISAE 3402). ISAE 3402 deals with assertion-based engagements that convey reasonable assurance.

Two limited assurance standards on review of historical financial information exist. The IAASB issued in 2005 a new standard on review of interim financial information performed by the auditor of the entity (ISRE 2410) to complement the standard on reviews of financial statements (ISRE 2400).[v] Review of historical financial information is discussed in the next section.

❖ REVIEW OF HISTORICAL FINANCIAL INFORMATION

LO5

Many non-public businesses do not choose to contract for an audit of their financial statements. This typically occurs because the entity is small, the owner is involved in the day-to-day operations, and there are no loan covenants or regulations requiring an audit. In some countries an audit is only required for public companies or public-interest entities. In most countries small private joint-stock companies and most personal ones are exempt from an audit requirement. Chapter 1 discusses situations where there is a demand for an audit when there are no regulations requiring an audit. Sometimes the parties prefer to have the financial statements *reviewed* rather than audited because a review is less costly than an audit. For example, the bank may request reviewed financial statements from loan applicants. In other situations the practitioner, ordinarily the entity's auditor, may be asked to review the entity's interim financial information, for example an engagement to review the quarterly financial reports issued by a listed company.

In a review the practitioner reduces the risk of expressing an inappropriate conclusion when the financial information is materially misstated to a moderate level. The scope of a review is substantially less than an audit. A review consists primarily of applying analytical procedures and making inquiries of members of management responsible for financial and accounting matters. Thus, a review brings significant matters affecting the financial information to the practitioner's attention, but it does not provide all of the evidence that would be required in an audit. The review provides a basis on which to express a conclusion whether anything has come to the practitioner's attention that causes the practitioner to believe that the financial information is not in accordance with the applicable financial reporting framework. This negative form of expression of the conclusion provides limited assurance for the users that the financial information is not materially misstated.

ISRE 2400 is directed towards the review of financial statements. ISRE 2410 is directed towards the review of interim financial information *performed by the auditor of the entity*. ISRE 2410 is written on the basis that the entity's auditor is able to use his or her audit-based knowledge of the entity to carry out a review of the financial information. ISRE 2400 and ISRE 2410 are to be applied, adapted as necessary in the circumstances, to engagements to review other historical financial information than financial statements and interim financial information.

To plan and conduct the review the practitioner should have a sufficient understanding of the entity and its environment to identify the types of potential material misstatement and to select the appropriate inquiries and analytical procedures. Table 20–2 gives examples of inquiries made during a **review engagement**.

Table 20–2   Examples of Inquiries Made During a Review Engagement
1.   Inquiries concerning the entity's accounting policies and practices.
2.   Inquiries concerning the entity's procedures for recording, classifying and summarizing transactions.
3.   Inquiries concerning actions taken at meetings of shareholders, the board of directors, and other meetings.

4.   Inquiries of persons having responsibility for financial and accounting matters concerning:
     •   Whether all transactions have been recorded.
     •   Whether the statements have been prepared in accordance with the basis of accounting indicated.
     •   Changes in the entity's business activities and accounting policies and practices.

5.   Inquiries about subsequent events up to the date of the review report that may require adjustments to or disclosure in the financial information.

When the auditor of the entity performs a review of interim financial information, the auditor primarily applies procedures to update his or her understanding.

Performing analytical procedures to identify relationships and individual items that appear to be unusual follows a similar process to that described for audits in Chapter 5. For example, the practitioner compares current financial information with relevant preceding information, anticipated results, ratios for entities in the same industry, or with non-financial information. The practitioner should obtain written representations from management on matters material to the financial information reviewed. Such matters are typically similar to those in an audit discussed in Chapter 17. Note that a review engagement does not require the auditor to test accounting records by performing detailed tests or corroborating inquiries, as would normally be done on an audit. However, if while conducting the review the auditor becomes aware of information that is incorrect, incomplete or misleading, he or she should perform any additional procedures necessary to provide limited assurance that no material modifications to the financial information are required.

A standard review report with an unmodified conclusion assumes that the financial information is in accordance with the identified financial reporting framework. Exhibit 20–2 gives an illustrative example of a review report on interim financial information with an unmodified conclusion.

Exhibit 20–2   Example of Report on Review of Interim Financial Information
Report on Review of Interim Financial Information
To the Shareholders of the Sierra Company
Introduction
We have reviewed the accompanying balance sheet of Sierra Company as of 31 March 2010 and the related statements of income, changes in equity and cash flows for the three-month period then ended and a summary of significant accounting policies and other explanatory information. Management is responsible for the preparation and presentation of this interim financial information in accordance with International Financial Reporting Standards. Our responsibility is to express a conclusion on this interim financial information based on our review.
Scope of Review
We conducted our review in accordance with International Standard on Review Engagements 2410, Review of Interim Financial Information Performed by the Independent Auditor of the Entity. A review of interim financial information consists of making inquiries of persons responsible for financial and accounting matters and applying analytical and other review procedures. A review is substantially less in scope than an audit conducted in accordance with International Standards on Auditing and consequently does not enable us to obtain assurance that we would become aware of all significant matters that might be identified in an audit. Accordingly, we do not express an audit opinion.
Conclusion
Based on our review, nothing has come to our attention that causes us to believe that the accompanying interim financial information does not present fairly, in all material respects, the financial position of the entity as at 31 March 2010, and the results of its operations and its cash flows for the three-month period then ended in accordance with International Financial Reporting Standards.
Auditor
Date
Address
Source: Adapted from ISRE 2410 *Review of Interim Financial Information Performed by the Independent Auditor of the Entity*, IAASB (2009).

Parallel to reporting in a financial statement audit, the practitioner should add an emphasis of matter paragraph to highlight a material uncertainty relating to an event or condition that may cast significant doubt on the entity's ability to continue as a going concern.

When the practitioner conducts a review, he or she may become aware of situations that require modification to the conclusion. The two particular situations are: (1) a departure from the financial reporting framework; and (2) limitation on the scope of the practitioner's work. The practitioner expresses a qualified conclusion for a scope limitation or departure from the applicable financial reporting framework when the matter is material, but not persuasive. Exhibit 20–3 provides an example of a review report on interim financial information with a qualified conclusion for a departure from IFRS.

Exhibit 20–3   Example of a Review Report on Interim Financial Information with a Qualified Conclusion for Departure from IFRSs

[Same wording as introduction and scope of review paragraphs of the review report with an unmodified conclusion]

Basis for Qualified Conclusion
Based on information provided to us by management, Nevada Company has excluded from property and long-term debt certain lease obligations that we believe should be capitalized to conform with International Financial Reporting Standards. This information indicates that if these lease obligations were capitalized at 31 March 2010, property and long-term debt would be increased by €116,791 and net income would be decreased by €1,512 for the three-month period then ended.

Qualified Conclusion
Based on our review, with the exception of the matter described in the preceding paragraph, nothing has come to our attention that causes us to believe that the accompanying interim financial information does not present fairly, in all material respects, the financial position of the entity as at 31 March 2010, and of the results of its operations and its cash flows for the three-month period then ended in accordance with International Financial Reporting Standards.

Source: Adapted from ISRE 2410 *Review of Interim Financial Information Performed by the Independent Auditor of the Entity*, IAASB (2009).

When the effect of the departure is material and pervasive an adverse conclusion is expressed. If a management-imposed scope limitation exists and management refuses to remove the limitation, the practitioner will be unable to complete the review and express a conclusion.

❖ ASSURANCE ENGAGEMENTS OTHER THAN AUDITS OR REVIEWS OF
LO6 HISTORICAL FINANCIAL INFORMATION

The IAASB framework for assurance engagement is discussed in a preceding section in this chapter. Recall that the framework defines and describes the elements and objectives of an assurance engagement, but does not establish procedural requirements for assurance engagements. As illustrated in Figure 20–1 the framework covers: (1) audits and reviews of historical financial information (ISAs and ISREs); and (2) other assurance engagements (ISAEs).

In 2003 the IAASB issued a general application standard on assurance engagements not covered by ISAs or ISREs; International Standard on Assurance Engagements (ISAE) 3000 *Assurance Engagements Other Than Audits or Reviews of Historical Financial Information*. ISAE 3000 is read in the context of the IAASB assurance framework and the standard covers many of the same elements as those covered by individual standards on auditing of financial statements. ISAE 3000, however, is more general in nature than the auditing standards. The basic elements in ISAE 3000 are:

- Ethical requirements.
- Quality control.
- Engagement acceptance and continuance.
- Agreeing on the terms of the engagement.
- Planning and performing the engagement.
- Using the work of an expert.
- Obtaining evidence.
- Considering subsequent events.
- Documentation.
- Preparing the assurance report.
- Other reporting responsibilities.

As for all assurance engagements, the practitioner should comply with the IFAC Code of Ethics for Professional Accountants, including independence requirements, and implement a system of quality control in accordance with ISQC 1 (refer to Chapter 19 for a discussion of the IFAC Code of Ethics and ISQC 1).

A practitioner may be requested to perform assurance engagements on a wide range of subject matters and subject matter information. Some subject matters may require specialized skills and knowledge beyond those ordinarily possessed by an individual practitioner. Those persons performing the engagement should collectively possess the necessary professional competencies. This may require the use of experts from professional disciplines other than accounting and auditing. For example, in an assurance engagement on reporting of an entity's environmental performance, engineering knowledge may be required. Due care must be exercised by the practitioners when an expert is used. The practitioner should be involved in the engagement and understand the work of the expert to an extent that is sufficient to enable the practitioner to accept responsibility for the conclusion on the subject matter information. The practitioner should also obtain sufficient appropriate evidence that the expert's work is adequate for the purposes of the assurance engagement. Table 20–3 provides other procedural requirements in an assurance engagement in accordance with ISAE 3000. The reader should observe that these basic procedural requirements are more general, but comparable to those governing an audit of financial statements.

Table 20–3 Selected Procedural Requirements in ISAE 3000

- Agree on the terms of the engagement with the engaging party.
- Plan the engagement so that it will be performed effectively.
- Obtain an understanding of the subject matter and other engagement circumstances, sufficient to identify and assess the risks of the subject matter information being materially misstated, and sufficient to design and perform further evidence-gathering procedures.
- Assess the appropriateness of the subject matter.
- Assess the suitability of the criteria to evaluate or measure the subject matter.
- Consider materiality and assurance engagement risk when planning and performing an assurance engagement.
- Reduce assurance engagement risk to an acceptably low level in the circumstances of the engagement.
- Obtain sufficient appropriate evidence on which to base the conclusion.
- Obtain representations from the responsible party, as appropriate.
- Consider the effect on the subject matter information and on the assurance report of events up to the date of the assurance report.
- Document matters that are significant in providing evidence that supports the assurance report and that the engagement was performed in accordance with ISAEs.
- Conclude whether sufficient appropriate evidence has been obtained to support the conclusion expressed in the assurance report.

The assurance report should be in writing and contain a clear expression of the practitioner's conclusion about the subject matter information. ISAE 3000 does not require a standardized format for reporting on all assurance engagements. Instead the standard identifies the basic elements the assurance report is to include:

- A title that clearly indicates the report is an independent assurance report.
- An addressee.
- An identification and description of the subject matter information and, when appropriate, the subject matter.
- Identification of the criteria.
- Where appropriate, a description of any significant, inherent limitation associated with the evaluation or measurement of the subject matter against the criteria.
- When the criteria used to evaluate or measure the subject matter are available only to specific intended users, or are relevant only to a specific purpose, a statement restricting the use of the assurance report to those intended users or that purpose.
- A statement to identify the responsible party and to describe the responsible party's and the practitioner's responsibilities.
- A statement that the engagement was performed in accordance with ISAEs.
- A summary of the work performed.
- The practitioner's conclusion.

- Where appropriate, the conclusion should inform the intended users of the context in which the practitioner's conclusion is to be read.
- In a reasonable assurance engagement, the conclusion should be expressed in the positive form. In a limited assurance engagement, the conclusion should be expressed in the negative form.
- Where the practitioner expresses a conclusion that is other than unmodified, the assurance report should contain a clear description of all the reasons.
- The assurance report date.
- The name of the firm or the practitioner, and a specific location, which ordinarily is the city where the practitioner maintains the office that has responsibility for the engagement.

The reader should observe that most of the elements of the assurance report bear close resemblance to those of an audit report. The format of assurance reports, however, is tailored to the specific engagements circumstances. The practitioner chooses a 'short form' or 'long form' style to facilitate effective communication with the intended users. 'Short form' reports ordinarily include only the basic elements. 'Long form' reports often describes in detail the terms of the engagement, the criteria being used, findings relating to particular aspects of the engagement and, in some cases, recommendations; as well as basic elements. Exhibit 20–4 is an example of an assurance report conducted in accordance with the ISAE 3000 provided by PwC to sustainability information reported by a large Australian mining and metal company (Rio Tinto).

Exhibit 20–4   Assurance Report to Rio Tinto on Selected Sustainability Development Performance Data

PRICEWATERHOUSE(COOPERS

Independent Assurance Report to the directors of Rio Tinto plc and Rio Tinto Limited on selected sustainable development performance data

For the purposes of this report, the Group comprises Rio Tinto plc and Rio Tinto Limited and the entities they control as at 31 December 2008 (hereafter "Rio Tinto").

We have been engaged to provide limited assurance on selected sustainable development performance data (the "selected data") included in the Sustainable development section of Rio Tinto's *Annual report* for the year ended 31 December 2008.

The selected data were chosen by Rio Tinto after considering the sustainable development risks that it assessed as material to the Company and after considering the areas of high importance identified by Rio Tinto management.

The selected 2008 data consists of the following:

- Total greenhouse gas emissions
- Total energy use
- Total freshwater withdrawn
- Number of fatalities
- All injury frequency rate
- Lost time injury frequency rate

Respective responsibilities of the directors and PricewaterhouseCoopers

The directors of Rio Tinto are responsible for preparing the selected data based on the Rio Tinto *Criteria for reporting on sustainable development performance indicators* (the "Reporting criteria"). The Reporting criteria are available on Rio Tinto's website at http://www.riotinto.com/ourapproach/

Our responsibility is to express a conclusion on the selected data based on our procedures. The procedures selected depend on our judgment, including an assessment of the risks of material misstatement of the selected data.

We read other information included within the Sustainable development section in the *Annual report* and consider whether it is consistent with the knowledge obtained through our procedures. We consider the implications for our report if we become aware of any apparent material inconsistencies with the selected data. Our responsibilities do not extend to any other information. Historic data has not been subject to assurance.

This report, including the conclusion, has been prepared for Rio Tinto to assist the directors in reporting Rio Tinto's sustainable development performance. We consent to

the inclusion of this report within the *Annual report* to enable Rio Tinto's members to verify that the directors have discharged their governance responsibilities by commissioning an independent assurance report in connection with the selected data. We do not accept or assume responsibility for our work or this report to anyone other than the directors as a body and to Rio Tinto save where terms are expressly agreed and with our prior consent in writing.

Inherent limitations

Non financial performance information is often subject to more inherent limitations than financial information, given the characteristics of the subject matter and the methods adopted for the definition and gathering of information. There are no generally accepted reporting standards applicable for sustainable development performance information. Qualitative interpretations of relevance, materiality and the accuracy of data are subject to individual assumptions and judgments. It is important to read the data in the context of Rio Tinto's Reporting Criteria.

Assurance work performed

We conducted our assurance engagement in accordance with International Standard on Assurance Engagements 3000 (Revised) – "Assurance Engagements other than Audits and Reviews of Historical Financial Information" issued by the International Auditing and Assurance Standards Board ("ISAE 3000"). Our procedures applied to the selected data primarily comprised:

- Making enquiries of relevant management of Rio Tinto
- Evaluating the design of the key processes and controls for managing and reporting the selected data
- Testing, on a selective basis, the preparation and collation of the selected data prepared by the management of Rio Tinto
- Undertaking analytical procedures over the reported data
- Reviewing a sample of relevant management information including reports to Rio Tinto's *Committee on social and environmental accountability*.

A limited assurance engagement is substantially less in scope than a reasonable assurance engagement under ISAE 3000. It excludes procedures such as testing controls effectiveness and corroborative data testing.

Conclusion

On the basis of our procedures, nothing has come to our attention which causes us to conclude that the selected data for the year

ended 31 December 2008 have not been prepared in all material respects in accordance with the Reporting criteria.

PricewaterhouseCoopers

PricewaterhouseCoopers
Liza Maimone, Partner

Melbourne
6 March 2009

Liability Limited by a scheme approved under Professional Standards Legislation

Source: Rio Tinto Annual Report 2008
(www.riotinto.com/annualreport2008/pdfs/p80_89SustainableDevelopment.pdf).

Before proceeding, review the exhibit and answer these questions. What are the subject matter and subject matter information? Who is the responsible party? What are the reporting criteria? Which assurance level is expressed by PwC?

ISAE 3000 provides a basis to provide assurance on a broad range of subject matters. Exhibit 20–5 illustrates how ISAE 3000 is applied to the assurance of compliance of De Beers with the Kimberley Process. De Beers is the largest diamond-producing and marketing company in the world; it produces more than 40 per cent of the world's diamonds by value. The Kimberley Process requires participants to certify that rough diamond shipments are conflict free. Conflict diamonds are rough diamonds used by rebel movements or their allies to finance conflict aimed at undermining legitimate governments.[vi]

Exhibit 20–5 Assurance Report to the Directors of De Beers Société Anonyme with regards to compliance with the Kimberley Process Introduction

Limited Assurance Report of the Independent Auditors to the Directors of De Beers Société Anonyme with regards to compliance with the Kimberley Process Introduction

We are the independent auditors of De Beers Société Anonyme (De Beers). We have been engaged to provide a limited assurance report on material compliance of the De Beers group with the terms of the diamond imports and exports undertakings governed by the Kimberley Process, and for no other purpose. To the fullest extent permitted by law, we do not accept or assume responsibility to anyone other than the De Beers group, for our work, for this report, or for the conclusions we have formed.

The Kimberley Process is a joint government, diamond industry and civil society initiative that require participants to certify that rough diamond shipments are conflict free. Compliance with the Kimberley Process is a legal requirement for participating countries. These requirements relate equally to the import and export of rough diamonds in and out of participant countries.

Directors' responsibility

The directors of the De Beers group are responsible for the design, implementation and effective operation of adequate systems of control over import and/or export transactions, for the maintenance of related supporting documentation that facilitates the prevention and detection of fraud and error, and for ensuring compliance with the terms of the diamond imports and exports undertakings with regard to the Kimberley Process. Please refer to the representation made by the Directors outlined on page 46 of this stakeholders report.

Auditors' responsibility

Our responsibility is to express our limited assurance conclusion to the directors about whether the De Beers group has materially complied with the rough diamond imports and exports undertakings governed by the Kimberley Process for the year ended 31 December 2007 and to report on material instances of non-compliance identified during our limited assurance engagement. We are not responsible for reporting on any diamond sales and purchases including import and export transactions beyond the period covered by our limited assurance engagement. For the purpose of our engagement, the De Beers group incorporates the subsidiaries, associates and joint ventures of De Beers excluding the Element Six group, De Beers Diamond Jewellers and the Hindustan Diamond Company.

Our independent limited assurance engagement, relating to diamond import and export transactions of the De Beers group in respect of the year ended 31 December 2007 was performed in accordance with the International Standard on Assurance Engagements (ISAE 3000), Assurance Engagements other than Audits or Reviews of Historical Financial Information. This standard requires us to comply with ethical requirements and to plan and perform our limited assurance engagement so that we obtain sufficient appropriate evidence regarding the subject matter of the engagement to support our limited assurance conclusion, which is stated below. As a limited assurance conclusion is expressed, our evidence-gathering procedures are more limited than they would be for a reasonable assurance engagement, and therefore less assurance is obtained than would be in a reasonable assurance engagement. Our engagement does not constitute an audit or review performed in accordance with International Standards on Auditing or International Standards on Review Engagements and consequently an audit or review opinion is not expressed.

Subject matter and criteria for evaluation of compliance

The subject matter and criteria for evaluation of compliance comprises the rough diamond sales and purchase including the import and export transactions conducted in accordance with the Kimberley Process including the industry self regulation System of Warranties, during the year ended 31 December 2007 and related supporting documentation required in terms of the diamond Imports and/or Exports Undertakings.

Limitations

Owing to the inherent limitations of a system of internal control and because of the characteristics of irregularities, including concealment through collusion and forgery, errors or fraud may not be prevented or detected, and a properly designed and performed limited assurance engagement may not necessarily detect all irregularities. Our procedures included the examination, on a test basis, of evidence supporting the amounts and transactions and were designed and performed to provide limited assurance that the De Beers group materially complies with the rough diamond sales and purchases including the imports and exports undertakings with regard to the Kimberley Process.

Summary of work performed

We have obtained an understanding of the entity and its environment, including its internal controls, and inspected, on a test basis, supporting Kimberley Process Certificates and warranties for the year ended 31 December 2007, sufficient to identify and assess the risks of material instances of non-compliance with the Kimberley Process whether caused by fraud or error.

Conclusion

Based on our examination of the evidence obtained, nothing has come to our attention that causes us to believe that the diamond imports and export transactions entered into by the De Beers group are not materially compliant with the requirements of the Kimberley Process.

Yours faithfully

Deloitte & Touche

Deloitte & Touche
Per Kevin Black
Partner
18 May 2008

Source: De Beers Report to Society 2007: Assurance Compliance Section
(www.debeersgroup.com/ImageVault/Images/id_1047/ImageVaultHandler.aspx).

Practitioners may also have been asked to provide assurance on the effectiveness of an entity's internal control. ISAE 3000 provides general guidance that could be used for assurance engagements on effectiveness of internal control. Criteria may be developed from the COSO framework and internal control considerations in auditing standards. Exhibit 20–6 is an example of an audit firm's standardized assurance report for engagement on internal control addresses where the audit committee is the intended user, the criteria is based on COSO and reasonable assurance is expressed.

Exhibit 20–6   Assurance Report on Internal Control

Independent Assurance Report to the Audit Committee of London plc

We refer to management's assessment of internal control over financial reporting as of 31 March 2009. As stated in their report, management's assessment is based on the Integrated Framework of the Committee of Sponsoring Organisations of the Treadway Commission (the COSO Framework).

Management is responsible for designing, implementing and maintaining effective internal control over financial reporting. The company's internal control over financial reporting includes those policies and procedures that (1) pertain to the maintenance of records that, in reasonable detail, accurately and fairly reflect the transactions and dispositions of the assets; and (2) provide reasonable assurance that transactions are recorded as necessary to permit preparation of financial statements in accordance with International Financial Reporting Standards.

Our responsibility is to independently conclude whether the assertion is fairly stated.

We draw to your attention that all financial reporting controls are dependent for their effectiveness on the diligence and propriety of those responsible for operating them. Our conclusion is not relevant to future periods due to the risk that the internal controls may become inadequate because of changes in conditions, or that the degree of compliance with policies or procedures may deteriorate.

Our work was performed in accordance with the International Standard on Assurance Engagements relating to reasonable assurance engagements.

In our opinion, management's assertion that internal control is effective, in all material respects, based on the COSO Framework, is fairly stated.

| Londinium House | **Londinium LLP** |
| London W1 1AA | Chartered Accountants |

Date

Source: Moore Stephens LLP, London (2009).

The IAASB is continually considering the demand for developing ISAEs to provide detailed assurance guidance on specific subject matter information, including reporting on sustainability, internal control, greenhouse gas, and pro forma financial information included in prospectuses. In 2009, the IAASB completed a standard on assurance reports on controls at a service organization and has announced its intention to revise the assurance standard on examination of prospective financial information.[vii] The next section discusses in more detail assurance on sustainability reporting that has become a viable service by practitioners and other assurance providers.

Assurance on Sustainability Reporting

Increasingly, companies report on sustainability information. The reports, also referred to as corporate social responsibility (CSR) reports, typically include information on the environmental, social and economic performance of the reporting entity. Thus, sometimes the term 'triple bottom line' reporting is used. Historically, companies with substantial environmental and social direct impact on the environment have been the most active in sustainability reporting, for example companies within the oil and gas industry, mining, chemical industry and forestry. Some of these companies command large resources and their activities affect the international community as well as a large number of local communities.

The sceptical user of sustainability reports may question the credibility of the information. For example, is the information complete? Specifically, is there a bias towards presenting favourable environmental and social information? Assurance provided by an independent third party adds credibility to sustainability reports.

Sustainability reporting and assurance are considerably less developed than financial reporting and audits of financial statements. One challenge has been the lack of authoritative criteria for reporting on sustainability and assurance standards. Today sustainability reporting guidelines issued by the Global Reporting Initiative (GRI) have gained considerable influence.[viii] The GRI's vision is to make sustainability reporting as routine and comparable as financial reporting. As shown in Table 20–4, the GRI guidelines cover principles and disclosure standards. Most of the principles are similar to concepts you are familiar with from audits of financial statements.

Table 20–4 Overview of Global Reporting Initiative (GRI) G3 Guidelines	
Principles and Guidance	**Standard Disclosures**
Apply the Reporting Principles and guidance to ensure your report is focused and of value for internal and external stakeholders.	There are three different types of measures that can be used to express strategic approach, management goals, and performance results.
• **Define report content** by applying the Principles of materiality, stakeholder inclusiveness, sustainability context, and completeness.	• **Profile** disclosures set the overall context for understanding performance – such as strategy and governance.
• **Ensure report quality** by applying the Principles of balance, comparability, accuracy, timeliness, reliability, and clarity.	• **Management Approach** disclosures explain how specific sustainability issues are managed, including goals and targets.
• **Set report boundary** by following the guidance provided to determine the range of entities that should be included in the report.	• **Performance Indicators** elicit comparable information on economic, environmental, and social performance.
Source: The GRI Guidelines (www.globalreporting.org/NR/rdonlyres/CF868D62–21F2–40DF-B090-F061BBB4AC3B/0/G3_Executive_Summary.pdf).	

Another visible initiative is AccountAbility (AA). Its AA1000 Assurance Standard covers assurance as well as aspects of sustainability performance reporting. The AA standard applies three basic principles for evaluating sustainability reports: inclusivity, materiality and responsiveness. Stakeholders' perspectives are at the core of these principles.[ix] Exhibit 20–7 shows an assurance report on the sustainability reporting of the Norwegian oil company StatoilHydro in accordance with ISAE 3000, which also refers to the GRI and AccountAbility.

Exhibit 20–7   Assurance Report on the Sustainability Reporting of StatoilHydro
Assurance report
To the stakeholders of StatoilHydro ASA
Scope of Engagement
We have been engaged by the corporate executive committee of StatoilHydro ASA to perform an independent assurance of the Sustainability Report ('the Report') as presented in the section 'Sustainable performance' in the StatoilHydro Annual and Sustainability Report 2008.
We have also been engaged by the corporate executive committee of StatoilHydro ASA to prepare an independent assurance report on the health, safety and environment (HSE) accounting for StatoilHydro ASA in 2008, as presented in the section 'HSE accounting' in the Report.

We have performed both assurance engagements in accordance with the SA 3000 (ISAE 3000), 'Assurance engagements other than audits or reviews of historical financial information'. The standard requires that we plan and execute procedures in order to obtain the following assurance levels:

- Reasonable assurance that the information in the section 'HSE accounting' is, in all material respects, an accurate and adequate representation of StatoilHydro HSE performance during 2008
- Reasonable assurance of the reliability of the consolidation process of the key performance indicators included in the HSE account and environmental data
- Limited assurance that the other information in the Report is, in all material respects, an accurate and adequate representation of the policy with respect to sustainability, business operations and events during 2008. The procedures performed in order to obtain limited assurance aim to verify the plausibility of information and probe less deeply than those performed for assurance engagements aimed at obtaining reasonable assurance.

Reporting criteria

As a basis for the HSE assurance engagement, we have used StatoilHydro ASA's internal reporting criteria specifically developed for HSE, as described in the section 'HSE accounting', together with relevant criteria in the sustainability reporting guidelines of the Global Reporting Initiative (GRI G3).

For the sustainability assurance engagement, we have used relevant criteria in the GRI G3 sustainability reporting guidelines, as well as the AA1000 Assurance Standard's principles of Materiality, Completeness and Responsiveness. We consider these reporting criteria to be relevant and appropriate to review the report.

The management's responsibility

StatoilHydro ASA's management is responsible for the HSE accounting. It is also responsible for selecting the information, collecting the data for presentation and preparing the Report. The choices made by the management, the scope of the report and the reporting principles, including the inherent specific limitations that might affect the reliability of the information are explained in the section 'About the report'.

The auditor's responsibility

Our task is to issue a statement on StatoilHydro's 2008 Sustainability Report and StatoilHydro's 2008 HSE accounting on the basis of the engagement outlined above. The content verified by us is marked with a text confirming the assurance engagement.

Assurance procedures for the HSE accounting

Our assurance of the HSE accounting is performed in accordance with the SA 3000 (ISAE 3000). The standard requires that we plan and execute procedures in order to obtain reasonable assurance that the HSE accounting as a whole is free of material misstatement.

Our work on the HSE accounting assurance has included:

- discussions with the corporate management for HSE on the content and aggregation of the HSE accounting
- site visits to selected entities, chosen based on an evalution of the entity's nature and significance, as well as general and specific risks. During site visits we have interviewed managers and personnel who participate in collecting the figures for the HSE accounting
- testing, on a sample basis, to evaluate whether HSE data which are included in the corporate performance indicators and environmental posters are reported, registered and classified according to StatoilHydro governing documents and in line with referred or recognized standards and methods
- review of whether systems used for registering, adapting, aggregating and reporting are satisfactory, and evaluating whether the reporting is complete and that the collection of data, adaptation and presentation of results in the HSE accounting is consistent
- an overall analyses of the figures compared with earlier reporting periods
- assessment of whether the overall information is presented in an appropriate manner in the HSE accounting

We have evaluated the HSE data's reliability, and whether the HSE performance is presented in an appropriate manner. Our objective has been to investigate:

- the acceptability and consistency of the reporting principles
- the reliability of the historical information presented in the HSE accounting section of the Report
- the completeness of the information and the sufficiency of the presentations

We believe that our procedures provide us with an appropriate basis to conclude with a reasonable level of assurance for StatoilHydro HSE accounting.

Assurance procedures for the Sustainability Report

Our assurance of the Report has been planned and performed in accordance with ISAE 3000 (limited assurance), and our conclusions have also been prepared against the main principles of the AA1000 Assurance Standard: Materiality, Completeness and Responsiveness.

Our review of the Report has involved the following activities:

- interviews with a selection of StatoilHydro's management and visits to four entities, as a representative sample of StatoilHydro's variety of activities, to gain an understanding of their approach to managing social, ethical and HSE issues that are covered in the Report
- interviews with a selection of StatoilHydro's management responsible for one selected area related to the content of the Report, to gain an understanding of their approach to the practical management of issues covered in the Report

- obtaining and considering evidence to support the assertions and claims made in the Report
- evaluation of the overall presentation of the Report, including the consistency of the information, based on the above-mentioned criteria
- evaluation of internal procedures for stakeholder inclusiveness and engagement
- review of StatoilHydro's report content against selected industry peers

Our review of the Report has not included assessing the implementation of policies. Only links referring to other sites included in the 'Sustainability Performance' parts of the Report are part of the assurance engagement. External links are not part of the assurance engagement.

Conclusion

On the basis of our procedures aimed at obtaining reasonable assurance, we conclude that in our opinion:

- The information in the HSE accounting presented in the section 'HSE accounting' of the Report is, in all material respects, an accurate and adequate representation of the policy and management with respect to HSE accounting during 2008, and that the HSE accounting includes information on all matters relating to HSE which are relevant to the StatoilHydro group as a whole
- the consolidation process that underlines the key performance indicators was, in all material respects, performed in a reliable manner, and that the information presented is consistent with the stated criteria
- the HSE performance indicators and environmental posters are in accordance with information submitted by the various entities, and illustrations of trends are in accordance with presented historical data

On the basis of our procedures aimed at obtaining limited assurance, nothing has come to our attention that causes us to believe that the information in the Report does not comply with the above mentioned reporting criteria. This also counts for StatoilHydro's declaration that the Report meets the requirements of the A application level of the GRI G3 sustainability reporting guidelines.

Stavanger, 17 March 2009
ERNST & YOUNG AS

Erik Mamelund
State authorised public accountant

Source: StatoilHydro Annual and Assurance Report 2008
(www.statoilhydro.com/AnnualReport2008/no/AboutThisReport/Documents/SignedAssuranceReport.pdf)

The assurance provider of sustainability reports may not be a practitioner. Non-accountant assurance providers include consultants, certification bodies, government bodies and non-governmental organizations (NGOs). For example, one of the pioneers in sustainability reporting, the oil company Shell, had the sustainability reports assured by its financial statement auditors in the period 1997–2004. In 2005 Shell started to use an External Review Committee to review its sustainability reports. Committee members in recent years have included representatives from Business for Social Responsibility, First Peoples Worldwide, Living Earth, the Institute for Business Ethics, the Energy and Resources Institute (TERI), and the International Institute of Sustainable Development (IISD). Committee members are occasionally rotated. For the reporting Shell uses the GRI G3 Guidelines and the Committee's review was guided by the AA1000 Assurance Standard (2008 Report).[x]

As sustainability reporting has become more widespread, the demand for assurance has increased. Practice continues to develop, albeit in some instances in an inconsistent manner. Legal requirements for sustainability reporting have been introduced in some countries, for example in France, the Netherlands and Denmark. One can envision a stronger rigour and regulation of sustainability reporting and assurance in the future. The IAASB's initiatives include a review of the Dutch professional institute Royal NIVRA assurance standard on sustainability reporting to determine whether it provides an appropriate basis for an international standard.

Investors and others may demand prospective financial information about the entity. The next section discusses assurance on prospective financial information.

Assurance on Prospective Financial Information

Prospective financial information contains financial information made up of either financial forecasts or financial projections. **Financial forecasts** are prospective financial information that presents an entity's *expectations*. They are based on assumptions reflecting conditions the responsible party *expects to exist* and the course of action it *expects to take* (best-estimate assumptions). **Financial projections** are prospective financial information based on *one or more hypothetical assumptions* about future events and the responsible party's actions. These assumptions may not reflect the most likely or expected conditions. The primary difference between the two is that the financial projection is based on hypothetical assumptions rather than what is actually expected and is intended to respond to a specific question, such as 'What would happen if the company were to outsource its customer support operations to India?' A financial projection is sometimes prepared to present one or more possible courses of action for evaluation.

Prospective financial information may be for either general use or limited use. *General use* of prospective financial information refers to the use of the information by persons with whom the responsible party is not negotiating directly. An example would be an offering statement containing prospective financial information for an entity's debt or equity securities. Because the intended users cannot question the responsible party, the appropriate basis of presentation is the *expected results*. Therefore, a financial *forecast* is appropriate for general use.

Limited use of prospective financial information refers to use of the information by the responsible party and third parties with whom the responsible party is directly negotiating. Examples of limited use include negotiations for a bank loan or submission to a regulatory body. In such cases, the third parties can question the responsible party about the prospective financial information and can question, understand, or even negotiate concerning the assumed conditions on which it is based. Thus, both financial forecasts and projections may be appropriate for limited use.

Management is responsible for the preparation and presentation of the prospective financial information, including the identification and disclosure of the assumptions on which it is based. The practitioners may be asked to provide assurance and report on the prospective financial information to enhance its credibility.

Assurance of prospective financial information normally involves four steps: (1) evaluating the preparation of the prospective financial information; (2) evaluating the support underlying the assumptions; (3) evaluating the presentation of the prospective financial information; and (4) issuing an assurance report. The accountant should be independent, have adequate professional competence to provide assurance on prospective financial information, and obtain sufficient appropriate evidence to issue an assurance report. The practitioners may also be asked to compile or perform agreed-upon procedures regarding prospective financial information.

ISAE 3000 provides the general principles the practitioners should apply where no specific ISAE is developed. For assurance of prospective financial information, ISAE 3400 *Examination of Prospective of Financial Information* exists. However, ISAE 3400 is considered outdated and therefore is not discussed further in this text. In 2009, the IAASB has announced its intention to revise the assurance standard on prospective financial information.

The EU Prospectuses Directive, which came into force 1 July 2005, intends to simplify the raising of capital in Europe. The new legal framework means that once a prospectus is authorized in one member state, it can be used in all others. There is a wide range of roles that a practitioner may be engaged in with respect to prospectuses. The Prospectuses Directive requires involvement of the practitioner to give assurance on historical and prospective information. This draws initiatives to establish assurance standards on practitioners' involvement in prospectuses.[xi]

The next section covers related services and completes the discussion of the IAASB engagement standards.

❖ RELATED SERVICES

LO7

The IAASB related services are either agreed-upon procedures regarding financial information or compilation of financial information. An agreed-upon procedures engagement is one in which a practitioner is engaged by a client to issue a report of findings based on specific procedures performed on the subject matter. In a compilation engagement the practitioner is engaged to use accounting expertise to collect, classify, and summarize financial information.

Related services are not covered by the IAASB's framework for assurance engagements. This is because the practitioner expresses no assurance when providing an agreed-upon procedures or compilation services in accordance with the International Standards on Related Services (ISRSs).

The practitioner and the firm should comply with the quality control standards and relevant parts of the IFAC Code of Ethics in an engagement of related services. However, a practitioner can perform an agreed-upon procedures engagements or a compilation engagement even though he or she is not independent of the entity. Where the practitioner is not independent, the lack of independence must be disclosed in practitioner's report. For example, the statement could be: 'We are not independent with respect to Learn Medical Services.'

Agreed-Upon Procedures

In an **agreed-upon procedures** engagement, a practitioner is engaged to carry out those procedures of an audit nature to which the practitioner and the entity and any appropriate third parties have agreed and to report on factual findings. As the practitioner simply provides a report of the factual findings of agreed-upon procedures, no assurance is expressed. The recipients of the report must form their own conclusions from the report by the practitioner. The report is restricted to those parties that have agreed to the procedures to be performed since others, unaware of the reasons for the procedures, may misinterpret the results.

ISRS 4400 *Engagements to Perform Agreed-Upon Procedures Regarding Financial Information* provides guidance on agreed-upon procedures engagements. An engagement to perform agreed-upon procedures may involve the practitioner in performing certain procedures concerning a complete set of financial statements or elements of financial statements such as a single financial statement (e.g. a balance sheet), specified accounts, elements of accounts or items in a financial statement (e.g. accounts payable, purchases from related parties, or sales and profits of a segment of an entity).

When the practitioner performs an agreed-upon procedures engagement, the practitioner should:

- Ensure with representatives of the entity and, ordinarily, other specified parties who will receive copies of the report of factual findings, that there is a clear understanding regarding the agreed procedures and the conditions of the engagement.
- Plan the work so that an effective engagement will be performed.
- Document matters which are important in providing evidence to support the report of factual findings, and evidence that the engagement was carried out in accordance with the ISRS 4400 and the terms of the engagement.
- Carry out the procedures agreed upon and use the evidence obtained as the basis for the report of factual findings.
- Report on the factual findings in accordance with ISRS 4400.

Exhibit 20–8 presents an example of a report in line with ISRS 4400 on the use of agreed-upon procedures for factual findings in connection with accounts payable. If the practitioner identifies errors or exceptions, these should be described in sufficient detail as part of the practitioner's actual findings.

Exhibit 20–8 Example of an Agreed-Upon Procedures Report for Accounts Payables

Report of Factual Findings

To the Boards of Directors of Exercise Company

We have performed the procedures agreed with you and enumerated below with respect to the accounts payable of Exercise Company as at 31 December 2009, set forth in the accompanying schedules (not shown in this example). Our engagement was undertaken in accordance with the International Standard on Related Services applicable to agreed-upon procedures engagements. The procedures were performed solely to assist you in evaluating the validity of the accounts payable and are summarized as follows:

1. We obtained and checked the addition of the trial balance of accounts payable as at 31 December 2009 prepared by Exercise Company, and we compared the total to the balance in the related general ledger account.
2. We compared the attached list (not shown in this example) of major suppliers and the amounts owing at 31 December 2009 to the related names and amounts in the trial balance.
3. We obtained suppliers' statements or requested suppliers to confirm balances owing at 31 December 2009.
4. We compared such statements or confirmations to the amounts referred to in item 2. For amounts which did not agree, we obtained reconciliations from Exercise Company. For reconciliations obtained, we identified and listed outstanding invoices, credit notes, and outstanding cheques, each of which was greater than €50. We located and examined such invoices and credit notes subsequently received and cheques subsequently paid and we ascertained that they should in fact have been listed as outstanding on the reconciliations.

We report our findings below:

(a) With respect to item 1 we found the addition to be correct and the total amount to be in agreement.
(b) With respect to item 2 we found the amounts compared to be in agreement.
(c) With respect to item 3 we found there were suppliers' statements for all such suppliers.
(d) With respect to item 4 we found the amounts agreed, or with respect to amounts which did not agree, we found Exercise Company had prepared reconciliations and that the credit notes, invoices, and outstanding cheques over €50 were appropriately listed as reconciling items with no exceptions.

Because the above procedures do not constitute either an audit or a review made in accordance with International Standards on Auditing or International Standards on Review Engagements, we do not express any assurance on the accounts payable as of 31 December 2009.

Had we performed additional procedures or had we performed an audit or review of the financial statements in accordance with International Standards on Auditing or International Standards on Review Engagements other matters might have come to our attention that would have been reported to you.

Our report is solely for the purpose set forth in the first paragraph of this report and for your information and is not to be used for any other purpose or to be distributed to any other parties. This report relates only to the accounts and items specified above and does not extend to any financial statements of Exercise Company, taken as a whole.

Auditor

Date

Address

Source: Adapted from ISRS 4400 *Engagements to Perform Agreed-Upon Procedures Regarding Financial Information*, IAASB (2009).

ISRS 4400 may provide guidance for engagements regarding non-financial information, provided that the practitioner has adequate knowledge of the subject matter in question and suitable criteria exist on which to base findings.

Compilation

In most countries small businesses are not required to have audited financial information. However, these entities may employ a practitioner to assist with preparing their financial statements, tax returns, or other financial documents, or to provide a *compilation* of financial information. A compilation engagement is directed towards presenting, ordinarily in the form of financial statements, information that is the representation of management or owners without undertaking to express any assurance on the information. The practitioner uses accounting expertise, as opposed to auditing expertise, to collect, classify and summarize financial information. The procedures employed are not designed and do not enable the practitioner to express any assurance on the financial information. However, users of the compiled financial information may derive some benefit as a result of the practitioner's involvement because the service has been performed with professional competence and due care. ISRS 4410 *Engagements to Compile Financial Statements* provides guidance for the performance of compilations.[xii]

In conducting a compilation, the practitioner should ensure that there is a clear understanding between the client and the practitioner regarding the terms of the engagement, plan the work so that an effective engagement will be performed, and document matters which are important in providing evidence that the engagement was carried out in accordance with ISRS and the terms of the engagement. The practitioner should obtain the following knowledge about the entity:

- General knowledge of the business and operations of the entity.
- Be familiar with the accounting principles and practices of the industry in which the entity operates.
- Be familiar with the form and content of the financial information that is appropriate in the circumstances.

Note that the practitioner is not required to conduct any inquiries or to perform any procedures to verify or corroborate any information supplied by the client. However, if the practitioner becomes aware that information supplied by management is incorrect, incomplete, or otherwise unsatisfactory, the practitioner should consider performing such procedures and request management to provide additional information. The practitioner should also read the compiled information and consider whether it appears to be appropriate in form and free from obvious material misstatements, such as mathematical or clerical mistakes or mistakes in the application of the identified financial reporting framework. If the practitioner becomes aware of material misstatements, the practitioner should try to agree appropriate amendments with the entity. If such amendments are not made and the financial information is considered to be misleading, the practitioner should withdraw from the engagement. The practitioner should also obtain an acknowledgement from management of its responsibility for the appropriate presentation of the financial information and of its approval of the financial information.

In all circumstances when a practitioner's name is associated with financial information compiled by the practitioner, the practitioner should issue a report. ISRS 4410 establishes the elements contained in a compilation report. Exhibit 20–9 provides an example of a report on an engagement to compile financial statements. The financial information compiled by the practitioner should contain a reference such as 'Unaudited', 'Compiled without audit or review', or 'Refer to the compilation report' on each page of the financial information or on the front of the complete set of financial statements.

Exhibit 20–9   Example of a Compilation Report

Compilation Report to the Boards of Directors

On the basis of information provided by management we have compiled, in accordance with the International Standard on Related Services applicable to compilation engagements, the balance sheet of Black & White Company as of 31 December 2009 and statements of income and cash flows for the year then ended. Management is responsible for these financial statements. We have not audited or reviewed these financial statements and accordingly express no assurance thereon.

Accountant

Date

Address

Source: Adapted from ISRS 4410 *Engagements to Compile Financial Statements*, IAASB (2009).

If a departure from the identified financial reporting framework exists, the practitioner should draw attention to the matter by adding a paragraph. An example of such an additional paragraph would be: 'We draw attention to Note 12 to the financial statements because management has elected not to capitalize the leases on plant and machinery which is a departure from International Financial Reporting Standards.'

A practitioner may provide other types of services, such as preparing a working trial balance, assisting in adjusting the account books, consulting on accounting, tax, and similar matters, preparing tax returns, and providing various manual or automated bookkeeping or data processing services, without having to comply with the standard for compilation.

❖ INTERNAL AUDITING

LO8

Up to this point, we have focused on non-audit assurance services and related services that are provided by practitioners. This section focuses on the role of, standards pertaining to, and services provided by internal auditors.

In many cases internal auditors have been instrumental in discovering financial statement fraud. For example, the largest financial statement fraud in the history of the USA may not have been discovered were it not for the persistent investigative efforts of Cynthia Cooper and her internal audit team (see Exhibit 14–2). Cynthia Cooper, the whistle-blower of the $9 billion WorldCom fraud, was head of internal audit at the communications giant at the time. According to the 2003 *Report of Investigation by the Special Investigative Committee of the Board of Directors of Worldcom, Inc.*, despite being ordered by the company's management to discontinue investigations in the areas where the fraud had been committed, Cooper's team aggressively pushed ahead and eventually uncovered the massive fraud.

After the recent years' long string of high-profile accounting frauds in some of the world's most respected companies increased emphasis has been placed on the importance of a viable internal audit function. The role of the internal auditor has become increasingly crucial to effective corporate governance and to the success of large organizations.[xiii]

Internal auditing can be a challenging and rewarding career path. Many professional accountants who work as external auditors eventually become internal auditors, and many internal auditors eventually become executives within their organizations. These opportunities arise because internal auditors are in a unique position to understand the organization from a perspective that is both broad and deep.

Internal Auditing Defined

The Institute of Internal Auditors (IIA), which oversees and sets standards for internal auditing internationally, defines *internal auditing* as follows:

Internal auditing is an independent, objective assurance and consulting activity designed to add value and improve an organization's operations. It helps an organization accomplish its objectives by bringing a systematic, disciplined approach to evaluate and improve the effectiveness of risk management, control, and governance processes.

This definition outlines the main goals of the profession and broadly states the methods whereby these goals may be achieved. The IIA has issued detailed and rigorous standards for the practice of internal auditing; however, there are several important differences between the internal and external auditing professions. Now that you know what internal auditing is, consider what attributes a good internal auditor should possess. How would these attributes be similar to or different from those a good external auditor would possess? How might the incentives and perspectives of internal and external auditors differ?

The Institute of Internal Auditors

Established in 1941, the IIA is an international professional association that serves as the global voice for the internal audit profession. The IIA has over 160,000 members in 165 countries, specializing in internal auditing, risk management, governance, internal control, IT audit, education, and security. The IIA is the recognized authority, principal educator, and acknowledged leader in certification, research, and technological guidance for the internal auditing profession worldwide. The Institute offers not only the general Certified Internal Auditor (CIA) certification but also specialty certifications in areas including government accounting and financial services.

IIA Standards

The IIA's professional guidance is organized into an *International Professional Practices Framework*. This framework consists of two broad categories of authoritative guidance:

Mandatory Guidance
- Definition of Internal Auditing.
- Code of Ethics.
- *Standards.*

Strongly Recommended Guidance
- Position Papers.
- Practice Advisories.
- Practice Guides.

The first of these areas provides mandatory guidance for IIA members and consists of the *Definition of Internal Auditing* (stated previously), the *Code of Ethics*, and the *International Standards for the Professional Practice of Internal Auditing*. The International Standards for the Professional Practice of Internal Auditing are in turn divided into three main areas: attribute standards; performance standards; and implementation standards.

Attribute standards address the characteristics of organizations and parties performing internal audit activities, and *performance standards* describe the nature of internal audit activities and provide criteria against which the performance of these services can be evaluated. Table 20–5 presents the IIA's attribute and performance standards. Given the substantial variation in internal audit environments across the world, attribute and performance standards are necessarily general; however, the third category of IIA standards, known as *implementation standards*, are more detailed, providing guidance applicable to specific types of engagements.

Table 20–5 International Standards for the Professional Practice of Internal Auditing	
Standard	*Definition*
Attribute Standards	
1000–Purpose, Authority, and Responsibility	The purpose, authority, and responsibility of the internal audit activity must be formally defined in an internal audit charter, consistent with the Definition of Internal Auditing, the Code of Ethics, and the *Standards*. The chief audit executive must periodically review the internal audit charter and present it to senior management and the board for approval.
1100–Independence and Objectivity	The internal audit activity must be independent, and internal auditors must be objective in performing their work.

1200–Proficiency and Due Professional Care	Engagements must be performed with proficiency and due professional care.
1300–Quality Assurance and Improvement Programme	The chief audit executive must develop and maintain a quality assurance and improvement programme that covers all aspects of the internal audit activity.
Performance Standards	
2000–Managing the Internal Audit Activity	The chief audit executive must effectively manage the internal audit activity to ensure it adds value to the organization.
2100–Nature of Work	The internal audit activity must evaluate and contribute to the improvement of governance, risk management, and control processes using a systematic and disciplined approach.
2200–Engagement Planning	Internal auditors must develop and document a plan for each engagement, including the engagement's objectives, scope, timing, and resource allocations.
2300–Performing the Engagement	Internal auditors must identify, analyse, evaluate, and document sufficient information to achieve the engagement's objectives.
2400–Communicating Results	Internal auditors must communicate the engagement results.
2500–Monitoring Progress	The chief audit executive must establish and maintain a system to monitor the disposition of results communicated to management.
2600–Management's Acceptance of Risks	When the chief audit executive believes that senior management has accepted a level of residual risk that may be unacceptable to the organization, the chief audit executive must discuss the matter with senior management. If the decision regarding residual risk is not resolved, the chief audit executive must report the matter to the board for resolution.

Practice Insight 20.2

The IIA's Internal Auditing Standards Board (IASB) approved a revision to Standard 1312 on external quality assessments that was implemented in January 2007. A 'quality assessment' is used to evaluate compliance with IIA standards, the internal audit activity and audit committee charters, the organization's risk and control assessment, and the use of successful practices. It is mandatory that every internal audit function have an external quality assessment at least once every five years to be in compliance with IIA standards. The potential need for more frequent external assessments should be assessed based on the size, complexity and industry of the organization in relation to the experience of the reviewer or review team (IIA Standard 1312).

Code of Ethics

As with most reputable professions, internal auditors must follow guidelines promoting ethical conduct (see Chapter 19 for a discussion of the IFAC Code of Ethics for Professional Accountants). The IIA Code of Ethics is important for internal auditors because the reliability of their work depends on a reputation for high levels of objectivity and personal integrity. The Code of Ethics specifies four main principles of ethical conduct and some associated rules that underpin the expected conduct of IIA members: integrity, objectivity, confidentiality and competency (see Tables 20–6 and 20–7).

Table 20–6	IIA Code of Ethics Principles
Principles	*Definition*
Integrity	The integrity of internal auditors establishes trust and thus provides the basis for reliance on their judgement.
Objectivity	Internal auditors exhibit the highest level of professional objectivity in gathering, evaluating, and communicating information about the activity or process being examined. Internal auditors make a balanced assessment of all the relevant circumstances and are not unduly influenced by their own interests or by others in forming judgements.
Confidentiality	Internal auditors respect the value and ownership of information they receive and do not disclose information without appropriate authority unless there is a legal or professional obligation to do so.
Competency	Internal auditors apply the knowledge, skills and experience needed in the performance of internal auditing services.

Table 20–7 IIA Rules of Conduct	
Principles	*Expectations*
Integrity	Internal auditors:
	1.1 Shall perform their work with honesty, diligence, and responsibility.
	1.2 Shall observe the law and make disclosures expected by the law and the profession.
	1.3 Shall not knowingly be a party to any illegal activity, or engage in acts that are discreditable to the profession of internal auditing or to the organization.
	1.4 Shall respect and contribute to the legitimate and ethical objectives of the organization.
Objectivity	Internal auditors:
	2.1 Shall not participate in any activity or relationship that may impair or be presumed to impair their unbiased assessment. This participation includes those activities or relationships that may be in conflict with the interests of the organization.
	2.2 Shall not accept anything that may impair or be presumed to impair their professional judgement.
	2.3 Shall disclose all material facts known to them that, if not disclosed, may distort the reporting of activities under review.
Confidentiality	Internal auditors:
	3.1 Shall be prudent in the use and protection of information acquired in the course of their duties.
	3.2 Shall not use information for any personal gain or in any manner that would be contrary to the law or detrimental to the legitimate and ethical objectives of the organization.
Competency	Internal auditors:
	4.1 Shall engage only in those services for which they have the necessary knowledge, skills, and experience.
	4.2 Shall perform internal auditing services in accordance with the *International Standards for the Professional Practice of Internal Auditing*.
	4.3 Shall continually improve their proficiency and the effectiveness and quality of their services.

Internal Auditors' Roles

Internal auditors are called 'internal' because they work within an individual entity and report the results of their work to management or (ideally) to the entity's audit committee or board of directors. They are not typically expected to report to the public or to parties outside the entity. However, internal audit functions differ widely in how they are managed and staffed. Some entities have internal audit functions that are staffed entirely 'in-house,' while others are 'co-sourced'. When an organization co-sources its internal audit function the entity typically hires an audit firm to provide internal audit services in conjunction with the entity's own internal auditors. This has become a significant source of revenue for many large audit firms. Ideally an entity will have a chief audit executive (CAE), whose role is to oversee the internal audit function (whether in-house or co-sourced) and to help coordinate the work of the internal and external auditors. You will recall from Chapter 19, however, that the IFAC Code of Ethics for Professional Accountants prohibits the external auditor from assuming audit client responsibility for internal control activities.

The roles played by internal auditors fall into two primary categories – *assurance services* and *consulting services.*

> Assurance services involve the internal auditor's objective assessment of evidence to provide an independent opinion or conclusions regarding a process, system or other subject matter. The nature and scope of the assurance engagement are determined by the internal auditor. There are generally three parties involved in assurance services: (1) the person or group directly involved with the process, system or other subject matter – the process owner; (2) the person or group making the assessment – the internal auditor; and (3) the person or group using the assessment – the user.

> Consulting services are advisory in nature, and are generally performed at the specific request of an engagement client. The nature and scope of the consulting engagement are subject to agreement with the engagement client. Consulting services generally involve two parties: (1) the person or group offering the advice – the internal auditor; and (2) the person or group

seeking and receiving the advice – the engagement client. When performing consulting services the internal auditor should maintain objectivity and not assume management responsibility.[xiv]

In general, an organization's internal audit function is most often deployed by management and the board of directors in the broad areas of evaluating risks, evaluating compliance, and performing financial and operational auditing. Through these activities, internal auditors contribute to effective *corporate governance* within an organization, which includes all management-administered policies and procedures to control risk and oversee operations within a company. Indeed, the IIA and other influential organizations identify the internal audit function as one of the cornerstones of effective corporate governance.

Evaluating Risks and Controls

As outlined by IIA Standard 2110, internal auditors should be directly involved in an entity's risk management process. In fact, IIA standards require internal auditors to conduct an evaluation of the organization's risk management process. Although the internal auditor's industry expertise allows him or her to stay abreast of general industry risks, it is his or her specific experience within the organization that enables him or her to accurately gauge risks relating to the integrity of financial and operational information, the safeguarding of assets, and compliance with laws and regulations. Internal auditors are often asked to determine the sources of these risks, and may sometimes be called on to recommend approaches to manage identified risks. Internal auditors have long been involved in evaluating and enhancing their organizations' system of internal control over financial reporting and over other areas of the organization.

Practice Insight 20.3

The IIA offers a Certification in Control Self-Assessment (CSA) designed for practitioners of control assessment. Professionals who hold the CSA designation include individuals from a variety of backgrounds. They use their knowledge about risk and controls to help their clients implement and maintain effective controls to achieve their objectives.

Reviewing Compliance

In many industries, compliance with relevant laws and regulations is an extremely complicated and important endeavour. For example, if a company fails to comply with health and safety regulations, significant fines and penalties can be levied against the offending company. Many other rules and regulations exist that must be followed by businesses and other organizations. This includes regulations related to products (e.g. drugs), competition (e.g. unfair competition), the environment (e.g. pollution), or employees (e.g. employees' rights). Internal auditors play an important role in helping management ensure that the organization complies with the laws, rules, and regulations that apply to the entity, as well as in ensuring that employees comply with organizational guidelines and rules.

Financial Auditing

Although the financial auditing performed by internal auditors involves many of the same concepts you have already studied in this text, it differs from the audits conducted by external auditors in several ways. For example, internal auditors tend to focus on specific financial issues as directed by management or the board rather than doing an audit of periodic financial statements. This is not, however, always the case. This is illustrated in Practice Insight 20.4 (see also Practice Insight 5.1).

Practice Insight 20.4

In Danske (Danish) Bank the internal auditors express an opinion on the bank's business procedures and internal control procedures as well as on the financial statements. The latter is in addition to the external auditors' opinion on the financial statements in their Independent Auditors' Report. View the Internal Audit's Report and Independent Auditors' Report in Danske Bank Annual Report 2008, pp. 172–173.

Source: www.danskebank.com/en-uk/ir/Documents/2008/Q4/Annualreport2008.pdf

The nature of internal auditors' audit report is different. Because the intention of the audit often relates to either very general or very specific factors, it is impossible to require a standardized internal audit report. Consequently, internal audit reports are normally uniquely composed to fulfil the requirements of the particular assignment. Exhibit 20–10 describes a real-life situation where an organization's internal auditor uncovered a fraud while evaluating a specific financial area at the request of the organization's management.

Exhibit 20–10   Internal Financial Audit Uncovers Employee Fraud

At a major research university, the internal audit team was called in to facilitate required budget cuts in the accounting department. The accounting department was understaffed and had only one staff member assigned to review procurement card transactions through the accounting office for staff and faculty. The internal auditor quickly identified some suspicious receipts that totalled €1,200. The investigation led to a single employee, and eventually over four van-loads of suspected unauthorized purchases were removed from the employee's home and personal vehicle. The fraud amounted to approximately €60,000 and led to the criminal prosecution of the suspect. The internal audit function saved the accounting department money immediately, but by identifying several deficiencies in the internal control system, it no doubt improved the efficiency and effectiveness of internal control for the entire university.

Source: Adapted from *Internal Auditor* (June 2004), pp. 97–99.

Operational Auditing

Due to their unique position in an organization, internal auditors typically achieve a thorough understanding of how the organization operates, and internal auditors are thus able to provide various types of services to improve the entities in which they work. An auditor should be prepared to recognize when enhancements could be made to align current operations with the entity's objectives. Operational audits serve a wide variety of purposes. They are primarily conducted to identify the causes of problems or to enhance the efficiency or effectiveness of operations. In many organizations, internal auditors spend most of their time performing operational audits. In fact, because they often spend relatively little of their time performing financial audits, the term *internal auditing* is often (incorrectly) used interchangeably with *operational auditing*.

Internal Audit Product Offerings

In order to illustrate the diversity of services offered by internal auditors, refer to Figure 20–4, which shows how DuPont decided to deploy its internal audit resources. The figure illustrates two important points. First, the management of risk is the central focus of internal audit at DuPont. Risk management is important because a successful company must be able to not only deal with current problems but also to anticipate and prepare for other potential obstacles. Second, the wheel in Figure 20–4 is not static, but contains several ongoing and interdependent processes. A modern internal audit function must be adaptable and able to keep up with the changing demands of the modern business environment in large and complex organizations such as DuPont. Exhibit 20–11 offers a more detailed description of each of the product categories outlined in DuPont's 'internal audit product wheel'.

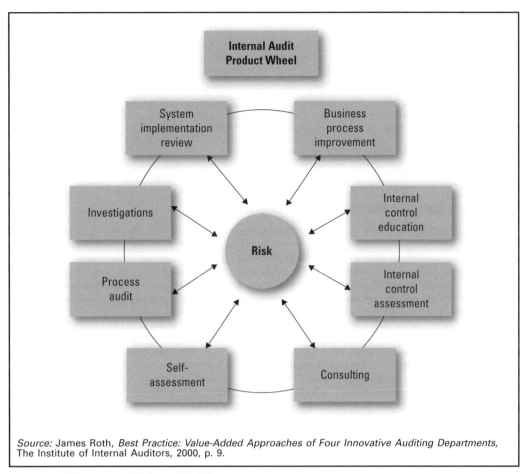

Source: James Roth, *Best Practice: Value-Added Approaches of Four Innovative Auditing Departments*, The Institute of Internal Auditors, 2000, p. 9.

Figure 20–4   DuPont's Uses of the Internal Audit Function

Exhibit 20–11   Definitions of the Services Provided by DuPont's Internal Auditors

Process Audits Internal auditing undertakes comprehensive analyses and appraisals of all phases of business activities and provides management with appropriate recommendations concerning the activities reviewed. This product includes business process audits, which appraise the adequacy and efficiency of accounting, financial, and operating controls; information systems audits, which focus on technical IS audit activities, system implementation and application reviews; reviews of emerging technology; and new site reviews which occur in the early stages of start-up operations, joint ventures, or acquisitions to ensure that cost-effective internal control is in place.

Special Investigation This service provides the client with an independent review of facts and circumstances surrounding an event or series of events and presents recommendations to management for appropriate resolution/action. Investigations are often associated with known or suspected wrongdoing, waste, fraud, abuse of company assets, other business ethics violations, and/or serious mismanagement.

System Implementation Review System implementation reviews are conducted as part of the prevention quadrant of internal auditing's products. The System Implementation Review promotes the inclusion of cost-effective controls into systems prior to implementation and assures that the controls will operate as intended when implemented.

Business Process Improvement In limited circumstances, internal auditing may initiate or participate in internal control-related business process improvement activities. This product is used to identify and minimize control deficiencies in business processes and is designed to assist organizations in making process changes that result in strengthened internal control and optimal performance.

Internal Control Education This offering assists the client organization to reduce risk through an enhanced understanding of the business value of internal control and business ethics. Instructional sessions may be conducted by internal auditing or by the client with internal auditing support.

Internal Control Assessment This product provides the client with an overall opinion or assessment of the current state of internal control and future risks. Internal control assessments are conducted periodically on a corporate, regional, SBU, and functional basis. The COSO model serves as the methodology for conducting these assessments.

Consulting This is an internal auditing activity normally provided in response to a request from management. It is designed to provide expertise in the resolution of internal control issues. Consulting may involve answering questions, developing solutions to problems, recommending courses of action, and/or formulating an opinion. Consulting may also involve the review of proposed procedures for internal control content.

Self-Assessment Self-assessments are performed by the client based upon a framework and facilitation provided by internal auditing. Internal auditing will be an active participant in self-assessment activities, which involve an assessment of risk and control activities within the business and/or function under review.

Source: James Roth, *Best Practices: Value-Added Approaches of Four Innovative Auditing Departments*, The Institute of Internal Auditors, 2000, pp. 9–10.

Interactions between Internal and External Auditors

The objectives and types of work performed by internal and external auditors are often quite different, but as you may imagine, there is varying degrees of overlap. External auditors do their work with the purpose of expressing an opinion as to whether the entity's financial statements are free of material misstatements. Because external auditors rely on the concept of materiality, they typically are not concerned with auditing a particular area in a great deal of depth – they gather evidence until they obtain reasonable assurance that no misstatements are present that would be considered significant in the context of the financial statements taken as a whole. They then report externally, outside of the organization being audited.

Internal auditors, on the other hand, assist management and the board of directors in evaluating and managing risk, assessing compliance with laws and regulations, assessing operational efficiency, and performing detailed financial audits of areas requiring particular attention. Because their objectives are often different from those of external auditors, the concept of materiality is usually quite different as well. For example, in auditing for employee fraud, the amounts involved are usually far from material in terms of the financial statements taken as a whole. However, internal auditors can reduce the incidence of employee fraud, saving money, and improving controls in the process.

Some of the work performed by internal auditors is directly relevant to the work of the independent auditor. For example, Chapter 5 briefly discusses the external auditor's use of work performed by the internal audit function in the context of the financial statement audit. Before a decision to use some of the work of internal auditors, the external auditor must evaluate the internal auditors' objectivity and competence. If the external auditor decides to use some of the internal audit work, the cost savings in terms of the reduction in the external audit fee can be significant.[xv]

🔒 Key Terms

Agreed-upon procedures. Specific procedures of an audit nature to which the auditor and the entity and any appropriate third parties have agreed to and report on factual findings.

Assurance engagement (IAASB). An engagement in which a practitioner expresses a conclusion designed to enhance the degree of confidence of the intended users other than the responsible party about the outcome of the evaluation or measurement of a subject matter against criteria.

Assurance engagement risk. The risk that the practitioner expresses an inappropriate conclusion when the subject matter information is materially misstated.

Assurance services (Elliott Committee). Independent professional services that improve the quality of information, or its context, for decision makers.

Audit engagement. A reasonable assurance engagement regarding historical financial information where the auditor expresses an opinion whether the financial statements are prepared, in all material respects, in accordance with an applicable financial reporting framework.

Compilation engagement. An engagement in which accounting expertise, as opposed to auditing expertise, is used to collect, classify and summarize financial information.

Financial forecasts. Prospective financial information prepared on the basis of assumptions as to future events which management expects to take place and the actions management expects to take as of the date the information is prepared (best-estimate assumptions).

Financial projections. Prospective financial information prepared on the basis of hypothetical assumptions about future events and management actions which are not necessarily expected to take place, or a mixture of best estimate and hypothetical assumptions.

Internal auditing. An independent, objective assurance and consulting activity designed to add value and improve an organization's operations. It helps an organization accomplish its objectives by bringing a systematic, disciplined approach to evaluate and improve the effectiveness of risk management, control and governance processes.

Limited assurance. A term that implies that engagement assurance risk is reduced to a level that is acceptable in the circumstances of the engagement, but where that risk is greater than for a reasonable assurance engagement.

Prospective financial information. Financial information based on assumptions about events that may occur in the future and possible actions by an entity. Prospective financial information can be in the form of a forecast, a projection or a combination of both.

Reasonable assurance. A term that implies that engagement assurance risk is reduced to an acceptably low level in the circumstances of the engagement.

Review engagement. An assurance engagement that enables an auditor to state whether, on the basis of procedures which do not provide all the evidence that would be required in an audit, anything has come to the auditor's attention that causes the auditor to believe that the financial information is not prepared, in all material respects, in accordance with an applicable financial reporting framework.

? Review Questions

LO1	20–1	Define *assurance services* in accordance with the Elliott Committee. Discuss why the definition focuses on decision making and information.
LO2	20–2	Explain the scope, hierarchy and relationship between IAASB engagement standards. Why are related services engagements not considered assurance engagements?
LO3	20–3	Define an *assurance engagement* in accordance with the IAASB framework. Explain the elements of the definition. What are meant by *appropriate* subject matters and *suitable* criteria?
LO4	20–4	Explain the two assurance levels provided by IAASB assurance engagement standards. How are the assurance levels expressed in the assurance report?
LO5	20–5	Why might an entity request a review report? How is the assurance level provided by the practitioner expressed in a review report?
LO6	20–6	Why is the nature of the basic elements, essential procedures and report in an assurance engagement (other than audits or reviews of historical financial information) comparable to those of an audit of financial statements? Which essential procedures should be applied if the assurance engagement requires use of specialized skill that the practitioner does not possess (use of an expert)?
LO6	20–7	What types of assurance services can be performed under ISAE 3000 (*Assurance Engagements Other Than Audits or Reviews of Historical Financial Information*)?
LO6	20–8	What is meant by sustainability reporting? Why would there be a demand for assurance of sustainability reports?
LO6	20–9	What are the two types of prospective financial information? How do they differ from each other?
LO7	20–10	Why is no assurance expressed in an agreed-upon procedure engagement?
LO7	20–11	Which expertise does the practitioner use to perform a compilation engagement? What type of knowledge must a practitioner possess about the entity in order to perform a compilation?
LO8	20–12	Explain why the internal audit function is one of the cornerstones of effective control.

Problems

LO5   **20–13**   Fleisher & Schmidt, independent auditors, has been engaged by their audit client Ajax Company to review the company's balance sheet for the six months ended 30 June 2009.

Required:

a   *Which procedures will be appropriate to apply to obtain sufficient appropriate evidence?*

b   *Prepare a draft of a review report with an unmodified conclusion.*

LO2,3,6   **20–14**   You have audited the financial statements of the Eastern Star Bank's (ESB) for the year ended 31 December 2009. Eastern Star Bank's management is required by the national banking supervisors to provide a report about the effectiveness of ESB's internal control over financial reporting. You have been engaged to assure management's report, which will be presented in a separate report. Management's report uses the criteria from the COSO framework.

Required:

a   *Prepare a draft of the assurance on management's report on the effectiveness of the EB's internal control. Assume that there are no significant deficiencies.*

b   *Draft the same report, except assume that the ESB has a significant deficiency in its loan application procedures for ensuring the adequacy of collateral for loans.*

LO7   **20–15**   Your client, Cheaney Rental Properties, has engaged you to perform a compilation of its income statement for a loan with the Mutual Bank.

Required:

a   *What will be your appropriate response if you became aware of a material misstatement in the income statement during the compilation?*

b   *Prepare a standard compilation report for Cheaney Rental Properties.*

Discussion Cases

LO2,3,6   **20–16**   *Environmental assurance* typically refers to the process of assessing compliance with environmental laws and regulations, as well as compliance with company policies and procedures. A practitioner provides assurance to assist users in evaluating management's written assertions about: (1) the entity's compliance with specified requirements; (2) the effectiveness of the entity's internal control over compliance; or (3) both.

Required:

a   *Discuss how a practitioner would conduct an assurance engagement to evaluate an entity's written assertion that it was in compliance with environmental laws and regulations.*

b   *Assume that this same entity maintained an internal control system that monitored the entity's compliance with environmental laws and regulations. Discuss how a practitioner would evaluate the effectiveness of the entity's internal control over compliance.*

LO6   **20–17**   Environmental and social reporting and its assurance are filled with controversies. Many of the companies reporting on sustainability are often criticized for their environmental and social behaviour. Sometimes criticism is raised directly on the assurance process. The following quote illustrates one such case:

'Oil giant Royal Dutch Shell faces damaging claims over its influence on a supposedly independent environmental audit to determine whether the world's biggest oil and gas project would receive vital bank funding.

Dozens of emails released by the government under the Freedom of Information Act show how Shell officials in London attempted to downplay and edit international environmental criticism of the $22bn Sakhalin II energy scheme off the east coast of Russia, which has subsequently been all but fully financed.

The exchange reveals anxiety from an unidentified party, thought to be a UK government agency, at how Shell was 'stage managing' the review conducted by AEA Technology, the one-time Atomic Energy Authority, now an environmental consultancy.

The report, published last November, was used by banks to assess whether funding Sakhalin II was consistent with environmental and social protocols.

...

A spokesman for Shell said: 'The opportunity for Sakhalin Energy and its shareholders to provide comments on a draft report of this kind is routine and designed to ensure accuracy. The findings contained in AEA Technology's report are entirely theirs.' (Observer, 31 August 2008)

Required:

a   *Why would reporting and assurance on environmental and social information be more challenging that financial reporting and audit of financial reporting?*

b   *Why would there be scepticism with regard to environmental and social reporting?*

c   *Discuss potential developments in the reporting and assurance on environmental and social information that can contribute to bridging the gap to such scepticism.*

⟳ Internet Assignments

LO2,3,6   20–18   Many international companies prepare sustainability reports. Audit firms and other entities provide assurance for some of these reports.

Required:

a   *Search on the Internet and find at least three companies that prepare sustainability reports that are accompanied by an assurance report. (Hint: Go to Global Reporting Initiative's home page www.globalreporting.org/.)*

b   *Which entity (or entities) provide(s) the assurance?*

c   *Which assurance guidance (e.g. ISAE 3000) is used?*

d   *Do the assurance reports include the basic elements of an assurance report as required by the ISAE 3000?*

LO2,3,6   20–19   Many oil companies provide sustainability information. Search for sustainability reports (or corporate responsibility reports) for oil companies such as BP, Chevron, Conoco Philips, Exxon, ENI, Repsol YPF, Shell, StatoilHydro and Total.

Required:

Prepare a report on your findings, including on criteria used for reporting, assurance provider, assurance standard(s) used and level of assurance provided (if applicable).

LO2,3,6   20–20   AccountAbility issues assurance standards. Go to AccountAbility's home site (www.accountability21.net/). (You can register for free.)

Required:

a *Learn about the AA1000 Assurance Standard.*

b *Compare AA1000 Assurance Standard and ISAE 3000.*

c *Learn about the Corporate Responsibility (CR) Report Award Winner (for example, the Vodafone Group won the CR Award 2008).*

LO6 20–21 KPMG International surveys corporate responsibility reporting globally.

Required:

Go to the KMPG website and learn about corporate responsibility reporting and assurance (www.kpmg.com/SiteCollectionDocuments/International-corporate-responsibility-survey-2008_v2.pdf).

LO8 20–22 The IIA maintains its own website containing useful information about the institute and the internal auditing profession in general. Visit the IIA's home page (www.theiia.org).

Required:

a *Follow the link to the official magazine of the IIA. What is the mission of this respected publication?*

b *Although the IIA does not require that its members obtain CIA certification, it is becoming popular worldwide. What advantages are afforded to those who certify, according to the IIA's website? Who might benefit from the CIA designation?*

NOTES

i   The scope of IAASB assurance engagements is comparable with that of AICPA attestation engagements. AICPA defines an attestation engagement as follows: '*Attest services occur when a practitioner is engaged to issue or does issue an examination, a review, or an agreed-upon procedures report on subject matter, or an assertion about subject matter, that is the responsibility of another party.*'
The AICPA's attestation standards provide for three types of engagements: *examination*; *agreed-upon procedures*; and *review*. An AICPA examination engagement provides the highest level of assurance and the practitioner must gather sufficient evidence to limit the attestation risk to a low level. The conclusion is expressed in the positive form. In an AICPA agreed-upon procedures engagement the level of assurance provided depends on the nature and scope of the procedures agreed upon with the specified parties. In an AICPA review engagement the practitioner expresses limited assurance and the conclusion is in the negative form. The PCAOB adopted the attestation standards along with the rest of the AICPA's professional standards on an interim basis in April 2003.
In practice many of the assurance services offered by audit firms in the USA are conducted in accordance with the AICPA attestation standards.

ii For more information on GRI see www.globalreporting.org/Home.

iii In an assertion-based engagement the responsible party may be responsible for the subject matter information only. This would be the case when a government organization has prepared a report to distribute to intended users about a private company's sustainability performance and the government organization engages a practitioner to perform an assurance engagement regarding the report.

iv Consulting typically involves some combination of activities relating to objective-setting, fact-finding, definition of problems or opportunities, evaluation of alternatives, development of recommendations including actions, communication of results, and sometimes implementation and follow-up. Reports (if issued) are generally written in a narrative style. Generally the work performed is only for the use and benefit of the client. The nature and scope of work is determined by agreement between the practitioner and the client.

v   The revision of ISRE 2400 is on the IAASB project timetable as of July 2009.

vi You can learn more about the Kimberley Process on www.kimberleyprocess.com/home/index_en.html.

vii The reader is encouraged to visit the IAASB's home site to learn about the status of the IAASB standard development process (www.ifac.org/IAASB/).

viii See note ii above.

ix   For more information on AccountAbility see www.accountability21.net/.

x   For more information on the Shell Sustainability Report and the External Review Committee see www.shell.com/home/content/responsible_energy/sustainability_reports/dir_shell_sustainability_reports.html.

xi   The Federation of European Accountants (FEE) issued in 2004, *Discussion Paper on the Auditor's Involvement with the New EU Prospectus Directive.* The IAASB project timetable as of July 2009 includes a project to develop an assurance standard on proper compilation of pro forma financial information included in prospectuses.

xii   The IAASB project timetable as of July 2009 includes a project to revise ISRS 4410.

xiii   Academic research confirms the importance of internal auditing. For example, a recent study indicates that high-quality internal auditing leads to more reliable externally reported earnings. (See D. Prawitt, J. Smith and D. Wood, 'Internal Audit Quality and Earnings Management', *The Accounting Review*, July 2009).

xiv   *Introduction to the International Standards for the Professional Practice of Internal Auditing* (www.theiia.org/).

xv   The IAASB project timetable as of July 2009 includes a revision of ISA 610, *Using the Work of Internal Auditors.*

Index

AccountAbility
  sustainability reporting assurance
    standard 631–633
accountant *see* professional accountant in
  business; professional accountants in public
  practice
accounting estimates 191
  auditing 102–103
  definition 105
  estimation uncertainty 102–103, 464
  evaluation of reasonableness 104–105
  management bias 104, 553
  risk of material misstatement 103–104
accounting fraud 4
  AIG Inc 484
  Enron 41
  forensic audits 58
  Parmalat 42
  revenue recognition 334
  Royal Ahold 377, 401
  WorldCom 469
accounting information system 62
accounting period
  accounts payable 398
  accounts receivable 358–359
  bank reconciliation 506–507
  cash disbursement transactions 391, 393
  cash receipt transactions 351, 353
  inventory transactions 449, 450
  payroll transactions 419
  payroll-related liabilities 424
  property management process 473
  purchase transactions 388, 390
  revenue transactions 348, 350
accounting policies
  auditors' evaluation 83
  definition 105
accounting records
  audit evidence, as 120–121
  definition 134
  electronic 121, 195
  IFAC Ethics Code on assisting client in
    preparing 596–597
accounting services 58
accounting systems
  flowcharts 201, 215–216
accounts payable 383
  auditing 394
  classification and understandability 399
  completeness 396–398
  confirmation process 399–401

cut-off 398
  evaluating audit findings 401
  existence assertion 398
  presentation and disclosure assertions 399
  rights and obligations 398
  substantive analytical procedures 394–395
  valuation 398–399
accounts payable subsidiary ledger 381
accounts receivable
  auditing 354–366
  classification and understandability 361
  completeness assertion 358
  confirmation process 362–366
  cut-off assertion 358–359
  evaluating audit findings 366–367
  existence assertion 359–360
  function 342
  presentation and disclosure assertions 361
  rights and obligations 360
  substantive analytical testing
    procedures 355–356
  valuation and allocation 360–361
accounts receivable subsidiary ledger 339
accrued expenses
  auditing 394
  completeness 396–398
  valuation 398–399
  see also accounts payable
accrued payroll liabilities *see* payroll-related
  liabilities
accuracy of records
  cash disbursements 391, 392
  cash transactions 351, 353
  inventory transactions 442, 443
  investments 513–514
  payroll transactions 418–419, 420
  purchase transactions 388, 389–390
  revenue transactions 348, 350
  stockholders' equity 490
adverse opinion 557, 560–562
  definition 568
advisory services 58
  definition 66
aged trial balance of accounts receivable 339–340
agents
  meaning 6
agreed-upon procedures engagement 50, 57,
  635–636
  definition 66, 644
AIG Inc
  derivative losses 484

American Institute of Certified Public
  Accountants (AICPA) 49
  Auditing Standards Board (ASB) 49
  Special Committee on Assurance Services
    (Elliott Committee) 616, 617
analytical procedures 52, 85, 126–127
  definition 66
  final procedures 168
  financial ratios useful as 172–175
  preliminary activities 154
  purposes 157–158
  substantive 158–168, 205–206
annual report 552
  definition 568
  see also financial statements
Apple Inc
  backdating of stock-options case 416
applicable financial reporting framework 11–12,
  57
  definition 21
appointments
  IFAC Ethics Code 588–589
arms length transactions 153
  definition 178
Arthur Andersen
  collapse 41
assertions 64–65, 115–120
  definition 66
  see also management assertions
assets
  impairment 474, 475
  inspection of tangible assets 125, 263
  misappropriation 91–92
  see also prepaid expenses; property, plant and
    equipment
Association of Certified Fraud Examiners
  (ACFE) 60, 334
  certification programme 60
assurance
  definition 10–11
assurance engagement
  assurance risks model 621
  definition 11, 618, 644
  IAASB Framework 50, 617–622
  IAASB standards 622–623, 625–630
  limited assurance 618
  reasonable assurance 618
  see also assurance services
assurance engagement risk
  definition 621
assurance report
  Shell sustainability report 633
  StatoilHydro ASA sustainability report 631–633
assurance services
  definition 616, 644
  example assurance reports 628–630, 631–633
  internal auditors performance of 640
  non-audit services 56–57
  prospective financial information, reporting
    on 633–634
  sustainability reporting 628, 631–633
  see also assurance engagement
assurance standards
  IAASB 622–623, 625–630
attribute sampling

applied to tests of controls 266–281
  definition 284
audit committee 61
  communications process 539–540
  definition 66
audit documentation
  achieved level of control risk 205–206
  archiving 133–134
  auditor's risk assessment and response 94–95
  content 128–130
  definition 134
  examples 130–131
  format 131–132
  internal control over financial reporting 241
  inventory management process 440–441
  objectives 128
  organization of 132
  ownership 132
  payroll system 417–418
  purchasing process 386
  retention 133–134
  retention period 539
  tick marks 132
  understanding of internal control 200–203
audit evidence 13–14, 114–135
  accounting records 120–121
  analytical procedures 52, 85, 126–127
  appropriateness 121–122
  computer-assisted audit techniques
    (CAATs) 126
  concepts 120–123
  confirmation 125–126, 263
  definition 21
  electronic documents 121, 195
  evaluation 99–101, 122–123
  evaluation on completing
    engagement 537–538
  final analysis on completing engagement 533
  inquiry 84–85, 88–90, 125
  inspection 85–86
  inspection of records or documents 123–124,
    263
  inspection of tangible assets 125, 263
  nature of 120–121
  observation 85–86, 124–125
  procedures for obtaining 123–127
  recalculation 126
  records or documents, reliability of 121–122
  relationship to audit report 114–115
  relevance 13–14, 121
  reliability 14, 121–122, 123
  reperformance 126, 263
  representation letter 536–537
  sampling 263–264
  scanning 127
  sufficiency 121–122
  types, reliability of 127
  vouching for occurrence 493–494
audit expense
  account analysis 493–494
audit file see audit documentation
audit firms
  composition 55–56
  fees 57
  organization 55–56

size 55
types of services 56–58
audit plan
    additional value-added services 154
    assessing compliance with laws and
        regulations 152–153
    assessing need for experts 152
    assessing risks 152
    client acceptance and continuance 146–147
    definition 178
    documenting 154–155
    engagement planning 151
    internal control over financial
        reporting 231–232
    related parties, identification of 153–154
audit procedures 14–18
    analytical 52, 85, 126–127
    audit engagement team discussions 88
    completion 527–541
    definition 135
    evaluation of internal auditors' work 150
    evidence *see* audit evidence
    inspection 85–86
    observation 85–86
    reasons for performing 120
    timing 206–208
    see also risk assessment procedures
audit report
    adverse opinion 557, 560–562
    comparative financial information 562–564
    departure from applicable financial reporting
        framework 556, 560–562
    disclaimer of opinion 557, 559
    emphasis of matter paragraph 554–556
    example of standard audit report with
        unmodified opinion 553–554
    going concern emphasis of matter
        paragraph 554–555
    internal auditors 642
    internal control over financial
        reporting 241–246
    issue 18
    materiality, effect of 557–558
    modified opinion 20, 552, 556–557, 558–562
    other information included with audited
        financial statements 564–565
    other matters paragraph 554–556
    pervasive effect of misstatement 555
    qualified opinion 557, 560–562
    relationship to audit evidence 114–115
    scope limitation 556, 558–560
    single financial statements/elements of
        financial statement 566
    special purpose financial statements 565–566
    special reporting issues 562–565
    summary financial statements 567
    unmodified opinion 18–20, 553–554
audit risk 12–13, 76–96
    definition 12
    see also risk assessment
audit risk model 77–80
    use of 78–80
audit sampling *see* sampling
audit strategy
    reliance strategy 195, 197, 344, 384

substantive strategy 195, 197
audit tests
    bank reconciliation 507
    dual-purpose tests 157
    evaluating results 93–94
    evaluating results on completing
        engagement 537–538
    financial ratios useful as analytical
        procedures 172–175
    hierarchy 168–171
    inventory management process 441–444
    payroll system 418–420
    petty cash fund 510–511
    prepaid insurance 462–464
    purchasing process 386
    substantive analytical procedures 158–168,
        205–206
    substantive procedures 156–157, 205–206
    tests of controls 156, 204
    tests of controls applying attribute sampling
        method 266–281
    timing of substantive procedures 206–208
    timing of tests of controls 207
    types 156–157
auditing
    assurance role 5–6
    definition 10–11
    role 6–7
    study of 5
auditing profession
    regulation 42–53
auditing standards 49–53
see also International Auditing and Assurance
    Standards Board (IAASB); International
    Auditing Practice Statements (IAPS);
    International Standards for the Professional
    Practice of Internal Auditing; International
    Standards on Assurance Engagements;
    International Standards on Auditing (ISAs)
auditor independence
    assisting client in accounting records and
        financial statement preparation 596–597
    business relationships 593
    corporate finance services 599
    employment with audit client 594
    ethics 151
    EU rules 602
    family and personal relationships 594
    fees size, overdue and contingent fees 599–600
    financial interest in audit client 592–593
    IFAC Ethics Code 591–595
    information technology services 598
    internal audit services 598
    legal services 598–599
    litigation support services 598
    litigation threat 600
    loans and guarantees 593
    opinion shopping 54
    provision of non-assurance services to audit
        clients 595–601
    quality control standards ISQC 1 603–605
    recruiting services 599
    taxation services 597–598
    temporary staff assignments to clients 594
    valuation services 597

auditor's business risk 77
auditor's expert
    assessing need for 152
    definition 178
    intangible asset valuation 464
auditors
    analogy to building surveyors 8–10
    forensic 60
    government 59–60
    legal liability 43–44
    responsibilities 53–54
    types 58–60
    see also external auditors; internal auditors;
        professional accountants in public practice
authorization
    cash disbursement transactions 391, 392
    cash discounts 351, 353
    credit 341
    inventory transactions 442, 443
    investments 513
    long-term debt 485, 486
    payroll transactions 418, 420
    property management process 470
    purchase transactions 388, 389
    revenue transactions 348, 349
    stockholders' equity 490
    write-offs 340
bank accounts
    branch accounts 503
    general cash account 502
    imprest cash accounts 503
    types 502–503
bank confirmation 506
bank reconciliation
    audit tests 507
    cut-off bank statement 506
    fraud-related audit procedures 507–508
    working paper 505–506
billing 341–342
board of directors 61
    communication with 539–540
    definition 66
    see also corporate governance
business processes
    audit 331–517
    categories 62–64, 115
    cycles 62, 115, 331
    definition 66
    effects of transactions on cash 501–502
    see also financing process; human resource
        management; inventory management
        process; purchasing process; revenue
        process
business risk 80–86
    definition 105
    final analysis on completing engagement 534
capital-stock accounts *see* equity capital accounts
cash
    auditing 501–502
    disclosure 511–512
    fraud-related audit procedures 507–510
    meaning 501
    petty cash fund 510–511
    proof of cash 508–509
    tests for kiting 509–510

cash disbursements
    accuracy of transactions 391, 392
    authorization 391, 392
    classification 391, 393
    completeness of transactions 390–391, 392
    control activities and tests of controls 390–393
    controls 504–505
    cut-off 391, 393
    fraud-related audit procedures 508–509
    occurrence assertion 390, 392
    segregation of duties 392
    substantive tests of details of
        transactions 504–505
cash disbursements journal 381
cash equivalents 501
    definition 501, 517
cash management
    bank accounts 502–503
    segregation of duties 503
cash receipts 342
    accuracy of transactions 351, 353
    authorization of cash discounts 351, 353
    classification 351, 353
    completeness of transactions 351, 352–353
    control activities and tests of controls 350–353
    controls 504–505
    cut-off of transactions 351, 353
    fraud-related audit procedures 508–509
    occurrence of transactions 351, 352
    substantive tests of details of
        transactions 504–505
cash receipts journal 340
cheques 381
classification
    accounts payable 399
    accounts receivable 361
    cash disbursement transactions 391, 393
    cash receipts 351, 353
    intangible assets 467
    inventory transactions 442, 444, 451–452
    investments 513–514
    long-term debt 485, 486
    payroll transactions 419, 420
    prepaid insurance 464
    property management process 473
    purchase transactions 390, 391
    revenue transactions 348, 350
client monies
    IFAC Ethics Code 590–591
clients
    acceptance 146–147, 588
    auditor independence 151
    confidentiality 147
    continuance 147
    new 146–147, 588
Code of Ethics (Institute of Internal
    Auditors) 639–640
Code of Ethics for Professional Accountants
    (IFAC) 54, 147, 151, 582–602
    conceptual framework 584–586
    conflicts of interest 589
    content 583
    corporate finance services 599
    custody of client assets 590–591
    definitions 584

fees and remuneration 589–590, 599–600
fees size, overdue and contingent fees 599–600
fundamental principles 584–586
gifts and hospitality 590, 600
independence requirements for audit and
    review engagements 591–595
information technology services 598
internal audit services 598
legal services 598–599
litigation support services 598
litigation threat 600
marketing professional services 590
objectivity 591
professional accountants in business 601–602
professional accountants in public
    practice 586–601
professional appointment 588–589
recruiting services 599
second opinions 589
taxation services 597–598
temporary staff assignments to clients 594
valuation services 597
collusion
    breakdown in internal control due to 202
commission
    IFAC Ethics Code 590
commitments 530–531
Committee of Sponsoring Organizations of the
    Treadway Commission (COSO)
    Enterprise Risk Management- Integrated
        Framework 227
    Internal Control- Integrated Framework 188,
        189–195, 227, 630
communications
    understanding the entity's 193, 199–200
    with those charged with governance 96, 150,
        539–540
    written by auditor to those charged with
        governance 539–540
comparative financial information
    audit report 562–564
comparative financial statements 562–564
    definition 568
compilation engagements 50, 57, 620, 636–637
    definition 66, 644
completeness
    accounts payable 396–398
    accounts receivable 358
    accrued expenses 397–398
    cash disbursement transactions 390–391, 392
    cash receipts transactions 351, 352–353
    equity capital accounts 491
    insurance policies 463
    inventory transactions 441–442, 443
    investments 513
    long-term debt 485, 486–487
    payroll-related liabilities 425
    property management process 472
    purchase transactions 387, 389
    revenue transactions 348, 349
completion of audit 527–541
component 175
    definition 178
component auditor 175
    definition 178

computer-assisted audit techniques (CAATs)
    audit evidence 126
    custom audit software 214
    definition 135
    generalized audit software 213–214
    test data 214–215
    testing internal control 204, 213–215
computers
    control activities 210–215
confidence bound 294
    definition 318
confidentiality
    client 147
confirmation 125–126, 263
    accounts payable 399–401
    accounts receivable 362–366
    bank 506
    blank 400
    compensating balances 511–512
    definition 135
    external 362
    long-term debt 489
    negative 363–364
    positive 362–363, 400
    procedures 364–365
    timing 364
    types 362–364
    zero-balance 400
conflicts of interest
    IFAC Ethics Code 589
    principal-agent relationship 6–7
consulting services
    internal auditors performance of 640–641
contingent fees
    definition 605
    IFAC Ethics Code 590, 600
contingent liabilities
    audit procedures for identifying 528–529
    commitments 530–531
    disclosure 527–529
    examples 527
    litigation and claims 529–530
    management's responsibilities 528
    tax 528
control activities 193–194, 200
    definition 216
control environment 190
    definition 216
    understanding 198–199
control risk
    achieved level 204–205
    assessing 203–204
    audit strategy 195–197
    definition 105
    tests 156, 204
corporate finance services
    IFAC Ethics Code on providing 599
corporate governance 61–62
    definition 66
    internal auditors' contributions to 641
    responsibility of those charged with
        governance 539–540
corporate social responsibility reporting *see*
    sustainability reporting
corresponding figures

definition 568
see also comparative financial information
cost accounting
inventory management 437
cost accumulation and variance report 436
credit approval form 338
credit authorization
revenue process function 341
credit memorandum 340
control activities and tests of controls 353–354
current assets *see* prepaid expenses
custody of client assets
IFAC Ethics Code 590–591
customer sales order 338
customer statement 339
data centre
control activities 210
debit memorandum 393
debt instruments 483
see also long-term debt
deduction forms 412
depreciation
property, plant and equipment 475
derivatives
AIG Inc losses 484
detection risk
definition 105
disbursements 382–383
dividends 491
human resource management 414
imprest cash accounts 503
see also cash disbursements
disclaimer of opinion 557, 559
definition 568
disclosure in financial statements
accounts payable 399
accounts receivable 361
assertions 119–120, 361
cash 511–512
compensating balances 511–512
contingent liabilities 527–528
human resource management process 425
investments 516–517
property, plant and equipment items 474–475
retained earnings 492
stockholders' equity 491
dividends
auditing 491
documentation
management's on internal control over
financial reporting 230
see also audit documentation
documents
electronic 121, 195
inspection 123–124, 263
inventory management process 435–436
payroll 411–413
purchasing process 379–381
reliability 121–122
revenue process 338–340
shipping 339, 436
see also audit documentation; records;
retention of documents
electronic commerce
definition 216

internal control 198
Electronic Data Interchange (EDI) 121, 195
definition 216
electronic documents
audit evidence, as 121, 195
electronic funds transfer 381
engagement letter 147–149
definition 178
sample 148–149
engagement of auditor
independence 151
preliminary activities 150
engagement partner 151
definition 178
engagement standards (IAASB) 50, 617–623
definition 66
Enron 41
environmental reporting *see* sustainability
reporting
equity capital accounts
auditing 490–491
completeness 491
occurrence 491
valuation 491
equity instruments 489
see also stockholders' equity
errors
auditor's responsibilities 53–54
breakdown in internal control due to 202
definition 105
information systems controls 207
misstatements caused by 81, 86–92
ethics
auditor engagement activities 151
definition 66, 579, 605
EC Recommendation on Statutory Auditors'
Independence in the EU 602
IFAC Code of Ethics *see* Code of Ethics for
Professional Accountants (IFAC)
Institute of Internal Auditors Code 639–640
theories of ethical behaviour 579–582
see also auditor independence
European Commission (EC)
auditors' legal liability 44
Recommendation on Statutory Auditors'
Independence in the EU 602
European Union (EU)
8th Directive on Statutory Audits 42, 48–49,
62, 602, 605
auditing regulation 48–49
auditor independence rules 602
compliance with international accounting and
auditing standards 44, 49
Prospectuses Directive 634
quality assurance programmes 605
expenses
definition 376
expert *see* auditor's expert
external auditors 59
interactions between internal and external
auditors 644
relationship with internal auditors 149–150
fair value
accounting estimates 102–103, 465
fees

audit firms 57
  contingent 590, 600
  IFAC Ethics Code 589–590, 599–600
  referral 590
  relative size 599–600
Financial Accounting Standards Board (FASB) 49
  Contingencies (ASC Topic 450) 225–226
financial forecasts
  assurance reporting 633–634
  definition 645
financial instruments
  debt instruments 483
  equity instruments 489
  see also investments; long-term debt;
    stockholders' equity
financial performance measures
  reliability for purpose of audit 84
financial projections
  assurance reporting 633–634
  definition 645
financial ratios
  activity ratios 173–174
  coverage ratios 175
  current ratio 173
  operating cash flow ratio 173
  profitability ratios 174–175
  quick ratio 173
  short-term liquidity ratios 173
  useful as analytical procedures 172–175
financial reporting
  fraudulent 89–92, 334
financial statement assertions 12, 115–120
  account balances at the period end 118
  definition 21
  presentation and disclosure 119–120
  see also management assertions
financial statements
  assertions about presentation and
    disclosure 361
  audit report for single financial
    statements/elements of financial
    statement 566
  definition 66
  evaluating presentation and disclosure 539
  group financial statements 175–177
  IFAC Ethics Code on assisting client in
    preparing 596–597
  independent engagement quality review 539
  other information 564–565
  test of selected account balances 493–494
financing process 63, 115
  auditing 501–517
  see also long-term debt
flowcharts
  internal control technique 201, 215–216
  symbols 215
forensic auditors 60
forensic audits 58
fraud
  auditor's responsibilities 53–54
  cash account audit procedures 507–510
  certified fraud examiners (CFEs) 60
  communicating to management 96
  definition 66
  financial reporting 89–92, 334

forensic auditors 60
forensic audits 58
inventory 439–440
misstatements caused by 81, 86–92
risk identification process 88–89
see also accounting fraud
fraud risk factors 89–92
  definition 105
general ledger
  human resource management 414
  inventory management process 437
  purchasing process 383
  revenue process 342
gifts
  IFAC Ethics Code 590, 600
Global Reporting Initiative (GRI)
  sustainability reporting guidelines 631
going concern
  emphasis of matter paragraph in audit
    report 554–555
  evaluation 534–535
goodwill 461
  definition 475
  see also intangible assets
governance
  communications with those charged with 96,
    150
  definition 178
  see also corporate governance
government auditors 59–60
group financial statements
  audit of 175–177
guarantees
  IFAC Ethics Code 593
hospitality
  IFAC Ethics Code 590, 600
human resource management 64, 115, 410–426
  collusion resulting in breakdown of internal
    control 202
  control risk assessment 416–418
  disbursement 414
  document and record types 411–413
  financial statement accounts affected by types
    of transactions 410–411
  functions 413–414
  general ledger function 414
  IFAC Ethics Code on recruiting services 599
  IFAC Ethics Code on temporary staff
    assignments to clients 594
  inherent risk assessment 416
  overview 410
  payroll processing 414
  personnel 413
  presentation and disclosure completeness
    assertion 425
  segregation of duties 194, 202, 342–343,
    353–354, 383–384, 392, 414–415, 437–438,
    470–471, 490, 514
  supervision 413
  timekeeping 414
  types of transactions 410–411
  see also payroll
IAASB *see* International Auditing and Assurance
  Standards Board
IFAC *see* International Federation of Accountants

impairment of assets 474
  disclosure 475
  investments 516
imprest accounts 503
  audit 510
  definition 517
income statement
  auditing 492–494
  substantive analytical procedures 493–494
  uses 492
industry-related factors
  purchasing process 384
  revenue process 344
information asymmetry
  definition 21
  principal-agent relationship 6–7
information risk
  meaning 7
information systems
  application controls 194, 211–213
  error controls 213
  general controls 193–194, 210–211
  internal control 193, 199–200
  output controls 213
  processing controls 212–213
  purchasing process 385–386
  understanding the entity's 199–200
information technology
  IFAC Ethics Code on providing services 598
  internal control, effect on 188–189
  see also computer-assisted audit techniques
    (CAATs); electronic commerce; information
    systems; software
inherent risk
  definition 105
inquiry
  confirmation 125–126
  definition 135
  of management and others 84–85, 88–89, 125
inspection 85–86
  definition 135
  different from 'observation' 125
  records or documents 123–124, 263
  tangible assets 124, 263
Institute of Internal Auditors (IIA) 59
  Code of Ethics 639–640
  membership 638
  standards 638–639
insurance, prepaid *see* prepaid insurance
intangible assets
  classification 467
  control risk assessment 465
  definition 475
  examples 464
  existence and completeness 466
  inherent risk assessment 464–465
  rights and obligations 466
  substantive procedures 465–467
  valuation 466
interest expense
  substantive analytical procedures 486
  see also long-term debt
interim financial statements
  review engagement 623–624
internal audit function

definition 178
internal audit services 640–644
  IFAC Ethics Code on providing 598
internal auditing 59, 637–644
  definition 59, 66, 645
Internal Auditing Standards Board (IASB) *see*
  Institute of Internal Auditors
internal auditors 59
  assurance services performed by 640
  certification 59, 641
  Code of Ethics 639–640
  consulting services performed by 640–641
  corporate governance, contributions to 641
  definition 178
  financial auditing 641–642
  interactions between external and internal
    auditors 644
  operational auditing 642
  relationship with external auditors 149–150
  reviewing compliance role 641
  risk assessment role 641
  role 640–642
  services performed by 640–644
internal control
  audit documentation 200–203
  audit strategy 195–197
  collusion resulting in breakdown of 202
  communication of deficiencies 209
  computer-assisted audit techniques
    (CAATs) 204, 213–215
  control activities 193–194, 200
  control risk assessment 203–204
  COSO Framework 188, 189–195, 227, 630
  deficiencies 209
  definition 216
  flowcharts 201, 215–216
  human errors or mistakes 202
  importance 187–188
  information systems and communications 193,
    199–200
  information technology, effect of 188–189
  limitations 202
  management override 202
  monitoring of controls 194–195, 200
  narrative memorandum 200
  policies and procedures 84
  procedures manuals and organizational
    charts 200
  questionnaires 201
  revenue process 345–346
  size of entity, effect of 202
  small entity 202
  system 62
  timing of substantive procedures 206–208
  timing of tests of controls 207
  understanding 198–200
  see also internal control over financial
    reporting
internal control over financial reporting
  (ICFR) 223–248
  auditor documentation 241
  auditor reporting 241–246
  deficiencies defined 225–226
  definition 224–225
  evaluating control deficiencies 238–240

management documentation 230
management's assessment process 226–230
performing an audit 230
planning the audit 231–232
Public Company Accounting Oversight Board
AS5 standard 224–248
remediation of a material weakness 240–242
Sarbanes-Oxley Act 2002 Section 404
requirements 223–224
testing controls 235–237
use of service organizations 247–248
using a top-down approach 233–235
using the work of others 232
walk-throughs 235
written representations 241
international accounting standards (IASs) *see*
international financial reporting standards
(IFRSs)
International Accounting Standards Board
(IASB) 44, 48
Framework for the Preparation and
Presentation of Financial Statements 376
International Auditing and Assurance Standards
Board (IAASB) 44, 49–53
assurance standards 622–623, 625–630
International Framework for Assurance
Engagements 50, 617–623
Quality Control for Firms that Perform Audits
and Reviews of Historical Financial
Information and Other Assurance and
Related Services Engagements (ISQC 1) 50,
133, 151, 603–605
reform of ISAs project 4, 51
see also International Standards on Auditing
(ISAs)
International Federation of Accountants (IFAC) 44
Code of Ethics *see* Code of Ethics for
Professional Accountants (IFAC)
International Auditing and Assurance
Standards Board *see* International Auditing
and Assurance Standards Board (IAASB)
membership 45
Public Interest Oversight Board (PIOB) 45
Quality Assurance (SMO 1) 605
quality assurance review programmes 605
Statement of Membership Obligation
(SMO) 605
structure and governance 45–47
international financial reporting standards
(IFRSs) 44, 48
Borrowing Costs (IAS 23) 474
Cash Flow Statements (IAS 7) 501
Financial Instruments: Disclosure (IFRS 7) 491,
512, 516
Financial Instruments: Disclosure and
Presentation (IAS 32) 512, 513
Financial Instruments: Recognition and
Measurement (IAS 39) 485, 491, 512, 513,
516
Impairment of assets (IAS 36) 474
Intangible assets (IAS 38) 465
Inventory (IAS 2) 446, 451
Presentation of Financial Statements (IAS
1) 376, 490, 534

Provisions, Contingent Liabilities and
Contingent Assets (IAS 37) 527
Related Party Disclosures (IAS 24) 153, 399
Revenue (IAS 18) 331–333
International Organization of Securities
Commissions (IOSCO) 44, 48
International Organization of Supreme Audit
Institutions (INTOSAI) 44, 48
International Standards for the Professional
Practice of Internal Auditing 638–639
International Standards on Assurance
Engagements (ISAEs)
Assurance Engagements Other Than Audits or
Reviews of Historic Financial Information
(ISAE 3000) 625–630
Examination of Prospective Financial
Information (ISAE 3400) 634
International Standards on Auditing (ISAs) 44,
51–53
Analytical Procedures (ISA 520) 52, 154, 533
Audit Considerations Relating to an Entity
Using a Service Organization (ISA 402) 208,
420
Audit Evidence (ISA 500) 52
Audit Evidence- Additional Considerations of
Specific Items (ISA 501) 447, 451, 559
Audit Sampling and Other Means of Testing
(ISA 530) 265
Auditing Accounting Estimates (ISA
540) 102–104, 332, 360, 399, 474, 491
The Auditor's Procedures in Response to
Assessed Risks (ISA 330) 93
The Auditor's Responsibility to Consider Fraud
in an Audit of Financial Statements (ISA
240) 53, 88, 93, 333, 507
Communicating Deficiencies in Internal
Control to Those Charged with
Governance and Management (ISA
265) 209
Communications of Audit Matters with Those
Charged with Governance (ISA 260) 150,
539
Comparative Information (ISA 710) 563
Consideration of Laws and Regulations in an
Audit of Financial Statements (ISA 250) 152
Considering the Work of Internal Auditing
(ISA 610) 52
Documentation (ISA 230) 128–129
Emphasis of Matter Paragraphs or Other
Matters Paragraphs in the Independent
Auditor's Report (ISA 706) 555, 560–561,
564
Engagements to Report on Summary Financial
Statements (ISA 810) 567
Evaluation of Misstatements in Performing an
Audit (ISA 450) 96, 100
External Confirmations (ISA 505) 126, 362
Going Concern (ISA 570) 534, 554–555
The Independent Auditor's Report on a
Complete Set of General Purpose Financial
Statements (ISA 700) 531–532, 562
Initial Engagements- Opening Balances (ISA
510) 556
list 51–52
Management's Representations (ISA 580) 536

Materiality in Planning and Performing an Audit (ISA 320) 96
Modifications to the Opinion in the Independent Auditor's Report (ISA 705) 557, 560, 561
Objective and General Principles Governing and Audit of Financial Statements (ISA 200) 151
Other Information in Documents Containing Audited Financial Statements (ISA 720) 564
Planning an Audit of Financial Statements (ISA 300) 155
Quality Control for Audits of Historical Financial Information (ISA 220) 151
quality control standards (ISQCs) 50, 133, 151, 603–605
reform project 4, 51
Special Considerations- Audits of Financial Engagements Prepared in Accordance with Special Purpose Frameworks (ISA 800) 565–566
Special Considerations- Audits of Group Financial Statements (including the Work of Component Auditors) (ISA 600) 175–177
Subsequent Events (ISA 560) 532, 533
Understanding the Entity and its Environment and Assessing the Risks of Material Misstatement (ISA 315) 65, 88, 93, 115
INTOSAI *see* International Organization of Supreme Audit Institutions
inventory
    auditing 444–453
    observation and physical count 447–448
    standard costs 446–447
inventory management process 64, 115
    audit documentation 440–441
    audit tests 441–444
    control activities and tests of controls 441–444
    control risk assessment 440–441
    cost accounting 437
    document and record types 435–436
    finished goods stores 437
    functions 436–437
    general ledger 437
    inherent risk assessment 438–440
    inventory management function 436–437
    manufacturing 437
    overview 433–434
    raw materials stores 437
    segregation of duties 437–438
    see also inventory transactions
inventory master file 436
inventory status report 436
inventory transactions
    accuracy 442, 443
    authorization 442, 443
    classification 442, 444
    classification and understandability 451–452
    completeness 441–442, 443
    cut-off 449, 450
    evaluating audit findings 452–453
    existence assertion 449, 450
    occurrence 441, 442–443
    presentation and disclosure assertions 452
    rights and obligations 449, 451

substantive analytical procedures 445–446
substantive procedures 444–446
valuation and allocation 449, 451
investments
    accuracy 513–514
    auditing 512
    authorization 513
    classification 513–514
    completeness 513
    control risk assessment 513–514
    disclosure 516–517
    existence 515–516
    impairment 516
    occurrence 513
    segregation of duties 514
    substantive analytical procedures 514
    substantive procedures 514–517
    valuation and allocation 515, 516
invoice processing 382
invoices
    sales 339
    vendor 380
IOSCO *see* International Organization of Securities Commissions
kiting 509–510
lapping 352
    definition 367
laws
    assessing compliance 152–153
    internal auditors' role in reviewing compliance 641
legal expense
    account analysis 493–494, 529
legal letters
    contents 529–530
    definition 541
    example 530
legal services
    IFAC Ethics Code on providing 598–599
liability
    contingent *see* contingent liabilities
    definition 376
lien 462
    definition 475
litigation
    legal letters 529–530
    types 529
litigation support services
    IFAC Ethics Code on providing 598
litigation threat
    IFAC Ethics Code 600
loan agreements
    restrictive covenants 489
loans
    IFAC Ethics Code 593
long-term debt
    analysis schedule 488
    auditing 483–484
    authorization 485, 486
    classification 485, 486
    completeness 485, 486
    confirmation 489
    control risk assessment 484–486
    occurrence 485, 486
    restrictive covenants 489

substantive procedures 486–489
types 483
valuation 485, 487
Madoff, Bernard 92
management
    auditor's inquiries of 84–85, 88–89, 125
    communicating fraud to 96
    communication of deficiencies in internal
        control to 209
    definition 178
    documentation on internal control over
        financial reporting 230
    governance role 539–540
    representation letter 536–537
    responsibilities concerning contingencies 528
management assertions 64–65, 115–120
    account balances at the period end 118
    accounts payable and accrued
        expenses 395–399
    accounts receivable 355–361
    by category 116–117
    cash balances 504
    cash disbursements 390–393
    cash receipts transactions 350–353
    classes of transactions 116–118
    financial statement presentation and
        disclosure 119–120
    inventory transactions 441–444
    investments 513–517
    long-term debt 485–487
    payroll transactions 418–420
    property management process 470, 471–475
    purchase transactions 387–390
    revenue transactions 346–350
    sales returns and allowances
        transactions 353–354
    stockholders' equity 489–490
management bias
    accounting estimates 104, 553
    definition 105
management letter 540
marketing
    professional services 590
materiality 13
    assessing 96–101
    audit report, effect on 557–558
    definition 21
    performance 97–98
materials requisition 435
Mintz, S M 579–580, 581
misstatement
    adjustment 537–538
    definition 13, 87
    detected in prior audits 469
    identified 96, 99
    misappropriation of assets 91–92
    types 87
    uncorrected 96, 99–100
    see also risk of material misstatement
monetary-unit sampling 265, 294–307
    advantages and disadvantages 295
    application 295–296
    computing sample sizes 298–299
    definition 285
    evaluation 301–307

expected misstatement 298
    performance 299–301
    planning 296–299
    projected misstatement 301
    risk of incorrect acceptance 297
    upper misstatement limit 301
new clients
    acceptance 146–147, 588
non-assurance services to audit clients
    assisting client in accounting records and
        financial statement preparation 596–597
    corporate finance services 599
    information technology services 598
    internal audit services 598
    legal services 598–599
    litigation support services 598
    recruiting services 599
    taxation services 597–598
    valuation services 597
non-compliance acts 152–153
    definition 178
observation
    activities and operations 85–86, 124–125
    definition 135
    different from 'inspection' 125
    inventory 447–448
open-order report 339
operational auditing
    internal auditors 642
opinion shopping 54
organizational charts 200
organizational structure of entity
    payroll transactions 417
    procedures manuals and charts 200
    purchasing process 385–386
other information included with audited financial
    statements
    auditors requirement to check for
        consistency 564–565
    definition 568
owner-manager relationship *see* principal-agent
    relationship
Parmalat Finanziaria S.p.A.
    accounting scandal 42
payroll
    accrued payroll liabilities 423–425
    accuracy of payroll transactions 418–419, 420
    audit documentation 417–418
    audit tests 418–420
    auditing payroll-related accounts 421–425, 510
    authorization of transactions 418, 420
    classification of transactions 419, 420
    control activities and tests of controls 418–420
    control risk assessment 416–418
    cut-off 419
    documents and records 411–413
    imprest cash accounts 503
    occurrence of transactions 418, 419–420
    processing 414
    substantive analytical procedures 421–422
    substantive procedures 421–425
payroll expense accounts
    evaluating audit findings 425
    substantive analytical procedures 423
payroll master file 412

payroll master file changes report 412
payroll register 412
payroll-related liabilities
    completeness 425
    cut-off 424
    evaluating audit findings 425
    existence and valuation 425
    substantive analytical procedures 421–425
performance materiality 97–98
    definition 106
performance reviews 193
periodic payroll reports 413
personnel records 412
petty cash fund
    audit tests 510–511
    auditing 510–511
    controls 510
Polaroid
    bankruptcy 439
practitioner *see* professional accountants in public
    practice
prepaid expenses
    auditing 461–464
    control risk assessment 462
    definition 476
    examples 461
    inherent risk assessment 461
    see also prepaid insurance
prepaid insurance
    classification 464
    existence and completeness 463
    rights and obligations 463
    substantive analytical procedures 462
    substantive procedures 462–464
    valuation 463–464
presentation of financial statements
    accounts payable 399
    accounts receivable 361
    assertions 119–120, 361
    human resource management process 425
    inventory transactions 452
principal-agent relationship
    conflict of interest 6–7
    information asymmetry 6–7
principals
    meaning 6
procedures manuals 200
production data information 436
production schedule 435
professional accountant
    definition in IFAC Ethics Code 583
professional accountant in business
    definition in IFAC Ethics Code 583
    IFAC Ethics Code 601–602
professional accountants in public practice
    conflicts of interest 589
    custody of client assets 590–591
    definition in IFAC Ethics Code 583
    fees and remuneration 589–590, 598–600
    gifts and hospitality 590, 600
    IFAC Ethics Code 586–601
    marketing professional services 590
    objectivity 591
    professional appointment 588–589
    second opinions 589

professional judgement 13, 53, 78
    definition 21
professional scepticism 53, 78
    definition 67
professional services
    definition in IFAC Ethics Code 583
    fees and remuneration 589–590, 598–600
    marketing 590
    non-assurance services to audit clients 595–601
    objectivity 591
professionalism
    definition 579
property, plant and equipment
    auditing 467–475
    authorization of transactions 470
    classification 474
    completeness of transactions 470
    complex accounting issues 468
    control risk assessment 470
    cut-off for the management process 473
    definition 476
    depreciation 475
    difficult-to-audit transactions 469
    disclosure issues 474–475
    evaluating audit findings 475
    existence 473–474
    inherent risk assessment 468–469
    occurrence of transactions 470
    overview of property management
        process 467–468
    rights and obligations 474
    segregation of duties for management
        process 470–471
    substantive analytical procedures 471
    substantive procedures 471–475
    types of transactions 467
    valuation and allocation 472, 474
prospective financial information
    assurance reporting 633–634
    definition 645
prospectuses
    EU Directive 634
public company
    definition 6
Public Company Accounting Oversight Board
    (PCAOB) 42, 49
    An Audit of Internal Control over Financial
        Reporting That is Integrated with an Audit
        of Financial Statements (AS5) 224–248
purchase commitments
    disclosure 399
purchase order 380
purchase requisition 379–380
purchase return transactions
    control activities and tests of controls 393
purchase transactions
    accuracy 388, 389–390
    authorization 388, 389
    completeness 387, 389
    control activities and tests of controls 387–390
    cut-off 388, 390
    occurrence 387, 388–389
purchases journal 380
purchasing function 382
purchasing process 63, 115, 375–402

accounts payable 383
audit documentation 386
audit tests 386
control risk assessment 384–386
disbursements 382
document and record types 379–381
financial statement accounts affected by types
    of transactions 379
functions 381–383
general ledger 383
information systems and
    communication 385–386
inherent risk assessment 384
invoice processing 382
overview 377
purchasing function 382
receiving 382
requisitioning 381–382
segregation of duties 383–384
substantive analytical procedures 394–395
substantive procedures 395–399
types of transactions 379
see also cash disbursements; purchase
    transactions
quality assurance review programmes 605
quality control
    IFAC Statements of Membership
        Obligation 605
    international standards (ISQCs) 50, 133, 151,
        603–605
    quality assurance review programmes 605
questionnaires
    internal control 201
reasonable assurance 12–13, 76, 553, 618
    definition 21, 645
recalculation 126
    definition 135
receivables
    audit 366
    see also accounts receivables
receiving function 382
receiving report 380, 435
records
    inspection 123–124, 263
    inventory management process 435–436
    payroll 411–413
    purchasing process 379–381
    reliability 123
    revenue process 338–340
    see also accuracy of records; completeness;
        documents; retention of documents
referral fee
    IFAC Ethics Code 590
regulations
    assessing compliance 152–153
    auditing profession 42–53
    internal auditors' role in reviewing
        compliance 641
related parties
    disclosure of purchase transactions
        between 399
    disclosure of sales transactions between 361
    identifying 153–154
    transactions with 153
related services 57

agreed-upon procedures engagement 50, 57,
    635–636
compilation engagements 50, 57, 620,
    636–637
relevance of evidence 13–14, 121
    definition 135
reliability of evidence 14, 121–122, 123
    definition 135
    records or documents 123
    types of evidence 127
remediation 240–241
    definition 248
remittance advice 340
remuneration
    IFAC Ethics Code 589–590, 598–600
reperformance 126, 263
    definition 135
representation letter
    audit evidence 536–537
    definition 541
    example 536–537
requisitioning function 381–382
retained earnings
    auditing 492
    disclosure 492
retention of documents
    audit documentation 133–134, 539
revenue process 64, 331–367
    accounts receivable function 342
    billing function 341–342
    cash receipts function 342
    control risk assessment 344–346
    credit authorization function 341
    document and record types 338–340
    financial statement accounts affected by types
        of transactions 335–338
    functions 340–342
    general ledger function 342
    inherent risk assessment 343–344
    internal control 345–346
    order entry function 341
    overview 334–335
    segregation of duties 342–343, 353–354
    shipping function 341
    substantive analytical procedures 355–356
    substantive procedures 354–361
    types of transactions 335–338
    see also accounts receivable; cash receipts;
        revenue transactions
revenue recognition 331–334
    complexity 344
    disclosure 361
revenue transactions
    accuracy 348, 350
    authorization 348, 349
    classification 348, 350
    completeness 348, 349
    control activities and tests of controls 346–350
    cut-off 348, 350
    occurrence 347, 349
    substantive analytical procedures 355–356
    see also accounts receivable; cash receipts
review engagement 50, 623–625
    definition 67, 645
review services 56–57

Rio Tinto
    assurance report on sustainability
        development performance data 628
risk assessment
    audit documentation 94–95
    auditor's response to results 92–93
    control risk 203–204
    control risk for long-term debt 484–486
    control risk for stockholders' equity 489–490
    control risk of the human resource
        management process 416–418
    control risk of the inventory management
        process 440–441
    control risk of investments 513–514
    control risk of prepaid expenses 462
    control risk of the property management
        process 470
    control risk of the purchasing process 384–386
    control risk of the revenue process 344–346
    definition 106
    inherent risk of the human resource
        management process 416
    inherent risk of the inventory management
        process 438–440
    inherent risk of prepaid expenses 461
    inherent risk of property management
        process 468–469
    inherent risk of the purchasing process 384
    inherent risk of the revenue process 343–344
    intangible assets 464–465
    internal auditors' role 641
    internal control over financial reporting 232
    material misstatement due to error or
        fraud 86–92
    see also risk assessment procedures
risk assessment procedures 80
    auditor's 84–86
    definition 106
    entity's 192, 199
    evaluation of the entity's 86
    types of test 156–157
risk of material misstatement 17
    accounting estimates 103–104
    and business risks 81
    definition 21
    due to error or fraud 86–92
Royal Ahold
    accounting scandal 377, 401
    disclosure for contingencies 527–528
safeguarding of assets 248
    definition 248
sales invoice 339
sales journal 339
sales order document 338
sales returns and allowances transactions
    control activities and tests of controls 353–354
sales transactions *see* revenue transactions
sampling 14
    audit evidence 263–264
    confidence bound 294
    confidence level 262
    definition of audit sampling 261
    non-sampling risk 262
    non-statistical 260, 264, 282–283, 307–312
    population 259–260

    population size 268–274, 284
    risk 261–262
    risk of an incorrect acceptance 261
    risk of an incorrect rejection 261
    statistical *see* statistical sampling
    tolerable and expected error 262–263
    types of 264–265
sampling unit 268, 294
    definition 285
Sarbanes-Oxley Act 2002 18, 44, 51
    Section 404 on internal control 223–224
scanning 127
    definition 135
scope of the audit 77, 79
    definition 106
second opinions
    IFAC Ethics Code 589
security
    computer 210–211
service organizations
    audit of internal control over financial
        reporting (ICFR) 247–248
    auditing accounting applications processed
        by 208–209
Shell
    assurance report to a sustainability report 633
shipping
    documents 339, 436
    function 341
significant risks 93, 464
    definition 106
small entity
    internal control 202
    review of financial information 623–625
software
    computer-assisted audit techniques
        (CAATs) 213–215
    control activities 210
    custom audit software 214
    generalized audit software 213–214
special purpose financial statements
    auditors' report on 565–566
    definition 569
standard costs
    auditing 446–447
statistical sampling 260
    allowance for sampling risk 293–294
    attribute sampling 266–281
    classical variables sampling 265, 312–318
    decline in use 312
    definition 285
    desired confidence level 262–263, 268–269
    evaluation 278–281
    expected population deviation rate 268, 270
    monetary-unit sampling *see* monetary-unit
        sampling
    non-statistical versus statistical sampling 264
    performance 274–277
    population 267–268
    population size 268–274, 284
    sample selection 274–277
    size of sample 268–274
    substantive tests 293–294
    tolerable deviation rate 269–272
    tolerable misstatement 293–294

types 265
StatoilHydro ASA
    assurance report on the sustainability
        report 631–633
stewardship
    meaning 6
stockholders' equity
    accuracy 490
    auditing 489–490
    authorization 490
    control risk assessment 489–490
    disclosure 491
    occurrence 490
    segregation of duties 490
    types of transactions 489
    valuation 490
subsequent events
    audit procedures 533
    auditor's responsibility 531–532
    definition 541
    examples 531
summary financial statements
    audit report 567
    definition 569
sustainability reporting
    AccountAbility assurance standard 631–633
    assurance services 628, 631–633
    Global Reporting Initiative guidelines 631
tangible assets
    inspection 124, 263
    see also property, plant and equipment
tax liabilities 528
taxation services 58
    IFAC Ethics Code on providing 597–598
tests
    definition 178–179
    see also audit tests
tick marks 132
time card 412
United States
    Public Company Accounting Oversight Board
        (PCAOB) 42, 49, 223–224
    Sarbanes-Oxley Act 2002 18, 42, 49, 223–224
    Securities and Exchange Commission (SEC) 49,
        226–227
unmodified opinion 553–554
    definition 569
valuation
    accounts payable 398–399
    accounts receivable 360–361
    accruals 398–399
    equity capital accounts 491
    intangible assets 465–466
    inventory 446
    investments 515, 516
    long-term debt 485, 487
    payroll-related liabilities 425
    prepaid insurance 463–464
    property, plant and equipment 472, 474
    standard costs 446–447
    stockholders' equity 490
valuation services
    IFAC Ethics Code on performing 597
value-added services 154
vendor invoice 380

vendor statement 381
voucher 380
voucher register 380
vouching 493–494
walk-throughs
    definition 248
    performing 235
    purchasing process 386
working papers
    bank reconciliation 505–506
    definition 541
    review 537
    see also audit documentation
WorldCom
    accounting fraud 469
write-off authorization 340
written communication
    auditor with those charged with
        governance 539–540
written representations
    as audit evidence 536–537
    audit of internal control over financial
        reporting 241
    example 536–537